CALAMARI AND PERILLO

ON

CONTRACTS

Fifth Edition

Joseph M. Perillo
Distinguished Professor of Law
Fordham University

HORNBOOK SERIES®

THOMSON
™
WEST

Mat # 40063469

COPYRIGHT © 1970, 1977, 1987 WEST PUBLISHING CO.

COPYRIGHT © 1998 By WEST GROUP

COPYRIGHT © 2003 By West, a Thomson business
     610 Opperman Drive
     P.O. Box 64526
     St. Paul, MN 55164–0526
     1–800–328–9352

ISBN 0–314–26485–X

TEXT IS PRINTED ON 10% POST CONSUMER RECYCLED PAPER

2nd Reprint — 2007

Preface to Fifth Edition

The First edition of this text by the late John D. Calamari and myself was published in 1970. This revision, like the fourth edition, was written without the aid of my late co-author; nonetheless it contains much of his learning and wisdom. Even where the words are mine alone, they reflect John's relation to me as a mentor and friend.

An attempt to introduce so vast a subject matter in a one volume text has obvious dangers. Over-simplifications are inevitable. Generalizations are always more dogmatic than the law in action. Nevertheless, the practitioner is aware and the student soon becomes aware of the uses and limitations of introductory texts. A text of this kind seeks to provide a guide to a deeper knowledge of the subject.

The four prior editions of this text have met with success beyond our expectations; not in a financial sense, as the royalties provide compensation at an hourly rate below what no practitioner would accept. We measure success by the many graduates of diverse law schools from the most prestigious to the least renowned, who have greeted us with thanks for having taught them contract law through the medium of this text. We also measure success by the very many reported decisions and scholarly works that have cited this text as support for their statements about contract law. The aspiration of the present author is that this edition will meet with comparable success.

We are grateful for the support of Fordham Law School's outstanding deans during our long tenure here–William Hughes Mulligan, Joseph M. McLaughlin, John D. Feerick, and now William M. Treanor.

JOSEPH M. PERILLO
CHELSEA, N.Y.

*

WESTLAW® Overview

Contracts offers a detailed and comprehensive treatment of the basic rules, principles, and issues relating to the law of contracts. To supplement the information contained in this book, you can access Westlaw, West's computer-assisted legal research service. Westlaw contains a broad array of legal resources, including case law, statutes, expert commentary, current developments, and various other types of information.

Learning how to use these materials effectively will enhance your legal research abilities. To help you coordinate the information in the book with your Westlaw research, this volume contains an appendix listing Westlaw databases, search techniques, and sample problems.

The instructions and features described in this Westlaw overview are based on accessing Westlaw via westlaw.com® at **www.westlaw.com**.

THE PUBLISHER

*

Summary of Contents

II.   SUFFICIENCY AND EFFECT OF A RECORD

III.   RESTITUTIONARY REMEDIES

IV.   ESTOPPEL

I.   CONSENSUAL DISCHARGES

II.   DISCHARGES BY OPERATION OF LAW

*

Table of Contents

CHAPTER 3. PAROL EVIDENCE AND INTERPRETATION

A. INTRODUCTION

B. THE PAROL EVIDENCE RULE

CHAPTER 5. INFORMAL CONTRACTS WITHOUT CONSIDERATION OR INJURIOUS RELIANCE

A. PAST CONSIDERATION AND MORAL OBLIGATION

B. CERTAIN COMMERCIAL AND WRITTEN CONTRACTS

H. DUTY TO READ

CHAPTER 10. RESERVED FOR FUTURE USE

CHAPTER 11. CONDITIONS, PERFORMANCE AND BREACH

A. INTRODUCTION

B. CONSTRUCTIVE CONDITIONS AND RELATED TOPICS

C. EXCUSE OF CONDITION

D. GOOD FAITH AND FAIR DEALING

E. ABUSE OF RIGHTS

CHAPTER 12. ANTICIPATORY BREACH AND PROSPECTIVE NON–PERFORMANCE

CHAPTER 14. DAMAGES

A. INTRODUCTION

I. AGREED DAMAGES

J. EFFICIENT BREACH THEORY

CHAPTER 15. RESTITUTION AS A REMEDY FOR BREACH

CHAPTER 16. SPECIFIC PERFORMANCE AND INJUNCTIONS

A. SUBSTANTIVE BASES FOR EQUITABLE RELIEF

B. ASSIGNMENTS—GENERAL BACKGROUND

C. DEVIANTS FROM THE NORM

D. NON–ASSIGNABLE RIGHTS

E. DEFENSES OF THE OBLIGOR

F. COUNTERCLAIMS, SET OFF, AND RECOUPMENT

G. OTHER POSSIBLE LIMITATIONS ON THE ASSIGNEE'S RIGHTS

H. RIGHTS OF THE ASSIGNEE AGAINST THE ASSIGNOR

I. DELEGATION

I. CONSENSUAL DISCHARGES

A. RESCISSION

B. DESTRUCTION OR SURRENDER

C. EXECUTORY ACCORD—ACCORD AND SATISFACTION— SUBSTITUTED AGREEMENT

D. THREE PARTY SITUATIONS

E. ACCOUNT STATED

F. RELEASE AND COVENANT NOT TO SUE

G. GIFTS AND REJECTION OF TENDER

H. MERGER

I. UNION OF RIGHT AND DUTY IN THE SAME PERSON

II. DISCHARGES BY OPERATION OF LAW

J. ALTERATION

K. BANKRUPTCY

L. PERFORMANCE

CHAPTER 22. ILLEGAL BARGAINS

CALAMARI AND PERILLO

ON

CONTRACTS

Fifth Edition

*

Chapter 1

INTRODUCTION

Table of Sections

---

§ 1.1   What Is a Contract?

No entirely satisfactory definition of the term "contract" has ever been devised. The difficulty of definition arises from the diversity of the expressions of assent which may properly be denominated "contracts" and from the various perspectives from which their formation and consequences may be viewed.

Every contract involves at least one promise that has legal consequences. The usual, but not the inevitable, legal consequence is that performance of the promise may be enforced in court by a money judgment, and sometimes by a decree ordering specific performance. The promissory element present in every contract is stressed in a widely quoted definition: "A contract is a promise, or set of promises, for breach of which the law gives a remedy, or the performance of which the law in some way recognizes as a duty."[1] This, like similar definitions, is

---

§ 1.1

1. 1 Williston, Contracts § 1:1 (4th ed. Lord 1990) [hereinafter Williston]; Restatement, Contracts § 1 (1932) [hereinafter Rs. 1st]. The definition is carried over into Restatement, Second, Contracts § 1 (1981) [hereinafter Rs. 2d]. Compare, 1 Corbin, Contracts § 1.3 (Perillo 1993) [hereinafter 1 Corbin].

somewhat misleading. While it is true that a promise, express or implied, is a necessary element in every contract, frequently the promise is coupled with other elements such as physical acts, recitals of fact, and the immediate transfer of property interests. In ordinary usage the contract is not the promise alone, but the entire complex of these elements. The definition also fails to point out that a contract usually requires the assent of more than one person. An additional criticism is that there are "voidable" and "unenforceable" contracts containing promises which at times may be dishonored with impunity. While promises contained in such contracts may have legal consequences, to say that the law recognizes them as duties is to stretch the concept of duty beyond its usual limitations.[2]

Another common definition of a contract is that it is a legally enforceable agreement. While this definition has the advantage of emphasizing that "agreement"[3] is at the core of the law of contracts, the troublesome fact is that there are certain kinds of contracts that may be formed without an agreement.[4] Also, like other definitions of the term "contract," it is unenlightening, and of little help in determining whether a given complex of words and acts are legally enforceable. In sum, knowledge of much of the law of contracts is a prerequisite to an understanding of what a contract is.

Professor Macneil has defined contract as "the relations among parties to the process of projecting exchange into the future."[5] One of the merits of this definition is that it stresses that a contract establishes an inter-relationship among the contracting parties that is broader than their promises and agreement. The agreement is fleshed out by its social matrix which includes such matters as custom, cognizance of the social and economic roles of the parties, general notions of decent behavior, basic assumptions shared but unspoken by the parties, and other factors in the particular and general context in which the parties find themselves. This definition also underscores that the economic core of contract is an exchange between at least two parties and that contract is an instrument for planning future action.

Apart from the difficulty, even when there is little or no substantive disagreement, of defining a legal term so as to achieve universal acceptance, it should be stressed that technical terms share an affliction in common with non-technical language. Words, carefully defined in one

---

2. "A duty is a legal relation that exists whenever certain action or forbearance is expected of an individual, and in default of it the representatives of organized society will act in some predetermined manner injurious to the defaulting individual." 2 Corbin § 7.12 (Perillo & Bender 1995). While the aggrieved party to an unenforceable or voidable contract sometimes has a remedy against the defaulting promisor, quite often there is none. Where there is no remedy for non-performance it seems inappropriate to speak of a "duty" of performance.

3. The term "agreement" may also be defined in various ways. The definition adopted by Rs. 2d § 3 is: "An agreement is a manifestation of mutual assent on the part of two or more persons." Cf. 1 Corbin § 1.9; 1 Williston § 1:3.

4. See ch. 5 infra.

5. Macneil, The New Social Contract 4 (1980).

context, have the frequently disagreeable habit of appearing in different contexts with widely divergent meanings. To illustrate, Article I, Section 10, of the United States Constitution, provides that "No State shall * * * pass any * * * Law impairing the Obligation of Contracts." The United States Supreme Court has held that this clause prohibits the Legislature of New Hampshire from modifying a charter granted by King George III to Dartmouth College.[6] A study of the treatises on the law of contracts would indicate clearly that this charter is not a contract as that term is used in the law of contracts. Nonetheless, by considering the purpose of the constitutional clause, and the presumed intention of the framers of the Constitution, the court held that the charter was a contract within the meaning of the Constitution. The re-defining of a term based on the purpose for which the term was used in its particular context is one of the subtle techniques of the legal art.[7]

Sometimes a legislative act will define terms used in the act in a manner different from standard definitions. The Uniform Commercial Code (UCC) in essence defines a contract as the total legal obligation created by a bargain.[8] Thus, by act of the legislature, the term "contract" for purposes of the UCC, has a somewhat different meaning than it has in transactions not governed by the Code, since the term "bargain" as used in legal parlance includes transactions in which no promise is made, such as the immediate sale of property without warranty in exchange for cash.[9]

The term "contract" is also used by lay persons and lawyers alike to refer to a document in which the terms of a contract are written. Use of the word in this sense is by no means improper so long as it is clearly understood that rules of law utilizing the concept "contract" rarely refer to the writing itself. Usually, the reference is to the agreement; the writing is merely a memorial of the agreement.

§ 1.2 Contracts Distinguished From Executed Agreements

The law gives effect to certain agreements other than contracts. These include barters, gifts, sales of goods, conveyances of interests in real property, and the creation of bailments.[1] The distinction is that a

---

6. Trustees of Dartmouth College v. Woodward, 17 U.S. (4 Wheat.) 518, 4 L.Ed. 629 (1819).

7. "The tendency to assume that a word which appears in two or more legal rules, and so in connection with more than one purpose, has and should have precisely the same scope in all of them, runs all through legal discussions. It has all the tenacity of original sin and must constantly be guarded against." Cook, Substance and Procedure in the Conflict of Laws, 42 Yale L.J. 333, 337 (1933).

8. See UCC § 1–201(11), read with § 1–201(3), substantially the same in the revised draft.

9. See Reporter's Note, Rs. 2d § 3. In addition, for purposes of Article 2 of the UCC § 2–106(1) (unchanged in the 2002 revision) specifically includes sales of goods within the term "contracts."

§ 1.2

1. See 1 Corbin § 1.3. A bailment is not necessarily formed by agreement. For example, a finder of personal property is a bailee. Brown, Personal Property § 3.1 (3d ed.1975).

contract is executory in nature. It contains a promise or promises that must be executed, that is, performed. For example, an agreement to sell a parcel of land is a contract; the sale of a parcel of land is not.

The distinction, like many legal distinctions, is helpful for the purpose of analysis, but is not rigid and is often artificial.[2] Looked at from a transactional perspective, probably most sales, conveyances and bailments are mixed transactions, involving both an executed transfer of property interests or possession and promises such as warranties or promises to surrender possession.

Even from a purely analytic point of view, the distinction between executed agreements and contracts is not firm. As noted in the preceding section, the UCC includes sales of goods and barters[3] within its definition of contract. This was not an arbitrary legislative decision. One of the basic purposes of Article 2 of the Code is to bring the rules governing sales of goods closer to the rules governing contracts to sell goods than had been true under the Uniform Sales Act which the Code has replaced.[4]

§ 1.3 Freedom of Contract

The law of contracts permeates every aspect of our society. Every day it reaches into the life of the individual, governing to some extent the individual's employment, purchase and sale of land and goods, the insuring of the individual's possessions and the financing of these transactions. On a vaster scale it enters into practically every aspect of domestic and international trade.

It was not always thus. In medieval England, contract law was rudimentary.[1] The protection of expectations engendered by promissory agreements was generally not regarded as important enough for the state to concern itself with. True, a remedy might be had in local courts, the proceedings of which we have few records.[2] The ecclesiastical courts took jurisdiction over some contract cases[3] and merchants and craftsmen

---

2. See Wagstaff v. Peters, 203 Kan. 108, 453 P.2d 120 (1969).

3. A barter was deemed a contract within the UCC definition in E & L Rental Equip. v. Wade Constr. Co., 752 N.E.2d 655 (Ind.App.2001).

4. See UCC § 2–106 cmt 1 (" * * * the rights of the parties do not vary according to whether the transaction is a present sale or a contract to sell unless the Article expressly so provides.")

§ 1.3

1. See Lindley, Contract, Economic Change, and the Search for Order in Industrializing America (1993); Simpson, A History of the Common Law of Contract (1975) (The 1987 paperback reprint contains valuable additional bibliography in the preface.) Teeven, A History of the Anglo–American

Common Law of Contract (1990); McGovern, Contract in Medieval England: The Necessity for Quid Pro Quo and a Sum Certain, 13 Am.J.Leg.Hist. 173 (1969); McGovern, The Enforcement of Oral Covenants Prior to Assumpsit, 65 Nw.U.L.Rev. 576 (1970); Pollock, Contracts in Early English Law, 6 Harv.L.Rev. 389 (1893), Selected Readings on the Law of Contracts 10 (1931) [hereinafter Selected Readings.]

2. See Fifoot, History and Sources of the Common Law: Tort and Contract 293–298 (1949).

3. Woodcock, Medieval Ecclesiastical Courts in the Diocese of Canterbury 89–102 (1952); Select Pleas from the Bishop of Ely's Court of Littleport, in Maitland and Baildon, The Court Baron 115–18, 125–26, 139, 144 (Volume 4 of the Selden Society Series 1891).

often utilized their own courts and arbitrators.[4] However, the central parts of the legal system—the courts of common law and the chancery—tended to regard the non-performance of promises as unworthy of the King's justice unless the promise was made pursuant to certain solemn forms.[5] The feudal society of the time assigned all persons to niches, statuses, which rather rigidly delineated the conduct expected of them and which they might expect from others. Enforcement of a voluntary assumption of duties of the kind we now call contractual tended to disrupt this status-oriented society.

No attempt will be made here to trace the step by step evolution of the law of contracts. The crux is that as England changed from a relatively primitive backwater to a commercial center with a capitalistic ethic, the law changed with it. As freedom became a rallying cry for political reforms, freedom of contract was the ideological principle for development of the law of contract. In Maine's classic phrase, it was widely believed that "the movement of the progressive societies has hitherto been a movement from *Status to Contract*."[6] Williston adds: "Economic writers adopted the same line of thought. Adam Smith, Ricardo, Bentham and John Stuart Mill successively insisted on freedom of bargaining as the fundamental and indispensable requisite of progress; and imposed their theories on the educated thought of their times with a thoroughness not common in economic speculation."[7]

In the twentieth century the tide turned away from the nineteenth century tendency toward unrestricted freedom of contract. Today, while the parties' power to contract as they please for lawful purposes remains a basic principle of our legal system, it is hemmed in by increasing legislative restrictions. Two areas of the law serve to illustrate this. Contracts of employment are controlled by a wide range of federal and state laws concerning minimum wages, hours, working conditions and required social insurance programs. Contracts of insurance, perhaps to a greater extent than labor contracts, are controlled by law. Often terms of the policy are dictated by statute.

Apart from legislative restrictions on freedom of contract, it seems likely that in the future there will be greater restrictions imposed by courts in the exercise of their function of developing the common law. There has been increasing recognition in legal literature that the bargaining process has become more limited in modern society. In purchasing a new automobile, for example, the individual may be able to dicker over price, model, color and certain other factors, but, in order to consummate the contract to purchase, the individual usually must sign the standard form prepared by the manufacturer (although the contract is with an independent dealer). The individual has no real choice and

4. Gross, Selected Cases Concerning the Law Merchant, A.D. 1270–1638, Vol. I (Volume 23 of the Selden Society Series 1908).

5. See Hazeltine, The Formal Contract of Early English Law, 10 Colum.L.Rev. 608 (1910), Selected Readings 1.

6. Maine, Ancient Law 165 (3rd American ed. 1873).

7. Williston, Freedom of Contract, 6 Cornell L.Q. 365, 366 (1921), Selected Readings 100, 101–102.

must take that form or leave it. Such contracts, called contracts of "adhesion,"[8] constitute a serious challenge to much of contract theory.

Most of contract law is premised upon a model consisting of two alert individuals, mindful of their self-interest, hammering out an agreement by a process of hard bargaining. The process of entering into a contract of adhesion, however " * * * is not one of haggle or cooperative process but rather of a fly and flypaper."[9] Courts, legislators and scholars have become increasingly aware of this divergence between the theory and practice of contract formation, and new techniques are evolving for coping with the challenges stemming from this divergence.[10]

§ 1.4 The Philosophical Foundations of Contract Law

Before the state, there was the family and the clan.[1] Before courts, there was the feud—private vengeance wreaked by members of the aggrieved party's extended family or the aggrieved party personally. It is well-recognized that the law of crimes and torts owe their origin to the state's desire to eliminate private vengeance and to minimize other forms of self-help. It is not as well known that contract law has the same genesis. Among the earliest executory contracts were compositions— agreements settling claims of personal injury or property damages. To the extent they were executory, performance was secured by the delivery of hostages to the promisee. In the event of breach, the hostage could be executed or enslaved.[2]

In modern law, where contract law refuses to enter, vengeance and self-help fill the vacuum. On nearly a daily basis, residents of our major cities are informed by the media of a "drug-related" murder or kidnapping. The relationship between the victim and the enforcer is usually that of debtor and creditor. Because the legal system will not aid in the collection of the debt formed by a criminal sale,[3] vengeance or hostage-taking substitutes for law. It is not only drug-related transactions that give rise to extra-legal punishment or enforcement. Take the example of a builder who went to a prospective lender for a loan. Not realizing the nature of the business of the person he was applying to, he inquired about the collateral the lender might want. He was told: "Your body is your collateral."[4]

Anthropology and history prove that a basis of contract law is the desire to keep the public peace. Nonetheless, contract law serves other functions and other rationales are given for its existence. For centuries,

8. See Kessler, Contracts of Adhesion— Some Thoughts About Freedom of Contract, 43 Colum.L.Rev. 629 (1943).

9. Leff, Contract as Thing, 19 Am. U.L.Rev. 131, 143 (1970).

10. See §§ 9.37 to 9.45 infra.

§ 1.4

1. See Perillo, Exchange, Contract and Law in the Stone Age, 31 Arizona L.Rev. 17 (1989).

2. Berger, From Hostage to Contract I, 35 Ill.L.Rev. 154, II, 35 Ill.L.Rev.281 (1940).

3. See ch. 22.

4. N.Y. State Comm. of Investigation, The Loan Shark Racket 11 (1965). See also the film "Rocky."

philosophers of the law have attempted to explain why, in addition to the keeping of the public peace, the legal system recognizes and enforces private agreements.[5] As is so frequently the case in philosophical discourse no consensus has been reached, but the range of disagreement, although significant, is surprisingly small. The exponents of different schools of thought have tended to focus variously on five factors: (a) the human will, either as a source of sovereignty or (b) as a source of moral compulsion, (c) private autonomy, (d) reliance, and (e) the needs of trade.

(a) The Sovereignty of the Human Will and (b) the Sanctity of Promise

In the heyday of the Enlightenment era, there was widespread belief in, and great stress was placed upon, the existence of inalienable rights which existed prior to, and independent of, government. Indeed, government itself was believed to be based upon a social contract that derived its binding force from the sovereignty of the individual wills of the contracting parties. The social contract theory was pithily put by an English lawyer in the mid 1600's. "[B]oth judge and prisoner have consented to a law that if either of them steal they shall be hanged." And again, "to know what obedience is due to the prince you must look into the contract betwixt him and the people; as if you would know what rent is due from the tenant to the landlord you must look into the lease."[6] An American exponent of this viewpoint, Chief Justice John Marshall, had this to say about the law of contract:[7]

> "If, on tracing the right to contract, and the obligations created by contract, to their source, we find them to exist anterior to, and

---

5. For further discussion of the topics discussed in this section, see Atiyah, Promises, Morals and Law (1981); Atiyah, The Rise and Fall of Freedom of Contract (1979); Barnett, A Consent Theory of Contract, 86 Colum.L.Rev. 269 (1986); Bentham, Theory of Legislation 192–194 (Odgen ed. 1931); Carswell & Schwartz, Foundations of Contract Law (1994) (economics anthology); Cohen, The Basis of Contract, 46 Harv.L.Rev. 553, 558–85 (1933); Cohen, Jewish and Roman Law, 78–79 (1966); Ehrlich, Fundamental Principles of the Sociology of Law 111 (Moll. trans. 1962); Farnsworth, The Past of Promise, 69 Colum.L.Rev. 576 (1969); Fried, Contract as Promise (1981); Fuller, Consideration and Form, 41 Colum.L.Rev. 799, 806–14 (1941); Grotius, The Rights of War and Peace, Book II, chs. 11, 12 (Whewell trans. 1853); Kant, The Philosophy of Law 134–144 (Albrecht trans. 1921); Kronman & Posner, The Economics of Contract Law (1979); Lorenzen, Causa and Consideration in the Law of Contracts, 28 Yale L.J. 621–44 (1919); Macneil, Efficient Breach of Contract: Circles in the Sky, 68 Va.L.Rev. 947

(1982); Pound, The Role of the Will in Law, 68 Harv.L.Rev. 1 (1954); Pufendorf, The Two Books on the Duty of Man and Citizen According to the Natural Law, Book I, ch. 9 § 3 (Moore trans. 1927); Radin, Contract Obligation and the Human Will, 43 Colum.L.Rev. 575 (1943); St. Thomas Acquinas, The Summa Theologica, Part II, Q. 88, Arts. 1, 2, 3, Q. 89, Art. 7 (Dominican trans. 1922); Sharp, Pacta Sunt Servanda, 41 Colum.L.Rev. 783–85 (1941); Vinogradoff, Reason and Conscience in Sixteenth Century Jurisprudence, 24 L.Q.Rev. 373 (1908); Willis, Rationale of the Law of Contracts, 11 Ind.L.J. 227 (1936). The flavor of contemporary debate is most easily approached by reading book reviews of the works of Atiyah and Fried supra.

6. Selden, Table–Talk (headings Equity and War).

7. Ogden v. Saunders, 25 U.S. (12 Wheat.) 213, 345, 6 L.Ed. 606 (1827). See Isaacs, John Marshall on Contracts: A Study in Early American Juristic Theory, 7 Va.L.Rev. 413 (1921).

independent of society, we may reasonably conclude that those original and pre-existing principles are, like many other natural rights brought with man into society; and, *although they may be controlled, are not given by human legislation.*"

Although, this natural law viewpoint could be logically consistent with other possible views, historically it was intertwined with the idea that, "I am bound because I intend to be bound." Intention is regarded as the keystone of contract law.

Although the Enlightenment concept of natural law was the natural law concept that had the most direct impact upon Anglo–American courts, it was preceded by canon law and rabbinical thinking about the sanctity of a promise. According to the canon lawyers and rabbinical scholars of the late middle ages and the Renaissance, promises were binding in natural law as well as in morality because failure to perform a promise made by a free act of the will was an offense against the Deity. Inasmuch as some training in theology was part of the education of every literate person during the formative era of the Anglo–American law of contracts, it is inferable that this doctrine had an impact upon the thinking of lawyers and judges as well as upon the teaching of philosophers. Indeed, it was often utilized by Enlightenment philosophers as an additional argument to support the notion of the sovereignty of the individual will. The difference was a shift in emphasis from a theological to a humanistic basis. This does not imply that the religious basis was abandoned. English college students in the 18th and 19th century were exposed to it in the many editions of Paley's Principles of Moral and Political Philosophy.[8] American college students received the same message from Paley or his principle American successor, Wayland.[9]

(c) Private Autonomy

A less radical analysis of the efficacy of the human will is made by the exponents of the theory of private autonomy. Simply put, the theory sees the foundation of contract law as a sort of delegation of power by the State to its inhabitants. Recognizing the desirability of allowing individuals to regulate, to a large extent, their own affairs, the State has conferred upon them the power to bind themselves by expression of their intention to be bound, provided, always, that they operate within the limits of their delegated powers.

> * * * [I]nsofar as the law of contract places the coercions of the legal order behind the terms of a contract settled by private parties, the legal order may and indeed should set socially approved limits to the support which it gives to the terms which one party is in a position to impose on the other.[10]

8. Book II, chs. I–III, Book III, chs. V–IX.

9. The Elements of Moral Science 260–64 (1835). A skeptical view of the influence of religion on contract law is expressed in Farnsworth, Parables About Promises: Religious Ethics and Contract Enforceability, 71 Fordham L.Rev. 695 (2002).

10. Stone, Social Dimensions of Law and Justice 253 (1966).

This power, it is argued, stems from the law of the State rather than the law of nature.

(d) Reliance

Proponents of the reliance theory of contracts profess to see the foundation of contract law not in the will of the promisor to be bound but in the expectations engendered by, and the promisee's consequent reliance upon, the promise. Although this idea is not in opposition to some aspects of the theories discussed under (a), (b) and (c) above, it is in opposition to a finding that the efficacy of a contract is based upon the power of the will of the promisor. It is significant that the earliest cases in which the courts of common law gave relief to promisees were those in which damage had been incurred in reliance upon a promise. On the other hand, it is clear that under modern law a contract, once made, is binding and an action for breach may be instituted although the contract is repudiated before it induces any action or inaction in reliance upon it.[11] We will see, however, that in many areas of contract law reliance by the promisee is often crucial.

(e) Economic Analysis and Critical Legal Studies

Some students of the law urge that contract law is based upon the needs of trade, sometimes stated in terms of the mutual advantage of the contracting parties, but more often of late in terms of a tool of the economic and social order. Such students find discussions of the efficacy of the will and competing notions to be irrelevant, or at least subordinate to what they perceive to be its main economic or social pillars. Consequently, proponents of these bases of the law of contracts do not necessarily exclude some validity to any of the theories discussed above.

In the period starting from about 1970 to the present, much of the literature about contracts has concentrated on the economic analysis of contract rules. Economists of the Chicago School have found traditional contract rules to be generally sound. This is fortunate because much of this literature is inaccessible to most lawyers and judges as it is laced with the jargon of economics instead of the jargon of law.[12] Professor Hillman offers in plain English this thumbnail summary of the views of legal economists of the Chicago School:[13]

> Neoclassical legal economists observe that people allocate society's scarce resources through the exchange process. Voluntary exchange occurs in a free-market setting because the parties, seeking to maximize their economic welfare, give up resources in return for

---

11. Hochster v. De La Tour, 118 Eng. Rep. 922 (Q.B.1853); Texaco, Inc. v. Penzoil Co., 729 S.W.2d 768 (Tex.App.1987).

12. One of the best of the law and economics scholars delivers a tale of woe. That is, law and economics scholarship has had little effect on the outcome of cases or in doctrinal analysis. Eric A. Posner, Economic Analysis of Contract Law After Three

Decades: Success or Failure?, <http://www.law.uchicago.edu/Lawyecon/index.html>.

13. Hillman, The Richness of Contract Law: An Analysis and Critique of Contemporary Theories of Contract Law 214 (1997).

more valuable resources. Such exchange is socially desirable because it moves resources to "higher valued uses," thereby increasing "allocative efficiency." By pursuing self-interest, then, people promote the interests of society. Skeptical of the capacity of lawmakers to improve on this "private" method of economic organization, neoclassical legal economists believe that contract law appropriately enforces voluntary exchange.

Proponents of contract as a tool of the economic order espouse broad autonomy for individuals to make their own market choices.

A school of thought known as Critical Legal Studies (CLS) is skeptical about many aspects of the legal system. Drawing some inspiration from literary deconstructionists, they tend to find that the rules of contract law are indeterminate and therefore the outcome of any contract dispute can be manipulated by the courts to reach any result. The courts tend, they assert, to reach results to perpetuate the status quo. In general, CLS offers no solution, no vision of a better system other than hints of communitarianism or utopian socialism.[14] Proponents are skeptical about treating consent as the basis of contractual obligation and see the role of the state as predominant.

(f) Synthesis

It cannot be said that any of the competing philosophic premises discussed above is officially enshrined in our law of contract. Each of them, together with the pervasive desire of the law to prevent unjust enrichment, coexists as part of our frequently utilized stock of legally acceptable arguments. The contradictions among them are rarely noticed. The premises were neatly synthesized by Sir Frederick Pollock.[15]

> The law of Contract may be described as the endeavor of the State, a more or less imperfect one by the nature of the case, to establish a positive sanction for the expectation of good faith which has grown up in the mutual dealings of men of average rightmindedness. * * * He who has given the promise is bound to him who accepts it, not merely because he had or expressed a certain intention, but because he so expressed himself as to entitle the other party to rely on his acting in a certain way.

Such a synthesis, while serving well for the generality of cases, breaks down when many difficult choices must be made. Illustrative of the questions which receive different answers depending upon which premise is accepted, are the following:

> (1) Should the law protect the interests of a person relying on the word of another person who at the same time disclaims any intention to be bound? The will premise and the reliance premise have produced conflicting decisions.[16]

14. A leading CLS article is Unger, The Critical Legal Studies Movement, 96 Harv. L.Rev. 561 (1983).

15. Pollock, Principles of Contract 9 (Preface to 4th ed. 1888).

16. See § 2.4 infra.

(2) Should a person who deliberately breaks a contract be treated differently from one who is merely negligent or unfortunate? Proponents of the moral basis of contract enforcement may answer the question differently from those who adopt the view that contract law is designed to meet the needs of trade.[17]

Questions such as the above permeate our law of contracts and receive no consistent or easily predictable reply. Different premises have been more strongly stressed and more dogmatically asserted in given historical eras than in others.[18] Readers of judicial opinions will note that rarely is a conscious choice made between competing theories, and perhaps this is to the good.[19] Each of the five theories are based upon values and interests which our legal system holds in high regard. We can, at the risk of oversimplification, draw the following equations:

Theory		**Underlying Social Value**
(1) Sovereignty of the Individual Will	=	Individual Responsibility of Promisors
(2) Sanctity of Promise	=	The Law Upholds Moral Values
(3) Private Autonomy	=	Freedom of the Private Sector With Controls Against Excesses
(4) Reliance	=	Fairness to Promisees
(5) Needs of Trade	=	Economic Efficiency

It seems unrealistic to expect our legal system to select one of these social values as the sole and exclusive basis of the law of contract. Realism aside, it is doubtful whether it would be desirable in each and every case to subordinate four of these values to any one of the five. It should also be reiterated that in many cases there is no irreconcilable clash among them.

---

17. For example, on the question of whether a party who has intentionally breached a contract may recover for the value of the benefits conferred upon the other party, compare the statements of New York's Chief Judge Cardozo with those of California's Chief Justice Traynor. Cardozo: "The willful transgressor must accept the penalty of his transgression * * *. The transgressor whose default is unintentional and trivial may hope for mercy if he will offer atonement for his wrong." Jacob & Youngs v. Kent, 230 N.Y. 239, 244, 129 N.E. 889, 891 (1921). Traynor: " * * * to deny the remedy of restitution because a breach is wilful would create an anomalous situation * * *." Freedman v. Rector, Wardens & Vestrymen of St. Mathias Parish, 37 Cal.2d 16, 22, 230 P.2d 629, 632, 31 ALR2d 1, 7 (1951). See § 11.22 infra. Compare further, the language of economic analysis: "Even if the breach is deliberate, it is not necessarily blameworthy. The promisor may simply have discovered that his performance is worth more to someone else. If so, efficiency is promoted by allowing him to break his promise, provided he makes good the promisee's actual losses. If he is forced to pay more than that, an efficient breach may be deterred and the law doesn't want to bring about such a result." Patton v. Mid–Continent Systems, 841 F.2d 742, 750 (7th Cir.1988). For another example of a split of authority turning on whether or not a contract breaker ought to be characterized as a "bad person," see Perillo, Restitution in a Contractual Context, 73 Colum.L.Rev. 1208, 1224 n. 104 (1973).

18. See generally Pound, Liberty of Contract, 18 Yale L.J. 454 (1909).

19. But see Barnett, Book Review, 97 Mich. L.Rev. 1413 (1999), supporting the desirability of a unifying theory.

With minor changes, this section appeared in the second edition of this text in 1977. Its basic thrust has been confirmed in a recent study by Professor Robert Hillman which examines the output of contract theoreticians of recent decades. It concludes: "Despite its many dimensions, contract law is a credible, if not flawless, reflection of the values of the surrounding society. A highly abstract unitary theory illuminates contract law, but it cannot explain the entire sphere."[20]

Hillman's study includes discussions of two lines of thought with which this section had not dealt—feminist legal theory and critical race theory. As to the first of these theories, there is no doubt that in the past the contours of contract law have been defined by men.[21] Women's voices are now being heard. There is, however, no one feminine voice, but among the voices two notes are clearly audible. One is influenced by psychologist Carol Gilligan.[22] The thrust of such scholarship is to identify the differences between feminine and masculine perspectives and to explore the implications of those differences for law. Feminists of this school of thought maintain that women see society and contractual relations within society in a relational tapestry rather than in sharply defined rights and wrongs.[23] Concerned that stressing differences might justify unequal treatment, other feminist scholars stress the importance of equality.[24] Among the innovative voices are those who argue for a greater role for enforceable contracts between spouses or between others in domestic arrangements.[25] They note that the law has traditionally treated issues that have mattered most to women as outside the law of contract. This criticism has had some impact on the courts and on legislatures.[26]

Critical race theory is another late 20th Century school of thought. It focuses on the status of non-whites as outsiders in a society dominated by Caucasians. While classical and most neoclassical contract law starts with the premise that free individuals are at liberty to give or withhold

---

20. Hillman, The Richness of Contract Law 6 (1997).

21. A notable exception was Soia Mentschikoff who was on the faculty of the University of Chicago from 1951 to 1974, when she became Dean of the University of Miami Law School. She continued as Dean until 1982, when she became Distinguished Professor Emeritus at that School. She worked with Karl Llewellyn on the revision of the Sales Act and ultimately the creation of the Uniform Commercial Code. She authored Commercial Transactions: Cases and Materials (1970), and co-authored, Soia Mentschikoff & Irwin P. Stotzky, The Theory and Craft of American Law: Elements (1981). The strength of her personality expressed as a teacher, lecturer, and advocate for the enactment of the Uniform Commercial Code is captured in Farnsworth, Foote, Huber & Swan, In Memoriam—Soia Mentschikoff, 16 U.Miami Inter–American L.Rev. 1 (1984).

22. Gilligan, In a Different Voice: Psychological Theory and Women's Development (1982).

23. For this, one can cite one quite accessible and strongly argued article. Frug, Rescuing Impossibility Doctrine: A Postmodern Feminist Analysis of Contract Law, 140 U.Pa.L.Rev. 1029 (1992).

24. E.g., Shaughnessy, Gilligan's Travels, 7 Law & Eq.L.J. 1, 9 (1988).

25. There are many such voices. See generally, Shultz, Contractual Ordering of Marriage: A New Model for State Policy, 70 Cal.L.Rev. 204 (1982). For others, see Hillman supra note 20 at 79–80.

26. E.g., Marvin v. Marvin, 18 Cal.3d 660, 134 Cal.Rptr. 815, 557 P.2d 106 (1976) (agreements between cohabitants); McKinney's N.Y. Dom.Rel.L § 236(B)(3) (agreements between spouses).

their consent to proposed contracts, critical race theory talks in terms "of the basic myths of American meritocracy," and the myth of the "color-blindness of law."[27] Racial, and not merely class barriers impede the notion of equality. For example, threats not to renew leases of African–Americans who have the audacity to vote cast doubt on notions of unfettered freedom to contract.[28] Race theorists have also commented extensively on how different cultural experiences have shaped different perceptions of the contracting process and contract itself.[29]

§ 1.5 Scope, Relevance and Adequacy of Contract Law

Contract Law interlocks with and overlaps all other legal disciplines. In particular, labor, sales, commercial financing, agency, suretyship, quasi contracts, insurance—to name but a few—are contract permeated subjects about which specialized treatises have been written.

It has been suggested that there is no law of contracts, or that if there is, it ought to be done away with. The thrust of the argument is that the variety of contractual contexts is so extensive and that the social and economic needs of each kind of transaction is so different that a disservice is done if one attempts to resolve transactional disputes by the application of supposed general principles of contract law.[1] Critics of contract law find additional support in the fact that when disputes arise in business and non-business transactions the parties involved usually resolve the dispute without reference to rules of law.[2] The latter argument is rather simple to dispose of. If neighboring children walk through one's yard as a short-cut to school one has the choice of greeting them with a welcome or with a snarl, and if one wishes, one may resort to a variety of legal remedies to punish or stop them from trespassing. The fact that in this context legal remedies are rarely resorted to hardly means that the law of property is irrelevant. Rather recourse to a legal remedy is the weapon of last resort when other methods of attaining one's goals fail. Similarly the reluctance of many to resort to law to resolve contract disputes may indicate a healthy social system rather than the irrelevance of contract law. To the extent that reluctance to employ legal remedies is based on the inadequacy of the legal system, the

27. Foreward to Critical Race Theory xiv, xx (Crenshaw, Gotanda, Peller & Thomas eds. 1995).

28. See U.S. v. Beaty, 288 F.2d 653 (6th Cir.1961) (such threats enjoined under the Civil Rights law). For the application of critical race theory to contract law, see Anthony R. Chase, Race, Culture and Contract Law: From the Cottonfield to the Courtroom, 28 Conn.L.Rev. 1 (1995); Morant, The Relevance of Race and Disparity in Discussions of Contract Law, 31 N. England L.Rev. 889 (1997); Symposium, 63 U.Cin.L.Rev. 269 (1994).

29. Williams, Alchemical Notes: Reconstructing Ideals from Deconstructed Rights, 22 Harv. CR–CL L.Rev. 401 (1987).

§ 1.5

1. See Atiyah, Contracts, Promises and the Law of Obligations, 94 L.Q.Rev. 193, 199–201 (1978); Mueller, Contract Remedies: Business Fact and Legal Fantasy, 1967 Wis.L.Rev. 833; see also Gilmore, The Death of Contract (1974). For a good analysis of this thesis, see Speidel, An Essay on the Reported Death and Continued Vitality of Contract, 27 Stanford L.Rev. 1161 (1975).

2. Friedman and Macaulay, Contract Law and Contract Teaching: Past, Present and Future, 1967 Wis.L.Rev. 805.

major flaw is not with the law of contracts, but with the expense and psychic pain of litigation.

The first argument is much more serious however. Can general principles be formulated to regulate adequately such diverse transactions as military enlistments,[3] credit card purchases,[4] collective bargaining agreements,[5] enrollment in private schools,[6] government construction contracts, maritime charters, house purchases, plea bargains,[7] cash for contraception,[8] and the wide variety of other consensual transactions? The answer is, and for centuries has been, a broad mixture of yes and no. There are legal questions common to all of these transactions, particularly those involving the nature of consent, capacity of parties, methods of interpretation, necessary formalities, the relationship between the parties' performances, rights of third parties, the discharge of obligations, as well as others. There are also questions unique to each kind of transaction; the business context of maritime charters requires that special rules should apply that do not apply to a contract for sale of a house.

Moreover, legislators and regulators have staked out various kinds of transactions for the enactment of special rules for the protection of the consumer, for economic regulation, or for other purposes. The coexistence of general rules common to all transactions and special rules for particular transactions was recognized in one of the earliest discussions of contracts available to us in English, by Hugo Grotius,[9] and continues to be recognized in most of the current American literature. Possibly surprising to some, the same general problems addressed by Grotius are addressed in much the same way in the recodification of contract law in Russia in the communist era,[10] and the post-communist era.[11] It is believed that the persistence of approaching general problems of contract, along with special rules for particular contracts, throughout the centuries and in countries with diverse economic systems, stems not from academic conservatism but from the persistency of similar problems that run through all consensual transactions. To study one kind of transaction in isolation from others would be to ignore the persistency of human behavior and the utility of generalizations.[12] Those who rebel at

---

3. Dilloff, A Contractual Analysis of the Military Enlistment, 8 U. Richmond L.Rev. 121 (1974).

4. Macaulay, Private Legislation and the Duty to Read—Business Run By IBM Machine, the Law of Contracts and Credit Cards, 19 Vand.L.Rev. 1051 (1966).

5. Summers, Collective Agreements and the Law of Contracts, 78 Yale L.J. 525 (1969).

6. See Annots., 47 ALR5th 1, 46 ALR5th 581.

7. U.S. v. Hyde, 520 U.S. 670, 678 (1997) (analogy); Griffin v. State, 756 N.E.2d 572 (Ind.App.2001); Note, 72 N.Y.U.L.Rev. 841 (1997).

8. Note, 43 Ariz.L.Rev. 205 (2001).

9. Grotius, The Rights of War and Peace, book II, chs. 11, 12 (Whewell trans. 1853).

10. Civil Code of the R.S.F.S.R., part III (Gray and Stults trans. 1965).

11. See Kozlow, The New Russian Civil Code of 1994.

12. "[I]n any intellectual enterprise * * * there must always be a certain difference between theory and practice or experience. A theory must certainly be simpler than the factual complexity or chaos that faces us when we lack the guidance which a general chart of the field affords us. A chart

generalizations might well be reminded of the tale of the empire whose exacting map makers produced a map so accurate that it coincided with the empire point by point.[13] Its uselessness was, of course, total.

Serious criticism has been leveled of late against the adequacy of contract law. The criticism is of two kinds. First, that contract law has not forged adequate tools for coping with contracts of adhesion. This is discussed elsewhere in this book.[14] The second criticism is made by Professor Ian Macneil in several challenging articles.[15] The thrust of the criticism is that traditional contract doctrine takes as its model the discrete transaction: the contract to sell a horse, a house, a plot of land, or short-term services. In today's world such transactions continue but are overshadowed by long-term relational contracts: franchises, collective bargains, long-term supply contracts and the like. The need in the future is to recast much of contract doctrine to consider more adequately the needs of on-going relational contracts. In this, he is surely right.

§ 1.6   Sources of Contract Law

Except in a few American jurisdictions the basic law of contracts is not codified. Contract law is thus primarily common law, embodied in court decisions. Many legislative enactments do, however, bear on the subject. Generally, only a few statutes purport to modify a principle running throughout contract law. For the most part legislatures have concentrated on regulating particular types of contracts such as insurance policies and employment contracts. Of particular relevance in twentieth century legislation is Article 2 of the UCC.[1]

For the guidance of the bench and bar, the American Law Institute in 1932 published a code-like document called the Restatement of Contracts. The Restatement, having been issued by a private organization, does not have the force of law. Nevertheless, it is highly persuasive authority. Leaders of the profession analyzed the often conflicting maze of judicial decisions, attempted to cull the sound from the less sound and to state the sounder views in systematic form.[2] The principal draftsman of the Restatement of Contracts was Samuel Williston.

---

or map would be altogether useless if it did not simplify the actual contours and topography which it describes. * * * No science offers us an absolutely complete account of its subject matter. It is sufficient if it indicates some general pattern to which the phenomena approximate more or less. For practical purposes any degree of approximation will do if it will lead to a greater control over nature than we should have without our ideal pattern. But for theoretic purposes we need the postulate that all divergences between the ideal and the actual will be progressively minimized by the discovery of subsidiary principles deduced from, or at least consistent with, the principles of our science." Cohen, Reason and Law 63–64 (Free Press ed. 1950).

13. Borges, A Universal History of Infamy 141 (di Giovanni trans., E. P. Dutton & Co. 1972).

14. See §§ 9.37 to 9.45 infra.

15. Macneil, The Many Futures of Contract, 47 So.Calif.L.Rev. 691 (1974); Macneil, Restatement (Second) of Contracts and Presentiation, 60 Va.L.Rev. 589 (1974); Symposium, 1985 Wis.L.Rev. 461.

§ 1.6

1. See § 1.7 infra.

2. For a fuller discussion, see Preface, Restatement of Contracts (1932).

After a passage of some thirty years, it was felt that there had been sufficient developments in the law for a new Restatement to be issued. In 1964 the first tentative draft of the initial portion of a second edition was circulated. The chief drafter of Chapters 1–9 of the second Restatement was Professor Robert Braucher, who resigned to serve as a Justice of the Supreme Judicial Court of Massachusetts. Subsequent chapters have been drafted primarily by Professor E. Allan Farnsworth. The final draft was approved in 1979 and published in 1981. It is fair to say that just as the first Restatement largely reflected the views of Professor Williston, the Second Restatement has drawn heavily on the views of Professor Arthur L. Corbin.[3]

The law of contracts is the subject of two of the best treatises in Anglo–American legal literature. The first edition of Professor Williston's treatise was published in 1920 and has had enormous impact on the law. Professor Corbin's, first published in 1950, has perhaps been more influential. Research into any contract problem necessarily requires consultation of both of these authors' views as well as the cases and statutes. Both treatises are masterful analyses. To capsulate the basic difference in approach of the two authors, requires an introduction to two schools of jurisprudence: the so-called positivist and realist schools.

Stated in its extreme form the positivist idea is this:

> "Justice is an irrational idea. * * * [T]hat only one of two orders is 'just' cannot be established by rational cognition. Such cognition can grasp only a positive order * * *. This order is positive law * * *. It presents the law as it is, without defending it by calling it just, or condemning it to call it unjust."[4]

The positivist usually believes that the legal system may be analyzed into component rules, principles and concepts and that any fact situation may be solved by the careful pigeonholing of the facts into the appropriate legal concepts, principles and rules. In other words, once the facts are determined, a carefully programmed computer would produce the correct decision. This approach has been criticized as "mechanical jurisprudence."[5]

The realist is skeptical whether decisions are in fact so arrived at and furthermore questions the propriety of such an approach. Again stated in extreme form, the realist believes:

> "[T]he law, with respect to any particular set of facts, is a decision of a court with respect to those facts so far as that decision

3. See Braucher, Freedom of Contract and the Second Restatement, 78 Yale L.J. 598, 616 (1969); Farnsworth, Ingredients in the Redaction of the Restatement (Second) of Contracts, 81 Colum. L. Rev. 1, 3 & 5 (1981).

4. Kelsen, General Theory of Law and State 13 (1961). Kelsen is the leading modern exponent of the positivist approach.

5. Pound, Mechanical Jurisprudence, 8 Colum.L.Rev. 605 (1908).

affects that particular person. Until a court has passed on those facts no law on that subject is yet in existence."[6]

The realist is also skeptical of the formulation of generalizations and definitions, believing that courts do in fact and should take into account the moral, ethical, economic and social situation in reaching a decision. This approach is subject to criticism in that it tends toward the creation of a legal system based on indeterminacy and to defeat society's expectations of order and certainty in legal relationships.

Neither Professor Williston nor Professor Corbin adopts either of the extreme positions just discussed. However, readers might find comprehension of their treatises enhanced if they realize at the outset that the former tends towards the positivist position and the latter towards the realist school.

The neophyte should also be apprised that although courts usually articulate their decisions in positivist terms, it is only the unsophisticated attorney who will phrase an argument purely in those terms without reference to social, economic and ethical considerations.

§ 1.7   The UCC, the United Nations Convention, and UNIDROIT Principles

The Uniform Commercial Code (UCC) is the product of a Permanent Editorial Board under the joint auspices of the American Law Institute and the National Conference of Commissioners on Uniform State Laws.[1] A draft was approved by these bodies in 1952. In 1953, it was enacted by Pennsylvania. No other state followed. In 1956, the New York Law Revision Commission recommended against enactment unless extensive amendments were made. Reacting to the New York report, the Permanent Editorial Board made extensive revisions. As so revised, it was enacted by all the states except Louisiana between 1957 and 1967. The enactments were not wholly uniform, as many of the states have varied from the uniform text at some points. In addition, the Code contained several optional provisions. These variations are noted in the "Uniform Laws Annotated" edition of the Code. Editions published in local state collections of statutes will usually indicate instances in which the local enactment varies from the uniform text.

The UCC originally contained nine articles.[2] Since its original enactment, two articles have been added and several have been thoroughly revised. Article 1 contains general provisions applicable to all transactions governed by the Code. Article 2 governs the sale of goods; Article

6. Frank, Law and the Modern Mind 46 (1930). See generally Fuller, American Legal Realism, 82 U.Pa.L.Rev. 429 (1934); Kalman, Legal Realism at Yale 1927–1960 (1986).

§ 1.7

1. See Schnader, A Short History of the Preparation and Enactment of the Uniform Commercial Code, 22 U. Miami L.Rev. 1 (1967); White and Summers, Uniform Commercial Code 1–21 (2d ed. 1980).

2. The citation "UCC § 2–238" indicates that the provision is in Article 2. The citation "UCC § 3–211" indicates the provision is in Article 3.

2A deals with the leasing of goods; Article 3 governs commercial paper; Article 4, bank deposits and collections; Article 4A, funds transfer; Article 5, letters of credit; Article 6, bulk transfers; Article 7, warehouse receipts, bills of lading and other documents of title; Article 8, investment securities; Article 9, secured transactions, including sales of accounts and chattel paper.

Most of the provisions of the Code do not affect basic contract law; those that do are mostly contained in Article 2, which deals with the sale of goods[3] and in Article 9 which deals, among other things, with the assignment (transfer) of some contract rights. As the most recent legislative statement of certain contract principles and rules, Article 2 of the Code has increasingly been looked to by courts for guidance in transactions other than the sale of goods.[4] As one court has stated: "While this contract is not controlled by the Code, the Code is persuasive here because it embodies the foremost legal thought concerning commercial transactions."[5]

The Code was published with official comments prepared by the Permanent Editorial Board. The "General Comment" introduction to the Code indicates that the purpose of the comments is to promote uniformity and "to aid in viewing the Act as an integrated whole, and to safeguard against misconstruction." The Act itself is law in the 49 states that have adopted the Code, but the comments are not since they have not been enacted by the legislatures.[6] The comments have, however, proved valuable. The courts have repeatedly turned to them in resolving issues. Of course, if the Code and a comment are in conflict, the Code must prevail.

The contract provisions of Article 2 of the Code make many changes in traditional contract law with the result that very often there is a different rule for "contracts for sale" than for other contracts such as for labor, services and the sale of land.[7] The Code does not change all the traditional rules; where it is silent, the traditional rules prevail even as to contracts for sale.[8] As indicated above,[9] there is a marked tendency to employ the Code by analogy, to transactions outside its coverage. In addition, the Restatement (Second) has recast many of the provisions of the original Restatement to harmonize them with the Code. The foreseeable result is that in future decades the principles underlying the

---

3. The term "goods" is defined in § 2–105, with a cross reference to § 2–107. This definition is discussed in § 19.16 infra.

4. See 1 Corbin § 1.22 (Perillo 1993) ("The Uniform Commercial Code as a Source of Common Law").

5. Vitex Mfg. Corp. v. Caribtex Corp., 377 F.2d 795, 799 (3d Cir.1967); see also Deisch v. Jay, 790 P.2d 1273 (Wyo.1990).

6. See Miller v. Preitz, 422 Pa. 383, 221 A.2d 320 (1966).

7. The result of having two sets of contract rules has been criticized. Williston,

The Law of Sales in the Proposed Uniform Commercial Code, 63 Harv.L.Rev. 561, 576 (1950); but see Corbin, The Uniform Commercial Code—Sales; Should it be enacted? 59 Yale L.J. 821 (1950).

8. UCC § 1–103 (2002 revision § 1–103(b)); see Jenkins, Preemption & Supplementation Under Revised 1–103: The Role of the Common Law and Equity in the New U.C.C., 54 SMU L.Rev. 495 (2001).

9. See note 4 supra.

contract provisions of Article 2 will be the law of the land even for contracts not governed by the Code.

As this edition of the text is being written, a revision of Article 2 of the UCC has been drafted. This textbook will cite many provisions of the revision draft. By the time this book is in print, the draft will probably have received final approval by the American Law Institute. Such approval will not transmute the draft into law. Before it is the law of a given state, it must be enacted by its legislature and signed by its governor. If it is not approved by the American Law Institute, it will probably be sent back to the drafters for revision. If that happens, readers can find the latest draft on the internet.[10] Thus, the current Article 2 will remain in effect for a considerable time. Indeed, the revision draft may never be enacted. The much shorter Article 1 of the Code has received approval by both the American Law Institute and the National Conference of Commissioners on Uniform State Law, but is not likely to be adopted by the legislatures separately from a revised Article 2. Article 1 has general provisions that are applicable to all other articles of the UCC.

Article 2 of the UCC Code governs contracts for the sale of goods, whether the seller is a merchant or a casual seller. However, some of its provisions treat merchants differently. The Code defines a merchant, as paraphrased in a leading case,[11] as follows:

> [A] person is a "merchant" if he (1) deals in goods of the kind, or (2) by his occupation holds himself out as having knowledge or skill peculiar to the *practices* involved in the transaction, or (3) by his occupation holds himself out as having knowledge or skill peculiar to the *goods* involved in the transaction, or (4) employs an intermediary who by his occupation holds himself out as having such knowledge or skill, and that knowledge or skill may be attributed to the person whose status is in question.

Despite the clarity of this definition, there are many borderline situations. For example, the courts are divided on the question of whether a farmer who sells a crop once a year is a merchant or a "casual seller." Contrary to the use of the term "merchant" in everyday speech, an interstate trucking company is a merchant in regards to its purchases of diesel oil.[12]

Frequently, a contract has a mixture of elements—goods are transferred but services predominate. Perhaps the thrust of an agreement may be the settlement of a dispute with the incidental transfer of goods.

---

10. Drafts are available at: <http://www.law.upenn.edu/library/ulc/ulc.htm>

11. Nelson v. Union Equity Co-op. Exch., 548 S.W.2d 352, 355, 95 ALR3d 471 (Tex.1977). See Smith v. General Mills, 291 Mont. 426, 968 P.2d 723 (1998) (farmer's agent is a merchant);. Harvest States Co-ops v. Anderson, 217 Wis.2d 154, 577 N.W.2d 381 (App.1998) (inexperienced farmer not a merchant); Dolan, 1977 Wash. U.L.Q. 1. Revision draft § 2–104(1) has substantially the same definition.

12. Ready Trucking v. BP, 248 Ga.App. 701, 548 S.E.2d 420 (2001).

In determining whether the UCC applies, most courts look to the predominant purpose or predominant factor of the agreement.[13]

Article 9, which is discussed in Chapter 18, has undergone a number of revisions. In 1999 a major revision of the Article was approved by the American Law Institute and the National Conference of Commissioners on Uniform State Law. Enactment by the states has been unusually prompt. To the extent relevant to the topic of this book, both the 1999 revision and the earlier text are discussed in Chapter 18.

Two international documents deserve mention. On October 9, 1986, the United States Senate, at the request of the President, consented to his ratification of the United Nations Convention on Contracts for the International Sale of Goods (CISG). Reference will be made to this Convention from time to time in this text. It governs many transactions for the sale of goods where the parties have places of business in different countries.[14] Many other major trading nations have also ratified it. The main exceptions are Japan and the United Kingdom. A companion document that does not have the force of law is the UNIDROIT Principles of International Commercial Contracts. It is broader in scope than CISG, but its legal effect is comparable to that of a Restatement. Neither of these documents will be covered in any detail in this text.

§ 1.8   Classification of Contracts

Contracts have been classified and distinguished in various ways for different purposes. Some of these classifications will be discussed here briefly.

(a) Formal and Informal Contracts

The distinction between formal and informal contracts is based on the method of the formation of the contract. Under the early common law a promise was not binding unless accompanied by certain formalities.[1] Three kinds of formal contracts are still important: (1) contracts under seal;[2] (2) recognizances;[3] and (3) negotiable instruments and letters of credit.[4]

---

13. Ogden Martin Systems of Indianapolis, Inc. v. Whiting Corp., 179 F.3d 523 (7th Cir.1999); Annot., 4 ALR4th 85.

14. For detailed treatment of CISG, see Jon O. Honnold, Uniform Law for International Sales Under the 1980 United Nations Convention (2d ed. 1991). Further data is available at <www.cisg.law.pace.edu>. Another database is the loose-leaf volume "Unilex."

§ 1.8

1. See Hazeltine, The Formal Contract of Early English Law, 10 Colum.L.Rev. 608 (1910), Selected Readings 1 (1931).

2. The seal has lost all or some of its effect in many jurisdictions. See ch. 7 infra.

3. A recognizance is made when the recognizor acknowledges in open court a duty to make a certain payment unless a specified condition is performed. Rs. 2d § 6 cmt c. Recognizances are discussed in 76 C.J.S. 73–104 (1952). In the federal court system, they are known as "personal appearance bonds." 18 U.S.C.A. § 3142(b).

4. Negotiable instruments and letters of credit are treated in specialized works. These are governed by Articles 3 and 5 of the UCC.

All other kinds of contracts are considered to be informal and are enforceable not because of the form of the transactions but because of their substance. Such contracts have also been called "simple" or "parol" contracts.

The historical usage is valuable only for understanding older cases and texts. Today, "formal contract" is a term in everyday usage that has no precise meaning. In common parlance, a "formal contract" would be understood to be a contract in writing, signed by an authorized officer of the party whose commitment is in question.

(b) Void, Voidable and Unenforceable Contracts

When a promisee is entitled to either a money judgment,[5] an injunction or specific performance[6] because of a breach, the contract is said to be enforceable.

A contract is void, a contradiction in terms, when it produces no legal obligation upon the part of a promisor. For example, an exchange of promises which lacks consideration is frequently said to be a void contract.[7] It would be more exact to say that no contract has been created.

A contract is voidable if one or more of the parties has the power to elect to avoid the legal relations created by the contract or by ratification to extinguish the power of avoidance. This power to avoid or ratify is sometimes given to an infant contracting party and to persons who have been induced to enter contracts by fraud, mistake or duress.[8]

Unenforceable contracts are those which have some legal consequences but which may not be enforced in an action for damages or specific performance in the face of certain defenses such as the Statute of Frauds and the statute of limitations. Certain contracts which are tainted by illegality but are neither wholly void nor voidable may also be classified as unenforceable,[9] as can be contracts with those governmental units which still retain a doctrine of sovereign immunity.[10] Unenforceable contracts share many of the features of voidable contracts, the main difference being that unenforceable contracts have a variety of legal consequences that voidable contracts do not share, including various methods of indirect enforcement.[11]

(c) Express and Implied Contracts—Quasi Contracts

When the parties manifest their agreement by words the contract is said to be express. When it is manifested by conduct it is said to be

---

5. A money judgment may be based on either the remedy of damages or of restitution, or both. See chs. 14, 15 infra.

  6. See ch. 16 infra.

  7. See ch. 4 infra.

  8. See ch. 9 infra.

  9. Rs. 2d § 8 cmt b.

10. Rs. 2d § 8 cmt c.

11. Rs. 2d § 8 ills. 2, 3, 4, 5; Corbin, Offer and Acceptance, and Some of the Resulting Legal Relations, 26 Yale L.J. 169, 179–181 (1917), Selected Readings 170, 178–77.

implied in fact.[12] If A telephones a plumber to come to A's house to fix a broken pipe, it may be inferred that A has agreed to pay the plumber a reasonable fee for the plumber's services although the parties did not talk about compensation. The contract is partly express and partly implied in fact. There are cases of contracts wholly implied in fact.[13] The distinction between this kind of contract and a contract expressed in words is unimportant: both are true contracts formed by a mutual manifestation of assent.[14]

A contract implied in law is not a contract at all but an obligation imposed by law to do justice even though it is clear that no promise was ever made or intended.[15] To illustrate, if a physician gives a child necessary medical care in the face of parental neglect, the physician may recover from the parents, in quasi contract, the value of the medical services.[16] There is nothing contractual about this at all. The quasi-contractual label arose from a procedural quirk. Since in the earlier law there was no writ for an obligation of this kind, courts permitted the use of the contractual writ of assumpsit and allowed the plaintiff to plead a fictitious promise. The crux is that a quasi contract is not a peculiar brand of contract. It is a non-contractual obligation that used to be treated procedurally as if it were a contract. The principal function of quasi contract is generally said to be that of prevention of unjust enrichment.[17]

Very often, however, quasi-contractual remedies are employed in contractual contexts. When the parties negotiate an agreement which fails because the subject matter is too indefinite, or because the agent for one of the parties had no power to bind the principal, or the parties each had a different reasonable understanding of the agreement, or because the agreement is illegal, it is the law of quasi contracts that is looked to for a determination of to what extent any performance rendered under the agreement, or other acts in reliance on the agreement, are to be compensated. Similarly, when a contract is made and avoided for incapacity, mistake, fraud, or duress or is unenforceable for non-conformity with form requirements, or discharged for impossibility or frustration, quasi contract is the body of law to which we look for the reallocation of gains and losses between the parties. It should be noticed that in the illustration given in the preceding paragraph, the law of quasi contract is the exclusive source of the plaintiff's rights and remedies. In the illustrations given in this paragraph any recovery is based on the interplay of rules of contract and quasi contract. When there is no agreement

12. Erickson v. Goodell Oil Co., 384 Mich. 207, 180 N.W.2d 798 (1970).

13. E.g., Day v. Caton, 119 Mass. 513 (1876).

14. Elias v. Elias, 428 Pa. 159, 237 A.2d 215 (1968); Bailey v. West, 105 R.I. 61, 249 A.2d 414 (1969).

15. Bradkin v. Leverton, 26 N.Y.2d 192, 309 N.Y.S.2d 192, 257 N.E.2d 643 (1970).

16. Greenspan v. Slate, 12 N.J. 426, 97 A.2d 390 (1953), noted in 39 Cornell L.Q.

337 (1954). It is only in very limited circumstances that a person can impose liability on another by volunteering services. See, e.g., Dailing v. Hall, 1 S.W.3d 490 (Mo.App. 1999) (landowner could not recover from neighbor for replacing a fence they owned in common).

17. Restatement, Restitution § 1 (1937).

between the parties, the basis of the plaintiff's recovery is the unjust enrichment of the defendant and the amount of recovery is measured on that basis. When there is an agreement which has failed from the start or because of subsequent avoidance or discharge, unjust enrichment, unjust impoverishment, relative fault, the allocation of risks in the failed agreement, and fairness of alternative risk allocations are all factors that go into the measure of recovery.[18]

18. See Perillo, Restitution in a Contractual Context, 73 Colum.L.Rev. 1208 (1973).

Chapter 2

OFFER AND ACCEPTANCE

Table of Sections

Table of Sections

A. INTENT TO CONTRACT

A. INTENT TO CONTRACT

Table of Sections

§ 2.1 Mutual Assent

Usually an essential prerequisite to the formation of a contract is an agreement: a mutual manifestation of assent to the same terms.[1] Ordinarily, this mutual assent is established by a process of offer and acceptance.[2] It is possible, however, to have mutual assent even though it is impossible to identify the "offer" and the "acceptance."[3] Thus if A and B are together and C suggests the terms of an agreement for them, there would be a contract without any process of offer and acceptance if A and B simultaneously agreed to these terms.[4]

Frequently, especially in transactions of considerable magnitude, the parties negotiate the terms of a proposed written contract. Then a final draft is typed or printed. The contract may be formed when the copies of the writing are signed and exchanged.[5] Again, neither an offer nor an acceptance can be identified in this circumstance. However, even in cases where the offer and acceptance cannot be identified, the conceptual model of offer and acceptance may be a helpful analytical tool.[6]

§ 2.2 Objective and Subjective Assent and Intent

A debate has raged as to whether the assent of the parties should be actual mental assent so that there is a "meeting of the minds"[1] or

---

§ 2.1

1. Russell v. Union Oil, 7 Cal.App.3d 110, 86 Cal.Rptr. 424 (1970); Quality Sheet Metal v. Woods, 2 Haw. App. 160, 627 P.2d 1128 (1981); Brown v. Considine, 108 Mich. App. 504, 310 N.W.2d 441 (1981); Christenson v. Billings Livestock Comm'n, 201 Mont. 207, 653 P.2d 492 (1982).

2. Dura–Wood Treating v. Century Forest Indus., 675 F.2d 745 (5th Cir.1982), cert. denied; Hahnemann Medical College & Hosp. v. Hubbard, 267 Pa.Super. 436, 406 A.2d 1120 (1979); Eisenberg v. Continental Cas., 48 Wis.2d 637, 180 N.W.2d 726 (1970).

3. Rs. 2d § 22 cmt a.

4. 1 Corbin § 1.12 (Perillo 1993).

5. Ibid. Contract obligations may, however, attach at an earlier stage. See § 2.8 infra.

6. See, for example, the problem of identical cross offers in § 2.11 infra. For an economic analysis of contract formation, see Katz, The Strategic Structure of Offer and Acceptance: Game Theory and the Law of Contract Formation, 89 Mich.L.Rev 215 (1990).

§ 2.2

1. Williston, Mutual Assent In the Formation of Contracts, in Selected Readings

whether assent should be determined solely from objective manifestations of intent—namely what a party says and does rather than what a party subjectively intends or believes or assumes.[2] The early common law had rigorously adopted an objective theory, but for a time in the early and mid-nineteenth century it flirted with a subjective theory. There were few consequences stemming from this change. When, however, the rules of evidence were changed in the mid-nineteenth century to allow parties to testify on their own behalf, the courts quickly retreated back to an objective approach.[3]

For more than a century the objective theory of contracts has been dominant.[4] Under this theory the mental intentions of the parties are irrelevant.[5] Still, even under the objective theory, the acts manifesting assent must be done either intentionally or negligently.[6] At the turn of the twenty-first century, although the objective theory still dominates, subjective elements are more freely considered.[7] We shall point out from time to time where such elements are relevant.

Another portion of the objectivists' credo is that objective manifestations of intent of the party should generally be viewed from the vantage point of a reasonable person in the position of the other party.[8] The phrase "in the position of the other party" means that the other party is charged not only with the knowledge of a reasonable person but also with what that party knows or should know because of that party's superior knowledge.[9] This will become clearer in the section that follows.

On the Law of Contracts 119 (1931). However even this theory requires that there be external acts indicating assent. Restatement of Contracts § 20 (1932). This is true in France where the subjective theory dominates thinking about contract. See 2 Formation of Contracts: A Study of the Common Core of Legal Systems 1316–19 (R. Schlesinger ed. 1968); Chloros, Comparative Aspects of the Intention to Create Legal Relations in Contract, 33 Tul.L.Rev. 607, 613–17 (1959).

2. See Williston, Freedom of Contract, 6 Cornell L.Q. 365 (1921), Selected Readings 100 (1931). The objective theory was reinforced by writings of Paley, the moral philosopher, and is referred to in nineteenth century cases as "Dr. Paley's Law." See Palmer, The Effect of Misunderstanding, 65 Mich.L.Rev. 33, 44–47 (1966). See also Ricketts v. Pennsylvania R.R., 153 F.2d 757, 761 n. 2 (2d Cir.1946); 2 Parsons on Contracts *498 n.(p) (9th ed. 1904).

3. See Perillo, The Origins of the Objective Theory of Contract Formation and Interpretation, 69 Fordham L.Rev. 427 (2000).

4. Judge Learned Hand stated the objective approach as follows, "A contract has,

strictly speaking, nothing to do with the personal, or individual, intent of the parties. A contract is an obligation attached by mere force of law to certain acts of the parties, usually words, which ordinarily accompany and represent a known intent." Hotchkiss v. National City Bank, 200 F. 287, 293 (S.D.N.Y.1911).

5. Fairway Center v. U.I.P., 502 F.2d 1135 (8th Cir.1974); Blackhawk Heating & Plumbing v. Data Lease Fin., 302 So.2d 404 (Fla.1974).

6. Whittier, 17 Calif.L.Rev. 441, 447–48 (1929). To act intentionally means to act with the intent to do the acts and not necessarily to desire the consequences.

7. The dialectic tension between objective and subjective elements in contract law is described in DiMatteo, Contract Theory: The Evolution of Contractual Intent (1998).

8. Ricketts v. Pennsylvania R.R., 153 F.2d 757, 760–61, 164 ALR 387 (2d Cir. 1946) (Frank, J., concurring opinion).

9. Sands v. Sands, 252 Md. 137, 249 A.2d 187 (1969); Embry v. Hargadine, McKittrick Dry Goods, 127 Mo.App. 383, 105 S.W. 777 (1907).

The same basic objective approach is taken in the United Nations Sales Convention.[10]

There are other versions of the objective approach[11] and even some more modern subjective approaches. These will be discussed in Chapter 3. In the meantime the approach outlined above will serve as an acceptable tentative test. A party's intention will be held to be what a reasonable person in the position of the other party would conclude the manifestation to mean.

§ 2.3 Must the Parties Be Serious?

If Pam and Dan enter into what appears to be a contract, but Dan asserts and proves that he was joking, would there be an enforceable contract? Under the subjective approach discussed in the preceding section, the answer would be, no. Under the tentative test proposed in the preceding section, the issue would be whether a reasonable person in the position of Pam would conclude from Dan's manifestations that Dan was serious. This, as we shall see, is ordinarily a question of fact.[1]

Under this test, if it is determined that Dan did not appear serious, there is no contract because Dan has in fact manifested an intention not to be bound by the apparent agreement.[2] If a reasonable person would conclude that Dan was serious, there is a contract unless Pam knows or should know Dan is not serious.[3] For example, if Dan appears to be serious to a reasonable bystander, there could still be no contract if Pam and Dan had joked about the matter under discussion many times before.[4] In that case Pam would be charged with superior knowledge of Dan's intent not to contract.[5]

If a purely objective theory were followed, Dan would not be permitted to testify that he was not serious but could only point to words and conduct that showed that he was not serious. Since the test is partially subjective, Dan would be permitted to testify that he was not serious because, if Pam knew or should have known that he was joking, there would be no contract.

The same rules would apply if Dan were to claim that he was not serious because he was angry or excited,[6] or because the entire matter

---

10. CISG Art. 8.

11. Chief among them is "Dr. Paley's law" pursuant to which the test is "the sense in which the person making the promise believed the other party to have accepted it." Weinstein v. Sheer, 98 N.J.L. 511, 120 A. 679, 680 (1923) (quoting 2 Kent, Commentaries on American Law 557).

§ 2.3

1. See § 2.7 infra.

2. Davis v. Davis, 119 Conn. 194, 175 A. 574 (1934); McClurg v. Terry, 21 N.J.Eq. 225 (1870).

3. Mears v. Nationwide Mut. Ins., 91 F.3d 1118 (8th Cir.1996); Lucy v. Zehmer, 196 Va. 493, 84 S.E.2d 516 (1954); Plate v. Durst, 42 W.Va. 63, 24 S.E. 580 (1896); 1 Corbin § 2.13 (Perillo 1993); 1 Williston § 3:5.

4. Smith v. Richardson, 31 Ky.L.R. 1082, 104 S.W. 705 (1907).

5. See § 2.2 supra.

6. Higgins v. Lessig, 49 Ill.App. 459 (1893).

was intended as a "frolic and banter."[7] Similarly, a unilateral intention not to be bound does not deprive the agreement of binding effect.[8] Very often, as indicated above, these issues are questions of fact rather than questions of law.[9]

§ 2.4 Must the Parties Intend to Be Bound?

The parties to a contract need not manifest an intent to be bound or think about any legal consequences that might flow from their agreement.[1] This is a sound rule because parties at the time of contracting rarely think about these matters or discuss them. Professor Corbin points out that if two ignorant persons agreed to exchange a horse for a cow there would be a contract even if the parties were unaware that society offers remedies for the breach of such an agreement.[2] This rule is consistent with the rule that mistake as to a rule of law does not necessarily deprive an agreement of legal effect.[3] The same result can be reached by employing the reasonable person test because "a normally constituted person" would know, however dimly, that legal sanctions exist.[4]

However, if, from the statements or conduct of the parties or the surrounding circumstances, it appears that the parties do not intend to be bound or do not intend legal consequences, then, under the great majority of the cases, there is no contract.[5] Under the classical rule, where the parties enter into an agreement regulating commercial relations but further agree that the agreement is to create no legal obligation, the agreement is not binding.[6]

There is, however, a strong current holding that, when the parties have acted under the agreement and it is unfair not to enforce the

---

7. Keller v. Holderman, 11 Mich. 248 (1863). See also Graves v. Northern N.Y. Pub., 260 A.D. 900, 22 N.Y.S.2d 537 (1940), app. dismissed.

8. "Contracts can be dangerous to one's well-being. That is why they are kept away from children. Perhaps warning labels should be attached * * *. Dr. Layton's comment that she considered the agreement a sham and never intended to be bound by it shows that she did not take it seriously. That is regrettable." Posik v. Layton, 695 So.2d 759, 763 (Fla.App.1997).

9. Theiss v. Weiss, 166 Pa. 9, 31 A. 63 (1895); Chiles v. Good, 41 S.W.2d 738 (Tex. Civ.App.1931), reversed on other grounds. On the distinction between questions of law and questions of fact, see § 2.7 infra.

§ 2.4

1. 1 Corbin § 2.13 (Perillo 1993); 1 Williston § 3:5; Rs. 2d § 21.

2. 1 Corbin § 2.13 (Perillo 1993).

3. Rs. 2d § 21 cmt a; see § 9.28 infra.

4. New York Trust v. Island Oil & Transport, 34 F.2d 655 (2d Cir.1929).

5. U.S. v. Aetna Cas. & Sur., 480 F.2d 1095 (8th Cir.1973); Nice Ball Bearing v. Bearing Jobbers, 205 F.2d 841 (7th Cir. 1953), cert. denied; New York Trust v. Island Oil Transport, 34 F.2d 655 (2d Cir. 1929); contra, 9 J. Wigmore, Evidence § 2406 (3d ed.1940). There have been cases where the sham arrangement has been enforced against a promisor by a third party on a theory of promissory estoppel. D'Oench, Duhme v. FDIC, 315 U.S. 447 (1942); Mt. Vernon Trust v. Bergoff, 272 N.Y. 192, 5 N.E.2d 196 (1936). See ch. 6 infra.

6. Smith v. MacDonald, 37 Cal.App. 503, 174 P. 80 (1918); Osgood v. Skinner, 211 Ill. 229, 71 N.E. 869 (1904); McNevin v. Solvay Process, 32 A.D. 610, 53 N.Y.S. 98 (1898), aff'd; Hirschkorn v. Severson, 319 N.W.2d 475 (N.D.1982); Rose & Frank v. J. R. Crompton, [1923] 2 K.B. 261 (C.A.); Annot., 42 ALR2d 461 (1955); Annot., 96 ALR 1093 (1935).

agreement, it should be enforced.[7] Such cases have been explained as instances where "the principle of reimbursing reliance is regarded as overriding the principle of private autonomy."[8] Failure to perform an agreement may result in unjust enrichment of the breaching party, presenting an additional ground for enforcement in contract or quasi contract.[9] Many of these cases have involved pension plans on which employers could reasonably expect employees to rely and which in fact did induce reliance. In addition, enforcement has occurred in bonus and employee death benefit cases.[10] Under the classical rule, no protection is available to an employee where the agreement explicitly states that it is non-contractual. This is one of the abuses the Pension Reform Act of 1974 has curtailed.[11]

The intent not to be bound or to intend legal consequences need not be explicitly stated; it may be inferred from the circumstances. Thus, if B accepts A's invitation to dinner and arrives at A's house at the appointed time and A is not there, B would not have a cause of action because it is a reasonable factual presumption that the parties intended that only a social obligation should result.[12] The inference is that the parties did not intend legal consequences with the result that the agreement is not binding. The result would be different if the parties had manifested an intent to be bound.

The same presumption that the parties do not intend to be bound exists when a husband and wife live together amicably and make an agreement with respect to a housekeeping allowance.[13] In this case, even if the parties expressly state that they intend legal consequences, there

---

7. Greene v. Howard Univ., 412 F.2d 1128 (D.C.Cir.1969); Tilbert v. Eagle Lock, 116 Conn. 357, 165 A. 205 (1933); Mabley & Carew v. Borden, 129 Ohio St. 375, 195 N.E. 697 (1935). See § 6.3(e) infra.

8. Fuller, Consideration and Form, 41 Colum.L.Rev. 799, 811 n. 16 (1941). Most of the cases, however, do not articulate their rationale in these terms, but use the fact of reliance as a predicate for often strained interpretation. In addition to the cases cited in the prior note, see Novack v. Bilnor Corp., 26 A.D.2d 572, 271 N.Y.S.2d 117 (1966). See also Fridman, Freedom of Contract, 2 Ottawa L.Rev. 1, 5–6 (1967) ("the parties are free to 'agree' without contracting, but only to the extent to which the courts permit them to do so. The courts could decide that their language or intentions did not have the effect of rendering the law of contract inapplicable.")

9. Cf. Schott v. Westinghouse Elec., 436 Pa. 279, 259 A.2d 443, 40 ALR3d 1404 (1969), 74 Dick.L.Rev. 798 (1970), 31 U.Pitt.L.Rev. 742 (1970). Other doctrines may also come into play. Rs. 2d § 21 cmt b.

10. See Annot., 28 ALR3d (1969); Annot., 42 ALR2d 461 (1955); § 6.3 infra.

11. Employee Retirement Income Security Act of 1974 § 2(c), 29 U.S.C.A. § 1101 et seq.

12. Mitzel v. Hauck, 78 S.D. 543, 105 N.W.2d 378 (1960). Absence of contractual intention will also be assumed when a candidate for public office makes preelection promises to the electorate. O'Reilly v. Mitchel, 85 Misc. 176, 148 N.Y.S. 88 (1914) (candidate for mayor promised not to change Civil Service Law). If contractual intention existed in such a case, however, the agreement so formed would doubtless be void on grounds of public policy. The Jewish marriage agreement known as the Ketubah creates no legal obligations; it is understood by modern participants to be a symbolic ritual rather than a contract. In re White's Estate, 78 Misc.2d 157, 356 N.Y.S.2d 208 (1974).

13. Balfour v. Balfour [1919] 2 K.B. 571 (C.A.). Separation agreements (where the parties are not living in amity) are ordinarily enforceable. Lacks v. Lacks, 12 N.Y.2d 268, 238 N.Y.S.2d 949, 189 N.E.2d 487 (1963).

are still questions of public policy to be considered. Many courts have refused to enforce such an agreement on the grounds that the courts would be flooded by such actions, or that the suits would interfere with family harmony, or that the agreements are unfair because changed circumstances may require a greater or lesser allowance. Indeed, the major vice of this sort of agreement is that frequently the economically dependent spouse agrees to surrender the legal right to maintenance during the marriage and, if the marriage ends in divorce, to alimony. Some jurisdictions have dealt with these questions by statute and others, by case law, and are developing flexible guidelines to enforce such agreements when they are fair and reasonable.[14]

Other kinds of cases can be discussed under this heading. If A promises B a gift, A's promise, absent further facts, is not binding. Courts in England tend to consider such cases to be based on the absence of contractual intent, while American cases have generally analyzed such cases in terms of the absence of consideration.

B.   OFFER

Table of Sections

§ 2.5   What Is an Offer?—Its Legal Effect

An offer, with minor exceptions discussed below, is a promise to do or refrain from doing some specified thing in the future conditioned on the other party's acceptance. A promise has been defined as "a manifestation of intent to act or refrain from acting in a specified way, so made as to justify a promisee in understanding that a commitment has been made."[1] An offer has also been defined as an assurance that a thing will

---

14. See, e.g., McKinney's N.Y. Dom. Rel.L. § 236(b); see generally H. Clark, Domestic Relations § 1.1 (2d ed. 1988).

§ 2.5

1. Rs. 2d § 2; accord, Day v. Amax, 701 F.2d 1258 (8th Cir.1983). To the effect that

an unaccepted offer is not a promise as that term is used in modern speech theory, see Tiersma, Reassessing Unilateral Contracts, 26 U.C.Davis L.Rev. 1 (1992).

or will not be done.[2] The promisor need not promise action on his or her part. "An assurance that it will rain tomorrow, or that a third person shall paint a picture" may be a promise.[3]

While the First Restatement included the word "promise" in its definition of offer, the Restatement (Second) does not, defining an offer as "a manifestation of willingness to enter into a bargain so made as to justify another person in understanding that * * * assent to that bargain is invited and will conclude it."[4] Apparently the reason that the Restatement (Second)'s definition of "offer" does not include the word "promise" is that it intends to include within the definition an offer to an executed sale or barter where no promise is made by the offeror or the offeree.[5] For example, assume that A says to B, "my car which is in your possession is yours if you pay me $4,000." If B pays the $4,000 there is an acceptance of the offer and a complete exchange without any promise being made. This situation should be compared with what is described below as a "reverse unilateral contract" another situation where the offeror does not make a promise; the offeree promises.[6]

One analyst, concludes that the omission of the word promise in the UCC is of great significance,[7] emphasizing that the Code instead stresses the word "agreement" and defines it as "the bargain of the parties in fact as found in their language or by implication from other circumstances including course of dealing or usage of trade or course of performance as provided in this Act * * *."[8] It is difficult to see how this definition undermines the importance of promise in determining the existence of an offer.[9]

Once it is decided that a party has made an offer; it follows that the offer invites an acceptance. An offer empowers the offeree to create a contract by accepting the offer.[10] The typical offer *is* promissory in character. The acceptance of a promissory offer transforms the offeror's promise into a contract[11] unless there is some other impediment to the existence of a contract.

---

2. Bowman v. Hill, 45 N.C.App. 116, 262 S.E.2d 376 (1980).

3. Holmes, The Common Law 298 (1881); see CBS v. Ziff–Davis, 75 N.Y.2d 496, 554 N.Y.S.2d 449, 553 N.E.2d 997, 7 ALR5th 1154 (1990) (warranty as a promise); Jay–Martin Sys. v. Ogilvy Group, 293 A.D.2d 410, 741 N.Y.S.2d 215 (2002) (service of named computer technician); Griffin–Amiel v. Frank Terris Orchestras, 178 Misc.2d 71, 677 N.Y.S.2d 908 (1998) (promise of a particular wedding singer); 1 Corbin § 1.14 (Perillo 1993).

4. Rs. 2d § 24.

5. Rs. 2d § 24 cmt a.

6. See § 2.10 infra.

7. Mooney, Old Kontract Principles and Karl's New Kode, 11 Vill.L.Rev. 213 (1966).

8. A synthesis of the Code's definition of contract and agreement is: Contract means the total obligation which results from the bargains of the parties in fact as found in their language or by implication from other circumstances as affected by rules of law. (UCC §§ 1–201(11), 1–201(3)). These are substantially unchanged in the revision.

9. See also Barndt, The Possible Words of Promise, 45 Tex.L.Rev. 44 (1966) (there cannot be a contract unless there is a promise). See also Sharp, Promissory Liability, 7 U.Chi.L.Rev. 1 (1939).

10. League Gen. Ins. v. Tvedt, 317 N.W.2d 40 (Minn.1982).

11. Philadelphia Newspapers v. Commonwealth Unemp. Comp. Bd. of Rev., 57 Pa.Cmwlth. 639, 426 A.2d 1289 (1981).

§ 2.6   Offers Distinguished From Statements That Are Not Offers

(a) Introduction

There are a number of kinds of expressions that border on, but are not, promises. To help distinguish among these expressions, the discussion will be subdivided into several somewhat arbitrary categories.

(b) Expressions of Opinion and Predictions

Because an expression of an opinion is not a promise it follows that it is not an offer. This distinction is often crucial, as illustrated by statements made by a physician in the doctor-patient relationship. It is generally held that a doctor is not liable in contract for breach of an implied promise to possess skill commensurate to that possessed by colleagues in similar localities. For a failure to live up to that standard it has generally been held that the patient is limited to a tort action for negligence, commonly known as malpractice.[1]

A physician, however, is free to enter into a binding express contract.[2] Thus, courts have held a physician liable for breach of a promise to cure,[3] or obtain a specified result,[4] or administer a prescribed treatment.[5] There is a minority view that such actions are contrary to public policy because they encourage the practice of defensive medicine and discourage a physician from reassuring the patient.[6] There are also a few cases requiring that as a condition to such an action, defendant's promise be supported by a consideration other than payment for services rendered.[7]

The issue in most cases is whether the doctor made a promise or merely stated an opinion or tried to buoy up the patient's spirits by uttering therapeutic words of confidence. How does one distinguish between the latter two situations and a promise? The cases are difficult to reconcile[8] and have been described as a "legal thicket."[9] For the most part the courts have held that the question is one of fact—the reasonable person test is employed.[10]

§ 2.6

1. Note, 24 De Paul L.Rev. 212, 214 (1974); Note, 54 N.C.L.Rev. 885, 887 (1976).

2. Note, 50 Ind.L.J. 361 (1975).

3. Hawkins v. McGee, 84 N.H. 114, 146 A. 641 (1929) (defendant guaranteed to make the hand one hundred percent perfect). But in the same case a statement that the patient would go back to work in a few days with a good hand was deemed to be an opinion.

4. Sullivan v. O'Connor, 363 Mass. 579, 296 N.E.2d 183, 99 ALR3d 294 (1973) (defendant promised to make plaintiff more beautiful).

5. Stewart v. Rudner, 349 Mich. 459, 84 N.W.2d 816 (1957) (defendant promised to perform a Caesarian section).

6. See Annot., 43 ALR3d 1221 (1972).

7. See, e.g., Gault v. Sideman, 42 Ill. App.2d 96, 191 N.E.2d 436 (1963); but see Cirafici v. Goffen, 85 Ill.App.3d 1102, 41 Ill.Dec. 135, 407 N.E.2d 633, 11 ALR4th 740 (1980).

8. De Paul Note, supra note 1, at 214–16.

9. N.C. Note, supra note 1, at 888.

10. See §§ 2.2 supra and 2.7 infra.

In determining the question of fact it is important to take into account not only what was said, but also the surrounding circumstances. For example, during an emergency situation it is less likely that the doctor's words should be taken as a promise. One case has tried to balance the competing views by stating that the action is a "little suspect" and therefore "clear proof" should be required. The case also suggests that the jury should be instructed that it is unlikely that a physician will make such a promise and that an optimistic statement of encouragement should not be taken as a promise when it is intended only as a therapeutic building of confidence.[11] At least one state has made such a promise subject to the writing or electronic record requirements of the Statute of Frauds.[12]

While the discussion has focused on the physician-patient relationship, similar problems confound other relationships; e.g., architect-owner and attorney-client relations. The borderland of contract and tort liability is difficult to map as the terrain is subject to constant shifts.

The issue is has there been a promise to attain a given result or to take specific action. If an attorney makes an express promise to attain a given result, the attorney is liable on the promise,[13] but in the absence of an express promise, no such promise is implied. In a case involving an architect, the court, however, distinguished attorney and physician cases stating: "A person who contracts with an architect or engineer for a building of a certain size and elevation has a right to expect an exact result."[14]

In another type of case the issue is whether the attorney or other professional has made an implied promise to exercise due care or is the liability solely based on the duty imposed by tort law to exercise due care.[15] The concrete concerns in such cases are such matters as the statute of limitations, and the measure of damages. Issues concerning the borderland of contract and tort are generally addressed in works on torts.[16]

At times, the attorney may address a client's creditor, requesting forbearance, using language that, in another context, might be regarded as engaging the attorney's personal credit. Because the attorney has no personal stake in having the obligation paid or in avoiding a law suit, it will not be lightly assumed that such language should be interpreted as a promise.[17] However, when a lawyer who is handling a tort claim, writes

11. Sullivan v. O'Connor, 363 Mass. 579, 296 N.E.2d 183 (1973).

12. See Gilmore v. O'Sullivan, 106 Mich.App. 35, 307 N.W.2d 695 (1981).

13. Jones v. Wadsworth, 791 P.2d 1013 (Alaska 1990).

14. Tamarac Dev. v. Delamater, Freund & Assoc., 234 Kan. 618, 675 P.2d 361, 365 (1984).

15. See Collins v. Reynard, 154 Ill.2d 48, 607 N.E.2d 1185, 180 Ill.Dec. 672 (1992) (attorney malpractice action can be brought as a tort or contract action or both). See Davis, The Illusive Warranty of Workmanlike Performance: Constructing a Conceptual Framework, 72 Neb.L.Rev. 981 (1983).

16. See Prosser & Keeton on Torts § 92 (5th ed.1984); Schlechtriem, The Borderland of Tort and Contract—Opening a New Frontier, 21 Cornell Int'l L.J. 467 (1988).

17. Sears Boston Emp. Federal Credit Union v. Cummings, 322 Mass. 81, 76 N.E.2d 150 (1947); Sefi Fabricators v. Tillim, 79 Misc.2d 213, 360 N.Y.S.2d 146

to the client's landlord, "if there is a favorable settlement or a verdict herein, I will protect your monies for you for this rent," the language is unmistakably a promise.[18]

In each of these cases the question is whether the defendant made an offer or merely expressed an opinion. Under the tentative standard adopted, this is determined by inquiring whether a reasonable person in the position of the plaintiff would conclude that the defendant made a promise or merely stated an opinion. Sometimes this is a question of law; at other times a question of fact.[19]

(c) Statements of Intention, Hopes and Desires and Estimates

If A says to B, "I'm going to sell my car for $450," and B replies, "Here is $450 I will take it," there is no contract because a reasonable person would conclude that A was stating an intention and made no promise.[20] Similarly, an announcement that an auction will be held is deemed to be a statement of intention,[21] despite the fact that "will" is a word commonly used as a promise. For example, if A says to B: "If you paint my house I will pay $5,000," it is clear that in context the words "I will pay" mean "I promise to pay." However, an internal memorandum from a corporate officer to its accounting department concerning compensation of an employee is not an offer, because an offer requires communication to the offeree.[22]

Businesses frequently sign "letters of intent." These documents are usually understood to be noncommittal statements preliminary to a contract. There is, however, no magic attached to the phrase "letter of intent" and a commitment may be found to have been made.[23] "Because of their susceptibility to unexpected interpretations, it is easy to understand why letters of intent have been characterized by at least one practitioner as 'an invention of the devil.' "[24] Also, in a modern business context, statements of intention to act in a given manner may often be regarded as statements of policy rather than promises.[25]

(1973) ("he is not liable unless he assumed a personal liability in clear and unmistakable language").

18. Scyoc v. Holmes, 192 W.Va. 87, 450 S.E.2d 784 (W.Va.1994).

19. See § 2.7 infra.

20. Cutler–Hammer v. U.S., 441 F.2d 1179 (Ct.Cl.1971); Pappas v. Bever, 219 N.W.2d 720 (Iowa 1974); Forbes v. Wells Beach Casino, 307 A.2d 210 (Me.1973); Pacific Cascade v. Nimmer, 25 Wn.App. 552, 608 P.2d 266 (1980); 1 Corbin § 1.15 (Perillo 1993); 1 Williston § 4:6.

21. Kinmon v. J. P. King Auction, 290 Ala. 323, 276 So.2d 569 (1973); Benjamin v. First Citizens Bank & Trust, 248 A.D. 610, 287 N.Y.S. 947 (1936) (plaintiff's assignor came from South Africa to attend an auction announced to be without reserve which was cancelled); cf. Peters v. Bower, 63 So.2d

629 (Fla.1953) (affidavit of intent to grade streets in a subdivision not binding).

22. Rosi v. Business Furniture, 615 N.E.2d 431 (Ind.1993).

23. Burbach Broadcasting v. Elkins Radio, 278 F.3d 401 (4th Cir.2002); Fru–Con Constr. v. KFX, 153 F.2d 1150 (10th Cir. 1998); Venture Assocs. v. Zenith Data Sys., 987 F.2d 429 (7th Cir.1993); 1 Corbin § 1.16 (Perillo 1993); compare Dunhill Sec. v. Microthermal Applications, 308 F.Supp. 195 (S.D.N.Y.1969) and Garner v. Boyd, 330 F.Supp. 22 (N.D.Tex.1970), aff'd, with Anderson (Arthur) v. Source Equities, 43 A.D.2d 921, 353 N.Y.S.2d 1 (1974).

24. Quake Constr. v. American Airlines, 141 Ill.2d 281, 319, 152 Ill.Dec. 308, 327, 565 N.E.2d 990, 1009 (1990).

25. Beverage Distrib. v. Olympia Brewing, 440 F.2d 21, 29 (9th Cir.1971), cert.

Statements of wishes, hopes, or desires are not promises or offers.[26] Similarly, an estimate is not generally an offer. A reasonable person would conclude that the party who is giving an estimate is not promising to do the job for the price named but thinks that the job can be completed for a sum in that neighborhood.[27] If the person who makes an offer based on an estimated price is asked whether he will agree to do the work at that price, the offeror will often state that a firm price must be higher in order to cover unknown contingencies. It should be clear, however, that the word "estimate" itself is not conclusive because "estimate" in context may be used in the sense of "offer." For example, if the party in response to an invitation to bid says "I estimate" such an amount, this may be deemed to be an offer.[28]

An estimate was held to be binding on a theory of equitable estoppel in U.S. v. Briggs Mfg. Co.[29] Equitable estoppel traditionally requires misrepresentation of *fact*, reliance and injury.[30] The reliance and injury were clear. The estimate was treated as a factual representation apparently because the "estimator" was or claimed to be an expert.[31] Other cases have also given some effect to price estimates.[32]

(d) Inquiry or Invitation to Make an Offer

If A writes to B asking, "Will you sell me your property on Rockledge Drive for $50,000?," this is not an offer but an inquiry. A question is not an offer because it seeks information and does not amount to a commitment. If B replied, "make me an offer," this obviously would be a statement inviting A to make an offer.

The same process is illustrated in the case of Owen v. Tunison.[33] Plaintiff wrote to defendant, "Will you sell me your store property * * * for the sum of $6,000?" This was an inquiry. Defendant answered, "it would not be possible for me to sell it unless I was to receive $16,000 cash." The court held that defendant had not made an offer to sell for $16,000; defendant was really saying, "I will not entertain an offer of less than $16,000." This was merely an invitation to make an offer.[34] A statement by a lender to the effect that it was "willing to discuss a

---

denied ("it is our intention that, if they show the ability and application required to make the business successful under reasonable direction of our organization, they shall have a reasonable amount of the new common stock, which will be issued exclusively to members of our organization." No promise here.); Martens v. Minnesota M. & M., 616 N.W.2d 732 (Minn.2000).

26. Bowman v. Hill, 45 N.C.App. 116, 262 S.E.2d 376 (1980); 1 Corbin § 1.15 (Perillo 1993).

27. Boise Cascade v. Reliance Nat. Indemn., 129 F.Supp.2d 41 (D.Me.2001); Denniston & Partridge v. Mingus, 179 N.W.2d 748 (Iowa 1970); Clark Sanitation v. Sun Valley Disposal, 87 Nev. 338, 487 P.2d 337 (1971).

28. See Parker v. Meneley, 106 Cal. App.2d 391, 235 P.2d 101 (1951); 1 Corbin § 2.2 (Perillo 1993).

29. 460 F.2d 1195 (9th Cir.1972).

30. See §§ 6.2, 11.29 infra.

31. See § 9.17 infra.

32. Hinson–Barr v. Pinckard, 292 S.C. 267, 356 S.E.2d 115 (1987) (invoice substantially higher than the estimate is a material alteration under UCC § 2–207).

33. 131 Me. 42, 158 A. 926 (1932).

34. Accord, Blakeslee v. Nelson, 212 A.D. 219, 207 N.Y.S. 676 (1925), aff'd. This line of reasoning is pursued to an extreme in Bourque v. FDIC, 42 F.3d 704 (1st Cir. 1994).

workout proposal'' along the lines previously discussed is merely an invitation to continue negotiations.[35]

(e) *Advertisements, Catalogs and Circular Letters.*

If a clothing store advertised a well-known brand of suit in the following terms, "nationally advertised at $440, today only at $250," and A came to the store in response to the advertisement, selected a suit and tendered $250, would there be a contract? The answer is, perhaps surprisingly, no.[36] Because the ad has not stated a quantity, and there is no language of commitment, the cases hold that the ad is only a statement of intention to sell or a preliminary proposal inviting offers.

Would the reasonable person so conclude?[37] While it would be onerous to interpret the ad as a commitment to sell an unlimited supply of the product, it could be argued that the merchant was impliedly promising to sell one to a customer or a reasonable number to a customer on a first come, first served basis so long as the supply lasts. Courts tend to use the reasonable person test to resolve cases of first impression which then serve as precedents in later cases. By this process certain hardened categories emerge. The newspaper advertisement cases relating to the sale of goods illustrate this process. Rightly or wrongly, at an early date it was decided[38] and the law is now settled that there is no offer in cases like the illustration just discussed. Consumer protection legislation may not have changed this contract rule. Generally, such legislation provides for administrative redress and is silent as to contract law. However, the expectations engendered by such legislation may affect how the consumer reasonably understands the legal effect of an ad.[39] The advertising rule may have some justification in the thought that a contrary rule would deter the publication of valuable market information. Sellers should have the ability to let it be known what wares they have; buyers should reap the valuable market information that advertisements contain.[40]

It does not follow, however, that an advertisement for the sale of goods never constitutes an offer. Consider the following department store ad: "1 Black Lapin Stole, Beautiful, Worth $139.50 * * * $1.00 FIRST COME FIRST SERVED." The plaintiff was the first in line when the store opened and tendered a dollar. The court held that this ad was

35. Travelers Ins. v. Westridge Mall, 826 F.Supp. 289 (D.Minn.1992), aff'd.

36. See Georgian Co. v. Bloom, 27 Ga. App. 468, 108 S.E. 813 (1921); Steinberg v. Chicago Medical School, 69 Ill.2d 320, 13 Ill.Dec. 699, 371 N.E.2d 634 (1977); O'Keefe v. Lee Calan Imports, 128 Ill.App.2d 410, 262 N.E.2d 758, 43 ALR3d 1097 (1970); Rhen Marshall, Inc. v. Purolator Filter Div., 211 Neb. 306, 318 N.W.2d 284 (1982); Craft v. Elder & Johnston, 38 N.E.2d 416 (Ohio App.1941); Rs. 2d § 26; Annot., 43 ALR3d 1102 (1972).

37. See Eisenberg, Expression Rules in Contract Law and Problems of Offer and Acceptance, 82 Cal. L.Rev. 1127, 1166–72 (1994).

38. Hall v. Kimball, Fed Cas. No. 5,938 (C.C.E.D.Mo.1874) (common understanding).

39. Consumer protection legislation was influential in finding an offer in Donovan v. RRL, 26 Cal.4th 261, 109 Cal.Rptr.2d 807, 27 P.3d 702 (2001).

40. See Klik, Mass Media and Offers to the Public, 36 Am.J.Comp.L. 235 (1988).

an offer.[41] The Restatement (Second) indicates that the basis of the decision is that the words "FIRST COME FIRST SERVED" are promissory, an element ordinarily lacking in advertisements for the sale of goods.[42] In addition, the ad made a statement of quantity (one).[43] "One" is not only a quantity but also a quantity per person. The existence of all of these factors appears to be important. Now suppose the ad had related to ten, rather than one, lapin stoles but listed a price per stole. Would there be an offer if the advertisement did not state the quantity allocated per person? There does not appear to be a ready answer to this question, but this hypothetical is much like the advertisement that has no quantity term.

If an advertiser announces that, "We will pay $100 for each share of the common stock of the XYZ Company tendered to us before July 1," an offer has been made.[44] Here again, there is a quantity, "each share" (every share), and also language of promise ("We will pay"). Note also that the ad calls for action by the offeree.

Another kind of ad is one which promises to pay a fixed sum to anyone who becomes ill from influenza after using a patent medicine. This kind of an ad makes an offer.[45] The problem here is quite different than the ad to sell a suit at a given price; it makes a promise and there is no problem with respect to quantity as in the typical advertisement for the sale of goods.

Even though an advertisement is not an offer, its terms may be tacitly included in a contract that is subsequently entered into by the parties.[46] When the customer makes an offer to purchase, the advertised terms may be an implicit part of the offer.

In the same category as advertisements for the sale of goods are catalogs,[47] circular letters,[48] price lists[49] and articles displayed in a win-

---

41. Lefkowitz v. Great Minneapolis Surplus Store, 251 Minn. 188, 86 N.W.2d 689 (1957).

42. Rs. 2d § 26 ill. 1.

43. An ad for the sale of a specific, unique automobile was held to be an offer in Donovan v. RRL, 26 Cal.4th 261, 109 Cal.Rptr.2d 807, 27 P.3d 702 (2001), but the ensuing contract was voidable because of a mistake in the ad.

44. R.E. Crummer & Co. v. Nuveen, 147 F.2d 3, 157 ALR 739 (7th Cir.1945); Chang v. First Colonial Sav. Bank, 242 Va. 388, 410 S.E.2d 928 (1991) (advertised return on deposit of $14,000).

45. Carlill v. Carbolic Smoke Ball Co., [1893] 1 Q.B. 256 (C.A.1892) (for the full story of the quackery that underlies this case see Simpson, 14 J.Leg.Studies 344 (1985)); accord, Minton v. F.G. Smith Piano, 36 App.D.C. 137 (1911); Whitehead v. Burgess, 61 N.J.L. 75, 38 A. 802 (1897).

46. Steinberg v. Chicago Medical School, 69 Ill.2d 320, 13 Ill.Dec. 699, 371 N.E.2d 634 (1977); Willis v. Allied Insulation, 174 So.2d 858 (La.App.1965); Rinkmasters v. Utica, 75 Misc.2d 941, 348 N.Y.S.2d 940 (City Ct.1973) (applying UCC). In Izadi v. Machado (Gus) Ford, 550 So.2d 1135 (Fla.App.1989), the court found an offer, but the case was really one of tacit incorporation of the terms of the ad.

47. Litton Microwave Cooking Prods. v. Leviton Mfg., 15 F.3d 790 (8th Cir.1994); Schenectady Stove v. Holbrook, 101 N.Y. 45, 4 N.E. 4 (1885).

48. Montgomery Ward & Co. v. Johnson, 209 Mass. 89, 95 N.E. 290 (1911); Moulton v. Kershaw, 59 Wis. 316, 18 N.W. 172 (1884).

49. 1 Corbin § 2.4 (Perillo 1993).

dow with a price tag.[50] But as a result of some exploding bottle cases, the law with respect to a display on a shelf, as for example in a supermarket, has become more complicated. Under the traditional rule such a display is held not to be an offer presumably because there is no language of promise or because no quantity is stated or at least no quantity per person.[51] There is, however, a trend holding that the display of goods in a supermarket does constitute an offer.[52]

These cases are based on the theory that placing the goods on the shelf with a unit price amounts to implied language of promise and that the quantity offered is the quantity on the shelf. But again, the question of how many to a customer must be answered. Under French law the advertisement is deemed to be a conditional offer which may be accepted by any member of the public subject to the offeror's power to reject an unreasonable acceptance.[53] This seems a satisfactory solution.

Professor Murray has suggested an alternative theory to explain the exploding bottle cases: the store display at a stated price should be treated as an irrevocable offer. The customer who removes the goods from the shelf becomes an option holder who exercises the option at the check-out. Meanwhile, while the goods are in the customer's possession, warranty protection attaches to the option.[54] At least one case, outside the bursting bottle context, has held that the display of goods in a self-service store constitutes an offer.[55]

The courts that have found contractual liability in the supermarket cases have stated that the acceptance occurs when the customer places the goods in the shopping cart, subject to the customer's power to terminate the contract before going through the check-out counter. This is strained reasoning; ordinarily an acceptance gives rise to a contract and a contract may not be terminated. Professor Murray's theory is intellectually more satisfactory.

(f) Auction Sales—Who Makes the Offer?

The auctioneer's query, "What am I bid?," is not an offer to sell. The query is merely an invitation for offers to purchase. The auctioneer can accept or reject the bids. The law so decided at an early date.[56] Even

50. Fisher v. Bell, [1960] 3 All E.R. 731.

51. Lasky v. Economy Grocery Stores, 319 Mass. 224, 65 N.E.2d 305, 163 ALR 235 (1946); Day v. Grand Union, 280 A.D. 253, 113 N.Y.S.2d 436 (1952), aff'd; Pharmaceutical Soc'y of Great Britain v. Boots Cash Chemists Ltd. [1953] 1 Q.B. 401.

52. Giant Food v. Washington Coca–Cola Bottling., 273 Md. 592, 332 A.2d 1, 78 ALR3d 682 (1975); Fender v. Colonial Stores, 138 Ga.App. 31, 225 S.E.2d 691, 693–94 (1976); Annot. 78 ALR3d 696 (1977).

53. 1 Formation of Contracts: A Study of the Common Core of Legal Systems 364–65 (R. Schlesinger ed. 1968).

54. Murray on Contracts § 36C (4th ed.); cf. McQuiston v. K–Mart, 796 F.2d 1346 (11th Cir.1986) (customer picked up merchandise for examination; no contract).

55. ProCD v. Zeidenberg, 86 F.3d 1447 (7th Cir.1996) (software).

56. Payne v. Cave, 100 Eng.Rep. 502 (K.B.1789). What is an auction? See Hawaii Jewelers Ass'n v. Fine Arts Gallery, 51 Haw. 502, 463 P.2d 914 (1970); Contreras, The Art Auctioneer, 13 Comm/Ent. L.J. 717 (1991); Gerstenblith, Picture Imperfect, 29 Wm. & Mary L.Rev. 501 (1988).

if the auctioneer announces that the goods will go to the highest bidder the cases generally hold that such a statement does not constitute an offer.[57] While the reasonable unsophisticated person might not understand this, auction-goers as a class understand these auction rules. However, as discussed below, the situation is different if the auction is announced to be "without reserve."[58]

The rules governing auction sales of goods,[59] are incorporated in the UCC[60] which continues the important distinction between auctions "with reserve" and auctions "without reserve." In an auction "with reserve" the bidder is the offeror and a contract is complete when the auctioneer so announces, often by the fall of the hammer.[61] The bidder may withdraw a bid before that time. A bid terminates all prior bids but a bidder's retraction does not revive any prior bids.[62] The auction is deemed to be "with reserve" unless otherwise indicated.[63]

Unusual rules govern auctions announced to be "without reserve." The UCC retains the common law rule that the auctioneer may not withdraw the article from sale after calling for a bid on the article (provided that a bid is received within a reasonable time),[64] but it permits the bidder to withdraw until the article is knocked down.[65] This rule diverges substantially from standard contract principles. It is difficult to identify the offeror. The auctioneer is deemed to have made an irrevocable offer; the bid is a conditional acceptance, subject to no higher bid being made and subject to the bidder's right to withdraw prior to the auctioneer's acceptance of the bid. It has been held that once the reserve price is reached, the rules governing auctions without reserve become applicable and the auctioneer is obligated to inform the bidders that the reserve price, if secret, has been reached.[66] It is doubtful whether this is done with any frequency.

---

57. Miami Aviation Serv. v. Greyhound Leasing & Fin., 856 F.2d 166 (11th Cir. 1988); Specialty Maintenance & Constr. v. Rosen Sys., 790 S.W.2d 835 (Tex.App.1990); Drew v. John Deere, 19 A.D.2d 308, 241 N.Y.S.2d 267 (1963); 1 Corbin § 4.14 (Perillo 1993).

58. To the effect that most participants in auctions are familiar with basic auction customs, see Eisenberg, supra § 2.6 n.37 at 1172–74.

59. There is a tendency to apply these rules in auction sales of real property. Chevalier v. Sanford, 475 A.2d 1148 (Me.1984); Hoffman v. Horton, 212 Va. 565, 186 S.E.2d 79 (1972); 1 Corbin § 1.22 (Perillo 1993) ("The Uniform Commercial Code as a Source of Common Law").

60. UCC § 2–328. The revision makes non-substantive changes.

61. In a judicial sale, the bid remains open until the auctioneer's acceptance is confirmed by the court. Well v. Schoenew-

eis, 101 Ill.App.3d 254, 56 Ill.Dec. 797, 427 N.E.2d 1343 (1981). If the auction is announced to be subject to the approval of the owner, no final sale is completed when the auctioneer accepts the high bid. Lawrence Paper v. Rosen & Co., 939 F.2d 376 (6th Cir.1991); see also Cuba v. Resolution Trust, 849 F.Supp. 793 (N.D.Ga.1994).

62. UCC § 2–328(2), (3) (inconsequential verbal changes in revision); Note, 12 B.U.L.Rev. 240 (1932).

63. Holston v. Pennington, 225 Va. 551, 304 S.E.2d 287 (1983).

64. Zuhak v. Rose, 264 Wis. 286, 58 N.W.2d 693, 37 ALR2d 1041 (1953); 1 Williston § 4:9.

65. UCC § 2–328(3). The rule may be different for judicial auctions. Commercial Federal S. & L. Ass'n v. ABA, 230 Neb. 317, 431 N.W.2d 613 (1988). See note 61 supra.

66. Worswick v. Switzer, 778 S.W.2d 226 (Ky.App.1989) (opinion withdrawn from bound volume).

Subsection 4 of § 2–328 reads:

If the auctioneer knowingly receives a bid on the seller's behalf or the seller makes or procures such a bid, and notice has not been given that liberty for such bidding is reserved, the buyer may at his option avoid the sale or take the goods at the price of the last good faith bid prior to the completion of the sale. This subsection shall not apply to any bid at a forced sale.

It would have been better if the word "reserved" in this subsection had been changed to "retained." Then there could have been no confusion with phrases "with reserve" and "without reserve" used in subsection 3. Clearly subsection 4 was not designed to change subsection 3.[67] Subsection 4 governs the rights of the parties where the auctioneer's agent or the agent of the seller (a shill) makes a bid and the auctioneer has not retained ("reserved") the right to have a shill makes such bids—a practice called "puffing."[68]

When puffing has occurred *the buyer* may * * * avoid the sale or take the goods at the price of the last good faith bid prior to the completion of the sale." This provision raises some difficult problems. Note first that only a "buyer" may use this subsection. Therefore, if the auction is "with reserve" the seller has the privilege of removing the goods from the auction block and, even if the seller accomplishes this removal through the subterfuge of having a shill make the high bid, the next highest bidder may not complain by virtue of this provision because the next highest bidder is not a buyer.[69] If the auction, however, is "without reserve" the highest legitimate bidder would be a "buyer" and have the option granted by subsection 4.

The next question is the meaning of the phrase "at the price of the last good faith bid prior to the completion of the sale." Suppose only B and A, a shill, bid. B makes the first bid of $40 and each party alternately raises the price by bidding $10 more until the price of $100 is bid by B and at that point the goods are knocked down to B. Note first that B is the buyer even if the auction is "with reserve." At what price may B claim the goods? Because the UCC provision was designed to protect B against puffing, it has been suggested that B should have the goods at $40 despite the fact that all of B's bids were literally in good faith, including the last.[70] But suppose that C, a legitimate bidder, had made the $90 bid? Although there has been puffing, a third person bid

---

67. UCC § 2–328 cmt 2.

68. The history of this ancient, if dishonorable, practice is colorfully traced in McMillan v. Harris, 110 Ga. 72, 35 S.E. 334 (1900).

69. Sly v. First Nat. Bank of Scottsboro, 387 So.2d 198 (Ala.1980); Feaster Trucking Service v. Parks–Davis Auctioneers, 211 Kan. 78, 505 P.2d 612 (1973); Drew v. John Deere, 19 A.D.2d 308, 241 N.Y.S.2d 267

(1963). This does not mean that the auctioneer may not encounter licensing difficulties or even criminal charges. See, e.g., McKinney's N.Y.Gen.Bus.Law § 24.

70. So held in Nevada Nat. Leasing v. Hereford, 36 Cal.3d 146, 680 P.2d 1077, 203 Cal.Rptr. 118, 44 ALR4th 101 (1984). Punitive damages were awarded. It is unclear whether there were other bidders.

$90. It has been suggested that, in order to protect C's interests, B, if B elects to buy, must pay $90.[71]

It is difficult to see, however, what legally protected interest C has or should have; the contest is now between B and the seller. Nevertheless, the suggestion that B should pay $90 for the goods may have some merit in that a third person in good faith valued the goods to be worth this sum and B valued them at a higher price. If B elects to avoid the sale, the election must be made promptly after B learns the facts; otherwise the buyer will be deemed to have ratified the sale.[72]

The UCC states that this subsection does not apply to a "forced sale." While the Code does not define "forced sale," it is an auction that takes place because the debtor has defaulted and the property must or may be sold to terminate the interest of the debtor or to satisfy the debt.[73] Both the secured party and the party whose interest is being foreclosed may bid.

Subsection 4 creates one additional problem. We have assumed that the existence of the shill has not been disclosed. But what if it is disclosed, for example, in an auction "without reserve" and the shill becomes the high bidder? Subsection 3 states that the goods may not be withdrawn and this should be equally true if the withdrawal is through the medium of a shill. Yet subsection 4 might be taken to say that the goods may be withdrawn from sale by knocking them down to an agent whose identity has been disclosed. The same type of problem can also arise in a forced sale. It would appear that the problem should be resolved in favor of the provisions of subsection 3.

The problems raised by the Statute of Frauds in an auction sale are discussed below.[74]

(g) Invitation to Bid—Bid

It is common for someone who wishes to build a large complex to send out invitations to bid to construction contractors. The invitation to bid will ordinarily specify in detail the work to be done and invites the recipient to state its price for the work. The situation is analogous to an auction "with reserve." The request to bid is not the offer; the bid itself is the offer.[75] Occasionally courts have held invitations to bid to be offers because of the unusual language contained in the invitation.[76] If so, the

71. See 1 W. Hawkland, A Transactional Guide to the Uniform Commercial Code 40 (1964) [hereinafter cited as Hawkland].

72. Vanier v. Ponsoldt, 251 Kan. 88, 833 P.2d 949 (1992); Berg v. Hogan, 322 N.W.2d 448 (N.D.1982). See Rs. 2d §§ 380, 381.

73. See UCC Art. 9, Part 6; State v. Lacey, 8 Wn.App. 542, 507 P.2d 1206 (1973), aff'd. The revision substitutes "an auction required by law" for the words "a forced sale." It is unclear whether a substantive change is intended.

74. See § 19.32 infra.

75. Carriger v. Ballenger, 192 Mont. 479, 628 P.2d 1106 (1981); 1 Corbin § 2.26 (Perillo 1993).

76. Short v. Sun Newspapers, 300 N.W.2d 781 (Minn.1980); Gulf Oil v. Clark County, 94 Nev. 116, 575 P.2d 1332 (1978); Jenkins Towel v. Fidelity–Philadelphia Trust, 400 Pa. 98, 161 A.2d 334 (1960).

bid is the acceptance. In such a case the analogy would be to an auction "without reserve."

The situation is more complicated when the invitation to bid is prepared by municipalities, states, or other governmental units. There is likely to be a statute stating that a contract shall be awarded to the lowest responsible bidder. If such a statute is read into the invitation to bid, it could be argued that the "invitation" is the offer and the bid is the acceptance, but this logic has not generally been followed. The bid is looked on as the offer and a contract is not formed until the lowest responsible bid is accepted. Even after the acceptance of the bid for a public contract, the law may require certain formalities, such as an integrated written contract, the checking of the creditworthiness and suitability of the bidder, the furnishing of a bond and the like. There may be no contract until these steps have been complied with. It is clear that the bid need not be accepted.

If for no adequate reason the governmental unit awards the contract to another bidder, does the disappointed low bidder have legal cause to complain? Because such statutes were deemed solely for the benefit of the public,[77] under the traditional rule the lowest bidder lacked standing to sue.[78] However a growing number of decisions have relaxed this traditional rule and have permitted the disappointed bidder to recover the costs of preparing a bid or to obtain an injunction preventing the contract from being awarded to another.[79] In this event new bids may be requested.[80] Statutes have been enacted to deal with the relief available.

(h) Price Quotations—Goods and Real Property

(1) Goods

A price quotation is usually a statement of intention to sell at a given unit price.[81] When the quotation is addressed to many people and this fact is disclosed, a quote is similar to an advertisement, circular letter, or catalog.[82] Even if the word "quote" is used in a communication addressed to an individual, it is commonly understood to mean that an offer is invited.[83] This, however, is far from a hard and fast rule; the word "quote" in some contexts may mean "offer." It is the communication as a whole rather than the label the party puts on it that must be interpreted.[84]

---

77. M.A. Stephen Constr. v. Borough of Rumson, 125 N.J.Super. 67, 308 A.2d 380 (1973), cert. denied.

78. Cf. Perkins v. Lukens Steel, 310 U.S. 113 (1940).

79. Merriam v. Kunzig, 476 F.2d 1233, 23 ALR Fed. 278 (3d Cir.1973), cert. denied; Scanwell Laboratories v. Shaffer, 424 F.2d 859 (D.C.Cir.1970). There has been some retreat from the liberal approach of Scanwell. See Look v. U.S., 113 F.3d 1129 (9th Cir.1997); Keyes, Government Contracts ch. 33 (1986).

80. 1 Williston § 4:10; see Clemens v. U.S., 295 F.Supp. 1339 (D.Or.1968), aff'd.

81. Rs. 2d § 26 cmt c.

82. See § 2.6(e) supra.

83. Interstate Indus. v. Barclay Indus., 540 F.2d 868 (7th Cir.1976); Thos. J. Sheehan Co. v. Crane Co., 418 F.2d 642 (8th Cir.1969); Rs. 2d § 26 cmt c.

84. Cannavino & Shea v. Water Works Supply, 361 Mass. 363, 280 N.E.2d 147 (1972); Nickel v. Theresa Farmers Co-op., 247 Wis. 412, 20 N.W.2d 117 (1945).

In a well-known case[85] the plaintiff asked for the defendant's price on 1000 gross of Mason green jars. The defendant answered, stating detailed terms including price, using the word "quote," but also stating that the price was "for immediate acceptance." The court decided that defendant's communication was an offer despite the use of the word "quote."

Three factors led the court to the conclusion that the word "quote" in this context meant "offer." First, defendant's communication came in response to an inquiry that obviously sought an offer. Second, the communication contained detailed terms and included by implication the quantity of 1000 gross that the plaintiff had inquired about. Finally, the communication used the words "for immediate acceptance."

What if one of these factors were missing? There is no easy answer to this question. As in other cases, the two key issues are whether there is language of commitment and whether the terms, especially quantity, are sufficiently definite.[86] The Restatement (Second) indicates that there would be an offer in the Mason green jar case even without the words "for immediate acceptance." It stresses the importance of detailed terms, and the fact that the communication was in response to an inquiry.[87]

In another case S wrote to B, "We quote Hungarian [flour] $5.40 [per barrel] car lots only and subject to sight draft with bill of lading. We would suggest your using wire [telegram] to order as prices are rapidly advancing that they may be beyond reach before a letter would reach us." The court held that this was not an offer because S's communication did not specify a quantity.[88] In this case if the word "offer" had been substituted for the word "quote" the result would still be the same because of the failure to specify quantity.[89]

Suppose S sent a letter to B saying, "We quote you two cars of Hungarian flour at $5.40 per barrel." Is this an offer? Williston indicates that it is, saying, "where the property to be sold is accurately defined and in the communication made states the price sought, and is directed not to the public generally but to one person individually, it seems more reasonable to interpret the expression as an offer to sell the property described for the price stated."[90] This statement does not appear to place sufficient emphasis on the question of promise or commitment.[91] Also it does not give sufficient importance to the question of whether the

---

85. Fairmount Glass Works v. Crunden–Martin Woodenware, 106 Ky. 659, 51 S.W. 196 (1899); accord, Gibson v. De La Salle Inst., 66 Cal.App.2d 609, 152 P.2d 774 (1944).

86. See, e.g., § 2.6(e) supra.

87. Rs. 2d § 26 cmt c ill. 3; see Nordyne, Inc. v. International Controls & Measurements, 262 F.3d 843 (8th Cir.2001).

88. Johnston Bros. v. Rogers Bros., 30 Ont. 150 (1899).

89. Earl M. Jorgensen Co. v. Mark Constr. Inc., 56 Haw. 466, 540 P.2d 978 (1975); Moulton v. Kershaw, 59 Wis. 316, 18 N.W. 172 (1884).

90. 1 Williston § 4.7. The prior edition of Williston was more emphatic, stating that no contrary reasonable interpretation seemed possible. 1 Williston § 27 (3d ed.).

91. See, e.g., Nebraska Seed v. Harsh, 98 Neb. 89, 152 N.W. 310 (1915).

communication is an initial communication as opposed to an answer to an inquiry.[92]

(2) Real Property

Although the problems in the real property cases are somewhat different, cases exist that are analogous to those discussed above. Two cases will illustrate this.

In Mellen v. Johnson[93] the defendant wrote the plaintiff that the price for certain property was $7,500 and that several other interested persons would be getting a similar letter. The plaintiff telegraphed an acceptance. The case is similar to the price quotation cases discussed above where the communication is addressed to many persons. The additional fact to be considered is that defendant made it clear that the defendant had only one piece of real property to sell. This is less likely to be the case where the subject matter is goods.

The court held that a reasonable person should have concluded that the defendant was not making an offer, especially because it would be unreasonable to assume that the defendant was willing to be bound by more than one contract. This is not to say that a person may not be held to have made offers to sell the same property to more than one offeree. If the owner is so unwise, each of the offerees who has accepted such an offer will have a remedy against the offeror.[94] An owner, when interested in disposing of real property, is likely to negotiate with more than one potential buyer. If in some way the owner indicates that proposals to sell have been addressed to others, in the absence of a clear promise to sell at given terms, this proposal is not reasonably construed as an offer. Rather, in this case it should be looked on as an invitation to make an offer or a mere price quotation.

In Harvey v. Facey[95] the plaintiff sent the following telegram to the defendant: "Will you sell us Bumper Hall Pen? Telegraph lowest cash price." (Bumper Hall Pen was a parcel of real property). The defendant answered, "Lowest price for Bumper Hall Pen £900." Plaintiff sent a telegram of acceptance. The court reasoned that, because the plaintiff's first question concerning the willingness to sell the property had not been answered, defendant's communication did not contain a promise to sell. But couldn't defendant's communication be reasonably understood to say, "Yes, I will sell you Bumper Hall Pen for £900?"

It is interesting to compare this case with the Mason green jar case above. In each case the plaintiff made an inquiry with respect to price and the defendant gave the price. The question in each case is whether the defendant promised to sell at that price. In the green jar case the

92. See, e.g., Cox v. Denton, 104 Kan. 516, 180 P. 261 (1919).

93. 322 Mass. 236, 76 N.E.2d 658 (1948).

94. See Tymon v. Linoki, 16 N.Y.2d 293, 266 N.Y.S.2d 357, 213 N.E.2d 661 (1965).

95. 1893 A.C. 552 (P.C.) (Jamaica). See also Courteen Seed v. Abraham, 129 Or. 427, 275 P. 684 (1929), 9 Or.L.Rev. 72 (1929).

word used in defendant's communication was "quote" but the communication also said "for immediate acceptance." According to the Restatement (Second), however, these words are not essential to the decision. Are the cases contradictory? The answer is, not necessarily.

There are additional facts in Harvey v. Facey that are important even though the court does not explicitly rely on them. The plaintiffs, who were solicitors in Kingston, dispatched their initial telegram the day after the City Council had publicly discussed an offer by the defendant to sell the premises to the City. Although the opinion does not state that the plaintiffs were aware of the Council meeting, the inference is clear that they were. This makes the case analogous to Mellen v. Johnson, discussed above; plaintiff was aware that the defendant was negotiating with others with respect to the same subject matter. Under the circumstances the failure to reply to the first question could well indicate that defendant did not intend to be committed to the plaintiffs.

Another possible explanation is that courts are quite properly reluctant to construe a communication as an offer unless it is quite clear that a promise has been made. Once a contract is made, courts tend to interpret language freely and, if justice seems to require, without finicky regard for grammatical nicety. However, they will not lightly determine that a person has taken the significant step of creating a power of acceptance unless that person quite clearly made a commitment.[96]

(i) Offer vs. Preliminary Negotiations—Factors to Consider

Preliminary negotiations can be defined to include any communication prior to the acceptance[97] or any communication prior to the operative offer in the case.[98] Because our topic is offers, the second definition is preferable for present purposes. Many of the types of communications already discussed are made in preliminary negotiations. These include statements of opinion, statements of intention, hopes and desires, estimates, inquiries, invitations to make offers, advertisements, catalogs, circular letters, invitations to make bids, and price quotations.

There is not always a clear answer to the question of whether a particular communication is preliminary to the offer or whether it is an offer. The essential difficulty is that, under the objective theory of contracts, the test is whether a reasonable person in the position of the plaintiff would conclude that the defendant had made a commitment. Under such a test, it is not surprising to find that there are often differences of opinion as to the correct result in a concrete case. Since the question is essentially one of the intent of the parties as gleaned

---

96. U.S. v. Braunstein, 75 F.Supp. 137, 139 (S.D.N.Y.1947), app. dismissed. ("It is true that there is much room for interpretation once the parties are inside the framework of a contract, but it seems that there is less in the field of offer and acceptance. Greater precision of expression may be required, and less help from the court given, when the parties are merely at the threshold of a contract."); accord, Henry Simons Lumber v. Simons, 232 Minn. 187, 44 N.W.2d 726 (1950). See Tiersma, The Language of Offer and Acceptance: Speech Acts and the Question of Intent, 74 Cal. L.Rev. 189 (1986).

97. 1 Corbin § 2.1 (Perillo 1993).

98. Rs. 2d § 26.

from the facts of a particular case, it is not surprising that the cases do not always appear to be in harmony.[99] The problem is further complicated by the distinction between questions of fact and questions of law—a topic discussed below.[100]

In determining whether a communication is an offer or not, some of the important factors are:

1) Whether the communication is an initial communication as opposed to an answer to an inquiry.[101] An answer to an inquiry is more likely to be an offer. The language of the inquiry is also important. Does the inquiry ask for an offer as in Fairmount?

2) The words used. Are the words generally associated with promise or are they noncommittal?

3) Are the terms detailed or are only a few terms included? Do they include the quantity and quality terms?

4) Selectivity of Communication—is it clear that the party who sends the communication is treating with other people with respect to the same subject matter?[102]

5) Does the case involve real property or goods? Courts are less likely to interpret a message about real property as an offer than a similar message about goods.

6) Relationship of the parties: husband and wife or other close bond.

7) Surrounding circumstances; for example, whether a physician is treating a patient under emergency conditions or not.

8) Usages of the trade, prior practices of the parties ("course of dealing") to be discussed later.[103]

C. OTHER MATTERS RELATING TO MUTUAL ASSENT

Table of Sections

99. 1 Corbin § 2.2 (Perillo 1993). See Alpen v. Chapman, 179 N.W.2d 585 (Iowa 1970).

100. See § 2.7 infra.

101. An unsolicited bid by a subcontractor to a contractor who was preparing a master bid was held to be an offer as it was foreseeable that the contractor would rely on it. Jaybe Constr. v. Beco, 3 Conn.Cir. 406, 216 A.2d 208 (1965).

102. This is stressed in CISG Art. 14.

103. See § 3.17 infra.

§ 2.7 Questions of Law and Fact

The distinction between questions of law and fact is analyzed in detail in treatises on procedure. Here it is sufficient to note that at the trial level, triers of fact, often a jury, determine questions of fact, and the trial judge determines questions of law. Appellate courts, subject to some exceptions, review only questions of law.[1]

To illustrate: Whether and to what extent subjective intention is relevant in making a particular determination is a question of law. Whether a person said "50" or "100" on a particular occasion is a question of fact. Whether a reasonable person in the position of the plaintiff would conclude that the defendant had made a commitment is a question of fact, unless the court rules that reasonable persons could reach only one reasonable conclusion.[2] Even where reasonable persons could reach different conclusions the question is often held to be one of law when it involves the interpretation of a writing or other record.[3] As Corbin points out "since two cases are never identical * * * the decision made in one of them can never be regarded as a conclusive precedent for the other."[4] It must also be remembered that the printed report never gives all of the facts and may well omit one of the decisive factors that led to the decision. There is also a tendency to rule as a matter of law in certain recurring situations, as in the advertising situation,[5] where the law has hardened as to the proper decision.

§ 2.8 Intent to Memorialize & Effect of Duplicate Originals

During negotiations, parties often manifest an intention that when an agreement is reached it will be formalized. Does a contract arise when the parties reach an otherwise binding agreement or is there no contract unless the formal document is adopted by both parties?

§ 2.7

1. U.S. ex rel. Howard Steel v. United Pac. Ins., 427 F.2d 366 (7th Cir.1970).

2. Construction Aggregates v. Hewitt-Robins, 404 F.2d 505 (7th Cir.1968), cert. denied.

3. General Dynamics v. Miami Aviation, 421 F.2d 416 (5th Cir.1970). Although the general rule is that the interpretation of a record is a question of law, it is no secret that logically the question is a question of fact. See § 3.15 infra.

4. 1 Corbin § 2.2 (Perillo 1993).

5. See § 2.6(e) supra.

The problem is another aspect of the question of intending legal consequences.[1] There are three possible scenarios. One, if the parties make it clear that they do not intend that there should be legal consequences unless and until a formal record is executed, there is no contract until that time.[2] Or two, if they make it clear that the prospective record is merely to be a convenient memorial of the agreement, it is binding even though a memorial is never adopted.[3] In this case, a party's refusal to execute the memorial constitutes a breach of contract.[4]

The difficult case is the third scenario where the parties have not expressly manifested their intent other than by the fact that they intended that there will be a record. Some of the cases have held that the parties are not bound until the record is executed.[5] Other cases, however, have concluded that the contract becomes binding when the agreement is reached.[6] This does not mean that there is a conflict in the cases even though at times they are difficult to reconcile.[7] The question involves the intention of the parties,[8] often a question of fact.[9] Some of the cases talk in terms of a presumption that the record is intended merely as a convenient memorial, while others indicate that the burden of proof is on the party who says that a formal document was required to complete the contract.[10] There is not a great deal of difference in these two formulations. There is, however, a third and contrary formulation to the effect that an understanding that the agreement will be reduced to writing or otherwise recorded raises a presumption that the parties did not intend the agreement to be binding.[11]

However, it may not be fruitful to analyze the problem in these

---

§ 2.8

1. See § 2.4 supra.

2. Warrior Constr. v. International Union, 383 F.2d 700 (5th Cir.1967); Golding v. Floyd, 261 Va. 190, 539 S.E.2d 735 (2001) ("subject to execution of a formal agreement").

3. Mesa Petroleum v. Coniglio, 629 F.2d 1022 (5th Cir.1980), cert. denied; 1 Corbin § 2.9 (Perillo 1993); 1 Williston § 4:8.

4. CitiSteel USA, Inc. v. Connell Ltd. Ptshp., 758 A.2d 928 (Del.2000); Rs. 2d § 27.

5. Wharton v. Stoutenburgh, 35 N.J.Eq. 266 (1882); Scheck v. Francis, 26 N.Y.2d 466, 311 N.Y.S.2d 841, 260 N.E.2d 493 (1970); Schwartz v. Greenberg, 304 N.Y. 250, 107 N.E.2d 65 (1952).

6. Barton v. Chemical Bank, 577 F.2d 1329 (5th Cir.1978); H.B. Zachry Co. v. O'Brien, 378 F.2d 423 (10th Cir.1967); Miles v. Wichita, 175 Kan. 723, 267 P.2d 943 (1954); Dohrman v. Sullivan, 310 Ky. 463, 220 S.W.2d 973 (1949); Peoples Drug Stores v. Fenton Realty, 191 Md. 489, 62 A.2d 273 (1948); Sanders v. Pottlitzer Bros.

Fruit, 144 N.Y. 209, 39 N.E. 75 (1894); see V'Soske v. Barwick, 404 F.2d 495 (2d Cir. 1968), cert. denied; cf. Sands v. Arruda, 359 Mass. 591, 270 N.E.2d 826 (1971).

7. 1 Corbin § 2.9 (Perillo 1993).

8. Smile, Inc. v. Moosehead Sanitary Dist., 649 A.2d 1103 (Me.1994); Smith v. Onyx Oil & Chem., 218 F.2d 104, 50 ALR2d 216 (3d Cir.1955); Mitchell v. Siqueiros, 99 Idaho 396, 582 P.2d 1074 (1978).

9. Babdo Sales v. Miller–Wohl, 440 F.2d 962 (2d Cir.1971); Texaco v. Pennzoil, 729 S.W.2d 768 (Tex.App.1987) (N.Y. law); Scott v. Ingle Bros. Pac., 489 S.W.2d 554 (Tex.1972), 26 Baylor L.Rev. 132 (1974); see Short v. Sunflower Plastic Pipe, 210 Kan. 68, 500 P.2d 39 (1972); 1 Corbin § 2.9 (1993).

10. Sanders v. Pottlitzer Bros. Fruit, 144 N.Y. 209, 39 N.E. 75 (1894).

11. Arcadian Phosphates v. Arcadian, 884 F.2d 69 (2d Cir.1989); Valjar, Inc. v. Maritime Terminals, 220 Va. 1015, 265 S.E.2d 734 (1980). Apparently contrary to Arcadian is Consarc v. Marine Midland Bank, 996 F.2d 568 (2d Cir.1993).

terms.[12] A better approach is to identify some of the important factors that influence the decisions of the courts.[13] The Restatement (Second) lists the following: "the extent to which express agreement has been reached on all terms to be included, whether the contract is a type usually put in writing [or otherwise recorded], whether it needs a formal writing or [record] for its full expression, whether it has few or many details, whether the amount involved is large or small, whether it is a common or unusual contract, whether a standard form of contract is widely used in similar transactions, and whether either party takes any action in preparation for performance during the negotiations."[14] In addition, if the agreement is reached by correspondence, it is likely that the parties intend to be bound when they reach agreement.[15]

The previous discussion assumed that the parties have manifested the same intent or have not manifested any intention. Obviously, however, in litigation, one party claims that there was no intention to be bound until there was a formal record. This issue is to be determined by the tentative test previously suggested. If a reasonable person in the position of the other party either knew or should have known that the other party did not intend to be bound in the absence of a formal agreement, there is no contract until a formal agreement is executed.[16]

When the parties do not intend to be bound before a formal document is duly executed, the question sometimes arises whether the contract is formed when both parties sign duplicate originals or only when the signed records are exchanged. The cases appear to be in hopeless conflict.[17] This is because a question of intention is being decided. This was recognized in Aspen Acres Association v. Seven Associates.[18] As stated there: "[T]he mere affixing of the signatures to the document did not conclusively prove that there was a binding contract. In addition, there must be a delivery, not in the traditional sense of a manual transfer, but in the sense that it was the intent of the parties to

---

12. 2 Formation of Contracts, supra § 2.2 n.1, at 1625.

13. Mississippi & Dominion S.S. v. Swift, 86 Me. 248, 29 A. 1063 (1894); Michigan Broadcasting v. Shawd, 352 Mich. 453, 90 N.W.2d 451 (1958).

14. Rs. 2d § 27 cmt c. See also 2 Formation of Contracts, supra § 2.2 n.1, at 1627–1632, identifying additional factors.

15. Sanders v. Pottlitzer Bros. Fruit, 144 N.Y. 209, 39 N.E. 75 (1894).

16. Rs. 2d § 27 cmt b. "[I]it is quite plain that if either of the parties manifests its intent not to be bound until a written contract is executed then the parties are not bound until that event occurs." Lizza & Sons v. D'Onfro, 186 F.Supp. 428, 432 (D.Mass.1959), aff'd; Advanced Marine Tech., Inc. v. Burnham Securities, 16 F.Supp.2d 375 (S.D.N.Y.1998). Compare the statement that the parties are bound by their agreement "in the absence of a positive agreement that it should not be binding until so reduced to writing and formally executed." Disken v. Herter, 73 A.D. 453, 455, 77 N.Y.S. 300, 302 (1902), aff'd. This statement is incorrect since it implies that the manifest intent of one of the parties may be ignored by the other. See Municipal Consultants v. Ramapo, 47 N.Y.2d 144, 417 N.Y.S.2d 218, 390 N.E.2d 1143 (1979).

17. Compare Schwartz v. Greenberg, 304 N.Y. 250, 107 N.E.2d 65 (1952) with Generes v. Justice Court, 106 Cal.App.3d 678, 165 Cal.Rptr. 222 (1980) and Whitley v. Patrick, 226 Ga. 87, 172 S.E.2d 692 (1970) and Besser v. K.L.T. Associates, 42 A.D.2d 725, 345 N.Y.S.2d 659 (1973), aff'd.

18. 29 Utah 2d 303, 508 P.2d 1179 (1973).

have the document become legally operative at some definite point in time, however such intent might be indicated."[19]

§ 2.9 Indefiniteness

We have already seen that indefiniteness in a communication is some evidence of an intent not to contract.[1] The more terms that are omitted the more likely it is that the parties do not intend to contract.[2] But, even if the parties intend to contract, if the content of their agreement is unduly uncertain no contract is formed.[3] This rule must be understood as a necessary limitation on freedom of contract because an agreement must be sufficiently definite before a court can determine if either party breached it.[4] The traditional rule is that if the agreement is not *reasonably* certain[5] as to its *material* terms there is a fatal indefiniteness and the agreement is void.[6] The rule does not supply a precise standard. Vagueness and indefiniteness are matters of degree.[7]

It is the contract, not the offer that must be definite. For example, assume A makes an offer to sell to B from 1 to 10 copies of a specified book at a certain price and adds "state the number in your acceptance." B replies "I'll take 5." B's acceptance creates a contract, although considered alone the offer might seem indefinite as to quantity. Also, a material term may be left to be determined by an outside standard, such as the royalty rate charged by the federal government,[8] or a price to be set by an appraiser.[9]

What are material terms? Material terms include subject matter, price, payment terms, quantity, quality, duration, the work to be done. Given the infinite variety of contracts, it is obvious that no precise list or definition can be articulated.[10] Indefiniteness as to an *immaterial* term is

19. Id. at 310–11, 508 P.2d at 1184; see also Cortlandt v. E.F. Hutton, 491 F.Supp. 1 (S.D.N.Y.1979); cf. 2 Formation of Contracts, § 2.2 n.1 supra, at 1584–86.

§ 2.9

1. Owen v. Owen, 427 A.2d 933 (D.C.App.1981); Hill v. McGregor Mfg., 23 Mich.App. 342, 178 N.W.2d 553 (1970). See § 2.6 supra.

2. Soar v. National Football League Players' Ass'n, 550 F.2d 1287, 1290 (1st Cir.1977) ("while an enforceable contract might be found in some circumstances if one or more of such questions were left unanswered, the accumulation in the instant case of so many unanswered questions is convincing evidence that there never was a consensus ad idem between the parties").

3. Ekedahl v. COREStaff, Inc.,183 F.3d 855 (D.C.Cir.1999); Rs. 2d § 33(1); 1 Corbin §§ 4.1–4.8 (Perillo 1993); 1 Williston §§ 4:18–4:29.

4. Snug Harbor Property Owners Ass'n v. Curran, 55 N.C.App. 199, 284 S.E.2d 752 (1981), rev. denied.

5. Coastland v. Third Nat'l Mtge., 611 F.2d 969 (4th Cir.1979).

6. Lawrence v. Jones, 124 Idaho 748, 864 P.2d 194 (App.1993); Werner v. Norwest Bank, 499 N.W.2d 138 (S.D.1993); Rs. 2d § 32. See § 1.8(b) supra.

7. Palmer v. Albert, 310 N.W.2d 169 (Iowa 1981).

8. Plateau Min. v. Utah Div. of State Lands & Forestry, 802 P.2d 720 (Utah 1990), coal royalties @ 15¢ per ton or rate charged by under federal leases, whichever is higher.

9. Penwell v. Barrett, 724 S.W.2d 902 (Tex.App.1987).

10. Rule v. Brine, 85 F.3d 1002 (2d Cir. 1996) ("fair royalty"); see 1 Corbin §§ 4.1–4.6 (Perillo 1993); 1 Williston §§ 4.18–4.29.

not fatal.[11]

If the agreement is reasonably certain, it is enforced even though the contract does not set forth its terms with "optimal specificity."[12] It is enough that the agreement is sufficiently explicit so that the court can perceive the respective obligations of the parties.[13] The requirement of definiteness cannot be pushed to extreme limits.[14] "What is reasonable in any case must depend on the subject matter of the agreement, the purpose for which it was entered into, the situation and relations of the parties and the circumstances under which it was made."[15] If, however, the agreement is fatally indefinite, any payments made for which a return performance has not been rendered must be disgorged.[16]

Three types of indefiniteness can be distinguished: 1) Where the parties purport to agree on a material term but have left it indefinite; 2) Where the parties are silent as to a material term; 3) Where the parties agree to agree later as to a material term. At common law each category is treated somewhat differently.

(a) The Common Law

(1) Indefinite Purported Agreement on a Material Term

If A says to B, "If you work for me for one year, I will pay you a fair share of the profits," it has been held that the promise is too vague and indefinite to be enforced.[17] If, however, B performs under the agreement, B may recover the reasonable value of services rather than by a share of the profits.[18] This recovery, known as "quantum meruit" is sometimes described as quasi-contractual and sometimes as a contract "implied in fact."[19] A promise to make a tailor-made suit for $500, where the fabric

11. Purvis v. U.S., 344 F.2d 867 (9th Cir.1965) (leaving open a $9,300 item in a construction contract involving $1,000,000 held immaterial); Yellow Run Coal v. Alma–Elly–Yv Mines, 285 Pa.Super. 84, 426 A.2d 1152 (1981); Estate of Eberle, 505 N.W.2d 767 (S.D.1993); Rs. 2d § 33 ill. 11.

12. Soar v. National Football League Players' Ass'n, 550 F.2d 1287, 1290 n. 6 (1st Cir.1977).

13. Id; Lambert Corp. v. Evans, 575 F.2d 132 (7th Cir.1978); Barry M. Dechtman, Inc. v. Sidpaul Corp., 89 N.J. 547, 446 A.2d 518 (1982); Berg Agency v. Sleepworld–Willingboro, 136 N.J.Super. 369, 346 A.2d 419 (A.D.1975).

14. V'Soske v. Barwick, 404 F.2d 495 (2d Cir.1968), cert. denied; Jack Richards Aircraft Sales v. Vaughn, 203 Kan. 967, 457 P.2d 691 (1969); Davco Realty v. Picnic Foods, 198 Neb. 193, 252 N.W.2d 142 (1977).

15. Marcor Housing Sys. v. First Am. Title, 41 Colo.App. 90, 92–93, 584 P.2d 86, 88 (1978), modified.

16. Aircraft Guar. v. Strato–Lift, 103 F.Supp.2d 830 (E.D.Pa.2000).

17. Varney v. Ditmars, 217 N.Y. 223, 111 N.E. 822 (1916); see also T'ai v. Kalso Systemet, 568 F.2d 145 (10th Cir.1977); Gray v. Aiken, 205 Ga. 649, 54 S.E.2d 587 (1949). A number of more liberal cases have enforced promises of this kind. Hodgkins v. NET, 82 F.3d 1226 (1st Cir.1996); Noble v. Joseph Burnett Co., 208 Mass. 75, 94 N.E. 289 (1911); Allan v. Hargadine–McKittrick Dry Goods, 315 Mo. 254, 286 S.W. 16 (1926). But the promise of a bonus, partly based on a formula and partly based on the employer's discretion, was held too indefinite. Arby's v. Cooper, 265 Ga. 240, 454 S.E.2d 488 (1995). The dissent makes greater sense.

18. Kearns v. Andree, 107 Conn. 181, 139 A. 695, 59 ALR 599 (1928); Varney v. Ditmars, 217 N.Y. 223, 111 N.E. 822 (1916); 1 Corbin § 4.5 (Perillo 1993).

19. Bergman v. DeIulio, 826 So.2d 500 (Fla.App.2002); ADP Marshall v. Brown University, 784 A.2d 309, 312 (2001) ("the fair and reasonable value of the work done").

is not specified, also suffers from indefiniteness.[20] Indefiniteness of this kind can be cured by the subsequent conduct of the parties.[21] If the tailor commences making the suit with a certain type of woolen cloth and the customer acquiesces in this, the indefiniteness is cured by the conduct of the parties.[22]

Indefiniteness can also be cured by agreement rather than by conduct. In Perreault v. Hall, the defendant promised to pay the plaintiff "well and enough." Later, on retirement, the defendant promised to give plaintiff a pension of $20 per week, an offer which plaintiff accepted. Thus, the indefiniteness was cured by the new agreement.[23] In the "fair share of the profits" case, in contrast, the indefiniteness was never cured and plaintiff was limited to recovery in quantum meruit; in the other two cases (tailor-made suit, pay "well and enough") the indefiniteness was cured and a contractual recovery was in order.[24]

That the question of reasonable certainty is relative may be shown by a comparison of two fact patterns. First, assume that the plaintiff, a contractor, agrees to build "a first class ranch house" for the owner for a stated price. Before there is any performance, one of the parties repudiates the agreement. On these bare facts, the agreement is too vague and indefinite to be enforced.[25] Contrast the case where plaintiff sold real property to defendant. In addition, to paying the owner's price, defendant promised to build a "first class theatre" on the site. Plaintiff, as the defendant knew, desired the theatre to enhance the value of plaintiff's other properties in the area. After the property was sold, defendant resold the property to a third party without having built the theatre. Plaintiff sued for damages and defendant argued fatal indefiniteness. The court rejected the defendant's indefiniteness contention and ruled for the plaintiff.[26]

---

20. Factor v. Peabody Tailoring Sys., 177 Wis. 238, 187 N.W. 984 (1922). Many cases have held an agreement to be void because of the indefiniteness of the subject matter. E.g., Greater Serv. Homebuilders' Inv. Ass'n v. Albright, 88 Colo. 146, 293 P. 345 (1930); see 1 Corbin § 4.6 (Perillo 1993).

21. Morris v. Ballard, 16 F.2d 175, 49 ALR 1461 (D.C.Cir.1926); Coyle's Pest Control v. Cuomo, 154 F.3d 1302 (Fed.Cir.1998) (payment for services actually rendered); Tattersall Club v. White, 232 Ga.App. 307, 501 S.E.2d 851 (1998); Dreazy v. North Shore Pub., 53 Wis.2d 38, 191 N.W.2d 720 (1971); 1 Corbin § 4.7 (Perillo 1993).

22. See 1 Corbin § 4.7 (Perillo 1993); Bremerton v. Kitsap County Sewer Dist., 71 Wn.2d 689, 430 P.2d 956 (1967). The question of forging a good unilateral contract out of a bad bilateral contract is discussed at § 4.12(b)(7) infra.

23. 94 N.H. 191, 49 A.2d 812 (1946); accord, Chase Nat. Bank v. Manufacturers Trust, 265 A.D. 406, 39 N.Y.S.2d 370 (1943); Rubin v. Adams, 368 S.W.2d 42 (Tex.Civ.App.1963); contra, Arby's v. Cooper, 265 Ga. 240, 454 S.E.2d 488 (1995) (facts as stated in dissent). The agreement might be viewed as a species of accord and satisfaction. See §§ 4.11, 21.4–21.6 infra.

24. 1 Corbin § 4.7 (Perillo 1993); 1 Williston § 4:29. In Highland Sewer & Water Auth. v. FHMA, 797 A.2d 385 (Pa.Cmwlth. 2002), a major sewerage project was built, but negotiations were never finalized. It was held that the plaintiff stated causes of action both for contract implied in fact and quasi contract.

25. See, for example, Hart v. Georgia Ry., 101 Ga. 188, 28 S.E. 637 (1897); Klimek v. Perisich, 231 Or. 71, 371 P.2d 956 (1962); but see Lawrence v. Saratoga Lake Ry., 36 Hun. 467 (N.Y.1885).

26. Bettancourt v. Gilroy Theatre, 120 Cal.App.2d 364, 261 P.2d 351 (1953).

The cases are not in conflict. In the theatre case, the court began with a statement made by a number of courts that "the law leans against the destruction of contracts because of uncertainty."[27] This is especially true, where, as here, there has been full or part performance by the plaintiff.[28] Perhaps the most significant factor in the case is that evidence of subjective understanding, and other evidence extrinsic to the writing, was admitted and helped explain what the words "first class theatre" meant to the parties. This type of evidence should be admissible in any case where the expression is ambiguous and the evidence can help resolve the problem.[29]

In addition, the purpose of the defendant was different in the two cases. In the "first class ranch house" case the detailed specifications would be of great importance to the owner because the owner wanted to use or sell it. In this case, the contract had to be much more definite than in the theatre case where any kind of first class theatre would meet the plaintiff's needs—enhancing the value of plaintiff's nearby properties.

Finally, the court stated another well-recognized rule to the effect that less certainty is required where the action is for damages than in an action for specific performance.[30] The reason for requiring greater certainty for specific performance is discussed elsewhere.[31]

(2) Where the Parties Are Silent as to a Material Term

The parties' silence is treated differently from the cases in which the parties have purported to agree on a material term and left it indefinite. If the parties are merely silent as to a material term or discuss the term but do not purport to agree on it, there is a strong possibility that a term may be either implied from surrounding circumstances or supplied by a court using a gap-filler.[32] The missing term may be implied from external sources, including standard terms, trade or local usages, a course of dealing between the parties prior to the agreement, and a course of performance after it.[33] The courts will assume that the parties contracted on the basis of these sources. For example, where standard forms, such as insurance policies are used, an agreement for the issuance of a fire

---

27. Id. at 367, 261 P.2d at 353; accord, In re Wonderfair Stores, 511 F.2d 1206 (9th Cir.1975); In re Sing Chong Co., 1 Haw. App. 236, 617 P.2d 578 (1980); Gift v. Ehrichs, 284 N.W.2d 435 (N.D.1979); Mag Constr. v. McLean County, 181 N.W.2d 718 (N.D.1970).

28. Butler v. Westgate State Bank, 3 Kan.App.2d 403, 596 P.2d 156 (1979), reversed on other grounds.

29. Kleinheider v. Phillips Pipe Line, 528 F.2d 837 (8th Cir.1975); 3 Corbin § 583. See ch. 3 infra.

30. Accord, Caisson Corp. v. Ingersoll–Rand, 622 F.2d 672 (3d Cir.1980); Rego v. Decker, 482 P.2d 834 (Alaska 1971); Davis v. Davis, 261 Iowa 992, 156 N.W.2d 870 (1968).

31. See § 16.8 infra.

32. Southwest Eng'r v. Martin Tractor, 205 Kan. 684, 473 P.2d 18 (1970); Flemming v. Ronson Corp., 107 N.J.Super. 311, 258 A.2d 153 (1969), aff'd.

33. Metro–Goldwyn–Mayer v. Scheider, 40 N.Y.2d 1069, 392 N.Y.S.2d 252, 360 N.E.2d 930 (1976); § 3.17 infra.

insurance policy is sufficiently definite because the parties are aware that the insurer's standard form will be used.[34]

A gap-filler, on the other hand, is a term courts supply either because the court thinks that the parties would have agreed on the term if it had been brought to their attention or because it is "a term which comports with community standards of fairness and policy."[35] Much legal scholarship in the U.S. has focused on what rationale should guide the legislator, judge, or scholar in the choice of default rules to fill in the parties' gaps. There are those who preach the sometimes discordant gospels of economic efficiency, the implementation of communitarian values, the inference of norms implicit in the parties' relationship, or implicitly consented to, and the rationale that the parties "are obligated in fairness to do their part to maintain the cooperative venture."[36] It cannot be said that the legal system has adopted any of these criteria as exclusive. The important point to remember, as elaborated below, is that it is difficult to know, without research, when the courts will or will not supply a gap-filler, and, if they will, how the gap will be filled.

In the language of one court, "[t]erms are implied not because they are just or reasonable, but rather for the reason that the parties must have intended them and have only failed to express them * * * or because they are necessary to give business efficacy to the contract as written, or to give the contract the effect which parties, as fair and reasonable [persons], presumably would have agreed if, having in mind the possibility of the situation which had arisen, they contracted expressly in reference thereto."[37] According to one persuasive source, in filling a gap the court should take into account "(a) the intention of the parties; (b) the nature and purpose of the contract; (c) good faith and fair dealing; and (d) reasonableness."[38]

Most gap-fillers, however, are based on the first of these four criteria—the intention of the parties. If A and B agree that A will perform a service for B and no mention is made of the price to be paid, a court will hold that the parties intended that a reasonable price should be paid and received.[39] Where one hires a contractor and no price is set,

34. Travel Stop v. Alliance General Ins., 950 P.2d 834 (Okla.1997).

35. Rs. 2d § 204 cmt d. That the Restatement's provision is sound from a sociological point of view, see E. Durkheim, The Division of Labor in Society 213–14 (Free Press ed. 1964).

36. The literature can be found in the notes to Steven J. Burton, Default Principles, Legitimacy and the Authority of Contract, 3 So. Cal. Interdisciplinary L. J. 115, 116–18 (1993). The quoted language expresses Professor Burton's rationale for default rules. It is similar to a view long espoused by Professor Hillman. See Hillman, Keeping the Deal Together After Material Breach—Common Law Mitigation

Rules, the UCC, and the Restatement (Second) of Contracts, 47 U. Colo. L. Rev. 553 (1976). A bibliography of contractarian and economic approaches to gap-filling can be found in Craswell & Schwartz, Foundations of Contract Law 27–30 (1994). See also Symposium: Void for Vagueness, 82 Cal. L.Rev. 487 (1994).

37. Barco Urban Renewal v. Housing Auth., 674 F.2d 1001, 1007 (3d Cir.1982).

38. UNIDROIT Principles of International Commercial Contracts Art. 4.8.

39. Charlotte Aircraft v. Braniff Airways, 497 F.2d 1016 (5th Cir.1974); A.M. Webb & Co. v. Robert P. Miller Co., 157 F.2d 865 (3d Cir.1946); S.F. Bowser & Co. v. F.K. Marks & Co., 96 Ark. 113, 131 S.W.

the term supplied is that the contractor is to be paid the usual charges for such work.[40] In a sale of goods where no price is stated, a court will hold that the parties meant a reasonable price and this rule has been continued by the UCC.[41] The rule has been applied even to a sale of real property.[42] A reasonable price may be measured by the market price;[43] where there is no market price the reasonable price may be determined by actual cost plus a reasonable profit[44] or other means of valuation.[45] If no time is stated for the delivery of goods,[46] or for the completion of a building contract,[47] or a transfer of real property,[48] or for making installment payments,[49] a reasonable time is assumed.

However, a gap-filler is not supplied to cover every material term with respect to which the parties have been silent. Thus, where the parties have omitted from their agreement the kind or quantity of goods[50] or the specifications of a building contract,[51] the courts have refused to fill the gap because no objective standard can ordinarily be found in such cases.[52]

334 (1910); Olberding Constr. v. Ruden, 243 N.W.2d 872 (Iowa 1976); Sitzler v. Peck, 162 N.W.2d 449 (Iowa 1968); Konitzky v. Meyer, 49 N.Y. 571 (1872); Dixon v. Kittle, 109 Ohio App. 257, 164 N.E.2d 806 (1959); but see Campbell v. WABC Towing, 78 Misc.2d 671, 356 N.Y.S.2d 455 (1974) (consumer protection legislation requires price to be revealed at outset of automobile repair contract; no recovery).

40. La Velle v. De Luca, 48 Wis.2d 464, 180 N.W.2d 710 (1970). But see Hemenover v. DePatis, 86 Ill.App.3d 586, 42 Ill.Dec. 9, 408 N.E.2d 387 (1980) (the contractor is entitled to the reasonable value of goods used and the customary price for labor).

41. UCC § 2–305 provides detailed rules for agreements in which the price has not been decided on, and the revision makes no substantive changes. For an analysis, see Note, 1 Val.U.L.Rev. 381 (1967); see Schmieder v. Standard Oil, 69 Wis.2d 419, 230 N.W.2d 732, 91 ALR3d 1231 (1975).

42. Shayeb v. Holland, 321 Mass. 429, 73 N.E.2d 731 (1947).

43. Credit Serv. v. Country Realty, 46 Or.App. 867, 612 P.2d 773 (1980).

44. Kuss Mach. Tool & Die v. El–Tronics, 393 Pa. 353, 143 A.2d 38 (1958) (decided under § 2–305 of the UCC); cf. Rs. 2d § 33 ill. 7.

45. Economic and legal methods of valuation are considered in D. Dobbs, Remedies 3.5, 5.15 and passim (2d ed 1993); C. McCormick, Damages ch. 6 (1935).

46. UCC § 2–309(1) (revision unchanged). Comment 5 requires that reasonable notice be given before a contract may

be treated as breached for failure to perform within a reasonable time. If the parties allow the reasonable time for delivery or demand to pass in silence, the reasonable time may be extended. At some point the contract may be considered tacitly rescinded. See § 21.2 infra.

47. American Concrete Steel v. Hart, 285 F. 322 (2d Cir.1922) (reasonableness of time sometimes a question of fact, sometimes of law). So also every contract of employment in the absence of a contrary agreement "includes an obligation to perform in a diligent and reasonably skillful workmanlike manner." Nash v. Sears, Roebuck & Co., 383 Mich. 136, 142, 174 N.W.2d 818, 821 (1970). Where a person contracts to perform work or render service, in the absence of a contrary agreement, that person promises to perform "in a workmanlike manner and to exercise reasonable care." Gilley v. Farmer, 207 Kan. 536, 542, 485 P.2d 1284, 1289 (1971). See Davis, The Illusive Warranty of Workmanlike Performance: Constructing a Conceptual Framework, 72 Neb.L.Rev. 981 (1993).

48. Rodin v. Merritt, 48 N.C.App. 64, 268 S.E.2d 539 (1980), rev. denied.

49. Sockwell & Assocs. v. Sykes Enter., 127 N.C.App. 139, 487 S.E.2d 795 (1997).

50. Burke v. Campbell, 258 Mass. 153, 154 N.E. 759 (1927); Guthing v. Lynn, 109 Eng.Rep. 1130 (K.B.1831).

51. Bissenger v. Prince, 117 Ala. 480, 23 So. 67 (1898); Peoples Drug Stores v. Fenton Realty, 191 Md. 489, 62 A.2d 273 (1948).

52. E.g., Wright v. Mark C. Smith & Sons, 283 So.2d 85 (La.1973); Klimek v.

(3) Duration Problems

There are situations where the courts disagree whether a gap should be filled. For example, in employment contracts, if no duration term is provided, most courts have held that either party may terminate at will even if the parties have set the compensation at a specified sum per month, day or year.[53] Some courts, however, have held that an agreement for a specified sum per day, month or year gives rise to a contract for such period in the absence of evidence to the contrary.[54] It is of course possible for the parties by use of appropriate language to bind themselves to an employment contract for a definite number of days, months or years.[55] If a hiring for a specified term is found, performance after the term expires usually gives rise to an inference that the parties have renewed their agreement on the same terms and for the same duration.[56] Evidence of a contrary intention, is, of course, admissible.[57]

There is a similar division in cases involving the duration of franchise agreements that are silent as to duration. This facet of the problem will be discussed below.[58] In other situations where the agreement is silent as to duration, most courts will decide that a reasonable time is intended.[59]

Perisich, 231 Or. 71, 371 P.2d 956 (1962); 1 Corbin § 4.6 (Perillo 1993).

53. Boatright v. Steinite Radio, 46 F.2d 385 (10th Cir.1931); Elliott v. Delta Air Lines, 116 Ga.App. 36, 156 S.E.2d 656 (1967); Feola v. Valmont Indus., 208 Neb. 527, 304 N.W.2d 377 (1981); Parker v. Borock, 5 N.Y.2d 156, 182 N.Y.S.2d 577, 156 N.E.2d 297 (1959); Plaskitt v. Black Diamond Trailer, 209 Va. 460, 164 S.E.2d 645 (1968); but see Elizaga v. Kaiser Foundation Hosp., 259 Or. 542, 487 P.2d 870 (1971) (misrepresentation theory). "[A] contract which is terminable upon the occurrence of an event is not terminable at will." Consolidated Labs. v. Shandon Scientific, 413 F.2d 208 (7th Cir.1969). Although a contract is terminable at will, an employee who is discharged without fault, is entitled to a proportionate share of a promised bonus. Sinnett v. Hie Food Prod., 185 Neb. 221, 174 N.W.2d 720 (1970). In many countries of the world, except for strictly seasonal labor, employees are entitled to job security. Unless they are dismissed for cause, they are entitled to a statutory period of notice and severance pay. See, e.g., 2 H. Blake, Business Regulation in the Common Market Nations 437 (1969).

54. Dennis v. Thermoid Co., 128 N.J.L. 303, 25 A.2d 886 (1942) (jury question); accord, Rs. 2d § 32 ill. 6.

55. Iniguez v. American Hotel Register Co., 820 So.2d 953 (Fla.App.2002); Pokora v. Warehouse Direct, 322 Ill.App.3d 870, 751 N.E.2d 1204, 256 Ill.Dec. 367 (2001). The determination that a contract of definite duration has been entered into may be inferred from all the facts and circumstances. School Committee v. Board of Regents, 112 R.I. 288, 308 A.2d 788 (1973).

56. Steed v. Busby, 268 Ark. 1, 593 S.W.2d 34 (1980); Steranko v. Inforex, 5 Mass.App.Ct. 253, 362 N.E.2d 222 (1977); Cinefot Int'l v. Hudson Photographic, 13 N.Y.2d 249, 246 N.Y.S.2d 395, 196 N.E.2d 54, 6 ALR3d 1347 (1963); Commonwealth v. Brozzetti, 684 A.2d 658 (Pa.Cmwlth.1996); Rs. 2d § 33 ill. 6. These are not all employment cases. Some statutes require that, even in the face of an automatic renewal provision, the dominant party must give notice to the subservient party. See, e.g., McKinney's N.Y. Gen'l Obl.Law § 5–903.

57. Temple Univ. Hosp. v. Healthcare Mgt., 764 A.2d 587 (Pa.Super.2000); Jurrens v. Lorenz Mfg., 578 N.W.2d 151 (S.D. 1998).

58. See § 4.12(b)(5) infra.

59. Compare Smith v. Smith, 375 So.2d 1138 (Fla.App.1979) with Shultz v. Atkins, 97 Idaho 770, 554 P.2d 948 (1976) and Haines v. New York, 41 N.Y.2d 769, 396 N.Y.S.2d 155, 364 N.E.2d 820 (1977) and East Coast Dev. v. Alderman–250, 30 N.C.App. 598, 228 S.E.2d 72 (1976). See also Keppy v. Lilienthal, 524 N.W.2d 436 (Iowa App.1994); Mann Bros. Logging v. Potlatch, 149 F.3d 790 (8th Cir.1998); but see Jespersen v. Minnesota M & M., 183

Frequently, an employer states that the employment will be "permanent." Most courts have thought that this term creates no commitment, it simply means that the employment is foreseen as steady rather than seasonal or for a particular project; thus, the employment is at will.[60] According to a minority view, however, if permanent employment is promised, the employee is entitled to work so long as the employee is able to do the work and the employer continues in the business for which the employee was hired.[61] If this is the express or implied agreement of the parties, there is no problem.[62]

Personnel manuals frequently make promises as to duration of employment, grounds or procedures for discharge, and promises of fringe benefits. Most courts have enforced the promises made in such manuals.[63] One court has outlined the circumstances in which such promises are enforceable, as follows:[64]

> First, the language of the policy statement must contain a promise clear enough that an employee would reasonably believe than an offer has been made. Second, the statement must be disseminated to the employee in such a manner that the employee is aware of its contents and reasonably believes it to be an offer. Third, the employee must accept the offer by commencing or continuing to work after learning of the policy statement.

Other courts have rejected the enforceability of such promises despite the fact that the employee's services exchanged in part for such promises

Ill.2d 290, 700 N.E.2d 1014, 233 Ill.Dec. 306 (1998) (at will).

60. Benson Co–op. Creamery Ass'n v. First Dist. Ass'n, 276 Minn. 520, 151 N.W.2d 422, 35 ALR 1417 (1967); Arentz v. Morse Dry Dock & Repair, 249 N.Y. 439, 164 N.E. 342, 62 ALR 231 (1928); Roberts v. Wake Forest Univ., 55 N.C.App. 430, 286 S.E.2d 120 (1982), rev. denied; but see Rooney v. Tyson, 91 N.Y.2d 685, 697 N.E.2d 571, 674 N.Y.S.2d 616, (1998) (trainer hired "for as long as the boxer fights professionally" is definite enough).

61. Boothby v. Texon, Inc., 414 Mass. 468, 608 N.E.2d 1028 (1993); 1 Williston § 4:20.

62. Stauter v. Walnut Grove Prods., 188 N.W.2d 305 (Iowa 1971); Toussaint v. Blue Cross & Blue Shield, 408 Mich. 579, 292 N.W.2d 880 (1980); Bobbitt v. Orchard, Ltd., 603 So.2d 356 (Miss.1992), 20 Am.J.Trial Advoc. 181 (1996); but see Architectural Metal Sys. v. Consolidated Sys., 58 F.3d 1227 (7th Cir.1995) (Michigan has backed away from *Toussaint* on grounds of vagueness); Fleming v. Mack Trucks, 508 F.Supp. 917 (E.D.Pa.1981).

63. Zuelsdorf v. University of Alaska, 794 P.2d 932 (Alaska 1990); Ex parte Graham, 702 So.2d 1215 (Ala.1997); Nickens v. Labor Agency, 600 A.2d 813 (D.C.App.

1991); Weiner v. McGraw–Hill, 57 N.Y.2d 458, 457 N.Y.S.2d 193, 443 N.E.2d 441, 33 ALR4th 110 (1982); (but see Sabetay v. Sterling Drug, 69 N.Y.2d 329, 514 N.Y.S.2d 209, 506 N.E.2d 919 (1987), drastically limiting the enforceability of such promises); King v. PYA/Monarch, 317 S.C. 385, 453 S.E.2d 885 (S.C.1995); Goodyear Tire v. Portilla, 879 S.W.2d 47 (Tex.1994). See 1 Corbin § 4.2 (Perillo 1993); Pettit, Modern Unilateral Contracts, 63 B.U.L.Rev. 551 (1983). Promises made in circulars and other non-manual form are equally enforceable. Irvin v. Community Bank, 717 So.2d 369 (Ala.Civ.App.1997).

64. Duldulao v. Saint Mary of Nazareth Hospital Center, 115 Ill.2d 482, 490, 106 Ill.Dec. 8, 12, 505 N.E.2d 314, 318 (1987). Some manuals contain language disclaiming any intention that the promises made will be enforceable. Bowen v. Income Producing Mgt., 202 F.3d 1282 (10th Cir.2000). Such disclaimers must be conspicuous and clear. Sellitto v. Litton Sys., 881 F.Supp. 932 (D.N.J.1994); Farnum v. Brattleboro Retreat, 164 Vt. 488, 671 A.2d 1249 (Vt.1995); some jurisdictions hold that to disclaim any described job security, the manual must explicitly state that the hiring is at will. These are described and criticized in Workman v. UPS, 234 F.3d 998 (7th Cir.2000).

quintessentially fits the mold of a unilateral contract.[65] The problems associated with the termination of offers to unilateral contracts also surface here with inconsistent results.[66]

Even under the majority view, some courts have held that the hiring is not at will if a consideration over and above the consideration supplied by the employee's services or promises of services is exchanged for the promise of permanent employment.[67] This approach gropes toward a fair result but confuses the questions of indefiniteness and consideration. It is possible to reach just results without confusing issues so diverse. Terms such as "permanent employment" have no immutable meaning. When used in different concrete situations by different individuals, different meanings may fairly be attached to the term. If the employee has paid—usually by forgoing a tort claim—for the promise of "permanent employment," it is likely that both parties understood that employment was to endure as long as the employee is able to perform the work for which the employee is hired.

The payment of a consideration is one evidentiary factor bearing on the proper interpretation of the parties' intention, but other evidentiary factors can perform the same function. In each case the court ought to consider all of the circumstances. Unfortunately, however, the courts have tended to deal with the question mechanically, as if *stare decisis* could provide the method by which the intention of the parties could be determined.

The same dichotomy exists in a promise of lifetime employment. Some cases hold that such a promise amounts to a hiring at will unless there are other factors such as an additional consideration being given.[68] But others take the position that the term should be accepted as written.[69] Despite the reluctance of the courts to take the terms "permanent" or "lifetime" literally, there are cases that have upheld perpetual obligations.[70] In the absence of an express agreement, however, the courts are reluctant to find that an obligation in perpetuity exists.[71]

65. See Pettit, supra note 62, at 560–61.

66. Asmus v. Pacific Bell, 23 Cal.4th 1, 96 Cal.Rptr.2d 179, 999 P.2d 71 (2000) (revocable on reasonable notice); Doyle v. Holy Cross Hosp., 186 Ill.2d 104, 237 Ill.Dec. 100, 708 N.E.2d 1140 (1999) (not revocable to employees who have commenced to perform).

67. Tobin v. Ravenswood Aluminum, 838 F.Supp. 262 (S.D.W.Va.1993); Satyshur v. General Motors, 38 F.Supp.2d 744 (N.D.Ind.1999), aff'd; Collins v. Parsons College, 203 N.W.2d 594, 60 ALR3d 218 (Iowa 1973); Humphrey v. Hill, 55 N.C.App. 359, 285 S.E.2d 293 (1982); see 1 Corbin § 4.2 (Perillo 1993); 2 Corbin § 6.2 (Perillo & Bender 1995); 3A Corbin § 684.

68. Page v. Carolina Coach, 667 F.2d 1156 (4th Cir.1982); McDole v. Duquesne Brewing., 281 Pa.Super. 78, 421 A.2d 1155

(1980); Smith v. Beloit Corp., 40 Wis.2d 550, 162 N.W.2d 585 (1968).

69. Ross–Simons v. Baccarat, 217 F.3d 8 (1st Cir.2000); Roberts v. Southern Wood Piedmont, 571 F.2d 276 (5th Cir.1978); Arentz v. Morse Dry Dock & Repair, 249 N.Y. 439, 164 N.E. 342 (1928).

70. Payroll Express. v. Aetna Cas. and Sur., 659 F.2d 285 (2d Cir.1981); Warner–Lambert v. John J. Reynolds, Inc., 178 F.Supp. 655 (S.D.N.Y.1959), aff'd; Holmgren v. Utah–Idaho Sugar, 582 P.2d 856 (Utah 1978).

71. Barton v. State, 104 Idaho 338, 659 P.2d 92 (1983); Haines v. New York, 41 N.Y.2d 769, 396 N.Y.S.2d 155, 364 N.E.2d 820 (1977); Carolina Cable Network v. Alert Cable TV, 316 S.C. 98, 447 S.E.2d 199 (1994); see also Baum Assocs. v. Society

The orthodox rule as to agreements terminable at will (or even on reasonable notice) has been that the agreement may be terminated "for good cause, for no cause or even for cause morally wrong."[72] The traditional reason given for this harsh rule is that it would not be good policy to keep the parties locked in the close relationship of employer-employee against the wishes of one of them,[73] but this rule is being overturned in many jurisdictions in cases where the discharge is contrary to public policy.

Federal legislation prohibits dismissal of employees because of union activity,[74] on grounds of racial discrimination,[75] or because of age;[76] a worker whose hiring is at will cannot be discharged in retaliation for filing a worker's compensation claim.[77] It has also been held that the manager of a consumer credit department whose employment was at will could not be discharged because the manager wished to adhere to the dictates of consumer protection legislation,[78] and that a tenancy at will cannot be terminated in retaliation for the tenant's complaint to the authorities about building violations.[79] The same rule applies if an employee is discharged solely to avoid paying pension benefits under ERISA.[80]

A New Hampshire[81] case has pushed the doctrine of these cases a giant step forward, holding that the firing of a female worker because she resisted the sexual advances of her foreman was wrongful, stating:

> "We hold that a termination by the employer of a contract of employment at will which is motivated by bad faith or malice or

Brand Hat, 477 F.2d 255 (8th Cir.1973); Gastonia v. Duke Power, 19 N.C.App. 315, 199 S.E.2d 27 (1973), cert. denied. Compare Southern Bell v. Florida East Coast Ry., 399 F.2d 854 (5th Cir.1968) (an agreement in 1917 for free passage of telephone lines over railroad property was held not perpetual but terminable on reasonable notice) with Gainesville v. Board of Control, 81 So.2d 514 (Fla.1955), (a promise by the City to provide free water to the University of Florida was held non-terminable so long as it remained in Gainesville because the promise had induced it to locate in Gainesville).

72. Payne v. Western & A. R. Co., 81 Tenn. 507, 519–20 (1884), overruled on other grounds Hutton v. Watters, 132 Tenn. 527, 179 S.W. 134 (1915); Kilbride v. Dushkin Pub. Group, 186 Conn. 718, 443 A.2d 922 (1982); accord, Brockmeyer v. Dun & Bradstreet, 113 Wis.2d 561, 335 N.W.2d 834 (1983). See Employment Law Issue, 43 Drake L.Rev. 292–377 (1994).

73. Blades, Employment at Will v. Individual Freedom, 67 Colum.L.Rev. 1404 (1967); Summers, Individual Protection Against Unjust Dismissal, 62 Va.L.Rev. 481 (1976); Note, 58 Tex.L.Rev. 991, 994 (1980).

74. 29 U.S.C.A. § 158(a)(3).

75. 42 U.S.C.A. § 2000(e)–(e)(2).

76. 29 U.S.C.A. §§ 621–34.

77. Frampton v. Central Indiana Gas Co., 260 Ind. 249, 297 N.E.2d 425, 63 ALR3d 973 (1973); Niesent v. Homestake Mining Co., 505 N.W.2d 781 (S.D.1993); accord, Smith v. Farmers Co–op. Ass'n, 825 P.2d 1323 (Okl.1992) (part-time mayor fired from his day job for declining to give a variance to a director of his employer).

78. Harless v. First Nat. Bank, 162 W.Va. 116, 246 S.E.2d 270 (1978); contra, Winters v. Houston Chronicle, 795 S.W.2d 723 (Tex.1990). See De Giuseppe, The Effect of the Employment-at-Will Rule, 10 Fordham Urban L.J. 1 (1981).

79. Robinson v. Diamond Housing, 463 F.2d 853 (D.C.Cir.1972), 18 Vill.L.R. 1119 (1973); 39 U.Cin.L.Rev. 712 (1970).

80. Moore v. Home Ins. Co., 601 F.2d 1072 (9th Cir.1979).

81. Monge v. Beebe Rubber, 114 N.H. 130, 316 A.2d 549, 551, 62 ALR3d 264, 268 (1974); accord, Siles v. Travenol Labs., 13 Mass.App.Ct. 354, 433 N.E.2d 103 (1982), rev. denied; see Blades, supra n. 73.

based on retaliation is not in the best interest of the economic system or the public good and constitutes a breach of the employment contract * * *. Such a rule affords the employee a certain stability of employment and does not interfere with the employer's normal exercise of his right to discharge, which is necessary to permit him to operate his business efficiently and profitably.''

A large number of cases are in accord with the public policy exception to the at-will rule,[82] but some have declined to follow this lead.[83] Some courts regard the firing in such case to constitute a tort. This characterization opens the door to punitive damages.[84] A government body that fires a public employee or government contractor for expressing critical political views has committed a constitutional tort.[85]

(4) Where the Parties Agree to Agree or Agree to Negotiate

The traditional rule is that an agreement to agree as to a material term prevents the formation of a contract.[86] Two reasons are given. First, such an agreement leaves a material term too vague and indefinite to be enforced.[87] Second, it shows a lack of present agreement.[88] Thus, an

82. Martin Marietta v. Lorenz, 823 P.2d 100 (Colo.1992); Carl v. Children's Hospital, 702 A.2d 159 (D.C.App.1997); Parsons v. United Technologies, 243 Conn. 66, 700 A.2d 655 (1997); Hodges v. Gibson Prods. Co., 811 P.2d 151 (Utah 1991); Kempfer v. Automated Finishing, 211 Wis.2d 100, 564 N.W.2d 692 (1997) (trucker refused to drive vehicle for which he had no license); see Rothstein, et al, Employment Law ch. 9 (1994). As to differing approaches to determining public policy, compare Gantt v. Sentry Ins., 1 Cal.4th 1083, 4 Cal.Rptr.2d 874, 824 P.2d 680 (1992).with Green v. Ralee Eng'g, 19 Cal.4th 66, 960 P.2d 1046, 78 Cal.Rptr.2d 16 (1998). As to retaliatory demotions, see Brigham v. Dillon Cos., 262 Kan. 12, 935 P.2d 1054 (1997). As to retaliation against an independent contractor, see Harvey v.Care Initiatives, 634 N.W.2d 681 (Iowa 2001) (collecting cases).

83. Green v. Amerada–Hess, 612 F.2d 212 (5th Cir.1980), reh. denied; Loucks v. Star City Glass Co., 551 F.2d 745 (7th Cir. 1977); Hoffman–La Roche v. Campbell, 512 So.2d 725 (Ala.1987); cf. Borse v. Piece Goods Shop, 963 F.2d 611 (3d Cir.1992) (Pa. law unclear); Amaan v. Eureka, 615 S.W.2d 414 (Mo.1981), cert. denied. To the effect that such a significant change should be made by the legislature, see Murphy v. American Home Products, 58 N.Y.2d 293, 461 N.Y.S.2d 232, 448 N.E.2d 86 (1983). The result is McKinney's N.Y.Labor L. § 740. Courts have held that the doctrine of prima facie tort should not be applied in this type of case. Cartwright v. Golub Corp., 51 A.D.2d 407, 381 N.Y.S.2d 901 (1976); but see Ivy v. Army Times Pub. Co., 428 A.2d

831 (D.C.App.1981); Parnar v. Americana Hotels, 65 Haw. 370, 652 P.2d 625 (1982).

84. Dillard Dept. Stores v. Beckwith, 115 Nev. 372, 989 P.2d 882 (1999).

85. Board of County Comm'rs v. Umbehr, 518 U.S. 668 (1996).

86. Joseph Martin, Jr., Deli. v. Schumacher, 52 N.Y.2d 105, 436 N.Y.S.2d 247, 417 N.E.2d 541 (1981); Prenger v. Baumhoer, 914 S.W.2d 413 (Mo.App.1996). This rule is criticized in Macneil, Contracts: Adjustment of Long–Term Economic Relations Under Classical, Neoclassical, and Relational Contract Law, 72 Nw.U.L.Rev. 854 (1978).

An agreement that contains a method of filling in the gap if the parties fail to agree is binding even under the traditional view. 166 Mamaroneck Ave. v. 151 E. Post Rd., 78 N.Y.2d 88, 571 N.Y.S.2d 686, 575 N.E.2d 104 (1991) (arbitration).

87. Willowood Condominium Ass'n v. HNC Realty, 531 F.2d 1249 (5th Cir.1976); Transamerica Equip. Leasing v. Union Bank, 426 F.2d 273 (9th Cir.1970); Western Airlines v. Lathrop Co., 499 P.2d 1013 (Alaska 1972); Burgess v. Rodom, 121 Cal. App.2d 71, 262 P.2d 335 (1953); Weil & Assocs. v. Urban Renewal Agency, 206 Kan. 405, 479 P.2d 875 (1971); Willmott v. Giarraputo, 5 N.Y.2d 250, 184 N.Y.S.2d 97, 157 N.E.2d 282 (1959); Deadwood Lodge v. Albert, 319 N.W.2d 823 (S.D.1982). Annot., 68 ALR2d 1221 (1959).

88. Rs. 1st § 33 cmt c. See, e.g., Martin v. Jack Yanks Constr., 650 So.2d 120 (Fla.

agreement to agree has been equated to a case where the parties purport to agree on a term and leave it indefinite. An agreement to agree can be distinguished from a situation where the parties agree to negotiate and to use reasonable efforts to reach agreement.[89] As will be shown below, however, modern courts have been holding that an agreement to agree carries with it an implied promise to negotiate in good faith. Such a duty also arises where the parties reach an "agreement in principle." In such a case there is also a duty to negotiate in good faith; failure to do so results in a breach.[90]

Some of the more modern cases (even without relying on the UCC and the Restatement (Second), discussed below) have recognized that agreements to agree serve a valuable commercial purpose and that the traditional rule may operate unfairly where a party uses the rule to defeat an agreement that the parties intended to be binding.[91]

An illustration of the modern cases is an option in a lease for the tenant to extend the lease at a rental fee to be agreed on. Some cases still follow the older view that the agreement to agree prevents the exercise of the option.[92] But, as one case has stated: "The better view, however, would hold that such a clause intends renewal at a 'reasonable' rent and would find that market conditions are ascertainable with sufficient certainty to make the clause specifically enforceable."[93] The result coincides with the intention of the parties and with fairness because the lessee has already paid for the option and should not be denied the benefit of the bargain.

The option case is only a small departure from the traditional rule. Let us now examine Kier v. Condrack, a case that takes a giant step away from the traditional rule.[94] Plaintiff entered into an arrangement with defendant whereby plaintiff obtained an option to buy a piece of real property for the sum of $23,500 "on payments and terms to be negotiated provided the same is exercised by June 1." On May 15, plaintiff sought to exercise the option. Plaintiff offered to pay $5,300 in

App.1995) ("Final price for restoration work to be worked out with * * * Insurance Company and the general contractor").

89. Tacoma v. U.S., 31 F.3d 1130 (Fed. Cir.1994); see Lake and Draetta, Letters of Intent and Other Precontractual Documents (2d ed. 1994); Farnsworth, Precontractual Liability and Preliminary Agreements, 87 Colum.L.Rev. 217 (1987).

90. Itek v. Chicago Aerial Indus., 248 A.2d 625 (Del.1968), on remand 257 A.2d 232 (Del.Super.1969). See Knapp, Enforcing the Contract to Bargain, 44 N.Y.U.L.Rev. 673 (1969); Temkin, When Does the "Fat Lady" Sing?: An Analysis of "Agreement in Principle" in Corporate Acquisitions, 55 Fordham L.Rev. 125 (1986).

91. Opdyke Inv. v. Norris Grain, 413 Mich. 354, 320 N.W.2d 836 (1982); Vigano v. Wylain, Inc., 633 F.2d 522 (8th Cir.1980)

(citing text); but see Viking Broadcasting v. Snell Pub. 243 Neb. 92, 497 N.W.2d 383 (1993); see also 1 Corbin § 2.8 (Perillo 1993), and Macneil, A Primer of Contract Planning, 48 S.Cal.L.Rev. 627, 662 (1975).

92. Walker v. Keith, 382 S.W.2d 198 (Ky.1964); Joseph Martin, Jr., Deli. v. Schumacher, 52 N.Y.2d 105, 436 N.Y.S.2d 247, 417 N.E.2d 541 (1981).

93. Moolenaar v. Co–Build Cos., 354 F.Supp. 980, 982 (D.V.I.1973); accord, Berrey v. Jeffcoat, 785 P.2d 20 (Alaska 1990); Carlson v. Bold Petroleum, 996 P.2d 751 (Colo.App.2000) (easement renewal); see Annot., 58 ALR3d 494 (1970).

94. Kier v. Condrack, 25 Utah 2d 139, 478 P.2d 327 (1970).

cash and to assume two mortgages in the combined amount of $18,200. Defendant refused to negotiate because defendant no longer wanted to sell. The court stated that plaintiff was free to suggest a method of payment, that the parties were obliged to negotiate in good faith, and that defendant breached this duty. The court concluded that plaintiff's proposal would satisfy a reasonable person (in any event plaintiff also offered to pay the entire $23,500 in cash) and therefore a Court of Equity could do what equity and good conscience requires, decree specific performance based on the offer of the plaintiff. It is obvious that here the court constructed a duty requiring the parties to negotiate in good faith even though there was no such provision in the contract.[95] Such duties have been constructed in other cases and the courts have exercised their equitable powers to order the parties to negotiate under court supervision.[96] Under these modern cases, an agreement to agree carries with it an implied promise to negotiate in good faith.

The Restatement (Second)[97] and the UCC[98] are in accord with the modern view on agreements to agree. A UCC comment expresses the modern philosophy as follows: "This article rejects * * * the formula that an agreement to agree is unenforceable * * * and rejects also defeating such agreements on the ground of 'indefiniteness.' Instead this article recognizes the dominant intention of the parties to have the deal continue to be binding on both."[99]

(b) The Uniform Commercial Code

The provisions of the UCC relating to indefiniteness are of two types. There are provisions relating to specific problems. Some of these, such as the provision relating to open price terms, have already been discussed.[100] They must be viewed in the light of the general provision on indefiniteness which is designed to prevent, where it is at all possible, a contracting party who is dissatisfied with a bargain from taking refuge in the doctrine to wriggle out of an agreement.[101] The guiding principle is:[102]

> "Even though one or more terms are left open a contract for sale does not fail for indefiniteness if the parties have intended to

95. See n.90 supra; see also Aviation Contractor Employees v. U.S., 945 F.2d 1568 (Fed.Cir.1991) ("the emerging view is that an agreement which specifies that certain terms will be agreed on by future negotiation is sufficiently definite, because it impliedly places an obligation on the parties to negotiate *in good faith*"); Yackey v. Pacifica Dev., 99 Cal.App.3d 776, 160 Cal.Rptr. 430 (1979).

96. Kenai v. Ferguson, 732 P.2d 184 (Alaska 1987); Oglebay Norton Co. v. Armco, Inc., 52 Ohio St.3d 232, 556 N.E.2d 515 (1990) (CEO's of the parties ordered to negotiate with the aid of a court-appointed

mediator). See also Unihealth v. U.S. Healthcare, 14 F.Supp.2d 623 (D.N.J.1998).

97. Rs. 2d § 33 ill. 8.

98. UCC §§ 2–305(1)(b) & 2–204(3) (revision unchanged).

99. UCC § 2–305 cmt 1.

100. UCC § 2–305 discussed above.

101. Rs. 2d § 33 cmt b. See, e.g., Kearns v. Andree, 107 Conn. 181, 139 A. 695, 59 ALR 599 (1928); Fairmount Glass Works v. Crunden–Martin Woodenware Co., 106 Ky. 659, 51 S.W. 196 (1899); Scammel v. Ouston, [1941] 1 All E.R. 14 (1940).

102. UCC § 2–204(3) (revision is unchanged).

make a contract and there is a reasonably certain basis for giving an appropriate remedy."

To satisfy this section the parties must intend to contract. Indefiniteness as to material terms does not prevent this intent from existing.[103] However, "when a dispute over material terms manifests a lack of intention to contract, no contract results."[104]

This section changes the traditional common law rules in all three types of cases discussed above. Under the UCC, contrary to common law, a gap-filler is available even though the parties agreed to agree or purported to agree on a term that was left indefinite. But the section goes beyond gap-fillers and permits a court to pursue a case-by-case approach and use any reasonably certain basis for giving an appropriate remedy. In this respect, Comment 3 points out:

"The test is not certainty as to what the parties were to do nor as to the exact amount of damages due the plaintiff. Nor is the fact that one or more terms are left to be agreed on enough of itself to defeat an otherwise adequate agreement. Rather, commercial standards on the point of 'indefiniteness' are intended to be applied, this act making provision elsewhere for missing terms needed for performance, open price, remedies and the like."

What is clear is that the omission of an important term or terms does not necessarily prevent a contract from arising.[105] What is not clear is when a court will find that "there is a reasonably certain basis for giving an appropriate remedy." The unwritten premise is that the court must be able to identify which party has breached. Thus, the key issues are *intent, remedy and breach.*

The approach envisaged is the type employed in the Kier case mentioned above.[106] This provision of the UCC offers an artful court wide scope to employ its ingenuity. The question of whether there is a reasonably certain basis for giving an appropriate remedy is one of law while the question of whether the parties intended to contract will ordinarily be one of fact. The Restatement (Second) is in accord with the UCC[107] and also considers questions of detrimental reliance in this context but we will defer this topic for later consideration.[108]

If part of an agreement is indefinite and part of it is not, should the part that is indefinite be disregarded and the remainder enforced? The

103. Pennsylvania Co. v. Wilmington Trust, 39 Del.Ch. 453, 166 A.2d 726 (1960). UCC § 2–204 cmt 3 on this point states: "The more terms the parties leave open, the less likely it is that they have intended to conclude a binding agreement, but their actions may be frequently conclusive on the matter despite omissions."

104. Kleinschmidt Div. of SCM v. Futuronics, 41 N.Y.2d 972, 975, 395 N.Y.S.2d 151, 152, 363 N.E.2d 701, 702 (1977).

105. Williston wished to limit the section to "minor" omissions. Williston, 63 Harv.L.Rev. 561 (1950). This recommendation was rejected. See Pennsylvania Co. v. Wilmington Trust, 39 Del.Ch. 453, 166 A.2d 726 (1960).

106. See n.94 supra.

107. Rs. 2d §§ 33, 34; Firstul Mtge. v. Osko, 604 P.2d 150 (Okl.App.1979).

108. Rs. 2d § 34 cmt d. See ch. 6 infra.

test is whether the parties would have entered into the agreement without the offending clauses.[109]

Sometimes a contract allows one of the parties to specify the details of the other's performance. Prior to the UCC such a provision presented grave difficulties. These difficulties are illustrated by the facts in Wilhelm Lubrication v. Brattrud.[110] The seller agreed to sell and the buyer agreed to buy five thousand gallons of "Worthmore Motor Oil SAE 10–70." The term "SAE 10–70" designates seven weights of oil. In this agreement the price for each weight was definite. Three weeks after the agreement was made and before any specifications were submitted, the buyer repudiated the agreement. The court held that the agreement was too vague and indefinite because of the indefiniteness of the assortment. Many cases were in accord holding that, unless the assortment is specified, the agreement was too vague and indefinite to be enforceable and perhaps an equal number of cases had held that agreement was sufficiently definite.[111] The latter cases ordinarily assessed damages on the alternative least onerous to the defendant.[112]

The UCC now resolves this problem by providing that, despite "the fact that the agreement leaves particulars of performance to be specified by one of the parties," there is a contract.[113] Under subsection 3 the contract would be breached if the buyer fails to specify the assortment or if the seller refuses to permit the buyer to specify the assortment. Although subsection 2 says that, unless otherwise agreed, the specifications of an assortment of goods are at the buyer's option, this does not mean that the buyer is free to specify or not specify, but rather has both the right and obligation. The problem of indefiniteness is solved by requiring the specification to be made in "good faith and within limits set by commercial reasonableness."[114]

§ 2.10 Unilateral, Bilateral and Reverse Unilateral Contracts and Some of Their Implications

(a) The Classical Approach

Every contract involves at least two contracting parties. In some contracts, however, only one party has made a promise and therefore only this party is subject to a legal obligation. Such a contract is said to be unilateral. In contrast, a contract where both parties have made promises is bilateral. If there are more than two parties, the contract is bilateral if one party is both a promisor and a promisee.

---

109. See, e.g., Eckles v. Sharman, 548 F.2d 905 (10th Cir.1977).

110. 197 Minn. 626, 268 N.W. 634, 106 ALR 1279 (1936), 37 Colum.L.Rev. 309 (1937).

111. The cases are collected in Annots., 106 ALR 1284 (1937), 105 ALR 1100 (1936) and are commented on in 11 Temp.L.Q. 250 (1936).

112. Rs. 1st § 344; 5 Williston § 1407. Remedies and damages in this type of case are discussed in 23 U.Chi.L.Rev. 499 (1956).

113. UCC § 2–311(1) (revision is unchanged).

114. Id.

If A says to B, "If you run in the New York Marathon and finish I will pay you $1,000," A has made a promise but has not asked B for a return promise. A has asked B to perform, not for a commitment to perform. A has thus made an offer looking to a unilateral contract.[1] B cannot accept this offer by promising to run in the race.[2] B must accept, if at all, by performing the act.[3] Because no return promise is requested, at no point is B bound to perform. If B does perform, a contract involving two parties is created, but the contract is classified as unilateral because only one party is ever under an obligation.

If A says to B: "If you promise to run in the Marathon and finish the race, I promise to pay you $1,000," A's offer requests B to make a commitment. A bilateral contract arises when the requisite return promise is made by B.[4] If B makes the promise both parties are bound.[5]

A contract would also arise if B made an implied promise. B's promise could be inferred if B started to run in the race in A's presence. However, if B started to run but not in A's presence, there would be no implied promise because the requisite communication would be lacking.[6] The rule is that where an offer to a bilateral contract is made, no contract is created unless B makes the requested promise either expressly or by implication.

All of these conclusions are premised on the notion that the offeror is "the master of the offer" and is thus free to indicate in what manner the offeree can assent.[7] There is perhaps one exception to this last statement. If the offeror asks for a promise and the offeree performs the act, instead of promising to perform the act, there is some authority to the effect that a contract is formed if the performance is completed while the offer is still open[8] and the requisite notice of performance is given.[9] Although this rule violates the notion that the offeror is master of the offer, it appeals to common sense in situations where the offeror is not

§ 2.10

1. See e.g., Multicare Medical Center v. State, 114 Wn.2d 572, 790 P.2d 124 (1990), en banc; Herschbach v. Corpus Christi, 883 S.W.2d 720 (1994). See generally, Pettit, Modern Unilateral Contracts, 63 B.U.L.Rev. 551, 560–61 (1983).

2. Suhre v. Busch, 343 Mo. 170, 120 S.W.2d 47 (1938); Rs. 2d § 59 ill. 2.

3. Becker v. State, 689 F.2d 763 (8th Cir.1982). Questioning the use of offer and acceptance concepts in unilateral contract analysis is Tiersma, Reassessing Unilateral Contracts: The role of Offer, Acceptance and Promise, 26 U.C.Davis L.Rev. 1 (1992).

4. Rs. 2d § 50(1) & ill. 3.

5. Judd Realty v. Tedesco, 400 A.2d 952 (R.I.1979).

6. Allied Steel & Conveyors v. Ford, 277 F.2d 907 (6th Cir.1960); U.S. ex rel. Wor-

thington Pump & Mach. v. John A. Johnson Contr., 139 F.2d 274 (3d Cir.1943), cert. denied; Vermillion v. Marvel Merchandising, 314 Ky. 196, 234 S.W.2d 673 (1950).

7. Wormser, The True Conception of Unilateral Contracts, 26 Yale L.J. 136 (1916).

8. Rs. 1st § 63; 1 Williston § 6.26.

9. On the question of notice see § 2.15 infra. This exception, based on the thought that performance is as desirable as a promise, has been eliminated in the Second Restatement. According to the Reporter's Note to Rs. 2d § 62, the need for this exception has been eliminated, but that is an exaggeration. See Braucher, Offer and Acceptance in the Second Restatement, 74 Yale L.J. 302, 307 (1964); Goble, 22 Ill. L.Rev. 789 (1928); Williston, 22 Ill.L.Rev. 791 (1928); cf. Crook v. Cowan, 64 N.C. 743 (1870).

adversely affected by receiving the performance rather than the promise.[10]

At times it is easy to decide whether an offer looks to a unilateral or a bilateral contract, but at other times the manifestations are ambiguous and the decision is not easy. The original Restatement espoused the presumption that the offer looked to a bilateral contract.[11] The reason given was that an offeror ordinarily wants the security of a promise to bind the offeree. This reasoning no longer prevails. As discussed below, unless it is crystal clear that the offeror prescribes a particular mode of acceptance, the offer may be accepted in any reasonable manner. At times an offer may be phrased so as expressly to permit an acceptance either by the making of a promise or by the rendering of a performance.[12]

In the usual unilateral contract, the promise is made by the offeror. However, in the unusual case of a reverse unilateral contract the offeree makes the only promise. For example, if A, a property owner, pays $500 to an insurance company asking for the company's promise to pay A $200,000 if A's house is destroyed by fire, A is the offeror but has made no promise. Rather A has requested a promise from B, the offeree. When B makes the promise a reverse unilateral contract is created.[13] The most common reverse unilateral contracts arise where the offeree silently accepts services that are rendered with the expectation of payment.[14]

Another preliminary question of some importance is the question of what is the act of acceptance called for by the offer to a reverse unilateral contract. For example, in the case above involving the insurance company, the act of acceptance was the insurance company's promise to pay, but if the facts were changed so that the insurance company is the offeror, the act of acceptance would be A's payment of the premium. The payment of the premium would create the unilateral contract, but the owner could not recover unless there was a fire. The occurrence of the fire is a condition precedent to the insurance company's obligation to pay. This distinction between an act necessary to the formation of a contract and an act or event that must occur before the performance of a contractual duty is due will be of importance in a number of contexts to be considered later.[15]

(b) The UCC

The UCC's § 2–206 has made extensive changes in the common law of offer and acceptance. Despite variations in language, the Restatement

---

10. Note, 52 S.Cal.L.Rev. 1917 (1979).

11. Rs. 1st § 31; see Craddock v. Greenhut Constr., 423 F.2d 111 (5th Cir.1970); Davis v. Jacoby, 1 Cal.2d 370, 34 P.2d 1026 (1934); Motel Services v. Central Maine Power, 394 A.2d 786 (Me.1978).

12. Ever–Tite Roofing v. Green, 83 So.2d 449 (La.App.1955); Koppers Co. v. Kaiser Aluminum & Chem., 9 N.C.App. 118, 175 S.E.2d 761 (1970); 49 Iowa L.Rev. 960 (1964); cf. Lazarus v. American Motors, 21 Wis.2d 76, 123 N.W.2d 548 (1963).

13. Rs. 2d § 55 ill. 1; Rs. 2d § 69, ill 1; 1 Corbin § 3.17 (Perillo 1993); 1 Williston § 4:4; see also Goble, The Non–Promissory Offer, 48 Nw.U.L.Rev. 590 (1953); Goble, Is an Offer a Promise?, 22 Ill.L.Rev. 567 (1928); Green, Is an Offer Always a Promise?, 23 Ill.L.Rev. 301 (1928); Stoljar, The Ambiguity of Promise, 47 Nw.U.L.Rev. 1 (1952).

14. See § 2.18 infra at notes 26–46.

15. See § 3.7(b) infra.

(Second) adopts the same basic approach. Subsections (1) and (2) of this Section reads as follows:[16]

"(1) Unless otherwise unambiguously indicated by the language or circumstances

(a) an offer to make a contract shall be construed as inviting acceptance in any manner and by any medium reasonable in the circumstances;

(b) an order or other offer to buy goods for prompt or current shipment shall be construed as inviting acceptance either by a prompt promise to ship or by the prompt or current shipment of conforming or non-conforming goods, but such a shipment of nonconforming goods does not constitute an acceptance if the seller seasonably notifies the buyer that the shipment is offered only as an accommodation to the buyer.

(2) Where the beginning of a requested performance is a reasonable mode of acceptance an offeror who is not notified of acceptance within a reasonable time may treat the offer as having lapsed before acceptance."

(1) Subsection (1)(a)

The word "manner" in subsection (a) relates to the distinction between a unilateral and a bilateral contract. At common law, except in unusual cases, an offer looked either to a bilateral or a unilateral contract. The classification as unilateral or bilateral determined the manner of acceptance. If the offer was ambiguous on this point it was presumed that the offer invited a promise,[17] but this section has substituted this presumption with the notion that in the vast majority of cases the offeror is indifferent as to the manner of acceptance. Thus, in most cases the offeree is free to proceed by performance or promise.[18]

When does an offeror "unambiguously indicate" an exclusive manner of acceptance? The Restatement (Second) furnishes some helpful illustrations that show that it will be an unusual case where the offeror has made such an unambiguous indication.[19] The use in the offer of unilateral words such as "deliver" is not enough to prevent an acceptance by promise.[20] Conversely the use of the word "promise" does not prevent an acceptance by performance.[21] However, where the buyer's order stated that "seller shall mail to purchaser a signed duplicate copy hereof," it was held that the offer unambiguously indicated that a promise by writing was the only manner of acceptance.[22]

16. No substantive change in revision.

17. See § 2.10(a) supra.

18. Murray, Contracts: A New Design for the Agreement Process, 53 Corn.L.Rev. 785 (1968).

19. Rs. 2d § 32.

20. Rs. 2d § 32 cmt a. An offer of reward would not be indifferent. Rs. 2d § 31 ill. 3.

21. Rs. 2d § 32 ills. 2 and 5; see also UCC § 2–206 cmt 2.

22. Southwestern Stationery & Bank Supply v. Harris Corp., 624 F.2d 168 (10th Cir.1980). The common law cases are split

(2) Subsection (1)(b)

Subsection (1)(b) is designed to accomplish two results. First if one reads up to the comma and ignores the word "non-conforming," the section "exemplifies" the more general provision of subsection 2–206(1)(a). It shows that an "indifferent" offer "to buy goods for prompt or current shipment" invites an acceptance either by performance or promise.[23] Parenthetically, it should be noted that if the offeree performs, UCC § 2–504(c) requires the prompt giving of notice of shipment. Under that provision failure to give notice is a ground for rejection only if there is a material delay in shipment or if loss ensues. The Restatement (Second) takes the position that notice is unnecessary.[24] This is an unfortunate mistake. The UCC will prevail because the situation involves a sale of goods.

This section was also designed to prevent the offeree from utilizing what Hawkland calls the "unilateral contract trick." At common law a shipment of non-conforming goods in response to an offer to purchase amounted only to a counter-offer. In contrast, under the UCC, even if the seller sends non-conforming[25] goods in response to an offer there is a contract. The non-conforming shipment is both the acceptance of the offer and simultaneously a breach.[26] However, there is no contract if "the seller seasonably notifies the buyer that the shipment is offered only as an accommodation to the buyer." In that event the shipment would be treated as a counter-offer.[27]

It is important to note that, under subsection 1(b), shipment is performance and not merely the beginning of performance. Loading goods on the seller's own truck is not shipment but it may be the beginning of performance.[28] Subsection 2, and not 1(b), applies to the beginning of performance.

(3) Subsection (2)

To understand subsection 2, which governs the effect of the beginning of performance, the common-law background must be recalled. Under the common law, if the offer looked to a unilateral contract there were three views on the effect of beginning performance. The prevailing view is that beginning performance does not bind the offeree but makes the offer irrevocable. The older view is that the beginning of performance has no effect.[29] In an offer looking to a bilateral contract the

on the question of whether similar language prescribes the method of acceptance. Compare, Allied Steel & Conveyors v. Ford., 277 F.2d 907 (6th Cir.1960) with Markoff v. New York Life Ins., 92 Nev. 268, 549 P.2d 330 (1976).

23. Hawkland § 1.1303.

24. Rs. 2d § 62 cmt b. The revision of UCC § 2–504(c) is unchanged.

25. Goods are conforming "when they are in accordance with the obligations under the contracts." UCC § 2–106(2) (revision unchanged).

26. Gilbride, The Uniform Commercial Code: Impact on the Law of Contracts, 30 Brooklyn L.Rev. 177, 185 (1964).

27. Weintraub, Disclaimer of Warranties and Limitation of Damages for Breach of Warranty under the UCC, 53 Texas L.Rev. 60 (1974).

28. UCC § 2–206 cmt 2.

29. See § 2.22 infra, where this is explained in detail.

beginning of performance was of no effect unless done with the knowledge of the offeror.[30]

The subsection starts out with the phrase, "where the beginning of performance is a reasonable mode of acceptance." If the beginning of performance is not a reasonable mode of acceptance, as for example where it is unambiguously clear that an express promise is sought, then this subsection is not applicable and we must consult the common law for solutions.

If, however, the beginning of performance is a reasonable mode of acceptance, the offeree is bound on commencement of performance provided that the beginning of performance unambiguously expresses the offeree's intent to commit to a contract.[31] In such a case the offeree's beginning of performance operates as if the offeree had made a promise to complete performance.

The net result is that bilateral contracts are favored over unilaterals. Even if the offeree is bound by starting to perform, the offeror is not bound to perform unless the offeree gives notice of beginning performance within a reasonable time. During the time between the beginning of performance and the reasonable time for giving notice, the offeror would not be free to revoke.[32] If timely notice is not given, the offeror, although not bound to perform, has the option to proceed as if there is a contract.[33] Again, the basic notion is that the offeror is not bound unless given notice, but the offeree is bound by beginning performance.

(c) Restatement (Second)

The Restatement (Second) follows the UCC in providing that unless the language or circumstances make it clear that only a promise or only a performance is requested as the acceptance, the offeree may choose any reasonable manner of acceptance.[34] If beginning performance is a reasonable mode of acceptance, then beginning performance constitutes acceptance unless the offeror knows or should know that the offeree does not intend to be bound. The Restatement adds that in such a case notice of the beginning of performance will ordinarily be required.[35] If the offeree

---

30. This is perhaps an overstatement. There is some authority to the effect that a contract is formed if the performance is *completed* while the offer is still open and the requisite notice of performance is given. See text at notes 8–10 supra.

31. UCC § 2–206 cmt 3. If the offeror reasonably should know that the offeree in starting to perform does not intend to be bound, the offeree is not bound. For example, the offeree may notify the offeror of non-acceptance within a reasonable time. Murray, Contracts: A New Design for the Agreement Process, 53 Cornell L.Rev. 785 (1968).

32. There is language in comment 3 to UCC § 2–206 that indicates that the revo-

cability of the offer is dependent on the common law of the concerned jurisdiction. This is one example of a number of instances where the language of the comment contradicts the text of the statute. See Murray, supra note 31. Often this occurs because the proposed statute is redrafted before enactment without redrafting the comment.

33. UCC § 2–206 cmt 3.

34. Rs. 2d §§ 30(2) & 32.

35. Rs. 2d § 54 cmt b, § 56. Notice would not be required, for example, if the offer itself or a prior course of dealing indicates that notice is not required. Rs. 2d § 56 ill. 1.

does not give the requisite notice, the offeror is discharged; however, the offeror may opt to hold the offeree to the bilateral contract that had already arisen.[36]

D. ACCEPTANCE

Table of Sections

---

36. Rs. 2d § 63.

§ 2.11 Must the Offeree Know of the Offer?

An offer creates a power of acceptance in the offeree. This power of acceptance permits the offeree to transform the offer into a contractual obligation.[1] Thus, an acceptance has been defined as "a voluntary act of the offeree whereby [the offeree] exercises the power conferred * * * by the offer and thereby creates the set of legal relations called a contract."[2] The acceptance of the offer terminates the power of revocation that the offeror ordinarily has.[3]

As a general proposition, a contract can only be formed if the offeree knew of the offer at the time of the alleged acceptance.[4] To create a contract the offeree must exchange a requested performance or promise for the offeror's promise.[5] Under the objective theory of contracts, however, it is possible that the offeree may be bound by an acceptance even without knowing of the offer. The appearance of a bargain in some circumstances is sufficient. For example, A mails an offer to B. Assume that B gets the offer, and without opening it and without suspecting that it is an offer, decides to confuse A by sending a letter stating, "I accept." Here, there would be a contract even though B did not know of the offer because A as a reasonable person could rely on B's promise.[6] The same principle operates to bind an offeree who signs a record which he knows or should know is an offer without reading it.[7]

The same result may obtain even without a signature. Thus, for example, the acceptance of documents such as bills of lading, passenger tickets, insurance policies and bank books gives rise to contracts based on the provisions contained in them which they may be reasonably expected to contain.[8] A different result has been reached as to provisions

---

§ 2.11

1. See § 2.5 supra.

2. Corbin, Offer and Acceptance, and Some of the Resulting Legal Relations, 26 Yale L.J. 169, 199–200 (1917), Selected Readings 170, 193 (1931); accord Cinciarelli v. Carter, 662 F.2d 73 (D.C.Cir.1981).

3. See § 2.20(d) infra.

4. 1 Corbin § 3.5 (Perillo 1993); 1 Williston §§ 4:13–4:16.

5. The exchange requirement is developed in ch. 4 infra.

6. Rs. 2d § 23 cmt b; see § 2.2 supra.

7. Paterson v. Reeves, 304 F.2d 950, 951 (D.C.Cir.1962) ("One who signs a contract which he had an opportunity to read and understand is bound by its provisions.")

See § 9.41 infra; 1 Corbin § 4.13 (Perillo 1993); 1 Williston § 4:16.

8. Regan v. Customcraft Homes, 170 Colo. 562, 463 P.2d 463 (1970); Polonsky v. Union Fed. Sav. & Loan Ass'n, 334 Mass. 697, 138 N.E.2d 115, 60 ALR2d 702 (1956); 1 Williston §§ 90A–90E (3d ed.). Thus, terms of a license contained in a box in which software is packed, may be binding on the purchaser. ProCD, v. Zeidenberg, 86 F.3d 1447 (7th Cir.1996). This rule may be subject to a requirement of legibility. Statutes sometimes provide that contracts must be printed in specified kinds of type. E.g., McKinney's N.Y.C.P.L.R. § 4544. Apart from statute, clauses that are virtually invisible are ineffective. See § 9.42 infra.

printed in small print on a parcel check because a person should not reasonably expect to find contract provisions on a parcel check.[9] The effect of signing or accepting a document which one does not read is discussed in more detail in §§ 9.41–9.45 infra.

The situation is quite different if the offer looks to a unilateral contract. If A mailed B an offer to a unilateral contract, and B performed the act called for, before opening the letter, B could not recover from A because B did not know of the offer; this would be the result even if B performed in the presence of A. Although B's performance in the presence of A may conceivably communicate a promise, the promise is a nullity because no promise was requested.[10] Thus, B may not recover. This result is often reached where an offer of reward has been made to the public; anyone who performed the act called for has no contractual claim[11] against the offeror unless the claimant knew of the offer.[12]

The principle that an offeree must know of the offer also gives rise to the rule that identical cross-offers do not create a contract. For example, suppose A mails an offer to B to sell a certain item at a certain price and in ignorance of this offer B mails an offer to buy the same item at the same price. No contract results.[13]

The Restatement (Second) adopts a fictionalized subversion of this rule. It asserts that the two offerors could assent in advance to cross-offers and suggests that such assent may be inferred when both parties think a contract has been made.[14] It would be better to say that identical cross-offers constitute a contract despite the objective theory because there is both subjective assent to the same deal and objective evidence of that subjective intent.[15] The Restatement (Second) takes precisely that approach in a similar problem discussed in the same section that discusses cross-offers.[16]

9. Klar v. H. & M. Parcel Room, 270 A.D. 538, 61 N.Y.S.2d 285 (1946), aff'd; Berguido v. Eastern Air Lines, 378 F.2d 369 (3d Cir.1967); see Hodgin, Fiction of the Cases, 23 No.Ire.L.Q. 174 (1972).

10. See § 2.10 supra.

11. In some states an offer for a reward made by a public agency is deemed to create a non-contractual liability toward a person performing the desired act. Sullivan v. Phillips, 178 Ind. 164, 98 N.E. 868 (1912); Smith v. State, 38 Nev. 477, 151 P. 512 (1915); Choice v. Dallas, 210 S.W. 753 (Tex. Civ.App.1919). In these jurisdictions knowledge of the offer is not a prerequisite to recovery. The reward is regarded as a grant rather than a contract.

12. Glover v. Jewish War Veterans, 68 A.2d 233 (D.C.Mun.App.1949); Fitch v. Snedaker, 38 N.Y. 248, 97 Am.Dec. 791 (1868); Broadnax v. Ledbetter, 100 Tex. 375, 99

S.W. 1111 (1907). Contra, Russell v. Stewart, 44 Vt. 170 (1872). See Annot., 86 ALR3d 1142 (1978).

13. Tinn v. Hoffman & Co., 29 L.T.R. (n.s.) 271 (Ex.1873).

14. Rs. 2d § 23 cmt d., ill. 5; cf. Morris Asinof & Sons v. Freudenthal, 195 A.D. 79, 186 N.Y.S. 383 (1921), aff'd; Perillo, Book Review, 37 Fordham L.Rev. 144, 148–49 (1968).

15. See Eisenberg, supra § 2.6 n.37 at 1152 (1994) ("mutually held subjective intent trumps objective interpretation"); Litvinoff, Offer and Acceptance in Louisiana Law: A Comparative Analysis: Part II Acceptance, 28 La.L.Rev. 153, 201 (1968).

16. See Rs. 2d § 23 cmt d, ill. 6. The illustration is based on the case of Mactier's Adm'rs v. Frith, 6 Wend. (N.Y.) 103, 21 Am.Dec. 262 (1830), discussed in § 2.23 infra.

When must the offeree know of the offer? Suppose, for example, that A offers a reward of $100 to anyone who finds and returns A's lost watch. B finds the watch, learns of the reward and returns it to A. Is B entitled to the reward? A number of authorities have concluded that B may not recover because B did not know of the offer before starting to perform.[17] As stated by the First Restatement, "the whole consideration requested by an offer must be given after the offeree knows of the offer."[18] The more modern view is that it is sufficient that the offeree completes performance with knowledge of the offer.[19] The theory of the second view is that it should be enough that the offer induces the completion of performance because this is the "common understanding" of the parties.[20] This paragraph applies only to unilateral contracts. When the offer is to a bilateral contract, the offeree's promise creates the contract and the question of when the offeree starts to perform is not usually relevant on the issue of acceptance.[21]

§ 2.12   Warranties in a Box; Shrinkwrap; Clickwrap

One of the controversial issues of today is the effect of a document packed with an appliance or other goods sealed in a box at the factory. Cases are divided on the binding effect on the purchaser of an arbitration clause contained in the limited warranty that accompanies the goods. The problem manifests itself where the purchaser is unaware that such a clause is contained in the document. In Hill v. Gateway 2000,[1] the court upheld the arbitration clause contained in a document packed in a carton containing a computer. The court said, "Payment before revelation of full terms is common * * * in many other endeavors," pointing out that airline tickets and insurance policies are frequently delivered a considerable time after contracting. Other courts have disagreed, holding that the packaged terms are not binding on the purchaser.[2] The reasoning in Gateway was flawed because that particular contract was made on the telephone and the terms in the box constituted additional terms that by the terms of the UCC do not become part of the contract.[3] Nonetheless, a direct seller such as Gateway can achieve the same result, without litigation, by merely having their sales clerks state at the time of purchase that there are terms and conditions in a booklet packed with their product and that, if the terms are unsatisfactory, the purchaser can return the product for a full refund.[4]

17. Rs. 1st § 53; Fitch v. Snedaker, 38 N.Y. 248, 97 Am.Dec. 791 (1868).

18. Rs. 1st § 53.

19. Rs. 2d § 51; Sharp Electronics v. Deutsche Fin. Services, 216 F.3d 388 (4th Cir.2000); Greene v. Heinrich, 59 Misc.2d 655, 300 N.Y.S.2d 236 (1969), aff'd.

20. Rs. 2d § 51 cmt b; accord 1 Corbin § 3.6 (Perillo 1993). See also Annot., 86 ALR3d 1142 (1978).

21. Rs. 2d § 51 cmt a; see also Rs. 1st § 53 cmt a.

§ 2.12

1. 105 F.3d 1147 (7th Cir.1997).

2. Klocek v. Gateway, 104 F.Supp.2d 1332 (D.Kan.2000); Licitra v. Gateway, 189 Misc.2d 721, 734 N.Y.S.2d 389 (Civ.Ct. 2001).

3. See § 2.21 infra.

4. While the revision draft (§ 2–313A), imposes a duty on the seller in favor of a remote buyer based on its "remedial promise" contained in or on packaging of its product, it does not impose duties on the

Gateway is a direct seller. It manufactures and sells directly to the customer. Most purchases are made from resellers. That situation is different. The limited warranty in the box is an offer by the manufacturer that the purchaser may accept during the warranty period. Would an arbitration clause relating to disputes between the buyer and the manufacturer be binding on the customer? It would seem clear that it would bind if the customer brought a contract action. The only privity between the manufacturer and the customer is created by the document in the box. If the claim is a tort claim based on products liability, the clause would be ineffective.

Another situation that has produced some confusion involves software licensing. Frequently, the customer purchases a disk or CD from a reseller to install in the buyer's computer. The shrinkwrap package containing the disk may contain a printed warning, "if you unwrap this disk, you will have consented to the terms of the license contained herein." Note that the message is not the reseller's. It is the message of the copyright holder. The message on the shrinkwrap is an offer to grant a license. The reseller has sold a product—a disk along with an option to the purchaser to contract with the copyright holder on the latter's terms. Opening the shrinkwrap would be an acceptance of the copyright holder's terms. Sometimes, instead, upon insertion of the disk into the computer, the user will be asked to click, "I agree," and does so. The user should be bound. But the cases are divided on these questions.[5] Where UCITA is enacted, the license terms are clearly binding on the licensee.[6]

Instead, the software may be furnished on the internet. On commencement of downloading the software, the furnisher will provide contractual terms. The customer scrolls down to the end of the terms and is asked to click "I agree" or "I disagree." If the customer clicks, "I disagree" or merely refuses to click at all, the downloading stops at that point. The cases hold that the clicking of "I agree" is a binding acceptance of the offered terms.[7]

§ 2.13   Must the Offeree Intend to Accept? When?

In accepting an offer, it is not enough that the offeree knows of the

buyer. However, the buyer's rights against the remote seller can be limited in accordance with the terms of the promise.

5. Holding that the license terms are binding: ProCD v. Zeidenberg, 86 F.3d 1447 (7th Cir.1996) (notice of license on exterior of box); Management Computer Controls v. Charles Perry Constr., 743 So.2d 627 (Fla. App.1999) (contract referenced license in package); M.A. Mortenson Co. v. Timberline Software, 93 Wn.App. 819, 970 P.2d 803 (1999), aff'd (purchaser was aware of license when contracting). Contra, Novell v. Network Trade Center, 25 F.Supp.2d 1218

(D.Utah 1997); cf. Step–Saver Data Sys. v. Wyse Tech., 939 F.2d 91 (3d Cir.1991) (distinguishable because contract was made on telephone).

6. UCITA is the acronym for the Uniform Computer Transactions Act, a pro-licensor statute enacted only in Maryland and Virginia.

7. Caspi v. Microsoft Network, 323 N.J.Super. 118, 732 A.2d 528 (App.Div. 1999); Rudder v. Microsoft, 1999 CarswellOnt 3195. The user must be made aware that the user's agreement is sought.

offer. The offeree also must manifest an intent to accept it.[1] When the offer looks to a bilateral contract, subjective intent to accept is usually irrelevant. A bilateral contract is formed when the offeree makes the requested promise even if the offeree did not subjectively intend to accept, unless the offeror knows or has reason to know that the offeree did not intend to accept.[2]

When the offer looks to a unilateral contract, the question is more complicated. If A says to B, "I will pay you $1,000 if you run in the New York Marathon and finish" and B enters and completes the Marathon, is there a manifestation of intent to accept? B may have raced in order to collect the $1,000, or to exercise, or from a combination of these two motives or even for other reasons. Thus, where the offer is to a unilateral contract, the performance of the requested act is ambiguous as to whether the offeree intended to accept. Consequently, the traditional view is that evidence of the offeree's subjective intention to accept or not to accept is relevant and admissible. The relevance of subjective intention in this situation is based on the view that subjective intention is relevant when a manifestation is ambiguous.[3] Thus, the offeree will prevail if the trier of fact believes the offeree's testimony that she intended to accept. If the offeree proves that several motives induced the activity, one of which was to receive the $1,000, again the offeree will prevail.[4] It is enough that the offer was some part of the reason for the offeree's performance.[5] Some cases have indicated the contrary.[6] A realistic reading of these cases, mostly involving offers of rewards, may indicate that they diverge from the norm because courts seem in reward cases, more than in others, to emphasize the ethical position of the particular claimant and public policy considerations. In many of these cases the act of acceptance was not voluntarily performed.[7]

A more modern view is that the offeree's testimony of subjective intention is irrelevant and inadmissible. The Restatement (Second), instead of allowing the offeree's testimony of subjective intention, holds that intent to accept is presumed in the absence of words or conduct indicating the contrary. The theory is that inquiry into the motives of the offeree is ordinarily unnecessary.[8] Because the intent to accept is only assumed, if the offeree manifests an intent not to accept before the

---

Specht v. Netscape, 306 F.3d 17 (2d Cir. 2002).

§ 2.13

1. 1 Corbin § 3.4 (Perillo 1993); 2 Williston §§ 6:3, 6:4.

2. Nationwide Resources v. Massabni, 134 Ariz. 557, 658 P.2d 210 (App.1982); see §§ 2.2, 2.11 supra.

3. See § 3.10 infra.

4. 1 Corbin § 3.4 (Perillo 1993).

5. Simmons v. U.S., 308 F.2d 160 (4th Cir.1962); Industrial America v. Fulton In-

dus., 285 A.2d 412 (Del.1971); Rs. 1st § 55 cmt b.

6. Reynolds v. Eagle Pencil, 285 N.Y. 448, 35 N.E.2d 35 (1941), reversing 260 A.D. 482, 23 N.Y.S.2d 101 (1940); Vitty v. Eley, 51 A.D. 44, 64 N.Y.S. 397 (1900); The Crown v. Clarke, 40 C.L.R. 227 (Austl.1927), 1 Austl.L.J. 287 (1928).

7. Sheldon v. George, 132 A.D. 470, 116 N.Y.S. 969 (1909).

8. Rs. 2d § 53 cmt c. See Industrial America v. Fulton Indus., 285 A.2d 412 (Del.1971); Braucher, Offer and Acceptance in Second Restatement, 74 Yale L.J. 302, 308 (1964).

offeror performs, the disclaimer is effective and renders the offeror's promise inoperative from the beginning.[9]

§ 2.14   Who May Accept the Offer?

As master of the offer, the offeror controls the person or persons in whom a power of acceptance is created.[1] An offer may be accepted only by the offeree or the offerees to whom it is made, or a duly authorized human or electronic agent.[2] Because the power of acceptance is personal to the offeree, it follows that the offeree may not transfer the power.[3] (After accepting the offer so that a contract is created, the offeree may have the power to transfer rights under the contract. This power is discussed below.)[4] The point made here is that, if A makes an offer to B, C may not accept. Also, if A makes an offer jointly to B and C, B or C alone may not accept.[5]

Ordinarily the identity of the offerees will be determined by the reasonable person test.[6] Thus, it has been determined that a reward offer may ordinarily be accepted by anyone who knows of the offer, but once the offer has been accepted no one else may accept.[7] On the other hand, an offer to pay a sum of money to anyone who uses a certain medicine and contracts influenza may be accepted by anyone who knows of the offer and by any number of persons.[8] Although in both cases the offer is made to the public, a reasonable person would reach different conclusions as to how many times each can be accepted.

None of the cases discussed above are particularly difficult, but there are more complicated situations. For example, if A individually is doing business under the trade name of "Acme Supply Co." and B sends in an order (offer) to "Acme Supply Co." and C, who buys out A including the name, fills the order, is there a contract? The question to be answered is whether C as a reasonable person would conclude that B manifested an intention to make the offer to "Acme Supply Co." irrespective of the ownership of the establishment or that B manifested an intention to make the offer to "Acme" only so long as A was the proprietor. The question may be one of fact.[9] If it is concluded that the

---

9. Rs. 2d § 53(3) & cmt c.

§ 2.14

1. 1 Corbin § 3.2 (Perillo 1993).

2. Boulton v. Jones, 157 Eng.Rep. 232 (Ex.1857); see Daru v. Martin, 89 Ariz. 373, 363 P.2d 61 (1961); Apostolic Revival Tab.v. Charles J. Febel, Inc., 131 Ill.App.2d 579, 266 N.E.2d 545 (1970); Trimount Bit. Prods. v. Chittenden Trust, 117 N.H. 946, 379 A.2d 1266 (1977); Wagner, 11 Vill. L.Rev. 95, 95–96 (1965).

3. Rs. 2d § 52.

4. See ch. 18 infra.

5. Mike Schlemer, Inc. v. Pulizos, 267 Ill.App.3d 393, 204 Ill.Dec. 738, 642 N.E.2d

200 (1994); Meister v. Arden–Mayfair, 276 Or. 517, 555 P.2d 923 (1976); see § 20.11 infra.

6. Rs. 2d § 29.

7. 1 Williston § 4:12. It has been argued that if a number of persons contribute to the performance of the requested act, the reward should be divided among them even though they were not acting in concert. 1 Corbin § 3.10 (Perillo 1993); 34 Mich. L.Rev. 854 (1936).

8. Carlill v. Carbolic Smoke Ball Co., [1893] 1 Q.B. 256 (C.A.1892).

9. See ch. 3 infra. The facts are suggested by Boulton v. Jones, 157 Eng.Rep. 232 (Ex.1857).

offer was not made to C, the question of a quasi-contractual recovery would have to be addressed.[10] Even if the offer was not made to C, but C delivered the goods and disclosed the change in ownership, there would be a contract if B accepted the goods. C made an offer which B accepted.[11]

§ 2.15 Must the Offeree Give Notice of Acceptance of an Offer to a Unilateral Contract?

When an offer to a unilateral contract is made the offeror has requested not words, but deeds. Consequently, the offeree need not give notice of an intent to perform,[1] but another question is whether the offeree must give notice of performance on completion.[2] Notice enables the offeror to avoid contracting with another for the same performance. In the credit guaranty cases it enables the guarantor to monitor the conduct of the principal debtor. On the other hand, if the offeror is in a position to learn of performance, notice should not be required.

The following illustration will clarify the issues. Suppose A, writes to C in a distant city as follows: "My brother, B, will ask you for credit. Please extend credit to him. If you do, I guaranty payment." The two Restatements take the position that a contract arises on performance— C's extension of credit to B—but if C, the offeree, has reason to know that the offeror has no adequate means of learning of the performance with reasonable promptness and certitude, the duty of the offeror is discharged unless the offeree exercises reasonable diligence to notify the offeror or the offeror otherwise learns of performance within a reasonable time, or the offer indicates that notification is not necessary.[3] There is a second view that is the same as above except that, if notice is required, no contract is consummated unless and until notice of performance has been communicated.[4]

The above illustration will help explain the difference between the two views. Assume A made the offer of guaranty on November 1, the act of acceptance occurred on November 2, A revoked the offer on November 3, and C sent notice of performance November 4. According to the second view there would be no contract because the revocation occurred prior to the act of acceptance. According to the two Restatements the revocation would not be effective because the acceptance had already occurred. However, the contract would be discharged, that is, its obli-

---

10. See Michigan Cent. R.R. v. State, 85 Ind.App. 557, 155 N.E. 50 (1927); Parker v. Dantzler Foundry & Mach. Works, 118 Miss. 126, 79 So. 82 (1918). There are related questions of agency, Kelly Asphalt Block v. Barber Asphalt Paving, 211 N.Y. 68, 105 N.E. 88 (1914), and possible questions of mistake. See 7 Corbin § 28.31 (Perillo 2002).

11. Orcutt v. Nelson, 67 Mass. (1 Gray) 536 (1854).

§ 2.15

1. Carlill v. Carbolic Smoke Ball, [1893] 1 Q.B. 256 (C.A.1892).

2. See generally 1 Williston §§ 6:5–6:9; Dole, Notice Requirements of Guaranty Contracts, 62 Mich.L.Rev. 57 (1963).

3. Rs. 1st § 56; Rs. 2d § 54.

4. Kresge Dep't Stores v. Young, 37 A.2d 448 (D.C.Mun.App.1944).

gations would come to an end, if notice is necessary and not given within a reasonable time. Even then, the contract would not be discharged if notice is otherwise received or dispensed with.

Under both views, one is faced with the question of under what circumstances does the offeree have "reason to know that the offeror has no adequate means of learning of performance with reasonable promptness and certitude." It is an exceptional case in which the offeror does not have means of ascertaining what has occurred.[5] The cases have imposed a duty of inquiry upon the offeror unless inquiry is not reasonably feasible and have placed the burden of proof on the offeror to show that inquiry is not reasonably feasible.[6] The Restatement gives an illustration of a case where it believes that the offeree carries this burden. It is a case where the offeror is a guarantor and a friend in another country makes the requested loan to the guarantor's brother.[7]

There is also a third view on the question of whether notice of performance must be given that at least has the merit of simplicity. Under this view notice is not required unless requested by the offer.[8]

§ 2.16 Acceptance of an Offer Looking to a Series of Contracts

The preceding discussion has been confined to offers looking to a single unilateral or bilateral contract. An offer may instead look to the formation of a series of contracts, unilateral or bilateral. For example, A on Jan. 1 writes to B: "In consideration of your advancing money from time to time over the next twelve calendar months, up to a total of $5,000, to X, at X's request, at your option, I hereby undertake to make good any losses you may sustain in consequence."[1] In reliance on the letter, B lends $1,000 to X on February 1, another $1,000 on March 1. A revokes the offer on March 15, but B makes an additional loan of $1,000 on April 1. A has made an offer looking to a series of unilateral contracts. The advance made on Feb. 1 gave rise to one unilateral contract and the advance on March 1 gave rise to a second unilateral contract.[2] The offer continues into the future but is effectively revoked and thus the alleged third acceptance, on April 1, is ineffective because of the earlier effective revocation.[3]

5. Rs. 1st § 56 cmt a.

6. Ross v. Leberman, 298 Pa. 574, 148 A. 858 (1930).

7. Rs. 2d § 54 ill. 5, based on Bishop v. Eaton, 161 Mass. 496, 37 N.E. 665 (1894).

8. Midland Nat. Bank v. Security Elevator, 161 Minn. 30, 200 N.W. 851 (1924); City Nat. Bank v. Phelps, 86 N.Y. 484 (1881) (dubbed the minority view in Dole, supra n.2, at 64).

§ 2.16

1. Based on Offord v. Davies, 142 Eng. Rep. 1336 (C.P.1862).

2. Rs. 1st § 30; Rs. 2d § 31 cmts a & b. Offers to guaranty the credit of another are usually held to look to a series of contracts and at times are referred to as "continuing guaranties." Walter E. Heller & Co. v. Aetna Bus. Credit, 158 Ga.App. 249, 280 S.E.2d 144 (1981).

3. Rs. 1st § 44; Rs. 2d § 47.

Offers looking to a series of bilateral contracts also exist. If A offers B stated quantities of certain goods as B may order from time to time during the next year at a fixed price, A has made an offer looking to a series of bilateral contracts. The series is bilateral because each time B places an order B impliedly promises to pay.[4] Each time an order is placed, one bilateral contract arises but as to the future the offer remains revocable.

Care must be taken to distinguish an offer looking to a series of contracts from an offer that looks to one acceptance with a number of performances.[5] Suppose A offers to sell B between 4,000 to 6,000 tons of a specified type of coal, deliveries to be made in equal monthly installments during the months of May, June, July and August, the acceptance to specify the quantity, the offer looks to one bilateral contract which will arise when B accepts and specifies the quantity. However, there will be four performances under the contract.[6]

Whether an offer looks to one contract or a series of contracts is a question of interpretation to be decided in the same way as any question of interpretation.[7] For example, A, a newspaper, requests B to discontinue distribution of a rival newspaper and promises to pay B $100 a week as long as B abstains from such distribution while A remains in business. It is conceivable that this offer could be viewed as an offer looking to a series of unilateral contracts. However, the court held that the offer looked to one unilateral contract with a series of performances.[8] The contract arose with the discontinuance of distribution but B would not become entitled to $100 until B had abstained from distributing the rival publication for a week. Thus not distributing for a week is a condition precedent to A's obligation to pay.

Thus far, it would seem that there is little practical difference between an offer looking to a series of unilateral contracts and an offer looking to one unilateral contract with a number of performances. But it would make a great difference if A wished to revoke the offer prospectively. A could do so if the offer looked to a series of unilateral contracts but not where there was only one unilateral contract with a series of performances.

Where there is an offer looking to series of unilateral contracts and it is assumed that notice of performance is required under one or more of the rules stated above,[9] there is authority that one notification may be sufficient even though there are multiple acceptances.[10]

4. Great Northern Ry. v. Withan, L.R., 9 C.P. 16 (1873); Strang v. Witkowski, 138 Conn. 94, 82 A.2d 624 (1951); 1 Corbin § 3.11 (Perillo 1993).

5. Hollidge v. Gussow, Kahn & Co., 67 F.2d 459 (1st Cir.1933).

6. Chicago and Great E. Ry. v. Dane, 43 N.Y. 240 (1870); Rs. 2d § 31 ill. 2.

7. See ch. 3 infra.

8. Based on Rague v. New York Evening Journal, 164 A.D. 126, 149 N.Y.S. 668 (1914) (there was no applicable antitrust law); see also American Pub. & Engraving v. Walker, 87 Mo.App. 503 (1901); Rs. 2d § 31 ill. 3, § 47 ill. 3, § 54 ill. 3.

9. See § 2.15 supra.

10. Rs. 2d § 31 cmt b, § 54 cmt d.

§ 2.17   The Necessity of Communicating Acceptance of an Offer to a Bilateral Contract

A unilateral contract arises on performance,[1] but for the creation of a bilateral contract, the general rule is that the offeree's promise must be communicated to the offeror.[2] Clearly the offeree, as a reasonable person, should understand that the offeror expects to know that the offeree has made the requested return promise so that the offeror may act accordingly.[3] Whether it is actually necessary for the communication to come to the offeror's attention is a matter discussed below.[4]

As master of the offer, the offeror may dispense with the requirement for communication.[5] In a recurring situation, A, an agent for B Corporation, presents C with a document that states the terms of a bilateral arrangement but adds that a contract will arise when approved by an executive officer of B Corporation. C signs the document setting forth the deal. Who is the offeror and who is the offeree? B Corporation has not made an offer because it has not committed itself to anything; it states that approval by an executive officer will be its commitment. C makes the offer by signing the document. C's offer includes the term relating to approval by an executive officer. Thus, we have an offer by C looking to a bilateral contract. Some cases have held that this offer is accepted by B Corporation when it indicates its assent even though the assent is not communicated.[6] The theory is that the language used (a contract will arise when approved by an executive officer of B Company) dispenses with the necessity for communication.[7] It is ironic that this dispensation comes about because the "offeror is master of the offer." The irony is that the offeree has written the script that the offeror—the supposed "master of the offer"—has adopted.

Even if the court concludes that the requirement of communication has been dispensed with, it would appear reasonable to require subsequent notice of acceptance by analogy to the rules established for giving notice of performance of a unilateral contract.[8] Such notice would not be necessary for the formation of the contract but the failure to give notice would discharge the obligation of the offeror and could amount to a

---

§ 2.17

1. See § 2.10 supra.

2. Zamore v. Whitten, 395 A.2d 435, 4 ALR4th 899 (Me.1978) (overruled on other grounds).

3. 1 Corbin § 3.13 (Perillo 1993); see Trounstine v. Sellers, 35 Kan. 447, 11 P. 441 (1886).

4. See § 2.23 infra.

5. Keller v. Bones, 260 Neb. 202, 615 N.W.2d 883 (2000).

6. Meekins–Bamman Prestress v. Better Constr., 408 So.2d 1071 (Fla.App.1982); Pacific Photocopy v. Canon U.S.A., 57 Or.App. 752, 646 P.2d 647 (1982), rev. denied.

7. International Filter v. Conroe Gin, Ice & Light, 277 S.W. 631 (Tex.Com.App. 1925). Cf. Iacono v. Toll Bros., 217 N.J.Super. 475, 526 A.2d 256 (A.D.1987), certif. denied. The seller's form provided: "This agreement shall not be binding upon seller unless signed by seller within 30 days." Failure to sign defeated the existence of the contract. Later proceedings determined that seller's silence coupled with buyer's change of position estopped the sellers from denying the existence of the contract and from asserting the Statute of Frauds. 225 N.J.Super. 87, 541 A.2d 1085 (1988).

8. See § 2.15 supra.

breach of the contract.[9] For example, even if the offer states that this order "will become a contract" when approved by an executive officer at the seller's home office, prompt notice of approval should be required.

In the fact pattern discussed above, what are the advantages and disadvantages to the corporation in doing business in such a fashion? One advantage is that such a form prevents an agent from exceeding the agent's authority.[10] A disadvantage is that the customer is free to withdraw the offer at any time until there is an acceptance by an executive officer.[11]

In some cases involving solicited offers that did not dispense with the need of communicating an acceptance, the offeree replied, with a statement such as "you may be assured of our very best attention to your order." The question is whether such language in context amounts to language of acceptance. The cases appear to conflict but different nuances in the facts may have justified differing results.[12] For example, merely communicating a tracking number assigned to an order is not acceptance.[13]

§ 2.18 Acceptance by Silence—Implied-in-Fact Contracts

An offer to a bilateral contract generally requires a communicated acceptance.[1] The question here is whether silence may amount to a promise. Offers can be made by silence or conduct, most of the cases have involved the question of acceptance by silence. At times, both the offer and the acceptance are implicit rather than explicit.[2] Ordinarily, silence does not give rise to an acceptance of an offer or a counter-offer,[3] but there are exceptions. The issue is whether the relationship of the parties and the circumstances justify the offeror's expectation of a negative reply if the offeree wishes to reject the offer.[4] When such

9. See Rs. 2d § 56 ill. 1; compare Neal–Cooper Grain v. Texas Gulf Sulphur, 508 F.2d 283 (7th Cir.1974) with Venters v. Stewart, 261 S.W.2d 444 (Ky.1953).

10. Carl Wagner & Sons v. Appendagez, 485 F.Supp. 762 (S.D.N.Y.1980).

11. West Penn Power v. Bethlehem Steel, 236 Pa.Super. 413, 348 A.2d 144 (1975).

12. Compare Hill's, Inc. v. William B. Kessler, Inc., 41 Wn.2d 42, 246 P.2d 1099 (1952) with Courtney Shoe v. E.W. Curd & Son, 142 Ky. 219, 134 S.W. 146 (1911). See Arnett v. Midwestern Enterprises, Inc., 95 Ohio App.3d 429, 642 N.E.2d 683 (1994) (no acceptance); Pace Communications v. Moonlight Design, 31 F.3d 587 (7th Cir. 1994) ("We are extremely pleased that you have decided to join our list of advertisers" constitutes acceptance).

13. Corinthian Pharm. Sys. v. Lederle Labs., 724 F.Supp. 605 (S.D.Ind.1989).

§ 2.18

1. Rs. 2d § 56.

2. An offer requesting forbearance can be made by conduct, see Citibank Int'l v. Mercogliano, 574 So.2d 1190 (Fla.App. 1991). For other cases of offers by conduct, see notes 26–28 infra.

3. Rs. 2d § 69 cmt a; Beech Aircraft v. Flexible Tubing, 270 F.Supp. 548 (D.Conn. 1967); Thomson v. U.S., 357 F.2d 683 (Ct. Cl.1966); Cincinnati Equip. v. Big Muddy River Consol. Coal, 158 Ky. 247, 164 S.W. 794 (1914); Bowen v. McCarthy, 85 Mich. 26, 48 N.W. 155 (1891); Royal Ins. v. Beatty, 119 Pa. 6, 12 A. 607 (1888); J.C. Durick Ins. v. Andrus, 139 Vt. 150, 424 A.2d 249 (1980); see Helen Whiting, Inc. v. Trojan Textile, 307 N.Y. 360, 121 N.E.2d 367 (1954); accord, CISG Art. 18(1). See Comment, 29 Yale L.J. 441 (1920); Laufer, 7 Duke B.A.J. 87 (1939).

4. R.A. Berjian, D.O. v. Ohio Bell, 54 Ohio St.2d 147, 375 N.E.2d 410 (1978);

expectation is justified, the offeror may reasonably conclude that silence is acceptance.[5] The same notion is expressed in a different way when it is stated that there is a duty to speak when silence "would be deceptive and beguiling."[6]

Generally, it is not incumbent on the offeree to reject an unwelcome offer. If A mails an unsolicited offer to B stating: "If I do not hear from you by next Tuesday, I shall assume you accept," all authorities agree that B need not reply because it would be unfair to impose such a burden.[7] However, it does not follow that B cannot accept. Certainly B can accept by communicating an acceptance. Indeed, there are cases holding that this is the only way to effectuate an acceptance.[8] Such holdings should be disapproved because the offeror has authorized the offeree to accept by remaining silent.

The Restatements take the position that because the offeree's silence is ambiguous (silence may indicate an intent to accept or the contrary) the offeree's subjective intent in remaining silent is relevant and admissible and a contract exists if the offeree intended to accept.[9] The case is analogous to the problem of intent to accept an offer looking to a unilateral contract. In that situation the First Restatement permitted the offeree to testify as to subjective intent.[10] Because the offeror is responsible for the existence of the ambiguity created by silence, the offeror should not be allowed to complain that the offeree's silence constitutes acceptance.[11]

To be distinguished from the case above is the situation where the parties have mutually agreed that silence will manifest assent. For example, A says to B, "I offer to sell you my Chevrolet for $5,000." B replies, "If you do not hear from me by next Tuesday you may assume I accept." A agrees. Here, by the agreement of both parties if B does not speak, B is bound in accordance with the agreement.[12]

Anderson Chevrolet/Olds v. Higgins, 57 N.C.App. 650, 292 S.E.2d 159 (1982); but see Discount Fabric House v. Wisconsin Tel., 117 Wis.2d 587, 345 N.W.2d 417 (1984).

5. John J. Brennan Constr. v. Shelton, 187 Conn. 695, 448 A.2d 180 (1982).

6. Brennan v. National Equitable Inv., 247 N.Y. 486, 490, 160 N.E. 924, 925 (1928); accord, Brooks Towers. v. Hunkin–Conkey Constr., 454 F.2d 1203 (10th Cir. 1972); Garcia v. Middle Rio Grande Conservancy, 99 N.M. 802, 664 P.2d 1000 (App. 1983), overruled on other grounds; Chorba v. Davlisa Enter., 303 Pa.Super. 497, 450 A.2d 36 (1982). The term "duty to speak," while eloquent, is inaccurate. A more accurate phrase is that there is a burden to reply. Hohfeld would say there is "no-right" to be silent. See Linzer, A Contracts Anthology 153–54 (1989).

7. William F. Klingensmith, Inc. v. D. C., 370 A.2d 1341 (D.C.1977); J.C. Durick

Ins. v. Andrus, 139 Vt. 150, 424 A.2d 249 (1980). Similarly no contract arises if the offeror says, "I shall conclude you accept if you watch the Giants' game on television this Sunday" and the offeree watches the game with no intent to accept.

8. Prescott v. Jones, 69 N.H. 305, 41 A. 352 (1898); Felthouse v. Bindley, 142 Eng. Rep. 1037 (C.P.1862).

9. Rs. 1st § 72(1)(b); Rs. 2d § 69(1)(b). Professor Farnsworth calls this rule a "throwback to subjectivism." Farnsworth, Contracts § 3.15 n.18 (3d ed.).

10. See § 2.13 supra.

11. Cavanaugh v. D.W. Ranlet Co., 229 Mass. 366, 118 N.E. 650 (1918).

12. SouthTrust Bank v. Williams, 775 So.2d 184 (Ala.2000); Attorney Grievance Comm'n v. McIntire, 286 Md. 87, 405 A.2d 273 (1979); 1 Williston § 6:53.

The burden of speaking may also arise by virtue of a prior course of dealing.[13] Suppose A on a number of occasions has without request sent goods to B who has always kept the goods and paid for them without protest. A makes an additional shipment of similar goods and B retains the goods for a long period of time without complaint. Has B accepted A's offer by retaining the goods in light of the prior course of dealing?[14] B's silence is concededly ambiguous. Thus, the question is whether B should be permitted to testify as to subjective intent or whether the case should be decided under the tentative objective test stated earlier. The Restatement (Second) explicitly takes the position that B may not testify as to his or her subjective intention[15] and thus the test is whether A as a reasonable person would conclude that B's silence under the circumstances amounted to an acceptance.[16] This is undoubtedly a jury question.[17]

It is important to note that the ambiguity here is the fault of B, the offeree, therefore B is not permitted to testify as to subjective intent. Whereas, in the case that introduced this section, the ambiguity was the fault of the offeror, who indicated that the offeree's silence would be deemed to be an acceptance, and thus the offeree was permitted to testify as to his or her subjective intent.

A similar problem arises when A, through a sales representative, has frequently solicited orders from B, which provide that the contract will arise when approved by A's home office. (As we have seen, in this situation B is the offeror and A the offeree.)[18] A has always shipped the goods to B without prior notification and has billed them after shipment. A's sales representative solicits and receives another order from B and A remains silent for a period of time.[19] As above, and for the same reasons, A's subjective intention is not relevant and so again, as above, the tentative objective test would be applied on the issue of whether the offeror (B) would conclude that A's silence indicated assent. Again, the issue is basically one of fact.[20]

According to the Restatement (Second), the contract is based on a true manifestation of assent and there is a contract even if B does not change position in reliance on A's silence, for example, by refraining

---

13. William F. Klingensmith, Inc. v. D. C., 370 A.2d 1341 (D.C.1977); 1 Corbin § 3.21 (Perillo 1993).

14. These are the facts of Hobbs v. Massasoit Whip, 158 Mass. 194, 33 N.E. 495 (1893). The same principle is involved in Krauss Bros. Lumber v. Louis Bossert & Sons, 62 F.2d 1004 (2d Cir.1933); Ballard v. Tingue Mills, 128 F.Supp. 683 (D.Conn. 1954); Holt v. Swenson, 252 Minn. 510, 90 N.W.2d 724 (1958).

15. Rs. 2d § 69(1)(c) cmt d.

16. The original Restatement made this question turn on the subjective understanding of the offeror. Rs. 1st § 72(1)(c).

17. See, e.g., William F. Klingensmith, Inc. v. D. C., 370 A.2d 1341 (D.C.1977); Terminal Grain v. Rozell, 272 N.W.2d 800 (S.D.1978).

18. See § 2.17 supra.

19. This is a recurring fact pattern. See, e.g., Ammons v. Wilson & Co., 176 Miss. 645, 170 So. 227 (1936); Ercanbrack v. Crandall–Walker Motor, 550 P.2d 723 (Utah 1976); Hendrickson v. International Harvester, 100 Vt. 161, 135 A. 702 (1927).

20. Again, the first Restatement made this question turn on the subjective understanding of the offeror. See notes 14–16 and accompanying text supra.

from buying elsewhere. Some cases have indicated that B should recover only if there was reliance involving a change of position—a theory of estoppel.[21] There are occasional cases which seem to place the entire doctrine of acceptance by silence on an estoppel theory.[22] But even these cases stress that silence is misleading rather than the other element of estoppel—an injurious change of position.[23]

Similar problems arise in connection with solicitation by insurance agents. As one court has stated: "It is the general rule that mere delay in passing upon an application for insurance is not sufficient in and of itself to amount to acceptance even though the premium is retained. * * * But an acceptance may be implied from retention of the premium and failure to reject within a reasonable time * * *. Having accepted and retained the premium paid upon an application solicited by its agent, the company was bound to act with reasonable promptitude."[24] It is significant to observe that the acceptance here is not predicated on a course of dealing. Conversely, where the insurer sends a renewal policy, the insured's silence may be construed as an acceptance.[25]

Another, and more common, instance of acceptance by silence arises where the offeree takes offered services with reasonable opportunity to reject them and with reason to believe that they are offered with expectation of compensation.[26] The burden of rejecting arises because it is impossible to return services that have been accepted. But again, that burden does not arise unless the offeree knows of the services and has "reason to believe that they are offered with expectation of compensation." The cases hinge primarily on the question of "expectation of compensation" and as usual, everything depends on the totality of the facts. Thus, if a reasonable person would conclude that the services are rendered gratuitously, there can be no recovery.[27] In such a case there is not even an offer. Where recovery is allowed, the obligation that is enforced is a reverse unilateral contract.[28]

21. Cole–McIntyre–Norfleet v. Holloway, 141 Tenn. 679, 214 S.W. 817, 7 ALR 1683 (1919); Hill's, Inc. v. William B. Kessler, 41 Wn.2d 42, 246 P.2d 1099 (1952).

22. See, e.g., Tanenbaum Textile v. Schlanger, 287 N.Y. 400, 404, 40 N.E.2d 225, 227 (1942) (dictum).

23. Laufer, 7 Duke B.A.J. 87 (1939).

24. American Life Ins. v. Hutcheson, 109 F.2d 424, 427–28 (6th Cir.1940), cert. denied; see State Farm Life Ins. v. Bass, 605 So.2d 908 (Fla.App.1992); but see, Joseph Schultz & Co. v. Camden Fire Ins., 304 N.Y. 143, 106 N.E.2d 273 (1952); 12 Appleman, Insurance Law & Practice § 7216–7223 (1981); Annots., 18 ALR4th 1115, 32 ALR2d 487. At times, the insurer is the offeror. Blumberg v. Paul Revere Life Ins., 177 Misc.2d 680, 677 N.Y.S.2d 412 (1998).

25. Golden Eagle Ins. v. Foremost Ins., 20 Cal.App.4th 1372, 25 Cal.Rptr.2d 242 (1993), rev. denied; Bohn Mfg. v. Sawyer, 169 Mass. 477, 48 N.E. 620 (1897).

26. Old Jordan Min. & Mill v. Societe Anonyme Des Mines, 164 U.S. 261 (1896); James v. P.B. Price Constr., 240 Ark. 628, 401 S.W.2d 206 (1966); Porter v. General Boiler Casing, 284 Md. 402, 396 A.2d 1090 (1979); Spencer v. Spencer, 181 Mass. 471, 63 N.E. 947 (1902); Day v. Caton, 119 Mass. 513 (1876); Stout v. Smith, 4 N.C.App. 81, 165 S.E.2d 789 (1969); Rs. 2d § 69(1)(a); Rs. 1st § 72(1)(a); see Minerals & Chem. v. Milwhite Co., 414 F.2d 428 (5th Cir.1969).

27. Lirtzman v. Fuqua Indus., 677 F.2d 548 (7th Cir.1982); Hobby v. Smith, 250 Ga.App. 669, 550 S.E.2d 718 (Ga.App.2001).

28. See supra § 2.10.

Many of the contested cases involve services rendered within the family or a close friendship.[29] In such relationships, the offeree ordinarily has no reason to conclude that compensation is expected. A family relationship can arise by consanguinity (blood) or affinity (marriage).[30] It may also arise by living as a family.[31] A family for this purpose has been defined "as a collective body of persons who form one household, under one head and one domestic government."[32] While this common definition reflects an obsolete patriarchal view, it is adaptable to modern times.[33] At times the two elements of relationship and living together in a common household co-exist and both factors will be considered in making the decision.

If services are rendered within the family relationship, there is a presumption that they were rendered without expectation of compensation.[34] If there is no family relationship the presumption is that compensation is expected.[35] In either case the presumption may be rebutted.[36] Whether a contract can be implied from the parties' conduct is ordinarily a question of fact.[37] The ultimate question is whether a reasonable person would conclude that the services were rendered with the expectation of compensation.[38]

One case has stated that, in order to demonstrate the existence of an implied-in-fact contract for services, "the party seeking payment must show that services were carried out under such circumstances as to give the recipient reason to understand that the services were rendered for the recipient and not for some other person * * * demonstrate the existence of such circumstances as to put the recipient on notice that the

29. In re Estate of Argersinger, 168 A.D.2d 757, 564 N.Y.S.2d 214 (1990).

30. There are changing conceptions of family. In Hall v. Mabe, 77 N.C.App. 758, 336 S.E.2d 427 (1985), it was held that the father-in-law was not a family member. See 1 Corbin § 3.17 (pocket part). For an innovative approach to promises within the family, see Leslie, Enforcing Family Promises: Reliance, Restitution and Relational Contracts, 77 N.C.L.Rev. 551 (1999).

31. When an unmarried couple live together, services rendered by the parties are presumtavely gratuitous. Morone v. Morone, 50 N.Y.2d 481, 429 N.Y.S.2d 592, 413 N.E.2d 1154 (1980). But see Marvin v. Marvin, 18 Cal.3d 660, 134 Cal.Rptr. 815, 557 P.2d 106 (1976) (a nonmarital partner may recover reasonable value for household services if it can be shown that such services were offered with expectation of monetary reward). Contra, Hewitt v. Hewitt, 77 Ill.2d 49, 31 Ill.Dec. 827, 394 N.E.2d 1204, 3 A.L.R.4th 1 (1979), holding that even an express contract between unmarried cohabitants with respect to support is void against public policy. Most case appear to enforce such express contracts. Estate of

Roccamonte, 174 N.J. 381, 808 A.2d 838 (2002); Doe v. Burkland, 808 A.2d 1090 (R.I.2002) (gay couple).

32. Annot., 7 ALR2d 8, 36 (1949); see Annots. 92 A.L.R.3d 726, 94 A.L.R.3d 552.

33. Estate of Jackson, 7 Neb.App. 427, 583 N.W.2d 82 (1998).

34. Worley v. Worley, 388 So.2d 502 (Ala.1980); In re Barnet's Estate, 320 Pa. 408, 182 A. 699 (1936); Estate of Steffes, 95 Wis.2d 490, 290 N.W.2d 697 (1980); McDowell, 45 B.U.L.Rev. 43 (1965). If the relationship is that of husband and wife or unmarried cohabitants, public policy questions may be engaged.

35. McKeon v. Van Slyck, 223 N.Y. 392, 119 N.E. 851 (1918).

36. Wilhoite v. Beck, 141 Ind.App. 543, 230 N.E.2d 616 (1967); Estate of Jackson, 7 Neb.App. 427, 583 N.W.2d 82 (1998).

37. Shapira v. United Medical Serv., 15 N.Y.2d 200, 257 N.Y.S.2d 150, 205 N.E.2d 293 (1965); see Sheldon v. Thornburg, 153 Iowa 622, 133 N.W. 1076 (1912).

38. Sturgeon v. Estate of Wideman, 608 S.W.2d 140 (Mo.App.1980).

services were not rendered gratuitously and prove that the services were beneficial to the recipient."[39]

The first and last factors mentioned are important in cases where medical services are rendered to a patient at the request of a third party. It has been stated that "the mere request to a medical practitioner or hospital to attend a third person to whom the person making such request is under no legal obligation to furnish such services [does] not raise an implied promise to pay therefor in the absence of an express undertaking to do so, or special circumstances justifying a proper inference of an intention to incur such liability."[40]

In a case where a party renders services to another not in a family relationship is it necessary that the offeror subjectively intend to be paid? This requirement has been posited in a number of the cases.[41] For example, if A's car is disabled and B, the owner of a tow truck begins to move the vehicle and the owner stands by and does or says nothing, there would be an implied in fact contract.[42] But what if the truck owner acted carelessly? Could B avoid contractual liability by showing that the assistance was gratuitous? Because any ambiguity resulted from the failure of the tow truck operator to mention gratuitous intent, subjective intent should not be considered.[43]

Another case where it is difficult to decode whether one should conclude that services were rendered gratuitously arises when a person seeks compensation for services rendered prior to the formation of an express contract, and no express contract is made. Much time and effort may be spent in preparing a presentation for a proposed contract. The question is whether it is reasonable to conclude that the claimant made these efforts gratuitously in hopes of obtaining the contract or whether the claimant expected to be paid for the preliminary work irrespective of obtaining the ultimate contract. The cases often turn on the usages of the trade or profession.[44] Often, the real grievance is that the work product of the claimant has been appropriated.[45] An offeror who necessarily must reveal valuable information or ideas to the offeree would be wise to obtain a confidentiality agreement prior to the revelation.[46]

39. H.G. Smithy Co. v. Washington Medical Center, 374 A.2d 891, 893 (D.C. 1977).

40. Annot., 34 ALR3d 176, 183 (1970).

41. See Wilhoite v. Beck, 141 Ind.App. 543, 230 N.E.2d 616 (1967); Bourisk v. Amalfitano, 379 A.2d 149 (Me.1977); Day v. Caton, 119 Mass. 513 (1876).

42. This hypothetical was verified by Crawford's Auto Center v. Commonwealth, 655 A.2d 1064 (Pa.Cmwlth.1995).

43. See Prince v. McRae, 84 N.C. 674 (1881).

44. Compare Arden v. Freydberg, 9 N.Y.2d 393, 214 N.Y.S.2d 400, 174 N.E.2d 495 (1961) (no compensation for insurance broker whose preparatory work was appropriated) and Vitale v. Russell, 332 Mass. 523, 126 N.E.2d 122 (1955) (no compensation for work done pending board approval) and Cronin v. Nat. Shawmut Bank, 306 Mass. 202, 27 N.E.2d 717 (1940) (no compensation for insurance broker) with Hill v. Waxberg, 237 F.2d 936 (9th Cir.1956) (compensation for architect); see Lehrer McGovern Bovis v. N.Y. Yankees, 207 A.D.2d 256, 615 N.Y.S.2d 31 (1994) (pre-construction management work—question of fact).

45. Compare Anisgard v. Bray, 11 Mass. App. 726, 419 N.E.2d 315 (1981) (recovery permitted) with the brokerage cases in the prior note.

46. Sikes v. McGraw-Edison, 665 F.2d 731 (5th Cir.1982).

§ 2.19 Acceptance by Conduct or an Act of Dominion

The preceding section discussed acceptance arising from silence and inaction. This section considers acceptance by affirmative conduct. If A, on passing a market, picks up an apple from a box marked "50 cents each" and holds it up so that the clerk sees it and nods assent, A has made an offer by conduct and B has accepted in the same way.[1] This is so because a reasonable person would conclude that there has been an offer and an acceptance. Thus, the UCC provides, "a contract for the sale of goods may be made in any manner sufficient to show agreement, including conduct by both parties which recognizes the existence of such a contract."[2] The proposed revision adds "including offer and acceptance * * * the interaction of electronic agents, or the interaction of an electronic agent and an individual." Neither the original UCC nor the proposed changes are at variance with the common law. As to conduct, one court has stated, "a contract implied in fact arises under circumstances which, according to the ordinary course of dealing and common understanding * * *, show a mutual intention to contract * * *. A contract is implied in fact where the intention is not manifested by direct or explicit words between the parties, but is to be gathered by implication or proper deduction from the conduct of the parties, language used or things done by them, or other pertinent circumstances attending the transaction."[3] Whether a promise will be implied under particular circumstances is ordinarily a question of fact.[4]

Another kind of conduct creates contracts irrespective of the intention of the parties. When one exercises dominion over the personal property of another, without authorization, one commits the tort of conversion.[5] Assume that goods are offered by A to B. Although B takes possession of them, B declares that "I reject the offer. I am a converter." Under an old rule of estoppel, A can treat B's actions as an acceptance of the offer, estopping B from claiming the status of a tortfeasor.[6] This rule can be invoked whenever the offeree's act of dominion is referable to the power of acceptance granted by the offeror.[7] A has the option of proceed-

§ 2.19

1. Rs. 2d § 4 ill. 2.

2. UCC § 2–204(1).

3. Miller v. Stevens, 224 Mich. 626, 195 N.W. 481 (1923); quoted in Schwartz v. Michigan Sugar, 106 Mich.App. 471, 308 N.W.2d 459 (1981). See also Pleines v. Franklin Constr., 30 Conn.App. 612, 621 A.2d 759 (1993); Bell v. Hegewald, 95 Wn.2d 686, 628 P.2d 1305 (1981).

4. Kane v. New Hampshire State Liquor Comm'n, 118 N.H. 706, 393 A.2d 555 (1978).

5. Prosser & Keeton, Torts § 15 (5th ed.).

6. Rs. 2d § 69 cmt e; UCC § 2–606(1)(c) (revision makes no substantive change); Raible v. Puerto Rico Indus. Dev., 392 F.2d 424 (1st Cir.1968); Louisville Tin & Stove v. Lay, 251 Ky. 584, 65 S.W.2d 1002 (1933); Ferrous Prods. v. Gulf States Trading, 160 Tex. 399, 332 S.W.2d 310 (1960). Similarly, a city will be estopped from claiming the status of a trespasser when it could have acted under an option contract. Hugie v. Shady Cove, 85 Or.App. 229, 736 P.2d 567 (1987), rev. denied.

7. Rs. 2d § 69 cmt e. But, according to this section, the offeree is not bound by the offered terms where these are manifestly unreasonable. See Wright v. Sonoma County, 156 Cal. 475, 105 P. 409 (1909); Schreiber v. Olan Mills, 426 Pa.Super. 537, 627 A.2d 806 (1993) (no mutual assent); Whittier, 17 Cal.L.Rev. 441, 452 (1929).

ing either on a contract, quasi contract, or tort theory.[8] Thus, where an insurer sends a check refunding a premium, stating that it is rescinding the policy for misrepresentation and the insured cashes the check, a mutual rescission is created.[9] This would be the result even if the insured notified the insurer that it regarded the policy to have continuing efficacy. The contractual characterization is a fiction because liability is not based on mutual assent. The rule is a vehicle for allowing a contractual remedy for what is essentially a tort. If, however, dominion is exercised *with* an intent to accept, a true contract is formed without communication to the offeror.[10]

Section 2–606(1)(c) of the UCC provides that there is an acceptance of goods when the buyer "does any act inconsistent with the seller's ownership; but if the act is wrongful as against the seller it is an acceptance only if ratified by him." The UCC rule is in accord with the common law.[11]

Illustrative of the section is F.W. Lang Co. v. Fleet.[12] The seller sent a freezer unit on approval to defendant who used the compressor of the freezer unit to operate an air-conditioner. The court held that the use made of the compressor amounted to an act of dominion. Therefore, the seller had the option of suing in tort or contract for the price of the entire unit.[13]

In order to discourage the unsolicited sending of goods to unwary customers, several states have enacted legislation making it unlawful to offer merchandise for sale by the unsolicited sending of goods and also providing that a person who receives such goods has a complete defense to an action for the price or for the return of the goods.[14] The Postal Reorganization Act of 1970[15] provides that one who receives "unordered merchandise"[16] by mail may treat the transaction as a gift.[17]

§ 2.20   Termination of the Power of Acceptance

A revocable offer creates a power of acceptance. That power may be terminated in a variety of ways prior to its exercise.[1]

(a) *Lapse of Time*

An offer may expire by the lapse of time. Some offers contain language indicating when the offer ends. Such language needs to be

8. Rs. 1st § 72 ill. 8; Rs. 2d 69 ill. 9.

9. Avemco Ins. Co. v. Northern Colo. Air Charter, 38 P.3d 555 (Colo.2002).

10. Rs. 2d § 56.

11. See Annot., 67 ALR3d 363 (1975).

12. 193 Pa.Super. 365, 165 A.2d 258 (1960).

13. See also Columbia Rolling Mill v. Beckett Foundry & Machine, 55 N.J.L. 391, 26 A. 888 (1893).

14. See, e.g., McKinney's N.Y.Gen.Obl. Law § 5–332; see Wehringer v. West Pub., 54 A.D.2d 638, 387 N.Y.S.2d 806 (1976); cf. Neb.Rev.Stat. § 63–101 (1936) (limited to newspapers and other publications).

15. 39 U.S.C.A. § 3009.

16. The statute defines the words "unordered merchandise" as "merchandise mailed without the prior expressed request or consent of the recipient." 39 U.S.C.A. § 3009 (1976).

17. See Note, 1970 Duke L.J. 991. At common law the recipient is an involuntary bailee and is required to keep the goods for a reasonable time before discarding them.

§ 2.20

1. For termination of irrevocable offers, see § 2.25 infra.

interpreted. For example, on Jan. 29 A sends a letter to B dated Jan. 29 which states "Will give you eight days to accept or reject." B receives the offer on Feb. 2 and on Feb. 8 sends a letter of acceptance which is received by A on Feb. 9. The offer lapses in eight days, but should the eight days be measured from Jan. 29 or from Feb. 2? Professor Williston suggests that because the offeree should realize that the offer is ambiguous and that the limitation is imposed for the benefit of the offeror, the eight days should be reckoned from Jan. 29 rather than Feb. 2.[2] Contrariwise, Corbin suggests that the ambiguity be construed against its author.[3] The case on which the illustration is based took the latter position.[4]

Another question is, how are the eight days calculated? The normal rule is that, in measuring eight days, the day from which the time is reckoned should be excluded.[5] Thus, eight days from Feb. 2 is Feb. 10. The same rule would apply if an act was to be done *within* 8 days.

Under the assumption that the eight days are to be measured from Feb. 2, the matter can be further complicated if there is a delay in the transmission of the offer. If the offeree knows or has reason to know of the delay, the eight days should be measured from the date it should have been received.[6] According to Corbin: "In most cases the offeree will have some indication of the delay from the date of the letter, the postmarks, the condition of the envelope, or statements of the messenger. All such indications must be considered."[7] Where a counter-offer was hand delivered on the afternoon of the 20th and provided that it expired on the 20th at noon, it was held that the late delivery waived the deadline.[8]

If the duration of the power of acceptance of the offer is not stated, it is deemed to be open for a reasonable time.[9] What amounts to a reasonable time is ordinarily a question of fact.[10] Factors considered are whether the transaction is speculative,[11] the manifest purpose of the

---

2. 1 Corbin § 2.14 (Perillo 1993); 1 Williston § 5:6. Accord, CISG Art. 20.

3. 1 Corbin § 2.14 (Perillo 1993).

4. Caldwell v. Cline, 109 W.Va. 553, 156 S.E. 55, 72 ALR 1211 (1930).

5. Clements v. Pasadena Fin., 376 F.2d 1005 (9th Cir.1967); Housing Auth. v. T. Miller & Sons, 239 La. 966, 120 So.2d 494 (1960); Barnet v. Cannizzaro, 3 A.D.2d 745, 160 N.Y.S.2d 329 (1957); Livesey v. Copps Corp., 90 Wis.2d 577, 280 N.W.2d 339 (1979). West's Ann. California Civ. Code § 10; McKinney's N.Y.Gen.Constr.L. § 20.

6. Rs. 1st § 51; Rs. 2d § 49.

7. 1 Corbin § 2.17 (Perillo 1993).

8. C.G. Schmidt, Inc. v. Tiedke, 181 Wis.2d 316, 510 N.W.2d 756 (App.1993), rev. dismissed. See also Gould v. Artisoft,

Inc., 1 F.3d 544 (7th Cir.1993) (offer required signing an "enclosed" covenant not to compete—failure to enclose it constituted a waiver).

9. Caldwell v. E.F. Spears & Sons, 186 Ky. 64, 216 S.W. 83 (1919); Rs. 1st § 41.

10. Kaplan v. Reid Bros., 104 Cal.App. 268, 285 P. 868 (1930); Starkweather v. Gleason, 221 Mass. 552, 109 N.E. 635 (1915); Orlowski v. Moore, 198 Pa.Super. 360, 181 A.2d 692 (1962).

11. Minnesota Linseed Oil v. Collier White Lead, 17 F.Cas. 447 (C.C.D.Minn. 1876) (No. 9635); Brewer v. Lepman, 127 Mo.App. 693, 106 S.W. 1107 (1908); Rs. 2d § 41 cmt f and ills. 7, 8.

offeror,[12] and according to the Restatement (Second), whether or not the offeree is acting in good faith.[13]

The offer may stipulate that the power of acceptance will terminate on the happening of a certain event. If the event occurs before the acceptance, the power of acceptance lapses even though the offeree is not informed that the event has occurred.[14] Utilizing this rule are many offers for the sale of realty or unique goods that contain the language "subject to prior sale."

Where an offer is made in a face to face or telephone conversation or in any situation where there are direct negotiations, the offer is deemed, in the absence of a manifestation of a contrary intention, to be open only while the parties are conversing.[15]

(b) Effect of a Late Acceptance

If an offer lapses before an acceptance becomes effective, it would seem to follow that the late acceptance is an offer which in turn can be accepted only by a communicated acceptance.[16] But this is only the classical view. A second view is that the offeror may treat the late acceptance as an acceptance by waiving the lateness.[17] This view should be followed only in cases where the offeror's subjective intent to enter into the contract is objectively manifested.[18] Under a third and intermediate view, if the acceptance is late but sent in what could plausibly be argued to be a reasonable time, the original offeror has a burden to reply within a reasonable time. If the offeror fails to do so, there is a contract. The theory is that, as in the first view, the late acceptance is an offer but here the original offeror accepts by remaining silent when it would be reasonable to reply because it is not clear to the offeree that the original acceptance was late.[19] Where an acceptance is late because of a delay in transmission that is apparent from the circumstances, the UN Convention on Sales provides that the offeror must inform the offeree that the acceptance is too late; otherwise the parties will be bound.[20]

---

12. In re Kelly, 39 Conn. 159 (1872); Mitchell v. Abbott, 86 Me. 338, 29 A. 1118 (1894); Loring v. Boston, 48 Mass. (7 Metc.) 409 (1844); Rs. 2d § 41.

13. Rs. 2d § 41 cmt f.

14. Oliphant, The Duration and Termination of an Offer, 18 Mich.L.Rev. 201 (1920).

15. Akers v. J.B. Sedberry, Inc., 39 Tenn.App. 633, 286 S.W.2d 617 (1955); Rs. 2d § 41 cmt d; 1 Corbin § 2.16 (Perillo 1993). See Eisenberg, supra § 2.6 n.37, questioning the rule, but endorsing it as a non-binding maxim.

16. Houston Dairy v. John Hancock Mut. Life Ins., 643 F.2d 1185 (5th Cir. 1981); Maclay v. Harvey, 90 Ill. 525 (1878); Ferrier v. Storer, 63 Iowa 484, 19 N.W. 288 (1884); Cain v. Noel, 268 S.C. 583, 235

S.E.2d 292 (1977); Wax v. Northwest Seed, 189 Wn. 212, 64 P.2d 513 (1937).

17. Sabo v. Fasano, 154 Cal.App.3d 502, 201 Cal.Rptr. 270 (1984); see 2 Williston § 6:55–6:66 (criticizing such cases as violating "significant principles of the law of contracts," namely the need for a communicated acceptance). The UN Sales Convention validates an acceptance if the offeror communicates a waiver. CISG Art. 21(1).

18. See Margaret H. Wayne Trust v. Lipsky, 123 Idaho 253, 846 P.2d 904, 39 ALR5th 817 (1993) (on receipt of late acceptance, offeror took steps in reliance on it and could not disavow the contract). Cf. Eisenberg, supra § 2.6 n.37 at 1152 n. 60.

19. Phillips v. Moor, 71 Me. 78 (1880).

20. CISG Art. 21(2).

Although the Restatement (Second) rejects the second view,[21] it is not clear whether it accepts the third view in a case where it could be plausibly argued that the late acceptance was timely. In Comment b, in discussing late acceptances and in particular the type of case under discussion, it states that "the failure of the original offeror to object to an acceptance and his subsequent preparation for performance may be evidence that the acceptance was made within a reasonable time."[22] This is not an adoption of the third view because it assumes that the acceptance was timely. Elsewhere the Restatement (Second) comes closer to the third view when its says, "But the original offeror may have a duty to speak, for example, if the purported acceptance embodies a plausible but erroneous reading of the original offer."[23] This statement embodies the theory of the third view but does not specifically relate it to a late acceptance because it speaks of an "erroneous reading" and the illustration used is discussed in terms of "ambiguity." But if an offer is open for a reasonable time, can't the offeree "misread" the time available and isn't a reasonable time to some extent indefinite?

A well known case has raised a difficult problem in this area of late acceptance.[24] A made an offer to B, stating no time limitation on acceptance. Consequently the power of acceptance was open for a reasonable time. B sent a letter of acceptance after a reasonable time had already expired. The acceptance, however, crossed a letter from A indicating that A regarded the offer as still open. B sent no other acceptance. Had B accepted after receiving A's second letter it would be easy to conclude that although the offer has lapsed it had been revived by the second communication and so was effectively accepted.[25]

The court decided that there was a contract and that the original offer was accepted. The court does not appear to apply any of the three views stated above. The basis of the decision may be that objective evidence of the offeror's state of mind, although not known to the offeree, was sufficient to show an agreement. The result appears to be just. The objective test is designed to do justice by protecting a person who puts a reasonable interpretation on the words of another. Where, however, there is clear objective evidence that the parties are in agreement, is not justice better served by application of a subjective test?[26] The Restatement (Second) approves the result on the theory that the second letter may be used in interpreting the duration of the original offer.[27] This case is related to the topic of identical cross offers, previously discussed.[28]

(c) Death or Lack of Capacity of the Offeror or Offeree

In most jurisdictions a power of acceptance is terminated when the offeror dies.[29] The rule refers only to death occurring between the

21. Rs. 2d § 70 cmt a.

22. Id. cmt b.

23. Id. cmt a.

24. Mactier's Adm'rs v. Frith, 6 Wend. 103, 21 Am.Dec. 262 (N.Y.1830).

25. Santa Monica Unified School Dist. v. Persh, 5 Cal.App.3d 945, 85 Cal.Rptr. 463

(1970); Livingston v. Evans, [1925] 4 D.L.R. 769 (Alberta).

26. Rs.2d § 201(1); Eisenberg, supra § 2.6 n.37.

27. Rs. 2d § 23 cmt d and ill. 6.

28. See § 2.11 supra.

making of the offer and the acceptance. Under the majority view the offer is terminated even if the offeree is unaware of the offeror's death.[30]

The rule is logical if the offeree is aware of the offeror's death because knowledge of death would be tantamount to a revocation, but if the offeree is not aware of the death, there does not seem any good reason to hold that the offer is terminated. This is the rationale of the minority view.[31] The majority view is a frequently criticized relic of the subjective theory. It does not conform to the objective theory because the offeree should be charged only with what the offeree knows or should know of the offeror's situation.[32] Despite the criticism it is still the majority rule.[33] If B accepts before A dies, there is a contract and the only question presented would be whether A's estate would have the defense of impossibility of performance.[34]

The same rule applies to offers to unilateral contracts, except in that situation there is the additional question of whether the offer has become irrevocable.[35] If the offer has become irrevocable, death can no longer terminate the offer.[36]

The problem with respect to incapacity of the offeror is more complicated and more limited. Here, as in the case of death, the discussion is confined to incapacity that arises between the making of the offer and the acceptance. Most of the cases in this area arise where there is an adjudication of mental illness or defect and, as a result, the property of the offeror is placed under guardianship. In such a case the supervening insanity terminates the offer whether or not the offeree is aware of the adjudication.[37] But, as in the case of death, there is a minority view to the effect that the offer is not terminated unless the offeree knows of the adjudication.[38] If there is no adjudication of insanity, the rule is that supervening mental incapacity terminates an offer if the offeree is or ought to be aware of the incapacity.[39]

29. New Headley Tobacco Warehouse v. Gentry's Ex'r, 307 Ky. 857, 212 S.W.2d 325 (1948); Jordan v. Dobbins, 122 Mass. 168 (1877); Jones v. Union Cent. Life Ins., 265 A.D. 388, 40 N.Y.S.2d 74 (1943), aff'd; Rs. 2d § 48.

30. Pearl v. Merchants–Warren Nat. Bank, 9 Mass.App.Ct. 853, 400 N.E.2d 1314 (1980); Stang v. McVaney, 44 P.3d 41 (Wyo. 2002); Rs. 2d § 48 cmt a.

31. Gay v. Ward, 67 Conn. 147, 34 A. 1025 (1895); 1 Corbin § 2.34 (Perillo 1993).

32. See § 2.2 supra; Oliphant, Duration and Termination of an Offer, 18 Mich. L.Rev. 201, 209–211 (1920).

33. Inroads have been made on the rule by statute and decisions in certain specific areas. Rs. 2d § 48 cmt a.

34. See § 13.7 infra.

35. See § 2.22 infra.

36. See § 2.25 infra.

37. Beach v. First Methodist Episcopal Church, 96 Ill. 177 (1880); Union Trust & Sav. Bank v. State Bank, 188 N.W.2d 300, 55 ALR3d 336 (Iowa 1971) (physical incapacity); Rs.2d § 48 cmt b.

38. Swift & Co. v. Smigel, 115 N.J.Super. 391, 279 A.2d 895 (1971) aff'd mem. The case involved an offer looking to a series of unilateral contracts and the court adverts to "the diminished business utility of continuing guarantees" under the majority rule. The case also states that the adjudication is only prima facie evidence of incapacity. This is also a minority view.

39. 1 Williston § 5:20.

What constitutes incapacity is discussed in chapter 8 below. The supervening death or incapacity of the offeree will prevent the offeree's representative from accepting the offer because only an offeree may accept.[40] The situation would be different if the representative had been made an additional offeree.

(d) Revocation

The most obvious way of terminating the power of acceptance created by a revocable offer is by revocation[41]—a manifestation of intent not to enter into the proposed contract.[42] A revocable offer may be revoked at any time prior to acceptance.[43] The question of whether the offeror's language revokes the offer is a question of interpretation. An offeror's statement that equivocates about the offeror's commitment acts as a revocation.[44]

The general rule is that a revocation is effective when received,[45] but some states have adopted the rule that a revocation is effective when sent.[46] A written communication is received "when the writing comes into the possession of the person addressed, or of some person authorized by him to receive it for him, or when it is deposited in some place which he has authorized as the place for this or similar communications to be deposited for him."[47] By terms of the offer, or by a subsequent amendment of the offer, the offeror can reserve the right to revoke the offer without notice. Of course, even in this situation the revocation will not be effective if it occurs after an acceptance.[48]

When an offer is made to a number of persons whose identity is unknown to the offeror as, for example, in a newspaper advertisement, it is impossible to revoke by sending a letter of revocation. In such a case the power of acceptance may be terminated by giving equal publicity to the revocation.[49] Normally this is accomplished by using the same medium for the revocation as was used for the offer.[50] Even then it should be necessary that the publication of the revocation continue for as

---

40. See § 2.14 supra; Rs. 2d § 48 cmt c, and ill. 3.

41. 1 Corbin § 2.18 (Perillo 1993); see Boston & M.R. v. Bartlett, 57 Mass. (3 Cush.) 224 (1849).

42. Rs. 1st § 42; Rs. 2d § 42.

43. Calvin v. Rupp, 471 F.2d 1346 (8th Cir.1973); K.L. House Constr. v. Watson, 84 N.M. 783, 508 P.2d 592 (1973); Leigh v. New York, 33 N.Y.2d 774, 350 N.Y.S.2d 414, 305 N.E.2d 493 (1973); R.J. Taggart, Inc. v. Douglas County, 31 Or.App. 1137, 572 P.2d 1050 (1977); Merritt Land v. Marcello, 110 R.I. 166, 291 A.2d 263 (1972); see generally, Wagner, 38 Notre Dame L.Rev. 138 (1963).

44. Hoover Motor Exp. v. Clements Paper, 193 Tenn. 6, 241 S.W.2d 851 (1951); Rs. 2d § 42 cmt d.

45. Patrick v. Bowman, 149 U.S. 411 (1893); L. & E. Wertheimer v. Wehle–Hartford, 126 Conn. 30, 9 A.2d 279, 125 ALR 985 (1939); Wheat v. Cross, 31 Md. 99 (1869).

46. See, e.g., West's Ann.Cal.Civ. Code § 1587.

47. Rs. 1st § 69; Rs. 2d § 68; accord, Howard v. Daly, 61 N.Y. 362 (1875); UCC § 1–201(26). The proposed revision § 1–202 is more elaborate, especially as to notification to an organization.

48. Rs. 2d § 42 cmt b.

49. Shuey v. U.S., 92 U.S. (2 Otto) 73 (1875); Rs. 2d § 46; Perillo, Screed for a Film and Pillar of Classical Contract Law, 71 Fordham L.Rev. 915 (2002).

50. Rs. 2d § 46.

long as the offer did, and in as prominent a location, and in at least the same size ad.[51] However, if the same medium is not available, the doctrine requires only the best means of notice available under the circumstances.[52] Should the offeror know the identity of a person who is taking action on the offer the offeror must, to have an effective revocation, communicate the revocation to that person.[53] If the attempted revocation actually comes to the attention of any offeree, this will amount to a revocation from the moment the offeree is aware of it.

An offer may also be terminated indirectly. In Dickinson v. Dodds[54] the defendant made an offer to sell specific real property to the plaintiff and, while the offer was still open, made an offer to sell the same property to Allan. Allan accepted the offer. Later the plaintiff, the first offeree, aware that Allan had accepted, gave the defendant a notice of acceptance. The court held that the offer to the plaintiff was revoked when the plaintiff received reliable information that Allan had accepted. The plaintiff reasonably should have concluded that the defendant offeror no longer wished the offer to be operative.

The case raises three questions. The first question is the scope of the rule. The original Restatement limited the doctrine to cases involving the sale of land and chattels.[55] The Restatement (Second) removes this limitation.[56] The second question is, what information is reliable. The cases hold that the information must be true and have come from a reliable source.[57] If the source is not reliable, the information may be ignored, but if it is reliable, reasonable inquiry should be made to ascertain its accuracy.

The most difficult question is what information should lead a reasonable person to conclude that the offeror wishes to terminate the offer? In Dickinson v. Dodds, the information was that Allan had accepted the offer. When plaintiff heard this reliable information, as a reasonable person, plaintiff should have understood that the offeror would not want the offer to continue. The same would be true if Dickinson had heard that the property had actually been sold.[58]

If Dickinson had heard only that an offer had been made to Allan, would there be a revocation? A reasonable person might reach two different conclusions. One is that the offeror would not want to make two offers because of the potential double liability. The other is that, because no revocation had been communicated, Dodds was willing to run

---

51.   See 1 Corbin § 2.21 (Perillo 1993).

52.   1 Corbin § 2.21 (Perillo 1993).

53.   Long v. Chronicle Pub., 68 Cal.App. 171, 228 P. 873 (1924); Rs. 2d § 46 ill. 1. The rule is one of reason.

54.   2 Ch.D. 463 (1876); see Bancroft v. Martin, 144 Miss. 384, 109 So. 859 (1926). On the issue of indirect acceptance, see Southern Nat. Bank v. Tri Financial, 317 F.Supp. 1173 (S.D.Tex.1970), modified.

55.   Rs. 1st § 43.

56.   Rs. 2d § 43 ill. 2; see also 1 Corbin § 2.20 (Perillo 1993); First Nat. Bankshares v. Geisel, 853 F.Supp. 1344 (D.Kan.1994).

57.   Berryman v. Kmoch, 221 Kan. 304, 559 P.2d 790 (1977); Coleman v. Applegarth, 68 Md. 21, 11 A. 284 (1887); Watters v. Lincoln, 29 S.D. 98, 135 N.W. 712 (1912); Frank v. Stratford–Handcock, 13 Wyo. 37, 77 P. 134 (1904).

58.   1 Corbin § 2.20 (Perillo 1993).

the risk of making two offers. The second conclusion is preferable.[59] Similarly if Allan, the second offeree, learned of the first offer, he could reasonably believe that the second offer was operative and could reasonably believe that the offeror was willing to run the risk of having two outstanding offers.

(e) Rejection—Counter–Offer

A rejection terminates the offeree's power of acceptance.[60] A counter-offer, because it is an implicit rejection, has the same effect.[61] According to the Restatement (Second) this result also carries out the usual understanding that a new proposal supersedes an earlier proposal.[62] A counter-offer includes a purported acceptance that adds qualifications or requires performance of conditions not contained in the offer.[63] But neither a rejection nor a counter-offer will operate to terminate an offer if the offeror or offeree manifests such an intention.[64] Thus, if the counter-offer states that the offeree is "keeping the offer under advisement" the power of acceptance is not terminated.[65] There is no implicit rejection in that statement. A rejection or a counter-offer does not terminate the power of acceptance until it is received.[66]

One can distinguish a counter-offer and a rejection from a counter-inquiry, a comment on the terms, a request for a modification of the offer,[67] a request for a modification of a contract, an acceptance plus a separate offer,[68] and even what has been referred to as a "grumbling assent."[69] The over-arching question is whether the offeror can reasonably understand that the offer is no longer alive; thus, an offer covering the same subject matter can be made to a third person. In the light of this test, the categories distinguished here are not rigid compartments, but convenient categories to test the offeree's expressions.[70] Regardless

---

59. 1 Corbin § 2.20 (Perillo 1993); Rs. 1st § 40.

60. Collins v. Thompson, 679 F.2d 168 (9th Cir.1982). But see Pepsi–Cola Bottling v. N.L.R.B., 659 F.2d 87 (8th Cir.1981) (applying a contrary rule to collective bargaining).

61. D'Agostino v. Bank of Ravenswood, 205 Ill.App.3d 898, 150 Ill.Dec. 759, 563 N.E.2d 886 (1990), app. denied; Logan Ranch v. Farm Credit Bank, 238 Neb. 814, 472 N.W.2d 704 (1991); Berg v. Lien, 522 N.W.2d 455 (N.D.1994); 1 Corbin § 3.35–3.36 (Perillo 1993); 1 Williston § 5:3.

62. Rs. 2d § 39 cmt a.

63. Gleeson v. Frahm, 211 Neb. 677, 320 N.W.2d 95 (1982). This common law rule and recent changes to it are discussed in § 2.21 infra.

64. Rs. 2d § 39.

65. Radford & Guise v. Practical Premium, 125 Ark. 199, 188 S.W. 562 (1916); Rs. 2d § 39 ill. 3.

66. Glacier Park Foundation v. Watt, 663 F.2d 882 (9th Cir.1981); Harris v. Scott, 67 N.H. 437, 32 A. 770 (1893); Rs. 2d § 40. Contra, Hunt v. Higman, 70 Iowa 406, 30 N.W. 769 (1886).

67. Berrey v. Jeffcoat, 785 P.2d 20 (Alaska 1990).

68. Rs. 2d § 39 cmt b.

69. Johnson v. Federal Union Sur., 187 Mich. 454, 153 N.W. 788, 792 (1915); see also Podany v. Erickson, 235 Minn. 36, 49 N.W.2d 193 (1951).

70. Cf. Eisenberg § 2.6 supra n.37 at 1161 ("the counter-offer rule is incongruent in many or most cases with the general principles of interpretation, is not supported by the accuracy of administrative justifications, is not based on any noninterpretive policy, does not serve as a coordinating device, and should be either dropped entirely or downgraded to the form of a maxim.")

of the form the expression takes, it is important to keep in mind that, among the categories discussed above, only counter-offers and rejections terminate the offeree's power of acceptance. In any of the other categories, the offeree can still accept the offer, even after having made, say, a counter-inquiry or a request for a modification.

If A makes an offer to B to sell an object for $5,000 and B replies, "I'll pay $4,800," this would be a counter-offer but if B said "will you take $4,800?," this could be considered a counter-inquiry.[71] "Your price is too high" seems to be a comment on the terms.[72] "Send lowest cash price" would be a request for a modification of the offer and not a rejection.[73] "I accept but I would appreciate it if you gave me the benefit of a 5% discount," would be an acceptance that requests a modification of the contract.[74] "I accept your offer and I hereby order a second object," is an acceptance coupled with a separate offer and not a counter-offer.[75] A "grumbling assent" has been described as an acceptance that expresses dissatisfaction at some terms "but stops short of dissent."[76] If an acceptance contains a term that is not expressly stated in the offer but is implied in it there is an acceptance and not a counter-offer.[77]

A counter-offer must also be distinguished from what could be termed a future acceptance.[78] For example, a general contractor who is about to make a bid may, in turn, receive a bid (offer) from a subcontractor. The general contractor may accept that offer provided that it is awarded the contract, a condition that the subcontractor agrees to.[79] The parties are not presently bound and therefore either party is entitled to

71. Rs. 1st, § 39 ills. 1 and 2. See King v. Travelers Ins., 513 So.2d 1023 (Ala.1987).

72. Rs. 2d § 39 cmt b.

73. Home Gas v. Magnolia Petroleum, 143 Okl. 112, 287 P. 1033 (1930); Stevenson, Jaques & Co. v. McLean, 5 Q.B.D. 346 (1880).

74. Kodiak Island Borough v. Large, 622 P.2d 440 (Alaska 1981); Culton v. Gilchrist, 92 Iowa 718, 61 N.W. 384 (1894); Collin v. Wetzel, 163 Md. 194, 161 A. 18 (1932); Butler v. Foley, 211 Mich. 668, 179 N.W. 34 (1920); Valashinas v. Koniuto, 308 N.Y. 233, 124 N.E.2d 300 (1954); Rucker v. Sanders, 182 N.C. 607, 109 S.E. 857 (1921); Rs. 2d § 61.

The case of Martindell v. Fiduciary Counsel, 131 N.J.Eq. 523, 26 A.2d 171 (1942), aff'd, is illustrative. In that case A gave B an option to purchase 27 shares of certain stock. Within the time specified in the option, the optionee wrote as follows: "I hereby exercise my option. I have deposited the purchase price with the Colorado National Bank to be delivered to you upon transfer of the stock. If you do not accept such procedure, I demand that you designate the time and place for the same." The court held that there was an acceptance and that the language relating to how the purchase

price would be paid did not give rise to a counter-offer because it merely suggested a way to perform the contract and the acceptance was otherwise unconditional.

75. 1 Corbin § 3.30 (Perillo 1993).

76. Johnson v. Federal Union Sur., 187 Mich. 454, 153 N.W. 788 (1915); 1 Corbin § 3.30 (Perillo 1993).

77. Suitts v. First Sec. Bank, 125 Idaho 27, 33, 867 P.2d 260, 266 (1993), rev. denied; Burkhead v. Farlow, 266 N.C. 595, 146 S.E.2d 802, 16 ALR3d 1416 (1966); Rs. 2d § 59 ill. 3; 1 Corbin § 3.32 (Perillo 1993); 2 Williston § 6:15. Contra, Phoenix Iron & Steel v. Wilkoff Co., 253 F. 165, 1 ALR 1497 (6th Cir.1918), and see Roth v. Malson, 67 Cal.App.4th 552, 79 Cal.Rptr.2d 226 (1998) (no additional terms, but use of the term "counter-offer" defeated acceptance).

78. Reed Bros. v. Bluff City Motor, 139 Miss. 441, 104 So. 161 (1925); Orr v. Doubleday, Page & Co., 223 N.Y. 334, 119 N.E. 552, 1 ALR 338 (1918); see 1 Williston § 6:14, where this type of acceptance is called "an acceptance in escrow."

79. Frederick Raff Co. v. Murphy, 110 Conn. 234, 147 A. 709 (1929).

withdraw before the future event occurs. Once that event occurs the parties are bound without the necessity for any further manifestation of intent. Fairness may require that the offeree give the offeror notice that the event has occurred.[80]

(f) Supervening Death, Destruction, or Illegality

The power of acceptance created by an offer is terminated by the death or destruction, prior to acceptance, of a person or thing essential to performance of the contract.[81] It is also terminated by illegality supervening between the making of an offer and its acceptance.[82]

§ 2.21 Acceptance Varying From Offer

(a) The Common Law Rule

The common law rule is that a purported acceptance that adds qualifications or conditions operates as a counter-offer and thereby a rejection of the offer.[1] This is so even if the qualification or condition relates to a trivial matter.[2] Courts have enforced this rule, sometimes called the "ribbon matching" or "mirror-image" rule, with a rigor worthy of a better cause.[3] In the words of one court, "acceptance [of an offer] must be 'positive, unconditional, unequivocal and unambiguous, and must not change, add to, or qualify the terms of the offer.' "[4] Rigid application of the rule has proved detrimental to commerce, particularly because business today is largely done on printed forms and the buyer's and seller's forms frequently clash as to ancillary terms of the transaction.[5] The UCC has sought to develop a more flexible rule. Even outside the UCC, a trend is developing to uphold acceptances that vary from offers in only immaterial details.[6]

Prior to the effective date of the UCC, a maxim, called "the last shot principle," determined the terms of the contract. If the buyer made an offer, and the seller's reply was a counter-offer, the purchaser's acceptance of delivery of the seller's shipment of the goods was deemed to be

80. See Craddock v. Greenhut Constr., 423 F.2d 111 (5th Cir.1970); Premier Elec. Constr. v. Miller–Davis, 422 F.2d 1132 (7th Cir.1970); Los Angeles Rams Football Club v. Cannon, 185 F.Supp. 717 (S.D.Cal.1960); Note, 24 Mich.L.Rev. 302 (1926).

81. Rs. 2d § 36.

82. Rs. 2d § 36 cmt c; Rs. 1st § 36.

§ 2.21

1. See § 2.20(e) supra; In re Pago Pago Aircrash, 637 F.2d 704 (9th Cir.1981); Rorvig v. Douglas, 123 Wn.2d 854, 873 P.2d 492 (1994), en banc.

2. Rs. 1st § 60; accord, Craddock v. Greenhut Constr., 423 F.2d 111 (5th Cir. 1970); Dickey v. Hurd, 33 F.2d 415 (1st Cir.1929), cert. denied; Rounsaville v. Van Zandt Realtors, 247 Ark. 749, 447 S.W.2d

655 (1969); Poel v. Brunswick–Balke–Collender, 216 N.Y. 310, 110 N.E. 619 (1915); see Llewellyn, On Our Case–Law of Contract: Offer and Acceptance I, 48 Yale L.J. 1, 30 (1938).

3. Dorton v. Collins & Aikman, 453 F.2d 1161 (6th Cir.1972).

4. Gyurkey v. Babler, 103 Idaho 663, 651 P.2d 928, 34 ALR4th 1199 (1982); Wagner v. Rainier Mfg., 230 Or. 531, 537, 371 P.2d 74, 77 (1962).

5. Macauley, Non–Contractual Relations in Business: A Preliminary Study, 28 Am. Soc.Rev. 55 (1963).

6. Hollywood Fantasy v. Gabor, 151 F.3d 203 (5th Cir.1998); Gresser v. Hotzler, 604 N.W.2d 379 (Minn.App.2000); Mazzella v. Koken, 559 Pa. 216, 739 A.2d 531 (1999); see also Rs. 2d § 59 cmt a.

an acceptance of the seller's terms.[7] The last set of terms placed on the table (the last shot) prior to the purchaser's acceptance (by exercise of dominion over the goods) governed the terms of the contract.[8] Usually these were the seller's terms. The frustrating fact is that, for purchases and sales in the ordinary course of business, the parties so frequently fail to read the conflicting forms,[9] and if they do, they fail to make the effort to iron out differences. The reasons for this are obvious. In a large organization, the routine use of forms is efficient. Any attempt to modify routine forms for a particular transaction often requires the approval of higher management. An attempt to seek such modification will involve delays, and the possible killing of the deal. Paralysis would often ensue.[10] Although it frequently happens that standard forms are not read by the employees who handle them, they were read and formulated by someone. Indemnity clauses, limitations of consequential damages, disclaimers of certain warranties and limitations under others all reflect decisions with respect to the contract price. Their importance should not lightly be disregarded.

(b) UCC § 2–207

This common law rule has been changed by § 2–207 of the UCC,[11] which reads as follows:

(1) A definite and seasonable expression of acceptance or a written confirmation which is sent within a reasonable time operates as an acceptance even though it states terms additional to or different from those offered or agreed upon, unless acceptance is expressly made conditional on assent to the additional or different terms.

(2) The additional terms are to be construed as proposals for addition to the contract. Between merchants such terms become part of the contract unless:

    (a) the offer expressly limits acceptance to the terms of the offer;

    (b) they materially alter it; or

---

7. See, e.g., Alaska Pacific Salmon v. Reynolds Metals, 163 F.2d 643 (2d Cir. 1947). The seller's disclaimer of warranty prevailed.

8. The last shot principle can apply in a non-UCC case. In Provident Life and Acc. Ins. Co. v. Goel, 274 F.3d 984 (5th Cir. 2001), a physician applied for a disability policy (the offer). The insurer issued a materially different policy (the counter-offer). The physician paid the premium and accepted the policy. His rights were determined by the materially different policy.

9. This is not universally true. "[I]t is customary practice in the industry to write a confirming letter if there are variations between the terms in the purchase orders and those in the acknowledgements." Reaction Molding Technologies v. General Electric, 588 F.Supp. 1280 (E.D.Pa.1984).

10. See Stewart Macaulay, Non–Contractual Relations in Business: A Preliminary Study, 28 Am.Sociological Rev. 55 (1963), where the author studied the battle of the forms as a sociological and legal phenomenon.

11. UCC § 2–207 is the subject of a vast amount of writing. A generally sound article is Caroline Brown, Restoring Peace in the Battle of the Forms, 69 N.C.L.Rev. 893 (1991). It contains an extensive bibliography; see also 1 Corbin § 3.37 (rev'd ed. Perillo).

(c) notification of objection to them has already been given or is given within a reasonable time after notice of them is received.

(3) Conduct by both parties which recognizes the existence of a contract is sufficient to establish a contract for sale although the writings of the parties do not otherwise establish a contract. In such cases the terms of the particular contract consist of those terms on which the writings of the parties agree, together with supplementary terms incorporated under any other provisions of this Act.

As is too often the case in attempts at law reform, this reform created far more problems than it solved. By far the most frequent question raised under the Uniform Commercial Code provision is not whether a contract exists but what are the contents of the contract. On the latter question, the UCC provision has proved to be a recipe for unadulterated chaos. Professor Gilmore aptly described the provision as "abominable," a "complete disaster," and a "miserable, bungled patched-up-job."[12]

(1) Subsection 1. Subsection 1 speaks of "a definite and seasonable expression of acceptance" but also speaks of a "confirmation which is sent within a reasonable time." Acceptance and confirmation are two separate and distinct concepts. Confirmations will be discussed toward the end of this analysis.

Subsection 1 assumes the existence of an offer[13] and raises two important questions on the issue of acceptance, that is, on the existence of mutual assent. The subsection assumes that the offer has arguably been accepted in a record that contains additional or different terms. The two critical questions are: 1) was the arguable acceptance *definite and seasonable*? 2) Is the arguable acceptance *expressly conditional on assent* to the additional or different terms?

(2) A Definite Expression of Acceptance. The adjective "seasonable" merely means that the acceptance must be made in timely fashion. In most cases there is no issue on the question of whether the expression of acceptance is "definite." But, for example, if the offeree's form indicates acceptance but shows a change in the quantity term, the purported acceptance is not a definite expression of acceptance.[14] This is because it is not a definite expression if it "diverges significantly as to a dickered term." Dickered terms include the description of the goods, price, quantity, and delivery terms.[15] One way of supporting this result is to

---

12. Grant Gilmore, Letter, in Speidel, Summers & White, Sales: Teaching Materials 93–94 (1987).

13. If the initial document is the seller's price quotation, or an order that is subject to acceptance by the buyer and the seller's home office, there is no offer. If the buyer follows up with a purchase order, the buyer's form will be the offer. See, e.g., Brown Machine, Division of John Brown v. Hercules, 770 S.W.2d 416 (Mo.App.1989); McCarty v. Verson Allsteel Press, 89 Ill.App.3d 498, 44 Ill.Dec. 570, 411 N.E.2d 936 (1980).

According to one court, this provision applies only to an offer in writing. ProCD v. Zeidenberg, 86 F.3d 1447, 1452 (7th Cir. 1996).

14. Duval & Co. v. Malcom, 233 Ga. 784, 214 S.E.2d 356 (1975); Dubrofsky v. Messer, 1981 Mass.App.Div. 55 (1981); see 1 Corbin § 3.37 n.16 (rev'd. ed.1993).

15. U.S. Indus. v. Semco Mfg., 562 F.2d 1061 (8th Cir.1977), cert. denied; White & Summers § 1–3.

reason from UCC § 2–204(3) to the effect that the parties must "have intended to make a contract." If the parties fail to agree as to a dickered term, they do not intend to make a contract, and do not have the commercial understanding that a deal has been closed.[16]

There are contrary cases. For example, in one case the seller's acceptance called for a 30% increase in price. Nevertheless, the court held that there was a definite and seasonable expression of acceptance.[17] Another relevant case is the Bosway Case[18] where the offer contained a delivery date but the acceptance stated a different delivery date. Yet the court held that the acceptance was definite. The court saw the problem as one of different terms. Certainly, the contrary could have been decided. This is one of many muddled issues under § 2–207 of the UCC.

(3) Is the Acceptance Expressly Conditional on Assent to the Additional or Different Terms? Assume that the expression of acceptance is definite enough, but it contains additional or different terms. The statute is designed to facilitate the finding that a contract has been formed despite this variance between the offer and acceptance. However, the offeree can prevent the formation of a contract if its definite expression of acceptance is conditioned on the offeror's assent to the additional or different terms in the expression of acceptance. For example, if the offeree's response states that the acceptance is expressly conditioned on the offeror's assent to all of the terms of the offeree's form, no contract is formed. However, the otherwise definite expression of acceptance may include an ambiguous term stating: "subject to all of the terms and conditions on the face and reverse side hereof, including arbitration, all of which are accepted by the [offeror]."[19] The introductory phrase "subject to" ordinarily is understood to introduce an express condition. Yet, to implement the general policy of finding that a contract has been formed, most courts have given such clauses narrow and literal interpretations. The quoted clause does not state that the acceptance is conditional on the offeror's *assent* to the additional or different terms contained in the acceptance. Consequently, the clause does not prevent the formation of a contract.[20] If the clause is in a non-standardized

16. Dorton v. Collins & Aikman, 453 F.2d 1161 (6th Cir.1972); Steiner v. Mobil Oil, 20 Cal.3d 90, 141 Cal.Rptr. 157, 569 P.2d 751 (1977); Kleinschmidt v. Futuronics, 41 N.Y.2d 972, 395 N.Y.S.2d 151, 363 N.E.2d 701 (1977); UCC § 2–207 cmt 2. Professor Murray argues that subsection 1 should not be read mechanically and the issue should be whether the parties should reasonably conclude that there was a deal or that a counter-offer was made. 39 Pitt. L.Rev. 597 (1978).

17. CBS v. Auburn Plastics, 67 A.D.2d 811, 413 N.Y.S.2d 50 (1979). See Stewart–Decatur Sec. Sys. v. Von Weise Gear, 517 F.2d 1136 (8th Cir.1975); Stanley–Bostitch, Inc. v. Regenerative Env. Eqpt., 786 A.2d 1063 (R.I.2001) (price adjustment clause);

31 Bus.Law. 1543–44 (1976); 37 Fordham L.Rev. 317, 322 (1969).

18. Bosway Tube & Steel v. McKay Mach., 65 Mich.App. 426, 237 N.W.2d 488 (1975).

19. Taken from Dorton v. Collins & Aikman, 453 F.2d 1161 (6th Cir.1972).

20. Dorton v. Collins & Aikman, 453 F.2d 1161 (6th Cir.1972). The Dorton case has been widely followed on this point. See Step–Saver Data Sys. v. Wyse Technology, 939 F.2d 91 (3d Cir.1991); Daitom, Inc. v. Pennwalt, 741 F.2d 1569 (10th Cir.1984); Idaho Power v. Westinghouse Electric, 596 F.2d 924 (9th Cir.1979); Reaction Molding Technologies v. General Electric, 588 F.Supp. 1280 (E.D.Pa.1984); Egan Mach. v.

record, it will not be given so narrow an interpretation, and the court will attempt to interpret its intended effect according to general principles of interpretation.[21]

(4) If the Records Form a Contract What Are the Terms? If the court concludes that the records form a contract, the vexing question is, what are the terms of the contract? The answer to this question is found in subsection 2 of § 2–207. The additional or different terms are treated as offers to modify the terms of the offer. The subsection then makes a distinction between merchants and non-merchants. If either party is a non-merchant, the terms of the offer constitute the contract without modification. The one exception is if the offeror expressly assents to the additional or different term. The offeror's silence will not normally be considered assent to the additional or different terms.[22]

(5) Additional Terms Between Merchants. Of course, it is possible for a merchant to expressly agree to a term in the acceptance that is additional to or different from the terms of the offer. Absent such agreement, Section 2–207(2) provides that between merchants[23] the additional terms become part of the contract unless: (a) the offer expressly limits acceptance to the terms of the offer,[24] (b) they materially alter it, or (c) notification of objection to them has already been given or is given within a reasonable time after notice of them is received. Drafters of forms have often availed themselves of the protective mechanisms of 2(a) and (c) to knock out additional or different terms that might be contained in an acceptance.

Mobil Chemical, 660 F.Supp. 35 (D.Conn. 1986); St. Charles Cable TV v. Eagle Comtronics, 687 F.Supp. 820 (S.D.N.Y.1988), affd; Brown Machine, Division of John Brown v. Hercules, 770 S.W.2d 416 (Mo. App.1989). See Annot., 22 ALR4th 939.

In Ralph Shrader, Inc. v. Diamond Int'l, 833 F.2d 1210 (6th Cir.1987), reh en banc den., the following language was deemed to be expressly conditioned on the buyer's assent: "The terms set forth on the reverse side are the only ones upon which we will accept orders."

In Dresser Indus. v. Gradall Co., 702 F.Supp. 726 (E.D.Wis.1988), the seller's acknowledgement form read, "Your order has been entered expressly subject to and conditioned on the understanding that our terms of sales stated on the front and reverse sides hereof and no others apply to this sale." It was held that "understanding" was the equivalent of "your assent" and that no contract was formed by the exchange of writings.

In Mace Indus. v. Paddock Pool Equipment, 288 S.C. 65, 339 S.E.2d 527, 530 (S.C.App. 1986), a purchase order constituted an acceptance despite the fact that it "contained on its reverse side (1) a notice that 'THE SELLER AGREES TO ALL OF THE FOLLOWING TERMS AND CONDITIONS' and (2) a provision that the order form shall constitute the entire agreement of the parties."

21. Air Master Sales v. Northbridge Park Co–Op, 748 F.Supp. 1110 (D.N.J. 1990). In response to an offer made by letter the offeree expressed assent but wrote, "This confirmation will be valid only when [offeree] receives a Purchase Order from [offeror] for the windows." No further correspondence or deliveries ensued. The offeree's attempt to enforce the alleged contract was unsuccessful.

22. Although Comment 6 talks in terms of acceptance by silence, it relates to a situation involving two merchants, and more specifically to the last part of 2(c). Dorton v. Collins & Aikman, 453 F.2d 1161 (6th Cir.1972); cf. Hohenberg v. Killebrew, 505 F.2d 643 (5th Cir.1974), rehearing denied.

23. Merchant is defined in § 1.7 supra.

24. See, e.g., CBS v. Auburn Plastics, 67 A.D.2d 811, 413 N.Y.S.2d 50 (1979).

If the offeror's form limits acceptance to the terms of the offer, or if it gives notification of objection to any additional or different terms, the offer provides the terms of the contract and the acceptance provides none of the terms. The same result would follow in the rare case where the offeror objects to the terms within a reasonable time after receipt of the acceptance. If the offeror does not take advantage of these opportunities, the additional term will be knocked out if it materially alters the terms of the offered contract. A primary criterion of materiality is "surprise." "Generally a material alteration is an addition or change to the contract which would result in surprise or hardship if incorporated without the express awareness by the other party."[25] Many of the cases involve the offeree merchant's inclusion of an arbitration clause in the acceptance, although arbitration was not mentioned by the offeror. The issue becomes whether the arbitration clause is a material alteration. The majority of courts have so ruled.[26] Others have held that the materiality of the arbitration clause is a question of fact that must be proved.[27]

If there is a trade usage that disputes are handled by arbitration but the offeror's form does not include it, and the offeree's acceptance does, does the arbitration clause become part of the contract by virtue of the usage or a course of performance or a course of dealing even though it would otherwise be deemed to be a material alteration? The cases are in conflict.[28] If a material alteration is assented to by the offeror it becomes part of the contract.[29]

(6) Different Terms Between Merchants. Again, we are assuming that the records of the parties have formed a contract, but the acceptance contains a term that is different from a term in the offer—a term that clashes with a term of the offer. But what if a term of the acceptance contradicts an implied term of the offer? Should it be deemed to be "different?" There is authority to that effect.[30]

Subsection 2 of § 2–207 is utterly silent about the fate of "different" terms. Thus, by elementary rules of interpretation it would appear that different terms do not become part of the contract unless the different terms are accepted by the offeror. However, Comment 3 to § 2–207

25. McMahan v. Koppers Co., 654 F.2d 380 (5th Cir.1981); UCC § 2–207 cmts 4 & 5.

26. Windsor Mills v. Collins & Aikman, 25 Cal.App.3d 987, 101 Cal.Rptr. 347 (1972); Andy Assocs. v. Bankers Trust, 49 N.Y.2d 13, 424 N.Y.S.2d 139, 399 N.E.2d 1160 (1979); Frances Hosiery Mills v. Burlington Indus., 285 N.C. 344, 204 S.E.2d 834, 72 ALR3d 466 (1974); Furnish, 67 Cal. L.Rev. 317 (1979).

27. Dorton v. Collins & Aikman, 453 F.2d 1161 (6th Cir.1972); Avedon Eng'r v. Seatex, 112 F.Supp.2d 1090 (D.Colo.2000).

28. See Baumgold Bros. v. Allan M. Fox Co., 375 F.Supp. 807 (N.D.Ohio 1973); Gay-

nor–Stafford Indus. v. Mafco Textured Fibers, 52 A.D.2d 481, 384 N.Y.S.2d 788 (1976); White & Summers § 1–3; see also Schubtex, Inc. v. Allen Snyder, Inc., 49 N.Y.2d 1, 424 N.Y.S.2d 133, 399 N.E.2d 1154 (1979), rearg. denied.

29. See Coastal Indus. v. Automatic Steam Products, 654 F.2d 375 (5th Cir. 1981).

30. Steiner v. Mobil Oil, 20 Cal.3d 90, 141 Cal.Rptr. 157, 569 P.2d 751 (1977); Air Prod. & Chem. v. Fairbanks Morse, 58 Wis.2d 193, 206 N.W.2d 414, 78 ALR3d 619 (1973); contra, JOM, Inc. v. Adell Plastics, 193 F.3d 47 (1st Cir.1999).

states that the rule that is applied to additional terms should be applied to different terms.[31] Under this approach, if one of the parties is a non-merchant, a different term will become part of the contract only if it is in turn accepted by the offeror. As to merchants, the different term would become part of the contract unless it is ejected under the provisions of subsection (2).[32] However, under Professor Summers' approach stated in note 32, the different term does not become part of the contract unless the offeror expressly agrees to the different term, as, for example, by signing and returning an expression of acceptance.[33]

Professor White[34] following the lead of the Bosway[35] case argues that different terms cancel each other out and the gap thus created should be filled with the gap-filling provisions of the Code. However, as White's co-author, Summers, correctly states, the Bosway case is not on point because it relates to confirmations.

Thus, there are three views as to the fate of different terms. One view is that a different term should be treated as an additional term. A second view is that the different terms cancel out and the gap-filler provisions of the Code should fill the void. A third view holds that different terms never become part of the contract unless the different terms are accepted by the offeror. Once again, UCC § 2–207 provides a recipe for confusion.

(7) If the Records Do Not Create a Contract. Even if no contract is formed by the exchange of documents, a contract can be formed by conduct. If the parties have behaved as though a contract had been formed, a contract exists. Subsection 3 determines the rights of the parties. As at common law, a contract can be formed by conduct, but the terms of the contract are determined in a different way. Under the common law, if the purported acceptance is a counter-offer, the offer is rejected and its terms are no longer relevant. If the goods are shipped and accepted, the common law's axiom was the "last shot principle," the last writing prior to performance determined the terms of the contract. Subsection 3, however, says, "The terms of the particular contract consist of those terms on which the writings of the parties agree, (including terms on which confirmations agree),[36] together with any

---

31. Boese–Hilburn v. Dean Mach., 616 S.W.2d 520, 22 ALR4th 925 (Mo.App.1981).

32. American Parts v. American Arb. Ass'n, 8 Mich.App. 156, 154 N.W.2d 5 (1967); Air Products & Chem. v. Fairbanks Morse, 58 Wis.2d 193, 206 N.W.2d 414 (1973). Prof. Summers suggests that this ejection would occur in every case by virtue of § 2–207(2)(c). White and. Summers, § 1–2.

33. N & D Fashions v. DHJ Indus., 548 F.2d 722 (8th Cir.1976); see Construction Aggregates v. Hewitt–Robins, 404 F.2d 505 (7th Cir.1968), cert. denied.

34. White & Summers, § 1–3 (4th ed). This was followed in Reilly Foam v. Rubber-maid, 206 F.Supp.2d 643 (E.D.Pa.2002) (asserting it is the majority view); Owens–Corning Fiberglas v. Sonic Dev., 546 F.Supp. 533 (D.C.Kan.1982). For a criticism, see Duesenberg, 34 Bus.L.Rev. 1477 (1979).

35. Bosway Tube & Steel v. McKay Mach., 65 Mich.App. 426, 237 N.W.2d 488 (1975).

36. Diamond Fruit Growers v. Krack, 794 F.2d 1440 (9th Cir.1986); Commerce & Indus. Ins. v. Bayer Corp., 433 Mass. 388, 742 N.E.2d 567 (2001).

supplementary terms incorporated under any other provisions of this act." The "act" referred to is the UCC, particularly its gap-filler provisions.

To illustrate, Seller made an offer. Buyer sent a fax, expressing assent but conditioned on one additional term. Thus, no contract was formed. Buyer then asked Seller to renew its offer. Seller complied. Buyer then caused a bank to issue a letter of credit to Seller on the terms of its counter-offer and Seller issued an internal work order and drawings for the product were drafted and sent to Buyer. Their conduct showed that in their commercial understanding a contract had been made.[37]

(8) Confirmations. At the beginning of this section we noted that subsection 1 dealing with acceptances also provides that "a written confirmation which is sent within a reasonable time operates as an acceptance even though it states terms additional to or different from those * * * agreed upon, * * *." It is strange and illogical to say that "a written confirmation" operates as an acceptance because a confirmation confirms the terms of a contract already formed. However, this part of the section is limited primarily to two situations: (1) "where an agreement has been reached either orally or by informal correspondence between the parties and is followed by one or both parties sending formal acknowledgements or memoranda embodying the terms so far agreed upon and adding terms not discussed."[38] The assumption in this quotation is that the terms are additional and that there is no conflict between the additional terms in the two memoranda or acknowledgements. Therefore, it is easy to understand that the rules governing "additional" terms in acceptances should apply. (2) Where there are "additional" terms in the memoranda sent and they conflict with each other, each party is deemed to object to the other party's terms "and the conflicting terms do not become part of the contract." The contract then consists of the terms originally expressly agreed to, terms on which the confirmations agree and terms supplied by the Act including subsection 2.

If a written confirmation contains terms that differ from (i.e., contradict) the agreement actually reached, the actual terms agreed on may be proved and will govern the transaction.[39] However, this situation also presents a problem with the parol evidence rule, discussed below.[40]

(9) Partly Oral, Partly Written. The Seventh Circuit has ruled that UCC § 2–207 has no application to a situation where an order is placed and accepted by telephone followed by the seller's sending of a record containing additional terms. It reasons that § 2–207 was designed for

37. Kvaerner, U.S. v. Hakim Plast Co., 74 F.Supp.2d 709 (E.D.Mich.1999).

38. UCC § 2–207 cmt 1.

39. Album Graphics v. Beatrice Foods, 87 Ill.App.3d 338, 42 Ill.Dec. 332, 408 N.E.2d 1041 (1980).

40. I.S. Joseph Co. v. Citrus Feed, 490 F.2d 185 (5th Cir.1974), reh. denied; UCC § 2–201(2) cmt 3; see ch. 3 infra.

the "battle of the forms" and the fact pattern involved only one form.[41] There is, however, disagreement on this point.[42] Indeed, such a writing meets the characteristics of a written confirmation, as described in Comment 1, that contains additional terms.

(10) CISG, UNIDROIT and UCITA. These documents do not follow the lead of the UCC. Nonetheless, to an extent, they depart from the Mirror–Image Rule. Under CISG, a trivial variation in the acceptance from the terms of the offer do not prevent a contract from being formed unless the offeror objects to the variation.[43] The UNIDROIT Principles distinguish between agreed terms and standard terms. If the parties agree on dickered terms a contract is formed on those terms and on the standard terms which they have in common. However, if one of the parties, prior to, or soon after, contracting objects to the knocking out of any of its standard terms, there is no contract.[44]

UCITA adopts a version of the last shot principle. Its Section 204(b) provides: "[A] definite and seasonable expression of acceptance operates as an acceptance, unless the acceptance materially alters the offer." Consequently, if the "acceptance" materially differs from the offer and the software is delivered, the terms of the counter-offer govern. There is no room in UCITA for confirmations of oral contracts, inasmuch as UCITA does not validate oral contracts. The ultimate written software license is the only operative expression of rights and liability.[45] UCITA can best be understood as a victory for software licensors.

(11) Proposed Revision of UCC. Revision of § 2–207 is a major goal of the revisors of Article 2. The revisors have made a major improvement by detaching the question of the formation of the contract from the question of what are the terms of the contract. A subsection (3) has been added to § 2–206 simply stating, "A definite and seasonable expression of acceptance in a record operates as an acceptance even if it contains terms additional to or different from the offer." Terminology has changed; no longer will it be correct to talk of "the battle of the forms." Instead we will have the "battle of the records." A record is either a writing or a retrievable information in a computer's memory, a computer disk, or the like.[46]

Revised Section 2–207 continues to be the provision that determines what terms become part of the contract. If a contract *is formed* by the process of offer and acceptance, the contract contains the terms in the records to the extent that the records agree. In other words, inconsistent

41. Hill v. Gateway 2000, 105 F.3d 1147 (7th Cir.1997); see Hillman, Rolling Contracts 71, Fordham Law Rev. 743 (2002); Post, The Gateway Thread, 16 Touro L.Rev. 1145 (2000); White, Autistic Contracts, 45 Wayne L.Rev. 1693 (2000); Comment, 95 Nw.U.L.Rev. 403 (2001).

42. Klocek v. Gateway, Inc., 104 F.Supp.2d 1332 (D.Kan.2000).

43. CISG Art. 19. For a comparative study of CISG, UCC and UNIDROIT provi-

sions, see Murray on Contracts § 50 L–M; Perales Viscasillas, 10 Pace Int'l L. Rev. 97 (1998).

44. Principles Art. 2.11

45. UCITA is law only in Maryland and Virginia. No attempt is made to describe its provisions in detail in this text.

46. Revised UCC § 1–201(33a).

terms are knocked out of both records and terms contained in only one party's record are also knocked out unless expressly agreed to by the other. Oral terms agreed to by both parties are also included subject to their admissibility under the parol evidence rule and the Statute of Frauds. Any gaps are filled by the normal gap-fillers of the UCC. Precisely the same formula determines the content of the contract even if the records of the parties *do not form a contract*, but a contract is formed by conduct.

Revised Section 2–207 clarifies an issue that has been unclear. Its terms determine the content of any contract formed by conduct whether or not there has been a battle of the records.[47]

Under revised § 2–207, if one or more parties send *confirmations*, the contract consists of the terms agreed to prior to the confirmations, and terms in the confirmations that agree with each other. Terms contained in one confirmation that do not materially vary the prior agreement and which are not seasonably objected to also enter the contract. Again, any gaps are filled by the normal gap-fillers of the UCC.

(12) Responses to Electronic Agents. Where an offer is made by an electronic agent, usually the agent is not programmed to respond to additional or different terms or even to queries. If an individual offeree has reason to know that it is communicating with a non-responsive program, any additional or different term stated by the offeree disappears into cyberspace and is ineffective. Similarly, if the individual makes an offer based on terms proposed by such an electronic agent, any new terms stated by the individual in the offer do not become part of the contract. This would be the common law result, but it is codified in UCITA and in the 2002 proposed revision of UCC Article 2.[48]

§ 2.22   Effect of Part Performance on an Offer to a Unilateral Contract

Can an offer to a unilateral contract be revoked (terminated) or changed after the offeree has partially performed?[1] The common law has had three views on the question. The classical view is that the offer may be revoked at any time before complete performance of the act requested by the offer.[2] The theory is that because the offeree is free not to complete performance the offeror should be free not to perform. In addition, the argument is made that it is logical because the definition of a unilateral contract includes the idea that the contract is formed upon complete performance.[3]

47. UCC § 2–207 cmt 1 (proposed).

48. Proposed § 2–211(4).

§ 2.22

1. A change in terms is tantamount to a revocation of the offer and the substitution of a new one. Sylvestre v. State, 298 Minn. 142, 214 N.W.2d 658 (1973).

2. Bartlett v. Keith, 325 Mass. 265, 90 N.E.2d 308 (1950); Petterson v. Pattberg, 248 N.Y. 86, 161 N.E. 428 (1928); Hummer v. Engeman, 206 Va. 102, 141 S.E.2d 716 (1965).

3. Wormser, The True Conception of Unilateral Contracts, 26 Yale L.J. 136 (1916), Selected Readings 307. But see Wormser, Book Review, 3 J.Legal.Educ. 145

But even if this is so, logic is not justice. And if logical deduction produces injustice, the premises must be reshaped. Clearly, once the offeree has relied on the offer by starting to perform, the offeree deserves protection from an arbitrary revocation. To provide such protection, a second and now obsolete view concludes that a bilateral contract arises when the offeree starts to perform,[4] but this view is both illogical and unjust because (1) the offeror did not ask for a promise and (2) the beginning of performance may not unequivocally indicate that the offeree intended to pursue performance to completion.[5]

The third and prevailing view stakes out a middle ground between the two. It holds that once the offeree begins to perform, the offer becomes irrevocable.[6] The term "irrevocable offer" is often used interchangeably with the expression used in the Restatement (Second)—"option contract." Under this view, the offeree does not become bound to complete performance, but the offeree will not be entitled to a contractual recovery unless performance is completed within the time allowable, or is excused. (For example, performance will be excused if the offeror repudiates the promise after the offeree has commenced performance. Even if the failure to complete performance is excused,[7] the offeree must prove a readiness, willingness and ability to have performed but for the repudiation.[8]) We need not discuss the measure of damages here but it is analogous to the measure for breach of a bilateral contract. Also, the aggrieved party must mitigate damages, usually by ceasing performance.[9]

We have two additional comments about this approach. One is that the offer becomes irrevocable only if the offeree actually starts to perform. Mere preparation is not enough.[10] The distinction between preparation for and commencement of performance is somewhat tenuous.[11] (It should be noted, however, that, under a generous application of

(1950); see also Stoljar, The False Distinction Between Bilateral and Unilateral Contracts, 64 Yale L.J. 515 (1954).

4. Los Angeles Traction v. Wilshire, 135 Cal. 654, 67 P. 1086 (1902). The current California view is expressed in Asmus v. Pacific Bell, 23 Cal.4th 1, 96 Cal.Rptr.2d 179, 999 P.2d 71 (2000), which however may be limited to offers made in personnel manuals. It holds that such offers may be revoked by giving a reasonable period of notice, presumably to give the affected employees an opportunity to find other employment.

5. See Ashley, Offers Calling for Consideration Other than a Counter Promise, 23 Harv.L.Rev. 159 (1910).

6. Holland v. Earl G. Graves Pub., 46 F.Supp.2d 681 (E.D.Mich.1998); Marchiondo v. Scheck, 78 N.M. 440, 432 P.2d 405 (1967); Motel Services v. Central Maine Power, 394 A.2d 786 (Me.1978); Harding v. Rock, 60 Wn.2d 292, 373 P.2d 784 (1962);

Rs. 2d § 45. For an interesting alternative approach based on speech theory, see Tiersma, Reassessing Unilateral Contracts, 26 U.C. Davis L.Rev. 1 (1992).

7. Rs. 2d § 45 cmt 3, wherein it is stated that performance is excused "for example if the offeror prevents performance, waives it or repudiates." See also Motel Services v. Central Maine Power, 394 A.2d 786 (Me.1978).

8. Rs. 2d § 45.

9. See § 14.15 infra.

10. See Bretz v. Union Cent. Life Ins., 134 Ohio St. 171, 16 N.E.2d 272 (1938); Peizer v. Bergeon, 111 Ohio App. 205, 164 N.E.2d 790 (1960); see also Doll & Smith v. A. & S. Sanitary Dairy, 202 Iowa 786, 211 N.W. 230 (1926); Rs. 2d § 45 cmt f; Comment, 5 Duq.L.Rev. 175 (1966).

11. See Rs. 2d § 45 cmt f, as to the many factors that must be considered in applying this distinction to a set of facts.

the doctrine of promissory estoppel, preparation for performance that is injurious could make the offer irrevocable.)[12] The second comment is that if performance requires the cooperation of the offeror and such cooperation is withheld, tender of part performance is the equivalent of part performance.[13]

The two comments can be clarified by one illustration. A makes an offer promising to pay B $500 if B appears at his child's birthday party and performs as a clown. Assume that, under all the circumstances, the offer is construed unambiguously to look to a unilateral contract. B arrives at the door ready, willing and able to perform and tenders his services. A sends B away. The first question is whether what B did prior to arriving at A's house, such as applying makeup, dressing for the role, and arriving at the scene, constitutes mere preparation for performance. If it is only preparation, then the second rule comes into play. The performance requires the cooperation of the offeror; without the offeror's permission to enter the premises, the offeree would be a trespasser. Thus, even if B has not commenced performance, B has tendered performance prior to revocation. The tender makes the offer irrevocable.

§ 2.23   Time of Acceptance of an Offer to a Bilateral Contract

(a) Parties at a Distance

A revocable offer to a bilateral contract may be revoked at any time prior to its acceptance. *A fortiori*, it may be withdrawn before the offeree receives it. Stated differently, the question in the caption is, when is an attempted acceptance effective? In a general way the answer is that it is effective when it is communicated.[1] As we have seen, a revocation and a rejection are effective when received.[2] This is generally true of other communications.[3]

An early case, however, held that an acceptance is effectively communicated when it is put out of the possession of the offeree as, for example, into a public mail box. This rule is sometimes referred to as the "mailbox rule" or the rule of Adams v. Lindsell.[4] This rule has been

---

12. Rs. 2d § 87(2).

13. Rs. 1st § 45 cmt d. It seems that the word "tendered" here is used in its technical significance as it was used by the majority in Petterson v. Pattberg, 248 N.Y. 86, 161 N.E. 428 (1928).

§ 2.23

1. See § 2.20 supra.

2. Lynch v. Webb City School Dist., 418 S.W.2d 608 (Mo.App.1967); Rs. 1st § 68. See § 2.20 supra.

3. See Hoch v. Hitchens, 122 Mich.App. 142, 332 N.W.2d 440 (1982); Sy Jack Realty v. Pergament Syosset, 27 N.Y.2d 449, 318 N.Y.S.2d 720, 267 N.E.2d 462 (1971);

§ 11.35 infra. But see Macke Laundry v. Mission Assocs., 19 Kan.App.2d 553, 873 P.2d 219 (Kan.App.1994) (notice of termination); Birznieks v. Cooper, 405 Mich. 319, 275 N.W.2d 221 (1979) (payment).

4. Adams v. Lindsell, 106 Eng.Rep. 250 (K.B.1818). For a critique see Macneil, Time of Acceptance: Too Many Problems for a Single Rule, 112 U.Pa.L.Rev. 947 (1964); Sharp, Reflections on Contract, 33 U.Chi.L.Rev. 211, 213–15 (1965). If the contract is governed by UCITA, an electronic acceptance is effective on receipt. UCITA § 203(4).

defended on the ground that at this point the offeree, having dispatched an acceptance, should be able to rely on the existence of a contract and should be protected against an intervening revocation.[5] The rule applies even if the communication is delayed or lost in transit.[6] The rule of Adams v. Lindsell prevails generally throughout the U.S.,[7] with the qualification that the acceptance must be dispatched in a proper manner.

The mailbox rule does not govern every case. When the offeror *prescribes* the exclusive place, time or medium of acceptance the offer controls.[8] No contract is formed unless the terms of the offer are followed.[9] If, for example, the offer states, "you must accept, if at all by telegram," a contract will be formed when the telegram is duly deposited with the telegraph company.[10] If the offeree uses another method of acceptance, no contract is formed; the offeree has made a counter-offer.[11]

Courts are reluctant to interpret language as calling for a prescribed medium or manner of acceptance. Thus, even though a medium of acceptance is stated in the offer, the tendency is to hold that the offeror has merely suggested, rather than prescribed, this form of acceptance.[12] If the suggested form of acceptance is not used, the question remains whether the medium actually used could be considered proper under the circumstances of the case.[13]

5. Rs. 2d § 63 cmt a.

6. Household Fire & Carriage Acc. Ins. v. Grant, 4 Ex.D. 216 (C.A.1879); Rs. 2d § 63 cmt b. But see Macneil note 4 supra. See also Llewellyn, Our Case Law of Contract: Offer and Acceptance (Pt. 2), 48 Yale L.J. 779, 795 n. 23 (1939).

7. Morrison v. Thoelke, 155 So.2d 889 (Fla.App.1963); Pribil v. Ruther, 200 Neb. 161, 262 N.W.2d 460 (1978); Marriage of Reich, 176 Or.App. 442, 32 P.3d 904 (2001) (acceptance mailed; fax revocation on the same day is ineffective); Scottish–American Mtge. v. Davis, 96 Tex. 504, 74 S.W. 17 (1903); Henthorn v. Fraser, [1892] 2 Ch. 27. Contra, Rhode Island Tool v. U.S., 128 F.Supp. 417 (Ct.Cl.1955) (relying on the privilege, under postal regulations to withdraw letter from the mails, but this position has not gained any substantial recognition); 38 Tul.L.Rev. 566 (1964). Even if the letter is actually withdrawn, it still amounts to an acceptance. Rs. 2d § 63 cmt c.

8. Eliason v. Henshaw, 17 U.S.(4 Wheat.) 225 (1819); Glenway Indus. v. Wheelabrator–Frye., 686 F.2d 415 (6th Cir. 1982); Golden Dipt v. Systems Eng'r & Mfg., 465 F.2d 215 (7th Cir.1972); Goode v. Universal Plastics, 247 Ark. 442, 445 S.W.2d 893 (1969); Brophy v. Joliet, 14 Ill. App.2d 443, 144 N.E.2d 816 (1957); Spratt v. Paramount Pictures, 178 Misc. 682, 35 N.Y.S.2d 815 (1942); Cochran v. Connell, 53 Or.App. 933, 632 P.2d 1385 (1981), rev.

denied; Rs. 2d § 58; Rs. 1st § 60. Where the method of acceptance is prescribed on the offeree's form, the offeree may waive compliance. Neal–Cooper Grain v. Texas Gulf Sulphur, 508 F.2d 283 (7th Cir.1974) ("Contract shall not be binding * * * until duly accepted at its New York Office.")

9. Lexington Housing Auth. v. Continental Cas., 210 F.Supp. 732 (W.D.Tenn. 1962); Lindsay v. Cooke County Elec. Co-op. Ass'n, 502 S.W.2d 117 (Tex.1973), cert. denied; see Brach v. Matteson, 298 Ill. 387, 131 N.E. 804 (1921).

10. Rs. 2d § 60 ill. 3.

11. Avila Group v. Norma J., 426 F.Supp. 537 (S.D.N.Y.1977); Executive Leasing Assocs. v. Rowland, 30 N.C.App. 590, 227 S.E.2d 642 (1976); Vaulx v. Cumis Ins. Society, 407 A.2d 262 (D.C.1979); Zinni v. Royal Lincoln–Mercury, 84 Ill.App.3d 1093, 40 Ill.Dec. 511, 406 N.E.2d 212 (1980).

12. Fujimoto v. Rio Grande Pickle, 414 F.2d 648 (5th Cir.1969); Allied Steel & Conveyors v. Ford, 277 F.2d 907 (6th Cir.1960); Mid–Continent Petroleum v. Russell, 173 F.2d 620 (10th Cir.1949); Manning v. Michaels, 149 A.D.2d 897, 540 N.Y.S.2d 583 (1989); Osprey L.L.C.v. Kelly–Moore Paint, 984 P.2d 194 (Okla.1999); Rs. 2d § 60 ill. 5.

13. Cf. In re Klauenberg's Estate, 32 Cal.App.3d 1067, 108 Cal.Rptr. 669 (1973).

The First Restatement, using a concept that a proper medium must be an *authorized* medium, states that, in the absence of contrary indications, the offer authorizes the means of communication used in transmitting the offer and any other means customary at the time and place received.[14] The test has resulted in conflicting decisions. Thus, it is often held that a telegram is an authorized method of accepting an offer sent by mail.[15] There are contrary decisions.[16] So also, an acceptance of a telegraphed offer by mail has been held to be authorized.[17] Again, there are contrary decisions.[18]

The UCC and the Restatement (Second), in addressing the question of proper manner, have changed the concept from what is *authorized* to what is *reasonable,* as has much case law.[19] If an offer is accepted by "any medium reasonable in the circumstances," it is effective when it is put out of the possession of the offeree.[20] The Restatement (Second) and the UCC make it clear that the concept of reasonability is intended to be flexible. They indicate that acceptance by mail is ordinarily reasonable where the parties are negotiating at a distance unless there is a reason for speed. It even may be reasonable where the offer is transmitted electronically. Acceptance of an offer made by mail by a more rapid means of communication would ordinarily be reasonable.[21]

Despite the emphasis on reasonableness, the offeror remains master of the offer and can insist on a particular medium of acceptance.[22] The offeror is free, despite the approach of the UCC, "to prescribe as many conditions, terms or the like as he may wish, including but not limited to, the time, place and method of acceptance."[23] Thus, the offeror continues to be master of the offer.

14. Rs. 1st § 65. It is also generally held that a letter which is properly addressed, stamped and mailed is presumed to have been delivered in due course of the post. Legille v. Dann, 544 F.2d 1 (D.C.Cir.1976). The presumption is rebuttable. Charlson Realty v. U.S., 384 F.2d 434 (Ct.Cl.1967); Meckel v. Continental Resources, 758 F.2d 811 (2d Cir.1985). For a more detailed statement of this rule, see Public Finance v. Van Blaricome, 324 N.W.2d 716 (Iowa 1982); see Wagner Tractor v. Shields, 381 F.2d 441, 24 A.L.R.3d 1423 (9th Cir.1967) (applying the same presumption to a telegram). However, proof of office practice may not be sufficient to give rise to the presumption. Pribil v. Ruther, 200 Neb. 161, 262 N.W.2d 460 (1978); but see Boomer v. AT & T, 309 F.3d 404 (7th Cir.2002).

15. Stephen M. Weld & Co. v. Victory Mfg., 205 F. 770 (E.D.N.C.1913).

16. Dickey v. Hurd, 33 F.2d 415 (1st Cir.1929); Lucas v. Western Union, 131 Iowa 669, 109 N.W. 191 (1906). But cf. Elkhorn–Hazard Coal v. Kentucky River Coal, 20 F.2d 67 (6th Cir.1927) (use of mail

for acceptance not authorized where written offer delivered in person).

17. Farmers' Produce v. McAlester Storage & Comm'n, 48 Okl. 488, 150 P. 483 (1915).

18. Richard v. Credit Suisse, 124 Misc. 3, 206 N.Y.S. 150 (1924), aff'd.

19. Fujimoto v. Rio Grande Pickle, 414 F.2d 648 (5th Cir.1969); Anderson Excavating & Wrecking v. Certified Welding, 769 P.2d 887 (Wyo.1988).

20. Albemarle Educ. Foundation v. Basnight, 4 N.C.App. 652, 167 S.E.2d 486 (1969); Rs. 2d § 63; UCC § 2–206(1)(a) (unchanged by revision).

21. Rs. 2d § 65 cmts b, c and d; see UCC § 2–206 cmt 1.

22. Empire Machinery v. Litton Business Tel. Sys., 115 Ariz. 568, 566 P.2d 1044 (1977).

23. Kroeze v. Chloride Group, 572 F.2d 1099, 1105 (5th Cir.1978); Southwestern Stationery & Bank Supply v. Harris Corp., 624 F.2d 168 (10th Cir.1980).

If the offeree uses an improper medium of acceptance, under the traditional rule the acceptance is effective when received rather than when sent.[24] The Restatement (Second), however, takes the position that even if an unreasonable method of acceptance is utilized, it is, nevertheless, effective when sent provided that it is seasonably[25] dispatched and provided it is received within the time a seasonably dispatched acceptance sent in a reasonable manner would normally have arrived.[26] A version of this rule has been applied to the mailing of a notice of termination.[27] The traditional view has been that if the offeree uses a proper means of communication, but fails to address it correctly, or to take other reasonable precautions to ensure safe transmission, the offeree loses the benefit of the mailbox rule. The acceptance in such a case is effective when received provided the offer is still open.[28] The Restatement (Second) has also changed this rule. It states that the acceptance is effective when sent provided that it is seasonably dispatched and provided that it is received within the time a seasonably dispatched properly stamped and addressed acceptance would normally have arrived.[29] Otherwise, it is effective on receipt if the offer is still open.

The offeror, it must be remembered, is master of the offer and has power to negate the mailbox rule. This can be done by framing the offer so as to require actual receipt of an acceptance as a precondition to the formation of the contract.[30] However, such a requirement must be clearly expressed.[31] The Restatement (Second) states that a condition to *performance*, not to *formation* of the contract, is normally implied "where the receipt of the notice is essential to enable the offeror to perform."[32]

The rule that an acceptance is effective when sent is troublesome when the offeree sends both an acceptance and a rejection. Remember, in

---

24. Rs. 1st § 67.

25. "Seasonably" means timely. UCC § 1–204 (revision § 1–205).

26. Rs. 2d § 67.

27. University Emergency Medicine v. Rapier Inv., Ltd., 197 F.3d 18 (1st Cir. 1999).

28. Rs. 1st § 67.

29. Rs. 2d § 67. In discussing the two problems raised by this paragraph, the Restatement (Second) makes a cross-reference to UCC § 1–201(38). The Reporter's Note states, "the provision that timely receipt has the effect of proper sending is also new; it conforms to UCC § 1–201(38) * * **." The UCC provision addresses improper sending: "* * * The receipt of any writing or notice within the time at which it would have arrived if properly sent has the effect of a proper sending." (Unchanged in revision). The provision does not relate to an unreasonable medium of acceptance. It applies to a misdi-rected acceptance. Even if applicable to an unreasonable medium, the rule is slightly different from the one announced in the Restatement. The Restatement talks about when a hypothetical seasonably dispatched acceptance would be received, whereas the UCC takes into account when the particular communication was actually sent in determining whether it arrives within the time at which it would have arrived if properly sent.

30. Union Interchange v. Sierota, 355 P.2d 1089 (Colo.1960); Holland v. Riverside Park, 214 Ga. 244, 104 S.E.2d 83 (1958); Lewis v. Browning, 130 Mass. 173 (1880); Western Union v. Gardner, 278 S.W. 278 (Tex.Civ.App.1925); 1 Williston § 6:40; Rs. 2d § 63 cmt b.

31. Vassar v. Camp, 11 N.Y. (1 Kern.) 441 (1854); 1 Williston § 6:40.

32. Rs. 2d § 63 cmt b.

contrast to an acceptance, a rejection is effective when received.[33] Consider the following sequences: (a) rejection sent, acceptance sent, rejection received, acceptance received; (b) rejection sent, acceptance sent, acceptance received, rejection received. The Restatement rule with respect to these two situations is that an acceptance dispatched after a rejection has been sent is not effective until received and only if received prior to the rejection.[34] Under this rule there is a contract in sequence (b)[35] but not in (a). In each case, the expectation of the offeror is protected. In sequence (a) the acceptance is regarded as a counter-offer.[36]

A more troublesome sequence arises in sequence (c): acceptance sent, rejection sent, rejection received, acceptance received. If the expectations of the offeror were followed, there would be no contract and some courts have so held.[37] However, there is significant authority, including the Restatement (Second), that a contract is formed.[38] Otherwise the offeree could speculate at the offeror's expense by seeing how the market went. If the market moved in the offeree's favor, the offeree would allow the acceptance to stand. If it moved in the offeror's favor, the offeree could use an earlier-arriving communication to undo the acceptance.[39] This would be unfair. If the offeror is bound by the offeree's communication, so should the offeree. This view is sometimes qualified by saying that if the offeror relies on the rejection before receiving the acceptance the offeree will be estopped from enforcing the contract.[40] Under the Restatement view, the over-taking rejection may be viewed as an offer to rescind the contract or a repudiation.[41] In sequence (c), if the acceptance arrived before the rejection, there would also be a contract.

(b) Parties in the Presence of One Another

When the parties are in the presence of each other an acceptance is operative only if the offeror hears it or is at fault in not hearing.[42] This rule is not consistent with the "mailbox rule" under which an undelivered acceptance can be effective. However, it would be an unusual case in which the offeror is at fault.[43] Even if the offeror is at fault in not hearing, there still would be no contract if the offeree knew or had reason to know that the offeror had not heard.[44]

Should a conversation conducted by telephone or similar medium be governed by the rules developed for face to face conversation? The text writers all but unanimously agree that these means of communication

33. Rs. 2d § 68.

34. Rs. 2d § 40.

35. Under this rule, in sequence (b) a revocation that became effective prior to the receipt of the acceptance would terminate the offer.

36. Rs. 2d § 40.

37. Dick v. U.S., 82 F.Supp. 326 (Ct.Cl. 1949); 1 Corbin § 3.41 (Perillo 1993).

38. Morrison v. Thoelke, 155 So.2d 889 (Fla.App.1963); Rs. 2d § 63 cmt c and ill. 7.

39. Rs. 2d § 63 cmt c.

40. E. Frederics, Inc. v. Felton Beauty Supply, 58 Ga.App. 320, 198 S.E. 324 (1938), overruled on other grounds; Rs. 2d § 63 cmt c.

41. Rs. 2d § 63 cmt c.

42. 1 Williston § 6:33.

43. 1 Corbin § 4.10 (Perillo 1993).

44. 1 Corbin § 3.25 (Perillo 1993).

should be governed by the rules governing parties who are in the presence of one another.[45] The majority of the cases are to the contrary, however, holding that the acceptance takes place when spoken by the offeree rather than when heard by the offeror, but these cases have arisen in the context of conflict of laws and concern the question of *where* the contract was formed rather than whether there was a contract.[46]

These cases do not involve a break in the connection. In such a case the Restatement argues that even if a court wished to apply the "at a distance" rule the issue of fault would have to be confronted. If the parties are equally blameless or equally at fault there would be no contract; otherwise the understanding of the least blameworthy party prevails.[47]

§ 2.24   Mistake in Transmission by an Intermediary

Suppose A intends to offer to sell a bike to B for $110, but inadvertently says "I offer to sell you my bike for $100," and B does not know or have reason to know of A's mistake. If B accepts the offer, a contract for the sale of the bike at $100 is formed.[1] If A's agent made the mistake, the same result would follow. But what if the mistake is made in transmission by an intermediary and not an agent? This problem arose in a number of cases that involve a mistake in transmission by a telegraph company. A majority of the cases have held that in such a case there is a contract based on the $100 figure.[2] The same result is generally reached if a newspaper makes a typographical error in printing an offer.[3] Where an advertiser was as negligent as the publisher in publishing the incorrect price in an offer for the sale of a specific unique automobile, a reader of the publication was able to accept and hold the advertiser to the terms of the offer.[4]

Three rationales are advanced for this result. One is that the telegraph company is A's agent.[5] But this is simply not true. The telegraph company is an independent contractor.[6]

A second rationale for the rule is that it results in better business convenience. This argument may have some validity but it is at most a debatable proposition.

45.   Id., 1 Williston § 6:34; Rs. 1st § 64.

46.   Perrin v. Pearlstein, 314 F.2d 863 (2d Cir.1963). Contra, Entores Ltd. v. Miles Far East, [1955] 2 Q.B. 327; but see Osprey v. Kelly–Moore Paint, 984 P.2d 194 (Okla. 1999) (mailbox rule applied to fax).

47.   Rs. 2d § 64 cmt b.

§ 2.24

1.   Wender Presses v. U.S., 343 F.2d 961 (Ct.Cl.1965); Rs. 1st § 71(c). Avoiding a contract for unilateral mistake is considered at § 9.27 infra.

2.   1 Corbin § 4.11 (Perillo 1993).

3.   Chang v. First Colonial Sav. Bank, 242 Va. 388, 410 S.E.2d 928 (1991).

4.   Donovan v. RRL, 74 Cal.App.4th 540, 88 Cal.Rptr.2d 143 (1999), reversed on grounds of mistake. 26 Cal.4th 261, 27 P.3d 702, 109 Cal.Rptr.2d 807 (2001).

5.   Des Arc Oil Mill v. Western Union., 132 Ark. 335, 201 S.W. 273, 6 ALR 1081 (1918).

6.   Butler v. Foley, 211 Mich. 668, 179 N.W. 34 (1920).

The third rationale is that the first party to utilize the telegraph company should bear the risk of loss because the use of the telegraph company makes the first party more responsible for the error.[7] But this reason is not consistent with a complete statement of the majority rule. The true majority view is that the message as transmitted is operative unless the other party knows or has reason to know of the mistake.[8] Thus, the offeree, who is the second to use the telegraph, would be bound by the acceptance of an offer that had been raised in price as a result of an error in transmission. Similarly, if the offeree had indicated an intent not to accept an offer but the telegraph company by a mistake in transmission sent an affirmative message, there would be a contract.

A minority view holds that no contract will arise where there is a mistake in transmission of an offer or acceptance.[9] This view is based on the notion that the telegraph company is an independent contractor, and the general rule is that a person who hires an independent contractor is not liable for the negligence of the contractor. It might be argued that the majority view is more consistent with the objective theory of contracts because the recipient of the erroneous telegram would normally take it at face value. But, for the objective theory to apply, the acts manifesting assent must be done either intentionally or negligently.[10] Here, there is no wrongful intentional or negligent conduct on the part of the sender of the message because the sender is not responsible for the negligence.

This section does not apply to a misdirected acceptance; in that case, the mailbox rule would apply. It applies to a message that has not been accurately transmitted.

Once it is determined which of the two innocent parties should suffer a loss as a result of a mistake in transmission, this party has an action against the telegraph company on a negligence theory and perhaps also for breach of contract.[11] However the remedy may prove to be unsatisfactory because telegraph companies by contract usually limit their liability. These limitations of liability clauses have been upheld and this question is governed by federal regulations.[12]

§ 2.25   Option Contracts—Irrevocable Offers

(a) What Makes an Offer Irrevocable

7. Ayer v. Western Union, 79 Me. 493, 10 A. 495 (1887).

8. 1 Corbin § 4.11 (Perillo 1993). If it is apparent from the face of the message, or otherwise, that an error has been made, no contract results. The addressee is not justified in relying on its contents. Germain Fruit v. Western Union, 137 Cal. 598, 70 P. 658 (1902).

9. Western Union v. Cowin & Co., 20 F.2d 103, 54 ALR 1362 (8th Cir.1927); see Rs. 2d § 64 cmt b.

10. See § 2.2 supra.

11. Webbe v. Western Union, 169 Ill. 610, 48 N.E. 670 (1897).

12. Western Union v. Priester, 276 U.S. 252 (1928); Annots., 20 ALR2d 761 (1951); 94 ALR 1056 (1935).

The term "option contract" is often used interchangeably with the term "irrevocable offer."[1] Although the two sets of words are not precisely interchangeable, any distinction does not carry any important implications.

Most offers are revocable. One of the classic ways of rendering an offer irrevocable is by the offeror's acceptance of a consideration in exchange for a promise to keep the offer open.[2] Such an offer is often called an "option contract." If A makes an offer to sell specific real property to B for a specified price and states that the offer is open for ten days, the offer is revocable even if A stated that the offer was irrevocable for ten days.[3] But if, for example, A bargained for and received $100 in exchange for A's promise to keep the offer open for ten days, the offer would be irrevocable because A's promise is supported by consideration.

An option may be binding even without consideration. Under the older common law, and still in some jurisdictions, an option is binding if the promise of irrevocability is under seal.[4] The Restatement (Second) would validate an option if it is in a signed writing and recites a purported consideration.[5] In addition, according to § 45 of the Restatements—old and new—an option contract arises when the offeree begins to perform the act requested in an offer to a unilateral contract.[6] Also, an offer may become irrevocable under the doctrine of promissory estoppel.[7]

Certain statutes permit the creation of irrevocable offers without consideration. For example, a New York statute set out in full in the note,[8] provides, in essence, that, if the offeror in a signed writing states that the offer is irrevocable, it is irrevocable despite the absence of consideration. There is a similar provision in the UCC.[9] The two statuto-

---

§ 2.25

1. See § 2.22 supra; Beall v. Beall, 291 Md. 224, 434 A.2d 1015 (1981).

2. Rs. 1st § 46; Crockett v. Lowther, 549 P.2d 303 (Wyo.1976).

3. Crowley v. Bass, 445 So.2d 902 (Ala. 1984); Amwest Surety Ins. v. RA–LIN & Assocs., 216 Ga.App. 526, 455 S.E.2d 106 (1995); Beall v. Beall, 291 Md. 224, 434 A.2d 1015 (1981); Board of Education v. James Hamilton Constr., 119 N.M. 415, 891 P.2d 556 (1994); Hummer v. Engeman, 206 Va. 102, 141 S.E.2d 716 (1965); 7 Wm. & Mary L.Rev. 186 (1966). See § 2.20(d) supra. This common law rule is criticized in Eisenberg, The Principles of Consideration, 67 Cornell L.Rev. 640, 653 (1982).

4. See ch. 7 infra.

5. Rs. 2d § 87 (1)(a); contra Berryman v. Kmoch, 221 Kan. 304, 559 P.2d 790 (1977).

6. See § 2.22 supra.

7. See § 6.3(b) infra. Accord, CISG Art. 16(2).

8. McKinney's N.Y.Gen.Obl.Law § 5–1109 provides:

"Except as otherwise provided in section 2–205 of the uniform commercial code with respect to an offer by a merchant to buy or sell goods, when an offer to enter into a contract is made in a writing signed by the offeror, or by his agent, which states that the offer is irrevocable during a period set forth or until a time fixed, the offer shall not be revocable during such period or until such time because of the absence of consideration for the assurance of irrevocability. When such a writing states that the offer is irrevocable but does not state any period or time of irrevocability, it shall be construed to state that the offer is irrevocable for a reasonable time."

9. UCC § 2–205 provides:

"An offer by a merchant to buy or sell goods in a signed ~~writing~~ *record* which by its terms gives assurance that it will be held open is not revocable, for lack of consideration, during the time stated or if no time is

ry formulations are compared in the notes.[10] Most courts have held that offers of settlement of litigation made pursuant to Federal Rule 68, or comparable state law, are irrevocable.[11] Under the UN Sales Convention, any offer that expressly or implicitly states that it is irrevocable would be irrevocable for the time stated or, if no time is stated, for a reasonable time.[12]

(b) Nature of an Option Contract

An option contract is a hybrid. It is a contract and an offer. Once it is determined that an option contract exists, the ordinary rules of offer and acceptance often apply.[13] For example, if the purported acceptance contains terms materially at variance with the offer, the acceptance is ineffective.[14] Nonetheless, some special rules apply, and the offer is less easily terminated.

(c) Termination of Irrevocable Offers

(1) Introduction

Like a revocable offer, an irrevocable offer is terminated by lapse of time, death or destruction of a person or thing essential for the performance of the contract, or supervening legal prohibition of the proposed contract. However, an irrevocable offer is not terminated by rejection, revocation, or supervening death or incapacity of the offeror or offeree.[15] The Sales Convention is to the contrary on the question of rejection.[16] An offer that would be irrevocable may be withdrawn prior to its receipt by the offeree.[17]

(2) Lapse of Time

Lapse of time terminates an irrevocable offer. Thus, it is frequently stated that time is of the essence for the acceptance of an irrevocable

---

stated for a reasonable time, but in no event may such period of irrevocability exceed three months; but any such term of assurance ~~on a form~~ *in a form record* supplied by the offeree must be separately signed by the offeror." Deleted matter is struck and new matter is italicised to conform to the proposed revision.

10. Four differences are rapidly perceptible. The UCC section is (1) limited to offers by merchants and (2) is limited to offers to buy and sell goods. Under the UCC, (3) the period of irrevocability may not exceed three months. The option may be renewed. UCC § 2–205 cmt 3. Finally, the UCC provides that (4) where the term of assurance is contained on a form supplied by the offeree, it must be separately signed by the offeror. For a critical comment on the necessity for such statutes, see Schultz, The Firm Offer Puzzle, 19 U.Chi. L.Rev. 237 (1952); Note, 53 Va.L.Rev. 1720 (1967).

11. Shelton v. Sloan, 127 N.M. 92, 977 P.2d 1012 (App.1999).

12. CISG Art. 16; Mather, Firm Offers Under the UCC and the CISG, 105 Dickinson L.Rev. 31 (2000).

13. Plantation Key Developers v. Colonial Mtge., 589 F.2d 164 (5th Cir.1979); Graham v. Anderson, 397 So.2d 71 (Miss. 1981); Northwestern Bell v. Cowger, 303 N.W.2d 791 (N.D.1981).

14. Civic Plaza Nat. Bank v. First Nat. Bank, 401 F.2d 193 (8th Cir.1968); Katz v. Pratt St. Realty, 257 Md. 103, 262 A.2d 540 (1970); Westinghouse Broadcasting v. New England Patriots, 10 Mass.App.Ct. 70, 406 N.E.2d 399 (1980); Schacht v. First Wyoming Bank, 620 P.2d 561 (Wyo.1980).

15. Rs. 2d § 37, § 48 cmt d.

16. CISG Art. 17.

17. Accord, CISG Art. 15(2).

offer.[18] One reason given for the application of a time-of-the-essence rule is that the offer is usually made irrevocable in exchange for a small consideration. But there are cases that have not followed this approach where a forfeiture would have resulted. These are not cases of mere options. Rather, these cases involve options that are connected to a contract of another kind, such as a lease containing an option to renew.[19]

(3) Death or Destruction etc. and Supervening Legal Prohibition

Because death or destruction of a person or thing essential for the performance of the contract discharges a contract on a theory of impossibility of performance, it follows that the same impossibility terminates an irrevocable offer. Because supervening legal prohibition also involves a question of impossibility of performance, the same rule applies.[20] In general, the rules governing discharge of contracts apply to option contracts.[21]

(4) Revocation and Rejection

By definition, revocation does not terminate an irrevocable offer.[22] However, the authorities are divided on the question of rejection. The earlier view was that rejection terminated an irrevocable offer,[23] but the more modern view is that rejection should not terminate an irrevocable offer because usually the offeree has paid a consideration for irrevocability[24] and contract rights are not generally lost by the rejection of a tendered performance.[25] If, however, the offeror injuriously relies on the rejection, the offeree should be estopped from accepting it later.[26] A counter-offer does not normally operate as a rejection where the offer is irrevocable.[27] However, a purported acceptance that varies the term of the offer is not a valid acceptance.[28]

(5) Supervening Death or Incapacity of the Offeror

Although supervening death or incapacity of the offeror or offeree does not terminate an irrevocable offer, death or incapacity creates a variety of other problems. These are discussed under the headings of Prospective Inability to Perform,[29] Impracticability,[30] and the Assignabili-

---

18. Western Sav. Fund v. Southeastern Pa. Transp. Auth., 285 Pa.Super. 187, 427 A.2d 175 (1981).

19. Loitherstein v. I.B.M., 11 Mass.App. Ct. 91, 413 N.E.2d 1146 (1980), rev. denied; 1 Corbin § 2.15 (Perillo 1993); 3 Corbin § 11.17 (Holmes 1996). See § 11.35 infra.

20. See Rs. 2d § 37 cmt b. See also § 13.5 & § 13.7 infra.

21. Rs. 2d § 37.

22. Smith v. Bangham, 156 Cal. 359, 104 P. 689 (1909); O'Brien v. Boland, 166 Mass. 481, 44 N.E. 602 (1896).

23. Rs. 1st § 44; Cozzillio, The Option Contract: Irrevocable not Irrejectable, 39 Catholic U.L.Rev. 491 (1990).

24. Rs. 2d § 37. McCormick v. Stephany, 61 N.J.Eq. 208, 48 A. 25 (1900); Silverstein v. United Cerebral Palsy Ass'n, 17 A.D.2d 160, 232 N.Y.S.2d 968 (1962); Humble Oil & Ref. v. Westside Inv., 428 S.W.2d 92 (Tex.1968).

25. Rs. 1st §§ 414–15; Rs. 2d § 277.

26. Rs. 2d § 36 ill. 2.

27. 1 Corbin § 3.38 (Perillo 1993).

28. Alliant Techsystems v. U.S., 178 F.3d 1260 (Fed.Cir.1999).

29. See § 12.2 infra.

30. See ch. 13 infra.

ty of Option Contracts.[31]

(d) When Acceptance of an Irrevocable Offer Is Effective

The rule that the acceptance of a revocable offer is ordinarily effective when sent[32] is designed to protect an offeree against revocation.[33] The offeree of an irrevocable offer does not require this protection. Thus, the weight of authority is that the acceptance of an irrevocable offer is operative when received by the offeror rather than when dispatched,[34] unless the option agreement otherwise provides.[35]

A binding right of first refusal supported by consideration or the equivalent is a conditional option; it creates in the holder only a right to purchase on the same terms, that are acceptable to the owner, offered by other parties.[36] As is the case with other offers, the acceptance must be unconditional to constitute an acceptance.[37]

§ 2.26   Common Law and CISG—Some Comparisons

Many of the leading trading nations, including some having such diverse legal systems as the U.S. and China, have ratified the United Nations Convention for the International Sale of Goods (CISG).[1] On the question of the effective moment of an acceptance when the parties communicate by other than instantaneous means, CISG takes a position in opposition to the traditional common law mailbox rule. The interrelationship among three rules in CISG needs to be examined. (1) An offer becomes irrevocable when an acceptance is dispatched,[2] but (2) the acceptance is effective only when and if it reaches the offeror.[3] (3) Article 22 of the Convention provides: "An acceptance may be withdrawn if the withdrawal reaches the offeror before or at the same time as the acceptance would have become effective."

These provisions represent a series of compromises between common law and civil law notions. In many civil law countries, offers are generally irrevocable for a stated or reasonable time. This rule favoring the offeree, contrasts with the common law's general pro-offeror rule permitting revocation of offers. To balance the common law's bias toward offerors on the issue of revocation, the common law developed the mailbox rule which shortens the period in which an offer may be

31. See § 18.32 infra.

32. See § 2.23 supra.

33. McAfee v. Brewer, 214 Va. 579, 203 S.E.2d 129 (1974).

34. Dynamics v. U.S., 389 F.2d 424 (Ct. Cl.1968); Santos v. Dean, 96 Wash.App. 849, 982 P.2d 632 (1999) (contrary cases cited); Rs. 2d § 63(b) and cmt f.

35. Jameson v. Foster, 646 P.2d 955 (Colo.App.1982).

36. Gyurkey v. Babler, 103 Idaho 663, 651 P.2d 928 (1982); DiMaria v. Michaels, 90 A.D.2d 676, 455 N.Y.S.2d 875 (1982);

Smith v. Mitchell, 301 N.C. 58, 269 S.E.2d 608 (1980).

37. Abraham Inv. v. Payne Ranch, 968 S.W.2d 518 (Tex.App.1998) (we would have ruled that the acceptance was unconditional with an offer to modify the contract).

§ 2.26

1. See § 1.7 supra.

2. CISG Article 16(1).

3. CISG Article 18(2). This provision, of course, does not affect acceptances that are properly made by performance rather than by promise. CISG Article 18(3).

revoked. To balance the civil law's bias toward offerees on the issue of revocability, the civil law developed a rule favoring the offeror on the question of when an acceptance takes effect. The Convention approximates the common law view on the question of revocability and the civil law view on the question of the time of acceptance.[4]

Professor Murray has constructed a worst-case scenario pursuant to which these CISG rules can be manipulated for speculation. Under this scenario the offeree may dispatch an acceptance by mail, thus making the offer irrevocable—if it was not irrevocable to start with. The offeree can later overtake the letter of acceptance with a withdrawal. During this period the offeree can speculate without risk. This is doubtless true, but in today's world, with its deteriorating postal systems, and its increasingly sophisticated means of electronic communication, it is seldom that offers are made in speculative matters by mail, and among the factors that go into determining whether an offer has been duly accepted within a reasonable time is the rapidity of the means of communication used by the offeror.[5] It may also be noted that under the rules of the Restatement (Second) of Contracts there is a similar ability to speculate with irrevocable offers.[6] It is, however, true that under the CISG rules there is an expansion in the grounds of irrevocability and therefore an expansion of situations in which the offeree can speculate without risk.

4. See John Honnold, Uniform Law for International Sales under the 1980 United Nations Convention §§ 157–163 (2d ed.).

5. UNIDROIT Principles of International Commercial Contracts Art. 27; see Perillo, Unidroit Principles of International Commercial Contracts: The Black Letter Text and a Review, 63 Fordham L.Rev. 281, 286 & 321 (1994).

6. Rs.2d § 63(2) and cmt f.

Chapter 3

PAROL EVIDENCE AND INTERPRETATION

Table of Sections

Table of Sections

A. INTRODUCTION

A.   INTRODUCTION

Table of Sections

§ 3.1   The Difficulty of the Subject Matter

Professor Thayer, aptly capturing the complexities of the parol evidence rule, observed, "Few things are darker than this, or fuller of subtle difficulties."[1] Much of the fog and mystery surrounding these subjects stems from the fact that there are basic disagreements as to the application of the parol evidence rule and as to the best method of ascertaining the intention of the parties—the process of contractual interpretation.[2]

The treatises of the contract giants and the cases tend to conceal this conflict. While frequently masking disagreement by using the same terminology, Professors Williston and Corbin are often poles apart in the meaning they attach to the same terms. Often starting from what superficially appear to be the same premises, they frequently advocate different results in similar fact situations. The polarity of their views reflects conflicting value judgments as to policy issues that are as old as our legal system and that are likely to continue as long as courts of law exist. Although many writers and courts have expressed their views on the subject and have made major contributions to it, concentration on

§ 3.1

1. J. Thayer, A Preliminary Treatise on Evidence at Common Law 390 (1898).

2. According to some analyses, the parol evidence rule also applies to exclude some or all types of extrinsic evidence offered in aid of interpretation. See § 3.16 infra.

the analyses of Professors Williston and Corbin will point up the fundamental bases upon which the conflicting cases and views rest.[3]

As one court has said, "To answer these two [parol evidence rule] questions, we, in Missouri, no different than the courts in most other jurisdictions, have used a variety of principles, chosen randomly with no consistency, from the common law, the treatises of Professor Williston and Corbin, and the First and Second Restatement of the Law of Contracts * * *. Thus, the random selection of principles * * * has made the parol evidence rule in Missouri, no different than in most other jurisdictions, a deceptive maze rather than a workable rule."[4]

In some ways, this is the most difficult and inaccessible chapter in this text. It will become obvious that intricate webs of rules have become constructed by various minds. It will become equally obvious that there is no unanimity as to the content of the parol evidence rule or the process called interpretation, and that the rules are complex, technical and difficult to apply. It would, however, be a mistake to suppose that the courts follow any of these rules blindly, literally or consistently.[5] As often as not the court chooses the standard or the rule that it thinks will give rise to a just result in the particular case.[6] We shall also see that, often under a guise of interpretation, a court will actually enforce its notions of good policy and justice.[7]

3. Articles include: Childres & Spitz, Status in the Law of Contracts, 47 N.Y.U.L.Rev. 1 (1971); Corbin, The Interpretation of Words and the Parol Evidence Rule, 50 Cornell L.Q. 161 (1965); Farnsworth, "Meaning" in the Law of Contracts, 76 Yale L.J. 939 (1967); Havighurst, 60 Nw.U.L.Rev. 599 (1965); Murray, The Parol Evidence Rule; A Clarification, 4 Duq.L.Rev. 337 (1966); Murray, The Parol Evidence Process and Standardized Agreements, 123 U.Pa.L.Rev. 1342 (1975); Patterson, The Interpretation and Construction of Contracts, 64 Colum.L.Rev. 833 (1964); Eric Posner, The Parol Evidence Rule, The Plain Meaning Rule and the Principles of Contractual Interpretation, 146 U.Pa.L.Rev. 533 (1998); Sweet, Contract Making and Parol Evidence: Diagnosis and Treatment of a Sick Rule, 53 Cornell L.Q. 1036 (1968); Young, Equivocation in the Making of Agreements, 64 Colum.L.Rev. 619 (1964).

4. Jake C. Byers, Inc.v. J.B.C. Investments, 834 S.W.2d 806 (Mo.App.1992).

5. The Restatement (Second)'s chapter on interpretation sets forth separate rules "with respect to various aspects of the process. Such separate statements may convey an erroneous impression of the psychological reality of the judicial process in which many elements are typically combined in a single ruling." Rs. 2d § 200, Introductory Comment.

It has been suggested that we are in a time of transition. In earlier days, objective criteria were utilized by courts as devices for creating order and stability in business practices. As other governmental agencies now have the primary function of regulating business practices, courts receive only a variety of specialized, nonrecurring issues for determination. Consequently, standardized interpretation is not seen as necessary for business stability. See Friedman, Law, Rules and the Interpretation of Written Documents, 59 Nw.U.L.Rev. 751, 774–80 (1965).

6. See, e.g., Crow v. Monsell, 200 So.2d 700 (La.App.1967), cert. denied. See Prince, Contract Interpretation in California: Plain Meaning, Parol Evidence and Use of the "Just Result" Principle, 31 Loyola L.A. L.Rev. 557, 563 (1998), quoting an earlier version of this statement and demonstrating its accuracy.

7. See Brezina Constr. v. U.S., 449 F.2d 372, 375 (Ct.Cl.1971) ("it is in cases such as this one, where the contract is ambiguous and where there are no extraneous aids to interpretation, that the courts are forced to resort to guidelines based on what is thought to be sound policy rather than on the intent of the contracting parties"); Rs. 1st § 230 cmt d.

B. THE PAROL EVIDENCE RULE

Table of Sections

§ 3.2 Introduction

A rule of substantive law states that whenever contractual intent is sought to be ascertained from among several expressions of agreement by the parties, an earlier tentative agreement will be rejected in favor of a later expression that is final.[1] More simply stated, the final agreement made by the parties supersedes tentative terms discussed in earlier negotiations. Consequently, in determining the content of the contract, earlier tentative agreements and negotiations are inoperative.[2] The analytic rationale for the parol evidence rule stems from this basic rule of substantive law.

The parol evidence rule comes into play only where the last expression is in writing[3] and is a binding contract.[4] The parol evidence rule has been stated in many ways but the basic notion is that a writing intended

---

§ 3.2

1. 3 Corbin § 573; McCormick, Evidence § 213 (1954) [hereinafter cited as McCormick]. The newer editions of McCormick do not deal with the parol evidence rule.

2. As to interpretation, see § 3.1 n.2 supra. In the meantime the emphasis here is on what terms outside of the writing may be considered to be part of the contract.

3. Rs. 2d § 213 cmt d and subd. (3); Rs. 1st § 228 cmt b, suggesting that the words of an oral agreement may be chosen with such precision that there is an equivalent of an integration. It adds that such a case is so unusual as not to require separate discussion. See 3 Corbin § 573 n.11; Rs. 2d § 215.

4. See § 3.7 infra.

by the parties to be a final embodiment of their agreement should be protected from certain kinds of evidence.[5] A writing that is final is an integration of the terms embodied in it. When it is final and complete it is a total integration. A writing that is final, but that does not completely express the parties' contract is a partial integration.[6]

Thus, a partial integration may not be contradicted by what has been called "parol" evidence. A total integration not only cannot be contradicted by the type of evidence in question but cannot even be supplemented by consistent (non-contradictory) additional terms.[7] A partial integration, being final and incomplete, may be supplemented by consistent additional terms. The important questions are whether the writing is integration, and if so, whether it is a total or only a partial integration. However, before taking up these questions, it would be helpful to consider a number of preliminary questions.

(a) Prior, Contemporaneous, and Subsequent Agreements

The parol evidence rule applies to terms[8] agreed upon *prior* to, or at the same time as, the integration regardless of whether the term is written or oral.[9] (Consequently, the term "parol" is an anachronistic misnomer; the term "extrinsic" would be better). The rule does not apply to *subsequent* agreements.[10]

Whether the rule applies to *contemporaneous* agreements is in dispute. Williston and the first Restatement take the position that contemporaneous oral terms should be treated in the same way as prior agreements but that a contemporaneous writing should be deemed to be a part of the integration and therefore be admissible into evidence.[11] Corbin argues that the terms are either prior or subsequent and that therefore the word "contemporaneous" merely clouds the issue.[12] This

---

5. See Farmers Co-op. Assn. v. Garrison, 248 Ark. 948, 454 S.W.2d 644 (1970); Ely Constr. v. S & S, 184 Neb. 59, 165 N.W.2d 562 (1969); 3 Corbin § 574.

6. 4 Williston § 636 (3d ed.). While Corbin is in agreement with the statement in the text, he advocates abandonment of the term "partial integration" and argues that parties rarely intend that an incomplete writing be considered final. 3 Corbin § 581; see Leyse v. Leyse, 251 Cal.App.2d 629, 59 Cal.Rptr. 680 (1967).

7. Rs. 2d § 210(1) and cmt a (1981).

8. § 1–201(42) of the UCC defines "term" as "that portion of an agreement which relates to a particular matter." (Substantially unchanged in the revision).

9. 3 Corbin § 576.

10. Thomas v. Garrett, 265 Ga. 395, 456 S.E.2d 573 (1995); Connell v. Diamond T. Truck, 88 N.H. 316, 188 A. 463 (1936). Some statutes, however, prevent any subsequent oral modification or rescission if such

an intent is expressed in the writing. See § 5.14 infra.

11. Rs. 1st § 237 cmt a; 4 Williston § 628 (3d ed.); Jenkins v. Watson–Wilson Transp. Sys., 183 Neb. 634, 163 N.W.2d 123 (1968); Sonfield v. Eversole, 416 S.W.2d 458 (Tex.Civ.App.1967); Hathaway v. Ray's Motor Sales, 127 Vt. 279, 247 A.2d 512 (1968). This position has been adopted by the UCC. The parol evidence provision applies to "evidence of any [oral, written or electronic] prior agreement or of a contemporaneous oral agreement." UCC § 2–202. The revision draft is substantially the same. A covering letter may be considered to be part of the integration. Sawyer v. Arum, 690 F.2d 590 (6th Cir.1982); Brown v. Financial Service, 489 F.2d 144 (5th Cir.1974).

12. 3 Corbin § 577. Corbin's position is adopted in Rs. 2d § 213 cmt a, but in § 241 the reference is to "prior or contemporaneous agreements or negotiations." See also 48 ALI Proceedings 449 (1971).

matter will again be mentioned at various places in the ensuing discussion.[13] It is sufficient to note here that Williston's approach is generally accepted on this issue,[14] as it should be. In the creation of a written transaction involving some complexity, it is common practice to separate the transaction into various components, each of which may be drawn up in a separate writing. None of those writing is barred by the parol evidence rule.

Thus, in a typical case, one of the parties offers into evidence a term that is not found in the writing but which the party alleges was orally agreed to prior to or contemporaneously with the writing. In Gianni v. R. Russell & Co.,[15] the landlord and tenant signed a two year lease. Under the terms of the writing, the tenant agreed not to sell tobacco products but was permitted to sell soft drinks. The tenant sought to introduce evidence showing that an oral agreement had been made prior to or contemporaneously with the writing. The alleged oral agreement was that, in consideration of the promise not to sell tobacco, the landlord promised the tenant an *exclusive* right to sell soft drinks on the premises and that the landlord breached this promise. The question was whether the oral exclusivity term could be received into evidence. Using a combination of the more conservative rules described below, the court excluded the evidence.

(b) Policy and Analytical Rationales

The policy behind the rule is to give the writing a preferred status so as to render it immune to perjured testimony and the risk of "uncertain testimony of slippery memory."[16] The rule also proceeds, at least in part, upon the analytical rationale that the offered term is excluded because it has been superseded by the writing, that is, it was not intended to survive the writing—a theory of merger.[17]

The rule is also designed to require parties to put their complete agreement (including oral contemporaneous agreements) in writing at the risk of losing the benefit of any term agreed upon that is not in writing.[18] The objective is to secure business stability.[19] Critics answer

---

13. See § 3.4(d) infra.

14. See 4 Williston § 628 (3d ed.); Rs. 1st § 237; North American Sav. Bank v. RTC, 65 F.3d 111 (8th Cir.1995) (Mo.Law); Hackel v. FDIC, 858 F.Supp. 289 (D.Mass. 1994); Rotelli v. Catanzaro, 686 A.2d 91 (R.I.1996); Hathaway v. Ray's Motor Sales., 127 Vt. 279, 247 A.2d 512 (1968); see also UCC § 2–202 (rule applies to "evidence of any prior agreement or of a contemporaneous *oral* agreement"). The revision draft is in accord.

15. 281 Pa. 320, 126 A. 791 (1924); accord, Borschow Hospital & Medical Supplies v. Cesar Castillo, Inc. 96 F.3d 10 (1st Cir. 1996).

16. McCormick, The Parol Evidence Rule as a Procedural Device for Control of

the Jury, 41 Yale L.J. 365, 366–67 & n.3 (1932); Wallach, The Declining "Sanctity" of Written Contracts—Impact of the UCC on the Parol Evidence Rule, 44 Mo.L.Rev. 651, 653 (1979); Binks Mfg. v. National Presto Indus., 709 F.2d 1109 (7th Cir.1983).

17. 3 A Corbin § 585.

18. 3 Corbin § 575; 4 Williston § 633 (3d ed.); Note, The Parol Evidence Rule, 44 N.Y.U.L.Rev. 972, 982 & n.54 (1969) [hereinafter Note, The Parol Evidence Rule].

19. See Cargill Comm'n v. Swartwood, 159 Minn. 1, 7, 198 N.W. 536, 538 (1924); S.W. Bridges & Co. v. Candland, 88 Utah 373, 380, 54 P.2d 842, 845 (1936).

that the rule has never had the effect of forcing people to reduce their entire agreement to writing and that commerce has nevertheless managed to survive.[20] The other major criticism is that the rule produces injustice because it may exclude as much truthful evidence as it excludes perjured testimony.[21] Another criticism is that the rule is simply too complicated and that it has not been applied consistently.[22]

Is the public better served by giving effect to the parties' entire agreement (written and oral) even at the risk of injustice caused by the possibility of perjury and the possibility that superseded agreements will be treated as operative? Or does the security of transactions require that, despite occasional injustices, persons adopting a formal writing be required, on the penalty of voidness of their side agreements, to put their entire agreement in the writing?[23]

The conflict is an old one. Rules excluding evidence on the ground that it is likely to be false are not strangers to the law. Formerly, parties and interested third parties were incompetent to testify on the ground that their testimony would be unworthy of belief.[24] The Statute of Frauds and the Statute of Wills embody similar considerations.[25] It is submitted, however, that the possibility of perjury is an insufficient ground for interfering with freedom of contract by refusing to effectuate the parties' entire agreement.

The whole thrust of our law for a century and a half has been directed to the eradication of exclusionary rules of evidence in civil cases. Thus the parties may now testify, their interest in the outcome affecting only the weight and not the admissibility of evidence.

Dissatisfaction with rigid application of the parol evidence rule has resulted in the strained insertion of fact situations into categories where the parol evidence rule is inapplicable. Thus to circumvent the rule fraud has been found[26] and reformation granted[27] in situations where those concepts are not normally deemed applicable. Moreover, whole categories of exceptions have been carved out, for example, a deed absolute may be shown to be a mortgage.[28] Thus, it is often stated that parol evidence is

---

20. E.g., Sweet, Contract Making and Parol Evidence: Diagnosis and Treatment of a Sick Rule, 53 Cornell L.Q. 1036 (1968) [hereinafter cited as Sweet I]; Note, The Parol Evidence Rule, supra n.18, at 983.

21. See 3 Corbin § 575, at 381; Note, The Parol Evidence Rule, supra n.18, at 974–75.

22. Professor Sweet describes the rule as a "maze of conflicting tests * * * and exceptions adversely affecting both the counseling of clients and the litigation process." Sweet I, supra n.20, at 1036. Note, The Parol Evidence Rule, supra n.18, at 973–74.

23. For the policy considerations involved, see 3 Corbin § 575; 4 Williston § 633 (3d ed.); McCormick §§ 210–16 (1954).

24. See McCormick § 65 (1954).

25. See 3 Corbin § 575.

26. E.g., Bareham & McFarland v. Kane, 228 A.D. 396, 240 N.Y.S. 123 (1930) (language sounding in warranty of performance held to be factual representation); see Sweet, Promissory Fraud and the Parol Evidence Rule, 49 Calif.L.Rev. 877, 896 (1961) ("It does not take much manipulation to classify a promise as either a warranty or a fact.")

27. E.g., Winslett v. Rice, 272 Ala. 25, 128 So.2d 94 (1960) (breach of oral collateral agreement constituted "fraud" justifying reformation).

28. Adrian v. McKinnie, 639 N.W.2d 529 (S.D.2002); Anderson v. Kimbrough, 741 So.2d 1041 (Miss.App.1999); 3 Corbin

admissible to show the true nature of the transaction between the parties.[29] Professor Thayer's observation concerning the parol evidence rule problem warrants repetition: "Few things are darker than this, or fuller of subtle difficulties."[30] When any rule of law is riddled through with exceptions and applications difficult to reconcile,[31] it is believed that litigation is stimulated rather than reduced.[32] If the policy of the parol evidence rule is to reduce the possibility of judgments predicated upon perjured testimony and superseded negotiations, it may be effectuated to a large extent by continuing to leave control over determining the question of intent to integrate in the hands of the trial judge.[33]

(c) The Role of the Judge and Jury

The parol evidence rule is generally stated in terms of the intent of the parties. Did the parties intend an integration and did they intend it to be total? Questions of intent are ordinarily questions of fact and

§ 587; 9 Wigmore § 2437 (Chadbourn rev.); 4 Williston § 635 (3d ed.); see Fogelman, The Deed Absolute as a Mortgage in New York, 32 Fordham L.Rev. 299 (1963). Parol evidence is also admissible to show that a mortgage absolute on its face was in fact intended to secure future advances. Gosselin v. Better Homes, 256 A.2d 629 (Me. 1969).

29. Mahoney v. May, 207 Neb. 187, 297 N.W.2d 157 (1980).

30. J. Thayer, supra § 3.1 n.1, at 390.

31. The Supreme Court of California has acknowledged that its decisions have not been consistent. It disapproved of the restrictive approach previously adopted in many cases. Masterson v. Sine, 68 Cal.2d 222, 65 Cal.Rptr. 545, 436 P.2d 561 (1968). Inconsistencies in the Virginia decisions are discussed in Note, 7 Wm. & Mary L.Rev. 189 (1966). Pennsylvania inconsistencies are discussed in 3 Corbin § 577 n. 34 (Supp.1971). Illinois inconsistencies in J & B Steel Contractors v. C. Iber & Sons, 246 Ill.App.3d 523, 187 Ill.Dec. 197, 617 N.E.2d 405 (1993), aff'd, 162 Ill.2d 265, 271, 642 N.E.2d 1215, 1219, 205 Ill.Dec. 98, 102 (1994) (inconsistencies denied).

An occasional jurisdiction appears to reach consistent results although on the most varied reasoning. For example, in Connecticut the leading cases appear to be State Finance v. Ballestrini, 111 Conn. 544, 150 A. 700 (1930) in which Williston's test is articulated but a result more consistent with Corbin's approach was reached; Harris v. Clinton, 142 Conn. 204, 112 A.2d 885 (1955), in which although he is not cited, the reasoning seems to be pure Corbin; Greenwich Plumbing & Heating v. A. Barbaresi & Son, 147 Conn. 580, 164 A.2d 405 (1960), in which parol evidence of a collateral agreement was admitted because the writing was ambiguous. The analysis, but not the result of this last decision is criticized in 3 Corbin § 582 n. 84 (Supp.1964).

A degree of consistency is shown in some jurisdictions which adopt a Willistonian approach. McDonough, The Parol Evidence Rule in South Dakota and the Effect of Section 2–202 of the Uniform Commercial Code, 10 S.D.L.Rev. 60 (1965); Comment, 27 Mo.L.Rev. 269, 279–82 (1962). New York is one such jurisdiction. Oxford Commercial v. Landau, 12 N.Y.2d 362, 239 N.Y.S.2d 865, 190 N.E.2d 230, 13 ALR3d 309 (1963), 49 Cornell L.Q. 311 (1964); Mitchill v. Lath, 247 N.Y. 377, 160 N.E. 646 (1928); Meadow Brook Nat. Bank v. Bzura, 20 A.D.2d 287, 246 N.Y.S.2d 787 (1964). This apparent consistency is often achieved by strained characterization of the facts to bring the case within one of the exceptions to the parol evidence rule. See e.g., People v. Kennedy, 16 A.D.2d 306, 227 N.Y.S.2d 971 (1962) (condition precedent to the formation of a contract); Bareham & McFarland v. Kane, 228 A.D. 396, 240 N.Y.S. 123 (1930) (fraud). For Washington, see Comment, 8 Gonzaga L.Rev. 88 (1972).

32. See 3 Corbin § 575; see also Fisch, New York Evidence § 64 (2d ed.1977): "Because the decisions are ineffective as guides to determine in advance whether or not the facts of any given transaction will come within one of the exceptions to the rule, the assumption, frequently enunciated in judicial opinions, that the rule is indispensable to business stability is specious * * *. The decisions as to these matters are valueless, contrary holdings being reached on almost identical facts."

33. See subsection (c) of this section.

would normally be submitted to a jury.[34] However, the courts have transmuted this question of intent, whether actual or presumed,[35] by legal alchemy into a question of law to be decided in the first instance by the trial judge and subject to appellate review.[36]

The policy of leaving this question to the trial judge is based on the belief that unsophisticated jurors would be easily beguiled by an artful presentation and would not give the writing the protection it deserved.[37] As stated by one commentator the policy gives the trial judge a polite means of keeping suspect oral evidence from the jury.[38] Making the question one of law strengthens the hand of an appellate court, because, ordinarily, appellate courts do not review questions of fact.[39] Some have criticized this policy. For example, they have pointed out that jurors routinely handle more complicated and sophisticated questions.[40] Others have observed that distrust of jurors is hardly a reason for excluding a prior written agreement[41] and that there are other ways in which juries can be controlled.[42]

A determination as to whether the parol evidence rule applies has several consequences. If the court decides that the rule applies, it will exclude the proffered term not because it was not agreed upon, but because it is legally immaterial. Conversely, if the court decides that the parol evidence rule does not apply, it admits the term into evidence. The jury will then determine the issue of fact as to whether the term was actually agreed upon.[43]

(d) Is the Rule One of Substantive Law or Procedure?

The earlier decisions had considered the parol evidence rule to be a rule of evidence, but Professor Thayer railed against this notion and argued—(apparently convincingly because almost all of the modern cases and texts seem to agree)—[44] that it is a rule of substantive law. A rule of evidence, he maintained, excludes relevant evidence and does not define

---

34. See § 2.8 supra.

35. See §§ 3.4(g) & 3.14 infra.

36. Rs. 2d § 210(3); McCormick, Evidence, at 380–82 (1954). Corbin generally agrees, but sees no harm in the judge's obtaining the aid of the jury on the issue. 3 Corbin § 595; accord, McCormick, at 378–79. The cases are in conflict. See Sullivan v. Massachusetts Mut. Life Ins., 611 F.2d 261 (9th Cir.1979) (discussing the conflict); see also Whitford, The Role of the Jury (and the Fact/Law Distinction) in the Interpretation of Written Contracts, 2001 Wisc.L.Rev. 931.

37. White & Summers, Uniform Commercial Code § 2–9 (4th ed.); McCormick, at 367.

38. Wallach, supra n.16, at 654.

39. See § 2.8 supra.

40. Sweet I, supra n. 20, at 1055 & n.86.

41. Murray, The Parol Evidence Rule: A Clarification, 4 Duq.L.Rev. 337, 342 (1965–1966) [hereinafter Murray I].

42. Other methods of jury control include the trial judge's comments on the evidence, the power of cross-examination, the judge's charge to the jury, and where the judge is convinced the jury reached an erroneous result, the granting of a motion for a new trial. Sweet I, supra n.20, at 1056.

43. 9 Wigmore § 2430 (Chadbourn rev. 1981).

44. E.g., Prophet v. Builders, Inc., 204 Kan. 268, 462 P.2d 122, 43 ALR3d 1378 (1969); Fogelson v. Rackfay Constr., 300 N.Y. 334, 90 N.E.2d 881 (1950), rearg. denied; O'Brien v. O'Brien, 362 Pa. 66, 66 A.2d 309 (1949); Adams v. Marchbanks, 253 S.C. 280, 170 S.E.2d 214 (1969); In re Spring Valley Meats, 94 Wis.2d 600, 288 N.W.2d 852 (1980); see 3 Corbin § 573.

obligations;[45] the rule is simply a statement of the substantive law principle that if the parties so intend their final expression will prevail over any antecedent expression of agreement.[46] This is true whether the final expression is oral or written. However, as Professor McCormick points out, making the question of intent to integrate a question of law gives the parol evidence rule a procedural function since the rule also has distrust of the jury as a basis.

The main consequence of the classification of the rule as substantive or evidentiary relates to whether the parol evidence question can be raised for the first time on appeal. Ordinarily, failure to object to any alleged error regarding the admission of evidence operates as a waiver of the right to object; the issue cannot be raised for the first time on appeal. However, because the parol evidence is a rule of substance, a different rule applies. Most cases hold that the question may be raised for the first time on appeal despite the failure to object.[47]

§ 3.3   Is the Writing Integrated?

The first issue in a parol evidence problem is whether the parties intended the writing to be a final embodiment of their agreement. If so, there is at least a partial integration and the writing may not be contradicted.[1] If a writing that appears to evidence a contract is not a *final* embodiment of the contract or some of its terms,[2] the parol evidence rule does not apply.[3] For example, a memorandum prepared by one party, but not shown to the other, is not an integration because it is not even assented to by the other party.[4] The writing is merely evidence of the agreement. Similarly, the parties may have intended their writings to be tentative and preliminary to a final draft.[5]

Confirmations are also documents prepared by only one party. Unlike a memorandum placed in one's own files, a confirmation is sent to the other party. Such a confirmation often is held to be an integration if the other party makes no response to it prior to performance.[6] However, an incomplete confirmation can only be a partial integration.[7]

45. J. Thayer, supra § 3.1 n.1, at 405–10.

46. Id.

47. Tahoe Nat. Bank v. Phillips, 4 Cal.3d 11, 92 Cal.Rptr. 704, 480 P.2d 320 (1971); Ruscito v. F–Dyne Elec., 177 Conn. 149, 411 A.2d 1371 (1979); Snow v. Winn, 607 P.2d 678 (Okl.1980); Poelker v. Jamison, 4 S.W.3d 611 (Mo.App.1999); Bulis v. Wells, 565 P.2d 487 (Wyo.1977); Annot., 81 ALR3d 249 (1977); Rs. 2d § 213 cmt a; but see Higgs v. De Maziroff, 263 N.Y. 473, 189 N.E. 555, 92 ALR 807 (1934).

§ 3.3

1. See § 3.2(a) supra.

2. Cornwell Quality Tools v. C.T.S., 446 F.2d 825 (9th Cir.1971), cert. denied.

3. Hechinger v. Ulacia, 194 A.D. 330, 185 N.Y.S. 323 (1920).

4. See Donald Friedman & Co. v. Newman, 255 N.Y. 340, 174 N.E. 703, 73 ALR 95 (1931); Hoots v. Calaway, 282 N.C. 477, 193 S.E.2d 709 (1973).

5. Rs. 2d § 209 ill. 1.

6. Petereit v. S.B. Thomas, Inc., 63 F.3d 1169 (2d Cir.1995), cert. denied; Tow v. Miners Memorial Hosp. Assn., 305 F.2d 73 (4th Cir.1962); Newburger v. American Surety, 242 N.Y. 134, 151 N.E. 155 (1926); Rs. 1st § 228 ill. 2; Rs. 2d § 209 ill. 2. The UCC rule is discussed in § 3.4(e) infra.

7. RFC v. Commercial Union of America, 123 F.Supp. 748 (S.D.N.Y.1954); Flavorland Indus. v. Schnoll Packing, 167 N.J.Super. 376, 400 A.2d 883 (1979); Hoots

Any relevant evidence is admissible to show that the writing was not intended to be *final*.[8] Although the question of finality is ordinarily characterized as one of law in order to remove it from the province of unsophisticated jurors, it is truly a question of fact—one of intention—that the trial judge determines in the first instance, subject to appellate review.[9]

What constitutes a final (integrated) writing? It need not be in any particular form and need not be signed. The crucial requirement is that the parties have regarded the writing as the final embodiment of their agreement.[10] Undoubtedly, the completeness of the agreement has some bearing on the question of finality; the more complete and formal the instrument is, the more likely that it is intended as final.[11]

§ 3.4   Is the Writing a Total Integration?

After the judge decides that the writing is an integration, the next issue is whether the writing is a total integration. An incomplete final statement of part of the agreement is only a partial integration, but if the writing is both final and *complete,* it is a total integration. It may not be contradicted or supplemented. In comparison, a partial integration can be supplemented by consistent additional terms.[1]

Whether the integration is total or partial is often the key issue in parol evidence disputes. Courts ordinarily treat the issue as a question of law even though they generally state that the issue involves the intention of the parties.[2] Many approaches are used to determine whether the integration is total and in many of them the intention of the parties is not the basis of the determination.[3] The leading tests employed to determine the existence of a total integration will now be briefly discussed.

v. Calaway, 282 N.C. 477, 193 S.E.2d 709 (1973); Levy v. Leaseway Sys., 190 Pa.Super. 482, 154 A.2d 314 (1959).

8. In re William Rakestraw Co., 450 F.2d 6 (9th Cir.1971); National Cash Register v. I.M.C., 260 Or. 504, 491 P.2d 211 (1971); Bullfrog Marina v. Lentz, 28 Utah 2d 261, 501 P.2d 266 (1972); 3 Corbin § 588; 4 Williston § 633 n. 13 (3d ed.); Rs. 1st § 228 cmt a; Rs. 2d § 209(2) and cmts b and c; id. § 214(a).

9. McCormick §§ 214–15. Corbin would allow greater participation by the jury. See 3 Corbin § 595; Rs. 2d § 209 cmt c.

10. Kitchen v. Stockman Nat. Life Ins., 192 N.W.2d 796 (Iowa 1971). Thus, even an offer may amount to an integration, if the parties both assent to it as an integration. Rs. 2d § 209 cmt b.

11. Antonellis v. Northgate Constr., 362 Mass. 847, 291 N.E.2d 626 (1973); Di Menna v. Cooper & Evans, 220 N.Y. 391, 397–98, 115 N.E. 993, 995 (1917); 3 Corbin

§ 581; Rs. 2d § 210 cmt c. "Where the parties reduce an agreement to a writing which in view of its completeness and specificity reasonably appears to be a complete agreement it is taken to be an integrated agreement unless it is established by other evidence that the writing did not constitute a final expression." Rs. 2d § 209(3). Ill. 3 of § 209 makes it clear that even if such a writing is not a total integration it ordinarily would be a partial integration.

§ 3.4

1. See § 3.2 supra.

2. Rs. 2d § 210(3); McCormick § 215; Hanslin v. Keith, 120 N.H. 361, 415 A.2d 329 (1980).

3. The courts are more likely to find the existence of a total integration in the case of a formal contract negotiated by attorneys or sophisticated parties. Childres & Spitz, Status In The Law of Contracts, 47 N.Y.U.L.Rev. 1, 7 (1972).

(a) The "Four Corners" Rule

The earliest view is the so-called "four corners" rule. Under that view, if the instrument appears complete on its face—a determination to be made by the trial judge by looking solely at the writing—the instrument is conclusively presumed to be a total integration.[4] This approach is in decline,[5] but still has much vitality.[6] The "four corners" rule is not only illogical but can produce harsh results since it is impossible to determine whether an agreement is complete on its face simply by looking at the writing.[7]

(b) The "Collateral Contract" Concept

In an attempt to obtain fairer results, the "collateral contract" concept was born. Under this approach, the existence of a total integration did not prevent "collateral agreements"—those that are independent of the writing—from being introduced so long as the main agreement was not contradicted.[8]

The collateral contract concept led to problems of application because courts applied the concept to logically distinct situations. To illustrate the first situation, suppose that S and B, in a signed writing, agreed to sell and buy a specific automobile for $20,000 and they contemporaneously orally agreed that B may keep the automobile in S's garage for one year in return for B's promise to pay $100 per month. The second agreement may be looked upon as being independent of the first agreement, because consideration is present on both sides of the agreement. Under the collateral contract concept (and *all* of the views discussed in this chapter), the ancillary agreement is admissible as it does not contradict the main agreement. Thus, the garage agreement is admissible even in the face of a merger clause.[9] It may be difficult to determine which is the main and which is the collateral agreement, but such a distinction is relevant only when the two agreements are contradictory.

If we change the facts of the garage illustration so that B seeks to prove that S promised to allow B to use the garage for no consideration other than the price of the car, the situation is quite different. Yet, under the "collateral contract" concept there were "many cases where parol evidence was admitted to prove the existence of a separate oral

---

4. Anchor Cas. v. Bird Island Produce, 249 Minn. 137, 82 N.W.2d 48 (1957).

5. White & Summers, Uniform Commercial Code § 2–10 (4th ed.).

6. Independent Energy v. Trigen Energy, 944 F.Supp. 1184 (S.D.N.Y.1996); Air Safety, Inc. v. Teachers Realty, 185 Ill.2d 457, 236 Ill.Dec. 8, 706 N.E.2d 882 (1999).

7. But see Note, The Parol Evidence Rule, supra § 3.2 n.18, at 975–6. Cases continue to hold that a writing is presumed to embody the final and entire agreement of the parties. See W.W.W. Assocs. v. Giancontieri, 77 N.Y.2d 157, 566 N.E.2d 639, 565

N.Y.S.2d 440 (1990) (completeness also barred parol evidence of meaning at variance with the writing).

8. Wallach, supra § 3.2 n.16, at 658; see Markoff v. Kreiner, 180 Md. 150, 154, 23 A.2d 19, 23 (1941); Buyken v. Ertner, 33 Wn.2d 334, 339–42, 205 P.2d 628, 633–36 (1949).

9. Gem Corrugated Box v. National Kraft Container, 427 F.2d 499 (2d Cir. 1970); Rs. 2d § 216(2) (a) and cmt c. Merger clauses are discussed in § 3.6 infra.

agreement as to any matter on which the document is silent and which is not inconsistent with its terms—even though the instrument appeared to state a complete agreement."[10] Wigmore seems to approve of this test.[11]

Under this approach, no writing could be considered more than a partial integration. However, many courts stated the "collateral contract" concept much more narrowly. For example, the Supreme Court stated:

> "Undoubtedly the existence of a separate oral agreement as to any matter on which the written contract is silent, and which is not inconsistent with its terms, may be proven by parol, if under the circumstances of the particular case it may properly be inferred that the parties did not intend the written paper to be a complete and final statement of the whole of the transaction between them. But such an agreement must not only be collateral, but must also relate to a subject distinct from that to which the written contract applies; that is, it must not be so closely connected with the principal transaction as to form part and parcel of it."[12]

The narrower view makes a distinction between promises that "are inherently and substantially collateral to the main purpose of the contract" and those "which directly relate to the main object." This distinction is unworkable.[13] Williston therefore suggested a new "reasonable person" test, discussed below. Since that time the "collateral contract" rule has been declining in popularity, although at times Williston's rules and the "collateral contract rule" are employed in the same case.[14] Despite its decline, the "collateral contract rule" is still alive, despite its amorphous nature.[15]

(c) Williston's Rules

Williston's rules have played a major role in the decision of parol evidence cases. His rules can be summarized as follows: (1) If the writing contains a "merger clause," a provision declaring that the writing contains the entire agreement of the parties,[16] this declaration conclusively establishes that the integration is total,[17] unless (a) the document

---

10. Masterson v. Sine, 68 Cal.2d 222, 65 Cal.Rptr. 545, 436 P.2d 561 (1968); see also Lee v. Kimura, 2 Haw.App. 538, 634 P.2d 1043 (1981); Crow–Spieker No. 23 v. Robinson, 97 Nev. 302, 629 P.2d 1198 (1981).

11. 9 Wigmore § 2430 (Chadbourn rev. 1981); Lanning Constr. v. Rozell, 320 N.W.2d 522 (S.D.1982).

12. Seitz v. Brewers' Refrigerating Mach., 141 U.S. 510 (1891).

13. See 4 Williston, § 638 (3d ed.). McCormick points out that the net result was that the courts could and did select the version of the rule that suited them in a particular case. McCormick, Evidence 372 (1954); see also Murray, The Parol Evi-

dence Process and Standardized Agreements Under the Restatement (Second) of Contracts, 123 U.Pa.L.Rev. 1342, 1349 (1975) [hereinafter Murray II].

14. See, e.g., Mitchill v. Lath, 247 N.Y. 377, 160 N.E. 646, 68 ALR 239 (1928) and Lee v. Joseph E. Seagram & Sons, 552 F.2d 447 (2d Cir.1977).

15. FMA Financial v. Hansen Dairy, 617 P.2d 327 (Utah 1980).

16. See § 3.6 infra.

17. See Benvenuti Oil v. Foss Consultants, 64 Conn.App. 723, 781 A.2d 435 (2001) (merger clause usually conclusive).

is obviously incomplete or (b) the merger clause was included as a result of fraud or mistake or any other reason sufficient to set aside a contract,[18] but even a merger clause does not prevent enforcement of a separate agreement supported by a separate consideration.[19] (2) In the absence of a merger clause, the determination is made by looking to the writing.[20] Consistent additional terms may be introduced if the writing is obviously incomplete on its face or if the writing is apparently complete but, as in the case of deeds, bonds, bills and notes, expresses the undertaking of only one party.[21] (3) Where the writing appears to be a complete instrument expressing the rights and obligations of both parties, it is deemed a total integration unless the alleged additional terms were such that parties in the position of those to the written agreement would naturally enter into a separate agreement with regard to the additional terms.[22] In such a case the writing is only a partial integration.[23]

The second rule makes clear that if the writing is obviously incomplete it cannot amount to more than a partial integration. This is a logical and generally accepted approach.[24] The second part of this rule is really a corollary of the third rule because it would be natural not to include all of the terms agreed upon in the type of instruments discussed—bonds, deeds, bills and notes, etc.[25]

It is the third rule that has had the greatest influence in the area of parol evidence. Williston found the "four corners" to be illogical and the "collateral contract" rule to be unworkable. He therefore selected the "reasonable person" approach embodied in the third rule as the basis of determining whether there was a total integration when the other two rules did not apply. Thus, when Williston talks about intent in this area, he is not talking about the actual intent of the parties but a presumed or fictitious intent.[26] More fully expressed, Williston's third rule states that when a term not found in the writing is offered into evidence by one of the parties and it would have been unnatural for the parties to have excluded that term from the writing, there is a total integration with respect to that term and the term may not be admitted into evidence even if it does not contradict the writing.

After the court has excluded such a term, suppose another alleged additional term were offered. It would be admitted if it would have been natural to exclude that particular term from the writing. Thus, the

---

18. 4 Williston § 633 (3d ed.); cf. 3 Corbin § 578; Hartsfield, The Merger Clause, 27 Tex.L.Rev. 361 (1949); Note, 19 Ala. L.Rev. 556 (1967).

19. See 3.4(b).

20. 4 Williston § 633 (3d ed.).

21. 4 Williston §§ 633, 636 (3d ed.); see Rs. 2d § 216 cmt c.

22. 4 Williston § 645 (3d ed.); 3 Corbin § 587; Rs. 2d § 216 cmt d.

23. 4 Williston §§ 638–39 (3d ed.); see Ratta v. Harkins, 268 Md. 122, 299 A.2d 777 (1973); Rs. 2d § 216(2) (b) and cmt d.

24. Chertkof v. Spector Baltimore Terminal, 263 Md. 550, 284 A.2d 215 (1971); Hatley v. Stafford, 284 Or. 523, 588 P.2d 603 (1978); Rs. 1st § 240.

25. Wallach, supra § 3.2 n.16, at 659.

26. See Murray II, supra n.13, at 1369–70; see also 3A Corbin § 587; 4 Williston § 645 (3d ed.).

concept of "total integration" is relative to the nature of the proffered term.

The question of whether it was natural to exclude the proffered term is answered by the court's conclusion of what reasonable parties similarly situated would naturally do with respect to the term.[27] It is obvious that there can be great difficulty in applying this test to a particular set of facts.[28]

Williston's rule was adopted by the First Restatement[29] and became and probably still is the majority rule in the country. But, in time, Williston was challenged by Corbin's bold new approach to the problem.

(d) Corbin's Approach

Earlier we discussed the question of whether the parol evidence rule applied to a contemporaneous agreement. We noted that Williston's view on this point is well-established. His view is that a contemporaneous written agreement becomes part of the integration but that a contemporaneous oral agreement is subject to the rule.[30] Under Corbin's view, the parol evidence rule does not apply to either kind of contemporaneous agreements. Corbin concludes that terms are either prior or subsequent to the writing and that the word "contemporaneous" merely clouds the issue.[31]

Despite our usual approval of Corbin's analysis of the parol evidence rule, we must note that Corbin here ignores the common business practice of preparing and executing more than one writing as a way of closing a transaction. For example, the purchaser of a business may make a number of promises to the seller. There may be one principal agreement concerning the purchase price, inventory control, the disposition of claims that may be made based on past transactions of the business, etc. A separate document may provide that the purchaser assumes the seller's lease. Why a separate document? A copy of the lease assumption may be sent to the landlord who need not be concerned with the other aspects of the transaction. Between the buyer and seller, the assumption agreement should be treated as part of the integration. Although both Williston and Corbin would admit the assumption agreement, Corbin's rejection of the idea of contemporaneous writings seems misguided.

However, Corbin agrees with Williston that the rule applies to prior agreements, whether written or oral, but Corbin rejects Williston's "reasonable person" approach and is determined to search out the actual intention of the parties. The issue for Corbin is whether the parties actually agreed or intended that the writing was a total and complete

27. 4 Williston § 633 (3d ed.).

28. Compare Gianni v. R. Russel & Co., 281 Pa. 320, 126 A. 791 (1924) with Masterson v. Sine, 68 Cal.2d 222, 65 Cal.Rptr. 545, 436 P.2d 561 (1968).

29. Rs. 1st § 240.

30. See 3.2(a) supra.

31. See 3.2(a) supra.

statement of their agreement;[32] the court determines whether the parties intended that the prior agreements should be merged.[33] According to Corbin, all relevant evidence should be considered on this issue of intent, including evidence of prior negotiations.[34] The very evidence whose admissibility is challenged is admissible on the issue whether there is a total integration.[35] It is clear that Corbin's approach undercuts the traditional parol evidence rule.[36] All that is left is that the judge, rather than the jury, ordinarily determines whether there has been an integration. The trend is now in the direction of Corbin[37] and will be accelerated by the Restatement (Second) which, as we shall see, has staked out a position similar to that of Corbin.[38]

(e) The UCC Rule

UCC section 2–202 contains the Code's Parol Evidence Rule. It provides:[39]

Final Written Expression: Parol or Extrinsic Evidence

Terms with respect to which the confirmatory memoranda of the parties agree or which are otherwise set forth in a writing intended by the parties as a final expression of their agreement with respect to such terms as are included therein may not be contradicted by evidence of any prior agreement or of a contemporaneous oral agreement but may be explained or supplemented:

(a) by course of dealing or usage of trade (Section 1–205) or by course of performance (Section 2–208); and

(b) by evidence of consistent additional terms unless the court finds the writing to have been intended also as a complete and exclusive statement of the terms of the agreement.

(1) Clause (b)

32. 3A Corbin § 577.

33. Wallach, supra § 3.2 n.16, at 664; 3A Corbin § 585; Sherman v. Mutual Benefit Life Ins., 633 F.2d 782, 784 (9th Cir. 1980); Bunbury v. Krauss, 41 Wis.2d 522, 164 N.W.2d 473, 476 (1969).

34. 3A Corbin § 582; see North American Sav. Bank v. RTC, 65 F.3d 111 (8th Cir.1995) (Mo. law); Bird Lakes Dev. v. Meruelo, 626 So.2d 234 (Fla.App.1993); Silver Syndicate v. Sunshine Mining, 101 Idaho 226, 611 P.2d 1011 (1979).

35. 3A Corbin § 582; Rs. 2d § 209(2); In re Eickman's Estate, 291 N.W.2d 308 (Iowa 1980); Alexander v. Snell, 12 Mass. App.Ct. 323, 424 N.E.2d 262 (1981).

36. 3A Corbin § 582; see also Wigmore § 2403(2) (Chadbourn rev.1981); Connell v. Aetna Life & Cas., 436 A.2d 408 (Me.1981); Rainbow Constr. v. Olsen, 64 Or.App. 699,

669 P.2d 814 (1983); In re Spring Valley Meats, 94 Wis.2d 600, 288 N.W.2d 852 (1980).

37. Ample authority for this proposition can be found in the cases relying upon Corbin's analysis and citations in 3 Corbin §§ 573–595. See also Aboussie v. Aboussie, 441 F.2d 150 (5th Cir.1971); U.S. v. Clementon Sewerage Auth., 365 F.2d 609 (3d Cir.1966) (New Jersey law); Masterson v. Sine, 68 Cal.2d 222, 65 Cal.Rptr. 545, 436 P.2d 561, (1968); 17 Cath.U.L.Rev. 489 (1968). Corbin's approach was adopted for admiralty in Battery Steamship v. Refineria Panama, 513 F.2d 735 (2d Cir.1975).

38. See § 3.4(g) infra.

39. The revision draft § 2–202 is substantially the same. The word "record" substitutes for "writing" and "memoranda."

Clause (b) deals with the parol evidence rule. It states the traditional rule that a total integration cannot be contradicted or supplemented. However, the section does not determine the existence of a total integration according to any of the rules previously discussed. Rather, it creates the presumption that the writing does not include all of the terms; the writing is presumed to be only a partial integration.[40] This presumption can be overcome if the parties actually intend the writing to be a total integration *or,* as stated in Comment 3, if it is *certain* that parties similarly situated would have included the offered term in the writing. In making these determinations the courts should be willing to receive all relevant extrinsic evidence.[41] There is some conflict as to what evidence is relevant based upon whether a purely objective or a partly subjective approach should be taken.[42]

The statute embraces Corbin's rule that the actual intention of the parties should be sought. The certainty test is a variation of Williston's reasonable person test. Under this alternative rule, there will be fewer total integrations than under Williston's rule[43] not to mention the four corners and the collateral contract rules. The effect of a merger clause will be discussed below.[44] Finally, it should be noted that the UCC follows Williston's rules with respect to contemporaneous agreements and that the integration question is treated as one of law.[45]

(2) Clause (a)

Under this clause, a course of dealing, usage of the trade, or a course of performance may be used to supply a consistent additional term even though the writing is deemed to be a total integration under the rule stated in clause (b) above.[46] Thus, under this rule, even a total integration is treated as if it were a partial integration in relation to this triad of evidence, and the only question to be decided is whether the evidence contradicts the writing. This sounds as if it makes an important change in the prior common law decisions that followed Williston's rules. However, under Williston's rules it would be natural for parties similarly situated not to include a course of dealing or the like in the writing. Thus, under Williston's rules the integration would be partial and the question would be whether the term offered is contradictory. This section would change the result under the "four corners rule."[47] Course

---

40. UCC § 2–202 cmt 3; revision cmts 1, 2 & 4; Wallach, § 3.2 n.16, at 666; cf. Rs. 2d § 209(3).

41. Cosmopolitan Fin. v. Runnels, 2 Haw. App. 33, 625 P.2d 390 (1981), cert.denied.

42. Wallach, supra § 3.2 n.16, at 674. Compare Hunt Foods & Indus. v. Doliner, 26 A.D.2d 41, 270 N.Y.S.2d 937 (1966) with Whirlpool v. Regis Leasing, 29 A.D.2d 395, 288 N.Y.S.2d 337 (1968).

43. Birsner v. Bolles, 20 Cal.App.3d 635, 97 Cal.Rptr. 846 (1971); Snyder v. Herbert Greenbaum & Assocs., 38 Md.App. 144, 380 A.2d 618 (1977); Hunt Foods & Indus. v. Doliner, 26 A.D.2d 41, 270 N.Y.S.2d 937 (1966).

44. See § 3.6 infra.

45. UCC § 2–202 cmt 3, revision cmt 4.

46. White & Summers § 2–10 (4th ed.).

47. UCC § 2–202 cmt 1(a), revision cmts 1,2 & 4.

of dealing, usage of the trade, and course of performance are discussed in more detail below.[48]

This subsection also deals with "confirmatory memoranda." At common law, a single confirmation often acts as a total integration if the other party makes no response to it prior to performance.[49] Is it possible under the UCC to have a total integration based upon a single confirmatory memorandum? It has been argued that because the UCC uses the words "confirmatory memoranda" such a result is no longer possible.[50] Professor Murray[51] and Professor Farnsworth disagree, arguing that a single confirmatory memorandum may operate as a total integration under the UCC.[52]

Under the UCC, even if there are "confirmatory memoranda" it does not follow that the result is a total integration. It will be a total integration only if the parties actually intended the writing to be an exclusive and total integration of their agreement or if the term offered in evidence would certainly have been included in the writing if it had been agreed upon.[53] This represents a change in the common law rule.

(f) CISG

The United Nations Convention on Contracts for the International Sale of Goods rejects the formalism of parol evidence rules and Statutes of Frauds. Article 11 provides: "A contract of sale need not be concluded in or evidenced by writing and is not subject to any other requirement of form. It may be proved by any means, including witnesses." This refreshingly modern point of view was subverted in the first case to consider the parol evidence rule in the context of a sale governed by the Convention. The Fifth Circuit, without discussion and apparently without argument on the point, applied the Texas parol evidence rule to such a sale.[54] It takes time for new legislation to be understood, and it was properly understood by the 11th Circuit.[55]

---

48. See § 3.17 infra.

49. See § 3.3 supra.

50. Album Graphics v. Beatrice Foods, 87 Ill.App.3d 338, 42 Ill.Dec. 332, 408 N.E.2d 1041 (1980).

51. Murray on Contracts 225 & n.9 (2d ed.); but see Murray on Contracts § 83 n.36 (3d ed.).

52. Farnsworth § 7–3 nn.9 & 18 (3d ed.). Section 2–202 has a cross-reference to § 2–316(1) (express warranty). It is generally held that an express warranty may not be introduced into evidence in the face of a total integration. S.M. Wilson & Co. v. Smith Int'l, 587 F.2d 1363 (9th Cir.1978). Broude, however, argues that printed form disclaimers do not become part of the agreement, and in any event § 2–316 cmt 2 clearly indicates that the section protects only against a "false" allegation of oral warranties. Therefore, an oral warranty which, in fact, has been made is admissible. Broude, The Consumer and the Parol Evidence Rule: Section 2–202 of the Uniform Commercial Code 1970 Duke L.J. 881. See also C. Birnbaum, L.A. Stahl, M.P. West, Standardized Agreements and the Parol Evidence Rule, 26 Arizona L.Rev. 793 (1984).

53. Paymaster Oil Mill v. Mitchell, 319 So.2d 652 (Miss.1975).

54. Beijing Metals & Minerals Import/Export v. American Business Ctr., 993 F.2d 1178 n. 9 (5th Cir.1993), holding defended in Note, 1995 B.Y.U.L.Rev. 1347.

55. MCC–Marble Ceramic Center v. Ceramica Nuova d'Agostino, 144 F.3d 1384 (11th Cir.1998), cert. denied.

(g) The Restatement (Second)

The Restatement (Second) formulates the parol evidence rule in a new way. Unfortunately, it has failed to make its position clear and has only added to the confusion. Its major premise is that Corbin's rule of ascertaining actual intent should be used in determining whether there is a total or partial integration,[56] but it does not stop there. It goes on to say that, even if this test leads to a determination of a total integration, consistent additional terms are still admissible if a) the alleged agreement is made for a separate consideration *or* b) the offered agreement is not within the scope of the integrated writing[57] (this seems to be a throwback to the more liberal cases under the collateral contract theory), *or* c) if the offered terms might naturally be omitted from the writing.[58] The bottom line of the Restatement (Second) is that it is impossible to have more than a partial integration.[59] Thus, the Restatement (Second) appears to have buried the parol evidence rule in a shallow grave of verbiage without even the accoutrements of a decent burial.

Finally, it should be noted that the Restatement (Second) does not take a clear position on the issue of contemporaneous agreements. Restatement (Second) § 239, comment a, appears to adopt Corbin's position that side agreements are prior or subsequent and the notion of contemporaneous agreements is unsound. However, § 241 refers to prior or contemporaneous agreements or negotiations.[60] The Restatement (Second) takes the position that integration is a question for the court, but with a nod toward Corbin's position that this is only ordinarily true.[61]

(h) Is the Intention of the Parties the Test?

It is obvious that the "four corners" and the "collateral contract" concepts do not determine the existence of a total integration on the basis of the intention of the parties. Instead, they concentrate on the words of the writing. In contrast, both Williston and Corbin assert that the existence of a total integration depends upon the intention of the parties. Williston does so primarily in a section entitled "Integration Depends Upon Intent."[62] Corbin's emphasis on intent runs throughout his entire discussion of the rule.[63] In this context, however, they use the term "intent" in ways that are remarkably dissimilar. A typical fact pattern will illustrate this. A agrees to sell and B agrees to purchase Blackacre for $100,000. The contract is in writing and in all respects appears complete on its face. Prior to the signing of the contract and in

---

56. Fortune Furniture Mfg. v. Pate's Elec., 356 So.2d 1176 (Miss.1978); FDIC v. First Mtge. Investors, 76 Wis.2d 151, 250 N.W.2d 362 (1977).

57. Professor Murray has sought to demonstrate that this notion is nebulous and probably unnecessary. See Murray II, supra n.13, at 1364–66.

58. For a detailed treatment of the position of the Restatement (Second) of Contracts, see Murray II, supra n. 13.

59. See Rs. 2d § 213 cmt a; see also Lane v. Pfeifer, 264 Ark. 162, 568 S.W.2d 212 (1978).

60. See 48 ALI Proceedings 226 (1971); Murray II, supra n.13, at 1362.

61. See Rs. 2d § 209 cmt c.

62. 5 Williston § 633 (3d ed.).

63. 3 Corbin §§ 573–596.

order to induce B's assent, A orally promises B, in the presence of a number of reputable witnesses, to remove an unsightly shack on A's land across the road from Blackacre if B will sign the contract. May this oral promise be admitted into evidence as part of the contract?[64] This depends upon whether the writing is a total integration.[65]

It is clear that the parties did not intend the writing to be a total integration. B did not subjectively intend a total integration. Under an objective test of B's reasonable understanding of A's intention, the parties have not manifested an intent to have a total integration. Williston argues that the evidence must be excluded because if the intention to have a total integration were to be determined by the ordinary process of determining intention, the parol evidence rule would be emasculated; the very existence of the collateral agreement would conclusively indicate that the parties intended only a partial integration;[66] the only question that would be presented is whether the alleged prior or contemporaneous agreement was made. Williston makes it clear that in determining the issue of total integration the fact of agreement is irrelevant and thus he excludes the evidence of prior and oral contemporaneous agreements in making this determination.[67] In addition, his rules for determining the existence of a total integration do not seek out the actual intention of the parties in determining whether the writing was a complete integration.[68]

Corbin's notion is to ascertain the actual manifested intention of the parties and he is willing to receive evidence of prior negotiations.[69] As we have seen, the UCC and the Restatement (Second) are substantially in accord with Corbin's approach.[70]

§ 3.5   Is the Offered Term Consistent or Contradictory?

Several times we have touched upon the rule that a partial integration may not be contradicted but may be supplemented by consistent additional terms. Is there always a clear distinction between a contradictory and a consistent term? For example, if a written real estate contract lists a number of obligations of the seller but the buyer offers proof that the seller orally assumed an additional obligation, would the term offered impliedly contradict the writing? Some cases have held the offered term is inconsistent because it contradicts an inference that all of the seller's obligations were listed in the contract;[1] such a holding converts the writing into a total integration.

---

64. Facts suggested by Mitchill v. Lath, 247 N.Y. 377, 160 N.E. 646, 68 ALR 239 (1928).

65. The possible application of promissory estoppel to cases of this kind is considered at § 6.1 infra.

66. 4 Williston § 633 (3d ed.).

67. 4 Williston § 633 (3d ed.).

68. See § 3.4(c) supra.

69. See § 3.4(d) supra.

70. See § 3.4(e) and (g) supra.

§ 3.5

1. See, e.g., Mitchill v. Lath, 247 N.Y. 377, 160 N.E. 646, 68 ALR 239 (1928); see also 4 Williston § 642 (3d ed.).

A more difficult problem is presented when the additional term contradicts not an explicit term but an implied in fact or an implied in law term. For example, if a writing is silent as to the time of performance, it is implied in law that the parties intended performance to be within a reasonable time. Under some of the cases, if a party offered evidence of an agreement that performance would take place at a particular time, the evidence would be excluded because it contradicts an implied term.[2] There is no clear distinction between implications of fact that in theory become part of the agreement by consent and rules of law that are read into the agreement by the court in order to fill its gaps.[3] Both Williston and Corbin appear to favor the rule that an implied in law term may be contradicted.[4] The cases under the UCC have taken the position that, to be inconsistent, a term must contradict an express term of the integration.[5] Many non-UCC cases disagree.[6]

Where the contradicted term is implied in law, courts, are less likely to exclude the proffered term than in the case of an implied in fact term.[7] Masterson v. Sine illustrates this problem.[8] D.M. and his wife had conveyed a ranch to D.M.'s sister and her husband. The deed contained an option to repurchase. In time, D.M. was adjudicated a bankrupt. D.M.'s trustee in bankruptcy sought to exercise the option to purchase on behalf of the creditors. D.M.'s sister and her husband asserted that there was a prior oral agreement that the option to purchase was personal to D.M. and his wife. If this agreement in fact was made and was proved, the option could not be exercised by the trustee in bankruptcy. The admissibility of this evidence was decided under Williston's rule. The majority concluded that it would have been natural not to include this term in the deed because of the close relationship of the parties and also because it would be natural not to include all of the terms agreed upon in a deed, typically a barebones instrument.[9] Thus, the majority concluded that there was only a partial integration, holding that the

---

2. See 4 Williston § 640 (3d ed.), but see 11 Williston § 1295 (3d ed.). Some courts, however, admit such evidence on the issue of what is a reasonable time. Sweet I, supra § 3.2 n.20, at 1039. Admitting evidence of an implied term in the face of a merger clause is Top of Track Assocs. v. Lewiston Raceways, 654 A.2d 1293 (Me.1995).

3. "There is no clear line between implications of fact and rules of law filling gaps; although fairly clear examples of each can be given, other cases will involve almost imperceptible shadings." Rs. 2d § 216 cmt b, § 204 cmt e, § 214 cmt c; Hayden v. Hoadley, 94 Vt. 345, 111 A. 343 (1920); 4 Williston § 640 (3d ed.); 4 Williston § 640 (3d ed.).

4. 3 Corbin § 593; 4 Williston § 640 (3d ed.).

5. Anderson & Nafziger v. G.T. Newcomb, Inc., 100 Idaho 175, 595 P.2d 709 (1979); Snyder v. Herbert Greenbaum &

Assoc., 38 Md.App. 144, 380 A.2d 618 (1977); Hunt Foods & Indus. v. Doliner, 26 A.D.2d 41, 270 N.Y.S.2d 937 (1966); Wallach, supra § 3.2 n.16, at 674–76. For an extended discussion as it relates to the UCC, see Broude, supra § 3.4 n.52.

6. McAbee Constr. v. U.S., 97 F.3d 1431 (Fed.Cir.1996) (contract permitting the deposit of waste; absence of a height restriction cannot be contradicted by term setting such a restriction); Storts v. Hardee's Food Sys., 919 F.Supp. 1513 (D.Kan.1996).

7. See 4 Williston § 640 (3d ed.) (collecting cases).

8. 68 Cal.2d 222, 65 Cal.Rptr. 545, 436 P.2d 561 (1968). For an excellent discussion of this area, see Hadjiyannakis, The Parol Evidence Rule and Implied Terms: The Sounds of Silence, 54 Fordham L.Rev. 35 (1986).

9. See § 3.4(c) supra.

non-assignability term was a consistent additional term even though it contradicted an implied in law term of the writing—namely the free assignability of the option.

The cases discussed above relate to whether an implied term or inference may be contradicted. It is equally difficult to determine whether an offered term contradicts an express term of the agreement. For example, is a demand note (a promissory note stating it is payable on demand) contradicted by evidence that it was to be paid only out of the proceeds of a sale? The cases are in conflict.[10] Is an agreement that calls for the sale of a specific quantity of goods contradicted by evidence of a custom to the effect that quantity terms in such contracts "are mere projections to be adjusted according to market, forces?" The court in *Columbia Nitrogen v. Royster Co.*,[11] held that there was no contradiction. In sum, there is little or no consistency on the question of what is contradictory and what is consistent. A UCC case has defined "inconsistency" as "the absence of reasonable harmony in terms of the language and respective obligations of the parties."[12]

§ 3.6 Merger Clauses

A merger clause states that the writing is a final, complete, and exclusive statement of all of the terms agreed on.[1] Williston's first rule, which is followed by most courts, is that a merger clause will ordinarily resolve the issue of total integration.[2] The only two exceptions are where the instrument is obviously incomplete on its face and where the merger clause was included in the instrument as a result of fraud or mistake or for any reason that is sufficient to set aside a contract.[3] Note that under these exceptions, the merger clause alone would be voidable whereas § 3.7 deals with the situation where the entire contract is voidable.[4]

Although Williston's position on merger clauses continues the traditional rule earlier established under the "four corners" and "collateral contract" concepts, and the vast majority of courts still follow it,[5] there is some motion in the other direction. There is now some authority to the effect that a merger clause is only one of the factors to be considered in determining whether there is a total integration.[6] The suggestion

---

10.   Compare Mozingo v. North Carolina Nat. Bank, 31 N.C.App. 157, 229 S.E.2d 57 (1976), rev. denied, with London & Lancashire Indem. v. Allen, 272 Wis. 75, 74 N.W.2d 793 (1956).

11.   451 F.2d 3 (4th Cir.1971).

12.   Luria Bros. & Co. v. Pielet Bros., Scrap Iron & Metal, 600 F.2d 103, 111 (7th Cir.1979); see also Anderson & Nafziger v. G.T. Newcomb, Inc., 100 Idaho 175, 595 P.2d 709 (1979).

§ 3.6

1.   White & Summers, Uniform Commercial Code § 2–12 (4th ed.).

2.   See § 3.4(c) supra.

3.   See § 3.4(c) supra.

4.   The distinction between voidability of the merger clause and voidability of the contract is not always observed; see e.g., White & Summers § 2–12.

5.   Hoeker v. Department, 171 Vt. 620, 765 A.2d 495 (2000); Wallach, supra § 3.2 n.16, at 677–78.

6.   See Corbin § 578; Murray on Contracts § 84(C) (2) (4thed.); see also Betz Labs. v. Hines, 647 F.2d 402 (3d Cir.1981); Luther Williams, Jr., Inc. v. Johnson, 229 A.2d 163 (D.C.1967); Zwierzycki v. Owens, 499 P.2d 996 (Wyo.1972).

gaining currency is that the merger clause should not have any effect unless the clause was actually agreed upon.[7] This approach is based upon notions ordinarily discussed under the headings of Duty to Read, Unconscionability and Contracts of Adhesion.[8] This is a sensible approach since it is logical to make a distinction between a "dickered" merger clause and one that is merely "boiler plate."[9]

A case discussed above indicates that a merger clause should not rule out evidence of a usage of the trade and a course of dealing[10] unless specific reference is made to this type of evidence. This seems clearly correct under the UCC. How specific must the clause be? For example, must the clause negate the usage being offered or only usages in general? It would seem to be necessary for the clause to exclude the specific usage or course of dealing. Otherwise the modernization of the law of evidence by UCC § 2–202 would easily be thwarted by boilerplate exclusions of all usages and courses of dealing.

§ 3.7   Rule Inapplicable Until It Is Decided That There Is a Contract

Parol evidence is admissible to show that a writing that appears to be a contract was never formed.[1] Even in the face of a merger clause, parol evidence is admissible to show that the agreement is void or voidable or to show grounds for granting or denying reformation, specific performance or other remedy.[2] A good example is duress; it may be shown that a party was forced into signing what is or appears to be an integrated writing.[3] All "defect in formation" cases are not equally simple and some require extended discussion.

(a) Writing Was Not Intended to Be Operative

A party may testify that what appears to be a total integration was never intended to be operative—in other words, that it was a sham or non-final agreement.[4] This rule is a logical emanation of the analytical

---

7. See Broude, supra § 3.4 n.52, at 897–99. Interestingly, comment 3 to UCC § 2–202 originally contained language referring to the effect of a merger clause "specifically agreed to by both parties." This language, however, was deleted between 1950 and 1952. See id. at 889 & n.36. See Betaco v. Cessna Aircraft, 32 F.3d 1126 (7th Cir. 1994) (merger clause is "strong evidence" of integration). The revision draft explicitly "takes no position on the evidentiary strength of a merger clause." Section 2–202 cmt 4.

8. Seibel v. Layne & Bowler, 56 Or.App. 387, 641 P.2d 668 (1982), rev. denied; see ch. 9 infra.

9. Rs. 2d § 216 cmt e; see O'Keeffe v. Hicks, 74 A.D.2d 919, 426 N.Y.S.2d 315 (1980).

10. Columbia Nitrogen v. Royster Co., 451 F.2d 3 (4th Cir.1971); accord, C–Thru

Container v. Midland Mfg., 533 N.W.2d 542 (Iowa 1995).

§ 3.7

1. Murray I, supra § 3.2 n.41, at 343–44; Wallach, supra § 3.2 n.16, at 654.

2. Branstetter v. Cox, 209 Kan. 332, 496 P.2d 1345 (1972); Broome Constr. v. Beaver Lake Recreational Ctr., 229 So.2d 545 (Miss.1969); Mitchell v. Kimbrough, 491 P.2d 289 (Okl.1971); Nat. Bank of Commerce v. Thomsen, 80 Wn.2d 406, 495 P.2d 332 (1972); Rs. 2d § 214(d), (e) & cmt c.

3. See §§ 9.1 to 9.8 infra; 4 Williston § 634 (3d ed.).

4. Johnston v. Holiday Inns, 565 F.2d 790 (1st Cir.1977); Arnold Palmer Golf v. Fuqua Indus., 541 F.2d 584 (6th Cir.1976); Drink, Inc. v. Martinez, 89 N.M. 662, 556

basis of the parol evidence rule, because a sham agreement is not a contract.[5] It is, however, at war with the notion that the parol evidence rule is designed to prevent perjury. A party who has decided to commit perjury may simply testify falsely that the purported agreement was a sham instead of testifying falsely as to the existence of an additional or contradictory term. If the testimony is believed, the perjurer will have succeeded in piercing the protective shield of the parol evidence rule. Here, there is a clash between the policy basis of the rule and the analytic rationale; the analytic rationale displaces the policy basis. The same observation applies to the subsections that follow.

(b) Contract Subject to an Express Condition

Where the parties agree that a condition precedent must occur before the contract is effective, it is generally agreed that the failure of the condition to occur may be shown despite a writing or other record that otherwise would be deemed a total integration.[6] This is because of the absence of finality. Thus, even if there is a merger clause,[7] it may be shown that the instrument was handed over to another with an oral condition attached to delivery.[8] The theory is that the agreement is not to take effect until the condition occurs and thus there is no contract to be added to or contradicted until that time.[9]

This rule presents a conceptual difficulty that is not encountered in the case of a defense such as duress; the condition precedent is a term of the parties' overall agreement and therefore arguably could be made subject to the parol evidence rule.[10] Some courts have made what appears to be a compromise. They have adopted the rule stated above, but do not apply it where the alleged condition precedent to the formation of the contract contradicts a specific term of the writing.[11] If conditions precedent to the formation of a contract are expressed in the writing, some courts refuse to permit evidence of other oral conditions precedent upon the theory of an implied contradiction.[12]

P.2d 348 (1976); Annot., 71 A.L.R.2d 382 (1960). There are, however, contrary negotiable instrument cases. See Houck v. Martin, 82 Ill.App.3d 205, 37 Ill.Dec. 531, 402 N.E.2d 421 (1980); Peacock Holdings v. Keefe & Keefe, 232 A.D.2d 331, 648 N.Y.S.2d 608 (1996); but see Long Island Trust v. International Inst. for Packaging Educ., 38 N.Y.2d 493, 381 N.Y.S.2d 445, 344 N.E.2d 377 (1976); Roberts v. Maze, 161 Or.App. 441, 985 P.2d 211 (1999).

5. See § 2.3 supra & 4.6 infra.

6. 3 Corbin, 589; Nord v. Herreid, 305 N.W.2d 337 (Minn.1981); Rs. 2d § 217 (1981); Rs. 1st § 241.

7. Luther Williams, Jr., Inc. v. Johnson, 229 A.2d 163 (D.C.App.1967); see also 1 N.Y. State Law Revision Comm'n, 1955 Report 683. Some cases disagree. See Broude supra § 3.4 n.52, at 897–98.

8. Paine v. Paine, 458 A.2d 420 (Me. 1983); Marquess v. Geuy, 47 Or.App. 351, 614 P.2d 142 (1980); Sweet I, supra § 3.2 n. 20, at 1039–40.

9. Hicks v. Bush, 10 N.Y.2d 488, 225 N.Y.S.2d 34, 180 N.E.2d 425 (1962); but see Bank of Suffolk v. Kite, 49 N.Y.2d 827, 404 N.E.2d 1323, 427 N.Y.S.2d 782 (1980) (negotiable instrument).

10. Wallach, supra § 3.2 n.16, at 654.

11. Mizuna, Ltd. v. Crossland Fed. Sav. Bank, 90 F.3d 650 (2d Cir.1996); Bank of Suffolk County v. Kite, 49 N.Y.2d 827, 427 N.Y.S.2d 782, 404 N.E.2d 1323 (1980).

12. E.g., Stafford v. Russell, 117 Cal. App.2d 326, 255 P.2d 814 (1953); Whirlpool v. Regis Leasing, 29 A.D.2d 395, 288 N.Y.S.2d 337 (1968); see Antonellis v. Northgate Constr., 362 Mass. 847, 291 N.E.2d 626 (1973); Hamon v. Akers, 159 W.Va. 396, 222 S.E.2d 822 (1976).

Frequently, the condition that is held to be a condition precedent to the formation of a contract operates logically as a condition precedent to the performance of the contract. A good illustration is the seminal case of Pym v. Campbell.[13] In Pym, the parties entered into an agreement to buy and sell a certain patent. The sale, however, was orally conditioned upon the approval of the patent by the purchaser's engineer. The court held that the oral condition was admissible because until the condition occurred no binding contract existed. Logically, however, there was a binding contract when the parties mutually agreed and thus the condition was actually a condition precedent to the performance of the contract. There is a binding contract because the purchaser has a duty to act in good faith in seeking the approval of the third party. If this is so, the case should have been decided under the rules stated in section 3.4 relating to the admissibility of evidence of additional oral terms to supplement a written contract.[14] Nonetheless, holdings of this type recur with some frequency.

(c) Fraud

The general rule is that a proof of fraud in the inducement may be shown to avoid the written agreement even in the face of a merger clause[15] and even if the evidence offered specifically contradicts the writing or a merger clause.[16] Some cases, however, hold that if the written contract includes a "specific disclaimer of the very representation later alleged to be foundation for rescission" the parol evidence rule will exclude the allegation of fraud.[17]

Promissory fraud occurs when a party makes a promise with the intent not to perform it. The majority of jurisdictions now hold that promissory fraud is a misrepresentation of fact, and constitutes fraud in the inducement that can give rise to an action for deceit, avoidance of the contract, or its reformation.[18] Nevertheless, the question remains

---

13. 6 El. & Bl. 370 (Q.B.1856). There were predecessors. Field v. Biddle, 2 Dall. 171 (Pa.1792).

14. Corbin provides an illustration of a genuine condition precedent to the formation of the contract: A makes a written offer to B and B is to accept by signing. A, however, had orally told B that the offer is to be operative only if a certain event happens. Here, the condition is clearly a condition precedent to the existence of the contract. 3 Corbin § 589, at 536–37; Rs. 2d § 217 ill. 1.

15. S.C. Johnson & Son v. Dowbrands, 167 F.Supp.2d 657 (D.Del.2001); Parker v. McGaha, 294 Ala. 702, 321 So.2d 182 (1975); 3 Corbin § 580; contra, Coram Healthcare v. Aetna U.S. Healthcare, 94 F.Supp.2d 589 (E.D.Pa.1999). Nor does the parol evidence rule prevent an action for reformation. See §§ 9.31 to 9.36 infra.

16. Keller v. A.O. Smith Harves. Prods., 819 P.2d 69 (Colo.1991); Barash v. Pennsylvania Terminal Real Estate, 26 N.Y.2d 77, 308 N.Y.S.2d 649, 256 N.E.2d 707 (1970); Marshall v. Keaveny, 38 N.C.App. 644, 248 S.E.2d 750 (1978); 3 Corbin § 580; contra, 1726 Cherry St. Ptshp. v. Bell Atlantic Properties, 439 Pa.Super. 141, 653 A.2d 663 (1995).

17. E.g., Grumman Allied Indus. v. Rohr Indus., 748 F.2d 729 (2d Cir.1984); Bank of America v. Pendergrass, 4 Cal.2d 258, 48 P.2d 659 (1935); Danann Realty v. Harris, 5 N.Y.2d 317, 184 N.Y.S.2d 599, 157 N.E.2d 597 (1959); Note, 1997 Colum. Bus L. Rev. 399.

18. U.S. v. 1,557.28 Acres of Land, 486 F.2d 445 (10th Cir.1973); Entron, Inc. v. General Cablevision, 435 F.2d 995 (5th Cir. 1970); Walker v. Woodall, 288 Ala. 510, 262 So.2d 756 (1972); Abbott v. Abbott, 188

whether such a promise may be shown by parol evidence in the face of a total integration. The cases are in utter confusion.[19] Ultimately the question is the weight to be given the policy underlying the parol evidence rule relative to the policy underlying the suppression of fraud.[20] It should be no contest. Fraud corrupts everything it touches.

A person who has signed what appears to be a contract may be able to establish a claim of fraud in the execution. Fraud in the *inducement* relates to false statements of fact that induce a party into contracting. Fraud in the *execution* relates to deception about the nature of the instrument. This may occur when one party tells the other that an document is a receipt, when, instead, it purports to be a contract.[21] The assumption, of course, is that the instrument appears to be an integration and the question is whether fraud in the execution may be shown in the face of that appearance. There are two views. One is that the failure to read the instrument precludes this evidence from being offered.[22] The modern view reaches the opposite conclusion on the theory that fraud is a greater evil than the failure to read.[23]

(d) Mistake

If there is a mistake recognized in law, an agreement induced by it is ordinarily voidable;[24] the parol evidence rule does not prevent a party from showing that a contract is void or voidable.[25] Alternatively, a party may claim that an integrated writing does not reflect the true agreement of the parties. The writing may be reformed to reflect the true agreement if certain conditions are met.[26] Compliance with the parol evidence rule is not one of these conditions.[27] In other words, the parol evidence

Neb. 61, 195 N.W.2d 204 (1972); Anderson v. Tri–State Home Improv., 268 Wis. 455, 67 N.W.2d 853 (1955); Rs. 2d § 171(2); Prosser & Keeton on Torts 763–65 (5th Ed.); 12 Williston § 1496 (3d ed.); Keeton, Fraud: Statements of Intention, 15 Tex. L.Rev. 185 (1937); Note, 38 Colum.L.Rev. 1461 (1938).

19. Professor Sweet has presented an outstanding analysis of the problem. Sweet, Promissory Fraud and the Parol Evidence Rule, 41 Cal.L.Rev. 877 (1961) [Sweet II]. According to Sweet, the majority of courts allow the evidence despite the parol evidence rule; a minority opt instead for excluding the evidence and strengthening the rule as a matter of public policy. Id. at 888–90. He also points out that admissibility may depend upon whether the promise is consistent with the writing, and upon what relief is sought. For example, on the basis of promissory fraud, rescission is more likely to be granted than reformation. Id. at 890–93. On the related question of promissory fraud and the Statute of Frauds, see Comment, 53 Fordham L.Rev. 1231 (1985).

20. Sweet II, supra n.20, at 888.

21. Whether this kind of fraud makes the agreement void or voidable is discussed in § 9.22 infra.

22. E.g., Mitchell v. Excelsior Sales & Imports, 243 Ga. 813, 256 S.E.2d 785 (1979); Knight & Bostwick v. Moore, 203 Wis. 540, 234 N.W. 902 (1931).

23. Belew v. Griffis, 249 Ark. 589, 460 S.W.2d 80 (1970); Estes v. Republic Nat. Bank, 462 S.W.2d 273 (Tex.1970); see § 9.22 infra.

24. For mistake, see §§ 9.25 to 9.30 infra.

25. E.g., F.R. Hoar & Sons v. McElroy Plumbing & Heating, 680 F.2d 1115 (5th Cir.1982); General Equip. Mfrs. v. Bible Press, 10 Mich.App. 676, 160 N.W.2d 370 (1968); Williams v. Glash, 789 S.W.2d 261 (Tex.1990); but see Paul's Rod & Bearing v. Kelly, 847 S.W.2d 68 (Mo.App.1991) (no parol evidence of misunderstanding).

26. See §§ 9.31 to 9.36 infra.

27. Sweet I, supra § 3.2 n. 20, at 1042; Central Transp. v. Board of Assessment App., 490 Pa. 486, 417 A.2d 144 (1980).

rule does not bar reformation even though the result is the enforcement of the alleged oral agreement.[28]

(e) *Illegality and Unconscionability*

Illegality may make a contract either void or voidable.[29] In either case, parol evidence is admissible to prove the illegality even though the evidence contradicts the integration.[30] For example, what the agreement describes as a liquidated damages clause may be shown to be a penalty. Thus, the clause is excised because it is contrary to public policy and the parol evidence rule does not prevent the process.[31] The same is true under modern notions of unconscionability.[32] Under this doctrine, a clause may, under some circumstances, be excised from an agreement because it is unduly oppressive or there was not "true assent" to a given term; the parol evidence rule will not deter a court from receiving parol evidence to show oppression or the lack of true assent.[33]

(f) *Consideration*

It is frequently said that the parol evidence rule does not preclude a showing of absence of consideration.[34] The issue arises in radically different fact patterns. First, suppose a written promise recites that it is in consideration of $1,000, in hand paid, receipt of which is acknowledged. A majority of the cases have held that a recital of consideration in the writing may be contradicted upon the theory that the rule does not bar the contradiction of recitals of fact.[35] A minority reaches an opposite conclusion upon the theory that the parties are estopped from contradicting the writing or that the recital gives rise to an implied promise to pay. The minority view is applied primarily in option and guaranty cases.[36] Because it is a factual question, parol evidence is admissible to show the identity of the contracting parties.[37]

However, the situation is somewhat different when there is an attempt to show that the only promise made by one party in what appears to be a binding total integration was not in fact made. A few

---

28. Neeley v. Kelsch, 600 P.2d 979 (Utah 1979).

29. § 22.2 infra.

30. 3 Corbin § 580; see Bunn v. Weyerhaeuser, 268 Ark. 445, 598 S.W.2d 54 (1980).

31. See §§ 14.31 to 14.34 infra; 3 Corbin § 580.

32. Mellon Bank v. Aetna Business Credit, 619 F.2d 1001 (3d Cir.1980).

33. See §§ 9.37 to 9.46 infra; Murray II, supra § 3.4 n.13, at 1343.

34. Sweet I, supra § 3.2 n. 20, at 1040. Weintraub v. Cobb Bank & Trust, 249 Ga. 148, 288 S.E.2d 553 (1982). Discussed here is lack of consideration, rather than failure of consideration. Failure of consideration

relates to performance of the contract rather than its formation and is thus unrelated to the parol evidence rule. Sweet I supra § 3.2 n. 20, at 1041 & n. 35; see § 11.21 infra.

35. 3 Corbin § 586.

36. See Smith v. Wheeler, 233 Ga. 166, 210 S.E.2d 702 (1974); Real Estate Co. v. Rudolph, 301 Pa. 502, 153 A. 438 (1930). The Rs. 2d takes the position that promises to keep an offer firm or guarantying credit are binding if they are in writing and contain a "recital of purported consideration." Rs. 2d §§ 87, 88; see § 4.6 infra.

37. Affordable Elegance v. Worldspan, 774 A.2d 320 (D.C.App.2001) (unclear which of several companies controlled by agent was a party).

cases have held that the writing may not be contradicted.[38] The majority view is to the effect that it may be contradicted because of the rule that the parol evidence rule does not apply until it is decided that there is a contract.[39]

The problem is reversed where a writing fails to show consideration on one or both sides of a writing. Here the rule is that it may in fact be shown that consideration exists even if the consideration takes the form of a promise. This does not create any serious theoretical problems because a look at the writing would indicate that it is not complete and thus at most it is a partial integration. The offered term is obviously not contradictory.[40]

(g) The Rule of Non-formation of Contract Under the UCC

The UCC makes no reference to the general rule that a party may show that there was no contract despite the existence of an integration. However, UCC § 1–103 provides that where the UCC is silent, the common law should be applied. This section has been applied to permit evidence of fraud in the inducement even though fraud is not mentioned in § 2–202, the parol evidence provision.[41] There have also been UCC cases in the area of "conditions precedent" discussed above.[42] The cases assumed that the doctrine was applicable even though § 2–202 does not mention it.[43] It may safely be assumed that the courts will apply all aspects of the non-formation rule to UCC cases.[44]

§ 3.8 Application of the Rule to Third Persons

Are non-parties bound by the parol evidence rule? The answer should be, yes, as to third party beneficiaries and assignees, because the policy of the rule should be the same whether a party or a third party claiming under the contract is seeking to defeat the integration.[1] There is generally no good reason to invoke the rule against strangers, such as tax collectors or others.[2] The holdings and generalizations in the cases

---

38. See W.P. Fuller & Co. v. McClure, 48 Cal.App. 185, 191 P. 1027 (1920); Schneider v. Turner, 130 Ill. 28, 22 N.E. 497 (1889); In re Emery's Estate, 362 Pa. 142, 66 A.2d 262 (1949); Lakeway v. Leon Howard, Inc., 585 S.W.2d 660 (Tex.1979); 4 Williston, § 642, at 1071 n. 15 (3d ed.); Annot., 100 ALR 17 (1936).

39. 3 Corbin §§ 577, 586; see § 3.2 supra; cf. Rs. 2d § 218.

40. Rs. 2d § 218; Rs. 1st § 214.

41. Associated Hardware Supply v. Big Wheel Distrib., 355 F.2d 114 (3d Cir.1965); George Robberecht Seafood v. Maitland Bros., 220 Va. 109, 255 S.E.2d 682 (1979). The revision comment 5 to § 2–202 explicitly states that evidence of fraud and the like are not barred by that Section.

42. See § 3.7(b) supra.

43. Whirlpool v. Regis Leasing, 29 A.D.2d 395, 288 N.Y.S.2d 337 (1968); Hunt Foods & Indus. v. Doliner, 26 A.D.2d 41, 270 N.Y.S.2d 937 (1966); see Broude, supra § 3.4 n.52, at 890–99.

44. White & Summers, Uniform Commercial Code § 2–11 (4th ed.).

§ 3.8

1. Mies Eqpt, Inc. v. NCI Bldg. Sys., 167 F.Supp.2d 1077 (D.Minn.2001); Cate v. Irvin, 44 Ark.App. 39, 866 S.W.2d 423, 486 (1993); Vu v. Pacific Ocean Marketplace, 36 P.3d 165 (Colo.App.2001); Ambrose Mar-Elia Co. v. Dinstein, 151 A.D.2d 416, 543 N.Y.S.2d 658, 660 (1989).

2. SIN, Inc. v. Department of Finance, 126 A.D.2d 339, 513 N.Y.S.2d 430, 434 (1987), affd; BRB Printing v. Buchanan, 878 F.Supp. 1049 (E.D.Mich.1995) (rule not

are in conflict.[3] Most of the cases involve releases[4] and should be read in the light of the history of some of the primitive rules governing the effect of a release on a joint tortfeasor.[5]

C. INTERPRETATION

Table of Sections

§ 3.9   Introduction

Interpretation of a promise or agreement is the "ascertainment of its meaning."[1] At times a distinction is drawn between interpretation and construction. Construction relates to the legal effect of the words used. The construction placed upon an agreement will not necessarily coincide with the meaning of the parties.[2] The distinction is, for the most part, not dwelled upon by the courts, with the result that it is difficult to tell which process is being employed.[3] For these reasons this distinction will not be pursued here.

In deciding what a communication means, there are two fundamental questions. First, whose meaning is to be given to a communication; some frame this question in terms of what standard of interpretation is to be used?[4] The second question is what evidence may be taken into

applicable to transaction with president of contracting party); Fulton v. L & N Consultants, 715 F.2d 1413 (10th Cir.1982) (broker); Cohan v. Sicular, 214 A.D.2d 637, 625 N.Y.S.2d 278 (1995) (broker).

3.   3 Corbin § 596; 4 Williston § 647 (3d ed.); Comment, 41 Fordham L.Rev. 945 (1973); Annot., 13 ALR3d 313 (1967); Habets v. Swanson, 303 Mont. 410, 16 P.3d 1035 (2000).

4.   Atlantic Northern Airlines v. Schwimmer, 12 N.J. 293, 96 A.2d 652 (1953); Oxford Commercial v. Landau, 12 N.Y.2d 362, 239 N.Y.S.2d 865, 190 N.E.2d 230, 13 A.L.R.3d 309 (1963).

5.   See §§ 21.10 to 21.11 infra.

§ 3.9

1.   Rs. 2d § 200; see also Rs. 1st § 226.

2.   Fashion Fabrics of Iowa v. Retail Investors, 266 N.W.2d 22 (Iowa 1978); 5 Corbin § 24.3 (Kniffin 1998) ; 4 Williston § 602 (3d ed.); Rs. 2d § 200 cmt c. Construction is a question of law. Farm Bureau Mut. Ins. v. Sandbulte, 302 N.W.2d 104 (Iowa 1981); Park View Manor v. Housing Authority, 300 N.W.2d 218 (N.D.1980).

3.   See generally Friedman, Law Rules and Interpretation of Written Documents, 59 Nw.U.L.Rev. 751 (1965); Patterson, The Interpretation and Construction of Contracts, 64 Colum.L.Rev. 833 (1964).

4.   The Rs. 1st § 227 lists six possible standards of interpretation, that is, six van-

account in applying the standard of interpretation selected. The second phase engages the parol evidence rule. Here, however, the issue relates to the admissibility of extrinsic evidence on the question of *meaning*. By way of contrast, in the preceding sections the discussion of the parol evidence rule related to the admissibility of *agreements* made prior to or contemporaneous with the writing or other record. Extrinsic evidence is a very broad term. It includes not only prior and contemporaneous statements, but also surrounding circumstances (e.g. market conditions), evidence of subjective intention, what the parties said to each other with respect to meaning, usages, course of dealing and course of performance.

Standard academic thinking, reflected in the treatises of Corbin,[5] Farnsworth,[6] Murray,[7] and Williston[8] is to the effect that the topic of the parol evidence rule is distinct from the topic of interpretation. The thought is that the parol evidence rule determines the provisions of the contract. Once the content of the contract has been established, the process of interpretation is a logically distinct step and the admissibility of parol evidence as an aid to interpretation is unrelated to the parol evidence rule. The logic of this dichotomy is unassailable, so is its impracticality. The very same words offered as an additional term that are rejected because the court deems the writing to be a total integration, can be offered as an aid to interpretation of an ambiguous written term. Able courts look at both proffers of evidence as governed by the "parol evidence rule."[9]

As in the case of the preceding discussion (sections 3.2 to 3.8) there is a wide variety of views and little consistency in results. It has been observed that there is no "lawyer's Paradise [where] all words have a fixed, precisely ascertained meaning, * * * and where, if the writer has been careful, a lawyer, having a document referred to him may sit in his chair, inspect the text, and answer all questions without raising his

tage points which might be used in the interpretation process. These standards are:

"1. The standard of general usage;

"2. A standard of limited usage, which would attach the meaning given to language in a particular locality, or by a sect or those engaged in a particular occupation, or by an alien population or those using a local dialect (the distinction between 1 and 2 is a difference in degree, since generality of usage does not necessarily imply universality);

"3. A mutual standard, which would allow only such meaning as conforms to an intention common to both or all parties, and would attach this meaning although it violates the usage of all other persons;

"4. An individual standard, which would attach to words or other manifestations of intention whatever meaning the person employing them intended them to express, or that the person receiving the communication understood from it;

"5. A standard of reasonable expectation, which would attach to words or other man-

ifestations of intention the meaning which the party employing them should reasonably have apprehended that they would convey to the other party;

"6. A standard of reasonable understanding, which would attach to words or other manifestations of intention the meaning which the person to whom the manifestations are addressed might reasonably give to them."

5.   3 Corbin § 579.

6.   Farnsworth ch.7(B) is entitled "Determining the Subject Matter to be Interpreted." Ch. 7(C) is captioned "Interpretation".

7.   Murray on Contracts § 82(A) (4th ed.).

8.   4 Williston § 631 (3d ed.); but see id. § 632.

9.   See § 3.16 infra.

eyes."[10] Despite the accuracy of this observation, there is a strong school of thought that has taken an approach that goes under the name of the Plain Meaning Rule.

§ 3.10   The Plain Meaning Rule and Ambiguity

The Plain Meaning Rule states that if a writing, or the term in question, appears to be plain and unambiguous on its face, its meaning must be determined from the four corners of the instrument without resort to extrinsic evidence of any kind.[1] As stated by one court, "When the language of the contract is clear, the court will presume that the parties intended what they expressed, even if the expression differs from the parties' intentions at the time they created the contract."[2] There are variations. Some plain-meaning jurisdictions allow evidence of surrounding circumstances.[3] The plain meaning rule has been properly condemned because the meaning of words varies with the "verbal context and surrounding circumstances and purposes in view of the linguistic education and experience of their users and their hearers or readers (not excluding judges)."[4] Meaning may not be ascertained simply by reading the document.[5] Although the Plain Meaning Rule has been condemned by the writers,[6] the UCC,[7] the Restatement (Second)[8] and an increasing number of courts,[9] the great majority of jurisdictions still employ the rule.[10] The dictionary is often used as a corroborating source.[11] Some

---

10.   Thayer, supra § 3.1 n.1, at 428–429 (1898).

§ 3.10

1.   W.W.W. Associates v. Giancontieri, 77 N.Y.2d 157, 565 N.Y.S.2d 440, 566 N.E.2d 639 (1990).

2.   Nicholson Air Services v. Allegany County, 120 Md.App. 47, 706 A.2d 124 (1998).

3.   Mobil Exploration and Producing v. Dover Energy Exploration, 56 S.W.3d 772 (Tex.App.2001).

4.   3 Corbin § 579, at 225 n.74 (1964 supp).

5.   Corbin, The Interpretation of Words and the Parol Evidence Rule, 50 Cornell L.Q. 161, 187 (1965). See generally Levie, The Interpretation of Contracts in New York Under the Uniform Commercial Code, 10 N.Y.L.F. 350 (1964). Supporters of the plain meaning rule sometimes acknowledge this. "If the contractual language is clear and unambiguous, we presume that the parties meant what they actually said, regardless of what they actually intended." Aetna Ins. v. Aaron, 112 Md.App. 472, 685 A.2d 858 (1996). For the proposition that evidence of the surrounding circumstances are essential to determine intent, see Florida East Coast Ry. v. CSX Transp., 42 F.3d 1125 (7th Cir.1994).

6.   5 Corbin § 24.7 (Kniffin 1998); 9 Wigmore §§ 2461–62 (Chadbourn rev. 1981); 4 Williston § 629 (3d ed.); Kniffin, A New Trend in Contract Interpretation: The Search for Reality as Opposed to Virtual Reality, 74 Or.L.Rev.643 (1995); Zamir, The Inverted Hierarchy of Contract Interpretation and Supplementation, 97 Colum.L.Rev. 1710 (1997); but see Scott, The Case for Formalism in Relational Contract, 94 Nw. L.Rev. 847 (2000).

7.   UCC § 2–202 cmt 2, revision cmt 6 states that it takes no position on this question

8.   Rs. 2d §§ 200–204.

9.   Mellon Bank v. Aetna Business Credit, 619 F.2d 1001 (3d Cir.1980) (Pa. law); Prichard v. Clay, 780 P.2d 359, 362 (Alaska 1989); Pacific Gas Elec. v. G.W. Thomas Drayage & Rigging, 69 Cal.2d 33, 69 Cal. Rptr. 561, 442 P.2d 641, 40 ALR3d 1373 (1968); Hilton Hotels v. Butch Lewis Productions, 107 Nev. 226, 808 P.2d 919 (1991); Mark V, Inc. v. Mellekas, 114 N.M. 778, 845 P.2d 1232, 1235 (1993); see also the U.N. Sales Convention Art. 8(3).

10.   E.g., Wonderland Shopping Center v. CDC Mortgage Capital, 274 F.3d 1085 (6th Cir.2001); Lion Oil v. Tosco, 90 F.3d 268 (8th Cir.1996) (Ark. law); Lambert v. Berkley South Condo. Assn., 680 So.2d 588

jurisdictions seem to have returned to a plain meaning approach after having adopted or flirted with more liberal approaches.[12]

Despite the dominance of the rule, there is a division of authority within jurisdictions that follow the plain meaning rule. The division concerns the question of whether extrinsic evidence is admissible to show that a term of the written agreement is ambiguous.[13] The more rigid approach is to bar evidence to demonstrate that what appears to be a plain meaning is actually ambiguous.[14] Although many jurisdictions rule that evidence is inadmissible to show the existence of an ambiguity, the apparent rigidity of this approach is mitigated by allowing a proffer of evidence. Counsel is permitted to inform the court what the nature of the alleged ambiguity is and what evidence is available to show the court the actual intended meaning.[15] Realistically viewed, such a proffer removes the blinders from the judge who is formally restricted to the four corners of the instrument.

Even in a plain meaning jurisdiction, if the term in question does not have a plain meaning it follows that the term is ambiguous, that is, it is susceptible to more than one meaning.[16] Thus, whether the attack on the World Trade Center was one insured "occurrence" is a question that cannot necessarily be determined solely from the four corners of an insurance binder.[17] It is for the court to say whether there is a "plain meaning" or whether an ambiguity exists.[18] Mere disagreement by the parties of the meaning of the contract at the time the dispute arises does not establish the existence of ambiguity.[19] Even a disagreement in the

(Fla.App.1996); Dawson v. Norfolk & Western Ry., 197 W.Va. 10, 475 S.E.2d 10 (1996); Burbank v. Wyodak Resources, 11 P.3d 943 (Wyo.2000).

11. Brown v. JMIC Life Ins., 222 Ga. App. 670, 474 S.E.2d 645 (1996); Krollman v. City of Hibbing, 550 N.W.2d 314 (Minn. App.1996); but see Bogle Farms v. Baca, 122 N.M. 422, 925 P.2d 1184 (1996) (whether sand and gravel are encompassed in the term "mineral" is to be determined on a case to case basis, depending on intent).

12. Nedlloyd Lines B.V. v. Superior Court, 3 Cal.4th 459, 11 Cal.Rptr.2d 330, 834 P.2d 1148 (1992); but see a narrow reading of this case in Kniffin, supra n.6, at 654–55 n.39; and see Prince supra § 3.1 n.5; Martin–Davidson, 25 Sw.U.L.Rev. 1 (1995); W.W.W. Associates v. Giancontieri, 77 N.Y.2d 157, 565 N.Y.S.2d 440, 566 N.E.2d 639 (1990).

13. Sumitomo Mach. v. AlliedSignal, 81 F.3d 328 (3d Cir.1996) (N.J. law) (evidence of circumstances admissible to show ambiguity); accord, R.T. Hepworth Co. v. Dependable Ins., 997 F.2d 315 (7th Cir.1993), cert. denied [but see Blue Cross & Blue Shield v. Blue Cross & Blue Shield Assn., 110 F.3d 318 (6th Cir.1997)]; Breslauer v. Fayston School Dist., 163 Vt. 416, 659 A.2d 1129 (1995); U.S. Life Credit Life Ins. v.

Williams, 129 Wn.2d 565, 919 P.2d 594 (1996).

14. Davenport Group MG v. Strategic Inv. Partners, 685 A.2d 715 (Del.Ch.1996); W.W.W. Assocs. v. Giancontieri, 77 N.Y.2d 157, 565 N.Y.S.2d 440, 566 N.E.2d 639 (1990); Doswell Ltd. Ptshp. v. Virginia Elec. & Power, 251 Va. 215, 468 S.E.2d 84 (1996); Wolter v. Equitable Resources Energy, 979 P.2d 948 (Wyo.1999).

15. See Donoghue v. IBC USA (Publications), 70 F.3d 206 (1st Cir.1995); American Flint Glass Workers v. Beaumont Glass, 62 F.3d 574 (3d Cir.1995).

16. Kaiser Aluminum v. Matheson, 681 A.2d 392 (Del.Supr.1996).

17. SR Int'l Business Ins. v. World Trade Center, 222 F.Supp.2d 385 (S.D.N.Y. 2002).

18. Id. It is no simple matter to reconcile the cases where the plain meaning rule has been applied with those holding that an ambiguity exists. Patterson, The Interpretation and Construction of Contracts, 64 Colum. L.Rev. 833, 839 (1964).

19. American States Ins. v. Hartford Cas. Ins., 950 F.Supp. 885 (C.D.Ill.1997); Fultz v. Shaffer, 111 Md.App. 278, 681 A.2d

case law concerning the meaning of a standard term does not necessarily make its meaning ambiguous.[20] Once it is found that an ambiguity exists, and conflicting extrinsic evidence is admitted, the jury determines the meaning.[21]

In the earlier cases, courts would admit extrinsic evidence to clarify a latent ambiguity but not a patent ambiguity.[22] These courts chose to decide what a patent ambiguity meant without the aid of extrinsic evidence.[23] Most of the modern cases, however, have abandoned the patent/latent distinction and hold that all relevant extrinsic evidence is admissible to clarify both types of ambiguities.[24] Williston's more enlightened approach, discussed next, undoubtedly had something to do with this change in attitude.

Even a plain meaning jurisdiction will admit parol evidence to define terms that, even if unambiguous, are not generally understood. For example, evidence may be taken of the meaning of "Amacid Blue Black KN."[25]

§ 3.11   Williston's Rules

(a) Interpreting Integrations

Williston does not follow the plain meaning rule, but he would not admit all types of extrinsic evidence and lays down different rules for integrations and for writings that are not integrations. As to integrated writings, Williston's standard of interpretation is the meaning that a reasonably intelligent person acquainted with all operative usages[1] and

568 (1996); Stuarts Draft Shopping Center v. S–D Assocs., 251 Va. 483, 468 S.E.2d 885 (1996).

20. O'Brien v. Progressive Northern Ins., 785 A.2d 281 (Del.2001).

21. Elam v. First Unum Life Ins., 346 Ark. 291, 57 S.W.3d 165 (2001).

22. Mass Appraisal Services v. Carmichael, 404 So.2d 666 (Ala.1981); McBaine, The Rule Against Disturbing Plain Meaning, 31 Calif.L.Rev. 145, 147 (1942). A patent ambiguity is one that is apparent on the face of the document, a latent ambiguity exists when the term in question appears clear but extrinsic evidence makes it ambiguous. St. Joseph Data Serv. v. Thomas Jefferson Life Ins., 73 Ill.App.3d 935, 30 Ill. Dec. 575, 393 N.E.2d 611 (1979); Hokama v. Relinc Corp., 57 Haw. 470, 559 P.2d 279 (1977). The best known illustration of a latent ambiguity is Raffles v. Wichelhaus, 159 Eng.Rep. 375 (Ex.1864) (the case of the two ships Peerless discussed below). In actuality, "[t]he old distinction between a patent and latent ambiguity was never more than 'an unprofitable subtlety.'" Thayer, supra § 3.1 n.1, at 424. The distinction is alive as applied to ambiguities in government contracts. Patent ambiguities are con-

strued against the contractor. P.R. Burke Corp. v. U.S., 277 F.3d 1346, 1355 (Fed.Cir. 2002). The distinction is made in Bourke v. Dun & Bradstreet, 159 F.3d 1032 (7th Cir. 1998), but the effect of the distinction is not as crucial as stated in the text.

23. McBaine, supra n.22, at 147; contra, Effinger v. Kenney, 115 U.S. 566 (1885) (U.S. or Confederate "dollar"); Reilly v. Insurance of North America, 32 A.D.2d 918, 302 N.Y.S.2d 435 (1969) (U.S. or Canadian "dollar"). For interpretation without the aid of parol evidence see § 3.13 infra.

24. Christopher v. Safeway Stores, 644 F.2d 467 (5th Cir.1981); Wigington v. Hill-Soberg Co., 396 So.2d 97 (Ala.1981); Cody v. Remington Elec. Shavers, 179 Conn. 494, 427 A.2d 810 (1980); Hokama v. Relinc Corp., 57 Haw. 470, 559 P.2d 279 (1977); but see Johnson Enterprises v. FPL Group, 162 F.3d 1290 (11th Cir.1998) (distinguishing patent and latent).

25. American Aniline Products v. Mitsui & Co., 190 A.D. 485, 489, 179 N.Y.S. 895, 898 (1920).

§ 3.11

1. On operative usages see § 3.17 infra.

knowing all of the circumstances prior to and contemporaneous with the making of the integration would attach to the integration or to any disputed term of the integration.[2] However, Williston would exclude what the parties said to each other about meaning (e.g. "buy" was to mean "sell") and what the parties subjectively believed the writing meant at the time of agreement.[3]

Williston's standards of interpretation may result in an interpretation that conforms to the intention of neither party.[4] For Williston the contract acquires a life and meaning of its own, separate and apart from the meaning the parties attach to their agreement. "It is not primarily the intention of the parties which the court is seeking, but the meaning of the words at the time and place when they were used."[5] He is explicit in stating why this should be so. "A facility and certainty of interpretation is obtained, which, though not ideal, is so much greater than is obtainable" by use of a less rigid standard.[6] The certainty so obtained is "more than adequate compensation for the slight restriction put upon the power to grant and contract."[7]

This rationale is the very heart of the divergence between the positions of Corbin and Williston. Corbin's position, as forcefully restated by Professor Murray, is that: "Any written expression of the agreement—whether it is not final, final, or final and complete—is nothing more than the manifestation of the agreement. It is not the agreement."[8] Williston's view has support in legal history where the distinction has been drawn between " 'carta' (a document which is the contract) and 'memoratorium' (a document which evidences a contract outside itself)."[9] The basic issue is whether the historical distinction rests on any sound basis in the modern world, or ought to be silently ignored, as it has been by Corbin and his supporters.

(b) Interpreting Non–Integrations

If the writing is not an integration and is not ambiguous, Williston's standard is the meaning that the party making the manifestation should reasonably expect the other party to give it—the standard of reasonable expectation, a test based primarily upon the objective theory of con-

2. Rs. 1st § 230.

3. Rs. 1st §§ 230, 231; First Nat. Bank in Dallas v. Rozelle, 493 F.2d 1196 (10th Cir.1974). There are a few limited exceptions to this statement that are also stated in these two sections.

4. 4 Williston §§ 607–607A (3d ed.); Rs. 1st § 230 ill. 1.

5. 4 Williston § 613, at 583 (3d ed.).

6. Id. § 612, at 577.

7. Id.

8. Murray, The Parol Evidence Process and Standardized Agreements under the Restatement (Second) of Contracts, 123 U.Pa.L.Rev. 1342, 1353 (1975).

9. Lucke, Contracts in Writing, 40 Austl. L.J. 265, 266 (1966). That Williston's approach is very much alive, see Rodolitz v. Neptune Paper Products, 22 N.Y.2d 383, 385, 292 N.Y.S.2d 878, 880, 239 N.E.2d 628, 630 (1968) ("While the Appellate Division's conclusion as to the real intent of the parties may be correct, the rule is well settled that a court may not, under the guise of interpretation, make a new contract for the parties or change the words of a written contract so as to make it express the real intentions of the parties if to do so would contradict the clearly expressed language of the contract * * * ").

tracts.[10] This should bring to mind the tentative working test we set up in § 2.2, where we state, "a party's intention will be held to be what a reasonable person in the position of the other party would conclude the manifestation to mean." In other words, if A says something to B, the meaning of what A said depends upon what a reasonable person in the position of B would conclude that A meant. The words "in the position of B" make it clear that what B knows or should know about A's intention should be taken into account. The tentative working test employs a standard of reasonable understanding (standard 6 in note 4 supra). However, Williston has chosen a slightly different standard than the tentative test advanced by us. Williston adopts the standard of reasonable expectation—the meaning that the party making the manifestation should reasonably expect the other party to give it. In the illustration given above, what A reasonably understood what B would understand the words to mean. In reaching this conclusion, the reasonable person should take into account what A knows or should know about B's knowledge.[11]

In the case of an unambiguous non-integration, all extrinsic evidence is admissible except evidence of subjective intention.[12] However, if a non-integration is ambiguous, even evidence of subjective intention is admissible.

When such evidence of subjective intent is introduced, its evaluation depends on certain factors. If the parties place the same meaning on the term, there is obviously a contract based on that meaning. If the evidence shows that the parties had conflicting understandings as to the meaning of a material term, there is a contract based on the meaning of the party who is justifiably unaware of the ambiguity. Finally, if the understandings conflict as to a material term and each party is guilty or blameless on the issue of knowledge or reason to know of the ambiguity, there is no contract.[13]

A good illustration of Williston's rule is Raffles v. Wichelhaus.[14] The seller agreed to sell cotton to the buyer, shipment to be made from Bombay on the ship Peerless. It so happened that there were two ships Peerless sailing from Bombay;[15] one was to sail in October and the other in December. The buyer meant the ship that sailed in October but the seller meant the ship that sailed in December. Under Williston's ap-

---

10. 4 Williston § 605 (3d ed.).

11. Sometimes the test is stated in terms of what a reasonable person in the position of the parties would have concluded. James v. Goldberg, 256 Md. 520, 261 A.2d 753 (1970).

12. 4 Williston § 605 (3d ed.); Rs. 1st § 235(d).

13. Jet Forwarding v. U.S., 437 F.2d 987 (Ct.Cl.1971); 4 Williston § 605 (3d ed.); Rs. 1st §§ 71 and 233. Williston does not employ the standard of reasonable expectation "where the law gives to certain words an established meaning" because "this

meaning is less readily controlled by the standard of interpretation * * * than is the meaning of other words." 4 Williston §§ 641, 615 (3d ed.); see Rs. 1st § 234.

14. 159 Eng.Rep. 375 (Ex.1864).

15. This case illustrates latent ambiguity. See § 3.10 supra. The doctrine was, however, applied to a patent ambiguities in Local Motion v. Niescher, 105 F.3d 1278 (9th Cir.1997); Sidwell Oil & Gas v. Loyd, 230 Kan. 77, 630 P.2d 1107 (1981) (terminology peculiar to petroleum leases).

proach, the question is whether one party knew or should have known of the ambiguity and the other did not. For example, if the seller knew or should have known of the ambiguity and the buyer did not, there would be a contract based upon the buyer's meaning—the ship Peerless that sailed in October. If neither party knew or had reason to know or if both parties knew or had reason to know, there would be no contract. If both parties meant the same ship Peerless, there would be a contract. What the parties know or should have known is ordinarily a question of fact. The same result would be appropriate under the plain meaning rule. Because there were two ships Peerless, there is no plain meaning.

Thus, in one employment case the parties had different reasonable meanings of the term, "gross receipts." There was no contract and compensation was based on reasonable value. When the parties again reached agreement and used the employer's same form contract, there was a contract based on the employer's understanding because this time the employee knew what the employer's intention was.[16]

§ 3.12   Corbin's Approach—Restatement (Second)—UCC–Reasonable Expectations

Under Corbin's approach, even if there is an unambiguous integration,[1] all relevant extrinsic evidence is admissible on the issue of meaning, including evidence of subjective intention and what the parties said to each other with respect to meaning.[2]

This is a partly subjective approach because in most cases evidence of what the parties intended the language to mean will be introduced. When such evidence is introduced the problem is similar to the case of the two ships Peerless discussed in the preceding section. Corbin and Williston do not resolve the problem in quite the same manner. They agree that if the parties meant the same ship, there is a contract based on that meaning, and that if both parties were blameless or equally at fault, there would be no contract. Corbin, however, unlike Williston, is willing to allow the court to weigh relative fault. Under his approach, if one of the parties is more guilty than the other for the difference in their meanings, the court should apply the meaning of the party who is less at fault.[3]

If evidence of subjective intention at the time of contracting is not introduced into evidence, the parties may still assert the meaning that

---

16. Krossa v. All Alaskan Seafoods, 37 P.3d 411 (Alaska 2001).

§ 3.12

1. 5 Corbin §§ 24.7 to 24.9 (Kniffin 1998); Corbin, The Interpretation of Words and the Parol Evidence Rule, 50 Cornell L.Q. 161, 189 (1965). Under Corbin's approach the parties may testify that they agreed that "buy means sell" and there is no special rule for words with an established meaning. Rs. 2d § 201 cmt c, and § 212 cmt b. The UCC is in accord. UCC § 2–202 cmt 1(a). See Peterson v. Wirum, 625 P.2d 866 (Alaska 1981); Mississippi State Highway Comm'n v. Dixie Contractors, 375 So.2d 1202 (Miss.1979).

2. 5 Corbin § 24.7 to 24.9 (Kniffin 1998); Mississippi State Highway Comm'n v. Dixie Contractors, 375 So.2d 1202 (Miss. 1979); Security Credit v. Jesse, 46 Or.App. 399, 611 P.2d 702 (1980).

3. 5 Corbin §§ 24.5; (Kniffin 1998); Rs. 2d § 201(2) & (3).

they now attach to the language in question. Corbin uses a standard based on the balance between the standard of reasonable expectations and the standard of reasonable understanding.[4] A contract exists in accord with the meaning the promisee could rely upon, provided the promisor had reason to foresee that the promisee had reason to attach this meaning. Actually this means that the issue is who is more responsible for the difference in meaning attached to the language in question.

Corbin tempers his more liberal rules by stating that the trial judge must initially decide whether the asserted meaning is one to which the language, taken in context, is reasonably susceptible in the light of all of the evidence.[5] If it is not, then that asserted meaning may not be attached to the language, and the jury will not be permitted to hear the proffered evidence of the asserted meaning.

The Restatement (Second) is generally in accord with Corbin.[6] Since the UCC has very little to say about interpretation, and its provisions concern primarily the admissibility of usage of the trade, course of performance, and course of dealing, we will delay that discussion until these topics are discussed below.[7]

Contract law is permeated by the notion that the law should take into account the reasonable expectations of contracting parties. The term "reasonable expectations," however, has taken on a specialized meaning in the interpretation of insurance policies, and, by extension, of standard form agreements in general. By analyzing various insurance cases that strayed from the classical mold–generous findings of ambiguity, unusual estoppels and reformations, and the like, Professor Keeton first formulated this rule: *"the reasonable expectations of applicants and intended beneficiaries will be honored even though a painstaking study of the policy provisions would have negated those expectations."* This formulation appeared in an article whose revealing title showed the foundation of the doctrine: "Insurance Law Rights at Variance with Policy Provisions."[8] The doctrine holds that the language of the contract will be

---

4. 5 Corbin § 24.5 (Kniffin 1998).

5. 3 Corbin § 579; Brobeck, Phleger & Harrison v. Telex, 602 F.2d 866 (9th Cir. 1979), cert. denied; International Brotherhood v. Hartford Acc. & Indem., 388 A.2d 36 (D.C.1978); Harrigan v. Mason & Winograd, 121 R.I. 209, 397 A.2d 514 (1979).

6. Rs. 2d §§ 210, 212, 215 cmt b.

7. See § 3.17 infra.

8. 83 Harv.L.Rev. 961 (1970); see Slawson, Binding Promises ch.3 (1996); Symposium, 5 Conn.Ins.L.J. (1998). A watered-down version appears in Rs.2d § 211. In Philadelphia Indem. Ins. v. Barerra, 200 Ariz. 9, 21 P.3d 395, 403 (2001), the court restated the doctrine as follows:

1. Where the contract terms, although not ambiguous to the court, cannot be understood by the reasonably intelligent consumer who might check on his or her rights, the court will interpret them in light of the objective, reasonable expectations of the average insured;

2. Where the insured did not receive full and adequate notice of the term in question, and the provision is either unusual or unexpected, or one that emasculates apparent coverage;

3. Where some activity which can be reasonably attributed to the insurer would create an objective impression of coverage in the mind of a reasonable insured;

4. Where some activity reasonably attributable to the insurer has induced a particular insured reasonably to believe that he has coverage, although such coverage is expressly and unambiguously denied by the policy.

ignored if it conflicts with the reasonable expectation of the promisee or what the promisor should reasonably expect the promisee to understand.

The doctrine has been embraced by some courts. Thus, where a commercial burglary policy contained a definition of burglary that required visible marks of forced entry, the court applied the doctrine.[9] It stated that although the language was "clear and precise," it was inconspicuous; it was an exclusion buried in the definitions section and defeated the reasonable understanding of the insured.

Others warily apply the the doctrine but limiting it to to ambiguities and inconspicuous language.[10] Many reject it.[11] Some make decisions that are consistent with the doctrine without expressly invoking it.[12]

§ 3.13   Aids to Interpretation; Rules of Preference

A considerable number of rules, often called "canons of construction," have been formulated to aid the courts in the task of interpretation. Sometimes these conflict with each other. Some seem devoid of any grounding in policy or common sense. For example, one canon states that if two terms in a writing conflict, the first term controls.[1] Why?

The goal of interpretation is to determine the common intention of the parties—if they had one.[2] But various rules, such as the plain meaning rule, that many jurisdictions employ to discourage or prevent the introduction of parol evidence obscure the discovery of this common intention. In contrast to those rules, the modern approach is to allow evidence of the surrounding circumstances to aid in interpretation.[3]

The principal purpose of the parties is of particular importance in determining meaning.[4] The purpose of the contract may often be gleaned from recitals of fact, often contained in the preamble to a written contract. Lord Esher stated the rule that is usually followed:[5] "If the recitals are clear and the operative part is ambiguous, the recitals govern the construction. If the recitals are ambiguous, and the operative part is clear, the operative part must prevail. If both the recitals and the operative part are clear, but they are inconsistent with each other, the

9.   Atwater Creamery v. Western Nat'l Mutual Ins., 366 N.W.2d 271, 52 ALR 4th 1217 (Minn.1985); see also Gordinier v. Aetna Cas. & Sur., 154 Ariz. 266, 742 P.2d 277, 283 (1987); Sparks v. St. Paul Ins. 100 N.J. 325, 495 A.2d 406, 412–14 (1985).

10.   Bank of the West v. Superior Court, 2 Cal.4th 1254, 10 Cal.Rptr.2d 538, 833 P.2d 545 (1992).; Max True Plastering v. U. S. Fidelity & Guar., 912 P.2d 861 (Okla. 1996).

11.   Deni Assocs. v. State Farm Fire & Cas., 711 So.2d 1135 (Fla.1998); Allen v. Prudential Property & Cas., 839 P.2d 798 (Utah 1992).

12.   See Slawson, note 8 supra at 60–62.

§ 3.13

1.   Homes of Legend v. McCollough, 776 So.2d 741 (Ala.2000): Vass v. Gainesville Bank & Trust, 224 Ga.App. 259, 480 S.E.2d 294 (1997).

2.   Rs. 2d § 201. If the parties misunderstood each other, the ruling may be that no contract was made. See § 3.11 supra.

3.   Rs. 2d § 202(1); cf. Rs. 1st § 235(d); see § 3.12 supra.

4.   Rs. 2d § 202 (1); Rs. 1st § 236(b); 6 Corbin § 24.20.

5.   Ex Parte Dawes, 17 Q.B.D. 275, 286 (1886).

operative part is to be preferred."[6] A descriptive caption is not part of the contract and may be disregarded if inconsistent with the terms of the contract.[7] Also, a contract that is in every respect a lease will be treated as a lease despite an express provision that it is "a residence agreement," not a lease.[8] To borrow someone else's phrase, if you put a Cadillac insignia on a Chevrolet, the car is still a Chevrolet.

A writing must be interpreted as a whole and no part should be ignored.[9] All of the writings that form a part of the same transaction should be interpreted together and, if possible, harmonized.[10] If no other intention is established, language is interpreted in accordance with its generally prevailing meaning.[11] This is a watered-down version of the plain meaning rule, but conforms to what is reasonable and logical. Similarly, terms used in a technical context are understood in accordance with their technical meanings, unless another intention is established,[12] as where there is a non-technical meaning and one party is a layperson.[13] The following, in their order of significance, are of great weight in determining intent: (a) course of performance, (b) course of dealing, and (c) trade usage.[14]

Three related latin maxims are sometimes invoked in the process of interpretation. *Ejusdem generis* ("of the same kind") is a canon that states that where a contractual clause enumerates specific things, general words following the enumeration are interpreted to be restricted to things of the same kind as those specifically listed.[15] *Noscitur a sociis* (known by one's associates), signifies that a word takes on coloration from the verbal context. Thus, a term requiring arbitration prior to an

6. See Notes, 41 Cornell L.Q. 126 (1955); 35 Colum.L.Rev. 565 (1935); United Va. Bank Nat. v. Best, 223 Va. 112, 286 S.E.2d 221 (1982), cert. denied; EMSI v. Kirschbaum, 927 P.2d 686 (Wyo.1996).

7. Swiss Bank v. Dresser Indus., 942 F.Supp. 398 (N.D.Ill.1996); Wayne J. Griffin Elec. v. Dunn Constr., 622 So.2d 314 (Ala. 1993).

8. M & I First Nat. Bank v. Episcopal Homes Mgt., 195 Wis.2d 485, 536 N.W.2d 175 (App.1995); see also Chemical Bank v. Meltzer, 93 N.Y.2d 296, 690 N.Y.S.2d 489, 712 N.E.2d 656 (1999) (party labeled as a "primary obligor" held to be a surety).

9. Tennessee Gas Pipeline v. FERC, 17 F.3d 98 (5th Cir.1994); Affiliated FM Ins. v. Owens–Corning Fiberglas, 16 F.3d 684 (6th Cir.1994); 5 Corbin § 24.21 (Kniffin 1998).

10. Rs. 2d § 202(2); Rs. 1st § 235(c); U.S. v. Basin Elec. Power Co-op., 248 F.3d 781 (8th Cir.2001); (even if they contain merger clauses); Wonderland Shopping Center v. CDC Mortgage, 274 F.3d 1085 (6th Cir.2001); Century Financial Services v. Bates, 934 S.W.2d 619 (Mo.App.1996);

Cadle Co. v. Harvey, 46 S.W.3d 282 (Tex. App.2001).

11. Rs. 2d § 202(3) (a); Rs. 1st § 235(a); McHugh v. United Service Automobile Ass'n, 164 .3d 451 (9th Cir.1999); Yount v. Acuff Rose–Opryland, 103 F.3d 830 (9th Cir.1996).

12. Rs. 2d § 202(3) (b); Rs. 1st § 235(b); Schneider Leasing, v. USAU, 555 N.W.2d 838 (Iowa 1996).

13. Rodriguez v. General Accident Ins., 808 S.W.2d 379, 382 (Mo.1991).

14. Rs. 2d § 202(4),(5); Rs. 1st § 235 (e) (course of performance); §§ 245–249 (usage); see § 3.17 infra.

15. Center Video Indus. v. Roadway Package Sys., 90 F.3d 185 (7th Cir.1996) (carrier's authority to accept on behalf of sender "cash, cashier's check, certified check, money order or other similar instrument" does not include a non-negotiable check); Smith v. Second Church of Christ, Scientist, 87 Ariz. 400, 351 P.2d 1104, 84 ALR2d 766 (1960) ("no barns, garages or other buildings whatsoever" does not include a church); Shatzer v. Globe American

employee being "disciplined, reprimanded, reduced in compensation or deprived of any professional advantage," does not encompass "dismissal" because all of the terms following "disciplined" indicate a lesser, not a greater, form of discipline.[16] *Expressio unius est exclusio alterius* ("expression of one thing is exclusion of another") is the third of these canons. Thus, a contract by a city to convey a bridge to the state that is silent as to funds that had been earmarked for bridge repair is interpreted to mean that the earmarked funds were not to be transferred with the bridge.[17]

Once all admissible evidence is placed on the record, and the rules of interpretation are applied, the court may still be in the dark as to the intended meaning of the parties. This sets the stage for the application of standards of preference—maxims that state, for example, that a lawful, reasonable interpretation is to be preferred over an unlawful or unreasonable interpretation.[18] Similarly, "if there are two reasonable interpretations of an agreement, preference should be given to that which renders the agreement enforceable."[19]

The dividing line—and the nature of the distinctions—that the Restatement (Second) has laid down between "rules in aid of interpretation" and "standards of preference," is murky indeed. The following "standards of preference" in that document seem instead to be excellent rules for getting at the parties' true intention. (1) If a term is added to a standard form, it is to be preferred over any conflicting term in the form.[20] (2) A specific term is to be preferred over any conflicting general term.[21] (3) Express terms have greater weight than course of performance, which in turn has greater weight than course of dealing, which has greater weight than trade usage.[22]

True standards of preference involve the role of the judge as a dispenser of equity. Some of these will be considered later in this text; e.g., if it is doubtful whether given language creates a condition or a promise, it should be interpreted as a promise.[23] Other standards of preference are considered here. Once the attempt to ascertain the true intention of the parties is exhausted and has proved unsuccessful, it may be appropriate to construe the language against the drafter, who, after all, is responsible for the lack of clarity.[24] A related rule of preference is

Cas., 639 N.W.2d 1 (Iowa 2001); 5 Corbin § 24.28 (Kniffin 1998).

16. Board of Education v. Barni, 66 A.D.2d 340, 412 N.Y.S.2d 908 (1979), reversed on other grounds.

17. State v. City of Davenport, 219 N.W.2d 503, 508 (Iowa 1974); see Payne v. Palisades Interstate Park, 226 A.D.2d 902, 640 N.Y.S.2d 683 (1996), app. denied.

18. Rs. 2d § 203(a); Rs. 1st § 236(a); 5 Corbin § 24.20.

19. Homes of Legend v. McCollough, 776 So.2d 741 (Ala.2000); Warden v. E.R. Squibb & Sons, 840 F.Supp. 203, 207 (E.D.N.Y.1993).

20. National Minority Supplier v. First Nat. Bank, 83 F.Supp.2d 1200 (D.Kan. 1999); Zygar v. Johnson, 169 Or.App. 638, 10 P.3d 326 (2000); Rs. 2d § 203(d), and cmt f; Rs. 1st § 236(e); 5 Corbin § 24.24.

21. Emily Towers Owners v. Carleton Emily Towers, 170 Misc.2d 82, 649 N.Y.S.2d 996 (1996), modified; Rs. 2d § 203(c), and cmt e; Rs. 1st § 236(c).

22. Rs. 2d § 203(b); but see § 5.14 supra (course of performance may create a modification).

23. See § 11.9 infra.

24. Rs. 2d § 206; Rs. 1st § 236(d); Kaiser Aluminum v. Matheson, 681 A.2d 392

that a deed is construed against the grantor[25] although the grantor is not necessarily responsible for its drafting. A guarantor is said to be a favorite of the law and the guaranty is narrowly construed.[26] Scores of such rules of preference can be found.

More general rules also abound. For example, if more than one reasonable meaning exists, and the public interest is involved, a meaning favoring that interest should be selected.[27] Any agreement should be interpreted to be consistent with the covenant of good faith and fair dealing that is incorporated into any contract,[28] as well as with notions of conscionability and decent behavior.[29] If a term is susceptible to more than one meaning, the court can select the fairest meaning, but cannot redraft the contract in the interests of fairness, absent a finding of unconscionability.[30]

Contracts treatises have generally downplayed the role of *stare decisis* in contractual interpretation. Such downplaying distorts reality. Where the rules in aid of interpretation and standards of preference fail to satisfy, courts frequently look to how other courts have interpreted the same or similar language. Thus, we have seen the standardized interpretation of the words "permanent employment."[31] Suppose that a covenant forbids the seller of a business from competing within a radius of five blocks. Where does the pencil of a compass go if there is a large park two blocks west and a river two blocks east of the center point? This and other ambiguities in provisions using the term "radius" in covenants not to compete are explored through the lens of prior court decisions.[32] Such holdings, based on *stare decisis* are appropriate where the parol evidence indicates the parties had not focused on the exact meaning of their covenant. The Restatement does not deal with the role of *stare decisis* in contract interpretation except in the context of standardized agreements,[33] where it quite rightly lays down the general rule that standardized forms should be interpreted so as to give every user of the form the same treatment with respect to the standardized terms.[34]

(Del.Supr.1996); Zimmerman v. Eagle Mtg., 110 Ohio App.3d 762, 675 N.E.2d 480 (1996). This rule is most frequently invoked against insurers. See, Key v. Allstate Ins., 90 F.3d 1546 (11th Cir.1996) (Fla. law); Queen City Farms v. Central Nat. Ins., 126 Wn.2d 50, 882 P.2d 703 (1994). An attorney-client contract is to be construed against the attorney. Untiedt v. Grand Labs., 552 N.W.2d 571 (Minn.App.1996).

25. Hart v. U.S., 945 F.Supp. 1009 (E.D.Tex.1996).

26. TMG Life Ins. v. Ashner, 21 Kan. App.2d 234, 898 P.2d 1145 (1995).

27. Rs. 2d. § 207; Rs. 1st § 236(b); 5 Corbin § 24.25 (Kniffin 1998).

28. See Rs. 2d § 205; see § 11.38 infra.

29. See §§ 9.37–9.40, 11.39 infra.

30. Calomiris v. Woods, 353 Md. 425, 727 A.2d 358 (1999).

31. See § 2.9 supra.

32. Annot., 10 ALR2d 605; see also Energynorth Natural Gas v. Continental Ins., 146 N.H. 156, 781 A.2d 969 (2001) ("accident").

33. Rs. 2d § 211; Dugan, Standardized Form Contracts—An Introduction, 24 Wayne L.Rev. 1307 (1978); Holmes & Thurmann, A New and Old Theory for Adjudicating Standardized Contracts, 17 Ga.J.Int'l & Comp.L. 323 (1987); Murray, The Parol Evidence Process and Standardized Agreements Under the Restatement (Second) of Contracts, 123 U.Pa.L.Rev. 1342 (1975).

34. Rs. 2d § 211(2); see also cmt e and ill.4. This is commonly done with insurance

It is often stated that existing rules of law are incorporated into contracts.[35] This is often an elliptical way of stating that the Constitution protects the validity of contracts under the Contract and Due Process clauses,[36] or that the common law does not favor retroactive termination of vested rights by legislative or administrative action.[37] However, the statement is not so limited. Mandatory provisions of law governing the kind of contract in question are read into the contract.[38] Moreover, interpretation often takes place in the shadow of the law. For example, a workers' compensation insurance policy can be best understood in the light of statutes mandating or authorizing such insurance coverage.[39] Also, a term, such as "beauty salon," that is defined by statute will generally be understood in terms of its statutory definition.[40] The parties may also incorporate statutory rules by reference.[41]

There are numerous canons and rules of interpretation and construction. How does the lawyer or judge know which to choose from the confusing thicket? This can be answered only by a metaphor: How does an oil painter armed with a palette of colors capture the sunset? The trained artist knows how. A Turner, however, may interpret the sunset differently from a Cezanne.

§ 3.14   Deciding Omitted Terms

Often a dispute arises where the parties have not agreed upon or even discussed a term covering the situation. The rules of interpretation provide no solution. The parties did not foresee the contingency that arose or they foresaw it but failed to make any provision with respect to it.[1] The ensuing gap is an "omitted term."

To illustrate, a ninety-nine year lease was entered into which provided that no rents were to accrue until the lessee had completed the planned construction of a shopping center.[2] Several years into the lease, during which no construction had commenced, the landlord brought an action for a declaration of rights. The court noted that there was no

policies. West American Ins. v. Band & Desenberg, 925 F.Supp. 758 (M.D.Fla.1996) (meaning of "absolute pollution exclusion"), but it also been held that boilerplate language common to trust indentures should be interpreted in the same way and parol evidence should not be taken. Kaiser Aluminum v. Matheson, 681 A.2d 392 (Del. 1996).

35.   Von Hoffman v. Quincy, 71 U.S.(4 Wall.) 535, 550 (1866) is the seminal case.

36.   Honeywell, Inc. v. Minnesota Life & Health Ins. Guar. Assn., 86 F.3d 766 (8th Cir.1996); see 5 Corbin § 24.26.

37.   Texas Workers' Comp. Ins. v. State Bd. of Insurance, 894 S.W.2d 49 (Tex.App. 1995); see Kainen, The Historical Framework for Reviving Constitutional Protection for Property and Contract Rights, 79 Cornell L.Rev. 87 (1993).

38.   Auction & Estate Reps. v. Ashton, 354 Md. 333, 731 A.2d 441 (1999).

39.   State Farm Fire & Cas. v. Workers' Comp. App. Bd., 16 Cal.4th 1187, 69 Cal. Rptr.2d 602, 947 P.2d 795 (1997). It is often said that statutory provisions form part of the contract. Western Waterproofing v. Springfield Housing Auth., 669 F.Supp. 901 (C.D.Ill.1987).

40.   Bentley v. Tsai, 198 Ga.App. 297, 401 S.E.2d 316 (1991).

41.   American Rock Salt v. Norfolk So., 180 F.Supp.2d 420 (W.D.N.Y.2001).

§ 3.14

1.   Farnsworth, Disputes over Omission in Contracts, 68 Colum.L.Rev. 860 (1968).

2.   Hunt v. First Nat. Bank, 381 So.2d 1194 (Fla.App.1980).

provision in the written lease concerning the rights of the parties in the event construction is not completed. This is an omitted term.

Another illustration that has recurred involves a percentage lease under which a retail merchant agrees to pay a stated percentage of its retail sales as rent. Subsequently, the retailer is franchised to sell lottery tickets or postage stamps and postal money orders. Are revenues derived from these sources "retail sales?" The courts have concluded that they are not, but a percentage of the retailer's commissions on such sales are subject to be calculated into the retail sales.[3]

In such situations, parol evidence will be admissible to determine if the parties had expressed any intention on the matter extrinsic to the writing. If the court finds that no intention has been expressed, and the rules in aid of interpretation and the rules of preference do not help, the court is dealing with an "omitted term."[4] It should supply a term that "comports with community standards of fairness and policy rather than analyze a hypothetical model of the bargaining process."[5] Many courts instead search for "what the parties would have included in their contract had they anticipated an occurrence which they in fact overlooked."[6] In so doing it is rare that they look to the relative bargaining strengths of the parties. Instead, they conclude that the parties would have agreed to the decent thing, thus arriving at the same conclusion as under a test of "community standards." Under these tests, courts have supplied terms such as "good faith," "best" or "reasonable efforts" and "reasonable notice."[7] Although additional promises or agreements between the parties as to the omitted term may be barred by the parol evidence rule, the term may be shown, "if relevant on the question of what is reasonable in the circumstances."[8]

Criteria other than community standards of fairness and policy are often used to fill in the gap that the omission has created. As one case states:[9]

> "Terms are implied not because they are just or reasonable, but rather for the reason that the parties must have intended them and have only failed to express them * * * or because they are necessary to give business efficacy to the contract as written, or to give the contract the effect which the parties, as fair and reasonable men, presumably would have agreed on if, having in mind the possibility of the situation which has arisen, they contracted expressly in reference thereto."

The problem of omitted terms arises in many areas of contract law, most notably in the areas of constructive conditions of exchange and under the doctrines of impracticability and frustration.[10]

---

3. Hartig Drug v. Hartig, 602 N.W.2d 794 (Iowa 1999).

4. Rs. 2d § 204 cmt b.

5. Rs. 2d § 204 cmt d.

6. Hunt v. First Nat. Bank, 381 So.2d 1194, 1196 (Fla.App.1980).

7. Farnsworth, Contracts § 7.17 (2d ed.).

8. Rs. 2d § 204 cmt e; see the discussion of implied terms in § 3.5 supra.

9. Barco Urban Renewal v. Housing Auth., 674 F.2d 1001 (3d Cir.1982).

10. See chs. 11 and 13. See also § 2.9 supra and § 4.12(b)(5) infra.

§ 3.15 Questions of Fact or Questions of Law?

Although the meaning of language is essentially a question of fact, the general rule is that the interpretation of a writing is treated as a question of law for the court.[1] Again, this rule reflects the unwillingness of the judicial system to trust unsophisticated jurors and the desire of judges to increase the scope of judicial review. Where, however, extrinsic evidence[2] is introduced,[3] in aid of interpretation of a writing, the question of meaning is left to the jury[4] except where, after taking the extrinsic evidence into account, the meaning is so clear that reasonable jurors could reach only one conclusion, in which event, the question is treated as one of law.[5] Where extrinsic evidence is not introduced, the question of the meaning of a writing is one of law. Even where the contract is oral, if the exact words used by the parties are not in dispute, the court will deal with the matter in the same way as if the contract were written.

§ 3.16 Parol Evidence Rule and Interpretation

The parol evidence rule has two components.[1] In part B of this chapter we dealt with the question of whether a *term* agreed upon prior to or contemporaneously with the writing or other record should be received in evidence when there is an integrated writing or other record. The second phase of the parol evidence rule (at least this is what it is called by the courts) relates to what, if any, extrinsic evidence is admissible in *interpreting* a writing or other record. The two phases are related because a basic notion of the traditional parol evidence rule (see B above) is that an integrated writing or other record may not be varied or contradicted.[2] A contradiction, however, may take place not only by

§ 3.15

1. Dillard & Sons Constr. v. Burnup & Sims Comtec, 51 F.3d 910 (10th Cir.1995) (error to allow jury to interpret unambiguous term); Langer v. Iowa Beef Packers, 420 F.2d 365 (8th Cir.1970); Levine v. Massey, 232 Conn. 272, 654 A.2d 737 (1995); Hartford Accident & Indem. v. Wesolowski, 33 N.Y.2d 169, 350 N.Y.S.2d 895, 305 N.E.2d 907 (1973); Stuarts Draft Shopping Center v. S–D Assocs., 251 Va. 483, 468 S.E.2d 885 (1996); Clint Hurt & Assocs. v. Rare Earth Energy, 198 W.Va. 320, 480 S.E.2d 529 (1996); Rs. 2d § 212 cmt d; 4 Williston § 616 (3d ed.); 5 Corbin § 24.30 (Kniffin 1998); Whitford, the Role of the Jury and the Fact/Law Distinction in the interpretation of Written Contracts, 2001 Wis.L.Rev. 931.

2. "Extrinsic Evidence" includes all evidence outside of the writing. See § 3.9 supra.

3. Under the Plain Meaning Rule no extrinsic evidence is received absent an ambiguity. See § 3.10 supra.

4. Rs. 2d § 212 cmt e; Anheuser–Busch v. John Labatt Ltd., 89 F.3d 1339 (8th Cir.1996), cert. denied; Hubbard v. Fidelity Fed. Bank, 91 F.3d 75 (9th Cir.1996); Kandlis v. Huotari, 678 A.2d 41 (Me.1996); Hernandez v. Exxon, 943 F.Supp. 740 (S.D.Tex. 1996).

5. See § 2.7 supra.

§ 3.16

1. See § 3.1 supra.

2. The Rs. 2d § 215 (Reporter's Note) suggests that the proper word is "contradict" because the word "vary" might include cases "where more than one meaning is reasonably possible."

offering into evidence a *term* that contradicts the writing or other record, but also by offering evidence as to *meaning* of the language of the agreement that contradicts the apparent meaning of the language.[3]

To what extent this can be done depends upon the various views discussed above. For example, under the Plain Meaning Rule, no contradiction is permitted if the court determines that the meaning is plain; extrinsic evidence of all types is excluded.[4] Williston obviously foresaw the possibility of undermining the parol evidence rule pertaining to additional or contradictory terms under the guise of interpretation and structured a rule for integrations that does not permit an integration to be contradicted by evidence of subjective intent or what the parties said to one another about the meaning of language in the written contract.[5]

Corbin and the Restatement (Second) disagree with Williston. They take the position that the parol evidence rule should have no effect on the question of interpretation—the meaning of language.[6] Corbin states that before the parol evidence rule may be invoked to exclude extrinsic evidence, the meaning of the writing or other record must be ascertained, since one may not determine whether a writing or other record is being contradicted or even supplemented until one knows what the writing or other record means.[7] There is a certain circularity of reasoning in this contention; the content of the contract to be interpreted cannot be known until the parol evidence rule has been consulted. Under Corbin's approach all relevant extrinsic evidence is admissible on the issue of meaning. The only limitation is that "the asserted meaning must be one to which the language of the writing or other record, read in context, is reasonably susceptible."[8] The UCC rule is discussed below.[9]

Corbin's discussion proceeds on the assumption that there is a clear-cut distinction between offering evidence of a consistent additional term and offering evidence on the issue of meaning. Nothing could be further from the truth.[10] For example, a written integrated contract between buyer and seller calls for the purchase and sale of "all cotton planted on 400 acres." If one party claims that the agreement meant 400 acres planted "solid" and the other said it meant 400 acres "however planted" it sounds as if there is an interpretation problem.[11] If the seller says that the parties in fact agreed on the "however planted" term and offers it in evidence, this would be looked upon as an additional term just as the exclusive right to sell soft drinks in the Gianni case was looked upon as

3. McBaine, supra § 3.10 n.22 at 145.

4. See § 3.10 supra.

5. See § 3.11 supra.

6. 5 Corbin, §§ 24.10, 24.11 (Kniffin 1998).

7. 5 Corbin § 24.10 (Kniffin 1998); Kitchen v. Stockman Nat. Life Ins., 192 N.W.2d 796 (Iowa 1971); Rs. 2d § 214 cmt b.

8. Rs. 2d § 215 cmt b.

9. The UCC rules of interpretation are for the most part limited to a course of dealing, course of performance and usage. See § 3.17 infra.

10. Some recent scholarship also takes the position that a hard parol evidence rule and a hard plain meaning rule are two aspects of the same rule. Eric Posner, supra § 3.1 n.3.

11. Based on Loeb & Co. v. Martin, 295 Ala. 262, 327 So.2d 711 (1976).

an additional term.[12] Generally speaking, and certainly under the rules of the Restatement (Second) and Corbin, it is to the advantage of the party offering the evidence to couch the offer of proof in terms of the parol evidence rule and interpretation.

§ 3.17 Course of Dealing, Course of Performance and Usage

We have previously mentioned course of performance, course of dealing, and trade usage. Here, our topic is to define these terms and to determine their effect. The topic is treated separately because it concerns both the addition of terms and the interpretation of terms.

The UCC is based on the premise that commercial usages and the parties behavioral patterns under prior contracts and under the contract are of enormous importance in interpreting and supplementing the contract. The Code has drawn a careful distinction among "trade usage," "course of dealing," and "course of performance" whereas the common law decisions often inartistically meshed the first two together under the classification of "custom" and the third under the heading of "practical construction." The UCC defines a course of dealing as "a sequence of previous conduct between the parties to a particular transaction which is fairly to be regarded as establishing a common basis of understanding for interpreting their expressions and other conduct."[1] A course of *dealing* relates to the conduct prior to the agreement in question. On the other hand, a course of *performance* involves conduct after the agreement has been made, as "where the contract for sale involves repeated occasions for performance by either party with knowledge of the nature of the performance and opportunity for objection to it by the other, any course of performance accepted or acquiesced in without objection shall be relevant to determine the meaning of the agreement."[2]

The UCC defines a usage of the trade as "any practice or method of dealing having such regularity of observance in a place, vocation or trade as to justify an expectation that it will be observed with respect to the transaction in question."[3] Under this definition, a trade usage may be

---

12. See § 3.2 at n.15.

§ 3.17

1. UCC § 1–205(1); (revision § 1–303 (2) (b)); Sinkwich v. E. F. Drew & Co., 9 A.D.2d 42, 189 N.Y.S.2d 630 (1959).

2. UCC § 2–208(1); accord, revision § 1–303(a). Under the Rs 1st, a course of performance is treated as a primary rule of interpretation: "If the conduct of the parties subsequent to a manifestation of intent indicates that all the parties placed a particular interpretation upon it, that meaning is adopted if a reasonable person could attach it to the manifestation." Rs. 1st § 235. See § 3.13. Sometimes it has been stated that

this type of evidence "is entitled to the greatest weight" or is referred to as "convincing evidence." R.F.C. v. Sherwood Distilling, 200 F.2d 672 (4th Cir.1952); Department of Revenue v. Jennison–Wright Corp., 393 Ill. 401, 66 N.E.2d 395 (1946); Martinson v. Brooks Equipment Leasing, 36 Wis.2d 209, 152 N.W.2d 849 (1967). Some courts have held that the parties are bound by a course of performance even though it did not conform to the contract. H.B. Deal Constr. v. Labor Discount Ctr., 418 S.W.2d 940 (Mo.1967).

3. UCC § 1–205(2), accord, revision draft § 1–303(c).

limited to a particular area or to a particular activity or both.[4] A course of performance or a course of dealing can be established by the testimony of the parties. A trade usage is usually established by expert testimony.

At early common law, a usage,[5] including a trade usage, had to be "(1) legal, (2) notorious, (3) ancient or immemorial and continuous, (4) reasonable, (5) certain, (6) universal and obligatory."[6] These requisites, however, even as a common law proposition, have been watered down.[7] To qualify under the UCC, the trade usage need not be ancient or immemorial[8] or universal.[9] The requirement of certainty is also eliminated.[10] Reasonableness is also abolished and substituted in its place is the requirement against "unconscionable contracts and clauses."[11] The notion that the custom be notorious is carried forward in the definition of usage in § 1–205(2) which requires "regularity of observance * * * as to justify an expectation that it will be observed with respect to the transaction in question." The Restatement (Second) generally follows the lead of the UCC in modernizing the law with respect to these matters and amplifies the criteria for the effectiveness of non-trade usage.[12]

4. UCC § 1–205(2); Rs. 2d § 219 cmt a.

5. Usages other than trade usages exist. These usages may be used in interpretation or to add terms or, under more modern authorities, to qualify an agreement even though it is integrated. Rs. 1st § 246; Rs. 2d §§ 220, 221. A usage is employed for these purposes (i) if both parties manifest assent that the usage shall be operative, or (ii) if one of the parties intends the usage to apply and the other knows or has reason to know of this intent or (iii) if each party knows or has reason to know of the usage but neither party manifests an intent with respect to it, unless one party knows or has reason to know that the other has an intent inconsistent with usage. Compare Rs. 1st § 247 with Rs. 2d §§ 220, 221. Thus, the rules as to trade usages set forth below are a particular application of the rules stated here. Rs. 2d § 222 cmt a.

6. Levie, Trade Usage and Custom Under the Common Law and the Uniform Code, 40 N.Y.U.L.Rev. 1101 (1965).

7. Richlands Flint Glass v. Hiltebeitel, 92 Va. 91, 22 S.E. 806 (1895); Rs. 2d § 222 cmt b.

8. UCC § 1–205 cmt 5, revision § 1–103 cmt 4.

9. Id. It is enough that it be "currently observed by the great majority of decent dealers." UCC § 1–205 cmt 5, revision § 1–103 cmt 4.

10. UCC § 1–205 cmt 9 states: "In cases of a well established line of usage varying from the general rules of this act where the precise amount of variation has not been worked out into a single standard, the party relying on the usage is entitled, in any event, to the minimum variation demonstrated. The whole is not to be disregarded because no particular line of detail has been established. In case a dominant pattern has been fairly evidenced, the party relying on the usage is entitled under this section to go to the trier of the fact on the question of whether such dominant pattern has been incorporated into the agreement." Accord, revision § 1–103 cmt 8.

11. UCC § 1–205 cmt 6. "The policy of this Act controlling explicit unconscionable contracts and clauses* * * applies to implicit clauses which restrain usage of the trade and carries forward the policy underlying the ancient requirement that a custom or usage must be reasonable. However, the emphasis is shifted. The very fact of commercial acceptance makes out a prima facie case that the usage is reasonable, and the burden is no longer on the usage to establish itself as being reasonable. But the anciently established policing of usage by the courts is continued to the extent necessary to cope with the situation arising if an unconscionable or dishonest practice should become standard." Accord, revision § 1–103 cmt 5.

12. Rs. 2d § 202 (5) (usage and course of performance and dealing) §§ 219–223 (usage); § 202(4) (course of performance).

Once a trade usage has been proved, the question remains whether the parties are bound by it. The general notion is that a party who is or should be aware of it is bound. A party engaged in a trade is bound by the usages of that trade even if ignorant of them, on the theory that everyone in the trade should know that trade's usage.[13] Of course, the parties by agreement may negate the usage.

Once a trade usage that binds the parties is proved, the trade usage may be used on the issue of meaning and also to add a term to the agreement. The Model Rules of Professional Conduct can supply implied terms, operating much like a statement of professional usages.[14] Under common law, in many jurisdictions, a trade usage (and a course of dealing) may be added as an additional term to a writing or other record "if the term is not inconsistent" with the agreement.[15] UCC § 2–202 adopts the same rule.[16] However, some common law cases continue to exclude evidence of usage, course of dealing and course of performance unless the written contract is ambiguous or contains a gap.[17]

However, as stated above, another phase of the parol evidence rule relates to interpretation. Under the modern common law rule, a trade usage (or a course of dealing) may be shown to contradict the plain meaning of the language. For example, a contract is made to sell 10,000 shingles. A usage is shown that 2 packs equals 10,000 even though they contain less than 10,000.[18] Comment 2 to § 2–202 continues this rule when it states, "such writings are to be read on the assumption that the course of prior dealings between the parties and the usages of the trade were taken for granted when the document was phrased. Unless carefully negated they become an element of the meaning of the word used."[19] While § 2–202 provides that trade usage and course of dealing are always admissible, UCC § 1–205(4) indicates that the evidence is not always controlling when it says, "the express terms of an agreement and an applicable course of dealing or trade usage shall be construed wherever reasonable as consistent with each other; but when such construction

13. UCC § 1–205(3); accord, revision draft § 1–303 cmts 3 & 4; see Valentine v. Ormsbee Exploration, 665 P.2d 452 (Wyo. 1983); Warren, Trade Usage and Parties in the Trade: An Economic Rationale for an Inflexible Rule, 42 U.Pitt.L.Rev. 515 (1981).

14. See Painter, Professional Responsibility Rules as Implied Contract Terms, 34 Ga.L.Rev. 953 (2000); Perillo, The Law of Lawyers' Contracts Is Different, 67 Fordham L.Rev. 443 (1998).

15. Rs. 1st § 246; Insurance Co. of N.A. v. NNR Aircargo, 201 F.3d 1111 (9th Cir. 2000); New England Rock Services v. Empire Paving, 53 Conn.App. 771, 731 A.2d 784 (1999); Valente v. Two Guys From Harrison, 35 A.D.2d 862, 315 N.Y.S.2d 220 (1970); El Reda v. Love Taxi, 202 A.D.2d 275, 608 N.Y.S.2d 656 (1994); contra, Hurst v. W. J. Lake & Co., 141 Or. 306, 16 P.2d 627 (1932); Rs. 2d § 220 cmts c, d.

16. See § 3.4(e) supra; Campbell Farms v. Wald, 578 N.W.2d 96 (N.D.1998) (no ambiguity needed); Rich Products v. Kemutec, Inc., 66 F.Supp.2d 937 (E.D.Wis.1999) (usage of no consequential damages).

17. Affiliated FM Ins. v. Constitution Rein., 416 Mass. 839, 626 N.E.2d 878 (1994); Insurance & Consulting Assocs. v. ITT Hartford, 48 F.Supp.2d 1181 (W.D.Mo. 1999); Killington, Ltd. v. Richards, 160 Vt. 641, 641 A.2d 340 (1993); contra Rs.2d § 222 cmt b.

18. Eie v. St. Benedict's Hospital, 638 P.2d 1190 (Utah 1981).

19. Allapattah Services v. Exxon, 61 F.Supp.2d 1300 (S.D.Fla.1999); see also Nanakuli Paving & Rock v. Shell Oil, 664 F.2d 772 (9th Cir.1981).

is unreasonable express terms control both course of dealing and trade usage and course of dealing controls usage of the trade."[20] It should be stressed that § 1–205(4) does not bar evidence; it provides the criteria for evaluating the evidence.

Course of performance is different in some respects from course of dealing. Since a course of performance is subsequent to the writing or other record, the aspect of the parol evidence rule that deals with additional terms does not apply to it. Thus, if a course of performance is used to add a term to the writing or other records, the issue is modification or waiver.[21] A course of performance may add a term to the agreement or subtract one.

A course of performance may also be relevant on the issue of meaning. At common law it is usually termed "practical construction."[22] Under UCC § 2–208(1) "any course of performance accepted or acquiesced in without objection shall be relevant to determine the meaning of the agreement" and a comment states that "a course of performance is always relevant to determine the meaning of the agreement."[23] This rule is supplemented by subsection 2 which states: "The express terms of the agreement and any such course of performance, as well as any course of dealing and usage of the trade, shall be construed whenever reasonable as consistent with each other; but when such construction is unreasonable, express terms shall control course of performance and course of performance shall control both course of dealing and usage of the trade."[24] This subsection provides criteria for evaluating the weight to be given a course of performance, not the admissibility of evidence.[25]

The UCC and the Restatement (Second) have given the trio (usage, course of dealing, course of performance) a major role in the interpretive process. An empirical study has questioned the wisdom of assigning such an important role to this trio.[26] The criticism points out first, the lack of uniform customs in many lines of business. Second, merchants frequently believe that if they readily grant concessions to keep relationships together, such concessions should not be imposed on them in the event a

---

20. The same rule is carried forward in revision draft § 1–303. A trade usage must be examined in its commercial setting to ascertain if the parties wished the trade usage to take priority over the writing or other record. See Krist, Usage of Trade and Course of Dealing, 1977 Ill.L.F. 811.

21. UCC § 2–208(3) & cmt 3. revision § 1–103(f); see Comment, 57 Iowa L.Rev. 215 (1971). Waiver is discussed in chapter 11.

22. Rs. 2d § 202(5); James v. Zurich–American Ins., 203 F.3d 250 (3d Cir.2000); Mayflower Corp. v. Davis, 655 So.2d 1134 (Fla.App.1994). Correspondence by the defendant to the plaintiff *after* the contract is made may provide evidence of the parties' intent. Urban Masonry v. N & N Contractors, 676 A.2d 26 (D.C.App.1996) (disingen-

uously characterized as "contemporaneous correspondence"); accord, Ophus v. Fritz, 301 Mont. 447, 11 P.3d 1192 (2000) (oral declarations); but see Continental Cas. v. Rapid–American, 80 N.Y.2d 640, 609 N.E.2d 506, 593 N.Y.S.2d 966 (1993) (practical construction not admissible if the contract is unambiguous).

23. Comment 2. In the revision, course of performance is integrated with course of dealing and trade usage. (§ 1–303).

24. UCC § 2–208(1); accord 1997 revision draft § 1–303.

25. Contra, Brooklyn Bagel Boys v. Earthgrains, 212 F.3d 373 (7th Cir.2000).

26. Bernstein, The Questionable Empirical Basis of Article 2's Incorporation Strategy, 66 U.Chi.L.Rev. 710 (1999).

relationship is ruptured. Third, standardized contracts incorporate trade customs and adherence to the written contract should not be undermined in a litigation setting. This criticism expresses a contrarian view and is based on data that may reflect the turmoil created by the emergence of national and international markets in the twentieth century.[27] The trio is often evaluated in the light of the court's judgment of the economic utility or conscionability of the alleged custom, course of dealing, or course of performance.[28]

---

27. Gillette, Harmonization and Stasis in Trade Usages for International Trade, 39 Va.J.Int'l.L. 707 (1999).

28. E.g., the court explained long delays as a "realistic necessity to operate in that market and thus vital to [the buyer's] ability to get large government contracts and to [the seller's] continued business growth." Nanakuli Paving & Rock v. Shell Oil, 664 F.2d 772, 780 (9th Cir.1981); see Carswell, "Do Trade Customs Exist?", in The Jurisprudential Foundations of Corporate and Commercial Law 118 (Kraus & Walt eds. 2000).

Chapter 4

CONSIDERATION

Table of Sections

---

§ 4.1 Introduction

Apparently no legal system has ever enforced all promises. Fundamentally, the idea is that the coercive power of the State will not be employed to impose sanctions on the defaulting promisor unless the law deems the enforcement of the promise socially useful.[1] In the words of one court, "consideration is the glue that binds the parties to a contract together."[2]

The starting point is that donative promises *generally* are not enforced.[3] This is a tenable position.[4] Both substantive and administrative reasons support this conclusion. In addition to difficulties of proof, the injury in this type of case is relatively slight; there are no significant costs on the part of the promisee and no enrichment on the part of the promisor at the expense of the promisee.[5] Furthermore, a donative promise may be made without sufficient deliberation and, even if deliberated, there might be reason not to enforce it if it was made improvidently or if the promisee showed ingratitude.[6] Another reason has been advanced:[7]

[T]he principle that simple donative promises are unenforceable does not show that the law fails to value donative promises. Just the opposite is true. * * * The world of gift is a world of our better selves, in which affective values like love, friendship, affection, gratitude, and comradeship are the prime motivating forces. These values are too important to be enforced by law and would be undermined if the enforcement of simple, affective donative promises were to be mandated by law.

However, historically, a formal donative promise—one made pursuant to a recognized form—has been enforceable.[8] Remnants of this

§ 4.1

1. Cohen, The Basis of Contract, 46 Harv.L.Rev. 553, 571–574 (1933). Many countries which have derived their legal systems from Roman law require either that contracts be made in solemn form or contain the elements of *causa*. See Friedmann, Legal Theory 525–27 (5th ed.1967); Von Mehren, Civil–Law Analogues to Consideration: An Exercise in Comparative Analysis, 72 Harv.L.Rev. 1009 (1959); Lorenzen, Causa and Consideration in the Law of Contracts, 28 Yale L.J. 621 (1919). On formal contracts in civil law systems, see Schlesinger, The Notary and the Formal Contract in Civil Law, 1941 Report of the New York Law Revision Commission 403.

2. Matter of Deed of Trust of Owen, 62 N.C.App. 506, 303 S.E.2d 351 (1983).

3. Thomas v. Omega Men, 714 So.2d 982 (Ala.App.1997); See 2 Corbin §§ 5.2, 5.3; Eisenberg, Donative Promises, 47 U.Chi.L.Rev. 1, 6 (1979). But see Wright,

Ought the Doctrine of Consideration to be Abolished from the Common Law?, 49 Harv.L.Rev. 1225, 1251–53 (1936). See § 4.5 infra.

4. Eisenberg, note 3, pp. 2–8. Compare C. Bufnoir, Proprieté et contrat 487 (2d ed.1924) (gift promises are sterile) with Posner, Economic Analysis of Law 96 (4th ed.1992) (the enforceability of gift promises would be efficient and value-enhancing).

5. Eisenberg, note 3 supra at pp. 2–6.

6. Eisenberg, note 3, pp. 5–6.

7. Eisenberg, The World of Contract and the World of Gift, 85 Cal.L.Rev. 821, 849 (1997).

8. See Hazeltine, The Formal Contract of Early English Law, 10 Colum.L.Rev. 608 (1910), Selected Readings 1; Maine, Ancient Law Ch. IX (5th ed. 1873); Perillo, The Statute of Frauds in the Light of the Functions and Dysfunctions of Form, 43 Fordham L.Rev. 39, 43–48 (1974).

notion are preserved in those jurisdictions still giving effect to the seal.[9] So also a gratuitous promise injuriously relied on by the promisee may be enforced under the doctrine of promissory estoppel.[10] Under certain circumstances, a gratuitous promise to make restitution for material benefits received in the past will be enforced, as will some other promises to fulfill a moral obligation.[11]

The end result is that an informal, unrelied-on gratuitous promise generally will not be enforced.[12] Note that the second paragraph of this section referred to "donative" promises, then the discussion shifted to "gratuitous" promises. A donative promise is a promise to make a gift. A gratuitous promise may, however, be made in a commercial relationship, as where a party gratuitously agrees to raise or lower the contract price to reflect changing market conditions. Such a promise is gratuitous but is not a promise of a gift. It is unfortunate that the law has lumped such commercial gratuitous promises into the same category as gift promises.

Consideration is generally required in executory agreements, but the lack of consideration is not grounds for avoiding an agreement that has been fully performed;[13] the promisor is not entitled to restitution after performing. At that point the promisor has made an effective transfer of money, property or services.

The doctrine of consideration contains certain oddities which, in the opinion of many, interfere with the needs of modern society.[14] The English Law Revision Commission recommended its abolition,[15] but Parliament has not followed its counsel. The question of whether the doctrine of consideration is essential for the policing of commercial transactions is addressed at the end of this chapter.[16]

Whatever the reasons, the common law usually requires that promises be made for a consideration if they are to be binding. The doctrine of consideration is a historical phenomenon and therefore in some of its aspects affected by fortuitous circumstances.[17] Despite the fact that the history of this requirement of consideration is tortuous, confused and wrapped in controversy,[18] a brief overview seems appropriate.

---

9. See ch. 7 infra.

10. See ch. 6 infra.

11. See ch. 5 infra.

12. Wilson v. Lynch & Lynch, 99 Ohio App.3d 760, 651 N.E.2d 1328 (1994), app. dismissed (fee splitting agreement void where attorney who claims a share provided no services).

13. Ope Shipping, Ltd. v. Allstate Ins., 687 F.2d 639 (2d Cir.1982), cert. denied; Zubik v. Zubik, 384 F.2d 267 (3d Cir.1967), cert. denied. But see § 4.10 infra.

14. See Farber & Matheson, Beyond Promissory Estoppel, 52 U.Chi.L.Rev. 903 (1985) (promises in furtherance of economic activity should be enforced); Gordon, Consideration and the Commercial–Gift Dichotomy, 44 Vanderbilt L.Rev. 283 (1991);

Wessman, Should We Fire the Gatekeeper?, 48 U.Miami L.Rev. 45 (1993) (demonstrating that the result in many cases of nonenforcement for lack of consideration is justified on other grounds).

15. See Chloros, The Doctrine of Consideration and the Reform of the Law of Contract, 17 Int. & Comp.L.Q. 137 (1968).

16. See § 4.16 infra.

17. See 2 Corbin § 5.1.

18. See Ames, The History of Assumpsit, 2 Harv.L.Rev. 1, 53 (1888), Selected Readings 33; Holdsworth, Debt, Assumpsit and Consideration, 11 Mich.L.Rev. 347 (1913); Ricks, The Sophisticated Doctrine of Consideration, 9 G. Mason L.Rev. 99 (2000); A. W. B. Simpson, A History of the

The history relates to the writs of covenant, debt and assumpsit. Covenant was used to enforce contracts made under seal.[19] A gratuitous promise under seal was enforced because the form would encourage deliberation and because the writing was deemed trustworthy evidence of the terms of the contract.[20] Debt was used to sue for a definite sum owing as a result of performance by the promisee. The theory was that the debt should be paid because the promisor had received a benefit.

The third writ, assumpsit, grew out of cases where a promisor had undertaken (assumpsit) to do something and had done it carelessly (misfeasance) to the detriment of the promisee. At the outset, assumpsit did not lie where the promisor simply did not perform (non-feasance). Later, the common law courts began to honor the writ of assumpsit in cases of non-performance but they postulated a requirement of detrimental reliance on the promise—as for example by a change of position in reliance on the promise. In time, an action in assumpsit was allowed for breach of a promise even though there was no change of position.

Eventually the writ of assumpsit supplanted the writ of debt. Before this occurred, the word "consideration" had already come into existence as a term of art. Several elements were included in the concept. It included the notion of the writ of debt that there must be a benefit to the promisor. It also included the notion of the writ of assumpsit that there must be detriment on the part of the promisee.

§ 4.2   What Is Consideration?

Three elements must concur before a promise is supported by consideration. When these three elements coexist in the facts, there is a "bargained-for exchange," a binding transaction.

(a) The promisee must suffer legal detriment; that is, do or promise to do what the promisee was not legally obligated to do;[1] or refrain from doing or promise to refrain[2] from doing what the promisee is legally privileged to do.[3] The use of the term detriment in this context is criticized because in plain English it seems silly to speak of "detriment"

Common Law of Contract (1975); Teeven. A History of the Anglo–American Law of Contract (1990).

19. See the text at n.9 supra and ch. 7 infra.

20. Fuller, Consideration and Form, 41 Colum.L.Rev. 799 (1941).

§ 4.2

1. Ragland v. Sheehan, 256 Mont. 322, 846 P.2d 1000 (1993) (a promise to pay $35,000 if promisee rejected an offer).

2. Habeck v. MacDonald, 520 N.W.2d 808 (N.D.1994) (forbearing from giving a notice of termination).

3. The Restatement (Second) takes the position that if the promisor bargains for an illegal act or promise and receives it, the promise is supported by consideration. Rs. 2d § 72 cmt d. The ensuing contract, however, will generally be unenforceable under the doctrine of illegality. See ch. 22 infra. The Restatement's approach is forward-looking, but unorthodox, and it may take considerable time to catch on. For the traditional approach, see Hartman v. Harris, 810 F.Supp. 82 (S.D.N.Y.1992), aff'd (promise to pay for the sale of stolen goods lacks consideration). The Restatement's approach is part of its laudable effort to remove extraneous doctrines such as unconscionability, duress and illegality from consideration analysis.

in cases involving no economic loss or other harm.[4] This criticism has merit, but similar criticism may be directed at legal terms such as "consideration" which frequently differ in meaning from use of the same words by non-lawyers. The term is so deeply ingrained in the case law[5] and the language of lawyers that this text continues its use.

(b) The detriment must induce the promise. The promisor must have made the promise because the promisor wishes to exchange it, at least in part, for the detriment to be incurred by the promisee. There, of course, must be a promise; incurrence of detriment that benefits another is not consideration if there is no promise to be enforced.[6]

(c) The promise must induce the detriment. This means as we have already seen, that the promisee must know of the offer and intend to accept.[7]

(a) The Promisee Must Incur Legal Detriment

There are two additional points to be made in relation to the rule that the promisee must incur detriment. First, although the rule was stated in terms of legal detriment incurred by the promisee, it is often stated in terms of "either legal detriment to the promisee or legal benefit to the promisor."[8] This phrasing connects with our historical discussion where it was pointed out that the concept of consideration borrowed elements of the writ of debt (benefit to the promisor) and of the writ of assumpsit (detriment to the promisee).[9] The result is the same no matter whether a detriment or a benefit approach is applied to a set of facts.[10] If the promisee incurs legal detriment, the promisor obtains a legal benefit.[11] In the balance of the chapter, the approach will be primarily in terms of detriment to the promisee.

The opening statement of the rule somewhat inaccurately speaks of legal detriment "to the promisee." It is well settled in the U.S. that the detriment may be given by a person other than the promisee and run to

---

4. Use of the term "detriment" has been avoided in the Rs. 2d. See § 79 cmt b. In revising volume 2 of Corbin, Professor Bender and the present writer continued Corbin's general avoidance of the term, but used it where Corbin had found it useful. Compare 2 Corbin § 5.10 with 2 Corbin § 7.2 (Perillo & Bender 1995). The difference between Corbin's terminology and this text is not a difference of substance; rather, it is a difference in vocabulary.

5. For a strong statement, see Adelvision v. Groff, 859 F.Supp. 797 (E.D.Pa. 1994).

6. Zip Lube v. Coastal Sav. Bank, 709 A.2d 733 (Me.1998).

7. See §§ 2.12, 2.13 supra.

8. Currie v. Misa, L.R. 10 Ex. 153, 162 (1875); Arledge v. Gulf Oil, 578 F.2d 130 (5th Cir.1978); Martin v. Federal Life Ins., 109 Ill.App.3d 596, 65 Ill.Dec. 143, 440 N.E.2d 998 (1982); Doggett v. Heritage Concepts, 298 N.W.2d 310 (Iowa 1980); Rickett v. Doze, 184 Mont. 456, 603 P.2d 679 (1979); Wells v. Hartford Accident & Indem., 459 S.W.2d 253 (Mo.1970); Hyde v. Shapiro, 216 Neb. 785, 346 N.W.2d 241 (1984); Albemarle Educ. Foundation v. Basnight, 4 N.C.App. 652, 167 S.E.2d 486 (1969); First Wisconsin Nat. Bank v. Oby, 52 Wis.2d 1, 188 N.W.2d 454 (1971); see Farnsworth, Contracts § 2.2 (3d ed. 1999).

9. See § 4.1 supra.

10. 3 Williston § 7:5. For a possible exception see § 4.9(d) infra.

11. 3 Williston § 7:4. For a possible exception see § 4.9(d) infra.

a person other than the promisor.[12] It does not matter from whom or to whom the consideration moves so long as it is bargained for and given in exchange for the promise.[13]

(b) Detriment Must Induce the Promise

The promise must be made to induce the conduct of the promisee. Another way of stating the same thought is that the promisor has manifested an offering state of mind looking to an acceptance rather than a gift-making state of mind. A gratuitous promise is not made with an offering (exchanging) state of mind and thus any detriment that ensues did not induce the promise.[14]

(c) The Promise Must Induce the Detriment

The promise must induce the promisee to exchange the promisee's conduct for the promise. This explains why the offeree must know of the offer and manifest an intent to accept; the offeree must actually or apparently be induced to act by the promise.[15] For example, surrendering a secure union-protected job and taking a management job with the same employer is not consideration for a promise unless the "promise was given as part of a bargained-for exchange for [the employee's] relinquishment of his union security."[16]

The essence of consideration, then, is legal detriment, that has been bargained for by the promisor, and exchanged by the promisee in return for the promisor's promise.[17]

A simple illustration will help clarify the concept of consideration. A says to B, "If you paint my house according to my specifications, I promise to pay you $5,000." B performs. A is the promisor and B the promisee. (a) The promisee (B) has incurred legal detriment. B has performed an act (painting) that B was not legally obligated to perform. (b) It is a reasonable conclusion that the promisor (A) was exchanging a promise to pay for the act of painting, and that (c) the offeree (B) painted knowing of the offer and intending to accept. The discussion in this section and this illustration are set up in terms of a unilateral arrangement in which there is only one promisor. In a bilateral contract

---

12. Rs. 1st § 75(2); Quattlebaum v. Gray, 252 Ark. 610, 480 S.W.2d 339 (1972); Cechettini v. Consumer Assocs., 260 Cal. App.2d 295, 67 Cal.Rptr. 15 (1968); Highland Park v. Grant–Mackenzie, 366 Mich. 430, 115 N.W.2d 270 (1962); Alamo Bank v. Palacios, 804 S.W.2d 291 (Tex.App.1991); Quazzo v. Quazzo, 136 Vt. 107, 386 A.2d 638 (1978); contra, Dunlap Pneumatic Tyre v. Selfridge & Co., [1915] A.C. 847.

13. Rs 2d § 71 cmt e; see, e.g., State v. Larsen, 515 N.W.2d 178 (N.D.1994) (loan to partnership guaranteed by partners); Harms v. Northland Ford Dealers, 602 N.W.2d 58 (S.D.1999) (promise to country club to provide prize to golfer who made a hole-in-one).

14. See § 4.5 infra.

15. As pointed out in §§ 2.12 & 2.13, at times this requirement is eliminated in a bilateral contract in order to protect the expectations of the offeror.

16. Taylor v. Canteen Corp., 69 F.3d 773 (7th Cir.1995).

17. Key Pontiac v. Blue Grass Savings Bank, 265 N.W.2d 906 (Iowa 1978); Baehr v. Penn–O–Tex Oil, 258 Minn. 533, 104 N.W.2d 661 (1960).

there are two promisors. This gives rise to some complications discussed below.[18]

Unlike the first Restatement, this text does not distinguish between "consideration" and "sufficient consideration." According to that terminology, there is "sufficient consideration" if all three elements listed above are present. If elements (b) and (c) are present but not (a) then there was "consideration" (exchange) but not "sufficient consideration."[19] The Second Restatement has wisely dropped this distinction.[20] Accordingly, when we say that there is consideration, it means that all three elements are present.

§ 4.3   Motive and Past Events Distinguished

If a mother says to one of her sons, "in consideration of the fact that you are not as wealthy as your brothers, I promise to pay you $5,000 within thirty days," this promise is not enforceable because the promisor has neither requested nor induced anything in exchange.[1] The promisor merely has stated the motive for a gratuitous promise and this motive is not consideration.[2] However, this is not to say that motive is irrelevant to the question of consideration. Motive may be evidence on the issue of whether an exchange is intended.[3] In the illustration, there was no detriment and therefore no consideration. If there were detriment, the motive of the promisor in entering into the transaction would have been important on the issue of consideration. The motive often is to induce action on the part of the promisee and conversely the motive of the promisee may be to gain what is offered by the promisor. The relationship between motive and consideration will be explored at greater length below.[4]

If the promisor had stated to her son, "in consideration of the fact that you have named your child after me, I promise to pay you $5,000 in thirty days," the promise is equally unenforceable because the promise did not induce the detriment.

The promisee neither knew of any offer nor had any intent to accept when the act was done.[5] Thus, it is frequently stated that past consideration is not consideration.[6] The term "past consideration" is a contradiction in terms. Consideration is essentially an exchange and parties cannot bargain or exchange for something that has already occurred.[7] In the illustration above, however, if the transaction had been prospective—

---

18. See § 4.12 infra.

19. Rs. 1st § 80.

20. Rs. 2d § 71, Reporter's Note.

§ 4.3

1. Fink v. Cox, 18 Johns. 145 (N.Y. 1820).

2. Lesnik v. Estate of Lesnik, 82 Ill. App.3d 1102, 38 Ill.Dec. 452, 403 N.E.2d 683 (1980); Rose v. Lurvey, 40 Mich.App. 230, 198 N.W.2d 839 (1972).

3. 2 Corbin § 5.7 (Perillo & Bender 1995).

4. See §§ 4.5—4.7 infra.

5. Lanfier v. Lanfier, 227 Iowa 258, 288 N.W. 104 (1939); 4 Williston § 8:9.

6. Amato v. Creative Confections, 97 F.Supp.2d 949 (E.D.Wis.2000); Estate of Lovekamp, 24 P.3d 894 (Okl.App.2001); 4 Williston § 8:9. There are exceptions. See the topic of Moral Obligation in Ch. 5.

7. 4 Williston § 8:9.

that is, if the promisor bargained for the naming of a child before the child was named and thereby induced the parents to name the child after the promisor, consideration would exist.[8]

The idea of "exchange" is central to the law of contracts, as it is to any advanced economic system.[9] Should it, however, set the boundaries of the law of contracts? One may question the adequacy of a legal system which refuses to enforce a promise such as this: "In consideration of your forty years of faithful service, you will be paid a pension of $200 per month."[10] It is not surprising that some legislatures[11] have turned their attention to promises of this kind which, if seriously made, deserve to be enforced. The requirement of an "exchange" may have seemed indispensable (with few exceptions)[12] to eighteenth and nineteenth century lawyers whose understanding of the proper role of contract law was conditioned by the pervasive influence of Adam Smith's theory of economics. Modern lawyers seem less inclined to ideological dogmatism of any school and more inclined to ask whether the community conscience would deem a particular promise worthy of enforcement. Although the exchange requirement still remains central to the law of contracts, lawyer-influenced legislation and the development of the doctrine of promissory estoppel[13] dispense with the exchange requirement in a number of instances. These instances will doubtless increase in the future

§ 4.4 Adequacy of Consideration

As a general rule the courts do not review the adequacy of the consideration. The parties make their own bargains.[1] Economic inadequacy of the detriment is, however, one of the factors to be considered in determining whether the promisor really exchanged the promise in return for a small detriment.[2] Courts, however, have believed that it would be an unwarranted interference with freedom of contract if they were to relieve an adult party from a bad exchange.[3] This reluctance to

8. Schumm by Whyner v. Berg, 37 Cal.2d 174, 231 P.2d 39, 21 ALR2d 1051 (1951).

9. Exchange is discussed in more detail in §§ 4.4—4.7 infra.

10. Cf. Bogley's Estate v. U.S., 206 Ct. Cl. 695, 514 F.2d 1027 (1975); Perreault v. Hall, 94 N.H. 191, 49 A.2d 812 (1946).

11. See §§ 5.12 to 5.18 infra.

12. See ch. 5 infra.

13. See ch. 6 infra.

§ 4.4

1. Sturlyn v. Albany, 78 Eng.Rep. 327 (K.B.1587) (promise to pay in exchange for showing proof of indebtedness); Ashby v. Ashby, 651 So.2d 246 (Fla.App.1995) (signing a satisfaction piece on receipt of pay-

ment); Hill v. Chubb Life American Ins., 182 Ariz. 158, 894 P.2d 701 (Ariz.1995) (submitting an application, taking a physical exam, etc. can be consideration for promise by insurer to process application promptly); Spaulding v. Benenati, 57 N.Y.2d 418, 456 N.Y.S.2d 733, 442 N.E.2d 1244 (1982). See Braucher, Freedom of Contract and the Second Restatement, 78 Yale L.J. 598 (1969).

2. See §§ 4.5 & 4.6 infra.

3. Black Indus. v. Bush, 110 F.Supp. 801, 805 (D.N.J.1953) ("Even if it were proved that the plaintiff was to have received a far greater profit than the defendants for a much smaller contribution, the defendants would nevertheless be bound by [the] agreement by the familiar rule that relative values of the consideration in a contract between [businesses] dealing at

interfere with economic freedom has been carried to its logical conclusion. Haigh v. Brooks illustrates this.[4] Defendant for a consideration had executed a guaranty of payment of a debt of £10,000 owed to the plaintiffs. The guaranty was legally ineffective at its inception because, among other reasons, it was unstamped and therefore worthless under then existing English law. Defendant subsequently promised to pay the stated sum if the plaintiffs would return the document. Plaintiffs performed. When sued on the promise, defendant argued that the surrender of the document—a worthless piece of paper—did not constitute detriment. Therefore, defendant argued, the promise was not binding. The court followed the traditional rule indicating that it was not the court's function to concern itself with the adequacy or the inadequacy of the detriment. The court also considered the question of what defendant bargained for and concluded on the facts that the defendant did bargain for the paper.[5]

This landmark case should be compared with another well-known case, Newman & Snell's State Bank v. Hunter,[6] in which a widow had promised the bank to pay the debt of her deceased husband's insolvent estate. In exchange, the bank returned the husband's note to the widow. The court, ruling in her favor, indicated that surrender of a worthless note did not constitute consideration. If the court meant that the surrender of the note was not legal detriment, the case is in radical opposition to the weight of authority. The case could have been sound if the court found that the widow bargained for the discharge of a supposed claim against her, rather than the note.[7] In any event, the case would be consistent with basic concepts of contract law if it were based on the ground that economic inadequacy may constitute some circumstantial evidence of fraud, duress, over-reaching, undue influence, unconscionability or mistake.[8]

The parties make there own contracts, but there is one kind of contract where the courts will review the balance between the value of consideration and the price charged for it—the lawyer-client retainer.

---

arm's length without fraud will not affect the validity of the contract."); Adelvision v. Groff, 859 F.Supp. 797 (E.D.Pa.1994); Guaranteed Foods v. Rison, 207 Neb. 400, 299 N.W.2d 507 (1980); Reliable Pharmacy v. Hall, 54 Wis.2d 191, 194 N.W.2d 596 (1972); Tsiolis v. Hatterscheidt, 85 S.D. 568, 187 N.W.2d 104 (1971); Patterson, An Apology for Consideration, 58 Colum.L.Rev. 929 (1958). The classic philosophical discussion supporting this point of view and which had enormous impact on law is Bentham, Defence of Usury: Showing the Impolicy of the Present Legal Restraints on the Terms of Pecuniary Bargains (Phila. 1796).

4. 113 Eng.Rep. 119 (K.B. 1839); Synergy Worldwide v. Long, Haymes, Carr, 44 F.Supp.2d 1348 (N.D.Ga.1998) (worthless credits from bankrupt airline); Mullen v.

Hawkins, 141 Ind. 363, 40 N.E. 797 (1895) (quitclaim deed from grantor who had no interest in the premises). See also Brooks v. Ball, 18 Johns. 337 (N.Y.1820). Compare, however, the situation where a recording act requires "valuable consideration." Hood v. Webster, 271 N.Y. 57, 2 N.E.2d 43, 107 ALR 497 (1936).

5. The question of what is bargained for in this kind of case is discussed in § 4.8 infra.

6. 243 Mich. 331, 220 N.W. 665, 59 ALR 311 (1928).

7. See § 4.8 infra.

8. Bowl–Opp v. Bayer, 255 Or. 318, 458 P.2d 435 (1969); Rs. 2d § 79 cmt e. Gross inadequacy of consideration is also an important factor on the issue of whether spe-

"Courts have a stake in attorney's fees contracts; the fairness of the terms reflect directly on the court and its bar."[9] Thus, the Tennessee Supreme Court struck down a fee arrangement that provided for a $2,500 retainer and a one-third contingency to secure a widower's rights in his deceased wife's estate. The probate court had limited the fee to a *quantum meruit* recovery of $12,500. The Supreme Court, however, held that the lawyer should get no compensation because such recoveries "would encourage attorneys to enter exorbitant fee contracts, secure that a safety net of *quantum meruit* is there in case of a subsequent fall."[10] Other lawyers have had disciplinary sanctions imposed for charging excessive fees.[11]

According to some authorities, there is one other kind of transaction in which the court will evaluate the economic adequacy of consideration. This involves a promise to exchange a specific amount of money or fungible goods for a lesser amount of money or goods at the same time and place.[12] Such transactions do not take place in the real world. The reasoning behind this exception is that in such a case the court takes judicial notice of the value of the things exchanged and cannot indulge in the supposed normal presumption of equivalence between the detriment and the promise.[13] The reasoning is a bit of medieval thinking that is at variance with several centuries of legal and economic thought.[14] This exception, if it exists, would not apply to an exchange of different currencies or an exchange for a rare coin since these are generally dealt with in the market place as commodities.[15] Williston extends the rule to a promise to exchange a specific sum of money or fungible goods for the same amount of money or goods at the same time and place,[16] giving as an illustration a bargain stated to be in consideration of one dollar by each to the other paid, where the one dollar was actually paid by each party.[17] Despite our disagreement with his reasoning, it would be ludicrous to assume that each party bargained for the dollar in question.[18] In any event, the Second Restatement of Contracts omits this exception on the ground that an agreement of this kind is highly unlikely to be made.[19]

cific performance will be decreed. See § 16.14 infra.

9. Rosquist v. Soo Line R.R., 692 F.2d 1107, 1111 (7th Cir.1982). On special rules of contract law for lawyers, see Perillo, The Law of Lawyers' Contracts is Different, 67 Fordham L.Rev. 443 (1998).

10. White v. McBride, 937 S.W.2d 796, 797 (Tenn.1996); accord, Brown & Sturm v. Frederick Rd. Ltd. Ptshp., 137 Md.App. 150, 768 A.2d 62 (2001) (disallowing agreed fee; no discussion of alternative fee).

11. In re Swartz, 141 Ariz. 266, 686 P.2d 1236 (1984).

12. Schnell v. Nell, 17 Ind. 29, 79 Am. Dec. 453 (1861); but see 2 Corbin § 5.16 (Perillo & Bender 1995).

13. American University v. Todd, 39 Del. (9 W.W. Harr.) 449, 1 A.2d 595 (Del.Super.1938); see 1 Corbin § 5.16 (Perillo & Bender 1995); 3 Williston § 7:21.

14. See James Gordley, Contract in Pre-Commercial Society and in Western History, VII Int'l Encyc. of Comp. L. ch.2 §§ 41–54 (1997); cf. Verplanck, An Essay on the Doctrine of Contracts 86–97 (1825).

15. 2 Corbin § 5.16 (Perillo & Bender 1995).

16. 3 Williston § 7:21.

17. 3 Williston § 7:21 p. 405–06.

18. 2 Corbin § 5.16 (Perillo & Bender 1995).

19. Rs. 2d § 72, Reporter's Note, citing Whittier, The Restatement of Contracts and

The cases discussed above are to be distinguished from a case in which a sum is exchanged for a promise to return a larger sum if a contingent event occurs. In one case, a party released from a mental institution solicited $50 from a friend for the purpose of traveling to Alaska to recover a gold mine, promising to repay the friend $10,000, if successful. It was held that since the loan was repayable only on the happening of a contingency there was sufficient consideration for this promise to pay two hundred times the amount received.[20]

Economic inadequacy, then, generally does not prevent any bargained-for detriment from constituting consideration. On the other hand, economic inadequacy may constitute some circumstantial evidence of fraud,[21] duress, over-reaching, undue influence, mistake,[22] or that the detriment was not in fact bargained for.[23] Relief from this harshly individualistic principle under the doctrine of unconscionability will be considered elsewhere in this volume.[24]

It should also be noted that the distinction between "sufficiency" of consideration and "adequacy" of consideration employed in the original Restatement is not used in this text or in the Second Restatement.[25]

§ 4.5   Conditions to Gift Distinguished

If A gratuitously says to B, "If it rains tomorrow I promise to pay you $10," B may not enforce the promise even if it rains. A has merely made an unenforceable conditional promise to make a gift.[1] In Kirksey v. Kirksey the defendant wrote to his widowed sister-in-law, promising her a place to raise her family, "If you will come down and see me."[2] In response to the promise she moved to the defendant's land, incurring certain losses and expenses. The court held that the defendant promised to make a gift and that the costs arising from the move were merely

Consideration, 18 Calif.L.Rev. 611, 623 (1930). But see Robertson v. Garvan, 270 F. 643 (S.D.N.Y.1920).

20. Embola v. Tuppela, 127 Wash. 285, 220 P. 789 (1923). See § 4.12(b)(6) infra.

21. Dreyer v. Dreyer, 48 Or.App. 801, 617 P.2d 955 (1980).

22. See text at n.8 supra; West Gate Bank v. Eberhardt, 202 Neb. 762, 277 N.W.2d 104 (1979).

23. See § 4.5 infra and 3 Williston § 7:18.

24. See §§ 9.37–9.40; Matter of Johnson's Will, 351 So.2d 1339 (Miss.1977).

25. Rs. 2d § 71, Reporter's Note. See § 4.2 supra.

§ 4.5

1. A gift ordinarily is ineffective until there has been delivery of the subject matter. See Brown, Personal Property 76–112

(3d ed.1975). In Hoffmann v. Wausau Concrete, 58 Wis.2d 472, 207 N.W.2d 80 (1973), the four elements of a gift were listed as: intent to give, actual or constructive delivery, termination of the donor's dominion and dominion in the donee. The statement in the text is not limited to promises to make gifts. See, e.g., U.S. v. Lewis 876 F.Supp. 308 (D.Mass.1994) (prosecutor's alleged promise not to question a witness about certain payments that would tie him to some bookmakers is not binding as there was no consideration).

2. Kirksey v. Kirksey, 8 Ala. 131 (1845). Compare Matter of Baer's Estate, 196 Misc. 979, 92 N.Y.S.2d 359 (Sur.Ct.1949) (in accord with Kirksey) with Maughs v. Porter, 157 Va. 415, 161 S.E. 242 (1931) (prize offered to anyone who would attend auction; attendance is sufficient detriment and was bargained for). See City Stores v. Ammerman, 266 F.Supp. 766 (D.D.C.1967), aff'd; Bredemann v. Vaughan Mfg., 40 Ill. App.2d 232, 188 N.E.2d 746 (1963), noted

necessary conditions to acceptance of the gift.[3] The defendant did not appear to be bargaining for the plaintiff's presence on his plantation; rather it appeared he wished to help her out of a difficult situation. The promisor made a gratuitous promise rather than an offer.[4] Two observations can be made with respect to this case. First, although adequacy of detriment is not important in itself, it is relevant in determining whether the promisor manifests a gift-making state of mind or a contract-making state of mind. The smallness of the detriment is one of the factors to be considered in determining whether the promisor has bargained for the named detriment or whether the detriment is merely a condition of a gift.[5]

Another factor to be considered in making this determination is whether the happening of the contingency would be a benefit to the promisor.[6] For example, if the defendant had wanted his sister-in-law to come to his house as a housekeeper the result doubtlessly would have been different.[7] Selfish benefit to the promisor is an indication of a contract-making state of mind, whereas if the benefit is merely the pleasure of altruism, a gift-making state of mind may be present. The distinction is not rigid and the test is not conclusive—merely one of the factors to be considered.

In another well-known case a promise was made by an uncle to his nephew to pay $5,000 if the nephew refrained from "drinking, using tobacco, etc., until he was twenty-one." The nephew fulfilled his uncle's requirements and the court held that there was sufficient evidence to sustain the lower court's finding that there was a contract.[8] Although it could be argued that the uncle was motivated by altruism, this factor did not turn the case. Ultimately this question is nothing more nor less than a question of interpretation; one could well conclude that the uncle was dangling his promise in exchange for controlling the nephew's conduct. The rules relating to subjective and objective intention and the dividing line between questions of law and fact again become relevant.[9]

To shift from family cases to commercial life, a case such as Bard v. Kent[10] is instructive. The lessor offered to extend a lease for an additional four years if the lessee promised to make improvements that would cost approximately $10,000. The offer was in writing and was in the

---

in 13 De Paul L.Rev. 158 (1964); Coder v. Smith, 156 Kan. 512, 134 P.2d 408 (1943).

3. Promissory estoppel in this kind of case is discussed in ch. 6.

4. See § 4.2 supra.

5. 3 Williston § 7:18.

6. 3 Williston § 7:18.

7. Davis v. Jacoby, 1 Cal.2d 370, 34 P.2d 1026 (1934); Brackenbury v. Hodgkin, 116 Me. 399, 102 A. 106 (1917).

8. Hamer v. Sidway, 124 N.Y. 538, 27 N.E. 256 (1891); see also Schumm by Whyner v. Berg, 37 Cal.2d 174, 231 P.2d 39, 21 ALR2d 1051 (1951) (naming a child after

actor Wallace Berry); Harris v. Time, 191 Cal.App.3d 465, 236 Cal.Rptr. 471, republished at 191 Cal.App.3d 449, 237 Cal.Rptr. 584 (1987) (opening an envelope); Davies v. Martel Lab. Services, 189 Ill.App.3d 694, 136 Ill.Dec. 951, 545 N.E.2d 475 (1989) (enrolling in an MBA program).

9. 3 Williston § 7:28; 2 Corbin § 5.34 (Perillo & Bender 1995). See ch. 3 and §§ 2.2 and 2.7 supra.

10. 19 Cal.2d 449, 122 P.2d 8, 139 ALR 1032 (1942). See Fisher v. Jackson, 142 Conn. 734, 118 A.2d 316 (1955); Stelmack v. Glen Alden Coal, 339 Pa. 410, 14 A.2d 127 (1940).

form of an option. Before the offer was made, the lessor suggested that the promisee retain an architect to check figures on the proposed improvements of the premises. This was done after the alleged option was created. One question in the case was whether the offer was made irrevocable (assuming that the offeror manifested an intent to make the offer irrevocable)[11] by engaging the architect. This was important because the offeror died prior to an acceptance and thus the power of acceptance was terminated unless there was consideration to make it irrevocable.[12] The court sustained the finding of fact made by the trial court that the hiring of the architect was not consideration because it was merely suggested and not bargained for. Thus, the offer was revocable and death terminated the power of acceptance. Cases such as this place the entire doctrine of consideration in disrepute and help explain the rules of the Restatement (Second) with respect to options discussed in the next section.

§ 4.6   Of Sham and Nominal Consideration

Will a pretense of consideration suffice as consideration? In the case of Bard v. Kent discussed immediately above, the instrument in question recited that the option was given in "consideration of ten dollars and other valuable consideration."[1] The $10 had not been paid. The question is whether this false (sham) recital[2] of consideration makes the offer irrevocable. There are a number of views.

The vast majority of cases have held that it may be shown that the consideration has not been paid and that no other consideration has been given.[3] This result does not contravene the parol evidence rule which permits the contradiction of a recital of fact.[4] There is a minority view—mostly involving options and guaranties—that reaches the opposite result either on the theory that the parties are estopped from contradicting the writing[5] or that the recital gives rise to an implied promise to pay.[6] Under the minority view, the pretended exchange is

---

11. The use of the term "option" by the offeror is a sufficient manifestation of such intent.

12. See § 2.25 supra.

§ 4.6

1. The words "for value received" raise a rebuttable presumption of consideration. Farrar v. Young, 158 W.Va. 977, 216 S.E.2d 575 (1975); Matter of Mingesz' Estate, 70 Wis.2d 734, 235 N.W.2d 296 (1975).

2. A recital of fact in a contract or agreement is prima facie evidence of that fact, subject, however, to refutation. Eastern Plank–Road v. Vaughan, 14 N.Y. 546 (1856). An Oregon statute makes the truth of recitals in a written instrument conclusive between the parties. See High v. Davis, 283 Or. 315, 584 P.2d 725 (1978). As to the relationship of recitals to the body of the instrument, see § 3.13 supra.

3. Bard v. Kent, 19 Cal.2d 449, 122 P.2d 8, 139 ALR 1032 (1942); Neils v. Deist, 180 Mont. 542, 591 P.2d 652 (1979); Komp v. Raymond, 175 N.Y. 102, 67 N.E. 113 (1903). See Ehrlich v. American Moninger Greenhouse Mfg., 26 N.Y.2d 255, 309 N.Y.S.2d 341, 257 N.E.2d 890 (1970); Lewis v. Fletcher, 101 Idaho 530, 617 P.2d 834 (1980) (citing text).

4. 3 Williston § 7:23. We have already discussed one aspect of the parol evidence rule as it relates to consideration in § 3.7(f) supra.

5. Real Estate Co. v. Rudolph, 301 Pa. 502, 153 A. 438 (1930); Hubbard v. Schumaker, 82 Ill.App.3d 476, 37 Ill.Dec. 855, 402 N.E.2d 857 (1980).

6. Baumer v. U.S., 580 F.2d 863 (5th Cir.1978) (Ga. law). The issue of sham consideration arises if there is a false recital of

accepted as if it were real.[7] For this reason, the Restatement (Second) says that in many cases the minority view is fictitious. As a result it takes a different conceptual approach[8] that singles out option contracts and credit guaranties for special treatment, reaching the same result as under the minority view

Section 87 provides, "an offer is binding as an option contract if it is in writing and signed by the offeror, recites a purported consideration for the making of the offer, and proposes an exchange on fair terms within a reasonable time * * *." There is a similar provision with respect to a guaranty. It reads, "A promise to be a surety for the performance of a contractual obligation made to the obligee is binding if the promise is in writing and signed by the promisor and recites a purported consideration."[9]

These sections are placed in topic 2 of Chapter 4 of the Restatement (Second) entitled "Contracts Without Consideration." Thus, the Restatement recognizes that these are enforceable transactions in which there is no exchange. The reason for giving special treatment to options and guaranties is their economic utility.[10] The form used also insures that there is sufficient reflection.[11] A recital of "for value received." should satisfy these sections.[12]

A related but quite different problem arises where the parties, having learned that a gratuitous promise is unenforceable, attempt to make a promise enforceable by cloaking the gratuitous promise with the form of a bargain. Thus, suppose that A wishes to make a binding contract to convey in the future property worth $100,000 to his daughter, B. A intends a gift, but being aware of the doctrine of consideration, drafts an instrument in which A promises to convey in return for B's promise to pay $10. If B knows or should know that the $10 is merely a token, should A's promise be enforced if B tenders the $10 in accordance with terms of the document? There are two views.

Since the exchange is only a charade used to circumvent the doctrine of consideration, one view is that the agreement should not be enforced because the exchange is a formality rather than a genuine intended bargain. The token payment was consideration in name only—nominal consideration.[13] The Restatement (Second) adopts this view.[14] The contrary view is supported by the original Restatement and some other authorities.[15]

fact. It arises in the face of a promise only if it is alleged that it was agreed the promise will not be carried out.

7. Lawrence v. McCalmont, 43 U.S. (2 How.) 426, 452, 11 L.Ed. 326 (1844).

8. Rs. 2d § 87(1) (a) & cmts b and c.

9. Rs. 2d § 88(a).

10. Rs. 2d § 88 cmt a.

11. Rs. 2d § 87 cmts a and c.

12. See n.1 supra.

13. Axe v. Tolbert, 179 Mich. 556, 562, 146 N.W. 418, 420 (1914); Wallace v. Figone, 107 Mo.App. 362, 81 S.W. 492 (1904).

14. Rs. 2d § 71 ill. 5. It should be recalled, however, that the Restatement (Second) has created special rules for options and guaranties under which a false recital of consideration binds the promisor.

15. Rs. 1st § 84 ill. 1; Holmes, The Common Law 293–95 (1881).

The question is one of philosophical approach. According to the first view, if a pretense is accepted as consideration then the doctrine of consideration is undermined. The other view argues that there ought to be a way to make a gratuitous promise binding especially since in many jurisdictions this can no longer be done through the mechanism of a seal.[16]

It is important to note in this situation that there is not a mixture of bargain and gift (the topic of the next section) but rather that there is only a gratuitous promise and a pretense of a bargained-for exchange rather than a bargain in fact.

§ 4.7   Mixture of Gift and Bargain

We have already seen that motive and consideration are not synonymous terms but that motive is related to consideration because the promisor in making the promise is ordinarily motivated by a desire to obtain the detriment sought.[1] It must be recalled, however, that the detriment to be surrendered by the promisee need not be the sole or even the predominant inducement,[2] but it must be enough of an inducement so that it is in fact bargained for.[3]

Suppose A is moved by friendship to promise to sell a horse to B for $1,000 but the horse is worth $5,000. Should the promise be enforced? If there is an element of exchange the answer is, yes, even though A's primary motive in entering into the transaction is friendship.[4] Such an agreement will be enforced.[5]

The ultimate question is how does one determine if there is a mixture of bargain and gift or whether any named consideration is not in fact bargained for. This should be treated as a question of fact unless reasonable jurors could reach only one reasonable conclusion.[6] The Restatement (Second) makes the following significant comment. "Even in the typical commercial bargain, the promisor may have more than one motive, and the person furnishing the consideration need not inquire into the promisor's motives. Unless both parties know that the purported consideration is a mere pretense, it is immaterial that the promisor's desire for consideration is incidental to other objectives and even that

---

16.   Note, 1 Val.U.L.Rev. 102 (1966); see generally Von Mehren, Civil Law Analogues to Consideration, 72 Harv.L.Rev. 1009 (1959).

§ 4.7

1.   See § 4.3 supra; 3 Williston § 7:17.

2.   Pasant v. Jackson Nat. Life Ins., 52 F.3d 94 (5th Cir.1995) (increased compensation was largely to reward past services but continued service supplied the consideration); see § 4.2 supra; 3 Williston § 7:17.

3.   2 Corbin § 5.4 (Perillo & Bender 1995).

4.   Rs. 2d § 71 cmt c; Thomas v. Thomas, 114 Eng.Rep. 330 (1842); Petition of Schaeffner, 96 Misc.2d 846, 410 N.Y.S.2d 44 (1978).

5.   Rs. 2d § 71 cmt c.

6.   Fischer v. Union Trust, 138 Mich. 612, 101 N.W. 852 (1904) ("To say that one dollar was the real, or such valuable consideration as would of itself sustain a deed of land with several thousand dollars, is not in accord with reason or common sense."); see also § 4.5 supra.

the other party knows this to be so."[7] But elsewhere the Restatement (Second) talks about the distinction between bargain and gift being a fine line and dependent on a number of factors.[8] Ultimately the Restatement (Second) takes the position that if the promisee does not know or does not have reason to know that the promisor is introducing detriment into the transaction as a pretense, then the promise should be enforced under the objective theory, but if it is clear from the facts that the consideration is merely pretense the promise will not be enforced.[9]

§ 4.8 Surrender of an Invalid Claim as Detriment

A promise to surrender a *valid* claim constitutes a detriment and, if bargained for, constitutes consideration.[1] There is no unanimity, however, with respect to the surrender of an invalid claim. Everyone has a duty not to assert a claim known to be unfounded and a contract entered into under threat of such a claim may well be set aside on the ground of duress, and restitution awarded to the aggrieved party.[2] If a party believes in the validity of the claim, however, should the surrender of an invalid claim still be considered non-detrimental? There are a number of views.

The earliest view is that the surrender of an invalid claim cannot constitute detriment because a person has no right to assert an unfounded claim.[3] This rule runs contrary to the policy of the law to favor settlements.[4] A more modern view, therefore, is that the surrender of an invalid claim serves as consideration if the claimant has asserted it in good faith and a reasonable person could believe that the claim is well founded.[5] Still other courts have held that the only requirement is good faith,[6] but some of these courts qualify the good faith requirement by insisting that the invalidity of the claim not be obvious; i.e. "unless the claim is so obviously unfounded that the assertion of good faith would affront the intelligence of the ordinary reasonable layman."[7] Under this

7. Rs. 2d § 81 cmt b.

8. Rs. 2d § 71 cmt c.

9. Rs. 2d § 79 cmt d, and ills 5 and 6.

§ 4.8

1. Mustang Equipment v. Welch, 115 Ariz. 206, 564 P.2d 895 (1977).

2. § 9.8 infra.

3. First Texas Sav. Ass'n v. Comprop Inv. Properties, 752 F.Supp. 1568, 1572 (M.D.Fla.1990) (Texas law); Renney v. Kimberly, 211 Ga. 396, 86 S.E.2d 217 (1955); Gunning v. Royal, 59 Miss. 45, 42 Am.Rep. 350 (1881).

4. Stanspec Corp. v. Jelco, Inc., 464 F.2d 1184 (10th Cir.1972); Rs. 2d § 74 cmt a.

5. Aviation Contractor Employees v. U.S., 945 F.2d 1568 (Fed.Cir.1991); Dick v. Dick, 167 Conn. 210, 355 A.2d 110 (1974); Dom J. Moreau & Son v. Federal Pac. Elec., 378 A.2d 151 (Me.1977); Wickman v. Kane,

136 Md.App. 554, 766 A.2d 241 (2001); Melotte v. Tucci, 319 Mass. 490, 66 N.E.2d 357 (1946); Rs. 1st § 76(b); 3 Williston § 7:45. See also Thompson v. Volini, 849 S.W.2d 48 (Mo.App.1993) (surrender of defense).

6. Ralston v. Mathew, 173 Kan. 550, 250 P.2d 841 (1952); Carter v. Provo, 87 N.H. 369, 180 A. 258 (1935); Byrne v. Padden, 248 N.Y. 243, 162 N.E. 20 (1928); Sanders v. Roselawn Memorial Gardens, 152 W.Va. 91, 159 S.E.2d 784 (1968); see 2 Corbin § 7.17 (Perillo & Bender 1995).

7. Murphy v. T. Rowe Price Prime Reserve Fund, 8 F.3d 1420 (9th Cir.1993) (good faith and "colorable" claim); Hall v. Fuller, 352 S.W.2d 559, 562 (Ky.1961), 51 Ky.L.J. 174 (1962); but see Duncan v. Duncan, 147 N.C.App. 152, 553 S.E.2d 925 (2001) (promise not to contest will is consideration although seemingly there were no grounds to contest).

view, even if there is good faith there is no detriment if "the plaintiff has not the shadow of a right as the basis of his claim."[8] When this qualification is added, this third view is very similar to the second view.[9] The Restatement (Second) takes the position that either good faith or objective uncertainty as to the validity of the claim is sufficient. The requirement of the first Restatement that a dispute be honest and reasonable was dropped in favor of the alternative test set forth by Professor Whittier[10] who pointed out that lawyers as well as laymen have great difficulty in determining whether a particular claim is reasonable and that one has a legal and moral right to assert honest claims that may be unreasonable.

The same rules that apply to surrender of the invalid claim also apply to forbearance to assert an invalid claim.[11] Some of the earlier decisions curiously had held that while a promise to forbear could constitute consideration, forbearance without a promise could not.[12] Where the forbearance is intended to be temporary so that a claim may be asserted later, there may be a question whether the forbearance is bargained for.[13]

A claim is invalid if there is a defense to it, for example, where the claim is made under a contract that is void, voidable or unenforceable. Is a worthless claim in the same category? For example, we previously discussed the case of Haigh v. Brooks where the defendant had guarantied an obligation of a third party in exchange for the return of a written document that was invalid under English law. The court not only held that the return of the document constituted detriment but also that its return was the bargained-for exchange.[14] It could, instead, have decided that the surrender of the claim embodied in the document was the bargained-for exchange and in that event the rules relating to invalid claims would apply. A clearer illustration of a case where a piece of paper is bargained for is a case where A, an owner of property, lost a prior deed from B, and promised to pay B $50 for a second deed in order to facilitate obtaining a mortgage loan.[15]

A word might also be said about the case of Newman & Snell's State Bank v. Hunter discussed in § 4.4. The husband died insolvent and was liable to the plaintiff bank on a note. The bank agreed to return the note in exchange for the widow's promise to pay her husband's obligation. The court improperly held that the surrender of the note was not

---

8. Sharp, Pacta Sunt Servanda, 41 Colum.L.Rev. 783, 787 (1941).

9. 2 Corbin § 7.17 (Perillo & Bender 1995).

10. Rs. 2d § 74. Whittier, The Restatement of Contracts and Consideration, 13 Calif.L.Rev. 611, 618–23 (1930). See Rs. 2d, Reporter's Note to § 73.

11. PMX Indus. v. LEP Profit Intern., 31 F.3d 701 (8th Cir.1994) (Iowa law); In re

All Star Feature, 232 F. 1004 (S.D.N.Y. 1916); Rs. 2d § 74 cmt d.

12. Shaw v. Philbrick, 129 Me. 259, 151 A. 423, 74 ALR 290 (1930); Reid–Strutt v. Wagner, 65 Or.App. 475, 671 P.2d 724 (1983) (implied promise to forbear).

13. Rs. 2d § 74 cmt d.

14. See § 4.4 supra.

15. See Rs. 2d § 74 cmt e and ill. 10.

detriment,[16] but assuming the existence of detriment, a number of problems are presented. First, the bank had a valid claim against the husband and therefore the topic of invalid claim can be relevant only if the claim can be treated as invalid simply because it is a worthless (uncollectible) claim. Assuming the invalid claim approach is not available, the question is what, if anything, did she bargain for—a worthless piece of paper, her husband's honor, or some other intangible benefit? The Restatement (Second) in discussing this case suggests as a possible explanation that plaintiff failed to sustain its burden of proof that the desire to secure the note motivated the promisor.[17] That is, it was not established that the widow bargained for the note.

It is important to ascertain what is being bargained for. For example, some authorities indicate that cases involving "worthless pieces of paper" and "invalid claims" should be kept distinct on the grounds that in one case the promisor is bargaining for the discharge of a duty,[18] and in the other case the bargain is for the piece of paper.[19] This means that if the promisor asks for possession of the paper he or she is bargaining for the paper, but if the promisor asks for the surrender of the claim, the promisor is bargaining for the surrender of the claim. The cases do not neatly fit this pattern and we believe these cases should be decided under the tests of good faith and reasonableness unless it is quite clear that the paper rather than the legal rights evidenced by the paper is the object of the bargain. Of course, if the promisor makes clear precisely what is bargained for, there is no problem.

§ 4.9   The Pre-existing Duty Rule

(a) Introduction

The pre-existing duty rule states that where a person performs or promises to perform a legal obligation, or promises to refrain from doing or refrains from doing what the person is not legally privileged to do, the person has not incurred detriment.[1] If a person performs a legal obligation (or less) the person is not incurring legal detriment; no legal privilege is surrendered.[2] Thus, if a landlord promises a tenant that it will refrain from evicting the tenant if the tenant pays past due rent, the landlord may proceed with the eviction even if the tenant pays the rent.[3]

16. See § 4.4 supra.

17. Rs. 2d § 79 ill. 6.

18. 2 Corbin § 5.14 n.6 (Perillo & Bender 1995) discussing Neikirk v. Williams, 81 W.Va. 558, 94 S.E. 947 (1918); Rs. 2d § 79 ill. 2.

19. 2 Corbin § 5.19 (Perillo & Bender 1995).

§ 4.9

1. GLS Development v. Wal–Mart Stores, 3 F.Supp.2d 952 (N.D.Ill.1998),

aff'd; Continental Ins. v. Rutledge & Co., 750 A.2d 1219 (Del.Ch.2000).

2. See § 4.2(a) supra; Hyatt v. Hyatt, 273 Pa.Super. 435, 417 A.2d 726 (1979); Hoffa v. Fitzsimmons, 673 F.2d 1345 (D.C.Cir.1982).

3. Brown v. Philadelphia Housing Auth., 159 F.Supp.2d 23 (E.D.Pa.2001).

The pre-existing duty rule has been the subject of debate. Although the rule is a logical consequence of the doctrine of consideration and its requirement for detriment, the rule can defeat the justifiable expectations of the parties. This is particularly true in the area of a modification of an existing contract where, under the modified agreement, one person is only doing what he or she was already legally obligated to do. Dissatisfaction with the rule has led to a number of exceptions, some of which are illogical or tenuous at best.[4] It is a rule in the process of decay and reformulation. In its homeland it has been abolished.[5]

(b) Pre-existing Duty Rule: Duties Imposed by Law

The pre-existing duty rule applies not only to a modification of an existing contract but to a duty that is not contractual in nature—a duty imposed by law.[6] Thus, for example, if one promises to pay his or her spouse $1,000 at the end of the year if the spouse carries out the obligations of the marriage, the spouse would not be entitled to the money.[7] A promise made to a witness who has been subpoenaed in consideration of his testimony is not enforceable.[8] Where a hotel was by statute required to provide a safe to store valuables, its written promise to do so was not consideration because of the pre-existing duty rule.[9] This conclusion in the context of the mutuality concept (§ 4.12(b) below) resulted in depriving the hotel guest from the benefit of the promise. Holdings such as this stand the pre-existing duty rule on its head. If the promise was supported by consideration, it should be enforceable; the guest should have rights both under the statute and under the promise.[10]

4. Discarding the rule are Quigley v. Wilson, 474 N.W.2d 277 (Iowa App.1991), aff'd. Winter Wolff & Co. v. Co–op. Lead & Chem., 261 Minn. 199, 111 N.W.2d 461 (1961); Angel v. Murray, 113 R.I. 482, 322 A.2d 630, 85 ALR3d 248 (1974); New England Rock Services v. Empire Paving, 53 Conn.App. 771, 731 A.2d 784 (1999); see also 2 Corbin § 7.1 (Perillo & Bender 1995); Patterson, An Apology for Consideration, 58 Colum.L.Rev. 929, 936 (1958); Snyder, The Law of Contract and the Concept of Change, 1999 Wisconsin L.Rev. 607, 612–24; Teeven, Development of Reform of the Preexisting Duty Rule and Its Persistent Survival, 47 Ala.L.Rev. 387 (1996).

5. Williams v. Roffey Bros & Nicholls (Contractors) Ltd., [1990] 1 All E.R. 512 (C.A. 1990). That rules of estoppel, duress, and good faith are beginning to penetrate the formal rules of contract in Australia, England, and New Zealand, see Gleeson, Innovations in Contract: An Australian Analysis, in 2 The Frontiers of Liability (Birks ed. 1994).

6. 3 Williston § 7:41; Keith v. Miles, 39 Miss. 442 (1860).

7. Salmeron v. U.S., 724 F.2d 1357 (9th Cir.1983); Lee v. Savannah Guano, 99 Ga.

572, 27 S.E. 159 (1896); Young v. Cockman, 182 Md. 246, 34 A.2d 428, 149 ALR 1006 (1943); Ritchie v. White, 225 N.C. 450, 35 S.E.2d 414 (1945); Blaechinska v. Howard Mission & Home, 130 N.Y. 497, 29 N.E. 755 (1892).

8. People v. Gumbs, 124 Misc.2d 564, 478 N.Y.S.2d 513 (1984).

9. Goncalves v. Regent Intern. Hotels, 58 N.Y.2d 206, 460 N.Y.S.2d 750, 447 N.E.2d 693 (1983), rearg. denied. See similar unsound reasoning in Adell Broadcasting v. Cablevision Indus., 854 F.Supp. 1280 n. 9 (E.D.Mich.1994). Assuming that the reasoning is not unsound, the promises should have been enforceable under the doctrine of forging. § 4.12(7) infra. A sound result was reached in Janda v. Madera Community Hospital, 16 F.Supp.2d 1181 (E.D.Cal.1998) (hospital's statutory duty to enact by-laws does not deprive them of binding force).

10. See 2 Corbin § 7.19 (Perillo & Bender 1995), entitled: "A Promise to Perform a Pre-existing Duty May be Binding Although It Does Not Constitute Consideration for the Other's Promise."

(c) Pre-existing Duty Rule: Contract Duties

Suppose, in August, B hires A at $900 per week for one year, the term to commence in November. In October, the parties agree to modify the agreement so that the salary is to be $1000 per week. B's promise to pay the additional $100 weekly is not enforceable because A has not incurred detriment. A is merely performing an existing duty.[11] This illustrates an attempted modification without consideration.[12] If, however, A assumed even a slight additional duty that was bargained for, there would be a binding modification.[13]

Instead, if the parties had rescinded their original contract by mutual agreement and subsequently entered into a new employment agreement at a salary of $1000 per week, the promise would be enforceable because A would have been under no obligation to B at the time the new agreement was entered into.[14] Note carefully that in this situation there are three separate and distinct agreements, each of which is supported by consideration. There is the initial agreement, the agreement of rescission by which each party gave up something, and finally the subsequent employment agreement. At the time of the subsequent agreement, there is no pre-existing duty on the part of either party because their duties were discharged by the agreement of rescission.

A number of cases have held the pre-existing duty rule does not apply where an existing agreement is subsequently rescinded by mutual agreement and the rescission and the new agreement are entered into simultaneously.[15] The courts, however, have resisted the invitation to find a rescission implied from the new agreement.[16] This is similar to the last case discussed above except there the rescission and the new agreement were not simultaneous but separated by an interval of time.

11. Ruffin v. Mercury Record Productions, 513 F.2d 222 (6th Cir.1975), cert. denied; Alaska Packers' Ass'n v. Domenico, 117 F. 99 (9th Cir.1902) [on which see Threedys, 2000 Utah L.Rev. 185]; Continental Cas. v. Wilson–Avery, 115 Ga.App. 793, 156 S.E.2d 152 (1967); see 15 Mercer L.Rev. 506 (1964); Insurance Agents v. Abel, 338 N.W.2d 531 (Iowa App.1983); Healy v. Brewster, 59 Cal.2d 455, 30 Cal. Rptr. 129, 380 P.2d 817 (1963); Rudio v. Yellowstone Merch., 200 Mont. 537, 652 P.2d 1163 (1982). See Corbin, Does a Pre-existing Duty Defeat Consideration, 27 Yale L.J. 362 (1918); Havighurst, Consideration, Ethics and Administration, 42 Colum.L.Rev. 1 (1942); Hillman, Contract Modification in Iowa, 65 Iowa L.Rev. 343 (1980). Before the consideration question is reached, it is necessary to see if there was an agreement. It is often stated that a modification agreement must be demonstrated by clear and/or satisfactory evidence. Grizzly Bar v. Hartman, 169 Colo. 178, 454 P.2d 788 (1969); St. Louis Fire & Marine Ins. v. Lewis, 230 So.2d 580 (Miss.1970).

12. See UCC § 2–209(1) which permits a modification of a sales contract without consideration, discussed in § 5.14 infra; the revision draft is substantially the same.

13. Care Travel v. Pan American World Airways, 944 F.2d 983 (2d Cir.1991); West India Indus. v. Tradex, 664 F.2d 946 (5th Cir.1981); Lugassy v. Independent Fire Ins., 636 So.2d 1332 (Fla.1994).

14. Leonard v. Downing, 246 Ark. 397, 438 S.W.2d 327 (1969); Jura v. Sunshine Biscuits, 118 Cal.App.2d 442, 258 P.2d 90 (1953); Rs. 1st § 406 ill. 1.

15. Martiniello v. Bamel, 255 Mass. 25, 150 N.E. 838 (1926); Schwartzreich v. Bauman–Basch, 231 N.Y. 196, 131 N.E. 887 (1921); cf. Frommeyer v. L. & R. Constr., 261 F.2d 879, 69 ALR2d 1040 (3d Cir.1958).

16. Armour & Co. v. Celic, 294 F.2d 432 (2d Cir.1961). See Patterson, An Apology for Consideration, 58 Colum.L.Rev. 929 (1958).

Where the rescission and the subsequent agreement are simultaneous, the pre-existing duty rule is violated because the parties clearly intend the rescission to be contingent on the new contract, which, in turn, is contingent on the rescission.[17] The Restatement (Second) rejects these cases as employing fictions.[18]

Although the pre-existing duty rule is generally followed,[19] there are many decisions in which ingenuity has been employed in circumventing the rule, often on tenuous grounds. These decisions show that the courts are not impressed with the fairness of the rule.[20] All that is needed to satisfy the consideration requirement is the slightest change in duties.[21] Indeed, there are cases holding that if the parties agree to an addendum to clarify their contract, no new consideration is required.[22]

Another exception to the pre-existing duty rule recognized by some jurisdictions is that a modification will be upheld even if it is without consideration if the modification is made after unforeseen difficulties have arisen in the performance of the prior agreement.[23] These decisions are inconsistent with the classical pre-existing rule unless the difficulties encountered amount to impossibility or impracticability of performance, in which event the excuse given by the law for non-performance would erase the pre-existing duty problem.[24] Suppose A agrees to excavate a building site for B for a stated price. When solid rock is unexpectedly encountered, A notifies B and they agree that A will complete the job and that B will pay double the contract price, which is reasonable in relation to the work to be done. Under the classical pre-existing duty rule, B's promise to pay double the price is not enforceable because the unforeseen difficulty did not amount to impossibility of performance and therefore did not excuse A from performing. In jurisdictions recognizing the exception, however, the promise would be binding.

The Restatement (Second) has adopted the spirit of the exception. Its rule has also been strongly influenced by UCC § 2–209(1), discussed below.[25] It regards the exception as being fair and useful because a

---

17. 3 Williston § 7:37; 2 Corbin § 7.15 (Perillo & Bender 1995).

18. Rs. 2d § 89 cmt b. But it reaches the same conclusion under § 89(a), see ill. 3.

19. Panasonic Comm. & Sys. Co. v. State, 691 A.2d 190 (Me.1997); Yerkovich v. AAA, 461 Mich. 732, 610 N.W.2d 542 (2000).

20. Angel v. Murray, 113 R.I. 482, 322 A.2d 630, 85 ALR3d 248 (1974).

21. Betterton v. First Interstate Bank, 800 F.2d 732 (8th Cir.1986).

22. Farmers Alliance Mut. Ins. v. Hulstrand Constr. Co., 632 N.W.2d 473 (N.D. 2001).

23. Pittsburgh Testing Lab. v. Farnsworth & Chambers, 251 F.2d 77 (10th Cir. 1958); Lange v. U.S., 120 F.2d 886 (4th Cir.1941); King v. Duluth, M. & N. Ry., 61 Minn. 482, 63 N.W. 1105 (1895); Watkins & Son v. Carrig, 91 N.H. 459, 21 A.2d 591, 138 ALR 131 (1941).

24. Rs. 1st § 76 ill. 8; Burton v. Kenyon, 46 N.C.App. 309, 264 S.E.2d 808 (1980); McGovern v. New York, 234 N.Y. 377, 138 N.E. 26, 25 ALR 1442 (1923); see 2 Corbin § 7.6 (Perillo & Bender 1995). Rs. 2d § 89 cmt c indicates that a decision such as the one in McGovern might in some states be based on "statutes or constitutional provisions [which] flatly forbid the payment of extra compensation to Government contractors." See Oneida v. Kennedy, 189 Misc.2d 689, 734 N.Y.S.2d 402 (2001).

25. See § 5.14 infra.

modification is "ancillary" to the original exchange and has utility.[26] It states that a promise to modify "under a contract not fully performed on either side is binding if the modification is fair and equitable[27] in view of circumstances not anticipated when the contract was made."[28] An event that is foreseen as a remote possibility may, according to the Restatement (Second), "be unanticipated for this purpose if it was not adequately covered in the agreement."[29] Whether the modification is fair and equitable depends on many factors.[30] Professor Eisenberg has suggested that it would have been better to remove the pre-existing duty rule from the Restatement and test modified contracts under the doctrine of unconscionability.[31]

There are a number of other theories adopted to defeat the pre-existing duty rule. The best known of these is based on the idea that a party incurs legal detriment in giving up the legal right to breach the contract.[32] This is unsound. Although a contracting party often can refuse to perform the agreement and respond in damages, the ability to breach the contract is neither a right nor a lawful exercise of power.[33] The mere fact that the business convenience of the promisor is served does not mean that the promisee has suffered a detriment or that the promisor has received legal benefit. The law has generally regarded a breach of contract to be as much a wrong as the commission of a tort,[34] although some economic analysts, who applaud "efficient breaches,"

26. Rs. 2d § 89 cmt a.

27. Guilford Yacht Club Ass'n v. Northeast Dredging, 438 A.2d 478 (Me.1981). See Horowitz, The Historical Foundations of Modern Contract Law, 87 Harv.L.Rev. 917 (1974). The reference to "fair and equitable" relates to the issues of duress and conscionability. Comment b states in part, "The limitation to a modification which is 'fair and equitable' goes beyond the absence of coercion and requires an objectively demonstrable reason for seeking a modification." UCC § 2–209 cmt 2 (dealing with duress). See § 5.14 infra.

28. Rs. 2d § 89(a) It is interesting to note that the position of the Second Restatement had been widespread in the nineteenth century. In Meech v. Buffalo, 29 N.Y. 198, 218 (1864), the following language appears. "The contractor, finding that the contract price must prove wholly inadequate on account of this hidden and wholly unforeseen obstacle, quitted the work and declined to proceed further without additional compensation. It was under these circumstances that the new agreement, providing for the additional compensation, was made; and the law will uphold it." One judge went further, saying, "It is conceded that the parties might have canceled the agreement, and, if they could do this, they could certainly modify it." 29 N.Y. at 213–14.

29. Rs. 2d § 89 cmt b.

30. Rs. 2d § 89 ills. 4 and 5.

31. See Eisenberg, The Principles of Consideration, 67 Corn.L.Rev. 640, 644 (1982).

32. Swartz v. Lieberman, 323 Mass. 109, 80 N.E.2d 5, 12 A.L.R.2d 75 (1948). In Lattimore v. Harsen, 14 Johns. 330 (N.Y. 1817), the court construed a contract containing a penalty clause as giving the defendant an option to perform or pay the penalty. The decision is clearly obsolete. Wirth & Hamid Fair Booking v. Wirth, 265 N.Y. 214, 192 N.E. 297 (1934); Bradshaw v. Millikin, 173 N.C. 432, 92 S.E. 161 (1917); Rs. 1st § 378; 11 Williston § 1444. And see Armstrong v. Stiffler, 189 Md. 630, 56 A.2d 808 (1948) ("Forfeiture and damage clauses are means to insure performance, not optional alternatives for performance.") 56 A.2d at 810.

33. Barbour, The "Right" to Breach a Contract, 16 Mich.L.Rev. 106 (1917), Selected Readings 500; Note, 55 L.Q.Rev. 1 (1939).

34. See Perillo, Misreading Oliver Wendell Holmes on Efficient Breach and Tortious Interference, 68 Fordham L.Rev. 1085, 1087 (2000); 2 Corbin § 7.12 (Perillo & Bender 1995).

regard this attitude as wrong.[35] In addition, a modifying promise that is not supported by consideration has been enforced under the Wisconsin rule which employs the fiction that the original consideration is imported into the new agreement.[36] A few jurisdictions have held that no consideration is required for a modifying agreement.[37] Still others have looked on the modification as an attempt to mitigate damages.[38] Some cases have held modifications to be binding on the theory of promissory estoppel.[39]

At the beginning of this section, the pre-existing duty rule was criticized on the ground that it is unreasonable for the law to prevent adult contracting parties from modifying their contractual obligations. In conflict with the reasonableness of this last proposition is the realization that modifications are frequently agreed to under conditions that approach duress. In a typical situation, the building contractor threatens to terminate operations if the price is not increased. The landowner succumbs rather than face the pitfalls of litigation and the difficulty of procuring a substitute contractor with dispatch. Although the courts have generally followed the pre-existing duty rule, there is a trend in the direction of making a modification without consideration binding.[40] At the same time the doctrine of duress is evolving to make it easier to set aside a modification on grounds of duress.[41]

(d) Pre-existing Duty Rule: Three Party Cases

As we have just seen, if A, a harness race driver, enters into a bilateral contract with B, the owner of a horse, to ride in a race for $1,000 and the contract is modified by the parties to provide for compensation of $1,500, under the majority view the promise to pay more is not supported by consideration because A will only be doing what A is legally obligated to do. But if C, an outsider, who does not have a right to performance under the contract, but owns the dam of B's horse and would receive a prize if B's horse wins, promises to pay a bonus of $500 to A if A rides, there are conflicting views as to whether C's promise is supported by consideration.[42]

35. See Posner, Economic Analysis of Law 118–120, 128–29 (4th ed. 1992). Judge Posner's efficient breach analysis is well-answered by Friedmann, The Efficient Breach Fallacy, 18 J.Legal Studies 1 (1989); Macneil, Efficient Breaches of Contract: Circles in the Sky, 68 Va. L.Rev. 947 (1982); and Woodward, Contractarians, Community, and the Tort of Interference with Contracts, 80 Minn.L.Rev. 1103 (1996); see § 14.36 infra.

36. Jacobs v. J.C. Penney, 170 F.2d 501 (7th Cir.1948); Everlite Mfg. v. Grand Valley Mach. & Tool, 44 Wis.2d 404, 171 N.W.2d 188 (1969); Holly v. First Nat. Bank, 218 Wis. 259, 260 N.W. 429 (1935); Mid–Century, Ltd. v. United Cigar–Whelan Stores, 109 F.Supp. 433 (D.D.C.1953). Minnesota and New Hampshire seem to be in accord. See Kramas v. Beattie, 107 N.H.

321, 221 A.2d 236 (1966) and Rye v. Phillips, 203 Minn. 567, 282 N.W. 459, 119 ALR 1120 (1938). See also § 4.10.

37. Industrial Dev. Bd. v. Fuqua Indus., 523 F.2d 1226 (5th Cir.1975) (Alabama law); see Shattuck, Contracts in Washington, 1937–1957, 34 Wash.L.Rev. 24, 58–59 (1959).

38. Scanlon v. Northwood, 147 Mich. 139, 110 N.W. 493 (1907); Evans v. Oregon & W. R.R., 58 Wash. 429, 108 P. 1095 (1910).

39. Canada v. Allstate Ins., 411 F.2d 517 (5th Cir.1969); see § 6.3 infra.

40. See §§ 5.13 & 5.14 infra.

41. See § 5.15 infra.

42. Bronaugh, A Secret Paradox of the Common Law, 2 L. & Philos. 193 (1983).

The classical view is that, because the harness race driver is merely promising to perform a contractual obligation, the agreement is void.[43] The result is different, even under this view, if the third party bargains for and causes the original contracting parties to refrain from rescinding their previous agreement; in that event A and B have incurred a detriment because together they have a legal right to rescind.[44] The same is true if A merely gives up the privilege to make such a proposal to B.[45] But in either case the question is whether this is what C bargained for.

A second and untenable view would enforce the promise of C if the contract between the driver and C is bilateral and not unilateral.[46] The fallacy in this is that it does not make any difference if the agreement is bilateral or unilateral because A's promise can be consideration only if the performance which is promised would be consideration; under the traditional view, it is not.[47]

The weight of modern authority holds that C's promise is enforceable whether or not C's arrangement with A is unilateral or bilateral.[48] This view is ordinarily justified on one of two grounds. One approach is that C's promise should be enforced because A's pre-existing duty was owed to B and not to C.[49] As a result A confers a benefit on C and some courts have held that a benefit conferred on the promisor is sufficient even if there is no detriment.[50]

The second justification is that there is less likelihood of duress or unfair pressure in the three party cases than in the two party cases.[51] Thus, the Restatements state that there is consideration for C's promise.[52] The Restatement (Second), however, refuses to apply its rule if the pre-existing duty is owed to the promisor as a member of the public.[53] For example, the public duty of a police officer would prevent the recovery of a reward for performing an act within the scope of the officer's employment.[54]

If the arrangement between the driver and the owner was an offer to a unilateral contract, the driver would not be under a duty to perform. Therefore, the promise would be binding on the performance of the

43. McDevitt v. Stokes, 174 Ky. 515, 192 S.W. 681 (1917); Arend v. Smith, 151 N.Y. 502, 45 N.E. 872 (1897).

44. De Cicco v. Schweizer, 221 N.Y. 431, 117 N.E. 807 (1917).

45. Rs. 2d § 73 cmt d.

46. Beale, Notes on Consideration, 17 Harv.L.Rev. 71 (1903); Pollock, Afterthoughts on Consideration, 17 L.Q.R. 415, 421 (1901).

47. See § 4.12 infra; 3 Williston § 7:39.

48. Patterson v. Katt, 791 S.W.2d 466 (Mo.App.1990); Perry M. Alexander Constr. v. Burbank, 83 N.C.App. 503, 350 S.E.2d 877 (1986); contra, In re Bennett, 154 B.R. 157 (N.D.N.Y.1993).

49. Rs. 2d § 73 cmt d.

50. Briskin v. Packard Motor Car, 269 Mass. 394, 169 N.E. 148 (1929); Neal v. Hagedorn Constr., 192 N.C. 816, 135 S.E. 120 (1926). See § 4.2 supra. See also Morgan, 1 Minn.L.Rev. 383 (1915), Selected Readings 491.

51. Morrison Flying Serv. v. Deming Nat. Bank, 404 F.2d 856 (10th Cir.1968), cert. denied; Rs. 2d § 73 cmt d.

52. Rs. 1st § 84(d); The Rs. 2d adds that B may be the party who is entitled to the additional payment on the theory that C's promise of payment to A is an interference with the employment relation. Rs. 2d § 73 ill 12.

53. Rs. 2d § 73 cmt b.

54. Rs. 2d § 73 ills. 1 and 2; Denney v. Reppert, 432 S.W.2d 647 (Ky.1968).

requested act. Thus, it is not uncommon for a person to earn multiple rewards for a single requested act, e.g., providing information leading to the arrest of a fugitive.

§ 4.10   Part Payment Cannot Satisfy a Debt

Thus far, we have examined consideration in the context of the enforceability of a promise. Here, we consider it in the context of the discharge of a debt. In Pinnel's Case, Lord Coke in dictum stated "that payment of a lesser sum on the [due] day in satisfaction of a greater, cannot be any satisfaction of the whole, because it appears to the judges that by no possibility, a lesser sum can be a satisfaction to the plaintiff for a greater sum."[1] Part payment by a debtor of an amount here and now undisputedly due is not consideration to support a promise by the creditor to discharge the entire amount due.[2] The same is true if there were a purported present discharge, as for example if the creditor delivered a release, not under seal, to the debtor.[3] This rule is a particular application of the pre-existing duty rule since the debtor in making part payment of an amount here and now undisputedly due is only doing what the debtor is legally obligated to do. Since consideration's primary function is to validate executory promises, the question of a present discharge of duties, as an original proposition could have been distinguished and exempted from the requirement of consideration.[4]

Lord Coke's dictum was not put to the test in an authoritative fashion until Foakes v. Beer[5] was decided in 1884. The plaintiff had obtained a judgment of some £2000 against the defendant. The parties agreed that the plaintiff would accept in full satisfaction of the judgment, £500 in cash and the balance in installments. There was no promise to pay interest. The defendant fully complied with the agreement and the amount of the judgment was fully paid. Plaintiff subsequently brought suit for interest on the judgment. The defendant argued that pursuant to the agreement he was fully discharged. The House of Lords ruled that payment, even if bargained for in satisfaction of an obligation, could not discharge the obligation to pay interest which attached as a matter of law because defendant had only performed a pre-existing legal obligation.[6]

§ 4.10

1. 77 Eng.Rep. 237 (1602).

2. Voight & McMakin Air Conditioning v. Property Redev., 276 A.2d 239 (D.C.App. 1971); In re Cunningham's Estate, 311 Ill. 311, 142 N.E. 740 (1924); Warren v. Hodge, 121 Mass. 106 (1876); Bunge v. Koop, 48 N.Y. 225, 8 Am.Rep. 546 (1872); 3 Williston § 7:26.

3. See § 21.10 infra.

4. Schiffman v. Atlas Mill Supply, 193 Cal.App.2d 847, 14 Cal.Rptr. 708 (1961); 15 Williston § 1851; see § 4.2 supra.

5. 9 App.Cas. 605 (1884).

6. See generally, Ames, Two Theories of Consideration, 12 Harv.L.Rev. 515, 521–531 (1899); Ferson, The Rule of Foakes v. Beer, 31 Yale L.J. 15 (1921); Hemingway, The Rule in Pennel's Case, 13 Va.L.Rev. 380 (1927); Gold, The Present Status of the Rule in Pinnel's Case, 30 Ky.L.J. 72, 187 (1942); Comment, 11 Ariz.L.Rev. 344 (1969).

Despite its overwhelming acceptance, the rule of Foakes v. Beer has been persistently criticized. In Frye v. Hubbell,[7] the rule was rejected and it was held that part payment of a debt, accepted in full payment, discharged liability for the balance. A small number of other cases have followed this minority view.[8] Other cases have held that if unforeseen hardships make full payment more onerous than anticipated, acceptance of part payment will discharge the balance. This would occur, for example, if there was an economic depression and an impecunious debtor has made a part payment in satisfaction of the whole.[9] The Restatement (Second) has adopted this rule.[10]

Even in jurisdictions that follow the rule of Foakes v. Beer, dissatisfaction with the rule has made the courts eager to ferret out some kind of detriment in the fact pattern. Lord Coke's dictum in Pinnel's Case indicated that delivery of a "horse, hawk or robe" in addition to or in place of part payment of the pre-existing debt would provide the necessary detriment to support the discharge of the debt. Of course the question of whether the detriment mentioned was bargained for must be examined and a pretense may not be enough.[11] Consideration has been found where the part payment was prior to the due date,[12] or was made at a place other than that stated in the agreement,[13] or if the debtor gives security in addition to the part payment,[14] or if the part payment is by a third person.[15] On the other hand it is generally held that the debtor's execution of the debtor's own promissory note or check is not sufficient consideration.[16] This holding is probably correct in most cases: the execution of a note or check, although a detriment, is rarely bargained for as such. If the creditor in fact bargained for the note or check to obtain evidence or secure facility of collection, consideration is present.[17]

More complicated problems have been presented where the debtor is insolvent. In making a part payment, the insolvent is only performing part of a legal obligation. Therefore, most courts have held that the insolvent is obligated to pay the balance.[18] But the situation is different if the debtor refrains from bankruptcy or insolvency proceedings at the

7. 74 N.H. 358, 68 A. 325 (1907), further explained in Watkins & Son v. Carrig, 91 N.H. 459, 21 A.2d 591, 138 ALR 131 (1941). This view was advanced in Rye v. Phillips, 203 Minn. 567, 282 N.W. 459, 119 ALR 1120 (1938) (dictum); cf. Winter Wolff & Co. v. Co-op. Lead & Chemical, 261 Minn. 199, 111 N.W.2d 461 (1961).

8. See cases cited in note 7.

9. Liebreich v. Tyler State Bank & Trust, 100 S.W.2d 152 (Tex.Civ.App.1936) (economic depression). Some courts have adopted the same rule with respect to a modification of an executory contract. See § 4.9(c) supra; Rs. 2d § 89.

10. Rs. 2d § 73 cmt c.

11. Rs. 2d § 71 cmt b.

12. Codner v. Siegel, 246 Ga. 368, 271 S.E.2d 465 (1980); Princeton Coal v. Dorth, 191 Ind. 615, 133 N.E. 386, 24 ALR 1471 (1921); see 3 Williston § 7:27 n.12.

13. 3 Williston § 7:27 n.14.

14. Jaffray v. Davis, 124 N.Y. 164, 26 N.E. 351 (1891).

15. Welsh v. Loomis, 5 Wn.2d 377, 105 P.2d 500 (1940).

16. Shanley v. Koehler, 80 A.D. 566, 80 N.Y.S. 679 (1903), aff'd; cf. § 3-303(a) (1) (1990); UCC § 3-408 (pre-1990).

17. Id.

18. 3 Williston § 7:26.

request of the creditor,[19] or if there is a composition agreement among creditors.[20]

There are decisions, even in states that follow the rule of Foakes v. Beer, which are difficult to reconcile with the rule. It is generally held that if a creditor agrees, in consideration of part payment, to discharge a retiring partner, the promise is binding.[21] There are occasional decisions holding that when a promisee is entitled to money payable in installments, as for example, under a lease or separation agreement, acceptance of a lesser sum in full payment discharges the debtor as to that installment despite the absence of detriment.[22] This would not be true as to any unpaid future installment. These cases should be carefully compared with a case such as McKenzie v. Harrison.[23] A lease called for payment of $1250 per quarter. The lessor subsequently agreed to accept and accepted $875 per quarter. On each payment the lessor gave the tenant a receipt marked "payment in full." On these facts alone, under the rule of Foakes v. Beer, the lessor would have the right to demand payment of the difference between the amount called for in the lease and the amount paid. The court, however, found that the lessor had a donative intent and the receipts constituted sufficient delivery of the gift.[24] As to future installments, the promise to accept reduced rental payments was not binding since gratuitous promises are not enforceable.

Injurious reliance on the creditor's promise to accept part payment in full satisfaction of an obligation could result in enforceability of the

19. Melroy v. Kemmerer, 218 Pa. 381, 67 A. 699 (1907); Brown Shoe v. Beall, 107 S.W.2d 456 (Tex.Civ.App.1937); Rs. 2d § 73, ill. 6.

20. Although composition agreements are invariably sustained, there has been a certain amount of difficulty in ascertaining the consideration which sustains them. As stated in Rs. 1st § 84, cmt d: "The consideration for which each assenting creditor bargains may be any or all of the following: (1) part payment of the sum due him; (2) the promise of each other creditor to forgo a portion of his claim; (3) forbearance (or promise thereof) by the debtor to pay the assenting creditors more than equal proportions; (4) the action of the debtor in securing the assent of the other creditors; (5) the part payment made to other creditors. Of these, number 1 is not a sufficient consideration; but each of the other four is sufficient. Numbers 4 and 5 are seldom bargained for in fact; but numbers 2 and 3 are practically always bargained for, by reasonable implication if not in express terms. Still other considerations may be agreed on in any case." See Massey v. Del–Valley, 46 N.J.Super. 400, 134 A.2d 802 (1957); White v. Kuntz, 107 N.Y. 518, 14 N.E. 423 (1887); A. & H. Lithoprint v. Bernard Dunn Adv., 82 Ill.App.2d 409, 226 N.E.2d 483 (1967).

21. Luddington v. Bell, 77 N.Y. 138, 33 Am.Rep. 601 (1879); 3 Williston § 7:29 (pointing out the possibility of detriment in the event of subsequent insolvency); see also J. Crane and A. Bromberg, Law of Partnership 450 (1968) who state that "Changing a joint obligation as partners into a separate obligation, thereby giving the creditor a parity with other creditors of the separate estate, will operate as consideration." Query, is this bargained for?

22. Julian v. Gold, 214 Cal. 74, 3 P.2d 1009 (1931); Russo v. De Bella, 220 N.Y.S.2d 587 (1961); see Annot., 30 ALR3d 1259 (1970); contra, Abbott v. Kiser, 654 So.2d 640 (Fla.App.1995) (alimony); Levine v. Blumenthal, 117 N.J.L. 23, 186 A. 457 (1936), aff'd; Pape v. Rudolph Bros., 257 A.D. 1032, 13 N.Y.S.2d 781 (1939), aff'd. This kind of case is discussed in more detail in ch. 21 infra. Cf. Rs. 1st § 416.

23. 120 N.Y. 260, 24 N.E. 458 (1890); see also Gray v. Barton, 55 N.Y. 68, 14 Am.Rep. 181 (1873).

24. See Rs. 2d § 275 cmt a ill. 2 and § 21.12 infra. But see Brown, Personal Property § 8.5 (3d ed. 1975).

promise[25] under the doctrine of promissory estoppel.[26]

Statutory changes in the rule of Foakes v. Beer, discussed below, have been made in a number of jurisdictions and by the UCC.[27]

§ 4.11 Consideration for an Accord and Satisfaction

(a) Introduction

Earlier, in § 4.8, the settlement of claims was discussed. The focus was on the surrender of, or forbearance from pursuing, an invalid claim as consideration for a promise made to the claimant. In this section we shall discuss the other side of the transaction. The claimant is asserting that the agreement to discharge a claim or the purported discharge of the claim is not supported by consideration.

(b) Discussion

The rule of Foakes v. Beer (§ 4.10) applies only to liquidated claims, that is, claims that are undisputed as to their existence and amount. If there is any dispute as to liability or the amount due or even as to some other question, for example the method of payment, the claim is unliquidated even if a party's assertion is incorrect, provided that the assertion is made in good faith and, according to some jurisdictions, if it is reasonably asserted.[1]

An accord is an offer to give or to accept a stipulated performance in the future in satisfaction or discharge of the obligor's existing duty plus an acceptance of that offer.[2] The performance of this stipulated performance is the satisfaction. If the agreement is not performed, then the special rules relating to breach of an accord apply. These rules are discussed below.[3] Also discussed at the same point is a more detailed discussion of how the rules of accord and satisfaction apply in a situation that does not involve the rule of Foakes v. Beer.

When a question of accord and satisfaction is presented, the analysis can be divided into three parts. 1) Have the parties gone through a process of offer and acceptance (accord)? 2) Has the accord been carried out (satisfaction)? The third question is whether the offer and acceptance is supported by consideration.[4] If so, there is a binding accord and satisfaction; if not, there is no accord and satisfaction.

---

25. Central London Property Trust v. High Trees House [1947] K.B. 130.

26. In re Stein's Estate, 50 Misc.2d 627, 271 N.Y.S.2d 449 (1966); see ch. 6.

27. See § 5.16 infra.

§ 4.11

1. Tanner v. Merrill, 108 Mich. 58, 65 N.W. 664 (1895); Fuller v. Kemp, 138 N.Y. 231, 33 N.E. 1034 (1893); Rs. 2d § 74 cmts b and c. See also Eames Vacuum Brake v. Prosser, 157 N.Y. 289, 51 N.E. 986 (1898);

Rs. 1st § 420; 3 Williston § 7:34; 2 Corbin § 7.17 (Perillo & Bender 1995).

2. Electra Ad Sign v. Cedar Rapids Truck Center, 316 N.W.2d 876 (Iowa 1982); Christensen v. Abbott, 595 P.2d 900 (Utah 1979).

3. See §§ 21.4–21.7 infra.

4. Geisco v. Honeywell, 682 F.2d 54 (2d Cir.1982).

An offer of accord must make it clear that the offeror seeks a total discharge. If this is not done, any payment made and accepted will be treated as part payment.[5] An acceptance of such an offer may take place by verbal assent or by conduct including the cashing of a check sent "in full payment" or according to some authorities by the retention of such check. All of these matters and others will be explored in greater detail below and clarified by a discussion of the following six fact patterns.

(c) Cases

Case 1. The debtor, D, owes C, the creditor, $100 here and now undisputably due; the claim is liquidated. D sends a check for $50 marked "paid in full" and C cashes the check.

We have already seen that the offer of accord must make it clear that the offeror is seeking a complete discharge. Do the quoted words achieve this result? According to most of the cases they do.[6] But there is a growing number of recent cases to the effect that this language is only one of the factors to be considered in determining whether an offer of accord has been made.[7] The debtor-offeror must make it clear to the creditor that the creditor is being asked to *agree* that the check will be accepted in full payment.[8] This means also that the language must be conspicuous.[9] The language need not be on the check; it could be in a letter of transmission.[10] It has also been held that the creditor must have been given notice of the dispute.[11] It should be very clear to the creditor that there is a dispute and an offer of settlement.[12]

Assuming the existence of an offer of accord, the second question would be one of acceptance. Most cases hold that the cashing (or depositing) of the check would amount to an acceptance.[13] Beyond that, some cases have held that the retention of the check for an unreasonable period is the same as cashing it and therefore operates as an accep-

---

5. See Calamari, The New York "Check Cashing" Rule, 1 N.Y.C.L.E. No. 2, p. 113 (1963); Scantlin v. Superior Homes, 6 Kan. App.2d 144, 627 P.2d 825 (1981); Pincus–Litman v. Canon U.S.A., 98 A.D.2d 681, 469 N.Y.S.2d 756 (1983); Hall GMC v. Crane Carrier, 332 N.W.2d 54 (N.D.1983). The burden of proof is on the party who asserts the existence of the accord and satisfaction. Bryson v. Kenney, 430 A.2d 1102 (Me. 1981). But see Sam Finley, Inc. v. Barnes, 147 Ga.App. 432, 249 S.E.2d 147 (1978).

6. Leonard v. Gray, 686 A.2d 1079 (Me. 1996); Calamari, supra note 5, at 113.

7. Ensley v. Fitzwater, 59 Or.App. 411, 651 P.2d 734 (1982); Kibler v. Frank L. Garrett & Sons, 73 Wn.2d 523, 439 P.2d 416 (1968).

8. Nationwide Mutual Ins. v. Quality Builders, 192 Mich.App. 643, 482 N.W.2d 474 (1992) ("Paid in full" insufficient notice of an offer); JRDM v. U.W. Marx Inc.,

252 A.D.2d 854, 675 N.Y.S.2d 691 (1998); Peterson v. Ramsey County, 563 N.W.2d 103 (N.D.1997); Hastings v. Top Cut Feedlots, 285 Or. 261, 590 P.2d 1210 (1979).

9. UCC § 3–311 (1990 revision) requires "a conspicuous statement to the effect that the instrument was tendered as full satisfaction of the claim."

10. Lincoln Nat. Life Ins. v. Prodromidis, 862 F.Supp. 10 (D.Mass.1994).

11. Trans World Grocers v. Sultana Crackers, 257 A.D.2d 616, 684 N.Y.S.2d 284 (1999).

12. Cadle Co. v. Hayes, 116 F.3d 957(1st Cir.1997); Zeller v. Markson Rosenthal & Co., 299 N.J.Super. 461, 691 A.2d 414 (1997).

13. Mobil Oil v. Prive, 137 Vt. 370, 406 A.2d 400 (1979); Malarchick v. Pierce, 264 N.W.2d 478 (N.D.1978). For some contrary cases, see 15 Williston § 1854 (3d ed.).

tance.[14] A second view is that the retention of the check does not amount to an acceptance.[15] Still other cases have held that the retention of the check creates a question of fact on this issue of acceptance.[16] It seems to us that if the check is uninvited, there should be no duty to speak. The creditor should be able to incinerate an uninvited offer. If, however, the check is a cashier's check or insurance draft, it is property—the commercial equivalent of cash—and any exercise of dominion over it constitutes a contract by the tort of conversion.

Assuming an offer and acceptance, the next issue is performance. The cashing of the check may operate not only as the necessary acceptance but also as the completion of performance.

In Case 1, the alleged accord and satisfaction is not supported by consideration because the debt is undisputably due. Thus, under the rule of Foakes v. Beer there is no consideration to support C's promise to take, or the actual taking, of a lesser amount in full satisfaction.[17] D is only doing what D was legally obligated to do. The rule stated here would not apply to the satisfaction of a judgment where the satisfaction is entered on the record.[18] Such a satisfaction requires no consideration.

Case 2. Assume the same facts as in Case 1, but further assume that there was a good faith dispute between the parties. C honestly tells D that C is entitled to $100 and D honestly replies that C is only entitled to $50, D then sends a check for $75 marked "payment in full." C cashes it.

The issues of offer, acceptance and performance are the same as in Case 1. There is consideration to support the accord and satisfaction because of the existence of the good faith dispute and a compromise which involved the surrender of detriment by both parties.[19]

What is the key difference between the two cases? In the first case the sum of $100 was "here and now undisputably due," while the second case involves a "good faith dispute."[20] Do the words "payment in full" without any other communication indicate the possibility of a good faith

---

14. Morris v. Aetna Life Ins., 160 Ga. App. 484, 287 S.E.2d 388 (1981); FCX v. Ocean Oil, 46 N.C.App. 755, 266 S.E.2d 388 (1980); Furgat Tractor & Equip. v. Lynn, 135 Vt. 329, 376 A.2d 760 (1977). So also if the check is cashed and not honored. Curran v. Bray Wood Heel, 116 Vt. 21, 68 A.2d 712, 717, 13 ALR2d 728 (1949). Cf. Peckham Indus. v. A.F. Lehmann, 49 A.D.2d 172, 374 N.Y.S.2d 144 (1975) (no accord and satisfaction where check was deposited and withdrawn).

15. Cole Assocs. v. Holsman, 181 Ind. App. 431, 391 N.E.2d 1196 (1979).

16. American Oil v. Studstill, 230 Ga. 305, 196 S.E.2d 847 (1973); Hoffman v. Ralston Purina, 86 Wis.2d 445, 273 N.W.2d 214 (1979).

17. See § 4.10 supra; Air Power v. Omega Equip., 54 Md.App. 534, 459 A.2d 1120

(1983); Adams v. B.P.C., 143 Vt. 308, 466 A.2d 1170 (1983).

18. Hazelwood Lumber v. Smallhoover, 500 Pa. 180, 455 A.2d 108 (1982).

19. In re Lloyd, Carr & Co., 617 F.2d 882 (1st Cir.1980); Flowers v. Diamond Shamrock, 693 F.2d 1146 (5th Cir.1982); Amino Bros. v. Twin Caney Watershed (Joint) Dist., 206 Kan. 68, 476 P.2d 228 (1970); Lafferty v. Cole, 339 Mich. 223, 63 N.W.2d 432 (1954); Farmland Service Coop. v. Jack, 196 Neb. 263, 242 N.W.2d 624 (1976); cf. Gottlieb v. Charles Scribner's Sons, 232 Ala. 33, 166 So. 685 (1936) (dispute related to the method rather than the amount of payment).

20. Grettenberger Pharmacy v. Blue Cross–Blue Shield, 98 Mich.App. 1, 296 N.W.2d 589 (1980).

dispute? One answer is that if there is no dispute this phrase does not create one, but if there is a basis for a dispute the words are sufficient to indicate a dispute even though the other party does not know its basis.[21] However, other cases have held that an accord and satisfaction will not arise unless the other party is aware of the basis of the dispute.[22] These seem sounder. It is hard to understand how a consensual discharge of a dispute comes about if one of the parties is unaware of the dispute.

Case 3. Assume the same facts as in Case 2 except that, while D admits to owing $50, D sends a check in that amount and C cashes the check. As above, there is offer, acceptance and performance.

This fact pattern, however, produces a division of authority on the issue of consideration. The majority of the courts have held that the claim is unliquidated and from this premise have concluded that there is consideration to support the accord and satisfaction.[23] A minority of courts have adopted the contrary position that D is only doing what D is legally obligated to do.[24] The majority view is preferable for supporting party autonomy and favoring the resolution of disputes.[25] D's admission of the $50 debt at the outset is not a binding admission.

The holdings under the majority view in Case 3 place the creditor on the horns of a dilemma. The creditor must either refuse the check, even though it is in an amount concededly due, or cash it and forgo the balance of the claim. Creditors have sought to avoid this result by striking out the words "payment in full" or by notifying the debtor that the check will be accepted in part payment, but to no avail.[26] For in cashing the check in violation of the conditions on which it was tendered, the creditor is held to assent to its terms much as in the cases where an offeree exercises dominion over unordered personal property sent the offeree.[27] Thus, assent is imputed rather than actual. Just as the offeree of a contract for the sale of goods can be estopped from claiming the status of a converter,[28] a creditor who cashes a check is estopped from claiming the status of a thief. This analysis was the subject of some doubt for a while, but has been restored by UCC § 3–311. In New York,

---

21. Gottlieb v. Charles Scribner's Sons, 232 Ala. 33, 166 So. 685 (1936).

22. Holm v. Hansen, 248 N.W.2d 503 (Iowa 1976); Matter of Leckie's Estate, 54 A.D.2d 205, 388 N.Y.S.2d 858 (1976); Trans World Grocers v. Sultana Crackers, 257 A.D.2d 616, 684 N.Y.S.2d 284 (1999); Hagerty Oil Company v. Chester County Security Fund, 248 Pa.Super. 456, 375 A.2d 186 (1977); Cannon v. Stevens School, 560 P.2d 1383 (Utah 1977).

23. Air Van Lines v. Buster, 673 P.2d 774, 42 ALR4th 1 (Alaska 1983); E.S. Herrick Co. v. Maine Wild Blueberry 670 A.2d 944 (Me.1996); Van Riper v. Baker, 61 Or. App. 540, 658 P.2d 537 (1983), rev. den.

24. Medd v. Medd, 291 N.W.2d 29 (Iowa 1980).

25. 6 Corbin § 1289.

26. Chrietzberg v. Kristopher Woods, 162 Ga.App. 517, 292 S.E.2d 100 (1982); Hannah v. James A. Ryder Corp., 380 So.2d 507 (Fla.App.1980); Goes v. Feldman, 8 Mass.App.Ct. 84, 391 N.E.2d 943 (1979); Olson v. Wilson & Co., 244 Iowa 895, 58 N.W.2d 381 (1953). But see 6 Corbin § 1279.

27. See Annot., 80 ALR 1052 (1932); RTL v. Manufacturer's Enterprises, 429 So.2d 855 (La.1983); T.B.M. Properties v. Arcon Corp., 346 N.W.2d 202 (Minn.App. 1984). See § 2.19 supra and 15 Williston § 1854 (3d ed).

28. See § 2.19 supra.

however, where this has not been enacted, cashing the check under protest may reserve the rights of the creditor.[29]

Case 4. Plaintiff (P) and defendant (D) entered into an agreement that specified the work to be done by P and that D would pay $6,000 when the work was completed. On completion, D honestly complained that there were certain defects in performance. The parties discussed the matter and agreed to settle the claim for $5,500 and D later sent P a check for $5,500 and P cashed it.

On these facts there is an accord and satisfaction. There is an express agreement of accord but, unlike Cases 1, 2, and 3, the offer and acceptance took place prior to the sending and cashing of the check and thus the sending and cashing do not involve offer and acceptance (that has already occurred) but involve the performance of the agreement. In the first three cases discussed above, the cashing of the check amounts both to the acceptance and the performance of the accord.[30]

Case 5. P owned a quantity of apples and requested D to obtain a purchaser, which D did, collecting the price. P claimed the service was to be gratuitous; D claimed that there was an agreement to pay D a 10% commission. P cashed a check for the reduced amount tendered in full payment by D but immediately protested to D that the deduction was erroneous and P subsequently brought suit for the amount of the deduction.

The jury found for P thus accepting P's version that the service was gratuitous. However, the court ruled that there was no accord and satisfaction, not because it disagreed with the majority rule in Case 3 above, but because it found that there is an important distinction between the two cases. In Case 3 the relationship between D and C was debtor-creditor. In this case the relationship between the plaintiff and defendant was principal and agent—a fiduciary relationship. The court articulates the importance of the distinction in two ways. First, a debtor paying the debtor's own money may attach conditions, but where, as here, an agent was accounting for money belonging to a principal, the agent may not lawfully impose any conditions. Second, to allow a fiduciary to proceed in this way would be to allow "a flagrant abuse of the opportunities and powers of a fiduciary position."[31]

Case 6. D in exchange for P's promise to do certain work promised P that P would receive ⅓ of the receipts of D's dairy. Prior to this arrangement, P had been working for D on a daily (per diem) basis under which there was concededly due to P the sum of $17.15. P received $17.15 from D and signed and delivered a receipt stating the $17.15 was received in "full of all accounts and demands to date."

29. Horn Waterproofing v. Bushwick Iron & Steel, 66 N.Y.2d 321, 497 N.Y.S.2d 310, 488 N.E.2d 56 (1985).

30. Sherwin–Williams v. Sarrett, 419 So.2d 1332, 42 ALR4th 89 (Miss.1982).

31. Hudson v. Yonkers Fruit, 258 N.Y. 168, 171, 179 N.E. 373, 374, 80 ALR 1052 (1932).

P brought an action for an amount allegedly due on the second contract. The trial court found that there was an accord and satisfaction and there is some logic to this conclusion because the case is similar to Case 3. This was reversed.[32] The appeals court could have said that there was no accord and satisfaction because D did not make it sufficiently clear that the offer related to both arrangements.[33] However, the court states a much broader proposition when it says: "The payment of an admitted liability is not a payment of or a consideration for an alleged accord and satisfaction of another and independent alleged liability."[34]

The important factor is not that there is an admitted liability because that is the situation in Case 3 where under the majority view there is a binding accord and satisfaction supported by consideration. Rather, there is no consideration because payment of a liquidated obligation is not consideration to support the surrender of a wholly distinct claim.[35] If the disputed claim is closely related to the undisputed claim, payment of the amount admittedly due on one claim may be consideration for the surrender of the two claims in the absence of unfair pressure or economic coercion.[36] Whether the claims are separate or not is a most obscure question, and actually the obscurity of the question serves as a safety-valve that a court can use to insure that justice is done in a particular case.

If the check is inadvertently cashed, the cases are split on the question of whether the effect of the cashing may be set aside for mistake.[37] Where a creditor's business is such that it receives a high volume of checks, these are generally handled by low-level personnel who are not empowered to contract for the creditor. The 1991 revision of Article 3 of the UCC provides detailed rules by which creditors can guard against full payment checks by preemptive notice, and by tendering the return of the funds represented by the checks. These protections do not apply where a person who has direct responsibility with respect to the disputed obligation knew that the instrument was tendered in full payment of the claim.[38]

A New York statute (Gen'l Obl.Law § 15–303) raises an interesting question. It provides that a release signed by a creditor is effective without consideration. Another Statute (Gen'l Obl. Law. § 5–1103) provides that a discharge is effective without consideration if it is expressed

32. Manse v. Hossington, 205 N.Y. 33, 98 N.E. 203 (1912).

33. Mademoiselle Fashions v. Buccaneer Sportswear, 11 Ark.App. 158, 668 S.W.2d 45 (1984); Messick v. PHD Trucking Service, 615 P.2d 1276 (Utah 1980).

34. Manse v. Hossington, 205 N.Y. 33, 98 N.E. 203 (1912).

35. 2 Corbin § 7.17 at n.51 (Perillo & Bender 1995).

36. Rs. 2d § 74 cmt c.

37. Relief on the grounds of mistake was granted in Dalrymple Gravel & Contr. v. State, 23 A.D.2d 418, 261 N.Y.S.2d 566 (1965), aff'd; cf. Hotz v. Equitable Life Assur., 224 Iowa 552, 276 N.W. 413 (1937); see also Teledyne Mid–America v. HOH, 486 F.2d 987 (9th Cir.1973); Kirk Williams Co. v. Six Industries, 11 Ohio App.3d 152, 463 N.E.2d 1266 (1983) (bookkeeper who made deposit lacked authority to contract); see McKinney's N.Y. State Finance Law § 145.

38. UCC § 3–311 (1991 revision). See Note, 26 Loy.Chi.L.J. 1 (1994).

in a writing signed by the creditor. We have previously seen that where D owes C a liquidated debt and D sends a check for a lesser amount the debt is not discharged even if D sends a check marked "payment in full" and C cashes it. Because D is only doing what D is legally obligated to do, there is no consideration. The alleged discharge is therefore invalid.[39] What is the result under the New York Statute? It could be argued that the language of full payment, written on the check, is a writing, the creditor's endorsement of the check is a signing, and therefore the liquidated debt is discharged. However, this argument has been rejected by the New York cases.[40] The apparent rationale is that such endorsement does not show the kind of circumspection and deliberation that the writing requirement was intended to ensure.[41]

§ 4.12   Problems Arising in Bilateral Contracts

(a) Consideration in Bilateral Contracts

It has sometimes been asserted that in a bilateral contract each party's promise is consideration for the promise of the other, since each party in making a promise is doing something the law does not require.[1] Closer analysis of decided cases, however, shows that the uttering of the promise does not supply the consideration; rather it is the promised performance that must be scrutinized to determine whether the promise constitutes consideration.[2] The cases hold that a promise in a bilateral agreement is consideration for the counter-promise only if the promised performance would be consideration.[3] For example, B says to A, "If you pay me the $50 you owe me, I promise to give you a hat worth $10." B's promise is not enforceable because A, if A performs, would merely be doing what A was legally obligated to do.[4] The result would be the same if B had asked for and received A's counter-promise to pay the amount admittedly due. Therefore, the mere utterance of words of promise does not constitute consideration in a bilateral contract.

It is possible to hypothesize a case in which one party bargains for the making of a promise rather than for its ultimate performance. For example, a nephew may, for past grievances, refuse to speak to his aunt. The aunt makes the following promise, "I will give you $1,000 if you say 'I promise to accept.' "If the nephew speaks the words of promise, he has

---

39. See Case 1 supra.

40. King Metal Products v. Workmen's Comp. Bd., 20 A.D.2d 565, 245 N.Y.S.2d 882 (1963).

41. On the various functions of writing requirements see, Perillo, The Statute of Frauds in the Light of Functions and Dysfunctions of Form, 43 Fordham L.Rev. 39, 43–69 (1974).

§ 4.12

1. Knack v. Industrial Commission, 108 Ariz. 545, 503 P.2d 373 (1972). See Ames,

Two Theories of Consideration, 12 Harv. L.Rev. 515 (1898), 13 Harv.L.Rev. 29 (1899), Selected Readings 320.

2. See 3 Williston § 7:6. See also Langdell, Mutual Promises as a Consideration for Each Other, 14 Harv.L.Rev. 496 (1900); Williston, Consideration in Bilateral Contracts, 27 Harv.L.Rev. 503 (1914).

3. Coca–Cola Bottling v. Kosydar, 43 Ohio St.2d 186, 331 N.E.2d 440 (1975).

4. See § 4.9 supra.

provided consideration in speaking them, but this is because the offer looks to a unilateral contract—the uttering of the words requested.

(b) Mutuality of Obligation

(1) Introduction

The meaning of the phrase "mutuality of obligation" is best explained by an illustration.[5] B here and now owes A a liquidated debt of $1,000. They agree that A will not seek to collect the debt for six months and B will pay the debt without interest at the end of this period.[6] If each side of the arrangement were approached as a unilateral arrangement, A's promise is not supported by consideration because B is only promising to do what B is already legally obligated to do. Conversely B's promise should be enforceable because A, in forbearing suit, is providing consideration and this is so even though B is only promising to do what B is legally obligated to do. But the theory of mutuality of obligation concludes that since A is free not to perform, B should equally be free not to perform.[7] Without mutuality of consideration, it is argued, there is a void bilateral agreement.[8]

The theory of mutuality of obligation is commonly expressed in the phrase that in a bilateral contract "both parties must be bound or neither is bound."[9] But this phrase is an over-generalization. The doctrine is not one of mutuality of obligation but rather one of mutuality of consideration.[10] Phrasing the rule in terms of mutuality of obligation rather than in terms of consideration has led to so-called exceptions and judicial circumventions to be discussed below. The concept of "mutuality of obligation" has been thoroughly discredited.[11] The Restatement (Sec-

---

5. The illustration is based on Hay v. Fortier, 116 Me. 455, 102 A. 294 (1917). Another aspect of this case is discussed at n.69 infra.

6. If under the agreement B was to pay interest, the majority view holds that B's promise would be detrimental since B is surrendering the privilege of discharging the debt and thereby terminating the running of interest. Hackin v. First Nat. Bank, 101 Ariz. 350, 419 P.2d 529 (1966); Adamson v. Bosick, 82 Colo. 309, 259 P. 513 (1927); Benson v. Phipps, 87 Tex. 578, 29 S.W. 1061 (1895); Rs. 2d § 73 ill. 8; cf. Rogers v. First Nat. Bank, 282 Ala. 379, 211 So.2d 796 (1968). A minority of jurisdictions have concluded that since interest accrues by operation of law on overdue debts, the debtor in promising to pay interest is merely promising to perform a pre-existing legal duty. Harburg v. Kumpf, 151 Mo. 16, 52 S.W. 19 (1899); Olmstead v. Latimer, 158 N.Y. 313, 53 N.E. 5 (1899); cf. Bier Pension Plan Trust v. Estate of Schneierson, 74 N.Y.2d 312, 545 N.E.2d 1212, 546 N.Y.S.2d 824 (1989). This reasoning overlooks that the debtor has surrendered the right to tender payment thereby stopping the fur-

ther accumulation of interest. 3 Williston § 7:27. There may be a question as to whether this was bargained for.

7. 2 Corbin § 6.1 (Perillo & Bender 1995).

8. Marcrum v. Embry, 291 Ala. 400, 282 So.2d 49 (1973); Pick Kwik Food Stores v. Tenser, 407 So.2d 216 (Fla.App.1981).

9. See Sala & Ruthe Realty v. Campbell, 89 Nev. 483, 515 P.2d 394 (1973); 3 Williston § 7:13.

10. R.S. Mikesell Assocs. v. Grand River Dam Auth., 627 F.2d 211 (10th Cir.1980); Consolidated Labs. v. Shandon Scientific, 413 F.2d 208 (7th Cir.1969); Marcrum v. Embry, 291 Ala. 400, 282 So.2d 49 (1973); S.J. Groves & Sons v. State, 93 Ill.2d 397, 67 Ill.Dec. 92, 444 N.E.2d 131 (1982) (overruled on other grounds); Acme Cigarette Services v. Gallegos, 91 N.M. 577, 577 P.2d 885 (App.1978); Jackson Hole Builders v. Piros, 654 P.2d 120 (Wyo.1982).

11. Smith v. Atlas Off–Shore Boat Service, 653 F.2d 1057 (5th Cir.1981); 2 Corbin § 6.1 (Perillo & Bender 1995); Murray

ond) goes beyond the abandonment of "mutuality of obligation" and abandons the idea that to have a valid bilateral contract both sides must provide consideration, taking the position that a non-binding promise constitutes consideration if its performance would be detrimental.[12] Remember that it is not the courts' function to weigh the adequacy of the consideration; If a promisor bargains for the non-binding promise, the promisor should be held to the promise. He or she will receive some protection from the second party's non-performance under the doctrine of constructive conditions.[13]

(2) Unilateral Contracts and Mutuality

In a unilateral contract there is no mutuality of obligation. At no time has the offeree been bound to do anything and, even if the offeree starts to perform, the offeree is not bound to complete the performance. Even if the offeree should promise to do the act called for, this unsolicited promise would be a nullity.[14] Only the promisor may become bound to perform; thus there is no possibility of mutuality of obligation. In most cases, if the offeree performs the act called for, the performance will constitute consideration. If the performance called for is detrimental and the offeror bargains for it, the offeree's performance is the bargained-for exchange.[15]

It would not make any difference if the promisor was only promising to perform a legal obligation; the doctrine of mutuality[16] was never applied to unilateral contracts. For example, assume A owed B $100 and A promised to pay B the $100, if B walked the Brooklyn Bridge. If B, in response, walked, B could sue on the original claim or on the unilateral contract but there could be only one recovery.[17]

(3) Voidable and Unenforceable Promises and Mutuality

If the theory of mutuality of obligation were to be accepted at face value (both parties must be bound or neither is bound), it would follow that a voidable or unenforceable promise on one or both sides of a bilateral contract would create a mutuality problem resulting in a void agreement. But, as we have seen, the issue in a bilateral contract is mutuality of consideration. It is well settled that a voidable or unenforce-

§ 90; Oliphant, Mutuality of Obligation in Bilateral Contracts at Law, 25 Colum.L.Rev. 705 (1925), 28 Colum.L.Rev. 907 (1928); Jackson Hole Builders v. Piros, 654 P.2d 120 (Wyo.1982).

12. Rs. 2d § 75 & ill. 5. See 2 Corbin § 6.1 (Perillo & Bender 1995).

13. Ch. 11 infra.

14. See § 2.10 supra.

15. See 2 Corbin §§ 6.1–6.2 (Perillo & Bender 1995); Adams County Record v. Greater North Dakota Ass'n, 564 N.W.2d 304 (N.D.1997); Jackson Hole Builders v. Piros, 654 P.2d 120 (Wyo.1982).

16. Chrisman v. Southern Cal. Edison, 83 Cal.App. 249, 256 P. 618 (1927).

17. Ward v. Goodrich, 34 Colo. 369, 372, 82 P. 701, 702 (1905) where it is said, "While it is settled that promising to do, or the doing of, that which the promisor is already legally bound to do, does not, as a rule, constitute consideration for a reciprocal promise, or support a reciprocal undertaking given by the promisee, it by no means follows that such promise may not be enforced against such promisor by the promisee, although its enforcement compels the performance of that which was already a legal obligation."

able promise is consideration for a counter-promise and thus there is mutuality of consideration even though one or both of the parties' promises is voidable or unenforceable.[18]

Why, for example, despite the infant's power to avoid the agreement, does the infant's promise serve as consideration to support the adult's promise? A number of explanations have been advanced. One is that an infant incurs legal detriment in making a promise that the infant must act affirmatively to avoid. Alternatively, it may be said that the infant's promise creates an expectation that the other party bargains for, and, generally, for consideration to exist the possibility of detriment rather than the absolute certainty of detriment is sufficient.[19] But in either case, is the detriment identified in these explanations really bargained for by the adult party?[20] The real explanation for the rule is grounded in the policy that it is desirable that the infant should be able to enforce the promise of the adult even though the infant has the power of avoidance. To achieve this result the law must say the promise of the infant is consideration. If the promise were not deemed to be consideration, the agreement would be void and the policy of the law in classifying certain promises as being voidable or unenforceable would be subverted.

(4) Illusory Promises

Under current orthodoxy, a bilateral contract is void if there is no mutuality of consideration. If the promise made by one or both parties is illusory or indefinite it does not constitute consideration.[21] An illusory promise is an expression cloaked in promissory terms, but which, on closer examination, reveals that the promisor is not committed to any act or forbearance. For example, the promise of a creditor made to a guarantor to forbear "until such time as I want my money" was held to be an illusory promise and rendered the bilateral agreement void under the doctrine of mutuality of consideration.[22] Courts are now quite willing

---

18. Rs. 2d § 80; see 3 Williston § 7:13. The essence of a voidable contract is that the law gives to a party (for example a minor) the option of avoiding the contract or of ratifying it. A contract may also be voidable for fraud, duress, mistake, etc. (See Chapters 8 and 9 and § 1.8(b) supra). An unenforceable contract may also be avoided, but it may not be ratified. Still it may produce some legal consequences. A contract may be unenforceable because of the Statute of Frauds or the Statute of Limitations (see § 1.08 supra and § 19.35 infra). An agreement is void when there is no consideration. For example, in cases of illusory promises or indefiniteness. See § 1.08 supra; but see also § 4.12(b)(7). There are other reasons why an agreement may be void, e.g., illegality.

19. Holt v. Ward Clarencieux, 93 Eng. Rep. 954 (K.B.1732); Atwell v. Jenkins, 163 Mass. 362, 40 N.E. 178 (1895) (insanity).

20. Compare Rs. 2d § 78 cmt a with 3 Williston § 7:13.

21. Penn v. Ryan's Family Steak Houses, 269 F.3d 753 (7th Cir.2001); 2 Corbin § 5.28 (Perillo & Bender 1995); For the related question of indefinite promises, see § 4.12(b)(7) infra.

22. Strong v. Sheffield, 144 N.Y. 392, 39 N.E. 330 (1895). Since a negotiable instrument was involved in this case, past consideration now supports the promise. UCC § 3–303 (former § 3–408); see Hardy v. Brookhart, 259 Md. 317, 270 A.2d 119 (1970); §§ 5.3, 5.18 infra. An employer's promises in a handbook are not consideration if the employer reserves the power to modify or revoke them at any time without notice. Trumbull v. Century Marketing, 12 F.Supp.2d 683 (N.D.Ohio 1998).

to consider the context of apparently illusory promises; thus, a promise to perform in the promisor's "sole, exclusive and complete discretion" has been held enforceable in the context of the particular set of facts.[23]

As a Texas court has stated, "the modern decisional tendency is against lending the aid of the courts to defeat contracts on technical grounds of want of mutuality."[24] These courts have recognized that countless bargains, freely entered into and openly arrived at, have been struck down because of zealous judicial concern that one party's promise appeared illusory. It mattered not that the party who made the illusory promise was prepared to carry out the bargain and that it was the other party who reneged, because under the theory of mutuality the other party is allowed free access to this escape hatch. Isn't it time to abolish this destructive doctrine of mutuality?

A death-blow could be aimed at the doctrine by the utilization of option analysis. According to the Restatement (Second), "an offer is binding as an option contract if it * * * is in writing and signed by the offeror, recites a purported consideration for the making of the offer, and proposes an exchange on fair terms within a reasonable time."[25] The party who has made the illusory promise has stated "a purported consideration." The other party's promise could be construed as an offer and should be enforced when the maker of the illusory promise indicates a willingness and ability to perform.[26]

(5) Consideration Supplied by Implied Promises

One of the methods of circumventing the illusory promise problem is interpolating into an agreement that otherwise seems illusory the requirement of good faith or reasonableness.[27] The leading case is Wood v. Lucy, Lady Duff–Gordon.[28] In an elaborate written instrument, defendant promised to give the plaintiff an exclusive agency and plaintiff promised to pay one-half of the profits resulting from the agency. If the plaintiff was not required to do anything that would bring about profits, plaintiff's promise was illusory. The court pointed out, however, that the plaintiff had an organization adapted to, and a financial self-interest in, carrying out the exclusive agency. It inferred a promise on plaintiff's part to use reasonable efforts to bring about profits. "It is true that he

23. Hodgkins v. New England Tel., 82 F.3d 1226 (1st Cir.1996).

24. Texas Gas Utilities v. Barrett, 460 S.W.2d 409 (Tex.1970).

25. Rs.2d § 87(1) (a); see § 4.6 supra.

26. See Eisenberg, Probability and Chance in Contract Law, 45 U.C.L.A. L.Rev 1020–23 (1998).

27. See, for example, Richard Bruce & Co. v. J. Simpson & Co., 40 Misc.2d 501, 243 N.Y.S.2d 503 (1963). But see Automatic Sprinkler v. Anderson, 243 Ga. 867, 257 S.E.2d 283 (1979); De Los Santos v. Great Western Sugar, 217 Neb. 282, 348 N.W.2d 842 (1984).

28. 222 N.Y. 88, 118 N.E. 214 (1917). The implication may vary from "reasonable" efforts to "good faith" efforts, to "best efforts." Whatever the adjective, heroic efforts are not implied. Compare Joyce Beverages of N.Y. v. Royal Crown Cola, 555 F.Supp. 271 (S.D.N.Y.1983), with Zilg v. Prentice–Hall, 717 F.2d 671, 43 ALR4th 1163 (2d Cir.1983), cert. denied. See also First Nat. Bank v. Gay, 694 So.2d 784 (Fla. App.1997); Laboratory Corp. v. Upstate Testing, 967 F.Supp. 295 (N.D.Ill.1997). The meaning of the term "best efforts" is explored in Martin v. Monumental Life Ins., 240 F.3d 223 (3d Cir.2001).

does not promise in so many words that he will use reasonable efforts to place the defendant's indorsements and market her designs. We think, however, such a promise is fairly to be implied. The law has outgrown its primitive stage of formalism when the precise word was the sovereign talisman, and every slip was fatal. It takes a broader view today. A promise may be lacking, and yet the whole writing, may be 'instinct with an obligation imperfectly expressed' * * *. If that is so there is a contract."[29]

The method of the case is to find a promise by inferences drawn from the facts. Under some circumstances the promise inferred is called an implied promise and in others it is referred to as a constructive promise. But whichever characterization is employed, the result is the same. An implied promise and a constructive promise are not treated differently. The difference between the two is that a constructive promise arises by construction of law only when justice requires it. A promise is implied in fact when the conduct of the parties reasonably indicates that a promise has been made.[30] The distinction between the two is obviously not precise, but the promise in the Lucy case was implied rather than constructive.[31] Constructive promises will be discussed later in a more appropriate context.[32]

The UCC adopts the reasoning of Wood v. Lucy, Lady Duff–Gordon; indeed, the UCC goes even further. It provides in § 2–306(2), (and the revision draft is unchanged):

> "A lawful agreement by either the seller or the buyer for exclusive dealing in the kind of goods concerned imposes unless otherwise agreed an obligation by the seller to use best efforts to supply the goods and by the buyer to use best efforts to promote their sale."

Of course the Code provision has reference only to exclusive dealings in "goods."[33] Thus, it would not be applicable to an agreement such as was involved in Wood v. Lucy, but the UCC adopts and extends its rationale by imposing the obligation of best efforts as a matter of legislative fiat rather than as a matter of interpretation. This approach had already been taken in a number of cases.[34] The reason is obvious. In an exclusive arrangement such as a sharecropping lease or mineral lease, it would be incredible to believe that the owner leased the premises without expecting a return. The same rationale applies to other exclusive relations.

The road opened by Wood v. Lucy has been much traveled, and not only in exclusive dealing cases. A good illustration is Furrer v. Interna-

---

29. 222 N.Y. 88, 90–91, 118 N.E. 214, 214 (1917); accord, Bailey v. Chattem, Inc., 684 F.2d 386 (6th Cir.1982), cert. denied; Licocci v. Cardinal Assocs., 445 N.E.2d 556 (Ind.1983).

30. Five requirements for finding an implied promise are stated in Brown v. Safeway Stores, 94 Wn.2d 359, 617 P.2d 704 (1980).

31. Farnsworth, Disputes over Omissions in Contracts, 68 Colum.L.Rev. 860, 865 (1968); see also 3A Corbin §§ 632 and 653.

32. See § 11.14 infra.

33. Goods are defined in UCC § 2–105.

34. See Mandel v. Liebman, 303 N.Y. 88, 100 N.E.2d 149 (1951).

tional Health Assurance Co.[35] There, a promise "to spend such time as he personally sees fit" in developing a business was held not to be illusory under the modern approach of implying a promise that the performance will be in good faith or will be reasonable. Some cases—usually older ones—do not go as far as Furrer.[36]

The new approaches that courts are taking to the illusory promise problem can be illustrated by cases where the promisor has the option to terminate. It should first be noted that where a party makes alternative promises, the rule is that each alternative must be detrimental, otherwise the promisor has not provided consideration.[37] Let us examine the traditional views in four fact patterns and then discuss the more modern approach.

Case 1. A and B enter into a bilateral agreement whereby A agrees to provide services for a year at a certain wage that B promises to pay. In addition, B retains the power to terminate the agreement on giving 30 days notice. Clearly, the agreement is supported by consideration. B has agreed either to pay the wages for one year or for 30 days. Since either alternative constitutes consideration, the rule with respect to alternative promises is satisfied.[38]

Case 2. Same facts as Case 1 except that B reserves the right to terminate the agreement at any time without notice. The cases traditionally have agreed that the promise is illusory.[39]

Case 3. Same facts as Case 2 except that B may exercise the power of termination simply by giving notice at any time. The older cases held that the alternative promise of giving notice is not detrimental and therefore B's promise is illusory.[40] But Corbin and the later decisions take the position that the requirement for notice, even though it may be given at any time, constitutes detriment.[41] Thus, each alternative is detrimental. The remaining question is whether notice is a bargained-for alternative, but this question seems to have been ignored in an effort to make the agreement enforceable.

Case 4. Same facts as Case 3 except that the language used is that the "contract may be terminated at any time," without stating whether

---

35. 256 Or. 429, 474 P.2d 759 (1970).

36. Flemming v. Ronson, 107 N.J.Super. 311, 258 A.2d 153 (1969), aff'd.

37. Osborn v. Boeing Airplane, 309 F.2d 99 (9th Cir.1962); Blish v. Thompson Automatic Arms, 30 Del.Ch. 538, 64 A.2d 581 (1948); Stopford v. Boonton Molding, 56 N.J. 169, 265 A.2d 657, 46 ALR3d 444 (1970); § 4.14 infra.

38. Daughtry v. Capital Gas, 285 Ala. 89, 229 So.2d 480 (1969); Ventanas Del Caribe v. Stanley Works, 158 Conn. 131, 256 A.2d 228 (1969); Long v. Foster & Assocs., 242 La. 295, 136 So.2d 48 (1961), 22 La.L.Rev. 872 (1962); Klug v. Flambeau Plastics, 62 Wis.2d 141, 214 N.W.2d 281

(1974); 2 Corbin § 6.13 (Perillo & Bender 1995); 3 Williston § 7:13.

39. Lynx Exploration & Production v. 4–Sight Operating, 891 S.W.2d 785 (Tex. App.1995); see note 42 infra; but see Water Street Dev. v. New York, 220 A.D.2d 289, 632 N.Y.S.2d 544 (1995), app. denied (retention of power to terminate by the City is in the public interest and the mutuality doctrine does not apply).

40. 2 Corbin § 6.12 (Perillo & Bender 1995); 3 Williston § 7:7; see Patterson, Illusory Promises and Promisors' Options, 6 Iowa L.Bull. 129 (1920).

41. 2 Corbin § 6.12 (Perillo & Bender 1995).

notice is required or not. Once the issue of notice is decided, the case will fall either into case (2) or (3). This issue is one of interpretation and the cases have gone both ways.[42]

For example, in Sylvan Crest Sand & Gravel Co. v. U.S.,[43] the government promised to purchase trap rock from the plaintiff. The agreement read, "cancellation by the Procurement Division may be effected at any time." The court could have read the quoted words as stating that the cancellation could be affected at any time without notice. Instead, it concluded that the government had promised to purchase trap rock, or alternatively to give notice of termination within a reasonable time. Under either alternative there was detriment. As the court interpreted the agreement, it brings the case within the boundaries of Case (3). Again, the court did not consider whether the notice was bargained for. The decision is explicable in part by the court's emphasis on the fact that the parties intended their agreement to be a contract and not a nullity.[44] If the parties intended to make a contract, that intent should not be frustrated by overly technical rules of law. The decision also undoubtedly accords with business convenience in that it fulfills the expectations of the parties. However, not all modern cases have followed this approach.[45]

Dispensing with the fiction, the Sylvan Crest case supports this proposition: "A promise is not rendered insufficient as consideration by reason of a power of termination reserved to the promisor."[46] The statement of the rule in these terms has the advantage of bringing the law governing a promisor's right to terminate into symmetry with the law governing contingent contracts generally and in particular with the rule governing unenforceable and voidable contracts.

Subsections (2) and (3) of UCC Section 2–309 also bear on this topic. Subsection (2) states that a contract that provides for successive performances but is indefinite in duration "is valid for a reasonable time but unless otherwise agreed[47] may be terminated at any time by either party." Subsection (3) states, "Termination of a contract by one party except on the happening of an agreed event requires that reasonable

---

42. Compare Miami Coca–Cola Bottling v. Orange Crush, 296 F. 693 (5th Cir.1924) with A.S. Rampell, Inc. v. Hyster, 3 N.Y.2d 369, 165 N.Y.S.2d 475, 144 N.E.2d 371 (1957).

43. 150 F.2d 642 (2d Cir.1945). See Gurfein v. Werbelovsky, 97 Conn. 703, 118 A. 32 (1922).

44. This is a recurrent theme in the modern cases. See e.g., Sonnenblick–Goldman v. Murphy, 420 F.2d 1169 (7th Cir. 1970); see also UCC § 2–204(3) discussed in § 2.9 supra.

45. See, for example, Zeyher v. S.S. & S. Mfg., 319 F.2d 606 (7th Cir.1963); Baber v. Lay, 305 S.W.2d 912 (Ky.1957).

46. This language is quoted in Flight Concepts Ltd. Ptnshp. v. Boeing Co., 819 F.Supp. 1535 (D.Kan.1993), aff'd; see also Cherokee Comm. v. Skinny's, 893 S.W.2d 313 (Tex.App.1994) ("A contract which provides for its termination at the option of one or either of the parties will be enforced if not contrary to equity and good conscience."); accord,. Albert v. NCR, 874 F.Supp. 1324 (S.D.Fla.1994); Orr v. Westminster Village North, 651 N.E.2d 795, 799 (Ind.App.1995), vacated on other grounds. A ten year lease terminable on notice was upheld in Lane v. Wahl, 101 Wash.App. 878, 6 P.3d 621 (2000).

47. Besco, Inc. v. Alpha Portland Cement, 619 F.2d 447 (5th Cir.1980).

notification be received by the other party and an agreement dispensing with notification is invalid if its operation would be unconscionable." The revision draft would add: "However a term specifying standards for the nature and timing of notice is enforceable if the standards are not manifestly unreasonable." The thought behind this sentence is probably already inherent in the UCC scheme that usually honors party autonomy.

These provisions are far from clear, but seem to stand for four propositions.

1) An agreement that is silent as to duration is valid but terminates after a reasonable time. In addition, it may be terminated by giving reasonable notice. One of the comments recognizes "that the application of principles of good faith and sound commercial practice normally call for such notification of the termination of a going contract relationship as will give the other party reasonable time to seek a substitute arrangement."[48]

2) If the agreement provides that it may be terminated "at any time" (Case 4 above), reasonable notice would still be required. *A fortiori*, the same result would apply in Case 3 above.

3) If the agreement specifically states that it may be terminated at "any time without notice" the issue is unconscionability. If it is unconscionable, the term should be stricken, and a reasonable time substituted. If the arrangement is not unconscionable, a court must nevertheless take into account the consideration problem.

4) If the time for giving notice is specified (e.g. 30 days as in Case 1, above), although there is no consideration problem, there may still be an issue of unconscionability. Unlike UCC 2–302 (substantially unchanged in the revision) which provides that unconscionability must be judged as of the time of the making of the contract, unconscionability under § 2–309 should be judged as of the time of termination.[49] The exercise of the power of termination is also subject to the rule of good faith inherent in every contract.[50]

This section applies to franchises for the resale of goods and should go a long way toward eliminating the unjust result previously reached in many franchise cases.[51] These cases had held that if the franchise agreement is silent as to duration, it may be terminated at will; they also held that a notice provision will be enforced as written.[52] There are contrary and sounder decisions. Some are based on the theory that the arrangement may be terminated only for good cause[53] and others holding

48. UCC § 2–309 cmt 8.

49. See UCC § 2–309 cmt 8.

50. Sons of Thunder v. Borden, 148 N.J. 396, 690 A.2d 575 (1997).

51. Note, 28 Miami L.Rev. 710 (1974).

52. 19 ALR3d 196; Comment, 1969 Duke Law Journal 959.

53. Shell Oil v. Marinello, 63 N.J. 402, 307 A.2d 598, 67 ALR3d 1291 (1973), cert. denied, noted 28 U.Miami L.Rev. 710 (1974), 45 Miss.L.J. 252 (1974). Contra, Division of Triple T Serv. v. Mobil Oil, 60 Misc.2d 720, 304 N.Y.S.2d 191 (1969).

that the franchisee is entitled to a reasonable time to recoup its investment and presumably to wind up its affairs and make other arrangements.[54] Special franchising rules for the protection of franchisees exist in many states by legislation and by regulation of the FTC.[55]

Although there is a strong trend toward limiting the concept of illusory promise by adopting a judicial or legislative construction or interpretation of the agreement which will sustain it,[56] the drafter of agreements would do well to take note of the many cases which have failed to sustain an inartful agreement despite the parties' intention to be bound.[57]

(6) Are Conditional and Aleatory Promises Illusory?

A promise to pay $500 is not illusory; but a promise to pay $500 "if I feel like it," is.[58] But if the happening of the condition is outside the control of the party who makes the promise, the promise is not illusory and does not fail for lack of consideration and can serve as consideration for a return promise.[59] Thus, if the condition is an event that is outside of the promisor's unfettered discretion, such as the promisee's nonperformance, or the happening of some event such as a strike, war, decline in business, etc., the promise is not illusory.[60]

An aleatory promise is conditional on the happening of a fortuitous event, or an event supposed by the parties to be fortuitous.[61] Thus an insurance company's promise to pay a sum of money in the event of fire or other casualty supplies consideration for the insured's payment of a premium even if no casualty occurs. Similarly a valid contract exists if in consideration of a payment of $50, a promise is made to repay $10,000 "if I recover my gold mine."[62] In each of these cases the promise is aleatory; it constitutes consideration because it is conditional on a fortuitous event that is not within the total control of the promisor.

The following fact pattern illustrates a promise conditioned on "an event supposed by the parties to be fortuitous." Suppose a man with two children, Pam and Dan, has made a will and Pam makes the following proposition to Dan: "You know how eccentric our father is. Let us agree now that no matter what his will contains, we will divide equally

---

54. McGinnis Piano & Organ v. Yamaha Intern., 480 F.2d 474 (8th Cir.1973); Bak–A–Lum v. Alcoa Bldg. Products, 69 N.J. 123, 351 A.2d 349 (1976). If reasonable notice is not given, damages for profits lost during the period of reasonable notice are available. Maytronics v. Aqua Vac Sys., 277 F.3d 1317 (11th Cir.2002).

55. See the loose-leaf services on Franchising published by CCH and Matthew Bender.

56. Jackson Hole Builders v. Piros, 654 P.2d 120 (Wyo.1982) (citing text).

57. See nn. 39 & 42 supra.

58. Call v. Alcan Pacific, 251 Cal.App.2d 442, 59 Cal.Rptr. 763 (1967); Endres v. Warriner, 307 N.W.2d 146 (S.D.1981) (cit-ing text); 2 Corbin § 6.15 (Perillo & Bender 1995); 3 Williston § 7:13.

59. Omni Group v. Seattle–First Nat. Bank, 32 Wn.App. 22, 645 P.2d 727 (1982).

60. 2 Corbin §§ 6.14–6.15 (Perillo & Bender 1995); 3 Williston § 7:13.

61. ASI Technologies v. Johnson Equipment, 75 S.W.3d 545 (Tex.App.2002) (defendants agree to split whatever verdict the jury brings in); Rs. 2d §§ 232 cmt c, 76 cmt c.

62. Embola v. Tuppela, 127 Wash. 285, 220 P. 789 (1923).

whatever he leaves to either of us." If the offer is accepted by Dan, there is consideration, even if it turns out that the father bequeathed all of his assets to Dan. Pam incurred no detriment, but she may enforce Dan's promise because Dan bargained against the possibility that Pam would be favored. The point is that the parties believed that the event was fortuitous.[63]

At times, an illusory promise problem is avoided by treating the express language of condition attached to the promise as carrying with it an implied promise. Typically, the issue arises in connection with a sale of real estate contingent on the purchaser's ability to obtain a specified mortgage loan. Although the promise by the buyer to pay the purchase price is not illusory, the condition would render the promise illusory if the buyer were not under any obligation to try to obtain the loan. The cases hold that the buyer has impliedly promised to use reasonable efforts to bring about the condition. The buyer's conditional promise is thus by no means illusory.[64] The same type of problem arises in sales of businesses contingent on the purchaser being able to obtain an extended lease from the landlord and in agreements to lease contingent on the lessee obtaining a license for the kind of business the lessee intends to engage in on the premises.[65]

Agreements of this kind serve a vital purpose. They are entered into with the understanding that both parties are firmly committed to the performance of the agreement provided that cooperation is forthcoming from a financial institution, landlord, or licensing authority. The agreement protects the purchaser or lessee, with the other party's consent, against the possibility that the purchaser or lessee will be unable to obtain the financing, lease or license.

In Di Bennedetto v. Di Rocco,[66] the court went further than have the courts in the cases just discussed. The agreement provided, "In the event that the buyer cannot make the settlement, he may cancel this agreement." The buyer's obligation was held not to be made illusory by virtue of the condition. The court reasoned that the word "cannot" meant objective inability, rather than subjective unwillingness. Therefore, the performance of the promise was not left to the whim of the buyer. The buyer was obliged to make a good faith effort to perform the agreement. This is a well-reasoned decision and the cases contrary in spirit of this case should be disapproved. Parties must be permitted to contract with

---

63. Minehan v. Hill, 144 A.D. 854, 129 N.Y.S. 873 (1911); see Beckley v. Newman, 24 Eng.Rep. 691 (Ch. 1723).

64. Brack v. Brownlee, 246 Ga. 818, 273 S.E.2d 390 (1980) (citing text); Lach v. Cahill, 138 Conn. 418, 85 A.2d 481 (1951); Carlton v. Smith, 285 Ill.App. 380, 2 N.E.2d 116 (1936); Eggan v. Simonds, 34 Ill.App.2d 316, 181 N.E.2d 354 (1962); Mezzanotte v. Freeland, 20 N.C.App. 11, 200 S.E.2d 410 (1973); but see Paul v. Rosen, 3 Ill.App.2d 423, 122 N.E.2d 603 (1954). For a more complete discussion, see § 11.11 infra. It is also important that the terms of the contemplated mortgage financing be agreed on. Otherwise the agreement may fail for indefiniteness. Burgess v. Rodom, 121 Cal. App.2d 71, 262 P.2d 335 (1953); Willmott v. Giarraputo, 5 N.Y.2d 250, 184 N.Y.S.2d 97, 157 N.E.2d 282 (1959); Gerruth Realty v. Pire, 17 Wis.2d 89, 115 N.W.2d 557 (1962); Note, 8 Ga.L.Rev. 186, 186–93 (1973).

65. Raner v. Goldberg, 244 N.Y. 438, 155 N.E. 733 (1927).

66. 372 Pa. 302, 93 A.2d 474 (1953).

flexibility to meet the complexities of modern life. Typical of the cases in which such flexibility serves a valuable economic need are requirements and output contracts to be discussed below.

(7) A Void Contract Is Not Necessarily a Nullity

We have seen that the prevailing view is that if there is no consideration on one side of a bilateral agreement, the entire agreement is void.[67] We have also seen that a void agreement produces no legal obligations.[68] However, where there has been performance under the void bilateral agreement, life may be breathed into it.

For example, in Hay v. Fortier,[69] the defendant was under an undisputed obligation to pay the plaintiff a liquidated debt. The parties entered into an agreement whereby the plaintiff agreed to forbear from suing on the obligation for six months, and defendant promised to pay the debt at the end of six months without interest. Under the pre-existing duty rule, the plaintiff's promise was unsupported by consideration and therefore not binding.[70] Under the theory of mutuality of consideration, plaintiff could not enforce defendant's promise and the court so stated.[71] However, the plaintiff did forbear for six months and then brought action not on the debt but on the defendant's promise to pay the debt. The court found for the plaintiff, despite the voidness of the bilateral contract, stating as follows: "If a contract, although not originally binding for want of mutuality, is nevertheless executed by the party not originally bound, so that the party asserting the invalidity of the contract has actually received the benefit contracted for, the latter will be estopped from refusing performance on his part on the ground that the contract was not originally binding on the other, who has performed."[72]

Although the court speaks in terms of estoppel,[73] an alternative analysis is that if there is performance under a void bilateral contract, the situation can be treated as if an offer looking to unilateral contract had been made to the party who performed.[74] Upon performance, there is a forging of a good unilateral contract out of a bad bilateral agreement.[75] Under such a concept, plaintiff's act was detrimental and the fact that defendant promised to do only what defendant was already bound to do is immaterial. On the facts, plaintiff could sue either on the original

---

67. See § 4.12 supra.

68. See § 4.12 supra.

69. 116 Me. 455, 102 A. 294 (1917). See discussion of this case at n.5 supra.

70. See § 4.9 supra.

71. See § 4.12(b)(1) supra.

72. 102 A. at 295 (quoting from an encyclopedia); First Wis. Nat. Bank v. Oby, 52 Wis.2d 1, 188 N.W.2d 454 (1971); contra, Comonwealth Dept. of Transp. v. First Pa. Bank, 77 Pa.Cmwlth. 551, 466 A.2d 753 (1983).

73. The relationship between this and promissory estoppel is discussed in ch. 6.

74. See Eisenberg, The Principles of Consideration 640, 649 (1982); Wright & Seaton v. Prescott, 420 So.2d 623 (Fla.App. 1982).

75. See Calamari, Forging a Good Unilateral or a Series of Good Contracts out of a Bad Bilateral Contract, 1961 Wash.U.L.Q. 367.

claim or on the subsequent promise but would be entitled to only one recovery.[76]

At least two requirements must be met before this forging can take place.[77] 1) All of the requisites of the law of offer and acceptance must be fulfilled including the requirement that the promise requested must have been given. Otherwise there would be no bilateral agreement rather than a void bilateral contract. 2) The act performed by the party seeking to enforce the contract must be detrimental. If this were not so, there would be no consideration to support the unilateral contract being forged.

This process of forging a good unilateral contract out of a bad bilateral is relevant in the case of any void bilateral contract. Thus, for example, it applies to a bilateral agreement that is too indefinite to be enforced. If the side of the agreement which was too indefinite becomes definite by performance, the other side of the agreement, although not originally enforceable, can become enforceable under the doctrine of forging a good unilateral contract out of a bad bilateral contract.[78] Thus, in an at-will employment relationship where the employee has worked, the employee has earned the contractual right to be paid and to be free of Civil Rights violations.[79]

For example, in a case involving the sale of goods, if the parties fail to agree on the quality of the goods but the seller sends a particular quality and the buyer accepts, there is a contract based on a theory of acquiescence,[80] or under the notion of forging a good unilateral contract out of a bad bilateral contract.[81]

Closely related to the doctrine of forging a good unilateral contract out of a bad bilateral contract is the doctrine of forging a series of good contracts out of a bad bilateral contract.[82] We have previously discussed the concept of an offer looking to a series of contracts.[83] The doctrine of forging a series of contracts is analogous. The point is that in a proper case a void bilateral contract is looked on as creating an offer looking to a series of contracts.

One illustration will suffice. In Rubin v. Dairymen's League Co–op. Ass'n.,[84] the defendant agreed to appoint the plaintiff as exclusive agent within a certain territory, in exchange for plaintiff's promise to develop a market for defendant's products. Plaintiff was to be paid a commission

---

76. Because of the number of obligors on the debt, there may have been procedural impediments to an action on the original debt. See §§ 20.1 to 20.5 infra.

77. See Calamari, supra n.75.

78. Swafford v. Sealtest Foods, 252 Ark. 1182, 483 S.W.2d 202 (1972); Hauser v. Rose Health Care Sys., 857 P.2d 524 (Colo. App.1993) (performance of an allegedly illusory promise); 1 Williston §§ 49, 104 (3d ed.).

79. Skinner v. Maritz, Inc., 253 F.3d 337 (8th Cir.2001).

80. See § 2.9 supra.

81. Continental Bank & Trust v. American Bonding, 605 F.2d 1049 (8th Cir.1979); Swafford v. Sealtest Foods, 252 Ark. 1182, 483 S.W.2d 202 (1972).

82. See Calamari, supra n.75.

83. See § 2.16 supra.

84. 284 N.Y. 32, 29 N.E.2d 458 (1940), rearg. denied.

on sales. No time was stated for the duration of the contract and the court held that the contract was terminable at will.[85] The court also held that although the contract was void because of indefiniteness, the plaintiff was entitled to be paid the commission for any sale plaintiff made—thus forging a series of good unilateral contracts out of a bad bilateral contract.[86]

Above it is stated that at a minimum there are two requirements for the process of forging. If these two elements are not present there can be no forging, but even if they are present it does not follow that forging will take place. Three illustrations will suffice. 1) In the case of indefiniteness, if only the promise which was originally definite is performed, even though the two requirements stated are met, the indefinite promise is still indefinite and therefore there is only the possibility of quantum meruit recovery.[87] 2) In a case such as Strong v. Sheffield,[88] where the plaintiff promised, in effect, to forbear for as long as the plaintiff felt like it, but forbore for two years, assuming that the two requisites are met, there is still a question of whether any period of performance is sufficient because no duration was stated in the agreement. Of course, it could be argued that forbearance for a reasonable time is sufficient, but this flies in the face of the plaintiff's own choice of words.[89] 3) Finally, suppose the party who seeks to use the doctrine has made the requisite promise, starts to perform and the other party attempts to revoke. Under the modern approach, the promise will have become irrevocable.[90]

One recurring situation has perplexed the courts. With some frequency, after being hired, sometimes years after the initial hiring, an employee is asked to sign a covenant not to compete. If the employee is under a hiring at will, some courts have held that there is no consideration to support the covenant; the employee could be fired instantly after the signing as the employer has made no commitment.[91] If the employee continues on the job for a considerable period of time, this does not constitute consideration, as it is not the bargained-for exchange; the employer could have fired the employee instantly. Other courts have disagreed and found that the covenant is supported by consideration if the employee is retained for a reasonable time after the covenant is entered into.[92] These cases can be explained as cases of forging.[93]

---

85. See § 2.9 supra; but see § 4.12(b)(5) discussing UCC § 2–309(2) & (3).

86. See § 4.12(b)(7) supra.

87. 1 Williston § 4:9. See § 2.9 supra.

88. 144 N.Y. 392, 39 N.E. 330 (1895), discussed in § 4.12(b)(4) supra.

89. The court avoided the problem by a reckless over-generalization, saying: "The consideration is to be tested by the agreement, and not by what was done under it." 144 N.Y. at 396, 39 N.E. at 331. Cf. Fun Motors v. Gratty, Inc. 51 S.W.3d 756, 762 (Tex.App.2001) reversed on other grounds ("the test for mutuality must be applied at the time enforcement is sought, not at the time when the promises were made.")

90. Ferguson v. Ferguson, 97 A.D.2d 891, 470 N.Y.S.2d 715 (1983) can be justified on this basis.

91. IKON Office Solutions v. Belanger, 59 F.Supp.2d 125 (D.Mass.1999); Zellner v. Stephen D. Conrad, 183 A.D.2d 250, 589 N.Y.S.2d 903 (1992); Poole v. Incentives Unlimited, 345 S.C. 378, 548 S.E.2d 207 (2001).

92. Central Adjustment Bureau v. Ingram, 678 S.W.2d 28 (Tenn.1984).

93. See 2 Corbin § 6.19 (Perillo & Bender 1995); Leibman & Nathan, The Enforceability of Post–Employment Noncompetition Agreements Formed After At–Will

As previously indicated, the Restatement (Second) has done away with the theory of mutuality of consideration even in bilateral contracts.[94] Illustration 4 to section 75 sets up a case in which A promises to forbear suit against B in exchange for B's promise to pay a liquidated debt to A. Under the rule of mutuality of consideration, even though A's promise was detrimental, A could not enforce B's promise. The conclusion of the Restatement (Second) is that A's promise is nevertheless consideration for B's promise but that "B's promise is conditional on A's forbearance and can be enforced only if the condition is met." The net result is that the Restatement (Second) reaches the same result that would be reached by employing the theory of forging a good unilateral contract out of a bad bilateral contract. Its theoretical basis, however, is different.

§ 4.13 Requirements and Output Contracts

(a) Introduction

In a typical *requirements* contract, the buyer expressly agrees to buy all of the buyer's requirements of a stated good from the seller who agrees to sell that amount to the buyer. Such a contract may, instead, arise by implication.[1] In a typical *output* contract, the seller agrees to sell all of its output of a certain item to the buyer and the buyer agrees to buy that output from the seller. In these situations the quantity term is measured by the requirements of the buyer (requirements contract) or by the output of the seller (output contract). If the buyer agrees to buy all of its requirements up to a specified amount from the seller, the contract is deemed by some courts to be a requirements contract,[2] but there are contrary cases.[3] The same problem can arise in the case of an output contract. Because the rules relating to output and requirements contracts are basically the same, as a matter of convenience emphasis will be on requirements contracts.

It is important to distinguish requirements and output contracts from continuing offers. A promise by X to bottle all milk produced by Y is merely an offer looking to a series of contracts and therefore revocable at will,[4] unless made irrevocable by payment of consideration or by compliance with statutory formalities. If however, a return promise by Y

Employment Has Commenced, 60 So.Cal. L.Rev. 1465 (1987); Comment, 54 Fordham L.Rev. 1123 (1988).

94. Rs. 2d § 79 cmt f.

§ 4.13

1. In re Modern Dairy, 171 F.3d 1106 (7th Cir.1999) (no implication); Indiana–American Water v. Town of Seelyville, 698 N.E.2d 1255 (Ind.App.1998) (implication found); Western Sign v. State, 180 Mont. 278, 590 P.2d 141 (1979);United Services Auto Ass'n v. Schlang, 111 Nev. 486, 894 P.2d 967, 65 ALR5th 787 (1995); Brem-

Rock v. Warnack, 28 Wn.App. 483, 624 P.2d 220 (1981).

2. Louisville v. Rockwell Mfg., 482 F.2d 159, 164 (6th Cir.1973). See UCC § 2–306 cmt 3 ("any maximum or minimum stated by the agreement.")

3. See 94 ALR5th 247 (2001); 96 ALR3d 1275, 1282 (1980).

4. Balsam Farm v. Evergreen Dairies, 6 A.D.2d 720, 175 N.Y.S.2d 517 (1958), rearg. and app. denied; see also Halloway v. Mountain Grove Creamery, 286 Mo. 489, 228 S.W. 451 (1920); § 2.16 supra.

to supply its output of milk is expressed or can be implied, a bilateral contract exists at least if it is assumed that a return promise was requested.

(b) Validity of Requirements Contracts

At one time requirements contracts were not enforced.[5] They were deemed illusory because the buyer might refrain from having requirements.[6] In time, the courts upheld requirements contracts on the theory that consideration could be found in the surrender of the buyer's privilege to purchase elsewhere.[7] Nevertheless, some courts refused to enforce the agreement when the buyer was entering into a new business or was a purchaser for resale.[8] The stated thinking was the lack of any basis for prediction of the amount of goods to be purchased rendered the agreement illusory or indefinite and thus void. Such reasoning is unsound in theory as each party has bargained away some of its freedom to deal with others.[9] Perhaps the real reason for striking down the agreement was the one-sidedness of the agreement. Nevertheless the business value of such agreements was recognized by many authorities and the subject has been regulated by the UCC. There is no doubt about their validity under modern law and the UCC has provided protection against one-sidedness.[10]

Output and requirements contracts involving the sale of goods are now governed by § 2–306 of the UCC, which provides (and the revision is unchanged):

> "A term which measures the quantity by the output of the seller or the requirements of the buyer means such actual output or requirements as may occur in good faith, except that no quantity unreasonably disproportionate to any stated estimate or in the absence of a stated estimate to any normal or otherwise comparable prior to output or requirements may be tendered or demanded."

This provision assumes the general validity of requirements contracts.[11] The Code makes clear that the "good faith" provision is designed to eliminate any lingering questions of indefiniteness and mutual-

---

5. See generally, Havighurst & Berman, Requirement and Output Contracts, 27 Ill. L.Rev. 1 (1932); Note, 78 Harv.L.Rev. 1212 (1965); Howard, 2 U.Tasmania L.Rev. 446 (1967).

6. Lima Locomotive & Mach. v. National Steel Castings, 155 F. 77 (6th Cir.1907); Simon Bros. v. Miller Brewing, 83 Wis.2d 701, 266 N.W.2d 369 (1978).

7. G. Loewus & Co. v. Vischia, 2 N.J. 54, 65 A.2d 604 (1949).

8. Oscar Schlegel Mfg. v. Peter Cooper's Glue Factory, 231 N.Y. 459, 132 N.E. 148, 24 ALR 1348 (1921). (The case may be read less broadly, since the buyer did not expressly promise not to purchase glue else-

where.); Nassau Supply v. Ice Service, 252 N.Y. 277, 169 N.E. 383 (1929), 43 Harv. L.Rev. 828 (1930) (The court may have thought the transaction fraudulent.); cf. McMichael v. Price, 177 Okl. 186, 58 P.2d 549 (1936).

9. Eisenberg, Probability and Chance in Contract Law, 45 U.C.L.A. L.Rev. 105, 1011–12 (1998).

10. But see Orchard Group v. Konica Medical Corp., 135 F.3d 421 (6th Cir.1998).

11. UCC §§ 2–306 cmt 2; Teigen Constr. v. Pavement Specialists, 267 N.W.2d 574 (S.D.1978); Note, 102 U.Pa. L.Rev. 654 (1954); 96 ALR3d 1275.

ity and is intended to include in the case of merchants the notion of "commercial standards of fair dealing."[12]

(c) How Much Is a Requirements Buyer Entitled to Demand?

At common law there were two views on this question. Under one view the buyer was entitled only to normal requirements; under the other to actual requirements, provided the buyer acted in good faith. At common law an estimate by the buyer had no effect except if made in bad faith in which event it operated as a maximum to the seller's liability.[13]

Under the UCC, the buyer is entitled to the buyer's good faith requirements. Insisting on unneeded goods is not good faith.[14] However, two limitations are placed on the rule of good faith. 1) If there is a stated estimate, the buyer is not entitled to any quantity unreasonably disproportionate to the estimate. Comment 3 states, "any maximum or minimum set by the agreement shows a clear limit on the intended elasticity." In similar fashion, it states, "the agreed estimate is to be regarded as a center around which the parties intend the variation to occur."[15] While at common law, in the absence of bad faith, an estimate was of little operative significance, under the Code the estimate limits the risk of the seller even though the buyer is making the demand in good faith.[16] 2) If there is no estimate or maximum or minimum stated in the contract, the buyer may demand only "any normal or otherwise comparable prior requirements."[17] This means an amount reasonably foreseeable at the time of contracting.[18] If the requirements are measured by a particular factory, a normal as opposed to a sudden expansion undertaken in good faith would ordinarily be proper. Where a requirements contract contains a fixed price, on the question of good faith one should always take into account whether the market price had increased greatly.[19]

(d) Diminution or Termination of Requirements

Can a requirements buyer go out of business so that it has no requirements, or change its way of doing business so that it has fewer or no requirements. At common law there were three views. 1) According to some courts, the buyer was free to go out of business with impunity and free to change the method of doing business at will.[20] It was this view

---

12. UCC § 2–306 cmt 2; see § 11.38 infra.

13. See Havighurst & Berman, supra n.5.

14. Homestake Mining v. WPPS, 476 F.Supp. 1162 (N.D.Cal.1979), aff'd.

15. Orange & Rockland Utilities v. Amerada Hess, 59 A.D.2d 110, 397 N.Y.S.2d 814, 96 ALR3d 1263 (1977).

16. McLouth Steel v. Jewell Coal & Coke, 570 F.2d 594 (6th Cir.1978), cert. dismissed.

17. See Note, 102 U.Pa.L.Rev. 654 (1954).

18. See UCC § 2–306 cmt 2.

19. UCC § 2–306 cmt 2; Orange & Rockland, supra n.15.

20. In re United Cigar Stores, 8 F.Supp. 243 (S.D.N.Y.1934), aff'd; cf. Dickey v. Philadelphia Minit–Man, 377 Pa. 549, 105 A.2d 580 (1954).

that had led some courts to believe that the buyer's promise was illusory. 2) Under a second view, the buyer was held liable if it went out of business or changed its method of doing business in bad faith.[21] Perhaps this test is best expressed in terms of whether the purchaser has used commercial judgment as opposed to an attempt to defeat the particular obligation.[22] 3) Under a third view, if the buyer went out of business or changed the way of doing business with the effect of lessening its requirements, it had to respond in damages.[23]

Under the UCC, the buyer may go out of business or change its method of doing business if it acts in good faith. It should be borne in mind that the seller has empowered the buyer with broad discretion. Even if the reductions are highly disproportionate to normal prior requirements or stated estimates, the issue in cases of reductions is only good faith.[24] It may be incumbent on the buyer to explain why it has changed its methods so as to eliminate its needs for the product.[25] Putting in more modern equipment so that the buyer has fewer requirements is not bad faith.[26] On this issue of good faith, Comment 2 states: "A shut down by a requirements buyer for lack of orders may be permissible when a shut down merely to curtail losses would not." But the case of Feld v. Henry S. Levy & Sons[27] appears to disagree with the comment when it states that an output seller may curtail losses if it acts in good faith and the losses are more than trivial.

A requirements contract is ordinarily an exclusive dealing contract.[28] Thus, § 2–306(2) would appear to apply and to impose on the buyer an obligation "to use best efforts to promote" the sale of the goods in question. However, it would seem obvious that if a requirements buyer

21. Fort Wayne Corrugated Paper v. Anchor Hocking Glass, 130 F.2d 471 (3d Cir.1942); Royal Paper Box v. E.R. Apt. Shoe, 290 Mass. 207, 195 N.E. 96 (1935); cf. New York Central Ironworks v. U.S. Radiator, 174 N.Y. 331, 66 N.E. 967 (1903) (requirements buyer may have ordered for speculation rather than to meet its needs).

22. Western Oil & Fuel v. Kemp, 245 F.2d 633 (8th Cir.1957); see also Rs. 2d § 205 illus. 1; cf. Cannonsburg Iron v. McKeever, 138 Pa. 184, 16 A. 97 (1888). (Buyer was privileged to convert to gas without being in breach of coal requirements contract.)

23. Texas Indus. v. Brown, 218 F.2d 510 (5th Cir.1955); Wigand v. Bachmann–Bechtel Brewing, 222 N.Y. 272, 118 N.E. 618 (1918); Wells v. Alexandre, 130 N.Y. 642, 29 N.E. 142 (1891); Humble Oil & Refining v. Cox, 207 Va. 197, 148 S.E.2d 756 (1966); cf. 407 East 61st Garage v. Savoy Fifth Avenue, 23 N.Y.2d 275, 296 N.Y.S.2d 338, 244 N.E.2d 37 (1968).

24. U & W Indus. Supply v. Martin Marietta Alumina, 34 F.3d 180 (3d Cir. 1994); R.A. Weaver & Assocs. v. Asphalt Constr., 587 F.2d 1315 (D.C.Cir.1978); Indiana–American Water v. Seelyville, 698 N.E.2d 1255 (Ind.App.1998). See Weistart, 1973 Duke L.J. 599; Note, 78 Harv.L.Rev. 1212, 1220 n. 34; 2 Corbin § 6.7 (Perillo & Bender 1995). The text of the UCC is less than clear on this point. One court holds that the plain meaning is that the buyer is in breach if it orders disproportionately less than the estimate. Simcala v. American Coal Trade, 821 So.2d 197 (Ala.2001).

25. Empire Gas v. American Bakeries, 840 F.2d 1333 (7th Cir.1988).

26. Southwest Natural Gas v. Oklahoma Portland Cement, 102 F.2d 630 (10th Cir.1939); see also Technical Assistance Int'l v. U.S., 150 F.3d 1369 (Fed.Cir.1998) (government bought more new vehicles, had less need for maintenance).

27. 37 N.Y.2d 466, 373 N.Y.S.2d 102, 335 N.E.2d 320 (1975); see Canusa Corp. v. A & R Lobosco, Inc., 986 F.Supp. 723 (E.D.N.Y.1997) (reduction in bad faith).

28. At times, the contract is for a percentage of requirements and thus non-exclusive. See Tigg Corp. v. Dow Corning, 962 F.2d 1119 (3d Cir.1992).

does not purchase the goods for resale (e.g. a contract to buy the household's requirements of oil), no such implication can be made. But if the buyer purchases for resale, comment 5 must be taken into account. That comment talks in terms of an "exclusive agent" who has an "exclusive territory." In such a case it is logical to imply such a promise.[29] But whether a promise should be implied when the buyer does not have an exclusive territory is more debatable. The same type of questions may also arise in connection with an output contract.[30]

(e) Non-exclusive Requirements Contracts

In Advent Systems Ltd. v. Unisys,[31] the court applied UCC § 2–306 to a contract that was not exclusive. Advent, in England, had developed the hardware and software for a document management system and contracted with Unisys whereby the latter would market the system in the U.S. It was exclusive on neither side. Unisys could market other systems and Advent could market through others. It involved a relationship, however, that was far more complex than a simple sales contract. Advent was obligated to provide sales and marketing material and manpower as well as technical personnel to work with employees of Unisys in building and installing the systems. Unisys breached the agreement upon deciding to produce its own system and argued that the agreement was unenforceable under the Statute of Frauds because it lacked a quantity term.

The court, however, relying on case law to the effect that "requirements" is a sufficient quantity term, found the contract to be enforceable as a "non-exclusive requirements contract." The reasons that support the sufficiency of "requirements" as a quantity term, also support the sufficiency of the description of the obligation of the parties in this case. It may be surprising that the parties intend a contract though they have not agreed on the quantity term. The quantity term is ordinarily thought of as central to a sale of goods contract. But in long-term relational contracts, of which a sales agency is an example, the parties, at the onset of their relationship, may have no way of predicting the quantity of goods which the sales agent will be able to sell.

Such long-term, often highly complex, relationships have many of the attributes of service contracts. Of course, unless there is a reasonable basis for granting a remedy, the contract will fail for indefiniteness.[32] But prior dealings, usage of trade, comparable dealings with others, and

---

29. See § 4.12(b)(5) supra; Tigg Corp. v. Dow Corning, 962 F.2d 1119, 1125–1127 (3d Cir.1992) (distinguishing bilateral exclusivity from other requirements contracts).

30. Feld v. Henry S. Levy & Sons, 37 N.Y.2d 466, 373 N.Y.S.2d 102, 335 N.E.2d 320 (1975).

31. 925 F.2d 670 (3d Cir.1991); accord PMC Corp. v. Houston Wire & Cable Co.,

147 N.H. 685, 797 A.2d 125 (2002) ("major share" of buyer's needs); see Goetz & Scott, Principles of Relational Contracts, 67 Va. L.Rev. 1089 (1981); but see Brooklyn Bagel Boys v. Earthgrains, 212 F.3d 373 (7th Cir. 2000) (requirements contract must be exclusive).

32. UCC § 2–204(3).

course of performance can be looked to in defining the obligations of the parties.[33]

§ 4.14   Must All of the Considerations Be Valid?

If a party to a bilateral agreement makes alternative promises, the rule is that each alternative must be detrimental.[1] Thus, if A promises to paint for B and in exchange B promises to do masonry work for A *or* to pay A the liquidated debt of $5,000 that B owes A, B has made alternative promises. Because one of the alternative promises is not detrimental, B's promises are not consideration for A's promise and thus there is a void bilateral contract. The Restatement (Second) qualifies this rule by stating that alternative promises are detrimental provided there is or appears to the parties to be a substantial possibility that events may eliminate the alternative that is not detrimental before the promisor makes a choice.[2] If the choice of alternatives is in the promisee, however, the alternative promises supply consideration for a counter-promise if any of the alternative performances is detrimental.[3] Thus in the illustration above, B's alternative promise is detrimental if A is free to choose to have B perform the masonry work.

The rule relating to conjunctive promises is quite different. Here the rule is that as long as one of the conjunctive promises is detrimental it will support a counter-promise.[4] For example, suppose A says to B, "I promise to give you my black Honda if you promise to pay me the liquidated debt of $500 you owe me *and* to paint my fence." Although in promising to pay the debt, B is not providing consideration, in promising to paint the fence, B is incurring detriment and thus is supplying consideration for A's counter-promise.[5]

A separate and distinct question that has no connection with the topic of consideration is what must B do to enforce A's promise. The answer is that B must paint and pay the debt. Even though the payment is not consideration, it is a condition that must be performed if B is to recover on A's promise.[6]

Suppose an uncle promises his nephew, "In consideration of your past good conduct and in consideration of your promise to refrain from smoking for a year, I will pay you $5,000." This promise would be supported by the consideration if the counter-promise were given. In this illustration, we have neither alternative nor conjunctive promises. The

33. See UCC §§ 1–205 & 2–208 (§ 1–103 of the revision). See generally, Bruckel [now Brown], Consideration in Exclusive and Nonexclusive Open Quantity Contracts Under the UCC: A Proposal for a New System of Validation, 68 Minn.L.Rev. 117, 206 (1983).

§ 4.14

1. Rs. 2d § 77(a) and cmt b.

2. Rs. 2d § 77(b).

3. Rs. 2d § 77 cmt c.

4. Rs. 2d § 80(2), 1 Corbin § 5.13 (Perillo & Bender 1995); 1 Williston § 134 (3d ed).

5. Spaulding v. Benenati, 86 A.D.2d 707, 446 N.Y.S.2d 543 (1982), subsequent history omitted.

6. 1 Williston § 134 (3d ed.).

rule that applies is that all of the considerations need not be valid.[7] The fact that part of the consideration is invalid (past consideration) does not prevent the valid part (promising to refrain from smoking) from operating as consideration. Thus, the situation is similar to conjunctive promises.

§ 4.15 One Consideration Will Support Many Promises

Sometimes, each party to a bilateral contract makes a single promise. But often the number of promises made by the two promisors need not be equal. For example, in consideration of an employee's promised services, the employer may promise a salary, a year-end bonus and other fringe benefits. All three promises of the employer are supported by the one promise of the employee. The rule is that one consideration will support many promises.[1] This rule is qualified by the rules governing alternative promises discussed in Section 4.14.

Similarly, one consideration will support the promises of more than one promisor. Thus, a lease executed by a lessor will support not only the tenant's promise to pay rent, but also the promise of a guarantor guarantying that the rent will be paid.[2]

§ 4.16 Afterthoughts on Consideration

Certain criticisms of the doctrine of consideration have been noted earlier in this chapter.[1] The UCC and other legislation have chipped away at the doctrine, without proclaiming its repeal. The UNIDROIT Principles of International Commercial Contracts, a restatement-like document, prepared by a group of experts, including experts from the U.S. and other common law countries, describes a set of principles that work well without a doctrine of consideration.[2] Commercial law can do without the doctrine. Indeed, it would do better without it.

To encourage the modernization of law, while working within the common law tradition, courts can find consideration where previously it was not sought. It is now generally recognized that in every contract there is a duty to exercise good faith in the performance and enforcement of every contract.[3] This check on the arbitrary will of the promisor

---

7. 2 Corbin § 5.13 (Perillo & Bender 1995); 1 Williston § 134 (3d ed).

§ 4.15

1. Rs. 2d § 80(1); 2 Corbin § 5.12 (Perillo & Bender 1995); 3 Williston § 7:49; Files v. Schaible, 445 So.2d 257 (Ala.1984); Martin v. World S. & L. Ass'n, 92 Cal. App.4th 803, 112 Cal.Rptr.2d 225 (2001); Hargrave v. Canadian Valley Electric Co-op., 792 P.2d 50 (Okla.1990); Howell v. Murray Mortgage, 890 S.W.2d 78 (Tex.App. 1994); contra Money Place v. Barnes, 349 Ark. 411, 78 S.W.3d 714 (2002) (arbitration clause considered separately from rest of contract).

2. John Mohr & Sons v. Apex Terminal Warehouses, 422 F.2d 638 (7th Cir.1970); Citizens Bank v. Pioneer Inv., 271 Or. 60, 530 P.2d 841 (1975).

§ 4.16

1. See, e.g., § 4.1. In § 4.9, we say of the pre-existing duty rule, "It is a rule in the process of decay and reformulation."

2. UNIDROIT Principles of International Commercial Contracts Art. 3.2 (1994).

3. See § 11.38 infra.

constitutes consideration.[4] Professor Caroline Brown (writing under her prior name of Bruckel) has persuasively argued that the obligation of good faith that permeates the Uniform Commercial Code provides consideration in every open quantity contract.[5]

> "[W]hen good faith serves * * * as a source of consideration all that need be understood is that its presence in an agreement represents a real commitment. Since the obligation is implied by law and is not subject to disclaimer, there is consideration in every open quantity contract."

What she says of quantity contracts, is equally applicable to *all* contracts. Still, two possible counter-arguments might be raised. The first is a boot-strapping argument. The second has to do with the necessity of a bargained-for exchange.

As to the first counter-argument, the common law generally regards consideration as necessary to the existence of a contract. Does it beg the question to state that the presence of an obligation of good faith in every contract provides the consideration that transforms a mere agreement into a contract? One answer is that it is no more question-begging than the implication of other terms that have been employed to support the existence of a contract. Consider the implication of obligations of best efforts, reasonable efforts, or good faith to support a promise that is alleged to be illusory.[6] Support for the proposition that the obligation of good faith implied in every contract, makes the agreement binding, is also found in the myriad cases where a party has conditioned its performance on personal satisfaction.[7] In short, the suggestion made here is well within the common-law tradition of contract law. If reasoning from these analogous cases does not give satisfaction, an argument can be made and justified that the obligation of good faith is implied in every offer.[8] Therefore, upon acceptance of the offer, it is a term of the contract constituting some or all of the consideration for the contract.

The second counter-argument is that the implied term of good faith is not bargained for. The same argument could be leveled unsuccessfully at the cases mentioned in the previous paragraph. Moreover, what does it mean when we say something is bargained for in exchange for a promise? For example, assume an employee bargains for a salary of $1,000 a week in exchange for the employee's services, and the employer bargains for the employee's services in exchange for the payment of $1,000 a week. Life is always more complex than simple hypotheticals. There are additional obligations of the employer imposed by law, e.g.,

---

4. Another check is the implication of a reasonable notice of termination in contracts of indefinite duration. See § 4.12(5) supra.

5. Bruckel [now Brown], Consideration in Exclusive and Nonexclusive Open Quantity Contracts Under the UCC: A Proposal for a New System Of Validation, 68 Minn. L. Rev. 117, 206 (1983).

6. See § 4.12(b)(5) supra.

7. See § 11.37 infra.

8. Gordon, Consideration and the Commercial—Gift Dichotomy, 44 Vand. L.Rev. 283, 310 (1991) ("the implied promise to act in good faith * * * is implied in an offer proposing an exchange.")

worker's compensation and social security payments, and usually additional obligations voluntarily assumed by the employer, e.g., paid vacation time and health insurance. These obligations may not have been discussed, but may have been contained in brochures or personnel manuals, or merely conveyed orally by co-workers who have preserved the institutional memory of company policy. In the plain English sense of the term, these obligations have not been "bargained for."

Occasionally, a court stumbles on the "plain meaning"[9] of "bargained-for" and holds that there is no consideration for the employer's undertaking to provide fringe benefits. Such a holding would disgrace any legal system. In contract law, the term "bargained for" does not connote dickering, haggling, or even discussion. Any terms contained in an agreement assented to by both parties are deemed to have been "bargained for." If any proof is needed of this proposition, consult the portion of this text discussing "duty to read," a doctrine that holds parties to the terms of written agreements that have not been read, much less discussed, dickered, or haggled over.[10]

---

9. See, e.g., Whitten v. Greeley–Shaw, 520 A.2d 1307 (Me.1987), noted in 2 Corbin § 5.21 n.15 (Perillo & Bender 1995); King v. Riveland, 125 Wn.2d 500, 886 P.2d 160 (1994).

10. See §§ 9.41 to 9.45 infra.

Chapter 5

INFORMAL CONTRACTS WITHOUT CONSIDERATION OR INJURIOUS RELIANCE

Table of Sections

Table of Sections

A. PAST CONSIDERATION AND MORAL OBLIGATION

§ 5.1   Introduction

Not all contracts require consideration. The distinction between formal and informal contracts is introduced in § 1.8. Formal contracts require no consideration. The formal contract under seal survives in some jurisdictions, as do recognizances and other kinds of specialties that are deemed to be formal contracts.[1] In addition, some informal contracts are exempt from the requirement of consideration. For example, promises that are enforceable because they have induced unbargained-for reliance are the subject of the next chapter on promissory estoppel. This chapter is concerned with informal promises enforceable without detrimental reliance or consideration. One group of promises of this kind, promises to perform a duty despite failure of a condition, will be discussed in chapter 11, where the context will make the discussion clearer.

Lord Mansfield, perhaps the greatest common law judge ever,[2] introduced revolutionary changes into the doctrine of consideration. These changes proved short-lived, but had certain residual effects on court decisions; also legislation has revived some of the ideas he espoused. In Pillans and Rose v. Van Mierop[3] he laid down two radical propositions. First, no consideration is required if a promise is expressed in writing. Second, no consideration is required in a commercial transaction. Although both of these propositions were quickly overruled,[4] they found limited acceptance in Twentieth Century legislation, as indicated in part B of this chapter. Perhaps the twenty-first century will awaken to the general soundness of the propositions he laid down.

---

§ 5.1

1. See ch. 7 infra.

2. His major achievement was the incorporation of the law merchant into the common law. In contracts, he is responsible for the doctrine of constructive conditions and substantial performance. He also introduced the Roman law idea of quasi contracts into the common law.

3. 3 Burr. 1663, 97 Eng.Rep. 1035 (K.B. 1765). A concurring judge remarked: "many of the old cases are strange and absurd; so also are some of the modern ones * * * "3 Burr. at 1671, 97 Eng.Rep. at 1039. The subject has hardly changed since.

4. Rann v. Hughes, 7 T.R. 350, 101 Eng. Rep. 1014 n. (Ex.1778).

The first part (part A) of this chapter will discuss the "moral obligation" question. In Lee v. Muggeridge,[5] another Mansfield took up certain *dicta* of his more famous namesake and ruled that a promise made in fulfillment of a previous moral obligation to pay for a benefit that had been conferred by the promisee was sufficiently supported by moral consideration. This ruling was well grounded in the older law.[6] The moral obligation that served as consideration was not the moral obligation created by the promise itself, but rather the antecedent moral obligation that induced the promise.[7] In time, this broad proposition was also overruled[8] but not entirely and not in every common law jurisdiction. This line of authority will be discussed first, followed by a discussion of statutes that, under certain circumstances, eliminate the necessity for consideration. The chapter will close with a brief discussion of stipulations, a category unto itself, which also dispense with the need for consideration.

§ 5.2   Past Consideration and Moral Obligation

The general rule is that past consideration is not consideration.[1] Although at early common law there was authority to the effect that a promise made in recognition of a moral obligation arising out of a benefit previously received is enforceable, today this notion is often rejected. The minority of jurisdictions which accept the moral obligation exception do so with a great deal of circumspection and qualification.

Cases that accept the moral obligation concept generally divide themselves into five categories. The common thread among these cases is that there is an exchange of values, even though in some of the cases the exchange is not bargained for in exchange for the promise that is enforced.[2] Another common thread is that a healthy moral sense dictates that the promise be enforced.[3] The five categories are: (1) Where the promise relates to a prior contractual or quasi-contractual debt that still exists as an enforceable obligation (§ 5.3); (2) where a material benefit was previously received by the promisor (§ 5.4); (3) where there was a prior legal obligation that was discharged by operation of law (§§ 5.5, 5.6, 5.7); (4) where there is a promise not to avoid an avoidable duty (§ 5.8); and (5) where there is a promise based upon a previous unen-

---

5. 2 Taunt. 36, 128 Eng.Rep. 599 (C.P. 1813).

6. E.g., Lampleigh v. Brathwait, Hobart 105, 80 Eng.Rep. 255 (C.P.1615). Occasionally a more modern case has stated the rule almost as broadly. In re Schoenkerman's Estate, 236 Wis. 311, 294 N.W. 810 (1940).

7. 3 Corbin §§ 9.21 to 9.30 (Holmes 1996). Although moral and legal obligations are commonly distinguished, it would be a mistake to regard moral obligations as devoid of legal consequences. For a list of fifteen legal consequences attaching to the existence of an unenforceable moral obligation, see Dias, The Unenforceable Duty, 33 Tulane L.Rev. 473, 483–88 (1959).

8. Eastwood v. Kenyon, 11 Ad. & E. 438, 113 Eng.Rep. 482 (Q.B.1840).

§ 5.2

1. See § 4.3 supra.

2. See Gordon, Consideration and the Commercial—Gift Dichotomy, 44 Vand. L.Rev. 283, 302–05 (1991).

3. There are those who place the law of contract on the moral obligation to keep a promise. Fried, Contract as Promise 14–17 (1981). To the effect that there is no general moral obligation to keep a promise, see Atiyah, Essays on Contract (1986), described in Perillo, Book Review, 34 N.Y.L.Sch.L.Rev. 563 (1989).

forceable obligation under the Statute of Frauds (§ 5.9). Section 5.10 discusses certain other promises not included in the categories listed above.

§ 5.3   Promises to Pay Pre-existing Debts

At early common law it was well settled that a pre-existing debt was consideration for a promise to pay the debt. Under this early common law rule, if C loaned D $1,000 which was to be repaid by D on January 2, 1600, and D failed to repay the debt when due, D's promise made on March 1, 1600, to repay the debt would be deemed to be supported by consideration. Under modern definitions of consideration, the promise is unsupported by consideration, since the past debt was not incurred in exchange for the subsequent promise. The rule that the pre-existing debt constitutes consideration had significant practical impact at that time. In an action on the promise to pay the pre-existing indebtedness, the writ of assumpsit was available under which the plaintiff was entitled to trial by jury. If the writ of debt was employed, defendant was entitled to trial by wager of law, pursuant to which the defendant could obtain judgment by swearing that he was not indebted and producing eleven persons who swore that they believed the defendant.[1]

Most modern authorities take the position that, if the past debt is still existing and enforceable, a promise to pay the debt is enforceable provided that the promise does not exceed the amount of the pre-existing debt.[2] Other authorities indicate that the promise is unenforceable.[3] The question is almost entirely of academic interest since the creditor may sue on the original obligation.[4] The primary context in which the new promise may become important is where the statute of limitations is in issue. Promises in this context, however, are governed by a particular set of rules, discussed below.[5] The UCC makes it clear that if the promise is made in an instrument, such as a note or a check governed by Article 3 of the Code, for a pre-existing indebtedness, no new consideration is required for the enforceability of the instrument.[6]

§ 5.4   Promises to Pay for Benefits Received

Under the early common law's writ system, if A requested B to perform a certain act without making an express promise in return,

§ 5.3

1. Ames, The History of Assumpsit, 2 Harv.L.Rev. 53 (1888), Selected Readings 33.

2. CIBC Bank and Trust v. Banco Central do Brasil, 886 F.Supp. 1105 (S.D.N.Y. 1995); 3 Corbin § 9.2 (Holmes 1996); Rs. 2d § 82(1). If the debtor promised to pay less, the promise is binding in accordance with its terms. 3 Corbin § 9.3 (Holmes 1996).

3. 4 Williston § 8:10.

4. An account stated (§ 21.9 infra) is enforceable without consideration and gives the claimant certain advantages of pleading

and proof. This is perhaps a result of the rule here discussed.

In Hood v. Birmingham, 562 So.2d 164 (Ala.1990), a city had entered into a written agreement acknowledging the decedent's services and itemized the fees due him. This document was treated as a contract governed by the six-year period of limitation and not a claim subject to a two-year notice of claim statute.

5. See § 5.7 infra.

6. 3–303(b) of the 1990 revision. (Former § 3–408). See Sverdrup v. Politis, 888 S.W.2d 753 (Mo.App.1994).

unlike the cases discussed in the preceding section, an action for debt would not lie because the obligation was not a liquidated sum certain. Assumpsit would not lie because A had made no express promise.[1] For example, if A requested B to paint A's house but made no express promise to pay for the services, A would not be liable to B either under the writ of debt or under the writ of assumpsit. To help overcome this unjust result, it was held that a subsequent express promise to pay for the acts performed was enforceable.[2] Later, it was even held that a promise to pay for services that had been rendered as a favor rather than in expectation of payment was enforceable.[3] Under modern law, however, this last point is controversial.

Today, it is clear that if A requests B to perform services, or A accepts services offered by B, unless the services were understood to be gratuitous, A will be liable on the implied promise to pay the reasonable value of the services.[4] A subsequent promise defining the amount which A is willing to pay for the services, assented to by B, is, of course, supported by consideration.[5]

If A promises to pay a fixed amount, but subsequently withdraws the promise prior to B's acceptance, no mutual assent and no consideration is present. A number of cases have held that there is no reason to enforce such a promise. Under this minority view, A's promise is at best a rebuttable evidentiary admission of the value of the services.[6] It is, nonetheless, much more commonly held that a new promise to pay a fixed sum in discharge of a pre-existing legal obligation arising from services or other material benefit rendered at request is enforceable without new consideration and without mutual assent. The rule does not apply where the promise is made in an offer that requires a return promise or performance by the promisee.[7] This is because the offer is a promise conditioned on acceptance.

Corbin takes the view that the promise will be enforced only to the extent that it is not disproportionate to the value of the services.[8] Under this view, the new promise is of little value except to the extent that it may be prima facie proof of the value of the prior acts. According to Williston's analysis, "the weight of authority supports the validity of a subsequent promise defining the extent of the promisor's undertaking," even if the promise is disproportionate to the value of the prior acts.[9] That is, the new promise will be enforced according to its terms.

§ 5.4

1. Ames, supra § 5.3 n.1.

2. Bosden v. Thinne, 80 Eng.Rep. 29 (K.B.1603).

3. Lampleigh v. Brathwait, 80 Eng.Rep. 255 (C.P.1615); contra, Moore v. Elmer, 180 Mass. 15, 61 N.E. 259 (1901) (Holmes, J.).

4. See § 2.18 supra; 3 Corbin § 9.24 (Holmes 1996); 4 Williston §§ 8:11–8:12.

5. There is consideration in an agreed liquidation of an unliquidated claim. See § 4.11 supra. However, the agreement may instead be an executory accord. See §§ 21.4 and 21.5–21.7.

6. See 4 Williston §§ 8:11.

7. Rs. 2d ch. 4, topic 2, intro. note.

8. 3 Corbin § 9.24 (Holmes 1996); accord, in dictum, Knight v. Board of Administration, 273 Cal.Rptr. 120, 144 n. 10 (Cal. App.1990), rev. denied, cert. denied.

9. 4 Williston § 8:11.

Although the cases appear to follow Williston's rule on this issue, many are analytically unsatisfactory in one respect. In many, if not most, of these cases, the facts show that the new promise was assented to by the promisee; the promise could equally have been treated as one side of an accord and satisfaction.[10] The point of the rule here discussed is that a promise is binding although, unlike an offer, the promise is not conditioned on the promisee's acceptance. The Restatement (Second) appears to avoid the question of whether a promise to pay more than the pre-existing debt is binding for the full amount promised.[11]

The discussion thus far involves a promise involving a bargained-for service that had already been performed with the expectation of payment. We now consider whether a promise to pay for services rendered at request, but as a favor, without expectation of payment, is enforceable. In a majority of jurisdictions, such a promise is *not* enforceable.[12] As discussed earlier, past consideration ordinarily will not support a promise.[13] Yet, a minority of jurisdictions follow Mansfield's ruling that the past consideration creates a moral obligation that supports a subsequent promise, even if the service was performed without the expectation of payment. Still, frequently, the decisions that follow the minority view are sustainable on other grounds.[14]

When a service or other benefit is conferred without request, a cause of action arises, in limited circumstances, to recover the reasonable value of those services under the rules of quasi contract.[15] When such a right exists, a promise to pay for benefits so received is governed by the same rules as govern a promise to pay for acts previously performed at request. In the ordinary case, however, receipt of unrequested benefits creates no legal obligation.[16] If a subsequent promise is made to pay for these benefits, the majority of cases hold that the promise is unenforceable.[17] A minority of cases, accepting the moral obligation concept, are to

10. E.g., In re Bradbury, 105 A.D. 250, 93 N.Y.S. 418 (1905); see n.5 supra.

11. Compare Rs. 2d § 82(1) with § 86(2)(b).

12. Moore v. Lawrence, 252 Ark. 759, 480 S.W.2d 941 (1972); Allen v. Bryson, 67 Iowa 591, 25 N.W. 820, 56 Am.Rep. 358 (1885); Moore v. Elmer, 180 Mass. 15, 61 N.E. 259 (1901); Pershall v. Elliott, 249 N.Y. 183, 163 N.E. 554 (1928).

13. See § 4.3 supra.

14. Old American Life Ins. v. Biggers, 172 F.2d 495, 8 ALR2d 781 (10th Cir.1949); Medberry v. Olcovich, 15 Cal.App.2d 263, 59 P.2d 551 (1936), app. denied; Sargent v. Crandall, 143 Colo. 199, 352 P.2d 676 (1960); Snow v. Nellist, 5 Wn.App. 140, 486 P.2d 117 (1971) (probably a duty to make restitution); In re Hatten's Estate, 233 Wis. 199, 288 N.W. 278 (1939) (the decision is supported by the majority view since payment for the services was promised prior to their complete rendition).

15. Chase v. Corcoran, 106 Mass. 286 (1871) (rescue and repair of a boat); Cotnam v. Wisdom, 83 Ark. 601, 104 S.W. 164, 12 LRA NS 1090 (1907) (medical services to an unconscious person); see Rs. 2d § 86 cmts b, c, d, e and f; Wade, Restitution for Benefits Conferred Without Request, 19 Vand.L.Rev. 1183 (1966).

16. Rs. Restitution § 112; see Dawson, The Self–Serving Intermeddler, 87 Harv. L.Rev. 1409 (1974).

17. In re Greene, 45 F.2d 428 (S.D.N.Y. 1930) ("the doctrine that past moral obligation is consideration is now generally exploded"); Mills v. Wyman, 20 Mass. (3 Pick.) 207 (1825) (father promised to pay for services rendered to ailing adult son; [see Watson, 17 Tulane L.Rev. 1749 (1997) for detailed facts and analysis of this case]; Estate of Voight, 95 N.M. 625, 624 P.2d 1022 (1981); Harrington v. Taylor, 225 N.C. 690, 36 S.E.2d 227 (1945) (plaintiff injured

the contrary,[18] and accept a doctrine of "promissory restitution."[19]

The more important part of the phrase "promissory restitution," is the word "promissory;" without the promise, there is no cause of action. The action is based on the terms of the promise and any conditions to the promise must be fulfilled for an action to lie. Despite suggestions by Corbin and the Restatement (Second) that enforcement of the promise may be limited, the holdings of the cases appear unanimously to grant full enforcement or none.[20]

The Restatement (Second) has accepted the minority view that a receipt of a material benefit with or without a prior request, followed by the receiver's promise to pay for the benefit, is enforceable without consideration "to the extent necessary to prevent injustice."[21] Despite the absence of a bargained-for exchange, the Restatement rightly takes the position that an expressed intention to be bound founded upon receipt of a material benefit ought to be enforced. The context assures that the promise is seriously meant; the past benefit creates a moral duty to pay. From the point of view of economics, the value of an enforceable promise is far greater than an unenforceable promise; therefore the promisor's goals can be accomplished at a lesser cost.[22] This combination justifies legal enforcement.

in saving promisor's life; promise to pay damages).

18. Webb v. McGowin, 232 Ala. 374, 168 So. 199 (1936) (plaintiff injured in saving defendant's life; promise to pay an annuity); Realty Assoc. v. Valley Nat. Bank, 153 Ariz. 514, 738 P.2d 1121 (App.1986) (owner promised to pay broker for finding buyer after listing had expired); Desny v. Wilder, 46 Cal.2d 715, 299 P.2d 257 (1956) (defendant promised to pay for plaintiff's idea which he was free to utilize without compensation); Worner Agency v. Doyle, 133 Ill.App.3d 850, 88 Ill.Dec. 855, 479 N.E.2d 468 (1985) (subsequent promise to pay for services as a finder); Holland v. Martinson, 119 Kan. 43, 237 P. 902 (1925), noted in 11 Cornell L.Q. 357 (1926); Brickell v. Hendricks, 121 Miss. 356, 83 So. 609 (1920), noted in 5 Cornell L.Q. 450 (1920); Patterson v. Katt, 791 S.W.2d 466 (Mo.App.1990); Edson v. Poppe, 24 S.D. 466, 124 N.W. 441, 26 LRA NS 534 (1910) (tenant orders well dug; landlord promised to pay well digger). The moral obligation doctrine was applied in the U. S. prior to its demolition (§ 5.1 supra) in England. E.g. Beach v. Lee, 2 U.S. (2 Dall.) 257, 1 L.Ed. 371 (Pa.1796). In Louisiana, the range of enforceable promises made because of moral obligation, is broader than under the Restatement. See Thomas v. Bryant, 639 So.2d 378 (La.App. 1994) (promise to pay for past drug abuse treatment of adult stepson); Azaretta v. Ma-

nalla, 768 So.2d 179, 98 A.L.R.5th 747 (La. App.2000).

At times the same result is reached by covert manipulation of consideration concepts. See, e.g., Griffin v. Louisville Trust, 312 Ky. 145, 226 S.W.2d 786 (1950) (conventional consideration found by a series of inferences); Yarwood v. Trusts & Guarantee, 94 A.D. 47, 87 N.Y.S. 947 (1904) (wealthy vagabond is taken in from the bitter cold; subsequently promises $5,000 for this apparently charitable act); Matter of Todd's Estate, 47 Misc. 35, 95 N.Y.S. 211 (Sur.Ct.1905) (same vagabond promises $5,000 for similar kindnesses).

19. The term "promissory restitution" appears to have been coined by Henderson, Promises Grounded in the Past: The Idea of Unjust Enrichment and the Law of Contract, 57 Va.L.Rev. 1115, 1118 n. 4 (1971). An economic justification for this doctrine appears in Kronman & Posner, The Economics of Contract Law 51–52 (1979); Kull, Reconsidering Gratuitous Promises, 21 J.Legal Stud 39 (1992).

20. See Thel & Yorio, The Promissory Basis of Past Consideration, 78 Va.L.Rev. 1045 (1992).

21. Rs. 2d § 86.

22. Posner, Gratuitous Promises in Economics and Law, 6 J.Leg.Stud. 411, 418 (1977).

The Restatement qualifies the right to recovery by refusing enforcement if "the promisee conferred the benefit as a gift or for other reasons the promisor has not been unjustly enriched."[23] It also provides that the promise will not be enforced "to the extent that its value is disproportionate to the benefit."[24] As the Restatement reporter for this section grants, the section "fairly bristles with unspecific concepts,"[25] such as "gift," "unjust enrichment" and "injustice." The primary thrust of the section is to provide for recovery on promises made to compensate for benefits received which are on the outer fringes of the law of quasi contract. The section comments and illustrations focus upon promises made because of benefits received in emergencies,[26] or in business settings,[27] and promises made to rectify mistakes.[28] Where the commentary dwells on "unjust enrichment," it is off the mark. For example, if A saves B's life, B is enriched, but there is no injustice in the enrichment.[29]

Corbin's treatise is generally in accord and suggests that the moral consideration concept is part of the legal resources of all jurisdictions to be utilized "as an escape from more hardened and definitely worded rules of law."[30] In New York, by statute, past consideration will support a written promise if certain formalities are complied with.[31] The statute is broader in scope than the Restatement rule. The Restatement indicates that a promise to pay an additional sum for benefits conferred under a contract would not be enforceable because no element of unjust enrichment would be present.[32] Under the New York statute such a promise would be enforceable as long as the required formalities are complied with.

23. Id. § 86(2)(a). In McMurry v. Magnusson, 849 S.W.2d 619 (Mo.App.1993), plaintiff was injured in a collision and her sister rendered nursing care. Plaintiff subsequently promised to pay the sister at the going rate. In an action against a tortfeasor, it was held to be a question of fact whether the services were a "gift," which would make the promise non-binding, thereby reducing the damages assessed against the tortfeasor.

24. Id. § 86(2)(b).

25. Braucher, Freedom of Contract and the Second Restatement, 78 Yale L.J. 598, 605 (1969). He also states that: "The new section seeks to draw a distinction between the cases involving moral obligations based on gratitude or sentiment and those cases which are on the borderline of quasi-contract or unjust enrichment, where the subsequent promise removes an objection which might otherwise bar quasi-contractual relief." Ibid.

26. Rs. 2d § 86 ills. 6, 7.

27. Id., ills. 8, 9, 10, 11. See Marnon v. Vaughan Motor, 184 Or. 103, 143–44, 194

P.2d 992, 1009–10 (1948) (prior disclosure of valuable business idea).

28. Id., ills. 4, 5.

29. Eisenberg, The Principles of Consideration, 67 Cornell L.Rev. 640, 664 (1982).

30. 3 Corbin § 9.21 (Holmes 1996); see also Fuller, Consideration and Form, 41 Colum.L.Rev. 799, 821–22 (1941); Grosse, Moral Obligation as Consideration in Contracts, 17 Vill.L.Rev. 1 (1971); Havighurst, Consideration, Ethics and Administration, 42 Colum.L.Rev. 1, 18–20 (1942); Henderson, § 5.4 n.19 supra; Kronman & Posner, The Economics of Contract Law 51–53 (1979); Thel & Yorio, supra n.20; cf. Von Mehren, Civil–Law Analogues to Consideration, 72 Harv.L.Rev. 1009, 1033–47 (1959).

31. See § 5.18 infra. Statutory formulations in California, Georgia and other Civil Code states are discussed in Henderson, § 5.4 n.19 supra, at 1129–35.

32. Rs. 2d § 86 cmt f; see 3 Corbin § 9.26 (Holmes 1996); but see cases such as Griffin v. Louisville Trust, 312 Ky. 145, 226 S.W.2d 786 (1950), n.18 supra.

§ 5.5 Promises to Pay Discharged Debts

For a considerable time it had been held that a promise to pay a debt discharged in bankruptcy, barred by the statute of limitations, or otherwise rendered unenforceable by operation of law[1] is enforceable without consideration. The rule with respect to bankruptcy has been drastically changed. (§ 5.6). The cases frequently articulate the rationale for enforcing such promises in terms that the debt coupled with the moral obligation to pay is sufficient consideration to support the new promise to pay.[2] Other cases speak in terms of the promise reviving a debt barred by operation of law.[3] Others adopt the rationale that the promise operates as a waiver of the debtor's defense; the right is said to have continued to exist, only the remedy having been barred.[4]

In truth, the basis of the rule is a historical one. The rule is a particular application of the old view that an antecedent debt is sufficient consideration for a subsequent promise to pay it. When this doctrine became unimportant, because the writ of debt became obsolete, courts generally agreed that promises to pay a debt discharged by operation of law should be enforced and treated these cases as a separate category.[5] That the reason for the rule is historical rather than purely logical is borne out by the cases holding that a promise to pay a tort claim barred by the statute of limitations is unenforceable despite the fact that the elements of waiver and moral obligation are equally strong as in a case in which a contract debt has become barred by the passage of time.[6] The survival of the moral obligation rule has been justified on the ground that the promisor "is only promising to do what [the promisor] should have done without a promise."[7] Economic theorists find utility in the rule because of the enhancement of the *promisor's* credit worthiness.[8]

§ 5.5

1. Other illustrations of this doctrine may be found in § 5.10 infra.

2. Stanek v. White, 172 Minn. 390, 215 N.W. 784 (1927); Herrington v. Davitt, 220 N.Y. 162, 115 N.E. 476, 1 ALR 1700 (1917); Kopp v. Fink, 204 Okl. 570, 232 P.2d 161 (1951).

3. See 4 Williston § 8:8.

4. Way v. Sperry, 60 Mass. (6 Cush.) 238, 52 Am.Dec. 779 (1851). Using this rationale, it is generally held that a payment made after the statute of limitations has run may not be recovered. Jordan v. Bergsma, 63 Wn.App. 825, 822 P.2d 319 (1992). It has also been held that even if the debt is time-barred, a mortgage given to secure the debt may be foreclosed. See De Anza Land and Leisure v. Raineri, 137 Ariz. 262, 669 P.2d 1339 (App.1983) (rejecting this view).

5. See § 5.3 supra; 4 Williston § 8:8; Stanek v. White, 172 Minn. 390, 215 N.W. 784 (1927); Carshore v. Huyck, 6 Barb. (N.Y.) 583 (1849); Rs. 2d §§ 82–83.

6. Marchetti v. Atchison T. & S.F. R.R., 123 Kan. 728, 255 P. 682 (1927) (negligence); Hollenbeck v. Guardian Nat. Life Ins., 144 Neb. 684, 14 N.W.2d 330 (1944) (fraud); Armstrong v. Levan, 109 Pa. 177, 1 A. 204 (1885) (but a promise made before the statute has run may be enforceable by estoppel); contra, Opitz v. Hayden, 17 Wn.2d 347, 135 P.2d 819 (1943) (promise for time-barred claim for seduction held enforceable). Even under the majority rule, the promise may be enforced under the doctrine of estoppel if the promisee relied upon the promise. See § 5.7 n.31 infra.

7. Fuller, supra § 5.4 n.30, at 821. Extending the doctrine from promises to pay money to a promise to cure defective construction is Potterton v. Ryland Group, 289 Md. 371, 424 A.2d 761 (1981).

8. Kronman & Posner, supra § 5.4 n.30, at 51.

§ 5.6　Promises to Pay Debts Discharged in Bankruptcy

By decree, a bankruptcy court can discharge a debtor's obligation. Not infrequently, after discharge, bankrupts promise one or more of their creditors that they will pay despite the discharge. Until enactment of the Bankruptcy Reform Act of 1978, such promises were binding and constituted perhaps the bulk of the past consideration cases. Because of perceived abuses by financing institutions, this Act bars enforcement of such promises except those made by a reaffirmation agreement in the bankruptcy proceeding itself.[1] Such agreements are most likely to be made where the creditor has a security interest in the property of the debtor.

§ 5.7　Effect of New Promise on Statute of Limitations

A promise to pay a contractual or quasi-contractual debt has the effect of starting the statute of limitations running anew.[1] From an economic point of view, this rule has the effect of increasing the promisor's creditworthiness[2] and, of course, increasing the promisee's wealth as well. This rule applies whether the promise is made before or after the debt has been barred by the passage of the statutory period.[3]

A promise not to plead the statute of limitations generally has the same effect as a promise to pay the debt,[4] but, in most jurisdictions if the promise is made in the original contract or before maturity of the debt, the promise is void as contrary to public policy.[5] Most cases invalidate attempts to provide for a longer period of limitations than provided for by statute,[6] as does the UCC.[7]

An acknowledgment of the existence of the debt is treated as an implied promise to pay,[8] unless there is an indication of a contrary

§ 5.6

1. 11 U.S.C.A. § 524(c).

§ 5.7

1. U.S. v. Upper Valley Clinic Hospital, 615 F.2d 302 (5th Cir.1980) (quasi-contractual action for medicare reimbursement); U.S. v. Illinois, 144 F.Supp.2d 990 (2001); Hood v. Birmingham, 562 So.2d 164 (Ala. 1990); Regan Farmers Union Co-op. v. Hinkel, 437 N.W.2d 845 (N.D.1989); Rs. 2d § 82; Kocourek, 18 Ill.L.Rev. 538 (1924).

2. Posner, supra § 5.4 n.22.

3. Harper v. Fairley, 53 N.Y. 442 (1873); 3 Corbin § 9.5 (Holmes 1996); 4 Williston § 8:21. For example, assume a six year period of limitation. If A lends B $1,000 on January 2, 1996, the money to be repaid on January 2, 1998, the statute of limitations begins to run in January of 1998. If B, on January 2, 1998, made a new promise to pay, the six year period would commence to run again from this date so that the debt would be barred in 2004. If instead, after the statute had run, B in 2003 promised to

pay, the statute would start to run again so that it will expire in 2009.

4. Rs. 2d § 82 cmt f; U. S. v. Curtiss Aeroplane, 147 F.2d 639 (2d Cir.1945); 4 Williston § 8:37. But if the debtor makes the promise but reserves the right to raise other defenses, there is no implied promise to pay the debt. The promise may, however, be enforced if supported by consideration or if the claimant injuriously relies on the promise. 4 Williston § 8:37.

5. 4 Williston § 8:37; Rs. 1st § 558; see McKinney's N.Y. C.P.L.R. 201.

6. E.L. Burns Co. v. Cashio, 302 So.2d 297, 84 ALR3d 1162 (La.1974); John J. Kassner & Co. v. New York, 46 N.Y.2d 544, 415 N.Y.S.2d 785, 389 N.E.2d 99 (1979).

7. UCC § 2–725(1) (revision draft retains this rule).

8. Banco do Brasil v. Antigua and Barbuda, 268 A.D.2d 75, 707 N.Y.S.2d 151 (2000). Some courts are reluctant to infer a promise. See American Multimedia v. Free-

intention. For example, a statement that "I know I owe the money * * * and I will never pay it," although an acknowledgment of the debt, rebuts any implication of a promise to pay.[9] Also, an offer of settlement is not such an acknowledgement as will create a cause of action.[10]

Statutes in most states require the subsequent promise to pay the debt or the acknowledgment of the debt to be in a signed writing or other record.[11] Part payment of principal or interest or the giving of collateral may have the same effect as an acknowledgment and be treated as the equivalent of a writing or other record.[12] To have this effect, the part payment must be voluntary.[13] Part payment tolls the statutory period on debts or contract damages owed to the U.S.[14]

The creditor's claim is based on the new promise and therefore is limited by the terms of the new promise.[15] Thus, the promise may be to pay in part or in installments[16] or on specified conditions.[17] The courts are divided as to whether the promise or acknowledgment must specify the amount of the debt.[18] A promise by one joint obligor does not bind the others if there is no agency relationship,[19] nor does it bind a surety.[20]

Historically, the rule enforcing new promises to pay debts barred by the statute of limitations was limited to antecedent obligations enforceable pursuant to the writ known as indebitatus assumpsit or general assumpsit.[21] Generally, this writ was available to enforce claims for

dom Distributing, 95 N.C.App. 750, 384 S.E.2d 32 (1989) ("we plan to pay" insufficient); Snyder v. Baltimore Trust, 532 A.2d 624 (Del.Super.1986) (promise to "take care" of the plaintiff for prior unpaid services, insufficient); see 3 Corbin § 9.7 (Holmes 1996); 4 Williston §§ 8:26–8:29. Some courts require that the communication contain directly or impliedly an expression by the debtor of the justness of the debt. Freeman v. Wilson, 107 Ariz. 271, 485 P.2d 1161 (1971); Rs. 2d § 82 cmt d.

9. A'Court v. Cross, 3 Bing. 329, 130 Eng.Rep. 540 (C.P.1825); see Garland Co. v. J.L. Miller & Sons, 395 Pa.Super. 532, 577 A.2d 917 (1990).

10. Sitkiewicz v. Sullivan, 256 A.D.2d 884, 681 N.Y.S.2d 677 (1998).

11. 4 Williston § 8:24; Rs. 2d § 82 cmt a; e.g., McKinney's N.Y. Gen'l Oblig. L. § 17–101; Manwill v. Oyler, 11 Utah 2d 433, 361 P.2d 177 (1961).

12. Skaneateles Savings Bank v. Modi Assocs., 239 A.D.2d 40, 668 N.Y.S.2d 819 (1998); Rs. 2d § 82 cmt e. The word "may" is used in the text because the question is whether the part payment is to be interpreted as an implied promise to pay the balance. Lew Morris Demolition v. Board of Ed., 40 N.Y.2d 516, 387 N.Y.S.2d 409, 355 N.E.2d 369, 10 ALR4th 925 (1976). This is often a question of fact. First Hawaiian Bank v. Zukerkorn, 2 Haw.App. 383, 633

P.2d 550 (1981); see also 3 Corbin § 9.8 (Holmes 1996); 4 Williston § 8:29. Where the payments are made sporadically, but without qualification, the statute of limitations is re-tolled with each payment. Greer Limestone v. Nestor, 175 W.Va. 289, 332 S.E.2d 589 (1985).

13. Security Bank v. Finkelstein, 160 A.D. 315, 145 N.Y.S. 5 (1913), aff'd; Rs. 2d § 82 cmt e; 4 Williston § 8:30.

14. 28 U.S.C.A. 2415(a). See U.S. v. Milam, 855 F.2d 739 (11th Cir.1988) (educational loan).

15. Tebo v. Robinson, 100 N.Y. 27, 2 N.E. 383 (1885).

16. Gillingham v. Brown, 178 Mass. 417, 60 N.E. 122, 55 LRA 320 (1901); Cross v. Stackhouse, 212 S.C. 100, 46 S.E.2d 668 (1948); 4 Williston § 8:32.

17. E.g., Big Diamond Mill. v. Chicago, M. & St. P. Ry., 142 Minn. 181, 171 N.W. 799, 8 ALR 1254 (1919); Andrews v. Cohen, 664 S.W.2d 826 (Tex.App.1984); Rs. 2d § 82 cmt c; see 1 Williston § 8:32.

18. See Annot, 21 ALR4th 1121 (1983).

19. Roth v. Michelson, 55 N.Y.2d 278, 449 N.Y.S.2d 159, 434 N.E.2d 228 (1982).

20. Gering State Bank v. Estrada, 1994 WL 380271 (Neb.App.1994).

21. Rs. 2d § 82 cmt b.

liquidated amounts or for the reasonable value of an executed performance.[22] New promises to pay obligations enforceable in special assumpsit or covenant were not enforced; the former writ was applicable to a breach of an executory contract and the latter was applicable to the enforcement of a sealed instrument or a judgment. Consequently, adopting the historical distinctions, the first Restatement stated the rule that a promise to pay all or part of any antecedent contractual or quasi-contractual obligation for the payment of money, whether liquidated or not, commences the running of the statute of limitations anew.[23] A promise to pay damages for breach of contract was not included in the class of promises that tolled the statute of limitations. The Restatement (Second) is in accord.[24]

This means, by way of illustration, that if A, a painter, painted B's house at B's request and B subsequently promised to pay for the services, B's subsequent promise will start the statute of limitations running anew even though the obligation is unliquidated, that is, even if it is not an uncontested sum certain.[25] However, if A and B entered into a bilateral contract for painting and B breached the contract before A performed, a subsequent promise by B to pay the damages caused by the breach will have no effect upon the statute of limitations.[26]

Another historical limitation on the enforceability of promises to pay involves formal contracts. With the abolition of the writ system a number of cases began to hold that the subsequent promise would have the effect of starting the obligation running anew even though the promise was to pay an obligation under seal or to pay a judgment.[27] The original Restatement took the position that the antecedent duty may be under seal but that "an antecedent duty under a judgment is not, however, included."[28] The Restatement Second takes no position with regard to sealed instruments or judgments.[29] It makes specific what appears to have been generally recognized: a promise to pay a tort claim has no effect upon the statute of limitations unless the tort claim involves unjust enrichment.[30] Such a promise may, however, be effective on a theory of estoppel where the promise lulls the promisee into a false feeling of security.[31]

---

22. See Shipman, Common Law Pleading 254–55 (1923).

23. Rs. 1st § 86; see Rs. 2d § 82.

24. Rs.2d § 82 (1).

25. Rs. 2d § 82(1) cmt b, but some cases have held that the indebtedness must be defined by the new promise. Bell v. Morrison, 26 U.S. (1 Pet.) 351, 7 L.Ed. 174 (1828).

26. 1 Williston § 188; Rs. 2d § 82 cmt b.

27. Spilde v. Johnson, 132 Iowa 484, 109 N.W. 1023, 8 LRA NS 439 (1906); Trustees of St. Mark's v. Miller, 99 Md. 23, 57 A. 644 (1904). Yes, a judgment has been conceived of as a kind of quasi-contract.

28. Rs. 1st § 86(1) cmt b; accord, Mutual Trust & Deposit v. Boone, 267 S.W.2d 751, 45 ALR2d 962 (Ky.1954). Williston asserts that there is no logical basis for this distinction (4 Williston § 8:34), and Corbin takes the position that a promise to pay a specialty debt or a barred judgment should be enforceable. 3 Corbin § 9.11 (Holmes 1996).

29. Rs. 2d § 82 cmt b.

30. Rs. 2d § 82 cmt b; 4 Williston § 8:33.

31. State Farm Mutual Auto. Ins. v. Budd, 185 Neb. 343, 175 N.W.2d 621, 44 ALR3d 476 (1970) (overruled on other grounds); Annot., 43 ALR3d 756 (1972).

§ 5.8   Promises to Perform Voidable Duties

If A is induced by fraud to promise to pay B $100 in return for property worth much less, the promise is voidable. If, upon discovering the fraud, A again promises to pay $100, or some lesser sum, the new promise is enforceable without fresh consideration,[1] provided of course, that the new promise is not itself voidable because of fraud or some other infirmity. However, if the second promise is made without knowledge of the fraud, it is not enforceable.[2]

The same analysis applies to contracts voidable on other grounds, such as duress, mistake and infancy. However it has not been generally applied to void agreements[3] although there is an occasional case to the contrary.[4]

The rule of law discussed here may also be explained on grounds other than the presence or absence of consideration. Voidable promises give promisors the power to avoid or to affirm their promises. In promising to make payment they have given notice of their decision not to exercise their powers of avoidance.[5]

§ 5.9   Effect of New Promise on the Statute of Frauds

As discussed in Chapter 19, the Statute of Frauds bars the enforcement of certain contracts that do not meet the Statute's requirement that there be a writing or electronic record evidencing it. If A and B enter into such a contract that is unenforceable because it does not meet the statutory requirement, should a subsequent oral promise based upon the previous unenforceable contract be enforceable? Assuming first that the arrangement within the Statute of Frauds is still executory, it might seem that the case is analogous to voidable contracts discussed above and that the subsequent oral promise should be enforceable despite the absence of fresh consideration.[1] However, an important difference is that enforcement of the subsequent oral promise would violate the policy of the Statute of Frauds which is to curtail perjured claims.[2] Consequently, the subsequent oral promise is not enforced.

A different problem is presented if the subsequent promise is in a writing or electronic record. Under the Statute of Frauds it is well settled that a memorandum subsequent to the agreement that sufficiently outlines the details of the transaction satisfies the Statute of Frauds

---

§ 5.8

1. Rs. 2d § 85.

2. Rs. 2d § 93. The promisor need only know the essential facts. According to the Restatement, it is not necessary that the promisor know that the facts create a legal power of avoidance or other remedy. But see § 8.5 infra as to infants; and see also 3 Black on Rescission § 591 (2d ed.1929).

3. Rs. 2d § 85.

4. Hansen v. Kootenai County, 93 Idaho 655, 471 P.2d 42, 47 ALR3d 1 (1970) (failure to call for public bids); Sheldon v. Haxtun, 91 N.Y. 124 (1883) (usury).

5. 4 Williston § 8:8.

§ 5.9

1. See § 5.8 supra.

2. Hill v. Dodge, 80 N.H. 381, 117 A. 728 (1922).

and it is immaterial that there is no consideration for the memorandum.[3] Thus, if the subsequent promise is contained in a sufficient memorandum it will be enforceable. But there is also some authority for the proposition that where the writing or other record definitely states the terms of the promise, as in a promissory note to pay a sum certain, it should be enforceable even though it does not serve as a sufficient memorandum.[4]

The situation is also different where the agreement that is unenforceable under the Statute of Frauds has been performed by one of the parties. Under these circumstances it is generally accepted that the party who has performed is entitled to a quasi-contractual recovery.[5] A subsequent promise to pay what is owing under this quasi-contractual obligation raises the problems discussed in section 5.4 above. Occasionally a statute is drawn in such a way as to forbid quasi-contractual recovery. In such a case the subsequent promise should be enforced unless the subsequent promise is included in the prohibition.[6]

If a party admits, in court proceedings, making the contract that is unenforceable under the Statute of Frauds there is a recent trend allowing enforcement.[7] In fact, if the contract is governed by the UCC, a party can be compelled under oath to admit or deny making the contract. If the party admits making the contract, it is enforceable.[8]

§ 5.10 Other Promises Supported by Moral Obligation

On moral obligation and related grounds a number of cases, not previously discussed, have enforced promises based on antecedent events. These include promises by sureties or indorsers whose obligations have been discharged on technical grounds,[1] promises to repay sums collected by force of an erroneous but valid judgment[2] and promises to pay for benefits received under an illegal bargain when the illegality does not involve moral turpitude,[3] as well as others.[4] The cases in this category are closely analogous in reasoning and rationale to the cases involving prior legal obligations discharged by the statute of limitations. Therefore, they should be authoritative even in jurisdictions that do not accept a broad view of moral obligation as an equivalent of consideration.

At common law, a father had no duty to support his children born out of wedlock. Yet, his promise of support made to the mother has often

---

3. See § 19.30 infra.

4. 4 Williston § 8:41; 3 Corbin § 9.29 (Holmes 1996). The Rs. 2d § 86 cmt g, states that "the new promise is binding if the policy of the statute is satisfied." See, e.g., Muir v. Kane, 55 Wn. 131, 104 P. 153, 26 LRA NS 519 (1909); Fellom v. Adams, 274 Cal.App.2d 855, 79 Cal.Rptr. 633 (1969); Bagaeff v. Prokopik, 212 Mich. 265, 180 N.W. 427, 17 ALR 1292 (1920).

5. See § 19.40 infra.

6. 3 Corbin § 9.29 (Holmes 1996).

7. See § 19.30(c) infra.

8. See § 19.34 infra.

§ 5.10

1. 3 Corbin § 9.15 (Holmes 1996).

2. Bentley v. Morse, 14 Johns. 468 (N.Y. 1817); 3 Corbin § 9.16 (Holmes 1996).

3. 3 Corbin § 9.27 (Holmes 1996).

4. 3 Corbin §§ 9.1–9.30 (Holmes 1996).

been enforced. This represents a singular case of a promise being enforced because the promisor has promised to do what he ought to do even though there has been no material benefit to the promisor.[5] It has been suggested that the enforcement of charitable subscriptions falls into the same class.[6]

§ 5.11   To Whom the Promise Must Be Made

A new promise to pay an antecedent obligation, to be enforceable, must be made to an obligee of the antecedent duty or a representative of the obligee.[1] A promise made to a stranger to the transaction has no operative effect unless it can be anticipated that this person will communicate the promise to the obligee.[2] In a few jurisdictions, where a mere admission of the indebtedness is sufficient to revive the debt, an admission or promise made to a third person is sufficient.[3]

B.   CERTAIN COMMERCIAL AND WRITTEN CONTRACTS

Table of Sections

§ 5.12   Scope of the Discussion

At common law, persons wishing to enter into a contract without consideration were empowered to resort to a sealed instrument.[1] In a majority of jurisdictions the legal effect of the seal has been abolished or substantially curtailed by legislation or judicial decision.[2] Partly in an attempt to fill the gap thus created, legislatures have reacted with a number of statutes providing that specified kinds of promises, if made in a signed writing or other record, are enforceable without consideration. The abolition of the seal was not the only motive for these statutes. Ever

---

5. See Thel & Yorio, supra § 5.4 n.20, at 1078–81; Annot., 20 ALR3d 500 § 9.

6. Thel & Yorio, supra § 5.4 n.20, at 1078–81.

§ 5.11

1. Fort Scott v. Hickman, 112 U.S. 150 (1884); Rs. 2d § 92; 4 Williston §§ 8:14, 8:38, esp. 8:36. Beneficiaries, sureties, assignees, and distributees are included in the term obligee. Rs. 2d § 92 cmts b and c.

2. Miller v. Teeter, 53 N.J.Eq. 262, 31 A. 394 (1895).

3. In re Stratman's Estate, 231 Iowa 480, 1 N.W.2d 636 (1942).

§ 5.12

1. See ch. 7 infra.

2. Id.

since Lord Mansfield's day[3] there has been a lingering feeling that written agreements show sufficient deliberation and that the requirement of consideration, as applied to them, tends, without sufficient justification, to defeat the expectations of the parties.[4] The doctrine sometimes seems to defeat commercial expectations without any countervailing benefit to the state's interest in regulating private contracts.

The most significant types of these statutes will be considered here. This text does not purport to attempt complete coverage of local variations.

§ 5.13 The Model Written Obligations Act

Pennsylvania is the only state that presently has on its books[1] the Model (formerly Uniform) Written Obligations Act.[2] This law provides:

> "A written release or promise, hereafter made and signed by the person releasing or promising, shall not be invalid or unenforceable for lack of consideration, if the writing or other record also contains an additional express statement, in any form of language, that the signer intends to be legally bound."

Under this statute, a written promise is not sufficient; there must be "an additional express statement" indicating the promisor's intent to be bound.[3] For example, the following language has been held to be insufficient to meet the statutory requirements:[4]

> "We, Pauline and Mike, release you from all obligations under the Lease, for the balance thereof, and will not hold you responsible whatsoever under the Lease if you sell to Mr. Brown."

Subsequent cases appear more ready to infer an intent to be bound from the use of legalistic language.[5]

§ 5.14 Modification of Contracts

(a) Consideration Not Required

Under the pre-existing duty rule, an enforceable agreement to modify a contract requires consideration.[1] Although a majority of jurisdictions follow the pre-existing duty rule, a number of states have

---

3. See § 5.1 supra.

4. For a contrary view, see Hays, Formal Contracts and Consideration, 41 Colum.L.Rev. 849, 852 (1941) ("deliberation, seriousness of purpose, intent to be legally bound, even if they were actually indicated by the formal device, are not, in themselves and apart from other factors, proper grounds for enforcing promises.")

§ 5.13

1. 33 Purdon's Statutes Ann. §§ 6–8.

2. 9C U.L.A. 378 (adopted 1925); see Note, 29 Colum.L.Rev. 206 (1929). The Act is criticized in Hays, § 5.12 n.4, at 850–52.

3. Gershman v. Metropolitan Life Ins., 405 Pa. 585, 176 A.2d 435 (1962) (words, "Approved by" followed by a signature is insufficient).

4. Fedun v. Mike's Cafe, 204 Pa.Super. 356, 204 A.2d 776 (1964), aff'd.

5. Paul Revere Protective Life Ins. v. Weis, 535 F.Supp. 379 (E.D.Pa.1981), aff'd; Fasco, A.G. v. Modernage, 311 F.Supp. 161 (W.D.Pa.1970).

§ 5.14

1. See § 4.9 supra.

mitigated the rule when unforeseen difficulties arise in the performance of the contract.[2] A distinct minority of jurisdictions have abandoned the rule by judicial decision.[3] There are also some statutes less sweeping than the Model Written Obligations Act that relate specifically to modifications or other special circumstances.

For example, a New York statute permits modifications without consideration, provided that the modification is in a signed writing or other record.[4] In the New York scheme, the writing or other record serves more than merely an evidentiary purpose. The requirement of a writing or other record is designed also to assure that the modification was a deliberate act of the will.[5] Consequently, unlike the requirements of the Statute of Frauds, the modification itself must be in a writing or other record; a memorandum of the modification is not sufficient.[6]

The UCC has also obviated the need for consideration in certain situations. The Sales Article provides in § 2–209(1): "An agreement modifying a contract within this Article needs no consideration to be binding."[7] The Code does not require written evidence of the modification except in two instances. First, a writing or other record may be required if the contract as modified is within the Statute of Frauds provision of the Code.[8] Also, a writing or other record may be required if the original contract by its terms excludes modification or rescission by mutual consent except by a signed writing or other record.[9]

As at common law, the modification under the UCC need not be express, it may be implied. In Mulberry–Fairplains Water Ass'n v. North Wilkesboro,[10] a town had contracted to sell water for forty years to the plaintiff for resale outside town limits. The contract included a schedule of prices and provisions for escalation that limited any rate increase to an amount proportional to the rates charged other customers. The contract further provided that the town would not be required to provide

---

2. See § 4.9 supra.

3. See § 4.9 supra.

4. McKinney's N.Y.Gen.Obl.L. § 5–1103, effective in 1936, Mich.Comp.L.Annot. § 566.1 is substantially the same. Compare such statutes as Mass.G.L.A. c. 4 § 9A, providing that an instrument reciting that it is a sealed instrument will be treated as a sealed instrument. Compare also such statutes as Miss.Code 1972, § 75–19–1 which appear to give the effect of a sealed instrument to all writing or other records. The effect of the statutes such as these depends on the effect seals have heretofore had in the particular jurisdiction. See § 7.9 infra.

5. Annual Report of the [N.Y.] Law Revision Commission 67, 172 (1936). ("Without undertaking to enforce all promises and agreements, the common law might conceivably establish a more comprehensive basis or theory for the enforcement of deliberate promises intentionally made when they are of a character ordinarily relied upon by

men in their economic or business dealings. The necessary deliberation, certainty and security could be insured by evidentiary and formal requirements.")

6. Cf. DFI Communications v. Greenberg, 41 N.Y.2d 602, 394 N.Y.S.2d 586, 363 N.E.2d 312 (1977), motion denied (decided under McKinney's N.Y.Gen.Oblig.L. § 15–301).

7. (Unchanged in the revision): see also Rs. 2d § 89, discussed in § 4.9 supra.

8. UCC § 2–209(3) (the revision substitutes "record" for "writing").

9. UCC § 2–209(2).

10. 105 N.C.App. 258, 412 S.E.2d 910 (1992), pet. denied; accord, Rosen Trust v. Rosen, 53 A.D.2d 342, 352, 386 N.Y.S.2d 491 (1976), aff'd; Ray v. Metropolitan Life Ins., 858 F.Supp. 626 (S.D.Tex.1994) (mailing address changed by course of performance).

in excess of fifteen million gallons of water per month. Despite this provision, for fifteen years the town had supplied the plaintiff, at the contract rate, almost twice as much water as the contract required. Suddenly, the town doubled the price of plaintiff's water and reduced the rates to most residents of the town. In partial justification for the rate increase, the town argued that it was supplying much more water than the contract required and therefore the contract did not regulate the price that could be charged. The court disagreed. The course of performance had given plaintiff a feeling of security that it had a good supply of water at the contract rate. This had led it to enter into contracts with water users in its market area. By supplying the excess water, the town had implicitly agreed to a modification of the contract and could not reinstate the fifteen million gallon limitation. The defendant waived the defense of the Statute of Frauds by failing to plead it. It is questionable whether the Statute should be available as a defense where a contract has been changed by a course of performance.[11] The conduct itself provides a sufficient evidentiary basis for enforcement of the modification.[12]

This section of the UCC which dispenses with the necessity for consideration and which does not generally require a writing or other record raises the question of whether there can be a modification without an express agreement and without a course of performance. In Gateway v. Charlotte Theatres[13] the parties had reduced their agreement to writing. In a cover letter, the buyer specified a completion date although none had been set in the original agreement. The seller ignored this and started performance but did not complete within the time specified by the buyer. The court held that the seller, by its conduct, had accepted the proposed modification.

Sales contracts can be modified even after the goods have been delivered and paid for. Warranties made after the transaction has closed are enforceable.[14] It has been held, however, that the mere mailing of the seller's limited warranty card by the purchaser of an airplane, after contracting, did not indicate assent to the seller's disclaimer of implied warranties, particularly the implied warranty of fitness.[15] Also, where the seller had informed the buyer of a price increase and the buyer replied that it could not absorb the additional costs and continued to pay at the original contract rate, there was no implicit acquiescence in the increase sought by the seller.[16]

---

11. "By delivering, pursuant to contract, approximately 36 truckloads of wheat to the elevator between March 27 and May 30, 1973, Anderson established a course of conduct sufficient to constitute a waiver of his right to assert a defense under the Statute of Frauds." Farmers Elevator v. Anderson, 170 Mont. 175, 552 P.2d 63, 66 (1976).

12. But see Hanson v. Signer Motors, 105 Or.App. 74, 803 P.2d 1207, 1210 (1990).

13. 297 F.2d 483 (1st Cir.1961).

14. Confer Plastics v. Hunkar Laboratories, 964 F.Supp. 73 (W.D.N.Y.1997); Bone Int'l v. Johnson, 74 N.C.App. 703, 329 S.E.2d 714 (1985); Estate of Upchurch, 62 Tenn.App. 634, 466 S.W.2d 886 (1970).

15. Van Den Broeke v. Bellanca Aircraft, 576 F.2d 582 (5th Cir.1978).

16. U.S. v. Santa Fe Engineers, 515 F.Supp. 512 (D.C.Colo.1981).

Skinner v. Tober Foreign Motors illustrates express modifications.[17] The defendant sold and delivered an airplane to the plaintiff who agreed to pay the purchase price at the rate of $200 per month. Soon after delivery, it was discovered that the engine was faulty. Apparently, the airplane was not warranted. Since the plaintiff would have to incur considerable expense in repairing the engine, defendant orally agreed that for one year plaintiff would have to pay only $100 per month toward the price. Several months later, defendant demanded that the payments be increased to $200. Plaintiff refused and defendant repossessed the aircraft. The court held that the modification was binding without consideration and that defendant was liable for substantial damages.[18]

Implicit modifications are common in construction contracts. If the parties fail to follow agreed-upon change order processes and a materially different project ensues, the contract is deemed to have been abandoned and the contractor's action is for quantum meruit.[19] Sometimes difficult to distinguish is the "cardinal change" doctrine where major changes are demanded and performed; for these cardinal changes the contractor is entitled to the contract price plus compensation for the reasonable value of the changes.[20]

(b) No–Oral–Modification Clauses; Statute of Frauds

Apart from statute, the majority common law rule is that "even where the contract specifically states that no non-written [modification] will be recognized, the parties may yet alter their agreement by parol."[21] This result stems from the notion that contracting parties cannot today restrict their own power to contract with each other tomorrow.[22] There are, however, contrary cases.[23] The UCC, however, recognizing that parties seek protection against false allegations of oral modifications,

---

17. 345 Mass. 429, 187 N.E.2d 669 (1963), 65 W.Va.L.Rev. 330 (1963).

18. The defendant did not plead the defense of Statute of Frauds. A discharge is involved here as well as a modification. There may be no distinction between these terms in this context; accepting $100 per month in place of $200 could be considered a modification even if there were no prior agreement. Anderson, The Part Payment Check under the Code, 9 Am.Bus.L.J. 103, 121 (1971).

19. Amelco v. Thousand Oaks, 27 Cal.4th 228, 115 Cal.Rptr.2d 900, 38 P.3d 1120 (2002).

20. Id.; L.K. Comstock & Co. v. Becon Constr. Co., 932 F.Supp. 906 (E.D.Ky.1993) ("abandonment" and "cardinal change" discussed but not found); Douglas Constr. v. Marcais, 239 A.D.2d 803, 657 N.Y.S.2d 835 (1997) ("abandonment" found).

21. Czapla v. Commerz Futures, 114 F.Supp.2d 715 (N.D.Ill.2000); Beach Higher Power Corp. v. Granados, 717 So.2d 563 (Fla.App.1998); Rule Sales & Service v. U.S. Bank Nat. Ass'n., 133 Idaho 669, 991 P.2d 857 (App.1999); Medina v. Sunstate Realty, 119 N.M. 136, 889 P.2d 171 (1995); Bennett v. Farmers Ins. Co., 332 Or. 138, 26 P.3d 785 (2001); King v. PYA Monarch, 317 S.C. 385, 453 S.E.2d 885 (1995); Pacific Northwest Group v. Pizza Blends 90 Wn.App. 273, 951 P.2d 826 (1998); but the result may be different if the oral modification is asserted against an assignee. Davis v. Avenue Plaza, 778 So.2d 613 (La.App.2000).

22. Rs. 2d § 283 cmt b.

23. Gerdes v. Russell Rowe Comm., 232 Ga.App. 534, 502 S.E.2d 352 (1998); Mathis v. Daines, 196 Mont. 252, 639 P.2d 503 (1982); Pantano v. McGowan, 247 Neb. 894, 530 N.W.2d 912 (1995). An intermediate position, is that, in the face of such a clause, an oral modification must be proved by clear and convincing evidence. Powers v. Miller, 127 N.M. 496, 984 P.2d 177 (1999).

gives effect, within limits, to clauses prohibiting oral modifications or rescissions.[24]

Under the UCC, if the contract is between a merchant[25] and a non-merchant, a term on the merchant's form requiring that modification or rescission be in a signed record must be separately signed by the non-merchant, otherwise the clause is ineffective.[26]

The UCC in Section 2–209 directly confronts the situation where an oral modification or rescission is made in violation of a clause forbidding such oral agreements. Subsection 4 provides that the attempted modification can operate as a waiver. A waiver is effective, but retractable by giving reasonable notification "unless the retraction would be unjust in view of a material change of position in reliance on the waiver."[27] In a confusing opinion, Judge Posner has stated that the term "waiver" in 2–209(4) means a waiver that has been relied upon.[28] Under this reading, § 2–209(5) becomes totally meaningless. Its fairly clear meaning is that an unrelied-on waiver can be retracted. The dissenting opinion is sounder.[29] The requirement of a writing or other record may also be overcome by a course of performance.[30] Section 2–209 seems clear enough, but its interpretation has vexed and confused the courts.[31]

If the oral modification is unretractable because of a change of position, would it bar an assignee who had no knowledge of the modification from insisting on the original terms? It has been held that if the assignee is a bona fide purchaser for value, the assignee could enforce the contract as written.[32]

A writing or other record is also required where the contract as modified is within the Statute of Frauds. While the UCC Statute of Frauds generally requires only that there be a sufficient record to make it plausible that a contract has been made, the majority of courts require that all the essential terms of a modification must be in a writing or other record.[33]

The UCC's provisions with respect to no-oral-modification clauses were patterned on a prior New York statute.[34] The New York statute is unclear on the question of the effect of part performance of an oral modification that violates a clause barring such modifications, but the

---

24. UCC § 2–209 cmt 3.

25. See § 1.7 supra.

26. UCC § 2–209(2).

27. UCC § 2–209(5).

28. Wisconsin Knife Works v. National Metal Crafters, 781 F.2d 1280 (7th Cir. 1986).

29. The dissent was approved in BMC Indus. v. Barth Indus., 160 F.3d 1322 (11th Cir.1998).

30. Brookside Farms v. Mama Rizzo's, 873 F.Supp. 1029 (S.D.Tex.1995); J.W. Goodliffe & Son v. Odzer, 283 Pa.Super. 148, 423 A.2d 1032 (1980).

31. See Hillman, Standards for Revising Article 2 of the UCC: The NOM Clause Model, 35 Wm. & Mary L.Rev. 1509, 1525–31 (1994).

32. Stoneybrook Realty v. Cremktco, 176 Misc.2d 589, 675 N.Y.S.2d 749 (1998) (under New York statute); but see § 18.17 infra.

33. Zemco Mfg. v. Navistar, 186 F.3d 815 (7th Cir.1999).

34. McKinney's N.Y. Gen.Oblig.L. § 15–301.

courts have interpreted it to conform to the UCC in most respects,[35] although points of difference may remain.[36] This is a sound interpretation inasmuch as conduct that makes the oral agreement unretractable is (1) highly probative of the oral modifying agreement and (2) good grounds for estopping a party from shielding itself against liability.

§ 5.15　Modifications Under Compulsion

The pre-existing duty rule, conceptually grounded on the idea that no promise is binding unless it is paid for by bargained-for detriment, also has had an important policy rationale—not allowing a party to take undue advantage of circumstances. In an early decision, a sailor who had signed for a voyage at a stipulated wage sued to recover for additional wages promised during the voyage. Lord Kenyon, in rendering his decision against the sailor, was little concerned about concepts of consideration. Rather, he said:

> "If this action was to be supported, it would materially affect the navigation of this kingdom * * * [I]f sailors were * * * in times of danger entitled to insist on an extra charge on such a promise as this, they would in many cases suffer a ship to sink, unless the captain would pay any extravagant demand they might think proper to make."[1]

Like Lord Kenyon, courts, in repeated instances, have defended the pre-existing duty rule as a salutary method of preventing the coerced modification of contracts.[2] But now that the UCC and other legislation permit a contractual modification without consideration, it seems clear that other approaches need to be developed to avoid the enforcement of coerced modifications.

Under the UCC, the request for modification without fresh consideration must be justified. The Code must be read as an integrated document. As the comments to § 2–209 make clear, the good faith standard of § 2–103 ("honesty in fact and the observance of reasonable commercial standards of fair dealing in the trade")[3] is applicable to a merchant's request for modification. Clearly, if unforeseen difficulties

---

35. Nassau Trust v. Montrose Concrete Prods., 56 N.Y.2d 175, 451 N.Y.S.2d 663, 436 N.E.2d 1265 (1982), Rose v. Spa Realty Assocs., 42 N.Y.2d 338, 397 N.Y.S.2d 922, 366 N.E.2d 1279 (1977). But, Georgia holds that a party has no right to rely on an oral modification of a contract containing a clause barring oral modifications. Gerdes v. Russell Rowe Comm., 232 Ga.App. 534, 502 S.E.2d 352 (1998).

36. E.g., the distinction between waiver and modification is stressed in Nassau Trust, cited in the prior note, where the court suggests that an estoppel will more readily be found in the case of an oral waiver than in the case of an oral modification. See also Fairchild Warehouse Assocs. v. United Bank of Kuwait, 285 A.D.2d 444,

727 N.Y.S.2d 153 (2001) (applying a part-performance rather than an estoppel rationale); Wechsler v. Hunt Health Sys., 186 F.Supp.2d 402 (S.D.N.Y.2002) (stringent requisites for estoppel or part performance doctrine).

§ 5.15

1. Harris v. Watson, 170 Eng.Rep. at 94 (K.B.1791); see also Stilk v. Myrick, 170 Eng.Rep. 1168 (C.P.1809); Bartlett v. Wyman, 14 Johns. (N.Y.) 260 (1817) (similar facts; cases decided on grounds of lack of consideration); see § 4.9 supra.

2. See, e.g., Lingenfelder v. Wainwright Brewery, 103 Mo. 578, 15 S.W. 844 (1891).

3. On "good faith" see 11.38 infra.

arise that are sufficient to excuse performance for failure of presupposed conditions,[4] a modification is permissible because detriment would exist in the surrender of the privilege not to perform. If unforeseen difficulties of a less significant kind arise, such as had led a minority of states, prior to enactment of the Code, to permit a modification without new detriment,[5] it is equally clear that a modification would be enforced under the Code. Indeed, the language permits a far broader permissibility of modifications unilaterally favorable to one party.[6]

As to modifications entered into under other statutory dispensations from the requirement of consideration, the common law doctrine of duress is relevant. The doctrine, in most jurisdictions has been rather narrow in scope. In the past, it had been held that a threat to break a contract does not constitute duress.[7] Of late, however, courts have begun to hold that various kinds of "business compulsion" constitute duress.[8] Only recently has this concept been expanded, to the point where a bad faith demand for modification, if coupled with other factors, will be treated as duress.[9] In this way the various statutory provisions permitting contractual modifications without consideration will be brought into harmony with the Code.

Under the UCC a modification assented to under protest may be set aside. [10]The protest is sufficient as an indicium of duress. There is common law authority to the same effect.[11]

§ 5.16 Release and Accord and Satisfaction

The pre-existing duty concept led to the rule that a voluntary discharge of a duty, except in an instrument under seal, is ordinarily ineffectual without consideration.[1] Section 1–107 of the UCC provides, however, that: "any claim of right arising out of alleged breach can be discharged in whole or in part by a written waiver or renunciation signed and delivered by the aggrieved party." The section relates to a

---

4. See §§ 13.2 & 13.22 infra.

5. See § 4.9 supra.

6. See Gross Valentino Printing v. Clarke, 120 Ill.App.3d 907, 458 N.E.2d 1027, 76 Ill.Dec. 373 (1983) (seller had under-estimated its costs); Iowa Fuel & Minerals v. Iowa State Bd. of Regents, 471 N.W.2d 859 (Iowa 1991) (price negotiated downward justified because of drop in the market price and some deficiencies in the product); Kelsey–Hayes v. Galtaco Redlaw Castings, 749 F.Supp. 794 (E.D.Mich.1990) (supplier was losing money—duress is question of fact where purchaser could find no other source). Duress is explored at greater length in § 9.6 infra. Duress in the modification context is discussed in Garvin, Adequate Assurance of Performance: Of Risk,

Duress, and Cognition, 69 U.Colo.L.Rev. 71 (1998).

7. Doyle v. Trinity Church, 133 N.Y. 372, 31 N.E. 221 (1892); but see Austin Instrument v. Loral, 29 N.Y.2d 124, 324 N.Y.S.2d 22, 272 N.E.2d 533 (1971).

8. See § 9.6 infra.

9. See § 9.6 infra.

10. UCC § 1–207.

11. U.S. Navigation Co. v. Black Diamond Lines, 124 F.2d 508 (2d Cir.1942), cert. denied; Harnett Co. v. New York State Thruway Auth., 3 Misc.2d 257, 257, 155 N.Y.S.2d 100 (1956); North Ocean Shipping Co. v. Hyundai Constr., [1979] Q.B. 705.

§ 5.16

1. See § 4.10 supra.

discharge by release; the word "renunciation" being a term of art used in connection with an oral discharge.[2]

The section is comparable to § 15–303 of the New York General Obligations Law which provides: "A written instrument which purports to be a total or partial release of any particular claim * * * shall not be invalid because of the absence of consideration or of a seal."[3] It should be noted that the Code section applies only to a claim or right arising out of an "alleged breach" whereas the New York statute covers the release of any claim or obligation even if there has been no actual or alleged breach. Both statutes merely dispense with the requirements of consideration. They do not make a release invulnerable to attack because of duress or other invalidating cause including the violation of the pervasive duty of good faith.[4] These statutes were designed to fill the vacuum left by the demise of the common law release under seal.[5] To be effective as a release, the writing or other record must contain an expression of present intention to renounce a claim.[6]

We have previously considered the recurring fact pattern where D, who owes C a liquidated debt, sends C a check for less than the debt and clearly marks it as "accepted as payment in full." When C cashes the check, no accord and satisfaction or release occurs because, under the pre-existing duty rule, D has furnished no consideration.[7] Would the statutes discussed in this section change the outcome? C, by indorsing the check, has signed a writing containing language of present discharge. Nevertheless, the New York courts have consistently ruled that no discharge results. The apparent rationale is that an indorsement does not show the kind of circumspection and deliberateness that the requirement was intended to ensure.[8]

§ 5.17 Firm Offers

As previously discussed, under the UCC and a number of other statutes, an offer may be made irrevocable without consideration, if the statutory formalities are met.[1]

§ 5.18 Moral Obligation and Guaranties of Pre-existing Debts

Past events do not constitute consideration, in the bargain sense, for a promise.[1] For example, a promise by C to guaranty payment of an

---

2. See §§ 21.10, 21.12 infra. The revision § 1–306, is in accord, but "record" replaces "writing," and delivery is not required.

3. Statutes similar to New York's are cited in 3 Williston § 7:26 n.6.

4. New Again Constr. v. New York, 76 Misc.2d 943, 351 N.Y.S.2d 895 (1974).

5. See Second Annual Report of the [N.Y.] Law Revision Commission 67 (1936).

6. Carpenter v. Machold, 86 A.D.2d 727, 447 N.Y.S.2d 46 (1982) (N.Y. statute).

7. See § 4.11 supra.

8. King Metal Products v. Workmen's Compensation Bd., 20 A.D.2d 565, 245 N.Y.S.2d 882 (1963).

§ 5.17

1. See § 2.25 supra.

§ 5.18

1. See § 4.3 supra.

existing debt owed by B to A, requires new consideration,[2] and a promise made after an employee's retirement to pay a pension, is unenforceable.[3] The New York General Obligations Law,[4] however, states that:

> "A promise in writing and signed by the promisor or by his agent shall not be denied effect as a valid contractual obligation on the ground that consideration for the promise is past or executed, if the consideration is expressed in the writing and is proved to have been given or performed and would be valid consideration but for the time it was given or performed."

Broader statutes, such as the Model Written Obligations Act, can produce similar results.[5]

The New York statute was designed primarily to permit recovery on a promise based on a prior moral obligation created by benefits conferred upon the promisor or a third person.[6] The writing requirement is expected to assure that the promise is made with deliberation.[7] The statute has been the subject of strong criticism[8] and has been applied infrequently. It was foreseen, and experience has borne out, that a principal application of this statute would be in cases where a promisor guaranties payment of a pre-existing debt of another.[9] The UCC has largely preempted this function of the statute, making it clear that no consideration is necessary to validate commercial paper governed by Article 3 of the Code if the instrument is given for an antecedent indebtedness.[10] Similarly no consideration is required to validate an indorsement made to guaranty payment of a pre-existing debt of another.[11]

---

2. Rohrscheib v. Helena Hosp. Ass'n, 12 Ark.App. 6, 670 S.W.2d 812 (1984); Sager v. Basham, 241 Va. 227, 401 S.E.2d 676 (1991); Baker v. Citizens State Bank, 349 N.W.2d 552 (Minn.1984); Moorcroft State Bank v. Morel, 701 P.2d 1159 (Wyo.1985).

3. Perreault v. Hall, 94 N.H. 191, 49 A.2d 812 (1946).

4. § 5–1105 (enacted in 1941, as since amended). E–Sign amends the writing requirement to include an electronic record. See § 19.1(b) infra.

5. See § 5.13 supra.

6. See 1941 Report of the [N.Y.] Law Revision Commission 345, 395–96. The legislature's failure to coordinate this section with other provisions relating to the effect on the statute of limitations of a new promise to pay a debt has caused confusion. See, as an expression of that confusion, Persico Oil v. Levy, 64 Misc.2d 1091, 316 N.Y.S.2d 924 (1970).

7. See 1941 Report of the [N.Y.] Law Revision Commission 345, 395–96.

8. Braucher, Freedom of Contract and the Second Restatement, 78 Yale L.J. 598, 605 ("This provision is too broad in scope and too restrictive in formal requirements; it does not seem to have had any significant effect."); 3 Corbin § 9.1 n. 1 (Holmes 1996) ("This is not a useful statute. Indeed, it is likely to do positive harm."). For criticism from the opposite direction, to the effect that this and other New York provisions do not go far enough, see Lloyd, Consideration and the Seal in New York—An Unsatisfactory Legislative Program, 46 Colum.L.Rev. 1 (1946) (gift promises ought to be enforceable). Another overall look at the New York statutory scheme is Comment, 46 Mich. L.Rev. 58 (1947).

9. 1941 Report of the [N.Y.] Law Revision Commission 345, 395–96; Hays, supra § 5.14 n.5, at 859. See Weyerhaeuser v. Gershman, 324 F.2d 163 (2d Cir.1963); Central State Bank v. Botwin, 66 Misc.2d 1085, 323 N.Y.S.2d 74 (1971) reversed on other grounds.

10. § 3–303(b) of the 1990 revision. (Former § 3–408). Article 3 governs commercial paper whether or not such paper is tied to a sales contract.

11. § 3–419 of the 1990 revision. (Former § 3–408 cmt 2).

The statute does not define the term "past consideration." From its legislative history it seems rather clear that past consideration includes past bargained-for detriment, even by a third person, and past material benefit received by the promisor even without request.[12] It is not clear whether past unbargained-for detriment would constitute past consideration. Suppose an uncle promises his niece $5,000 in a signed writing "in consideration of the fact that you have refrained from using tobacco and alcohol for five years." It is doubted whether such a promise would be enforceable. If it were to be, any gift promise could be made enforceable by searching out past unbargained-for detriment and reciting it in a signed writing. This would stretch the statute beyond its legislative purpose. The courts have been insistent that the record contain an "unequivocal" promise.[13] In view of the gratuitous nature of the promise, this construction of the statute seems sound.[14]

C. STIPULATIONS

Table of Sections

§ 5.19   Stipulation Defined

A stipulation is a promise or agreement with reference to a pending judicial proceeding, made by a party to the proceeding or an attorney for a party.[1] Stipulations are favored by the courts. They tend to relieve court congestion and place the settlement of litigation or details of litigation on the litigants where it primarily belongs.

§ 5.20   Consideration and Formality in Stipulations

Generally, statutes or rules of court provide that a stipulation should be in writing or other record or made in open court.[1] If made in open court and a record of the stipulation is made by the court reporter, the Statute of Frauds is inapplicable.[2] Stipulations are enforced without regard to consideration[3] but, as in the case of any other kind of contract,

---

12. See Report, supra note 9.

13. Umscheid v. Simnacher, 106 A.D.2d 380, 482 N.Y.S.2d 295 (1984).

14. Perillo, The Statute of Frauds in the Light of the Functions and Dysfunctions of Form, 43 Fordham L.Rev. 39, 55–56, 79 (1974).

§ 5.19

1. See Rs. 2d § 94; 4 Williston § 8:43.

§ 5.20

1. Id. "Open court" does not include judge's chambers. Matter of Dolgin Eldert, 31 N.Y.2d 1, 334 N.Y.S.2d 833, 286 N.E.2d

228 (1972). However, an unrecorded settlement reached in court may be binding on ordinary contract principles. Monaghan v. SZS 33 Assocs., 875 F.Supp. 1037 (S.D.N.Y. 1995), aff'd.

2. Estate of Eberle, 505 N.W.2d 767 (S.D.1993).

3. Connors v. United Metal Products, 209 Minn. 300, 296 N.W. 21 (1941); Rs. 2d § 94.

fraud or other vitiating circumstances can be shown to avoid their legal effect.[4] Indeed, if there is no prejudice to the other party, a court has power to relieve a party from a stipulation for reasons such as inadvertence, improvidence or excusable neglect.[5] A unilateral stipulation may merely be an offer and, if so, may be revoked until accepted.[6]

An oral stipulation made out of court is not a nullity. It is dishonorable for an attorney to avoid performance of an oral agreement and courts will enforce oral stipulations upon which parties rely to their injury.[7]

4. 4 Williston § 8:43.

5. Hester v. New Amsterdam Cas., 268 F.Supp. 623 (D.S.C.1967); Matter of Frutiger's Estate, 29 N.Y.2d 143, 324 N.Y.S.2d 36, 272 N.E.2d 543 (1971). But if a party relies on it, as by discontinuing the action, no relief is available to the other party. Lowe v. Steinman, 284 A.D.2d 506, 728 N.Y.S.2d 56 (2001).

6. Kocinski v. Home Ins., 154 Wis.2d 56, 452 N.W.2d 360 (1990).

7. Em-Co Metal Prods. v. Great Atlantic & Pacific Tea, 280 S.C. 107, 311 S.E.2d 83 (1984); Rs. 2d § 94(c).

Chapter 6

PROMISSORY ESTOPPEL AS A SUBSTITUTE FOR CONSIDERATION AND MUCH ELSE

Table of Sections

---

§ 6.1 Introduction

The concept of promissory estoppel, and perhaps the term itself, was coined by Samuel Williston in the 1920 edition of his treatise where he pulled together an assortment of cases where promises without consideration had been enforced on one theory or another. The common thread through these cases was that the promisee had relied on the promise.[1] In 1932, through the combined efforts of Williston and Corbin,[2] Section 90 of the Restatement of Contracts adopted the concept as an orthodox doctrine of contract law. Since its adoption by the Restatement, the courts have greeted it with broad support. Although in its original formulation, it was a substitute for (or the equivalent of) consideration, it has since grown from a consideration substitute to a doctrine that provides a remedy for many promises or agreements that fail the test of enforceability under many traditional contract doctrines, including indef-

---

§ 6.1

1. 1 Williston on Contract § 139 (1st ed. 1920).

2. See Perillo, Twelve Letters from Arthur L. Corbin to Robert Braucher Annotated, 50 Wash. & Lee L.Rev. 755, 768–69 (1993).

initeness, failure to comply with the Statute of Frauds,[3] non-compliance with the parol evidence rule[4] and more.[5] Promissory estoppel may now be viewed as a mender of ailing contracts. The Restatement (Second) has embraced and enlarged the concept.

The key difference between a promise supported by consideration and a gratuitous promise supported by promissory estoppel is that in the former case the detriment is bargained for in exchange for the promise; in the latter, there is no bargain. The injury is a consequence of the promise but does not induce the making of the promise.[6] Justice Holmes, in arguing for strict adherence to the concept of consideration, said, "[i]t is not enough that the promise induces the detriment or that the detriment induces the promise if the other half is wanting."[7] Elsewhere Holmes lamented that the courts "have gone far" in losing sight of this fact.[8] The modern law has tended to hold firm to Holmes' view of consideration and to develop a separate doctrine of promissory estoppel from the cases which he had criticized as stretching the doctrine of consideration beyond its conceptual boundaries.[9] Surprisingly, courts now frequently base a decision on promissory estoppel grounds when conventional consideration is present.[10]

Section 90 of the first Restatement stated the doctrine in the following terms: "A promise which the promisor should reasonably expect to induce action or forbearance of a definite and substantial character on the part of the promisee and which does induce such action

---

3. See § 19.48 infra.

4. Johnson Enterprises v. FPL Group, 162 F.3d 1290 (11th Cir.1998) (inducement exception to parol evidence rule); Prudential Ins. Co. v. Clark, 456 F.2d 932, 937 (5th Cir.1972); Darner Motor Sales v. Universal Underwriters Ins. Co., 140 Ariz. 383, 682 P.2d 388 (1984) (equitable estoppel); Young v. State Farm Mutual Auto. Ins. Co., 127 Idaho 122, 898 P.2d 53 (1995). This is not a universal development. See Coll v. PB Diagnostic Sys., 50 F.3d 1115 (1st Cir.1995); DeJong v. Sioux Center, 980 F.Supp. 1010 (N.D.Iowa 1997); Prentice v. UDC Advisory Serv., 271 Ill.App.3d 505, 207 Ill.Dec. 690, 648 N.E.2d 146 (1995); Davis v. Univ. of Montevallo, 638 So.2d 754 (Ala.1994); Banbury v. Omnitrition Int'l, 533 N.W.2d 876 (Minn.App.1995); Metzger, The Parol Evidence Rule: Promissory Estoppel's Next Conquest?, 36 Vand.L.Rev. 1383 (1983). Cases finding promissory estoppel in this context do not always discuss the parol evidence rule. E.g., Williams v. Workers' Comp. Appeals Board, 33 Cal.Rptr.2d 753 (Cal.App.1994) subsequently depublished (insurance company estopped to deny workers' compensation coverage where property owner was assured he had full coverage); Chrysalis Health Care v. Brooks, 65 Ohio Misc.2d 32, 640 N.E.2d 915 (1994); see Bill

Brown Constr. Co. v. Glens Falls Ins. Co., 818 S.W.2d 1 (Tenn.1991) (estoppel can extend coverage); 3 Corbin § 8.11 (Holmes 1996).

5. See Williams, What To Do When There's No "I Do", 70 Wash.L.Rev. 1019 (1995) (promissory estoppel should be employed to redress breach of promises to marry).

6. Youngman v. Nevada Irr. Dist., 70 Cal.2d 240, 74 Cal.Rptr. 398, 449 P.2d 462 (1969).

7. Wisconsin & Mich. Ry. Co. v. Powers, 191 U.S. 379, 386 (1903).

8. Holmes, The Common Law 292 (1881).

9. A legal system that does not impose a requirement of consideration has little need for a doctrine of promissory estoppel. See Comment, 31 La.L.Rev. 84 (1970). Nonetheless, the fact of reliance plays an important role in other legal systems. A seminal article, Fuller & Perdue, The Reliance Interest in Contract Damages (pts 1 & 2), 46 Yale L.J. 52 & 373 (1936–37) is replete with references to the German Civil Code.

10. E.g., Daigle Commercial Group v. St. Laurent, 734 A.2d 667 (Me.1999) (a routine brokerage commission case).

or forbearance is binding if injustice can be avoided only by the enforcement of the promise.''

First, a promise is necessary to create promissory estoppel.[11] Thus, a statement of intent to take future action is not sufficient,[12] nor is a precatory remark.[13] Similarly, an estimate is not generally sufficient.[14] It is possible, however, to base a promissory estoppel claim on an implied promise,[15] but generally courts are not receptive to finding such implied promises.[16] The content of the promise must be clear.[17] Second, the promise must be one which the promisor should reasonably anticipate will lead the promisee to act or to forbear;[18] this requirement takes into account the expectations of the promisor. In addition, the promisee must be reasonable in relying on the promise.[19]

Furthermore, the reliance of the promisee must be of a definite and substantial character. "Substantiality" is a quantitative factor.[20] The conduct in reliance must be foreseeable. Williston illustrated this by the example of a promise of $1,000 with which to buy an automobile; it would be binding if it induced the purchase of a car whereas a promise of $1,000 for no specific purpose would not be binding if it induced similar action. In other words, the conduct in reliance must not only be reasonable but also must be foreseeable.[21] Corbin also identifies the

11. Lockheed Missile & Space Co. v. Hughes Aircraft Co., 887 F.Supp. 1320 (N.D.Cal.1995) (no promise in on-going negotiations); Burst v. Adolph Coors Co., 650 F.2d 930 (8th Cir.1981); U.S. Jaycees v. Bloomfield, 434 A.2d 1379 (D.C.App.1981); Irwin Concrete v. Sun Coast Properties, 33 Wn.App. 190, 653 P.2d 1331 (1982). The promise may be implied rather than express. Masso v. United Parcel Service, 884 F.Supp. 610 (D.Mass.1995).

12. School Dist. No. 69 v. Altherr, 10 Ariz.App. 333, 458 P.2d 537 (1969); Pappas v. Bever, 219 N.W.2d 720 (Iowa 1974). A hedged promise does not justify reliance. W.R. Grace & Co. v. Taco Tico Acquisition Corp., 216 Ga.App. 423, 454 S.E.2d 789 (1995); Faimon v. Winona State Univ., 540 N.W.2d 879 (Minn.App.1995).

13. Woodmere Academy v. Steinberg, 41 N.Y.2d 746, 395 N.Y.S.2d 434, 363 N.E.2d 1169, 97 A.L.R.3d 1047 (1977).

14. Robert Gordon, Inc. v. Ingersoll–Rand, 117 F.2d 654 (7th Cir.1941); cf. Leo F. Piazza Paving v. Bebek & Brkich, 141 Cal.App.2d 226, 296 P.2d 368 (1956). But see U.S. v. Briggs Mfg., 460 F.2d 1195 (9th Cir.1972).

15. Wright v. Newman, 266 Ga. 519, 467 S.E.2d 533 (1996).

16. Trans-World Int'l v. Smith–Hemion Prods., 972 F.Supp. 1275 (C.D.Cal.1997).

17. Gellerman v. Oleet, 164 Misc.2d 715, 625 N.Y.S.2d 831 (1995); see Annot.,

Promissory Estoppel of Lending Institution Based on Promise to Lend Money, 18 ALR 5th 307. Although the promise must be unambiguous, it may be inferred from conduct and words. Decker v. Andersen Consulting, 860 F.Supp. 1300, 1309 (N.D.Ill. 1994).

18. Smith v. Boise Kenworth Sales, 102 Idaho 63, 625 P.2d 417 (1981); Dial v. Deskins, 221 Va. 701, 273 S.E.2d 546 (1981).

19. Landess v. Borden, Inc., 667 F.2d 628 (7th Cir.1981); Atlanta Nat. Real Estate Trust v. Tally, 243 Ga. 247, 253 S.E.2d 692 (1979); Coll v. PB Diagnostic Sys., 50 F.3d 1115 (1st Cir.1995) (unreasonable to rely on prehire discussions not included in written offer); State v. Law Offices, 663 So.2d 650 (Fla.App.1995) (unreasonable to rely on oral promise of state official); cf. King v. Riveland, 125 Wn.2d 500, 886 P.2d 160 (1994) (reliance on promise of state officer was justified); Malaker Corp. Stockholders Protective Comm. v. First Jersey Nat. Bank, 163 N.J.Super. 463, 395 A.2d 222 (1978), certif. denied.

20. First Nat. Bankshares v. Geisel, 853 F.Supp. 1344 (D.Kan.1994) (refraining from leaving well-paid employment is not "substantial" detriment).

21. 4 A.L.I. Proceedings at 92–93; see RCM Supply Co. v. Hunter Douglas, Inc., 686 F.2d 1074 (4th Cir.1982); Levitt Homes v. Old Farm Homeowner's Ass'n, 111 Ill. App.3d 300, 67 Ill.Dec. 155, 444 N.E.2d 194

question as one of foreseeability, but argues that the test should be what a reasonable person in the position of the promisor could have foreseen,[22] rather than follow Williston's idea that the promise itself must indicate the way in which the promisee can rely.

Finally, the promise will be enforced if injustice can be avoided only by the enforcement of the promise.[23] To some extent this relates to Williston's notion (implicit in the First Restatement) that any recovery under the doctrine of promissory estoppel will be a full contractual recovery and not be limited to reliance damages. Under this approach, in deciding what is just, one must consider this premise of full recovery and this premise is probably the reason for including the provisions for definite and substantial reliance.[24] The question of avoidance of injustice is one of law; the other elements raise questions of fact.[25]

The authorities are not in accord on the precise meaning of the injustice requirement. Some courts have ruled that it is sufficient that the reliance be detrimental in the consideration sense; others have insisted that the reliance be injurious to the promisee.[26] Logically, injury is required; without injury there would be no injustice in not enforcing the promise.[27] As Judge Posner has indicated, the doctrine requires that the promisee incur a real cost.[28]

Section 90 of the Restatement Second has made four important changes in the formulation of the doctrine. (1) It has excised the words "of a definite, and substantial character" from the text of the section.[29] (2) It added a new sentence permitting flexibility of remedy; for example, a promise that is reasonably relied on need not be enforced by granting

(1982); Yorio & Thel, The Promissory Basis of Section 90, 101 Yale L.J. 111, 125 (1991); Barnett & Becker, Beyond Reliance: Promissory Estoppel, Contract Formalities, and Misrepresentations, 15 Hofstra L.Rev. 443 (reliance helps establish promisor's intent to be bound).

22. 3 Corbin § 8.9 (Holmes 1996); see Sanders v. Arkansas–Missouri Power Co., 267 Ark. 1009, 593 S.W.2d 56 (App.1980).

23. Rs. 2d § 90.

24. Eisenberg, Donative Promises, 47 U.Chi.L.Rev. 1, 23 (1979).

25. R. S. Bennett & Co. v. Economy Mech. Indus., 606 F.2d 182 (7th Cir.1979).

26. See Northern State Constr. Co. v. Robbins, 76 Wn.2d 357, 457 P.2d 187 (1969). But see Henderson, Promissory Estoppel and Traditional Contract Doctrine, 78 Yale L.J. 343 (1969).

27. It is argued in Farber & Matheson, Beyond Promissory Estoppel: Contract Law and the "Invisible Handshake," 52 U.Chi. L.Rev. 903, 910–14 (1985), that the courts have deemphasized the requirement of reli-

ance, giving two cases as examples. Both are clear-cut cases of unilateral contracts based on a bargained-for exchange, mistakenly decided under the rubric of promissory estoppel. Nonetheless, the principle they forward that promises made in furtherance of economic activity should be enforced, vague as it is, is the thrust of modern contract law. For further development of this idea, see Barnett, The Death of Reliance, 46 J.Leg.Ed. 518 (1996).

28. Cosgrove v. Bartolotta, 150 F.3d 729 (7th Cir.1998).

29. However, Rs. 2d § 90 cmt b makes it clear that the definite and substantial nature of the reliance is one of the factors to be considered. The comment lists a number of other factors to be considered and concludes, "The force of particular factors varies in different types of cases: thus reliance need not be of a substantial character in charitable subscription cases, but must in cases of firm offers and guaranties." The Rs. 2d thus provides not only for a flexible approach on remedies but also as to the substantive doctrine itself.

damages based on the expectation interest.[30] This new provision on flexibility of remedy contributed to the omission of the words "of a definite and substantial character."[31] (3) It has also provided for the contingency of reliance by a third party on a promise.[32] (4) It provides that a charitable subscription or a marriage settlement is binding without proof that the promise induced action or forbearance.[33]

§ 6.2 The Roots of Promissory Estoppel

Historically, promissory estoppel has been an expansion of equitable estoppel,[1] but traditionally, estoppel *in pais*, also known as equitable estoppel has been limited to cases in which one party has misrepresented a *fact* to another who injuriously relies on the representation. In such cases the court bars the party who made the representation from contradicting it.[2] Traditionally, an equitable estoppel could not be created by reliance on a promise,[3] but the doctrine was later expanded to encompass promises. The equitable origins of the doctrine are recognized in decisions holding that there is no constitutional right to trial by jury on the issue of promissory estoppel,[4] because the constitutional right to a jury trial is limited to actions at common law.

30. Reliance damages, however, may include lost opportunity costs. Oscar Productions v. Zacharius, 893 F.Supp. 250 (S.D.N.Y.1995).

31. See Rs. 2d § 90 Reporter's Note.

32. An illustration of a third party reliance is found in the case of Mount Vernon Trust Co. v. Bergoff, 272 N.Y. 192, 5 N.E.2d 196 (1936). At the request of B, a bank, D gave B a note in the sum of $35,000. At the same time B gave D a written statement to the effect that D would not be held liable on the note. The note, however, was treated on B's books as an asset of B and was shown to bank examiners. The bank became insolvent. The court held that the bank's liquidators could enforce the note against D because of reliance by the examiners. Better known is the similar case of D'Oench Duhme & Co. v. FDIC, 315 U.S. 447 (1942), which has been codified and expanded in 12 U.S.C.A. § 1823(e); see Echevarria, A Precedent Embalms a Principle: The Expansion of the *D'Oench, Duhme* Doctrine, 43 Cath.U.L.Rev 745 (1994); Galves, Might Does Not Make Right: The Reform of the Federal Government's D'Oench, Duhme, 88 Minn.L.Rev. 1323 (1996). On the separate question of enforcement by a third party beneficiary based upon reliance by the promisee, see Broxson v. Chicago Milwaukee, St. Paul & P.R. Co., 446 F.2d 628 (9th Cir.1971); Metzger & Phillips, Promissory Estoppel and Third Parties, 42 Southwestern L.J. 931 (1988); Note, 6 Val.U.L.Rev. 352 (1972); see also Rs. 2d § 90 cmt c.

33. See § 6.2(d) infra. For an extensive discussion of the Restatement (Second), see Knapp, Reliance in the Revised Restatement, 81 Colum.L.Rev. 52 (1981).

§ 6.2

1. " '*Estoppe*' cometh of the French word *estoupe*, from whence the English word stopped: and it is called an estoppel, or conclusion, because a man's owne act or acceptance stoppeth or closeth up his mouth to alleage or plead the truth * * *." *Coke Upon Littleton* 352.a.

2. See § 11.29 infra. This ancient doctrine is very much alive. See, e.g., Council Bros., Inc. v. Tallahassee, 634 So.2d 264 (Fla.App.1994).

3. Henderson, supra § 6.1 n.26, at 376; Commonwealth v. School Dist., 49 Pa. Cmwlth. 316, 410 A.2d 1311 (1980); see Rs. 2d § 90 cmt a. A promise, at times, has been looked upon as a misrepresentation if the party who made it did not intend to carry it out when it was made. See § 9.19 infra.

4. Merex A.G. v. Fairchild Weston Sys., 29 F.3d 821 (2d Cir.1994), cert. denied; C & K Engineering Contractors v. Amber Steel Co., 23 Cal.3d 1, 587 P.2d 1136, 151 Cal. Rptr. 323 (1978). For the same reason, it has been held that punitive damages are not available in a promissory estoppel case. Blanton Enterprises v. Burger King, 680 F.Supp. 753, 776 n. 24 (D.S.C.1988). Not all cases agree. See Becker Promissory Estoppel and Damages, 16 Hofstra L.Rev. 131 (1987).

In addition to its equitable estoppel ancestry, promissory estoppel has been extracted as a general principle from a number of recurring decisions where promises were enforced under conditions which were difficult, and sometimes impossible, to explain in terms of the doctrine of consideration.[5] We now briefly consider these historical antecedents.

(a) Promises in the Family

In Devecmon v. Shaw,[6] an uncle promised his nephew that, if the nephew would take a trip to Europe, the uncle would reimburse the nephew's expenses. The nephew made the trip but the uncle died and his executor[7] refused to make payment. The court concluded that the uncle's promise was supported by consideration. Surely there was detriment, but the court did not consider whether the detriment was bargained for in exchange for the promise.

The court came to grips with the conceptual problem in Ricketts v. Scothorn.[8] A man had given his granddaughter a promissory note, indicating that it was for the purpose of freeing her from the necessity of working. It was clear that he was not demanding that she cease working in exchange for the note, but she did quit her job. The court recognized that there was no consideration for the note but enforced the note anyway on the grounds of estoppel *in pais*. The court in Ricketts extended the doctrine of estoppel to a promissory expression.

Recognition of the doctrine of promissory estoppel as an independent ground for enforcing intrafamily promises can lead to a profitable reexamination of many similar cases decided on grounds of consideration.[9]

(b) Promise to Make a Gift of Land

Cases involving a promise to make a gift of land generally arise in a family context and thus are related to the cases discussed in the preceding sub-section. If the promise is oral, the case involves non-compliance with the writing requirements of the Statute of Frauds[10] as well as the absence of consideration. Such promises have an historical background somewhat different from other kinds of intrafamily promises.

A promise to give land, standing alone, is unenforceable as a gift because of the lack of delivery of a conveyance to complete the gift. Not infrequently, however, acting in reliance on the gratuitous promise to

---

5. See § 6.1 supra.

6. 69 Md. 199, 14 A. 464 (1888).

7. How often it is in these cases that the promise is not repudiated by the promisor. Frequently, it is the executor, conscious of the possibility of being surcharged, who refused the payment.

8. 57 Neb. 51, 77 N.W. 365, 42 LRA 794 (1898); see In re Estate of Bucci, 488 P.2d

216 (Colo.App.1971) (applying promissory estoppel).

9. E.g., Kirksey v. Kirksey, 8 Ala. 131 (1845); Hamer v. Sidway, 124 N.Y. 538, 27 N.E. 256 (1891). See § 4.5 supra for a discussion of these cases.

10. The Statute of Frauds generally requires that a contract to create or the creation of an interest in land be in writing. See §§ 19.14–19.15 infra.

convey land, the promisee, with the knowledge and assent of the promisor, takes possession of the land and makes improvements. In such circumstances courts of equity in almost all states have granted the promisee specific performance, ordering the promisor to deliver a conveyance[11] or have granted other equitable remedies[12] even though the oral promise was made without consideration and contravenes the Statute of Frauds.[13] Traditionally, courts have expressed their rationales of these decisions in two different ways. Sometimes, the court has relied on an analogy from the law of gifts, treating the entry on the land and the making of improvements as the equivalent of physical delivery of a chattel.[14] Of course, by definition, a gift requires no consideration. Perhaps more frequently the courts have said that the taking of possession and the making of improvements constitute "good consideration in equity."[15] Under modern ideas of the relationship between law and equity, it is indeed anomalous that a different definition of consideration should prevail in the equity and law sides of the court. The true ancestry of this line of cases is the ancient practice of "livery of seisin,"[16] but it is now recognized that the decisions enforcing promises to give land are justified on the basis of promissory estoppel.[17]

(c) Gratuitous Agencies and Bailments

The early case of Coggs v. Bernard[18] has been highly influential in this area of gratuitous agencies and bailments. A carter, who agreed to transport a keg of brandy for the plaintiff free of charge, negligently damaged it. The court held that an action for breach of contract would lie for the carter's breach of the implied promise to use requisite care. The court reasoned that the "bare being trusted with another man's goods, must be taken to be a sufficient consideration."[19] It is clear, however, that the carter, as a gratuitous bailee, did not bargain for the privilege of being entrusted with the goods. Consequently, the decision is not in accord with modern ideas of consideration.[20] Courts, in cases such as Coggs, employed a distinction between nonfeasance and misfeasance. If the gratuitous promisor takes possession of the goods and fails to carry

---

11. Seavey v. Drake, 62 N.H. 393 (1882); Freeman v. Freeman, 43 N.Y. 34, 3 Am.Rep. 657 (1870); cf. Miller v. Lawlor, 245 Iowa 1144, 66 N.W.2d 267, 48 ALR2d 1058 (1954). Some courts have distinguished between a promise to make a gift in the future and a purported present gift, stating that the former is not enforceable. Prior v. Newsom, 144 Ark. 593, 223 S.W. 21 (1920); Burris v. Landers, 114 Cal. 310, 46 P. 162 (1896); Hagerty v. Hagerty, 186 Iowa 1329, 172 N.W. 259 (1919).

12. King's Heirs v. Thompson, 34 U.S. (9 Pet.) 204 (1835) (equitable lien); see Frady v. Irvin, 245 Ga. 307, 264 S.E.2d 866 (1980). In addition, an action for restitution at law or equity is available. Carter v. Carter, 182 N.C. 186, 108 S.E. 765, 17 ALR 945 (1921); see also Tozier v. Tozier, 437 A.2d

645 (Me.1981). Of course, an action in damages should also be available.

13. See Annot., 83 ALR3d 1294 (1978).

14. Roberts–Horsfield v. Gedicks, 94 N.J.Eq. 82, 118 A. 275 (1922), aff'd.

15. Young v. Overbaugh, 145 N.Y. 158, 163, 39 N.E. 712, 713 (1895); see Lindell v. Lindell, 135 Minn. 368, 371, 160 N.W. 1031, 1032 (1917) ("The promise to give is no longer *nudum pactum.* It has become a promise upon a consideration.")

16. See § 19.15 infra.

17. Greiner v. Greiner, 131 Kan. 760, 293 P. 759 (1930).

18. 92 Eng.Rep. 107 (K.B.1703).

19. Id. at 114.

20. See § 4.2 supra.

out the promise to use requisite care, there would be misfeasance and liability has traditionally been found to exist.[21] If, however, the gratuitous promisor fails to take possession, traditionally there would be nonfeasance and no liability for breach of the gratuitous promise.[22]

A similar distinction between nonfeasance and misfeasance has been made in cases of gratuitous agencies. Here, the influential case has been Thorne v. Deas.[23] The parties were co-owners of a brig. On the day it was to sail, the defendant promised his co-owner to procure insurance for the voyage insuring the interests of both. Ten days later, the defendant told the plaintiff that no insurance had been procured. The plaintiff, upset at this revelation, said he would procure insurance himself. The defendant, however, told the plaintiff to "make himself easy" and that he would procure coverage that very day. Defendant failed to act and the brig was wrecked in the Bermuda triangle. It was held that the defendant was not liable since there was no consideration for the promise and no liability for mere nonfeasance pursuant to a gratuitous promise. If, however, the defendant had negligently procured insurance that was somehow defective, he would have been guilty of misfeasance and liable in contract.[24]

The gratuitous agency and bailment cases coalesced in the case of Siegel v. Spear & Co.[25] The defendant agreed to store plaintiff's furniture (on which defendant held a mortgage) free of charge and also agreed to procure insurance at the plaintiff's expense, stating that he could obtain the insurance at a cheaper rate than could the plaintiff. The defendant failed to procure the insurance but did take possession of the furniture. The uninsured furniture was destroyed by fire. It was held that the defendant was liable. The court characterized the case as one of gratuitous bailment, indicating that once possession of the goods was taken by the bailee, failure to carry out the promise to insure was misfeasance.

In accord with the approach stated in the Restatements,[26] courts have largely abandoned the distinction between misfeasance and nonfeasance in gratuitous agency cases.[27] These cases recognize that there is a potential for injurious reliance, not only in the misfeasance cases, but also in the nonfeasance cases. While some of these cases have involved a promise to procure insurance, the Restatement (Second) points out that this type of case should be approached with caution because the promi-

21. Siegel v. Spear & Co., 234 N.Y. 479, 138 N.E. 414, 26 ALR 1205 (1923); 4 Williston § 8:1.

22. Tomko v. Sharp, 87 N.J.L. 385, 94 A. 793 (Sup.Ct.1915).

23. 4 Johns. 84 (N.Y.1809), followed in Comfort v. McCorkle, 149 Misc. 826, 268 N.Y.S. 192 (1933).

24. Barile v. Wright, 256 N.Y. 1, 175 N.E. 351 (1931); Elam v. Smithdeal Realty & Ins. Co., 182 N.C. 599, 109 S.E. 632, 18 ALR 1210 (1921).

25. 234 N.Y. 479, 138 N.E. 414 (1923), noted in 23 Colum.L.Rev. 573 (1923), 32

Yale L.J. 609 (1923); accord Schroeder v. Mauzy, 16 Cal.App. 443, 118 P. 459 (1911).

26. See § 6.1 supra.

27. Northern Commercial v. United Airmotive, 101 F.Supp. 169 (D.Alaska 1951); Graddon v. Knight, 138 Cal.App.2d 577, 292 P.2d 632 (1956); Franklin Investment Co. v. Huffman, 393 A.2d 119 (D.C.App.1978); Spiegel v. Metropolitan Life Ins., 6 N.Y.2d 91, 188 N.Y.S.2d 486, 160 N.E.2d 40 (1959); Shoemaker v. Commonwealth Bank, 700 A.2d 1003 (Pa.Super.1997); East Providence Credit Union v. Geremia, 103 R.I. 597, 239 A.2d 725 (1968). See Rs. 2d of Agency § 378.

sor is in effect treated as an insurer and thus exposed to a large liability. It suggests that at times the promisee may not be justified in relying on the promise or that such reliance may be justified only for a short time.[28]

The distinction between misfeasance and nonfeasance is untenable and the issue under the modern view is injurious reliance. To some extent this traditional distinction appears to be traceable to the writ system.[29] The writ of assumpsit rose late in the life of the writ system and grew out of cases similar to Coggs v. Bernard where the emphasis was on a physical injury to person or property as a result of negligently carrying out a consensual arrangement. These decisions initially did not go far enough to impose liability for nonfeasance.[30] Despite the ultimate development of the writ of assumpsit to encompass generally any action for breach of promise, the distinction still plagues us in these cases— further proof that the writs still rule us from the grave.[31] Although the Restatements have rejected the distinction, some case law continues it.

(d) Charitable Subscriptions and Marriage Settlements

With great frequency, but not with complete uniformity, charitable subscriptions have been enforced in this country.[32] There are cases in which the promise to give money to a charity is supported by consideration in the strict sense of the term. For example, the promisor may have bargained for and received a commitment from the charity that the "gift" be employed in a specified way or that a memorial be built bearing the promisor's name.[33]

In the usual case, however, there is no bargain in fact and the promisor manifests a gift-making state of mind.[34] Courts have, however, purported to find consideration on various tenuous theories. They have found consideration on the theory that the donee impliedly promises to use the promised gifts for charitable purposes,[35] but the charity has a duty to use its funds for charitable purposes, and the performance of a pre-existing duty generally does not constitute consideration. Other cases have found consideration in the purported exchange of promises

28. Rs. 2d § 90 cmt f; but see Verschoor v. Mountain West Farm Bureau Mutual Ins. Co., 907 P.2d 1293 (Wyo.1995) (insurer of employer promised to pay plaintiff's medical bills, and in reliance he underwent costly surgery).

29. Shattuck, Gratuitous Promises—A New Writ?, 35 Mich.L.Rev. 908, 917 (1937).

30. A. Simpson, A History of the Common Law of Contract (1975). See generally Holdsworth, Debt, Assumpsit and Consideration, 11 Mich.L.Rev. 347 (1913).

31. F. Maitland, The Forms of Action at Common Law 2 (1936) (written 1909).

32. Billig, The Problem of Consideration in Charitable Subscriptions, 12 Cornell L.Q. 467 (1927); Page, Consideration: Genuine and Synthetic, 1947 Wis.L.Rev.

483; Shattuck, Gratuitous Promises—A New Writ?, 35 Mich.L.Rev. 908 (1937). In England, unsealed charitable subscriptions generally are not enforced. In re Hudson, 54 L.J.Ch. 811 (1885).

33. Rogers v. Galloway Female College, 64 Ark. 627, 44 S.W. 454 (1898) (locating a college in a particular town); American Legion v. Thompson, 121 Kan. 124, 245 P. 744 (1926) (building a particular building); Woodmere Academy v. Steinberg, 41 N.Y.2d 746, 395 N.Y.S.2d 434, 363 N.E.2d 1169 (1977) (naming of building).

34. Floyd v. Christian Church Widows & Orphans Home, 296 Ky. 196, 176 S.W.2d 125, 151 ALR 1230 (1943); In re Taylor's Estate, 251 N.Y. 257, 167 N.E. 434 (1929).

35. In re Griswold's Estate, 113 Neb. 256, 202 N.W. 609, 38 ALR 858 (1925).

among the subscribers.[36] If such an exchange actually is bargained for and actually occurs, consideration exists.[37] E.g., "I will give one million dollars to *alma mater* if you will match my gift." This is hardly what occurs in many large fund-raising campaigns. A subscriber may be motivated by the fact that others have given or will give but there is ordinarily no element of exchange among the various promisors. Motive and consideration are not equivalents.[38] Moreover, the prior subscriptions are past and therefore cannot constitute consideration.[39] A number of cases have held that the subscription is an offer to a unilateral contract which is accepted by the charity's performance or starting to perform the terms of the subscription.[40] Since the terms of the subscription are often "in consideration of continuing your humanitarian work," or language to that effect, such holdings appear to run afoul of the pre-existing duty rule.

This wide variation in reasoning indicates the difficulty of enforcing a charitable subscription on grounds of consideration. Yet, the courts have generally striven to find grounds for enforcement, indicating the depth of feeling in this country that private philanthropy serves a highly important function in our society.[41] Of late, courts have tended to abandon the attempt to utilize traditional contract doctrines to sustain subscriptions and have placed their decisions on the grounds of promissory estoppel.[42] Surprisingly, however, if promissory estoppel in its traditional form is the doctrine under which subscriptions are to be tested, fewer subscriptions are likely to be enforced than previously. Promissory estoppel requires substantial injurious reliance, an element that the charity would not be able to show in the majority of the cases. Typically, the charity would need to show that it did something differently than it would have done without the promise.[43] This would appear

---

36. First Presbyterian Church v. Dennis, 178 Iowa 1352, 161 N.W. 183 (1917); Congregation B'Nai Sholom v. Martin, 382 Mich. 659, 173 N.W.2d 504 (1969).

37. Floyd v. Christian Church, 296 Ky. 196, 176 S.W.2d 125 (1943); 4 Williston §§ 8:5.

38. See § 4.3 supra.

39. See § 4.3 supra.

40. I. & I. Holding Corp. v. Gainsburg, 276 N.Y. 427, 12 N.E.2d 532, 115 ALR 582 (1938), 39 Colum.L.Rev. 283 (1939), 7 Fordham L.Rev. 264 (1938), 12 St. John's L.Rev. 339 (1938). See § 2.10 supra.

41. Danby v. Osteopathic Hosp. Ass'n, 34 Del.Ch. 427, 104 A.2d 903 (1954); but see Maryland Nat. Bank v. United Jewish Appeal, 286 Md. 274, 407 A.2d 1130 (1979).

42. Danby v. Osteopathic Hosp. Ass'n, 34 Del.Ch. 427, 104 A.2d 903 (1954); Estate of Timko v. Oral Roberts Evangelistic

Ass'n, 51 Mich.App. 662, 215 N.W.2d 750 (1974); Allegheny College v. National Chautauqua County Bank, 246 N.Y. 369, 159 N.E. 173, 57 ALR 980 (1927) (dictum); but see I. & I. Holding Corp. v. Gainsburg, 276 N.Y. 427, 12 N.E.2d 532 (1938) (reverting to unilateral contract analysis and applying Rs. 1st § 45). Neither promissory estoppel nor a unilateral contract theory was held to support a charitable subscription, at least in the absence of demonstrable reliance, in the case of Jordan v. Mount Sinai Hosp., 276 So.2d 102 (Fla.App.1973), aff'd 290 So.2d 484 (Fla.1974), 26 Baylor L.Rev. 256 (1974). The doctrine was not applied in a case where the charity assured the subscriber that the pledge was not binding. Pappas v. Hauser, 197 N.W.2d 607 (Iowa 1972). The doctrine is rejected in Virginia School for the Arts v. Eichelbaum, 254 Va. 373, 493 S.E.2d 510 (1997).

43. Salsbury v. Northwestern Bell Tel. Co., 221 N.W.2d 609 (Iowa 1974).

to be true even in a case where the first subscriber has promised to pledge a large sum if others would pledge an equal amount.[44]

The Restatement (Second) appears to have reached a similar conclusion by providing that, "A charitable subscription * * * is binding * * * without proof that the promise induced action or forbearance."[45] The Restatement recognizes that courts have favored charitable subscriptions and have found consideration where none existed and thus sets forth a rule stating that a charitable subscription is enforceable without consideration and without injurious reliance.[46] Recognition of such a rule puts an end to needless litigation created by the caution of executors and administrators who, for self-protection against surcharging, will not pay out on a subscription without a court decree.

Marriage settlements pose a problem similar to charitable subscriptions. Courts have adopted a policy in favor of sustaining marriage settlements and this had led them to find consideration by the use of strained reasoning.[47] A good illustration is the case of DeCicco v. Schweizer.[48] There, Judge Cardozo concluded that the father of the bride bargained for the marriage of his daughter and her fiancé. However, in the Allegheny College case Cardozo suggested that the real basis for the decision was promissory estoppel. However, there was nothing in the facts as stated in the court's opinion to indicate that the couple would not have married even if the father had not made the promise. Thus, there was no proof of injurious reliance. For this reason and to carry out the public policy to sustain marriage settlements, the Restatement (Second) has classified marriage settlements with charitable subscriptions as enforceable "without proof that the promise induced action or forbearance."[49]

(e) Other Roots of the Doctrine

Other roots of promissory estoppel include cases where an obligor has promised, without consideration, not to plead the statute of limitations.[50] Cases involving gratuitous licenses for the use of real property

---

44. At times, the promise of the "bellwether" has been enforced on a consideration theory. Congregation B'Nai Sholom v. Martin, 382 Mich. 659, 173 N.W.2d 504 (1969).

45. Rs. 2d § 90(2). Of course, any condition stated in the promise qualifies the enforceability of the promise in accordance with its terms. See Annot., 97 ALR3d 1054.

46. Rs. 2d § 90 cmt c, ill. 7. For a suggestion that the moral obligation of the pledgor to give to charity is the true rationale for enforcing charitable pledges, see Thel & Yorio, The Promissory Basis of Past Consideration, 78 Va.L.Rev. 1045, 1080–81 (1992) ("Charitable subscriptions are another group of promises that are powerful because the promisor makes a commitment

to do what she recognizes that she ought to do.").

47. Phalen v. U.S. Trust Co., 186 N.Y. 178, 78 N.E. 943 (1906); Rs. 2d § 90 cmt c, ill. 8.

48. 221 N.Y. 431, 117 N.E. 807 (1917).

49. Rs. 2d § 90(2).

50. If the promise is made to pay an existing debt, no reliance is needed. See § 5.7 supra. The rule here discussed is primarily applied in non-contract cases. Randon v. Toby, 52 U.S. (11 How.) 493 (1850); State Farm Mut. Auto. Ins. Co. v. Budd, 185 Neb. 343, 175 N.W.2d 621, 44 ALR3d 476 (1970) (overruled on other grounds); see McKinney's N.Y. Gen. Oblig.L. § 17–103.

also precede the general recognition of promissory estoppel.[51] Such gratuitous promises and licenses continue to be enforced. The whole topic of waiver of condition is permeated with estoppel reasoning, sometimes promissory in form.[52]

§ 6.3   The Modern Evolution of Promissory Estoppel

(a) As a Consideration Substitute

Although Section 90 on promissory estoppel of neither edition of the Contracts Restatement mentions the term "consideration," these sections are in subchapters devoted to contracts without consideration. Therefore, it is not surprising that promissory estoppel's first conquest has been cases of promises without consideration such as those mentioned in § 6.2. Thus, Section 90 of the Restatement has been applied to a promise to make a gift of land,[1] promises relating to gratuitous bailments and agencies,[2] charitable subscriptions,[3] and promises not to plead the statute of limitations in tort cases.[4] However, currently, promissory estoppel is not limited to the types of cases listed above. The present tendency is to use the doctrine as a substitute for consideration in cases of gratuitous promises in just about any case where all of the elements for promissory estoppel are present.[5] Cases speak "of the widespread acceptance of the doctrine as formulated by the two Restatements."[6]

Since the kinds of gratuitous promises that are likely to induce reliance are as varied as human ingenuity, no exhaustive listing of the cases will be attempted.[7] The doctrine has been applied to a promise that prior service of an employee would be included for certain purposes,[8] to a promise by an insurance company that it would give the plaintiff a full and complete settlement,[9] to a promise by an insurance company to notify a bank of a premium default,[10] to gratuitous advice given by an attorney,[11] to a gratuitous promise to pay an employee a pension[12] and to

51.   4 Williston § 8:4.

52.   See §§ 11.29–11.32 infra.

§ 6.3

1.   Greiner v. Greiner, 131 Kan. 760, 293 P. 759 (1930).

2.   Lusk–Harbison–Jones v. Universal Credit Co., 164 Miss. 693, 145 So. 623 (1933).

3.   Danby v. Osteopathic Hosp. Ass'n, 34 Del.Ch. 427, 104 A.2d 903 (1954).

4.   Jackson v. Kemp, 211 Tenn. 438, 365 S.W.2d 437 (1963).

5.   Wroten v. Mobil Oil, 315 A.2d 728 (Del.Super.1973); Kirkpatrick v. Seneca Nat. Bank, 213 Kan. 61, 515 P.2d 781 (1973); Fretz Constr. Co. v. Southern Nat. Bank, 626 S.W.2d 478 (Tex.1981).

6.   Chapman v. Bomann, 381 A.2d 1123 (Me.1978); see also Knapp, Reliance in the Revised Restatement: The Proliferation of

Promissory Estoppel, 81 Colum.L.Rev. 52 (1981).

7.   For an exhaustive state by state listing of the cases see 3 Corbin § 8.12 (Holmes 1996).

8.   Schmidt v. McKay, 555 F.2d 30 (2d Cir.1977); Alix v. Alix, 497 A.2d 18 (R.I. 1985).

9.   Huhtala v. Travelers Ins. Co., 401 Mich. 118, 257 N.W.2d 640 (1977).

10.   Northwestern Bank of Commerce v. Employers' Life Ins. Co., 281 N.W.2d 164 (Minn.1979).

11.   Togstad et al. v. Vesely, Otto, Miller & Keefe, 291 N.W.2d 686, 693 (Minn.1980).

12.   Hessler, Inc. v. Farrell, 226 A.2d 708 (Del.1967); Feinberg v. Pfeiffer Co., 322 S.W.2d 163 (Mo.App.1959).

a gratuitous promise to guaranty payment of a debt.[13] It has also been applied to the discharge of an obligation.[14]

Although initially there was some authority to the effect that the doctrine of promissory estoppel should be limited to enforcing gratuitous promises and should not be applied in transactions contemplating a bargain,[15] the trend today is in the other direction.[16] This is made clear by consideration of the representative cases discussed below. Moreover, promissory estoppel has come to be a doctrine employed to rescue failing contracts where the cause of the failure is not related to consideration.

(b) Reliance on Offers

In a recurring fact pattern, a general contractor receives a low bid from a subcontractor and uses that bid in preparing its own bid on a project. The bid of the subcontractor is an offer to a bilateral contract.[17] Under the traditional common law rule, the offer may be withdrawn prior to acceptance, even though in submitting its own bid the general contractor has relied on the subcontractor's offer.[18] Does the contractor's justifiable injurious reliance render the offer irrevocable? Yes, according to the majority of courts that have considered the issue since 1958.[19] The Restatement (Second) has explicitly adopted this approach.[20] Of course, there must be something on which the contractor may justifiably rely.

13. W.B. Saunders Co. v. Galbraith, 40 Ohio App. 155, 178 N.E. 34 (1931); Rs. 2d § 88. See also Baehr v. Penn–O–Tex Oil Corp., 258 Minn. 533, 104 N.W.2d 661 (1960); cf. Glitsos v. Kadish, 4 Ariz.App. 134, 418 P.2d 129 (1966).

14. Fried v. Fisher, 328 Pa. 497, 196 A. 39, 115 ALR 147 (1938).

15. See, e.g., James Baird Co. v. Gimbel Bros., 64 F.2d 344 (2d Cir.1933); see also Fridman, Promissory Estoppel, 35 Can. B.Rev. 279 (1957); 28 Ill.L.Rev. 419 (1933); 22 Minn.L.Rev. 843 (1938); 20 Va.L.Rev. 214 (1933).

16. Universal Computer Sys. v. Medical Servs. Ass'n, 628 F.2d 820 (3d Cir.1980). On the invasion of promissory estoppel into the commercial area, see Metzger & Phillips, The Emergence of Promissory Estoppel as an Independent Theory of Recovery, 35 Rutgers L.Rev. 472, 513–28 (1983); Farber & Matheson, Beyond Promissory Estoppel: Contract Law and the Invisible Handshake, 52 U.Chi.L.Rev. 903 (1985); Cyberchron Corp. v. Calldata Sys. Dev., 47 F.3d 39 (2d Cir.1995).

17. See § 2.6(g) supra.

18. See § 2.6(g) supra.

19. Montgomery Indus. Intern. v. Thomas Constr. Co., 620 F.2d 91 (5th Cir. 1980); Reynolds v. Texarkana Constr. Co.,

237 Ark. 583, 374 S.W.2d 818 (1964), 18 Ark.L.Rev. 351 (1965); Drennan v. Star Paving Co., 51 Cal.2d 409, 333 P.2d 757 (1958); Pavel Enterprises v. A.S. Johnson Co., 342 Md. 143, 674 A.2d 521 (1996) (insufficient reliance); Branco Enterprises v. Delta Roofing, 886 S.W.2d 157 (Mo.App. 1994); Seater Constr. Co. v. Rawson Plumbing, 239 Wis.2d 152, 619 N.W.2d 293 (App. 2000); Rs. 2d § 87, ill. 6; cf. Harris v. Lillis, 24 So.2d 689 (La.App.1946) (bid irrevocable pursuant to local custom); contra, R.C.Constr. Co. v. National Office Sys., 622 So.2d 1253 (Miss.1993); B.D. Holt Co. v. OCE, 971 S.W.2d 618 (Tex.App.1998) (subcontractor relieved on grounds of mistake); see Gergen, Liability for Mistake in Contract Formation, 64 S.C.al. L.Rev. 1 (1990); Kostritsky, Reshaping the Precontractual Liability Debate: Beyond Short Run Economics, 58 U.Pitt.L.Rev. 325 (1997); Katz, When Should an Offer Stick: The Economics of Promissory Estoppel in Preliminary Negotiations, 105 Yale L.J. 1249 (1996).

20. Rs. 2d § 87. See also M.L. Closen & D.G. Weiland, The Construction Bidding Cases, 13 John Marshall L.Rev. 565 (1980). This restatement provision receives strong criticism in Kniffin, Innovation or Aberration: Recovery for Reliance on an Offer as Permitted by the New Restatement (Second) Contracts, 62 U.Detroit L.Rev. 23 (1984).

An estimate is not enough[21] and if the subcontractor's bid is so palpably low as to indicate that it is based on a mistake, reliance is not justified.[22]

In addition, the seminal case has stated: "It bears noting that a general contractor is not free to delay acceptance after he has been awarded the general contract in the hope of getting a better price nor can he reopen bargaining with the subcontractor and at the same time claim a continuing right to accept the original offer."[23] In other words, "bid shopping" and "bid chiseling" by the general contractor will terminate the option contract.[24]

In cases of reliance on a subcontractor's bid, although the subcontractor is bound, the general contractor is not bound to accept the bid. The general contractor has not made any promise on which the subcontractor relies.[25]

When an offer looks to a bilateral contract it would be unusual for the offer to become irrevocable under the doctrine of promissory estoppel. Ordinarily the offeree is not justified in relying on an offer.[26] Normally, an offeree must accept the offer before relying on it.[27] This is not true in the subcontractor cases.[28]

21. Robert Gordon, Inc. v. Ingersoll–Rand Co., 117 F.2d 654 (7th Cir.1941); Leo F. Piazza Paving Co. v. Bebek & Brkich, 141 Cal.App.2d 226, 296 P.2d 368, 371 (1956).

22. Robert Gordon, Inc. v. Ingersoll–Rand Co., 117 F.2d 654 (7th Cir.1941).

23. Drennan v. Star Paving Co., 51 Cal.2d 409, 333 P.2d 757, 760 (1958). This view is adopted by the Rs. 2d § 87(2). Although the cases allow an expectancy measure of damages, the section talks of a recovery that would "avoid injustice."

24. Preload Technology v. A.B. & J. Constr. Co., 696 F.2d 1080 (5th Cir.1983), reh. denied. For a discussion of these practices, see Comment, 18 U.C.L.A. L.Rev. (1970).

25. Seacoast Elec. Co. v. Franchi Bros. Constr. Corp., 437 F.2d 1247 (1st Cir.1971); Cortland Asbestos Prods. v. J. & K. Plumbing & Heating Co., 33 A.D.2d 11, 304 N.Y.S.2d 694 (1969); Southern California Acoustics Co. v. C.V. Holder, Inc., 71 Cal.2d 719, 79 Cal.Rptr. 319, 456 P.2d 975 (1969). "In contrast, the subcontractor does not rely on the general and suffers no detriment. A subcontractor submits bids to all or most of the general contractors that it knows are bidding on a project." * * * "The two situations are very different." Holman Erection Co. v. Orville E. Madsen & Sons, 330 N.W.2d 693 (Minn.1983).

A number of commentators and some courts have disagreed with this view. See, e.g., Closen & Weiland, The Construction Industry Building Cases, 13 John Marshall

L.Rev. 565 (1980); Note, Another Look at Construction Bidding and Contracts at Formation, 53 Va.L.Rev. 1720 (1967). Under this approach the general contractor becomes bound by using the bid provided the general contractor's bid is accepted. This would be so even if the subcontractor's name is not listed in the bid of the general contractor. The result is different under the Subletting and Subcontracting Fair Practices Act which requires the listing of the subcontractor; the contractor may not without the consent of the owner substitute another subcontractor for the one listed. Cf. Air Technology Corp. v. General Elec. Co., 347 Mass. 613, 199 N.E.2d 538 (1964).

Where a contractor accepts a bid before it is awarded the general contract, the contractor may be held to a bilateral contract, although it is possible to find an implied condition that the general contract be awarded to the general contractor. Bogue v. Sizemore, 241 Ill.App.3d 250, 181 Ill.Dec. 772, 608 N.E.2d 1246 (1993).

26. Friedman v. Tappan Development Corp., 22 N.J. 523, 126 A.2d 646 (1956) (query if on the facts reliance was not justified); Hill v. Corbett, 33 Wn.2d 219, 204 P.2d 845 (1949).

27. Berryman v. Kmoch, 221 Kan. 304, 559 P.2d 790 (1977).

28. See generally Schultz, The Firm Offer Puzzle, 19 U.Chi.L.Rev. 237 (1952) (business practice indicates to the author that subcontractor's bid should not be treated as irrevocable); Sharp, Promises,

The situation is quite different in the case of an offer looking to a unilateral contract. We saw earlier that part performance in response to an offer for a unilateral contract renders the offer irrevocable under Section 45 of both Restatements.[29] If the offeree merely prepares to perform, Section 45 does not protect against a revocation.[30] However, under the doctrine of promissory estoppel, preparation may render the offer irrevocable.[31]

(c) Promissory Estoppel Under an Indefinite Agreement

In Wheeler v. White[32] the plaintiff owned some land with rental buildings but wanted to construct new rental properties on it. Plaintiff entered into an agreement with the defendant by the terms of which defendant was either to lend plaintiff $70,000 or obtain the loan from a third party. Defendant was to be paid $5,000 plus 5% of the rent of tenants procured by defendant. The loan was to be payable in monthly installments over fifteen years with interest of not more than 6%. After the agreement was signed, defendant assured plaintiff that the money would be available and urged plaintiff to demolish the buildings presently on the site. Plaintiff complied.

The court held that the loan arrangement was too vague and indefinite to be enforced because of the payment terms of the loan. It was a void bilateral agreement.[33] The court did not consider the possibility of forging a good unilateral contract out of a bad bilateral, properly so, because the plaintiff's actions amounted to preparation rather than the beginning of performance.[34] The court, however, applied promissory estoppel and allowed a reliance measure of damages based on the value of the improvements destroyed and the lost rental.[35]

There are other cases of promissory estoppel salvaging indefinite contracts. In Grouse v. Group Health Plan,[36] plaintiff applied for a position with the defendant as a pharmacist. After several interviews, he was offered the job and he accepted. It was agreed that he would resign

Mistakes and Reciprocity, 19 U.Chi.L.Rev. 28 (1952); Note, 53 Va.L.Rev. 1720 (1967).

29. See § 2.22 supra.

30. See § 2.22 supra.

31. Abbott v. Stephany Poultry Co., 44 Del. 513, 62 A.2d 243 (Super.Ct.1948); Kucera v. Kavan, 165 Neb. 131, 84 N.W.2d 207 (1957); Spitzli v. Guth, 112 Misc. 630, 183 N.Y.S. 743 (1920); Rs. 2d § 87 cmt e.

32. 398 S.W.2d 93 (Tex.1965), noted in 18 Baylor L.Rev. 546 (1966); see also Neiss v. Ehlers, 135 Or.App. 218, 899 P.2d 700 (1995) (agreement to agree); Metzger & Philips, Promissory Estoppel and Reliance on Illusory Promises, 44 Sw. L.J. 841 (1990).

33. See § 2.9 supra.

34. See § 4.12(b)(7) supra. The two doctrines may be applied in the case of void bilateral contracts. The main difference is that in forging, the act done must be detrimental in the consideration sense while in the case of promissory estoppel, injurious reliance is necessary.

35. But see Bickerstaff v. Gregston, 604 P.2d 382 (Okl.App.1979) (injurious reliance on a void agreement creates no rights under promissory estoppel because reliance on a void contract is unreasonable); see also Bixby v. Wilson & Co., 196 F.Supp. 889 (N.D.Iowa 1961), 47 Iowa L.Rev. 725 (1962); Clark v. Kellogg Co., 205 F.3d 1079 (8th Cir.2000) ("permanent employment" cases).

36. 306 N.W.2d 114 (Minn.1981); accord, Goff–Hamel v. Obstetricians, 256 Neb. 19, 588 N.W.2d 798 (1999); Humphreys v. Bellaire Corp., 966 F.2d 1037, 1042 (6th Cir.1992).

from his present position, giving two weeks notice. After accepting, he turned down another offer. When he showed up for work, he was told that someone else had been hired. Because the hiring was at will, he had no action for breach based on a conventional contract. He was granted damages based on promissory estoppel, measured by his lost opportunity costs—what he lost by quitting and by turning down another job offer.[37] He was not awarded what he would have earned under the contract, which in this case would have been zero, because the hiring was at will.

(d) Promises Made During Preliminary Negotiations

In the cases discussed above the parties intended to contract, had reached agreement and believed that they had entered into a contract. Yet for some reason there was a legal defect in the formation of the contract. The situation in cases involving promises made in preliminary negotiations is different. The assumption is that the parties were still negotiating, had not as yet reached agreement and did not expect to be bound until some later time.

Although there are a number of cases[38] that fit this mould, the best known example is Hoffman v. Red Owl Stores.[39] The plaintiff was assured that if he took certain steps and raised $18,000 worth of capital he would be granted a supermarket franchise. In compliance with the recommendation of the defendant, he sold his bakery, purchased a grocery store to gain experience, resold it, acquired an option on land for building a franchised outlet, and moved his residence nearby. He raised the necessary capital by borrowing the major portion of it from his father-in-law. This arrangement was approved by the defendant's agent. Later, however, the defendant's more highly placed agents insisted that plaintiff's credit standing was impaired by his loan and demanded that the plaintiff procure from his father-in-law a statement that these funds were an outright gift. Plaintiff refused and sued. The court ruled for the plaintiff on the theory of promissory estoppel, limiting recovery to the amounts expended in reliance on the promise.[40]

37. Accord, Jarboe v. Landmark Community Newspapers, 644 N.E.2d 118 (Ind. 1994); Ravelo v. Hawaii, 66 Haw. 194, 658 P.2d 883 (1983), noted 8 U. Haw. L.Rev. (1986).

38. See, e.g., Midwest Energy v. Orion Food Sys., 14 S.W.3d 154 (Mo.App.2000); De Bourgknecht v. Cianci, 846 F.Supp. 1057 (D.R.I.1994); Where one party to a renegotiation of a contract floated proposals that would benefit the other, with the intent to lull the other into a false sense of security while making alternative arrangements, never intending to reduce the proposals to writing as it promised, a promissory estoppel case had been made out. Moore v. Missouri–Nebraska Exp., 892 S.W.2d 696 (Mo. App.1994); see also Greenstein v. Flatley, 19 Mass.App.Ct. 351, 358, 474 N.E.2d 1130, 1134 (1985) ("conduct beyond the toleration even of persons inured to the rough and tumble of the world of commerce."); Bercoon, Weiner, Glick & Brook v. Mfrs. Hanover Trust Co., 818 F.Supp. 1152, 1159–61 (N.D.Ill.1993).

39. 26 Wis.2d 683, 133 N.W.2d 267 (1965), discussed in Katz, When Should an Offer Stick: The Economics of Promissory Estoppel in Preliminary Negotiations, 105 Yale L.J. 1249 (1996).

40. But see Smith v. Boise Kenworth Sales, 102 Idaho 63, 625 P.2d 417 (1981) ("the doctrine of promissory estoppel is intended as a substitute for consideration * * * and not as a substitute for an agreement * * * ").

As the court pointed out, the contract was indefinite; the parties had not agreed on the "size, cost, design and layout of the store building, and the terms of the lease with respect to rent, maintenance, renewal, and purchase options."[41] In this respect the case is like Wheeler v. White discussed above, but here not only was there indefiniteness, there was nothing more than preliminary negotiations.

The court held that promissory estoppel can sustain a cause of action despite the absence of an intent to be bound. In the court's view, promissory estoppel is more than an equivalent of or substitute for consideration. The doctrine is the basis of a cause of action that is not contract, tort, or quasi-contract.[42] The court's result is close in spirit to the doctrine of *culpa in contrahendo* recognized in a number of Civil Law countries, under which, where justice demands, recovery is awarded for losses sustained as a result of unsuccessful negotiations.[43]

Another case involving liability for promises made during preliminary negotiations is Arcadian Phosphates v. Arcadian Corp.[44] The parties were negotiating for the sale of the defendant's business to the plaintiff. They reached agreement on most of the important terms of a contract for purchase and sale. Their agreement, however, expressly contained terms referring to the possibility of the failure of negotiations. Nonetheless, plaintiff occupied offices in the defendant's premises, its principals were introduced by the defendant to others as the new owners, and plaintiff spent funds improving defendant's physical facilities. Abruptly, the market for the defendant's product improved and defendant demanded a dramatic improvement in the terms of the sale. The court held that although there was no contract of sale, defendant had breached an obligation to negotiate in good faith. For breach of such an obligation, defendant was adjudged liable for damages on a theory of promissory estoppel. The court limited the recovery to the costs incurred by plaintiff in reliance upon the negotiations.

(e) Agreements Disclaiming Legal Consequences

Frequently employers have offered pension plans, death benefits or other fringe benefits while retaining the power to withdraw or modify

41. Hoffman v. Red Owl Stores, 26 Wis.2d 683, 687, 133 N.W.2d 267, 274 (1965). In a similar, but distinguishable case, the court awarded lost profits. The terms had basically been established. Walters v. Marathon Oil Co., 642 F.2d 1098 (7th Cir.1981).

42. The decision may be read as indicating that "Section 90 should serve as a distinct basis of liability without regard to theories of bargain, contract, or consideration. The criteria which justify and limit the application of promissory estoppel are to be determined exclusively by what Section 90 says about the effects of nonperformance of promises." Henderson, supra

§ 6.1 n. 26, at 359. See also Debron Corp. v. National Homes Constr. Corp., 493 F.2d 352 (8th Cir.1974), 40 Mo.L.Rev. 163 (1975); Metzger & Phillips, The Emergence of Promissory Estoppel as an Independent Theory of Recovery, 35 Rutgers L.J. 472 (1983).

43. See Kessler & Fine, *Culpa in Contrahendo*, Bargaining in Good Faith, and Freedom of Contract: A Comparative Study, 77 Harv.L.Rev. 401 (1964); Mirmina, A Comparative Survey of *Culpa in Contrahendo*, 8 Ct.J.Int'l L. 77 (1992).

44. 884 F.2d 69 (2d Cir.1989).

the offer at will.[45] Such a promise can be classified as illusory or as an instance where the parties do not intend legal consequences.[46] Yet, some courts, by a process of interpretation, have held inapplicable the clause disclaiming legal consequences, so as to preclude withdrawal or modification after the employee has retired[47] or died.[48] Injurious reliance on the promise doubtlessly is a primary factor in impelling the courts to so interpret the offer. More recently, courts have overtly applied promissory estoppel to personnel manuals that disclaim legal consequences.[49]

Once it is decided that a void bilateral agreement may be the basis for promissory estoppel, the possibilities are almost limitless. For example, the Restatement (Second) has specific sections covering (1) modifications without consideration,[50] and (2) promises of sureties inducing injurious reliance.[51]

In the first situation, a modification is binding "to the extent that justice requires enforcement in view of a material change of position in reliance on the promise."[52] The reason for the special rule is the "presumptive utility" of a modification without consideration. Thus even though the promise is not binding when made, it may become binding by reliance, but the terms of the original contract may be reinstated as to the future by reasonable notification unless this would be unfair because of a change of position.[53]

The Restatement uses the case of Central London Property Trust, Ltd. v. High Trees House[54] to illustrate the point. "A is the lessee of an apartment house under a 99 year lease from B at a rent of $10,000 per year. Because of war conditions many of the apartments became vacant, and in order to enable A to stay in business B agrees to reduce the rent to $5,000. The reduced rent is paid for five years. The war being over, the apartments are then fully rented, and B notifies A that the full rent called for by the lease must be paid. A is bound to pay the full rent only from a reasonable time after the receipt of the notification." Under the

45. See Notes, 23 U.Chi.L.Rev. 96 (1955), 56 Colum.L.Rev. 251 (1956).

46. See § 4.12(4) and § 2.4.

47. West v. Hunt Foods, 101 Cal.App.2d 597, 225 P.2d 978 (1951); Kari v. General Motors, 79 Mich.App. 93, 261 N.W.2d 222 (1977), reversed 402 Mich. 926, 282 N.W.2d 925 (1978); Schofield v. Zion's Co–op. Mercantile Inst., 85 Utah 281, 39 P.2d 342, 96 ALR 1083 (1934).

48. Stopford v. Boonton Molding Co., 56 N.J. 169, 265 A.2d 657, 46 ALR3d 444 (1970); Mabley & Carew Co. v. Borden, 129 Ohio St. 375, 195 N.E. 697, 100 ALR 511 (1935) (death benefit); see Annot. 46 ALR3d 464 (1972). Following the orthodox view is Abelson v. Genesco, 58 A.D.2d 774, 396 N.Y.S.2d 394 (1977). See also, Note, Public Employee Benefits—A Promissory Estoppel Approach, 10 Wm. Mitchell L.Rev. 287 (1984).

49. Greene v. Howard Univ., 412 F.2d 1128 (D.C.Cir.1969); Cronk v. Intermountain Rural Elec. Ass'n, 1992 WL 161811 (Colo.App.). The same result is sometimes reached by a process of interpretation. See, e.g., Aiello v. United Air Lines, 818 F.2d 1196 (5th Cir.1987); cf. McDonald v. Mobil Coal Producing, 820 P.2d 986 (Wyo.1991) (some judges base the decision on promissory estoppel; others on interpretation); but see Hatfield v. Board of County Com'rs, 52 F.3d 858 (10th Cir.1995).

50. Rs. 2d § 89.

51. Rs. 2d § 88.

52. Rs. 2d § 89 cmt a.

53. Rs. 2d § 89 cmt d; see also UCC § 2–209(4) and (5).

54. [1947] K.B. 130; Rs. 2d § 89 ill. 7.

pre-existing duty rule the modification is without consideration and the assumption is that the reliance, although not detrimental in the consideration sense, is injurious. B is allowed to reinstate the $10,000 term as to the future because there has been no change of position that would make reinstatement unfair.

The Restatement (Second) takes a similar approach toward a guaranty. The provision is directed to a situation where the surety guaranties payment after the creditor has already furnished the consideration to the principal debtor; therefore there is no consideration for the surety's promise. If the creditor relies on the promise of the surety, as for example by refraining from bringing action against the principal at a time when the amount due could have been recovered, the promise may be enforced.[55]

It is also possible to use promissory estoppel to enforce an unenforceable agreement, as for example a case involving the Statute of Frauds.[56] Presumably promissory estoppel could be used in cases involving voidable contracts but the rules employed in the area of voidable contracts take into account the element of reliance together with the policy to be attained.[57]

§ 6.4   Flexibility of Remedy

The unspoken premise of the First Restatement is that if the elements of promissory estoppel are present a contract is formed and therefore ordinary remedies for breach of promise would be available.[1] As Williston explained, either a contract was formed or it was not, "you have to take one leg or the other."[2] This conceptual approach very likely has hindered full judicial acceptance of the doctrine.

Some courts, however, broke the conceptual barrier and have decided that the remedy need not be as broad as that which would be available for breach of a contract founded in consideration.[3] Only reliance damages were awarded in the cases of Wheeler v. White, Hoffman v. Red Owl Stores, and Arcadian Phosphates v. Arcadian Corp., discussed above.[4] Such flexibility is to be encouraged.[5] If reliance on an extremely valuable promise is moderate, courts should not be compelled to choose

---

55. Rs. 2d § 88 cmts a and d, and ills. 2 and 3.

56. See § 19.48 infra. The promissory estoppel doctrine can be used to overcome the parol evidence rule, see § 6.1 n.4 supra.

57. See generally ch. 9.

§ 6.4

1. See § 6.1 supra.

2. Williston, IV American Law Institute Proceedings, Appendix p. 103 (1926); but see 3 Corbin § 8.8 (Holmes 1996).

3. Grouse v. Group Health Plan, 306 N.W.2d 114 (Minn.1981). See the thorough

discussion in Comment, 37 U.Chi.L.Rev. 559 (1970); see also Seavey, Reliance on Gratuitous Promises or Other Conduct, 64 Harv.L.Rev. 913 (1951); Shattuck, Gratuitous Promises—A New Writ?, 35 Mich. L.Rev. 908 (1936). But see Note, 13 Vand. L.Rev. 705 (1960).

4. See also RCM Supply Co. v. Hunter Douglas, Inc., 686 F.2d 1074 (4th Cir.1982).

5. Associated Tabulating Serv. v. Olympic Life Ins. Co., 414 F.2d 1306 (5th Cir. 1969).

between full contractual recovery or none at all.[6] Nonetheless, in the overwhelming majority of cases employing promissory estoppel as a consideration substitute, expectation damages have been granted.[7] Where it acts to salvage aspects of an indefinite contract, expectation damages are not awardable under the analysis given in § 14.9 below or because the case bears a closer relationship to tort-based liability than to traditional contract liability.[8]

The Restatement (Second) states that the remedy for breach of a contract based on promissory estoppel should be flexible.[9] It is proper in a given case to award reliance damages to protect the reliance interest but "full-scale enforcement by normal remedies is often appropriate."[10] It is not a simple matter to determine in a given case which remedy is appropriate.[11] Also, there may be many difficult problems in determining how reliance damages are "to be measured in the donative-promise context."[12] Because promissory estoppel is basically an extension of contract law, damages for mental distress are not awardable.[13]

Some light on flexibility of remedy can be obtained through the lens of history. Professor Eric Mills Holmes has examined perhaps every promissory estoppel case decided in the last two centuries.[14] His analysis shows that the development of the doctrine can be divided into three stages. In the first stage, the earliest cases applied the yet unnamed doctrine defensively, as where it was applied to estop a party from pleading the statute of limitations. The second stage of the doctrine's development involved the creation of a cause of action in which the estoppel was raised to enforce a promise made without consideration. The relief given in such cases involved the protection of the promisee's expectancy interest by granting expectancy damages or specific performance. Courts generally continue the protection of the expectancy interest in such cases.[15] Some jurisdictions remain in this stage, and perhaps two jurisdictions linger in the first stage, but most have woven a more complex tapestry. Virginia, however, has rejected the doctrine.[16]

---

6. Fuller and Perdue, The Reliance Interest in Contract Damages, 46 Yale L.J. 373, 405 (1937).

7. Becker, Promissory Estoppel Damages, 16 Hofstra L.Rev. 131 (1987); Yorio & Thel, The Promissory Basis of Promissory Estoppel, 101 Yale L.J. 111 (1991). This analysis of the results is challenged by Eisenberg, The World of Contract and the World of Gift, 85 Cal.L.Rev. 821 (1997).

8. See Becker, supra, at 134–35, 155–63; Becker & Barnett, Beyond Reliance, 15 Hofstra L.Rev. 443 (1987); but see Kelly, The Phantom Reliance Interest in Contract Damages, 1992 Wis.L.Rev. 1775.

9. See § 6.1 supra.

10. Rs. 2d § 90 cmt d (Reporter's Note).

11. See Rs. 2d § 90 cmt d, ills. 8, 11.

12. Eisenberg, supra § 6.1 n.24, at 26–31. See also Seavey, Reliance upon Gratu-

itous Promises or Other Conduct, 64 Harv. L.Rev. 913 (1951); Comment, 37 U.Chi. L.Rev. 559 (1970).

13. Deli v. University of Minnesota, 578 N.W.2d 779 (Minn.App.1998).

14. 3 Corbin §§ 8.11–8.12 (Holmes 1996). Later versions are Holmes, The Four Phases of Promissory Estoppel, 20 Seattle U.L.Rev. 45 (1996); Holmes, Restatement of Promissory Estoppel, 32 Willamette L.Rev. 263 (1996).

15. See Kostritsky, A New Theory of Assent–Based Liability Emerging Under the Guise of Promissory Estoppel, 33 Wayne L.Rev. 895 (1987); Barnett, The Death of Reliance, 46 J.Leg.Ed. 518 (1996); Yorio & Thel, The Promissory Basis of Section 90, 101 Yale L.J. 111 (1991).

16. W.J. Schafer Assoc. v. Cordant, 254 Va. 514, 493 S.E.2d 512 (1997).

The third stage involves the creation of an independent claim for injurious reliance where tort-like reliance damages are granted. These include cases such as Red Owl, Arcadian, and Wheeler v. White,[17] where the reliance was on a promise that was too indefinite to be enforceable, or which was for some reason, other than the lack of consideration, was non-binding under traditional contract theory. This third stage, which some jurisdictions have entered is the adoption of a truly equitable and flexible doctrine that amalgamates all of the prior stages.[18] Does such an approach produce too much uncertainty? All "equitable" doctrines, to some extent, increase the law's uncertainty. Long ago, Francis Bacon addressed this issue.

> "But to this Objection it may be answered in general that where Conscience is to direct the Judge, that Court cannot with any Propriety of Sense or Speech, be said to be arbitrary. The Judge knows and is sensible that he sits there, not to dictate according to his Will and Pleasure, but to be guided by that infallible Monitor within his own Breast; and surely he who is bound to determine according to the original and eternal Rules of Justice, is no more arbitrary, than he that is bound to judge according to positive Laws and Statutes."[19]

Bacon exaggerated. No judge has "an infallible monitor within his [or her] own breast." But, as the other rules of the common law, and the rules of equity, have evolved from experience and precedent and the responses of able judges to the *mores* of their time, so too will the doctrine of promissory estoppel. Just as the original Restatement gave great impetus to promissory estoppel, it may be expected that the Second Restatement with its liberalization of the doctrine will give added impetus to its utilization.[20] Promissory estoppel may be used in any context in order to do justice. As one court has stated, the doctrine of promissory estoppel is "an attempt by the courts to keep remedies abreast of increased moral consciousness of honest and fair representations in all business dealing. * * * "[21]

17. See supra § 6.4(c) & (d).

18. Professor Feinman argues that "[i]t is time for a paradigm shift." Feinman, The Last Promissory Estoppel Article, 61 Fordham L.Rev. 303 (1992). But the paradigm has been continuously shifting for centuries.

19. Sir Francis Bacon, Maxims of Equity 1 (1978 photo reprint of a 1727 printing) (1623).

20. Knapp, Reliance in the Revised Restatement: The Proliferation of Promissory Estoppel, 81 Colum.L.Rev. 52 (1981) ("The revised Restatement provides a useful summary of the current status of the section 90 principle, but it is not likely to be the end of the story. Indeed, by the time its force is finally felt, section 90 may well have transformed the face of contract law in ways undreamt by its drafters—or its revisers."); Knapp, Rescuing Reliance: The Perils of Promissory Estoppel, 49 Hastings L.Rev. 1191 (1998).

21. Peoples Nat. Bank v. Linebarger Constr. Co., 219 Ark. 11, 17, 240 S.W.2d 12, 16 (1951).

Chapter 7

CONTRACTS UNDER SEAL

Table of Sections

---

§ 7.1   Introduction

Centuries before the doctrine of consideration was developed and long before informal contracts[1] were enforced, contracts under seal were enforced.[2] A contract under seal is a formal contract;[3] indeed, the prevalent kind of formal contract from the late middle ages down to recent times, at least in non-commercial transactions.[4] Even after the development of consideration, the sealed instrument required no consideration,[5] although, at times, courts, losing sight of its historical origins, have said that the seal "imports a consideration."[6] The promise under

§ 7.1

1. See § 1.8 supra on formal and informal contracts.

2. 3 Corbin § 10.14 (Holmes 1996); 1 Williston § 2:2. See generally, Backus, The Origin and Use of Private Seals under the Common Law, 51 Am.L.Rev. 369 (1917); Crane, The Magic of Private Seal, 15 Colum.L.Rev. 598 (1915), Selected Readings 598; Holmes, Stature and Status of a Promise Under Seal as a Legal Formality, 29 Willamette L.Rev. 617 (1993); Praeger, The Distinction between Sealed and Unsealed Instruments, 74 Cent.L.J. 172 (1912); Riddell, The Mystery of the Seal, 4 Can.B.Rev. 156 (1926); N. Y. Law Revision Commission Reports: 1936 p. 287ff., 1940 p. 173ff.; Comment, 15 Wake Forest L.Rev. 251 (1979).

3. See § 1.8 supra. The efficacy of the seal has not been limited to contracts. Tra-

ditionally, many executed transactions such as conveyances and releases have been under seal.

4. This is not to say that sealed instruments have not been used in mercantile transactions, but other forms of formal instruments are more important in commercial law; e.g., negotiable instruments and letters of credit.

5. Milde v. Harrison, 162 Ga.App. 809, 293 S.E.2d 56 (1982); Johnson v. Norton Housing Auth., 375 Mass. 192, 375 N.E.2d 1209 (1978).

6. See discussion of this terminology in Hartford–Connecticut Trust Co. v. Divine, 97 Conn. 193, 116 A. 239, 21 ALR 134 (1922); Hensel v. U.S. Electronics Corp., 262 A.2d 648 (Del.Super.1970); Twining v. National Mtg. Corp., 268 Md. 549, 302 A.2d

seal is enforced because of the form of the instrument. The three required formalities are: a sufficient writing, a seal, and delivery. In addition, the promisor and promisee must have legal capacity and the contract must not be void as, for example, because of illegality. Also, if the promisee is to render some performance under the contract, such performance may be required as a condition precedent to enforcement of the promise under the same rules as are applicable to a contract without a seal (an informal contract).[7]

Although a sealed instrument did not require consideration, a court of equity may take into account the absence of consideration in determining whether an equitable remedy such as specific performance should be granted.[8]

Formalities serve important functions in many legal systems,[9] particularly in relatively primitive societies. Important among these is the evidentiary function. Compliance with formalities provides reliable evidence that a given transaction took place. Formalities also serve a cautionary function. The ceremony of melting sealing wax onto parchment followed by impressing the melted wax with a signet ring was imposing. Before performing the required ritual, the promisor had ample opportunity to reflect and deliberate on the wisdom of the act. Therefore the legal system could accept the document as a serious act of volition. A third function of formalities is one of an earmarking or channeling. The populace is made aware that the use of a given device will attain a desired result. When the device is used, the judicial task of determining the parties' intentions is facilitated. A fourth function of formalities is clarification. When the parties reduce their transaction to writing (and a contract under seal must be in writing) they are more likely to work out details not contained in their oral agreement. In addition, form requirements can serve regulatory and fiscal ends, to educate the parties as to the full extent of their obligations, to provide public notice of the transaction, and also to promote management efficiency in an organizational setting.

The legal effect of the seal has been abolished or downgraded in most jurisdictions.[10] Despite the numerous advantages to formal requirements, in time the disadvantages outweighed the advantages. Perhaps more importantly, the ceremony of sealing degenerated to such an extent that it lost its almost magical power to impress the parties with the

---

604 (1973); Minch v. Saymon, 96 N.J.Super. 464, 233 A.2d 385 (1967); Thomason v. Bescher, 176 N.C. 622, 97 S.E. 654, 2 ALR 626 (1918).

7. See ch. 11 infra; Venners v. Goldberg, 133 Md.App. 428, 758 A.2d 567 (2000); Thomas v. Webster Spring Co., 37 Mass. App.Ct. 180, 638 N.E.2d 51 (1994); In re Conrad's Estate, 333 Pa. 561, 3 A.2d 697 (1938).

8. Capital Investors Co. v. Estate of Morrison, 584 F.2d 652 (4th Cir.1978), cert. denied; see Rs. 1st. § 366; Rs. 2d § 95,

reporter's note. An offer under seal that promises irrevocability is irrevocable for the time stated, or for a reasonable time if no time is stated. O'Brien v. Boland, 166 Mass. 481, 44 N.E. 602 (1896); Clark on Contracts 43 (4th ed. 1931).

9. See, generally, Perillo, The Statute of Frauds in the Light of the Functions and Dysfunctions of Form, 43 Fordham L.Rev. 39, 43–69 (1974).

10. See § 7.9 infra.

seriousness of their conduct.[11] There are those, however, who lament the weakened condition of the seal.[12]

§ 7.2 Sufficiency of the Writing or Other Record

An instrument under seal was known as a deed. "[E]arly law generally required that a deed be written on paper or parchment, but now an instrument written or printed on any substance capable of receiving and retaining legible characters, would probably have equal validity."[1] Today, an electronic record has the status of a writing.[2] Although today sealed instruments are invariably signed, a signature is not a requirement for the efficacy of the instrument.[3] The instrument must contain a promise which is sufficiently definite as to be capable of performance.[4] In addition, the promisor and the promisee must be named or sufficiently described in the instrument so as to be capable of identification.[5] Thus, for example, the rule of agency law that a principal may sue or be sued on a contract, although the contract by its terms appears to be made with the agent, is inapplicable to sealed instruments.[6] Some courts, however, have circumvented this rule in part by holding that if the contract was such that no seal is required, it will be treated as an informal contract.[7]

§ 7.3 What Constitutes a Seal?

For some period in history seals were required to consist of wax affixed to the parchment or paper on which the terms of the instrument were written. The wax was required to have an identifiable impression made upon it.[1] Usually this was made by a signet ring.

Ordinary people did not have signet rings. When literacy became widespread, it was to be expected that the law would accept substitutes for the traditional seal. Thus, today it would be generally accurate to say that a seal may consist of wax, a gummed wafer, an impression on the paper, the word "seal," the letters "L.S." (locus sigilli) or even a pen scratch.[2] Corporate seals are designed to authenticate instruments. The

11. See Cardozo, The Paradoxes of Legal Science 70–72 (1928).

12. Posner, Economic Analysis of Law 96 (4th ed.1992) ("its disappearance is a puzzle.")

§ 7.2

1. 1 Williston § 2:3.

2. See § 19.1(b) infra.

3. Rs. 2d § 95 cmt c; Parks v. Hazlerigg, 7 Blackf. 536, 43 Am.Dec. 106 (Ind.1845).

4. On definiteness, see § 2.13 supra.

5. Rs. 2d § 108.

6. Crowley v. Lewis, 239 N.Y. 264, 146 N.E. 374 (1925); 1 Williston § 2:12.

7. Harris v. McKay, 138 Va. 448, 122 S.E. 137, 32 ALR 156 (1924); contra, New England Dredging Co. v. Rockport Granite Co., 149 Mass. 381, 21 N.E. 947 (1889).

§ 7.3

1. Coke, 3 Institutes 169 (1812 ed.). See 3 Corbin §§ 10.2–10.3 (Holmes 1996); 1 Williston § 2:4.

2. Milford Fertilizer Company v. Hopkins, 807 A.2d 580 (Del.Super.2002).(Recital in testimonium clause of promissory note that it was being signed under seal, and presence of the word "SEAL" to right of maker's signature, were sufficient to establish that note was under seal.) Woodbury v. U.S. Cas. Co., 284 Ill. 227, 120 N.E. 8 (1918); Loraw v. Nissley, 156 Pa. 329, 27 A. 242 (1893); Rs. 2d § 96; 3 Corbin § 10.2–10.3 (Holmes 1996); 1 Williston § 2:4.

mere affixing of a corporate seal without a recital of sealing or other evidence of an intent to have a sealed instrument, does not create an instrument under seal.[3]

To have a sealed instrument, in addition to the formalities mentioned above, it must appear that the party executing it intended it to be a sealed instrument.[4] The most common way in which this intent is shown is by a witnessing clause—a clause stating: "In Witness Whereof I Have Hereunto Set My Hand and Seal" or words to that effect. Some cases have held that a recital is necessary at least where the seal is other than a wax impression.[5] Others, contrary to the formerly prevailing view that one must determine from the face of the instrument whether it is sealed, have admitted extrinsic evidence to show the necessary intention.[6] The Restatement (Second) adopts the approach that a recital of sealing is neither required nor conclusive.[7] Generally, however, an objective test of sealing is incorporated in its definition of a seal as "a manifestation in tangible and conventional form of an intention that a document be sealed."[8] The Restatement recognizes, however, that extrinsic evidence should be freely admitted to determine whether or not there was a manifestation of intention to seal.[9]

§ 7.4   The Adoption of a Seal Already on the Instrument

Often the parties adopt a pre-printed form upon which the word "seal," or some other form of seal has been printed or otherwise affixed, or they adopt a form prepared by the attorney for one of the parties. The promisor need not personally attach the seal,[1] and one seal may serve for several persons;[2] a seal that is on the instrument may be adopted. Since the question of adoption is one of intent and the writing is seldom unambiguous, extrinsic evidence is ordinarily admissible to determine

3. AT & T v. Harris Corp., 1993 WL 401864 (Del.Super.1993).

4. Empire Trust Co. v. Heinze, 242 N.Y. 475, 152 N.E. 266 (1926). However, there are cases indicating that the intent to seal is sufficient, as for example, where there is a clause which says "In Witness Whereof, I have hereunto set my hand and seal," not accompanied by a seal. Beach v. Beach, 141 Conn. 583, 107 A.2d 629 (1954).

5. Alropa Corp. v. Rossee, 86 F.2d 118 (5th Cir.1936); Dawsey v. Kirven, 203 Ala. 446, 83 So. 338, 7 ALR 1658 (1919); Bradley Salt Co. v. Norfolk Imp. & Exp. Co., 95 Va. 461, 28 S.E. 567 (1897).

6. Jackson v. Security Mut. Life Ins. Co., 135 Ill.App. 86 (1907), aff'd (1908); Matter of Pirie, 198 N.Y. 209, 91 N.E. 587 (1910), modified 199 N.Y. 524, 91 N.E. 1144 (1910). There is no need, however, for the party to know the legal effect of the seal. Jacoby v. D'Amico, 1989 WL 7038 (Del.Ch. 1989).

7. Rs. 2d § 100.

8. Rs. 2d § 96(1); contra, Mobil Oil Corp. v. Wolfe, 297 N.C. 36, 252 S.E.2d 809 (1979) (recital conclusive).

9. Rs. 2d § 100 cmt b: "A recital may give meaning to a manifestation of intention, indicating that a dash or scrawl after a signature is intended as a seal or that the promisor intends to adopt a seal affixed by another party. * * * [R]ecitals are often false and their falsity may be shown by any relevant evidence."

§ 7.4

1. Commonwealth v. Gutelius, 287 Pa. 441, 135 A. 214 (1926); Van Domelen v. Westinghouse Elec. Corp., 382 F.2d 385 (9th Cir.1967).

2. Rs. 2d § 99; McNulty v. Medical Service, 176 A.2d 783 (D.C.App.1962).

this issue of adoption.[3] If the instrument contains a recital of sealing and some form of seal, all who signed will be presumed to have adopted the seal,[4] regardless of whether or not they knew the legal effect of the seal.[5]

§ 7.5 Delivery of a Sealed Instrument

Delivery of a sealed instrument is required for its validity.[1] The earlier cases seemed to have assumed that when the promisor placed the instrument in the possession of the promisee or of some third person as agent of the promisee, delivery was effectuated.[2] It soon became recognized, however, that possession of the paper could be relinquished without an intent that the obligation should exist as, for example, where it is given merely for inspection. Consequently, it was held that, in addition to the surrendering of possession, an intent to deliver is required.[3] Under the more modern cases, the only requirement for an intent to deliver is a manifestation of intent by the promisor that the document be immediately operative, even where the instrument has never left the promisor's possession.[4] This view is not sufficiently widespread, however, to cause the Second Restatement to depart from the traditional rule that the promisor must part with possession.[5]

§ 7.6 Effect of Acceptance by the Promisee

Some cases have stated that an expression of assent by the other party is necessary to complete a delivery.[1] However, if the instrument expresses an obligation only on the part of the promisor, the promisee need not express assent.[2] It has sometimes been said that the promisee's assent is presumed absent a disclaimer. A more direct statement is that the instrument is effective upon delivery without assent, but that it may be disclaimed by the promisee within a reasonable time after learning of the existence of the instrument.[3]

3. FDIC v. Barness, 484 F.Supp. 1134 (E.D.Pa.1980); Rs. 2d § 98; 1 Williston § 2:5.

4. Cammack v. J.B. Slattery & Bro., 241 N.Y. 39, 148 N.E. 781 (1925); Branton v. Martin, 243 S.C. 90, 132 S.E.2d 285 (1963); contra, McCalla v. Stuckey, 233 Ga.App. 397, 504 S.E.2d 269 (Ga.App.1998).

5. Jacoby v. D'Amico, 1989 WL 7038 (Del.Ch.1989).

§ 7.5

1. Rs. 2d § 95(1)(b). Where the record is silent on the question of delivery, a prima facie case for a contract under seal has not been made. Tallent v. Meredith, 1988 WL 40182 (Del.Super.1988).

2. If the instrument is transferred to an agent or custodian of the promisor, there is no delivery by virtue of the transfer. 3 Corbin § 10.6 (Holmes 1996).

3. The delivery must be voluntary and not induced by fraud. Tallent v. Meredith,

1988 WL 40182 (Del.Super.1988). On delivery see generally, Gavitt, The Conditional Delivery of Deeds, 30 Colum.L.Rev. 1145 (1930); Corbin, Delivery of Written Contracts, 36 Yale L.J. 443 (1926); Patterson, The Delivery of a Life Insurance Policy, 33 Harv.L.Rev. 198 (1919).

4. Maciaszek v. Maciaszek, 21 Ill.2d 542, 173 N.E.2d 476 (1961); McMahon v. Dorsey, 353 Mich. 623, 91 N.W.2d 893 (1958).

5. Rs. 2d § 102 cmt b.

§ 7.6

1. Bowen v. Prudential Ins., Co., 178 Mich. 63, 144 N.W. 543 (1913); 1 Williston § 2:10.

2. Rs. 2d § 104.

3. Branton v. Martin, 243 S.C. 90, 132 S.E.2d 285 (1963); Rs. 2d § 104(2); 1 Williston § 2:10; 3 Corbin § 10.7 (Holmes 1996).

The situation is different if the instrument delivered by the promisor calls for a return promise. In order for the promisee to be bound by a sealed promise, the promisee must seal and deliver the instrument (or another instrument). If the promisee does not seal and deliver, but makes the required return promise, the parties are bound by a bilateral contract. The original promisor is bound by a promise under seal and the second promisor is bound by the informal promise.[4] It is sometimes held, however, that acceptance of the sealed instrument containing a return promise justifies a holding that the party accepting the instrument is liable on the instrument by adoption or estoppel.[5] Since such a transaction involves consideration, the effects of the distinction between action on a sealed promise and on an informal promise are primarily two: (1) where common law pleading survives, the action of the sealed promise is in covenant rather than assumpsit; and (2) in many jurisdictions the statutory period of limitations is appreciably longer in the case of an action on a sealed instrument.[6]

Under any view of the matter, if the sealed instrument calls for a return promise, the delivery is deemed conditional until the return promise is made as the promisor has no intent to deliver until there is an expression of assent by the other party.[7]

§ 7.7 Delivery in Escrow—Conditional Delivery

We have already seen that the transfer of possession to a third party other than an agent of the promisor can constitute delivery. The question here is the effect of such a delivery when instructions are given to the third party to deliver the instrument to the grantee or promisee only upon the occurrence of a condition not specified in the instrument itself. The function of the conditional delivery is to make the promisor bound upon the instrument in the sense that, unless the power of revocation is reserved, the instrument is irrevocable;[1] however, the promisor is not bound to perform until the condition takes place.[2] When the condition occurs the promisor is bound even though the third party does not

---

4. Rs. 2d § 107; 3 Corbin § 10.17 (Holmes 1996); 1 Williston § 211.

5. Atlantic Dock Co. v. Leavitt, 54 N.Y. 35, 13 Am.Rep. 556 (1873); 1 Williston § 211. In Blass v. Terry, 156 N.Y. 122, 50 N.E. 953 (1898), the court has held that sufficient delivery of a deed so as to vest title in the grantee did not necessarily result in a sufficient manifestation of assent to a mortgage assumption clause in the deed. The grantee had not been given the opportunity to read the deed. Under ordinary circumstances, the grantee who accepts a deed is chargeable with its contents whether the grantee reads it or not. See § 9.42 infra.

6. See the statutory note preceding Rs. 2d § 95 which compiles the relevant statutes. See also, e.g., Georgia Receivables v. Maddox, 216 Ga.App. 164, 454 S.E.2d 541 (Ga.App.1995) (20 years); State v. Regency Group, 598 A.2d 1123 (Del.Super.1991) (20 years).

7. Diebold Safe & Lock Co. v. Morse, 226 Mass. 342, 115 N.E. 431 (1917).

§ 7.7

1. Moore v. Downing, 289 Ill. 612, 124 N.E. 557 (1919); Rs. 2d § 103.

2. Sunset Beach Amusement Corp. v. Belk, 31 N.J. 445, 158 A.2d 35 (1960); as to conditional delivery of conveyances, see Aigler, Is a Contract Necessary to Create an Effective Escrow, 16 Mich.L.Rev. 569 (1918).

deliver the instrument.[3] The parol evidence rule presents the main legal problem in this fact pattern. However, the weight of authority is to the effect that the parol evidence rule is no bar to proof that the delivery was conditional.[4] Indeed, if the writing is not a total integration, parol evidence of additional terms is admissible under the same conditions as in an action on an informal contract.[5]

A similar problem arises where the instrument is delivered not to a third person but to the promisee and is delivered subject to the occurrence of a condition not stated in the instrument. Many of the older cases, particularly those involving conveyances, held that the condition not stated in the writing should be disregarded because of the parol evidence rule.[6] The weight of authority under the modern cases is to the contrary.[7]

Of course it is possible that the condition is one which prevents any delivery from taking place so that the instrument is not effective in any way. For example, if A hands B a sealed instrument which contains a promise in favor of B and says "hold this for me until tomorrow," there is no delivery and therefore the instrument is not effective.[8] At times it is difficult to determine whether the condition imposed prevents a delivery or whether it is merely a condition to performance. "Without doubt, interpretations have been variable and inconsistent."[9]

§ 7.8   Some Effects of the Seal

The rule on discharge or modifications of sealed contracts has changed considerably. At early common, law courts held that the discharge or modification of a sealed contract could be accomplished only by another sealed instrument.[1] Later it was held that a sealed instrument could be discharged or modified by an accord and satisfaction but not by an unperformed executory bilateral contract.[2] The more modern view is that a sealed instrument may be modified or rescinded in the same manner as any other instrument.[3]

3. Gardiner v. Gardiner, 36 Idaho 664, 214 P. 219 (1923).

4. Rs. 2d § 103; Corbin, Conditional Delivery of Written Contracts, 36 Yale L.J. 443, 455 (1927); 3 Corbin §§ 10.10–10.12; 1 Williston § 2:9.

5. Husband (P.J.O.) v. Wife (L.O.), 418 A.2d 994 (Del.Super.1980).

6. Hume v. Kirkwood, 216 Ala. 534, 113 So. 613 (1927).

7. 3 Corbin § 10.11 (Holmes 1996); 1 Williston § 2:9; Notes, 18 Mich.L.Rev. 314 (1920), 5 Minn.L.Rev. 287 (1921).

8. See § 7.5 supra.

9. 3 Corbin § 10.12 at 398 (Holmes 1996); see also, Puckett v. Hoover, 146 Tex. 1, 202 S.W.2d 209 (1947); 1 Williston § 2:9.

§ 7.8

1. See 3 Corbin § 10.15 (Holmes 1996).

2. Tussing v. Smith, 125 Fla. 578, 171 So. 238 (1936).

3. Husband (P.J.O.) v. Wife (L.O.), 418 A.2d 994 (Del.Super.1980); Koth v. Board of Education, 141 S.C. 448, 140 S.E. 99, 55 ALR 682 (1927); Rs. 1st. § 407. See generally, Costigan, Waiver, Alteration or Modification by Parol of Contracts under Seal, 6 Ill.L.Rev. 280 (1911). At early common law many other defenses that could be raised against simple contracts could not be raised against sealed instruments, necessitating the intervention of equity to stay the unconscionable exercise of the promisee's legal right to enforce the sealed instrument despite the defense of fraud, payment or the like. See Ames, Specialty Contracts and Equitable Defenses, 9 Harv.L.Rev. 49 (1895).

There are other effects of the seal. Under the traditional rule, an undisclosed principal cannot sue on a sealed instrument, but this rule is also changing.[4] Also, although there was an initial reluctance to permit a suit by a third party beneficiary upon a sealed contract, the prevailing view today is that there is no greater obstacle to such an action than in the case of informal contracts.[5] Finally, in some jurisdictions, causes of actions arising from instruments under seal enjoy a longer statute of limitations.[6]

§ 7.9   Statutory Changes Affecting the Seal

In its original conception, the sealing of an instrument was surrounded by impressive solemnity. Individuals who owned signet rings or similar devices guarded them as they would guard treasure. The community was aware of the consequences of the ceremony of sealing and delivery. As times changed and the ceremony was abandoned and supplanted by the mere presence on a printed form of the word "seal" or the initials "L.S."[1] on or near the signature line, the community lost its awareness of the distinction between sealed and unsealed instruments. This is not to say that there are not some jurisdictions, such as Delaware, where the seal enjoys much of its pristine power, validating contracts without consideration.[2]

Taking cognizance of the change in community expectations, many legislatures have enacted statutes affecting the seal.[3] Some statutes make private seals wholly inoperative.[4] The UCC is in this class. It "makes clear that every effect of the seal which relates to 'sealed instruments' is wiped out insofar as contracts for sale are concerned."[5] In some states where the effectiveness of the seal has been abolished, it has been deemed necessary to enact statutory substitutes to perform one or more of its functions, particularly the function of sustaining a transaction without consideration.[6]

Statutes that have abolished the effectiveness of the seal represent only one group of statutes that have impacted on the old system. A

4. See § 7.9 infra.

5. Wilmington Housing Auth. v. Fidelity & Deposit Co., 43 Del. (4 Terry) 381, 47 A.2d 524, 170 ALR 1288 (1946); Coster v. City of Albany, 43 N.Y. 399 (1871); 3 Corbin § 10.16 (Holmes 1996); Rs. 2d § 303.

6. Birmingham v. Cochrane Roofing & Metal Co., 547 So.2d 1159 (Ala.1989); AT & T v. Harris Corp., 1993 WL 401864 (Del.Super.1993); Georgia Receivables v. Maddox, 216 Ga.App. 164, 454 S.E.2d 541 (Ga.App. 1995).

§ 7.9

1. The abandonment of the ceremony apparently occurred early in American history. See Alexander v. Jameson, 5 Bin. 238, 244 (Pa.1812), quoted in Loraw v. Nissley, 156 Pa. 329, 27 A. 242 (1893).

2. Fox v. Christina Square Assoc., 1994 WL 146023 (Del.Super.1994); Tallent v. Meredith, 1988 WL 40182 (Del.Super.1988).

3. The courts had previously taken cognizance of the deterioration of the ceremony of sealing. Their piecemeal attempts to deal with the problem, however, tended to place the law in confusion. See Crane, The Magic of the Private Seal, 15 Colum.L.Rev. 24 (1915), Selected Readings 598.

4. See the statutory note preceding Rs. 2d § 95. Another statutory classification appears in 1 Williston § 2:17. The statutes are analyzed in Holmes, supra § 7.1 n.2.

5. § 2–203 cmt 1; (revision draft substantially unchanged). A seal, however, may have the effect of a signature. Id. cmt 2.

6. See ch. 5(B) supra.

second group of statutes has abolished the distinction between sealed and unsealed instruments but provide that any written promise is rebuttably presumed to be supported by consideration.[7] A third group of statutes provide that a seal is only presumptive evidence of consideration on executory instruments, generally leaving unchanged the effect of the seal on executed instruments such as releases. This discussion does not contain an exhaustive list of the relevant kinds of statutes. In addition to the groups above there exist additional statutes of miscellaneous types. Also there are variations within these general groups.

Not all statutes of the same type have received similar interpretations. For example, the New Jersey legislature enacted legislation to the effect that the seal is merely presumptive evidence of consideration. This was held not to deprive a sealed gratuitous promise of its efficacy if no bargained-for exchange was intended.[8] A subsequent statutory change was enacted to the effect that in an action on a sealed promise, the defendant may prove the absence of consideration with the same effect as if the instrument were not sealed. In the face of this statute the court still adhered to its view that no consideration is necessary on a sealed instrument.[9]

It is apparent that the different kinds of statutes may give rise to different results. Thus, for example, if a jurisdiction has not overruled the common law principle that a sealed instrument may only be modified or rescinded by an instrument under seal,[10] a statute abolishing the effect of a seal would obliterate this rule, but a statute which modifies the effect of a seal by providing that it is presumptive evidence of consideration would have no direct effect on this rule.

The same analysis would apply in the case of the common law rule that an undisclosed principal may not sue or be sued upon a sealed instrument. Under a statute providing that the seal gives rise to a presumption of consideration, this common law rule would not be changed. (Of course, the courts could change the common law rule as has been done by courts in other jurisdictions).[11] Indeed, the legislative policy to reduce the sanctity of a sealed instrument should be given effect even as to rules such as this. A similar analysis is applicable to the rules

---

7. Two states, Mississippi and New Mexico, have statutes which appear to have elevated all written contracts to the level of sealed instruments. In each state, however, the court decisions must be consulted to determine the interpretation given to the local statute.

The rebuttable presumption of consideration conferred on all written promises can have a significant impact upon the decision of a concrete case. See Patterson v. Chapman, 179 Cal. 203, 176 P. 37, 2 ALR 1467 (1918).

8. Aller v. Aller, 40 N.J.L. 446 (1878); see 3 Corbin § 10.18, at 424 (Holmes 1996); 1 Williston § 2:16. Cf. Cochran v. Taylor,

273 N.Y. 172, 7 N.E.2d 89 (1937), decided under the former New York statute that a seal created a presumption of consideration. It was held that the parties were estopped from contradicting a recital of $1.00 as consideration. An estoppel is not created in New York by such a recital on an unsealed instrument. See § 4.6 supra.

9. Zirk v. Nohr, 127 N.J.L. 217, 21 A.2d 766 (1941); but see Linder v. Commissioner of Internal Revenue, 68 T.C. 792 (1977).

10. See § 7.8 supra.

11. See Nalbandian v. Hanson Restaurant & Lounge, 369 Mass. 150, 338 N.E.2d 335 (1975).

retained in some jurisdictions that a third party beneficiary may not sue on a sealed instrument[12] and that an agent's authority to execute a sealed instrument must be granted by a sealed instrument.[13]

12. See § 7.8 supra.

13. Restatement, Second, Agency § 28 cmt g.

Chapter 8

CAPACITY OF PARTIES

Table of Sections

Table of Sections

§ 8.1   Introduction

There are certain classes of persons whose contractual capacity is limited. Their agreements are either void, or more often, voidable. These classes include infants and persons suffering from mental infirmity.[1] In addition, there are limitations upon one's ability to contract with oneself.

A.   INFANTS

Table of Sections

§ 8.1

1. Other classes exist. Formerly, the agreements of married women were void. This disability has largely been eliminated by statutory enactments. The statutes are compiled in 5 Williston §§ 11:5. Some disabilities of married women may continue to exist in various jurisdictions. See Rs. 2d § 12 cmt d.

In a number of jurisdictions a spendthrift may be placed under guardianship. The ward's contracts are voidable. See Lilienthal v. Kaufman, 239 Or. 1, 395 P.2d 543 (1964).

Convicts are under disabilities which vary from state to state. See 5 Williston § 11:12; Note, 14 Colum.L.Rev. 592 (1914); Note, 5 Cornell L.Q. 320 (1920).

The problem of capacity to contract arises as to corporations in connection with the doctrine of *ultra vires;* that is, in relation to agreements entered into outside the scope of the powers of the corporation. This doctrine is extensively discussed in works on corporation law. For summary treatment, see 2 Williston § 11:10. As to defunct corporations, see Animazing Entertainment v. Louis Lofredo Assocs., 88 F.Supp.2d 265 (S.D.N.Y.2000).

A related problem exists in relation to the contracts of municipal corporations and other public agencies. Public contracts not awarded pursuant to the procedures provided by law are void or voidable. There is much disagreement in the cases as to whether and under what circumstances the private party who has performed under such a contract may recover in quasi contract. Extensive discussion and citations will be found in American–LaFrance v. Philadelphia, 183 Miss. 207, 184 So. 620 (1938); Hudson City Contracting v. Jersey City Incinerator Auth., 17 N.J. 297, 111 A.2d 385 (1955); Federal Paving v. Wauwatosa, 231 Wis. 655, 286 N.W. 546 (1939). Some jurisdictions will in almost no case grant such relief. See Seif v. Long Beach, 286 N.Y. 382, 387–88, 36 N.E.2d 630, 632 (1941); but see Gerzof v. Sweeney, 22 N.Y.2d 297, 292 N.Y.S.2d 640, 239 N.E.2d 521, 33 ALR3d 387 (1968). See also Haight, 14 Syracuse L.Rev. 426 (1963). Others are quite liberal. See Campbell v. Tennessee Val. Auth., 421 F.2d 293 (5th Cir.1969). See also 10A McQuillin The Law of Municipal Corporations (3d ed. 1990); Gitleman, 20 Ark.L.Rev. 292 (1967); Vaubel, 2 Akron L.Rev. 20 (1968); Note, 19 S.Dak.L.Rev. 485 (1974).

§ 8.2 Introduction

The law often preserves archaic terminology. In everyday language we distinguish between adults and minors. Lawyers, however, refer to minors as "infants." If this label were changed, volumes of digests, texts and encyclopedias would immediately become obsolete. The age of majority has been changed in the last half of the twentieth century. At common law, a person remained an infant until the age of twenty-one.[1] However, legislation enacted mostly in the 1970's has set the age of majority at eighteen in almost all jurisdictions.[2] There are two other rules concerning the length of infancy. In accordance with the maxim that the law often disregards fractions of a day, it is commonly held that one's infancy ends at the very first moment of the day preceding one's eighteenth birthday.[3] Thus if A was born on September 14, 2001, A's infancy will end after the stroke of midnight on the morning of September 13, 2019. Emancipation of the infant does not enlarge capacity to contract.[4]

Like the age of majority, the legal effect of contracts that infants have entered into has changed over the years. Formerly, the rule was that such contracts were void.[5] Later, it was held that they were voidable but that certain kinds of transactions entered into by an infant such as the appointment of an agent, the execution of a promissory note, and an agreement to be surety were void.[6] It is now almost everywhere agreed that even such transactions are merely voidable rather than void.[7] Not

§ 8.2

1. Gastonia Personnel v. Rogers, 276 N.C. 279, 172 S.E.2d 19, 41 ALR3d 1062 (1970); Rs. 2d § 14 cmt. a.

2. The Legal Status of Adolescents 1980 (U.S.Dept. of Health and Human Services 1981) p. 41.

3. Turnbull v. Bonkowski, 419 F.2d 104 (9th Cir.1969); Nelson v. Sandkamp, 227 Minn. 177, 34 N.W.2d 640, 5 ALR2d 1136 (1948); Rs. 2d § 14. In several jurisdictions, an infant attains majority at the first moment of the eighteenth anniversary of birth. See In re Harris, 5 Cal.4th 813, 21 Cal. Rptr.2d 373, 855 P.2d 391 (1993); 5 Williston § 9:3; but see Fields v. Fairbanks North Star, 818 P.2d 658 (Alaska 1991) (start counting the day after one's birth).

4. Commonwealth v. Graham, 157 Mass. 73, 31 N.E. 706 (1892); Daubert v. Mosley, 487 P.2d 353, 56 ALR3d 1328 (Okl. 1971); Schoenung v. Gallet, 206 Wis. 52, 238 N.W. 852, 78 ALR 387 (1931). Emancipation occurs upon the express or implied parental renunciation of their right of control over the infant and particularly of the infant's obligation to provide the parent with services and to turn earnings over to them. See Katz, Schroeder & Sidman, Emancipating Our Children, 7 Family L.Q.

211 (1973). Emancipation may also relieve the parent of the duty to support. See Accent Service v. Ebsen, 209 Neb. 94, 306 N.W.2d 575 (1981); Note, 31 Idaho L.Rev. 205 (1994). In most jurisdictions emancipation also occurs by operation of law upon marriage. See 5 Williston § 9:4; but see Berks County Children and Youth Services v. Rowan, 428 Pa.Super. 448, 631 A.2d 615 (1993). In some jurisdictions it is also held that contractual capacity is attained upon marriage, but this is a distinctly minority view. Succession of Hecker, 191 La. 302, 185 So. 32 (1938).

Several jurisdictions permit judicial emancipation upon the petition of the minor and the decree may also remove in whole or in part the lack of capacity. See 1938 Report of the New York Law Revision Commission 139, for discussion of such statutes.

5. For the historical development of this rule, see the learned opinion in Henry v. Root, 33 N.Y. 526 (1865); 5 Williston § 9:5.

6. There are statutory exceptions making certain contracts void. See Moran v. Williston Co-op. Credit Union, 420 N.W.2d 353 (N.D.1988).

7. See Casey v. Kastel, 237 N.Y. 305, 142 N.E. 671, 31 ALR 995 (1924); 5 Williston § 9:5; Rs. 2d § 14.

only an executory contract, but also an executed transaction, such as a sale, conveyance or release[8] may be avoided.[9]

The power of avoidance resides only in the infants[10] or in their heirs, administrators or executors.[11] An adult party to a transaction cannot avoid the contract on the ground of the other's infancy.[12] Occasional decisions permitting a parent or other guardian to disaffirm the infant's contract can, however, be found and are sound if the infant is not emancipated.[13]

Because of the one-sided power of avoidance held by the infant it might seem anomalous to speak in terms of the limited capacity of infants. To some observers it has seemed that the infant has capacity to contract coupled with an additional power of disaffirmance. It has been said that "the law confers a privilege rather than a disability."[14] This, however, represents but one side of the coin. Adult parties frequently will refuse to contract with or sell to infants because an infant is incapable of giving legal assurance of non-disaffirmability.[15] From this point of view the infant is under both a legal and practical disability.[16] Protection, as is so often the case, involves "limitations on the individual liberty of the protected person."[17] Some have strenuously argued that the price of this protection is too high and that the interests of infants of any age would be best served by granting them full freedom of contract.[18]

8. Addario v. Sandquist, 1998 WL 161176 (Conn.Sup.); Mitchell v. Mitchell, 963 S.W.2d 222 (Ky.App.1998) (release by married minor); Dilallo v. Riding Safely, 687 So.2d 353 (1997) (pre-injury release); Y.W. v. National Super Markets, 876 S.W.2d 785 (Mo.App.1994).

9. Even a sheriff's sale was held to be voidable in G.M.A.C. v. Stotsky, 60 Misc.2d 451, 303 N.Y.S.2d 463 (1969).

10. Quality Motors v. Hays, 216 Ark. 264, 225 S.W.2d 326 (1949) (father cannot disaffirm for son); Oliver v. Houdlet, 13 Mass. 237, 7 Am.Dec. 134 (1816) (guardian may not disaffirm for ward); Dostal v. Magee, 272 Wis. 509, 76 N.W.2d 349 (1956) (father cannot ratify for son).

11. Gendreau v. North American Life & Cas., 158 Minn. 259, 197 N.W. 257 (1924); Eagan v. Scully, 29 A.D. 617, 51 N.Y.S. 680 (1898), aff'd; cf. Kline v. L'Amoureux, 2 Paige Ch. 419 (N.Y.1831).

12. Holt v. Ward Clarencieux, 93 Eng. Rep. 954 (K.B.1732); Shaw v. Philbrick, 129 Me. 259, 151 A. 423, 74 ALR 290 (1930). For the relationship between this rule and the doctrine of "mutuality of obligation," see § 4.12 supra.

A contract between two infants is voidable at the option of either. Hurwitz v. Barr, 193 A.2d 360 (D.C.App.1963) (sale of motor scooter).

13. Crockett Motor v. Thompson, 177 Ark. 495, 6 S.W.2d 834 (1928); Hughes v. Murphy, 5 Ga.App. 328, 63 S.E. 231 (1908) (action brought by guardian to disaffirm sale permissible although infant objected); Boudreaux v. State Farm, 385 So.2d 480 (La.App.1980); Champa v. New York Central Mut. Relief Ass'n, 57 Ohio App. 522, 15 N.E.2d 172 (1936).

14. Simpson, Contracts 216 (2d ed. 1965).

15. As a practical matter the adult party may refuse to contract with the infant unless the infant's parent or other responsible adult agrees to become jointly liable with the infant. In such a case, disaffirmance by the infant does not discharge the co-obligor. Campbell v. Fender, 218 Ark. 290, 235 S.W.2d 957 (1951); 10 Williston § 1214; but if the contract has been avoided and the status quo restored, the co-obligor may be discharged. Allen v. Small, 129 Vt. 77, 271 A.2d 840, 44 ALR3d 1412 (1970).

16. See Warner Bros. Pictures v. Brodel, 31 Cal.2d 766, 192 P.2d 949, 3 ALR2d 691 (1948), cert. denied.

17. Dicey, Law and Public Opinion in England 151 (2d ed. 1962).

18. Holt, Escape from Childhood, 172, 236–37 (1974); see also, Navin, 50 N.Car. L.Rev. 517, 544–45 (1972) (suggesting age of majority of fourteen years); Mehler, 11

A comprehensive enactment in New South Wales goes very far in this direction although it retains some protection for infants regarding contracts that are not beneficial to them.[19]

After the infant has exercised the power to avoid the contract, the transaction is treated for many purposes as if it were void from the beginning. Thus, by disaffirming a conveyance the infant may reclaim the real property from a subsequent purchaser who purchased in good faith and without notice of the fact that an infant had preceded the vendor in the chain of title.[20] So also an infant may disaffirm liability on a negotiable instrument even as to a holder in due course.[21] But this rule does not apply to sales of goods. The Uniform Sales Act provided that an infant's power of disaffirmance had no effect on a subsequent bona fide purchaser who obtained the goods for value.[22] The UCC has continued this rule.[23] On the other hand, an infant has no power to grant an irrevocable discharge. Thus, where an insurance company paid an infant beneficiary of a life insurance policy, it had to pay again when she attained her majority.[24]

Where the minor's employment required a work permit, a contract in violation of that requirement was held to be illegal and adult guarantor of the infant's performance was held not to be liable.[25]

§ 8.3   Transactions That the Infant Cannot Avoid

There are certain situations where the infant cannot avoid the contract.[1] No clear-cut test can be formulated except to state that the infant cannot disaffirm certain contracts because public policy so requires, or because a statute so provides, or because the infant has done or promised to do something which the law would compel, even in the absence of the contract.[2] Thus, if a minor male contracts to support his out-of-wedlock child, this promise cannot be disaffirmed as he is under a legal obligation to support his children.[3] Also, an infant employee's promise not to utilize secret customer lists will be enforced by injunction because the promise merely defines the scope of a legal duty existing

U.Kan.L.Rev. 361, 373 (1963); Edge, 1 Ga. L.Rev. 205 (1966); Note, 57 UMKC L.Rev. 145 (1988).

19. See Harland, 7 Sydney L.Rev. 41 (1973); Pearce, 44 Austl.L.J. 269 (1970).

20. Ware v. Mobley, 190 Ga. 249, 9 S.E.2d 67 (1940) (collecting cases); but see Matter of LeBovici, 171 Misc.2d 604, 655 N.Y.S.2d 305 (1997) (assignee of mortgagee takes free of the defense of mental illness).

21. UCC § 3–305(a)(1)(i) (1990 revision). But the infant may not assert any claim against a holder in due course predicated upon infancy. UCC § 3–202 (1990 revision).

22. Uniform Sales Act § 24; see Jones v. Caldwell, 216 Ark. 260, 225 S.W.2d 323, 16

ALR2d 1416 (1949), 28 Chi.-Kent L.Rev. 253 (1950).

23. UCC § 2–403.

24. Iverson v. Scholl, 136 Ill.App.3d 962, 483 N.E.2d 893, 91 Ill.Dec. 407 (1985).

25. Metropolitan Model Agency v. Rayder, 168 Misc.2d 324, 643 N.Y.S.2d 923 (1996).

§ 8.3

1. Rs. 2d § 14 cmt b.

2. 5 Williston § 9:6; see e.g., McKinney's N.Y. Gen'l Oblig. L. §§ 3–101 to 3–109.

3. Gavin v. Burton, 8 Ind. 69 (1856); Bordentown v. Wallace, 50 N.J.L. 13, 11 A. 267 (1887).

apart from the express contractual provision.[4] It has been held that a minor who was an employee cannot on termination of employment disaffirm an arbitration clause.[5] Minors are liable for the necessities of life supplied to their children. Consequently, a 17 year old mother was held liable for necessary medical care for her child.[6] Infants are generally held liable on their bail bonds on the ground that public policy would otherwise be offended.[7] A small number of cases hold an infant contractually liable if the infant has received benefits under the contract.[8]

By statute, most jurisdiction have created certain exception to the general rule of the voidable nature of infant's contract. Insurance legislation, banking laws, educational loan statutes, federal and state legislation regarding military enlistments,[9] and the like, must be consulted. Some statutes provide that a contract made by an infant may not be disaffirmed when it has been approved by a court.[10] Generally speaking, court approval is required for the settlement of tort claims.[11]

To be distinguished from legislation permitting infants to contract are statutes permitting a guardian to sell the property of an infant under specified conditions. Usually a court order is required to effectuate such a sale, and when made pursuant to the statutory procedure, the sale is not disaffirmable.[12] To facilitate gifts of securities to minors, almost all jurisdictions have enacted the Uniform Transfer to Minors Act which permits a custodian of property given to the minor pursuant to the terms of the Act to sell the infant's property and to reinvest the proceeds with great freedom and without the possibility of disaffirmance.[13]

Although parents lack the general ability to release their childrens' tort claims without court approval, it has been held that a parent can bind a child to a pre-injury exculpation clause to enable the child to participate in amateur sports, ski trips, and the like.[14] This, however, seems to be a distinctly minority view.[15]

4. Mutual Milk & Cream v. Prigge, 112 A.D. 652, 98 N.Y.S. 458 (1906) (decided on other grounds); Career Placement v. Vaus, 77 Misc.2d 788, 354 N.Y.S.2d 764 (1974).

5. Sheller v. Frank's Nursery & Crafts, 957 F.Supp. 150 (N.D.Ill.1997).

6. Ex Parte Odem, 537 So.2d 919 (Ala. 1988).

7. Commonwealth v. Harris, 11 Pa.D. & C. 2, 77 U.Pa.L.Rev. 279 (1928).

8. See § 8.9 infra.

9. See U.S. v. Williams, 302 U.S. 46 (1937), 12 St. John's L.Rev. 346 (1938).

10. West's Ann.Cal.Civ.Code § 36(2) (contracts of employment as an entertainer or athlete); West's Ann.Cal.Labor Code § 1700.37 (contracts with theatrical employment agencies and artists' managers); McKinney's N.Y. Arts & Cult. Affairs L § 35.03 (contracts with infant athletes or artists). See also Deville v. Federal Sav. Bank, 635 So.2d 195 (La.1994). In several

states, a court may in whole or in part remove the disabilities of infants. See § 8.2 n.4 supra.

11. See, e.g., McKinney's N.Y.C.P.L.R. 1207.

12. See 4 Tiffany, Real Property § 1244 (3d ed. 1939).

13. Where enacted, the Act supersedes the Uniform Gifts to Minors Act. see, Allison, Uniform Transfer to Minors Act—New and Improved, but Shortcomings Still Exist, 10 U. Ark. L.R. L.J.339 (1987); Comment, 66 N.C.L.Rev. 1349 (1988). The Act treats 21 as the age of majority.

14. Zivich v. Mentor Soccer Club, 82 Ohio St.3d 367, 696 N.E.2d 201 (1998).

15. Holding such exculpations to be void: Cooper v. Aspen Skiing, 48 P.3d 1229 (Colo.2002); Meyer v. Naperville Manner, 262 Ill.App.3d 141, 634 N.E.2d 411, 199 Ill.Dec. 572 (1994); Alexander v. Kendall

§ 8.4 Avoidance and Ratification

As we have seen, the general rule is that an infant's contract is voidable by the infant. The exercise of this power of avoidance is often called disaffirmance. The effective surrender of this power is known as ratification. An effective ratification obviously cannot take place prior to the attainment of majority; any purported ratification prior to that time suffers from the same infirmity of voidability as the contract itself.[1]

An infant may disaffirm a contract at any time prior to ratification. A disaffirmance of a contract is irrevocable.[2] Except as to conveyances of real property, it is clear that a disaffirmance may effectively be made during infancy and once made is irrevocable. It seems to be the weight of authority, however, that a conveyance of real property executed by an infant may be disaffirmed only after majority,[3] but sound modern authority permits disaffirmance during minority.[4] The older rule, based on a desire to protect the infant's interests, has a tendency to keep land unmarketable for an excessive period.

No particular form of language or conduct is required to effectuate a disaffirmance. Any manifestation of unwillingness to be bound by the transaction is sufficient.[5] It may be oral.[6] Often disaffirmance is manifested for the first time by a plea of infancy as a defense,[7] or by the commencement of an action to set aside the transaction.[8]

The entire contract must be avoided. The infant is not entitled to enforce portions that are favorable, and at the same time disaffirm other portions that are burdensome.[9] An infant who is a third party beneficiary cannot disaffirm portions of a contract while claiming benefits under it.[10]

Central School Dist., 221 A.D.2d 898, 634 N.Y.S.2d 318 (1995); Scott v. Pacific West Mountain Resort, 119 Wn.2d 484, 834 P.2d 6 (1992).

§ 8.4

1. Elkhorn Coal v. Tackett, 261 Ky. 795, 88 S.W.2d 943 (1935); Morris v. Glaser, 106 N.J.Eq. 585, 151 A. 766 (1930), aff'd.

2. Smith v. Wade, 169 Neb. 710, 100 N.W.2d 770 (1960); McNaughton v. Granite City Auto Sales, 108 Vt. 130, 183 A. 340 (1936). Michigan appears to stand alone in holding that no effective disaffirmance may occur until majority. Poli v. National Bank, 355 Mich. 17, 93 N.W.2d 925 (1959).

3. 5 Williston § 9:13.

4. New Domain Oil & Gas v. McKinney, 188 Ky. 183, 221 S.W. 245 (1920) (infant's action to set aside conveyance). Even in jurisdictions in which it is held that the infant may not disaffirm during minority it has been held that the infant may enter onto the land to take profits or recover the income of the premises conveyed. Sims v. Bardoner, 86 Ind. 87, 44 Am.Rep. 263

(1882); Bool v. Mix, 17 Wend. 119, 31 Am. Dec. 285 (N.Y.1836).

5. Tracey v. Brown, 265 Mass. 163, 163 N.E. 885 (1928); McNaughton v. Granite City Auto Sales, 108 Vt. 130, 183 A. 340 (1936).

6. But see Ray v. Acme Finance, 367 So.2d 186 (Miss.1979) (statutory writing requirement).

7. Lesnick v. Pratt, 116 Vt. 477, 80 A.2d 663 (1951).

8. Del Santo v. Bristol County Stadium, 273 F.2d 605 (1st Cir.1960) (disaffirmance of release accomplished by bringing suit on underlying negligence claim); accord, Slaney v. Westwood Auto, 366 Mass. 688, 322 N.E.2d 768, 89 ALR3d 433 (1975).

9. Power v. Allstate Ins., 312 S.C. 381, 440 S.E.2d 406 (1994) (cannot disaffirm rejection of uninsured motorist coverage while keeping policy coverage); Dairyland County Mut. Ins. v. Roman, 498 S.W.2d 154 (Tex.1973).

10. Leong v. Kaiser Foundation Hosps., 71 Haw. 240, 788 P.2d 164 (1990).

Ratification may take place in three ways: failure to make a timely disaffirmance, express ratification, and conduct manifesting an intent to ratify. No consideration is required to create an effective ratification.[11]

(a) Failure to Make a Timely Disaffirmance

Leaving aside for the moment special rules in connection with conveyances, an infant may disaffirm contracts until a reasonable time after reaching majority.[12] Failure to do so is a ratification. What is a reasonable time is often a question of fact dependent on such circumstances as whether there has been any performance by either or both parties, the nature of the transaction and the extent to which the other party has been prejudiced by any extensive delay in disaffirming.[13]

A good many cases speak in terms of a firm rule that distinguishes between executory and executed contracts. According to these cases, executed contracts are automatically ratified and thus binding if not disaffirmed within a reasonable time after majority, but executory contracts are not binding unless ratified by words or conduct after majority.[14] The rule is a carryover from the older view than an infant's executory contract is void rather than voidable.[15] It is apparent, however, that this "rule" as to executory contracts is not applied when the infant's failure to disaffirm within a reasonable time after attaining majority works injustice on the other party.[16]

Ordinarily, however, if the infant has obtained no benefits under the contract[17] as will usually be the case if the contract is wholly executory or executed only by the infant, there is no reason to bar the infant from disaffirming at any time up until the time the statute of limitations has run. Where it has been executed by the adult or by both parties, it will ordinarily be inequitable to permit the infant to retain the benefits of the contract for a long time and then disaffirm. However, for example, it has been pointed out that where pursuant to contract the infant received and paid for services during minority, there is no reason not to permit the infant to disaffirm long after reaching majority as the infant's

---

11. Rs. 2d § 85; see § 5.8 supra.

12. In some jurisdictions this is the rule by statute and is applicable to executory and executed transactions. See Pottawatomie Airport & Flying Serv. v. Winger, 176 Kan. 445, 271 P.2d 754 (1954). Similar statutory provisions exist elsewhere. 1938 Report of the New York Law Revision Commission 132–137.

13. Harrod v. Kelly Adjustment, 179 A.2d 431 (D.C.App.1962); Adamowski v. Curtiss–Wright Flying Serv., 300 Mass. 281, 15 N.E.2d 467 (1938); Johnson v. Storie, 32 Neb. 610, 49 N.W. 371 (1891); International Text–Book v. Connelly, 206 N.Y. 188, 99 N.E. 722 (1912); Merchants' Credit Bureau v. Kaoru Akiyama, 64 Utah 364, 230 P. 1017 (1924); and see Wooldridge v. Lavoie,

79 N.H. 21, 104 A. 346 (1918), where disaffirmance at trial was deemed reasonable.

14. Nichols & Shepard v. Snyder, 78 Minn. 502, 81 N.W. 516 (1900); Warwick Mun. Employees Credit Union v. McAllister, 110 R.I. 399, 293 A.2d 516 (1972).

15. See Henry v. Root, 33 N.Y. 526 (1865), where the court traces the historical changes in the law of infants' contracts.

16. E.g., Jones v. Godwin, 187 S.C. 510, 198 S.E. 36 (1938) (in reliance upon a mortgage executed by infant, creditor advanced money to infant's father after infant attained majority).

17. Whether or not the infant had received any benefit was said to be the test in Cassella v. Tiberio, 150 Ohio St. 27, 80 N.E.2d 426, 5 ALR2d 1 (1948).

inaction constituted neither benefit to the infant nor prejudice to the other.[18] In summary, the true rule, reflecting what the courts have done in fact, has been expressed in a Texas case in terms of "the effect which mere nonaction by the minor has upon the respective rights or interest of the parties, rather than upon arbitrary test of whether the contract be regarded as executed or executory in whole or in part."[19]

In a good number of cases often cited as announcing a rule on the question, close reading of the opinion indicates that the court merely held that there were sufficient facts to sustain the verdict of the jury or findings of fact of the trial court,[20] and ordinarily the question is the factual one of whether, because of the passage of time after attaining full legal capacity, it is unreasonable to disaffirm. However, if different inferences cannot reasonably be drawn from the facts it becomes a question of law.[21]

It is the general rule that conveyances of real property are ratified if not disaffirmed within a reasonable time after reaching majority,[22] but many cases hold that in the absence of estoppel, the former infant has the right to avoid the conveyance until the statute of limitations has run.[23]

(b) Express Ratification

In addition to ratification by failing to disaffirm, a contract can be explicitly ratified. Unless a statute indicates otherwise, an express ratification cam be oral.[24] It has been said frequently that "ratification depends upon intent"[25] and, as to contracts not yet performed by the former infant, many cases hold that a mere acknowledgment of the

18. Terrace v. Calhoun, 37 Ill.App.3d 757, 347 N.E.2d 315 (1976); Adamowski v. Curtiss–Wright Flying Serv., 300 Mass. 281, 15 N.E.2d 467 (1938).

19. Walker v. Stokes Bros. & Co., 262 S.W. 158 (Tex.Civ.App.1924); and see Terrace v. Calhoun, 37 Ill.App.3d 757, 347 N.E.2d 315 (1976).

20. Adamowski v. Curtiss–Wright Flying Serv., 300 Mass. 281, 15 N.E.2d 467 (1938); Johnson v. Storie, 32 Neb. 610, 49 N.W. 371 (1891); International Text–Book v. Connelly, 206 N.Y. 188, 99 N.E. 722 (1912).

21. Nationwide Mut. Ins. v. Chantos, 25 N.C.App. 482, 214 S.E.2d 438 (1975), cert. denied.

22. Sims v. Everhardt, 102 U.S. (12 Otto) 300 (1880); Martin v. Elkhorn Coal, 227 Ky. 623, 13 S.W.2d 780 (1929); Sprecher v. Sprecher, 206 Md. 108, 110 A.2d 509 (1955); Muncey v. Norfolk & Western Ry., 106 W.Va. 348, 145 S.E. 581 (1928); cf. 5 Williston § 9:17.

23. Gibson v. Hall, 260 Ala. 539, 71 So.2d 532 (1954); Walker v. Ellis, 212 Ark. 498, 207 S.W.2d 39 (1947); Mott v. Iossa,

119 N.J.Eq. 185, 181 A. 689 (1935). Of course, many of the same factors which go into a finding of whether there is an estoppel are the same as those which go into a determination under the majority rule of whether a reasonable time has elapsed. The equitable doctrine of laches can also be applicable and much the same factors as create an estoppel give rise to the application of that doctrine. Curtis v. Curtis, 398 Ill. 442, 75 N.E.2d 881 (1947). Very often it is unclear which rule the court is applying. E.g., Green v. Green, 69 N.Y. 553, 25 Am. Rep. 233 (1877).

24. Statutes requiring that a ratification be in writing were enacted in Arkansas, Kentucky, Maine, Mississippi, Missouri, New Jersey, South Carolina, Virginia and West Virginia. See 1938 Report of the New York Law Revision Commission 139.

25. International Text–Book v. Connelly, 206 N.Y. 188, 99 N.E. 722 (1912). If ratification occurs because of failure to make a timely disaffirmance, it is obvious that subjective intention is immaterial.

contract is not enough[26] and that nothing less than a promise will suffice to expressly ratify a contract.[27] Still, a jury may be entitled to find that a promise can reasonably be implied from the language and circumstances.[28] It has been pointed out in an able opinion that the requisite that there be a new promise is an erroneous carryover from the obsolete view that the contracts of infants are void,[29] and that therefore a ratification must, by analogy, meet the requisites of a new promise to pay a debt discharged by operation of law.[30]

The authorities agree that if the contract is fully executed, an acknowledgment or other words consistent with an intention to stand on the transaction is sufficient to constitute a ratification.[31]

(c) Ratification by Conduct

Ratification by failure to make a timely disaffirmance, previously discussed, may be considered a kind of ratification by conduct, at least if inaction be deemed conduct. But other types of conduct may give rise to a ratification, and frequently the question is for the jury to decide. Retention and enjoyment of property received pursuant to contract for more than a reasonable time after attaining majority involves both kinds of conduct, that is, active use of the property coupled with a failure to disaffirm. Under such circumstances, a ratification will often be found to have occurred.[32] Also, receipt of performance from the other party after attaining majority will be normally considered to be a ratification.[33] On the other hand, part payment or other performance by the infant, without more, will not ordinarily be deemed a ratification.[34] Frequently, the question is for the jury to determine.

§ 8.5 Effect Upon Ratification of Ignorance of Law or Fact

Ratification is ineffective unless the former infant knows the facts

26. E.g., Lee v. Thompson, 124 Fla. 494, 168 So. 848 (1936). See 2 Page, Contracts § 1372 (2d ed. 1920): "By the weight of authority the rule in ratification of an infant's contract * * * is that mere acknowledgment that the obligation has been incurred, or even a part payment thereon is not a ratification. Even payment of interest, part payment of principal, and a mere acknowledgment of the debt, or a statement, 'I owe a debt and you will get your pay' was held not to be a ratification." (Citations omitted).

27. Thus, it is generally held that part payment made by an infant after attaining majority is not, without more, a ratification. International Accountants Soc'y v. Santana, 166 La. 671, 117 So. 768, 59 ALR 276 (1928).

28. Camp v. Bank of Bentonville, 230 Ark. 414, 323 S.W.2d 556 (1959); Sanchez v.

Sanchez, 464 So.2d 1009 (La.App.1985); Hook v. Harmon Nat. Real Estate, 250 A.D. 689, 295 N.Y.S. 249 (1937), amended.

29. Henry v. Root, 33 N.Y. 526 (1865). Inconsistent language in subsequent New York opinions should be disapproved.

30. On these requisites, see § 5.7 supra.

31. E.g., Lee v. Thompson, 124 Fla. 494, 168 So. 848 (1936).

32. Jones v. Dressel, 623 P.2d 370 (Colo. 1981); Fletcher v. Marshall, 260 Ill.App.3d 673, 632 N.E.2d 1105, 198 Ill.Dec. 494 (1994) (lease ratified by occupancy for 1½ months after majority); Bobby Floars Toyota v. Smith, 48 N.C.App. 580, 269 S.E.2d 320 (1980); and see notes 16–19 supra.

33. Turner v. Little, 70 Ga.App. 567, 28 S.E.2d 871 (1944); Clark v. Kidd, 148 Ky. 479, 146 S.W. 1097 (1912).

34. See notes 25–27 supra.

upon which liability depends,[1] but the cases are in conflict as to whether there must be knowledge that the law grants the power to avoid the original contract. Perhaps the majority of cases have applied the maxim that everyone is presumed to know the law and have held that lack of knowledge of the law is immaterial.[2] A significant number of cases, however, have held that there can be no ratification without full knowledge of the legal consequences.[3]

§ 8.6 Obligations of Restitution Upon Disaffirmance

A variety of questions and a number of conflicting views exist as to the adjustment of the economic relations of the parties after an infant has disaffirmed. If either or both parties have rendered some performance, questions of restitution may arise.[1] The analysis often depends on whether the infant is the plaintiff or the defendant.

(a) Infant as Defendant

Suppose A, an infant, has purchased on credit an automobile from B.[2] A makes some payments but at some point effectively disaffirms this contract and B brings an action for the balance of the price. A's avoidance is an affirmative defense.[3] It would be an obvious injustice, however, if the infant defendant were to be allowed to retain the automobile while escaping the obligation to pay. Thus, it is everywhere recognized that the infant is under an obligation to return any consideration which the infant has received and still possesses.[4] But this rule applies only in situations where the infant still possesses the consideration. If the infant no longer has the consideration, there in no obligation to return it. This is true even if it has been squandered, wasted or negligently destroyed.[5] Also, because services received cannot be re-

---

§ 8.5

1. An infant partner who continued to accept partnership benefits after minority was held not to have ratified outstanding bad checks of which the partner was unaware. Tobey v. Wood, 123 Mass. 88, 25 Am.Rep. 27 (1877).

2. Shepherd v. Shepherd, 408 Ill. 364, 97 N.E.2d 273 (1951); Campbell v. Sears, Roebuck, 307 Pa. 365, 161 A. 310 (1932); Annot., 5 ALR 137 (1920).

3. Trader v. Lowe, 45 Md. 1 (1876); International Text–Book v. Connelly, 206 N.Y. 188, 99 N.E. 722 (1912). An intermediate position was taken in Ogborn v. Hoffman, 52 Ind. 439 (1876), where it was held that the presumption that everyone knows the law is rebuttable.

§ 8.6

1. See Rs. 2d § 14 cmt c; Rs. Restitution §§ 61–62.

2. It is assumed here that the automobile is not a necessary. If it is a necessary other rules come into play. See § 8.8 infra.

3. Clark, Code Pleading 611, 621 (2d ed. 1947).

4. It is generally agreed that the infant need not tender restitution of the consideration as a condition precedent to a defensive plea of infancy. 5 Williston § 9:16.

"When property is bought by an infant on credit, and being sued for the price, he pleads infancy, the seller may recover at law the property, the title being revested in him by the result of the suit for the price * * *" Evans v. Morgan, 69 Miss. 328, 329, 12 So. 270, 270–71 (1891) (citations omitted).

5. Terrace v. Calhoun, 37 Ill.App.3d 757, 347 N.E.2d 315 (1976) (because services cannot be returned, no duty of restitution); Drude v. Curtis, 183 Mass. 317, 67 N.E. 317, 62 LRA 755 (1903) (rule applied where both parties were infants); Webster St. Ptshp. v. Sheridan, 220 Neb. 9, 368 N.W.2d 439 (1985) (apartment lease); but see Wheeless v. Eudora Bank, 256 Ark. 644, 509 S.W.2d 532 (1974) (statute requiring full restitution by infant).

turned, there is no obligation to return or account for the services.[6] Thus, the infant purchaser of the automobile on credit is not accountable for the automobile if it has been wrecked.[7] The rule absolving the infant of the obligation to return the consideration is subject to one exception. If the infant has exchanged or sold the property and still possesses the property received in the exchange, the infant will be liable for such portion of it as is represented by the exchange or investment.[8]

(b) Infant as Plaintiff

Suppose that instead of purchasing an automobile on credit, the infant purchases the automobile for $25,000, pays cash and proceeds to wreck it. If the infant then disaffirms and brings an action for restitution to recover the purchase price, application of the rule that an infant need account only for that part of the consideration still retained would seem to dictate that the infant may have full recovery of the $25,000 upon return of the wreck. This is the traditional view.[9] Many courts, however, do not follow this approach, distinguishing between cases where the infant is the plaintiff from those where the infant is the defendant. They have ruled that the infant's recovery will be offset by the value of the use of the automobile or the amount of depreciation in value of the vehicle.[10] Thus, the infant who disaffirmed the contract of purchase could recover only for the value of the wreck. Although the texts have not usually emphasized the distinction in result based upon

---

6. Mitchell v. Mizerski, 1995 WL 118429 (Neb.App.1995).

7. 5 Williston § 9:16; see Swalberg v. Hannegan, 883 P.2d 931 (Utah App.1994) (infant need not account for depreciation or value of use of truck).

8. MacGreal v. Taylor, 167 U.S. 688 (1897) (subrogation theory); Whitman v. Allen, 123 Me. 1, 121 A. 160, 36 ALR 776 (1923) (infant had proceeds of sale); Evans v. Morgan, 69 Miss. 328, 12 So. 270 (1891) (infant in business purchased goods from plaintiffs on credit and goods were intermingled with other stock; plaintiffs could execute on entire stock).

9. Quality Motors v. Hays, 216 Ark. 264, 225 S.W.2d 326 (1949) (wrecked automobile); Weisbrook v. Clyde C. Netzley, Inc., 58 Ill.App.3d 862, 16 Ill.Dec. 327, 374 N.E.2d 1102 (1978); Carpenter v. Grow, 247 Mass. 133, 141 N.E. 859 (1923); Star Chevrolet v. Green, 473 So.2d 157 (Miss.1985) (dealer gets no credit for collision insurer's payment to the minor); Rotondo v. Kay Jewelry, 84 R.I. 292, 123 A.2d 404 (1956) (burden of proof on adult party that infant still has the consideration); Halbman v. Lemke, 99 Wis.2d 241, 298 N.W.2d 562 (1980); Annots., 16 ALR 1475 (1922); 36 ALR 782 (1925). The traditional view does not always hold if the infant misrepresented his or her age. See § 8.7 infra.

On the manner of evaluation of the consideration supplied by the infant when the infant supplies goods rather than money, see Robertson v. King, 225 Ark. 276, 280 S.W.2d 402, 52 ALR2d 1108 (1955).

10. Myers v. Hurley Motor, 273 U.S. 18, 50 ALR 1181 (1927) (depreciation caused by negligent use of automobile); Worman Motor v. Hill, 54 Ariz. 227, 94 P.2d 865, 124 ALR 1363 (1939); Creer v. Active Automobile Exchange, 99 Conn. 266, 121 A. 888 (1923) (value of depreciation deducted from infant's recovery but not value of use); Marceiliac v. Stevens, 206 Ky. 383, 267 S.W. 229 (1924) (rental value of house; alternate ground as house was also a necessary); Latrobe v. Dietrich, 114 Md. 8, 78 A. 983 (1910); Berglund v. American Multigraph Sales, 135 Minn. 67, 160 N.W. 191 (infant must account for benefits received); Wooldridge v. Lavoie, 79 N.H. 21, 104 A. 346 (1918) (infant must account for benefit received from use but not depreciation caused by negligence); Rice v. Butler, 160 N.Y. 578, 55 N.E. 275, 47 LRA 303 (1899); Pettit v. Liston, 97 Or. 464, 191 P. 660, 11 ALR 487 (1920) (value of use of motorcycle); Dodson v. Shrader, 824 S.W.2d 545 (Tenn.1992) (deduction for value of use, depreciation, damage). See also Annot., 12 ALR3d 1174 (1967).

whether the infant is the plaintiff or defendant in the action, it explains a good many cases which otherwise appear contradictory. The distinction has been recognized explicitly in some of the decisions.[11]

A distinction in result based upon the procedural position of the parties may seem arbitrary, but to some extent the distinction reflects the risks foreseeable to the parties. A seller on credit assumes legal and practical risks of nonpayment. A seller for cash would usually be astounded if the law required restoration of the price paid without a requirement that the goods be returned. There is rough justice in holding that an infant who takes a flight from New York to Los Angeles and pays cash cannot demand the return of the fare after taking the flight,[12] but where the same infant flies on the "pay later plan," it seems just that the party extending the credit bear the risk of nonpayment. What is involved is an attempt to protect an infant from improvident commitments but not from improvident cash expenditures, at least where protection of the infant would result in a harsh forfeiture against the other party. This approach, pioneered in New Hampshire, has led to a complete breakthrough in the ordinary rules relating to infancy in that jurisdiction.[13] Another suggested approach is that each contract be judged by criteria of fairness, and that restitutionary principles, based on concepts of conscionability, be applied on a case by case basis.[14]

§ 8.7 Torts Connected With Contracts

Very often tort liability is intimately connected with a contractual relation. Infants are liable for their torts.[1] At least three kinds of problems arise from the interplay of tort and contract liability in cases involving infants.

(a) Infants' Torts Stemming From Contracts

The other party to a contract cannot sue the infant for tort if the tort is in essence a breach of contract. While it is possible in some jurisdictions to frame an action for negligence in respect to a bailment in terms of tort or in terms of breach of contract,[2] the almost universal holding is that the action cannot be brought against the infant no matter how it is couched.[3] It is believed that to allow such an action would in

---

11. The distinction is suggested in 2 Kent's Commentaries *240. Many of the cases making the distinction rely upon and cite these influential commentaries. E.g., Rice v. Butler, 160 N.Y. 578, 55 N.E. 275, 47 LRA 303, and Pettit v. Liston, 97 Or. 464, 191 P. 660, 11 ALR 487 (1920).

12. Vichnes v. T. & W. Air, 173 Misc. 631, 18 N.Y.S.2d 603 (App.Term 1940), 15 St. John's L.Rev. 98 (1940); contra, Adamowski v. Curtiss–Wright Flying Serv., 300 Mass. 281, 15 N.E.2d 467 (1938), criticized 27 Georgetown L.J. 233 (1938), 7 Fordham L.Rev. 445 (1938).

13. § 8.9 infra.

14. Navin, supra § 8.2 n.18 (as to infants over age fourteen).

§ 8.7

1. See Prosser & Keeton, Torts § 134 (5th ed. 1984).

2. Although a bailment is not a contract, it is often formed by a contract, (see § 1.2 supra) and as a common law proposition, "assumpsit" could be brought for negligence in relation to a bailment.

3. Jones v. Milner, 53 Ga.App. 304, 185 S.E. 586 (1936); Eaton v. Hill, 50 N.H. 235, 9 Am.Rep. 189 (1870); Brunhoelzl v. Brandes, 90 N.J.L. 31, 100 A. 163 (1917);

effect be enforcing the contract in circumvention of the protective contract rule of infancy. The same analysis is made as to breach of warranty. Although such a breach may often give rise to an action in tort, because it stems from a contract, it is not maintainable against an infant.[4]

Infants, however, are liable for conversions of chattels since this kind of wrong is deemed to be independent of the contract, rather than a breach of an implied promise not to convert.[5]

(b) False Representations by the Infant

Infants who wilfully misrepresent their ages, under the majority view, may nevertheless exercise their powers of avoidance.[6] However, it often has been held that in equity the rule is different and infants who disaffirm under these circumstances must restore the other party to the status quo ante.[7]

Despite the general recognition of the rule that a misrepresentation of age does not inhibit the infant's power of avoidance, there is a marked split of authority whether an infant is liable in tort for the deceit of willful misrepresentation of age. The division stems from the rule that a tort action will not lie against an infant if in essence it involves the enforcement of a contract. Some courts assert that ultimately the fraud action is based on the contract.[8] Others take the position that the tort is sufficiently independent of the contract and that the granting of tort relief does not involve indirect enforcement of the contract.[9] A case can be made for either point of view. The basic dispute is as to what extent

contra, Daggy v. Miller, 180 Iowa 1146, 162 N.W. 854 (1917).

4. Collins v. Gifford, 203 N.Y. 465, 96 N.E. 721, 38 LRA NS 202 (1911).

5. Williams v. Buckler, 264 S.W.2d 279 (Ky.1954); Young v. Muhling, 48 A.D. 617, 63 N.Y.S. 181 (1900); Vermont Acceptance v. Wiltshire, 103 Vt. 219, 153 A. 199, 73 ALR 792 (1931).

6. Myers v. Hurley Motor, 273 U.S. 18, 50 ALR 1181 (1927); Del Santo v. Bristol County Stadium, 273 F.2d 605 (1st Cir. 1960); Creer v. Active Automobile Exchange, 99 Conn. 266, 121 A. 888 (1923); Sternlieb v. Normandie Nat. Sec., 263 N.Y. 245, 188 N.E. 726, 90 ALR 1437 (1934); Gillis v. Whitley's Discount Auto Sales, 70 N.C.App. 270, 319 S.E.2d 661 (1984); contra, Nichols v. English, 223 Ga. 227, 154 S.E.2d 239, 29 ALR3d 1265 (1967); La Rosa v. Nichols, 92 N.J.L. 375, 105 A. 201, 6 ALR 412 (1918); Haydocy Pontiac v. Lee, 19 Ohio App.2d 217, 250 N.E.2d 898 (1969), 31 Ohio St.L.J. 403 (1970). In some jurisdictions the estoppel is mandated by statute. Thosath v. Transport Motor, 136 Wn. 565, 240 P. 921 (1925). See, Miller, 15 U.Pitt.L.Rev. 73 (1953).

7. Lewis v. Van Cleve, 302 Ill. 413, 134 N.E. 804 (1922); Stallard v. Sutherland, 131 Va. 316, 108 S.E. 568, 18 ALR 516 (1921); contra, Sims v. Everhardt, 102 U.S. (12 Otto) 300 (1880); Watson v. Billings, 38 Ark. 278, 42 Am.Rep. 1 (1881). In line with the usual flexibility of equitable doctrine, however, the decisions have varied with questions such as whether the infant is the plaintiff or defendant and whether the contract is executed or executory. See Note, 20 Iowa L.Rev. 785, 790–91 (1935).

8. Drennen Motor Car v. Smith, 230 Ala. 275, 160 So. 761 (1935); Slayton v. Barry, 175 Mass. 513, 56 N.E. 574 (1900); Sternlieb v. Normandie Nat. Sec., 263 N.Y. 245, 188 N.E. 726, 90 ALR 1437 (1934); Greensboro Morris Plan v. Palmer, 185 N.C. 109, 116 S.E. 261 (1923).

9. Keser v. Chagnon, 159 Colo. 209, 410 P.2d 637 (1966) (adult may counterclaim for fraud in infant's action for restitution); Byers v. LeMay Bank & Trust, 365 Mo. 341, 282 S.W.2d 512 (1955); Wisconsin Loan & Finance v. Goodnough, 201 Wis. 101, 228 N.W. 484, 67 ALR 1259 (1930). See Miller, note 6 supra.

the law's policy of protecting infants should apply to a fraudulent infant. The same kind of split of authority exists as to other kinds of fraudulent statements made by infants in connection with their contracts.[10]

It is recognized that the infant's fraudulent misrepresentation as age or other material facts will permit the other party to avoid the contract on grounds of fraud.[11]

(c) Torts and Agency Relationships

Under the doctrine of respondeat superior, principals are liable for the torts committed by their agents within the scope of their employment. However, the situation is more complicated where the principal is an infant armed with the power of disaffirmance. An infant may appoint an agent but such an appointment is subject to disaffirmance. Accordingly, the majority view is that infants may avoid their liabilities for the torts of their agents,[12] at least insofar as the tort liability stems from respondeat superior.[13]

§ 8.8 Liability of an Infant for Necessaries

An infant is liable in quasi-contract for necessaries furnished the infant but the infant may disaffirm an executory contract for necessaries.[1] As a consequence of the quasi-contractual nature of the action, the infant is not liable for the contract price, but for the reasonable value of the necessaries furnished.[2]

The concept of "necessaries" is relative to the infant's status in life.[3] It would seem clear that the range of what is necessary is considerably larger if the infant is emancipated, and larger yet if married,[4] as compared with what is necessary for an unemancipated infant. Thus, it is a somewhat fruitless quest to analyze the cases to determine, for

---

10. Not liable: Collins v. Gifford, 203 N.Y. 465, 96 N.E. 721, 38 LRA NS 202 (1911); Lesnick v. Pratt, 116 Vt. 477, 78 A.2d 487 (1951), rearg. Liable: Wisconsin Loan & Finance v. Goodnough, 201 Wis. 101, 228 N.W. 484, 67 ALR 1259 (1930).

11. Beardsley v. Clark, 229 Iowa 601, 294 N.W. 887 (1940), 39 Mich.L.Rev. 1417 (1941); Neff v. Landis, 110 Pa. 204, 1 A. 177 (1885); Fredeking v. Grimmett, 140 W.Va. 745, 86 S.E.2d 554, 50 ALR2d 1346 (1955). See Miller, note 6 supra and appendix thereto.

12. Payette v. Fleischman, 329 Mich. 160, 45 N.W.2d 16 (1950); Hodge v. Feiner, 338 Mo. 268, 90 S.W.2d 90, 103 ALR 483 (1936); Covault v. Nevitt, 157 Wis. 113, 146 N.W. 1115, 51 LRA NS 1092 (1914) (infant businessman not liable for negligence of his janitor); contra, Scott v. Schisler, 107 N.J.L. 397, 153 A. 395, 44 Harv.L.Rev. 1292 (1931). See Gregory, 5 Wis.L.Rev. 453 (1930).

13. Cf. Sikes v. Johnson, 16 Mass. 389 (1820) (infant procured another to commit a battery).

§ 8.8

1. Gregory v. Lee, 64 Conn. 407, 30 A. 53, 25 LRA 618 (1894); Wallin v. Highland Park, 127 Iowa 131, 102 N.W. 839 (1905).

2. Sceva v. True, 53 N.H. 627 (1873); see 5 Williston §§ 9:18–9:21; Woodward on Quasi Contracts § 202.

3. "The word 'necessaries' as used in the law is a relative term, except when applied to such things as are obviously requisite for the maintenance of existence, and depends on the social position and situation in life of the infant as well as upon his own fortune and that of his parents." International Text–Book v. Connelly, 206 N.Y. 188, 195, 99 N.E. 722, 725 (1912).

4. Ragan v. Williams, 220 Ala. 590, 127 So. 190, 68 ALR 1182 (1930); Spaulding v. New England Furniture, 154 Me. 330, 147 A.2d 916 (1959).

example, whether an automobile is a necessary.[5] When reasonable persons would differ, the question is for the jury. It is obvious, however, that food,[6] shelter,[7] and clothing[8] are necessaries. But the kind of food,[9] shelter,[10] and clothing[11] is another question. Medical services can generally be considered as necessaries.[12] Legal services are necessaries in many instances, particularly for the enforcement or defense of tort claims and criminal prosecutions,[13] but are often not considered such if the attorney is retained to protect property rights. This result is reached on the ground that a guardian should be appointed to protect such rights and the attorney should contract with the guardian.[14] However, if the legal services result in a money judgment or settlement, the attorney may be compensated from the funds paid to the infant's guardian.[15]

Education is necessary, but the kind of education which is necessary depends upon the circumstances of the infant. While a basic public school education is recognized as a necessary, it appears that generally a college education has not been deemed to be,[16] but education in a trade has been said to qualify as a necessary.[17] The language of the decisions

---

5. Generally the cases have held that the automobile was not a necessary under the facts of the particular case. See Harris v. Raughton, 37 Ala.App. 648, 73 So.2d 921 (1954), 6 Hastings L.J. 112 (1954) (pointing out the changing place of the automobile in society); Star Chevrolet v. Green, 473 So.2d 157 (Miss.1985). Contra, Ehrsam v. Borgen, 185 Kan. 776, 347 P.2d 260 (1959); Bancredit v. Bethea, 65 N.J.Super. 538, 168 A.2d 250 (1961) (remanded for jury determination); Daubert v. Mosley, 487 P.2d 353, 56 ALR3d 1328 (Okl.1971).

6. O'Donniley v. Kinley, 220 Mo.App. 284, 286 S.W. 140 (1926) (loan to purchase groceries).

7. Ragan v. Williams, 220 Ala. 590, 127 So. 190, 68 ALR 1182 (1930) (house rental for married infant); Gregory v. Lee, 64 Conn. 407, 30 A. 53, 25 LRA 618 (1894) (lodging for Yale student); but see Moskow v. Marshall, 271 Mass. 302, 171 N.E. 477 (1930) (lodging for Harvard student).

8. Lynch v. Johnson, 109 Mich. 640, 67 N.W. 908 (1896).

9. Kline v. L'Amoureux, 2 Paige Ch. 419 (N.Y.1831); L'Amoureux v. Crosby, 2 Paige Ch. 422, 22 Am.Dec. 655 (1831) (liquor not a necessary).

10. The purchase of a house was held to be a necessary in Johnson v. Newberry, 267 S.W. 476 (Tex.Com.App.1924), 13 Georgetown L.J. 416 (1925), although this would not ordinarily be the case.

11. Lefils & Christian v. Sugg, 15 Ark. 137 (1854) (cologne, cravats, kid gloves, and walking canes not necessaries).

12. Ex Parte Odem, 537 So.2d 919 (Ala. 1988); Scott County School Dist. v. Asher, 263 Ind. 47, 324 N.E.2d 496 (1975) (child jointly and severally liable with parents); Johns Hopkins v. Pepper, 346 Md. 679, 697 A.2d 1358 (1997) (child liable only if parents are unable to pay); Cole v. Wagner, 197 N.C. 692, 150 S.E. 339, 71 ALR 220 (1929); Annot., 53 ALR4th 1249.

13. Crafts v. Carr, 24 R.I. 397, 53 A. 275 (1902); Plummer v. Northern Pac. Ry., 98 Wn. 67, 167 P. 73, 7 ALR 104 (1917). See Annot., 13 ALR3d 1251 (1967).

14. Grissom v. Beidleman, 35 Okl. 343, 129 P. 853 (1912); 5 Williston § 9:19; but see a 900 page symposium "Ethical Issues in the Legal Representation of Children," 64 Fordham L. Rev. 1281–2132 (1996).

15. Statler v. Dodson, 195 W.Va. 646, 466 S.E.2d 497 (1995) (court rejects test of necessaries and adopt test of reasonably necessary to protect the infant's interests).

16. Moskow v. Marshall, 271 Mass. 302, 171 N.E. 477 (1930); La Salle Extension Univ. v. Campbell, 131 N.J.L. 343, 36 A.2d 397 (1944); Hawley v. Doucette, 43 A.D.2d 713, 349 N.Y.S.2d 801 (1973); Middlebury College v. Chandler, 16 Vt. 683, 42 Am.Dec. 537 (1844); see also N.J. Dist. Kiwanis Int'l v. Gandhi, 284 N.J.Super. 102, 663 A.2d 661 (1994), aff'd (educational trip; parent liable).

17. Mauldin v. Southern Shorthand & Bus. Univ., 126 Ga. 681, 55 S.E. 922 (1906) (stenography may qualify, but not under the facts); Curtiss v. Roosevelt Aviation School, 5 Air L.Rev. 382 (Mun.Ct.N.Y.1934) (mechanical training course). In Siegel &

shows sufficient flexibility, however, to allow for changing community standards in this regard.[18]

Business and employment expenses have received variable treatment,[19] but a North Carolina case has broken with the ordinary strictures as to what constitutes a necessary, holding a married infant liable for the reasonable value of an employment service fee, stating:

> "In our view, the concept of 'necessaries' should be enlarged to include such articles of property and such services as are reasonably necessary to enable the infant to earn the money required to provide the necessities of life for himself and those who are legally dependent upon him."[20]

If the infant borrows money for the purpose of purchasing necessaries and so uses it, the infant is liable to the lender as if the lender had supplied the necessaries.[21] The same result should follow if a loan is in fact used for necessaries although there was no agreement with the lender as to the use to which the money is to be put.[22] If the funds are advanced for the purpose of purchasing necessaries but are squandered for other purposes, the cases are divided as to the infant's liability.[23]

The liability of infants for necessaries is relative not only to their status in life but also depends on whether the infant has an existing supply of necessaries, or parents or guardians who are able and willing to supply the necessities of life.[24] The mere fact that the goods or services are in general considered necessaries does not make them necessary to the particular infant if the infant is already supplied with them.[25] Also an infant who has not been emancipated cannot be liable for necessaries

Hodges v. Hodges, 20 Misc.2d 243, 191 N.Y.S.2d 984 (1959), aff'd, it was held that voice training could constitute a necessary for a ten year old prodigy who made many television appearances, but that a parent could not recover from the child, as the primary duty of furnishing the necessaries is upon the parent. See also Siegel v. Hodges, 15 A.D.2d 571, 222 N.Y.S.2d 989 (1961). It was subsequently held that whether a third person could recover for managerial and coaching services as necessaries was a question of fact for the jury. Siegel v. Hodges, 24 A.D.2d 456, 260 N.Y.S.2d 405 (1965).

18. See International Text–Book v. Connelly, 206 N.Y. 188, 195, 99 N.E. 722, 725 (1912). Cases in other contexts, e.g., family court support orders, petitions for invasion of trust funds, welfare program administration, etc., have indicated that a college education can be a necessary. 1961 Report of the New York Law Revision Commission 283–84.

19. Bancredit v. Bethea, 65 N.J.Super. 538, 168 A.2d 250 (1961); Annot. 56 ALR3d 1335 § 4 (1974). For a special situation, see Beane, The Role of an Infant as a Member of a Partnership, 87 Commercial L.J. 622 (1982). By statute in New York an infant

who is in business is bound by provident business-related contracts.

20. Gastonia Personnel v. Rogers, 276 N.C. 279, 172 S.E.2d 19, 24, 41 ALR3d 1062 (1970); but see Fisher v. Cattani, 53 Misc.2d 221, 278 N.Y.S.2d 420 (1966).

21. Norwood Nat. Bank v. Allston, 152 S.C. 199, 149 S.E. 593, 65 ALR 1334 (1929), 43 Harv.L.Rev. 498 (1930). Sometimes this result is attained by the equitable doctrine of subrogation by which the lender is placed in the position of the party who supplied the necessaries. Price v. Sanders, 60 Ind. 310 (1878).

22. 5 Williston § 9:20 argues strongly for this position.

23. The infant was held to be liable in Norwood Nat. Bank v. Allston, 152 S.C. 199, 149 S.E. 593, 65 ALR 1334 (1929), 43 Harv.L.Rev. 498 (1930). A strong contrary dictum appears in Randall v. Sweet, 1 Denio 460 (N.Y.1845).

24. 5 Williston § 9:21.

25. Conboy v. Howe, 59 Conn. 112, 22 A. 35 (1890); Trainer v. Trumbull, 141 Mass. 527, 6 N.E. 761 (1886).

unless the parents or guardians refuse (or are unable) to supply them, and broad discretionary latitude is granted the parent or guardian in determining the manner to best meet the needs of the child or ward.[26] Moreover, even if all other tests of what is necessary are met it must appear that the goods or services were supplied on the credit of the infant and not on that of the parent, guardian or third person.[27] Therefore, the mere fact that the creditor has supplied necessaries to the family unit of which the infant is a part does not render the infant liable unless the infant contracted for the necessaries.[28] Thus, the liability, although quasi-contractual, requires that there be a contract with the infant. The basis of this liability is thus considerably different from the liability of *parents* for necessaries furnished their children.[29]

§ 8.9　Infants' Liability for Benefits in New Hampshire

Many jurisdictions now require that an infant who as plaintiff seeks to disaffirm a contract and obtain restitution must return or account for the benefits received under the contract.[1] If, however, the infant is a defendant and sets up a defense of infancy, the infant is liable only for necessaries[2] or for the value of tangible consideration still retained.[3] In New Hampshire, however, the courts have taken the position that it is immaterial whether the infant is the plaintiff or defendant. Under the New Hampshire approach, if the infant has received benefits, whether necessaries or not, the infant is liable in an action for restitution for the value of the benefits. Thus, it has been held that an infant dealer in milk is liable for the value of milk supplied in the course of business,[4] and that an infant orphan is liable for the reasonable value of legal services received to contest the appointment of a particular guardian, the court

---

26. Mauldin v. Southern Shorthand & Bus. Univ., 126 Ga. 681, 55 S.E. 922 (1906); International Text–Book v. Connelly, 206 N.Y. 188, 99 N.E. 722 (1912). "It would be subversive of parental authority and dominion if interested third persons could assume to judge for the parent, and subject him to liability for their unauthorized interference in supplying the supposed wants of the child." Lefils & Christian v. Sugg, 15 Ark. 137, 140 (1854).

27. McManus v. Arnold Taxi, 82 Cal. App. 215, 255 P. 755 (1927); Scott County School Dist. 1 v. Asher, 263 Ind. 47, 324 N.E.2d 496 (1975), (allowing infant to recover necessary medical expenses against a tortfeasor on theory infant is bound to pay when parents cannot); Garay v. Overholtzer, 332 Md. 339, 631 A.2d 429 (1993) (similar); Foster v. Adcock, 161 Tenn. 217, 30 S.W.2d 239, 70 ALR 569 (1930); but see Gardner v. Flowers, 529 S.W.2d 708 (Tenn. 1975). "A third party had no right to usurp the rights and duties of the guardian." McKanna v. Merry, 61 Ill. 177, 180 (1871).

28. Foster v. Adcock, 161 Tenn. 217, 30 S.W.2d 239, 70 ALR 569 (1930).

29. See § 1.8 supra; A father is liable for an infant's educational expenses where the father assents to the educational program. New Jersey Dist. Kiwanis Int'l v. Gandhi, 284 N.J.Super. 64, 663 A.2d 642 (1995); Madison General Hosp. v. Haack, 124 Wis.2d 398, 369 N.W.2d 663, 53 ALR4th 1235 (1985) (mother liable for minor daughter's expenses in giving birth). A seventeen year-old parent is bound by a contract to supply necessary medical services to her child. Ex Parte Odem, 537 So.2d 919 (Ala.1988).

§ 8.9

1. See § 8.6 supra.

2. Id.

3. Id.

4. Bartlett v. Bailey, 59 N.H. 408 (1879).

deeming it irrelevant to determine whether or not the services were necessary.[5]

The New Hampshire approach makes good sense as it protects the infant from executory contracts, and transactions which are not beneficial.[6] At the same time, it recognizes the legitimate interests of those who have dealt with the infant. Arizona has followed New Hampshire's lead, allowing recovery for the value of repairs obtained by an infant truck owner who engaged in a profitable trucking business.[7] Similarly, in West Virginia, where legal services were rendered to an infant's share in a decedent's estate, recovery was allowed.[8]

B. THE MENTALLY INFIRM

Table of Sections

§ 8.10 Introduction

According to older authority, transactions of the mentally infirm[1] are void,[2] but under the overwhelming weight of modern authority, with one exception, the contracts and executed transactions of the mentally infirm are merely voidable.[3] The exception, adopted in many jurisdic-

5. Porter v. Wilson, 106 N.H. 270, 209 A.2d 730, 13 ALR3d 1247 (1965); Hall v. Butterfield, 59 N.H. 354, 47 Am.Rep.209 (1879); Wooldridge v. Lavoie, 79 N.H. 21, 104 A. 346 (1918). Accord, under a statute, Spencer v. Collins, 156 Cal. 298, 104 P. 320 (1909). Similar reasoning is found in Pankas v. Bell, 413 Pa. 494, 198 A.2d 312, 17 ALR3d 855 (1964), 42 U.Det.L.J. 218 (1964), in enjoining a former infant employee from violation of a covenant not to compete, and in Cidis v. White, 71 Misc.2d 481, 336 N.Y.S.2d 362 (Dist.Ct.1972) (infant required to pay for contact lenses which she ordered but did not receive). See also Frank v. Volkswagenwerk, 522 F.2d 321 (3d Cir. 1975). A similar approach has been taken in New South Wales by statute. See § 8.2 supra; but see CBS v. Tucker, 412 F.Supp. 1222, 1226 (S.D.N.Y.1976).

6. See Notes, 12 S.Dak.L.Rev. 426 (1967); 43 N.Dak.L.Rev. 89 (1966); 19 Hastings L.J. 1199 (1968).

7. Valencia v. White, 134 Ariz. 139, 654 P.2d 287 (App.1982). The court mistakenly views itself as aligning itself with New

Hampshire and Minnesota. But Minnesota has not granted affirmative relief to adults against infants under the benefit theory.

8. Statler v. Dodson, 195 W.Va. 646, 466 S.E.2d 497 (1995).

§ 8.10

1. See Allen, Ferster & Weihofen, Mental Impairment and Legal Incompetency (1968); Cotton, Agreements of the Mentally Disabled, 3 Rutgers–Camden L.J. 241 (1971); Comment, 57 Mich.L.Rev. 1020 (1959). On the question of the effect of supervening mental disability on offers, see § 2.20 supra.

2. Hovey v. Hobson, 53 Me. 451, 89 Am.Dec. 705 (1866); Shoals Ford v. Clardy, 588 So.2d 879 (Ala.1991); Shepard v. First American Mtge., 289 S.C. 516, 347 S.E.2d 118 (App.1986) (void where grantee did not give value).

3. Atwell v. Jenkins, 163 Mass. 362, 40 N.E. 178 (1895) (Holmes, J.); Levine v. O'Malley, 33 A.D.2d 874, 307 N.Y.S.2d 919

tions, holds that if the person so afflicted has been adjudicated an incompetent and a guardian of property has been appointed prior to entering into the transaction, the transaction is deemed void.[4] Commitment to an asylum is not equivalent to the appointment of a guardian of property[5] nor is the voluntary appointment of a conservator.[6] The law with respect to an agent's power to continue as agent after the principal's incompetence sets in is to a large extent controlled by statute and will not be discussed here.[7] Related to the subject of this chapter is an incompetent's ability to waive the right to counsel and to divulge information after receiving Miranda warnings.[8] The relationship between attorneys and their mentally impaired clients presents many difficult issues beyond the scope of this chapter.[9]

Although the problems we are now considering are ordinarily grouped under the heading of "Contracts of Insane Persons, "or similar headings,[10] a significant number of the cases do not deal with insanity,

(1969); see 5 Williston §§ 10:1–10:4. As one consequence of this rule, as in the case of infancy, a bona fide purchaser of personal property takes free of the incompetent's interest in the property. See 5 Williston § 10:4; see also Matter of LeBovici, 171 Misc.2d 604, 655 N.Y.S.2d 305 (1997) (assignee of mortgagee takes free of defense of incompetency).

As to real property, unlike in the case of infants, the majority rule protects the bona fide purchaser on the basis of the rule requiring restoration of the status quo, discussed in the next section. See Note, 47 Colum.L.Rev. 675 (1947), but see Shepard v. First American Mtge., 289 S.C. 516, 347 S.E.2d 118 (1986) (where deed was void, bona fide mortgagee took no rights from grantee).

4. Rs. 2d § 13; Church v. Rosenstein, 85 Conn. 279, 82 A. 568 (1912); Dupont v. Dupont, 308 So.2d 512 (La.App.1975) (Mississippi law); Hughes v. Jones, 116 N.Y. 67, 22 N.E. 446, 5 LRA 632 (1889); Fixico v. Fixico, 186 Okl. 656, 100 P.2d 260 (1940) (despite acquiescence of guardian); Huntington Nat. Bank v. Toland, 71 Oh.App.3d 576, 594 N.E.2d 1103 (1991) (but guardian can ratify); Note, 41 Harv.L.Rev. 536 (1928); but seeIn re Estate of Cline, 250 Iowa 265, 93 N.W.2d 708 (1958) (voluntary guardianship). An adjudication without appointment of a guardian is merely evidence of incompetency. McCormick v. Littler, 85 Ill. 62, 28 Am.Rep. 610 (1877). An appointment of a guardian is prima facie evidence that the person was incapable of contracting just prior to the adjudication but is not conclusive. Hughes v. Jones, 116 N.Y. 67, 22 N.E. 446, 5 LRA 632 (1889); cf. L'Amoureux v. Crosby, 2 Paige Ch. 422 (N.Y. 1831) (judgment entered by confession void

where judgment creditor knew incompetency proceedings were pending against judgment debtor).

It is often held that if the guardianship falls into disuse because the ward has regained sanity, the ward's contracts are enforceable. Fugate v. Walker, 204 Ky. 767, 265 S.W. 331 (1924); Schultz v. Oldenburg, 202 Minn. 237, 277 N.W. 918 (1938); Rs. 2d § 13 cmt d. See Note, 1967 Wash.U.L.Q. 545.

5. Finch v. Goldstein, 245 N.Y. 300, 157 N.E. 146 (1927); Rs.2d § 13 ill. 2.

6. Board of Regents v. Davis, 14 Cal.3d 33, 120 Cal.Rptr. 407, 533 P.2d 1047 (1975) (superseded by statute); but see Edmunds v. Equitable S. & L., 223 A.2d 630 (D.C.App.1966); Citizens State Bank & Trust v. Nolte, 226 Kan. 443, 601 P.2d 1110 (1979); Jones v. Kuhn, 59 Or.App. 135, 650 P.2d 999 (1982).

7. See Meiklejohn, Incompetent Principals, Competent Third Parties, and the Law of Agency, 61 Ind.L.J. 114 (1986).

8. See People v. Newton, 175 Misc.2d 887, 671 N.Y.S.2d 601 (1998).

9. See Bray & Ensley, Dealing with the Mentally Incapacitated Client: Ethical Issues Facing the Attorney, 33 Family L. Q. 329–348 (1999); Novak & Novak, Clear Today, Uncertain Tomorrow: Competency and Legal Guardianship, and the role of the Lawyer in Serving the Needs of Cognitively Impaired Clients, 74 N.D.L.Rev. 295 (1998). A Symposium, Ethical Issues in Representing Older Clients, 62 Fordham L.Rev. 961 (1994) contains many references to the issues of dealing with incapacitated clients.

10. E.g., 5 Williston ch. 10 (4th ed.) ("Capacity of Parties–Mentally Ill and Intoxicated Persons.")

but with other forms of mental infirmity,[11] such as senility,[12] mental retardation,[13] temporary delirium deriving from physical injuries,[14] intoxication,[15] and the side effects of medication.[16]

It is generally held that incapacity exists where a party does not understand the nature and consequences of what is happening at the time of the transaction.[17] This test, as well as subsidiary tests of whether the person was rational except for "insane delusions" as to the particular transaction in question, has been attacked as unscientific.[18] Some observers have pointed out, however, that not using psychiatric tests has enabled the courts to work out just results.[19] In other words, if the contract is fair and beneficial to the alleged incompetent there will be a great tendency to find sanity; otherwise; the tendency is to find lack of capacity.[20] Of course, a tendency must not be confused with doctrine, and there must be some arguable basis for a determination of incompetency and this tendency merely reflects judicial treatment of borderline cases. It is clear, however, that incompetency may be proved by circumstantial

---

11. See B.C. White, Competence to Consent (1994) (focusing on competence to consent to medical treatment).

12. E.g., Lloyd v. Jordan, 544 So.2d 957 (Ala.1989); Farnum v. Silvano, 27 Mass. App.Ct. 536, 540 N.E.2d 202 (1989); Smith v. Smith, 574 So.2d 644 (Miss.1990); Estate of Obermeier, 150 A.D.2d 863, 540 N.Y.S.2d 613 (1989); cf. JML Inv. v. Hilton, 231 A.D.2d 493, 647 N.Y.S.2d 244 (1996) ("some impaired mental processes").

13. E.g., Edmunds v. Chandler, 203 Va. 772, 127 S.E.2d 73 (1962); see Sears, Mental Retardation and Unconscionability, 13 Law & Psych. Rev. 77 (1989).

14. E.g., Kilgore v. Cross, 1 Fed. 578 (E.D.Ark.1880); Hauer v. Union State Bank, 192 Wis.2d 576, 532 N.W.2d 456 (1995) (brain damage from motorcycle accident).

15. Hunt v. Golden, 271 Or. 321, 532 P.2d 26 (1975) (wine and Demerol); see § 8.14 infra.

16. Saret–Cook v. Gilbert et al., 74 Cal. App.4th 1211, 88 Cal.Rptr.2d 732 (1999) (demerol); Faulkenberry v. Elkins, 213 Ga. App. 472, 445 S.E.2d 283 (1994); Wolkoff v. Villane, 288 N.J.Super. 282, 672 A.2d 242 (medication and pain raised a question of fact as to competency); cf. Sharpe, 35 N.Car.L.Rev. 380 (1957).

17. Cundick v. Broadbent, 383 F.2d 157 (10th Cir.1967), cert. denied; Shoals Ford v. Clardy, 588 So.2d 879 (Ala.1991); Kruse v. Coos Head Timber, 248 Or. 294, 432 P.2d 1009 (1967); In re Estate of Erickson, 202 Mich.App. 329, 508 N.W.2d 181 (1993); Ridings v. Ridings, 55 N.C.App. 630, 286 S.E.2d 614 (1982). See Guttmacher and Weihofen,

Mental Incompetency, 36 Minn.L.Rev. 179 (1952). See also Forman v. Brown, 944 P.2d 559 (Colo.App.1996), stressing the mental state at the time of the transaction.

18. See Comment, "Civil Insanity," 44 Cornell L.Q. 76, 88–93 (1958).

19. A series of articles by Green demonstrates that the legal fact of insanity or sanity tends to be determined by the finding which will better serve the interests of alleged incompetents or their heirs. The courts are primarily concerned, he demonstrates, with the question of whether the transaction was abnormal, tending to determine the question of sanity by that criterion. Green, 43 Colum.L.Rev. 176 (1943); Green, 38 Mich.L.Rev. 1189 (1940); Green, 6 Mo.L.Rev. 141 (1941); Green, 21 Tex. L.Rev. 554 (1943); Green, 53 Yale L.J. 271 (1944). See also Virtue, 26 N.Y.U.L.Rev. 132 and 291 (1951).

20. E.g., in discussing the contests surrounding life support contracts frequently entered into by aged persons, one observer concludes "if it was a reasonable contract and the recipient was a worthy object of trust and faith, then that shows sufficient capacity to uphold the contract; but if support was not given, or if there was fraud, then the grantor was incapacitated because no one in his right mind would have made such a contract." Virtue, supra note 19, at 151. It is to be noted that in many of such cases, it is the heirs of the alleged incompetent who are attempting to set aside the contract or conveyance, thereby seeking to frustrate a bargain which was beneficial to the deceased.

evidence[21] including disparity of value in the considerations exchanged.[22]

No doubt the application of the rules as to the mentally infirm vary with the context.[23] Contract law focuses primarily on commercial exchanges, but an enormous number of cases involving the mentally infirm are in the context of family and social relations. In the noncommercial cases, as in cases of undue influence,[24] an unnatural transaction resulting in the enrichment of the admittedly competent party at the expense of the alleged incompetent is an indicium of a voidable transaction. Courts scrutinize the relationship between the parties in the past to determine whether the transaction is unnatural.[25]

The Restatement (Second) accepts the cognitive test "of ability to understand," but it, in addition, has adopted the position that the contract is also voidable if the party "by reason of mental illness or defect * * * is unable to act in a reasonable manner in relation to the transaction and the other party has reason to know of this condition."[26] This approach makes it easier for parties to disaffirm a contract as it permits disaffirmance of contracts made by persons who understand what they are doing but cannot control their behavior in a rational manner.

Although there has been debate about the appropriate test to determine incompetency, the apparently unanimous assumption has been that incompetents, properly defined, require protection from their own actions. A psychiatrist and a legal scholar have made a forceful attack against that assumption.[27] Among the points made is that protection of the incompetent, in effect, masks protection of the relatives of the incompetent at the expense of the incompetent's freedom of action. "The result of such solicitude can easily be that the contractor is protected into a straitjacket, both figuratively and literally." Further, they argue that the setting aside of transactions "is punishment for deviancy, not protection against helplessness."[28] Deprivation of contractual capacity also deprives a psychiatric patient of the power to withhold consent from

21. Bragdon v. Drew, 658 A.2d 666 (Me. 1995)

22. Gindhart v. Skourtes, 271 Or. 115, 530 P.2d 827 (1975); Bach v. Hudson, 596 S.W.2d 673 (Tex.Civ.App.1980).

23. See Meiklejohn, Contractual and Donative Capacity, 39 Case Wes.R.L.Rev. 307 (1989); see Stefan, Silencing the Different Voice: Competency Feminist Theory and Law, 47 U. Miami L.Rev. 763, 766 (1993) ("I assert that questions of competence arise only as a function of a relationship between two or more people and that this relationship is necessarily a hierarchical one.")

24. See § 9.10 infra.

25. See Meiklejohn, note 23 supra, for a detailed discussion.

26. § 15; accord, Ortelere v. Teachers' Retirement Board, 25 N.Y.2d 196, 303 N.Y.S.2d 362, 250 N.E.2d 460 (1969), 36 Brooklyn L.Rev. 145 (1969), 45 N.Y.U.L.Rev. 585 (1970), 16 Wayne L.Rev. 1188 (1970). For further facts and analysis of this case, see Danzig, The Capability Problem in Contract Law 148–204 (1978). The Restatement's and Ortelere's insistence that the incapacity be a product of "mental disease or defect" is criticized in Hardisty, 48 Wn.L.Rev. 735 (1973). Mississippi allows avoidance for "weakness of intellect" or "great weakness of mind." Smith v. Smith, 574 So.2d 644 (Miss.1990).

27. Alexander & Szasz, From Contract to Status Via Psychiatry, 13 Santa Clara L.Rev. 537 (1973).

28. Id. at 546.

lobotomy or electro-shock treatment or even therapy that consists of battering and bruising the patient.[29]

This criticism of the protective policy of the law may be more severe than the existing state of the law merits, but, as in the case of infants' contracts, a comprehensive review of the policy bases and operative rules applicable to the contracts of the mentally infirm seems appropriate.[30]

§ 8.11 Requirement of Restitution

To some extent the rationales of the rules concerning the transactions of infants and incompetents coincide. In both cases, the law desires to protect these classes of persons from their own presumed improvidence. But, as to incompetents, an additional factor is present. Contracts are based on mutual assent. A person incapable of rational volition cannot give intelligent assent. Under a purely subjective test, such contracts would be void. But under a purely objective test, the inquiry would be whether the individual appeared to a reasonable person in the position of the other party to be capable of rational assent. This purely objective approach, however, conflicts with the policy of protecting the incompetent from improvident transactions.

Under the majority view, a kind of compromise has evolved. Two kinds of contracts are automatically voidable: executory contracts,[1] and contracts based upon grossly inadequate consideration.[2] In addition, a second class of contracts is voidable if the incompetent can place the other party in the status quo ante.[3] This second class of voidable contracts consists of executed contracts where the other party took no advantage of the incompetent and had no reason to know of the infirmity. If the incompetency would be obvious to a reasonable person, there is no obligation upon the incompetent to make restitution if the

---

29. Id. at 548–52.

30. See Id. at 557–59 for some suggestions in this regard.

§ 8.11

1. Cundell v. Haswell, 23 R.I. 508, 51 A. 426 (1902). The English rule is contrary. Where the other party did not take advantage of the incompetent and had no reason to know of the mental infirmity the executory contract is enforceable. York Glass v. Jubb, 134 L.T.R.(N.S.) 36 (C.A.1925); Note, 25 Colum.L.Rev. 230 (1925).

2. Alexander v. Haskins, 68 Iowa 73, 25 N.W. 935 (1885) (land conveyed for about one third of its value).

3. Rs. 2d § 15(2); Knighten v. Davis, 358 So.2d 1022 (Ala.1978); Sparrowhawk v. Erwin, 30 Ariz. 238, 246 P. 541, 46 ALR 413 (1926); Coburn v. Raymond, 76 Conn. 484, 57 A. 116 (1904); Perper v. Edell, 160 Fla. 477, 35 So.2d 387, 47 Mich.L.Rev. 269 (1948) (incompetent must pay real estate

broker's commission); Atlanta Banking & Savings v. Johnson, 179 Ga. 313, 175 S.E. 904, 95 ALR 1436 (1934); cf. Georgia Power v. Roper, 201 Ga. 760, 41 S.E.2d 226 (1947); Verstandig v. Schlaffer, 296 N.Y. 62, 70 N.E.2d 15 (1946), 47 Colum.L.Rev. 675 (1947); Edmunds v. Chandler, 203 Va. 772, 127 S.E.2d 73 (1962). Restoration of the status quo ante often requires a complex evaluation of the equities and a complex accounting. See Virtue, supra § 8.10 n. 19, esp. at 291–320. If that status cannot be returned to, the party seeking to avoid must make "meaningful restitution." Pappert v. Sargent, 847 P.2d 66, 70 (Alaska 1993).

The modern tendency is to bring the rules regarding infants' contracts into harmony with those governing the contracts of mental incompetents. See § 8.6 supra as to infants' obligations to make restitution.

consideration has been consumed or dissipated.[4] Under a minority view, the appearance of sanity is immaterial and the incompetent need restore the consideration only if the incompetent still has it.[5] More broadly, it has been stated, "the contractual act of an incompetent is voidable by the incompetent only if avoidance accords with equitable principles."[6]

§ 8.12　Avoidance and Ratification

As in the case of infants' contracts, the competent party to the contract has no power of avoidance.[1] The power of avoidance and ratification is reserved to the incompetent and, after death, to the incompetent's heirs or personal representative.[2] If a guardian is appointed, the power is vested in the guardian.[3]

Once the incompetent recovers, he or she may ratify the contract. As in the case of infants' contracts, a ratification is irrevocable and can be effected by conduct or words.[4] After ratification, the former incompetent or guardian may, however, have an action for compensatory and punitive damages if exploitation of the incompetent amounted to actionable fraud.[5]

§ 8.13　Liability for Necessaries

As in the case of infants, even if they may avoid their contracts, mental incompetents are liable in a quasi-contractual actions for the

4. Spence v. Spence, 239 Ala. 480, 195 So. 717 (1940); Metter Banking v. Millen Lumber & Supply, 191 Ga.App. 634, 382 S.E.2d 624 (1989); Hauer v. Union State Bank, 192 Wis.2d 576, 532 N.W.2d 456 (App.1995) (jury returned a verdict that lending bank acted in bad faith); Rs. 2d § 15 cmt e.

5. The leading case is Seaver v. Phelps, 28 Mass. (11 Pick.) 304 (1831).

6. Hauer v. Union State Bank, 192 Wis.2d 576, 532 N.W.2d 456 (Wis.App. 1995).

§ 8.12

1. Atwell v. Jenkins, 163 Mass. 362, 40 N.E. 178 (1895). If the contract is executory, the competent party, upon discovery of the incompetency of the other, may refuse to perform until a guardian is appointed. Rattner v. Kleiman, 36 S.W.2d 249 (Tex. Civ.App.1931).

The competent party could obtain a declaration of nullity of a transaction entered into with an incompetent under guardianship as such a transaction is void rather than merely voidable.

2. Orr v. Equitable Mtge., 107 Ga. 499, 33 S.E. 708 (1899); 5 Williston § 10:5. See also Reed v. Brown, 215 Ind. 417, 19 N.E.2d

1015 (1939) (administrator prevailed over adversary grantee-heir); Bullard v. Moor, 158 Mass. 418, 33 N.E. 928 (1893) (administrator's ratification binding on heirs).

Some jurisdictions permit creditors of the incompetent to attack transfers of property. Chandler v. Welborn, 156 Tex. 312, 294 S.W.2d 801 (1956).

3. Finch v. Goldstein, 245 N.Y. 300, 157 N.E. 146 (1927) (ratification); Kline v. L'Amoureux, 2 Paige Ch. 419 (N.Y.1831) (avoidance); 5 Williston § 10:5; contra, Gingrich v. Rogers, 69 Neb. 527, 96 N.W. 156 (1903).

Strangers cannot generally avail themselves of the incompetency of a party to the transaction. Safe Deposit & Trust v. Tait, 54 F.2d 383 (D.Md.1931) (Commissioner of Internal Revenue).

4. First Nat. Bank v. Bunker, 494 F.2d 435 (8th Cir.1974); Norfolk Southern v. Smith, 262 Ga. 80, 414 S.E.2d 485 (1992); Saret–Cook v. Gilbert et al., 74 Cal.App.4th 1211, 88 Cal.Rptr.2d 732, 735 (1999); Hauer v. Union State Bank, 192 Wis.2d 576, 532 N.W.2d 456 (1995).

5. Hunt v. Golden, 271 Or. 321, 532 P.2d 26 (1975).

reasonable value of necessaries furnished them[1] or their dependents.[2] Roughly the same classes of goods and services, including money advanced to procure necessaries, are necessaries for incompetents.[3] Obviously, the incompetent's needs for nursing and medical attention are salient.[4] Also legal services availed of to procure release from custody and guardianship, whether or not successful, are ordinarily compensable.[5] Legal expenses of the party petitioning to have a person placed under guardianship can also be necessaries.[6]

§ 8.14 Intoxicated Persons

Intoxication by alcohol or the influence of narcotics can render a party legally incompetent. If the person does not understand the nature and consequences of the transaction in issue, the legal effect is much the same as in the case of any other kind of mental infirmity having the same effect.[1] Since the incompetency is self-induced, however, there is a different emphasis in the cases. Particularly in the older cases, the courts voiced a good deal of moral indignation at the intoxicated person[2] or the person supplying liquor.[3] Cases permitting avoidance for intoxication alone are rare. This may be explainable on grounds that it would be unusual for the admittedly competent party to contract unknowingly with a person who is so intoxicated as not to understand the nature and consequences of the transaction.[4] Under the rule that the Restatement

§ 8.13

1. Coffee v. Owens' Adm'r, 216 Ky. 142, 287 S.W. 540 (1926), 15 Ky.L.J. 361 (1927).

2. Dalton v. Dalton, 172 Ky. 585, 189 S.W. 902 (1916); Linch v. Sanders, 114 W.Va. 726, 173 S.E. 788 (1934).

3. Bank of Rector v. Parrish, 131 Ark. 216, 198 S.W. 689 (1917); Henry v. Knight, 74 Ind.App. 562, 122 N.E. 675 (1919).

4. Landmark Medical Center v. Gauthier, 635 A.2d 1145 (R.I.1994); In re Weber's Estate, 256 Mich. 61, 239 N.W. 260 (1931), 17 Cornell L.Q. 502 (1932).

5. Kay v. Kay, 53 Ariz. 336, 89 P.2d 496, 121 ALR 1496 (1939); Carr v. Anderson, 154 Minn. 162, 191 N.W. 407, 26 ALR 557 (1923); Carter v. Beckwith, 128 N.Y. 312, 28 N.E. 582 (1891); In re Weightman's Estate, 126 Pa.Super. 221, 190 A. 552 (1937), 85 U.Pa.L.Rev. 852 (1937). An application made three months after an unsuccessful prior application was held not to be a necessary legal service. Guardianship of Hayes, 8 Wis.2d 32, 98 N.W.2d 430 (1959).

6. Penney v. Pritchard & McCall, 255 Ala. 13, 49 So.2d 782, 22 ALR2d 1430 (1950).

§ 8.14

1. Reiner v. Miller, 478 S.W.2d 283 (Mo. 1972). See Poole v. Hudson, 46 Del. (7 Terry) 339, 83 A.2d 703 (Super.1951); First

State Bank of Sinai v. Hyland, 399 N.W.2d 894 (S.D.1987) (ratification when sober); Seminara v. Grisman, 137 N.J.Eq. 307, 44 A.2d 492 (1945); Lucy v. Zehmer, 196 Va. 493, 84 S.E.2d 516 (1954).

See, McCoid, Intoxication and its Effect upon Civil Responsibility, 42 Iowa L.Rev. 38 (1956); Annot. 36 ALR 619 (1925); 5 Williston §§ 10:5–10:15. Chronic alcoholism is grounds in many jurisdictions for an adjudication of incompetency and for the appointment of a guardian.

2. See Cook v. Bagnell Timber, 78 Ark. 47, 94 S.W. 695 (1906), expressing a minority view that intoxication per se is never a defense. If coupled with fraud by the other, the transaction is voidable on grounds of fraud. Accord, Burroughs v. Richman, 13 N.J.L. 233, 23 Am.Dec. 717 (1832). See also Somers v. Ferris, 182 Mich. 392, 148 N.W. 782 (1914); Christensen v. Larson, 77 N.W.2d 441 (N.D.1956).

3. See L'Amoureux v. Crosby, 2 Paige Ch. 422 (N.Y.1831), where the Chancellor expressed regret that he did not possess the power of the English Chancellor to commit plaintiff innkeeper to Fleet Prison.

4. See 5 Williston § 10:11.

(Second) has laid down, contracts made by an intoxicated party are voidable only if the other party has reason to know that the intoxicated party is unable to act in a reasonable manner in relation to the transaction or lacks understanding of it.[5] This limitation is not generally found in the language of the cases. Where the other party is aware of the intoxication, the rules alluded to in the next section also come into play.

§ 8.15   Exploitation of Alcoholics and Weak Minded Persons

Mental infirmity, feebleness of intellect or intoxication may exist to a lesser degree than required by law for the avoidance of a contract. Persons so afflicted are bound by their contracts if no other ground for avoidance exist. The cases, however, frequently reveal exploitation of such persons. The law offers a number of other doctrines for their protection. It is obvious that where a feeble-minded illiterate woman is made to execute a conveyance at pistol point the transaction is voidable on grounds of duress.[1] The woman's mental powers are barely relevant in such circumstances. The fact patterns, however, usually involve more subtle forms of duress, fraud, undue influence or overreaching. To ply an alcoholic with liquor and then induce the alcoholic to enter into a contract for a grossly inadequate consideration has been deemed a species of fraud.[2] Such cases are not decided on grounds of lack of capacity, but on the ground that the victim's limited mental ability is coupled with unconscionable exploitation by the other. This is further illustrated by cases holding that a hard bargain aggressively pressed upon a sober alcoholic by a party who knows of the consuming desire for cash to obtain liquor is voidable for overreaching.[3]

The situation in which persons who suffer from some infirmity, but who are not legally insane, and have been exploited are as varied as the expressions of human avarice. Typical situations which recur involve deeds extracted from the aged bedridden,[4] and releases extracted from

---

5. Rs. 2d § 16.

§ 8.15

1. Suggested by Phillips v. Bowie, 127 S.W.2d 522 (Tex.Civ.App.1939).

2. Thackrah v. Haas, 119 U.S. 499 (1886); Tubbs v. Hilliard, 104 Colo. 164, 89 P.2d 535 (1939); Ealy v. Tolbert, 209 Ga. 575, 74 S.E.2d 867 (1953); Matthis v. O'Brien, 137 Ky. 651, 126 S.W. 156 (1910).

3. Kendall v. Ewert, 259 U.S. 139 (1922), 3 Tenn.L.Rev. 84 (1925); Harlow v. Kingston, 169 Wis. 521, 173 N.W. 308, 6 ALR 327 (1919); see § 9.9 to 9.12 infra.

4. An analysis of 123 cases involving contracts and conveyances with aged persons attacked for want of capacity leads one observer to conclude that in addition to evidence of the extent of the infirmity and the fairness of the bargain the courts place emphasis on whether there is a fiduciary relationship, secrecy or unkindness. Of the 62 transactions which were set aside, undue influence and fraud rather than want of capacity seems to have been the basis of most of the decisions. The observer concludes: "These are perhaps the most difficult cases of all for the courts, which are virtually without doctrinal guidance, and must base their decisions solely on the individual equities, as disclosed by witnesses who are usually deeply involved emotionally in some variant of the King Lear situation." Virtue, § 8.10 n.19, at 298–99. As to wills in similar circumstances, see Langbein, Book Review, 103 Yale L.J. 2039 (1994); Moller, Undue Influence and the Norm of Reciprocity, 26 Idaho L.Rev. 275 (1989). See also ch 9 C, infra.

injured persons suffering great shock or pain.[5] In each case, the court has the difficult task of sifting through the facts. Some degree of infirmity coupled with the unfairness of the bargain will often result in a finding of fraud, undue influence, overreaching or even mental incapacity.[6] The recent enlargement of the doctrine of unconscionability offers another and more forthright approach to cases of this kind.[7]

C. SELF–DEALING

Table of Sections

§ 8.16 Contracting With Oneself

Although the issue discussed here often has serious consequences, a less-than-serious illustration will illuminate the larger legal issues. If Dan promises himself that if he abstains from smoking for one year he will spend $4,000 on a Caribbean vacation for himself, the promise, although accepted in accordance with its terms, creates no legal duty.[1] The same result would follow even if the promise were made in a formal document containing a recital of an intention that the promise be legally binding. Perhaps no better illustration than this exists to demonstrate that intention to be bound is not the exclusive basis of contract law. From illustrations such as this, large generalizations have been drawn. The First Restatement adamantly asserted: "It is not possible under existing law for a man to make a contract with himself."[2] Such a transaction has been said to be void.[3] This statement of the rule ought to be tempered by an awareness that the needs of concrete cases requires greater flexibility than such a rule suggests.[4]

On the ground that one cannot contract with oneself it has been said that dealers in mobile homes who purportedly contracted to sell mobile homes to themselves on credit and who, as sellers, purported to retain security interests in the homes, created no change in legal relations. Certainly if they were suing themselves such an analysis would be appropriate. But to hold that a purchaser of the business who agreed to

---

5. Union Pacific Ry. v. Harris, 158 U.S. 326 (1895) (release signed under the influence of morphine); Carr v. Sacramento Clay Products, 35 Cal.App. 439, 170 P. 446 (1918). For additional cases, see Virtue, supra § 8.10 n.19, at 296–97.

6. Williamson v. Matthews, 379 So.2d 1245 (Ala.1980); McPheters v. Hapke, 94 Idaho 744, 497 P.2d 1045 (1972); Patterson v. Ervin, 230 So.2d 563 (Miss.1970).

7. See §§ 9.37 to 9.40 infra; see also Ryan v. Weiner, 610 A.2d 1377 (Del.Ch.

1992) (application of traditional equity unconscionability doctrine).

§ 8.16

1. 1 Corbin § 3.1; 1 Williston § 3.2; Rs. 2d § 9.

2. Rs 1st § 15 cmt. a.

3. Rs. 1st § 15 ill. 2; Schmaeling v. Schmaeling, 127 Misc.2d 763, 487 N.Y.S.2d 494 (1985); Ackerman v. McMillan, 314 S.C. 268, 442 S.E.2d 618 (App.1994).

4. See Rs. 2d § 9 cmt a.

take an assignment of all the rights and to assume all the liabilities of the business would not be protected and limited by the terms of the "contracts" of sale that the prior owners of the business made with themselves would be palpably unfair.[5] Entrepreneurs tend to conceive of their business assets as something other than their personal assets. When they deal with them on such a basis, interested third parties have a right to hold them to their promises, even if originally the promises were made to themselves.

At times a person has more than one legal capacity.[6] Can Pamela Jones contract with the same Pamela Jones in her capacity as executrix of the estate of John Smith, or as president of XYZ Corporation, or both? Suppose Jones, as executrix of Smith's estate has title to certain equipment and wishes to transfer the equipment on a credit sale to XYZ Corporation which she heads, and also agrees personally to guarantee payment of the price. This may be a sensible transaction for the benefit of all concerned. A lawyer would advise Jones to arrange the transaction through a strawperson, transferring the equipment to Y, who would then transfer to XYZ. But if Jones is not guided by a lawyer, should the transaction be struck down merely because of the notion that one cannot contract with oneself? Certainly not. A more important question is, shouldn't the transaction be struck down because of Jones' conflict of interest? As seller is she likely to get the best possible price for the equipment by bargaining with herself? The answer is that the transaction ought to be treated as voidable at the election of the beneficiaries of the estate. Indeed, it is unlikely that a transaction of the type here hypothesized would be entered into without the consent of the beneficiaries or the probate court.

The same problem is shown in a somewhat clearer light when we consider multi-divisional entities such as banks. May a bank, acting as executor for an estate, contract with its loan division to borrow money for estate purposes? There is authority to the effect that this may be done.[7] Statutes have been enacted explicitly to govern aspects of multi-department banking, permitting contracts between departments.[8]

In a significant case, the U.S. appointed the defendant steamship company as its agent for the management of a government owned merchant ship. As agent, the company contracted with its stevedoring division for the loading and unloading of the ship. Despite the company's subsequent contention that it could not contract with itself, the court ruled that the contract was binding on the defendant upon ratification of the contract by the U.S.[9] A contrary result based upon the supposed incapacity of a company to contract with itself would clearly have sacrificed a sound result from an overgeneralized rule. The case is in

---

5. Cf. Forest Investment v. Chaplin, 55 Ill.App.2d 429, 205 N.E.2d 51 (1965).

6. Rs. 2d § 9 cmt b.

7. Breedlove v. Freudenstein, 89 F.2d 324, 112 ALR 777 (5th Cir.1937), cert. denied; 51 Harv.L.Rev. 351 (1937).

8. See Bogert, Trusts & Trustees § 598, pp. 487–98 (rev'd 2d ed. 1980).

9. U.S. v. Alaska S.S., 491 F.2d 1147 (9th Cir.1974).

tune with the same realistic approach which permits one department of the executive branch of government to sue another department of the executive branch.[10]

§ 8.17 Contracting With Oneself and Another

Courts of equity have long enforced contracts between an individual and a group of individuals which includes the individual. Thus a member of an unincorporated club may contract with the club[1] and a partner may contract with the partnership.[2] In each of these instances, the member is both a promisor and a promisee in the contractual relation.[3]

---

10. U.S. v. Nixon, 418 U.S. 683 (1974).

§ 8.17

1. Anderson v. Amidon, 114 Minn. 202, 130 N.W. 1002, 34 LRA NS 647 (1911).

2. Forsyth v. Butler, 152 Cal. 396, 93 P. 90 (1907).

3. See Rs. 2d § 11; 1 Williston § 3:2; 1 Corbin § 3.1.

Chapter 9

AVOIDANCE OR REFORMATION FOR MISCONDUCT OR MISTAKE

Table of Sections

Table of Sections

A. INTRODUCTION

A. INTRODUCTION

Table of Sections

§ 9.1 Scope of This Chapter and Rationale

Even though parties who have contractual capacity have expressed mutual assent and their agreement is supported by consideration or one of its equivalents, the agreement may be void, voidable, or reformable because it is contaminated by duress, undue influence, misrepresentation, mistake, or unconscionability.

The law of contracts presupposes that individuals contract for mutual gain. S agrees to sell Blackacre for $200,000 because S values that sum more than S values Blackacre. S would prefer to have the money than to have the land. B agrees to pay that sum because B values Blackacre more than the value he or she places on $200,000. B would rather have the land than the money. Yet, B's preference or apparent preference may have been expressed at the point of a gun, or induced by S's lies about future planned developments in the vicinity. The assumption of mutual gain from the transaction is a false one. It is false, not because one party's judgment was unsound, but because the party's judgment was distorted by wrongful conduct of the other. Cases of mistake do not always fit this rationale, but in those cases where relief is granted, the usually shared assumption that both will gain from the transaction is thwarted.[1]

B. DURESS

Table of Sections

§ 9.2 The History and Elements of Duress

Few areas of the law of contracts have undergone such radical changes[1] in the nineteenth and twentieth centuries as has the law

---

§ 9.1

1. See Eptstein, Simple Rules for a Complex World 80–82 (1995).

§ 9.2

1. So characterized in Tallmadge v. Robinson, 158 Ohio St. 333, 338–340, 109

governing duress. In Blackstone's time (c. 1776) relief from an agreement on grounds of duress was a possibility only if the agreement was coerced by actual (not threatened) imprisonment or fear of loss of life or limb. "A fear of battery * * * is no duress; neither is the fear of having one's house burned, or one's goods taken away or destroyed," Blackstone wrote, "because in these cases, should the threat be performed, a man may have satisfaction by recovering equivalent damages: but no suitable atonement can be made for the loss of life, or limb."[2]

Today the general rule is that any wrongful act or threat which overcomes the free will of a party constitutes duress.[3] This simple statement of the law, however, conceals a number of questions, particularly as to the meaning of "free will" and "wrongful." Also, as in the case of all contractual rules that make reference to mental processes, we must ask whether the test is objective or subjective. This last is the easiest of the questions posed. In contrast to earlier cases, the overwhelming weight of modern authority uses a subjective test. Thus, the issue now is whether the will of the particular person has been overcome,[4] and not, as the earlier cases had held, whether a brave person would be put in fear or whether the will of a person of ordinary firmness would be overcome.[5] Evidence showing whether a reasonable person would be put in fear is relevant, however, as circumstantial evidence of whether the person's free will was overcome.[6]

Still, an objective test governs certain situations. Where the coercion involves economic pressure rather than threat of physical injury, courts continue to apply an objective element. In the face of a threat of "either

---

N.E.2d 496, 499 (1952). For the history, see 13 Williston §§ 1601–1602 (3d ed.).

2. 1 Blackstone's Commentaries * 131. The rule in England seems to have been relaxed but slightly, until the 1980's and 90's when there was a burst of development. See Birks, 1990 Lloyd's Marit. & Comm. L.Q. 341; O'Dair, 1992 Lloyd's Marit. & Comm. L.Q. 145. The doctrine of undue influence had been expanded to fill part of the void. See Cheshire, Fifoot & Furmston, The Law of Contract 312–21 (12th ed.1991). Blackstone was not strictly correct; the doctrine of duress of goods already had been originated. See § 9.5 infra.

3. Kaplan v. Kaplan, 25 Ill.2d 181, 185, 182 N.E.2d 706, 709 (1962); Austin Instrument v. Loral, 29 N.Y.2d 124, 130, 324 N.Y.S.2d 22, 25, 272 N.E.2d 533, 535 (1971). See 2 Palmer on Restitution § 9.2 (1978).

4. Kaplan v. Kaplan, 25 Ill.2d 181, 186, 182 N.E.2d 706, 709 (1962); Silsbee v. Webber, 171 Mass. 378, 50 N.E. 555 (1898) (classic exposition by Holmes); Rubenstein

v. Rubenstein, 20 N.J. 359, 120 A.2d 11 (1956); 13 Williston § 1605 (3d ed.); but see Three Rivers Motors v. Ford Motor, 522 F.2d 885 (3d Cir.1975). To the effect that the subjective theory of contract was victorious in the area of grounds for avoidance, see Perillo, The Origins of the Objective Theory of Contract Formation and Interpretation, 69 Fordham L.Rev. 427, 466–74 (2000).

5. Young v. Hoagland, 212 Cal. 426, 298 P. 996, 75 ALR 654 (1931). At times the "mind of a person of ordinary firmness" rule is stated, but usually in a case where the precise test is not really in issue. See, e.g., Bata v. Central–Penn Nat. Bank, 423 Pa. 373, 224 A.2d 174 (1966), cert. denied, where the old rule is stated but in a context where "we find it inconceivable that appellant was subject to any degree of restraint or danger." 224 A.2d at 180. The test is. however, repeated in Strickland v. University of Scranton, 700 A.2d 979 (Pa.Super.1997).

6. Rs. 1st § 492 cmt b; Rs. 2d § 175 cmt b.

* * * or," did the person threatened have some reasonable third alternative? For example, was there a judicial proceeding that could have produced prompt and adequate relief? If so, a case for duress would not be made out.[7] Clearly, economic interests receive a different level of protection than interests of personality.

The idea of "free will" requires some elaboration. This, of course, is not the place to deal with the millennia-old concern of philosophers as to whether free will exists, but contract law is very much premised on its existence.[8] Older doctrine was often premised on the idea that an agreement made under duress lacks "real" consent and produces only apparent assent. However, as has been pointed out, when parents pay a kidnapper to save their daughter's life, they may be expressing "the most genuine, heartfelt consent."[9] The consent is real enough; the vice of it is that it was coerced in a manner that society brands as wrongful and is therefore not deemed the product of free will.

Consequently, in determining whether a transaction may be avoided for duress, the main inquiry is to ascertain what acts or threats are branded as wrongful. It is, of course, important in every case to inquire not only whether the act or threat was wrongful but also whether the transaction was in fact induced by the wrong.[10] In addition, another factor, not generally articulated as a rationale in the cases or treatises, is often emphasized in the court's review of the facts—the degree of economic imbalance in the transaction.[11] Duress will generally not be found to exist unless the party exercising the coercion has been unjustly enriched.[12] As stated by a court, "where there is adequacy of consideration, there is generally no duress."[13] Remedies for duress are primarily

---

7. Leeper v. Beltrami, 53 Cal.2d 195, 1 Cal.Rptr. 12, 347 P.2d 12, 77 ALR2d 803 (1959); Austin Instrument v. Loral, 29 N.Y.2d 124, 324 N.Y.S.2d 22, 272 N.E.2d 533 (1971); Gibson v. Wal–Mart, 181 F.3d 1163 (10th Cir.1999); Dalzell, Duress by Economic Pressure II, 20 N.C.L.Rev. 341, 367–82 (1942).

8. See for an introduction, Macneil, The Many Futures of Contracts, 47 S.Cal.L.Rev. 691, 701–06 (1974).

9. Dalzell, Duress by Economic Pressure I, 20 N.C.L.Rev. 237, 237–238 (1942); see also 13 Williston § 1627A (3d ed); Sharp, The Ethics of Breach of Contract, 45 Int'l J. of Ethics, 27, 30–31 (1934); Notes, 38 Or. L.Rev. 246, 248 (1959), 26 Harv.L.Rev. 255 (1912). The classic statement of this analysis is by Justice Holmes in Union Pac. R.R. v. Public Service Comm'n, 248 U.S. 67 (1918). Similar analysis, in a broader discussion of the idea of liberty, is found in Hale, Bargaining, Duress and Economic Liberty, 43 Colum.L.Rev. 603 (1943).

10. U.S. v. Bethlehem Steel, 315 U.S. 289 (1942); Hellenic Lines v. Louis Dreyfus, 372 F.2d 753 (2d Cir.1967). The fear must

induce the contract, but need not be the sole cause. Rs. 1st § 492 cmt f.

11. This is the primary thrust of the analysis in Dawson, Economic Duress—An Essay in Perspective, 45 Mich.L.Rev. 253 (1947); see also Dawson, Unconscionable Coercion: The German Version, 89 Harv. L.Rev. 1041 (1976); Dawson, Duress through Civil Litigation I, II, 45 Mich. L.Rev. 571, 679 (1947); Dawson, Economic Duress and Fair Exchange in French and German Law, 11 Tul.L.Rev. 345 (1937). Another commentator argues that lack of balance is merely evidence of coercion and not a substantive basis for a finding of duress. Dalzell, Duress by Economic Pressure I, 20 N.C.L.Rev. 237, 263 (1942).

12. First Data Resources v. Omaha Steaks Int'l, 209 Neb. 327, 307 N.W.2d 790 (1981) (coercion must result in a contract that is illegal, unjust or unconscionable). See Andreini v. Hultgren, 860 P.2d 916 (Utah 1993) (surgeon refused to proceed unless plaintiff signed a release).

13. Campbell Soup v. Desatnick, 58 F.Supp.2d 477, 482 (D.N.J.1999), quoting N.J. Supreme Court.

aimed at the cancellation of unjust gain.[14] Of course, where the coercion is extreme the legal system's interest in the protection of individual freedom will prevail regardless of any inquiry into the unfairness of the transaction itself.[15]

One commentator, focusing on the means of coercion, rather than its result, has argued that the law of duress has developed to control the bargaining process. Inasmuch as the state allows the exchange process to be handled through the mechanism of contracts, the state has an interest in regulating that mechanism of exchange.[16] This view appears to be based on the premise that the power to contract exists by state delegation to private parties. This text, however, takes the position that the state exists as a delegation of power from contracting parties, rather than vice-versa.

The two possible vantage points—(1) the end result of the coercion and (2) the means of coercion—help explain some of the confusion surrounding differing views concerning coerced modifications of contracts, discussed in § 9.6 below.

§ 9.3 Wrongful Acts or Threats—Abuse of Rights

Violence and threats of violence are wrongful but, although not as rare as one would hope,[1] such wrongs no longer make up the bulk of duress cases. The law has evolved so as to permit relief for duress in a vast variety of situations. These roughly may be categorized into four principal classes:[2]

1. Violence or threats of violence.

2. Imprisonment or threats of imprisonment.

3. Wrongful seizing or withholding, or threats wrongfully to seize or withhold, goods or lands.

14. 2 Palmer on Restitution § 9.4 (1978); Dawson, Economic Duress—An Essay in Perspective, 45 Mich.L.Rev. 253, 283–285 (1947); Rs. 2d § 176, see § 9.8 infra.

15. Dawson, supra note 14, at 284–285; Rs. 2d § 176(1); cf. Pound, Interests of Personality, 28 Harv.L.Rev. 343, 357–359 (1915) (duress doctrine is about freedom of will).

16. Carlston, Restitution—The Search for a Philosophy, 6 J.Leg.Ed. 330, 336–38 (1954). For a similar discussion to the effect that "moralistic" arguments "prevent serious analysis," i.e., in terms of the functioning of the market. 2 Dobbs, Remedies § 10.1; see Eisenberg, The Bargain Principle and its Limits, 95 Harv.L.Rev. 741 (1982). Another analysis, but focusing on duress as a defense in criminal law, is Hill, A Utilitarian Theory of Duress, 84 Iowa L.Rev. 275 (1999).

A release executed by a person under arrest in exchange for a prosecutor's agreement to dismiss charges has been held against public policy because of the inherently coercive nature of the bargaining context. Boyd v. Adams, 513 F.2d 83 (7th Cir.1975); see Annot., 86 ALR3d 1230; but see Newton v. Rumery, 480 U.S. 386 (1987) (no constitutional violation on similar facts).

§ 9.3

1. Williams v. Macchio, 69 Misc.2d 94, 329 N.Y.S.2d 405 (1972); Rubenstein v. Rubenstein, 20 N.J. 359, 120 A.2d 11 (1956); Quazzo v. Quazzo, 136 Vt. 107, 386 A.2d 638 (1978).

2. See, e.g., Rs. 1st § 493 (Restatement categories (a) and (c) are merged in our category No. 1). Rs. 2d § 176 contains a longer list.

4. Other wrongful acts.

It will be helpful to the discussion if the miscellaneous category of "other wrongful acts" is discussed first. This category, of course, includes such criminal conduct as blackmail.[3] The evolving case law, however, has for the most part dealt, instead, with threats to exercise legal rights in oppressive or abusive ways. Perhaps a better term would be "other coercive acts."[4] For example, a threat to bring a law suit is a legitimate form of coercion protected by the common law and the Constitution. However, where a husband threatens his wife with a suit demanding custody of their children on grounds of her adultery unless she transfers certain shares of stock to him, it is at least a jury question whether the assignment is voidable for duress. In the words of the court:

> The weight of modern authority supports the rule, which we here adopt, that the act done or threatened may be wrongful even though not unlawful, per se; and that the threat to instigate legal proceedings, criminal or civil, which might be justifiable, per se, becomes wrongful, within the meaning of this rule, if made with the corrupt intent to coerce a transaction grossly unfair to the victim and not related to the subject of such proceedings.[5]

Similarly, at-will employees may be fired without cause. However, a threat to fire the employees unless they agree to sell their shares of stock in the employing corporation back to the employer constitutes an abuse of the employer's rights and the employee who succumbs to the threat may recover the shares if the trier of fact finds that the employee had been coerced by the threat.[6] On the other hand, a threat to fire unless the employee signs an arbitration agreement or a covenant not to compete will not generally be a predicate for a finding of duress.[7] To summarize, in the context of duress, an act or threat is wrongful if it is "an abuse of the powers of the party making the threat; that is, any threat the purpose of which was not to achieve the end for which the right, power, or privilege was given."[8] Looked at from the point of view

3. This would include also lesser tortious threats such as a threat to use one's influence to cause a lender to refuse to consummate a loan, Criterion Holding v. Cerussi, 140 Misc. 855, 250 N.Y.S. 735 (1931), and a threat to induce a person's employer to fire him. Wise v. Midtown Motors, 231 Minn. 46, 42 N.W.2d 404, 20 ALR2d 735 (1950); Tindall v. Konitz Contr., 240 Mont. 345, 783 P.2d 1376 (1989).

4. Northern Fab. v. Unocal, 980 P.2d 958 (Alaska 1999).

5. Link v. Link, 278 N.C. 181, 194, 179 S.E.2d 697, 705 (1971). For a contrarian view, see Note, 73 Tex. L.Rev. 629 (1995).

6. Laemmar v. J. Walter Thompson, 435 F.2d 680 (7th Cir.1970); but see Vines v. General Outdoor Advertising, 171 F.2d 487 (2d Cir.1948); see also Mitchell v. C.C.

Sanitation, 430 S.W.2d 933 (Tex.App.1968) (duress where employer threatens to fire employee unless employee signed release); Annots., 20 ALR2d 743 (1951); 30 ALR4th 294 (1984).

What of the situation where, when threatened with being fired, the employee accedes to the employer's threats and is soon thereafter fired? See McCubbin v. Buss, 180 Neb. 624, 144 N.W.2d 175 (1966) (coerced agreement may be rescinded).

7. Gibson v. Wal–Mart, 181 F.3d 1163 (10th Cir.1999); Campbell Soup v. Desatnick, 58 F.Supp.2d 477 (D.N.J.1999). Of course, there may be other grounds for attacking such agreements. See §§ 16.19 to 16.22 infra.

8. Dalzell, Duress by Economic Pressure II, 20 N.C.L.Rev. 341, 364 (1942); see also

of the coerced party, one may ethically protect oneself by making a contract one has no intent to keep in order to save oneself from the abusive invasion or threatened invasion of rights. Such self-protection is justified by the general principle that allows self defense.[9]

It should be noted, however, that where there is a good faith dispute, a refusal to pay under a contract until a dispute is settled or adjudicated, does not constitute duress.[10] A party's refusal to settle does not constitute a wrongful threat.[11] When an employee is offered the chance of being fired for cause or resigning, it will usually be held that the resignation cannot be avoided,[12] unless the threat to fire is made for bad faith reasons or is accompanied by threats to ruin the reputation of the employee.[13] Conditioning a marriage on the signing of a pre-marital agreement is not duress.[14] In short, absent a *wrongful* threat, the driving of a hard bargain is not duress.[15] This is true even if one party benefits from the financial distress of the other.[16]

§ 9.4 Threats of Imprisonment or Criminal Prosecution

Civil imprisonment or the threat of it, if caused or threatened in good faith and allowed by law, cannot normally justify a finding of duress. It may be coercive, but such behavior is not wrongful. On the other hand if the law does not allow the imprisonment or the imprisonment is oppressively exercised or threatened so as to constitute an abuse of rights, there is sufficient foundation for a finding of duress.[1] Similarly, a threat of a legitimate civil suit coupled with threats to ruin the other party by enmeshing the party in difficulties with licensing and regulatory authorities may be the basis for a finding of duress.[2]

When a transaction is induced by a threat of arrest, criminal prosecution, or criminal imprisonment, the most varied reasoning and results are found.[3] Few generalizations can be made. The reason for the

---

13 Williston § 1607 (3d ed.); Rs. 1st § 492 cmt g.

9. See Sharp, § 9.2 n.9, at 34.

10. Selmer v. Blakeslee–Midwest, 704 F.2d 924 (7th Cir.1983); LaBeach v. Beatrice Foods, 461 F.Supp. 152 (S.D.N.Y. 1978); Landers v. State, 56 A.D.2d 105, 391 N.Y.S.2d 723 (1977), aff'd.

11. Wiesen v. Short, 43 Colo.App. 374, 604 P.2d 1191 (1979). Otherwise, if the claim is in bad faith. Adams v. Crater Well Drilling, 276 Or. 789, 556 P.2d 679 (1976); see also International Underwater Contr. v. New England Tel. and Tel., 8 Mass.App. 340, 393 N.E.2d 968 (1979).

12. Miami v. Kory, 394 So.2d 494 (Fla. App.1981), rev. denied.

13. Humana v. Fairchild, 603 S.W.2d 918 (Ky.App.1980).

14. Marriage of Barnes, 324 Ill.App.3d 514, 258 Ill.Dec. 139, 755 N.E.2d 522 (2001).

15. Selmer v. Blakeslee–Midwest, supra § 9.3 n.10; Grand Motors v. Ford Motor, 564 F.Supp. 34 (W.D.Mo.1982).

16. Chouinard v. Chouinard, 568 F.2d 430 (5th Cir.1978); First Texas Sav. Assn. v. Dicker Center, 631 S.W.2d 179 (Tex.App. 1982).

§ 9.4

1. Rs. 1st § 493 cmt b. Cases are collected and discussed in Dawson, Duress through Civil Litigation 1, 45 Mich.L.Rev. 571, 586–91 (1947); 13 Williston §§ 1609–1610 (3d ed.).

2. Jamestown Farmers Elevator v. General Mills, 552 F.2d 1285 (8th Cir.1977).

3. See generally 2 Palmer on Restitution § 9.11; 13 Williston §§ 1609–1615 (3d ed.); Woodward, Quasi Contracts §§ 141–142, 214–215; Dawson, Economic Duress—An Essay in Perspective, 45 Mich.L.Rev. 253, 285–287 (1947). As to a release of

confusing disparity of results can perhaps be understood by examining a typical fact pattern. A principal charges a fiduciary with embezzlement, and threatens to turn the fiduciary over to the authorities unless the fiduciary makes restitution. Induced by the threat, the fiduciary produces part of the demand in cash and signs a promissory note for the balance, co-signed by a concerned relative. The following propositions can be stated, some of which tug in a different direction than others. The first two propositions point to a finding of duress. (1) Although the principal has a legal right to report suspicions to the authorities, the threat to exercise this right solely for private gain constitutes an abuse of this right. (2) The threat is coercive and capable of inducing a settlement against the free will of the fiduciary and the relative.[4] Whether it induced the settlement is a question of fact. A third proposition points, however, to an opposite result. If the fiduciary was in fact guilty, the principal is not unjustly enriched by the fiduciary's performing or promising to perform a legal obligation.[5]

A fourth proposition must be injected into the equation, if, as so frequently occurs, the principal agrees not to prosecute a criminal proceeding against the fiduciary. Such an agreement is emphatically illegal.[6] As to illegal agreements the general proposition is that the court will leave the parties where it finds them.[7] If this proposition stood alone the court would neither enforce the promissory note nor would it compel restitution of the amount paid. This result, however, is placed in doubt by a fifth proposition. A party who is pressured into an illegal bargain by duress is deemed not to be equally guilty with the party exercising the pressure and generally will be awarded restitution.[8]

claims of false arrest exchanged for a prosecutor's dismissal of charges see § 9.2 n.16 supra. A threat to turn one's claim over to one's attorney for prosecution does not justify an inference of a threat of criminal prosecution. Rivervalley v. Deposit Guaranty Nat. Bank, 331 F.Supp. 698 (N.D.Miss. 1971).

4. Some courts distinguish between the accused and his relative, expressing a greater willingness to consider a claim of duress where the party coerced is a relative. Kronmeyer v. Buck, 258 Ill. 586, 101 N.E. 935 (1913). Others disagree. Union Exchange Nat. Bank of New York v. Joseph, 231 N.Y. 250, 131 N.E. 905, 17 ALR 323 (1921).

There must be a threat. A statement to the accused that he could be subject to a penitentiary offense was held not to be a threat. Buhrman v. International Harvester, 181 Neb. 633, 150 N.W.2d 220 (1967); but see Germantown Mfg. v. Rawlinson, 341 Pa.Super. 42, 491 A.2d 138 (1985) (implied threat).

5. If a finding of duress is made and there is no complicating factor of illegality,

the recovery is frequently limited to the excess of the amount paid over the amount of the indebtedness. Merrel v. Research & Data, 3 Kan.App.2d 48, 589 P.2d 120 (1979); see also cases cited by Dawson, Economic Duress—An Essay in Perspective, 45 Mich.L.Rev. 253, 285–87 (1947). For similar reasons, courts which are unwilling to allow duress to be raised as a defense or as a basis for an action for restitution where the settlement is fair, are willing to allow the claim of duress to be proved where the settlement is out of proportion to the legal obligation. Kronmeyer v. Buck, 258 Ill. 586, 101 N.E. 935 (1913).

6. If there is no such agreement and the withholding of prosecution is merely an unbargained-for result of the settlement, the transaction is not illegal. Rs. 1st § 548 ill. 1; Blair Milling v. Fruitager, 113 Kan. 432, 215 P. 286, 32 ALR 416 (1923). Apparently, an agreement to withhold prosecution is not illegal in Florida. Smith v. Paul Revere Life Ins., 998 F.Supp. 1412 (S.D.Fla.1997)

7. See § 22.1 infra.

8. See § 22.7 infra.

In view of the tensions among these propositions it is not surprising that courts have reached differing results. At times the decisions show a sophisticated awareness of the nature of the choice to be made.[9] Frequently, however, the competing factors are submerged beneath dubious reasoning.[10]

§ 9.5 Duress of Property: Assertion of Liens

A wrongful threat to detain or the detention of the property of another amounts to duress if two factors are present: (1) it coerces the assent of the other to a transaction and (2) the party coerced had no reasonable alternative but to assent.[1]

A wrongful action may arise from the exercise of a legal right. Often one may have a legal right to assert a retaining lien on property of another, to obtain an attachment of goods, to foreclose a mortgage, etc. The exercise of such rights is inherently coercive even if scrupulously employed. If a legal right is employed in a particularly oppressive manner or is employed to force a settlement disproportionate to what is owed, the exercise of the right constitutes duress unless the coerced party could have obtained judicial or other relief that would have been reasonably prompt and efficacious under the circumstances.[2]

The classic case is Chandler v. Sanger,[3] where a creditor whose claim had been discharged in bankruptcy procured a writ of attachment and attached the plaintiff's ice wagon in the pre-dawn hours after they had been loaded with ice. To dissolve the attachment the plaintiff paid the creditor's claim. The alternative was to move in court that the attachment be dissolved and a bond posted. Plaintiff was advised, however,

---

9. See Union Exchange Nat. Bank v. Joseph, 231 N.Y. 250, 131 N.E. 905, 17 ALR 323 (1921) (no enforcement of note against accused's brother-in-law and no restitution; restitution perhaps available if criminal charge is asserted in bad faith) ("there is to be no traffic in the privilege of invoking the public justice of the state."); contra, and equally cognizant of competing state interests, Gorringe v. Read, 23 Utah 120, 63 P. 902 (1901) ("as civilization has advanced the law has tended much more strongly than it formerly did to overthrow everything which is built on violence and fraud.") Rs. 2d § 176 cmt c, takes the position that duress renders executory transactions of this kind voidable. It takes no position on the question of restitution of money paid pursuant to a threat.

10. See, e.g., Harrell v. Allen, 439 F.2d 1005 (5th Cir.1971) (as a matter of law a threat of arrest cannot overcome free will).

§ 9.5

1. The doctrine of duress of goods originated with the case of Astley v. Reynolds, 2 Strange 915, 93 Eng.Rep. 939 (K.B.1732)

where a pledgee refused to surrender pledged property to the pledgor except on payment of an unjustified bonus. The pledgor payed and recovered the excess payment, the court stating the owner "might have such an immediate want of his goods, that an action of trover would not do his business." For a modern application, see S.P. Dunham & Co. v. Kudra, 44 N.J.Super. 565, 131 A.2d 306 (1957), 32 Tul.L.Rev. 512 (1958).

2. See generally, 13 Williston §§ 1616–1619 (3d ed.); Dalzell, Duress by Economic Pressure I, II, 20 N.C.L.Rev. 237, 341 (1942); Dawson, Duress Through Civil Litigation I, II, 45 Mich.L.Rev. 571, 679 (1947).

3. 114 Mass. 364, 19 Am.Rep. 367 (1874); accord, Fenwick Shipping v. Clarke Bros., 133 Ga. 43, 65 S.E. 140 (1909) (attachment of baggage of a traveler when he has abundant other assets within the jurisdiction); Rs. 2d § 176, ill. 7; compare the tort doctrine of abuse of process. Prosser & Keeton, Torts § 121 (5th ed. 1984).

that three days would be required to obtain such relief, by which time the ice would have melted and, perhaps, the ice business crippled.

The facts of Chandler easily give rise to a finding of duress. Note that the property chosen for attachment was deliberately selected to deprive the plaintiff of freedom of choice and that the claim was known to be unfounded as the bankruptcy court had already discharged the claim. Where these elements co-exist in the same fact pattern duress can easily be found. But, of course, duress can be found even where all of these elements are not present.

The bad faith assertion of a claim is a key element. Where the oppression is no greater than that which is inherent in the typical attachment or assertion of a lien, but the claim is made in bad faith, a finding of duress is generally indicated if the evidence shows that the pressured party was indeed coerced by the lien and had no reasonable alternative but to agree to the offered terms.[4] Where the claim is made in good faith but is factually unfounded, or the claim although in good faith is in excess of what is in fact owed, a claim of duress is extremely difficult to sustain.[5] Strong judicial policies favor the settlement of disputes and encourage the use of the courts where settlement can not satisfactorily be attained. On the other hand, there is increasing willingness to realize that liens asserted, even in good faith, have the power to coerce unjustified settlements resulting in unjust enrichment. In what is perhaps the leading modern case, plaintiff acceded to the defendant's demands for payment of repairs to plaintiff's motor boat in order to secure release of the boat.[6] The court found duress and allowed recovery of the overcharges without making reference to the presence or absence of the defendant's good faith. In addition, the court made no reference to whether the plaintiff had any reasonable alternative (e.g., posting a bond pending litigation) to acceding to defendant's demands. Professor Epstein explained the court's reasoning. Defendant has put plaintiff to a choice between plaintiff's boat or plaintiff's money. Defendant has forced plaintiff to abandon one right to protect another. The recovery is designed to protect both.[7]

§ 9.6   Coerced Settlements or Contract Modifications

The doctrine of duress has tended to be compartmentalized into various categories: rules governing threats of imprisonment, duress of property, etc., often being treated as separate doctrines rather than separate manifestations of common legal principles. Among these categories are threats to breach contracts and the traditional rule has been

4. First Nat. Bank v. Pepper, 454 F.2d 626 (2d Cir.1972) (attorney's retaining lien); Leeper v. Beltrami, 53 Cal.2d 195, 1 Cal.Rptr. 12, 347 P.2d 12, 77 ALR2d 803 (1959) (threatened foreclosure); Kilpatrick v. Germania Life Ins., 183 N.Y. 163, 75 N.E. 1124 (1905) (mortgagee's refusal of tender by mortgagor).

5. See Annot., 18 ALR 1233 (1922).

6. Murphy v. Brilliant, 323 Mass. 526, 83 N.E.2d 166 (1948); compare Hensel v. Cahill, 179 Pa.Super. 114, 116 A.2d 99 (1955). See Joannin v. Ogilvie, 49 Minn. 564, 52 N.W. 217, 16 LRA 376 (1892).

7. Epstein, Unconscionability: A Critical Reappraisal, 18 J.L. & Econ. 293, 296 (1975).

that a threat to breach a contract does not constitute duress,[1] except in coercive situations in which the government, a common carrier or a public utility made the threat.[2] Hackley v. Headley[3] has been regarded as a leading case. The defendant admittedly owed the plaintiff $4,260, and knowing that the plaintiff was in great need of money and could be financially ruined if he were not quickly paid, offered the plaintiff his note for $4,000 on a take it or sue me basis. The plaintiff took the note and signed a release demanded by the defendant. The plaintiff later sought to avoid the release, but the court held that there was no duress. The courts are open to compel payment of debts, reasoned the court, and the fact that plaintiff was in dire financial straits and needed relief more quickly than could be supplied by the courts was not pressure supplied by the defendant.[4] Consequently, the inadequacy of the judicial remedy was due to subjective factors personal to the plaintiff.[5]

Note two points about Hackley. First, the case is inconsistent with the subjective approach to duress dominating the law today.[6] Second, the case is squarely inconsistent with a persuasive case in which duress was

§ 9.6

1. 2 Palmer on Restitution § 9.12; Dalzell, Duress by Economic Pressure I, 20 N.C.L.Rev. 237, 255–276 (1942). An example of survival of a version of this rule is Degenhardt v. Dillon, 543 Pa. 146, 669 A.2d 946 (1996) (There can be no economic duress if the party had an opportunity to consult counsel.)

2. Id. at 254–55. The government contract exception was based on the inadequacy of remedy against the government. Now that in most jurisdictions sovereign immunity no longer presents a significant barrier to actions against the government, a plea of duress is nonetheless available. The federal standards are restated in Loral v. U.S., 193 Ct.Cl. 473, 434 F.2d 1328, 1332–1333 (1970); and Urban Plumbing & Heating v. U.S., 187 Ct.Cl. 15, 408 F.2d 382 (1969), cert. denied; compare state standards stated in Pearlman v. State, 18 Misc.2d 494, 191 N.Y.S.2d 422 (1959). The carrier and utility cases are based on the monopolistic position of the public service company. See Woodward, Quasi Contracts §§ 220–21 (1913).

3. 45 Mich. 569, 8 N.W. 511 (1881).

4. If the plaintiff had urgent need for cash, why did he accept the note? Presumably the note would be used as collateral security for a loan or, as was customary in the nineteenth century, discounted at a bank, or used as a medium of exchange. Promissory notes served many of the functions of money. See Lincoln Nat. Bank of Lincoln, Ill. v. Perry, 66 F. 887, 894 (8th Cir.1895) ("as notes and bills are designed to circulate freely, and to take the place of money in commercial transaction."); see

also Bakken, Contract Law in the Rockies, 1850–1912, 18 Am.J.Leg.Hist. 33, 41 (1974).

5. Compare Selmer v. Blakeslee–Midwest, 704 F.2d 924 (7th Cir.1983) with Totem Marine Tug & Barge v. Alyeska Pipeline Service, 584 P.2d 15, 9 ALR4th 928 (Alaska 1978). See also Rich & Whillock v. Ashton Dev., 157 Cal.App.3d 1154, 204 Cal. Rptr. 86 (1984). Arguing for the position that exploitation of hardship not caused by the other party should never invalidate the contract is Epstein, Unconscionability, 18 J.L. & Econ. 293, 297 (1975). Cases such as Long's Marine v. Boyland, 899 S.W.2d 945 (Mo.App.1995), agree.

6. See § 9.2 supra. On the question of the pressure of circumstances taken advantage of by one party, see 13 Williston § 1608 (3d ed.). If the wrongful pressure is exerted by a third party unbeknownst to the party benefiting from the pressure, duress will not generally be a defense. The party benefiting will normally be in the position of a bona fide purchaser for value. U.S. v. Bond, 322 Md. 170, 586 A.2d 734 (1991) (but would be a defense if there were an absence of consent (§ 9.8 n.2 infra)); see Rs. 2d § 175(2); 13 Williston § 1622A (3d ed.). Contra, Barry v. Equitable Life Assur. Soc., 59 N.Y. 587 (1875), and see Resolution Trust v. Ruggiero, 977 F.2d 309 (7th Cir. 1992) (D'Oench, Duhme doctrine applied).

Where a party alleges duress by the party's own attorney to settle a case, the court will show little sympathy. Evans v. Waldorf–Astoria, 827 F.Supp. 911 (E.D.N.Y.1993), aff'd; Lee v. Lee, 44 S.W.3d 151 (Tex.App. 2001).

deemed well pleaded where it was alleged that a liquidated obligation of $157,000 was released for $5,000 where money was immediately required to prevent foreclosure of a mortgage on the coerced party's house and repossession of personal property.[7] Third, in both of the cases just described the coerced parties were entitled to relief under the doctrine of consideration instead of duress.[8] The persistence of the pre-existing duty rule has relieved the pressure for expansion of the doctrine of duress to cases of threatened contractual breach. However, the decline of the doctrine of consideration under the UCC and certain other statutes, and its deemphasis in the Restatement (Second),[9] have given an additional impetus for the expansion of the duress doctrine into the areas of threatened breach.[10]

Thus, cases[11] now hold that a threat to breach a contract constitutes duress if the threatened breach would, if carried out, result in irreparable injury because of the absence of an adequate legal or equitable remedy[12] or other reasonable alternative.[13] In such situations, the threatened breacher enjoys monopoly power.

According to the Restatement (Second),[14] the threatened breach must be a "breach of the duty of good faith and fair dealing." The

---

7. Capps v. Georgia Pacific, 253 Or. 248, 453 P.2d 935 (1969). If the debt was unliquidated, it is unlikely that duress would be found. Northern Fabrication v. Unocal, 980 P.2d 958 (Alaska 1999). On releases by employees, see Annot., 30 ALR4th 294 (1984).

8. In subsequent litigation the release in Headley v. Hackley was held void for want of consideration. Headley v. Hackley, 50 Mich. 43, 14 N.W. 693 (1883). In Capps v. Georgia Pacific, Justice Denecke, concurring specially, was of the opinion that the doctrine of duress was inapplicable but the release would be void for want of consideration if the facts were as alleged. See Note, Unbalanced Transactions under Common and Civil Law, 43 Colum.L.Rev. 1066 (1943) (focusing on consideration doctrine).

9. See § 4.9 & 5.14 supra.

10. See § 5.15 supra.

11. Thompson Crane & Trucking v. Eyman, 123 Cal.App.2d 904, 267 P.2d 1043 (1954), 28 So.Cal.L.Rev. 317 (1955); Ross Sys. v. Linden Dari–Delite, 35 N.J. 329, 173 A.2d 258 (1961) (refusal to pay overcharges would result in loss of source of supply); Austin Instrument v. Loral, 29 N.Y.2d 124, 324 N.Y.S.2d 22, 272 N.E.2d 533 (1971) (overcharges by sub-contractor where substitute components were unavailable on the market); compare New Again Constr. v. New York, 76 Misc.2d 943, 351 N.Y.S.2d 895 (1974) (purported release of claims without consideration under statute denied effect because of City's "bad faith"); Equity Funding v. Carol Management, 66 Misc.2d 1020, 322 N.Y.S.2d 965 (1971), aff'd

(coerced increase in rent). Some of the above cases, although classified as "threatened" breaches could be viewed as actual breaches by anticipatory repudiation. (See ch. 12 infra). In Pecos Constr. v. Mortgage Inv., 80 N.M. 680, 459 P.2d 842 (1969), plaintiff was awarded restitution for amounts paid because of duress plus damages for breach caused by delay between the time of defendant's unjustified demand and the time of the coerced settlement. See also, Gilbert Kobatake, Inc. v. Kaiser Hawaii–Kai Dev., 56 Haw. 39, 526 P.2d 1205 (1974); Wurtz v. Fleischman, 97 Wis.2d 100, 293 N.W.2d 155, 12 ALR4th 1254 (1980).

12. On what constitutes an adequate remedy in this context, see Dalzell, Duress by Economic Pressure II, 20 N.C.L.Rev. 341, 367–382 (1942).

13. For example, getting the goods from another supplier (Kelsey–Hayes v. Galtaco Redlaw Castings, 749 F.Supp. 794 (E.D.Mich.1990); Walbern Press v. C.V. Communications, 212 A.D.2d 460, 622 N.Y.S.2d 951 (1995)) or retaining another contractor. Tri–State Roofing v. Simon, 187 Pa.Super. 17, 142 A.2d 333 (1958). But cf. Windham v. Alexander, Weston & Poehner, 887 S.W.2d 182 (Tex.App.1994) (attorney allegedly threatened to abandon the client at the final stages of a divorce action unless the client signed a note for an allegedly excessive fee; question of fact). See MacDonald, 1989 J.Bus.L. 460 (English law).

14. Rs. 2d § 176(1)(d); for a criticism of the Restatement approach, see Snyder, The

Restatement (Second) follows the UCC in this respect. Although the UCC permits modifications and releases without consideration, it requires that a request for a modification or release be made in good faith. The Restatement (Second) gives this illustration,[15] which conceals as many problems as it clarifies:

> A contracts to excavate a cellar for B at a stated price. A unexpectedly encounters solid rock and threatens not to finish the excavation unless B modifies the contract to state a new price that is reasonable but is nine times the original price. B, having no reasonable alternative, is induced by A's threat to make the modification by a signed writing that is enforceable by statute without consideration. A's threat is not a breach of his duty of good faith and fair dealing, and the modification is not voidable by B. See Illustration 1 to § 89.

If we assume that nine times the original price meets only A's costs and a reasonable profit, we might conclude that A is not unjustly enriched. We are, however, told nothing about B's situation. Suppose B is a general contractor working under a fixed price contract with C. Clearly the modification is induced by coercion. Unless C is willing to modify the contract price upward with B, the coercion has resulted in B's unjust impoverishment. If B cannot get relief under the doctrine of duress, can B get protection under the doctrine of unconscionability? As indicated earlier, there have been two different vantage points from which the doctrine of duress has been analyzed: (1) unjust enrichment and (2) policing the bargaining process.[16] The Restatement (Second) has concentrated on the first,[17] while some commentators focus on the second.[18] A leading case under the UCC also focused on the second vantage point and held that coercive conduct itself is bad faith, unless it is justified by the contract.[19] Dishonest conduct also constitutes bad faith.[20]

Under the UCC, the party who is subjected to coercion has an additional vehicle for setting aside a coerced modification or settlement. The coerced party may agree, but simultaneously indicate that the agreement is under protest. This preserves the party's rights.[21] There

Law of Contract and the Concept of Change, 1999 Wisc.L.Rev. 507.

15. Rs. 2d § 176, ill. 8.

16. See § 9.2 supra.

17. As has its reporter. Farnsworth, Coercion in Contract Law, 5 U.Ark.Little Rock L.J. 329 (1982).

18. Brody, Performance of a Pre–Existing Contractual Duty as Consideration, 52 Denv.L.J. 433 (1975); Hillman, Contract Modification Under the Restatement (Second) of Contracts, 67 Cornell L.Rev. 680 (1982); Hillman, A Study of UCC Methodology: Contract Modification Under Article Two, 59 N.C.L.Rev. 335 (1981); Hillman, Policing Contract Modifications Under the UCC, 64 Iowa L.Rev. 849 (1979); Mather,

Contract Modification Under Duress, 33 S.Car.L.Rev. 615 (1982); Medina, Economic Duress as a Means of Avoiding Settlement Agreements in Oklahoma, 15 Okl.City L.Rev 255 (1990). On developments in England, see Halson, 107 L.Q.Rev. 649 (1991); MacDonald, 1989 J.Bus.L. 460. Compare Robison, Enforcing Extorted Contract Modifications, 68 Iowa L.Rev. 699 (1983).

19. Roth Steel Products v. Sharon Steel, 705 F.2d 134 (6th Cir.1983).

20. Palmer v. Safe Auto Sales, 114 Misc.2d 964, 452 N.Y.S.2d 995 (1982).

21. UCC § 1–207; § 1–308 of the revision. See U.S. Nav. v. Black Diamond Lines, 124 F.2d 508 (2d Cir.1942), cert. denied (a pre-UCC case in accord); E.H. Oftedal &

will be occasions when the coercing party will insist that the protest be withdrawn. Under such circumstances, a withdrawn protest should act as a protest. Outside of the Code, protest is merely some evidence of duress.[22]

There are conflicting policies at work in this area. Modifications and settlements are encouraged. Such transactions will be discouraged, however, if they are easily upset. At the same time, coercion, unjust enrichment and unjust impoverishment are not favorites of the law. Neither the UCC nor the Restatement (Second) offer much guidance on how to reconcile these policies. The courts are likely to continue to balance the competing concerns in arriving at decisions in concrete cases. However, a modification coerced by a wrongful threat to breach under circumstances in which the coerced party has no reasonable alternative should prima facie be voidable absent the reasonable possibility of passing on the additional costs downstream. If the increased cost cannot be passed on, it should be immaterial that the party exercising coercion has a good business reason for its wrongful demands.[23]

§ 9.7   Business Compulsion

There has been a tendency to categorize cases involving threatened contract breaches and other forms of economic pressure as something other than duress. Cases involving economic pressure have been grouped under the heading of "business compulsion" restricting duress to its nineteenth-century categories of duress to person and property.[1] There is little justification for this tendency and the two in-depth scholarly analyses of this area have not accepted it.[2] Cases recognizing economic pressure as grounds for setting aside a transaction have adopted the principles of duress and have modernized them but have created no separate doctrine.

§ 9.8   Remedies for Duress—Ratification

Normally, duress renders a transaction voidable at the election of the coerced party.[1] In highly unusual situations, however, duress would render the transaction void. These situations involve the absence of consent rather than coerced consent. An example would be where a

---

Sons v. State, 308 Mont. 50, 40 P.3d 349 (2002) (contract signed under protest); 2 Corbin § 7.21 (Perillo & Bender 1995).

22. 2 Palmer on Restitution § 9.17; in England, protest provides a strong basis for relief. North Ocean Shipping v. Hyundai Constr. Co., [1979] 1 Q.B. 705.

23. See Snyder, The Law of Contract and the Concept of Change: Public and Private Attempts to Regulate Modification, Waiver, and Estoppel, 1999 Wisconsin L.Rev. 607, 674–685, who would substitute a rule of reasonableness for the "no reasonable alternative" analysis.

§ 9.7

1. E.g., Ramp Buildings v. Northwest Building, 164 Wn. 603, 4 P.2d 507, 79 ALR 651 (1931).

2. Dalzell, Duress by Economic Pressure I, II, 20 N.C.L.Rev. 237, 341 (1942); Dawson, Economic Duress—An Essay in Perspective, 45 Mich.L.Rev. 253 (1947).

§ 9.8

1. Rs. 1st § 496; 13 Williston §§ 1624, 1627 (3d ed.); cf. Lanham, 29 Modern L.Rev. 615 (1966). On the availability of reformation for duress, see § 9.35 infra.

party is made to sign an instrument at gun point without knowledge of its contents.[2]

A transaction that is voidable for duress may be ratified. Where coercion induces consent, the coerced party's behavior, once the coercion is removed,[3] may constitute ratification. The coerced party may ratify the voidable transaction by recognizing its validity, by acting on it, accepting benefits under it, or merely failing to avoid it with reasonable promptness.[4] According to some authorities, avoidance requires the tender back of the benefits received under the contract.[5] Tender of restoration should not be required, however, where money has been received and the party alleging duress claims that additional money should be paid. Where, however, the initial coercion continues for a period of time, it has been held that the wrong is a continuing one and the statute of limitations does not commence to run until the coercion ceases.[6]

Normally, the remedy for duress is a quasi-contractual action for "money had and received." Because the principal economic function of duress has been to redress unjust enrichment, the normal recovery is limited to the amount paid by the party to the coercing party in excess of the amount that was fairly owed.[7] Where the plaintiff has not parted with money but with property or services, the recovery is the market value of the property or services with an offset for any money received by the coerced party.[8] Alternatively, the plaintiff may be able to invoke the equity arm of the court to assert a constructive trust or equitable lien on the property handed over, or an equitable lien on the property the services have benefitted.[9] Indeed, the aid of equity may be essential to cancel a deed of record.[10]

Professor Woodward has made a persuasive argument that, as in the case of fraud, the plaintiff who has a restitutionary action based on duress ought to be able to elect instead to bring a tort action.[11] In certain cases this could be highly advantageous.[12] Yet, the tort of duress has

2. Rs. 1st § 495; Rs. 2d § 174; 13 Williston § 1624 (3d ed.).

3. There is no ratification if the coerced party has no reasonable alternative but to acquiesce in the transaction. Sosnoff v. Carter, 165 A.D.2d 486, 568 N.Y.S.2d 43 (1991).

4. Dorn v. Astra, USA, 975 F.Supp. 388 (D.Mass.1997); Capstone Enterprises v. County of Westchester, 262 A.D.2d 343, 691 N.Y.S.2d 574 (1999); Gallon v. Lloyd–Thomas, 264 F.2d 821, 77 ALR2d 417 (8th Cir. 1959); Keshishian v. CMC Radiologists, 142 N.H. 168, 698 A.2d 1228 (1997); see Williston § 1627 (3d ed.). Also, where the transaction is merely voidable, the party who obtains property by duress can transfer good title to a bona fide purchaser for value. See § 9.6 n. 6 supra.

5. Harless v. Research Inst. of America, 1 F.Supp.2d 235 (S.D.N.Y.1998).

6. Pierce v. Haverlah's Estate, 428 S.W.2d 422 (Tex.App.1968), reh. denied. On the statute of limitations, see Annot., 77 ALR2d 821 (1961).

7. First Nat. Bank v. Pepper, supra § 9.5 n.4; Jamestown Farmers Elevator v. General Mills, supra § 9.4 n.2; Dawson, supra § 9.7 n.2, at 283–285 (1947); Rs. Restitution § 150.

8. Rs. Restitution §§ 151–152.

9. Rs. Restitution § 51 cmt g; § 152 cmt a.

10. See 1 Pomeroy, Equity Jurisprudence §§ 110, 171 (1918); 2 id. § 950.

11. Woodward, The Law of Quasi Contracts § 211 (1913); Note, 53 Iowa L.Rev. 892 (1968).

12. See Note, 39 Harv.L.Rev. 108 (1925).

been recognized only in "odd cases,"[13] and cases in which counsel argued for such a doctrine also appear to be very rare.[14] To be distinguished of course are cases where the coercion itself involves a battery, false imprisonment or other traditional tort. In such a case, an independent tort action for damages may be brought in addition to an action in quasi contract for restitution.[15]

While duress is often the basis of an action for restitution, the doctrine may be raised by way of an affirmative defense to an action on the executory portion of the agreement.[16] If the action brought is for specific performance, less coercion and oppression is required to sustain a defense than in a case seeking relief at law.[17] This stems from the discretionary nature of the remedy of specific performance.[18] If the instrument executed under duress is a release or its equivalent, duress may be raised by way of reply in a case where the coerced party brings an action on the underlying claim and the release is raised by defense.[19]

C.　UNDUE INFLUENCE

Table of Sections

§ 9.9　Background of Undue Influence

Undue influence is a concept that courts of equity originated as a ground for setting aside a transaction that a dominant party had imposed on a subservient party.[1] In the nineteenth century courts of

13.　Prosser & Keeton, Torts 121 (5th ed. 1984); see also Dawson, Economic Duress—An Essay in Perspective, 45 Mich. L.Rev. 253, 285 n.80; Notes, 53 Iowa L.Rev. 892, 901 n.57, 38 Or.L.Rev. 246, 257–258 (1959). In addition to the cases cited by these sources, the tortious nature of duress may be induced from those cases holding that in addition to restitution the plaintiff may recover punitive damages. Edquest v. Tripp & Dragstedt, 93 Mont. 446, 19 P.2d 637 (1933); Adams v. Crater Well Drilling, supra § 9.3 n.11; Southwestern Gas & Elec. v. Stanley, 123 Tex. 157, 70 S.W.2d 413 (1934).

14.　The argument was made unsuccessfully in Davis v. Hargett, 244 N.C. 157, 92 S.E.2d 782, 58 ALR2d 494 (1956).

15.　Prosser & Keeton, Torts 121 (5th ed. 1984).

16.　Austin Instrument v. Loral, 29 N.Y.2d 124, 324 N.Y.S.2d 22, 272 N.E.2d 533 (1971); Great American Indem. v. Ber-

ryessa, 122 Utah 243, 248 P.2d 367 (1952) (burden of proof of this affirmative defense on the defendant.)

17.　Scheinberg v. Scheinberg, 249 N.Y. 277, 164 N.E. 98 (1928).

18.　See § 16.7 infra.

19.　Wise v. Midtown Motors, 231 Minn. 46, 42 N.W.2d 404, 20 ALR2d 735 (1950); Fleming v. Ponziani, 24 N.Y.2d 105, 299 N.Y.S.2d 134, 247 N.E.2d 114 (1969) (useful discussion of burden of proof in such a case). Similarly, duress may be raised by way of estopping the defendant from asserting other affirmative defenses. Bayshore Indus. v. Ziats, 232 Md. 167, 192 A.2d 487 (1963), overruled in part (employee failed to file timely worker's compensation claims because of employer's threats).

§ 9.9

1.　Early cases are cited by Dawson, supra § 9.7 n.2, at 262 (1947).

equity expanded the concept to allow relief on grounds akin to duress but which failed to come within the rigid Blackstonian definition of duress that the common law employed. As stated in one case: "Undue influence * * * is 'any improper or wrongful constraint, machination, or urgency of persuasion, whereby the will of a person is overpowered, and he is induced to do or forbear an act which he would not do, or would do if left to act freely.' "[2]

When at the beginning of the twentieth century, the common law doctrine of duress was expanded to provide relief for coercion irrespective of the means of coercion,[3] much of the work of undue influence became unnecessary. Today, undue influence has a much more specialized role, although the precedents decided under the older approach are cited and quoted often enough to confuse the profession.[4] Today the gist of the doctrine is unfair persuasion rather than coercion. Often, but certainly not always, the state of mind of the party unduly influenced is euphoria, not fear.[5] In such cases, the emphasis is on the unfairness of the advantage to the party who exerts the influence rather than on the want of consent of the victim.[6]

§ 9.10 Elements of Undue Influence

(a) Non–Attorney Cases

There are two broad classes of undue influence cases, and a third category involving attorneys. In the first, one party uses a dominant psychological position in an unfair manner to induce the subservient party to consent to an agreement to which the other party would not otherwise have consented.[1] The doctrine requires neither threats nor deception although often enough one or the other is present. In the second class, one uses a position of trust and confidence, rather than dominance, to unfairly persuade the other into a transaction.[2] Very often the line between these two categories is blurred, as when the dominant party dominates by virtue of the trust and confidence, rather than the subservience, engendered. The rules are elusive. The primary problem is centered on the definition of "unfair" persuasion. Most statements of the problem focus on the means of persuasion, but Professor Dawson has

2. Smith v. Henline, 174 Ill. 184, 203, 51 N.E. 227, 233 (1898). 2 Pomeroy, A Treatise on Equity Jurisprudence § 951 (4th ed. 1918); see also 1 Story, Commentaries on Equity Jurisprudence § 239 (13th ed. 1886).

3. The turning point appears to have been Holmes' opinion in Silsbee v. Webber, 171 Mass. 378, 50 N.E. 555 (1898).

4. See note, 22 Baylor L.Rev. 572 (1970).

5. For psychological studies, see Shaffer, 45 Notre Dame Law. 197 (1970); Fingarette, 42 W. & L.L.Rev 65 (1985); Comment, 25 Loy.L.A.L.Rev. 499 (1992).

6. Smith v. Ellison, 171 Or.App. 289, 15 P.3d 67 (2000).

§ 9.10

1. Rs. 1st § 497; see e.g., In re Kaufmann's Will, 20 A.D.2d 464, 247 N.Y.S.2d 664 (1964), aff'd.

2. Rs. 1st § 497; Rs. 2d § 177 cmt a; see e.g., Schroeder v. Ely, 161 Neb. 252, 73 N.W.2d 165 (1955) (unfairness in not revealing facts to friend who trusted implicitly). Cases such as this are often treated under fraudulent non-disclosure rather than undue influence. See § 9.20 infra.

indicated that the key is perhaps not the means, but the results.[3] The foremost indicator of undue influence is an unnatural transaction resulting in the enrichment of one of the parties at the expense of the other.[4]

If the party exerting the influence induces the other to contract with a third party, e.g., to borrow money from a bank, the contract cannot be avoided unless the third party is aware of the undue influence; if the third party is not so aware, it is in the position of a bona fide purchaser for value.[5]

Many, perhaps most, undue influence cases arise after the death of the person alleged to have been unduly importuned. Typically, disappointed relatives seek to set aside a will[6] or inter vivos transfer. Since unfair persuasion normally takes place in privacy, its proof must normally be made by circumstantial evidence. Though many cases have required less, evidence of four elements are sufficient to make out a prima facie circumstantial case of undue influence.[7] First, facts showing the susceptibility of the party influenced. Mental and physical weakness and psychological dependency tend to show susceptibility. Second, there must be evidence of the opportunity to exercise undue influence. The existence of a confidential relationship is strong evidence of such an element. Confidential relationships include husband-wife,[8] parent-child, trustee-beneficiary, guardian-ward, administrator-legatee, physician-patient, pastor-parishioner, and fiance-fiancée.[9] Third, there must be evidence of a disposition to exercise undue influence. Such a disposition may be shown by evidence that the alleged influencer took the initiative in the transaction. Also, many cases stress the following factual elements: whether the influenced party had reasonable access to independent advice.[10] Fourth, evidence must show the unnatural nature of the transaction. Evidence of inadequacy of consideration or neglect of the natural objects of the transferor's or testator's bounty may establish this element. Evidence of the fairness of the transaction may rebut a prima facie

---

3. Dawson, supra § 9.7 n.2, at 264; compare the discussion with respect to the mentally infirm § 8.15 supra.

4. For a discussion of what is unnatural, see Tetrault v. Mahoney, Hawkes & Goldings, 425 Mass. 456, 681 N.E.2d 1189 n. 11 (1997)

5. CIBC Mtge.s v. Pitt, [1993] 4 All E.R. 417 (H.L.); see Clements, Lending on the Security of Co–Owned Homes, Suretyship and Undue Influence, [1995] 3 Web JCLI.

6. A study of cases of wills concludes that "undue influence doctrine disproportionately injures women." Note, 19 Women's Rts. L.Rep. 97, 103 (1997).

7. See Note, 41 Colum.L.Rev. 707, 717–23 (1941); Note, 1968 Wis.L.Rev. 569, 571–585; other elements are listed in Caudill v. Smith, 117 N.C.App. 64, 450 S.E.2d 8 (1994); contra, Blackmer v. Blackmer, 165 Mont. 69, 525 P.2d 559 (1974), 37 Mont. L.Rev. 250 (1976).

8. See Clements supra note 5; Matter of Lutz, 563 N.W.2d 90 (N.D.1997) (pre-marital agreement; court defines "fiduciary relationship" to encompass confidential relationship).

9. Note, 49 Notre Dame Law. 631, 632 (1974); Wenzel–Gosset v. Nickels, 575 N.W.2d 425 (N.D.1998) (house-keeper in confidential relation with employer); see also Ferguson v. Jeanes, 27 Wn.App. 558, 619 P.2d 369 (1980). In Womack v. Womack, 622 N.E.2d 481 (Ind.1993), it was held that the presumption of undue influence in a transaction between spouses, where one spouse benefits at the other's expense, is antiquated and overruled.

10. 13 Williston § 1625 (3d ed.); 2 Black, Rescission of Contracts and Cancellation of Written Instruments § 244 (2d ed. 1929) [hereinafter Black].

case of undue influence.[11] Of course, any relevant evidence may rebut the presumption.[12]

Many cases ease the proof requirements even further. On proof of the existence of a confidential relationship and of a transaction benefitting the person in whom trust and confidence is reposed, the burden of proof is placed on the party benefitted to show that the transaction was not procured by undue influence.[13] At times, the benefitted party is required to carry this burden by clear and convincing evidence.[14] The decision is preeminently one of fact and rarely is the finding of the trial court reversed.[15]

(b) Attorney–Client Cases[16]

In the words of one court, *"although it is not advisable*, a lawyer may also contract with a client with respect to matters not involving legal services, or in addition to legal services * * *. "[17]Unlike in the case of a retainer agreement, the client cannot terminate such an agreement without cause.[18] Then, why is it "not advisable" for a lawyer to contract with a client? The reason is that, because of the fiduciary duty that the lawyer owes the client, there is a heavy burden of proof on the lawyer to show that the transaction is free of undue influence.[19] "Lawyers cannot act like other people, at least not when doing business."[20] They share this disability with other fiduciaries.[21]

11. Kase v. French, 325 N.W.2d 678 (S.D.1982); Simmons v. Foster, 622 S.W.2d 838 (Tenn.App.1981).

12. Wenzel–Mosset v. Nickels, 575 N.W.2d 425 (N.D.1998).

13. Francois v. Francois, 599 F.2d 1286 (3d Cir.1979), cert. denied; McCollough v. Rogers, 431 So.2d 1246 (Ala.1983); Matter of Dunn, 784 So.2d 935 (Miss.2001); JML Investors v. Hilton, 231 A.D.2d 493, 647 N.Y.S.2d 244 (1996); Ruggieri v. West Forum, 444 Pa. 175, 282 A.2d 304 (1971); but see Moser v. DeSetta, 527 Pa. 157, 589 A.2d 679 (Pa.1991). Frequently it is unclear whether the court is laying down a rule concerning the burden of proof in the sense of burden of persuasion or the burden of going forward with the evidence. 2 Dobbs, Remedies § 10.3 (1993). For a sophisticated discussion, see In re Wood's Estate, 374 Mich. 278, 132 N.W.2d 35, 5 ALR3d 1 (1965), overruled on other grounds; see also, Note, 41 Colum.L.Rev. 707, 711–16 (1941); Under the rule shifting the burden of proof, it is not surprising that frequently the main trial battle concerns whether there is a confidential relation. See, e.g., Clyde v. Hodge, 460 F.2d 532 (3d Cir.1972); Woodbury v. Pfliiger, 309 N.W.2d 104 (N.D. 1981); Estate of Till, 458 N.W.2d 521 (S.D. 1990), 36 S.D.L.Rev. 211 (1991).

14. Atkinson v. McHugh, 250 A.D.2d 560, 671 N.Y.S.2d 684 (1998).

15. E.g., Robert O. v. Ecmel A., 460 A.2d 1321 (Del.1983), overruled on other grounds; Kase v. French, supra § 9.10 n.11. For a statistical sampling, see Note, 1968 Wis.L.Rev. 569.

16. This subsection is based on Perillo, The Law of Lawyers' Contracts Is Different, 67 Fordham L.Rev. 443 (1998). The article provides a more thorough discussion of the rationale for the rules laid down here and also considers law-partnership liability for undue influence exercised by one of its members.

17. Greene v. Greene, 56 N.Y.2d 86, 451 N.Y.S.2d 46, 436 N.E.2d 496, 499 (1982) (emphasis supplied).

18. Id.

19. Bauermeister v. McReynolds, 254 Neb. 118, 575 N.W.2d 354 (1998). Exceptions are made for routine transactions such as where the lawyer makes a purchase in the ordinary course of business from a client who is a storekeeper.

20. Barry S. Martin, The Evils of Lawyer–Client Deals, 8 Cal. Law. 53 (Dec. 1987).

21. Thus if a trustee sells trust property to himself individually, "the consent of the beneficiary to the sale will not prevent him from setting aside the sale, * * * if the price and all other conditions of the sale

If the transaction is called into question, the lawyer must show: (1) that the transaction was fairly and equitably conducted; (2) that the lawyer fully informed the client of the nature and consequences of the transaction; (3) fully revealed the lawyer's own interest in the matter; and (4) saw to it that the client obtained independent advice or gave the client the kind of advice a disinterested lawyer would have given the client.[22] Other courts dispense with the need for undue influence, and hold that if the lawyer "got the better of the bargain," the agreement can be invalidated unless the lawyer "can show that the client was fully aware of the consequences and that there was no exploitation of the client's confidence."[23]

There is no lack of other formulations,[24] but at bottom, under all of them, a business transaction between lawyer and client is presumptively "invalid", *i.e.*, voidable,[25] as is a testamentary provision in favor of the lawyer who prepared the will.[26] Thus, a loan by a lawyer to the client is presumptively voidable and if the presumption is not rebutted, the client must repay only the principal and the cost of the money to the lawyer.[27] Courts in some cases have held that the presumption can only be rebutted by clear and convincing evidence. As stated by the New Jersey Supreme Court, the presumption "can be overcome only by the clearest and most convincing evidence showing full and complete disclosure of all facts known to the lawyer and absolute independence of action on the part of the client."[28]

Aside from the possible voidability of the transaction with the client, the lawyer may face disciplinary charges,[29] and even disbarment.[30] The

were not fair and reasonable." Austin W. Scott, The Fiduciary Principle, 37 Cal. L. Rev. 539, 542 (1949). Note, however, that Scott discusses dealings with trust property, not with a contract between trustee and beneficiary concerning matters outside the trust relationship.

22. Israel v. Sommer, 292 Mass. 113, 197 N.E. 442 (1935); Cleary v. Cleary, 427 Mass. 286, 692 N.E.2d 955 (1998) (even when the client is a close family member).

23. Greene v. Greene, 56 N.Y.2d 86, 451 N.Y.S.2d 46, 436 N.E.2d 496, 499 (1982).

24. E.g., Bell v. Ramirez, 299 S.W. 655, 659 (Tex.App.1927) ("presumed to be fraudulent"); Walker v. Weinstock, 173 Misc.2d 1, 658 N.Y.S.2d 167 (1997), aff'd ("unconscionable").

25. P & M Enterprises v. Murray, 293 N.J.Super. 310, 680 A.2d 790 (A.D.1996). Although the courts speak of "invalidity," they tend to use the term loosely. Since the legal foundation is "undue influence," such transactions are merely voidable at the election of the client. See §§ 9.9–9.12 supra; Rs. of the Law Governing Lawyers § 207, cmt. a (Proposed Final Draft No.1, 1996).

26. Krischbaum v. Dillon, 58 Ohio St.3d 58, 567 N.E.2d 1291 (Ohio 1991).

27. P & M Enterprises v. Murray (agreed interest rate was 16.5%; cost of money to the lender was presumably less); but see Fanaras Enterprises v. Doane, 423 Mass. 121, 666 N.E.2d 1003 (Mass. 1996), where the loan was from the client to the lawyer who was on retainer. The court held that loan was not part of the lawyer-client relation. Thus, the lawyer's malpractice insurer was not liable for the lawyer's nonpayment.

28. In re Gavel, 22 N.J. 248, 125 A.2d 696, 703 (1956) (disciplinary case); but see Franciscan Sisters Health Care v. Dean, 95 Ill.2d 452, 69 Ill.Dec. 960, 448 N.E.2d 872 (1983) (will contest; once contrary evidence is introduced, presumption disappears and evidence is evaluated neutrally); cf. Monco v. Janus, 222 Ill.App.3d 280, 164 Ill.Dec. 659, 583 N.E.2d 575 (1991) (the burden of persuasion shifts to the client only after clear and convincing evidence has rebutted the presumption).

29. In re Harper, 326 S.C. 186, 485 S.E.2d 376 (1997) (60 day suspension for questionable property transaction where there no evidence that client had any understanding of the nature of the transaction).

promulgated standards governing lawyer-client contracts do not have the force of contract law,[31] and some courts have rejected their applicability to civil litigation,[32] but others have applied them to civil disputes, either as directly applicable standards[33] or as evidence of proper contractual conduct.[34] Nonetheless, the cases involving disciplinary action and the cases involving contract remedies use remarkably similar reasoning and the Restatement of the Law Governing Lawyers appears to synthesize them into a coherent whole.[35] Sir Francis Bacon wrote to the effect that clients entrust lawyers, as counselors, "with the whole" of their being.[36] It is in the context of the lawyer-client business contract that the observation has the greatest resonance.

There is no *per se* rule prohibiting lawyers from contracting with their clients in matters beyond the rendering of legal services.[37] In a proper case, the court will even grant specific performance to the lawyer.[38] However, even if the transaction is valid and violates no

30. In re Wolk, 82 N.J. 326, 413 A.2d 317 (1980), cert. denied (counseled client "to make a hopeless investment in a building in which he had an interest, and concealed material information from her, including the fact of a foreclosure").

31. Rule 1.8(a) of the ABA Model Rules of Professional Conduct (1983) provides:

A lawyer shall not enter into a business transaction with a client or knowingly acquire an ownership, possessory, security or other pecuniary interest adverse to a client unless:

(1) the transaction and terms on which the lawyer acquires the interest are fair and reasonable to the client and are fully disclosed and transmitted in writing to the client in a manner which can be reasonably understood by the client;

(2) the client is given a reasonable opportunity to seek the advice of independent counsel in the transaction; and

(3) the client consents in writing thereto.

The ABA Model Code of Professional Responsibility has a similar, but less detailed, rule. DR 5–104(A) provides:

A lawyer shall not enter into a business transaction with a client if they have differing interests therein and if the client expects the lawyer to exercise his professional judgment therein for the protection of the client, unless the client has consented after full disclosure.

32. Garwood v. Johnson, 1994 WL 138434 p.4 (Ohio App.) ("Appellee relies heavily on the violation of two disciplinary rules contained in the Code of Professional Responsibility as a ground for vacating the judgment against him. However, we point

out that these violations, if they in fact occurred, are not defenses and furthermore they are not even counterclaims."); see also Buffalo v. Blackmon, 1994 WL 14583 (Ark. App.1994); Mozzochi v. Beck, 204 Conn. 490, 529 A.2d 171, 176 n. 8 (1987); Smith v. Bitter, 319 N.W.2d 196, 198 (Iowa 1982).

33. Schlanger v. Flaton, 218 A.D.2d 597, 631 N.Y.S.2d 293 (1995).

34. Cornell v. Wunschel, 408 N.W.2d 369, 376–79 (Iowa 1987).

35. Rs. (Third) of the Law Governing Lawyers § 207 (Proposed Final Draft No. 1, 1996).

36. The greatest Trust, betweene Man and Man, is the Trust of *Giving Counsell.* For in other Confidences, Men commit the parts of life; Their Lands, their Goods, their Children, their Credit, some particular Affaire: But to such, as they make their *Counsellours*, they commit the whole: By how much the more, they are obliged to all Faith and integrity. Sir Francis Bacon, *Of Counsell*, in The Essayes or Counsel, Civil and Moral 63 (Michael Kiernan ed. 1985).

37. Howard v. Murray, 38 N.Y.2d 695, 382 N.Y.S.2d 470, 346 N.E.2d 238 (1976) (although lawyer got the better of the bargain, trial court findings that the lawyer had dealt openly and frankly with the client bind the appellate court).

38. Clifton Country Road Assocs. v. Vinciguerra, 195 A.D.2d 895, 600 N.Y.S.2d 982 (1993) (lawyer did not have "unclean hands" when professional relationship was tenuous, no confidential information was abused, and was not guilty of wrongdoing); Alala v. Peachtree Plantations, 292 S.C. 160, 355 S.E.2d 286 (1987).

disciplinary rule, the contract will be strongly construed against the lawyer who drafted it.[39]

At least one case, has held that an insurance adjuster who advises an accident victim, is engaged in the practice of law and is held to the standard of an attorney.[40]

§ 9.11   Undue Influence: No Confidential Relationship

Although the great majority of twentieth century cases that have upheld a finding of undue influence[1] have involved confidential relationships, there has been no stated requirement that such a relationship exist. In a significant California case, undue influence was found where no such relationship existed.[2] The transaction in question was the resignation of a school teacher who had been arrested on charges, later dismissed, of homosexual activity. After 40 hours without sleep and soon after his release on bail, school officials visited him and persuaded him that it was in his best interests to resign. The court set aside the resignation. In so doing the court laid down the following criteria for distinguishing between legitimate persuasion and excessive pressure.

"However, overpersuasion is generally accomplished by certain characteristics which tend to create a pattern. The pattern usually involves several of the following elements: (1) discussion of the transaction at an unusual or inappropriate time, (2) consummation of the transaction in an unusual place, (3) insistent demand that the business be finished at once, (4) extreme emphasis on untoward consequences of delay, (5) the use of multiple persuaders by the dominant side against a single servient party, (6) absence of third-party advisers to the servient party, (7) statements that there is no time to consult financial advisers or attorneys. If a number of these elements are simultaneously present, the persuasion may be characterized as excessive."[3]

§ 9.12   Remedies for Undue Influence

We know of no case in which undue influence has been deemed to constitute a tort. In courts of equity where the doctrine originated, the remedy given was cancellation of any instrument contaminated by undue influence, avoidance of the transaction and restoration of the status quo

---

39. Shaffer v. Terrydale Management, 648 S.W.2d 595 (Mo.App.1983) (although he was not in the usual sense an employee, the lawyer-stockholder was held to be an employee within the meaning of the contract he drafted); Rogers v. Niforatos, 57 A.D.2d 984, 394 N.Y.S.2d 473 (1977).

40. Jones v. Allstate, 146 Wn.2d 291, 45 P.3d 1068 (2002).

§ 9.11

1. See 49 Notre Dame Law. 631, 632–33.

2. Odorizzi v. Bloomfield School District, 246 Cal.App.2d 123, 54 Cal.Rptr. 533 (1966).

3. Id. at 133, 54 Cal.Rptr. at 541; see Note, 49 Notre Dame Law. 631 (1974). See also Methodist Mission Home of Tex. v. N__ A__ B__, 451 S.W.2d 539 (Tex.App.1970).

ante.[1] Today, in a jurisdiction where law and equity have been merged and all that is sought is a money judgment, a quasi-contractual action may be brought at law.[2]

Where enforcement is sought by the party exercising overpersuasion, undue influence may be raised as an affirmative defense. If the relief sought is specific performance, the defense of undue influence can be successful even if the unfair persuasion would not have been sufficient to set aside an executed transaction.[3]

As undue influence merely renders the transaction voidable, ratification is an issue. Once the party having the power to avoid the transaction has knowledge of the essential facts, and is free of the other's influence he or she may ratify the transaction. The power to disaffirm may be lost by an implicit ratification.[4]

D. MISREPRESENTATION AND NON–DISCLOSURE

Table of Sections

§ 9.13 Elements of Misrepresentation

Whenever a party has fraudulently induced another to enter into a transaction under circumstances giving the latter the right to bring a tort action for deceit, the deceived party may instead elect to avoid the transaction and claim restitution.[1] The converse, however, is not true.

---

§ 9.12

1. 2 Dobbs, Remedies § 10.3 (1993) (constructive trust, equitable lien, or accounting); see also 2 Black § 239. Punitive damages were awarded in Kennedy v. Thomsen, 320 N.W.2d 657 (Iowa App.1982).

2. Woodbury v. Woodbury, 141 Mass. 329, 5 N.E. 275 (1886); Eldridge v. May, 129 Me. 112, 150 A. 378 (1930).

3. This stems from the discretionary nature of the remedy of specific performance.

Scheinberg v. Scheinberg, 249 N.Y. 277, 164 N.E. 98 (1928). See § 16.7 infra.

4. 3 Black §§ 610–615; Rs. Restitution § 70 cmt a.

§ 9.13

1. Pursuant to certain statutes no election is necessary and both remedies may be pursued. See § 9.23 infra. On some occasions the remedy of reformation is available. See § 9.35 infra. On rare occasions the transaction is void and avoidance is not needed. See § 9.22 infra.

Misrepresentation or non-disclosure may render a transaction voidable even if there would be no tort cause of action for fraud.

Tortious fraud—the action of deceit—involves five elements, each of them, although tersely stated, is quite complex: (1) representation, (2) falsity, (3) scienter, (4) deception, and (5) injury.[2] The tort law of fraud[3] is not within the scope of this book but reference will be made to these elements as they relate to the remedy of restitution that follows after the avoidance of a contract. Inasmuch as this remedy is designed merely to restore the situation that existed prior to the transaction, it is not surprising that the requisites necessary to make out a case for restitution are far less demanding than those necessary to make out a tort action.[4] Nonetheless, neither law nor morality require that all lies made in negotiations be redressed.[5]

A number of jurisdictions use the out of pocket rule to measure damages for deceit. That rule is an essentially restitutionary measure of damages designed to restore the status quo ante rather than to compensate for loss of bargain. Even in such jurisdictions however, consequential damages are frequently awarded. Such damages are generally not available in an action for restitution.

Where a contract requires a party to provide information to the other, e.g., a "rent roll," a negligent misrepresentation constitutes a breach of contract.[6] If it is material, it is also grounds for cancelling the contract.[7] However, such a representation if intentionally made can be redressed as a tort and serve as a predicate for punitive damages.[8] Punitive damages have also been granted in other instances of tortious misrepresentation.[9]

The misrepresentation must be by the other party or someone on the other party's behalf. Thus if a debtor fraudulently induces the promisor to guaranty a debt, without the creditor's knowledge, the guaranty cannot be avoided.[10]

§ 9.14 Scienter and Materiality

In a tort action, to establish the scienter element of deceit, the deceived party in most contexts would need to show that the deceiving

---

2. Reno v. Bull, 226 N.Y. 546, 124 N.E. 144 (1919); see Prosser & Keeton, Torts 727–29 (5th ed. 1984).

3. See generally Prosser & Keeton supra; James & Gray, Misrepresentation, 37 Md.L.Rev. 286 (1977), Part II, 37 Md.L.Rev. 488 (1978).

4. See Tralon v. Cedarapids, 966 F.Supp. 812 (N.D.Iowa 1997).

5. See Strudler, Incommensurable Goods, Rightful Lies, and the Wrongness of Fraud, 146 U.Pa.L.Rev. 1529 (1998).

6. Linden Partners v. Wilshire Linden Assocs., 62 Cal.App.4th 508, 73 Cal.Rptr.2d 708 (1998).

7. Lincoln Benefit Life v. Edwards, 45 F.Supp.2d 722 (D.Neb.1999) (court spoke of rescission for fraud and duress).

8. Gregory v. Chemical Waste Management, 38 F.Supp.2d 598 (W.D.Tenn.1996) (fraudulent calculation of royalties).

9. E.g., Chrysler v. Schiffer, 736 So.2d 538 (Ala.1999) (representing a repaired car as "new").

10. National Union Fire Ins. v. Worley, 257 A.D.2d 228, 690 N.Y.S.2d 57 (1999).

party made the representation with the knowledge of its falsity, and with an intent to deceive and that the misrepresentation shall be acted on in a certain way.[1] Less rigorous tests are employed in some contexts and tort liability for negligent and even innocent misrepresentation is not unknown.[2] In tort law the question is quite complex,[3] but it has long been the rule in equity that avoidance and restitution are available for a negligent and even an innocent misrepresentation[4] and the same rule now prevails in quasi-contractual actions for restitution at law.[5] There is perhaps one qualification in some jurisdictions. A few scattered cases have followed the English view that avoidance for nonfraudulent misrepresentation will not be available if the contract is fully performed on both sides.[6] In England, this view has been overturned by statute.[7]

Frequently, one distinction is made between intentional and unintentional misrepresentation. For avoidance to be available for an unintentional misrepresentation it is usually held that the fact misrepresented must be material.[8] Where the misrepresentation is intentional, however, avoidance is available even if the fact represented is immaterial. The different tests are the consequence of different standards. In cases of unintentional misrepresentation, the standard is an objective one and the focus is on materiality. However where the misrepresentation is intentional, the standard is a subjective one and materiality is irrelevant.

Materiality exists whenever the misrepresentation would be likely to affect the conduct of a reasonable person or if "the maker of the representation knows that the recipient is likely to regard the fact as

§ 9.14

1. Where the misrepresentation is egregious, it may be the basis of avoiding an insurance policy even beyond the two year period of the standard incontestability clause. Fioretti v. Massachusetts Gen. Life Ins., 53 F.3d 1228 (11th Cir.1995), cert. denied (HIV positive sent an imposter to provide blood for testing).

2. E.g., Mortarino v. Consultant Engineering Services, 251 Va. 289, 467 S.E.2d 778 (1996) (innocent or negligent misrepresentation can constitute "constructive fraud.")

3. See Prosser & Keeton, supra § 9.13 n.2, at 748–49; Keeton, Fraud: The Necessity for an Intent to Deceive, 5 UCLA L.Rev. 583 (1958). Prosser's analysis of innocent misrepresentation as a tort is severely criticized in Hill, Breach of Contract as a Tort, 74 Colum.L.Rev. 40 (1974).

4. Smith v. Richards, 38 U.S. (13 Pet.) 26 (1839); see Berger v. Cantor Fitzgerald Securities, 967 F.Supp. 91 (S.D.N.Y.1997) (elements described); Groothand v. Schlueter, 949 S.W.2d 923 (Mo.App.1997); 1 Story, Commentaries on Equity Jurisprudence

§ 193 (13th ed. 1866); 1 Black §§ 102, 106; 2 Parsons, The Law of Contracts * 786 (6th ed. 1873).

5. Kessler v. National Enter., 238 F.3d 1006 (8th Cir.2001); Liebling v. Garden State Indm., 337 N.J.Super. 447, 767 A.2d 515 (A.D.2001), cert. denied; Seneca Wire & Mfg. v. A.B. Leach & Co., 247 N.Y. 1, 159 N.E. 700 (1928); Rs. 2d § 164 cmt b; see 12 Williston § 1500 (3d ed.). Prosser & Keeton, supra § 9.13 n.2, at 729–33; 1 Palmer on Restitution § 3.19.

6. E.g., Thompson v. Jackson, 24 Va. (3 Rand.) 504, 15 Am.Dec. 721 (1825). Such decisions stem from the general idea that equity will deny specific performance more readily than it will award restitution.

7. Misrepresentation Act of 1967 § 7(b); see Cheshire, Fifoot & Furmston, The Law of Contract 294–95 (12th ed. 1991).

8. Clyde A. Wilson Int'l Investigations v. Travelers Ins., 959 F.Supp. 756 (S.D.Tex. 1997) (federal common law); Rs. 2d § 164(2) and cmt b; Rs. Restitution § 9(2). Materiality is also required for a tort action. Restatement, Torts § 538(1) and cmt g.

important" although a reasonable person would not.[9] (This objective requisite is to be contrasted with the subjective test employed in cases of duress).[10] Where the misrepresentation is intentional, however, a subjective test is employed and avoidance is available even if the fact represented is immaterial,[11] because in this last case the wrongdoer has accomplished the intended purpose, whereas one who innocently misstates an unimportant fact has no reason to know that the statement will cause action.[12] Here, as elsewhere in the law, principals are responsible for the misrepresentations of their agents.[13]

§ 9.15   Deception and Reliance

To recover for misrepresentation, the deceived party must establish causation. It must be proved that the party was in fact deceived by the misrepresentation and relied on it in entering into the transaction.[1] The party to whom a falsehood is addressed who did not believe it cannot later use the falsehood as a ground for avoidance.[2] There has been no deception, but a material misrepresentation gives rise to a rebuttable presumption of deception and reliance.[3] To be distinguished are cases where a party warrants the accuracy of its representation. In such a case the warranty is paid for, and no-fault contractual liability attaches.[4]

There are two main issues in the area of reliance: (1) Did the person deceived have a right to rely? (2) Did the party in fact rely? On the question of one's right to rely on the representation of another, in the absence of a confidential relationship, the nineteenth and earlier twentieth century cases were quite strict. Many cases took the position that it was the duty of every person to take notice of obvious facts and to investigate the truth of representations.[5] The credulous were deemed to have invited their own misfortunes. Although there were many qualifications of the rule,[6] there were frequent harsh applications. But the tide turned. The Vermont Court proclaimed that "the law will afford relief

9. Rs., Torts § 538(2)(b). Accord, Rs. 2d § 162(2).

10. See § 9.2 supra. A subjective test is stated in 2 Parsons on Contracts *769.70 (6th ed. 1873) ("if the fraud be such, that, had it not been practiced, the contract would not have been made, or the transaction completed, then it is material to it.") Parsons makes no distinction for this purpose between intentional and unintentional misrepresentations. This test has been quoted or paraphrased in many cases.

11. Rs. 2d § 162(1); Rs. Restitution § 9 cmt b; 12 Williston § 1490 (3d ed.). On what constitutes an intentional misrepresentation, see Rs. 2d § 162 and cmt b.

12. Rs. 2d § 162 cmt c.

13. VRT v. Dutton–Lainson, 247 Neb. 845, 530 N.W.2d 619 (Neb.1995) (attorney falsely represented to assignee that a patent application had been filed).

§ 9.15

1. Eslamizar v. American States Ins., 134 Or.App. 138, 894 P.2d 1195 (1995); Rs. 2d § 167; 12 Williston §§ 1515–1515C (3d ed.); 1 Black, §§ 109–111.

2. Woodtek v. Musulin, 263 Or. 644, 503 P.2d 677 (1972) (some officers of plaintiff were aware of misstatements); Lundy v. Palmetto State Life Ins., 256 S.C. 506, 183 S.E.2d 335 (1971); M & A Constr. v. Akzo Nobel Coatings, 936 P.2d 451 (Wyo.1997).

3. Miller v. Celebration Mining Co., 29 P.3d 1231 (Utah 2001); Rs. 2d § 107 cmt b.

4. CBS v. Ziff–Davis Publishing, 75 N.Y.2d 496, 554 N.Y.S.2d 449, 553 N.E.2d 997, 7 ALR5th 1154 (1990).

5. 1 Black § 113.

6. Id. §§ 118–120, 122–125.

even to the simple and credulous who have been duped by art and falsehood."[7] The same court stated, "no rogue should enjoy his ill-gotten plunder for the simple reason that his victim is by chance a fool."[8]

As Vermont went, so has gone the nation. It is the exceptional case today where, especially in the face of an intentional misrepresentation,[9] relief will be denied on the ground of the undue credulity or negligence of the defrauded party.[10] The nineteenth century attitude is particularly relaxed where the relief sought is restitution rather than tort damages. On the other hand, the old approach is often reasserted,[11] but seemingly with little consistency.[12] One frequently receives the impression that when the old rule is applied, the court is covertly acting on its conviction that the trier of fact erred in its finding of reliance.[13] Misrepresentation of the contents of a written proposal is discussed under "Duty to Read."[14]

The question of whether the party did in fact rely on representation is preeminently a question of fact. Normally it is so treated. But where the party receiving the representation in fact makes a personal investigation, many courts have ruled that, as a matter of law, there is no reliance.[15] But a perfunctory investigation by a non-expert does not rule out a finding of reliance.[16]

§ 9.16 Injury

A necessary element of the tort of deceit is pecuniary injury, but this requirement does not apply to the avoidance of a contract. In the

---

7. Kendall v. Wilson, 41 Vt. 567, 571 (1869).

8. Chamberlin v. Fuller, 59 Vt. 247, 9 A. 832, 836 (1887).

9. Investors Eq. Exch. v. Whiteley, 269 Or. 309, 524 P.2d 1211 (1974); Black § 124; Rs. 2d § 164 cmt b, § 169(c), § 172.

10. See 12 Williston § 1515B (3d ed.); Spyder Enter. v. Ward, 872 F.Supp. 8 (E.D.N.Y.1995) ("it is no excuse for a culpable misrepresentation that the means of probing it were at hand."); Azam v. M/I Schottenstein Homes, 761 So.2d 1195 (Fla. App.2000) (case by case analysis).

11. Patell Industrial Mach. v. Toyota Machinery U.S.A., 880 F.Supp. 96 (N.D.N.Y.1995) (tort action); Gladstone Hotel v. Smith, 487 P.2d 329 (Wyo.1971).

12. Compare with the prior note, Weaver Org. v. Manette, 41 A.D.2d 138, 341 N.Y.S.2d 631 (1973), order modified. "The older rule that the buyer is generally required to make an independent inspection or investigation wherever possible and is put upon notice of and bound by any knowledge that a reasonable inspection or investigation would have revealed * * * has been cast aside in favor of a more elastic requirement of inspection and investigation which

has been altered, reshaped, and somewhat distorted from year to year and case to case." (footnotes omitted). Comment, 3 Willamette L.J. 183, 184 (1965). For an attempt to rationalize the cases in terms of "the implied rules of the business game" and "community-wide assumptions in connection with business practices," see Harper & McNeely, 32 Minn.L.Rev. 939, 1006–07 (1938). The Rs. 2d § 172 makes the inquiry turn on whether the person duped failed "to act in good faith and in accordance with reasonable standards of fair dealing."

13. For additional comments, see § 9.24 infra.

14. See § 9.42 infra.

15. McCormick & Co. v. Childers, 468 F.2d 757 (4th Cir.1972); Gary v. Politte, 878 S.W.2d 849 (Mo.App.1994); Copland v. Diamond, 164 Misc.2d 507, 624 N.Y.S.2d 514 (1995); but see Fisher v. Mr. Harold's Hair Lab, 215 Kan. 515, 527 P.2d 1026 (1974); Gibb v. Citicorp Mtge., 246 Neb. 355, 518 N.W.2d 910 (1994) (tort action permitted); Rs. 2d § 167 ill. 1.

16. Groothand v. Schlueter, 949 S.W.2d 923 (Mo.App.1997).

nineteenth century, leading text writers appear to have uncritically cited tort cases for the proposition that injury was an element of the power to avoid a contract for fraud.[1] The courts followed, and in the late nineteenth and early twentieth centuries a large number of courts stated their agreement.[2] Yet, the statement of the rule was often so qualified as almost to eradicate the requirement. A frequently cited case stated that whenever a misrepresentation is material, damage will be presumed.[3] Such holdings, which in essence cancel out the requirement, led to the rule stated in both editions of the Restatement that it is not relevant whether damage was caused.[4] The Restatements undoubtedly go a little further than the cases. An in depth analysis has shown that the cases dealing with the injury requirement can readily be divided into three categories:[5] (1) the defrauded party obtains what is bargained for but because of the misrepresentation it is worth less than the party had reason to expect; (2) the defrauded party obtains something substantially different from what the party was led to expect; (3) the defrauded party obtains what is bargained for and it is as valuable as the party was led to expect.

In the first two classes the defrauded party has been deprived of reasonable expectations and this is sufficient harm on which to base an avoidance.[6] In the last case, the court may find that the social interest in the security of transactions outweighs any social interest in redress for the trick played on the defrauded party.[7] Another court, however, may balance the scales differently.[8] Certain situations reoccur. Suppose that Pam knows that Dan will not deal with her, and misrepresents her identity or acts through an undisclosed agent. Most courts have been willing to set aside such a transaction even if a fair exchange has been agreed on.[9] On the other hand, where the misrepresentation causes the other to perform a legal duty, or to sign a promissory note for a

§ 9.16

1. McCleary, Damage as Requisite to Rescission for Misrepresentation, 36 Mich. L.Rev. 1, 20–23 (1937).

2. Id. at 17.

3. Stuart v. Lester, 49 Hun. 58, 1 N.Y.S. 699 (1888).

4. Rs. 1st § 476 cmt c; Rs. 2d §§ 164 cmt c, 165. Gross v. State Cooperage Export Crating & Shipping, 32 A.D.2d 540, 299 N.Y.S.2d 773 (1969).

5. McCleary, Damage as Requisite to Rescission for Misrepresentation II, 36 Mich.L.Rev. 227 (1937).

6. Id. at 258; Kelsey v. Nagy, 410 N.E.2d 1333 (Ind.App.1980).

7. See the curious case of Mott v. Tri-Continental Fin., 330 F.2d 468 (2d Cir. 1964) (avoidance would be futile where defrauded party has sold at no loss what he has received). This case may also illustrate

a proposition that avoidance will be denied where the remedy would be of no practical value. McCleary, Damages as Requisite to Rescission for Misrepresentation II, 36 Mich.L.Rev. 227, 251–53 (1937).

8. See Earl v. Saks & Co., 36 Cal.2d 602, 226 P.2d 340 (1951) (avoidance allowed where plaintiff got what in economic terms was worth more than he bargained for); but see Reed v. King, 145 Cal.App.3d 261, 193 Cal.Rptr. 130 (1983) (pecuniary loss required for avoidance based on nondisclosure).

9. McCleary, Damages as Requisite to Rescission for Misrepresentation II, 36 Mich.L.Rev. 227, 245–248 (1937). McCleary includes in this category cases where a purchaser misrepresents the purpose for the purchase of land but the cases generally do not support this proposition unless the defrauded party owns other land that will be adversely affected by the purchaser's use. See Finley v. Dalton, 251 S.C. 586, 164 S.E.2d 763, 35 ALR3d 1364 (1968).

preexisting debt, the equities are weighed differently and the transaction cannot be avoided.[10]

§ 9.17   Fact Versus Opinion

Misrepresentations of fact render a contract voidable; erroneous statements of opinion do not.[1] There are some exceptions to this rule, and the distinction between fact and opinion is extremely tenuous. Statements such as, "it is hot today" contain both a factual element—a statement about the temperature and the speaker's characterization of the temperature—a characterization that may well differ from that of the reasonable person who has been reared in the tropics.

The distinction between fact and opinion has long been regarded by keen analysts as a logical absurdity.[2] At bottom, a "fact" is an opinion that is not open to question.[3] The opinion rule doubtless arose as a means of denying relief to persons who unjustifiably (by community standards) relied on sellers' "puff" or "trade talk." Courts have deemed descriptions of what a seller puts on the market as "best buys," "finest quality," etc. not to be the kind of statement that, if false, ought to be redressed by the legal system.[4] There have been three ways of analyzing such language so as to deny relief. Trade talk could be deemed "immaterial;" second, it could be said that one has "no right to rely" on such puffery;[5] third, it could be deemed a statement of opinion.[6] Yet, if the court's sympathies are sufficiently with the party who relies on a used car salesman's statement that a car is in "A–1 shape" and "mechanically perfect," the court may find that the opinion line has crossed into the area of fact.[7] And, although statements of value are usually deemed to be opinions,[8] where a farmer is induced by a confidence man to exchange a homestead for a store with a represented inventory value of $9,000 to

---

10. First State Bank v. Moen Enterprises, 529 N.W.2d 887 (N.D.1995); McCleary, 36 Mich.L.Rev. 227, 251–52 (1937).

§ 9.17

1. Great Lakes Chemicals v. Pharmacia, 788 A.2d 544 (Del.Ch.2001); Keeton, Fraud: Misrepresentations of Opinion, 21 Minn. L.Rev. 643 (1937); 12 Williston §§ 1491–1494 (3d ed.); Rs. 2d § 168; Rs. 1st § 474; Black §§ 76–88.

2. See 7 Wigmore, Evidence § 1919 (3d ed.1940); Keeton, supra note 1, at 656–57.

3. Sharp, The Ethics of Breach of Contract, 45 Int'l J.of Ethics 41 (1934).

4. To the effect that the legal standards must be less stringent than the demands of morality, see 2 Parsons, The Law of Contracts *768–69 (6th ed.1873). A contrary view is expounded by Verplanck, An Essay on the Doctrine of Contracts 170 (1825).

A more recent example of puffery is this: "A driver is 100 times more likely to benefit from a vehicle's crash-avoidance capabilities (such as anti-lock brakes) than from its crash-survival capabilities (such as air bags)." In re GM Anti–Lock Brake Products Liability Litigation, 966 F.Supp. 1525, 1531 (E.D.Mo.1997).

5. Anderson v. Bungee Int'l Mfg., 44 F.Supp.2d 534 (S.D.N.Y.1999) ("premium quality").

6. See Keeton, supra note 1, at 667–68.

7. Wat Henry Pontiac v. Bradley, 202 Okl. 82, 210 P.2d 348 (1949). "A–1" was deemed to be language of opinion in Deming v. Darling, 148 Mass. 504, 20 N.E. 107 (1889), but a statement that a car was "mechanically sound," "in good condition" and had "no problems" created an express warranty in Weng v. Allison, 287 Ill.App.3d 535, 678 N.E.2d 1254, 223 Ill.Dec. 123 (1997); see also Morehouse v. Behlmann Pontiac, 31 S.W.3d 55 (Mo.App.2000) ("excellent condition," "reliable").

8. Fifty Assocs. v. Prudential Ins., 450 F.2d 1007 (9th Cir.1971).

$11,000, the farmer may avoid the contract when the inventory value is found to be $2,500.[9] On the other hand, other litigants have not been so fortunate. One observer notes:

> "And then there is always the friendly doctrine of sellers' puff to shield the advertiser from liability. If such statements as, 'these second hand tires are as good as new,' 'this suit of clothes will wear like iron,' 'these bicycles are unsurpassable, having been subjected to severe and practical tests; we are in a position to guarantee them to be all that is claimed for them, perfect of their kind,' or 'this article will give first class satisfaction, it is the best upon the market, it will sell like hot cakes and will be the best drawing card ever handled,' are regarded as puffs, then all the copy writer has to do is to give free rein to his fancy and avoid any useful information about the article. The facts besides being dull do not sell the article and may involve liability. (Citations omitted)."[10]

Some opinions are in the nature of predictions as to future events. A statement to a potential shareholder that shares priced at $8.00 will be worth $25.00 in a year has been held to be a statement of opinion, not "susceptible of knowledge."[11] The same court, however, held that representations that a chicken-raising franchise would "return to the careful broiler raiser an income roughly equal to half as much as is obtained from an average size farm in the Midwest—and it will do so for about 6 hours of one person's attention daily," together with related "highly colored" and "overly optimistic" statements were actionable.[12] Wherein lies the distinction? In an early and philosophical American discussion of fraud, the author lamented, "whilst I had little difficulty in deciding on the morality of a single given case, I found it much less easy to lay down any general rules or definitions, at once comprehending all that strict integrity enjoined, and not requiring too much."[13]

Sharing the author's embarrassment, we can point not to rules, but to factors that justify the differing results in the two cases. Among the factors are that in the second case the representations were not oral, but printed in a glossy brochure; the business experience of the representee was far more in the first case than in the second; and unlike the representor in the first case, the representor in the second case had an aura of expertise as the representations in the second case were part of a regional selling campaign.[14]

9. Foote v. Wilson, 104 Kan. 191, 178 P. 430 (1919).

10. Handler, False and Misleading Advertising, 39 Yale L.J. 22, 25–26 (1929) (footnotes omitted); see also Prosser & Keeton, Torts § 109 (5th ed.1984); Nordstrom, Sales § 70 (1970).

11. Kennedy v. Flo–Tronics, 274 Minn. 327, 143 N.W.2d 827 (1966). Where a distributor tells a dealer that a particular customer will pay its bills, this is a prediction not a representation of present or past fact.

Widmark v. Northrup King, 530 N.W.2d 588 (Minn.App.1995).

12. Hollerman v. F.H. Peavey & Co., 269 Minn. 221, 130 N.W.2d 534 (1964). Compare Clements Auto v. Service Bureau, 298 F.Supp. 115 (D.Minn.1969), aff'd in part, reversed in part.

13. Verplanck, supra § 9.17 n.4, at 101.

14. Another case in which avoidance of a transaction was permitted when representations of value were made pursuant to a sophisticated and well organized "hard

Some of the factors relevant to a decision of opinion cases are sometimes stated as rules of law; that is, as exceptions to the general rule of no relief for reliance on an opinion. These exceptional circumstances include: (1) where there is a relation of trust and confidence between the parties;[15] (2) where the representor is or claims to be an expert;[16] (3) where the representor has superior access to knowledge of facts making the opinion false;[17] (4) where the opinion is stated by a third person posing as a disinterested person;[18]and (5) where the opinion intentionally varies so far from reality that no reasonable person in the representor's position could have such an opinion.[19] Consistent application of these "exceptions" would signal the death knell of the opinion rule as a significant barrier to relief. Furthermore, in doubtful cases, whether or not a statement is a representation of fact or opinion can be a question of fact,[20] further weakening the general rule.

To the extent that the fact-opinion dichotomy of prior law is still viable, it is continued by the UCC.[21]

§ 9.18   Fact Versus Law

Two contradictory rationales provided the basis for the traditional rule that misrepresentations of law do not render a contract voidable. (1) Everyone is presumed to know the law.[1] (2) A statement of the law governing a given set of facts is merely the expression of an opinion: no lawyer or layman ought to rely on such an opinion without further research. Based on either or both of these contradictory rationales, the rule has been stated that: "One cannot rescind a contract or withdraw

sell" is Vertes v. G A C Properties, 337 F.Supp. 256 (S.D.Fla.1972). Under Rs. 2d § 168, if it purports to be based on knowledge rather than judgment, it is more than a statement of opinion.

15. Rs. 2d § 169; Keeton, supra note 1, at 645–47.

16. Id. at 647–48; Vokes v. Arthur Murray, 212 So.2d 906, 28 ALR3d 1405 (Fla. App.1968); Rs. 1st § 474(a); Rs. 2d § 169(b). Where both parties are experts, there is generally no reason why the party to whom a representation of value is addressed should be entitled to rely on it. Fifty Assocs. v. Prudential Ins., 450 F.2d 1007 (9th Cir.1971).

17. Ryan v. Glenn, 489 F.2d 110 (5th Cir.1974); Keeton, supra note 1, at 648–54.

18. Keeton, supra note 1, at 654–56; cf. Farnsworth v. Feller, 256 Or. 56, 471 P.2d 792 (1970) (forged appraiser's report).

19. Rs. 1st § 474(b).

20. Russell v. Royal Maccabees Life Ins., 193 Ariz. 464, 974 P.2d 443 (App.1998) (representation that applicant had not been a convicted felon); Condas v. Adams, 15 Utah 2d 132, 388 P.2d 803 (1964).

21. UCC § 2–313(2) provides " * * * an affirmation merely of the value of the goods or a statement purporting to be merely of the value of the goods or a statement purporting to be merely the seller's opinion or commendation of the goods does not create a warranty." If the word "merely," repeated thrice in this provision, is stressed, the opinion rule is further weakened. The quoted language is unchanged but moved to § 2–313(3) in the revision. On the relationship between representations and warranties, see §§ 9.20, 9.23 infra.

§ 9.18

1. "The maxim 'a man is presumed to know the law,' is a trite, sententious saying, 'by no means universally true.'" Municipal Metallic Bed Mfg. v. Dobbs, 253 N.Y. 313, 317, 171 N.E. 75, 76, 68 ALR 1376, 1378 (1930); but see Platt v. Scott, 6 Blackf. 389, 390, 39 Am.Dec. 436 (Ind.1843) ("It is considered that every person is acquainted with the law, both civil and criminal, and no one can, therefore, complain of the misrepresentations of another respecting it.") Platt v. Scott is the ancestor of hundreds of decisions on point.

from an obligation into which he was induced to enter by representations made to him by the other party, however false and fraudulent, when such representations related to a matter of law * * * * ''[2] In so far as this rule has its foundation in the opinion rule, it shares the same logical absurdity. Does a representation that a given college has the legal authority to award the dental degree of D.M.D. represent fact or law?[3]

The traditional rule also shares with its opinion counterpart common exceptions,[4] the most important of which is the expertise exception. If the representor is a lawyer expressing an opinion about the law of the state in which the lawyer practices, the representee may normally rely on that opinion,[5] even if the representee is an adversary rather than a client.[6] Other situations of trust and confidence or supposed superior knowledge of the representor will be treated on the same basis.[7] Some jurisdictions may have abolished the law-fact distinction.[8]

An additional exception, over and above the exceptions generally involved in the opinion category, exists in the misrepresentation of law category. A misrepresentation of the law of another state or country is treated as a misrepresentation of fact.[9] This originates from the rule, now changed in many jurisdictions, that for purposes of pleading and proof the law of another jurisdiction is a fact.[10] There was little logic in importing the rule into the context of misrepresentation. Yet, any relief from the broad generalization that misrepresentation of law is not grounds for avoidance is to be welcomed.

§ 9.19   Fact Versus Intention and Promise

If an issuer of bonds misrepresents the purpose to which the issuer intends to put the proceeds, has a fact been misrepresented? Yes, said

2. Black § 71; see Spitzmueller v. Burlington Northern R.R., 740 F.Supp. 671 (D.Minn.1990); Bowles v.All Counties Inv. Corp., 46 S.W.3d 636 (Mo.App.2001); 12 Williston § 1495 (3d ed.); Rs. 2d § 170; Prosser & Keeton, Torts 758–60 (5th ed.1984).

3. Kerr v. Shurtleff, 218 Mass. 167, 105 N.E. 871 (1914) (fact); see Note, 32 Colum.L.Rev. 1018, 1021–23 (1932).

4. Rs. 2d § 170 cmt b. See § 9.17 supra.

5. See the authorities cited supra § 9.17 n.17. Where a releasor signed a release and her attorney did not disclose that her rights against a joint tortfeasor would also be discharged, there was no basis for avoiding the release. The tortfeasors were not responsible for her attorney's failure to disclose. Flynn v. Lockhart, 526 N.W.2d 743 (S.D. 1995).

6. Sainsbury v. Pennsylvania Greyhound Lines, 183 F.2d 548, 21 ALR2d 266 (4th Cir.1950).

7. Note, 32 Colum.L.Rev. 1018, 1023–25 (1932); Lynch v. Cruttenden & Co., 18 Cal.

App.4th 802, 22 Cal.Rptr.2d 636 (1993) (customer can rely on stockbroker's representation); cf. Farnsworth v. Feller, 256 Or. 56, 471 P.2d 792 (1970) (seller concealed his knowledge of zoning ordinances).

8. Peterson v. First Nat. Bank, 162 Minn. 369, 375, 203 N.W. 53, 55, 42 ALR 1185 (1925) ("useless duffle of an older and more arbitrary day"); National Conversion v. Cedar Building, 23 N.Y.2d 621, 627–28, 298 N.Y.S.2d 499, 504, 246 N.E.2d 351, 355 (1969) ("the law has outgrown the oversimple dichotomy between law and fact in the resolution of issues of deceit."); cf. Curtin v. United Airlines, 275 F.3d 88 (D.C.Cir.2001) (misrepresentation based on a reasonable misinterpretation of law).

9. Bernhan Chemical & Metal v. Ship-A-Hoy, 200 A.D. 399, 193 N.Y.S. 372 (1922), aff'd in part, reversed in part; 22 Colum.L.Rev. 591 (1922);12 Williston § 1495 (3d ed.); 1 Black § 72; but see American Fracmaster v. Richardson, 71 S.W.3d 381 (Tex.App.2001).

10. Cf. 30 Mich.L.Rev. 301 (1931).

the court, giving this classic answer: "The state of a man's mind is as much a fact as the state of his digestion."[1] Note, however, that frequently a representation of purpose is of no great importance to the representee and would be deemed immaterial.[2] Moreover, a person's intentions may change over time and a change of mind is not a misrepresentation.[3]

A majority of jurisdictions now hold that making a promise with an intent not to perform it constitutes a misrepresentation of fact.[4] This is not surprising since a promise is merely a statement of intention coupled with a commitment to act in accordance with that statement.[5] The rationale is that: "Every promise involves an implied representation that the promisor intends to carry out the promise at the time it is made."[6] Under some penal codes, promissory fraud can be the crime of larceny by false promise.[7] Where the alleged promise is oral and is contradicted by the express terms of a written agreement, a claim of fraud will meet with grave difficulty.[8]

Special problems exist when the promise would be void or unenforceable on the grounds of lack of consideration, the parol evidence rule, the Statute of Frauds, illegality, etc. The courts are far from unanimous on the resolution of these problems.[9] Some take the position that such contractual doctrines, although applicable in an action to enforce a

§ 9.19

1. Edgington v. Fitzmaurice, L.R., 29 Ch.D. 459, 483 (1885); cf. "In an ancient case, Y.B. 17 Edw. IV, 2, Brian, C.J., remarked, perhaps erroneously, that 'the devil himself knoweth not the thought of man.' " 7 Corbin § 28.27 n. 13 (Perillo 2002).

2. See generally, Keeton, Fraud: Statements of Intention, 15 Tex.L.Rev. 185 (1937); Note, 38 Colum.L.Rev. 1461 (1938); 12 Williston § 1496 (3d ed.); Prosser, Torts 762–65 (5th ed. 1984); 1 Black §§ 89–91; Rs. 2d § 171.

3. Kassebaum v. Kassebaum, 42 S.W.3d 685 (Mo.App.2001).

4. See n.2; U.S. v. 1,557.28 Acres of Land, 486 F.2d 445 (10th Cir.1973) (promise by federal agent); Entron v. General Cablevision, 435 F.2d 995 (5th Cir.1970) (reason to know of inability to carry out the promise is sufficient); SNCB Corporate Finance v. Schuster, 877 F.Supp. 820, 828 (S.D.N.Y.1994), aff'd; Florida Software Sys. v. Columbia/HCA Healthcare, 46 F.Supp.2d 1276 (M.D.Fla.1999), aff'd; Tyson Foods v. Davis, 347 Ark. 566, 66 S.W.3d 568 (2002); Engalla v. Permanente Medical Group, 15 Cal.4th 951, 938 P.2d 903, 64 Cal.Rptr.2d 843 (1997); Graubard Mollen Dannett & Horowitz v. Moskovitz, 86 N.Y.2d 112, 629 N.Y.S.2d 1009, 653 N.E.2d 1179 (1995); Formosa Plastics v. Presidio Eng'rs & Contractors, 960 S.W.2d 41 (Tex.1998). Contra,

Hinchey v. NYNEX, 979 F.Supp. 40 (D.Mass.1997), aff'd. Adhering to the view that a promise is not a representation, but carving out exceptions, is Fayette v. Ford Motor Credit, 129 Vt. 505, 282 A.2d 840 (1971). Promissory fraud was, perhaps disingenuously, characterized as the representation of a present fact in R.R.S. II Enterprises v. Regency Assocs., 646 N.E.2d 56 (Ind.App.1995), because Indiana does not redress promissory fraud. See, e.g., Anderson v. Indianapolis Indiana AAMCO Dealers Advertising Pool, 678 N.E.2d 832 (1997).

5. See §§ 2.5, 2.6 supra.

6. Keeton, Fraud: Statements of Intention, 15 Tex.L.Rev. 185, 195 (1937).

7. See People v. Norman, 85 N.Y.2d 609, 627 N.Y.S.2d 302, 650 N.E.2d 1303 (1995).

8. Stone v. Schulz, 231 A.D.2d 707, 647 N.Y.S.2d 822 (1996).

9. See Prosser & Keeton, Torts 763–64 (5th ed. 1984). Keeton, Fraud: Statements of Intention, 15 Tex.L.Rev. 185, 200–16 (1937); Sweet, Promissory Fraud and the Parol Evidence Rule, 49 Cal.L.Rev. 877 (1961); Notes, 7 Buffalo L.Rev. 332 (1958); 38 Colum.L.Rev. 1461, 1465–72 (1938); 53 Fordham L.Rev. 1231 (1985); York v. Golden Poultry, 883 F.Supp. 32 (E.D.N.C.1995) (statute of frauds is no bar), reversed on other grounds.

promise, have no relevance in an action for restitution or deceit.[10] Other courts are of the opinion that to allow a restitutionary or tort action would open the gate to circumvention of these contract doctrines by artful recasting of the facts in pleadings and testimony,[11] or, if the question is lack of consideration, circumvention of the old rule that one has no right to rely on a promise made without consideration, a rule which is now pretty well exploded by acceptance of the doctrine of promissory estoppel.[12]

The above abstract exposition can be illustrated by two variations on one case. X, Inc. was negotiating to sell to Y its ownership interest in a subsidiary. Because the negotiations were not producing the sort of price X wanted, it approached Z with a proposal to negotiate the sale to Z. At the commencement of negotiations, Z extracted a written agreement that X would not negotiate with anyone else with respect to the proposed sale. X never intended to honor that promise. Had the promise been made orally, collateral to a written contract, it would have been unenforceable under the Statute of Frauds and also barred by the parol evidence rule. Could it have been the basis of a fraud action? The court adopted the point of view that where the contract is in writing, the intention not to perform one of the promises expressed in writing does not constitute actionable fraud. But the intent not to perform a "collateral" promise that is *not* contained in the writing does constitute fraud.[13]

§ 9.20　Non–Disclosure; Implied Warranty

Information is valuable. Possession of it frequently permits an individual to enter into a transaction that is profitable precisely because the individual is acting on the information not possessed by the other party. To what extent must a contracting party share information with the other party when that information bears on the relative exchange of values? Poker players do not share information concerning the content of their hands. Is this an apt analogy to a bargaining transaction? The answer is complex. The kinds of information that affect values are many. Means of gathering information are multiple. The circumstances surrounding the negotiation of contracts vary greatly, and the relationships between negotiating parties are diverse.

10. In a parol evidence rule case the court said: "Objectivity and certainty in the law of contracts are desirable, but at times they are too weak to protect legitimate expectations of fair dealing." Abbott v. Abbott, 188 Neb. 61, 66, 195 N.W.2d 204, 208 (1972). See also § 9.21 infra on disclaimers. A Statute of Frauds case in accord is Burgdorfer v. Thielemann, 153 Or. 354, 55 P.2d 1122, 104 ALR 1407 (1936); contra, Caplan v. Roberts, 506 F.2d 1039 (9th Cir.1974).

11. Scott v. Minuteman Press Int'l, 68 F.3d 481 (9th Cir.1995) (Cal.Law), but see analysis of California law in Comment, 37 Santa Clara L.Rev. 1031 (1997).

12. See ch. 6 supra.

13. International CableTel v. Le Groupe Videotron, 978 F.Supp. 483 (S.D.N.Y.1997); Shred–It USA v. Mobile Data Shred, 202 F.Supp.2d 228 (S.D.N.Y.2002). For a variation on this approach, see Scott v. Minuteman Press, 68 F.3d 481 (9th Cir.1995). A contrary approach is that an oral fraudulent promise that contradicts a written promise is inadmissible because of the parol evidence rule. Columbia Gas Transmission v. Ogle, 51 F.Supp.2d 866 (N.D.Ohio 1997), aff'd.

Every schoolkid learns that the Battle of New Orleans took place after a treaty of peace had been signed in Ghent ending the War of 1812. Every lawyer ought to be familiar with a case that had its genesis soon thereafter, which articulated the general rule that there is no duty to disclose information. The British blockade, which ended with the peace treaty, had drastically curtailed the export of tobacco, depressing its price in this country. Plaintiff, through special circumstances, learned of the treaty of peace before news of it had reached the general public in New Orleans. Plaintiff called on the defendant seller soon after sunrise at defendant's New Orleans trading company, and purchased a large quantity of tobacco. Within hours the news of the treaty became public, the market price rose substantially and the defendant seller sought to avoid the sale. The purchaser naturally sought to enforce the contract. Chief Justice Marshall, finding for the purchaser, stated that:[1]

> The question in this case is, whether the intelligence of extrinsic circumstances, which might influence the price of the commodity, and which was exclusively within the knowledge of the vendee, ought to have been communicated by him to the vendor? The court is of the opinion, that he was not bound to communicate it. It would be difficult to circumscribe the contrary doctrine within proper limits * * *.[2]

In short, the bargaining process was treated as if it were a poker game. On the question of whether the decision conforms to community expectations of good faith and fair dealing, one observer has noted: "If those facts were given to the normal person, as an abstract question, he would probably say that the buyer's conduct was unethical; on the other hand, if the same individual were given the opportunity the buyer had * * * he would do precisely the same thing."[3] This case is very likely good law on its facts[4] and can be cited for the general rule that in a bargaining transaction there is generally no duty to disclose information.[5]

This rule contains numerous exceptions. The first exception or group of exceptions is where a statute or regulation requires disclosure. The number of such statutes perhaps attests to the inadequacy of common law disclosure rules. The Securities Act,[6] Truth-in-Lending,[7]

---

§ 9.20

1. Laidlaw v. Organ, 15 U.S. (2 Wheat.) 178 (1817).

2. Id. at 194.

3. Keeton, Fraud—Concealment and Non-disclosure, 15 Tex.L.Rev. 1, 32 (1936). For a contemporary criticism of the decision, see Verplanck, supra § 9.17 n.4, passim, and the suggested contrary rule at 125–26, 227.

4. But see Palmer, Mistake and Unjust Enrichment 83–4 (1962) ("Today, I believe many courts would reach the opposite conclusion.") The ruling is supported by Bar-

nett, Rational Bargaining Theory and Contract, 15 Harv.J.L. & Pub.Pol. 783 (1992).

5. Schaller Tel. v. Golden Sky, 298 F.3d 736 (8th Cir.2002); Fisher Development v. Boise Cascade, 37 F.3d 104 (3d Cir.1994); Cambridge Engineering v. Robertshaw Controls, 966 F.Supp. 1509 (E.D.Mo.1997); Stoner v. Anderson, 701 So.2d 1140 (Ala. App.1997); Houdashelt v. Lutes, 282 Mont. 435, 938 P.2d 665 (1997). See generally, Keeton, supra § 9.20 n.3; 12 Williston §§ 1497–99 (3d ed.); 1 Black § 41.

6. See generally, Loss, Fundamentals of Securities Regulation (3d ed.1995).

The Interstate Land Sales Full Disclosure Act,[8] The Truth-in-Negotiation Act,[9] and Federal Rules regarding discovery[10] are some of the more prominent legislation in this field displacing the common law. All of these statutes govern transactions where one party is in possession of information which can be obtained by the other, if at all, only by extremely expensive means *and* where abuses of the information monopoly frequently took the form of false or misleading statements. Similarly, flouting court rules requiring disclosure of even damaging information in discovery proceedings, contaminates a settlement agreement procured by non-disclosure.[11]

A second exception or qualification of the general rule is the distinction made between non-disclosure and concealment. Positive action designed to hide the truth or to stymie the other party's investigation constitutes misfeasance that can result in liability for misrepresentation.[12]

A third exception is that where partial disclosure is made, lack of full disclosure (a half truth) may constitute misrepresentation.[13] Thus where one party reads a suggested contract to another, leaving out portions, the reader's actions have run afoul of this exception.[14] Where a resident of the Philippines was offered a job in Oregon, without disclosure that the existence of the job slot is under review, non-disclosure was deemed fraudulent and damages were awarded when the slot was canceled as of the date of the promised employment.[15]

A fourth exception is where a party has made a true statement in good faith, but supervening events make it no longer true.[16] Or, after making the statement, the party discovers new information demonstrating that the statement was not true when made. There is a duty to

---

7. See generally, Clontz, Truth–In–Lending Manual (1997).

8. See on this act: 27 Ark.L.Rev. 65 (1973); 47 Notre Dame Law. 267 (1971); 51 Or.L.Rev. 381 (1972); 24 S.Car.L.Rev. 331 (1972); 25 Stan.L.Rev. 605 (1973). Related state legislation is discussed in 60 Ill.B.J. 16 (1971); 9 Ga.St.B.J. 369 (1973).

9. This Act, applies to federal contracts, see 2 Pub.Cont.L.J. 88 (1968).

10. E.I. DuPont de Nemours & Co. v. Florida Evergreen Foliage, 744 A.2d 457 (Del.1999).

11. Fuku–Bonsai v. E.I. DuPont de Nemours & Co., 187 F.3d 1031 (9th Cir. 1999).

12. Keeton, supra note 3, at 2–6; 1 Black § 43. E.g., covering over a defect in a machine with paint. Kuelling v. Roderick Lean Mfg., 183 N.Y. 78, 75 N.E. 1098, 2 LRA NS 303 (1905). See also Rs. 2d § 160.

13. Cambridge Plating v. NAPCO, 876 F.Supp. 326 (D.Mass.1995), aff'd in part,

vacated in part; Norton v. Poplos, 443 A.2d 1 (Del.1982); Russ v. Brown, 96 Idaho 369, 529 P.2d 765 (1974); Krause v. Eugene Dodge, 265 Or. 486, 509 P.2d 1199 (1973) ("new car" had 5,000 miles of use); 12 Williston § 1497 n. 4 (3d ed.). "Half the Truth is often a great Lie." Benjamin Franklin, Poor Richard: 1758. The problem of concealed information in a letter of reference from a prior employer is the subject of Comment, 32 U.S.F. L. Rev. 405 (1998).

14. Ten–Cate v. First Nat. Bank, 52 S.W.2d 323 (Tex.App.1932). Additional "half-truth" cases in Prosser & Keeton, Torts 736–40 (5th ed. 1984); 1 Black § 67; see also Coral Gables v. Mayer, 241 A.D. 340, 271 N.Y.S. 662 (1934), subseq. history omitted.

15. Elizaga v. Kaiser Foundation Hosps., 259 Or. 542, 487 P.2d 870 (1971). See also Rs. 2d § 159 cmt b.

16. In re Williams, 314 Or. 530, 840 P.2d 1280 (1992) (attorney disciplined for failing to disclose that tenant had now vacated premises).

disclose the truth if representor knows that the other is relying on it.[17] Similarly, if one party becomes aware that the other is operating under a mistake as to a basic assumption on which the negotiations are based,[18] that party has a duty to correct the mistake even if that party did not cause it.[19] Under this heading come the numerous cases holding that the seller of goods, lands or securities is under an obligation to disclose latent defects. This is very old doctrine, though its history is not smooth. The doctrine was prevalent in the early nineteenth century. "A sound price warrants a sound commodity" was the maxim.[20] But later in that century the phrase *caveat emptor* had thoroughly eradicated the earlier maxim.[21] Although the dust has not settled, it may safely be said that the older law once again prevails as to latent defects in consumer transactions and single family housing[22] although some citadels of *caveat emptor* remain. Thus, in Massachusetts a seller of a house need not disclose that the house is infested with termites,[23] although the seller must disclose conditions dangerous to health and safety.[24] In general, *caveat emptor* remains as a viable doctrine in commercial realty and transactions between merchants.[25] Under modern legislation the owner of land is responsible for the cleaning up of hazardous wastes on the land. Does the vendor who knows of the presence of such wastes have a duty to inform the vendee of their presence? Generally, in the sale of commercial property the answer has been, no.[26] Often, this is dictated by the wording of the contract. Does one have a duty to disclose that a house is haunted by ghosts? Yes, says the court; one cannot inspect, or hire a professional inspector, for this condition.[27]

17. Rs. 1st § 472 (similarly where he knowingly tells an untruth not expecting the other to rely and discovers that he is relying); Keeton, n.3 supra, at 6; 12 Williston §§ 1497, 1499 (3d ed.). See also Rs. 2d § 161(a).

18. Rs. 2d § 161(b).

19. Brinkerhoff v. Campbell, 99 Wash. App. 692, 994 P.2d 911 (2000); Davis v. Reisinger, 120 A.D. 766, 105 N.Y.S. 603 (1907); Rs. 1st § 472(b); 12 Williston §§ 1497, 1499 (3d ed.).

20. See Horwitz, The Historical Foundations of Modern Contract Law, 87 Harv. L.Rev. 917, 926 (1974), and authorities there cited; Cowen, A Treatise on the Civil Jurisdiction of a Justice of the Peace in the State of New York 146–147 (1821).

21. By 1873 a leading text could state that the maxim "a sound price implies a sound article" is peculiar to South Carolina. 2 Parsons, The Law of Contracts, *775 n. j (6th ed.1873).

22. Neuman v. Corn Exchange Nat. Bank & Trust, 356 Pa. 442, 51 A.2d 759 (1947); 12 Williston § 1498 (3d ed.); 3 Williston, Sales § 631 (1948); Prosser & Keeton, supra § 9.20 n.14, at 736–40.

23. Swinton v. Whitinsville Sav. Bank, 311 Mass. 677, 42 N.E.2d 808, 141 ALR 965 (1942); accord, Williams v. Dudley Trust Foundation, 675 A.2d 45 (D.C.App.1996) (rotted roof); contra, Hill v. Jones, 151 Ariz. 81, 725 P.2d 1115 (1986); see also Weintraub v. Krobatsch, 64 N.J. 445, 317 A.2d 68 (1974) (roaches); Greenberg v. Glickman, 50 N.Y.S.2d 489 (1944), subseq. history omitted (duty to disclose sub-surface water conditions); Lawson v. Citizens & Southern Nat. Bank, 259 S.C. 477, 193 S.E.2d 124 (1972) (filled earth); Ollerman v. O'Rourke, 94 Wis.2d 17, 288 N.W.2d 95 (1980).

24. Cutter v. Hamlen, 147 Mass. 471, 18 N.E. 397 (1888) (child of prior tenant died of diphtheria because of defective drains); accord, Cesar v. Karutz, 60 N.Y. 229, 19 Am.Rep. 164 (1875) (prior tenant died of smallpox).

25. See Note, 70 S.Cal.L.Rev. 1571 (1997).

26. Annot., 12 ALR5th 630.

27. Stambovsky v. Ackley, 169 A.D.2d 254, 572 N.Y.S.2d 672 (1991).

In sale of goods cases, usually the question of non-disclosure is of no relevance, inasmuch as the UCC supplies an array of implied warranties granting the purchaser relief for defects in the goods whether or not these are known to the seller.[28] Thus, the question of whether non-disclosure constitutes a misrepresentation becomes significant primarily in those cases where warranties have been effectively disclaimed,[29] where the non-disclosure is by a buyer rather than by a seller,[30] and perhaps on the question of consequential damages for breach of warranty.[31]

Although at common law there were no warranties attaching to a sale of real property other than those recited in the deed, there is a modern trend recognizing an implied warranty of habitability in the sale of new housing.[32] There is also an increasing trend toward recognition of such a warranty in the leasing of new or old housing.[33]

A fifth exception centers on the nature of the transaction. Contracts of suretyship[34] and insurance[35] are transactions in which, by long established precedent, broad duties of disclosure are required.[36]

A sixth exception focuses on the relationship of the parties. If there is a fiduciary or confidential relation between the parties, there is a duty of disclosure of material facts.[37] This may include the relationship between the parties who enter into a pre-nuptial agreement.[38] Indeed, the duty extends somewhat beyond such relationships. Whenever one party to a transaction justifiably believes the other is looking out for his or her interests, a duty of disclosure arises.[39]

28.   UCC §§ 2–312 to 2–318 (same numeration in revision).

29.   UCC § 2–316 (some major changes in revision).

30.   It is only rarely that a buyer is held to be under a duty to disclose. Keeton, supra § 9.20 n.3, at 22–27. If the buyer fails to disclose material facts, however, specific performance will be denied. See infra § 9.20 n.44.

31.   Undisclosed knowledge of a defect gives the seller reason to know of consequential damages and inhibits the purchaser from minimizing injury. See § 14.5 infra.

32.   Tassan v. United Development, 88 Ill.App.3d 581, 43 Ill.Dec. 769, 410 N.E.2d 902 (1980); Yepsen v. Burgess, 269 Or. 635, 525 P.2d 1019 (1974); see 12 Williston § 1506A (3d ed.); Demko, 71 Ill.B.J. 724 (1983); Moskowitz, 62 Cal.L.Rev. 1444 (1974); Note, 23 U.Fla.L.Rev. 626 (1971).

33.   Green v. Superior Court, 10 Cal.3d 616, 111 Cal.Rptr. 704, 517 P.2d 1168 (1974); Berzito v. Gambino, 63 N.J. 460, 308 A.2d 17 (1973); Love, Landlord's Liability for Defective Premises: Caveat Lessee, 1975 Wis.L.Rev. 19; Notes, 2 Fordham Urb. L.J. 433 (1974); 28 Stan.L.Rev. 729 (1976).

34.   Simpson, Suretyship 86–93 (1950).

35.   Certain Underwriters v. Montford, 52 F.3d 219 (9th Cir.1995); Vance, Insurance 368–86 (3d ed.1951).

36.   Long ago, an observer argued that a distinction between insurance and other transactions rested on no logical basis and that the insurance rule ought to to encompass all business dealings. Verplanck, supra § 9.17 n.4, ch. 7.

37.   Benevento v. Life USA Holding, 61 F.Supp.2d 407 (E.D.Pa.1999) (insurance sales agents); Rs. 2d § 161(d); Keeton, supra § 9.20 n.3, at 11–14; 12 Williston § 1499 (3d ed.); 1 Black §§ 48–58. This rule is closely tied to and overlaps the doctrine of undue influence. See § 9.10 supra. See e.g., Burnsville v. Westwood, 290 Minn. 159, 189 N.W.2d 392 (1971); Jackson v. Seymour, 193 Va. 735, 71 S.E.2d 181 (1952) (constructive fraud; could have been based on innocent misrepresentation).

38.   Randolph v. Randolph, 937 S.W.2d 815 (Tenn.1996); 27 U.Mem.L.Rev 1021 (1997).

39.   Rs. 1st § 472(c); 1 Black § 49; contra, requiring a confidential relationship, Grow v. Indiana Retired Teachers, 149 Ind. App. 109, 271 N.E.2d 140 (1971).

A special category is an attorney's duty to disclose certain information to an adversary. Where an attorney makes changes in a document that has been pre-approved by the parties or is sent to the attorney for the client's signature, the attorney has a duty to disclose that changes were made. Failure to make such disclosure can result in disciplinary action[40] and civil liability.[41]

In the law of medical malpractice, a rule of "informed consent" to therapy has evolved. One statement of the doctrine is that "true consent to what happens to one's self is the informed exercise of a choice, and that entails an opportunity to evaluate knowledgeably the options available and the risks attendant upon each."[42] Disclosure of the risks by the physician is a necessary precondition to the patient's ability to evaluate knowledgeably whether to accept the proposed therapy. It would indeed be salutary if the doctrine of "informed consent" were adapted to the general law of contracts so as to require disclosure of all facts which "if known, would so affect the value of the thing sold or done, in the general estimation of those whose use or estimation fixes the market price of similar things, as to make the price of the actual subject of the contract vary materially from that of other things of the same nature or use."[43] The adoption of such a principle would bring the law with respect to avoidance into harmony with the rule governing the remedy of specific performance, where the governing principle is that "equity only compels the specific performance of a contract which is fair and open, and in regard to which all material matters known to each have been communicated to the other."[44] The U.S. Court of Claims appears to have gone far toward adoption of such a principle. A government agency is required to disclose information possessed by it "which it knew that bidders did not have and would need in order to make an intelligent appraisal of the

40. In re Rothwell, 278 S.C. 391, 296 S.E.2d 870 (1982).

41. Wright v. Pennamped, 657 N.E.2d 1223, modified 664 N.E.2d 394 (Ind.App. 1996). For these and other attorney nondisclosure cases, see Crystal, 87 Ky.L.J. 1055 (1999).

42. Karp v. Cooley, 493 F.2d 408, 419 (5th Cir.1974), reh. denied.

43. Verplanck, supra § 9.17 n.4, at 228; see also Holmes, A Contextual Study of Commercial Good Faith, 39 U.Pitt.L.Rev. 381 (1978). Such a rule is approximated in some jurisdictions.

"It is now settled in California that where the seller knows of facts materially affecting the value or desirability of the property which are known or accessible only to him and also knows that such facts are not known to, or within the reach of the diligent attention and observation of the buyer, the seller is under a duty to disclose them to the buyer."

Lingsch v. Savage, 213 Cal.App.2d 729, 29 Cal.Rptr. 201, 204, 8 ALR3d 537, 543 (1963); accord, Ollerman v. O'Rourke, 94 Wis.2d 17, 288 N.W.2d 95 (1980); see also Sage v. Broadcasting Publications, 997 F.Supp. 49 (D.D.C.1998) (equipment lessee did not inform lessor of its precarious financial circumstances); Kaas v. Privette, 12 Wn.App. 142, 529 P.2d 23, 80 ALR3d 1 (1974). Compare Sharp, The Ethics of Breach of Contract, 45 Int'l Journal of Ethics 27, 45 (1934). See Carlson v. General Motors, 883 F.2d 287 (4th Cir.1989), cert. denied (where durational limits on implied warranty are inadequate and seller is aware of problems with its diesel engine, a case of unconscionability may be present).

44. Rothmiller v. Stein, 143 N.Y. 581, 592, 38 N.E. 718, 721 (1894); cf. Amend v. Hurley, 293 N.Y. 587, 59 N.E.2d 416 (1944); McClintock, Equity § 73 (2d ed.1948). Barnett, supra § 9.20 n.4, however, supports the efficiency of keeping much information to oneself.

problems and costs that would be involved in the performance of the proposed contract."[45]

Despite the desirability of a broad rule of disclosure an exception must, however, be made for collateral information deliberately acquired at some cost in time or money such as by scientific market research or careful investment analysis. The nondisclosure of such information is no breach of the obligation of good faith and fair dealing.[46]

§ 9.21 Disclaimers; Merger Clauses; "As Is"

Contracts frequently contain merger clauses stating that the writing contains the entire contract and that no representations other than those contained in the writing have been made. Despite the existence of a merger clause, parol evidence is admissible for purposes of demonstrating that the agreement is void or voidable or for proving an action for deceit.[1] *Fraus omnia corrumpit:* fraud vitiates everything it touches.

New York, however, makes a peculiar distinction based on the specificity of the merger clause. While a general merger clause does not bar parol evidence of misrepresentations, a specific merger clause disclaiming specific representations does bar such evidence.[2] The distinction is more subtle than practical and has produced the proverbial flood of litigation. There is tension between two seemingly reasonable propositions: parties by agreement ought to be able to provide that a purchaser is relying solely on the purchaser's inspection and the also reasonable proposition that a party ought not by the use of magic words exorcize fraud. The distinction doubtless causes drafters of standard forms to draft lengthier, more verbose merger clauses. A sounder distinction, if, indeed, any is needed, would be between a negotiated clause and a standard form clause.[3]

45. T.F. Scholes, Inc. v. U.S., 174 Ct.Cl. 1215, 357 F.2d 963, 970 (1966), followed in J.A. Jones Constr. v. U.S., 182 Ct.Cl. 615, 390 F.2d 886 (1968).

46. See Kronman & Posner, The Economics of Contract Law 116–121 (1979); L & N Grove v. Chapman, 291 So.2d 217 (Fla.App.1974), cert. dismissed.

§ 9.21

1. 3 Corbin § 580; 1 Palmer on Restitution § 3.20; 5 Williston § 811 (3d ed); Associated Hardware Supply v. Big Wheel Distrib., 355 F.2d 114, 17 ALR3d 998 (3d Cir. 1965); Sound Techniques v. Hoffman, 50 Mass.App. 425, 737 N.E.2d 920 (2000), cert. denied (but bars evidence of negligent misrepresentation); Greenfield v. Heckenbach, 144 Md.App. 108, 797 A.2d 63 (2002) (does not bar evidence of negligent misrepresentation); Davis, Licensing Lies, 33 Val. U.L.Rev. 485 (1999); Sweet, Promissory

Fraud and the Parol Evidence Rule, 49 Cal. L.Rev. 877 (1961).

2. Danann Realty v. Harris, 5 N.Y.2d 317, 184 N.Y.S.2d 599, 157 N.E.2d 597 (1959); see Note 1997 Colum. Bus.L.Rev. 399; cf. Cohan v. Sicular, 214 A.D.2d 637, 625 N.Y.S.2d 278 (1995) (merger clause protected vendor and attorney, but not broker); Circle Centre v. Y/G Indiana, 762 N.E.2d 176 (Ind.App.2002) (clause stating that tenant did not rely on any representations bars evidence of misrepresentations).

3. The disclaimer in the Danann case was a typewritten rider to a printed form. Brief for Defendant p. 10. The distinction suggested in the text is considered in Citibank, N.A. v. Plapinger, 66 N.Y.2d 90, 495 N.Y.S.2d 309, 485 N.E.2d 974 (1985). The distinction was made in Great Lakes Chemical v. Pharmacia, 788 A.2d 544, 555 (Del. Ch.2001).

Even under the majority rule, a merger clause may not be entirely ineffective. If the clause states that no representations have been made and that the purchaser relies on nothing but purchaser's own inspection, the clause, although not conclusive, is at least an evidentiary admission by the purchaser.[4] If the clause states that the company's agents have no authority to make representations, it places the other party on notice of the agent's lack of authority. There are holdings applying this concept rather rigidly.[5] Under the Restatement view, a compromise has been put forward, permitting a party who has relied on unauthorized representations of an agent to rescind and have restitution but not to recover damages.[6]

Expressions such as "as is" are commonly understood to exclude all implied warranties,[7] but do not bar an action for deceit or restitution.[8]

§ 9.22   Fraud in the Factum or Fraud in the Inducement

In the great majority of cases, actionable misrepresentation renders a transaction voidable rather than void. There is some loose language in the cases on this score, for seldom is the distinction of importance. However, the distinction becomes of crucial importance if property has been transferred by virtue of the misrepresentation. If the property has been subsequently transferred to a bona fide purchaser for value, the defrauded party may recover the property only if the initial transaction is void.[1] The void-voidable dichotomy also has an effect on the burden of proof. The defrauded party normally has the burden of proof on matters of avoidance; the party seeking to enforce the contract has the burden of establishing the existence of the contract.[2]

On the question of what kind of misrepresentation renders a transaction void, the House of Lords in 1970[3] laid down a twofold criteria.

4. Omar Oil & Gas v. MacKenzie Oil, 33 Del. 259, 289, 138 A. 392, 398 (1926); Abbott v. Abbott, 188 Neb. 61, 195 N.W.2d 204 (1972).

5. E.g., Holland Furnace v. Williams, 179 Kan. 321, 295 P.2d 672 (1956) (furnace salesman untruthfully told customer his present furnace emitted carbon monoxide into his house); contra, Gibb v. Citicorp Mtge., 246 Neb. 355, 518 N.W.2d 910 (1994) (lies about extent of termite damage; tort action permitted).

6. Rs. Agency 2d § 260 (1958); Herzog v. Capital, 27 Cal.2d 349, 164 P.2d 8 (1945); cf. Anderson v. Tri–State Home Improvement, 268 Wis. 455, 67 N.W.2d 853 (1955), reh. denied (damages for deceit allowed where representor was the corporate president).

7. UCC § 2–316(3)(a) (some change in revision); Chamberlain v. Bob Matick Chevrolet, 4 Conn.Cir. 685, 239 A.2d 42, 24 ALR3d 456 (1967).

8. Lingsch v. Savage, 213 Cal.App.2d 729, 29 Cal.Rptr. 201, 8 ALR3d 537 (1963) (non-disclosure); New England Foundation v. Elliott A. Watrous, Inc., 306 Mass. 177, 27 N.E.2d 756 (1940); Packard–Dallas v. Carle, 163 S.W.2d 735 (Tex.App.1942); Stemple v. Dobson, 184 W.Va. 317, 400 S.E.2d 561, 8 ALR5th 957 (1990); Annot. id. at 312.

§ 9.22

1. 1 Palmer on Restitution § 3.2; Rs. 2d § 163 cmt c. See Pedersen v. Bibioff, 64 Wn.App. 710, 828 P.2d 1113 (1992) (mortgagee has no interest in property obtained by mortgagor by fraud in the execution).

2. Boxberger v. New York, N.H. & H.R., 237 N.Y. 75, 142 N.E. 357 (1923).

3. Gallie v. Lee, [1969] 1 All E.R. 1062 (C.A.); Saunders v. Anglia Building Soc., [1970] 3 All E.R. 961 (H.L.), aff'g sub nom; Note, 87 L.Q.Rev. 145 (1971).

First, the party asserting that the contract is void must have signed an instrument that is radically different from that which he or she was led to believe. Second, this party must have acted without negligence in the sense that a reasonable person would have signed it under the circumstances of the case. When these two factors coexist, the party may claim *non est factum:* it is not my deed. The decision of the House of Lords is also an accurate restatement of American common law.[4]

Article 3 of the UCC has laid down a similar test. Commercial paper is void even against a holder in due course if the paper is vitiated by "fraud that induced the obligor to sign the instrument with neither knowledge nor reasonable opportunity to obtain knowledge of its character or its essential terms."[5] Where a stockbroker tells a customer not to bother reading the form agreement containing an arbitration clause because the documents are mere formalities for the opening of an account, the customer is not bound by the clause because the customer is unaware that the form is a contract.[6] Where management introduces evidence that a union negotiator switched written proposals after management had read and agreed to a proposal and was distracted by another union negotiator and then, unaware of the switch, signed the substituted proposal, it made out a prima facie case of fraud in the execution.[7]

An attorney who participates in something of this sort is in violation of disciplinary rules. Thus, an attorney was reprimanded where a deed was sent to him for his client's signature and the attorney added a new term to the deed, oversaw its signature and returned it to the other party, without comment, for recording.[8]

§ 9.23　Remedies—Election, Express Warranty, Restitution, Measurement

If the fraud constitutes the tort of deceit, the defrauded party may elect to stand on the transaction, keep what was received, and sue for damages.[1] Instead, the victim may choose to avoid the transaction and claim restitution.[2] In many cases restitutionary recovery has included

---

4. Rs. 2d § 163; Trustees of the ALA–Lith. Pension Plan v. Crestwood Printing, 141 F.Supp.2d 406 (S.D.N.Y.2001); Operating Eng'rs Pension v. Gilliam, 737 F.2d 1501 (9th Cir.1984); Curtis v. Curtis, 56 N.M. 695, 248 P.2d 683 (1952) (wife signed separation agreement on representation it was a property division for income tax purposes); Whipple v. Brown Bros., 225 N.Y. 237, 121 N.E. 748 (1919).

5. UCC § 3–305(a)(1)(iii)(1990).

6. Lynch v. Cruttenden & Co., 18 Cal. App.4th 802, 22 Cal.Rptr.2d 636 (1993), cert. denied; but see Houlihan v. Offerman & Co., 31 F.3d 692 (8th Cir.1994).

7. Hetchkop v. Woodlawn at Grassmere, 116 F.3d 28 (2d Cir.1997).

8. In re Rothwell, 278 S.C. 391, 296 S.E.2d 870 (1982).

§ 9.23

1. Phipps v. Winneshiek County, 593 N.W.2d 143 (Iowa 1999) (settlement induced by fraud). The measure of damages is discussed at § 14.21 infra.

2. A third remedy, reformation, is considered at §§ 9.31 to 9.36 infra. A number of authorities permit a restitution action to be brought against all participants in the fraud even as to those who are not contracting parties. Metge v. Baehler, 762 F.2d 621 (8th Cir.1985), cert. denied; Gordon v. Burr, 506 F.2d 1080 (2d Cir.1974).

reliance damages.[3] Under statutes in some states,[4] and under the sales article of the UCC,[5] no election is necessary. The defrauded party may pursue and obtain both remedies so long as items of recovery are not duplicated. For example, where plaintiff was induced to purchase a horse by a representation that it was a stallion, when it was discovered that the horse was a gelding, plaintiff was permitted to return the horse, and recover the price plus expenses for food, maintenance and veterinary care.[6] This case also illustrates another rule of the UCC. The factual representation that the horse is a stallion is deemed an express warranty;[7] an absolute undertaking that the representation is true. When pursuing a remedy for breach of warranty, questions such as the seller's knowledge of the falsity of the representation disappear.[8] The only requisite is that the representation be "part of the basis of the bargain," which appears to mean that reliance in some broad, vague sense is required, although some courts have held no reliance is required.[9]

Election must be distinguished from ratification or avoidance. As a substantive law matter, a party who has discovered that it has been induced by fraud to enter into a contract may by words or conduct indicate that it will proceed with the transaction despite the fraud. This is a ratification, also known as affirmance.[10] At this point the party's only remedy is in tort.

The defrauded party may, instead, indicate that it will not continue with the execution of the transaction. At this point, under the common law rule, it has a right to elect between an action for deceit and an action for restitution. This can be looked at as a procedural decision, although it has substantive effects. There is a great diversity of views about what constitutes an election and when it must be made.[11] The older view demanded a prompt and irrevocable election.[12] This is still the present

---

3. Hammac v. Skinner, 265 Ala. 9, 89 So.2d 70 (1956); Jennings v. Lee, 105 Ariz. 167, 461 P.2d 161 (1969); Mock v. Duke, 20 Mich.App. 453, 174 N.W.2d 161 (1969); see 1 Palmer on Restitution § 3.9.

4. E.g., McKinney's N.Y.C.P.L.R. 3002(e).

5. UCC § 2–721 (unchanged in revision).

6. Grandi v. LeSage, 74 N.M. 799, 399 P.2d 285 (1965). See acute analysis in Monserud, Rescission and Damages for Buyer Due to Seller's Fraudulent Inducement of an Article 2 Contract for Sale, 1998 Colum.Bus.L.Rev. 331.

7. UCC § 2–313(1)(a), (b) (unchanged in revision); see also Steadman v. Turner, 84 N.M. 738, 507 P.2d 799 (1973) (warranty as to real property).

8. A number of jurisdictions allow an action against a manufacturer based on breach of warranty even where there is no privity of contract and no personal injuries.

Generally, however, restitution is not allowed. Voytovich v. Bangor Punta Operations, 494 F.2d 1208 (6th Cir.1974). Some courts, however, have held that a buyer may revoke acceptance of goods against a manufacturer that has expressly warranted the goods to the ultimate buyer. Gochey v. Bombardier, Inc., 153 Vt. 607, 611, 572 A.2d 921, 923 (1990).

9. See Rogath v. Siebenmann, 129 F.3d 261 (2d Cir.1997) (discussing several approaches to the reliance factor in warranty law); White & Summers, Uniform Commercial Code § 9.4–9.6 (4th ed.).

10. Rs. 2d § 380 (words or conduct); § 381 (delay); Dean v. Garland, 779 A.2d 911 (D.C.2001), cert. denied.

11. 1 Palmer on Restitution § 3.10.

12. The view persists. SMR Tech. v. Aircraft Parts Int'l, 141 F.Supp.2d 923 (W.D.Tenn.2001); G. Mansour, Inc. v. Mansour's, Inc., 233 Ga.App. 7, 503 S.E.2d 304 (1998).

tendency if the remedy sought is restitution and the other party would be prejudiced by delay.[13] Otherwise, the time at which the election must be made varies with local practice, but the modern tendency is to allow an election even after the pleading stage of a lawsuit.[14] Still, there are cases requiring an election prior to bringing suit.[15]

Avoidance and restitution on grounds of misrepresentation was originally an equitable remedy.[16] The common law courts, however, also opened the courts of law to claimants for restitution by development of the law of quasi contracts, restitution being based on the fictional promise to refund that which had been obtained by fraud. Today in many jurisdictions, equity has ceded its power except in cases where equitable relief is required to provide relief other than a money judgment, as where the cancellation of a written instrument is required for complete relief.[17] In an equitable action, it is not essential for the plaintiff to tender restoration of what was received as a precondition of relief. The flexibility of the equity decree is such that relief can be conditioned on restoration, or the value of what has been received may be offset from the relief granted.[18]

Where restitution is sought at law, the general rule is that as a precondition to relief the defrauded party must offer to return what was received under the contract.[19] Strictly applied, it has been held that failure to tender restoration prior to commencement of an action is grounds for dismissal.[20] It is certainly arguable that the equity rule should, in all states where law and equity are merged, be applied at law.[21] In New York, a statute explicitly achieves this result.[22] In other jurisdictions a tendency towards adoption of the equity rule can be

13. Johns Hopkins Univ. v. Hutton, 488 F.2d 912 (4th Cir.1973), cert. denied; Moore v. Farm & Ranch Life Ins., 211 Kan. 10, 505 P.2d 666 (1973). If after discovery of the fraud, some modification of the contract is agreed on, it is likely that this will be deemed to release any claims for tort damage as well as the power to rescind. United Forest Products v. Baxter, 452 F.2d 11 (8th Cir.1971). If after discovery of the fraud, the defrauded party merely continues to accept the other's performance, he may be deemed to have released the fraud claim unless it would be economically unreasonable to terminate the relationship, or there has been substantial performance. Clements Auto v. Service Bureau, 444 F.2d 169 (8th Cir.1971).

14. Moore, Federal Practice §§ 8.31[2] (1984).

15. Wender & Roberts v. Wender, 238 Ga.App. 355, 518 S.E.2d 154 (1999).

16. 2 Pomeroy, Equity Jurisprudence §§ 910–915 (4th ed.1918).

17. Herrick v. Robinson, 267 Ark. 576, 595 S.W.2d 637 (1980); Schank v. Schuchman, 212 N.Y. 352, 106 N.E. 127 (1914), or where specific restitution is appropriate. Rs. 1st § 489; § 15.5 infra. See generally, 1 Palmer on Restitution § 3.7.

18. Knaebel v. Heiner, 663 P.2d 551 (Alaska 1983); Jennings v. Lee, 105 Ariz. 167, 461 P.2d 161 (1969); Limoli v. Accettullo, 358 Mass. 381, 265 N.E.2d 92 (1970); Rs. 1st § 481; Rs. 2d § 372; 3 Black § 625.

19. Stefanac v. Cranbrook Educational Comm., 435 Mich. 155, 458 N.W.2d 56 (1990); Rs. 2d § 384; see 3 Black §§ 616–637; 12 Williston §§ 1529–1530 (3d ed.); see also Patterson's studies in N.Y. Law Rev. Comm'n Rep. 31–78 (1946); 339–54 (1952).

20. Wittorf v. Shell Oil, 37 F.3d 1151 (5th Cir.1994); Bennett v. Coors Brewing, 189 F.3d 1221 (10th Cir.1999) (Colo.); Stefanac v. Cranbrook Educ. Community, 435 Mich. 155, 163, 458 N.W.2d 56, 60 (1990); Haller v. Borror Corp., 50 Ohio St.3d 10, 552 N.E.2d 207, 210 (1990); 3 Black § 625.

21. 12 Williston § 1529 n. 3 (3d ed.); but see Barker v. Ness, 587 N.W.2d 183 (N.D.1998) (discussing variance between legal and equitable actions).

22. McKinney's N.Y.C.P.L.R. 3004.

discerned, primarily by the proliferation of exceptions to the well eroded general rule requiring an offer to restore.[23] Some of the stated exceptions are where the defrauded party is a governmental unit,[24] where what has been received was wholly worthless, has become worthless because of the fault of the other party or because of the absence of represented qualities,[25] where what has been received consists of money which can be credited to the plaintiff's claim,[26] etc.[27] In essence, these and other exceptions state that an offer to restore is unnecessary where it would be useless or unfair to insist on it. Nonetheless, it is everywhere the rule that, if on discovering the truth the aggrieved party fails to act with reasonable promptness to avoid the contract, the contract will be deemed ratified, thus destroying the power of avoidance. The victim is then relegated to a tort action, if any.[28]

The offer to restore need only be conditional; that is conditioned on the return of what the offeror parted with.[29] If the offer is rejected, the plaintiff must retain as bailee what plaintiff has received.[30]

"Restitution" is an ambiguous term, sometimes referring to the disgorging of something which has been taken and at times referring to compensation for injury done.[31] Often, the result under either meaning of the term would be the same. If the plaintiff has been defrauded into paying $1,000 to the defendant, plaintiff's loss and the defendant's gain coincide. Where they do not coincide, as where the plaintiff is out of pocket more than the defendant has gained and the defendant's conduct is tortious, the plaintiff will recover the loss in a quasi-contractual or equitable action for restitution.[32] Unjust impoverishment as well as unjust enrichment is a ground for restitution.[33] If the defendant is guilty of a non-tortious misrepresentation, the measure of recovery is not rigid[34] but, as in other cases of restitution, such factors as relative fault, the agreed on risks, and the fairness of alternative risk allocations not agreed on and not attributable to the fault of either party need to be weighed.[35]

23. See generally, 1 Palmer on Restitution § 3.11–3.12.

24. Rs. 1st § 480(1).

25. Rs. 1st § 384(2)(a); Rs. Restitution § 65(d).

26. Rs. 1st § 480(2)(c); Rs. Restitution § 65(f); but see Bennett v. Coors Brewing, 189 F.3d 1221 (10th Cir.1999).

27. Rs. 1st § 480(2)(d), (e); Rs. 2d § 384; Rs. Restitution § 65(a), (b), (e); § 66(3), (4), (5).

28. Gannett v. The Register Pub., 428 F.Supp. 818 (D.Conn.1977); Herrick v. Robinson, supra § 9.23 n.17; Rs. 2d §§ 380–381.

29. Rs. 1st § 480(3); Rs. 2d § 384.

30. Rs. Restitution § 67.

31. See Perillo, Restitution in a Contractual Context, 73 Colum.L.Rev. 1208, 1219–22 (1973).

32. See Rs. Restitution pp. 595–96 (topic note) and §§ 151–153; Jennings v. Lee, 105 Ariz. 167, 461 P.2d 161 (1969); Groothand v. Schlueter, 949 S.W.2d 923 (Mo.App. 1997) (no bright line rule on the availability of consequential damages in connection with rescission).

33. Rs. Restitution § 154 ill. 1; see also supra § 9.23 n.3.

34. No opinion on the question is expressed by Rs. Restitution § 155, Caveat to Subsection 1.

35. Perillo, supra § n.31, at 1224–25. In Remediation Services v. Georgia–Pacific, 209 Ga.App. 427, 433 S.E.2d 631 (1993), an owner avoided a construction contract for fraud. The contractor was entitled to restitution measured by the value of the work to the defendant, rather than the plaintiff's costs.

Where the fraudulent party's gains have increased in value, the most appropriate remedy is the imposition, by a court of equity, of a constructive trust on what the fraudulent party has received or its proceeds, thus permitting the defrauded party to recover the enhanced value.[36]

A misrepresentation may also give rise to an estoppel, preventing the party who made the representation from denying the truth of the assertion. Contrary to a widely quoted statement that estoppel is merely the basis of a defense and not of a cause of action,[37] estoppel may be raised affirmatively. For example, prior to any legislation on the point, a good number of jurisdictions had ruled that a carrier or warehouse-keeper was estopped from denying the accuracy of a receipt for goods as against a bona fide purchase for value, consequently allowing affirmative relief to the bona fide purchaser.[38] Estoppel is a doctrine, though never exclusively equitable, which has acquired a good deal of its sustenance from equitable principles; therefore, even an innocent misrepresentation can provide the basis of an estoppel.[39]

Fraud may also be used as an affirmative defense to an action to enforce the contract. At times, the defense is based on after-acquired evidence. For example, suppose an employee sues for breach of contract. The employer may investigate, determine that the employee falsified information on the initial job application and use such falsification as a defense.[40] If the remedy sought is specific performance, the court may deny relief although the fraud would not constitute grounds for avoidance.[41] This rule stems from the discretionary nature of the remedy of specific performance.[42] At the option of the plaintiff, however, the court may compel specific performance with an abatement of the price.[43]

As is the case with any kind of voidable transaction, the aggrieved party may affirm the contract thereby ratifying it. The ratification may be express or it may occur by actions inconsistent with disaffirmance after acquisition of facts that give notice that a misrepresentation has been made,[44] for example, an insurance company's acceptance of premi-

36. Janigan v. Taylor, 344 F.2d 781 (1st Cir.1965) (constructive trust measure applied at law), cert. denied; Sher v. Sandler, 325 Mass. 348, 90 N.E.2d 536 (1950), 63 Harv.L.Rev. 1463 (1950); Falk v. Hoffman, 233 N.Y. 199, 135 N.E. 243 (1922).

37. "Estoppel is only a rule of evidence; you cannot found an action upon estoppel." Low v. Bouverie, [1891] 3 Ch. 82, 105 (Bowen, L.J.).

38. See Ewart, Principles of Estoppel 235–36 (1900); Williston, Liability for Honest Misrepresentation, 24 Harv.L.Rev. 415, 423–27 (1911); Vu v. Prudential Prop. & Cas. Ins., 26 Cal.4th 1142, 113 Cal.Rptr.2d 70, 33 P.3d 487 (Cal.2001) (misrepresentation that deductible exceeded the loss estops the defendant from pleading the one-year contractual period of limitations).

39. Ewart, supra § 9.23 n.38, at 85–97; Williston § 9.23 n.36, at 424; Atiyah, Misrepresentation, Warranty and Estoppel, 9 Alberta L.Rev. 347 (1971).

40. Schiavello v. Delmarva Sys., 61 F.Supp.2d 110 (D.Del.1999).

41. Clayburg v. Whitt, 171 N.W.2d 623 (Iowa 1969) (equity rule applied to law action for the price).

42. See § 16.7 infra.

43. Stoll v. Grimm, 681 N.E.2d 749 (Ind.App.1997).

44. Citicorp Real Estate v. Smith, 155 F.3d 1097 (9th Cir.1998); Sears, Roebuck & Co. v. Meadows, 878 S.W.2d 171 (Tex.App. 1993), reversed on other grounds; Barrier Systems v. A.F.C. Enterprises, 264 A.D.2d

ums after learning of a misrepresentation precludes it from avoiding the policy.[45] Whether particular conduct constitutes ratification is often a question of fact.[46]

§ 9.24 Adequacy of the Case Law of Fraud

The rules governing fraud are quite elastic. Seemingly erratic approaches toward the issues of materiality, reliance, non-disclosure and the fact-opinion distinction often mask appellate judges' covert imposition of control over the findings of fact of the court below. In addition, there is ideological tension between rules forged in the nineteenth century in an era where risk taking and self-reliance were extolled and judicially applied in the maxim of *caveat emptor,*[1] and recognition that individuals and even companies often have no real alternative but to rely on statements made by sellers in today's mass, impersonal, global market.

Some have defended the elasticity and lack of definiteness of the law of fraud on the ground that fraud is too multifarious to be reduced to firm rules.[2] This may be true but it makes the business of advising clients difficult. Perhaps the main difficulty with the law of fraud in modern society is that much fraud is aimed at the public generally and aggrieved members of the public are unable to investigate the representations made, and when injured, it is often by a lesser sum than it would cost in legal expenses to obtain redress. In addition, unsophisticated members of the public are often unable to comprehend aspects of the transaction—such as true interest rates—when cloaked in obfuscating language. It is to problems such as these that the doctrine of unconscionability (§§ 9.37 to 9.40) and consumer protection legislation address themselves.

E. MISTAKE

Table of Sections

432, 694 N.Y.S.2d 440 (1999); Rs. 2d §§ 380, 381; 1 Palmer on Restitution § 3.10.

45. Scalia v. Equitable Life Assurance Soc., 251 A.D.2d 315, 673 N.Y.S.2d 730 (1998).

46. Akins v. Couch, 271 Ga. 276, 518 S.E.2d 674 (1999).

§ 9.24

1. "It is one of that tribe of anonymous Latin maxims that infest our law * * * they fill the ear and sound like sense, and to the eye look like learning; while their main use is to supply the place of either or both." Verplanck, supra § 9.17 n.4, at 218. On the history (by no means ancient) of the maxim as a rule of law, see Hamilton, The Ancient Maxim Caveat Emptor, 40 Yale L.J. 1133 (1931).

2. 2 Parsons, The Law of Contracts *769 (6th ed.1873).

§ 9.25   Subject of This Discussion

Certain kinds of error may prevent the formation of contracts. These errors include misunderstandings and mistake in transmission, topics dealt with elsewhere.[1] Here we are primarily concerned with mistake as a ground for *avoiding* a transaction.[2] The existence of a mistake is often internal to the workings of the minds of the contracting parties. Nowhere in the law of contracts do objective elements supporting the certainty and stability of transactions and subjective elements supporting fairness and the autonomy of the will clash as frequently as in the subject matter of mistake.[3] Notions of subjective assent borrowed from civil law countries have found their way into the objective matrix of the common law.[4]

§ 9.26   Mutual Mistake

Not long ago it was a common statement of the law that while relief is available for certain kinds of mutual mistake, it is unavailable for unilateral mistake unless the other party knew or had reason to know of the mistake.[1] This statement is no longer entirely accurate and it has been strongly argued that the distinction between mutual and unilateral mistake should be dropped.[2] This argument may be accepted in the long run, but for the present, the distinction is so embedded in the cases that it cannot be ignored.[3]

Mutual mistake can render a transaction voidable. Where both parties share a common assumption about a vital existing fact on which they based their bargain and that assumption is false, the transaction may be avoided under certain circumstances. If, because of the mistake,

---

§ 9.25

1. For misunderstanding, see § 3.11 supra; for mistake in transmission, see § 2.24 supra.

2. The remedy of reformation is discussed at §§ 9.31 to 9.36 infra.

3. For discussions of mistake in the framework of objective and subjective theories of contracts, see McKeag, Mistake in Contract 127–132 (1905); Patterson, Equitable Relief for Unilateral Mistake, 28 Colum.L.Rev. 859, 861–67 (1928); Sabbath, Effect of Mistake in Contracts, 13 Int. & Comp.L.Q. 798 (1964).

4. See Ricks, American Mutual Mistake: Half Civilian Mongrel, Consideration Reincarnate, 58 La.L.Rev. 663 (1998).

§ 9.26

1. Foulke, Mistake in Formation and Performance of a Contract, 11 Colum.L.Rev. 197, 224 (1911); Rs. 1st § 503; Rs. Restitution § 12.

2. See Rabin, A Proposed Black–Letter Rule Concerning Mistaken Assumptions in Bargain Transactions, 45 Tex.L.Rev. 1273, 1277–79 (1967).

3. See 7 Corbin § 28.39 (Perillo 2002).

a quite different exchange of values occurs from the exchange of values the parties contemplated, the transaction can be avoided, unless the risk of such a mistake is otherwise allocated by agreement, custom or law.[4] The same rule holds if the parties are operating under differing mistakes about the same vital fact.[5] It is immaterial whether the mistake relates to factors traditionally stressed as most likely to be vital such as to the identity of the subject matter. The important thing is that it be a basic assumption on which both parties acted.[6] Normally, for example, tax considerations are important factors entering into the calculations of each party to a bargain. That the parties are mistaken in their belief of these tax consequences will be grounds for setting the bargain aside if a mutual error as to tax liability was a basic assumption on which they proceeded.[7] With the understanding that the following categories represent typical fact patterns rather than legally distinct compartments, we shall examine several classes of cases.

(a) Existence, Ownership, or Identity of the Subject Matter

Absent a contrary assumption of the risk, if at the time of contracting for the sale of specific goods, unbeknownst to the parties, the goods never existed or are no longer in existence, no contract is made.[8] Where the seller is negligent in having a mistaken belief, however, liability may be found on an implied warranty of existence or a negligence theory.[9]

If the question involves ownership of goods, the question is resolved by an implied warranty of title which the seller makes to the buyer under the UCC.[10] Where the transfer carries no implied warranty, as may be the case with a transfer of a patent, the problem may be dealt with under mistake. Absent an assumption of the risk by the transferee, it may be held that if the patent is found to be invalid, the transferee

---

4. Rs. 2d § 152; see Palmer, Mistake and Unjust Enrichment 38–40, 47 (1962). Where the mistake does not affect the exchange of values, it is unlikely to be material and will not be grounds for relief. Fada v. Information Sys. and Networks, 98 Ohio App.3d 785, 649 N.E.2d 904 (1994).

5. Rs. 1st § 503; cf. Rs. 2d § 152 cmt h. Where the parties are mistaken about different facts, it is a case of two unilateral mistakes. Alden Auto Parts Warehouse v. Dolphin Equipment Leasing, 682 F.2d 330 (2d Cir.1982).

6. Rs. 2d § 152 cmt a.

7. Future Plastics v. Ware Shoals Plastics, 407 F.2d 1042 (4th Cir.1969) (stipulation); West Los Angeles Inst. v. Mayer, 366 F.2d 220 (9th Cir.1966), cert. denied (decided under related doctrine of frustration), noted 42 Notre Dame Law. 557 (1967); Stone v. Stone, 319 Mich. 194, 29 N.W.2d 271, 174 ALR 1349 (1947); accord, Dover Pool & Racquet Club v. Brooking, 366 Mass. 629, 322 N.E.2d 168 (1975) (mistake

as to zoning); cf. Walton v. Bank of California, Nat. Assoc., 218 Cal.App.2d 527, 32 Cal.Rptr. 856 (1963) (mistake not inducing cause of transaction).

8. Rs. 2d § 266; 7 Corbin § 28.30 (Perillo 2002); 13 Williston §§ 1561–62 (3d ed.). If the goods are in existence at the time of contracting and are destroyed subsequently, the question is one of risk of loss and impossibility of performance. See §§ 13.3, 13.24 infra.

9. McRae v. Commonwealth Disposals Comm'n, 84 Commw.L.R. 377 (Austl.1951); In re Zellmer's Estate, 1 Wis.2d 46, 82 N.W.2d 891 (1957); see Krasnowiecki, Sale of Non–Existent Goods, 34 Notre Dame Law. 358 (1959); Nicholas, Rules and Terms—Civil Law and Common Law, 48 Tul.L.Rev. 946, 966–72 (1974).

10. UCC § 2–312 (some changes in revision); cf. Rs. 2d § 152 cmt g ("A buyer usually finds it more advantageous to rely on the law of warranty than on the law of mistake").

may have restitution.[11] Where a life insurance policy is surrendered after the insured is dead, but before the death is known to the parties, the surrender can be retracted because of the mistaken assumption on which the parties acted.[12]

Where the parties are mistaken as to the identity of the subject matter, the contract may be avoided. For example, if both A and B mistakenly believe that a cask that actually contains sand, is instead a cask of lime and enter into an agreement on that basis, the agreement would be avoidable for mistake.[13] Under the UCC, if the seller describes the cask as containing lime, the seller has made an express warranty to that effect.[14] Although the Code thus throws the risk on the seller that the description is accurate, it does not foreclose the possibility that the warranty itself can be avoided for mistake.[15] The extent to which this will be allowed is not at all clear. It is assumed that barring very exceptional circumstances it will be deemed that the seller has assumed the risk that the description is accurate.

(b) Qualities of the Subject Matter and Conscious Uncertainty

Two famous cases illuminate the law with respect to mistaken qualities. In Sherwood v. Walker[16] a cow of good breeding stock, Rose 2d of Aberlone, was believed to be sterile and the owner contracted to sell her at a price far under that which she would have brought if fertile. Before she was delivered, however, it was discovered that she was fertile and thereby worth about ten times the sales price. The court ruled that the transaction was voidable, saying, "Yet the mistake was not of the mere quality of the animal, but went to the very nature of the thing. A barren cow is substantially a different creature than a breeding one. There is as much difference between them * * * as there is between an ox and a cow * * *."[17] One explanation for the decision is that in any contract parties take certain risks, but do not take risks of the existence

11. Herzog v. Heyman, 151 N.Y. 587, 45 N.E. 1127 (1897); cf. 1 Black §§ 87, 157. Where an owner of securities owned American Israeli Paper Mills, Ordinary B shares, but thought he owned American Israeli Paper Mills, American shares (listed on a stock exchange) and ordered them sold, it was held the mistake was unilateral and no relief was available. A sounder ground was that the defendant broker would not have been restored to the status quo ante. Morris Speizman v. Williamson, 12 N.C.App. 297, 183 S.E.2d 248, 48 ALR3d 504 (1971), cert. denied; cf. Ohio Co. v. Rosemeier, 32 Ohio App.2d 116, 288 N.E.2d 326, 61 O.O.2d 105 (1972).

12. Riegel v. American Life Ins., 153 Pa. 134, 25 A. 1070 (1893); accord, Duncan v. New York Mut. Ins., 138 N.Y. 88, 33 N.E. 730 (1893) (policy surrendered after insured ship had been lost).

13. Cf. Conner v. Henderson, 15 Mass. 319, 8 Am.Dec. 103 (1818).

14. UCC § 2–313; (substantially unchanged in revision).

15. UCC § 1–103 (revised as 1–103(b)); see Nordstrom, Sales 173 (1970); Kavanagh, 1 Ottawa L.Rev. 113 (1966); Rs. 2d § 152 cmt g.

16. 66 Mich. 568, 33 N.W. 919 (1887), reexamined and questioned in Lenawee County Board v. Messerly, 417 Mich. 17, 331 N.W.2d 203 (1982).

17. 66 Mich. at 577, 33 N.W. at 923. See Smith v. Zimbalist, 2 Cal.App.2d 324, 38 P.2d 170 (1934) (violin was assumed to be a Stradivarius); Beachcomber Coins v. Boskett, 166 N.J.Super. 442, 400 A.2d 78 (A.D. 1979) (counterfeit coin).

of facts materially affecting their bargain which both shared as a common pre-supposition.[18] In deciding which facts are vital and basic to their bargain one must search the facts for unexpected, unbargained-for gain on the one hand and unexpected, unbargained-for loss on the other. A perceptive analyst of the case states, "Here the buyer sought to retain a gain that was produced, not by a subsequent change in circumstances, nor by the favorable resolution of known uncertainties when the contract was made, but by the presence of facts quite different from those on which the parties based their bargain."[19]

In Wood v. Boynton[20] the plaintiff found a small pretty stone and sold it for one dollar to the defendant after two conversations in which the parties expressed their ignorance of the nature of the stone and guessed it to be a topaz. However, when the stone turned out to be an uncut diamond worth from $700 to $1,000, the court refused to allow avoidance. The court made three points. First, the action was at law and not in equity, expressing no opinion on the question of whether the more liberal equity approach to mistake would produce a contrary decision.[21] Second, that the subject matter of the sale was a particular stone and there was no mistake as to which stone was sold. Third, and most fundamental, there was no mistake about the nature of the stone; there was conscious uncertainty. Therefore, each party took the risk that it was something more or less valuable than the agreed price.[22]

Where there is conscious uncertainty there is an assumption of the risk that the resolution of the uncertainty may be unfavorable.[23] This principle is particularly noticeable in cases involving settlements by insurers. Where both the insured and insurer act under a mistaken belief that a given death or casualty loss has occurred, the settlement of the policy can be avoided.[24] Where, however, there is conscious doubt whether the death or casualty loss has occurred, the settlement stands.[25]

18. 7 Corbin § 28.35 (Perillo 2002). For an economic analysis, see Kronman, Mistake, Disclosure, Information and the Law of Contracts, 7 J.Leg.Stud. 1, 2–9 (1978). In Gould v. Board of Ed., 81 N.Y.2d 446, 599 N.Y.S.2d 787, 616 N.E.2d 142 (1993), both parties mistakenly assumed that the plaintiff teacher was untenured. She was advised that she would be terminated. In reaction, she resigned. It was held that the resignation could be disaffirmed.

19. Palmer, supra § 9.26 n.4, at 16–17.

20. 64 Wis. 265, 25 N.W. 42 (1885).

21. See 13 Williston § 1579 (3d ed.) as to the continued viability of the law-equity dichotomy as to mistake.

22. Nelson v. Rice, 198 Ariz. 563, 12 P.3d 238 (App.2000) (paintings sold for $60 were resold for $1 million); Knutson v. Bitterroot Int'l Sys., 300 Mont. 511, 5 P.3d 554 (2000) (mistake in valuation of stocks).

23. Rs. 2d § 154(b); Backus v. MacLaury, 278 A.D. 504, 106 N.Y.S.2d 401 (1951),

appeal denied (conscious uncertainty as to potency of a bull). Where there is conscious ignorance and an opportunity to investigate the facts, *a fortiori* avoidance is not permitted. Southern Nat. Bank v. Crateo, 458 F.2d 688 (5th Cir.1972); Copland v. Diamond, 164 Misc.2d 507, 624 N.Y.S.2d 514 (1995) (proceeding in conscious ignorance after investigation showed potential problem). The distinction between ignorance and mistake is discussed in Culbreath v. Culbreath, 7 Ga. 64, 70, 50 Am.Dec. 375 (1849); see Rs. 2d § 154 cmt c.

24. Continental Cas. v. Van Deventer, 277 A.D. 553, 101 N.Y.S.2d 342 (1950).

25. New York Life Ins. v. Chittenden & Eastmen, 134 Iowa 613, 112 N.W. 96 (1907); Sears v. Grand Lodge, AOUW, 163 N.Y. 374, 57 N.E. 618, 50 LRA 204 (1900); contra, Phoenix Indem. v. Steiden Stores, 267 S.W.2d 733 (Ky.1954), 40 Cornell L.Q. 618 (1955). In Harbor Ins. v. Stokes, 45 F.3d 499 (D.C.Cir.1995), the parties settled

The application of the leading precedents on the question of the basic nature of particular assumptions is most difficult. It may be quite obvious that a fire insurance binder issued when neither party knows that the insured premises are afire is avoidable because of mistake.[26] That a fire was in progress is not a risk assumed by the insurer. Put another way, a house ablaze is as different in kind from a house not ablaze as a barren cow is from a pregnant cow. On the other hand, consider the case of a settlement of a paternity suit. Paternity is one of the risks assumed by the male party to such a settlement and, if scientific evidence becomes available that he is not the father of the child, the settlement nonetheless stands.[27] It is not clear, however, whether the settlement involves the assumption of the risk that the pregnancy is a false one.[28]

The House of Lords decided a similarly difficult case.[29] Defendants were the chairman of the board and a director of a subsidiary of Lever Brothers, a major corporation. When the subsidiary was merged with another corporation, defendants agreed to release their rights under their employment contracts in return for a payment of £50,000. Soon thereafter, Lever Brothers became aware that defendants had committed breaches of trust and could have been fired without compensation.[30] Lever Brothers sought restitution on grounds of mistake. The court ruled for the defendants, saying, in effect, a contract to rescind a breached contract is not different in kind from a contract to rescind a contract not breached.

The difference "in kind" test should not be taken literally. Such a test can be criticized as overly metaphysical,[31] but courts have generally employed the test more in a metaphorical than metaphysical sense. When the court rules that there must be a difference in kind between the state of facts and the facts the parties had assumed to be true, it is employing an analogy to the early cases allowing avoidance for a mistake in identity of the subject matter, and suggesting that the mistake must be about as vital as in those early cases. Metaphors, however, are dangerous for there are those who will take them literally. It would be

a personal injury case after the appellate court had affirmed a judgment for the plaintiff but before this was communicated to the parties. It was held that this was a case of conscious uncertainty rather than mistake.

26. Powderly v. Aetna Cas. & Sur., 72 Misc.2d 251, 338 N.Y.S.2d 555 (1972); accord, Richardson Lumber v. Hoey, 219 Mich. 643, 189 N.W. 923 (1922) (sale of lumber which neither party knew was in imminent danger of fire).

27. Fiege v. Boehm, 210 Md. 352, 123 A.2d 316 (1956).

28. Rheel v. Hicks, 25 N.Y. 289 (1862) (mistake a good defense; pregnancy a vital fact not in issue); cf. Heaps v. Dunham, 95 Ill. 583, 590 (1880); Thompson v. Nelson,

28 Ind. 431 (1867). Of course, if the claim is asserted in bad faith, there is no consideration. See § 4.8 supra.

29. Bell v. Lever Bros., [1932] A.C. 161; criticized, Palmer, supra § 9.26 n.4, at 92–94.

30. Cf. Hadden v. Consolidated Edison of New York, 45 N.Y.2d 466, 410 N.Y.S.2d 274, 382 N.E.2d 1136 (1978) (plaintiff was under suspicion of wrongful conduct when he retired with pension).

31. Palmer, supra § 9.26 n.4, at 46. The author favors a test of whether the mistake is "objectively basic." Id. at 47, 92. The court abandoned the "difference in kind" test in Lenawee County Board v. Messerly, supra § 9.26 n.16.

beneficial if the rule were stated to be that for relief to be granted for mistake as to quality, the mistake must relate to a vital fact on which the parties based their bargain.[32]

(c) Mistake in Acreage—Realty Contracts

A fact pattern which recurs with remarkable frequency involves a contract to convey or a conveyance of land under a mistake as to the number of acres in the parcel. If the acreage is materially at variance with what was believed, the aggrieved party may avoid the contract.[33] In such a case it is unimportant whether the sale was in gross or on a per acre basis. Such a distinction matters where the aggrieved party seeks relief other than avoidance. If the sale is in gross, generally no relief other than avoidance of the entire transaction for a material variance is available.[34] If the sale is on a per acre basis, the purchaser may have pro rata restitution of the purchase price for any missing acres[35] and the seller has an action for additional payment for any excess acres.[36] It is often difficult to determine whether the sale is on an in gross or per acre basis. Among the factors to consider is whether the purchase price is an equimultiple of the acreage, whether the property is described by a name, as the XYZ ranch, or by acreage, whether the acreage had a uniform value, and whether personal property has been included in the sale price.[37]

(d) Releases—Mistake as to Injuries

A release of a personal injury claim is not a commercial transaction.[38] Social policies favoring the assumption of entrepreneurial risks as a means of improving market efficiency are not present. Instead, a policy of adequate compensation for injury tortiously done is strong. Thus, boilerplate release forms releasing all injuries, known and unknown, present and future are not automatically honored.[39] The main tool for

32. For such an approach, see Davey v. Brownson, 3 Wn.App. 820, 478 P.2d 258, 50 ALR3d 1182 (1970) (termites); Faria v. Southwick, 81 Idaho 68, 337 P.2d 374 (1959) (parties wrongly assumed productivity of leasehold); Hinson v. Jefferson, 24 N.C.App. 231, 210 S.E.2d 498 (1974), modified; Knudsen v. Jensen, 521 N.W.2d 415 (S.D.1994) (latent structural defect); Vermette v. Andersen, 16 Wn.App. 466, 558 P.2d 258 (1976).

33. McGeorge v. White, 295 Ky. 367, 174 S.W.2d 532, 153 ALR 1 (1943); D'Antoni v. Goff, 52 A.D.2d 973, 383 N.Y.S.2d 117 (1976); Enequist v. Bemis, 115 Vt. 209, 55 A.2d 617, 1 ALR2d 1 (1947); 13 Williston § 1571 (3d ed.); Comment, 49 Marquette L.Rev. 767 (1966); cf. Christian v. All Persons, 144 F.Supp.2d 420 (D.Vi.2001) (mistake not material); Bowling v. Poole, 756 N.E.2d 983 (Ind.App.2001) (same).

34. See Branton v. Jones, 222 Va. 305, 281 S.E.2d 799, 801 (1981). Granting an

abatement in price contrary to the general rule is Glover v. Bullard, 170 Ark. 58, 278 S.W. 645 (1926).

35. State v. Regency Group, 598 A.2d 1123 (Del.Super.1991); Rs. 2d § 158 ill. 1.

36. Lyons v. Keith, 316 S.W.2d 785 (Tex.App.1958), ref. n.r.e. A good discussion is in Lawrence v. Staigg, 8 R.I. 256 (1866); see Rs. 2d § 158 ill. 2. Contra, Ford v. Delph, 203 Mo.App. 659, 220 S.W. 719 (1920).

37. Speedway Enterprises v. Hartsell, 75 Ariz. 36, 251 P.2d 641 (1952).

38. See Ricketts v. Pennsylvania R., 153 F.2d 757, 767–68, 164 ALR 387 (2d Cir. 1946) (Frank, J., concurring).

39. See generally Dobbs, Conclusiveness of Personal Injury Settlements, 41 N.Car. L.Rev. 665 (1963); Havighurst, Problems Concerning Settlement Agreements, 53 Nw. U.L.Rev. 283 (1958); Keefe, Validity of Re-

avoiding them is a doctrine of mistake somewhat more flexible than is employed in commercial transactions.[40] Most of the cases involve mistake as to existence, nature or gravity of personal injuries.[41]

There appear to be at least four views on the problem. The most strict view refuses to distinguish between personal injury and commercial releases.[42] Next in the spectrum is a view that makes relief for mistake available for unknown injuries but not for unknown consequences of known injuries.[43] This test has been erratically applied. Where an injured party's symptom was a bruise on a foot, a settlement for $275 was allowed to stand despite the fact that the injury subsequently required amputation of the leg. The amputation was deemed the consequence of a known injury.[44] On the other hand, knowledge of superficial injury to the knee was held not knowledge of serious bone injury.[45]

A third view, often indistinguishable from the second, but somewhat more relaxed, allows recovery for mistake as to the nature and *extent* of an injury but not for mistake as to its future course.[46] Diagnosis is distinguished from prognosis.

A fourth approach, most favorable to the injured party, is difficult to synthesize. This view operates from the general principle allowing relief for vital mistake rather than from any particular formulation. Thus a vital mistake as to prognosis is grounds for setting aside the release.[47]

(e) Releases—Sailors and Other Employees

A special rule governs seamen, who, as wards of admiralty receive paternalistic treatment. A release will not be sustained unless it is fair, just and reasonable.[48] "The tender consideration of admiralty for those 'favorites' of the court who are 'a class of persons remarkable for their rashness, thoughtlessness and improvidence' "[49] is the asserted basis for this rule.

leases Executed Under Mistake of Fact, 14 Fordham L.Rev. 135 (1945); Annots., 71 ALR2d 82, 13 ALR4th 686; 9 Wigmore, Evidence § 2416; Rs. 2d § 154 cmt f.

40. Of course, releases are frequently also attacked on grounds of duress, misrepresentation and mistake of law.

41. Other cases involve (a) mistake as to the nature of the instrument executed or (b) mistake as to the contents of the instrument. Keefe, supra § 9.26 n.39, at 136–40.

42. Oliver v. Kroger, 872 F.Supp. 1545 (N.D.Tex.1994); Bernstein v. Kapneck, 290 Md. 452, 430 A.2d 602 (1981).

43. La Fleur v. C.C. Pierce, 398 Mass. 254, 496 N.E.2d 827 (1986); Mangini v. McClurg, 24 N.Y.2d 556, 301 N.Y.S.2d 508, 249 N.E.2d 386 (1969).

44. Mack v. Albee Press, 263 A.D. 275, 32 N.Y.S.2d 231 (1942), aff'd.

45. Lockrow v. Church of the Holy Family, 5 A.D.2d 959, 171 N.Y.S.2d 622 (1958), aff'd; cf. Simmons v. Blauw, 263

Ill.App.3d 829, 200 Ill.Dec. 262, 635 N.E.2d 601 (1994) (doctor, patient, & lawyer believed the injury was to soft tissue, but later a herniated disc manifested itself; release stands).

46. Newborn v. Hood, 86 Ill.App.3d 784, 42 Ill.Dec. 96, 408 N.E.2d 474, 13 ALR4th 681 (1980); Poti v. New England Road Mach., 83 N.H. 232, 140 A. 587 (1928).

47. Witt v. Watkins, 579 P.2d 1065 (Alaska 1978); Reed v. Harvey, 253 Iowa 10, 110 N.W.2d 442 (1961); Sloan v. Standard Oil, 177 Ohio St. 149, 203 N.E.2d 237, 29 O.O.2d 355 (1964), 16 West Res.L.Rev. 1004 (1965).

48. Harden v. Gordon, 11 Fed.Cas. 480 (No. 6,047) (C.C.D.Me.1823) (Story, J); Garrett v. Moore–McCormack, 317 U.S. 239 (1942).

49. Bonici v. Standard Oil, 103 F.2d 437, 438 (2d Cir.1939) cert denied, quoting from Mr. Justice Story in Brown v. Lull, 4

The release of a federal statutory right, such as a right under Title VII of the Civil Rights law must be "voluntary and knowing."[50] In making this subjective determination, a frequently utilized test takes into account the following factors:[51] 1) the employee's education and business experience; 2) the amount of time the employee has possession of or access to the agreement before signing it; 3) the role of the employee in deciding the terms of the agreement; 4) the clarity of the agreement; 5) whether the employee was represented by or consulted with an attorney; 6) whether the consideration given in exchange for the waiver exceeds the benefits to which the employee was already entitled by law; and 7) whether the employer encouraged or discouraged the employee to consult an attorney.

These factors are circumstances that will corroborate or rebut the employee's testimony that the release was involuntary or not understood. Of course, in jurisdictions which require a release to be supported by consideration, the 6th factor could by itself be determinative.[52] Under the Older Workers Benefit Protection Act, the voluntary and knowing standard is enacted into legislation. In addition to factors such as the judicially constructed factors listed in the previous paragraph, the worker must be given at least 45 days to mull over the proffered release, and 7 days after signing it to revoke acceptance.[53] Some courts have ruled, on several theories, that an employee who signs a release may bring an action for age discrimination seeking to disaffirm the release without tendering back the benefits received from the employer.[54]

(f) Mistaken Predictions

The doctrine of mistake concerns itself with mistaken understandings of existing facts.[55] If the mistake relates to future events, relief is available, if at all, only under the doctrines of impracticability or frustration.[56]

§ 9.27 Unilateral Mistake

The common generalization has been that avoidance is not available for unilateral mistake except for a palpable mistake, that is, a mistake

Fed.Cas. 407, 409 (No. 2018) (C.C.Mass. 1836).

50. Alexander v. Gardner–Denver, 415 U.S. 36, 52 (1974). Even if these criteria are not met, the release can be ratified by conduct. Hogan v. Eastern Enterprises/Boston Gas, 165 F.Supp.2d 55 (D.Mass.2001).

51. Gorman v. Earmark, 968 F.Supp. 58, 62 (D.Conn.1997) (claims under ERISA (pension), age amd disability discrimination statutes and comparable state law).

52. On consideration and releases, see § 20.10 infra.

53. 29 U.S.C. § 626(f).

54. Long v. Sears, Roebuck & Co., 105 F.3d 1529 (3d Cir.1997), cert. denied.

55. Dairyland Power Co-op. v. U.S., 16 F.3d 1197 (Fed.Cir.1994); George Backer Management v. Acme Quilting, 46 N.Y.2d 211, 413 N.Y.S.2d 135, 385 N.E.2d 1062 (1978); Lakes of the Meadow v. Arvida/JMB Partners, 714 So.2d 1120 (Fla.App.1998) (release of contractor; latent defects were later discovered).

56. Metropolitan Life Ins. v. Kase, 718 F.2d 306 (9th Cir.1983), on reh. 720 F.2d 1081 (9th Cir.1983); but see Alcoa v. Essex Group, 499 F.Supp. 53, 71 (W.D.Pa.1980), criticized in Wabash v. Avnet, 516 F.Supp. 995 (N.D.Ill.1981), distinguished in Louisiana Power & Light v. Allegheny Ludlum Indus., 517 F.Supp. 1319 (E.D.La.1981).

the existence of which the other party knows or has reason to know.[1] (Relief in such cases is readily available.)[2] But, "the decisions that are inconsistent with it are too numerous and too appealing to the sense of justice to be disregarded."[3] Since those words were written, an increasing number of cases have permitted avoidance where only one party was mistaken. Today avoidance is generally allowed if two conditions concur: 1) enforcement of the contract against the mistaken party would be oppressive, or, at least, result in an unconscionably unequal exchange of values,[4] and 2) avoidance would impose no substantial hardship on the other.[5] The rule permitting avoidance for palpable mistake also continues in effect.[6]

The most frequent fact pattern in which relief for unilateral mistake is sought involves a mistaken bid by a construction contractor, usually caused by computational error or misconstruction of the invitation to bid. Decades ago, relief generally was not allowed unless the error was palpable, that is, known or obvious to the party receiving the bid.[7] Modern cases are, however, to the contrary, permitting relief even for impalpable mistake in bidding.[8] Relief has even been given to a mortgagee whose agent mistakenly underbid at a foreclosure auction.[9] It is quite apparent that if liberally applied, such a rule would erode, if not totally deluge, the prevailing objective theory of contracts.[10]

§ 9.27

1. Foulke, Mistake in the Formation and Performance of a Contract, 11 Colum.L.Rev. 197, 299 (1911); Rs. 1st § 503; Rs. Restitution § 12. Such statements continue to be found in many cases. E.g., Cohen v. Merrill, 95 Idaho 99, 503 P.2d 299, 304 (1972). But frequently in one jurisdiction one finds the generalization repeated, but specific cases to the contrary. See, e.g., Comment, 18 U.Miami L.Rev. 954 (1964).

2. Speckel v. Perkins, 364 N.W.2d 890 (Minn.App.1985); Lanci v. Metropolitan Ins., 388 Pa.Super. 1, 564 A.2d 972 (1989).

3. 3 Corbin § 608, at 675 (1960). The existence of such cases had been noted by some earlier authorities but dismissed as aberrations. One saying, "the doctrine is opposed by the great preponderance of the authorities." 1 Black § 128, at 397; cf. 1 Page, The Law of Contracts § 256 (2d ed. 1920).

4. Mariah Investments v. McCabe, 163 Or.App. 91, 986 P.2d 1209 (1999), rev. denied, (4–4 opinion; besides mistake, facts border on unconscionability and undue influence).

5. Rs. 2d § 153(a) and cmt d; Maryland Casualty v. Krasnek, 174 So.2d 541, 544 (Fla.1965); Gethsemane Lutheran Church v. Zacho, 258 Minn. 438, 104 N.W.2d 645 (1960); Da Silva v. Musso, 53 N.Y.2d 543,

444 N.Y.S.2d 50, 428 N.E.2d 382 (1981); cf. Beatty v. Depue, 78 S.D. 395, 103 N.W.2d 187, 1 ALR3d 531 (1960) (less restrictive approach); 13 Williston §§ 1577–1578 (3d ed.).

6. Parrish v. United Bank of Arizona, 164 Ariz. 18, 790 P.2d 304 (App.1990).

7. See Lubell, 16 Minn.L.Rev. 137 (1932); cf. Centex Constr. v. James, 374 F.2d 921 (8th Cir.1967) (ambiguous specifications); Patterson, 28 Colum.L.Rev. 859, 884–94 (1928). In this text, as in the Restatement, the question of mistake of one party known to the other is dealt with under the heading of misrepresentation and non-disclosure. See § 9.20 supra.

8. National Fire Ins. v. Brown & Martin, 726 F.Supp. 1036 (D.S.C.1989), aff'd (collecting cases); Annot., 2 ALR4th 991. The cases allow withdrawal, not amendment of the bid. Hemphill Constr. Co. v. Laurel, 760 So.2d 720 (Miss.2000).

9. Burge v. Fidelity Bond & Mtge., 648 A.2d 414 (Del.Super.1994); contra, Crossland Mtge. v. Frankel, 192 A.D.2d 571, 596 N.Y.S.2d 130 (1993), lv. denied.

10. See 13 Williston § 1579 (3d ed.). As to gifts given under mistake there is no such danger in granting relief, and such relief is granted with liberality. Deskovick v. Porzio, 78 N.J.Super. 82, 187 A.2d 610 (A.D.1963); In re Agnew's Will, 132 Misc.

It is therefore not surprising that there are strict limitations on the right to avoid a contract for unilateral impalpable mistake. First, relief is not available unless the agreement is entirely executory or the other party can be placed in the status quo ante.[11] Second, the mistake must be vital.[12] If the mistake is large enough that it should be obvious, then the mistake is classified as palpable and relief is easily given.[13] If, on the opposite end, the mistake is not substantial, relief is not given.[14] Therefore, if the mistake involved is impalpable, it must be substantial, but not astronomical. The test of substantiality is probably met in the bidding cases if the mistake swallows up the allocation made in the bid for profit.[15] A third restriction is that the mistake must be of a clerical or computational error or a misconstruction of the specifications or something of that sort. Avoidance is not allowed for a mistake of judgment.[16] Many of the cases routinely state that the error should not have been negligent. But, of course, the essence of the holdings is that there must have been negligence of a particular sort. When this is realized, courts have floundered with "culpable" versus ordinary negligence, "bad faith" versus "good faith" negligence and other such nonsense.[17] As in tort law, the question should be whether the carelessness caused any injury to the other party. Also, however, relief will be denied if the mistaken party had easy access to the information about which he or she was mistaken.[18]

Unilateral mistake is grounds for avoidance by the mistaken party. It cannot be invoked by the other party.[19]

The remedy of specific performance is a discretionary one and unilateral mistake may be raised as a defense under circumstances in which an action for restitution would not be permitted.[20] It has been urged that the rule applicable to specific performance be applied to

466, 230 N.Y.S. 519 (1928); Comment, 58 Mich L.Rev. 90 (1959).

11. Monarch Marking System v. Reed's Photo Mart, 485 S.W.2d 905 (Tex.1972); contra, Crenshaw County Hosp. Bd. v. St. Paul Fire & Marine Ins., 411 F.2d 213 (5th Cir.1969) (other party's expectations are to be compensated).

12. Lakes of the Meadow v. Arvida/JMB Partners, 714 So.2d 1120 (Fla.App.1998) (release of contractor and later discovery of latent defects).

13. Syracuse v. Sarkisian Bros., 87 A.D.2d 984, 451 N.Y.S.2d 945 (1982), aff'd. If the bidder notifies the other party before the bid is accepted, even if a statute makes the bid irrevocable, the mistake becomes palpable and avoidance is allowed. Ruggiero v. U.S., 190 Ct.Cl. 327, 420 F.2d 709 (1970); M.F. Kemper Constr. v. Los Angeles, 37 Cal.2d 696, 235 P.2d 7 (1951); B.D. Holt Co. v. OCE, 971 S.W.2d 618 (Tex.App.1998). Such cases actually support relief for unilateral mistake, since the mistake is used as a basis for relief from the irrevocable offer which is itself a contract.

14. Fields, 32 Ins.Couns.J 259, 260 (1965).

15. Boise Junior College Dist. v. Mattefs Constr., 92 Idaho 757, 450 P.2d 604 (1969).

16. Mt. St. Mary's College v. Aetna Cas. & Sur., 233 F.Supp. 787 (D.Md.1964), aff'd.

17. See Fields, § 9.27 n.14, at 260–61; Annot. 52 ALR2d 792 (1957). See E.H. Oftedal & Sons v. State, 308 Mont. 50, 40 P.3d 349 (2002) (recognizing that mistakes stem from negligence); Murray v. Laugsand, 179 Or.App. 291, 39 P.3d 241 (2002) (gross negligence bars relief despite inequitable conduct).

18. Hillcrest Realty v. Gottlieb, 234 A.D.2d 270, 651 N.Y.S.2d 55 (1996) (stipulation of settlement made several months after the appeal had been decided).

19. U.S. v. Systron–Donner, 486 F.2d 249 (9th Cir.1973).

20. Bailey v. Musumeci, 134 N.H. 280, 591 A.2d 1316 (1991); Panco v. Rogers, 19 N.J.Super. 12, 87 A.2d 770 (Ch.Div.1952) (avoidance and specific performance denied).

restitution.[21] Not surprisingly, proponents of extension of relief for unilateral mistake are much attached to the will theory of contracts[22] and opponents tend to regard the will theory as an outlandish transplant into American law.[23]

§ 9.28   Mistake of Law

The once-nearly-universal rule on the effect of a mistake of law was itself based on a mistake of law of sorts. In 1802 Lord Ellenborough mistakenly ruled that, because ignorance of the law is no excuse, money paid under a mistake of law that a debt was owed need not be repaid.[1] A number of earlier cases confuted his broad principle that relief is not available for mistake of law.[2] Nonetheless, the plausibility of the principle, imported from the criminal law, was such that almost all of the jurisdictions in the U.S. adopted it. Connecticut[3] and Kentucky,[4] were apparently the only exceptions. Others have since joined them;[5] some have done so by statute.[6]

Today, the rule denying relief for mistake of law has little vitality. It has been eroded by so many qualifications and exceptions,[7] varying from jurisdiction to jurisdiction. It is common to find cases where the issue is not even raised.[8] The Restatement (Second) expressly treats the old rule as non-existent and the Restatement of Restitution regards the rule as surviving only as to payments made pursuant to an honest demand under a mistaken belief of law that payment was owed.[9] The most

21. Newman, Relief for Mistake in Contracting, 54 Cornell L.Rev. 232, 237–48 (1969).

22. The theory that contract is based on the sovereignty of the will appears in § 1.4 supra. For relationship between mistake and the will theory, see Sharp, Williston on Contracts, 4 U.Chi.L.Rev. 30, 31–39 (1936).

23. Patterson, 28 Colum.L.Rev. 859 (1928).

§ 9.28

1. Bilbie v. Lumley, 2 East 469, 102 E.R. 448 (K.B.1802); see generally 7 Corbin §§ 28.49–28.54 (Perillo 2002); 13 Williston §§ 1581–1592 (3d ed.); 1 Black §§ 147–153; Woodward, On Quasi Contracts §§ 35–44; Comment, 19 Hastings L.J. 1225 (1968). A defense of the rule of no recovery for mistake of law may be found in Sutton, Kelly v. Solari, 2 N.Z.U.L.Rev. 173 (1966); Note, 45 Harv.L.Rev. 336 (1931). It is followed in Commonwealth Dep't of General Services v. Collingdale Millwork, 71 Pa.Cmwlth. 286, 454 A.2d 1176 (1983); Webb v. Webb, 171 W.Va. 614, 301 S.E.2d 570 (1983).

2. See Ireton, 67 U.S.L.Rev. 405 (1933); Comment, 4 Fordham L.Rev. 466 (1935).

3. Northrop's Ex'rs v. Graves, 19 Conn. 548 (1849).

4. Ray v. Bank of Ky., 42 Ky. (3 B.Mon.) 510, 39 Am.Dec. 479 (Ky.1843).

5. Gayle Mfg. v. FSLIC, 910 F.2d 574 (9th Cir.1990) (Cal.); Gartner v. Eikill, 319 N.W.2d 397 (Minn.1982); McFarland v. Stillwater County, 109 Mont. 544, 98 P.2d 321 (1940); contra, Thompson v. Volini, 849 S.W.2d 48 (Mo.App.1993); Marriott Fin. Services v. Capitol Funds, 23 N.C.App. 377, 209 S.E.2d 423 (1974).

6. E.g., McKinney's N.Y.C.P.L.R. 3005 (" * * * relief shall not be denied merely because the mistake is one of law rather than one of fact.") Other state statutes are considered in Report of the [N.Y.] Law Rev. Comm. 27 (1942); see statute applied in Mattson v. Rachetto, 591 N.W.2d 814 (S.D. 1999).

7. 13 Williston §§ 1581–1592 (3d ed.); Smith, 9 Tex.L.Rev. 309 (1931); Comment, 4 Fordham L.Rev. 466, 471–75 (1935); Note, 30 Mich.L.Rev. 301 (1931). Cf. misrepresentation of law, § 9.18 supra.

8. 4500 Suitland Rd. v. Ciccarello, 269 Md. 444, 306 A.2d 512 (1973) (zoning ordinance); State v. Robinson, 249 Wis.2d 553, 638 N.W.2d 564 (2002) (plea bargain).

9. Rs. 2d § 151 cmt b; Rs. Restitution, Intro. Note to Ch. 2, Topic 3, p. 179.; Putnam v. Time Warner, 255 Wis.2d 447, 649 N.W.2d 626 (2002).

common fact pattern to which this rule is applicable is distinctly non-contractual. It involves the payment of taxes or fees to a public agency which are subsequently determined to be unconstitutional or otherwise illegal. Mistake of law is not grounds for relief in such cases[10] although, on occasion, duress may be, as where one would be forced to discontinue doing business if a license fee is not paid.[11]

§ 9.29   Mistake in Performance

A party may mistakenly hold a belief as to the nature of the obligations under an existing contract. When a valid and enforceable contract exists between the parties and one of the parties pays money to the other in the mistaken belief that the payment is required by the contract, the payment may be recovered.[1] The same rule holds true if excess payment is made.[2] If something other than money has been transferred to the other, generally the same rule holds.[3] The transferor may recover the value of what has been transferred,[4] and, under proper circumstances, have specific restitution. Relief for mistake in performance is given far more readily than in cases of mistake in formation of a contract. It matters not that the mistake is merely unilateral and that it is negligent.[5] This is because the contract itself defines the rights of the parties, and mistaken overpayment or the equivalent involves the unjust enrichment of the payee and unjust impoverishment of the payor.[6] A "voluntary payment" doctrine needs to be distinguished. "Money voluntarily paid in the face of a recognized uncertainty as to the existence or extent of the payor's obligation to the recipient may not be recovered, on the ground of "mistake," merely because the payment is subsequently revealed to have exceeded the true amount of the underlying obligation."[7]

10. Video Aid v. Town of Wallkill, 85 N.Y.2d 663, 628 N.Y.S.2d 18, 651 N.E.2d 886 (1995) (despite statute quoted supra § 9.28 n.6). Canadian taxpayers appear to be more fortunate. See Crawford, 17 U. Toronto L.J. 344 (1967). For a qualification of the rule, see Brookside Memorials v. Barre City, 702 A.2d 47 (Vt.1997).

11. Manufacturer's Cas. Ins. v. Kansas City, 330 S.W.2d 263, 80 ALR2d 1035 (Mo. App.1959); Five Boro Elec. Contrs. Assn. v. New York, 12 N.Y.2d 146, 237 N.Y.S.2d 315, 187 N.E.2d 774 (1962). If the payment is stated to be "under protest," this is usually treated as sufficient evidence of duress in this context.

§ 9.29

1. Bank of N.Y. v. Spiro, 267 A.D.2d 339, 700 N.Y.S.2d 207 (1999); Rs. Restitution § 18; see generally, 13 Williston §§ 1574–1575 (3d ed.); Woodward, supra § 9.28 n.1, § 179; Foulke, 11 Colum.L.Rev. 299, 303–319 (1911).

2. WH Smith Hotel Services v. Wendy's, 25 F.3d 422 (7th Cir.1994); Talley v. Talley, 566 N.W.2d 846 (S.D.1997); State v. Unisys, 637 N.W.2d 142 (Iowa 2001); Rs. Restitution § 20.

3. Rs. Restitution §§ 39–40; Annot. 10 ALR4th 524 (1984) (mistaken payments by banks).

4. Some of the difficulties involved in calculating "value" in this context are suggested by Findlay v. State, 113 Tex. 30, 250 S.W. 651 (1923) (conveyance of excess land).

5. Rs. Restitution § 59.

6. See Chiang, Payment by Mistake in English Law, 11 Fla.J.Int'l L. 91 (1996).

7. Rs.3d Restitution and Unjust Enrichment § 6 cmt e; Dillon v. U–A Columbia Cablevision, 292 A.D.2d 25, 740 N.Y.S.2d 396 (2002) (appeal pending); Note 16 Ga. L.Rev. 893 (1982).

Although most of the cases involve mistaken payments, the doctrine is not limited to such cases. For example, if a party takes advantage of the fact that the other has forgotten, or overlooked, or is mistaken about, material provisions of their contract, it has breached the obligation of good faith and fair dealing.[8] The consequences of such a breach, however, do not lead to avoidance and restitution; rather, they engage the remedies for breach.

There are exceptions to the mistake in performance rule. If the person who pays or transfers something is under a moral obligation to do so, restitution is not available.[9] Thus if the obligation is unenforceable under the statute of limitations, or is barred by another legal rule that does not discharge the moral obligation, restitution is not available.[10] An important exception is where at the direction of the creditor, payment is made to a third person to whom the creditor is indebted.[11] The receiver of the funds stands in the position of a bona fide purchaser for value.

As in the case of mistake in formation of a contract, conscious ignorance must be distinguished from mistake.[12] For example, where both the insured and the insurer act under a mistaken belief that a given death or casualty has occurred, the payment made is recoverable,[13] but if there is conscious doubt whether the death or casualty loss has occurred, the settlement stands.[14] Also to be distinguished is the rule discussed in the previous section with respect to payments made under a mistaken belief of law that payment is owed and payment is demanded in good faith by the payee.

§ 9.30   Estoppel, Ratification, Assumption of the Risk

Suppose because of mistake in formation of a contract or mistaken overpayment, one party has been unjustly enriched, but has subsequently spent the money or otherwise disposed of what has been received. Should not the payor be estopped from claiming restitution? The answer in general terms is that it depends. A detrimental change of position by the payee in reliance on an overpayment may raise such an estoppel,[1] but merely spending the money may not be a detrimental change of position if it is not shown that the expenditure would not have been made from

---

8. Market Street Assoc. v. Frey, 941 F.2d 588 (7th Cir.1991).

9. Rs. Restitution § 61; Equilease v. Hentz, 634 F.2d 850 (5th Cir.1981).

10. On the legal meaning of "moral obligation," see ch. 5 supra.

11. Kull, Defenses to Restitution: The Bona Fide Creditor, 81 B.U.L.Rev. 919 (2001); contra Wilson v. Newman, 463 Mich. 435, 617 N.W.2d 318 (2000).

12. Estate of Hatch, 270 A.D.2d 590, 704 N.Y.S.2d 340 (2000) (payment of royalties when liability was uncertain).

13. Continental Cas. v. Van Deventer, 277 A.D. 553, 101 N.Y.S.2d 342 (1950).

14. New York Life Ins. v. Chittenden & Eastmen, 134 Iowa 613, 112 N.W. 96 (1907); contra, Phoenix Indemnity v. Steiden Stores, 267 S.W.2d 733 (Ky.1954), 40 Cornell L.Q. 618 (1955).

§ 9.30

1. Alden Auto Parts v. Dolphin Equipment Leasing, supra § 9.26 n.5; Lake Gogebic Lumber v. Burns, 331 Mich. 315, 49 N.W.2d 310, 40 ALR2d 993 (1951); Rs. Restitution § 69; see Scott, Restitution from an Innocent Transferee who is Not a Purchaser for Value, 62 Harv.L.Rev. 1002 (1949).

other funds. For example, where the payee used funds paid to her by mistake to pay off the mortgage on her house, she was not deemed to have engaged in a detrimental change of position.[2] Her net worth increased as a result of the mistaken overpayment. Similarly, if an insurance company mistakenly calculates—in favor of the annuitant— payments to be made under an annuity policy, the mistake can be cured by reformation provided that the annuitant has not reasonably changed position in reliance on the miscalculation.[3]

Other defenses to avoidance for mistake include ratification of the transaction after knowledge of the mistake[4] and undue delay in manifesting an intent to avoid the transaction.[5] The need by the avoiding party to offer to restore what the party has received is governed by essentially the same principles as in the case of avoidance for misrepresentation.[6]

As previously indicated, the underlying rationale for avoidance for mistake is that the risk of the particular unknown fact was not consciously assumed by, and is not reasonably allocable to, the party who has been disadvantaged by the mistake.[7] The parties can expressly allocate the risk of mistake in the contract.[8] For example, it has been held that an "as is" clause allocated to the purchaser the risk of mutual mistake as to the usability and legality of the vendor's sewerage system,[9] and a disclaimer of warranty may have the same effect.[10]

F. REFORMATION

Table of Sections

§ 9.31 Introduction to Reformation for Mistake

Misrepresentation, duress, misunderstanding, or mistake can result in a record that does not reflect the parties' agreement. Reformation is the remedy by which records are rectified to conform to the actual agreement of the parties.[1] At the simplest level it is the mechanism for

---

2. Ohio Co. v. Rosemeier, 32 Ohio App.2d 116, 288 N.E.2d 326 (1972); see Watson Clinic v. Verzosa, 816 So.2d 832 (Fla.App.2002).

3. Freeman v. MBL Life Ass., 60 F.Supp.2d 259 (S.D.N.Y.1999).

4. Rs. 2d § 380(2).

5. Rs. 2d § 381(2).

6. Rs.2d § 384; see § 9.23 supra.

7. See § 9.26 supra.

8. Rs. 2d § 154(a).

9. Lenawee County Board of Health v. Messerly, supra § 9.26 n.16.

10. Alaska Division of Agriculture v. Carpenter, 869 P.2d 1181 (Alaska 1994).

§ 9.31

1. See generally, 3 Palmer on Restitution §§ 13.1–13.19. In England the remedy is known as "rectification." See Powell–Smith, 120 New L.J. 330 (1970).

the correction of typographical[2] and other similar inadvertent errors in reducing an agreement to a record. Reformation is the quintessential equitable remedy that is sometimes now available at law.[3]

In addition to inadvertent errors, mistakes, misunderstandings, misrepresentation, and duress can provide a basis for reformation.[4] The substantive requisites vary with the basis. The standard of proof for reformation, clear and convincing evidence, is a higher standard of proof than is normal in civil cases.[5] Because the remedy was created by courts of equity, the parol evidence rule has no application in reformation cases.[6]

Note the limited scope for reformation. Contracts are not reformed for mistake; records are. The distinction is crucial. With rare exceptions, courts have been tenacious in refusing to remake a bargain entered into because of mistake.[7] They will, however, rewrite a record that does not express the bargain. Stated another way, courts give effect to the expressed wills of the parties; they will not second-guess what the parties would have agreed to if they had known the facts.

At times the distinction is very difficult to apply. Suppose Ms. X owns Blackacre including the mineral interests therein, but mistakenly believes that she owns only 50% of the mineral interests. She informs a prospective purchaser that she has a 50% mineral interest and that she will convey her entire interest with the land. Acting under this mutual mistake as to the extent of her ownership, she conveys Blackacre together with all her mineral rights in Blackacre to the purchaser.[8] On discovery of the mistake, may she have reformation? (She would have a good shot at avoidance, but she would rather keep the purchase price plus 50% of the mineral interests than disgorge the purchase price and return to the status quo ante). Was the agreement to convey her entire

---

2. Corcoran v. Supertel, 159 F.Supp.2d 1321 (D.Kan.2001); Traggis v. Shawmut Bank, 72 Conn.App. 251, 805 A.2d 105 (2002); Vasilakos v. Gouvis, 296 A.D.2d 668, 745 N.Y.S.2d 132 (2002).

3. Rs. 2d § 155 cmt a; Peterson v. First State Bank, 737 N.E.2d 1226 (Ind.App. 2000).

4. On misunderstanding, see Palmer, 65 Mich.L.Rev. 33, 51–56 (1966).

5. Rs. 2d § 155 cmt c; Berezin v. Regency Savings Bank, 234 F.3d 68 (1st Cir. 2000); Resort of Indian Spring v. Indian Spring Country Club, 747 So.2d 974 (Fla. App.1999); Estate of Shaw, 202 A.D.2d 433, 608 N.Y.S.2d 707 (1994) ("clear, positive and convincing"); Pepsi–Cola Bottling v. Peerson, 471 P.2d 924 (Okl.1970). This standard of proof is relaxed when there is a confidential relationship between the parties. Hardy v. Hendrickson, 27 Utah 2d 251, 495 P.2d 28 (1972). See § 9.10 supra.

6. Berezin v. Regency Savings Bank, 234 F.3d 68 (1st Cir.2000).

7. U.S. v. Williams, 198 F.3d 988 (7th Cir.1999) (plea bargain); Davenport Bank & Trust v. State Central Bank, 485 N.W.2d 476 (Iowa 1992); Perea v. Snyder, 117 N.M. 774, 877 P.2d 580 (N.M.App.1994). Deviations from this principle are to be found in the U.S. Court of Claims. See National Presto Indus. v. U.S., 167 Ct.Cl. 749, 338 F.2d 99 (1964), cert. dismissed, discussed at § 13.17 infra; Paragon Energy v. U.S., 645 F.2d 966 (Ct.Cl.1981), aff'd (reformation for mistake in bidding); Annot., 19 ALRFed. 645 (1974). Where reformation is sought on grounds of unconscionability, the court can reshape the bargain. See §§ 9.37 to 40 infra.

8. This hypothetical is digested from Malone, The Reformation of Writings for Mutual Mistake of Fact, 24 Geo.L.J. 613, 634 (1936). For a similar dilemma, see Yeargan v. Bank of Montgomery, 268 Ark. 752, 595 S.W.2d 704 (1980).

interest or to convey a 50% mineral interest in Blackacre? Courts have reached contradictory results in cases such as this, some being of the opinion that the mistake was one which induced the bargain and others that the mistake was in articulating the bargain.[9]

The requisites for reformation on grounds of mistake are three, although four are often stated.[10] First, there must have been an agreement between the parties. Second, there must have been an agreement to put the agreement into a record. Third, a variance between the prior agreement and the record exists. The often-stated fourth requisite is that the mistake be mutual. However, except in cases of misrepresentation, every unintended variance between the prior agreement and the record is deemed to constitute a mutual mistake.[11] Consequently, except in misrepresentation cases, the fourth element is included in the third. When courts speak of mutuality of the mistake, they usually mean that a mistaken belief by one party alone that the record will contain a given provision is not a ground for reformation.[12] This, however, is encompassed in the requisite that there be a prior agreement that the provision be included in the record. Thus, the mutual-unilateral mistake dichotomy adds nothing to the analysis of reformation problems. Some scholars and courts have recognized this fact.[13]

Parties to the contract are not the only ones who can obtain reformation. A third party beneficiary may obtain reformation[14] even under circumstances where the beneficiary is mistakenly excluded from the record.[15] Reformation against an assignee, however, is another matter. If the assignee is a bona fide purchaser for value, under general equitable principles, the obligor's right to reformation is lost.[16]

It has been held that reformation of a deed relates back to the time of the mistaken deed thus establishing priority over intervening liens.[17]

§ 9.32 The Prior Agreement

It is not a prerequisite to an action for reformation that the antecedent agreement be a contract. It may have merely been an agreement to the effect that if a contract is made and recorded it would

9. Malone, supra n.8, at 634. In addition, see Metzler v. Bolen, 137 F.Supp. 457 (D.N.D.1956) (reformation denied); Continental Oil v. Doornbos, 386 S.W.2d 610 (Tex.App.1964), reversed 402 S.W.2d 879 (1966).

10. The analysis which follows owes a large debt to Malone, supra § 9.31 n.8.

11. Id. at 618; Fidelity & Guaranty v. Global Tech., 117 F.Supp.2d 911 (D.Minn. 2000).

12. See, e.g., American Family Mutual Ins. v. Bach, 471 S.W.2d 474 (Mo.1971).

13. Alaska Foods v. American Mfrs. Mut. Ins., 482 P.2d 842 (Alaska 1971); Travelers Ins. v. Bailey, 124 Vt. 114, 197 A.2d 813 (1964); Palmer, Mistake and Unjust Enrichment 78–79 (1962); 3 Palmer on Restitution § 13.5; but see Rs. 2d § 155.

14. Wilhide v. Keystone Ins., 195 F.Supp. 659 (M.D.Pa.1961).

15. In re CS Assocs., 121 B.R. 942 (Bkrtcy.Pa.1990); Line Lexington Lumber & Millwork v. Pennsylvania Pub., 451 Pa. 154, 301 A.2d 684 (1973). So also, the mistaken inclusion of a person as a grantee can be excised. Eisenhart v. Lobb, 11 Neb.App. 124, 647 N.W.2d 96 (2002).

16. Hill v. Imperial Savings, 852 F.Supp. 1354 (W.D.Tex.1992) (D'Oench, Duhme doctrine).

17. Monroe v. Martin, 726 So.2d 701 (Ala.App.1998).

contain a particular provision.[1] It may have been a provision contained in a tentative agreement of the type that will not bind the parties until an integration is executed.[2] If by error, rather than by subsequent modification,[3] the record is at variance with the prior agreement, the record may be reformed.

§ 9.33 Intentional Omissions and Misstatements

With some frequency, for a multitude of reasons, usually unsound, parties knowingly fail to include an agreed term in their record. Under some circumstances, e.g., the final record is not a total integration, the parol evidence rule will not bar evidence of that term in an action at law and there is no need for reformation.[1] There is grave danger, however, that the court will deem the record to be an integration that bars extrinsic evidence of the term.[2] Although the parol evidence rule is not a defense in an action for reformation, reformation is not available for an intentional omission because there was no agreement to put the term into the record.[3] Similarly, if the parties intentionally misstate a term of their agreement, reformation is not available,[4] although if the parties agreed that the record would be inoperative, a declaratory judgment that the agreement is a sham and therefore a nullity may be available.[5]

§ 9.34 The Variance—Mistake Cases

The variance between the original agreement and the record may take any one of an infinity of conceivable forms. Typically, there "is the insertion of an incorrect description of the subject matter; street numbers, survey numbers, boundary lines," etc.[1] Computational errors are frequent.[2] Drafters of contracts or releases sometimes copy language from similar documents previously prepared and import language that is inappropriate for the present document. In a typical case, a ten-year annuity was part of an informal settlement agreement. When the formal settlement document was prepared, language from another settlement providing a lifetime annuity was copied. Reformation was granted.[3] Often, the mistake is as to the legal effect of the record. The parties' agreement called for a particular legal result. The record, however, if

§ 9.32

1. Rs. 2d § 155 cmt a; Joscelyne v. Nissen, 1 All E.R. 1213 (C.A.1969), 120 New L.J. 330.

2. 7 Corbin § 28.45 (Perillo 2002).

3. See Mid–States Underwriters v. Leonhard, 48 Wis.2d 176, 179 N.W.2d 914 (1970).

§ 9.33

1. See ch. 3 supra.

2. See § 3.3 supra.

3. Frantl Industries v. Maier Constr., 68 Wis.2d 590, 229 N.W.2d 610 (1975); see Abbott, 23 Harv.L.Rev. 608, 618 (1910); Palmer, 65 Mich.L.Rev. 833, 842–44 (1967).

4. Grubb v. Rockey, 366 Pa. 592, 79 A.2d 255 (1951) criticized in Palmer, supra n.3, at 840–42, 849–50.

5. See § 3.7 supra.

§ 9.34

1. 7 Corbin § 28.45 p. 291 (Perillo 2002); Donohue v. Picinich, 852 F.Supp. 144 (D.Conn.1994).

2. DR Lakes v. Brandsmart U.S.A., 819 So.2d 971 (Fla.App.2002); Ballard v. Chavez, 117 N.M. 1, 868 P.2d 646 (N.M.1994); Covington, 1964 U.Ill.L.F. 548, 552–53.

3. U.S. Fidelity & Guar. v. Burress, 844 F.Supp. 1475 (D.Kan.1994).

enforced, produces a different result. Reformation is available.[4] In one case a party who owned property as trustee signed a contract for sale in her individual capacity. Because she and the buyer had the mistaken belief that she owned in her individual capacity, reformation was granted.[5] The case pushes the boundaries of the remedy.

At times, the parties disagree as to the meaning of a record. Plaintiff takes the position that either plaintiff's interpretation is the correct one, properly restating the prior agreement, or, if this interpretation is incorrect, the record ought to be reformed. Such pleading in the alternative is generally permitted under modern practice.[6] While parol evidence is freely admitted on the reformation count,[7] it must satisfy rules concerning the admissibility of parol evidence for purposes of interpretation.[8]

§ 9.35   Reformation for Misrepresentation or Duress[1]

Where, because of mistake, a record fails accurately to state the agreement of the parties, reformation is usually the exclusive remedy. If the record is inaccurate because of misrepresentation, the alternative remedies of reformation and avoidance are available.[2] It is not every misrepresentation that gives rise to a right of reformation. The misrepresentation must relate to the content or legal effect of the record.[3] Misrepresentations concerning the qualities of the subject matter or other factors which affect the desirability of the bargain or the economic equivalence of the exchange are not grounds for reformation. Such relief would require the court to remake the agreement itself. Deviations from this principle have been few.

Critics have singled out one case, Brandwein v. Provident Mutual Life Ins.,[4] for such alleged deviation. Plaintiff signed a written agree-

---

4. Pasotex Petroleum v. Cameron, 283 F.2d 63 (10th Cir.1960); Franz v. Franz, 308 Mass. 262, 32 N.E.2d 205, 135 ALR 1448 (1941); 7 Corbin § 28.52 (Perillo 2002); Rs. 2d § 155 cmt a; Thompson, Reformation of Written Instruments in Iowa, 23 Drake L.Rev. 327, 334 (1974).

5. Yates v. Hill, 761 A.2d 677 (R.I.2000).

6. Klemp v. Hergott Group, 267 Ill. App.3d 574, 204 Ill.Dec. 527, 641 N.E.2d 957 (1994); Metro Office Parks v. Control Data, 295 Minn. 348, 205 N.W.2d 121 (1973). See Thompson, supra n.4, at 337–38; Comment, 37 Mo.L.Rev. 54, 57 (1972); cf. General Discount v. Sadowski, 183 F.2d 542 (6th Cir.1950) where reformation was granted after plaintiff had lost an action at law based on his interpretation. Such trial strategy runs into the danger in some jurisdictions of running afoul of the plea of res judicata. Annot., 49 ALR 1513 (1927).

7. Rs. 2d § 214(d). On the Statute of Frauds and reformation, see § 19.28 infra.

8. See Palmer, supra § 9.33 n.3, at 840 n. 27.

§ 9.35

1. Reformation to purge a contract of illegality is discussed at § 22.2(e) infra.

2. Rs. 2d § 166 cmt b. Reformation was coupled with an award of punitive damages in Hedworth v. Chapman, 135 Ind.App. 129, 192 N.E.2d 649 (1963).

3. Rs. 2d § 166 cmt b; In re Cendant, 72 F.Supp.2d 498 (D.N.J.1999); International Milling v. Hachmeister, 380 Pa. 407, 110 A.2d 186 (1955). Cf. E.H. Oftedal & Sons v. State, 308 Mont. 50, 40 P.3d 349 (2002) (unilateral mistake in pricing that should have been known by the state).

4. 3 N.Y.2d 491, 168 N.Y.S.2d 964, 146 N.E.2d 693 (1957), criticized 44 Cornell L.Q. 124 (1958); 37 Mo.L.Rev. 54, 68–69 (1972); 27 Fordham L.Rev. 125 (1958). Other cases alleged to deviate from the general rule are cited in McClintock, Equity § 100

ment on the fraudulent promise that additional promises omitted from the writing would be recorded in the corporate promisor's records. The court upheld plaintiff's complaint requesting reformation. Although this may be fraud in the inducement rather than fraud as to the content of the record, it does not go to the desirability of the bargain, rather, it goes toward its transcription. Thus, it appears to be sound.

Non-disclosure is treated as the equivalent of misrepresentation where one party knows that the record does not express the intention of the other and knows the other's intention.[5]

Duress is normally a ground only for setting a transaction aside. Where, however, because of duress, for example a lender forces a borrower to assent to a mortgage on terms different from those that had earlier been contractually agreed on, reformation of the mortgage to conform to the prior contract is an appropriate alternative.[6]

§ 9.36   Defenses to Reformation

The courts will not grant reformation if its effect would be to curtail the rights of a bona fide purchaser for value or others who have relied on the record.[1] Normally reformation will not be given against a donor of a gratuitous conveyance or other instrument of gift.[2]

Many tortured opinions have been written on the question of the negligence of the claimant to reformation. Where one party carelessly believes that a record contains a certain clause or produces a given result and this belief is neither shared nor induced by the other, the temptation is to deny relief on the ground of the petitioner's negligence.[3] A sounder ground, however, is that the record does not misstate the prior agreement. The weight of authority is that if the requisites of reformation are met, negligence is not a bar to reformation unless the negligence has in some way harmed the other, non-negligent, party.[4]

As is the case with avoidance, ratification can terminate the right to reformation.[5] And, since reformation is an equitable remedy, equitable defenses such as unclean hands and laches are, of course, applicable. As

---

(2d ed. 1948). McClintock's analysis is challenged in Comment, 37 Mo.L.Rev. 54, 69 n.89 (1972).

5. Line Lexington Lumber & Millwork v. Pennsylvania Pub., 451 Pa. 154, 301 A.2d 684 (1973); Rs. 1st § 505; cf. Palmer, Mistake and Unjust Enrichment 76 (2d ed. 1962).

6. Leben v. Nassau Sav. & Loan Assn., 40 A.D.2d 830, 337 N.Y.S.2d 310 (1972), aff'd.

§ 9.36

1. Holton State Bank v. Greater Milwaukee Food Merchants Assn., 9 Wis.2d 95, 100 N.W.2d 322, 79 ALR2d 1176 (1960); Rs. 2d § 155 cmt f.

2. Rs. 2d § 155 cmt b; Clark, Equity §§ 258–59 (1954).

3. E.g., Harris v. Uhlendorf, 24 N.Y.2d 463, 301 N.Y.S.2d 53, 248 N.E.2d 892 (1969).

4. Anderson, Clayton & Co. v. Farmers Nat. Bank, 624 F.2d 105 (10th Cir.1980); Ruff v. Charter Behavioral Health Sys., 699 N.E.2d 1171 (Ind.App.1998); Maland v. Houston Fire & Cas. Ins., 274 F.2d 299, 81 ALR2d 1 (9th Cir.1960); Woodriff v. Ashcraft, 263 Or. 547, 503 P.2d 472 (1972); Rs. 1st § 508; cf. Rs. 2d § 157; Clark, Equity § 271 (1954); Comment, 37 Mo.L.Rev. 54, 85–90 (1972).

5. Clark, Equity § 274 (1954).

in the case of equity decrees generally, the court may impose such conditions to its decree as it deems equitable.[6] The Statute of Frauds does not apply to actions for reformation.[7]

G. UNCONSCIONABILITY

Table of Sections

§ 9.37 The UCC Provision on Unconscionability

Few, if any, sections of the UCC[1] have attracted more attention than its provision on unconscionability.[2] The provision that governs contracts that were unconscionable at the time they were made reads as follows:

> (1) If the court as a matter of law finds the contract or any clause of the contract to have been unconscionable at the time it was made the court may refuse to enforce the contract, or it may enforce the remainder of the contract without the unconscionable clause, or it may so limit the application of any unconscionable clause as to avoid any unconscionable result.

> (2) When it is claimed or appears to the court that the contract or any clause thereof may be unconscionable the parties shall be afforded a reasonable opportunity to present evidence as to its commercial setting, purpose and effect to aid the court in making the determination.

6. Mader v. Hintz, 186 N.W.2d 897 (N.D.1971).

7. See § 19.28 infra.

§ 9.37

1. UCC § 2–302. The concept of unconscionability is also operative in UCC §§ 2–309(3) (termination) and 2–719(3) (limitations on consequential damages). These differ in providing the vantage of point of the time of application rather than the time of contracting. (The revision draft makes no substantial changes in any of these provisions).

2. Much of the law review literature centers on Leff, Unconscionability and the Code: The Emperor's New Clause, 115 U.Pa.L.Rev. 485 (1967), an intensive study of the various drafts of this Code provision and an often brilliant analysis of the problems of its interpretation and application, but often idiosyncratic in its "value judgments, lamentations, and prophecies of doom." Braucher, 31 U.Pitt.L.Rev. 337, 338 (1970). Among the more helpful articles are Craswell, 60 U.Chi.L.Rev. 1 (1993); Ellinghaus, 78 Yale L.J. 757 (1969); Eisenberg, 95 Harv.L.Rev. 741 (1982); Epstein, 18 J.Law & Ec. 293 (1975); Fort, 9 Loy.U.Chi. L.J. 765 (1978); Hillman, 67 Cornell L.Rev. 1 (1981); Hunter, 68 N.D.L.Rev. 145 (1992); Jordan, 62 Minn.L.Rev. 813 (1978); Pizzimenti, 72 Marquette L.Rev. 151 (1989); Prince, 46 Hastings L.J. 459 (1995); Schwartz, 63 Va.L.Rev. 1053 (1977); Rakoff, 96 Harv.L.Rev. 1173 (1983); Spanogle, 117 U.Pa.L.Rev. 931 (1969); Speidel, 31 U.Pitt.L.Rev. 359 (1970); Wisner, 51 U.Toronto Fac.L.Rev. 396 (1993). An acute but rather narrow reading of the intent of the section is Murray, Unconscionability: Unconscionability, 31 U.Pitt.L.Rev. 1 (1969). The balance of the literature, much of very high quality, is vast. For a recent review, see Swanson, Unconscionable Quandry, 31 N.M.L.Rev. 359 (2001).

The primary purpose of the section is illuminated by the following language in the official comment.

"This section is intended to make it possible for the courts to police explicitly against the contracts or clauses which they find to be unconscionable. In the past such policing has been accomplished by adverse construction of language, by manipulation of the rules of offer and acceptance or by determinations that the clause is contrary to public policy or to the dominant purpose of the contract. This section is intended to allow the court to pass directly on the unconscionability of the contract or particular clause therein and to make a conclusion of law as to its unconscionability."

The official comment then articulates a two-pronged test for unconscionability under the UCC.

The basic test is whether, in the light of the general commercial background and the commercial needs of the particular trade or case, the clauses involved are so one-sided as to be unconscionable under the circumstances existing at the time of the making of the contract. Subsection (2) makes it clear that it is proper for the court to hear evidence upon these questions. *The principle is one of the prevention of oppression and unfair surprise* (Cf. Campbell Soup Co. v. Wentz, 172 F.2d 80 (3d Cir.1948)) and not of disturbance of allocation of risks because of superior bargaining power." (Emphasis supplied).

"Oppression" is quite distinct from "surprise." Professor Leff labeled the two kinds of unconscionability as "substantive" and "procedural," distinguishing the content of the contract (substantive oppression) and the process by which the allegedly offensive terms found their way into the agreement (procedural surprise).[3] Many authorities have adopted this terminology.[4] Some cases hold that the defense of unconscionability cannot be invoked unless the contract or clause is both procedurally and substantively unconscionable,[5] but there is no basis in the text of the statute for such a conclusion,[6] and cases of purely substantive unconscionability exist.[7]

---

3. Leff, supra § 9.37 n.2, at 487.

4. E.g., Nelson v. McGoldrick, 73 Wn. App. 763, 871 P.2d 177 (1994), reversed for a plenary hearing on unconscionability, 127 Wn.2d 124, 896 P.2d 1258 (1995).

Professor Schwartz has suggested that the word, "nonsubstantive," be substituted for "procedural," because some non-procedural factors, such as the status of the parties, are often decisive on the issue of unconscionability. Schwartz, supra § 9.37 n.2, at 1054–55; Sears, Mental Retardation and Unconscionability, 17 Law & Psych. Rev. 77 (1989).

5. Marin Storage v. Benco Contracting, 89 Cal.App.4th 1042, 107 Cal.Rptr.2d 645 (2001); Hubscher & Son v. Storey, 228 Mich.App. 478, 578 N.W.2d 701 (1998); Burch v. Second Judicial District, 49 P.3d 647 (Nev.2002); see citations in Prince, supra note 2, at 472 n.66.

6. See Brower v. Gateway 2000, 246 A.D.2d 246, 676 N.Y.S.2d 569 (1998) (stating that both are generally required but substantive unconscionability will suffice).

7. Rodziewicz v. Waffco Heavy Duty Towing, 763 N.E.2d 491 (Ind.App.2002).

§ 9.38   Historical Background

Although the concept of unconscionability has deep roots[1] both in law and equity, the concept was developed primarily in equity. Indeed, Chief Justice Stone exaggerated only a bit in describing the concept of unconscionability as underlying "practically the whole content of the law of equity."[2] There are numerous examples of the application of the unconscionability doctrine in equity in such categories as mortgages, trusts, and penalties. On the ground that a contrary result would involve the "unconscionable exercise of a legal right," mortgagees were and are enjoined from insisting on a default when the mortgagor tenders late payment.[3] Holders of legal title to land who agree to hold it for the benefit of another were and are enjoined from utilizing the land for their own benefit, for such utilization would involve the unconscionable exercise of legal title.[4] Also equity enjoined the enforcement of penalty clauses on the ground that such remedial relief would be the result of unconscionable insistence on one's legal remedy.[5] Thus, equity has a long history of concern with the *substantive* conscionability of the exercise of rights given by agreement.[6]

Gradually, each of the categories alluded to above became a recognized doctrine with general rules, exceptions and variations. This hardening of the categories was never complete and to the time of enactment of the UCC equity continued, and doubtless will continue, to exercise its generalized power to refuse to enforce oppressive bargains on grounds of substantive unconscionability even outside of distinct doctrines relating to mortgages, trusts, penalties and other matters of special equitable cognizance.[7] Where equitable relief is denied on the

§ 9.38

1. The same problems confronted by the doctrine of unconscionability arise in other legal systems. For comparative studies, see Welfarism in Contract Law (Brownsord et al eds.); Symposium, 14 Loyola L.A.Int'l & Comp.L.J. 435 (1992); Comment, 25 U.C.Davis L.Rev. 229 (1991).

2. Stone, Book Review, 12 Colum.L.Rev. 756, 756 (1912); see Teeven, Decline of Freedom of Contract Since the Emergence of the Modern Business Corporation, 37 St. Louis U.L.J. 117, 136–40 (1992).

3. Osborne, Mortgages 12–15 (2d ed. 1970). For application of unconscionability doctrine in such a case beyond the general rules developed in this area, see Domus Realty v. 3440 Realty, 179 Misc. 749, 40 N.Y.S.2d 69 (1943), aff'd. Equity doctrine and UCC unconscionability provisions were applied to relieve from an automobile forfeiture in Urdang v. Muse, 114 N.J.Super. 372, 276 A.2d 397 (1971).

4. Bogert, Trusts 9–10 (5th ed. 1973); Scott, Abridgment of the Law of Trusts §§ 1.1–1.6 (1960).

5. The rule of non-enforcement of penalty clauses has been borrowed by law from equity and equitable relief from such a clause is now unnecessary. See § 14.31 infra; 1 Pomeroy, Equity Jurisprudence §§ 72, 434 (4th ed. 1918). Pre–UCC cases at law expressly placing non-enforcement of penalties on grounds of unconscionability include Marshall Milling v. Rosenbluth, 231 Ill.App. 325, 336 (1924); Greer v. Tweed, 13 Abb.Pr., N.S. 427 (N.Y.C.P.1872). The Indian Claims Commission Act of 1946 provides redress based on agreements between tribes and the U.S. based on "unconscionable consideration." 60 Stat. 1049.

6. See Julius Stone, Human Law and Human Justice, ch. 3 § 10 (1965).

7. Campbell Soup v. Wentz, 172 F.2d 80 (3d Cir.1948), cert. denied (noted in several law reviews); Weeks v. Pratt, 43 F.2d 53 (5th Cir.1930); Ryan v. Weiner, 610 A.2d 1377 (Del.Ch.1992) (collecting real property cases); Chewning v. Brand, 230 Ga. 255, 196 S.E.2d 399 (1973); McKinnon v. Benedict, 38 Wis.2d 607, 157 N.W.2d 665 (1968), and see Comment, 44 Can.Bar Rev. 142 (1966).

generalized doctrine of unconscionability the right to enforce the contract at law is frequently preserved,[8] although often this right is of little use.[9]

Equity has through the centuries also been concerned with procedural *(nonsubstantive)* conscionability. Agreements are set aside or enforcement is refused in the presence of undue influence,[10] misrepresentation,[11] and other kinds of nonsubstantive unconscionability. Indeed, in one of the more frequently cited cases involving a discussion of unconscionability,[12] the court adopted the equitable doctrine in a law case and helped establish the doctrine of relief for unilateral palpable mistake.[13] The case is an excellent illustration of how certain categories of relief originally based on the generalized concept of unconscionability emerge and are subsequently discussed without regard for their origin. Despite the emergence of such categories, equity continues to apply the original generalized concept of unconscionability when circumstances warrant, refusing to enforce a contract unless it "is fair and open, and in regard to which all material matters known to each have been communicated to the other."[14]

Prior to the enactment of the UCC, the use and definition of unconscionability at law has been quite different. On rare occasions courts of law have explicitly refused to grant normal contractual enforcement on grounds of unconscionability, stating that an unconscionable agreement is one "such as no man in his senses and not under delusion would make on the one hand, and as no honest and fair man would accept on the other."[15] In general, however, courts of law did not directly condemn a contract as unconscionable but resorted to imaginative flanking devices to defeat the offending contract.[16] The law courts searched for and found (even though not present under ordinary rules) failure of consideration,[17] lack of consideration,[18] lack of mutual assent,[19] duress or

---

8. Pope Mfg. v. Gormully, 144 U.S. 224 (1892). See also Kleinberg v. Ratett, 252 N.Y. 236, 169 N.E. 289 (1929). Equity, however, would and will frequently order the avoidance of contracts on grounds of misrepresentation and the like, rendering the contract unenforceable even at law.

9. See Frank and Endicott, Defenses in Equity and "Legal Rights," 14 La.L.Rev. 380 (1954).

10. See §§ 9.9 to 9.12 supra.

11. See §§ 9.13 to 9.24 supra.

12. Hume v. U.S., 132 U.S. 406 (1889).

13. See § 9.27 supra.

14. Rothmiller v. Stein, 143 N.Y. 581, 592, 38 N.E. 718, 721 (1894); see also West Kentucky Coal v. Nourse, 320 S.W.2d 311 (Ky.1959).

15. Hume v. U.S., 132 U.S. 406 (1889), quoting Earl of Chesterfield v. Janssen, 2 Ves.Sen. 125, 155, 28 Eng.Rep. 82, 100 (Ch. 1750). For other instances of findings of

unconscionability at law, see 1 Page, Contracts § 636 (2d ed. 1920).

16. See Note, 45 Iowa L.Rev. 843 (1960).

17. See Laitner Plumbing & Heating v. McThomas, 61 S.W.2d 270, 272 (Mo.App. 1933), in which the court said the seller of refrigeration equipment which broke down several times a month would not be permitted to recover the price of the equipment, not because a disclaimer of warranties was ineffective, but because the jury could find equipment to have no value other than the material of which it was composed.

18. Faced with a contract which required that a borrower pay the lender, a bank president, $100 monthly so long as the borrower remained in business in addition to 8% interest, an Indiana court was able to discard the unconscionable provision by finding that the $5000 loan was consideration for the interest and that there was

misrepresentation,[20] inadequacy of pleading,[21] lack of integration in a written contract[22] or a strained interpretation after finding ambiguity where little or no ambiguity existed.[23] These approaches, although producing justice in individual cases, were highly unreliable and unpredictable.

The conflict between what courts said they were doing and what they were in fact doing has had an unsettling effect on the law, giving the sensitive a feeling of lawlessness, the logician a feeling of irrationality and the average lawyer a feeling of confusion.[24] The tension "produced by the contrary pulls of dogmatic prescriptions and the inherent requirements of individual cases"[25] made unpredictable which of the competing pulls would prevail. "Covert tools," said Karl Llewellyn, principal architect of the UCC, "are never reliable tools."[26]

Against this background, the Code provision on unconscionability was designed to do two things: (1) encourage courts to openly strike down provisions of the type which had previously been denied enforcement at law largely through covert means; (2) achieve a substantive merger[27] of equity doctrine into law.[28] The evidence points to the UCC's

no consideration for the promise to pay the $100 monthly. Stiefler v. McCullough, 97 Ind.App. 123, 174 N.E. 823 (1931).

19. We have previously seen the general rule that in the absence of misrepresentation one who does not choose to read a contract before signing it is bound by the contract. See also § 9.41 infra; Moreira Constr. v. Moretrench, 97 N.J.Super. 391, 235 A.2d 211 (1967), aff'd. We have also seen that this rule has been circumvented at times by a finding that there was no mutual consent to a contract or to the terms of a contract. See §§ 9.41 to 9.45 infra. This finding has been made most often in contracts of adhesion. See § 9.43 infra.

20. In McCoy v. Gas Engine & Power, 135 A.D. 771, 119 N.Y.S. 864 (1909), the court had to assume that a legal fraud had been perpetrated because of a lawyer's unexplained $153,000 contingent fee, due to the lack of a doctrine of unconscionability to which to turn.

21. See Davis Motors, Dodge and Plymouth v. Avett, 294 S.W.2d 882 (Tex.App. 1956).

22. In V. Valente v. Mascitti, 163 Misc. 287, 295 N.Y.S. 330, 335 (City Ct.1937), a buyer of a shortwave radio who was told by the plaintiff's salesman that it "could get Rome easily," was not compelled to pay for the radio despite the lack of any warranty as to the radio's capabilities in the written contract which generally would be considered integrated.

23. See Patterson, The Delivery of a Life Insurance Policy, 33 Harv.L.Rev. 198, 222 (1919), which indicates prime examples of the way language in insurance contracts

is occasionally strained "out of its meaning." The rule of interpretation to the effect that language in contracts placing one party at the mercy of the other is not favored by the courts, Tibbetts Contracting v. O & E Contracting, 15 N.Y.2d 324, 258 N.Y.S.2d 400, 206 N.E.2d 340 (1965), can be used to reach the same result.

24. The statement of an Eastern sage may here be apposite:

"Now if names of things are not properly defined, words will not correspond to facts. When words do not correspond to facts, it is impossible to perfect anything. Where it is impossible to perfect anything, the arts and institutions of civilization cannot flourish. When the arts and institutions of civilization cannot flourish, law and justice do not attain their ends; and when law and justice do not attain their ends, the people will be at a loss to know what to do."

Confucius, The Analects, xiii, 3. We are indebted for this reference to Jackson, 53 L.Q.Rev. 525, 536 (1937).

25. Von Mehren & Trautman, The Law of Multistate Problems 78 (1965).

26. Llewellyn, The Common Law Tradition 365 (1960).

27. Procedural merger of law and equity has taken place in many jurisdictions since 1848. Nevertheless, the tendency has been to keep the substantive doctrines separate and apart. See McClintock on Equity § 78 (2d ed. 1948).

28. At least two scholars have argued that there is no intent to adopt the equity

twofold purpose. First, the official comment refers specifically to the prior covert activities of law courts in achieving conscionable results by indirection. Second, the comment cites to a then recent and celebrated equity case denying specific performance of an unconscionable contract. Third, the UCC defines a large number of terms, but refrains from a definition of unconscionability. This omission points to a legislative intent to utilize a term in the same general sense in which it has been employed in the legal system in the past.[29] A major difference is that in an action at law the courts are empowered to exercise the power that once was almost exclusively within the jurisdiction of courts of equity. The substantive merger of law and equity is long overdue.[30]

§ 9.39   The Emerging Law of Unconscionability

Since the enactment of the UCC, the unconscionability concept has developed along several discernable lines. First, and perhaps most significant, the provision has entered the general law of contracts and has been applied to numerous transactions outside the coverage of Article 2 of the UCC.[1] It has been deemed applicable or, at least, relevant, in cases involving a contract to construct asphalt plants,[2] home improvement contracts,[3] equipment leases,[4] real estate brokerage contracts,[5] hiring a hall for a Bar Mitzvah,[6] a contract opening a checking account,[7] an

approach at law. Murray on Contracts § 96 (4th ed.2001); Leff, supra § 9.37 n.2, at 528–41. Murray's insistence on divorcing equity from UCC unconscionability is tied to his reading the UCC provision in a narrow fashion, tying it to the idea of assent rather than to ideas of fairness. His analysis shows an awareness that equity unconscionability doctrine goes far beyond what he is willing to grant to the UCC. Professor Leff argues that equity is primarily concerned with "presumptive sillies like sailors and heirs and farmers and women" and others who if not crazy are "pretty peculiar." Leff at 532–33. This is simply not so. See, e.g., Weeks v. Pratt, 43 F.2d 53 (5th Cir.1930) (inventive genius). He also argues that equity is concerned with "only one form of substantive unconscionability—overall imbalance." Leff at 533. This is simply not so. Consider equity's treatment of penalty clauses and mortgages, and employees' covenants not to compete. See §§ 16.19 to 16.22 infra. Equity will relieve against unconscionability of specific clauses as well as gross overall imbalance.

29. Indeed, the evidence is overwhelming that this was the legislative intent. Leff, supra § 9.37 n.2, at 528 n.166.

30. Newman, The Renaissance of Good Faith in Contracting in Anglo–American Law, 54 Cornell L.Rev. 553, 561–565 (1969).

§ 9.39

1. It has been accepted as a general doctrine of contract law by the American Law Institute. Rs. 2d § 208.

2. County Asphalt v. Lewis Welding & Engineering, 444 F.2d 372 (2d Cir.1971), cert. denied.

3. American Home Imp. v. MacIver, 105 N.H. 435, 201 A.2d 886, 14 ALR3d 324 (1964).

4. Fairfield Lease v. Pratt, 6 Conn.Cir. 537, 278 A.2d 154 (1971); Industralease Auto. & Scientific Eqpt. v. R.M.E. Enterprises, 58 A.D.2d 482, 396 N.Y.S.2d 427 (1977); Electronics v. Lear Jet, 55 Misc.2d 1066, 286 N.Y.S.2d 711 (1967).

5. Ellsworth Dobbs, Inc. v. Johnson, 50 N.J. 528, 236 A.2d 843 (1967); cf. Kaye v. Coughlin, 443 S.W.2d 612 (Tex.App.1969).

6. Lazan v. Huntington Town House, 69 Misc.2d 1017, 332 N.Y.S.2d 270 (1969), aff'd.

7. David v. Manufacturers Hanover, 59 Misc.2d 248, 298 N.Y.S.2d 847 (1969).

apartment house lease,[8] a release,[9] a contract for a motion picture idea,[10] an arbitration provision in a contract of employment,[11] a security transaction,[12] a filling station lease,[13] the settlement of a will contest dispute,[14] and, coming full circle to its equitable origins, to a problem relating to a spendthrift trust.[15]

Second, although consumers will be the primary beneficiaries of the unconscionability doctrine, and businesses are expected to be able to look out for their own interests to a far greater extent than consumers,[16] businesses, particularly small businesses, can be victimized by unconscionable contracts and will receive judicial protection.[17] There has been much litigation by businesses whose listings have been omitted or misplaced in the Yellow Pages. The businesses have alleged that the publishers of the telephone directories use a form contract that limits their liability to refunding the amount paid for the listing, and that such a limitation is unconscionable. Although most of the cases have found such limitations of liability not to be unconscionable,[18] a contrary trend has begun.[19] If such limitations of liability are held to be unconscionable, the cost of the increased liability will almost certainly be passed on to the advertisers. Businesses are the primary beneficiaries of the unconscionability provision of UCC § 2–309(3).[20]

Third, courts have heeded the admonition in UCC § 2–302(2) that the parties shall be afforded a reasonable opportunity to present evidence as to the commercial setting, purpose and effect of the contract or clause alleged to be unconscionable. Many cases have held that the

---

8. Seabrook v. Commuter Housing, 72 Misc.2d 6, 338 N.Y.S.2d 67 (1972).

9. Kelly v. Widner, 236 Mont. 523, 771 P.2d 142 (1989).

10. Buchwald v. Paramount Pictures, unreported, but printed as Appendix B to O'Donnell & McDougal, Fatal Subtraction (Doubleday 1992) (unconscionable accounting terms).

11. Armendariz v. Foundation Health Psychcare Services, 24 Cal.4th 83, 99 Cal. Rptr.2d 745, 6 P.3d 669 (2000). Many other cases could be cited.

12. Unico v. Owen, 50 N.J. 101, 232 A.2d 405 (1967); but see In re Advance Printing & Litho., 277 F.Supp. 101 (W.D.Pa. 1967), aff'd; Hernandez v. S.I.C. Finance, 79 N.M. 673, 448 P.2d 474 (1968).

13. Weaver v. American Oil, 257 Ind. 458, 276 N.E.2d 144, 49 ALR3d 306 (1971).

14. Abbott v. Abbott, 188 Neb. 61, 195 N.W.2d 204 (1972).

15. In re Estate of Vought, 70 Misc.2d 781, 334 N.Y.S.2d 720 (1972), aff'd.

16. Riesett v. W.B. Doner & Co., 293 F.3d 164 (4th Cir.2002); Dow Corning v. Capitol Aviation, 411 F.2d 622 (7th Cir. 1969); Vitex Mfg. v. Caribtex, 377 F.2d 795

(3d Cir.1967); County Asphalt v. Lewis Welding & Engineering, 323 F.Supp. 1300 (S.D.N.Y.1970), aff'd; P & O Containers v. Jamelco, 94 Ohio App.3d 726, 641 N.E.2d 794 (1994); K & C v. Westinghouse Elec., 437 Pa. 303, 263 A.2d 390 (1970); cf. Kaye v. Coughlin, 443 S.W.2d 612 (Tex.App.1969) (lawyer).

17. Luick v. Graybar Elec., 473 F.2d 1360 (8th Cir.1973); Fairfield Lease v. Pratt, 6 Conn.Cir. 537, 278 A.2d 154 (1971); Architectural Cabinets v. Gaster, 291 A.2d 298 (Del.Super.1971); Weaver v. American Oil, 257 Ind. 458, 276 N.E.2d 144, 49 ALR3d 306 (1971); Steele v. J.I. Case, 197 Kan. 554, 419 P.2d 902 (1966) (large farm); Wilson Trading v. David Ferguson, 23 N.Y.2d 398, 297 N.Y.S.2d 108, 244 N.E.2d 685 (1968); see Goldberg, 58 Wash.L.Rev. 343 (1983); Jordan, 62 Minn.L.Rev. 813 (1978); Mallor, 40 Sw.L.J. 1065 (1986).

18. PK's Landscaping v. New England Tel. & Tel., 128 N.H. 753, 519 A.2d 285 (1986).

19. Pigman v. Ameritech Pub., 650 N.E.2d 67 (Ind.App.1995); Rozeboom v. Northwestern Bell, 358 N.W.2d 241, 47 ALR4th 869 (S.D.1984).

20. Some changes in the revision draft.

provision mandates an evidentiary hearing or a full fledged trial on the merits.[21] However, a more reasonable interpretation of the section would be to require such a hearing only if the parties have raised real issues of fact in their motion papers.[22] Otherwise, the unconscionability defense will become the primary dilatory defense in contract litigation.

Fourth, the UCC makes clear that the court and not the jury should decide the issue of unconscionability.[23] This is constitutional on the ground that the issue of conscionability is an equitable issue for which no constitutional right to a jury trial exists.[24]

Fifth, the courts have fully exercised, and, indeed, may have expanded the flexibility which the Code has endowed the courts in granting remedies to an aggrieved party. The Code permits the court to refuse to enforce the contract, to excise an unconscionable clause or to limit the application of such a clause. In most of the cases in which unconscionability has been found, nonenforcement of a clause has been the result.[25] In others, the contract was not enforced.[26] An earlier draft of the Code had expressly permitted courts to reform contracts by remaking the bargain for the parties.[27] Although the final draft did not include this provision, courts have been remaking bargains by reducing price terms,[28]

21. Luick v. Graybar Elec., 473 F.2d 1360 (8th Cir.1973); Williams v. Walker–Thomas Furniture, 350 F.2d 445, 18 ALR3d 1297 (D.C.Cir.1965) (for the aftermath of this case, see 34 Conn.L.Rev 625 (2002)); Food Assocs. v. Capital Assocs., 491 So.2d 345 (Fla.App.1986); Zicari v. Joseph Harris, 33 A.D.2d 17, 304 N.Y.S.2d 918 (1969), app. denied; Schroeder v. Fageol Motors, 86 Wn.2d 256, 544 P.2d 20 (1975); see also Wilson Trading v. David Ferguson, 23 N.Y.2d 398, 297 N.Y.S.2d 108, 244 N.E.2d 685 (1968) (leaving question open); Central Ohio Co-op. v. Rowland, 29 Ohio App.2d 236, 281 N.E.2d 42, 58 O.O.2d 421 (1972).

22. Bishop v. Washington, 331 Pa.Super. 387, 480 A.2d 1088 (1984); Architectural Aluminum v. Macarr, Inc., 70 Misc.2d 495, 333 N.Y.S.2d 818 (1972); Jeffery v. Weintraub, 32 Wn.App. 536, 648 P.2d 914 (1982); see Golden Reward Min. v. Jervis B. Webb, 772 F.Supp. 1118 (D.S.D.1991) (informal hearing satisfies the statute); Nelson v. McGoldrick, 73 Wn.App. 763, 871 P.2d 177 (1994) ("a hearing on a motion for summary judgment provides a reasonable opportunity to present evidence").

23. UCC § 2–302(1) (slight stylistic change in revision).

24. County Asphalt v. Lewis Welding & Engineering, 444 F.2d 372 (2d Cir.1971), cert. denied.

25. A & M Produce v. FMC, 135 Cal. App.3d 473, 186 Cal.Rptr. 114 (1982) (dis-

claimer of warranty and consequential damages); Architectural Cabinets v. Gaster, 291 A.2d 298 (Del.Super.1971) (confession of judgment); Weaver v. American Oil, 257 Ind. 458, 276 N.E.2d 144, 49 ALR3d 306 (1971) (indemnity clause); Steele v. J.I. Case, 197 Kan. 554, 419 P.2d 902 (1966) (limitation of damages); Unico v. Owen, 50 N.J. 101, 232 A.2d 405 (1967) (waiver of defenses); Industralease Auto. & Scientific Eqpt. v. R.M.E. Enterprises (disclaimer of warranty), supra § 9.39 n.4; Antz v. GAF Materials, 719 A.2d 758 (Pa.Super.1998) (limitation on express warranty).

26. A lease was cancelled in Seabrook v. Commuter Housing, 72 Misc.2d 6, 338 N.Y.S.2d 67 (1972). Suits for deficiency judgments were dismissed in Fairfield Lease v. Pratt, 6 Conn.Cir. 537, 278 A.2d 154 (1971); Urdang v. Muse, 114 N.J.Super. 372, 276 A.2d 397 (1971).

27. 63 Yale L.J. 560 (1953).

28. Toker v. Westerman, 113 N.J.Super. 452, 274 A.2d 78 (1970); Jones v. Star Credit, 59 Misc.2d 189, 298 N.Y.S.2d 264 (1969). Further developments in the Star Credit case are in Star Credit v. Ingram, 75 Misc.2d 299, 347 N.Y.S.2d 651 (1973) ($15,-000 punitive damages assessed on plaintiff for continued fraudulent and unconscionable conduct). Price terms were scrutinized in Perdue v. Crocker Nat. Bank, 38 Cal.3d 913, 216 Cal.Rptr. 345, 702 P.2d 503 (1985).

increasing a duration term,[29] and reducing interest rates.[30] Most significantly, unconscionability has been held to constitute "fraud" within the meaning of consumer protection legislation empowering the state attorney-general to sue to enjoin the offering of contracts on unconscionable terms.[31] However, unconscionability does not create a cause of action for damages.[32]

§ 9.40 What Is Unconscionable?

"Unconscionable" is a word that defies lawyer-like definition.[1] It is a term borrowed from moral philosophy and ethics. As close to a definition as we are likely to get is "that which 'affronts the sense of decency.'"[2] The purpose of the doctrine is to prevent two evils: *"oppression and unfair surprise."*[3] Although this twofold purpose has led to a distinction between "substantive" (oppression) and "procedural" (unfair surprise) unconscionability,[4] the cases do not neatly fall into these two divisions. More frequently elements of both are present. Indeed, some courts have said that both elements *must* ordinarily be present before a finding of unconscionability can be made.[5] Nonetheless, the courts have ruled that gross excessiveness of price is itself unconscionable (oppressive).[6] Significantly, however, in these cases it was clear that the purchaser was not aware that the price was exorbitant. Consequently, these cases may be viewed as examples of oppressive terms combined with unfair surprise. It has also been held that an arbitration clause providing for a forum with

29. Shell Oil v. Marinello, 120 N.J.Super. 357, 294 A.2d 253 (1972) (franchise cannot be cancelled without just cause), modified 63 N.J. 402, 307 A.2d 598 (1973).

30. In re Elkins–Dell Mfg., 253 F.Supp. 864 (E.D.Pa.1966) (dictum).

31. Kugler v. Romain, 58 N.J. 522, 279 A.2d 640 (1971). Some state legislation explicitly grants this authority to the attorney-general in cases of unconscionability. E.g., McKinney's N.Y.Exec. Law § 63(12). The Uniform Consumer Sales Practices Act would grant similar power to state officials as well as the power to sue for damages on behalf of injured consumers. U.C.S.P.A. § 9.

32. Mitchell v. Ford Motor, 68 F.Supp.2d 1315 (N.D.Ga.1998).

§ 9.40

1. The great 17th century lawyer, John Selden, was as troubled by this in his day as some lawyers are troubled today. "One Chancellor has a long foot, another, a short foot, a third an indifferent foot: 'tis the same thing in the Chancellor's conscience." Selden, Table Talk, under the heading "Equity." See also id., under the heading "Conscience."

2. Gimbel Bros. v. Swift, 62 Misc.2d 156, 307 N.Y.S.2d 952 (1970). The dictionary has little to add: " * * * lying outside the limits of what is reasonable or acceptable: shockingly unfair, harsh, or unjust * * *." Webster's Third Unabridged. Judicial definitions include "an absence of meaningful choice on the part of one of the parties together with contract terms which are unreasonably favorable to the other party." Williams v. Walker–Thomas Furniture, 350 F.2d 445, 449 (D.C.Cir.1965). See also text at § 9.38 n.15 supra.

3. UCC § 2–302 cmt 1 (emphasis supplied) (substantially unchanged in revision).

4. Leff, supra § 9.37 n.2, at 487.

5. E.g., Gillman v. Chase Manhattan Bank, 73 N.Y.2d 1, 10, 534 N.E.2d 824, 828, 537 N.Y.S.2d 787, 791 (1988) ("some showing of an 'absence of meaningful choice on the part of one of the parties together with contract terms which are unreasonably favorable to the other party'") quoting Williams v. Walker–Thomas Furniture, 350 F.2d 445, 449.

6. Ahern v. Knecht, 202 Ill.App.3d 709, 150 Ill.Dec. 660, 661, 563 N.E.2d 787, 788 (1990); Sho–Pro v. Brown, 585 N.E.2d 1357 (Ind.App.1992); American Home Imp. v. MacIver, 105 N.H. 435, 201 A.2d 886, 14 ALR3d 324 (1964); Kugler v. Romain, 58 N.J. 522, 279 A.2d 640 (1971); Rossi v. 21st Century Concepts, 162 Misc.2d 932, 618 N.Y.S.2d 182 (1994); but see Morris v. Capitol Furniture & Appliance, 280 A.2d 775 (D.C.App.1971). See Darr, Unconscionability and Price Fairness, 30 Houston L.Rev 1819 (1994).

excessively high fees is unconscionable in a consumer transaction with a relatively small amount in issue.[7] Employment contracts containing arbitration clauses binding only on the employee have been found to be unconscionable.[8] Similarly, a forum selection clause was, on particular facts, found to be substantively and procedurally unconscionable.[9]

A number of scholars have suggested several analytic frameworks for analyzing unconscionability cases.[10] These theories appear to have had little impact on the courts. Certain cases involve exchanges that are unconscionable per se. These include cases where the exchanges are grossly unequal.[11] Holdings along this line are rare because contracts involving grossly unequal exchanges almost always involve some impropriety in the negotiating process or disability of a party. Outside of the unconscionable *per se* cases are cases "[W]here an aggrieved party is ignorant of the risk involved, ignorant of the contract terms which transfer or allocate that risk and/or lacks alternative terms for that risk allocation, the contract or clause may be unconscionable and unenforceable."[12]

Typically the cases in which courts have found unconscionability involve gross overall one-sidedness or gross one-sidedness of a term disclaiming a warranty, limiting damages, or granting procedural advantages. In these cases, one-sidedness is often coupled with the fact that the imbalance is buried in small print and often couched in language unintelligible to even a person of moderate education. Often the seller deals with a particularly susceptible clientele.[13] In what may prove to be a leading case, the court indicated that if a clause places great hardship or risk on the party in the weaker bargaining position it must be shown that "the provisions were explained to the other party and came to his knowledge and there was in fact *a real and voluntary meeting of the minds and not merely an objective meeting.*"[14] A Code comment states that UCC § 2–302 is not intended to cause a "disturbance of allocation

---

7. Ball v. SFX Broadcasting, 165 F.Supp.2d 230 (N.D.N.Y.2001); Brower v. Gateway 2000, 246 A.D.2d 246, 676 N.Y.S.2d 569 (1998); Mendez v. Palm Harbor Homes, 111 Wn.App. 446, 45 P.3d 594 (2002) (employment), but the arbitration clause need not specify the fees. Green Tree v. Randolph, 531 U.S. 79 (2000). An arbitration clause that unduly restricts the powers of the arbitrator may be unconscionable. State v. Berger, 211 W.Va. 549, 567 S.E.2d 265 (2002), cert. denied.

8. Armendariz v. Foundation Health, 24 Cal.4th 83, 99 Cal.Rptr.2d 745, 6 P.3d 669 (2000). Most cases are contra. Pridgen v. Green Tree, 88 F.Supp.2d 655 (S.D.Miss. 2000).

9. First Fed. Fin. v.Derrington's Chevron, 230 Wis.2d 553, 602 N.W.2d 144 (App. 1999).

10. Fort supra § 9.37 n.2.

11. Id. at 771–75.

12. Id at 798. The Kansas Supreme Court has listed ten factors relevant to an unconscionability determination. Wille v. Southwestern Bell, 219 Kan. 755, 549 P.2d 903 (1976). Colorado lists seven. Davis v. M.L.G., 712 P.2d 985, 991 (Colo.1986).

13. See Kugler v. Romain, 58 N.J. 522, 279 A.2d 640 (1971) ("sales solicitations were consciously directed toward minority group consumers and consumers of limited economic means * * *. Sales among these people were thought to be 'easier.' ")

14. Weaver v. American Oil, 257 Ind. 458, 464, 276 N.E.2d 144, 49 ALR3d 306 (1971) (emphasis in original); but see Max Oil v. Shell Oil, 945 F.Supp. 241 (M.D.Ala. 1996), aff'd.

of risks because of superior bargaining power,"[15] but cases such as the one just quoted make it clear that inequality of bargaining power is an important element in an unconscionability determination.

Superior bargaining power is not in itself a ground for striking down a resultant contract as unconscionable. There must be additional elements, as for example, a lack of meaningful choice as in the case of an industry-wide form contract heavily weighted in favor of one party and offered on a take it or leave it basis,[16] or a situation where freedom of contract is exploited by a stronger party who has control of the negotiations due to the weaker party's ignorance, feebleness, unsophistication as to interest rates or similar business concepts, or general naiveté.[17] Unconscionability, however, may exist even where the parties are on "about equal footing" or even where the oppressor is inexperienced compared to the oppressed.[18] One approach to non-consumer transactions is to analyze the "totality of the circumstances." These include unfair surprise, conspicuousness of the term, the presence or absence of negotiations, custom, trade usage, and course of dealing.[19]

Section 2–302 on unconscionability should be considered in conjunction with the obligation of good faith that the UCC imposes at several places. For example § 1–203 (§ 1–304 of the revision) provides that "every contract or duty within this Act imposes an obligation of good faith in its performance or enforcement."[20] Although § 1–203 applies

---

15. UCC § 2–302 cmt 1; see Schwartz, Seller Unequal Bargaining Power and the Judicial Process, 49 Ind.L.J. 367 (1974).

16. See, e.g., Campbell Soup v. Wentz, 172 F.2d 80 (3d Cir.1948); Carlson v. General Motors, 883 F.2d 287 (4th Cir.1989), cert. denied (lack of competition among automobile manufacturers as to warranty terms); Brunsman v. DeKalb Swine Breeders, 138 F.3d 358 (8th Cir.1998) (parties were free to go elsewhere); Hooters v. Phillips, 39 F.Supp.2d 582 (D.S.C.1998), aff'd (arbitration clause where forum is controlled by employer); Iwen v. U.S. West, 293 Mont. 512, 977 P.2d 989 (1999) (one-sided arbitration clause); Henningsen v. Bloomfield Motors, 32 N.J. 358, 161 A.2d 69, 75 ALR2d 1 (1960); Larned v. First Chicago, 264 Ill.App.3d 697, 201 Ill.Dec. 572, 636 N.E.2d 1004 (1994) (plaintiff could choose other Visa cards that did not have the clause plaintiff found oppressive).

17. See supra § 9.40 n.10; see also Williams v. Walker–Thomas Furniture, 350 F.2d 445, 18 ALR3d 1297 (D.C.Cir.1965), 51 Cornell L.Q. 768 (1966), in which the court indicated that relief might be owing to a consumer who had entered into an extremely harsh installment sales contract with a furniture company. The contract had a tie-in clause designed so that the company could repossess all items purchased over a number of years on default in payment of the price of any one of them.

In Frostifresh v. Reynoso, 52 Misc.2d 26, 274 N.Y.S.2d 757 (1966) reversed in part 54 Misc.2d 119, 281 N.Y.S.2d 964 (1967), a poor Spanish speaking person was persuaded into promising to pay $1145 for a $348 appliance.

See also State by Lefkowitz v. ITM, 52 Misc.2d 39, 275 N.Y.S.2d 303 (1966), in which the defendant company, which received up to $658 for $80 broilers by selling them on time, was warned to tell consumers of the contract terms "in language the least educated person can understand." Compare Lundstrom v. RCA, 17 Utah 2d 114, 405 P.2d 339, 14 ALR3d 1058 (1965).

18. Miller v. Coffeen, 365 Mo. 204, 280 S.W.2d 100 (1955); see also Pope Mfg. v. Gormully, 144 U.S. 224 (1892).

19. Puget Sound Fin. v. Unisearch, 146 Wn.2d 428, 47 P.3d 940 (2002).

20. § 1–201(19) defines good faith as "honesty in fact in the conduct or transaction concerned." In the case of a merchant it "means honesty in fact and the observance of reasonable commercial standards of fair dealing in the trade." § 2–103(1)(b).

specifically to the performance of a contract rather than its formation, it has been suggested that good faith should be considered in determining unconscionability.[21]

The Uniform Consumer Sales Practices Act, released in 1970, and not widely adopted, also condemns unconscionable contracts. It provides six illustrative circumstances which a court should consider in an unconscionability determination. Certainly, even under the UCC, these circumstances should be relevant. These circumstances are that the supplier has reason to know:[22]

> "(1) that he took advantage of the inability of the consumer reasonably to protect his interests because of his physical infirmity, ignorance, illiteracy, inability to understand the language of an agreement, or similar factors;
>
> "(2) that when the consumer transaction was entered into the price grossly exceeded the price at which similar property or services were readily obtainable in similar transactions by like consumers;
>
> "(3) that when the consumer transaction was entered into the consumer was unable to receive a substantial benefit from the subject of the transaction;
>
> "(4) that when the consumer transaction was entered into there was no reasonable probability of payment of the obligation in full by the consumer;
>
> "(5) that the transaction he induced the consumer to enter was excessively one-sided in favor of the supplier; or
>
> "(6) that he made a misleading statement of opinion on which the consumer was likely to rely to his detriment."

Another guide is found in the Uniform Consumer Credit Code of 1974 which states: "The competence of the buyer, lessee, or debtor, any deception or coercion practiced upon him, the nature and extent of the legal advice received by him, and the value of the consideration are relevant to the issue of unconscionability."[23] In addition, this Code lists a series of factors that must be considered in consumer credit transactions. These are similar to those found in the Uniform Consumer Sales Practices Act.[24]

---

21. Llewellyn, The Common Law Tradition 369 (1960); cf. 1955 N.Y.Law Rev. Comm'n, vol. 1, 658; see Standard Oil of Texas v. Lopeno Gas, 240 F.2d 504 (5th Cir.1957); Kugler v. Romain, 58 N.J. 522, 279 A.2d 640 (1971); Flash v. Powers, 99 N.Y.S.2d 765 (1950), which in attempting to define unconscionability have dwelled on the element of lack of good faith.

22. Uniform Consumer Sales Practices Act § 4. A similar listing appears in McKinney's N.Y. City Administrative Code § 2203d–2.0(b), which adds: "the degree to which terms of the transaction require consumers to waive legal rights."

23. Uniform Consumer Credit Code § 1.107 (the context is unconscionable settlement agreements regarding disputes arising under the Code).

24. Uniform Consumer Credit Code § 6.111(3); see Hersbergen, The Improvident Extension of Credit as an Unconscionable Contract, 23 Drake L.Rev. 225 (1974).

H.   DUTY TO READ*

Table of Sections

§ 9.41   Introduction: The Traditional Rule

Aspects of this topic have been discussed under the heading of Offer and Acceptance.[1] However, since the topic is also directly related to some of the topics discussed immediately above—misrepresentation, mistake, unconscionability—coverage here permits comprehensive treatment.

The duty to read is based on the objective theory of contracts. Thus, if A sends an offer to B who, without opening it and without suspecting that it is an offer, decides to confuse A by sending a letter stating "I accept," there would be a contract because A reasonably believed that B assented to the offer.[2] Under the objective theory of contracts a party is bound by the reasonable impression the party creates.[3] The same principle applies here:[4] a party who signs an instrument manifests assent to it and may not later complain about not reading or not understanding.[5] A typical case states that "one having the capacity to understand a written document who reads it, or, without reading it or having it read to him,

---

* This material is based on Calamari, Duty to Read—A Changing Concept, 43 Fordham L.Rev. 341 (1974).

§ 9.41

1. See ch. 2 supra.

2. See ch. 2 supra.

3. Ricketts v. Pennsylvania R.R., 153 F.2d 757, 760 (2d Cir.1946) (L. Hand, J.); Rs. 2d § 20 cmt d; 1 Williston §§ 3:4–3:5; see Whittier, The Restatement of Contracts and Mutual Assent, 17 Calif.L.Rev. 441 (1929).

4. Strictly speaking, the "duty" to read is not an obligation. Rather, a party may be bound by what he fails to read. The theory of the recording acts is based on analogous reasoning. But see Fli–Back v. Philadelphia Mfrs. Mut. Ins., 502 F.2d 214, 217 (4th Cir.1974) which indicates that a failure to read may support claims of contributory negligence and failure to mitigate damages.

5. Walker v. MDM Services, 997 F.Supp. 822 (W.D.Ky.1998); Clyde A. Wilson Int'l v. Travelers, 959 F.Supp. 756 (1997); Copelco v. Eyerman, 855 F.Supp. 1049 (E.D.Mo. 1994); Richardson Greenshields v. Metz, 566 F.Supp. 131 (S.D.N.Y.1983); Green Tree Agency v. White, 719 So.2d 1179 (Ala. 1998); Peterman v. Clegg, 641 A.2d 867 (Me.1994) (parties whose signatures appeared on personal guarantee bound even though they contended they never intended to sign a personal guarantee and did not recall signing it); Caspi v. Microsoft, 323 N.J.Super. 118, 732 A.2d 528 (A.D.1999) (on-line contract terms); Border States Paving v. South Dakota, 574 N.W.2d 898 (S.D. 1998); Webber v. State Farm, 49 S.W.3d 265 (Tenn.2001) (insured bound by policy limitations although his mother-in-law negotiated the policy); Yakima County v. Yakima, 122 Wn.2d 371, 858 P.2d 245 (1993).

signs it, is bound by his signature.''[6] The thought is that no one could rely on a signed document if the other party could avoid the transaction by not reading or not understanding the record.[7]

The same rule applies even without a signature if the acceptance of a document which purports to be a contract implies assent to its terms.[8] Thus, for example, the mere acceptance of documents such as bills of lading, passenger tickets, insurance policies, bank books and warehouse receipts may give rise to contracts based on the provisions contained therein.[9] The recipient has a duty to read.

§ 9.42 Traditional Qualifications to the Traditional Rule

Most of the qualifications to the duty to read rule are not truly exceptions. Instead, they are based on the conclusion that there was in fact no intentional or apparent manifestation of assent to the document or the term or terms in question.[1]

(a) Document or Provision Not Legible

If the document is not legible it is easy to conclude that there was no assent.[2] Thus the cases generally agree that a party is not bound by fine print[3] or by other circumstances that make the document or clause in question illegible. Describing such a document, one court stated: "The compound, if read by him, would, unless he were an extraordinary man, be an inexplicable riddle, a mere flood of darkness and confusion. * * * [I]t was printed in such small type, and in lines so long and so crowded, that the perusal of it was made physically difficult, painful, and injurious."[4] Frequently, statutes make provision with respect to the size of the type to be used in certain clauses of common contracts.[5]

---

6. Rossi v. Douglas, 203 Md. 190, 192, 100 A.2d 3, 7 (1953); see also Pers Travel, Inc. v. Canal Square Assocs., 804 A.2d 1108 (D.C.App.2002); Dunn v. Dunn, 786 So.2d 1045 (Miss.2001); Scotland Vet Supply v. ABA Recovery Service, 1998 S.D. 103, 583 N.W.2d 834 (1998).

7. For the policy considerations, see Macaulay, Private Legislation and the Duty to Read, 19 Vand.L.Rev. 1051 (1966).

8. Regan v. Customcraft Homes, 170 Colo. 562, 565, 463 P.2d 463, 464 (1970).

9. 1 Williston §§ 6:42–6:45. The word "may" is used because the cases are far from harmonious. Compare George v. Bekins Van & Storage, 33 Cal.2d 834, 205 P.2d 1037 (1949) and D'Aloisio v. Morton's, 342 Mass. 231, 234, 172 N.E.2d 819, 821 (1961) with Voyt v. Bekins Moving & Storage, 169 Or. 30, 127 P.2d 360 (1942) (all warehouse receipt cases). See UCC §§ 7–202 to 7–204; Ruud, 16 Ark.L.Rev. 81 (1961).

The rule stated generally applies to bills of lading. 1 Williston § 6:45; UCC § 7–309. Although bank depositors generally are held bound by conditions stated on signature cards and in passbooks, Chase v. Waterbury Sav. Bank, 77 Conn. 295, 299–300, 59 A. 37, 39 (1904), they may not be bound by unusual conditions. Los Angeles Inv. v. Home Sav. Bank, 180 Cal. 601, 182 P. 293, 298 (1919). See Annot., 5 ALR Fed. 394 (1970) (passenger tickets); 30 Tex.L.Rev. 634 (1952) (insurance policies).

§ 9.42

1. Cf. supra § 9.41 n. 8.

2. Compare this statement with the cases of blind and illiterate persons at text accompanying notes 34 & 35 infra.

3. Dessert Seed v. Drew Farmers Supply, 248 Ark. 858, 861, 454 S.W.2d 307, 309 (1970); Baker v. Seattle, 79 Wn.2d 198, 484 P.2d 405 (1971); Note, 63 Harv.L.Rev. 494 (1950).

4. De Lancey v. Rockingham Farmers' Mut. Fire Ins., 52 N.H. 581, 588 (1873). As a result of decisions such as this, standardized drafts of certain insurance policies have become common. See Vance, Insur-

(b) Terms Insufficiently Called to the Attention of a Party

Even when the term is legible it may be placed in such a way that it is not likely to come to the attention of the other party. When this occurs a party should not be bound by the term.[6] No rule can be stated to determine when consent is present. All that can be said is that whether a contractual provision is sufficiently called to the attention of a party depends on whether a reasonable person, considering all circumstances of the case, would know that the terms in question were intended to be part of the proposed agreement.[7] As one court noted, "failure to read an instrument is not negligence per se but must be considered in light of all surrounding facts and circumstances."[8] If the agreement is not read, the party is bound by "the provisions in the form over which the parties actually bargained and such other provisions that are not unreasonable in view of the circumstances surrounding the transaction."[9]

This situation occurs frequently in cases involving printed notices on letterheads, catalogues, or tags,[10] and on packaging,[11] and even in the package.[12] In a similar vein a number of cases have suggested that a party is not bound by burdensome and unexpected clauses printed on the reverse side of a document which the party signs unless they are called to the attention of the adhering party.[13] Similar problems arise when the document attempts to incorporate other provisions by reference.[14]

ance 56–62 (3d ed. Anderson 1951); Kimball & Pfennigstorf, Legislative and Judicial Control of the Terms of Insurance Contracts: A Comparative Study of American and European Practice, 39 Ind.L.J. 675 (1964).

5. See, e.g., McKinney's N.Y.C.P.L.R. 4544.

6. Egan v. Kollsman Instrument, 21 N.Y.2d 160, 168–69, 287 N.Y.S.2d 14, 19, 234 N.E.2d 199, 202–03 (1967), cert. denied (passenger ticket).

7. Mellinkoff, How to Make Contracts Illegible, 5 Stan.L.Rev. 418, 430–31 (1953); see also § 9.22 supra.

8. Chandler v. Aero Mayflower Transit, 374 F.2d 129, 136 (4th Cir.1967) (bill of lading).

9. One Stop Supply v. Ransdell, 1996 WL 187576 (Tenn.App.)

10. 1 Williston § 6:47. However, here again, the cases are not harmonious.

11. Even here, if the provision is plainly stamped, it may be binding on the buyer. 1 Williston § 6:48. ProCD, Inc. v. Zeidenberg, 86 F.3d 1447 (7th Cir.1996); Willard Van Dyke Productions v. Eastman Kodak, 12 N.Y.2d 301, 239 N.Y.S.2d 337, 189 N.E.2d 693 (1963) (print on film package limiting liability not binding on buyer because of its ambiguity).

12. Hill v. Gateway 2000, Inc., 105 F.3d 1147 (7th Cir.1997), cert. denied (contract terms in a box are binding) ("Payment before revelation of full terms is common * * * in many other endeavors"); contra, Klocek v. Gateway, 104 F.Supp.2d 1332 (D.Kan.2000); see Thompson v. Anderson, 824 P.2d 712 (Alaska 1992) (shipper bound by DHL airbill although shipper did not have opportunity to read it.)

13. Allstate Ins. v. La Perta, 42 A.D.2d 104, 108, 345 N.Y.S.2d 138, 141–42 (1973); Tri–City Renta–Car & Leasing v. Vaillancourt, 33 A.D.2d 613, 304 N.Y.S.2d 682 (1969); Cutler v. Latshaw, 374 Pa. 1, 97 A.2d 234 (1953). The notion that a surprising clause must be brought to the attention of the other party is gaining currency and is consistent with the cases discussed in § 9.43 infra; see also § 9.40 supra; see, e.g., Birmingham Television v. Water Works, 292 Ala. 147, 290 So.2d 636 (1974) (warehouse receipt); but see Samson Plastic Conduit & Pipe Corp. v. Battenfeld, Extrusionstechnik GMBH, 718 F.Supp. 886 (M.D.Ala. 1989), forum selection clause in German on back of form held binding.

14. In Paper Exp., Ltd. v. Pfankuch Maschinen GmbH, 972 F.2d 753 (7th Cir.

Closely related are cases in which a purported contractual provision is posted on a desk or wall. For example, in one case, a sign containing such a provision was posted at the reception desk of a garage. The court held the provision not binding on the customer unless, prior to contracting, the customer had actually observed the sign, or the sign was posted so prominently that the customer must have known of its existence and assented to its terms.[15] Lachs v. Fidelity & Casualty[16] went even further. In Lachs an air traveler purchased from a vending machine an insurance policy which limited coverage to flights on "scheduled airlines." A large sign posted in the area listed the names of non-scheduled airlines. The passenger bought a ticket on a non-scheduled flight and was killed when it crashed. In the subsequent suit by the beneficiary, the court held that it was a question of fact whether the passenger had been given sufficient notice of the limitation,[17] but that the sign was of little or no significance in making this determination.[18]

The question of whether the contractual provisions are sufficiently called to the attention of a party also arises where a person accepts an instrument in which the person would not reasonably expect to find contractual provisions.[19] The most common illustration is a limitation of liability clause printed on the tag one receives when checking-in a parcel or coat. The majority of courts have held that the average person would consider the tag to serve merely as evidence of the right to a return of goods and would not reasonably expect it to contain contractual provisions.[20] This result is actually a manifestation of the fundamental rule that if a person, without fault, assents to a document believing that it is something other than what it is, the instrument is void.[21]

(c) Fraud and Mistake

There is a relationship between the issue of assent and the concepts of duty to read, fraud, and mistake.[22] For example, what is the result if a

---

1992) The phrase "Warranty: six months according to the rules of VDMA" was held to incorporate by reference the forum selection provision of those rule which were in German. Compare Level Export v. Wolz, Aiken & Co., 305 N.Y. 82, 86–87, 111 N.E.2d 218, 220 (1953) (incorporation by reference held enforceable) with Riverdale Fabrics v. Tillinghast–Stiles, 306 N.Y. 288, 118 N.E.2d 104 (1954) (incorporation by reference held unenforceable).

15. Mendelssohn v. Normand, [1969] 3 W.L.R. 139 (C.A.); accord, Brummett v. Jackson, 211 Miss. 116, 51 So.2d 52 (1951).

16. 306 N.Y. 357, 118 N.E.2d 555 (1954).

17. Id. at 365, 118 N.E.2d at 558–559.

18. Id. at 364, 118 N.E.2d at 558. Other insurance cases requiring exclusions to be conspicuous and clear: Daburlos v. Commercial Ins., 521 F.2d 18 (3d Cir.1975); Ponder v. Blue Cross, 145 Cal.App.3d 709, 193 Cal.Rptr. 632 (1983). See § 3.12 supra.

19. 1 Williston § 6:44.

20. Kergald v. Armstrong Transfer Express, 330 Mass. 254, 113 N.E.2d 53 (1953); Klar v. H. & M. Parcel Room, 270 A.D. 538, 542–43, 61 N.Y.S.2d 285, 289 (1946), aff'd. Tickets issued by a parking lot often are treated the same way. Parkrite Auto Park v. Badgett, 242 S.W.2d 630 (Ky.1951), 44 Ky.L.J. 233 (1956); cf. Ellish v. Airport Parking, 42 A.D.2d 174, 345 N.Y.S.2d 650 (1973), aff'd. The cases are divided on the issue of whether contract provisions on an ordinary baggage check are binding. 1 Williston § 6:44, at 301. On limiting liability by filing tariffs, see Annot., 68 ALR2d 1350, 1359–1363 (1959); Shirazi v. Greyhound, 145 Mont. 421, 401 P.2d 559 (1965).

21. 1 Williston § 6:59.

22. Duress, which also relates to the issue of assent, seems irrelevant in a discussion of the duty to read. As to undue influence, see Dauer, Contracts of Adhesion in

party misrepresents the terms of a record and the other party, relying on the misrepresentation, signs without having read the document?[23] The courts disagree, taking one of three positions. Some courts, given the facts of a particular case have held that there was no justification for relying on the misrepresentation and thus have held the deceived party bound.[24] Other courts have disagreed, based on one of two grounds: either there is a lack of mutual assent or the party who misrepresents is guilty of fraud.[25] Those courts which follow the fraud theory have allowed the defrauded party to avoid the contract or, at times, on a theory of estoppel or reformation, to claim that there is a contract based on the terms as they were represented to the innocent party.[26] Other courts have allowed claims based on negligent misrepresentation.[27]

The Restatement (Second) adopts the view that fraudulent representation of the contents of a record overcomes the duty to read.[28] Both Restatements give this illustration: "A says to B, 'I offer to sell you my horse for $100.' B, knowing that A intends to offer to sell his cow, not his horse for that price, and that the use of the word 'horse' is a slip of the tongue, replies, 'I accept.' "[29] The first Restatement concludes that "[t]here is no contract for the sale of either the horse or the cow."[30] The Restatement (Second) concludes "[t]here is a contract for the sale of the cow and not of the horse."[31] Thus, the Restatement (Second) expresses the view that B's conduct is fraudulent and that, even if A is negligent, a fraudulent party is more guilty than a negligent party; consequently, there is a contract based on the understanding of the more innocent party.[32] The original Restatement, however, either refused to weigh one fault (negligence) against the other (fraud), or relies on the rule: "If either party knows that the other does not intend what his words or other acts express, this knowledge prevents such words or other acts from being operative as an offer or an acceptance."[33]

Light of the Bargaining Hypothesis, 5 Akron L.Rev. 1, 29–30 (1972).

23. The discussion here is without reference to the parol evidence rule which is considered infra at notes 38 to 40.

24. Coddington Enterp. v. Werries, 54 F.Supp.2d 935 (W.D.Mo.1999). The rule generally has been condemned. In the words of one court: "Is it better to encourage negligence in the foolish, or fraud in the deceitful? Either course has most obvious dangers. But judicial experience exemplifies that the former is the least objectionable, and least hampers the administration of pure justice." Western Mfg. v. Cotton & Long, 126 Ky. 749, 754, 104 S.W. 758, 760 (1907); see § 9.15 supra; Comment, 34 Mich.L.Rev. 705 (1936).

25. E.g., Buckmasters v. Action Archery, 915 F.Supp. 1188 (M.D.Ala.1996); Quillen v. Twin City Bank, 253 Ark. 169, 485 S.W.2d 181 (1972); Loden v. Drake, 881

P.2d 467 (Colo.App.1994);Toker v. Perl, 103 N.J.Super. 500, 247 A.2d 701 (1968), aff'd; Bixler v. Wright, 116 Me. 133, 100 A. 467 (1917); Phillips Petroleum v. Roth, 186 Minn. 173, 242 N.W. 629 (1932), 31 Mich. L.Rev. 568 (1933); Whipple v. Brown Bros., 225 N.Y. 237, 121 N.E. 748 (1919).

26. See supra n.23.

27. Heard v. Sexton, 243 Ga.App. 462, 532 S.E.2d 156 (2000).

28. Rs. 2d § 20.

29. Rs. 1st § 71. ill. 2; Rs. 2d § 20 ill. 5.

30. Rs. 1st § 71 ill. 2.

31. Rs. 2d § 20 ill. 5.

32. See id. § 20 cmt d. There is also a suggestion that A may avoid the contract. See also Rs. 2d § 157 cmt b.

33. Rs. 1st § 71(c) & cmt a; see §§ 3.11, 3.12 supra.

A good and recurring illustration of the duty to read issue involves a person who is blind, illiterate or unfamiliar with the language in which the contract is written and who has signed a document without having anyone read it aloud or explaining it.[34] There is all but unanimous agreement that the party is bound by the general rule. Therefore, except possibly in the case of an emergency, the party must employ self-protection by procuring someone to read aloud, explain, or translate the record. However, if the other party is deceitful about its contents, the problem is the one discussed above—the effect of fraud on a failure to read. Most of the cases have held that such a contract may at least be avoided.[35] Under the theory of the Restatement (Second),[36] the defrauded party also would have the option to sue on the contract as it was described. The same result is obtained as if the remedy of reformation were sought.[37]

The problem of a party misrepresenting the contents of the record to one who has failed to read is more complicated when one takes into account the parol evidence rule. For example, if a party signs a document that contains a merger clause to the effect that no representations have been made other than those stated in the record (so that the instrument is presumably integrated), may the party who has failed to read show that the prior oral agreement: (1) contained a misrepresentation which was relied on and which was intended to be included in the record, and (2) that the other party fraudulently represented that the record contained this representation?[38] There are cases which hold that a failure to read the integration precludes a party from introducing a representation despite an allegation of fraud in the execution of the instrument.[39] A better view, however, is repeated in an Arkansas case[40] as follows:

> It is well settled that a written contract which one party induced another to execute by false representations as to its contents is not enforceable, and the party so defrauded is not precluded from contesting the validity of the contract, by the fact that he failed to read it before attaching his signature.[41]

---

34. MCC–Marble Ceramic Center v. Ceramica Nuova d'Agostino, 144 F.3d 1384 (11th Cir.1998), cert. denied (contract in Italian); Paredes v. Princess Cruises, 1 F.Supp.2d 87 (D.Mass.1998) (parties could not read English); Weiss v. La Suisse, 154 F.Supp.2d 734 (S.D.N.Y.2001) (contract in German); Smith v. Standard Oil, 227 Ga. 268, 180 S.E.2d 691 (1971); Ellis v. Mullen, 34 N.C.App. 367, 238 S.E.2d 187 (1977); Salinas v. Beaudrie, 960 S.W.2d 314 (Tex. App.1997) (party could not read English); see Gesualdi v. Miranda, 110 R.I. 694, 296 A.2d 676 (1972). See also Comment, "No Hablo Ingles," 11 San Diego L.Rev. 415 (1974). British Commonwealth cases may be more flexible. See Date–Bah, Illiterate Parties and Written Contracts, 3 Rev. of Ghana Law 181 (1971).

35. Pimpinello v. Swift & Co., 253 N.Y. 159, 170 N.E. 530 (1930); 7 Corbin § 28.37—27.38 (Perillo 2002).

36. See text at notes 23 to 26 supra.

37. See § 9.35 supra.

38. It has been said that a party presenting a document for signature represents that its contents conform to the terms of the agreement previously reached. See, e.g., Bixler v. Wright, 116 Me. 133, 136, 100 A. 467, 469 (1917).

39. Knight & Bostwick v. Moore, 203 Wis. 540, 234 N.W. 902 (1931).

40. Belew v. Griffis, 249 Ark. 589, 460 S.W.2d 80 (1970); see also Estes v. Republic Nat. Bank, 462 S.W.2d 273 (Tex.1970).

41. 249 Ark. at 591–92, 460 S.W.2d at 82, quoting earlier cases. This discussion

When signing a document without reading it, the signer may be operating under a mistake as to the contents of the document.[42] However, avoidance of the contract is not normally permitted.[43] Nonetheless, the situation is different if the record does not reflect the agreement previously made and the term was not omitted by agreement. In such a situation, most courts have granted reformation for mutual mistake despite the negligence involved in failing to read the document,[44] the parol evidence rule,[45] and the Statute of Frauds.[46]

Assuming a case where there is no mistake or wrongdoing on the part of the other party,[47] a claim of mistake of fact might still exist in favor of the party who signs an instrument mistakenly thinking that he or she know its contents. In such a case, however, avoidance for unilateral mistake traditionally would be denied.[48] Today, however some jurisdictions will allow avoidance even for unilateral mistake, if two conditions concur: (1) enforcement of the contract against the mistaken party would be oppressive (or at least result in an unconscionably unequal exchange of values); and (2) avoidance would impose no substantial hardship on the other party.[49] In considering whether to grant the discretionary remedy of specific performance against a party who has failed to read, some courts have denied the remedy.[50]

(d) Fiduciary Relationship

If there is a fiduciary duty on the part of the party proffering the document to the signer, the law goes beyond the qualifications stated in (a) through (c) above. As one court has pithily stated, there is an exception to the general rule that placed a burden of reading on the signing party, "where a person is induced to sign a legal document by

relates primarily to fraud in the execution rather than to fraud in the inducement. The general rule is that proof of fraud may be shown, even if it contradicts an integration. See 3 Corbin § 580; Rs. 2d § 214(d). See also § 9.21 & § 3.7(c) supra. Some courts have held that promissory fraud contradicting the integration may not be shown. See Sweet, Promissory Fraud and the Parol Evidence Rule, 49 Cal.L.Rev. 877 (1961). It has been suggested that under the UCC, an express warranty contradicting an integration may be shown. Broude, The Consumer and the Parol Evidence Rule: Section 2–202 of the UCC, 1970 Duke L.J. 881. See also Associated Hardware Supply v. Big Wheel Distributing, 355 F.2d 114 (3d Cir. 1965).

42. 7 Corbin § 28.37–28.38 (Perillo 2002).

43. Id.

44. See §§ 9.31 to 9.36 supra; Annot., 81 ALR2d 7, 37–39 (1962); Rs. 2d § 157 cmt b.

45. Rs. 2d § 214(d). See also Rs. 2d § 157 cmt b.

46. See § 19.28 infra.

47. If one party is mistaken as to the contents of the document and the other has actual knowledge of this fact, the mistaken party may avoid the contract. 7 Corbin § 28.38 (Perillo 2002); Rs. 2d § 157 cmt a.

48. See Sanger v. Yellow Cab, 486 S.W.2d 477, 481 (Mo.1972) (mutual mistake distinguished from unilateral failure to read); Hampshire v. Hampshire, 485 S.W.2d 314, 316 (Tex.App.1972) (absent fraud, failure to read sales contract held not to justify avoidance).

49. Gethsemane Lutheran Church v. Zacho, 258 Minn. 438, 443, 104 N.W.2d 645, 649 (1960); cf. Beatty v. Depue, 78 S.D. 395, 103 N.W.2d 187 (1960); Annot., 1 ALR3d 531 (1960). See § 9.27 supra; 13 Williston §§ 1577–78; 7 Corbin § 28.38 (Perillo 2002).

50. 13 Williston § 1577.

one standing in a fiduciary relation to that person and where the fiduciary has an interest in the document's execution. In such a case, the document can generally be avoided by its signer on a showing merely that the fiduciary failed to make him aware of the legal significance of the signing of the document, provided that the rights of innocent third persons have not intervened."[51]

§ 9.43 Contracts of Adhesion—Exculpation and Indemnity Clauses

There has been a tendency, particularly in cases involving the duty to read,[1] to treat contracts of adhesion or standard form contracts differently from other contracts.[2] There is nothing inherently wrong with a contract of adhesion. Most of the transactions of daily life involve such contracts that are drafted by one party and presented on a take it or leave it basis. They simplify standard transactions such as obtaining or using a credit card.[3] There is a growing body of case law subverting the traditional duty to read concept in adhesion or other standard form contracts, on three different grounds: 1) there was not true assent to a particular term, 2) even if there was assent, the term is to be excised from the contract because it contravenes public policy[4] or 3) the term is unconscionable and should be stricken.[5] At times, the same decision may employ all three rationales. This modern approach to the problem and the meaning of true assent may be shown best by a brief examination of three of the leading cases on the subject.

A significant case, Weaver v. American Oil Co.,[6] involved a lease by an oil company to a filling station operator. The lessee signed, without reading, a lease which provided that the lessee would indemnify the lessor for damages caused by the lessor's negligence. The court first

51. Markell v. Sidney B. Pfeifer Foundation, Inc., 9 Mass.App.Ct. 412, 440, 402 N.E.2d 76, 93 (1980), overruled on other grounds, Cleary v. Cleary, 427 Mass. 286, 692 N.E.2d 955 (1998).

§ 9.43

1. Ehrenzweig, Adhesion Contracts in the Conflict of Laws, 53 Colum.L.Rev. 1072 (1953); Note, Contract Clauses in Fine Print, 63 Harv.L.Rev. 494 (1950); see Wilson, Freedom of Contract and Adhesion Contracts, 14 Int'l & Comp.L.Q. 172 (1965).

2. Kessler, Contracts of Adhesion—Some Thoughts About Freedom of Contract, 43 Colum.L.Rev. 629 (1943). In the Kessler article, as here, the terms "contract of adhesion" and "standardized contract" are used interchangeably, but the two concepts are not always treated as coextensive. See Sheldon, Consumer Protection and Standard Contracts, 22 Am.J.Comp.L. 17, 18 (1974).

3. There is a tendency for some lawyers and judges to use the term "contract of adhesion" to refer to a contract that is not only adhesive but also grossly unfair. E.g., Klos v. Polskie Linie Lotnicze, 133 F.3d 164 (2d Cir.1997). This misuse of the term creates confusion. Probably most contracts of adhesion are simple and reasonable.

4. Particularly if the exculpation covers intentional torts. McQuirk v. Donnelley, 189 F.3d 793 (9th Cir.1999) (defamation).

5. The notion of condemning clauses as illegal or contrary to public policy is hardly new. However, it is being used today more often and in a wider variety of circumstances. See, e.g., von Hippel, The Control of Exemption Clauses—A Comparative Study, 16 Int'l & Comp.L.Q. 591 (1967). Unconscionability is discussed in §§ 9.37 to 9.40 supra.

6. 257 Ind. 458, 276 N.E.2d 144 (1971); Annot., 49 ALR3d 306 (1973). See also Frame v. Merrill Lynch, Pierce, Fenner & Smith, Inc., 20 Cal.App.3d 668, 97 Cal.Rptr. 811 (1971).

stated that the duty to read rule had no application to the case because "the clause was in fine print and contained no title heading * * *."[7] This conclusion would have ended the matter under the rules discussed above, but the court seemed anxious to break new ground, for it also brought in issues of unconscionability, public policy, and lack of true assent. The court said:[8]

> When a party show[s] that the contract, which is * * * to be enforced, was * * * an unconscionable one, due to a prodigious amount of bargaining power on behalf of the stronger party, which is used to the stronger party's advantage and is unknown to the lesser party, the contract provision, or the contract as a whole, if the provision is not separable, should not be enforceable on the grounds that the provision is contrary to public policy. The party seeking to enforce such a contract has the burden of showing that the provisions were explained to the other party and came to his knowledge and there was in fact a real and voluntary meeting of the minds and not merely an objective meeting.

The above quotation combines three different concepts: unconscionability, violation of public policy, and lack of true assent.[9] The court's ultimate approach appears to be that the contract is unconscionable because an objective assent which flows from a duty to read is not sufficient (despite the objective theory of contracts) to bind a party to clauses which are unusual or unfair unless the clauses are at least brought to the adhering party's attention and explained.[10] The theory is that since such clauses impose a great hardship or risk on the weaker party, who is at the mercy of the stronger, an informed and voluntary consent should be required.[11] A party might be considered to be capable of self-protection if the party has bargaining power relatively equal to that of the other party, or if insurance was available to protect against a known risk.

The court in Henningsen v. Bloomfield Motors,[12] employed the same approach, although the case arose under the Uniform Sales Act, rather than its successor, the UCC.[13] In Henningson, a consumer brought an

7.   257 Ind. at 462, 276 N.E.2d at 147.

8.   Id. at 464, 276 N.E.2d at 148.

9.   The Weaver opinion also proceeded on a warranty analogy when it stated: "The burden should be on the party submitting such 'a package' in printed form to show that the other party had knowledge of any unusual or unconscionable terms contained therein. The principle should be the same as that applicable to implied warranties, namely, that a package of goods sold to a purchaser is fit for the purposes intended and contains no harmful materials other than that represented." Id., 276 N.E.2d at 147–48. See also C. & J. Fertilizer v. Allied Mut. Ins., 227 N.W.2d 169 (Iowa 1975).

10.   See § 9.40. Under this approach a party who carefully reads the proposed con-

tract is in a worse position than one who does not. Carr v. Hoosier Photo Supplies, 441 N.E.2d 450 (Ind.1982).

11.   See, e.g., Vitex Mfg. v. Caribtex, 377 F.2d 795, 799–800 (3d Cir.1967); Johnston, The Control of Exemption Clauses: A Comment, 17 Int'l & Comp.L.Q. 232 (1968).

12.   32 N.J. 358, 161 A.2d 69 (1960); Annot., 75 ALR2d 39 (1961).

13.   If the case had arisen under the UCC, the court could have noted the Code provision that, in the case of a disclaimer of the warranty of merchantability, the word merchantability must be used and the disclaimer must be conspicuous. UCC § 2–316(2) (same in revision). The term "conspicuous" is defined in UCC § 1–201(10)

action for personal injuries against both the vendor and manufacturer of an automobile. Relying on a clause stating that its express warranty was in lieu of all other warranties express or implied, the defendants argued that the plaintiff's action should be limited to a claim for defective parts. The heart of the Henningsen decision, with its reliance on the imbalance of bargaining position, appears in a paragraph near the end of the opinion:[14]

> True, the Sales Act authorizes agreements between buyer and seller qualifying the warranty obligations. But quite obviously the Legislature contemplated lawful stipulations (which are determined by the circumstances of a particular case) arrived at freely by parties of relatively equal bargaining strength. The lawmakers did not authorize the automobile manufacturer to use its grossly disproportionate bargaining power to relieve itself from liability and to impose on the ordinary buyer, who in effect has no real freedom of choice, the grave danger of injury to himself and others that attends the sale of such a dangerous instrumentality as a defectively made automobile.

Although there was some discussion about mutual assent, the ultimate holding was based on the conclusion that such a clause, under the circumstances of the case (clause on reverse side, small print, disparity of bargaining power, clause on a take-it-or-leave-it basis and included by all major car manufacturers), was invalid as unconscionable. This was made clear when the court further stated that it was not required to consider whether a particular charge which related to mutual assent was correct because "the disclaimer is void as a matter of law."[15]

Another leading case illustrating the same approach is Williams v. Walker–Thomas Furniture[16] There, an installment sales agreement had a

(reworded in the revision). A disclaimer in small print preceded by the word "NOTE" printed in the large type was held to be conspicuous in Velez v. Craine & Clarke Lumber, 41 A.D.2d 747, 341 N.Y.S.2d 248 (1973), reversed on other grounds. But see Tennessee Carolina Transp. v. Strick, 283 N.C. 423, 196 S.E.2d 711 (1973). For an emphatically conspicuous disclaimer, see Brunsman v. DeKalb Swine Breeders, 138 F.3d 358 (8th Cir.1998).

Even more to the point is UCC § 2–719(3) (unchanged in revision). It provides: "Consequential damages may be limited or excluded unless the limitation or exclusion is unconscionable. Limitation of consequential damages for injury to the person in the case of consumer goods is prima facie unconscionable but limitation of damages where the loss is commercial is not." See also UCC §§ 2–316(1), 2–719(1) & (2).

Professor Murray takes the position that even if the disclaimer is conspicuous it must, in addition, be negotiated, and comprehensible to the buyer. See Murray, supra § 9.37 n.2, at 48–49. Contra, Leff, supra § 9.37 n.2, at 523–24. There are, as usual, cases which support each position. Compare Belden–Stark Brick v. Morris Rosen & Sons, 39 A.D.2d 534, 331 N.Y.S.2d 59 (1972), aff'd, with Dobias v. Western Farmers Assn., 6 Wn.App. 194, 491 P.2d 1346 (1971). Professor Broude suggests that under §§ 2–202 and 2–316 printed form disclaimers of warranties, even though they are contained in an integration, should not be considered to be part of the agreement because they are not truly assented to. Broude, The Consumer and the Parol Evidence Rule: Section 2–202 of the UCC, 1970 Duke L.J. 881. Professor Rakoff goes further, arguing that all non-dickered terms in an adhesion contract be treated as presumptively invalid. Rakoff, supra § 9.37 n.2.

14.   32 N.J. at 404, 161 A.2d at 95.

15.   Id. at 405, 161 A.2d at 95.

16.   350 F.2d 445 (D.C.Cir.1965), noted in 79 Harv.L.Rev. 1299 (1966).

provision resulting in "a balance due on every item purchased until the balance due on all items, whenever purchased, was liquidated."[17] As a result, in the event of a default on any one item, all items could be repossessed. The court in concluding that the fairness of the clause needed to be tested at trial stated:

> When a party of little bargaining power, and hence little real choice, signs a commercially unreasonable contract with little or no knowledge of its terms, it is hardly likely that his consent, or even an objective manifestation of his consent, was ever given to all the terms. In such a case the usual rule that the terms of the agreement are not to be questioned should be abandoned and the court should consider whether the terms of the contract are so unfair that enforcement should be withheld.[18]

The three cases discussed above do not expunge the duty to read rule, but create an exception if the terms (or a term) of the contract are unfair under the circumstances. In such a case, the ordinary manifestation of assent implicit in signing or accepting a document is insufficient because the assent is not reasoned and knowing. Such consent involves an understanding of the clause in question[19] and a reasonable opportunity to accept or decline.[20] Even then, if the clause is sufficiently odious, it will be struck down as unconscionable or contrary to public policy.

Having established the nature of the new approach, the question becomes how it has been applied. Cases relating to promises to indemnify a person against the consequences of that person's own negligence, and to exculpate another for the other's negligence, serve as excellent illustrations.

While Weaver[21] held that a promise to indemnify was not binding under the circumstances of the case, it can hardly be said that there is a general rule that promises to indemnify are objectionable.[22] On a similar set of facts, a New York case, Levine v. Shell Oil,[23] reached a conclusion directly opposite to that of Weaver.[24] The court paid lip service to the rules announced in the cases discussed above when it stated:

---

17. 350 F.2d at 447. See Uniform Consumer Credit Code § 3.302; UCC § 9–204 (protecting consumers against such clauses).

18. 350 F.2d at 449–50 (footnotes omitted).

19. See, e.g., Henningsen v. Bloomfield Motors, 32 N.J. 358, 399–400, 161 A.2d 69, 92 (1960).

20. Id. at 390, 161 A.2d at 87. But what is the choice discussed? In the Henningsen case it was clear that a person could not buy a new car from a major manufacturer without submitting to the clause in question. But in Weaver there was no evidence that the lessee could not have obtained a similar lease from another oil company without the offending clause.

By now it should be clear that the assent discussed in § 9.41 supra, is not the same type of assent being discussed here under the label "true assent."

21. See text accompanying note 6 to 11 supra.

22. Messersmith v. American Fidelity, 232 N.Y. 161, 133 N.E. 432 (1921); Annot., 19 ALR 879 (1921); Corbin §§ 1471, 1472; Rs. 1st § 572.

23. 28 N.Y.2d 205, 321 N.Y.S.2d 81, 269 N.E.2d 799 (1971); see also Max Oil v. Shell Oil, 945 F.Supp. 241 (M.D.Ala.1996).

24. A reading of the briefs tends to reinforce this conclusion.

Lastly, there has been no showing that the agreement involved herein is either a contract of adhesion or an unconscionable agreement and we need not now pass upon the question whether an indemnification clause in a contract of that nature would be void for those reasons. * * * In this arm's length transaction the indemnification provision was a part of [sic] business relationship between the parties. If [the lessee] had reservations as to the scope of the agreement, he should have insisted on a different indemnification clause or refused to give his assent to the contract. * * *[25]

Notice, however, that while the Levine court emphasized that it was not dealing with a contract of adhesion, the dissenting opinion in Weaver criticized the majority for incorrectly relying on cases involving adhesion contracts instead of following the more traditional rule.[26] One has the impression that the facts in Weaver and Levine are similar but opposite results were reached.

The intermediate appellate court in Weaver held that a provision in a contract by which one party agreed not to hold the other liable for negligence is contrary to public policy in the absence of an understanding of the provision and true assent to it.[27] Although, this cannot be considered to be the traditional view,[28] that view does recognize a public

---

25. 28 N.Y.2d at 213, 321 N.Y.S.2d at 86–87, 269 N.E.2d at 803 (citation omitted).

26. This raises the problem of what is a contract of adhesion. A standardized agreement has been described as one which is dictated by a predominant party to cover transactions with many people rather than with an individual, and which resembles an ultimatum or law rather than a mutually negotiated contract. Siegelman v. Cunard White Star, 221 F.2d 189, 206 (2d Cir.1955). It is characterized by a lack of negotiation. Cohen, The Basis of Contract, 46 Harv. L.Rev. 553, 588–90 (1933); Llewellyn, What Price Contract?—An Essay in Perspective, 40 Yale L.J. 704, 731–34 (1931); Meyer, Contracts of Adhesion and the Doctrine of Fundamental Breach, 50 Va.L.Rev. 1178, 1179–86 (1964); Oldfather, Toward a Usable Method of Judicial Review of the Adhesion Contractor's Lawmaking, 16 U.Kan. L.Rev. 303, 305–07 (1968); Slawson, Standard Form Contracts and Democratic Control of Lawmaking Power, 84 Harv.L.Rev. 529, 531 (1971); Note, 111 U.Pa.L.Rev. 1197, 1205–06 (1963). See also K & C v. Westinghouse Elec., 437 Pa. 303, 308–09, 263 A.2d 390, 393 (1970).

The New York court in Levine assumed that the lessee had a choice and could bargain with respect to the clause. Would the Weaver court agree? See supra § 9.43 notes 4 to 9. It should also be noted that the plaintiffs in the Henningsen and Williams cases are consumers while the lessee in Weaver is not. See, e.g., 15 U.S.C.A.

§ 1602(a)–(h); Uniform Consumer Credit Code § 1.301(11); Model Consumer Credit Act § 1.410. How important this factor should be is still unclear. Certainly as a matter of fact, it may usually be assumed that a consumer has little or no bargaining power. In any event, there are other cases which have taken the Weaver approach even though consumers were not involved. See, e.g., Chandler v. Aero Mayflower Transit, 374 F.2d 129 (4th Cir.1967); Standard Oil v. Perkins, 347 F.2d 379 (9th Cir.1965).

27. Weaver v. American Oil, 261 N.E.2d 99, 104 (Ind.App.1970), modified 262 N.E.2d 663 (1970), modified 257 Ind. 458, 276 N.E.2d 144 (1971). See Ransburg v. Richards, 770 N.E.2d 393 (Ind.App.2002) (residential lease exculpating landlord from negligence is against public policy).

Exculpatory clauses are often circumvented by a process of interpretation. See e.g., Willard Van Dyke Productions v. Eastman Kodak, 12 N.Y.2d 301, 189 N.E.2d 693, 239 N.Y.S.2d 337 (1963).

28. Johnston, The Control of Exemption Clauses, 17 Int'l & Comp.L.Q. 232 (1968); von Hipple, The Control of Exemption Clauses, 16 Int'l & Comp.L.Q. 591 (1967); Note, 42 Chi.-Kent L.Rev. 82 (1965). However there is a different rule for willful, wanton, reckless, gross or intentional negligence. Winterstein v. Wilcom, 16 Md.App. 130, 136, 293 A.2d 821, 824 (1972). The courts have shown a greater hostility to

policy exception in cases of public servants involved in the performance of their public duties for compensation.[29] The primary illustration of such a public servant is a common carrier.[30] Some jurisdictions, however, have a blanket ban on the validity of pre-injury exculpation agreements.[31] Opinions in some jurisdictions appear incoherent.[32]

Cases involving private voluntary transactions, however, are not harmonious. While the intermediate court in Weaver held the indemnity clause invalid,[33] a number of cases involving indemnity or exculpation clauses have indicated the contrary.[34] Here again, the problem is discussed not only from the perspective of public policy, but also from the point of view of mutual assent.[35] For example, in Ciofalo v. Vic Tanney Gyms,[36] a patron of a gymnasium operated by the defendant agreed in a membership contract to assume the risk of injuries arising out of the defendant's negligence. The court did not find the clause in opposition to public policy, adding: "Here there is no special legal relationship and no overriding public interest which demand that this contract provision, voluntarily entered into by competent parties, should be rendered ineffectual."[37] Although the court stated that the plaintiff had voluntarily assented, the facts here were not sufficiently delineated to allow a

exculpatory clauses than to indemnification agreements. See Allison v. Bank One–Denver, 289 F.3d 1223 (10th Cir.2002); Jamison v. Ellwood Consol. Water, 420 F.2d 787, 789 (3d Cir.1970); Haynes v. County of Missoula, 163 Mont. 270, 280–282, 517 P.2d 370, 377 (1973).

29. Tunkl v. Regents of the Univ. of Calif., 60 Cal.2d 92, 98–102, 383 P.2d 441, 445, 447, 32 Cal.Rptr. 33, 37–39 (1963) extended to services to the public in Dalury v. S–K–I, 164 Vt. 329, 670 A.2d 795 (1995) (ski lift).

30. There also have been a number of statutes dealing with the topic of exculpation. See e.g., 6 Del.Code § 2704; Ill.—Smith–Hurd Ann. ch. 80, ¶ 91; McKinney's N.Y.Gen.Obli.Law §§ 5–321 to 5–325 (concerning leases; caterers; building service and maintenance contracts; architects; engineers; surveyors; garages and parking lots).

31. Coles v. Jenkins, 34 F.Supp.2d 381 (W.D.Va.1998).

32. See Comment, 81 Marq.L.Rev. 1081 (1998) (Wisconsin).

33. See 261 N.E.2d at 101; accord, Dixilyn Drilling v. Crescent Towing & Salvage, 372 U.S. 697 (1963); Bisso v. Inland Waterways, 349 U.S. 85 (1955); Kansas City Power & Light v. United Tel., 458 F.2d 177, 179 (10th Cir.1972); Fitzgerald v. Newark Morning Ledger, 111 N.J.Super. 104, 267 A.2d 557 (1970) (such a clause not favored but question is one of public policy and

answer depends on position of the parties). See also Rogers v. Dorchester Assocs., 32 N.Y.2d 553, 564, 347 N.Y.S.2d 22, 30, 300 N.E.2d 403, 409 (1973).

34. Royal Typewriter, Division Litton Business Sys. v. M/V Kulmerland, 346 F.Supp. 1019 (S.D.N.Y.1972), aff'd; Cree Coaches v. Panel Suppliers, 384 Mich. 646, 186 N.W.2d 335 (1971); Great Northern Oil v. St. Paul Fire & Marine Ins., 291 Minn. 97, 189 N.W.2d 404 (1971); Stamp v. Windsor Power House Coal, 154 W.Va. 578, 177 S.E.2d 146 (1970). See also Rs. 1st § 574. These authorities do not necessarily conflict with the cases cited in note 29, since the underlying rationale of all these cases is that the questions are about assent and public policy.

35. The leading case is probably Tunkl v. Regents of Univ. of Calif., 60 Cal.2d 92, 32 Cal.Rptr. 33, 383 P.2d 441 (1963) (hospital admission); see also Eelbode v. Chec, 97 Wash.App. 462, 984 P.2d 436 (1999) (pre-employment physical).

36. 10 N.Y.2d 294, 177 N.E.2d 925, 220 N.Y.S.2d 962 (1961).

37. 10 N.Y.2d at 297–98, 177 N.E.2d at 927, 220 N.Y.S.2d at 965. There has been much discussion concerning the language required for an exculpatory clause to be effective irrespective of any question of public policy. See Levine v. Shell Oil, 28 N.Y.2d 205, 269 N.E.2d 799, 321 N.Y.S.2d 81 (1971); Cason v. Geis Irrigation, 211 Kan. 406, 507 P.2d 295 (1973).

determination of whether there was the true, voluntary, understanding assent required by Weaver and a number of other cases.[38] Most cases dealing with recreational activities are in accord,[39] although the quoted case has been overturned by legislation.[40] Although exculpation and indemnity clauses are generally upheld, most courts will not allow a party to contract away its liability for gross negligence.[41] Many cases bypass the issues by holding that the contested clause lacks sufficient clarity to attain its aim,[42] or is insufficiently conspicuous,[43] or does not apply to claims of misrepresentation.[44]

The indemnity and exculpation cases are changing, in a gradual but perceptible way.[45] Freedom of contract, laissez-faire, and black letter law are giving way to notions of what is fair under the particular circumstances of the case, even if the result is not strictly in compliance with the objective theory of contracts.[46] These cases also illustrate the modern attack on the duty to read rule. First, there are findings of a lack of true mutual assent. Second, even if there is a finding of true assent, the challenged clause may be stricken. A combination of notions of public policy and conscionability lead to holdings to the effect that a party should not be permitted to shift the burden of the party's wrongdoing to a weaker party or to deprive the injured party of the right to recover for the wrong done.[47]

A Minnesota court has summarized the trend as follows:

An examination of the cases demonstrates the emergence of a two-prong test used by the courts in analyzing the policy considerations. Before enforcing an exculpatory clause, both prongs of the test are

38. Winterstein v. Wilcom, 16 Md.App. 130, 293 A.2d 821 (1972); Van Noy Interstate v. Tucker, 125 Miss. 260, 87 So. 643 (1921); Joseph v. Sears Roebuck & Co., 224 S.C. 105, 77 S.E.2d 583, 40 ALR2d 742 (1953); Dodge v. Nashville, C. & St. L.R.R., 142 Tenn. 20, 215 S.W. 274 (1919).

39. YMCA v. Superior Court, 55 Cal. App.4th 22, 63 Cal.Rptr.2d 612 (1997); Schmidt v. U.S., 912 P.2d 871 (Okl.1996) (horseback riding); Cooper v. Aspen Skiing Co., 48 P.3d 1229 (Colo.2002) (parents cannot release on behalf of child); U. S. Auto Club v. Smith, 717 N.E.2d 919 (Ind.App. 1999); Hardy v. St. Clair, 739 A.2d 368 (Me.1999) (but release does not bar loss of consortium claim); Holzer v. Dakota Speedway, 610 N.W.2d 787 (S.D.2000); contra Berlangieri v. Running Elk Corp., 132 N.M. 332, 48 P.3d 70 (App.2002) (horseback riding). The release must, however, clearly cover the conduct that caused the injury. Moore v. Hartley Motors, 36 P.3d 628 (Alaska 2001).

40. McKinney's N.Y. Gen'l Obl. L. § 5-326.

41. Royal Ins. v. Southwest Marine, 194 F.3d 1009 (9th Cir.1999); cf. Sparks v. Re/

Max Allstar Realty, 55 S.W.3d 343 (Ky.App. 2000) (can exculpate against gross negligence, but not "willful and wanton" negligence); McQuirk v. Donnelley, 189 F.3d 793 (9th Cir.1999) (cannot exculpate against intentional torts).

42. Marsh v. Dixon, 707 N.E.2d 998 (Ind.App.1999); Gates v. Sells Rest Home, 57 S.W.3d 391 (2001); Steele v. Mt. Hood Meadows, 159 Or.App. 272, 974 P.2d 794 (1999).

43. Sale v. Slitz, 998 S.W.2d 159 (Mo. App.1999) (funeral arrangements); Littlefield v. Schaefer, 955 S.W.2d 272 (Tex. 1997).

44. Sear–Brown Group v. Jay Builders, 244 A.D.2d 966, 665 N.Y.S.2d 162 (1997).

45. See, e.g., Smith v. Kennedy, 43 Ala. App. 554, 195 So.2d 820 (1966), cert. denied, which according to the casenote in 19 Ala.L.Rev. 484, 486 (1967) makes a substantial change in Alabama law. See also 4 Duq.U.L.Rev. 475 (1966).

46. W. Friedmann, Law in a Changing Society 93–94 (1959).

47. See text accompanying notes 1 to 5 supra.

examined, to-wit: (1) whether there was a disparity of bargaining power between the parties (in terms of a compulsion to sign a contract containing an unacceptable provision and the lack of ability to negotiate elimination of the unacceptable provision) and (2) the types of services being offered or provided (taking into consideration whether it is a public or essential service).[48] (Citations omitted)

The summary is largely accurate but fails to take into account more radical cases that emphasize the presence or absence of true assent.[49]

Despite such trends, one must take into account the realities of each situation. Burglar alarm companies generally demand that the user of its services agree to exculpate them from liability. In this context, the exculpation makes sense as the customer normally will insure its goods. If the clauses were not upheld, the alarm company would be cast in the role of a reinsurer.[50]

§ 9.44 Duty to Read and Restatement (Second)

Somewhat curiously, unlike the first Restatement,[1] the Restatement (Second) does not state a general rule with respect to the duty to read. Instead, it sets forth in the chapter on interpretation, in § 211, a rule primarily for standardized agreements.[2] The section provides:

(1) Except as stated in Subsection (3), where a party to an agreement signs or otherwise manifests assent to a writing and has reason to believe that like writings are regularly used to embody terms of agreements of the same type, he adopts the writing as an integrated agreement with respect to the terms included in the writing.

(2) Such a writing is interpreted wherever reasonable as treating alike all those similarly situated, without regard to their knowledge or understanding of the standard terms of the writing.

(3) Where the other party has reason to believe that the party manifesting such assent would not do so if he knew that the writing contained a particular term, the term is not part of the agreement.

The rule has a dual thrust. First, it recognizes that standardized agreements serve a useful purpose because most contracts are concluded between a party who bargains, if at all, only with respect to certain limited terms, and by an agent of a business who has limited under-

---

48. Schlobohm v. Spa Petite, 326 N.W.2d 920, 923 (Minn.1982); see Stanley v. Creighton, 911 P.2d 705 (Colo.App.1996) (exculpatory clause in residential lease).

49. See Krohnert v. Yacht Sys. Hawaii, 4 Haw. App. 190, 664 P.2d 738 (1983) where true assent is made a third prong.

50. See, e.g., Sasco, Inc. v. Wells Fargo Alarm Services, 969 F.Supp. 535 (E.D.Mo. 1997).

§ 9.44

1. The rule of the original Restatement is set forth in § 70 which is in basic conformity with the general rule discussed in § 9.41 supra. The Rs. 2d § 211 cmt b, suggests some recognition of the general rule and cmt d covers to some extent the same ground as § 9.41 hereof.

2. There is no definition of standardized agreement. See supra § 9.43 n.26; see also Rs. 2d § 157 cmt b.

standing of the terms and limited authority to vary them.[3] Second, the rule follows the lead of cases such as Weaver v. American Oil[4] by stating that parties "are not bound to unknown terms which are beyond the range of reasonable expectation."[5] The rationale is that if the drafter of the form knows or has reason to know that "the adhering party would not have accepted the agreement if he had known that the agreement contained the particular term" then the adhering party should not be deemed to have assented.[6]

Although the Restatement (Second) speaks of assent it seems that it is not using the word assent in its ordinary connotation for it indicates that all persons who sign a standardized agreement should be treated alike, even though a more sophisticated individual customer might give the type of informed assent required by some of the cases discussed above. Thus, the Restatement position is that if the ordinary reasonable person would not expect such a clause it should be read out of the contract.[7] The Restatement in essence is applying the unconscionability notion of "unfair surprise."[8] It recognizes this when it states that the rule of § 211 "is closely related to the policy against unconscionable terms."[9]

Two of the factors to be considered in determining whether a reasonable person would expect a particular provision in the agreement are: (1) whether "the term is bizarre or oppressive,"[10] and (2) whether "it eviscerates the non-standard terms explicitly agreed to, or * * * eliminates the dominant purpose of the transaction."[11]

The Restatement (Second) thus recognizes the utility of standard agreements but refuses to allow them to be used unfairly. This seems a reasonable resolution of the problem and is in general accord with the rule of some of the cases discussed above that even an objective manifestation of assent stemming from a failure to read should not preclude consideration of whether there is true assent to unfair or unexpected terms.

§ 9.45   Conclusion

The underlying philosophy of the objective theory of contracts is to enshrine a record as sacrosanct and inviolate. This result is achieved by rules that exclude or minimize the true subjective intention of the

---

3. Rs. 2d § 211 cmts a & b.

4. 257 Ind. 458, 276 N.E.2d 144 (1971); see text in § 9.42 supra at nn. 6 to 11.

5. Rs. 2d § 211 cmt f.

6. Id.

7. Id. at § 211(2). However, in Comment f it is stated that one of the factors to be considered is whether the adhering party ever had an opportunity to read the term.

8. UCC § 2–302 cmt 1; see § 9.40 supra; cf. Clark, Equity 247 (1954).

9. Rs. 2d § 211 cmt f; see § 9.40 supra.

10. Rs. 2d § 211 cmt f.

11. Id.; see Meyer, Contracts of Adhesion and the Doctrine of Fundamental Breach, 50 Va.L.Rev. 1178 (1964). See also Fairbanks, Morse & Co. v. Consolidated Fisheries, 190 F.2d 817 (3d Cir.1951); Weisz v. Parke–Bernet Galleries, 67 Misc.2d 1077, 325 N.Y.S.2d 576 (1971); reversed 77 Misc.2d 80, 351 N.Y.S.2d 911 (1974); Karsales (Harrow) v. Wallis [1956] 2 All E.R. 866 (C.A.).

parties. The policy is that a party to a written agreement may safely rely on the written document.[1] These results are achieved, for example, under the traditional parol evidence rule and traditional rules of interpretation including the plain meaning rule. It might be noted that all of these rules are presently under serious attack.[2]

The duty to read rule is yet another fortification thrown up by the objective theory of contracts to make a record impregnable.[3] It is based on the realities of the bargaining practices of the past, when the self-reliance ethic was strong and standardized agreements were rare. Under such circumstances, it may have been realistic to expect each party to read and understand the agreement. However, in the current era of mass marketing, a party may reasonably believe that an attempt to read a standardized document would be met with impatience since so few adhering parties do. In such circumstances an imputation that the adhering party assents to all of the terms in the document is dubious. An assertion that the customer is bound by them would place a premium on an artful draftsman who is able to put asunder what the salesman and the customer have joined together.[4]

Thus, some of the more modern cases search not only for apparent objective assent but also for a true subjective assent. Under this view, true assent does not exist unless there is a genuine opportunity to read the clause in question and its impact is explained by the dominant party and understood by the other party who has a reasonable choice, under the circumstances, of accepting or rejecting the clause.[5] Thus, the printed form that implicitly suggests that it should not be challenged or even read loses some of its apparent authority.[6] The Restatement (Second) goes one step further when it indicates that what is important, at least

---

§ 9.45

1. D. Hume, A Treatise of Human Nature 523–26 (Silby–Bigge ed. 1888); Whittier, The Restatement of Contracts and Mutual Assent, 17 Calif.L.Rev. 441 (1929); cf. 1 Williston §§ 21 & 35 (3d ed.).

2. See, e.g., Rs. 2d ch. 9.

3. The Weaver case recognized the relationship between the objective theory of contracts and the duty to read when it stated: "The parole evidence rule states that an agreement or contract, signed by the parties, is conclusively presumed to represent an integration or meeting of the minds of the parties. This is an archaic rule from the old common law. The objectivity of the rule has as its only merit its simplicity of application which is far outweighed by its failure in many cases to represent the actual agreement, particularly where a printed form prepared by one party contains [sic] hidden clauses unknown to the other party is submitted and signed. The law should seek the truth or the subjective understanding of the parties in this more enlightened age. The burden should be on the party submitting such 'a package' in printed form to show that the other party had knowledge of any unusual or unconscionable terms contained therein," 257 Ind. at 463–64, 276 N.E.2d at 147 (emphasis deleted).

It also has been suggested that the party who prepared the standardized form should shoulder the burden of proving that an opportunity for bargaining existed. Wilson, Freedom of Contract and Adhesion Contracts, 14 Int'l & Comp.L.Q. 172, 186 (1965).

4. See generally Dauer, Contracts of Adhesion in Light of the Bargain Hypothesis: An Introduction, 5 Akron L.Rev. 1 (1972); Mellinkoff, How to Make Contracts Illegible, 5 Stan.L.Rev. 418 (1953); Slawson, Standard Form Contracts and Democratic Control of Lawmaking Power, 84 Harv. L.Rev. 529 (1971).

5. See § 9.43 supra.

6. Shuchman, Consumer Credit by Adhesion Contracts, 35 Temp.L.Q. 125 (1962).

in contracts of adhesion, is whether a reasonable person would have expected to find such a clause in the contract. If not, the clause is considered to be oppressive, unfair or indecent.[7] This, of course, carries one into the doctrine of substantive unconscionability which in turn is related to the question of whether a particular clause should be struck down as contrary to public policy.[8] The Restatement (Second) seems to be suggesting a new kind of objective approach to standardized agreements. Rather than seeking out true assent on a case by case basis, it places the duty on the courts to consider the essential fairness of the printed terms, both from the viewpoint of surprise and inherent one-sidedness.

Not only is there inconsistency in the authorities regarding which theory should be applied, but apparently opposite results are being reached in cases with substantially similar fact patterns.[9] This should not come as a surprise to any student of the law. New law is evolving in this area and it will be many years, if ever, before any semblance of uniformity will be achieved.

The ultimate result may be a radically different set of rules for transactions in which all major aspects of the agreement are negotiated and those in which standard forms are used. If the industries that employ standard forms do not police themselves so as to insure inherent fairness of forms, it is likely that the courts will increasingly refuse legal effect to non-negotiated terms of a contract and that standardized forms, as in the case of insurance policies, will be dictated by legislatures or administrative agencies.[10]

7. K. Llewellyn, The Common Law Tradition: Deciding Appeals 370 (1960).

8. See § 9.43 supra.

9. See § 9.43 supra.

10. See, e.g., Sales, Standard Form Contracts, 16 Mod.L.Rev. 318, 337–38 (1953); Sheldon, Consumer Protection and Standard Contracts: The Swedish Experiment in Administrative Control, 22 Am.J.Comp.L. 17 (1974); Comment, Administrative Regulation of Adhesion Contracts in Israel, 66 Colum.L.Rev. 1340 (1966). See also Speidel, Unconscionability, Assent and Consumer Protection, 31 U.Pitt.L.Rev. 359 (1970).

Chapter 10

RESERVED FOR FUTURE USE

Chapter 11

CONDITIONS, PERFORMANCE AND BREACH

Table of Sections

Table of Sections

A. INTRODUCTION

A. INTRODUCTION

Table of Sections

§ 11.1 Relationship of Conditions to Offer and Acceptance

This chapter deals primarily with the *performance* rather than the *formation* of a contract.[1] A bilateral contract arises when the offeree makes the promise requested by the offeror.[2] In a sense, offer and acceptance are conditions to the performance of the contract because if the contract is not formed, there is no need to perform it. Once a bilateral contract has been created, questions relating to its performance arise, and it is in this context that the word "condition" is used.[3]

A unilateral contract is different. Assume A says to B, "If you walk across the Brooklyn Bridge, I'll pay you $100." Walking the Bridge creates a unilateral contract.[4] It is both the acceptance of the offer and an express condition precedent to A's duty to perform the promise to pay $100. What is an "express condition precedent?"

§ 11.2 Definition of a Condition

The basic concept of a condition is that it is an act or event that qualifies a promised performance. Thus, in the Brooklyn Bridge case, B's failure to walk the bridge is a failure of condition relieving A of the promise to pay. Traditionally, a condition is defined as an act or event other than a lapse of time, which, unless it is excused, affects a duty to render a promised performance.[1] The Restatement (Second) defines a condition as "an event, not certain to occur, which must occur, unless its non-occurrence is excused, before performance under a contract becomes due."[2]

The major difference in the two definitions is their scope. The first definition uses the words "*affects* a duty to render a promised performance." The second definition talks in terms of an event which must occur "*before* performance under a contract becomes due." The Restatement (Second) definition is limited to what is referred to below as a condition precedent.[3] The first definition is broad enough to include both a condition precedent and a condition subsequent.[4]

§ 11.1

1. Rs. 2d § 224 cmt c.

2. See § 2.10 supra.

3. See § 2.10 and n.1 supra.

4. See § 2.10.

§ 11.2

1. Rs. 1st § 250.

2. Rs. 2d § 224; First Nat. Bank v. National Bank, 249 Ga. 216, 290 S.E.2d 55 (1982).

3. See § 11.5 infra.

4. See § 11.5 and § 11.7 infra.

A better definition may be that a condition is an act or event, other than a lapse of time, which, unless the condition is excused, must occur before a duty to perform a contractual promise arises (condition precedent), or which discharges a duty of performance that has already arisen (condition subsequent). This definition has two merits. It covers both conditions precedent and conditions subsequent and suggests the basis for the distinction. Secondly, it makes it clear that a condition affects a contractual promise in some way.

Not all promises are conditional. A promise may be unconditional (independent, absolute). If on July 1, A promises to pay B $100 on July 15, A's promise is unconditional because the duty to perform arises after the time stated has elapsed, and lapse of time is not treated as a condition because it is looked on as an event certain to occur.[5] In contrast, a promise made on July 1, to pay $100 on July 15, if it rains on July 2, is by definition conditional.

§ 11.3 Classification of Conditions

Conditions may be classified in at least two different ways. One classification is based on the time when the conditioning event is to happen in relation to the promisor's duty to perform a promise. Under this classification, conditions are labeled as conditions precedent, conditions concurrent and conditions subsequent. A second classification is based on the manner in which the condition arises, that is, whether it is imposed by the parties or whether it is created by law. Under this division conditions are divided into express conditions and constructive conditions.

§ 11.4 The Time Classification

When conditions are divided into conditions precedent, concurrent and subsequent, these terms are used in relation to a particular moment when a duty to perform a particular promise in the agreement arises.[1] With this idea firmly in mind, we shall now briefly discuss each of the three categories.

§ 11.5 Conditions Precedent

A condition precedent is an act or event, other than a lapse of time, which must exist or occur before a duty to perform a promise arises.[1] If

5. Corbin, Conditions in the Law of Contract, 28 Yale L.Rev. 739, 742 (1919), Selected Readings 871, 874. This rationale is not entirely convincing. The writers are seemingly unanimous in this view that a mere lapse of time cannot be a condition. It is said that a condition must be "future and uncertain." Ashley, Conditions in Contract, 14 Yale L.J. 424, 425 (1905), Selected Readings 866, 867; see also Rs. 2d § 224 cmt b; 13 Williston § 381–38–2 (4th ed.). Consider, this term: "You may take possession on my death." All would agree that this term

makes death a condition. Yet, there is no uncertainty that death will occur.

§ 11.4
1. Harnett & Thornton, The Insurance Condition Subsequent, 17 Fordham L.Rev. 220 (1948).

§ 11.5
1. Internatio–Rotterdam v. River Brand Rice Mills, 259 F.2d 137 (2d Cir.1958), cert. denied; Ross v. Harding, 64 Wn.2d 231, 391 P.2d 526 (1964); Rs. 1st § 250(a).

the condition does not occur and is not excused, the promised performance need not be rendered.[2] For example, if A has promised for a consideration to pay B $100 if a specified ship arrives in port before a certain date, A's duty to pay does not arise unless and until the ship arrives. If the ship does not arrive within the time specified, A need not pay.

It should be stressed that in this chapter the term "condition" is ordinarily used to describe acts or events which must occur before a party is obliged to perform a promise made in an *existing contract*.[3] Such a situation must be distinguished from a condition precedent to the existence of a contract usually called a condition precedent to the formation of a contract. In that situation, the contract itself does not arise unless and until the condition occurs.[4] This means that each party is free to retreat from the transaction until the condition occurs and a contract is formed.[5]

This concept of a condition precedent to the formation of a contract has already been mentioned in connection with the parol evidence rule.[6] It is difficult in a concrete case to distinguish a condition precedent to the formation of a contract from a condition precedent to the performance of a contract.[7] This is because the distinction is highly artificial.[8]

It is also possible that in the case of a condition precedent to the *performance* of a contract, the event that operates as a condition may have occurred before or at the time of the formation of the contract.[9] For example, this could occur in the case of a marine policy that insures against a loss that already occurred at the time of contracting.[10]

§ 11.6 Concurrent Conditions

Concurrent conditions exist where the parties are to exchange performances at the same time.[1] It is conceivable that the law could provide that if neither party performed at the appointed time, each could sue the other. However, although this was the law initially, it was changed by the doctrine of constructive conditions—a topic to be discussed below.[2]

An illustration will help clarify the existing law. S agrees to sell and B agrees to buy a certain book at a fixed time and place. In the absence of an agreement to the contrary, payment and delivery are concurrent conditions. As a result, if B fails to tender the price, S must make conditional tender of the book or show that tender is excused, to put B in

2. Rs. 2d § 225(2).

3. See § 11.1 supra.

4. Hicks v. Bush, 10 N.Y.2d 488, 225 N.Y.S.2d 34, 180 N.E.2d 425 (1962).

5. Edmund J. Flynn v. Schlosser, 265 A.2d 599 (D.C.App.1970).

6. See § 3.7 supra.

7. See, e.g., M.K. Metals v. Container Recovery, 645 F.2d 583 (8th Cir.1981).

8. See § 3.7 supra.

9. Rs. 2d § 224 cmt b.

10. Rs. 2d § 224 cmt b.

§ 11.6

1. Rs. 1st § 251.

2. See ch. 11B infra.

default. The converse is also true. In order for B to put S in default, B must make conditional tender of the price or show that tender is excused.[3]

A concurrent condition is a particular kind of condition precedent.[4] In the illustration, unless tender is excused, a party must perform or tender performance *before* the party has a claim.[5] Concurrent conditions principally occur in contracts for the sale of goods[6] and contracts for the conveyance of land.[7]

§ 11.7 Conditions Subsequent

A condition subsequent is any event the existence of which, by agreement of the parties, discharges a duty of performance that has arisen.[1] For example, assume that an insurance company promises to pay up to $1 million to the insured if a fire occurs and if the insured files proof of loss within sixty days after the loss. The occurrence of the fire and the filing of the proof of loss with the insurance company are conditions precedent to the insurance company's performance of its promise to pay.[2] If these are the only two conditions precedent to the insurance company's obligation to pay, the company is obliged to pay on fulfillment of these conditions. The insurance company's failure to pay amounts to a breach.

However, the result would be different if the policy also provided that the insurer's obligation to pay is discharged if the insured fails to sue within one year of the filing of proofs of loss, and the insured did not sue within that time. This clause provides for a condition subsequent because the failure to sue within the time specified discharges a duty to pay that had already arisen.[3]

3. Vidal v. Transcontinental & Western Air, 120 F.2d 67 (3d Cir.1941); Rubin v. Fuchs, 1 Cal.3d 50, 81 Cal.Rptr. 373, 459 P.2d 925, (1969); Rs. 2d § 238 and cmt a; see Ocean Air Tradeways v. Arkay Realty, 480 F.2d 1112 (9th Cir.1973); McFadden v. Wilder, 6 Ariz.App. 60, 429 P.2d 694 (1967); 8 Corbin § 30.8; § 11.20 infra. Under the traditional notion of tender, the parties must be face to face. See Petterson v. Pattberg, 248 N.Y. 86, 161 N.E. 428 (1928). Under a more modern version, tender "as used in this connection means" "a readiness and willingness to perform in case of *concurrent* performance by the other party, with present ability to do so, and notice to the other party of such readiness." 6 Williston § 833 (3d ed.) quoted in Monroe St. Properties v. Carpenter, 407 F.2d 379 (9th Cir.1969). See also UCC § 2–503(1) (substantively unchanged in revision); See 13 Williston §§ 38:1–38:2 (4th ed.). On excuse of tender, see Owens v. Idaho First Nat. Bank, 103 Idaho 465, 649 P.2d 1221 (App. 1982).

4. Rs. 1st § 251.

5. Vidal v. Transcontinental & Western Air, 120 F.2d 67 (3d Cir.1941).

6. UCC §§ 2–503(1), 2–507, 2–511, 2–709.

7. It is possible for concurrent conditions to exist in a unilateral contract. For example A says to B, "If you pay me $50, I will give you my watch." B may condition tender of the $50 on the conditional tender of the watch. See Turner v. Goodwin, 92 Eng.Rep. 796 [K.B. 1711].

§ 11.7

1. Rs. 1st § 250.

2. Lawson v. American Motorists Ins., 217 F.2d 724 (5th Cir.1954); Harris v. North British & Mercantile Ins., 30 F.2d 94 (5th Cir.1929), cert. denied. For such a provision in an employment contract, see Inman v. Clyde Hall Drilling, 369 P.2d 498, 4 ALR3d 430 (Alaska 1962), 14 Syracuse L.Rev. 109 (1963).

3. Berman v. Palatine Ins., 379 F.2d 371 (7th Cir.1967); Barza v. Metropolitan Life

Conditions precedent are quite common while true conditions subsequent are very rare.[4] From a substantive point of view, the characterization of a condition as precedent or subsequent is not important. However, the distinction is procedurally important because it controls the burden of proof.[5] The party who wishes to sue on a promise has the burden of proving that the conditions precedent attached to that promise arose, otherwise there would be no breach of that promise.[6] A party claiming that a duty that has already arisen has been discharged has the burden of proof on that issue.

Thus, in the insurance illustration, the insured would have the burden of proving that a fire occurred and that proof of loss was given within sixty days. The insurer would have the burden on the question of whether the action has been duly commenced within one year.

The distinction between the different types of conditions is also a factor in the application of the parol evidence rule. While a condition precedent to formation of a written contract can be proved by parol, a condition subsequent cannot be so proved.[7]

Although true conditions subsequent are very rare, there are many cases that have treated what is by definition a condition precedent as a condition subsequent because the language used was in the form of a condition subsequent. An illustration is Gray v. Gardner.[8] Defendant

Ins., 281 Mich. 532, 275 N.W. 238, 112 ALR 1283 (1937). Although this characterization is made by the writers of law books and Restatements, the courts have not always labeled such a condition as a condition subsequent. E.g., Graham v. Niagara Fire Ins., 106 Ga. 840, 32 S.E. 579 (1899) (characterized as condition precedent); see Harnett and Thornton, § 11.4 n.1. A condition subsequent creates affirmative defense and this provision is similar in operation to the defense of statute of limitations.

In some jurisdictions contractual clauses curtailing the statute of limitations are invalid, see Annot., 112 ALR 1288 (1938), or regulated by Statute. E.g., McKinney's N.Y.Ins.Law §§ 164(3)(A)(11), 168(6). But such clauses frequently are utilized even outside the insurance field and are generally upheld. Soviero Bros. Contracting v. New York, 286 A.D. 435, 142 N.Y.S.2d 508 (1955), aff'd; Rs. 1st § 218; 4 Williston § 8:37 (4th ed.). The UCC regulates such clauses, allowing a reduction to not less than one year. § 2–725(1).

4. Kindler v. Anderson, 433 P.2d 268 (Wyo.1967).

5. Holmes, The Common Law, 316–318 (1881).

6. That this is sometimes a matter of great importance is demonstrated by McGowin v. Menken, 223 N.Y. 509, 119

N.E. 877, 5 ALR 794 (1918), in which the executor of the wife was unable to show that the wife survived when the husband and wife perished in a common disaster. Formerly, the party to whom the duty is owed (usually the plaintiff) also had the burden of alleging the occurrence of all conditions precedent. Shipman, Common Law Pleading 246–49 (3d ed.1923). Under Code pleading, a general allegation of due compliance with all conditions precedent is generally sufficient. Clark, Code Pleading 280–82 (2d ed.1947); 5 Williston § 674 (3d ed.). Under modern procedural enactments even this requirement is dispensed with. The simplification of pleading requirements does not, however, change the burden of proof. Although the burden is placed on the defendant to deny the occurrence of a condition precedent, once the defendant has made the denial, the burden is placed on the plaintiff to prove its occurrence. Fed. R.Civ.Pro. 9(c); McKinney's N.Y.C.P.L.R. 3015. To the effect that allocation of the burden of proof is not automatically turned by the traditional rule stated here, see McCormick on Evidence § 337 (4th ed. 1992) (enumerating policy factors).

7. Gottlieb v. Cinema Equities, 30 N.Y.2d 553, 330 N.Y.S.2d 613, 281 N.E.2d 556 (1972).

8. 17 Mass. 188 (1821). For additional facts in this case, see Nyquist, A Contract

promised to pay 60 cents per gallon for oil that had been delivered, and also promised to pay an additional 25 cents per gallon in the future with a proviso. The second promise would be void if a greater quantity of oil should arrive in whaling vessels at Nantucket and New Bedford on or before the first day of April and the first day of October both inclusive, than had arrived at these ports within the same time the previous year.

Two points are clear. The first promise was unconditional and the second promise was not to be performed if a greater quantity of oil arrived during the specified period. The non-arrival of a greater quantity of oil during the specified period was, by definition, a condition precedent to defendant's obligation to perform the second promise.[9] However, the court decided that the condition was a condition subsequent primarily because the word "void" suggests that a duty that has already arisen is being discharged.

Whether this was a condition precedent or a condition subsequent was important on the issue of burden of proof, because there was a conflict in the evidence on the issue of whether a certain vessel arrived at Nantucket on October 1, 1819. Since the court found that the condition was subsequent, the burden of proof on this issue was placed on the defendant.

Conditions subsequent in form but precedent by definition are particularly common in insurance policies and surety bonds, e.g., bail bonds. In these cases, perhaps more often than not, courts will, for purposes of pleading and burden of proof, treat the condition as if it were a condition subsequent. There is no universal consistency and a good deal of subtlety has gone into the refinements of the problem,[10] without, however, resulting in any satisfactory resolution.[11]

At times what is by definition a condition precedent is treated as a condition subsequent, so that the burden of proof is placed on the party with better access to the facts.[12] Such treatment may be called a "functional" approach.

Although the Restatement (Second) disapproves of the term "condition subsequent" as confusing, it follows the basic notions but not the vocabulary used here.[13]

Tale from the Crypt, 30 Hous.L.Rev. 1205 (1993).

9. Rs. 2d § 227 cmt d and ill. 13.

10. 13 Williston §§ 38:10, 38:26 (4th ed.); see Clark, Code Pleading 280–83 (2d ed.1947). Parol evidence may illuminate whether a condition is precedent or subsequent. Loyal Erectors v. Hamilton & Son, 312 A.2d 748 (Me.1973).

11. Compare, 8 Corbin §§ 39:11–39:13 (McCauliff 1999) with the authorities in the preceding note. Corbin appears to argue that, unless social policy dictates another conclusion, the burden of proof should be allocated in accordance with whether or not the condition is a true condition subsequent and that the form in which the condition is couched should be disregarded.

12. Buick Motor v. Thompson, 138 Ga. 282, 75 S.E. 354 (1912); Esterces & Assocs. v. Coastal Communications, 271 A.D.2d 286, 707 N.Y.S.2d 62 (2000); but see Tallman Pools v. Fellner, 160 Ga.App. 722, 288 S.E.2d 46 (1981).

13. Rs. 2d § 224 cmt e & ill. 8. The Restatement adds that as a matter of interpretation there should be a preference in favor of a condition precedent rather than a

§ 11.8 The Other Classification of Conditions

Another way to classify conditions is based on how the condition arises. Express conditions are created by agreement of the parties.[1] In contrast constructive conditions are imposed by law to do justice. These are sometimes called conditions implied in law.[2]

In addition to conditions implied in law (constructive conditions), there are also conditions implied in fact. Such a condition is treated as an express condition. However, an implied in fact condition is not spelled out in words but rather is "gathered from the terms of the contract as a matter of interpretation."[3]

The distinction between express conditions and implied in fact conditions is not terribly important. The same general rule applies to both—the condition must be strictly complied with.[4] Since there is no difference in consequences, implied in fact conditions and conditions set forth in words are both denominated as express (true) conditions.[5]

The dividing line between an express condition (especially implied in fact conditions) and constructive conditions is often quite indistinct.[6] Yet, the distinction is often of crucial importance. The general rule governing an express condition, is that it must be strictly performed. The general rule as to constructive conditions is that substantial compliance is sufficient.[7] This distinction and its ramifications are pursued in the sections that follow.

§ 11.9 Express Conditions and Promises Compared

The distinction between a condition and a promise is critical. While failure to perform a promise, unless excused, is a breach, failure to comply with a condition is not a breach. For example, A says to B, "If you walk across the Brooklyn Bridge I will pay you $100." B's walking the Bridge is an express condition precedent to A's obligation to pay. If B does not fully perform (and performance is not excused), A will not be obliged to pay. The general rule is that an express condition must be strictly complied with,[1] but if B does not walk the Bridge, B will not be liable because B did not promise to walk.[2] One cannot be liable for breach of contract unless one breaches a *promise.*

condition subsequent. Rs. 2d § 227(3) and cmt e.

§ 11.8

1. Rs. 1st § 252; Corbin, Conditions in the Law of Contracts, 28 Yale L.J. 739 (1919).

2. Rs. 1st § 253; Rs. 2d § 226 cmt c.

3. Costigan, The Performance of Contracts 50 (2d ed. 1927). For an illustration of an implied in fact condition, see Cadwell v. Blake, 72 Mass. (6 Gray) 402 (1856) where an obligation to instruct in the art of making paper was treated as an implied in fact condition to the duty to pay in paper.

4. Jungmann & Co. v. Atterbury Bros., 249 N.Y. 119, 163 N.E. 123 (1928); Ram Dev. v. Siuslaw Enterprises, 283 Or. 13, 580 P.2d 552 (1978).

5. Rs. 1st § 258.

6. 13 Williston, § 38:11 (4th ed.).

7. See § 11.18(b) infra.

§ 11.9

1. See § 11.8 supra.

2. U.S. v. O'Brien, 220 U.S. 321 (1911); Hale v. Finch, 104 U.S. (14 Otto) 261 (1881); Arizona Land Title & Trust v. Safe-

Suppose, instead, A had said to B, I promise to pay you $100 if you promise to walk the Bridge and provided you in fact walk the Bridge. B promises. We have the same express condition, but, in addition, B has made a promise to walk the Bridge. If B does not walk, A need not pay the $100 because B has failed to comply with the express condition precedent to A's promise to pay. In addition, since B has made a promise to walk the Bridge, B will be liable for breach of the promise.

In these illustrations, the conditions and the promises are clearly labeled. Often, however, it is difficult to tell whether particular language is language of promise or language of condition. The result in a particular case is a matter of the intention of the parties,[9] and all of the rules of interpretation apply.[1]

In a borderline case, the courts prefer the interpretation that particular language is language of promise rather than language of condition.[5] In one case,[6] the parties entered into an agreement whereby plaintiff agreed to do certain work for the defendant and defendant agreed to pay a fixed amount and to reimburse plaintiff for labor costs over 4 cents per square foot. Provisions in the contract stated that plaintiff would furnish defendant with an itemized cost breakdown. This was not done. Had furnishing the cost breakdown been looked on as an express condition precedent to defendant's promise to pay additional labor costs, defendant would not have been obliged to pay these costs because the express condition was not performed. If the language was a promise on the part of plaintiff to furnish itemized costs, the plaintiff would be guilty of a breach of this promise but this would not defeat plaintiff's claim because the breach would be immaterial.[7]

The court relied on the presumption in favor of finding that the language in question is language of promise and added that the presumption is particularly strong when a finding that there is a condition and not a promise would lead to a forfeiture on the part of a party who has done the work.[8]

way Stores, 6 Ariz.App. 52, 429 P.2d 686 (1967).

3. Cramer v. Metropolitan S. & L. Ass'n, 401 Mich. 252, 258 N.W.2d 20 (1977), cert. denied; Partlow v. Mathews, 43 Wn.2d 398, 261 P.2d 394 (1953).

4. Rs. 2d § 226 cmt b and § 227; Rs. 1st § 258; Chirichella v. Erwin, 270 Md. 178, 310 A.2d 555 (1973).

5. Sahadi v. Continental Ill. Natl. Bank & Trust, 706 F.2d 193 (7th Cir.1983); Howard et al. v. Federal Crop Ins., 540 F.2d 695 (4th Cir.1976); Home Sav. Assoc. v. Tappan, 403 F.2d 201 (5th Cir.1968); N.Y. Bronze Powder v. Benjamin Acquisition, 351 Md. 8, 716 A.2d 230 (1998); Rs. 1st § 261; Rs. 2d § 227(2) and cmt d. The First Restatement also set forth a presumptive test based on whose words are being interpreted. If they purport to be the words of the party to do

the act they are presumed to be language of promise. If they purport to be the words of the party who is not to do the act, then they are language of condition. Rs. 1st § 260. This rule, which was helpful only in special contexts, was not included in the Second Restatement. Rs. 2d § 227.

6. Pacific Allied v. Century Steel Prods., 162 Cal.App.2d 70, 327 P.2d 547 (1958); but see A.H.A. General Constr. v. N.Y.C. Housing Authority, 92 N.Y.2d 20, 699 N.E.2d 368, 677 N.Y.S.2d 9 (1998) (provision was assumed to be a condition).

7. See § 11.18(b) infra.

8. Forfeiture, as used here, goes beyond the concept of divestiture of property. It also includes a situation where a party loses the "right to an agreed exchange after he has relied substantially on the expectation

§ 11.10　Conditions Compared to Time References

In a recurring fact pattern, a general contractor agrees to pay a sub-contractor "as money is received from the owner" or language to that effect. The subcontractor completes the work, but the owner fails to pay the general contractor. The question is whether the term creates an express condition or merely sets the time of payment.[1] If it is a condition, the subcontractor is not entitled to payment, because the condition has not been met. Some cases have concluded it is language of condition.[2] Others have concluded that language does not create a condition; it is language of time. According to these courts, the language is intended to set a convenient time for payment and if the event does not occur then the obligation is to pay within a reasonable time.[3]

The question is one of interpretation. Most of the modern cases lean to the view that this is not an express condition and, in the absence of extrinsic evidence to the contrary, reach the conclusion that, as a matter of law, a clause of this kind refers merely to the time of payment.[4] Some courts have ruled that a condition to the effect a contractor will pay the subcontractor when the owner pays the contractor is void because it is against the legislative policy promulgated in mechanics' lien statutes,[5] but others give effect to a clearly worded "pay when paid" condition.[6]

The notion behind the modern view is that when personal services are rendered it will not lightly be assumed that payment is contingent on the happening of an event outside the control of the party rendering services.[7] If, however, the services are of a kind that are frequently rendered on a contingent fee basis, the result will be otherwise. Thus, a promise to pay a brokerage commission "on closing of title" will be held to be expressly conditioned on the closing of title.[8]

A large number of cases are concerned with the interpretation of a promise to pay "when able." Although there is said to be a "majority

of that exchange, as by preparation for performance." Rs. 2d § 227 cmt b.

§ 11.10

1. See Rs. 2d § 227.

2. J.J. Shane, Inc. v. Aetna Cas. & Sur., 723 So.2d 302 (Fla.App.1998) (unambiguous expression of intention); Mascioni v. I.B. Miller, 261 N.Y. 1, 184 N.E. 473 (1933) (parol evidence showed that this was the intent).

3. North Am. Graphite v. Allan, 184 F.2d 387 (D.C.Cir.1950); De Wolfe v. French, 51 Me. 420 (1864); Grossman Steel and Aluminum v. Samson Window, 54 N.Y.2d 653, 442 N.Y.S.2d 769, 426 N.E.2d 176 (1981).

4. Main Elec. v. Printz Serv., 980 P.2d 522 (Colo.1999); Brown & Kerr v. St. Paul Fire & Marine Ins., 940 F.Supp. 1245

(N.D.Ill.1996); Mignot v. Parkhill, 237 Or. 450, 391 P.2d 755 (1964); Rs. 2d § 227 cmt b ills. 1 and 2.

5. Wm. R. Clarke v. Safeco Ins., 15 Cal.4th 882, 64 Cal.Rptr.2d 578, 938 P.2d 372 (1997); West–Fair Elec. Contractors v. Aetna Cas. & Sur., 87 N.Y.2d 148, 638 N.Y.S.2d 394, 661 N.E.2d 967 (1995); accord, Brown & Kerr, in the previous note (dictum).

6. J.J. Shane, Inc. v. Aetna Cas. & Sur., 723 So.2d 302 (Fla.App.1998). Where the language of condition is unclear, enforcement is withheld. Koch v. Construction Technology, 924 S.W.2d 68 (Tenn.1996).

7. Harry W. Applegate, Inc. v. Stature Elec., Inc., 275 F.3d 486 (6th Cir.2001) (sales commission).

8. Amies v. Wesnofske, 255 N.Y. 156, 174 N.E. 436, 73 ALR 918 (1931).

rule," interpreting this language as language of condition,[9] and a "minority rule" interpreting such language as a promise that payment will be made in a reasonable time,[10] it is likely that many of the seemingly conflicting cases can be reconciled if it is realized that in each case the language must be interpreted in its verbal and factual context. If, as is often the case, the promise to pay "when able" is a new promise to pay a debt that otherwise would be barred by operation of law, it is gratuitous, and interpretation of the language as a condition would seem to be justified.[11] Similarly, if a major stockholder renders services to the corporation on the understanding that the services will be paid for "as the financial condition of the corporation permits out of profits," it can readily be inferred from the relationship of the parties that the corporation's promise was intended to be conditional.[12] Where, however, the promise is to pay for services rendered to strangers, goods delivered, or property conveyed, in the absence of special circumstances, it would be reasonable to assume that the promisee intended no more than to allow the promisor a reasonable time in which to effectuate payment.[13]

In drafting a contract, a party who wishes to obtain the benefits of the rule of strict compliance with an express condition should use clear language of express condition. Thus, a provision of a contract stating that filing of a notice of claim with the other contracting party within thirty days after any claim arises "shall be a condition precedent to recovery" creates an express condition precedent in the most explicit fashion.[14] As a rule of thumb, provisions commencing with words such as "if,"[15] "on condition that,"[16] "subject to,"[17] and "provided"[18] create conditions precedent.[19] However, this result cannot be guaranteed because of the presumption in favor of language of promise and because all language requires interpretation.[20]

9. Zane v. Mavrides, 394 So.2d 197 (Fla. App.1981).

10. See 14 Williston § 42:9 (4th ed); Annot., 94 ALR 721 (1935). A promise to pay "when able to effect a sale" requires the promisor to bring the event about or pay within a reasonable time. Duncan Box & Lumber v. Sargent, 126 W.Va. 1, 27 S.E.2d 68, 148 ALR 1072 (1943); see 8 Corbin § 31.3 (McCauliff 1999). Some cases take an intermediate position, holding that the promisor is obligated at least to use reasonable efforts to become able to pay.

11. Tebo v. Robinson, 100 N.Y. 27, 2 N.E. 383 (1885).

12. Booth v. Booth & Bayliss Comm. School, 120 Conn. 221, 180 A. 278, 99 ALR 1517 (1935).

13. Sanford v. Luce, 245 Iowa 74, 60 N.W.2d 885 (1953) (construction work); Mock v. Trustees of First Baptist Church,

252 Ky. 243, 67 S.W.2d 9, 94 ALR 716 (1934) (architectural services).

14. Inman v. Clyde Hall Drilling, 369 P.2d 498 (Alaska 1962).

15. Guerrette v. Cheetham, 289 Mass. 240, 193 N.E. 836 (1935).

16. Hale v. Finch, 104 U.S. (14 Otto) 261 (1881).

17. Rubin v. Fuchs, 1 Cal.3d 50, 81 Cal. Rptr. 373, 459 P.2d 925 (1969); Barbara Oil v. Patrick Petroleum, 1 Kan.App.2d 437, 566 P.2d 389 (1977).

18. Goodwin v. Jacksonville Gas, 302 F.2d 355 (5th Cir.1962); Hamilton Constr. v. Board of Public Inst., 65 So.2d 729 (Fla. 1953).

19. Rs. 2d § 226 cmt a.

20. See, e.g., Southern Sur. v. MacMillan, 58 F.2d 541 (10th Cir.1932).

§ 11.11 Language of Condition May Imply a Promise

Not only is it difficult to determine whether particular language is language of condition or language of promise (discussed immediately above), but the problem is further complicated because express language of condition may in addition be implied language of promise[1] (discussed in this section). The converse is also true. Express language of promise may give rise to an implied in fact or constructive condition (to be discussed in the next two sections).

To illustrate, A and B enter into a contract for the sale and purchase of real property. The contract contains a clause that performance is "contingent on B obtaining" a described mortgage loan.[2] The phrase in the quotation is language of condition. B is not obliged to perform[3] if the financing is not obtained after reasonable efforts.[4] However this would be the result only if B fails to obtain the financing after reasonable efforts. B has impliedly promised to use reasonable efforts to cause the condition to occur.[5] Failure to use such efforts would be a breach of contract.[6]

The issue of control is important. In the same transaction, if B conditioned the promise on the Dow Jones average reaching 12,000 at some point between the time of signing the contract and the time for performance, B would not be bound to perform if the condition did not arise and in addition, B is not impliedly promising to use reasonable

§ 11.11

1. Rs. 2d § 225(3) cmt d; Rs. 1st § 257; Stewart v. Griffith, 217 U.S. 323 (1910); Green County v. Quinlan, 211 U.S. 582, 29 S.Ct. 162, 53 L.Ed. 335 (1909); Shakey's Inc. v. Covalt, 704 F.2d 426 (9th Cir.1983); Western Hills v. Pfau, 265 Or. 137, 508 P.2d 201 (1973).

2. If the loan terms are not sufficiently described there could be an indefiniteness problem. See, e.g., Aiken, 43 Marq.L.Rev. 265 (1960).

3. Although the clause is a condition precedent to B's obligation to proceed with the underlying contract, it is not a condition precedent to A's obligation to proceed if B was ready, willing and able to tender the money even though B did not obtain the mortgage loan. De Freitas v. Cote, 342 Mass. 474, 477, 174 N.E.2d 371, 373 (1961). In other words the condition is for the benefit of B only and B alone may waive it. Rs. 2d § 226 ill. 4; see § 11.30.

A slightly different question is presented in such a case if, when B is unable to obtain a mortgage loan, A offers to take a purchase money mortgage from B to finance B's purchase. The vendee was held to be under a duty to accept the purchase money mortgage financing in Marino v. Nolan, 24 A.D.2d 1005, 266 N.Y.S.2d 65 (1965), aff'd,

but in Glassman v. Gerstein, 10 A.D.2d 875, 200 N.Y.S.2d 690 (1960), the vendee was held not to be obliged to accept such financing because the contract language referred to obtaining a loan from a "lending institution." See also Simms v. Wolverton, 232 Or. 291, 375 P.2d 87 (1962); but see Kovarik v. Vesely, 3 Wis.2d 573, 89 N.W.2d 279 (1958).

4. Sheldon Builders v. Trojan Towers, 255 Cal.App.2d 781, 63 Cal.Rptr. 425 (1967); Mecham v. Nelson, 92 Idaho 783, 451 P.2d 529 (1969); cf. Lane v. Elwood Estates, 28 N.Y.2d 620, 320 N.Y.S.2d 79, 268 N.E.2d 805 (1971). In this situation the vendor does not suffer a forfeiture as that term is defined in § 11.35. Although the vendor may be deprived of an expectancy interest, there is no unjust enrichment and there is no reliance injury. See § 11.10 n.8.

5. Lach v. Cahill, 138 Conn. 418, 85 A.2d 481 (1951); Eggan v. Simonds, 34 Ill. App.2d 316, 181 N.E.2d 354 (1962); Carlton v. Smith, 285 Ill.App. 380, 2 N.E.2d 116 (1936). But see Paul v. Rosen, 3 Ill.App.2d 423, 122 N.E.2d 603 (1954).

6. Internatio–Rotterdam v. River Brand Rice Mills, 259 F.2d 137 (2d Cir.1958), cert. denied. See generally Patterson, Constructive Conditions in Contracts, 42 Colum.L.Rev. 903, 928–42 (1942).

efforts to cause the condition to occur.[7] In the mortgage illustration, it was within B's control to use reasonable efforts to obtain the loan; but in the case involving the Dow Jones average, it was not in B's power to cause the average to rise to 12,000. A related question is discussed in § 11.28.

§ 11.12 A Promise May Create an Implied or Constructive Condition

In modern times, the performance of a promise may be an implied or constructive condition.[1] That was not true at early common law when the English courts were very literal minded. If a contract contained only language of promise, the court would say that no conditions were present. If S agreed to sell and B agreed to buy 100 cases of apples, S without tendering performance could sue B for breach. Conversely, B without tendering performance could sue S.[2] Finally in the late 1700's the courts held that such express mutual promises gave rise to constructive concurrent conditions.[3] This means that, although the contract does not expressly condition either party's promise on performance by the other, the law, to do justice, constructs a condition that performance, or tender of performance, by one party is a condition precedent to the liability of the other.[4] At first, the courts called such conditions "implied," but modern courts realize that often such conditions were not contemplated by the parties, but are constructed by the courts in the interests of justice. Constructive conditions are discussed in more detail below.[5]

§ 11.13 Constructive Conditions and Implied in Fact Conditions

Courts prefer to find constructive conditions rather than implied in fact conditions.[1] The reason is that, as we saw in § 11.8, implied in fact conditions are treated the same way as express conditions and therefore the general rule with respect to these conditions is that they must be strictly performed. Constructive conditions need only be substantially performed. The doctrine of substantial performance is a more flexible instrument for justice than a rule that requires literal compliance.

Constructive conditions and implied in fact conditions are difficult to distinguish as both ordinarily arise from language of promise. The courts

---

7. Connor v. Rockwood, 320 Mass. 360, 69 N.E.2d 454 (1946); Simpson, Contracts 307.

§ 11.12

1. See § 11.8. At times, a constructive condition may be imposed by law unrelated to language of promise. See Hadden v. Consolidated Edison, 34 N.Y.2d 88, 356 N.Y.S.2d 249, 312 N.E.2d 445 (1974).

2. Nichols v. Raynbred, 80 Eng.Rep. 238 (K.B. 1615).

3. See § 11.6 supra, which anticipated this discussion.

4. Kingston v. Preston, Lofft 194, 2 Doug. 684 (K.B.1773). See § 11.6 supra.

5. See 11B infra.

§ 11.13

1. Gold Bond Stamp v. Gilt–Edge Stamps, 437 F.2d 27 (5th Cir.1971); Orkin Exterminating v. Harris, 224 Ga. 759, 164 S.E.2d 727 (1968).

are becoming more and more inclined to limit implied in fact conditions to situations involving cooperation. Where A's promise is incapable of performance unless B performs, B's performance is an implied in fact condition to A's duty to perform.[2] For example, assume A promised to paint B's house and B promised to supply the paint. By the terms of the contract, A cannot perform without B supplying the paint Thus, supplying the paint is an implied in fact condition to A's duty to paint.

§ 11.14 Constructive Promises—Omitted Terms

Courts construct promises as well as conditions.[1] The topic of omitted terms was discussed in Chapter 3[2] and in the discussion of indefiniteness,[3] and will also be mentioned in the chapter on Impracticability and Frustration.[4] All of these matters, including constructive conditions, can be subsumed under the heading of "omitted terms," a phrase designed to convey the notion that, when parties fail to cover a term, the court, in the interests of justice, may supply a term.[5]

To illustrate: A wrote a book and sold the right to use the book to B as the basis of a play. Before the play was produced, talking pictures were invented and A sold the rights to use the book as the basis of a movie. The court constructed a promise that A would not grant "talkie" rights as this would destroy the value of the license that A had granted to B.[6] Omitted terms are often supplied by looking through the lens of the covenant of good faith and fair dealing.[7] Even though a constructive promise is created by a court to do justice, once it is created by the court it is a full fledged promise; its operation is not in any way diminished by the fact that it is a constructive promise. A judgment for a large sum was entered against A.

§ 11.15 Distinguishing Between Express and Constructive Conditions

We have already adverted to the importance of the distinction between an express (including an implied in fact) condition and a constructive condition. An express condition must be strictly performed while a constructive condition need only be substantially performed.[1] We have also adverted to the fact that very often it is difficult to determine

2. 8 Corbin § 31.2 (McCauliff 1999); Rs. 2d § 226 cmt c; Mainieri v. Magnuson, 126 Cal.App.2d 426, 272 P.2d 557 (1954); Cadwell v. Blake, 72 Mass. (6 Gray) 402 (1856).

§ 11.14

1. See § 4.12 supra.

2. See § 3.14 supra.

3. See § 2.9 supra.

4. See Ch. 13 infra.

5. See Farnsworth, Disputes over Omission in Contracts, 68 Colum.L.Rev. 860 (1968).

6. Kirke La Shelle v. Paul Armstrong, 263 N.Y. 79, 188 N.E. 163 (1933). According to Rs. 2d § 204 cmt d, when constructing an omitted promise "the court should supply a term which comports with community standards of fairness and policy rather than analyze a hypothetical model of the bargaining process."

7. Oregon RSA No. 6 v. Castle Rock Cellular, 840 F.Supp. 770 (D.Or.1993); see § 11.38.

§ 11.15

1. See § 11.8 supra.

whether particular language is language of express condition or language of promise, or both.[2] The purpose of this section is to show the results that follow in a concrete case once this determination has been made. It also introduces the concepts of material breach and substantial performance.

Assume that A is the owner in possession of a vessel in England. In a bilateral contract A agrees to charter the vessel to B who is in the U.S. A agrees to supply the vessel and B to pay for it when it arrives. The critical clause in the agreement is: "The vessel to sail from England on or before the 4th day of February." The vessel did not sail by the 4th but sailed on the 5th.[3]

The quoted language is ambiguous as to its intended legal effect. It could be interpreted in three ways, 1) as an express condition to B's obligation to pay, 2) as a promise by A to cause the vessel to sail on or before the 4th, and 3) both as an express condition to B's obligation to pay and as a promise by A to cause the vessel to sail by the 4th.[4]

The interpretation of the ambiguous clause governs the legal position of the parties. If the clause is interpreted as an express condition to B's obligation to pay, B would be free not to proceed with the contract because as a general proposition an express condition must be strictly complied with.[5] At the same time, A would not be liable for breach of contract because by hypothesis A has not made a promise to cause the vessel to sail by February 4th.[6]

If the term was not a condition but a promise that was breached by the late sailing, the question becomes whether the breach is a material one. If the breach is found to be material, B would be free not to proceed but also could sue for a total breach or could elect to continue with the contract and hold A liable for a partial breach.[7] If the breach is immaterial, B would be required to perform and could only assert a claim for a partial breach.[8]

Whether an aggrieved party can withhold partial payment for the other's partial breach is a matter about which there are differences of opinion. Withholding is authorized by the UCC,[9] and some common law cases,[10] but at least one prominent court in a non-UCC case has regarded

---

2. See §§ 11.9 and 11.12 supra.

3. The fact pattern is suggested by Glaholm v. Hayes, 133 Eng.Rep. 743 (C.P. 1841).

4. As suggested above, the preferred interpretation would be that this was language of promise. However, for reasons we need not now consider, the court decided that sailing by the 4th was an express condition; therefore B was justified in canceling the contract.

5. B could elect to continue with the contract by waiving the condition. See § 11.32.

6. Contract liability is based solely on breaches of promises. The failure to per-

form a condition has other consequences. For example, it may discharge the duty of the other party to the contract.

7. See § 11.18(a).

8. Phillips & Colby Constr. v. Seymour, 91 U.S. (1 Otto) 646 (1875). This is the terminology adopted by the Restatement (Second). See Reporter's Notes to § 236. See 11.18(a).

9. UCC § 2–717, substantially unchanged in the revision.

10. E.g., K & G Constr. v. Harris, 223 Md. 305, 164 A.2d 451 (1960); see Comment, 62 Fordham L.Rev. 163 (1993).

such self-help as a material breach,[11] a decision bereft of commercial reality.

What if A sued B for breach when B refused to take the vessel because it sailed one day late? Under the assumption that sailing by February 4 was not an express condition, the case should be approached under the doctrine of constructive conditions. A is to perform before B is to perform and, therefore, A's performance is a constructive condition precedent to B's obligation to pay.[12] The question, then, is whether A has tendered substantial performance of the contract. If A has, A is entitled to any payment that is due less any damages B may have incurred because of the late sailing.[13]

Substantial performance and material breach are often opposite sides of the same coin. If a party has substantially performed, it follows that any breach by the party is immaterial. Conversely, if a party has committed a material breach, any performance by the party cannot be substantial. Thus, the way in which the issue is stated is usually not of great importance, but the distinction is important for clarity of thought.[14] Generally speaking, there are two scenarios where the distinction will arise. If the plaintiff claims that plaintiff has performed, the issue is substantial performance, but if plaintiff claims justification in not performing because of a breach by the defendant, the issue is whether the defendant is guilty of a material breach.[15]

The principal reason for distinguishing between material breach and substantial performance is breach by delay. Assume a contract to convey Blackacre on February 4th. The vendor is unprepared to convey on that date, but will be able to tender performance on the 5th. On the 4th the vendor has not substantially performed, but in the usual case will not have materially breached.[16]

B. CONSTRUCTIVE CONDITIONS AND RELATED TOPICS

Table of Sections

---

11. ARP Films v. Marvel Entertainment Group, 952 F.2d 643 (2d Cir.1991).

12. See § 11.18(b).

13. See § 11.18(b).

14. Rs. 2d § 237 cmt d.

15. Austin v. Parker, 672 F.2d 508 (5th Cir.1982).

16. See § 11.18 infra.

§ 11.16 Introduction

Constructive conditions are created by courts in order to do justice.[1] They are constructed in bilateral contracts.[2] In bilateral contracts, the parties exchange promises with the understanding that there will also be an exchange of performances.[3] This is true even when the performances are not to be exchanged simultaneously.[4] Bilateral contracts are presumed to involve promises exchanged for an exchange of performance and thus, involve constructive conditions of exchange.[5]

Where promises are exchanged looking toward an exchange of performances, the failure of one party to perform may have an effect on the obligation of the other party to perform. If the parties have not agreed to express conditions covering the matter, that effect is expressed in terms of constructive conditions. Constructive conditions also determine, for example, the order of performance in a bilateral contract, whether one party's performance of some but not all of the promises undertaken entitles that party to performance by the other party, what effect failure or delay in performing by one party has on the rights and duties of the other party, and the effect of present or prospective inability or unwillingness to perform. Most of these matters and others are discussed in the sections that follow and will help clarify the concepts discussed in this section. The question of prospective inability or unwillingness is discussed in Ch. 12.

§ 11.17 Order of Performance in a Bilateral Contract

In a bilateral contract, the parties often neglect to state the order in which their promises are to be performed. Constructive conditions fill these gaps.[1] Fortunately the way in which these gaps are filled is based on common sense, or at least the average person is familiar with them by reason of business experience.

§ 11.16

1. See § 11.8 supra.

2. See § 11.12 supra. The fact that express conditions are also present in the contract does not prevent constructive conditions from arising. Rs. 2d § 231 cmt c.

3. Rs. 2d & its Ch. 10 Introductory Note.

4. Rs. 2d § 231 cmt b.

5. Rs. 2d § 231 cmt a and its Ch. 10 Introductory Note. The first Restatement used the term "promises for an agreed exchange." Rs. 1st § 266.

§ 11.17

1. Rochester Distilling v. Geloso, 92 Conn. 43, 101 A. 500 (1917).

The first and simplest rule is that, unless otherwise agreed,[2] a party who is to perform work over an extended period of time must substantially perform before becoming entitled to payment.[3] Performance of the work is a constructive condition precedent to the duty to pay. Periodic payments are not implied.[4]

If, however, periodic payments have been agreed on, a different situation is presented. A series of alternating constructive conditions precedent exist. Performance is a constructive condition precedent to the first periodic payment, and the first payment is a condition precedent to the next stage of the work, and so on.[5]

Assume a case where defendant makes a contract with plaintiff for the erection of 19 houses on the defendant's land. There is an agreement for progress payments according to a formula. Plaintiff finishes a portion of the work and defendant, without any justification, fails to pay the amount allotted to the installment. This failure gives rise to two separate questions: is plaintiff justified in suspending performance, and, if so, would the plaintiff also be justified in canceling the contract?[6] The answer to the first question is, yes. The answer to the second question depends on an additional factor: whether and at what point there exists an uncured material breach.[7] The moment at which a failure to pay becomes a material breach is ordinarily a question of fact.[8]

Where the promised acts are capable of simultaneous performance, unless otherwise agreed, each duty of performance is constructively conditioned on conditional tender of the other.[9] The primary application of this rule is in contracts for the sale of personal or real property.[10] In

2. Clark v. Gulesian, 197 Mass. 492, 84 N.E. 94 (1908).

3. Bright v. Ganas, 171 Md. 493, 189 A. 427, 109 ALR 467 (1937) (for years of faithful performance plaintiff was to receive $20,000 out of employer's estate, but with employer on his death bed plaintiff wrote a love letter to employer's wife, i.e., was unfaithful and thus there was not substantial performance); Coletti v. Knox Hat, 252 N.Y. 468, 472, 169 N.E. 648, 649 (1930) ("when the performance of a contract consists in doing (faciendo) on one side, and in giving (dando) on the other side, the doing must take place before the giving."); Rs. 2d § 234(2) and cmt e. This rule arises primarily in service contracts such as employment and construction contracts. Id. § 234 cmt f; Rs. 1st § 270.

4. Smoll v. Webb, 55 Cal.App.2d 456, 130 P.2d 773 (1942); Le Bel v. McCoy, 314 Mass. 206, 49 N.E.2d 888 (1943); Kelly Constr. v. Hackensack Brick, 91 N.J.L. 585, 103 A. 417, 2 ALR 685 (1918); Stewart v. Newbury, 220 N.Y. 379, 115 N.E. 984, 2 ALR 519 (1917).

5. Guerini Stone v. P.J. Carlin Constr., 248 U.S. 334 (1919); K & G Constr. v.

Harris, 223 Md. 305, 164 A.2d 451 (1960); Turner Concrete Steel v. Chester Constr. & Contracting, 271 Pa. 205, 114 A. 780 (1921); Pelletier v. Masse, 49 R.I. 408, 143 A. 609 (1928). The same is true of a divisible contract. Rs. 1st § 272 ill. 2. But see Palmer v. Watson Constr., 265 Minn. 195, 121 N.W.2d 62 (1963); Zulla Steel v. A & M Gregos, 174 N.J.Super. 124, 415 A.2d 1183 (A.D.1980).

6. Rs. 1st § 276 ill. 5; Harton v. Hildebrand, 230 Pa. 335, 79 A. 571 (1911); Rs. 2d § 237 ill. 1.

7. See § 11.18(a) infra.

8. 9 Corbin § 35.6 (McCauliff 1999); Darrell J. Didericksen & Sons v. Magna Water, 613 P.2d 1116 (Utah 1980).

9. Rs. 2d § 234(1). The rule also applies where simultaneous performances are possible in part. Id. §§ 233(2), 234 and cmt b.

10. Rubin v. Fuchs, 1 Cal.3d 50, 81 Cal. Rptr. 373, 459 P.2d 925 (1969). The UCC is explicit on the point. UCC § 2–507(1) provides: "Tender of delivery is a condition to the buyer's duty to accept the goods and, unless otherwise agreed, to his duty to pay

such cases, constructive concurrent conditions will normally be imposed in the following circumstances:

(a) the same time is fixed for the performance of each promise; or

(b) a fixed time is stated for the performance of one of the promises and no time is fixed for the other; or (c) no time is fixed for the performance of either promise; or (d) the same period of time is fixed within which each promise shall be performed.[11]

Where each party is to perform an act which takes time, the performances are concurrent at least in the sense that one need not proceed with the performance unless the other performance is proceeding apace.

§ 11.18 Material Breach and Substantial Performance

(a) Material Breach

Where a party fails to perform a promise, it is important to determine if the breach is material.[1] If the breach is material, and there is no cure forthcoming, the aggrieved party may cancel the contract[2] and may sue for total breach. A successful suit requires a showing that the plaintiff would have been ready, willing and able to perform but for the breach.[3] However, the aggrieved party also has the option to continue with the contract and to sue for a partial breach.[4] If the breach is immaterial, the aggrieved party may not cancel the contract[5] but may sue for a partial breach.[6]

When an aggrieved party is entitled to cancel a contract and does so, there is to be no further performance under the contract and thus damages are assessed on the premise that the breaching party will not perform. The aggrieved party is permitted to recover all damages under the contract. When the breach is partial, the contract continues, but the

for them. Tender entitles the seller to acceptance of the goods and to payment according to the contract." UCC § 2–511(1) provides: "Unless otherwise agreed tender of payment is a condition to the seller's duty to tender and complete any delivery." (Unchanged in the revision). See also Rs. 2d § 234 cmt a. As to Real Property, see McFadden v. Wilder, 6 Ariz.App. 60, 429 P.2d 694 (1967).

11. Rs. 1st § 267; See also Rs. 2d § 234 cmt b.

§ 11.18

1. See § 11.15 supra. In international trade, the term "fundamental non-performance" has been put forward to substitute for "material breach." It looks to a very aggravated breach before a contract can be put to an end. This is so because goods or services may have been tendered or performed at an enormous distance and the consequences of rejection or cancellation may be far more serious than in domestic cases. See Perillo, UNIDROIT Principles of International Commercial Contracts, 63 Fordham L.Rev. 281, 307 (1994).

2. Daugherty v. Bruce Realty & Dev., 892 S.W.2d 332 (Mo.App.1995). Until the aggrieved party cancels, the contract remains in effect. Bocchetta v. McCourt, 115 Ill.App.3d 297, 71 Ill.Dec. 219, 450 N.E.2d 907 (1983).

3. Malani v. Clapp, 56 Haw. 507, 542 P.2d 1265 (1975).

4. Cities Service Helex v. U.S., 543 F.2d 1306 (Ct.Cl.1976).

5. See § 11.15 supra.

6. See § 11.15 supra.

aggrieved party may recover damages that were caused by the particular breach.[7]

Under the terminology of the Second Restatement, the term "material" breach is a breach that justifies the suspension of performance, and term "total" breach describes a breach that justifies cancellation of the contract. It provides that after the aggrieved party has suspended performance, the breaching party may cure the breach by remedying the defect, if it is remediable, until there is a "total" breach that justifies the aggrieved party to cancel the contract.[8] While a rule that requires the aggrieved party to itemize defects and to allow cure is consistent with civilized norms of behavior, many common law cases hold that the breaching party has no right to cure unless the contract expressly provides for such a right.[9]

There is no simple test to ascertain whether or not a breach is material.[10] Among the factors to be considered are: 1) to what extent, if any, the contract has been performed at the time of the breach.[11] The earlier the breach the more likely it will be regarded as material.[12] 2) A willful breach is more likely to be regarded as material than a breach caused by negligence or by fortuitous circumstances.[13] 3) A quantitatively

---

7. Rs. 2d § 236; Rs. 1st § 313.

8. Rs. 2d § 237. For a criticism of this section see Lawrence, Cure After Breach of Contract Under the Restatement (Second), 70 Minn.L.Rev. 713 (1986).

9. Southland v. Froelich, 41 F.Supp.2d 227 (E.D.N.Y.1999); Dynacon Builders v. Janowitz, 892 S.W.2d 807 (Mo.App.1995).

10. See 4 Corbin §§ 945–46; 15 Williston §§ 43:1–45:19 (4th ed); Andersen, A New Look at Material Breach in the Law of Contracts, 21 U.C.Davis L.Rev. 1073 (1988); Gibson v. Cranston, 37 F.3d 731 (1st Cir. 1994).

11. The more a party has performed the more likely it is that there will be a forfeiture. The less the performance the more likely it is that the injured party will be deprived of reasonable expectations. Rs. 2d § 241(a) and (c) and cmts b and d.

12. A breach occurring at the very beginning is more likely to be deemed material even if it is relatively small. See Note, The Breach in Limine Doctrine, 21 Colum.L.Rev. 358 (1921); Leazzo v. Dunham, 95 Ill.App.3d 847, 51 Ill.Dec. 437, 420 N.E.2d 851 (1981). The reason for this is that it is fair in determining the materiality of the breach, to consider what has been done and the benefits which the non-breaching party has received. At times the same problem arises in another form where there is a breach which is excused. Thus, if a school teacher is absent for five weeks at

the beginning of school due to illness, although the teacher's performance is excused under the doctrine of impossibility, nevertheless the employer is free to discharge the teacher if the employer is deprived of an important part of what it bargained for. Hong v. Independent School Dist., 181 Minn. 309, 232 N.W. 329, 72 ALR 280 (1930); Poussard v. Speirs, 1 Q.B.D. 410 (1876); cf. Bettini v. Gye, 1 Q.B.D. 183 (1876). See also Rs. 2d § 237 cmt a.

13. Combustion Engineering v. Miller Hydro Group, 13 F.3d 437 (1st Cir.1993); First Capital v. Country Fruit, 19 F.Supp.2d 397 (E.D.Pa.1998). Since the basic question in determining materiality of the breach is one of fairness, it is obvious that whether the breaching party was guilty of willful or negligent behavior is relevant. Thus where an employee absented himself from the job for one day to care for his own business, and where permission has been denied by the employer, the breach was deemed willful and material. Jerome v. Queen City Cycle, 163 N.Y. 351, 57 N.E. 485 (1900); but see Midway School Dist. v. Griffeath, 29 Cal.2d 13, 172 P.2d 857 (1946). The result would have been different if the employee had been ill and probably, even if he had been ill as a result of intoxication. Insubordination by an employee amounts to a material breach. Rudman v. Cowles Communications, 35 A.D.2d 213, 315 N.Y.S.2d 409 (1970), modified on appeal.

serious breach is more likely to be considered material.[14] In addition, the consequences of the determination must be taken into account. The degree of hardship on the breaching party is an important consideration particularly when considered in conjunction with the extent to which the aggrieved party has or will receive a substantial benefit from the promised performance and the adequacy with which damages may compensate for partial breach.[15] Materiality of breach is ordinarily a question of fact.[16] The goal is to assure that the aggrieved party gets what was bargained for. If a breach makes prospects of getting this from the other party seem doubtful, the aggrieved party should be free to look elsewhere for the performance.[17]

Perhaps the most frequent question raised in this area is whether delay in performance constitutes a material breach.[18] A party need not perform on the precise day stated in the contract unless time is made of the essence.[19] If time is not of the essence, reasonable delay in performing does not constitute a material breach. Unreasonable delay constitutes a material breach.[20]

If time is of the essence, any delay will constitute a material breach.[21] When is time of the essence? There is no mechanical test to make this determination. The trier of fact must determine the intention of the parties in the light of the instrument itself and all the surrounding circumstances, including the parties' words, actions and interpretation of their agreement.[22] Of course, the easiest way in which to make time of the essence is to state in the contract that "time is of the essence."[23] When this has been done, most cases have concluded that

14. The ratio of the part performed to the part to be performed is an important question in determining substantial performance and so also an important question in determining material breach. However, it is equally true that a breach which might ordinarily be insignificant could be deemed material if it prevents the other party from obtaining what was bargained for. However, in the case of a sale of goods under a non-installment contract the buyer need not take any number less than called for in the contract. See § 11.20(e).

15. Rs. 2d § 241(b) and cmt c. The same section adds that the likelihood that the breaching party will perform should be taken into account as well as whether this party is acting in good faith and dealing fairly. Rs. 2d § 241(d) & (e) and cmts e & f. Also to be taken into account is the difficulty of calculating damages for a total breach. Rs. 2d § 243 cmt d. See generally, Rs. 1st § 275; 4 Corbin §§ 945–46; 8 Corbin §§ 36.1–36.11 (McCauliff 1999).

16. Coxe v. Mid–America Ranch & Recreation, 40 Wis.2d 591, 162 N.W.2d 581 (1968); Coleman v. Shirlen, 53 N.C.App. 573, 281 S.E.2d 431 (1981). A breach may be material even if the breaching party is unaware of the facts giving rise to the

breach. Rs. 2d § 237 cmt c; Pots Unlimited v. U.S., 600 F.2d 790 (Ct.Cl.1979).

17. See Andersen, supra note 10.

18. Rs. 2d § 242 and cmts a, b, c and d.

19. Edward Waters College v. Johnson, 707 So.2d 801 (Fla.App.1998): Tator v. Salem, 81 A.D.2d 727, 439 N.Y.S.2d 497 (1981); but see Pinewood Realty v. U.S., 617 F.2d 211 (Ct.Cl.1980).

20. Keller v. Hummel, 334 N.W.2d 200 (N.D.1983).

21. E.E.E. v. Hanson, 318 N.W.2d 101 (N.D.1982).

22. Blaustein v. Weiss, 409 So.2d 103 (Fla.App.1982); Allard & Geary v. Faro, 122 N.H. 573, 448 A.2d 377 (1982); Whitney v. Perry, 208 A.D.2d 1025, 617 N.Y.S.2d 395 (1994); Cahoon v. Cahoon, 641 P.2d 140 (Utah 1982). Thus, it is possible for time to be of the essence even though this is not specifically so stated. Arnhold v. Ocean Atlantic, 132 F.Supp.2d 662 (N.D.Ill.2001); Barker v. Johnson, 591 P.2d 886 (Wyo. 1979).

23. Where there are various times stated in the contract, e.g., time for obtaining financing and time for closing, it may be

time is of the essence.[24] There is a school of thought, however, that "such stock phrases" do not necessarily have this effect, although they are to be considered along with other circumstances in determining the effect of delay.[25]

The rules stated above do not apply to contracts for the sale of goods which are discussed in the next section.[26]

(b) Substantial Performance

Substantial performance is the antithesis of material breach. If a breach is material, it follows that substantial performance has not been rendered. Just as the question of materiality of breach depends on many factors, the question of substantial performance depends to a large extent on the same factors.[27] The question of substantial performance is ordinarily a question of fact.[28]

The doctrine of substantial performance is a natural outgrowth of the doctrine of constructive conditions. If a constructive condition had to be strictly performed, as does a true condition, the doctrine of constructive conditions which was developed as an instrument for justice would have been a vehicle for injustice. Therefore, it was soon held that a constructive condition requires only substantial performance.[29] As one court has explained, "The 'substantial performance' doctrine provides that where a contract is made for an agreed exchange of two performances, one which is to be rendered first, substantial performance rather than exact, strict or literal performance by the first party of the terms of the contract is adequate to entitle the party to recover on it."[30]

As this quotation indicates, the doctrine is generally applicable to bilateral contracts for an agreed exchange of performances.[31] One exception is a contract for the sale of goods.[32] The doctrine has been applied

necessary to be explicit as to which time is of the essence. Gaskill v. Jennette Enterprises, Inc., 147 N.C.App. 138, 554 S.E.2d 10 (2001).

24. Elda Arnhold and Byzantio v. Ocean Atlantic, 284 F.3d 693 (7th Cir.2002); Linan–Faye Constr. v. Housing Authority, 995 F.Supp. 520 (D.N.J.1998); Goldston v. AMI Investments, 98 Nev. 567, 655 P.2d 521 (1982); Corbray v. Stevenson, 98 Wn.2d 410, 656 P.2d 473 (1982).

25. Rs. 2d § 242 cmt d; Foundation Dev. v. Loehmann's, 163 Ariz. 438, 788 P.2d 1189 (1990); Nash v. Superior Court, 86 Cal.App.3d 690, 150 Cal.Rptr. 394 (1978), overruled on other grounds; Vermont Marble v. Baltimore Contractors, 520 F.Supp. 922 (D.D.C.1981); Pederson v. McGuire, 333 N.W.2d 823 (S.D.1983); Driver Pipeline Co. v. Mustang Pipeline Co., 69 S.W.3d 779 (Tex.App.2002).

26. 8 Corbin §§ 37.6–37.7 (McCauliff 1999); 15 Williston 46:7 (4th ed); Walton v. Denhart, 226 Or. 254, 359 P.2d 890 (1961).

27. 8 Corbin § 36.1 (McCauliff 1999); Rs. 2d § 237 cmt d. Nordin Constr. v. Nome, 489 P.2d 455 (Alaska 1971); Hadden v. Consolidated Edison, 34 N.Y.2d 88, 356 N.Y.S.2d 249, 312 N.E.2d 445 (1974).

28. Pisani Constr., Inc. v. Krueger, 68 Conn.App. 361, 791 A.2d 634 (2002); Little Thompson Water Ass'n v. Strawn, 171 Colo. 295, 466 P.2d 915 (1970).

29. Boone v. Eyre, 126 Eng.Rep. 160 (K.B.1779). For new insights into this case and Kingston v. Preston, see Oldham, Detecting Non–Fiction: Sleuthing among Manuscript Case Reports for What was Really Said, *in* Law Reporting in Britain ch. 9 (Stebbings ed. 1995).

30. Brown–Marx Assocs. v. Emigrant Sav. Bank, 703 F.2d 1361 (11th Cir.1983).

31. See § 11.16 supra.

32. See § 11.20.

with particular emphasis to building contracts where a considerable default is sometimes treated as immaterial,[33] but it is applicable in other contexts, such as a contract to convey real property,[34] and service contracts.[35]

For the doctrine of substantial performance to apply, the part unperformed must not destroy the value or the purpose of the contract.[36] However, if more than one promise is made, each promise does not have to be substantially performed. Overall substantial performance is sufficient.[37]

There is a great deal of authority to the effect that substantial performance does not apply where the breach is willful. "The willful transgressor must accept the penalty of his transgression."[38] The word willful in this context is not easily defined.[39] An intentional variation from the contract, even if made with good motives, is deemed by some courts to be willful.[40] However, there are contrary cases.[41] In recent years, this strict approach to the doctrine of willful breach has been softened by a number of authorities. The notion is that a willful breach does not prevent substantial performance, it is only one of the factors to be considered.[42] As stated in Vincenzi v. Cerro,[43] "[t]he pertinent inquiry is not simply whether the breach was 'wilful' but whether the behavior of the party in default 'comports with standards of good faith and fair dealing. . . .' Even an adverse conclusion on this point is not decisive but is to be weighed with other factors, such as the extent to which the owner will be deprived of a reasonably expected benefit and the extent to which the builder may suffer forfeiture, in deciding whether there has been substantial performance." Under any view, trivial defects, even if

33. Chinigo v. Ehrenberg, 112 Conn. 381, 152 A. 305 (1930) (default involved about one-third of the value of the promised performance); Jardine Estates v. Donna Brook, 42 N.J.Super. 332, 126 A.2d 372 (1956); but see Schieven v. Emerick, 220 A.D. 468, 221 N.Y.S. 780 (1927) (five per cent deviation; no substantial performance). Nor is there substantial performance where there is a structural defect. Spence v. Ham, 163 N.Y. 220, 57 N.E. 412 (1900). That there is no simple solution to the problem based on a ratio between monetary loss to the injured party and the contract price, see Rs. 2d § 241 cmt b. Illinois judges charge the jury as follows: "I mean a performance in good faith of almost all that the contract required with only slight deviations. Such performance does not materially affect the benefits a party would have received from full performance." IPI Civil 3d § 700.12 (July 1993).

34. Schaefer v. Rivers, 965 S.W.2d 954 (Mo.App.1998) (contract required that all corners be flagged; flagging of 12 of 14 was substantial).

35. Phipps v. Skyview Farms, 259 Neb. 492, 610 N.W.2d 723 (2000).

36. Mac Pon v. Vinsant Painting & Decorating, 423 So.2d 216 (Ala.1982); Shaeffer v. Kelton, 95 N.M. 182, 619 P.2d 1226 (1980); Klug & Smith v. Sommer, 83 Wis.2d 378, 265 N.W.2d 269 (1978).

37. Rs. 2d § 232 cmt b.

38. Jacob & Youngs v. Kent, 230 N.Y. 239, 244, 129 N.E. 889, 891, 23 ALR 1429 (1921).

39. 8 Corbin § 36.8 (McCauliff 1999); 15 Williston § 44:57 (4th ed.).

40. Shell v. Schmidt, 164 Cal.App.2d 350, 330 P.2d 817, 76 ALR2d 792 (1958), cert. denied.

41. See Annot., 76 ALR2d 792 (1958).

42. Rs. 2d § 241 ill. 7 (based on Mathis v. Thunderbird Village, 236 Or. 425, 389 P.2d 343 (1964)); Hadden v. Consolidated Edison, 34 N.Y.2d 88, 356 N.Y.S.2d 249, 312 N.E.2d 445 (1974).

43. 186 Conn. 612, 442 A.2d 1352, 1354 (1982) (Citations omitted).

willful, are to be ignored under the doctrine of de minimis non curat lex.[44] This maxim also applies to express conditions.[45]

Substantial performance is not full performance and the party who relies on the doctrine has breached, and consequently, is liable in damages to the aggrieved party.[46] Thus, the party who has substantially performed is limited to the contract price less appropriate allowance "for the cost of completing omissions and correcting defects."[47] Under the majority view, the burden of proof on the cost of completion is on the party who claims to have rendered substantial performance.[48]

There are situations where a party is not proceeding with performance in accordance with the terms of the contract but is not yet guilty of a material breach. Under these circumstances, the other party may, by a proper notice, set a reasonable time for performance and specify that time is of the essence. If a reasonable period of time is provided in the notice that time is of the essence, failure to perform by the specified date is a material breach of contract.[49] If less than a reasonable time is allowed, the notice is ineffective and insistence on it is a repudiation.[50]

§ 11.19   Successive Lawsuits—Risk of Splitting a Claim

An illustration will help clarify the topic of splitting a claim. A agrees to build five cottages at staggered intervals for B who agrees to pay $500,000 on completion of the entire contract. The first cottage is completed several months after the date provided for in the contract. Assuming the breach was not material, B sues and recovers for a partial

44. 8 Corbin § 36.8 (McCauliff 1999); Van Clief v. Van Vechten, 130 N.Y. 571, 29 N.E. 1017 (1892).

45. Oppenheimer & Co. v. Oppenheim, Appel, Dixon & Co., 205 A.D.2d 412, 613 N.Y.S.2d 622 (1994). In reversing, however, the Court of Appeals held that the substantial performance doctrine does not apply to express conditions. 86 N.Y.2d 685, 636 N.Y.S.2d 734, 660 N.E.2d 415 (1995)

46. Cox v. Fremont County Pub. Bldg. Auth., 415 F.2d 882 (10th Cir.1969); Reynolds v. Armstead, 166 Colo. 372, 443 P.2d 990 (1968).

47. Mirisis v. Renda, 83 A.D.2d 572, 441 N.Y.S.2d 138 (1981).

48. Treiber v. Schaefer, 416 S.W.2d 576 (Tex.App.1967). However, many cases place the burden of proof on the other party. See, e.g., Hopkins Constr. v. Reliance Ins., 475 P.2d 223 (Alaska 1970); Silos v. Prindle, 127 Vt. 91, 237 A.2d 694 (1967). Assuming substantial performance, some courts hold that the measure of damages is the difference between the value of the structure as built and the value it would have had had it been constructed according to the contract. White v. Mitchell, 123 Wn. 630, 213 P. 10

(1923); Venzke v. Magdanz, 243 Wis. 155, 9 N.W.2d 604 (1943). On the other hand there are jurisdictions which hold that ordinarily the defaulting party will be allowed to recover the contract price less the cost of correction of the defects or finishing the work. Bellizzi v. Huntley Estates, 3 N.Y.2d 112, 164 N.Y.S.2d 395, 143 N.E.2d 802 (1957). But where this measurement would be unfair, as where correction of a usable structure containing no structural defect would require substantial tearing down of the structure and its rebuilding, the deduction will be for the difference between the value of the structure had it been built according to specifications and its value as constructed. Jacob & Youngs v. Kent, 230 N.Y. 239, 129 N.E. 889 (1921); see Annot., 76 ALR2d 805 (1961) & § 14.29. It should also be noted that these formulae are also used in determining whether there is substantial performance.

49. 8 Corbin § 37:10; Blaustein v. Weiss, 409 So.2d 103 (Fla.App.1982); Zev v. Merman 134 A.D.2d 555, 521 N.Y.S.2d 455 (1987), aff'd mem.

50. Beckman v. Kitchen, 599 N.W.2d 699 (Iowa 1999); Miller v. Almquist, 241 A.D.2d 181, 671 N.Y.S.2d 746 (1998).

breach.[1] A subsequently abandons the work. At this point there is a material breach.[2] The question is whether B's prior action for a partial breach precludes a second action for total breach on a theory of splitting an indivisible cause of action.

Logically, B should be permitted to institute another action for additional damages and should not be barred from recovery of those damages that could not have been recovered in the initial action.[3] There is a minority view, based on the theory of splitting an indivisible cause of action. Under this view, there can be only one claim for the breach of one indivisible contract[4] and as a practical matter, the aggrieved party should defer bringing the action until the consequences of the breach are clear because if it should turn out that the breaching party will not perform, the plaintiff will be precluded from bringing a second action. Under this approach, the exercise of a legal right in bringing an action for partial breach becomes a snare for the innocent. Nevertheless, there are some cases that have reached this conclusion.[5]

One rationale for the rule against splitting an indivisible claim is that multiple actions on the same claim would be unjust and vexatious to the defendant.[6] However, the theoretical basis for the rule is found in the law of judgments. The effect of a judgment is to extinguish the claim on which the judgment was based. The claim is merged in the judgment with the result that the judgment creditor is precluded from bringing a second action on the same claim.[7] The definition of the term "claim" or "cause of action" is critical. However, there is no "consistent and commonly accepted definition."[8]

In any event, a problem exists under the minority view stated above. The same type of problem exists when there is a material breach and the non-breaching party elects to treat it as a partial breach. There is also the same split of authority.[9] The same type of problem also occurs in installment contracts which are entire rather than divisible.[10] However,

---

§ 11.19

1. See § 11.18(a) supra.

2. See § 11.18(a) supra.

3. Rs. 1st § 449 cmt e; Restatement, Judgments § 62 cmt h; cf. Clark, Code Pleading § 74 (2d ed. 1947).

4. 11 Williston § 1293 (3d ed.). None of the cases cited by this authority supports this broad a proposition. With the exception of Pakas v. Hollingshead, see § 11.19 n.10, all of the cited cases involve either dictum or a clear repudiation by the breaching party. In the case of a repudiation there is usually no power to elect to continue performance and sue for partial breach. See § 12.8. But see §§ 12.9 & 12.10.

5. See n.4 supra.

6. 4 Corbin § 950; Clark, Code Pleading § 73 (2d ed. 1947); Clark, Joinder and Split-

ting of Causes of Action, 25 Mich.L.Rev. 393 (1926).

7. 11 Williston § 1293 (3d ed.).

8. 4 Corbin § 955; cf. Restatement, Judgments, Ch. 3 Introductory Note Topic 2, Title D (1942) which indicates that the meaning of these terms varies with the context.

9. See also Rs. 2d § 243 cmt d. Compare, Rs. 1st § 449 cmt e and Restatement, Judgments § 62 cmt h with 11 Williston § 1294 (3d ed).

10. The leading case espousing the minority view is Pakas v. Hollingshead, 184 N.Y. 211, 77 N.E. 40 (1906); cf. Perry v. Dickerson, 85 N.Y. 345, 39 Am.Rep. 663 (1881). Goodwin v. Cabot Amusement, 129 Me. 36, 149 A. 574 (1930), is representative of the majority view. The UCC has adopted the majority view as to installment con-

when the contract is divisible, it seems generally to be agreed that a breach of the severable portion gives rise to a separate cause of action.[11]

Closely related in policy to the rule against splitting a cause of action is the rule that even though there are successive breaches, the plaintiff must sue for all of the breaches that have occurred prior to the commencement of the action or lose the right to any cause of action not included.[12] This rule is not generally deemed to apply to separate and distinct contracts.[13] However, if separate and distinct contracts constitute a running account,[14] then the general rule applies. A suit on less than all of the breaches which have occurred will result in the loss of those claims not joined in the action.[15]

§ 11.20   Sales of Goods—The Perfect Tender Rule

The doctrine of substantial performance which is almost universally applied[1] does not apply to contracts for the sale of goods.[2] Instead, the perfect tender rule developed with respect to sales contracts in the nineteenth century. Under the rule, the buyer is free to reject the goods unless the tender conforms in every respect to the contract—not only in quantity and quality but also the details of shipment.[3] In the words of Learned Hand: "There is no room in commercial contracts for the doctrine of substantial performance."[4] The rule has been criticized[5] and is particularly unfair when it is impractical for the seller to resell the rejected goods, for example, because the goods were specially manufactured.[6]

tracts. UCC § 2–612(3) and cmt 6 (substantially unchanged in the revision).

11.   4 Corbin § 949.

12.   Thomas v. Carpenter, 123 Me. 241, 122 A. 576 (1923); See v. See, 294 Mo. 495, 242 S.W. 949, 24 ALR 880 (1922); 11 Williston § 1294.

13.   Lozier Auto. Exch. v. Interstate Cas., 197 Iowa 935, 195 N.W. 885 (1923). Negotiable bills and notes have long been regarded as separate contracts. 4 Corbin § 952.

14.   Whether or not there is a running account appears to be a question of intent, often manifested by submission and acceptance of a consolidated bill for multiple purchases or services rendered. Corey v. Jaroch, 229 Mich. 313, 200 N.W. 957 (1924).

15.   Kruce v. Lakeside Biscuit, 198 Mich. 736, 165 N.W. 609 (1917).

§ 11.20

1.   At times a rule equivalent to the perfect tender rule has been applied to contracts for the sale of realty where the action is for damages at law. Smyth v. Sturges, 108 N.Y. 495, 15 N.E. 544 (1888).

2.   Applying a rule of substantial performance, erroneously citing the 2d edition of this text, is Curt Ogden Equipment v. Murphy Leasing, 895 S.W.2d 604 (Mo.App. 1995). The decision is, however, justified by the duty of a buyer to pay for each commercial unit that is accepted. UCC §§ 2–601, 2–709 (substantially unchanged in the revision).

3.   Norrington v. Wright, 115 U.S. 188 (1885); Filley v. Pope, 115 U.S. 213 (1885).

4.   Mitsubishi Goshi Kaisha v. J. Aron & Co., 16 F.2d 185, 186 (2d Cir.1926). That Learned Hand may be in error is shown by the adoption of the United Nations Convention for the International Sale of Goods. Its Article 25 sets a standard of "fundamental breach," rather than perfect tender. The UNIDROIT Principles of International Commercial Contracts adopts a standard of "fundamental non-performance" in Article 7.3.1.

5.   Honnold, Buyer's Right of Rejection, 97 U.Pa.L.Rev. 457 (1949).

6.   Ellison Furniture & Carpet v. Langever, 52 Tex.Civ.App. 50, 113 S.W. 178 (1908). Another objection to the perfect tender rule is that "buyers in a declining mar-

Nevertheless, the UCC has retained the perfect tender rule albeit with a number of significant exceptions.[7] Section 2–601 of the UCC states, unless otherwise agreed,[8] "if the goods or the tender of the delivery fail in any respect to conform to the contract, the buyer may

(a) reject the whole; or

(b) accept the whole; or

(c) accept any commercial unit or units and reject the rest."

The UCC has, however, limited the perfect tender rule by engrafting on the rule a number of exceptions.[9] These exceptions, in fact, represent a new rule, supplanting the perfect tender rule, and despite § 2–601, the UCC frequently applies the doctrine of substantial performance to sales contracts.[10] The cases are generally in accord with the notion that the perfect tender rule is still alive but that the Code, through its exceptions, "strikes a different balance."[11] Before discussing these exceptions one should not lose sight of the pervasive role of good faith in the UCC. Rejection of goods that fail to conform to the perfect tender rule has been held to be a breach where the motive for the rejection was to take advantage of falling market prices.[12]

(a) Cure

The general notion of the perfect tender rule is that the buyer may reject goods if they are non-conforming in any respect.[13] Although the power to reject continues under the UCC,[14] the buyer's rejection does not

ket would reject goods for minor non-conformities and force the loss on surprised sellers." Ramirez v. Autosport, 88 N.J. 277, 440 A.2d 1345 (1982).

7. See Priest, Breach and Remedy for the Tender of Nonconforming Goods Under the Uniform Commercial Code: An Economic Approach, 91 Harv.L.Rev. 960 (1978).

8. For example, if the contract provides that the seller's obligations are limited to replacement of defective items or if a trade usage is inconsistent with the perfect tender rule.

9. For example, while § 2–503(1) of the Code states: "[t]ender of delivery requires that the seller put and hold conforming goods at the buyer's disposition and give the buyer any notification reasonably necessary to enable him to take delivery," § 2–504 limits the perfect tender rule in a shipment contract when it provides that a failure to give notice pursuant to 2–503(1) is not a grounds for rejection if no material delay or loss results.

10. J. White & R. Summers, Uniform Commercial Code § 8–3 at 301–02 (4th ed.).

11. Ramirez v. Autosport, 88 N.J. 277, 440 A.2d 1345 (1982); Rs. 2d § 241 cmt b.

12. T.W. Oil v. Consolidated Edison, 57 N.Y.2d 574, 457 N.Y.S.2d 458, 443 N.E.2d 932, 36 ALR4th 533 (1982); Oil Country Specialists v. Philipp Bros., 762 S.W.2d 170 (Tex.App.1988); see also Cambee's Furniture v. Doughboy Recreational, 825 F.2d 167 (8th Cir.1987) (cancellation for breach would, if merely a pretextual reason, violate the covenant of good faith and fair dealing); accord, Neumiller Farms v. Cornett, 368 So.2d 272 (Ala.1979); Printing Center of Texas v. Supermind Pub., 669 S.W.2d 779 (Tex.App.1984); contra, Crim Truck & Tractor v. Navistar Int'l Transp., 823 S.W.2d 591, 52 ALR5th 919 (Tex.1992) (no general duty of good faith in performance of contracts).

13. See generally Schwartz, Private Law Treatment of Defective Products in Sales Situations, 49 Ind.L.J. 8 (1983); Whaley, Tender, Acceptance, Rejection and Revocation, the UCC's "Tarr" baby, 24 Drake L.Rev. 52 (1974).

14. There has been an occasional suggestion that because some defects can be cured under the rules stated below, rejection is not justified. Gindy Mfg. v. Cardinale Trucking, 111 N.J.Super. 383, 268 A.2d 345 (1970). This suggestion was rejected in Ra-

necessarily discharge the contract because the UCC grants to the seller a right to cure in two specific situations.[15] The UN Sales Convention and UNIDROIT Principles of International Commercial Contracts heavily emphasize cure; both adopt a policy of keeping the contract intact if at all feasible. The UCC permits cure in two situations.

(1) When the Time for Performance Has Not Expired

If the buyer rejects a seller's defective tender before the time for performance has expired, the seller has an unconditional right to cure by making a conforming delivery within the contract time.[16] There is some question as to whether the cure may consist of repair of the defective goods.[17] Some courts have stated that the right to cure should not be extended to defects that substantially impair value.[18]

(2) When the Time for Performance Has Expired

When the buyer rejects a non-conforming tender, the seller also has a right to cure after the time for performance has passed provided two conditions are met. One, the seller had reasonable grounds to believe that the tender would be accepted "with or without money allowance;"[19] and, two, "the seller * * * seasonably notifies the buyer" of the intention to cure and cures the non-conforming tender within "a further reasonable time."[20]

The statute is not limited to situations where the seller knowingly makes a defective tender.[21] The overall aim of the UCC is to encourage the parties to amicably resolve their own problems.[22]

(b) Rejection and Acceptance of Goods

mirez v. Autosport, 88 N.J. 277, 440 A.2d 1345 (1982).

15. UCC § 2–508 (some clarifying changes in revision). If the cure takes place before the rejection, the right to reject is lost, but the buyer retains the right to damages under UCC § 2–714.

16. UCC § 2–508(1). See Note, 69 Mich. L.Rev. 130 (1970). The revision also grants the right to cure in a non-consumer transaction if the buyer revokes acceptance. Under the unrevised UCC, it is unclear whether the right to cure extends to revocation of acceptance. Linscott v. Smith, 3 Kan.App.2d 1, 587 P.2d 1271 (1978).

17. Note, 52 Minn.L.Rev. 937 (1968). Compare, Zabriskie Chevrolet v. Smith, 99 N.J.Super. 441, 240 A.2d 195 (1968), with Newmaster v. Southeast Equip., 231 Kan. 466, 646 P.2d 488 (1982).

18. Linscott v. Smith, 3 Kan.App.2d 1, 587 P.2d 1271 (1978); Johannsen v. Minnesota Valley Ford Tractor, 304 N.W.2d 654 (Minn.1981); Pavesi v. Ford Motor, 155 N.J.Super. 373, 382 A.2d 954 (1978),

squarely overruled on this point by Ramirez v. Autosport, 88 N.J. 277, 440 A.2d 1345 (1982); Oberg v. Phillips, 615 P.2d 1022 (Okl.App.1980).

19. White & Summers, Uniform Commercial Code § 8–5 (4th ed.).

20. UCC § 2–508(2). The revision extends the right to cure, in non-consumer sales, to revocations of acceptance. There is some question as to whether a price adjustment given by the seller amounts to a cure. See White & Summers, Uniform Commercial Code § 8–5 (4th ed.). The revision indicates that cure must be made by tender of conforming goods.

21. T.W. Oil v. Consolidated Edison, 57 N.Y.2d 574, 457 N.Y.S.2d 458, 443 N.E.2d 932 (1982).

22. The seller's right to cure is even more expansive under the UN Sales Convention and the UNIDROIT Principles. See Perillo, supra § 11.18 n.1 at 303.

Ordinarily, when non-conforming goods are tendered, the buyer has a choice between accepting or rejecting them.[23] But the buyer's power of rejection does not last forever. Once the buyer accepts, the right to reject is lost. The buyer also loses the right to reject if the rejection is not made, "within a reasonable time after their delivery or tender" or if the buyer fails to "seasonably" notify the seller of their rejection.[24] Note that this is not a matter of contract formation, but of acceptance or rejection of goods that have been tendered in the performance of a bilateral contract or in the creation of a unilateral contract.

After the seller is properly notified of rejection, the seller often has a right to cure.[25] Consequently, the Code provides that, when rejecting, the buyer must state all defects discoverable by reasonable inspection. If this isn't done, the buyer may not justify rejection on any unstated nonconformity that the seller could have cured had the seller been given seasonable notice.[26] This rule does not apply when both the buyer and the seller are merchants.

Between merchants, a more drastic rule prevails. When a seller requests in writing a full and final statement of all defects on which buyer prepares to rely on as grounds for rejection, the buyer cannot rely on unstated defects (irrespective of their curability) that reasonably could have been discovered.[27] If a rejection is wrongful (e.g. rejection of conforming goods), the buyer is liable for the wrongful rejection.[28]

There are three ways in which a buyer accepts goods; one is by failing to make an effective rejection, just discussed. The second is an express acceptance. This is an acceptance where "the buyer after a reasonable opportunity to inspect the goods[29] signifies to the seller that the goods are conforming or that he will take or retain them in spite of their non-conformity."[30] The third way a buyer accepts goods is by doing

---

23. UCC § 2–601 (substantially unchanged in the revision). For a critical analysis, see Kraus, Decoupling Sales Law from the Acceptance–Rejection Fulcrum, 104 Yale L.J. 129 (1994) (too many issues turn on this "Fulcrum").

24. UCC § 2–602(1) (unchanged in the revision); Liberty Steel v. Franco Steel, 57 F.Supp.2d 459 (N.D.Ohio 1999); Bead Chain Mfg. v. Saxton Prods., 183 Conn. 266, 439 A.2d 314 (1981); G & H Land & Cattle v. Heitzman & Nelson, 102 Idaho 204, 628 P.2d 1038 (1981); Konitz v. Claver, 287 Mont. 301, 954 P.2d 1138 (1998). If the buyer pays against documents without reserving rights and there are "defects apparent on the face of the documents," the buyer may not recover payment because of the existence of such defects. UCC § 2–605(2) and cmt 4 (substantially unchanged in revision).

25. See § 11.20(a).

26. UCC § 2–605. The revision extends the rule to also govern revocations of acceptance.

27. UCC § 2–605(1). The revision substitutes "record" for "writing."

28. White & Summers, Uniform Commercial Code § 8–3 (4th ed.).

29. For example, a buyer who signs a seller's form stating that the goods have been inspected and are conforming has not accepted under this rule unless there was a genuine opportunity to perform more than a cursory inspection. See T.J. Stevenson & Co. v. 81,193 Bags of Flour, 629 F.2d 338 (5th Cir.1980), reh. denied; Jakowski v. Carole Chevrolet, 180 N.J.Super. 122, 433 A.2d 841 (1981). The basic section of the Code governing inspection is § 2–513. See also §§ 2–310(b) and 2–321(3).

30. UCC § 2–606(1)(a) (substantially unchanged in the revision); Plateq v. Machlett Labs., 189 Conn. 433, 456 A.2d 786 (1983). Subsection (2) of this section also provides, "acceptance of a part of any commercial unit is acceptance of that entire unit."

"any act inconsistent with the seller's ownership; but if such act is wrongful as against the seller it is an acceptance only if ratified by him."[31]

What is consistent or inconsistent with the seller's ownership is a difficult question.[32] Use after rejection or revocation is generally wrongful,[33] but may be reasonable if the seller will not accept the buyer's decision.[34] The words "ratified by him" indicate that an act inconsistent with the seller's ownership is an acceptance if the seller treats it as an acceptance. The seller also has the option of treating it as a conversion.[35]

Once there has been an effective rejection, a buyer who has possession of the goods owes a duty to hold them at the seller's disposition and to exercise reasonable care.[36] A merchant buyer owes additional duties. Among them is the duty to sell perishable goods for the seller's account if the seller has no agent at the location.[37]

Acceptance not only precludes rejection but requires the buyer to pay at the contract rate.[38] In addition, acceptance of the goods shifts the burden of proof to the buyer "to establish any breach with respect to the goods accepted."[39] Even though the buyer is required to pay at the contract price after acceptance, if the goods are non-conforming, the buyer is still entitled to recover damages for breach provided that the buyer gives proper notice of non-conformity.[40] In fact, such a notice must be sent even if the seller is aware of the non-conformity. The point is that the seller must be aware that the buyer will assert its right to a remedy.[41]

31. UCC § 2–606(1)(c) (substantially unchanged in the revision).

32. See White & Summers, Uniform Commercial Code, § 8–2 (4th ed.); Jacobs v. Rosemount Dodge–Winnebago, 310 N.W.2d 71 (Minn.1981); Steinmetz v. Robertus, 196 Mont. 311, 637 P.2d 31 (1981).

33. UCC § 2–602(2)(a); Shokai Far East v. Energy Conservation Sys., 628 F.Supp. 1462 (S.D.N.Y.1986).

34. CPC Int'l v. Techni–Chem, 660 F.Supp. 1509 (N.D.Ill.1987) (continued use was reasonable as it mitigated damages); Aluminum Line Prods. v. Rolls–Royce Motors, 98 Ohio App.3d 759, 649 N.E.2d 887 (1994). Revised § 2–608(4) would expressly authorize reasonable use.

35. See § 2.19 supra.

36. UCC § 2–602(2)(b) (substantially unchanged by the revision).

37. UCC § 2–603 (some clarifying changes in the revision). In Kysar v. Lambert, 76 Wn.App. 470, 887 P.2d 431 (1995), the buyer rejected perishable goods and sold them for more than the contract price. The buyer was required to pay the seller the net proceeds.

38. UCC § 2–607(1) (unchanged in the revision); Unlaub v. Sexton, 568 F.2d 72 (8th Cir.1977); Borges v. Magic Valley Foods, 101 Idaho 494, 616 P.2d 273 (1980); Montana Seeds v. Holliday, 178 Mont. 119, 582 P.2d 1223 (1978).

39. UCC § 2–607(4) (unchanged in the revision); Liberty Steel v. Franco Steel, 57 F.Supp.2d 459 (N.D.Ohio 1999). It is possible to have an acceptance after a revocation. Cardwell v. International Housing, 282 Pa.Super. 498, 423 A.2d 355 (1980).

40. UCC § 2–607(3) provides: "When a tender has been accepted (a) the buyer must within a reasonable time after he discovers or should have discovered any breach notify the seller of breach or be barred from any remedy." See also UCC § 2–714; Maybank v. S.S. Kresge, 302 N.C. 129, 273 S.E.2d 681 (1981); See Notes, 70 Cornell L.Rev. 525 (1985), 25 U.Fla.L.Rev. 520 (1973). The revision preserves the notice requirement, but mitigates the effects of failure to give notice, barring a remedy only "to the extent the seller is prejudiced."

41. Aqualon Co. v. Mac Equipment, Inc., 149 F.3d 262, 89 ALR5th 721 (4th Cir.1998).

(c) Revocation of Acceptance

Even if goods have been accepted, the buyer may, in a proper case, revoke the acceptance.[42] The first requirement for revocation of an acceptance of a lot or commercial unit is that its non-conformity substantially impairs its value to the buyer. This is a question of fact.[43] The question may be phrased in terms of the seller's substantial performance. If the seller has substantially performed, the buyer cannot revoke.[44] The question could also be phrased in terms of whether the seller materially breached; if so, the buyer may revoke.[45] The result will almost always be the same under either formulation.[46]

The phrase "impairs its value to him" seems to suggest a subjective test. Comment 2 to § 2–608 seems to be in accord with this suggestion when it states: "The question is whether the non-conformity is such as will in fact cause a substantial impairment of the value to the buyer though the seller had no advance knowledge as to the buyer's particular circumstances."[47]

When the seller has materially breached or not substantially performed, the buyer may revoke by satisfying one of two requisites set forth in section 2–608. The buyer must show either that the acceptance was (a) "on the reasonable assumption that its non-conformity would be cured and it has not been seasonably cured;" or (b) even if the buyer did not discover such non-conformity at the time of acceptance, "if his acceptance was reasonably induced either by the difficulty of discovery before acceptance or by the seller's assurances."[48]

In order to revoke effectively, the buyer must do so "within a reasonable time after the buyer discovers or should have discovered the ground for it and before any substantial change in condition of the goods which is not caused by their own defects."[49] "[S]hould have discovered" is directed to the requirement that the buyer make a reasonable inspection.[50] The revocation is not effective until the buyer notifies the seller of

42. UCC § 2–608(1); Cissell Mfg. Co. v. Park, 36 P.3d 85 (Colo.App.2001); Phillips, 75 Comm.L.J. 354 (1970); Annots., 65 ALR3d 388, 65 ALR3d 354 (1975).

43. Erling v. Homera, 298 N.W.2d 478 (N.D.1980); contra Chmill v. Friendly Ford–Mercury, 144 Wis.2d 796, 424 N.W.2d 747 (App.1988).

44. See Note, 69 Mich.L.Rev. 130 (1970).

45. White & Summers, Uniform Commercial Code § 8–4 (4th ed.); but see Murray v. D & J Motor, 958 P.2d 823 (Okla. App.1998) (revocation as to car sold "as is").

46. See § 11.18 supra.

47. The cases are not all in accord. See, e.g., Black v. Don Schmid Motor, 232 Kan. 458, 657 P.2d 517 (1983); Champion Ford Sales v. Levine, 49 Md.App. 547, 433 A.2d

1218 (1981); Bergenstock v. Lemay's G.M.C., 118 R.I. 75, 372 A.2d 69 (1977); see also Note, 32 U.Pitt.L.Rev. 439 (1971); Annot., 98 ALR3d 1183 (1980).

48. UCC § 2–608(1)(a), (b) (substantially unchanged by the revision); Four Sons Bakery v. Dulman, 542 F.2d 829 (10th Cir. 1976); Grand St. Marketing v. Eastern Poultry Distributors, 63 Ark.App. 123, 975 S.W.2d 439 (1998); Lynx v. Ordnance Prods., 273 Md. 1, 327 A.2d 502 (1974).

49. UCC § 2–608(2) (substantially unchanged by the revision); Conte v. Dwan Lincoln–Mercury, 172 Conn. 112, 374 A.2d 144 (1976); Michigan Sugar v. Jebavy Sorenson Orchard, 66 Mich.App. 642, 239 N.W.2d 693, 93 ALR3d 357 (1976); Desilets Granite v. Stone Equalizer, 133 Vt. 372, 340 A.2d 65 (1975).

50. Lynx v. Ordnance Prods., 273 Md. 1, 327 A.2d 502 (1974).

the revocation.[51] No particular form of notice is required.[52] The effect of a valid revocation of acceptance is that the buyer has the same rights and duties with regard to the goods as in the case of a rejection.[53] Most courts, however, hold that the seller has no right to cure, but the seller's efforts to cure may extend the reasonable time for the buyer to revoke.[54]

Continued possession and reasonable use of property after the buyer has notified the seller of revocation of acceptance does not necessarily amount to a waiver of the right to revoke acceptance.[55]

(d) Installment Contracts

The perfect tender rule does not apply to an installment contract; the installment buyer may not reject a tender merely because it is not perfect. Such a buyer is justified in rejecting a delivery and canceling the whole contract only where a non-conformity with respect to one or more installments substantially impairs the value of the whole contract—a material breach.[56] However, if the non-conformity of an installment impairs the value only of that installment, the buyer must accept the installment if it can be cured and the seller gives adequate assurance of its cure.[57]

For example, B contracted to buy 20 carloads of plywood from S. Nine percent of the first carload consisted of non-conforming plywood. B canceled the contract. S sued. The court held that B was liable for breach of contract because the non-conformity did not substantially impair the value of the entire contract.[58] Moreover, it is doubtful whether B could have rejected the first carload. Although 91% of performance would not ordinarily meet the criterion for substantial performance, in an installment contract it may because there are continuing opportunities to cure. Even if the value of that installment was impaired, S would still be entitled to attempt a cure. As Professor Quinn points out: "It is tough to reject any single installment under an installment contract and even tougher to get rid of the rest of the whole contract."[59]

An installment contract is one in which separate lots are to be delivered and separately paid for and accepted.[60] There is a presumption

51. UCC § 2–608(2) (substantially unchanged by the revision).

52. Peckham v. Larsen Chevrolet–Buick–Oldsmobile, 99 Idaho 675, 587 P.2d 816 (1978).

53. UCC § 2–608(3) (substantially unchanged by the revision). See (b) in this section for the rights and duties when the goods are rejected. Volkswagen of America v. Novak, 418 So.2d 801 (Miss.1982).

54. Bland v. Freightliner, 206 F.Supp.2d 1202 (M.D.Fla.2002); Head v. Phillips Camper Sales, 234 Mich.App. 94, 593 N.W.2d 595 (1999).

55. O'Shea v. Hatch, 97 N.M. 409, 640 P.2d 515 (1982); Wilk Paving v. Southworth–Milton, 162 Vt. 552, 649 A.2d 778 (1994).

56. UCC § 2–612(3) (substantially unchanged by the revision); Note, 7 Willamette L.J. 107 (1971).

57. UCC § 2–612(2) (minor change in the revision); Kirkwood Agri–Trade v. Frosty Land Foods, 650 F.2d 602 (5th Cir. 1981). This is consistent with prior law. Monroe v. Diamond, 279 Pa. 310, 123 A. 817 (1924).

58. Continental Forest Prods. v. White Lumber Sales, 256 Or. 466, 474 P.2d 1 (1970).

59. T. Quinn, U.C.C. Commentary and Digest, § 2–612[A][5].

60. UCC § 2–612(1) (unchanged in the revision).

that goods are to be delivered in one lot.[61] However, this presumption may be rebutted by the express language of the contract or may be inferred from the circumstances.[62] When the parties intend an installment contract, this will not be changed by a clause to the effect that "'each delivery is a separate contract' or its equivalent."[63] A buyer's breach under an installment contract is also tested by the substantial impairment test, but a failure to pay is very serious.[64]

(e) The Perfect Tender Rule and the Buyer

We have discussed the effect of a non-conforming tender by the seller. But, instead, the buyer may make a non-conforming tender. In an installment contract, if the buyer fails to make a conforming payment, the perfect tender rule does not apply and the issue is material breach.[65] However, the UCC regards late payment of a non-installment contract as a material breach.[66] The buyer may also breach by failing to accept goods pursuant to the terms of the contract even though payment is not yet due.[67] The buyer must also "furnish facilities reasonably suited to the receipt of the goods."[68]

The Code provides that payment ordinarily need not be made in cash and that a check will suffice. It provides: "Tender of payment is sufficient when made by any means or in any manner current in the ordinary course of business unless the seller demands payment in legal tender and gives any extension of time reasonably necessary to procure it."[69]

§ 11.21 "Failure of Consideration"

The term "failure of consideration" simply means a failure to perform[1] and is only obliquely related to the term "consideration" as used in Chapter 4. It does not relate to the formation of a contract but to

---

61. UCC § 2–307 (unchanged in the revision); see also Rs. 2d § 233(2) and ill. 3 and Reporter's Note.

62. UCC § 2–307 and cmt 2 (unchanged in revision).

63. UCC § 2–612(1) (unchanged in the revision).

64. L & M Enterprises v. BEI Sensors, 231 F.3d 1284 (10th Cir.2000).

65. Cherwell–Ralli v. Rytman Grain, 180 Conn. 714, 433 A.2d 984 (1980). This was also the rule prior to the Code. See Helgar v. Warner's Features, 222 N.Y. 449, 119 N.E. 113 (1918). Failure to pay for the first installment justifies the withholding of further deliveries. C.T. Chemicals (U.S.A.) v. Vinmar Impex, 81 N.Y.2d 174, 613 N.E.2d 159, 597 N.Y.S.2d 284 (1993).

66. UCC § 2–703. "Creditors are a superstitious sect, great observers of set days and times." Benjamin Franklin, Poor Richard: 1737. Revised § 2–703 is more elaborate but makes no substantive change.

67. Eastern Air Lines v. Hartford Acc. & Indem., 437 F.2d 449 (5th Cir.1971), cert. denied.

68. UCC § 2–503(1)(b) (unchanged in the revision); Valero Marketing & Supply v. Kalama Int'l, 51 S.W.3d 345 (Tex.App.2001) (inappropriate barge for methanol.)

69. UCC § 2–511(2) (unchanged in the revision); accord, Rs. 2d § 249.

§ 11.21

1. Murray, Contracts § 108(A) (4th ed.); Rs. 2d § 237 cmt a. But see 3 Williston § 7:11 (4th ed.) (favoring the use of the term).

its performance.[2] To illustrate, C promises to build a structure for O and O promises to make payment when the work is completed. There is consideration on both sides. Therefore a contract was *formed* on the exchange of promises.[3] If C fails to perform, the result is sometimes described as a "failure of consideration."

The use of the term "failure of consideration" in this sense appears to be an unnecessary invitation to confusion because the word consideration is used in two different senses. Fortunately, this phrase is gradually falling into disuse. Its use is, however, still sufficiently widespread to be mentioned here.[4] It sometimes appears as a misnomer for "lack of consideration." This volume does not utilize "failure of consideration" as an operative concept.

§ 11.22   Quasi–Contractual and Statutory Relief

A plaintiff who has breached but has substantially performed is ordinarily entitled to a recovery based on the terms of the contract.[1] But a defaulting plaintiff who has not substantially performed may be entitled to restitution in a quasi-contractual action.

Two early cases involving employment contracts have forcefully stated the two contrasting approaches that have been taken to this problem. In Stark v. Parker,[2] the plaintiff was hired to work for one year for the sum of $120. Before the end of the year, the plaintiff without cause left the defendant's employment. Plaintiff framed the complaint for services rendered in the quasi-contractual form of action known as indebitatus assumpsit. The Supreme Judicial Court found the plaintiff's complaint "strange" and "repugnant" saying:

> "The law indeed is most reasonable in itself. It denies only to a party an advantage from his own wrong. It requires him to act justly by a faithful performance of his own engagements before he exacts the fulfillment of dependent obligations on the part of others. It will not admit of the monstrous absurdity, that a man may voluntarily and without cause violate his agreement and make the very breach of that agreement the foundation of an action which he could not maintain under it."[3]

Although this case probably still reflects the weight of authority,[4] the contrary reasoning of another old and still widely cited case contin-

---

2. Lord Simon in Fibrosa Spolka Akcyjna v. Fairbairn Lawson Combe Barbour, 1943 A.C. 32, [1942] 2 All E.R. 122 (H.L.); Converse v. Zinke, 635 P.2d 882 (Colo. 1981); Franklin v. Carpenter, 309 Minn. 419, 244 N.W.2d 492 (1976).

3. See § 4.2 supra.

4. E.g., Resolution Trust v. Forest Grove, 33 F.3d 284 (3d Cir.1994).

§ 11.22

1. See § 11.18(b). There are other instances where a defaulting plaintiff, who has not substantially performed, is entitled to a contractual recovery. See §§ 11.23 to 11.26.

2. 19 Mass. (2 Pick.) 267 (1824).

3. Id. at 275.

4. 1 G. Palmer, Law of Restitution § 5.13 (1978); see Lee, The Plaintiff in Default, 19 Vand.L.Rev. 1023 (1966).

ues to make converts and to influence legislation. In a nearly identical fact pattern, the Supreme Court of New Hampshire in Britton v. Turner[5] ruled that the defaulting plaintiff, although unable to recover on the contract, could recover under a quasi-contractual theory for the reasonable value of the services less any damages suffered by defendant. The Court stressed the injustice of the defendant's retention without payment of benefits received under the contract.[6] Also, the court noted that the general understanding of the community is that payment should be made for services actually rendered.

The conflict of authority extends beyond employment to all kinds of contracts. Some jurisdictions permit quasi-contractual relief under a building or other service contract, even where the performance is less than substantial, minus damages for breach.[7] The same split of authority is found when a defaulting purchaser of land seeks to recover a down payment.[8] In the case of a buyer of goods, the UCC permits a defaulting buyer to obtain restitution of payments minus one of two figures: $500 or 20% of the buyer's obligation if the latter is less than $500.[9] The buyer's claim for restitution is subject to a further offset in the amount of the seller's actual damages and the value of benefits received by the buyer as a result of the contract.[10] The buyer's rights may be curtailed or expanded by a valid liquidated damages clause.[11]

For example, B contracts to purchase furniture from S for $2,100, paying $700 of the purchase price. B repudiates and sues for restitution of the down payment. B obtains restitution of $700 minus the lesser of $500 or 20% of the price ($420). Since $420 is less than $500, B is entitled to $700–$420, that is, $280. This sum will be reduced to the extent of the seller's damages and the value of benefits received by the buyer.

5. 6 N.H. 481, 26 Am.Dec. 713 (1834).

6. See Ashley, 24 Yale L.J. 544 (1915); Corman, (pts. I & II) 38 Marq.L.Rev. 61, 139 (1954–55); Laube, 20 Minn.L.Rev. 597 (1936); Laube, 83 U.Pa.L.Rev. 825 (1935); Laube, 84 U.Pa.L.Rev. 68 (1935); Williston, id. at 68.

7. Mills v. Denny Wiekhorst Excavating, 206 Neb. 443, 293 N.W.2d 112 (1980); Lynn v. Seby, 29 N.D. 420, 151 N.W. 31 (1915) (contract to thresh grain); Lancellotti v. Thomas, 341 Pa.Super. 1, 491 A.2d 117 (1985) (contract to purchase a business and build an addition); Bailey–Allen v. Kurzet, 876 P.2d 421 (Utah App.1994); see Nordstrom & Woodland, 20 Ohio St.L.J. 193 (1959). Although generally substantial performance permits recovery on the contract, in some jurisdictions only quasi-contractual relief is permitted. Allen v. Burns, 201 Mass. 74, 87 N.E. 194 (1909).

8. 32 Beechwood v. Fisher, 19 N.Y.2d 1008, 228 N.E.2d 823, 281 N.Y.S.2d 843 (1967) (majority refuses restitution); contra,

Freedman v. Rector, 37 Cal.2d 16, 230 P.2d 629, 31 ALR2d 1 (1951) (minority); Shanghai Inv. v. Alteka, 92 Hawai'i 482, 993 P.2d 516 (2000); Huckins v. Ritter, 99 N.M. 560, 661 P.2d 52 (1983) (the issue is whether there is a forfeiture or such unfairness as shocks the conscience of the court); see also Ponderosa Pines Ranch v. McBride, 197 Mont. 301, 642 P.2d 1050 (1982) (no restitution where claimant has been grossly negligent, willful, or fraudulent).

9. UCC § 2–718(2)(b). The revision drops the formula; the buyer may have restitution to the extent that its payments exceeds both the seller's damages and benefits the buyer has received.

10. UCC § 2–718(3) (unchanged in the revision). The same subtraction was made in non-UCC cases. Ducolon Mechanical v. Shinstine/Forness, 77 Wn.App. 707, 893 P.2d 1127 (1995).

11. UCC § 2–718(2)(a); revision § 2–718(1). On the validity of liquidated damages clauses, see §§ 14.31–14.34.

The modern trend in the law is that a party in substantial default should not be treated as an outlaw. This is being accomplished by case law[12] and legislation. For example, In addition to the UCC provision, most states have labor legislation requiring the payment of wages to workers at periodic intervals, and the payment of accrued wages at the termination of employment regardless of any contractual provision to the contrary.[13] Also, the Restatement (Second) "is more liberal in allowing recovery" than the first Restatement.[14] Nonetheless, there is a substantial division as to whether a willful breach should prevent the granting of restitution.[15]

Despite the inroads of statutes and fairly wide acceptance of the doctrine of Britton v. Turner, the majority of jurisdictions appear to adhere to the general principle that a defaulting party has no remedy notwithstanding the degree of hardship and forfeiture. The general principle is punitive, but not rational in meting out punishment. The penalty is not fashioned to meet the specific wrong. Rather, the amount of penalty depends on the fortuitous circumstances of the transaction. Paradoxically, the more the defaulting party has performed, the greater the forfeiture and the greater the unearned enrichment of the other party.[16] Other rules of forfeiture avoidance are considered in § 11.35.

§ 11.23   Recovery by a Party in Default: Divisibility

Some contracts are said to be "entire" while others are said to be "divisible." A contract is said to be divisible if "performance by each party is divided into two or more parts" and "performance of each is divided into two or more parts, the number of parts due from each party being the agreed exchange for a corresponding part by the other party."[1] It is often said that whether a contract is divisible is a question of

12. 5A Corbin § 1123; see Judge Clark's able discussion in Amtorg Trading v. Miehle Printing Press & Mfg., 206 F.2d 103 (2d Cir.1953) (prophesizing a change in New York law. The prophesy has not been fulfilled. Collar City P'shp v. Redemption Church, 235 A.D.2d 665, 651 N.Y.S.2d 729 (1997)); see also Kitchin v. Mori, 84 Nev. 181, 437 P.2d 865 (1968) (asserting that the weight of authority now permits a party in default to recover the value of performance less the aggrieved party's damages).

13. Rs. 2d § 265 cmt a; see Annot, 18 ALR5th 577.

14. Rs. 2d § 374 Reporter's Note; Perillo, Restitution in the Second Restatement of Contracts, 81 Colum.L.Rev. 37 (1981).

15. Compare, Harris v. The Cecil N. Bean, 197 F.2d 919 (2d Cir.1952) with Begovich v. Murphy, 359 Mich. 156, 101 N.W.2d 278 (1960) and Rs. 2d § 374 and cmt b. See also Combustion Engineering v. Miller Hydro Group, 13 F.3d 437 (1st Cir. 1993) (no recovery under Me. law).

16. In Freedman v. Rector, 37 Cal.2d 16, 230 P.2d 629, 31 ALR2d 1 (1951), the court in granting restitution to a defaulting purchaser of land stated that the majority rule, in effect, grants punitive damages to the non-breaching party. But this award has no "rational relationship to its purpose. * * * It not only fails to take into consideration the degree of culpability but its severity increases as the seriousness of the breach decreases." 37 Cal.2d at 22, 230 P.2d at 632.

§ 11.23

1. Howard University v. Durham, 408 A.2d 1216 (D.C.App.1979); see Scavenger, Inc. v. GT Interactive, 273 A.D.2d 60, 708 N.Y.S.2d 405 (2000); Hogan v. Coyne Int'l Enter., 996 S.W.2d 195 (Tenn.App.1998); Rs. 2d § 240 and cmts a & d; Rs. 1st § 266 cmt e; 15 Williston § 45:1 (4th ed.); 8 Corbin § 35.8 (McCauliff 1999).

interpretation or one of the intention of the parties.[2] However, the process of interpretation and the search for intention is result-oriented.[3] It is easier to understand the distinction between divisible and entire contracts if one understands the consequences of the determination.

If A and B agree that A will act as B's secretary for one year at a salary of $1,000 per week, the contract is said to be divisible.[4] Once A has worked for a week, A becomes entitled to $1,000 irrespective of any subsequent events.[5] Thus, even if A breaches the contract by wrongfully quitting, A is nonetheless entitled to $1,000 less whatever damages were caused by the material breach.[6] In effect, for the purpose of payment, the contract is deemed to be divided into 52 exchanges of performances. However, if the secretary failed, without justification, to work for four days out of a particular week and the employer wished to discharge the secretary, the question would be materiality of the breach. On this issue, the divisibility of the contract would be irrelevant because the question of materiality of the breach would be decided on the ratio of four days to a year rather than four days to a week.[7]

Not only must one inquire for *what purposes* a contract is divisible, one must also ascertain *how* the contract is divisible. A good illustration is Gill v. Johnstown Lumber.[8] Plaintiff agreed to drive logs for the defendant. The contract provided that plaintiff would receive $1 per thousand feet for logs of oak delivered to the Johnstown Boom. Thus, the contract was divisible into 1,000 feet segments. A flood made full performance impossible. The plaintiff was entitled to be paid $1 for each delivery of 1,000 feet of logs of oak or whatever amounted to substantial performance of 1,000 feet. Could plaintiff recover for driving other logs very close to the boom, if, at the last moment the logs were swept away by the flood? The court held that there could be no recovery. The contract was not divisible by the distance traversed.

2. Blakesley v. Johnson, 227 Kan. 495, 608 P.2d 908 (1980); Gaspar v. Flott, 209 Neb. 260, 307 N.W.2d 500 (1981); Matter of Wilson's Estate, 50 N.Y.2d 59, 427 N.Y.S.2d 977, 405 N.E.2d 220 (1980); Management Servs. v. Development Assocs., 617 P.2d 406 (Utah 1980).

3. It is also often stated that a contract should be treated as entire when by a consideration of its terms, nature and purposes each and all of the parts appear to be interdependent and common to one another and to the consideration. Singleton v. Foreman, 435 F.2d 962 (5th Cir.1970); First S. & L. Ass'n v. American Home Assurance, 29 N.Y.2d 297, 327 N.Y.S.2d 609, 277 N.E.2d 638 (1971). Custom and usage are important in making the determination as are the surrounding circumstances. George v. School Dist., 7 Or.App. 183, 490 P.2d 1009 (1971); see also Rs. 2d § 240 cmt e; Village Inn Pancake House v. Higdon, 294 Ala. 378, 318 So.2d 245 (1975). At times it is said that the question is one of law. L.D.A. v.

Cross, 167 W.Va. 215, 279 S.E.2d 409 (1981). Other courts have indicated that it is a question of fact. Studzinski v. Travelers Ins., 180 N.J.Super. 416, 434 A.2d 1160 (1981).

4. White v. Atkins, 62 Mass. (8 Cush.) 367 (1851); Wrightsman v. Brown, 181 Okl. 142, 73 P.2d 121 (1937).

5. A secretary who substantially performed a divisible part of such a contract would be entitled to $1,000 less whatever damages were caused by the failure to work a full week. See Lowy v. United Pac. Ins., 67 Cal.2d 87, 60 Cal.Rptr. 225, 429 P.2d 577 (1967).

6. See Rs. 2d § 240 cmt a (state statutes requiring frequent periodic payment of wages have reduced the importance of the doctrine of divisibility in employment contracts).

7. Rs. 2d § 240 cmt b.

8. 151 Pa. 534, 25 A. 120 (1892).

In another case[9] the plaintiff agreed to make extensive alterations to the defendant's property for $3,075, payable in installments: $150 on signing the contract, $1,000 on delivery of the material and starting to work, $1,500 on completion of the rough carpentry and $425 on the completion of the work. Plaintiff completed the rough carpentry, but the owner failed to pay. Plaintiff sued for the entire price, but the lower courts entered judgment for $1,500 on a theory of divisibility. This was held to be erroneous as the contract was entire. The provision for progress payments was not for payment of the equivalent work.[10] The $1,500 was not an "agreed exchange" for the rough carpentry, just as $150 was not the "agreed exchange" for its signature. It could, however, be argued that the contractor could have treated the unpaid progress payment as a debt owed to him, forgoing an action for total breach.[11] However the contractor in this case sued for total breach, and was required to prove its damages.

Despite the supposed reliance on intention, it is rare that the parties express an intention on the issue of divisibility. The test ultimately appears to be whether, had the parties thought about it as fair and reasonable people, they would be willing to exchange the performance in question irrespective of what transpired subsequently or whether the divisions made were merely for the purpose of requiring periodic payments as the work progresses.[12] The results reached depend largely on the kind of contract involved. Building contracts are generally entire.[13] This is especially so where the owner makes progress payments, with, however, a retainage of, say, 15%, to be paid on completion.[14] Employment contracts are, however, generally held to be divisible. The rules of the UCC relating to installment contracts are discussed above.[15]

§ 11.24   Divisibility: Other Uses of the Concept

The concept of divisibility is, perhaps, employed primarily in connection with the problem of whether a party in default may recover as discussed immediately above. However, the concept is also used in other contexts. It is used to determine whether a contract tainted with illegality can be severed into a legal and enforceable portion and an

9. New Era Homes v. Forster, 299 N.Y. 303, 86 N.E.2d 757, 22 ALR2d 1338 (1949).

10. Bridgeport v. T.A. Scott, 94 Conn. 461, 109 A. 162 (1920); Pennsylvania Exch. Bank v. U.S., 170 F.Supp. 629 (Ct.Cl.1959).

11. 8 Corbin § 35.11, at 325 (McCauliff 1999).

12. Tipton v. Feitner, 20 N.Y. 423 (1859).

13. New Era Homes v. Forster, 299 N.Y. 303, 86 N.E.2d 757, 22 ALR2d 1338 (1949). But see Lowy v. United Pac. Ins., 67 Cal.2d 87, 60 Cal.Rptr. 225, 429 P.2d 577 (1967), which combined the doctrines of divisibility and substantial performance. The contract provided that contractor was to excavate and improve the street; a unit price was allocated to each phase. The contract was divisible and the contractor recovered for substantial performance of the first phase, despite defaulting entirely on the second phase and in part as to the first phase. In a case of the construction of 35 houses each house was deemed to be divisible. Carrig v. Gilbert–Varker, 314 Mass. 351, 50 N.E.2d 59, 147 ALR 927 (1943).

14. Bridgeport v. T.A. Scott, 94 Conn. 461, 109 A. 162 (1920).

15. See § 11.20(d) supra.

illegal and unenforceable portion.[1] The concept is also used to determine allocation of risks where performance of contractual duties in part becomes impossible.[2] The question of divisibility may be raised in connection with the running of the Statute of Limitations[3] and the applicability of the Statute of Frauds,[4] as well as with the question of whether the aggrieved party has one cause of action or several.[5]

Given the wide variety of contexts in which the question of divisibility is raised, it is fairly obvious that the contours of the concept will be reshaped to provide a just result in the particular context in which the concept is raised.[6]

§ 11.25   Independent Promises

A promise is independent[1] (unconditional) if it is unqualified or if nothing but the lapse of time is necessary to make the promise presently enforceable.[2] An independent promise must be performed even though the other party has not performed.[3] For example, A promises to build a house for B and B promises to pay X dollars when the house is completed. B's promise is constructively conditioned on A's performance. A must perform before B is required to do anything.[4] Thus, A's promise is, by definition, independent (unconditional) with the result that if A is guilty of a material breach, B may cancel and sue for a total breach, although B has not performed. B need only prove that he or she would have been ready, willing and able to pay had A performed.[5] Even though A's promise is by definition independent, events may occur which would relieve A of the duty to perform the promise. For example, if B repudiated the contract, A would not be obliged to perform.[6]

Promises that were originally independent may become conditional with the passage of time. For example, in a transaction for the sale and purchase of real property B agrees to pay the purchase price in three

---

§ 11.24

1. See § 22.6 infra. However, as we shall see, the word is not necessarily used in the same sense in which it is used here.

2. See Rs. 1st § 463; ch. 13.

3. See Rich v. Arancio, 277 Mass. 310, 178 N.E. 743, Annot., 82 ALR 313 (1931); see also In re Payless Cashways, 203 F.3d 1081 (8th Cir.2000) (timeliness of filing of mechanics's lien).

4. See U.S. Rubber v. Bercher's Royal Tire Serv., 205 F.Supp. 368 (W.D.Ark. 1962).

5. See Armstrong v. Illinois Bankers Life Ass'n, 217 Ind. 601, 29 N.E.2d 415, 131 ALR 769 (1940), reh. denied.

6. Rs. 2d § 240 cmt e.

§ 11.25

1. The Restatements prefer not to use the term "independent promise." See Rs. 2d § 231 Reporter's Note.

2. See § 11.2 supra.

3. Orkin Exterminating v. Harris, 224 Ga. 759, 164 S.E.2d 727 (1968); Orkin Exterminating v. Gill, 222 Ga. 760, 152 S.E.2d 411 (1966); Guglielmi v. Guglielmi, 431 A.2d 1226 (R.I.1981); Hanks v. GAB Business Servs., 644 S.W.2d 707 (Tex.1982), reversing 626 S.W.2d 564 (Tex.App.1981). But cf. Kaye v. Orkin Exterminating, 472 F.2d 1213 (5th Cir.1973); Associated Spring v. Roy F. Wilson & Avnet, 410 F.Supp. 967 (D.S.C.1976).

4. See § 11.17 supra.

5. See § 11.17 supra. B's promise is constructively conditional on A's substantial performance.

6. See § 12.8 infra.

installments and S agrees to convey at the time of the payment of the final installment. The buyer's promises to pay the first two installments are unconditional (independent) but the promise to pay the last installment is concurrently conditional on the tendering of the deed.[7] However, if B has not paid the first two installments when the third installment becomes due, S may not, under the majority view, sue for the first two installments without tendering a deed or showing that such tender is excused.[8] Thus, a promise which was originally unconditional, by definition, becomes conditional in an attempt to do justice.[9]

Except in the situation where by the terms of the contract one party must perform before the other, there is a strong presumption that a promise in a contract is not intended to be independent, "unless a contrary intention is clearly manifested."[10] The result is that very few promises are independent.[11]

While the promise of an insurance company is always conditioned on the insured event (e.g. fire) and thus its promise is conditional and not independent, it may be independent of the insured's payment of the premium. At times the insured will make a promise to pay premiums. If the doctrine of constructive conditions applied, one would expect that the insurance company's obligation would be constructively conditioned on the payment of the premiums so that the insured could not recover if the premium was not paid. However under the cases, the insured may recover even if the premium is unpaid because the promise of the insurance company is deemed to be "independent of" the payment of premiums.[12] It should be noted that this is not a question of substantial performance, but rather the courts simply refuse to apply the doctrine of constructive conditions. To avoid this result, the insurance company may and does expressly condition its promise on payment of the premium or includes a clause providing for cancellation in the event of nonpayment.

It is often stated that a lease illustrates a true independent promise.[13] A lease is a peculiar instrument. It acts as a conveyance of a leasehold interest in real property. Usually it also is a bilateral contract in which the tenant agrees to pay rent and the landlord agrees to make

---

7. Kane v. Hood, 30 Mass. (13 Pick.) 281 (1832).

8. See § 11.6.

9. Jozovich v. Central California Berry Growers Ass'n, 183 Cal.App.2d 216, 6 Cal. Rptr. 617 (1960); Beecher v. Conradt, 13 N.Y. (3 Kern.) 108 (1855). But cf. Gray v. Meek, 199 Ill. 136, 64 N.E. 1020 (1902) (all but last installment may be recovered without tender). See also Rs. 2d § 234 cmt d & ill. 8.

10. Rs. 2d § 232 and cmt a; K & G Constr. v. Harris, 223 Md. 305, 164 A.2d 451 (1960).

11. Rs. 2d § 232; Gold Bond Stamp v. Gilt–Edge Stamps, 437 F.2d 27 (5th Cir. 1971).

12. Dwelling–House Ins. v. Hardie, 37 Kan. 674, 16 P. 92 (1887); Rs. 1st § 293; but see McDuffie v. Criterion Cas., 214 Ga. App. 818, 449 S.E.2d 133 (1994). The Restatement (Second) achieves the same result on totally different reasoning. It states that the insurance company may terminate for non-payment of premium but it must do so before the insured event occurs; otherwise it will be deemed to have elected to continue the contract. Rs. 2d § 379; see § 11.32 infra.

13. Restatement (Second) of Property, (Landlord & Tenant) § 7.1 Reporter's Note (1977) and Ch. 7 Introductory Note.

repairs or provide other services. Courts have generally focused on the property rather than the contract aspects of the lease.[14] As a result of this orientation, it has generally been held that the tenant's duty to pay is independent of the landlord's promise to repair or to provide services,[15] a result which contributed to the decay of urban housing and to the phenomenon of the "rent strike."[16] The rule is mitigated by holding that if the landlord's non-performance is extreme it may amount to a "constructive eviction" justifying cancellation of the lease by the tenant, and in recent years a number of courts have applied the contract rules of constructive conditions to leases, particularly residential leases.[17]

§ 11.26 Dependency of Separate Contracts

Where the parties have entered into two written contracts at substantially the same time, the question arises whether they are part of the same exchange. If they are not, a breach of one will have no effect on the other. If they are part of the same exchange, the question will be the overall materiality of the breach.[1] This is a question of intention, but the making of two separate contracts ordinarily indicates an intent that a failure to perform one contract will have no effect on the other.[2]

C. EXCUSE OF CONDITION

Table of Sections

14. Rock County Sav. & Trust v. Yost's, 36 Wis.2d 360, 153 N.W.2d 594 (1967); see also Rs. 2d § 231 cmt e.

15. Rs. 1st § 290; Means v. Dierks, 180 F.2d 306 (10th Cir.1950); Thomson–Houston Elec. v. Durant Land Improvement, 144 N.Y. 34, 39 N.E. 7 (1894). This conclusion does not prove that the tenant's promise is unconditional (independent) because tenant need not pay if the landlord does not have title.

16. See Simmons, 15 Buffalo L.Rev. 572 (1966); Comment, 54 U.Cin.L.Rev. 1035 (1986).

17. Charles E. Burt v. Seven Grand, 340 Mass. 124, 163 N.E.2d 4 (1959); see McKinney's N.Y. Real Prop. Law § 235–b (providing that every lease contains a warranty of habitability); Quinn & Phillips, The Law of Landlord–Tenant: A Critical Evaluation of

the Past With Guidelines For the Future, 38 Fordham L.Rev. 225 (1969).

§ 11.26

1. Rs. 1st § 231 cmt d.

2. Greenberg v. Dowdy, 930 S.W.2d 512 (Mo.App.1996); Rudman v. Cowles Communications, 30 N.Y.2d 1, 330 N.Y.S.2d 33, 280 N.E.2d 867, 63 ALR3d 527 (1972). Accord, National Union Fire Ins. v. Clairmont, 231 A.D.2d 239, 662 N.Y.S.2d 110 (1997) (fraud as to one contract does not infect another); But see Murphy v. Chitty, 739 So.2d 697 (Fla.App.1999); Brooks v. Towson Realty, 223 Md. 61, 162 A.2d 431 (1960) (specific performance of one of two related contracts refused unless plaintiff also performed the other); Talley v. Talley, 566 N.W.2d 846 (S.D.1997); Countryside Ortho. v. Peyton, 261 Va. 142, 541 S.E.2d 279 (2001).

§ 11.27   Introduction

So far in this chapter, we have seen how a party' s duty to perform depended on the occurrence of certain conditions. But this dependence will not always exist. Sometimes a party must perform even though the condition did not occur. This is because the condition is excused. In a general way, it can be said that a condition will be excused when it would be unjust to insist on the fulfillment of a condition, express or constructive.[1] Some of the reasons why a condition may be excused will now be discussed.

§ 11.28   Prevention, Hindrance, or Failure to Cooperate

May a plaintiff who has failed to perform a condition precedent to defendant's obligation recover on the contract when the performance has been wrongfully prevented or hindered by the conduct of the defendant? Only the law of the jungle would say that plaintiff's failure to perform should not be excused.[1] The major question is, what is wrongful conduct?[2]

An illustration will help clarify the question. Plaintiff agreed to care for his granduncle until the uncle died, in exchange for a payment to be made when the uncle died.[3] Plaintiff was prevented from doing so when, without cause, the uncle ordered him to leave at gunpoint. Plaintiff had not fulfilled the constructive condition precedent to the uncle's obligation to pay. However, he successfully relied on a theory of excuse of condition because the uncle's conduct was wrongful and prevented the condition from occurring.

The case raises a number of questions. The first is what does it mean when one says that a condition is excused? It means that even

§ 11.27

1. Hubler Rentals v. Roadway Exp., 637 F.2d 257 (4th Cir.1981); Propst Constr. v. North Carolina Dep't of Transp., 56 N.C.App. 759, 290 S.E.2d 387 (1982).

§ 11.28

1. Rohde v. Massachusetts Mut. Life Ins., 632 F.2d 667 (6th Cir.1980); Rs. 2d § 245 and cmt a. Wrongful prevention not only excuses conditions, but acts as a breach. Sunshine Steak, Salad & Seafood v.

W.I.M. Realty, 135 A.D.2d 891, 522 N.Y.S.2d 292 (1987).

2. Rs. 1st § 315.

3. Barron v. Cain, 216 N.C. 282, 4 S.E.2d 618 (1939). In Haft v. Dart Group, 877 F.Supp. 896 (D.Del.1995), there was no gun, but the plaintiff was fired in breach of contract and told his stock options were terminated. This relieved him of the condition of giving a notice of exercise of the options.

though the condition did not take place, the plaintiff may recover *on the contract* provided it is proved that plaintiff would have been ready, willing and able to perform but for the prevention.[4]

A potential question involves causation. H and W entered into an ante-nuptial agreement. H promised W that H's executor would pay her $20,000 at H's death, if she survived him. H intentionally killed W. Upon H's death, is W's executor entitled to the $20,000?[5] W's survival is an express condition precedent to H's obligation to pay and H's conduct was wrongful. The question is whether H's wrongful conduct was the proximate cause of W's failure to survive H. Would W, in the normal course of events, have survived H? Under the First Restatement, the test was whether "the condition would have occurred * * * except for such prevention or hindrance."[6] The Restatement (Second) applies a more liberal approach. It states that the condition will be excused if the wrongful conduct "substantially contributed to the non-occurrence of the condition" and puts the burden of proof on this issue on the defendant.[7]

One of the difficult questions is what constitutes *wrongful* prevention, *wrongful* hindrance, or *wrongful* failure to cooperate. In Amics v. Wesnofske,[8] plaintiff's right to a brokerage commission from the vendor was, by agreement, conditioned "on closing of title."[9] The vendee defaulted but the vendor took no legal action. Instead, the vendor settled by agreement with the vendee under which he retained the down payment. The broker insisted on payment of a commission, arguing that the occurrence of the condition was excused because of the vendor's failure to bring an action for specific performance against the vendee. This would bring about the closing of title. It was held that the vendor's duty to cooperate did not extend to bringing an action for specific performance.[10] The broker would be entitled to a commission, however, if the seller agreed with the buyer to rescind the contract when there had been no breach on the part of the buyer.[11] This would be affirmative conduct preventing the condition from occurring.[12]

---

4. Rs. 2d § 225 cmt c.

5. Foreman State Trust & Sav. Bank v. Tauber, 348 Ill. 280, 180 N.E. 827 (1932).

6. Rs. 1st § 295.

7. Rs. 2d § 245 cmt b and ill. 5. The case did not discuss this problem.

8. 255 N.Y. 156, 174 N.E. 436, 73 ALR 918 (1931).

9. When this condition is not imposed by the contract, the broker is entitled to a commission when the broker produces a buyer who is ready, willing and able to buy. Turner v. Minasian, 358 Mass. 425, 265 N.E.2d 371 (1970); Kaelin v. Warner, 27 N.Y.2d 352, 267 N.E.2d 86, 318 N.Y.S.2d 294 (1971). The purchaser is not ordinarily liable to the broker. Geller v. New England Indus., 535 F.2d 1381 (2d Cir.1976); Annot., 30 ALR3d 1395 (1970); but see Ellsworth Dobbs v. Johnson, 50 N.J. 528, 236 A.2d

843, 30 ALR3d 1370 (1967); 1 Corbin § 2.30 (Perillo 1993).

10. Accord, Ellsworth Dobbs v. Johnson, 50 N.J. 528, 236 A.2d 843, 30 ALR3d 1370 (1967); Beattie–Firth v. Colebank, 143 W.Va. 740, 105 S.E.2d 5, 74 ALR2d 431 (1958); see also Barbetta Agency v. Sciaraffa, 135 N.J.Super. 488, 343 A.2d 770 (A.D. 1975). Contra, Tarbell v. Bomes, 48 R.I. 86, 135 A. 604, 51 ALR 1386 (1927). A seller who refuses to convey without cause will be liable to the broker. Hillis v. Lake, 421 Mass. 537, 658 N.E.2d 687 (1995); Westhill Exports v. Pope, 12 N.Y.2d 491, 240 N.Y.S.2d 961, 191 N.E.2d 447 (1963).

11. Cf. Levy v. Lacey, 22 N.Y.2d 271, 292 N.Y.S.2d 455, 239 N.E.2d 378 (1968).

12. Is a marketing agent entitled to commissions resulting from his efforts, but actual sales agreements were made after

The determination of what constitutes wrongful prevention does not depend on any mechanical rule. Rather, the court's instinct for the commercial setting, the ethical position of the parties, the probable understanding that they would have reached had they considered the matter and many other factors enter into the determination.[13]

Let us compare two other cases with some additional wrinkles. In Patterson v. Meyerhofer,[14] plaintiff agreed to sell, and the defendant agreed to buy certain real property. Plaintiff informed defendant that he did not have title to the property but expected to acquire it at a foreclosure sale. The defendant outbid the plaintiff at the foreclosure sale. The defendant's conduct was wrongful because it violated the implied covenant not to engage in conduct that intentionally prevents the other party from performing. Two results followed from the wrongful prevention of the defendant. First, plaintiff was excused from the inability to convey because of wrongful prevention, and second, since an affirmative obligation had been violated, plaintiff was entitled to damages.

The limits of the doctrine of prevention are set by Iron Trade Products v. Wilkoff Co.[15] Plaintiff entered into a contract with the defendant for the purchase of 2,600 tons of section relaying rails. Defendant failed to deliver and alleges as a defense that the supply of such rails was very limited and that the plaintiff during the term of the contract bought and agreed to buy large quantities of rails from the two parties from whom defendant was planning to buy, thus enhancing the price. The defendant was seeking to be excused from the promise to sell the rails and argued that the wrongful prevention excused the promise.[16] The court held that plaintiff's conduct was not wrongful because this was a foreseeable commercial risk which any short-seller assumes.[17] Because the defendant assumed this risk, plaintiff's conduct could not be wrongful.[18] The result would be different if the buyer exhausted what the buyer knew to be the seller's only source of supply. The seller would likely have had the defense of impossibility of performance.

The Amies brokerage case involved the question of the degree of cooperation contracting parties owe each other. The question comes up in a number of other contexts. If the contract requires the owner to provide specifications for completion of a building, the failure of the contractor to comply with a time-is-of-the-essence clause will be excused if completion was impeded by the owner's delay in providing specifications.[19] Failure to cooperate can also result in a breach from which

the agent was fired? Harold Wright v. E.I. Du Pont De Nemours & Co., 49 F.3d 308 (7th Cir.1995) (questions of fact are present, but default rule would be yes).

13. Patterson, Constructive Conditions in Contracts, 42 Colum.L.Rev. 903, 928–42 (1942).

14. 204 N.Y. 96, 97 N.E. 472 (1912).

15. 272 Pa. 172, 116 A. 150 (1922).

16. See Ch. 13.

17. See U.S. v. Fidelity & Deposit, 152 Fed. 596 (2d Cir.1907); 6 Corbin § 1264.

18. Keystone Bus Lines v. ARA Serv., 214 Neb. 813, 336 N.W.2d 555 (1983); Rs. 2d § 245 cmt a.

19. Bruson Heights v. State, 281 A.D. 371, 120 N.Y.S.2d 73 (1953) (owner was to select fixtures for the building); Levicoff v.

damages flow,[20] or as a failure of condition.[21] Implied duties of cooperation are frequently present when government approvals are required[22] and in commercial leases where rent is based on a percentage of revenues. Unless the lease provides for a substantial minimum rent, it is generally held that the tenant has an obligation to use reasonable efforts to maximize revenues.[23] Similar analysis can be applied to a trademark license.[24]

In a remarkable case, the court held that a lessee had a duty to remind a sophisticated lessor that the denial of a request for financing by the lessor triggered an option to purchase at very favorable terms.[25] The rationale was expressed as follows:

> Before the contract is signed, the parties confront each other with a natural wariness. Neither expects the other to be especially forthcoming, and therefore there is no deception when one is not. Afterwards the situation is different. The parties are now in a cooperative relationship the costs of which will be considerably reduced by a measure of trust. So each lowers his guard a bit, and now silence is more apt to be deceptive.

The court looked at the failure to cooperate as a question of whether the lessee had breached the covenant of good faith and fair dealing. It is not alone in this approach.[26]

Richard I. Rubin & Co., 413 Pa. 134, 196 A.2d 359 (1964) (lessee neglected to provide plans for store which lessor was to build). A general contractor must take reasonable measures to insure that subcontractors are not delayed. McGrath v. Electrical Constr., 230 Or. 295, 364 P.2d 604 (1961).

20. Kehm v. U.S., 93 F.Supp. 620 (Ct. Cl.1950) (the government failed to supply the proper tail assemblies for bombs to be made by the plaintiff); Van Valkenburgh, N. & N. v. Hayden Pub., 30 N.Y.2d 34, 330 N.Y.S.2d 329, 281 N.E.2d 142 (1972) (publisher sabotaged sales of books written by one of its authors); Fairfax County v. Worcester Bros., 257 Va. 382, 514 S.E.2d 147 (1999). If a party's duty is subject to governmental approval, failure to apply for approval will excuse the condition and make it liable for damages. Bradford Dyeing Ass'n v. J. Stog Tech, 765 A.2d 1226 (R.I. 2001)

21. Myers, Smith & Granady v. N.Y. Property Ins. Underwriting Assoc., 85 N.Y.2d 832, 623 N.Y.S.2d 840, 647 N.E.2d 1348 (1995).

22. Bradford Dyeing Ass'n v. J. Stog Tech, 765 A.2d 1226 (R.I.2001).

23. Swartz v. War Memorial Commission, 25 A.D.2d 90, 267 N.Y.S.2d 253 (1966)

(material breach occurred where concessionaire on a percentage contract in sports arena refused to apply for a license to sell beer); Stop & Shop v. Ganem, 347 Mass. 697, 200 N.E.2d 248 (1964) (closing store is no breach of percentage lease where there is a substantial minimum rent); Olympus Hills Shopping Center v. Smith's Food & Drug Centers, 889 P.2d 445 (Utah App. 1994) (jury question whether radically different use was a breach of the duty of good faith and fair dealing); Frederick Business Properties v. Peoples Drug Stores, 191 W.Va. 235, 445 S.E.2d 176 (1994) (no implied covenant of continuous operation).

24. Emerson Radio v. Orion Sales, 253 F.3d 159 (3d Cir.2001).

25. Market St. Assocs. v. Frey, 941 F.2d 588 (7th Cir.1991) (Posner, J.).The holding has been conceptualized as creating a duty to warn, a subset of a duty to rescue. Eisenberg, The Duty to Rescue in Contract Law, 71 Fordham L.Rev. 647, 666–70 (2002).

26. See Seaward Constr. v. Rochester, 118 N.H. 128 383 A.2d 707 (1978), as explained by Souter, J., in Centronics v. Genicom, 132 N.H. 133, 141, 562 A.2d 187, 192 (1989); see also 511 West 232nd Owners Corp. v. Jennifer Realty Co., 98 N.Y.2d 144, 746 N.Y.S.2d 131, 773 N.E.2d 496 (2002).

§ 11.29   Waiver, Estoppel and Election

(a) Introduction

Waiver, estoppel and election are concepts utilized in many contexts in the fabric of the law. Here we are concerned with them only as they relate to excuse of contractual conditions. We also briefly consider here the topic of renunciation of a right to damages.[1]

(b) Estoppel Defined

Equitable estoppel, also known as estoppel *in pais,* is a progenitor of the doctrine of promissory estoppel.[2] In its traditional form, equitable estoppel applies when a party (1) misrepresents or conceals a fact, (2) on which the other party justifiably relies, (3) injuriously. The party is estopped from denying the utterances or acts to the injury of the other party.[3]

Often additional factors are required. There is a substantial body of law to the effect that not only must the representation be false but that the party to be estopped must be shown to have known that the representation was false. In addition, under this view, it must be shown that the party to be estopped must have intended that the representation be acted on or at least must so act that the party asserting the estoppel has a right to believe that it was so intended.[4] Contrary to the traditional view of equitable estoppel, some of the more modern cases state that a misrepresentation of fact is not necessary for the doctrine to apply,[5] and that fraud, bad faith or intent to deceive are not essential.[6]

A promise is sometimes said to be sufficient to form the basis of an equitable estoppel.[7] Such holdings, of course, are invoking promissory estoppel in disguise. For example, if a party promised before breach to accept a late payment, the promisor would be estopped from asserting the lateness of the payment unless the promise was withdrawn in time.[8]

§ 11.29

1. See § 11.33 infra.

2. See Ch. 6.

3. 4 Williston § 8:3 (4th ed.)

4. Beverage v. Harvey, 602 F.2d 657 (4th Cir.1979); Strong v. Santa Cruz, 15 Cal.3d 720, 125 Cal.Rptr. 896, 543 P.2d 264 (1975); Bettendorf Educ. Ass'n v. Bettendorf Community, 262 N.W.2d 550 (Iowa 1978); Scotts Bluff v. Hughes, 202 Neb. 551, 276 N.W.2d 206 (1979); Albuquerque Nat. Bank v. Albuquerque Ranch Estates, 99 N.M. 95, 654 P.2d 548 (1982).

5. A misrepresentation of fact includes nondisclosure when there is a "duty" to speak. Stratmann v. Stratmann, 6 Kan. App.2d 403, 628 P.2d 1080 (1981); Wynn v. Farmers Ins. Group, 98 Mich.App. 93, 296 N.W.2d 197 (1980); Cheqer, Inc. v. Painters and Decorators Joint Committee, 98 Nev.

609, 655 P.2d 996 (1982); In re Allstate Ins., 179 N.J.Super. 581, 432 A.2d 1366 (1981); Williams v. Stansbury, 649 S.W.2d 293 (Tex.1983). See § 9.20 supra.

6. Arctic Contractors v. State, 564 P.2d 30 (Alaska 1977); Town of West Hartford v. Rechel, 190 Conn. 114, 459 A.2d 1015 (1983); Pino v. Maplewood Packing, 375 A.2d 534 (Me.1977); Addressograph—Multigraph v. Zink, 273 Md. 277, 329 A.2d 28 (1974); Triple Cities Constr. v. Maryland Cas., 4 N.Y.2d 443, 176 N.Y.S.2d 292, 151 N.E.2d 856 (1958).

7. Novelty Knitting Mills v. Siskind, 500 Pa. 432, 457 A.2d 502 (1983).

8. Dreier v. Sherwood, 77 Colo. 539, 238 P. 38 (1925); see UCC § 2–209(5) (substantially unchanged in revision).

The promise is enforced even though there is no consideration for it.[9] This is a species of promissory estoppel except that the term promissory estoppel is ordinarily used in reference to the *formation* of a contract and not to the *performance* of a contract.[10] Nonetheless, this promise is effective on a theory of estoppel whether it be denominated equitable or promissory.[11]

It is often stated that equitable estoppel is an affirmative defense that must be established by clear and convincing evidence and that its existence is ordinarily a question of fact.[12] The rules of equitable estoppel are applied somewhat differently to a government.[13] The theory is that one should not rely on statements made by governmental officials unless the statement is made in accordance with authorized governmental procedures.

(c) Waiver and Election

A waiver, which may be express or implied,[14] is generally defined as a voluntary and intentional relinquishment of a known right.[15] As the subsequent sections will show, there are few, if any, more erroneous definitions known to the law. For one thing, waiver is far more multifaceted than this definition would allow for. Moreover, even as far as it goes, it is totally misleading. It strongly implies that the waiving party intends to give up a right. In reality, many, if not most waivers are unintentional and frequently do not involve a "right" that the party is aware of. Finally, contractual *rights* are not waivable, *conditions* are.

The party waiving must know or have reason to know the facts giving rise to the failure of condition.[16] However, knowledge of the law is

---

9. The explanation for this result and the limitations placed on it are explained in § 11.31.

10. Williams v. FNBC Acceptance, 419 So.2d 1363 (Ala.1982); Morgan v. Maryland Cas., 458 S.W.2d 789 (Ky.1970); Leonard v. Sav–A–Stop Serv., 289 Md. 204, 424 A.2d 336 (1981); Perkins v. Kerby, 308 So.2d 914 (Miss.1975); Clark & Enersen v. Schimmel Hotels, 194 Neb. 810, 235 N.W.2d 870 (1975); Commonwealth v. School Dist., 49 Pa.Cmwlth. 316, 410 A.2d 1311 (1980); Klinke v. Famous Recipe Fried Chicken, 94 Wn.2d 255, 616 P.2d 644 (1980).

11. Moline I.F.C. Finance v. Soucinek, 91 Ill.App.2d 257, 234 N.E.2d 57 (1968); Arrow Lathing & Plastering v. Schaulat Plumbing Supply, 83 Ill.App.2d 394, 228 N.E.2d 209 (1967); Dart v. Thompson, 261 Iowa 237, 154 N.W.2d 82 (1967); American Bank & Trust v. Trinity Universal Ins., 251 La. 445, 205 So.2d 35 (1967); Triple Cities Constr. v. Maryland Cas., 4 N.Y.2d 443, 176 N.Y.S.2d 292, 151 N.E.2d 856 (1958).

12. Coachmen Indus. v. Security Trust & Sav. Bank, 329 N.W.2d 648 (Iowa 1983); Stevan v. Brown, 54 Md.App. 235, 458 A.2d

466 (1983); Mundy v. Arcuri, 165 W.Va. 128, 267 S.E.2d 454 (1980). However there are cases saying that equitable estoppel may be the basis of a cause of action as is true of promissory estoppel. Janke Construction v. Vulcan Materials, 527 F.2d 772 (7th Cir.1976).

13. See, e.g., Saltzman, Estoppel Against the Government, 45 Fordham L.Rev. 497 (1976).

14. Goldenberg v. Corporate Air, 189 Conn. 504, 457 A.2d 296 (1983), overruled on other grounds; James v. Mitchell, 159 Ga.App. 761, 285 S.E.2d 222 (1981).

15. Realty Growth Investors v. Council of Unit Owners, 453 A.2d 450 (Del.1982); Babb's v. Babb, 169 N.W.2d 211 (Iowa 1969); Cohler v. Smith, 280 Minn. 181, 158 N.W.2d 574 (1968).

16. Mobley v. Estate of Parker, 278 Ark. 37, 642 S.W.2d 883 (1982); Realty Growth Investors v. Council of Unit Owners, 453 A.2d 450 (Del.1982); Alsens Am. Portland Cement Works v. Degnon Contracting, 222 N.Y. 34, 118 N.E. 210 (1917); Rs. 2d § 93.

immaterial.[17] Whether and to what extent a waiver is effective is the subject matter of the next three sections. These sections examine waiver contemporaneous with the formation of the contract, waiver after formation of the contract, but before failure of condition, and waiver after failure of condition. A waiver after failure of condition is often referred to as an election. Waiver is ordinarily a question of fact.[18]

§ 11.30   Waiver at the Formation of the Contract

The doctrine of waiver has sometimes been applied to events prior to or contemporaneous with the formation of the contract. If an insurance policy provides that the policy is void if the same property is covered by other insurance and an authorized agent "waives" this condition by a statement contemporaneous with the issuance of the policy, the issue is one of the admissibility of evidence of this promise (waiver) under the parol evidence rule. There is no consideration problem because that promise is supported by the same consideration as supports the other promises of the insurer. Under the parol evidence rule, it would appear that the policy is a total integration and that the oral promise contradicts the integration. Some courts have followed this logic.[1] Many, however, on a variety of theories, especially on the grounds of equitable estoppel, have held that the parol evidence rule does not bar proof of the "waiver."[2] Other cases have proceeded on the theory that reformation of the instrument is available even in an action at law.[3]

Whatever the analytic grounds advanced to support these cases, the courts have been influenced by the relative bargaining positions of the parties and have attempted to mitigate the "take it or leave it" nature of printed form policies.[4] Statutory enactments in a number of states have put this problem on a new basis. The power of the insurer is reduced by requiring the policy to conform to statutory standards; at the same time, the insured's right to rely on oral waivers is removed or severely restricted.[5]

This theory of "waiver" has also been applied in non-insurance cases but much more sparingly. A good illustration is Ehret Co. v. Eaton,

---

17. Rs. 2d § 84 cmt b & § 93.

18. Riverside Dev. v. Ritchie, 103 Idaho 515, 650 P.2d 657 (1982); Travelers Indem. v. Fields, 317 N.W.2d 176 (Iowa 1982).

§ 11.30

1. Lumber Underwriters v. Rife, 237 U.S. 605 (1915); Northern Assurance v. Grand View Bldg. Ass'n, 183 U.S. 308 (1902).

2. Annot., 63 ALR5th 427. Note that the estoppel here is promissory in nature. This once again demonstrates that promissory estoppel is not merely a substitute for consideration, since the "waiver" is supported by consideration.

3. Wilhide v. Keystone Ins., 195 F.Supp. 659 (M.D.Pa.1961); Grand View Bldg. Ass'n v. Northern Assurance, 73 Neb. 149, 102 N.W. 246 (1905), aff'd. For the availability of reformation at law, see Rs. 2d § 155 cmt a; Rs. 1st § 507.

4. See 14 Williston § 41:8 (4th ed.).

5. Metropolitan Life Ins. v. Alterovitz, 214 Ind. 186, 14 N.E.2d 570, 117 ALR 770 (1938); Johnson v. Mut. Benefit Health & Acc. Ass'n, 5 A.D.2d 103, 168 N.Y.S.2d 879 (1957), modified; see 14 Williston § 41:12 (4th ed.).

Yale & Towne.[6] A franchisee (A) was presented by B (franchisor) with a written franchise agreement that contained a 30 day termination clause. A balked at the termination provision but signed it after B orally promised that A could rely on fair treatment. Under the parol evidence rule this evidence normally would be excluded except possibly under the doctrine of promissory fraud. However, the court allowed the evidence on a theory of "waiver." The provision of the form contract had been waived by the franchisor. The waiver induced the franchisee's acceptance of the contract, and the franchisor is estopped from attempting to enforce the printed termination clause.[7]

§ 11.31 Waiver After Formation of the Contract

There are three important rules with respect to a waiver of a condition before failure of condition. The most important rule is that a waiver of a material part of the agreed exchange is ineffective.[1] Only an immaterial part of the agreed exchange may be waived. (There is an analogous rule with respect to aleatory contracts).[2] For example, conditions which merely fix the time or manner of performance or provide for giving notice or the supplying of proofs may be waived.[3]

Suppose Vendor, for a consideration gave Purchaser an option to purchase Blackacre for $100,000, exercisable only by a tender of $100,000 in cash or certified check. Purchaser's tender of the purchase price is an express condition precedent to Vendor's obligation. Suppose, before expiration of the option, Vendor told purchaser that the payment of the price is waived and Vendor will convey Blackacre anyway. The waiver would be ineffective. A related rule renders ineffective a waiver of an aleatory condition. Thus, if Insurer promises to pay up to $100,000 for any fire loss Owner's home suffers, Insurer's waiver of the condition that there be a fire would be ineffective.

The second rule is that even if an immaterial part of the agreed exchange is waived, the waiver may be withdrawn or modified if the withdrawal or modification does not operate unfairly.[4] Suppose A agrees to complete a structure for B by January 1 and time is made of the essence. Suppose further that B, before there is a failure of condition, waives the January 1 deadline by a promise that the work may be completed later. Such a waiver is effective because the completion date is not a material part of the agreed exchange.[5] However, as a matter of

6. 523 F.2d 280 (7th Cir.1975), cert. denied, overruled on other grounds.

7. See, e.g., Miller v. Lawlor, 245 Iowa 1144, 66 N.W.2d 267, 48 ALR2d 1058 (1954).

§ 11.31

1. For express conditions: Rs. 2d § 84(1); Rs. 1st § 297 cmt c; for constructive conditions Rs. 2d § 246; Rs. 1st § 297; Rennie & Laughlin v. Chrysler, 242 F.2d

208 (9th Cir.1957); Industrial Machinery v. Creative Displays, 344 So.2d 743 (Ala.1977).

2. Rs. 2d § 84(1)(b).

3. Rs. 2d § 84 cmt d; Spaulding v. McCaige, 47 Or.App. 129, 614 P.2d 594 (1980).

4. 8 Corbin § 40.1 (McCauliff 1999); Rs. 2d § 84 cmt f; Imperator Realty v. Tull, 228 N.Y. 447, 127 N.E. 263 (1920).

5. 8 Corbin § 40.1 (McCauliff 1999). It is, of course, true that failure to perform on

fairness, the limitation once waived may be reimposed if there has been no change of position in reliance on the waiver.[6] Even if there has been such reliance, a new limitation may be set by B, provided that a reasonable time is allowed.[7] Even if B sets no time limit, performance within a reasonable time from the time of the waiver is still required.[8]

The third rule is that the condition must be solely for the benefit of the party waiving it.[9] At times, it is difficult to determine whether the condition is for the benefit of the party waiving it or is for the benefit of the other party or, what is more likely, for the benefit of both parties. In the last case it cannot be unilaterally waived by either party.[10] A frequent issue in this area is the application of the parol evidence rule. Where the contract provides that on the happening or non-happening of a condition the contract shall be "void" or that "either party shall have the right to cancel," may it be shown that the condition was meant only to benefit one party? "Plain meaning" courts disagree with courts that attempt to determine from parol evidence why the condition was agreed upon.[11]

How does a waiver differ from a modification? A modification requires mutual assent, and consideration, or a statutory equivalent of consideration, or injurious reliance.[12] A waiver, however, is ordinarily unilateral in character. To be effective, a waiver of an immaterial part of the agreed exchange need not be supported by consideration, or its equivalent.[13] Thus, waiver is a very limited exception to the requirement of consideration. An important difference between waiver and modification is that where there is a binding modification the parties are not free

time when there is a time of the essence clause would amount to a material breach. However, in waiving the time of the essence clause, B is not waiving any of the work agreed on.

6. According to Judge Posner, the existence of an estoppel is required as an evidentiary basis for proving the existence of the waiver. Bank v. Truck Ins. Exch., 51 F.3d 736 (7th Cir.1995). Others think of estoppel as the basis for the injustice of retracting the waiver.

7. Rs. 2d § 84 and cmt f. UCC § 2-209(5) provides: "A party who has made a waiver effecting an executory portion of the contract may retract the waiver by reasonable notification received by the other party that strict performance will be required of any term waived, unless the retraction would be unjust in view of a material change of position in reliance on the waiver." (Stylistic changes in revision). See Salvatore v. Trace, 109 N.J.Super. 83, 262 A.2d 409 (1969), aff'd.

8. Barker v. Leonard, 263 Ill.App.3d 661, 200 Ill.Dec. 507, 635 N.E.2d 846 (1994); 8 Corbin § 40.5 (McCauliff 1999). Ordinarily a waiver of condition does not

amount to a renunciation of a right to damages for breach. See § 11.33 infra.

9. Brotman v. Roelofs, 70 Mich.App. 719, 246 N.W.2d 368 (1976); Bliss v. Carter, 26 Mich.App. 177, 182 N.W.2d 54 (1970); Goebel v. First Fed. S. & L. Ass'n, 83 Wis.2d 668, 266 N.W.2d 352 (1978).

10. Wallstreet Properties v. Gassner, 53 Or.App. 650, 632 P.2d 1310 (1981).

11. W.W.W. Assocs. v. Giancontieri, 77 N.Y.2d 157, 566 N.E.2d 639, 565 N.Y.S.2d 440 (1990) (plain meaning); BPL Dev. v. Cappel, 86 A.D.2d 591, 446 N.Y.S.2d 134 (1982) (for benefit of purchaser). Although these were cases of waiver after failure of condition, the same issue applies to waiver before failure. Wyler Summit P'shp v. Turner Broadcasting, 135 F.3d 658 (9th Cir. 1998) (question of fact; dissent stresses plain meaning).

12. See Chs. 4, 5 and 6.

13. Nassau Trust v. Montrose Concrete Prods., 56 N.Y.2d 175, 451 N.Y.S.2d 663, 436 N.E.2d 1265 (1982), rearg. denied; Wachovia Bank & Trust v. Rubish, 306 N.C. 417, 293 S.E.2d 749 (1982), reh. denied.

to terminate the modification except by mutual agreement. In the case of an effective waiver, however, the party waiving may withdraw it if the withdrawal does not operate unfairly.

§ 11.32 Waiver After Failure of Condition: Election

In previous sections, we saw how, before a condition was due to happen, a party could choose to excuse the happening of that condition. Here we focus on the excuse of the condition after the condition has failed, but the other party chooses to excuse the failure. That is an election.

Consider the following illustrations. Assume first a contract in which A, in England, promises to charter a vessel to B who is in the U.S. and who promises to pay when the vessel arrives. B successfully negotiates for an express condition that the vessel must sail from England "on or before Feb. 4," but the vessel sails on Feb. 5th. Since the express condition has not been strictly performed, B may elect to terminate the contract or elect to continue with the contract.[1]

The second illustration involves a constructive condition that arises out of a bilateral contract. A, a contractor who has promised to erect a structure for B, has failed to render substantial performance in timely fashion, but has not abandoned the project. B may elect to terminate the contract and sue for a total breach or continue with the contract and hold A liable for damages for a partial breach.[2] If the owner elects to continue the contract, the contractor would still have to perform within a reasonable time. The owner can set a reasonable date and make time of the essence.[3] Note the similar discussion in the topic of waiver before failure of condition.[4] However, there is this difference: once a party elects to continue after a failure of condition, the election cannot be retracted.[5]

An election may be made by express promise or by conduct.[6] Such conduct will take one of two forms. One, the innocent party continues to perform after failure of condition (e.g. the Feb. 4th case above), the other, the innocent party allows the other party to continue to perform after a material breach (e.g. the construction case).[7]

Under the majority view, an election may not be withdrawn even if the other party has not relied on it.[8] Many of cases included in the majority view are cases involving insurance policies.[9] Under a small

§ 11.32

1. See § 11.18 supra.

2. § 11.18 supra.

3. See § 11.31 supra.

4. See § 11.31 supra.

5. Times Mirror v. Field & Stream, 103 F.Supp.2d 711 (S.D.N.Y.2000), aff'd.

6. Stephens v. West Pontiac–GMC, 7 Ark.App. 275, 647 S.W.2d 492 (1983); Rs. 1st § 309; 8 Corbin § 40.4 (McCauliff 1999).

7. S.S. Steiner, Inc. v. Hill, 191 Or. 391, 230 P.2d 537 (1951); Rs. 2d § 84.

8. Chilton Ins. v. Pate & Pate Enterprises, 930 S.W.2d 877 (Tex.App.1996); Rs. 2d § 84.

9. Rs. 2d § 84 cmt d; Rs. 1st § 309 (estoppel needed only if waiver is without knowledge of the facts); AIG Hawaii Ins. v. Smith, 78 Haw. 174, 891 P.2d 261 (1995) (liability insurer by beginning the defense is estopped to deny lack of coverage); Utica Mut. Ins. Co. v. 215 West 91st St., 283 A.D.2d 421, 724 N.Y.S.2d 758 (2001).

minority view (which is consistent with the rule on waiver discussed above) the election may be withdrawn if it would be fair to do so.[10]

In the case of a waiver of condition *before* failure of condition, the rule is that all that can be waived is an immaterial part of the agreed exchange.[11] In the case of an election after a failure of condition, may the non-breaching party "elect" to perform, for example, by making a binding promise to pay despite the failure of condition? We must divide the answer into two parts. If the failure of condition does not involve a breach of duty, the election is not effective if the condition is a material part of the agreed exchange.[12]

Suppose, however, the failed condition is also an incurable material breach of promise. May the party who is protected by the condition elect to perform? To illustrate, suppose a contractor contracts to build a structure on the owner's property. The owner, despite knowing of a material breach, moves into the structure. Unlike a case involving the sale of goods,[13] the owner does not lose the privilege of refusing to pay, because, in moving in, the owner does not concede that there is substantial performance. The owner may refuse to pay and can sue for a material breach. This is because the defective performance is attached to the owner's property and cannot be removed without material injury.[14]

The situation is different if the owner manifests an intent to pay the contract price despite the known defects. In that event, the owner is electing to pay despite the material breach and is limited to an action for partial breach. Since the owner can collect damages for partial breach for the unperformed or defective portion, the owner is not "electing" to eliminate a material part of the agreed exchange by way of gift. Conceptually, the owner owes the price but has a claim for breach. Procedurally, the contractor has an action for the price and the owner a claim for damages. In a practical context, where litigation is a last resort, this means the owner may withhold enough money to compensate for the breach—in the jargon of the construction trade, "backcharge" the contractor.

If there were material defects of which the owner was justifiably not aware,[15] the owner may withhold payment despite an earlier election to pay.[16]

Another question in this area is the effect of repeated waivers. The same rules apply to waivers prior to failure of condition and election waivers. By far, most of the cases involve an election to accept late

---

10. Coleman Furn. v. Home Ins., 67 F.2d 347 (4th Cir.1933).

11. See § 11.31 supra.

12. Rs. 2d § 84(1)(a). A similar rule exists for aleatory contracts. Rs. 2d § 84(1)(b).

13. A buyer who accepts goods, knowing of defects that would justify rejection, must pay the price and is limited to an action for partial breach or may resort to self help by

deducting damages from the price. See § 11.20 supra.

14. Cawley v. Weiner, 236 N.Y. 357, 140 N.E. 724 (1923); Nees v. Weaver, 222 Wis. 492, 269 N.W. 266, 107 ALR 1405 (1936); Rs. 2d § 246(2).

15. Ting–Wan Liang v. Malawista, 70 A.D.2d 415, 421 N.Y.S.2d 594 (1979).

16. Rs. 2d § 246 ill. 7.

payments. However, cases of repeated waivers in advance of the failure of condition exist. It has been held that repeated progress payments made by the owner to the contractor prior to performance of the condition requiring payment will not prevent the owner from insisting on fulfillment of the condition precedent to the next progress payment.[17] At times, however, the repeated waivers may be such as to cause the contractor justifiably to change position so that a demand for compliance with future conditions would be manifestly unjust. In such a case, an estoppel will be raised against the owner who will be held to have effectively waived the right to insist on compliance with future conditions of the same kind, unless a reasonable period of notice is granted that strict compliance will be demanded.[18]

Ultimately, the question of whether repeated waivers are effective as to future performances depends on whether the other party justifiably believes that subsequent performances will be accepted in spite of similar defects.[19]

Another question is how repeated waivers are affected by a "no waiver" clause that states that no waiver of a breach or any term or condition shall be a waiver of any other or subsequent breach of the same or any other term or condition. Some cases have given effect to such clauses.[20] Other cases do not where elements of estoppel are present.[21] At least one court has forthrightly held that enforcement of such a clause would be unconscionable in the face of previous repeated waivers.[22]

Repeated waivers may constitute a course of performance and thus operate as a modification.[23] In most cases, there would be no consider-

---

17. Cases are collected in 8 Corbin § 40.3 n. 36 (McCauliff 1999). Waiver by a road commission of a condition in one contract with the plaintiff does not estop the commission from insisting on compliance with a similar condition in another contract. W.P. Harlin Constr. v. Utah State Road Commission, 19 Utah 2d 364, 431 P.2d 792 (1967). Making payments on the purchase of an interest in real property prior to delivery of a deed does not waive the condition of delivery as to future payments. Gail v. Gail, 127 A.D. 892, 112 N.Y.S. 96 (1908).

18. Kummli v. Myers, 400 F.2d 774 (D.C.Cir.1968) (mortgagee who has consistently waived lateness of payments may not without prior reasonable notice refuse a late payment and institute foreclosure proceedings); Burger King v. Family Dining, 426 F.Supp. 485 (E.D.Pa.1977), aff'd; Moe v. John Deere, 516 N.W.2d 332 (S.D.1994); Porter v. Harrington, 262 Mass. 203, 159 N.E. 530 (1928); A.P. Dev. v. Band, 113 N.J. 485, 550 A.2d 1220 (1988); Stinemeyer

v. Wesco Farms, 260 Or. 109, 487 P.2d 65 (1971). See 8 Corbin § 40.3 n.39 (McCauliff 1999).

19. Rs. 2d § 247; Iversen v. Kiger, 48 Or.App. 873, 617 P.2d 1386 (1980). Acceptance of one late payment may not be a sufficient basis for estopping the creditor from rejecting a subsequent late payment. Isaacson v. DeMartin Agency, 77 Wn.App. 875, 893 P.2d 1123 (1995).

20. Universal C.I.T. Credit v. Middlesboro Motor Sales, 424 S.W.2d 409 (Ky. 1968); Jefpaul Garage v. Presbyterian Hosp., 61 N.Y.2d 442, 474 N.Y.S.2d 458, 462 N.E.2d 1176 (1984) (late acceptance of rent waives ability to evict, but not the condition to an option to renew where there is such a clause).

21. Bott v. J.F. Shea Co., 299 F.3d 508 (5th Cir.2002); Bethpage Theatre v. Shekel, 133 A.D.2d 62, 518 N.Y.S.2d 408 (1987).

22. Porter v. Harrington, 262 Mass. 203, 159 N.E. 530 (1928).

23. See § 3.17 supra.

ation to support the modification.[24] However, under the UCC a modification is binding without consideration.[25]

§ 11.33   Effect of Election on Damages

An immaterial breach does not justify the cancellation of the contract but justifies an action for partial breach.[1] In the case of a material breach, the aggrieved party may elect to continue the contract and sue for a partial breach.[2] However, an election to continue with the contract does not foreclose a suit for a partial breach. For example, if a building contract contains a promise by the contractor that the structure will be completed by January 1 and time is made of the essence, failure to complete by January 1 is a failure of an express condition and simultaneously is a material breach. If the work is not finished on January 1, and the owner allows the contractor to continue with the work and the contractor subsequently finishes the work within a reasonable time from the time of the election, the owner is still entitled to damages for partial breach because of the late completion.[3] The language or conduct of the aggrieved party, however, may indicate not only an election to continue the contract but also a renunciation of rights to damages.[4]

The UCC has two provisions that apply to this. One provision requires a buyer to give notice of breach or "be barred from any remedy."[5] Notice is required even if the seller is aware of the breach. Its purpose is to make the seller aware of potential litigation, as well as opportunities to cure, investigate, offer a settlement, and possibly assert claims against suppliers.[6] The other provision permits a renunciation of damages without any consideration provided that the renunciation is "signed and delivered by the aggrieved party."[7] Whether or not it

---

24. See §§ 4.2 & 4.9 supra.

25. See § 5.14 supra; UCC § 2–209(1) (unchanged in the revision).

§ 11.33

1. See § 11.18 supra.

2. See § 11.18 supra

3. Phillips & Colby Constr. v. Seymour, 91 U.S. 646 (1875); Glen Cove Marina v. Little Jennie, 269 F.Supp. 877 (E.D.N.Y. 1967); Dunn v. Steubing, 120 N.Y. 232, 24 N.E. 315 (1890); Chilton Ins. v. Pate & Pate Enterprises, 930 S.W.2d 877 (Tex.App. 1996). Contra, Minneapolis Threshing Mach. v. Hutchins, 65 Minn. 89, 67 N.W. 807 (1896). The distinction between waiver of condition and discharge of a right to damages is sometimes lost sight of. See Western Transmission v. Colorado Mainline, 376 F.2d 470 (10th Cir.1967), where the court, although reaching a correct result, assumed that plaintiff's continued acceptance of defendant's performance after breach ordinarily results in a waiver of a right to damages. The court found a supposed exception to this supposed rule. For

sounder analyses, see Sitlington v. Fulton, 281 F.2d 552 (10th Cir.1960); Robberson Steel v. Harrell, 177 F.2d 12 (10th Cir. 1949).

4. See § 21.12 infra.

5. UCC § 2–607(3)(a): "the buyer must within a reasonable time after he discovers or should have discovered any breach notify the seller of breach or be barred from any remedy." See § 11.20. This provision applies to accepted goods. The revision would continue the notice requirement, but failure to notify would have less drastic consequences. Remedies would be barred only to the extent the seller is prejudiced. For the rule as to rejected goods, see UCC § 2–605. The revision would extend the rule of that section to revocations of acceptance.

6. Aqualon v. MAC Equipment, 149 F.3d 262 (4th Cir.1998); Connick v. Suzuki Motor, 174 Ill.2d 482, 221 Ill.Dec. 389, 675 N.E.2d 584 (1996).

7. UCC § 1–107; the revision in § 1–306 would dispense with the delivery requirement; see § 5.16, and substitutes a "record" for a writing.

represents a codification of common law or a departure from common law will be discussed subsequently.[8]

§ 11.34 Giving Incomplete Reasons for Non–Performance

Ordinarily, a party is not required to give reasons for rejecting or objecting to the other party's performance. However, if the aggrieved party gives one or more reasons but fails to state other reasons which the party knows or should know,[1] and the other party reasonably understands that the reasons stated are exclusive, then the party who has failed to state all of the reasons will be estopped from asserting the unstated reasons if the other party has injuriously relied on the exclusivity of the reasons stated.[2] Thus, if an owner lists defects in construction and a contractor cures these defects, the owner cannot claim that the contractor did not substantially perform or was guilty of a material breach by showing known curable unstated defects.[3]

§ 11.35 Excuse of Conditions Involving Forfeiture

The rule that an express condition must be strictly performed can lead to a forfeiture (loss of property or denial of compensation for something done, i.e., loss of reliance interest) and to unjust enrichment, improperly permitting a party to obtain a benefit and not pay for it (a restitutionary interest).[1] Sometimes, courts will excuse the failure of condition to prevent forfeiture, though it would be an overstatement to say that "virtually all contemporary American contract decisions refuse to give effect"[2] to the rule that express conditions must be strictly performed.[3]

One way in which the rule of strict compliance is circumvented is by an excuse of condition to avoid a forfeiture. The first Restatement[4] generalized as follows:

---

8. See § 21.12 infra. A renunciation of damages for partial breach does not require consideration. This rule applies to damages for total breach unless there has been full performance on the other side creating a debt. Rs. 1st §§ 410–411. The Rs.2d § 277 requires a signed writing or the acceptance of a further performance by the aggrieved party.

§ 11.34

1. In re Nagel, 278 F. 105 (2d Cir.1921). For the UCC rules, see § 11.20. See generally, 14 Williston §§ 40:4 (4th ed.).

2. Rs. 2d § 248.

3. New England Structures v. Loranger, 354 Mass. 62, 234 N.E.2d 888 (1968).

§ 11.35

1. Rs. 2d § 227 cmt b and § 229 cmt b. For the more restrictive English view of forfeiture, see Pawlowski, The Scope of Eq-

uity's Jurisdiction to Relieve against Forfeiture, 1994 J.Bus.L. 372.

2. Childres, Conditions In the Law of Contracts, 45 N.Y.U.L.Rev. 33 (1970).

3. Cases giving drastic effect to express conditions, see, S.B. v. Hartford Acc. & Indem., 880 F.Supp. 751 (D.Nev.1995); Hall v. JFW, 20 Kan.App.2d 845, 893 P.2d 837 (1995); Coppi v. West Am. Ins., 247 Neb. 1, 524 N.W.2d 804 (1994); Oppenheimer & Co. v. Oppenheim, Appel Dixon & Co., 86 N.Y.2d 685, 636 N.Y.S.2d 734, 660 N.E.2d 415 (1995); Harwell v. State Farm Mut., 896 S.W.2d 170 (Tex.1995); but see New England Extrusion v. American Alliance Ins., 874 F.Supp. 467 (D.Mass.1995).

4. Rs. 1st § 302.

A condition may be excused without other reason if its requirement

(a) will involve extreme forfeiture or penalty, and

(b) its existence or occurrence forms no essential part of the exchange for the promisor's performance.[5]

Before the condition is excused, the courts will balance the equities, taking into account the ethical position of the party who seeks to have the condition excused (e.g. was the conduct willful?) and the injury suffered by the other party.[6] Some cases inquire into the purpose and materiality of the condition.[7] Even though few courts have explicitly relied on this Restatement rule, the Second Restatement adopts the same rule except that it asks whether there would be a "disproportionate forfeiture."[8] It points out the relationship of this rule to the doctrine of unconscionability.[9] Unconscionability is tested as of the time of the formation of the contract, while this rule relates to a forfeiture arising "because of ensuing events."[10] The Restatement provisions are not a recent innovation. In the 1600's Lord Coke wrote: "Accident, as when a servant of an obligor, mortgagor, etc., is sent to pay money on the [due] day, and he is robbed, etc., the remedy is to be had in this court against the forfeiture."[11]

Many of the cases involving excuse of condition as a result of forfeiture have been option cases. A leading case is Holiday Inns of America v. Knight.[12] Plaintiff entered into a contract with the defendant for an option to purchase certain real property for the sum of $198,633. The option could be exercised at any time but not later than April 1, 1968. The contract was signed on September 30, 1963, when an initial payment of $10,000 was made as consideration for the option. Under its terms, to keep the option open, plaintiff was required to make additional payments of $10,000 on or before July 1, 1964, 1965, 1966 and 1967.

5. This statement parallels one of the requirements listed for a "waiver" before failure of condition. See § 11.31. The Section is based on the maxim that "equity abhors a forfeiture." Jefferson Chemical v. Mobay Chemical, 267 A.2d 635 (Del.Ch. 1970). In a jurisdiction where there is a merger of law and equity the relief may be given at law. McCombs Realty v. Western Auto Supply Co., 10 Neb.App. 962, 641 N.W.2d 77 (2002); Sharp v. Holthusen, 189 Mont. 469, 616 P.2d 374 (1980); Jackson v. Richards 5 & 10, 289 Pa.Super. 445, 433 A.2d 888 (1981). One of the illustrations under the Section, based on Jacob & Youngs v. Kent, 230 N.Y. 239, 129 N.E. 889 (1921), seems to excuse a material part of the agreed exchange. However, as pointed out above, there would be a corresponding right to damages for a partial breach. See Rs. 2d § 229 ill. 1.

6. See, e.g., Xanthakey v. Hayes, 107 Conn. 459, 140 A. 808 (1928).

7. Acme Markets v. Federal Armored Exp., 437 Pa.Super. 41, 648 A.2d 1218 (1994).

8. Rs. 2d § 229 cmt b explains the meaning of "disproportionate forfeiture." "In determining whether the forfeiture is 'disproportionate', a court must weigh the extent of the forfeiture by the obligee against the importance to the obligor of the risk from which he sought to be protected and the degree to which that protection will be lost if the non-occurrence of the condition is excused to the extent required to prevent forfeiture."

9. Rs. 2d § 229 cmt a.

10. Id.

11. 4 Co. Inst. 84.

12. 70 Cal.2d 327, 74 Cal.Rptr. 722, 450 P.2d 42 (1969).

Time was stated to be of the essence. These payments were not to be applied to the purchase price. On June 30, 1966, plaintiff mailed a check for $10,000. The check was received on July 2. Defendant rejected the late payment. Plaintiff sought a declaration that the option was still effective. The court granted the relief sought based on a California statute[13] relating to forfeitures. The court pointed to the "economic realities of the transaction." It stated, "On the basis of risk allocation, it is clear that each payment of $10,000 was partially for an option to buy the land during that year and partially for installment renewal of the option for another year up to a total of five years. With the passage of time, plaintiffs have paid more and more for the right to renew, and it is this right that would be forfeited by requiring payment strictly on time. At the time the forfeiture was declared, plaintiff had paid the substantial part of $30,000 for the right to exercise the option during the last two years. Thus, they have not received what they bargained for and they have lost more than the benefit of their bargain. In short, they will suffer a forfeiture of that part of the $30,000 attributable to the right to exercise the option during the last two years."[14]

The case involves a late installment payment rather than a late exercise of an option. In the latter situation the court states that the time within which an option must be exercised "cannot be extended beyond" the time stated in the contract.[15] The Restatement (Second) appears to be in accord on the theory that if the condition were excused, the optionee would receive "a more extensive option than that on which the parties agreed."[16]

Where the option is contained in a lease or other bilateral contract, the courts have been liberal in allowing the late exercise. This is because the lessee's rental payments during the term of the lease have been in part payments for the option, and very often, the lessee in reliance on the right to renew or to purchase, has made substantial improvements that would revert to the landlord.[17]

§ 11.36 Other Bases for Excusing Conditions

As we have seen, conditions may be excused by a tortured interpretation, such as treating express language of condition as language of promise.[1] A condition may also be excused if it is contrary to public

---

13. There is no reason to believe that the result in the case would be different if the statute (Civil Code of California § 3275) had not existed.

14. Holiday Inns at 331–32, 75 Cal.Rptr. at 725, 450 P.2d at 45.

15. Id. at 330, 74 Cal.Rptr. at 724, 450 P.2d at 44.

16. Rs. 2d § 229 ill. 5. If the relief is granted the optionee would have additional time to speculate at the expense of the optionor. See, e.g., Cummings v. Bullock, 367 F.2d 182 (9th Cir.1966).

17. R & R of Conn. v. Stiegler, 4 Conn. App. 240, 493 A.2d 293 (1985); Donovan Motor Car v. Niles, 246 Mass. 106, 140 N.E. 304 (1923); J.N.A. Realty v. Cross Bay Chelsea, 42 N.Y.2d 392, 397 N.Y.S.2d 958, 366 N.E.2d 1313 (1977); 1 Corbin § 2.15. (Perillo 1993); but see SDG Macerich Prop. v. Stanek, 648 N.W.2d 581 (Iowa 2002).

§ 11.36

1. §§ 11.9 & 11.11 supra.

policy,[2] unconscionable,[3] or if there is no duty to read the particular provision.[4] A condition may also be excused on a theory of impossibility; this discussion is reserved for later consideration when the doctrine of impossibility is considered in all of its aspects.[5]

§ 11.37   The Satisfaction Cases

(a) Introduction

The satisfaction cases are discussed here because they also relate to excuse of conditions because of forfeiture.[1] They are treated in a separate section because there are a significant number of cases under this heading, and express conditions of satisfaction are sometimes treated differently than other express conditions. One of the key issues in most cases is whether the provision in the contract calls for personal (actual) satisfaction or only reasonable satisfaction.[2] The discussion is divided into two parts—the satisfaction of a party to the contract and the satisfaction of a third person.

(b) Satisfaction of a Party to the Contract

Assume a case where an artist promised to paint a portrait of a celebrity who promised to pay for it only if she is personally satisfied with the portrait. The contract calls for the personal satisfaction of the celebrity. However, where there is doubt or ambiguity, the preferred interpretation is that the contract calls for an objectively satisfactory performance.[3] The Restatement (Second) is in accord, but makes it clear that personal satisfaction is required if the "agreement leaves no doubt that it is only honest satisfaction that is meant,"[4] or if it is the type of case in which it is impracticable to apply a reasonable person test.[5] It is important to note that the cases deal with express conditions of satisfaction; a condition of satisfaction is not implied.[6]

In a case of where a party is to be satisfied, the courts tend to group the cases into two categories.

(1) Those which involve taste, fancy or personal judgment, the classical example being a commission to paint a portrait. In such cases the promisor is the sole judge of the quality of the work, and his right to reject, if in good faith, is absolute and may not be

---

2. Inman v. Clyde Hall Drilling, 369 P.2d 498 (Alaska 1962); see ch. 22.

3. Id.; see §§ 9.37 to 9.40.

4. C & J Fertilizer v. Allied Mut. Ins., 227 N.W.2d 169 (Iowa 1975); see §§ 9.41 to 9.46.

5. See § 13.10 infra.

§ 11.37

1. See § 11.35 supra.

2. Rs. 2d § 228.

3. Handy v. Bliss, 204 Mass. 513, 90 N.E. 864 (1910); Hawkins v. Graham, 149

Mass. 284, 21 N.E. 312 (1889); Rs. 1st § 265; Brook, Conditions of Personal Satisfaction in the Law of Contracts, 27 N.Y.L.Sch.L.Rev. 103 (1981).

4. Rs. 2d § 228 cmt a.

5. Western Hills Oregon v. Pfau, 265 Or. 137, 508 P.2d 201 (1973) (satisfactory development plan of real estate).

6. Incomm v. Thermo–Spa, 41 Conn. Supp. 566, 595 A.2d 954 (1991).

reviewed by court or jury.[7] (2) Those which involve utility, fitness or value, which can be measured against a more or less objective standard. In these cases, although there is some conflict, we think the better view is that performance need only be "reasonably satisfactory," and if the promisor refuses the proffered performance, the correctness of his decision and the adequacy of his grounds are subject to review.[8]

The quotation would have you believe that once it is decided into which category the case fits, the problem is solved. This is not true. For example, in the portrait case, although it involves taste and fancy, the parties could agree that the defendant was entitled only to reasonable satisfaction and the agreement would be honored.[9]

The quoted statement is a rule of construction where the parties have not unequivocally indicated the legal effect of the satisfaction clause. But it goes beyond a rule of construction. If the contract unequivocally calls for personal satisfaction, the courts frequently refuse to give effect to such a provision. For example, would a promise to paint a barn to the personal satisfaction of the promisee be honored? There are many cases which have responded to questions of this sort in the negative.[10] The court's tendency to remake the contract for the parties in cases involving mechanical fitness, utility or marketability can be criticized on the ground that under the guise of interpretation the courts ignore the manifest intention of the parties. In many of the cases such interference with freedom of contract is based on the notion that literal compliance with the contract would result in unjust enrichment and/or forfeiture.[11] If this is the basis of the decisions, it is submitted that forthright recognition should be given to this underlying rationale and a distinction drawn between cases involving unjust enrichment and/or forfeiture on the one hand, and cases in which these elements are not present.

7. Illustrations of this type of case include contracts to provide a work of art, Davis v. General Foods, 21 F.Supp. 445 (S.D.N.Y.1937); valet services, Fursmidt v. Hotel Abbey Holding, 10 A.D.2d 447, 200 N.Y.S.2d 256 (1960), rearg. denied; household drapes, Scott v. Erdman, 9 Misc.2d 961, 173 N.Y.S.2d 843 (1957), app. denied; contracts conditioned on one party's satisfaction with the financial status or credit rating of another, Jackson v. Roosevelt Fed. S. & L. Ass'n, 702 F.2d 674 (8th Cir.1983); and a lease satisfactory to the purchaser, Mattei v. Hopper, 51 Cal.2d 119, 330 P.2d 625 (1958); but see General Inv. & Dev. v. Guardian S. & L. Ass'n, 862 F.Supp. 153 (S.D.Tex.1994) (government approval "in a manner that is satisfactory" to vendor is construed as reasonable satisfaction).

8. Johnson v. School Dist. No. 12, 210 Or. 585, 590–91, 312 P.2d 591, 593 (1957); see also Action Engineering v. Martin Marietta Aluminum, 670 F.2d 456 (3d Cir. 1982).

9. Fitzmaurice v. Van Vlaanderen Mach., 110 N.J.Super. 159, 264 A.2d 740 (1970), certif. granted.

10. Loma Linda Univ. v. District–Realty Title Ins., 443 F.2d 773 (D.C.Cir.1971); American Oil v. Carey, 246 F.Supp. 773, 774 (E.D.Mich.1965) ("obtain * * * permits satisfactory to purchaser,"); Alper Blouse v. E.E. Connor & Co., 309 N.Y. 67, 127 N.E.2d 813 (1955) (sale of goods); Doll v. Noble, 116 N.Y. 230, 22 N.E. 406 (1889) (rubbing and staining woodwork); Duplex Safety Boiler v. Garden, 101 N.Y. 387, 4 N.E. 749 (1886) (modernization of a boiler). Contra, Thompson–Starrett v. La Belle Iron Works, 17 F.2d 536 (2d Cir.1927) (contract to build houses—reasonableness of honest dissatisfaction immaterial); Gerisch v. Herold, 82 N.J.L. 605, 83 A. 892 (1912) (taste or fancy of owner may be an important element in satisfaction involving a dwelling house).

11. Handy v. Bliss, 204 Mass. 513, 90 N.E. 864 (1910).

Once it is decided that personal satisfaction is called for, the issue is the good faith of the party to be satisfied.[12] This does not mean that a party's statement must be accepted. Such an agreement would be illusory.[13] The dissatisfaction must be actual and not merely simulated.[14] Under the good faith test, plaintiff must show that the defendant is, in fact, satisfied with the performance rendered or tendered and has other motives for testifying to dissatisfaction. Plaintiff may establish defendant's true state of mind by evidence showing that that defendant made statements giving other reasons for rejecting the performance,[15] that the defendant refused to examine performance,[16] or has a motive to simulate dissatisfaction, for example, because there has been a change of circumstances.[17] According to some authorities, evidence of the unreasonableness of the defendant's expressed dissatisfaction is admissible, but not conclusive, to justify an inference of bad faith.[18]

(c) Satisfaction of a Third Party

In the construction industry, it is quite common to have a provision in the contract expressly conditioning the owner's promise to make progress payments, or at least the final payment, on the personal satisfaction or approval of a named architect or engineer, evidenced by a certificate. Although the third person is usually retained by the party for whom the structure is to be built, the parties have agreed to rely on the professional integrity of the named individual.[19]

Generally, courts have applied the same standard to this type of express condition precedent that has been applied to other express conditions.[20] Strict compliance with the condition is the rule.[21] The court

12. The burden of proof is on the party asserting bad faith. Hortis v. Madison Golf Club, 92 A.D.2d 713, 461 N.Y.S.2d 116 (1983).

13. See § 4.12(4). However, it has been held that the absence of good faith is irrelevant where a contract provides for "absolute discretion." Automatic Sprinkler v. Anderson, 243 Ga. 867, 257 S.E.2d 283 (1979). This is the equivalent of upholding a clause stating "our discretion may be exercised in bad faith." Such a clause would be invalid if the UCC governed. UCC § 1–102(3); accord, revised § 1–302(b). Also holding that the obligation cannot be disclaimed is Scribner v. Worldcom, 249 F.3d 902 (9th Cir.2001); Ainsworth v. Franklin County Cheese, 156 Vt. 325, 331–32, 592 A.2d 871, 874–75 (1991).

14. Tow v. Miners Memorial Hosp. Ass'n, 305 F.2d 73 (4th Cir.1962); Mattei v. Hopper, 51 Cal.2d 119, 330 P.2d 625 (1958).

15. Rs. 1st § 265, ill. 1.

16. Rs. 1st § 265, ill. 2; Frankfort Distilleries v. Burns Bottling Mach. Works, 174 Md. 12, 197 A. 599 (1938).

17. Thompson–Starrett v. La Belle Iron Works, 17 F.2d 536, 541 (2d Cir.1927), cert. denied.

18. 6A Corbin § 645. Plaintiff can prevail by proving that the promisor is dissatisfied with the bargain rather than with the performance. Thompson–Starrett v. La Belle Iron Works, 17 F.2d 536 (2d Cir. 1927), cert. denied. Dissatisfaction cannot be based on facts known before the signing of the contract. Western Hills, Oregon v. Pfau, 265 Or. 137, 508 P.2d 201 (1973).

19. Devoine v. International, 151 Md. 690, 136 A. 37 (1927); Misano di Navigazione v. U.S., 968 F.2d 273 (2d Cir.1992).

20. Rs. 2d § 228 cmt b. In the usual case the third party is not in the employ of the owner. Some courts have followed the same notion even though the third party is in fact an employee of the employer. See, e.g., Frankfort Distilleries v. Burns Bottling Mach. Works, 174 Md. 12, 197 A. 599 (1938).

21. Pope v. King, 108 Md. 37, 69 A. 417 (1908); cf. Rs. 1st § 303. See 8 Corbin §§ 31.9—31.14 (McCauliff 1999); 13 Williston §§ 38:6, 38:22–38:25 (4th ed.).

will not substitute the approval or satisfaction of judge or jury for that of the chosen expert.[22] Nevertheless, if it can be established that the expert acted in bad faith, the condition that the expert express approval will be excused.[23] Gross mistake is treated as the equivalent of bad faith unless this risk has been assumed.[24] The expert's misconduct is a question of fact and the burden of proof is on the party who alleges it. Although unreasonableness may be circumstantial evidence of dishonesty,[25] in most jurisdictions the mere fact that the refusal is unreasonable is insufficient grounds for excusing the condition.[26]

There is, however, a contrary minority view. There are a number of cases, especially in New York, which go far in remaking the contract of the parties. In Nolan v. Whitney,[27] plaintiff, a builder, sued for $2,700, the final payment in a building contract. An express condition to the payment of the final installment was the issuance of an architect's certificate of satisfaction. The architect refused to issue the certificate because some of the plastering was defective. The evidence showed that it would cost $200 to remedy this condition.

Under the majority view, discussed above, the condition calling for personal satisfaction would be excused only if the architect acted in bad faith or the like. The court did not discuss the issue of good faith but instead examined the question of whether the architect acted unreasonably, deciding that the architect acted unreasonably and stated "an unreasonable refusal to give the certificate dispenses with its necessity."[28] The court held that since the plaintiff had substantially performed, plaintiff could recover the final payment less $200.

This is a decision that defies logic. Why was the architect unreasonable in refusing to issue a certificate when the work was defective? Under the terms of the contract, the owner was entitled to the personal satisfaction of the agreed-upon expert. The majority view would have upheld the express terms of the contract under which the issue of substantial performance is irrelevant in the case of an express condition.

The court was manipulating concepts in order to achieve a result.[29] The case was subsequently more adequately explained as resting "on the

---

22. Second Nat. Bank v. Pan–Am. Bridge, 183 F. 391 (6th Cir.1910); contra Casa Linda Tile & Marble Installers v. Highlands Place 1981, 642 So.2d 766 (Fla. App.1994).

23. Rizzolo v. Poysher, 89 N.J.L. 618, 99 A. 390 (1916); Zimmerman v. Marymor, 290 Pa. 299, 138 A. 824, 54 ALR 1252 (1927) (collusion); Rs. 1st § 303.

24. Rs. 2d § 227 cmt c; Anthony P. Miller v. Wilmington Housing Auth., 179 F.Supp. 199 (D.Del.1959).

25. 8 Corbin § 31.7 (McCauliff 1999).

26. Hebert v. Dewey, 191 Mass. 403, 77 N.E. 822 (1906); Gerisch v. Herold, 82 N.J.L. 605, 83 A. 892 (1912); see also Chil-

dres, Conditions in the Law of Contracts, 45 N.Y.U.L.Rev. 33, 42–44 (1970).

27. 88 N.Y. 648 (1882); accord, Coplew v. Durand, 153 Cal. 278, 95 P. 38 (1908); Casa Linda Tile and Marble Installers v. Highlands Place 1981, 642 So.2d 766 (Fla. App.1994); Richmond College v. Scott–Nuckols, 124 Va. 333, 98 S.E. 1 (1919). For an extended criticism see Mehler, Substantial Performance Versus Freedom of Contract, 33 Brooklyn L.Rev. 196 (1967); see also Ashley, 4 Colum.L.Rev. 423, 425 (1904).

28. Nolan v. Whitney, at 650.

29. While quasi-contractual recovery would be permitted in this type of case in some jurisdictions, this is not available to a

basis that enforcement of the contract according to its strict terms would cause forfeiture of compensation for work done or materials furnished."[30] Since the basis of the decision is forfeiture (and if the plaintiff was working on defendant's property, unjust enrichment), the same court applied the majority view to a case involving the sale of goods where the contract made the sale subject to the personal satisfaction of a named expert.

The Nolan rule was further restricted by an Appellate Division decision that stated:

> "Substantial performance might make compliance with an express condition unnecessary, but only when the departure from full performance is an inconsiderable trifle having no pecuniary importance."[31]

Often a contract that makes payment expressly conditional on the personal satisfaction of an architect, engineer, or other expert will contain a provision that any finding of fact by the named party is final. The question is to what extent can the findings of fact made by the third party be reviewed by a court? The answer to this question has been formulated in many ways. Under federal procurement law, a statute provides that a court may review whether the third party is "capricious or arbitrary or so grossly erroneous as necessarily to imply bad faith, or is not supported by substantial evidence."[32] Under this statute, a court may review the findings to see if the third party was guilty of fraud. Most state courts will review the third party's determination for fraud. In a state that limits the review to fraud, the courts may evade the rule by finding that there is constructive fraud.[33]

At times, a contract is signed, subject to approval of the attorney of one of the parties. In these cases it is generally held that the attorney's disapproval for any reason is final.[34]

D. GOOD FAITH AND FAIR DEALING

Table of Sections

breaching party in New York. See § 11.22 supra. Sometimes the problem is avoided by interpreting the language as calling for the reasonable satisfaction of the third party. Vought v. Williams, 120 N.Y. 253, 24 N.E. 195 (1890).

30. Van Iderstine v. Barnet Leather, 242 N.Y. 425, 434, 152 N.E. 250, 252, 46 ALR 858 (1926).

31. Witherell v. Lasky, 286 A.D. 533, 536, 145 N.Y.S.2d 624, 627 (1955).

32. 41 U.S.C.A. §§ 321–322 is referred to as the Wunderlich Act because the statute was in response to the restrictive deci-

sion in U.S. v. Wunderlich, 342 U.S. 98 (1951). See Annot., 2 ALRFed. 691.

33. Anthony P. Miller v. Wilmington Hous. Auth., 179 F.Supp. 199 (D.Del.1959); see also Rs. 2d § 227 ill. 8. Under some views the court may also reverse the third party if the determinations are based on an "error of law." J.J. Finn Elec. Serv. v. P & H Gen. Contractors, 13 Mass.App.Ct. 973, 432 N.E.2d 116 (1982).

34. Indoe v. Dwyer, 176 N.J.Super. 594, 424 A.2d 456, 15 ALR4th 752 (1980); Stevens v. Manchester, 128 Ohio App.3d 305, 714 N.E.2d 956 (1998).

§ 11.38 Good Faith

(a) Introduction

Despite a promising beginning in the eighteenth century, "the common law has traditionally been reluctant to recognize, at least as overt doctrine, any generalized duty to act in good faith toward others in social intercourse."[1] This approach was solidified with the development, "during the late nineteenth century, of the pure theory of contract characterized by notions of volition, *laissez-faire,* freedom of contract, judicial nonintervention and bargained-for-exchange."[2] In the twentieth century doctrines of promissory estoppel, unconscionability and modern theories of quasi-contract have changed these rigid notions.[3] As part of the same development, "modern contract law appears to support and promote good-faith conduct based on reasonable standards in the formation, performance and discharge of contracts."[4] The UCC and Second Restatement have been influential in bringing about this result.[5]

The concept of good faith has been mentioned many times in this text. A few illustrations: in the area of indefiniteness where "a contract confers on one party a discretionary power affecting the rights of the other, a duty is imposed to exercise the discretion in good faith and in accordance with fair dealing."[6] The concept of good faith is used in the chapter on consideration with respect to the termination of an agreement,[7] illusory promises,[8] the surrender of an invalid claim[9] and output and requirements contracts.[10] The rules relating to the duty not to prevent the other party's compliance with conditions are emanations of the duty of good faith.[11] Cases where the satisfaction of a party is a condition also engage the concept.[12] The concept is also used in the area of duress.[13] In promissory estoppel doctrine, the notion of culpa in contrahendo is based on a duty to bargain in good faith.[14]

Perhaps the largest number of good faith cases arise in the context of an implied in fact or a constructive promise to act in good faith.[15] A

---

§ 11.38

1. Holmes, A Contextual Study of Commercial Good Faith: Good–Faith Disclosure in Contract Formation, 39 U.Pitts.L.Rev. 381, 384 (1978).

2. Id. at 384–5.

3. Id. at 389–90.

4. Id. at 381.

5. Id. at 384.

6. Perdue v. Crocker Nat. Bank, 38 Cal.3d 913, 216 Cal.Rptr. 345, 702 P.2d 503 (1985), Cox v. CSX Intermodal, 732 So.2d 1092 (Fla.App.1999), rev. denied; Oil Exp. v. Burgstone, 958 F.Supp. 366 (N.D.Ill. 1997); see § 2.9 n.109.

7. See § 4.12 supra.

8. See § 4.12 supra.

9. See § 4.8 supra.

10. See § 4.13 supra.

11. See § 11.28 supra.

12. See § 11.37 supra; see White Stone Partners v. Piper Jaffray Cos., 978 F.Supp. 878 (D.Minn.1997) (decided by the implied covenant).

13. See § 5.15 supra and ch. 9.

14. See § 6.3(d).

15. This discussion relates back to § 11.14 supra, and involves constructive promises and omitted terms.

much quoted phrase is "that in every contract there exists an implied covenant of good faith and fair dealing."[16] Normally, a violation of such a duty is treated as a breach of contract.[17] There is a tendency, however, in violations of insurance contracts by insurers[18] and in abusive discharges of at-will employees[19] to treat violations of the duty of good faith and fair dealing as torts. The distinction is important. Characterization as a tort opens the door to punitive damages and difficulties in choosing the applicable statute of limitations. Although there is an obligation of good faith implicit in all contracts, there is nothing to prevent the parties from having an explicit provision elaborating the scope of the duty.[20] Because the requirement of good faith is designed to help fulfill the reasonable expectations of the parties, parol evidence of those expectation is necessarily admissible.[21]

(b) *The Meaning of Good Faith*

UCC § 1–203 states "Every contract or duty within this Act imposes an obligation of good faith in its performance or enforcement."[22] The comment adds: "This section sets forth a basic principle running throughout this Act. The principle involved is that in commercial transactions good faith is required in the performance and enforcement of all agreements or duties."

UCC § 1–201(19) defines "good faith" as "honesty in fact in the conduct or transaction concerned."[23] This Article 1 section applies to the entire Code. The definition "makes negligence irrelevant to good faith." The test is "subjective" and is known as the rule of "the pure heart and the empty head."[24] The subjective nature of this test has been severely

16. Kirke La Shelle v. Paul Armstrong, 263 N.Y. 79, 87, 188 N.E. 163, 167 (1933); Rs. 2d § 205. The concept of good faith is embodied in UCC § 1–203 (revision § 1–304). As to government contracts, see Claybrook, 56 Md.L.Rev. 555 (1997).

17. Duffield v. First Interstate Bank, 13 F.3d 1403 (10th Cir.1993); Jo–Ann's Launder Center v. Chase Manhattan Bank, 854 F.Supp. 387 (D.Vi.1994); Crowley v. F.D.I.C., 849 F.Supp. 124 (D.N.H.1994); cf. Carmichael v. Adirondack Bottled Gas, 161 Vt. 200, 635 A.2d 1211 (Vt.1993) (because the duty is imposed by law, it is "really is no different than a tort action.").

18. See Richmond, An Overview of Insurance Bad Faith Law and Litigation, 25 Seton Hall L.Rev. 74 (1994); Speidel, The Borderland of Contract, 10 N.Ky.L.Rev. 163 (1983); Symposium, 72 Tex.L.Rev. 1203 (1994); Note 43 Ark.L.Rev. 789 (1990); see Trinity v. Tower Ins. Co., 251 Wis.2d 212, 641 N.W.2d 504 (2002) (bad faith refusal to reform policy).

19. See Murphy v. American Home Prods., 58 N.Y.2d 293, 461 N.Y.S.2d 232, 448 N.E.2d 86 (1983) (Meyer, J., dissenting and collecting authorities)

20. See Adler & Mann, Good Faith, 28 Akron L.Rev. 31 (1994) (a contract could provide for a higher standard than an arm's length transaction but less than a fiduciary or confidentiality standard).

21. Seidenberg v. Summit Bank, 348 N.J.Super. 243, 791 A.2d 1068 (2002).

22. Revised § 1–304. The good faith requirement does not apply to contract formation, but applies to a modification; a modification relates to the performance of a contract. The UN Sales Convention has an equivocal provision of good faith, while the later UNIDROIT Principles require good faith in negotiation and performance of contracts. See Perillo, supra § 11.18 n.1 at 287–88.

23. The revision states, " 'Good faith' except as provided in Article 5, means honesty in fact and the observance of reasonable commercial standards of fair dealing." § 1–201(19). See also Wendling v. Cundall, 568 P.2d 888 (Wyo.1977).

24. Braucher, The Legislative History of the Uniform Commercial Code, 58 Colum.L.Rev. 798 (1958).

criticized. There is a strong feeling that the test should have an objective component.[25]

However, for merchants in goods, the Code has a different definition. Section 2–103 states: "Good faith" in the case of a merchant means honesty in fact and the observance of reasonable commercial standards of fair dealing in the trade. This definition includes the subjective test supplied by § 1–201, but adds an objective element. Section 1–201(19) of revised Article 1 adopts the merchant definition for all parties, except as to Article 5 dealing with letters of credit.

The Restatement (Second) provides that: "Every contract imposes upon each party a duty of good faith and fair dealing in its performance and its enforcement."[26] The Comment acknowledges that the meaning of the phrase "varies somewhat with the context." According to the Comment, "Good faith performance or enforcement of the contract emphasizes faithfulness to an agreed common purpose and consistency with the justified expectations of the other party; it excludes a variety of types of conduct characterized as involving 'bad faith' because they violate community standards of decency, fairness, or reasonableness."

Comment d elaborates on what is "good faith" and what is "bad faith." It states: "Subterfuges and evasions violate the obligation of good faith in performance even though the actor believes his conduct to be justified. But the obligation goes further: bad faith may be overt or may consist of inaction, and fair dealing may require more than honesty. A complete catalogue of types of bad faith is impossible, but the following types are among those which have been recognized in judicial decisions: evasion of the spirit of the bargain, lack of diligence and slacking off, willful rendering of imperfect performance, abuse of power to specify terms, and interference with or failure to cooperate in the other party's performance." This catalogue contains both subjective and objective criteria.[27]

The Restatement section has been quoted in detail to show that the concept of good faith is amorphous.[28] A wide variety of attempts to give it

25. See, e.g., Farnsworth, Good Faith Performance and Commercial Reasonableness under the Uniform Commercial Code, 30 U.Chi.L.Rev. 666 (1963).

26. Rs. 2d § 205.

27. The comment is largely based on Robert S. Summers, The General Duty of Good Faith—Its Recognition and Conceptualization, 67 Cornell L. Rev. 810, 818–821 (1982); see also Summers, 54 Va.L.Rev. 195 (1968). A monistic view of good faith is expressed in Burton, Breach of Contract and the Common Law Duty to Perform in Good Faith, 94 Harv.L.Rev. 369 (1980) and Burton, Good Faith Performance of a Contract within Article 2 of the Uniform Commercial Code, 67 Iowa L.Rev. 1 (1981). Un-

der this view, bad faith consists of depriving the other part of the fruits of the contract. 94 Harv.L.Rev. at 973. Often, this is by exercising discretion in a manner the other party would not have agreed to. See, e.g., Tolbert v. First Nat. Bank, 312 Or. 485, 823 P.2d 965 (1991), noted 29 Willam.L.Rev. 597 (1993). For good faith in enforcement, see Andersen, Good Faith in the Enforcement of Contracts, 73 Iowa L.Rev. 299 (1988). Their views are further developed in Burton & Andersen, Contractual Good Faith (1995).

28. Eisenberg, Good Faith Under the Uniform Commercial Code—A New Look at an Old Problem, 54 Marq.L.Rev. 1 (1971).

flesh and substance can be found in the literature.[29] What is or is not good faith is ordinarily a question of fact.[30] Many, many cases where the courts have found implied terms are based on the inherent obligation of good faith in performance.[31]

Comment c states that this section does not apply to the formation of a contract. Therefore, it does not apply to negotiations. Pre-contractual bad faith may, however, be redressed under rules regulating fraud,[32] duress,[33] undue influence, and promissory estoppel.[34]

Closely related to the topic under discussion is the doctrine of tortious bad faith breach of contract.[35] The Silberg case cited in note 35 states that the insurer's duty is "to give the interests of the insured at least as much consideration as it gives to its own interests."[36] This approaches the standard of a fiduciary duty. Outside of the insurance context, a "duty of good faith does not mean that a party vested with a clear right is obligated to exercise the right to his own detriment for the purpose of benefitting another party to the contract."[37]

An important application of the concept of good faith is Fortune v. National Cash Register,[38] involving a hiring at will which reserved to the parties an explicit power to terminate the contract without cause. The employer terminated to prevent the sales representative from collecting bonuses on goods already sold. The court found that the termination was a violation of an implied duty of good faith, stating:

> "We do not question the general principles that an employer is entitled to be motivated by and to serve its own legitimate business interests; that an employer must have wide latitude in deciding whom it will employ in the face of the uncertainties of the business world; and that an employer needs flexibility in the face of changing circumstance. We recognize the employer's need for a large amount of control over its work force. However, we believe that where, as

---

29. See n.27 and Eisenberg,.

30. Huang v. BP Amoco, 271 F.3d 560 (3d Cir.2001); Sons of Thunder v. Borden, 148 N.J. 396, 690 A.2d 575 (1997); Eisenberg, note 28, at 15.

31. E.g., 511 West 232nd Owners Corp. v. Jennifer Realty Co., 98 N.Y.2d 144, 773 N.E.2d 496, 746 N.Y.S.2d 131 (2002).

32. See Ch. 9D.

33. See Ch. 9B.

34. See Ch. 6.

35. See note 18 supra, and Silberg v. California Life Ins., 11 Cal.3d 452, 113 Cal. Rptr. 711, 521 P.2d 1103 (1974).

36. Silberg at 460, 521 P.2d at 1109, 113 Cal.Rptr. at 716–717. See also Holmes, Is There Life After Gilmore's Death of Contract—Introductions from a Study of Commercial Good Faith in First Party Insurance Contracts, 65 Cornell L.Rev. 330, 360–7 (1980).

37. Rio Algom v. Jimco, 618 P.2d 497 (Utah 1980); see White, Good Faith and the Cooperative Antagonist, 54 SMU L.Rev. 679 (2001); Burton, Good Faith in Articles 1 and 2 of the U.C.C., 35 Wm. & Mary L.Rev. 1533 (1994). It is generally held that the concept of good faith "may not be used to override explicit contractual terms," Grand Light & Supply v. Honeywell, 771 F.2d 672, 679 (2d Cir.1985); accord Sawyer v. Guthrie, 215 F.Supp.2d 1254 (D.Wyo.2002); Storek & Storek, Inc. v. Citicorp Real Estate, 100 Cal.App.4th 44, 122 Cal.Rptr.2d 267 (2002); but see Wakefield v. Northern Telecom, 769 F.2d 109 (2d Cir.1985).

38. 373 Mass. 96, 364 N.E.2d 1251 (1977). The specific holding is probably preempted by ERISA. See Nealy v. U.S. Healthcare HMO, 844 F.Supp. 966 (S.D.N.Y.1994).

here, commissions are to be paid for the work performed by the employee, the employer's decision to terminate its at will employee should be made in good faith. NCR's right to make its decisions in its own interest is not, in our view, unduly hampered by a requirement of adherence to this standard."[39]

The concept of "good faith" can be used in any situation to right a wrong that created by bad faith if the traditional rule were applied.[40] Somewhat enigmatically, the Permanent Editorial Board and some cases have stated that the UCC's provision on good faith and fair dealing does not "create a separate duty of fairness and reasonableness which can be independently breached."[41] Certainly, the obligation does not create a general duty to rescue the other party from disadvantageous contract provisions, but it does require that any right or condition created by any contract term or by the applicable law be exercised with honesty and decency. Thus, rejection of goods that fail to conform to the perfect tender rule is a breach where the motive for the rejection was to take advantage of falling market prices.[42] An alternative explanation for such a holding is that the rejection is an abuse of the buyer's rights, a topic discussed in the next section.

E. ABUSE OF RIGHTS

Table of Sections

§ 11.39 Abuse of Rights

The concept of abuse of rights overlaps the doctrine of good faith in the sense that some cases decided under the concept of good faith might

---

39. Fortune, 373 Mass. at 101, 364 N.E.2d at 1256.

40. Rs. 2d § 205. Its reporter has since written "fairness" says all that needs to be said. Farnsworth, Good Faith in Contract Performance, in Good Faith and Fault in Contract Law 153, 165 (Beatson & Friedmann eds. 1995); Cadle Co. v. Vargas, 55 Mass.App.Ct. 361, 771 N.E.2d 179 (2002); Table Steaks v. First Premier Bank, 650 N.W.2d 829 (S.D.2002).

41. UCC § 1–203 cmt added in 1994 and retained in revised § 1–304; see APS Sports Collectibles v. Sports Time, 299 F.3d 624 (7th Cir.2002) (accord in non-UCC case); U & W Indus. Supply v. Martin Marietta Alumina, 34 F.3d 180 (3d Cir.1994); Indian Harbor Citrus v. Poppell, 658 So.2d 605 (Fla.App.1995). For a critique of this point of view, see Farnsworth, note 40, at

165; Black Horse Lane v. Dow Chemical, 228 F.3d 275 (3d Cir.2000) (under N.J. law, good faith is an independent obligation); Wells Fargo Bank v. Arizona Laborers, etc., 201 Ariz. 474, 491, 38 P.3d 12, 29 (2002) (same).

42. T.W. Oil v. Consolidated Edison, 57 N.Y.2d 574, 457 N.Y.S.2d 458, 443 N.E.2d 932 (N.Y. 1982); Oil Country Specialists v. Philipp Bros., 762 S.W.2d 170 (Tex.App. 1988). See also Cambee's Furniture v. Doughboy Recreational, 825 F.2d 167 (8th Cir.1987) (cancellation for breach would, if merely a pretextual reason, violate the covenant of good faith and fair dealing); accord, Neumiller Farms v. Cornett, 368 So.2d 272 (Ala.1979); Printing Center of Texas v. Supermind Pub., 669 S.W.2d 779 (Tex.App.1984).

be better understood through the lens of "abuse of rights." It is both narrower and broader than the concept of bad faith. Narrower, because some cases of bad faith have nothing to do with abusing a right. For example, if a contract modification is procured by coercion and deception, bad faith justifies the denial of enforcement;[1] abuse of rights has nothing to do with the matter. Broader, because abuse of rights explains the voidability of some contracts, and some tort and criminal liability where the covenant of good faith and fair dealing is not involved. For example, assume a property owner is legally privileged to erect a fence, but does so solely to spitefully deprive a neighbor of light and air. In most jurisdictions, a court will decree the dismantling of the fence.[2]

Before attempting a definition, it may be useful to set the scene by providing an illustration. Several days before the great Chicago fire of October 8–10, 1871, the plaintiff obtained fire insurance coverage from the defendant insurer terminable by the insurer on notice and on the return of the premium. As the fire raged and neared the insured property, an agent of the company notified the plaintiff of termination of the policy and tendered the return of plaintiff's premium. The court upheld a judgment for the plaintiff enforcing the insurance policy, saying, "[i]t cannot be claimed that an insurer against fire can, when the fire is approaching the property insured, cancel the policy.... Of what avail would it be, to take a policy against fire to permit its cancellation when the fire is approaching?"[3]

No doctrine was invoked; the court merely thought that cancellation under such circumstances was unthinkable. It might have invoked a doctrine of reasonable expectations or a doctrine of bad faith. There are those, however, who would argue that the reasonable expectations were only those engendered by the policy language and would also question whether the insurer's exercise of a power expressly given by the contract could ever be bad faith. Most would, however, agree that the decision was just. The doctrine of abuse of rights justifies the court's overriding the express terms of the policy.

Three kinds of abusive actions are condemned by the doctrine. These are where (1) the predominant motive for the action is to cause harm; or (2) the exercise of a right is totally unreasonable given the lack of any legitimate interest in the exercise of the right and its exercise harms another; or (3) the right is exercised for a purpose other than that for which it exists.

(a) Malicious Motive

We have previously seen the development of the doctrine of abusive discharge which holds that it is a legal wrong to discharge an employee

§ 11.39

1. Roth Steel Prods. v. Sharon Steel, 705 F.2d 134 (6th Cir.1983).

2. See Perillo, Abuse of Rights: A Persuasive Legal Concept, 27 Pac.L.J. 37, 44–47 (1995).

3. Home Ins. v. Heck, 65 Ill. 111, 114 (1872).

for a malicious motive.[4] Let us consider the alternative. In Comerford v. International Harvester,[5] plaintiff alleged that he had been dismissed in retaliation for his wife's refusal to show affection to his immediate supervisor. The court echoed early American cases when it stated that: "if one does an act which is legal in itself [firing an at-will employee] and violates no rights of another, the fact that this rightful act is done from bad motives or with bad intent toward the person so injured thereby does not give the latter a right of action against the former."[6] As demonstrated earlier, this *does not* represent the modern rule as to abusive discharges. It is quite clear today that the exercise of a power of termination granted by the parties' explicit agreement or by a rule of law cannot, without liability, be exercised for a malicious reason in an employment or any other relation.[7]

(b) Exercise of a Right Is Unreasonable and Without any Legitimate Interest

Courts applying classical contract law hold that a lessor, franchisor, or manufacturer can withhold consent to an assignment of a lease, distributorship, or franchise without any liability. In a typical case, the tenant wished to vacate commercial space under a lease that had a clause forbidding subletting or assignment without the consent of the landlord.[8] The landlord refused to approve the assignment to the Post Office, a willing assignee. One may speculate that a landlord may have good reason not to want the Post Office as a tenant, but such speculation does not explain the conduct in this case, inasmuch as "it was stipulated that the postmaster general of the United States was 'in all respects a highly satisfactory, desirable, and suitable subtenant.' "[9] One might speculate further as to why the landlord withheld consent. Did the landlord want to capture an increase in rental value by dealing directly with a new tenant?[10] Not so. The tenant vacated the premises. The premises remained vacant and the landlord brought an action for rent. The court framed the issue as follows: "[t]he only issue presented for determination is whether under the lease clause above quoted plaintiffs could arbitrarily refuse to accept the suitable subtenant proffered by defendant."[11] It answered with candor that the landlord can arbitrarily

---

4. See § 2.9 supra.

5. 235 Ala. 376, 178 So. 894 (1938).

6. 178 So. at 895.

7. Contra, Tuf Racing Prods. v. American Suzuki Motor, 223 F.3d 585 (7th Cir. 2000).

8. Gruman v. Investors Diversified Servs., 247 Minn. 502, 78 N.W.2d 377 (1956); accord, Pacific First Bank v. New Morgan Park, 319 Or. 342, 876 P.2d 761 (1994); Dobyns v. South Carolina Dept. of Parks, 325 S.C. 97, 480 S.E.2d 81 (1997).

9. Gruman, 78 N.W.2d at 379.

10. Truschinger v. Pak, 513 So.2d 1151 (La.1987), a tenant found a sublessor who was willing to assume the lease and pay $80,000 to boot. The landlord refused to consent to the sublease unless one-half of the $80,000 were to be paid to him. This was held not to be an abuse of right. The landlord's economic motive was legitimate, violated no moral rules, was not in bad faith or in violation of elementary fairness.

11. Gruman, 78 N.W.2d at 379. The court cited cases from a score of jurisdictions that were in accord. In the bankruptcy proceeding of In re Bellanca Aircraft, 850

refuse to approve a subletting and may arbitrarily refuse to mitigate damages. If one function of contract law is to be in the service of the commercial economy, is a standard of "arbitrary" discretion an appropriate commercial standard?

Many courts, however, have thought that arbitrariness is not an appropriate standard. According to the California court, "[a] growing minority of jurisdictions now hold that where a lease provides for assignment only with the prior consent of the lessor, such consent may be withheld *only where the lessor has a commercially reasonable objection to the assignment*." (Emphasis by the court).[12] Such a rule is consistent with an evolutionary change in other areas of contract law. Most contracts are imbedded in a commercial context. If naked words have been stripped from the context, their meaning is distorted. Classic contract law imposed such distortion. Modern contract law is seriously concerned with the context of the words.

A non-lease Louisiana case illustrates the utility of the abuse of rights doctrine. In Sanborn v. Oceanic Contractors,[13] the plaintiff had worked for the defendant Oceanic in Dubai in the United Arab Emirates. Some months after the employment terminated, plaintiff was offered a job in Dubai with Scimitar, another employer. The immigration regulations in the Emirates provided that he was eligible for entry only if the former employer "released his work visa." Oceanic refused to supply such a release. Plaintiff brought this action for tortious interference with a contract. The lower court dismissed the complaint, ruling that plaintiff had failed to show any duty on the part of Oceanic to provide a release. The Supreme Court of Louisiana remanded with instructions to allow the plaintiff to amend his complaint to allege that Oceanic had abused its right not to provide a release. The doctrine of abuse of right, as applied to these facts, was framed in the following fashion:[14]

> Also, even if Oceanic had the right afforded by laws of the United Arab Emirates, not to consent to plaintiff's employment with Scimitar, the exercise of that right, without any benefit to Oceanic . . . might constitute an actionable abuse of rights which would support an award of damages.

Franchise cases replicate the question of one contracting party's veto of the other's wish to assign rights to a third party. In Walner v. Baskin–Robbins Ice Cream, the court expressed the classical view of a franchisor's power to disapprove the assignment of a franchise. "Once it is established that [the franchisor] possessed the right to disapprove a transfer, contract law permits [the franchisor] to exercise that right

F.2d 1275 (8th Cir.1988), the issue was the value of two agreements licensing the bankrupt to manufacture and market two kinds of aircraft. Both contracts had clauses prohibiting assignability without the consent of the licensor. The court held that under Minnesota law the contracts had no value because the licensors could arbitrarily and irrationally withhold consent.

12. Kendall v. Ernest Pestana, 40 Cal.3d 488, 496, 709 P.2d 837, 841, 220 Cal.Rptr. 818, 822 (1985); accord, Economy Rentals v. Garcia, 112 N.M. 748, 819 P.2d 1306 (1991).

13. 448 So.2d 91 (1984).

14. Id., 448 So.2d at 94.

without regard to good faith or motive,"[15] but this view has been challenged. In Larese v. Creamland Dairies,[16] a franchise agreement provided that it could not be assigned without the consent of the franchisor. Acting under this provision, the franchisor refused to consent to the franchisee's sale of the business, arguing that its right to withhold consent was absolute. The court disagreed, holding that the franchisor had a duty to act in good faith and in a commercially reasonable manner. A contrary result could be reached only by the implication of a covenant that the franchisor could withhold consent in bad faith and unreasonably. The court refused to pass on the hypothetical question of the effect of a provision "expressly granting the right to withhold consent unreasonably."[17]

(c) The Right Is Exercised for an Illegitimate Purpose

Some abusive discharges, discussed above, are wrongful because of the malicious nature of the decision to fire the employee. Others are wrongful because the discharge serves an illegitimate purpose. Similarly, the withholding of compensation pursuant to the terms of a contract can be wrongful. In Fortune v. National Cash Register,[18] the plaintiff, a sales representative, received a notice of termination the day after his employer received a $5 million order that he had procured. The parties had a written agreement that expressly provided for an at-will duration. Under the terms of the writing, plaintiff was entitled to a substantial "bonus" commission only if he remained in defendant's employ. Bad faith consists of, *inter alia*, the attempt to deprive the other contracting party of the fruits of the contract that he or she bargained for[19] and the jury found that the dismissal was in bad faith. The court held that the plaintiff had a contractual cause of action, based on the implied covenant of good faith and fair dealing that is present in every contract. Other cases have followed suit. The implication of a covenant of good faith and fair dealing, however, is frequently a fiction, if one views the implication as an implication of fact. Instead, the concept of abuse of rights operates as a rule of law, restraining the employer from a misuse of power. It is a more forthright way of explaining the abusive discharge decisions. As has been written elsewhere "[r]ules of basic dignity whether based on legislation or not have been incorporated into the employment relation."[20] Such rules are not necessarily based on the intention of the parties. Louisiana adheres to the abusive discharge concept rule by application of the abuse of rights concept.[21]

---

15. 514 F.Supp. 1028, 1031 (N.D.Tex. 1981).

16. 767 F.2d 716, 717 (10th Cir.1985) (Colorado law).

17. Id., 767 F.2d at 718; accord, Dunfee v. Baskin-Robbins, 221 Mont. 447, 720 P.2d 1148, 1153–54 (1986). Contra, Hubbard Chevrolet v. General Motors, 873 F.2d 873 (5th Cir.1989) (no room for the covenant of good faith and fair dealing when contract language on the issue of relocation is clear).

18. 373 Mass. 96, 364 N.E.2d 1251 (1977).

19. Burton, Breach of Contract and the Common Law Duty to Perform in Good Faith, 94 Harv. L. Rev. 369, 373 (1980).

20. 1 Corbin 561 (Perillo 1993).

21. See Clark v. Glidden Coatings & Resins, 666 F.Supp. 868 (E.D.La.1987); see also the Sanborn case discussed at n.13.

In Automatic Sprinkler of America v. Anderson,[22] the issue as framed by the court was "the question of whether good faith is a prerequisite in the exercise of an absolute discretion to withhold incentive compensation." The plaintiff had been a sales representative of the defendant under a contract containing detailed formulas for the computation of incentive compensation.[23] He resigned[24] and requested payment of the deferred incentive earned under the contract. The employer, giving no reason, refused. It relied on language in the contract to the effect that such payment to terminated employees "will rest completely in the absolute and final discretion of the Compensation Committee of the Board of Directors."[25] Based on this language, the trial court awarded summary judgment to the defendant. The intermediate court reversed, saying that the defendant's good faith presented a factual issue. The Supreme Court, reinstated the judgment of the trial court, and held that the presence or absence of good faith was irrelevant. Absolute discretion, said the court, means absolute discretion. It would not imply a term to the effect that "our discretion will be exercised in good faith," but seemingly found an implicit term that "our discretion may be exercised in bad faith." Some,[26] but not all, courts have disagreed with this case on the meaning of the term "absolute discretion."[27] As one

22. 243 Ga. 867, 257 S.E.2d 283 (1979).

23. The contract terms are quoted at length in the opinion of the intermediate appellate court. Anderson v. Automatic Sprinkler of America, 147 Ga.App. 236, 248 S.E.2d 507 (1978).

24. This fact appears in the intermediate court's opinion. Anderson, 248 S.E.2d at 508.

25. Id.

26. In VTR v. Goodyear Tire & Rubber, 303 F.Supp. 773, 777 (S.D.N.Y.1969), an "absolute discretion" case, the court states that the general rule to the effect that there is a covenant of good faith and fair dealing in every contract is "subject to the exception that the parties may, by express provisions of the contract, grant the right to engage in the very acts and conduct which would otherwise have been forbidden by an implied covenant of good faith and fair dealing." Cf. UCC § 1–102(3) "the obligations of good faith, diligence, reasonableness and care prescribed by this Act may not be disclaimed by agreement." Accord, § 1–302(b) of the revision. See also Wagenseller v. Scottsdale Memorial Hospital, 147 Ariz. 370, 381, 710 P.2d 1025, 1036 (1985) (en banc) ("[f]iring for bad cause—one against public policy articulated by constitutional, statutory, or decisional law—is not a right inherent in the at-will contract, or in any other contract, *even if expressly provided*.") (emphasis supplied). If one deems that a bad faith action is against public policy, the

quoted phrase is applicable to the kind of case under discussion.

See also, a sales representation case, A.W. Fiur v. Ataka & Co., 71 A.D.2d 370, 422 N.Y.S.2d 419, 422 (1979) ("Although the contract conferred upon [Ataka] America the 'absolute and exclusive right to reject any orders for any reason whatsoever,' such a contract does not import the right arbitrarily to refuse to accept orders.")

In Newmac/Bud Light Team Bass Circuit v. Swint, 486 So.2d 255 (La.App.1986), the court held that a fishing contest rule which provided that all interpretations of rules and final decisions would rest with the tournament director was not a potestative condition because the director had a duty to exercise sound judgment in interpreting the rules and to award prizes to those catching the most poundage of fish. A potestative condition is one that is entirely within the control of a party and a finding that it was such a condition would invalidate the contract on grounds similar to the common law notion of illusory promise.

See Martin v. Prier Brass Mfg., 710 S.W.2d 466, 473 (Mo.App.1986) (employer had the right to terminate the insurance plan, but it was bad faith to terminate without notice).

27. Richard Bruce & Co. v. J. Simpson & Co., 40 Misc.2d 501, 243 N.Y.S.2d 503 (1963). The plaintiff, a securities underwriter, had the power to terminate, "if prior to the effective date the Underwriter, in its

court stated a century ago: "[i]f one party to a contract has the unrestrained power to say what it means, the other has no right except by sufferance.... and human language is not strong enough to place them in that situation."[28]

If a concept of abuse of rights were generally adopted, the discussion would be conducted in a different framework. A court would ask, what is the *purpose* of awarding incentive compensation? If it is designed to instill employee loyalty and act as an incentive for the employee's remaining with the company and to work harder at his assigned tasks, the result reached by the court would be appropriate.[29] If, instead, it is designed to withhold earnings until the project is completed and paid for, abuse of rights analysis would conclude that the discretion had been abused.[30]

Justice Scalia engaged in much this kind of reasoning when he was sitting on a similar case as a D.C. Circuit Court judge. In Tymshare v. Covell,[31] the employer, Tymshare, was empowered to retain a portion of the sales representatives' earnings in a reserve fund. The earnings were calculated in part based on a sales quota assigned to each of the representatives. The quota could be raised or lowered from time to time and "management reserves the right to change ... individual quota and reserve payments at any time during the quota year within their sole discretion."[32] Covell argued that a retroactive increase in his quota at the time of his termination was in bad faith. The employer urged that "sole discretion" precluded inquiry into its motives. Scalia stated that the phrase was "not necessarily the equivalent of 'for any reason whatsoever, no matter how arbitrary or unreasonable.' "[33] The trial court had found that the employer had breached the contract by manipulating the quota plan. As understood by the Circuit Court, this means the trial court found "that in using its quota adjustment authority (combined with its termination authority) to reduce Covell's compensation, Tyms-

absolute discretion, shall determine that market conditions or the prospects of the public offering are such as to make it undesirable or inadvisable to make or continue the public offering hereunder." It was argued that the agreement was not binding because the underwriter's promise was illusory. The court disagreed, saying: "[t]he term 'absolute discretion' must be interpreted in context and means under these circumstances a discretion based upon fair dealing and good faith—a reasonable discretion." See also Seymour Grean & Co. v. Grean, 274 A.D. 279, 82 N.Y.S.2d 787 (1948) ("sole judgment").

28. Industrial & General Trust v. Tod, 180 N.Y. 215, 225, 73 N.E. 7, 9 (1905).

29. In Walker v. American Optical, 265 Or. 327, 509 P.2d 439 (1973) (en banc), American's sales incentive plan promised bonuses to employees exceeding a certain quota provided they were still working for American at the time of distribution. Walker far exceeded his quota, but voluntarily left American before distribution. He sued for his bonus. The court affirmed a judgment for American, reasoning that an employer's duty to pay a bonus which is subject to a condition precedent of performance arises only when the condition is fulfilled. Here the purpose of the plan was to secure the continued services of employees producing high levels of sales. The promise of a bonus helps advance that purpose, so does the denial of a bonus to an employee who leaves the company.

30. See Burton, Breach of Contract note 19, at 379–85. "The purpose of the discretion exercising party is a key factor." Id. at 385 n.74.

31. 727 F.2d 1145 (D.C.Cir.1984).

32. Id., 727 F.2d at 1148.

33. Id. at 1154.

hare was not acting for any of the purposes implicitly envisioned by the contract. . . . [W]e agree that this would be a proper basis for judgment against Tymshare."[34] A theory of abuse of rights is being employed.

As Scalia states: "even the permissible act performed in bad faith is a breach only because acts in bad faith are not permitted under the contract."[35] This sentence is framed in the language of abuse of rights. The trial court was given a mandate to inquire into the purposes for which the employer retroactively raised Covell's quota at the time of the termination of his employment. If it was done to deprive him of his earned compensation, it was in bad faith and he was entitled to damages. This reasoning is perfectly consistent with abuse of rights analysis.[36] Indeed, a Louisiana case, on similar facts, states that "the exercise of a right without legitimate and serious interest, even where there is neither alleged nor proved an intent to harm, constitutes an abuse of right which courts should not countenance."[37]

Results similar to the modern abusive discharge cases have been reached in cases involving retaliatory cancellation of insurance policies, as where a dentist's malpractice policy is canceled in retaliation for his testimony against another dentist insured by the insurer,[38] or a landlord seeks to evict a tenant for the exercise of the tenant's rights in the landlord-tenant relationship,[39] or even in retaliation for the tenant's exercise of voting rights.[40] In all of of these cases, the court held that the use of an admitted right to achieve an improper purpose was an abuse of that right and the court struck down such conduct. Delaware courts are particularly receptive to the civilized idea that if a contract or statutory right is sought to be exercised for an improper purpose, the courts will not assist such an exercise.[41] "Delaware case law clearly teaches that

---

34. Id. at 1154–55.

35. Id., 727 F.2d at 1150 n.3.

36. Similar reasoning is employed in Wakefield v. Northern Telecom, 769 F.2d 109 (2d Cir.1985), where an incentive compensation plan contained an express condition that the employee be employed by the company on the date that the payment is due. The Second Circuit remanded with instructions that the jury be charged to determine if the defendant discharged the plaintiff for the purpose of avoiding the payment of the incentive commissions. See also Wyss v. Inskeep, 73 Or.App. 661, 699 P.2d 1161 (1985), rev. denied, a "sole discretion" case, where the court stresses that the purpose of the bonus program was to retain key personnel and succeeded in keeping plaintiff on the job. The plaintiff's dismissal and denial of a bonus were for reasons unrelated to performance of the job and therefor a breach of the promise of a bonus. See also Hainline v. General Motors, 444 F.2d 1250, 1255 (6th Cir.1971) (a bonus case, "discretion may not be abused by those to whom it

is entrusted."); Holderman v. Huntington Leasing, 19 Ohio App.3d 132, 483 N.E.2d 175 (1984) (bonus, "any controversy regarding this plan shall be decided exclusively by employer in its sole discretion."). But see Stinger v. Stewart & Stevenson Serv., 830 S.W.2d 715 (Tex.App.1992) (incentive compensation case, "this arrangement may be modified or changed upwards or downwards at any time at the Company's discretion;" held that Company had discretion to go downwards to zero).

37. Morse v. J. Ray McDermott & Co., 344 So.2d 1353, 1369 (La.1976).

38. L'Orange v. Medical Protective, 394 F.2d 57 (6th Cir.1968).

39. See Roger A. Cunningham, William B. Stoebucke & Dale A. Whitman, The Law of Property § 6.9 (1984); Annot., 23 ALR5th 140 (1994).

40. U.S. v. Beaty, 288 F.2d 653 (6th Cir.1961).

41. Schwartzberg v. CRITEF Assocs. Ltd. P'shp, 685 A.2d 365 (Del.Ch.1996).

even complete compliance with the mandate of a statute does not, in every case, make the action valid in law."[42]

Certain decisions relating to covenants not to compete also reflect the concept of abuse of rights. These are discussed in § 12.10 below.

---

42. Singer v. Magnavox, 380 A.2d 969, 975 (Del.1977), overruled on other grounds.

Chapter 12

ANTICIPATORY BREACH AND PROSPECTIVE NON–PERFORMANCE

Table of Sections

---

§ 12.1   Introduction

This chapter discusses two related concepts—prospective failure of condition and anticipatory breach.[1] Prospective failure of condition is subdivided into two classes: prospective inability to perform and prospective unwillingness to perform. In this chapter we employ the new terms just mentioned and some other new terminology which we will introduce by variations on a simple hypothetical.

Suppose Jane Actress contracts to play the leading role in a stage show. Rehearsals are to begin on March 1 and the show is scheduled to open on April 1. On February 15 she is severely injured while a passenger in a car which crashes. Her physician expresses the opinion

§ 12.1

1. Prospective failure of condition logically might have been discussed in Chapter 11 because it is the basis of a constructive condition. However, the prospective failure of condition and anticipatory breach frequently appear in the same fact pattern. Therefore it seems preferable to integrate their discussion. A few words will also be said about a repudiation that accompanies a present breach.

that she cannot return to work until about June 1 and her agent communicates this opinion to the employer. She is prospectively unable to perform. This *prospective inability* gives her employer several options, including the option to cancel the contract and hire a replacement. If, after the employer had hired a substitute, Jane miraculously presented herself ready to work on March 1, the employer would have this defense: your prospective inability to perform acted as a failure of constructive condition, justifying my cancellation of the contract.

Suppose the accident did not occur, but instead, on February 15, she auditioned for a part in a motion picture that was to be filmed in a distant city at the same time the play was to run, and her employer learns of this audition. Her conduct is an indication of *prospective unwillingness* to perform. Again, the employer is given certain options to protect its interests, although cancellation at this stage is likely to be too precipitous a reaction.

Suppose instead, on February 15, she informs her employer that she has accepted an offer to appear in a motion picture in a distant city at the same time the play was to run. Two consequences flow from her statement. She has expressed grave *prospective unwillingness*, which acts as a failure of constructive condition. Her statement is also a *repudiation* of the contract—an unequivocal statement of unwillingness to perform. The repudiation is an *anticipatory repudiation* because it occurs before any performance is due. This repudiation has the legal effect of creating an *anticipatory breach*. Such a breach does not have all the characteristics of a present breach, the type of breach discussed in Chapter 11.[2]

§ 12.2   Prospective Inability and Unwillingness

(a) The First Restatement and Other Traditional Approaches

The First Restatement discussion of this topic is concerned with inability or unwillingness that arises before the party who is unable or unwilling to perform is obliged to perform.[1] The permissible reaction of the other party depends on how serious the prospective inability or unwillingness is. Under some circumstances where there is prospective non-performance the other party may be justified only in suspending performance; at other times the situation may justify cancellation of the contract, or proceeding as if the contract no longer exists and changing position.[2] The course which may be taken ultimately depends upon

---

2. Local 92 v. B & B Steel Erectors, 850 F.2d 1551 (11th Cir.1988); Bill's Coal v. Board of Pub. Utilities, 682 F.2d 883 (10th Cir.1982), cert. denied. The differences are pointed out in § 12.8.

§ 12.2

1. If there is serious prospective inability or unwillingness to perform coupled with a present breach, it is all but certain that there would be a material breach. See § 12.3 infra. The withdrawal or cure of prospective inability or unwillingness to perform is discussed below. See § 12.7 infra.

2. See generally Rs. 1st §§ 280–87; 6 Corbin §§ 1259–1261; 6 Williston §§ 875–79 (3d ed.); 5 Williston § 699 (3d ed.).

whether there is reasonable probability that a party will not or cannot substantially perform.[3] If substantial performance is still possible, the most that the other party can do is suspend performance. However, if performance is also an express condition, the question is not substantial performance, but rather, is there a reasonable probability that the condition will be satisfied.

Prospective inability, or unwillingness to perform may be manifested by words or conduct,[4] destruction of the subject matter,[5] death or illness of a person whose performance is essential under the contract,[6] encumbrance or lack of the title in a contract vendor at the time of the making of the contract, or a sale of the property to another subsequent to the making of the contract,[7] existing or supervening illegality of a promised performance,[8] insolvency of a party[9] and defective performances rendered under other contracts between the parties or even under a contract with third parties.[10] What follows is a brief discussion of each of these topics as well as the topic of demanding assurances in the face of prospective inability or unwillingness.

Assume that S agrees to sell and B agrees to buy a specific used car, delivery to be made and title to pass on June 1, and B agrees to pay the purchase price on May 1. If the car is destroyed by fire on April 25th, B could not successfully enforce the contract against S, for as we shall see S would almost certainly have the defense of impossibility of performance.[11] Although B's promise is originally independent of any performance on the part of S, B's performance is excused because S's apparent ability to perform is a constructive condition precedent to B's duty to perform;[12] S has the defense of impossibility and B has the defense of prospective inability to perform.

But suppose that in the same case the car does not burn, but rather S on April 26 unconditionally sells the car to X. (Here, impossibility of performance is not a defense). B on April 27th buys a substitute car. Because of S's prospective non-performance, B is justified in changing position by buying a different car and therefore was not obliged to buy on May 1. B was discharged from all obligations under the contract.[13] In

---

3. At times in the subsequent discussion, this is referred to as "serious" prospective inability or unwillingness.

4. Rs. 1st § 280. If there is an anticipatory breach, *a fortiori* there is prospective unwillingness. Courts frequently speak of "anticipatory breach," even where the words or conduct are being raised defensively. E.g., Eschenbacher v. Anderson, 306 Mont. 321, 34 P.3d 87 (2001). The issue then is whether a constructive condition should be raised rather than whether a cause of action is created. See, e.g., Truman L. Flatt & Sons. v. Schupf, 271 Ill.App.3d 983, 649 N.E.2d 990, 208 Ill.Dec. 630 (1995), app. denied.

5. Rs. 1st § 281.

6. Rs. 1st § 282.

7. Rs. 1st §§ 283–84.

8. Rs. 1st §§ 285–86.

9. Rs. 1st § 287.

10. UCC § 2–609 cmt 3; Creusot–Loire In'l v. Coppus Engineering Corp., 585 F.Supp. 45 (S.D.N.Y.1983).

11. Dexter v. Norton, 47 N.Y. 62, 7 Am. Rep. 415 (1871). See § 13.3 infra.

12. Rs. 1st § 282, ill. 4.

13. Brimmer v. Salisbury, 167 Cal. 522, 140 P. 30 (1914); Fort Payne Coal & Iron v. Webster, 163 Mass. 134, 39 N.E. 786 (1895); James v. Burchell, 82 N.Y. 108 (1880).

addition, B would have a cause of action for a total breach of the contract. Because S's conduct is a repudiation, B has a cause of action.[14]

Assume, however, that B did not buy another car on April 27th but merely told S that because of S's conduct the contract was cancelled. Assume further, that S on April 28 re-acquired the car. A more difficult question is presented.[15] Some authorities indicate that B was justified in canceling the contract. Therefore, B is no longer bound despite S's re-acquisition and despite the lack of change of position by B.[16] Because the sale of cars is governed by the UCC, it is clear that simply notifying the seller would cancel the contract.[17]

Assume that instead of selling the car, S on April 25 tells B that under no circumstances will the car be delivered. B immediately changes position by buying a substitute automobile. B would not be bound to pay on May 1 and would be discharged from all obligation under the contract.[18] This discussion applies equally well to a contract to sell real property or to render services.[19]

Death or illness of a person whose performance is essential under the contract may give rise to prospective inability to perform. A good illustration is Poussard v. Spiers.[20] Defendant (D) agreed to employ plaintiff (P) to play the lead in a particular opera for a period of three months at a specified salary. The first performance was to take place on November 28th. On November 23rd P became ill during a rehearsal. At this time the length of her incapacity was indefinite and unknown. D hired the only other available substitute performer to take P's place. The substitute insisted on being hired for the entire performance. P was ready to perform on Dec. 4th and tendered her services, which were refused. The jury found as a fact that the engagement of the substitute was reasonable.

Clearly, there was prospective inability to perform of an unknown duration. D changed position which would discharge D's obligations under the contract if the change of position was justified. Whether the change of position was justified depends upon how serious the prospective inability was. The finding of fact made by the jury was the equivalent of a finding that there was reasonable probability that P would not or could not substantially perform. Therefore, the prospective inability was serious; D was justified in changing position and D's obligations under the contract were discharged. P was not guilty of any breach because P had the defense of impossibility of performance.[21]

---

14. See § 12.4(b) infra.

15. If S did not reacquire the automobile, there can be no doubt that S's probable non-performance would justify B in not paying the purchase price on May 1 even if B had not cancelled the contract.

16. Somerville v. Epps, 36 Conn.Supp. 323, 419 A.2d 909 (1980).

17. UCC § 2–611(1).

18. Windmuller v. Pope, 107 N.Y. 674, 14 N.E. 436 (1887). Not only would there be a discharge but B could sue immediately under a theory of anticipatory repudiation. See § 12.3 infra.

19. See Rs. 1st § 284.

20. 1 Q.B.D. 410 (1876); See also Rs. 2d § 262 cmt a; cf. Bettini v. Gye, 1 Q.B.D. 183 (1876).

21. See § 13.7 infra.

Some relevant cases involve contracts for the sale of realty where the vendor did not have title to the property at the time the contract of sale was entered into, a serious prospective inability to perform. The rule is that the vendee may invoke the doctrine of prospective inability (change position, etc.) unless the vendor has the right to acquire title or has a justifiable expectation of becoming owner in time to perform under the terms of the contract[22] or unless the vendee had knowledge of the lack of title when the contract was signed.[23]

A similar problem arises when the vendor has title to the property but the title is encumbered by a defect that would render title unmarketable. The First Restatement announced the same rule with respect to this situation as in the case where the vendor does not have title.[24] However, there is another view, probably a majority view, which takes a different approach. It states that when time is not of the essence and the vendor has the power to remedy the defect within a reasonable time after the property should have been conveyed, the vendee does not have the right to change position and cancel the contract.[25] As has been stated, "The question must resolve itself into one of degree and probability."[26] In this situation the vendee must advise the seller of curable title defects—that is, defects that can be cured within a reasonable time.[27]

Obviously, insolvency will also raise the question of prospective inability to perform. It does not normally involve prospective unwillingness to perform or repudiation because insolvency is usually involuntary, and thus it amounts only to prospective inability to perform.[28] What constitutes insolvency? UCC § 1–201(23) lists three situations that constitute insolvency: (1) ceasing to pay debts in the ordinary course of business; (2) inability to pay debts as they mature; (3) insolvency within the meaning of the Federal Bankruptcy Act—that is, where a party's debts are greater than the party's assets. The Restatement (Second) is in accord as is revised Article 1.[29] Although mere doubts as to solvency are not enough,[30] if a reasonable person would conclude that a party is insolvent that is sufficient. For example, unsatisfied judgments would lead a reasonable person to such a conclusion.[31]

Now, assuming a party is insolvent, the question is what are the rights and obligations of a party who is dealing with an insolvent? For

---

22. Caporale v. Rubine, 92 N.J.L. 463, 105 A. 226 (1918); Clark v. Ingle, 58 N.M. 136, 266 P.2d 672 (1954); Rs. 1st § 283.

23. Tague Holding v. Harris, 250 N.Y. 422, 165 N.E. 834 (1929).

24. Rs. 1st § 283 cmt a; see Breuer–Harrison v. Combe, 799 P.2d 716 (Utah App.1990) (incurable cloud on title justifies cancellation).

25. Schilling v. Levin, 328 Mass. 2, 101 N.E.2d 360 (1951); Cohen v. Kranz, 12 N.Y.2d 242, 238 N.Y.S.2d 928, 189 N.E.2d 473 (1963) (vendor could have cured title by moving a fence; vendee not justified in cancelling contract.)

26. 6 Williston § 879 (3d ed.).

27. First Nat. Bank v. Ron Rudin Realty, 97 Nev. 20, 623 P.2d 558 (1981); Ilemar v. Krochmal, 44 N.Y.2d 702, 405 N.Y.S.2d 444, 376 N.E.2d 917 (1978).

28. See § 12.6 infra.

29. Rs. 2d § 252(2); revised Article 1–201(23).

30. Hall v. Add–Ventures, Ltd., 695 P.2d 1081 (Alaska 1985).

31. Leopold v. Rock–Ola Mfg., 109 F.2d 611 (5th Cir.1940).

example, if S agrees to sell and deliver certain goods to B on May 1, for which B is to pay on August 1, and on April 30 B is insolvent,[32] must S deliver the goods according to terms of the contract?

UCC § 2–702 lists four courses that seller may follow. Of these, the course that relates most directly is subdivision (1) which states, "where the seller discovers the buyer to be insolvent he may refuse delivery except for cash including payment for all goods theretofore delivered under the contract, * * *."[33] The Restatement (Second), however, allows the insolvent to give security rather than pay cash and thus become entitled to the other party's performance.[34] Of course, this provision does not overturn the UCC in goods cases. In either case, under the majority view, the failure of the insolvent party to make the necessary tender within a reasonable time discharges the duty of the solvent party altogether.[35]

(b) UCC and the Restatement (Second) Innovations

UCC § 2–609 introduced into the law the notion that where a party to a contract manifests a serious prospective inability or unwillingness to perform, the other party may make a demand for "adequate assurances of due performance."[36]

There was no such common law procedure,[37] although it is not uncommon for contractual provisions to require a response to a demand

---

32. If the seller were insolvent, the insolvency would be immaterial because the rules being discussed relate only to the insolvency of a party receiving credit. Rs. 1st § 287, ill. 3.

33. Subsection (1) ends with the words "and stop delivery under this article." The section continues: "(2) Where the seller discovers that the buyer has received goods on credit while insolvent he may reclaim the goods upon demand made within ten days after the receipt, but if misrepresentation of solvency has been made to the particular seller in writing within three months before delivery the ten day limitation does not apply. Except as provided in this subsection the seller may not base a right to reclaim goods on the buyer's fraudulent or innocent misrepresentation of solvency or of intent to pay. (3) The seller's right to reclaim under subsection (2) is subject to the rights of a buyer in ordinary course or other good faith purchaser under this Article (section 2–403). Successful reclamation of goods excludes all other remedies with respect to them." Revised Article 1, deletes the clause concerning the misrepresentation of solvency.

34. Rs. 2d § 252(1). Revised Article 1 excepts from the insolvency definition the cessation of the payment of debts "other than as a result of a bona fide dispute as to

them." This exception is inherent in the present text.

35. Leopold v. Rock–Ola Mfg., 109 F.2d 611 (5th Cir.1940); Hanna v. Florence Iron, 222 N.Y. 290, 118 N.E. 629 (1918); but cf. Keppelon v. W. M. Ritter Flooring, 97 N.J.L. 200, 116 A. 491 (1922) (the solvent party must tender or at least inquire whether the insolvent party can furnish the required security or cash).

36. (Revised Article 1 makes no substantive change.) See Garvin, Adequate Assurance of Performance, 69 U.Colo.L.Rev. 71 (1998). UCC § 2A–401 is similar. CISG Art. 71 is also similar, but probably requires a higher threshold of insecurity. UNIDROIT Principles Art. 7.3.4 seems to relax the threshold. Labor arbitrators have often ordered reinstatement of employees on condition that they give assurances of a particular type, for example, participation in a substance abuse program. Elkouri & Elkouri, How Arbitration Works 939–43 (4th ed. 1997).

37. McCloskey & Co. v. Minweld Steel, 220 F.2d 101 (3d Cir.1955); 1973 ALI Proc. 232 (1974). However, failure to grant assurances may be some evidence that the repudiation is unequivocal and positive. O'Shanter Resources v. Niagara Mohawk Power, 915 F.Supp. 560 (N.D.N.Y.1996).

for assurances. This UCC section provides, (and the revision makes only stylistic changes):

"Right to Adequate Assurance of Performance

(1) A contract for sale imposes an obligation on each party that the other's expectation of receiving due performance will not be impaired. When reasonable grounds for insecurity arise with respect to the performance of either party the other may in writing demand adequate assurance of due performance and until he receives such assurance may if commercially reasonable suspend any performance for which he has not already received the agreed return.

(2) Between merchants the reasonableness of grounds for insecurity and the adequacy of any assurance offered shall be determined according to commercial standards.

(3) Acceptance of any improper delivery or payment does not prejudice the aggrieved party's right to demand adequate assurance of future performance.

(4) After receipt of a justified demand failure to provide within a reasonable time not exceeding thirty days such assurance of due performance as is adequate under the circumstances of the particular case is a repudiation of the contract."[38]

The Code innovation in this section is to impose an obligation on each party to the contract to respond to a demand for assurances, provided the demanding party has reasonable grounds for insecurity. According to Comment 1, reasonable grounds for insecurity exist when the willingness or the ability of a party to perform materially declines between the time of contracting and the time for performance.[39] Implicit in this is the notion that the insecurity must be based on matters not known to the party demanding assurances at the time of contracting and as to which the risk was not assumed.[40] Under the Code the insecurity may be based upon defaults under other contracts between the parties[41] and even upon defaults with third parties.[42]

This section provides three remedies. First, in a proper case, the aggrieved party is permitted to suspend performance, and second, is entitled to receive adequate assurance. Third, under subdivision 4, failure to supply adequate assurance may create an anticipatory repudia-

---

38. Revised § 2–609 is substantively unchanged.

39. The Restatement (Second) provides on this point, "In any case, in order for the section to apply, the ground for insecurity must call into question the obligor's willingness or ability to perform without a breach that would so substantially impair the value of the contract as to the obligee as to give him a claim for total breach." Rs. 2d § 251 cmt c. It has been suggested that the UCC provision is not that limited. Rosett, Contract Performance: Promises, Conditions and the Obligation to Communicate, 22 U.C.L.A. L.Rev. 1083, 1087, n.5. (1975).

40. Field v. Golden Triangle Broadcasting, 451 Pa. 410, 305 A.2d 689 (1973), cert. denied (1974); UCC § 2–609 cmt 3; Rs. 2d § 251 cmts a and c.

41. Smyers v. Quartz Works, 880 F.Supp. 1425 (D.Kan.1995).

42. UCC § 2–609 cmt 3; accord Rs. 2d § 251 cmt c.

tion and thus give rise to all of the remedies available for such a repudiation.[43] Thus, this section creates a constructive repudiation.

Although the term "adequate assurance" is left intentionally vague, the Code comment indicates that standards of commercial reasonableness are involved, and depending upon the nature of the insecurity and the reputation of the parties, these standards may at one extreme be satisfied by a simple letter stating an intention to perform, and at the other extreme may require posting of a guaranty.[44] An inadequate response is a breach.[45] When a party has reasonable grounds for insecurity is ordinarily a question of fact.[46]

UCC § 2–609 applies only to a contract involving sale of goods unless it is extended by analogy. The Restatement (Second) adopts a similar, but not identical, rule and applies it to all types of contracts in § 251.[47] Some differences do not appear to be very important. For example, the Restatement (Second) does not require that the demand for assurances be in writing.[48] Again, while the Code requires assurances to be given within a reasonable time, not to exceed thirty days, the Restatement speaks of a reasonable time.[49]

However, some significant differences between the two documents also exist. An important question is whether the procedure for demanding assurances created by the UCC supplants the prior common law which permitted the insecure party to change position, or is it in addition to the responses previously permitted by the common law that the First Restatement had incorporated.

The Restatement (Second) rejects the approach of the First Restatement and has replaced all of that learning with the section on assurances. Under the Second Restatement, the insecure party may no longer, for example, change position. The insecure party must proceed by way of a demand for assurances,[50] unless the prospective unwillingness can be characterized as a repudiation. The UCC is silent on this question. It has been suggested that the procedure of demanding assurances is merely authorized by the Code and not required.[54] If this is so, the insecure party may still resort to the responses previously discussed. Another

---

43. UCC § 2–609 cmt 2. See § 12.8 infra.

44. See Comment, 50 Fordham L.Rev. 1292, 1306 (1982).

45. Land O'Lakes v. Hanig, 610 N.W.2d 518 (Iowa 2000).

46. AMF v. McDonald's, 536 F.2d 1167 (7th Cir.1976).

47. Judge Posner applied it to a construction contract in C.L. Maddox, Inc. v. Coalfield Services, 51 F.3d 76 (7th Cir. 1995); see also Nashville Lodging v. Resolution Trust, 59 F.3d 236 (D.C.Cir.1995); Norcon Power Partners v. Niagara Mohawk, 92 N.Y.2d 458, 682 N.Y.S.2d 664, 705 N.E.2d 656 (1998) (electric power supply).

48. Rs. 2d § 251 cmt d. Under the UCC, an oral demand for assurances has been held insufficient, but there is contrary authority. See DLA v. D.F. Shoffner Mechanical Contractors, 1991 WL 73940 (Tenn. App.) (collecting cases).

49. Rs. 2d § 251 cmts e and f.

50. Reporter's Note to § 251. Applying the traditional view, allowing a contractor to suspend performance for non-payment of a progress payment, without demanding assurances, is Hart & Son Hauling v. MacHaffie, 706 S.W.2d 586 (Mo.App.1986).

54. In Scott v. Crown, 765 P.2d 1043 (Colo.App.1988), a suspension without a written demand for assurance was held to be a breach.

important difference between the UCC and the Restatement (Second) is that under the Restatement (Second) the insecure party need not treat the failure to provide assurances as a repudiation.[55] Unlike in the case of a repudiation, wrongful refusal to grant assurances does not require the aggrieved party to cease performance.[56]

The Restatement (Second)'s new approach of demanding assurances has rescued the insecure party from a difficult choice but not in all situations. Without such a procedure the insecure party has to make a perilous choice. For example, previously if the insecure party changed position with justification, there would be no liability. If, however, a jury determined that the prospective inability was not sufficiently serious to permit a change of position, then the insecure party would be subjected to an action for a total breach. Does this new approach of demanding assurances spare the insecure party from this unhappy choice? Assume that a party unjustifiably demands assurances and ceases performance. The other party properly fails to give them. The party who feels insecure refuses to proceed. This conduct amounts to a repudiation by the party demanding assurance.[57] Nonetheless, the procedure fosters communications that often will be productive by clearing up misunderstandings and uncertainty.

§ 12.3   Anticipatory Repudiation—History and Analysis

Where a party repudiates the contract before the time for performance arises, the issue of anticipatory repudiation is presented. Historically, the courts had difficulty finding a breach because no express promise has as yet been breached. The effect of such a repudiation has received the attention of the courts and writers.[1]

All discussion of the problem revolves around the case of Hochster v. De La Tour.[2] In April 1852 the plaintiff and the defendant entered into a contract by the terms of which plaintiff was to work for a fixed period commencing on June 1, 1852. On May 11, 1852, defendant repudiated by unequivocally stating that he would not perform. The plaintiff brought an action for breach of contract on May 22 at which time defendant had not breached any express promise. The defendant resisted the suit on the grounds that the action was premature because there was no breach.

---

55. Rs. 2d § 251(2).

56. Rs.2d § 251 cmt a; see § 12.8 infra.

57. Pittsburgh–Des Moines Steel v. Brookhaven Manor Water, 532 F.2d 572 (7th Cir.1976); Deville Court Apts. v. FHLMC, 39 F.Supp.2d 428 (D.Del.1999); CT Chemicals (U.S.A.) v. Vinmar Impex, 81 N.Y.2d 174, 597 N.Y.S.2d 284, 613 N.E.2d 159 (1993).

§ 12.3

1. Leading articles are Ballantine, Anticipatory Breach and the Enforcement of Contractual Duties, 22 Mich.L.Rev. 329 (1924); Limburg, Anticipatory Repudiation of Contracts, 10 Cornell L.Rev. 135 (1925);

Vold, The Tort Aspect of Anticipatory Repudiation of Contracts, 41 Harv.L.Rev. 340 (1928); Rosett, Partial, Qualified and Unequivocal Repudiation of Contract, 81 Colum.L.Rev. 93 (1981); Rowley, A Brief History of Anticipatory Breach in American Contract Law, 69 U.Cincinnati L.Rev. 565 (2001); Vold, Withdrawal of Repudiation after Anticipatory Breach of Contract, 5 Tex. L.Rev. 9 (1926); Wardrop, Prospective Inability in the Law of Contracts, 20 Minn. L.Rev. 380 (1936); Williston, Repudiation of Contracts, 14 Harv.L.Rev. 317, 421 (1901).

2. 118 Eng.Rep. 922 (1853).

The court disagreed. It reasoned erroneously that unless plaintiff was free to sue immediately he would have to wait for an actual breach (which under the court's analysis could not occur before June 1)[3] before suing or even before changing his position by, for example, getting another position. As the court saw the problem unless the plaintiff were permitted to sue immediately he would be caught in a dilemma: to remain idle and hope in the future for a favorable court judgment or to obtain other employment thereby forfeiting his rights against defendant since he would not be able to show that he was ready, willing and able to perform at the agreed time. The court overlooked the doctrine of prospective unwillingness to perform, discussed in the preceding section. Under that doctrine, he was free to change his position, as for example by obtaining other employment. In any event on the facts, as previously explained, he could have successfully sued on June 1 if he could show not that he *was* ready, willing and able to perform at that time but that he *would have been* ready, willing and able to perform *but for* the repudiation.[4]

Although based on erroneous premises, the doctrine of anticipatory breach, or more properly, breach by anticipatory repudiation, has been followed in England and in the U.S.[5] Since the case which introduced the doctrine was based on erroneous premises, the doctrine has been hostilely received by many influential writers. Partly as a result of this academic hostility[6] a number of limitations which are not inherent in the nature of the doctrine have been accepted by the courts.

The following quotation from Professor Terry of Columbia will illustrate the depth of this hostility. In a book review complimenting Professor Williston's treatment of the doctrine, he states that the "fearlessness with which the author stamps in no uncertain terms and with clearness of logic and irrefutable argument those vicious errors which have crept in, in one way or another, but which should be extirpated for the everlasting good of the science, can be illustrated in no better way than by his attack upon the false doctrine of 'anticipatory breach.' That

---

3. Under the facts it might be argued that the defendant would not commit a present breach until he was required by the contract to make the first payment. However, a breach would have occurred on June 1, if the defendant on that date refused to permit the plaintiff to perform the services for which he was engaged as this would have been a breach of the defendant's duty of cooperation. Indeed, it could be argued that a repudiation may constitute a breach of a duty of cooperation even before any performance is due. See 11 Williston § 1316 (3d ed.). For a suggestion that a repudiation always has this effect, see Equitable Trust v. Western Pac. Ry., 244 F. 485, 501–02 (S.D.N.Y.1917), aff'd 250 F. 327 (2d Cir. 1918), cert. denied. This question is discussed in more detail below in this section.

4. See the preceding section. The meaning of the "but for" clause is explored in § 12.7 infra.

5. See Holiday Inns of America v. Peck, 520 P.2d 87 (Alaska 1974); Rs. 2d § 253(1) cmt a; 4 Corbin § 959; 11 Williston § 1312 (3d ed.).

6. Judicial hostility is expressed in Daniels v. Newton, 114 Mass. 530, 19 Am.Rep. 384 (1874). However, Massachusetts has accepted the doctrine of prospective unwillingness as a ground for cancellation of a contract. E.g., Nevins v. Ward, 320 Mass. 70, 67 N.E.2d 673 (Mass.1946), and permits an action for specific performance to be brought immediately. Cavanagh v. Cavanagh, 33 Mass.App. 240, 598 N.E.2d 677 (1992).

doctrine, as the author well demonstrates, is not and never has been defensible * * *. There can be no fine-spun reasoning which will successfully make that a breach of promise which, in fact, is not a breach of promise * * *. To say that it may be broken by anticipation is to say that which, in the nature of things, cannot be so."[7]

Is it indeed possible that a doctrine which in a few generations swept practically the entire common law world is so illogical as to violate the "nature of things?" On the contrary, the doctrine does not offend logic and is supported by practical wisdom. As far as logic goes, a contract is usually formed by promises, but the obligation of a contract is the sum of duties thrust by law on the promisor or promisors. There is no lack of logic in the law's imposition of a duty not to repudiate, as, for example, it has imposed constructive conditions and duties of cooperation on the contracting parties. This duty not to repudiate imposed by law may be breached although no express promise has been breached.[8] Whether this duty is articulated in terms of an implied promise that neither party "will do anything to the prejudice of the other inconsistent with that [contractual] relation"[9] or in terms that "the promisee has an inchoate right to performance of the bargain * * * he has a right to have the contract kept open as a subsisting and effective contract,"[10] there is no lack of power in a common law court to develop the law by imposing duties. The exercise of this power does not offend logic, or "the nature of things."

Also there is much wisdom in imposing a duty not to repudiate. Very often a repudiation is made because the repudiator believes that cancellation is justified. The sooner this issue is resolved, the better. Let it be resolved when memories are fresh and witnesses available. From a more substantive point of view, a right to a future performance has present economic value. Usually, it may be dealt with in the market as an asset, either by outright assignment or by assignment as security for a loan. Apart from this possibility, its presence or absence on a balance sheet affects credit standings. A repudiated right, however, has little value on the market or on an honest financial statement since the statement usually must indicate that the right in question is contested. Moreover, a promisee has a valuable interest, trite as it may seem, in peace of mind. Will the promisee's expectation of a future benefit materialize? The sooner the community enables the promisee to obtain an answer, the sooner it will have performed one of the most valuable functions the law can serve.

A repudiation that occurs simultaneously with or subsequent to a breach by nonperformance (a "present repudiation") is not necessarily governed by the same rules that relate to an anticipatory repudiation. For example, where there is a "present repudiation," there is actually a

7. Book Review, 34 Harv.L.Rev. 891, 894 (1921), Selected Readings, 1259, 1263.

8. See Ballantine, supra note 1.

9. Hochster v. De La Tour, 118 Eng. Rep. 922, 926 (1853).

10. Frost v. Knight, L.R., 7 Ex. 111 (1872).

breach and that breach is treated as is any other breach. That is to say the breach may be considered total or partial, but ordinarily the breach will be total.[11] It is total where the repudiation is of a performance the loss of which substantially impairs the value of the contract to the other party. Relief for a present repudiation historically preceded relief for anticipatory repudiation.[12]

§ 12.4 What Constitutes a Repudiation?

In the preceding section the emphasis was on the anticipatory nature of the doctrine. Here, the stress is on the word "repudiation."[1] Not every prospective unwillingness to perform amounts to a repudiation.[2]

The first Restatement of Contracts lists three actions that constitute repudiation.[3] These are "(a) a positive statement to the promisee or other person having a right under the contract[4] indicating that the promisor will not or cannot substantially perform his [or her] contractual duties;[5] (b) transferring or contracting to transfer to a third person an interest in specific land, goods or in any other thing essential for the substantial performance of his [or her] contractual duties;[6] (c) any voluntary affirmative act which renders substantial performance of his [or her] contractual duties impossible or apparently impossible."[7]

(a) A Positive Statement, etc.

Many authorities have addressed the question of what constitutes a "positive statement." The traditional rule is that the statement must be so unequivocal that the intent not to be bound by the terms of the contract must be beyond question.[8] Thus a statement to the effect that

---

11. Rs. 2d § 253 cmt b; Rs. 1st § 317 cmt b. "The breach will be considered partial only if it does not substantially impair the value of the contract to the injured party." Rs. 2d § 243(4). This test appears in UCC § 2–610 (the revision adopts the same test); see Cargill v. Storms Agri Enterprises, 46 Ark.App. 237, 878 S.W.2d 786 (1994) (repudiation of deliveries of 14 out of 17 truckloads substantially impairs the value of the contract).

12. Newcomb v. Brackett, 16 Mass. 161 (1819); Masterton & Smith v. City of Brooklyn, 7 Hill 61 (N.Y.1845).

§ 12.4

1. The word "repudiation" carries with it the connotation that the party is not justified. If the other party has materially breached, the "repudiation" would be justified and would not be wrongful.

2. See § 12.2 supra n.11.

3. Rs. 1st § 318. The UCC contains no definition of repudiation. The Restatement (Second)'s definition is much like that of the first Restatement, but collapses the cat-

egories into two instead of three. Rs. 2d § 250. CISG deals with anticipatory breach in Arts. 72 & 73, the UNIDROIT Principles in 7.3.3.

4. This refers to a third party beneficiary or an assignee. Rs. 2d § 250 cmt b.

5. UCC § 2–610 has a similar provision as does Rs. 2d § 250. See Fairfax v. Washington Met. Area Transit Auth., 582 F.2d 1321 (4th Cir.1978), cert. denied; Fredonia Broadcasting v. RCA, 481 F.2d 781 (5th Cir.1973).

6. See also Rs. 2d § 250 cmt a.

7. Gilman v. Pedersen, 182 Conn. 582, 438 A.2d 780 (1981); see also Rs. 2d § 250 cmt a. The UCC has added to this list a type of constructive repudiation. See § 12.2 supra. It might also be noted that for some purposes an adjudication of bankruptcy is treated as the equivalent of a repudiation. See § 12.6 infra.

8. McDonnell Douglas v. U.S., 35 Fed. Cl. 358, 377 (1996); Link v. Weizenbaum, 229 Va. 201, 326 S.E.2d 667 (1985); see

"I doubt that I will perform" is not a repudiation.[9] In addition, under the traditional rule, it is not a repudiation if the promisor states that performance will be withheld unless a specified condition is met, even though the event is not likely to occur.[10] For example, under that view, a statement such as "I will not perform unless you provide financing" is not a repudiation even if the contract does not require the other party to provide financing.

The more modern rule is found in the Restatement (Second). It provides that the statement "must be sufficiently positive to be reasonably interpreted that a party will not or cannot substantially perform." The Restatement adds: "However, language that under a fair reading 'amounts to an intention not to perform except on conditions which go beyond the contract' constitutes a repudiation."[11] The rule of the UCC in this respect is generally in accord with the Restatement (Second). Its commentary contains the language of the "However" clause above and states, "[r]epudiation can result from action which reasonably indicates a rejection of the continuing obligation."[12] Revised Article 2 has explicit language based on the Restatement (Second)'s formulation. Revised § 2–610(2) reads: "Repudiation includes language that a reasonable party would interpret to mean that the other party will not or cannot make a performance still due under the contract or voluntary, affirmative conduct that would appear to a reasonable party to make a future performance by the other party impossible." A proposed comment states that

Wallace Real Estate Inv. v. Groves, 124 Wn.2d 881, 881 P.2d 1010 (1994) (difference between a statement that one "may" not perform and "cannot" perform). While the English rule is much the same, its application appears confusing. See Whincup, 146 New L.J. 674 (1996). At times, the question is treated as a question of fact. Minidoka Irrigation Dist. v. Dept. of the Interior, 154 F.3d 924 (9th Cir.1998).

9. Rs. 2d § 250 cmt b; SMF Realty, v. Consolini, 903 F.Supp. 656 (S.D.N.Y.1995). However, it should be recalled that this language amounts to prospective unwillingness to perform and would justify a demand for assurances. See § 12.2 supra; but see Jones v. Solomon, 207 Ga.App. 592, 428 S.E.2d 637 (1993) ("I want to keep my options open," does not justify a demand for assurances). A suggestion for a modification does not amount to a repudiation. Unique Systems v. Zotos Int'l, 622 F.2d 373 (8th Cir.1980). An attorney who advises a client that an equivocal expression is a repudiation, justifying cancellation of the contract, may be guilty of malpractice. Drake v. Wickwire, 795 P.2d 195 (Alaska 1990).

10. Dingley v. Oler, 117 U.S. 490, (1886); 2401 Pennsylvania Ave. v. Federation of Jewish Agencies, 507 Pa. 166, 489

A.2d 733 (1985); but note that it may justify a demand for assurances. Lane Enterprises v. L.B. Foster, 700 A.2d 465 (Pa.Super.1997).

11. Rs. 2d § 250 cmt b (e.g., a statement by a contractor that it will not perform unless the other party advances money to it, where there is no duty to make such an advance). E.g., Millis Constr. v. Fairfield Sapphire Valley, 86 N.C.App. 506, 358 S.E.2d 566 (N.C.App. 1987) (statement of inability to continue without earlier payment than contract provides; jury question whether this was a repudiation); see also Chamberlin v. Puckett Constr., 277 Mont. 198, 921 P.2d 1237 (1996); Created Gemstones v. Union Carbide, 47 N.Y.2d 250, 417 N.Y.S.2d 905, 391 N.E.2d 987 (1979).

12. UCC § 2–610 cmt 2; see Aero Consulting v. Cessna Aircraft, 867 F.Supp. 1480 (D.Kan.1994). Some of the cases do not appear to have taken the comment too seriously. See, e.g., Tenavision v. Neuman, 45 N.Y.2d 145, 408 N.Y.S.2d 36, 379 N.E.2d 1166 (1978). The Code does not attempt a formal definition of repudiation, but it has added an additional form of repudiation to those known under prior law, by its provisions concerning a demand for assurances. See § 12.2 supra.

this "does not purport to be an exclusive statement of when a repudiation has occurred."

Thus, under the modern approach, insistence on an incorrect interpretation of an agreement and refusing to perform except on that interpretation is a repudiation.[13]

It should be stressed that, subject to the rules stated below, a party's inability to perform is not a repudiation.[14] This is consistent with the requirement that there be positive language that the party will not or cannot substantially perform.[15]

Even though the language used is not sufficiently positive to amount to a repudiation, if the language is accompanied by an actual breach, this combination of language and conduct may be a repudiation.[16] This would be a "present repudiation" rather than an "anticipatory repudiation."[17]

(b) Transferring Specific Property.

In Section 12.2(a) above, an illustration relating to the sale of goods was discussed. S agreed to sell and B agreed to buy a specific car, delivery to be made and title to pass on June 1; B agreed to pay the price on May 1. This illustration was used as the basis of a discussion of the doctrine of prospective inability or unwillingness to perform. Under one variation of this illustration, S sold the car to a third party. At that point the question of prospective inability and unwillingness was highlighted.[18] Here we pursue the analysis further. The sale to the third party was also an anticipatory repudiation creating an immediate cause of action against S upon a theory of anticipatory breach.[19]

(c) Other Voluntary Acts

As the First Restatement stated, a "voluntary affirmative act" by a party "which renders substantial performance of his contractual duties impossible, or apparently impossible," amounts to a repudiation. If A agrees to work for B for one year starting on June 1, in exchange for B's promise to pay, and on May 25th A embarks on an ocean voyage around the world, A has demonstrated not only prospective inability and unwillingness to perform, but has also repudiated.[20] Surrender of one's license

---

13. IBM Credit Financing v. Mazda Motor Mfg. (USA), 92 N.Y.2d 989, 706 N.E.2d 1186, 684 N.Y.S.2d 162 (1998).

14. Rs. 1st § 318 cmt h.

15. Sometimes, actions speak in positive terms, e.g., returning a purchaser's down payment. Blue Lakes Apts. v. George Gowing, Inc., 464 So.2d 705 (Fla.App.1985).

16. Rs. 2d § 250 cmt b.

17. See § 12.3 supra.

18. See § 12.2 supra.

19. Miller v. Baum, 400 F.2d 176 (5th Cir.1968); Wilson Sullivan Co. v. International Paper Makers Realty, 307 N.Y. 20,

119 N.E.2d 573 (1954); Pappas v. Crist, 223 N.C. 265, 25 S.E.2d 850 (1943); Red River Commodities v. Eidsness, 459 N.W.2d 811 (N.D.1990); Lazarov v. Nunnally, 188 Tenn. 145, 217 S.W.2d 11 (1949); Petersen v. Intermountain Capital, 29 Utah 2d 271, 508 P.2d 536 (1973); Allen v. Wolf River Lumber, 169 Wis. 253, 172 N.W. 158, 9 ALR 271 (1919).

20. Rs. 2d § 250, ill. 7. For a case in which the death of a contracting party, coupled with the inability of the representatives of the decedent to perform, constituted a repudiation, see Bonebrake v. Cox, 499 F.2d 951 (8th Cir.1974); Taylor v. Johnston, 15 Cal.3d 130, 123 Cal.Rptr. 641, 539 P.2d

to do business is a repudiation of contracts related to that business.[21] Where a public entity exhausts its spending limit by paying the wrong party, it has repudiated.[22]

§ 12.5   Repudiation and Good Faith

Frequently a party, with honorable motives, states reasons for refusing to perform or takes some action which objectively constitutes a repudiation. In good faith the party believes that the contract justifies the refusal or that there is a lawful excuse for the action. There is respectable authority to the effect that a good faith refusal to perform is not a repudiation.[1] The prevailing view, however, is that the test should be objective and that the good faith of the repudiator is immaterial.[2] It should be remembered, however that an offer to perform under a misinterpretation of the contract will generally not constitute an unequivocal repudiation.[3]

§ 12.6   Bankruptcy as the Equivalent of Repudiation

Although insolvency may create prospective inability, it does not amount to a repudiation. The reason is that insolvency is not voluntarily caused.[1] However, filing a petition in bankruptcy amounts to an anticipatory repudiation if the trustee in bankruptcy—the person appointed by the court to manage the bankrupt's property—does not adopt the contract within a statutory period.[2] This conclusion is not based on the definition of repudiation. The rule was adopted by statute so that unmatured claims would be "provable claims" under the Bankruptcy Act and thus be dischargeable in the bankruptcy proceeding. The failure of the promisee to prove the claim in the bankruptcy proceeding will discharge all rights against the bankrupt.[3]

425 (1975); Fairfax County v. Ecology One, 219 Va. 29, 245 S.E.2d 425 (1978).

21.   In re C & S Grain, 47 F.3d 233 (7th Cir.1995).

22.   Solano v. Vallejo Redev. Agcy., 75 Cal.App.4th 1262, 90 Cal.Rptr.2d 41 (1999).

§ 12.5

1.   New York Life Ins. v. Viglas, 297 U.S. 672, (1936); Peter Kiewit Sons' v. Summit Constr., 422 F.2d 242 (8th Cir.1969). The assertion of an erroneous interpretation of a contract was held not to be a repudiation in Blackfeet Tribe Res. v. Blaze Constr., 108 F.Supp.2d 1122 (D.Mont.2000).

2.   Walker & Co. v. Harrison, 347 Mich. 630, 81 N.W.2d 352 (1957); York Agents v. Bethlehem Steel, 36 A.D.2d 62, 318 N.Y.S.2d 157 (1971), aff'd; Rs. 2d § 250 cmt d; Rs. 1st § 318; 4 Corbin § 973; 11 Williston § 1323 (3d ed.); cf. IBM Credit Financ-

ing v. Mazda Motor Mfg. (USA), 92 N.Y.2d 989, 706 N.E.2d 1186, 684 N.Y.S.2d 162 (1998) (insistence on untenable interpretation constitutes repudiation). However, good faith does appear to be important on the issue of material breach. See § 11.18(a) supra.

3.   Zurich American Ins. v. Superior Court, 205 F.Supp.2d 964 (N.D.Ill.2002).

§ 12.6

1.   See the discussion in § 12.2 supra; see also Rs. 1st § 324; 4 Corbin § 985.

2.   11 U.S.C.A. § 365(d)(1) (currently 60 days); see Central Trust v. Chicago Auditorium Assn., 240 U.S. 581 (1916); In re Marshall's Garage, 63 F.2d 759 (2d Cir.1933); Rs. 2d § 250 cmt c; Rs. 1st § 324 cmt a.

3.   Rs. 1st § 324 ill. 3. But cf. Rs. 1st § 324 ill. 2 (relating to certain obligations which are not discharged in bankruptcy).

If a petition in bankruptcy is filed but does not result in an adjudication of bankruptcy, the legal effect is similar to that of a withdrawal of a repudiation[4]—to be discussed immediately below.

§ 12.7 Retractions: Anticipatory and Present Repudiations Distinguished

Section 2–611(1) of the UCC entitled "Retraction of Anticipatory Repudiation" states: "Until the repudiating party's next performance is due he can retract his repudiation unless the aggrieved party has since the repudiation cancelled or materially changed his position or otherwise indicated that he considers the repudiation final."[1] This is in general accord with the common law rule that an anticipatory repudiation may be retracted until the other party has commenced an action, or has otherwise changed position.[2] In addition, the Code is explicit that no other act of reliance is necessary where the aggrieved party indicates that the repudiation will be considered to be final.[3]

Retraction of a repudiation is ordinarily written or verbal;[4] but where the repudiation consists of an act (or failure to act) inconsistent with the contract, the retraction may consist in the repudiator's regaining the ability to perform.[5] To be effective, however, this fact must come to the attention of the other party.[6]

At common law it is generally held, somewhat anomalously, that if an anticipatory breach is withdrawn in time there is no breach.[7] The UCC has changed this rule. It provides: "Retraction reinstates the

---

4. Rs. 1st § 324 cmt a.

§ 12.7

1. The revision makes only stylistic changes.

2. See generally, Roehm v. Horst, 178 U.S. 1 (1900); Truman L. Flatt & Sons v. Schupf, 271 Ill.App.3d 983, 649 N.E.2d 990, 208 Ill.Dec. 630 (1995); Carr v. Carr, 751 S.W.2d 781 (Mo.App.1988). The change of position need not be communicated. Lumbermens Mut. Cas. v. Klotz, 251 F.2d 499 (5th Cir.1958); Bu–Vi–Bar Petroleum v. Krow, 40 F.2d 488, 69 ALR 1295 (10th Cir.1930). The same rule is applied in the area of prospective inability and unwillingness.

3. UCC § 2–611; see Neptune Research & Dev. v. Teknics Indus. Sys., 235 N.J.Super. 522, 563 A.2d 465 (A.D.1989) (no retraction allowed after cancellation, even the same day). The majority of the common law cases appear to be in accord. U.S. v. Seacoast Gas, 204 F.2d 709 (5th Cir.1953), cert. denied; Rs. 2d § 256(1) & cmt c. Similar rules apply to a cure of prospective inability or unwillingness to perform. See § 12.2 supra, and this section below; Rs. 2d § 251 cmt b; Keltner v. Sowell, 926 S.W.2d 528 (Mo.App.1996).

4. Rs. 2d § 256 cmt b.

5. Rs. 2d § 256(2); 11 Williston § 1335 (3d ed.).

6. Rs. 2d § 256(2); Rs. 1st § 319. UCC § 2–611(2) provides: "Retraction may be by any method which clearly indicates to the aggrieved party that the repudiating party intended to perform, but must include any assurance justifiably demanded under the provisions of this Article (§ 2–609)." It has been held that a repudiation is effective when and where mailed. Auglaize Box Board v. Kansas City Fibre Box., 35 F.2d 822 (6th Cir.1929), cert. denied; Rs. 1st § 321.

7. Rs. 1st § 319 cmt a. The result is different if there is a present repudiation. Rs. 2d § 256 cmt a. Another peculiarity of the anticipatory breach doctrine is that the courts hold that the statute of limitations does not begin to run until there is a failure to perform. Romano v. Rockwell Int'l, 14 Cal.4th 479, 59 Cal.Rptr.2d 20, 926 P.2d 1114 (1996); Ga Nun v. Palmer, 202 N.Y. 483, 96 N.E. 99 (1911); High Knob Assocs. v. Douglas, 249 Va. 478, 457 S.E.2d 349 (1995); Rs. 1st § 322; 4 Corbin § 989.

repudiating party's rights under the contract with due excuse and allowance to the aggrieved party for any delay occasioned by the repudiation."[8]

Retraction may take place at any time before the injured party has changed position, or has indicated that the repudiation is final or has commenced a law suit.[9] UCC § 2–611(1) however limits the retraction of an anticipatory repudiation "until the repudiating party's next performance is due." This limitation is based on the notion that once the repudiating party's next performance is due the repudiation is no longer anticipatory. There is now a present breach accompanied by a repudiation. There is a present material breach.[10] However, as we shall see in the next section, there is an important distinction between repudiations and other material breaches.

§ 12.8   Responses to an Anticipatory Repudiation

Basically there are three possible responses to an anticipatory repudiation. One has already been discussed. The injured party may bring an immediate action for a total breach.[1] Part of plaintiff's case is to show that she or he would have been ready, willing and able to perform but for the repudiation.[2] When the plaintiff brings an action for damages or restitution in response to the repudiation, the plaintiff's duties under the contract are discharged.[3] Of course the injured party need not sue immediately but failure to do so creates the risk of the repudiation being retracted.[4] Whenever the injured party sues, even if it is after the time for performance arrives, there must be a showing of plaintiff's readiness, willingness and ability to have performed but for the repudiation.[5] The

---

8. UCC § 2–611(3) (unchanged in the revision). See Wallach, 13 UCC L.J. 48 (1980). See Rs. 2d § 256 cmt a.

9. Rs. 2d § 256(1) & cmt c.

10. Riess v. Murchison, 329 F.2d 635 (9th Cir.1964), cert. denied; Rs. 2d § 243(2).

§ 12.8

1. As in the case of other total breaches, the aggrieved party has the option of damages, restitution and specific performance. Far West Bank v. Office of Thrift Supervision, 119 F.3d 1358 (9th Cir.1997).

2. See § 12.3 supra; see also Madison Investments v. Cohoes Assocs., 176 A.D.2d 1021, 574 N.Y.S.2d 980 (1991), lv. dismissed; but see General Electric Supply v. Gulf Electroquip, 857 S.W.2d 591 (Tex.App. 1993), and the puzzling case of American List v. U.S. News & World Report, 75 N.Y.2d 38, 550 N.Y.S.2d 590, 549 N.E.2d 1161 (1989).

3. In re Estate of Weinberger, 203 Neb. 674, 279 N.W.2d 849 (1979).

4. See § 12.7 supra; Space Center v. 451 Corp., 298 N.W.2d 443, 13 ALR4th 912 (Minn.1980). However, the repudiation may not be retracted if there is a change of position or a statement of cancellation by the innocent party.

5. Rs. 2d § 255 cmts a and b. For example, assume in Hochster v. De La Tour, § 12.3 supra, that after the repudiation plaintiff suffered a severe injury that prevented him from serving any part of the period provided for by the contract. Plaintiff would not have been able to show that he would have been ready, willing and able to perform but for the repudiation. The repudiation would not have been the proximate cause of the non-performance and thus he could not have recovered. If he had obtained another position after the repudiation, then the repudiation would have been the cause of his non-performance and he could have recovered. See also Iowa–Mo Enterprises v. Avren, 639 F.2d 443 (8th Cir. 1981); Hospital Mtge. Group v. First Prudential Dev., 411 So.2d 181 (Fla.1982).

repudiation, however, relieves the party of any need to tender performance.[6]

The second possible response by the aggrieved party is to urge or
insist that the other party perform—to urge the repudiating party to
retract the repudiation. The effect of this response is tied into the topic
of election. Some of the early English cases interpreted the doctrine as
granting the promisee the power to elect to keep the contract in force or
to cancel it.[7] The modern and better view is that there is no right of
election in the face of repudiation.[8]

To illustrate, in Bernstein v. Meech,[9] plaintiff had contracted to
perform in December at the defendant's theater. In August, plaintiff
wrote that he would not honor the engagement unless the promised
remuneration was increased. Defendant replied insisting the plaintiff
comply with the contract. Defendant heard nothing further from the
plaintiff and booked other entertainers for the period in question. In
December, plaintiff appeared at the theater and tendered his services
which, because a substitute had been hired, were refused.

The court, applying the election theory, held that defendant, by
insisting upon performance, had elected to keep the contract alive and
therefore was liable for breach of contract. The case and the election
theory have been strongly criticized. Fortunately, the weight of authority,[10] the Restatements,[11] and the UCC take a position contrary to this
decision. The Code specifically states that the non-repudiating party may
"resort to any remedy for breach * * * even though he has notified the
repudiating party that he would await the latter's performance and had
urged retraction."[12]

The topic of election is also related to the third possible response.
The question is, may the aggrieved party elect to ignore the repudiation
and proceed with performance or does the repudiation prevent the
exercise of the normal power of election that the injured party has when
there is a material breach?[13]

---

6. Stanwood v. Welch, 922 F.Supp. 635
(D.D.C.1995); Capozzola v. Oxman, 216
A.D.2d 509, 628 N.Y.S.2d 777 (1995).

7. See, e.g., Johnstone v. Milling, 16
Q.B.D. 460, 472 (1886).

8. 4 Corbin § 981.

9. 130 N.Y. 354, 29 N.E. 255 (1891).
Subsequent cases have overruled this case
by implication. See, e.g., De Forest Radio v.
Triangle Radio Supply, 243 N.Y. 283, 153
N.E. 75 (1926); but see Mundinger v. Clark,
240 A.D.2d 714, 660 N.Y.S.2d 27 (1997); see
also Dillon v. Anderson, 43 N.Y. 231 (1870)
(mitigation principle applied).

10. Renner Co. v. McNeff Bros., 102
F.2d 664 (6th Cir.1939), cert. denied; Tri–
Bullion Smelting & Dev. v. Jacobsen, 233 F.
646 (2d Cir.1916); Canda v. Wick, 100 N.Y.

127, 2 N.E. 381 (1885); Carvage v. Stowell,
115 Vt. 187, 55 A.2d 188 (1947); 11 Williston §§ 1333–34 (3d ed.).

11. Rs. 2d § 257 and cmt a; Rs. 1st
§ 320.

12. UCC § 2–610(b) and cmt 4 (revision
makes a stylistic change.) This rule can on
occasion be rather harsh on the repudiating
party. However, repudiators are responsible
for their own plight. Lagerloef Trading v.
American Paper Products, 291 F. 947 (7th
Cir.1923), cert. denied; Sawyer Farmers Co-
op. v. Linke, 231 N.W.2d 791 (N.D.1975).

13. When there is a material breach the
non-breaching party ordinarily may elect to
continue with the contract. See § 11.18(a)
supra. As indicated below there is a different rule as to an anticipatory or present
repudiation.

For example, if the promisor contracts to pay for the construction of a bridge but repudiates in advance of any performance by the promisee, may the promisee elect to proceed with construction? Under the election theory, a number of earlier American cases held that the promisee may elect to perform.[14] The modern cases, representing the overwhelming weight of authority, hold that the duty to mitigate damages overrides the concept of election.[15] The promisee may not continue to perform if the effect of performance would be to enhance damages. Conversely, if the contractor repudiated, the owner must mitigate damages, for example, by securing another contractor.[16]

How soon must the non-repudiating party act to mitigate damages? Section 2–610(a) of the UCC, provides that the aggrieved party may "for a commercially reasonable time await performance by the repudiating party." Comment 1 to the section adds: "But if he awaits performance beyond a commercially reasonable time he cannot recover resulting damages which he should have avoided."[17] This rule was apparently placed in the Code to overcome the rule employed by some cases that the aggrieved party may ignore an anticipatory repudiation until there was a breach by non-performance.[18] However, the general common law rule is that the injured party must act promptly after learning of the repudiation.

§ 12.9 An Exception: Unilateral Obligations

The rule of Hochster v. De La Tour does not apply under all circumstances. It is well established in almost all jurisdictions that no action will lie for the present or anticipatory repudiation of a unilateral obligation to pay money at a future time or in future installments.[1] This has to do with obligations to pay that were unilateral in their inception and obligations that have become unilateral because of full performance on one side of a bilateral contract.

---

14. Reliance Cooperage v. Treat, 195 F.2d 977 (8th Cir.1952); John A. Roebling's Sons v. Lock–Stitch Fence, 130 Ill. 660, 22 N.E. 518 (1889). Many of the cases relying on this reasoning are sustainable on other grounds. See e.g., Barber Milling v. Leichthammer Baking, 273 Pa. 90, 116 A. 677, 27 ALR 1227 (1922) (dealer in goods need not sell at time of buyer's repudiation to minimize damages; this rule is explained at §§ 14.15 to 14.17 infra.).

15. Bu–Vi–Bar Petroleum v. Krow, 40 F.2d 488, 69 ALR 1295 (10th Cir.1930); Fowler v. A & A, 262 A.2d 344 (D.C.1970); Cameron v. White, 74 Wis. 425, 43 N.W. 155 (1889). Other cases are collected in 4 Corbin § 983; 11 Williston §§ 1301–1303 (3d ed.). Problems concerning mitigation and anticipatory breach are also considered in the chapter on Damages at § 14.15 to 14.17 infra. A contract can be drafted to circumvent this rule. See West Texas Utili-

ties v. Exxon Coal USA, 807 P.2d 932 (Wyo. 1991).

16. The rules stated here also apply to a "present repudiation." See § 12.3 supra and Rs. 2d § 243(2). Comment b to this section points out that, if the repudiator agrees, the other party may continue to perform.

17. Accord, Trinidad Bean & Elev. v. Frosh, 1 Neb.App. 281, 494 N.W.2d 347 (1992); Roye Realty & Dev. v. Arkla, 863 P.2d 1150 (Okla.1993).

18. Reliance Cooperage v. Treat, 195 F.2d 977 (8th Cir.1952).

§ 12.9

1. Scherer v. Equitable Life, 190 F.Supp.2d 629 (S.D.N.Y.2002); Starling v. Still, 126 N.C.App. 278, 485 S.E.2d 74 (1997); Rs 2d § 253(1) (anticipatory breach); Rs. 2d § 243(3) (present breach and repudiation).

The reason for the exception is historical. Within months of the Hochster decision, a petition was addressed to Chief Justice Taney in his capacity as a trial judge in the Maryland Circuit. A vendor had sued for damages for breach of a contract for the sale of property. The lawsuit had been brought before the first payment was due and the case had been dismissed for that reason. The petition, based on the Hochster decision, essentially was a motion to allow the case to be appealed to the Supreme Court. In ruminating on the decision, he stated:[2]

> It has never been supposed that notice to the holder of a bond, or a promissory note, or bill of exchange, that the party would not (from any cause) comply with the contract, would give to the holder an immediate cause of action, upon which he might sue before the time of payment arrived. If, therefore, the case in the queen's bench trial had been decided previously to the trial in the circuit court, it would not have influenced the decision, and furnishes no sufficient ground for this application.

Thus was born an indefensible exception to the rule that an action lies for an anticipatory breach. For one thing, the plaintiff's action was for damages and not for the price. Thus, the statement was dictum.

An illustration will clarify the implications of the exception. If B says to A, "If you walk across Brooklyn Bridge I'll pay you $100 one year after you finish walking" and A walks and B repudiates his obligation, A cannot bring an immediate action for the $100. The anticipatory repudiation does not justify an immediate action because of the exception discussed here.[3] The same would be true if the arrangement were bilateral and A had performed.[4]

Assume that A lends B $12,000 and B promises to pay $1,000 per month starting one month from the making of the loan. Before the time for the first payment arrives, B repudiates. Under the general rule allowing an action for a total breach when the promisor repudiates, A should be entitled to $12,000 (plus interest) minus an adjustment if there is an early payment. However, the majority of courts do not permit such an action and permit A to sue for an installment only after that installment becomes due.[5] A may recover only $1,000, and may not recover for the other installments until they severally mature.[6] Two factors coexist in this case. First, the plaintiff has completely performed and second, the plaintiff is entitled to a fixed payment of money at one time or in installments.[7] For the exception to apply, the first factor must

2. Greenway v. Gaither, Taney 227, 10 Fed.Cas. 1180, 1182 (No. 5788) (C.C.D.Md. 1853).

3. Rs. 2d § 277 cmt b and § 268 cmt c.

4. Rs. 2d § 243(3) & § 253(1); 4 Corbin §§ 962–969; 11 Williston §§ 1326–1330 (3d ed.). Texas is in a distinct minority to the contrary. See Jenkins v. Jenkins, 991 S.W.2d 440 (Tex.App.1999); 11 Williston § 1330 (3d ed.). Florida has joined Texas.

National Education Centers v. Kirkland, 635 So.2d 33 (Fla.App.1993).

5. Rs. 1st § 318 (amended in 1946); 4 Corbin §§ 962–969; 1 Williston §§ 1326–1330 (3d ed.).

6. Phelps v. Herro, 215 Md. 223, 137 A.2d 159 (1957).

7. This relates not only to performance of all promises but also to compliance with all conditions. For example, in a life insur-

always be present. Some courts have expanded the second requirement by applying the exception to promises not involving an obligation to pay.[8] The Restatement (Second) would allow such expansion in the case of an anticipatory breach,[9] but not where there is a present breach coupled with the repudiation.[10] The distinction appears to be based on the original fallacy in Hochster to the effect that in the case of an anticipatory breach the allowance of a present action is necessary to relieve the injured party of obligations under the contract. Where there is a present breach no such action is necessary to discharge the aggrieved party.

No one has articulated a sound logical or practical ground for the rule that no action lies for a repudiation of a unilateral obligation to pay money at a fixed time or times. Professor Williston, expressing hostility to the entire doctrine of anticipatory breach, states that the rule as to unilateral obligations is justified because "it seems undesirable to enlarge the boundaries of the doctrine."[11] Such reasoning seems as sound as stating that the doctrine should exclude contracts made on Thursdays. He continues his argument by asserting that to permit such an action "is truly nothing but a direct bonus to the promisee beyond what he was promised and a direct penalty to the promisor."[12] By this is meant that to grant enforcement of the promise prior to maturity would be to remake the contract to the benefit of the promisee and to the injury of the promisor. If this argument were sound, it would be sound in any case in which damages are granted for breach of a contract involving performances to be rendered in the future. In an action for damages, however, the promise is not enforced as such, but a remedy is granted for breach of the obligations contained in the contract. There is no reason why the granting of the remedy of damages is any more of a bonus and penalty in this context than in any other.

Another reason for the rule has been advanced: "The reason why a contract to pay money at a definite time in the future is an exception to the rule is that money is not a commodity which is sold and bought in the market and the market value of which fluctuates, as is the case with grain, stocks, and other similar articles."[13] This argument also misses its mark. Although, inflation aside, money does not fluctuate in value, the

---

ance policy the insured does not normally promise to pay premiums. However, the payment of premiums is a condition. If the insurance company repudiates, the insured has not fully performed and thus may sue for a total breach because the exception does not apply. American Ins. Union v. Woodard, 118 Okla. 248, 247 P. 398, 48 ALR 102 (1926). But there is a minority view which refuses to permit an action for total breach because the insured's rights can be protected in an action in equity for a declaratory judgment. However, even under the minority view, an action for restitution would be available. Kelly v. Security Mut. Life Ins., 186 N.Y. 16, 78 N.E. 584 (1906).

Some courts have held that the insured may sue for a total breach. Stephenson v. Equitable Life, 92 F.2d 406 (4th Cir.1937).

8. See Diamond v. Univ. of Southern Cal., 11 Cal.App.3d 49, 89 Cal.Rptr. 302 (1970).

9. Rs.2d § 253 ill. 4.

10. Rs. 2d § 243(3).

11. 11 Williston § 1326 at p. 150 (3d ed.).

12. Ibid.

13. Alger–Fowler v. Tracy, 98 Minn. 432, 437, 107 N.W. 1124, 1126 (1906).

creditor's right to payment does fluctuate in value and, when repudiated by the debtor becomes nearly valueless as an asset.

Because, more often than not, creditors draft loan agreements, such agreements typically contain acceleration clauses, for example, to the effect that missing one payment will make all payments immediately payable and that repudiation of the obligation to pay will make all payments immediately payable. The Uniform Commercial Code even authorizes provisions permitting acceleration by a creditor "at will" or "when he deems himself insecure." Clauses of this type, however, may be exercised "only if he in good faith believes that the prospect of payment or performance is impaired."[14]

One class of debtors, however, do the drafting—insurance companies. Repudiation by the insurer often provides difficult questions. A problem arises in a disability insurance policy where the insurance company, claiming that the insured is not disabled, refuses to make a monthly or a weekly payment, and states that it will not make any further payments. Here again the majority of the cases have held that the insured even though disabled may sue only for installments that are presently due.[15] In the cases involving disability insurance and other contracts for the payment of installments for life, it has been argued that it would be much too speculative to award damages as the duration of the disability and the duration of the plaintiff's life cannot be proved with absolute certainty.[16] While this is a plausible argument, such obstacles are routinely surmounted in tort cases and cases involving breach, anticipatory or otherwise, of executory bilateral contracts.

Long Island R.R. v. Northville Industries[17] is a case that attempted to put this topic on a rational basis but, alas, fell into a logical fallacy. The plaintiff gave the defendant a license to install and use an oil pipeline along the railroad's right of way. The defendant agreed to pay plaintiff a minimum of $20,000 per year for twenty years plus additional sums based upon use. The defendant repudiated the agreement and the repudiation was anticipatory. The issue was whether to apply the exception concerning unilateral obligations to pay money, or whether to apply the general rule that an anticipatory repudiation created a breach. The case turned upon whether there had been full performance by the

---

14. UCC § 1–208 (revised § 1–309); see Van Horn v. Van De Wol, 6 Wn.App. 959, 497 P.2d 252, 61 ALR3d 241 (1972).

15. N.Y. Life Ins. v. Viglas, 297 U.S. 672 (1936); contra, Federal Life Ins. v. Rascoe, 12 F.2d 693 (6th Cir.1926), cert. denied; see 4 Corbin § 969; 11 Williston § 1329 (3d ed.). In a number of cases the court, although limiting the plaintiff's recovery to installments due at the time of commencement of the action (or in some jurisdictions, at the date of judgment), also issued a decree for specific performance as to payment of future installments. First State Bank v. Jubie, 86 F.3d 755 (8th Cir.1996) (pension plan); John Hancock Mut. Life Ins. v. Cohen, 254 F.2d 417 (9th Cir.1958); Amend v. Hurley, 293 N.Y. 587, 59 N.E.2d 416 (1944); contra, Brotherhood of Locomotive Firemen & Enginemen v. Simmons, 190 Ark. 480, 79 S.W.2d 419 (1935). Other courts have granted a declaratory judgment on installment judgments or restitution. Rs. 2d § 268 cmt c.

16. 11 Williston § 1329 (3d ed.); and see Mabery v. Western Cas. & Sur., 173 Kan. 586, 250 P.2d 824 (1952).

17. 41 N.Y.2d 455, 393 N.Y.S.2d 925, 362 N.E.2d 558 (1977).

plaintiff. The court decided that the plaintiff had not fully performed. The court claimed that railroad had continuing obligations under the contract because it was under a duty not to abandon the property and not to sell to one who would use the property in such a way as to prevent the construction of the pipeline.[18] The fallacy of this claim is that under the doctrine of prospective failure of condition triggered by the prospective unwillingness of defendant to perform, the plaintiff was discharged of its obligations by the repudiation. The judgment for the plaintiff, despite the fallacy, did substantial justice, but it would have been an apt occasion to overrule the exception. It should be noted that under the bankruptcy act where the petition requests liquidation of the debtor, unilateral obligations to pay money in the future are accelerated.[19]

At times the element of the exception that is missing is the fixed payment of money either at one time or in installments. For example, A transfers a farm to B in consideration of B's promise to support A for life but, prior to the time for performance, B repudiates. A may bring an action for total breach based upon the anticipatory repudiation. Although A has completely performed there is no fixed amount for each payment to be made.[20]

§ 12.10   Another Exception: Independent Promises

The above discussion should not be confused with a situation where one party repudiates and the other party has breached an independent promise. For example, A and B enter into an employment contract for five years. A, the employee, promises not to engage in the same business for a designated period after the termination of employment. The contract provides that this promise is independent. After A starts to perform, B repudiates the contract. According to the Restatement (Second), A is still liable on the promise; if A breaches the promise B may sue for breach of this covenant even though B has repudiated.[1]

This answer has logic behind it, but reeks of injustice. Elsewhere, one of us has written on this topic:[2] "Covenants not to compete ancillary to employment contracts are not favorites of the law. They deprive the public of the competitive services of the employee. Also, they frequently act harshly on the employee. There is no intent to discuss here the many facets of the legal problems affecting such covenants. The topic here is limited to the employee who has entered a *valid* covenant that meets the tests of consideration and public policy and suffers from no infirmity such as fraud. If such an employee is discharged without cause, will the covenant be enforced? Would not such enforcement be unconscionably

---

18. Notice that the case involves a bilateral contract. There is some question as to whether the exception applies in the case of a unilateral contract. See 11 Williston § 1305 (3d ed.). Compare 4 Corbin § 962 with Sodus Mfg. v. Reed, 94 A.D.2d 932, 463 N.Y.S.2d 952 (1983).

19. 11 U.S.C.A. § 502(b).

20. Rs. 1st § 317, ill. 6; see 4 Corbin § 970; 11 Williston § 1326 (3d ed.).

§ 12.10

1. Rs. 2d § 232, ill. 3.

2. Perillo, Abuse of Rights: A Pervasive Legal Concept, 27 Pac.L.J. 37, 88–89 (1995) (footnotes renumbered).

abusive? The answer of classical contract law is that a valid contract exists and should be enforced.[3] Yet, very many cases have employed flanking devices such as artful interpretation,[4] the exercise of equitable discretion,[5] and even stretching the equitable doctrine of 'unclean hands.'[6] Other courts basically have sputtered that enforcement would be unjust.[7] A recognized doctrine of abuse of rights would explain why such a covenant will not be enforced by either law or equity where the employee is discharged for the convenience of the employer. The shared purpose of an employment agreement containing a covenant not to compete is to protect the employer from conduct that is in the penumbra

3. Torrington Creamery v. Davenport, 126 Conn. 515, 12 A.2d 780 (1940). (New owners discharged defendant. The court enjoined a violation of a covenant not to compete, but thought it significant that the plaintiff requested that defendant be enjoined from competing only in two towns.) Robert S. Weiss & Assocs. v. Wiederlight, 208 Conn. 525, 546 A.2d 216 (1988) (expiration of the contract activated the covenant); Orkin Exterminating v. Harris, 224 Ga. 759, 164 S.E.2d 727, 728–29 (1968) (The agreement provided: "[t]hese covenants (restrictive) on the part of the employee shall be construed as an agreement independent of any other provision in this agreement * * *"); Gomez v. Chua Medical, 510 N.E.2d 191, 195 (Ind.App.1987) (holding that where an at-will employment was terminated by the employer the covenant would be enforced even if the firing were "essentially arbitrary").

The court in Vermont Elec. Supply v. Andrus, 132 Vt. 195, 315 A.2d 456, 458 (1974), said of an employee who voluntarily quit, "[h]e was not placed in the double bind of being both fired and subject to five years of employment restraint."

4. In Derrick, Stubbs & Stith v. Rogers, 256 S.C. 395, 182 S.E.2d 724, 726 (1971), it was held that termination of the contract of employment also terminated the covenant. Many covenants are written to prevent such a holding. In Grant v. Carotek, 737 F.2d 410 (4th Cir.1984), very strict construction was given to the covenant making it unreasonable and unenforceable.

5. Frierson v. Sheppard Bldg. Supply, 247 Miss. 157, 154 So.2d 151, 155 (1963) ("Had the chancellor found that appellant's discharge was arbitrary, capricious, or in bad faith, he could have refused to lend the aid of equity in enforcing the contract.") Ma & Pa v. Kelly, 342 N.W.2d 500 (Iowa 1984) (the cause for the termination is only one factor in determining whether an injunction should issue); Security Services v. Priest, 507 S.W.2d 592, 595 (Tex.Civ.App. 1974) ("equity may deny enforcement of

the covenant if the employer acts arbitrarily and unreasonably in discharging the employee. . . . ")

6. Chicago Towel v. Reynolds, 108 W.Va. 615, 152 S.E. 200 (1930). The employee was discharged without notice because his salary was too high. Injunction denied on the basis of "unclean hands."

7. In Bailey v. King, 240 Ark. 245, 398 S.W.2d 906, 908 (1966), the court said: "Of course, if an employer obtained an agreement of this nature from an employee, and then, without reasonable cause, fired him, the agreement would not be binding. In other words, an employer cannot use this type of contract as a subterfuge to rid himself of a possible future competitor."

In Post v. Merrill, Lynch, Pierce, Fenner & Smith, 48 N.Y.2d 84, 421 N.Y.S.2d 847, 849, 397 N.E.2d 358, 361 (1979), the court said "[w]here the employer terminates the employment relationship without cause, however, his action necessarily destroys the mutuality of obligation on which the covenant rests as well as the employer's ability to impose a forfeiture. An employer should not be permitted to use offensively an anticompetition clause coupled with a forfeiture provision to economically cripple a former employee and simultaneously deny other potential employers his services." The attempt to base the result on mutuality of obligation is like the flailing of a non-swimmer. First, mutuality of obligation is an obsolete and abandoned doctrine. See supra § 4.12(c); 2 Corbin ch. 6 (Perillo & Bender 1995). Second, in the typical at-will employment, there is no obligation on the employee, except perhaps the covenant itself. A theory of abuse of rights is inherent in the rest of this quotation.

In Dutch Maid Bakeries v. Schleicher, 58 Wyo. 374, 131 P.2d 630, 636 (1942) the court said that the employer's conduct "savored with injustice." See also Hopper v. All Pet Animal Clinic, 861 P.2d 531 (1993) (enforceability depends in part on whether termination was in good faith).

of unfair competition while assuring the employee a means of practicing the trade or profession for which the employee is trained. The employee's purpose in agreeing to the covenant is to practice this trade or profession with the employer who has now destroyed the assurance of a job while seeking to prevent the employee from working at such a job elsewhere. Such enforcement would be a grave abuse of rights.''

Although in a lease of real property the tenant's duties are sometimes treated as independent of the landlord's obligations, it has been held that a lease where the landlord has duties other than delivery of possession, a tenant's repudiation acts as a breach by repudiation.[8]

8. Pitcher v. Benderson–Wainberg Assocs., 277 A.D.2d 586, 715 N.Y.S.2d 104 (2000). Under the terminology of this chapter, the landlord's lock-out of the tenant was a justifiable reaction to the tenant's prospective unwillingness to perform.

Chapter 13

IMPRACTICABILITY AND FRUSTRATION

Table of Sections

§ 13.1 Impracticability of Performance: Introduction

Sometimes an event occurs after the formation of a contract that makes it impossible to perform a contractual promise.[1] The harsh

§ **13.1**   § 13.11.
1. For existing impracticability, see

traditional common law rule was "pacta sunt servanda;"[2] promises must be kept though the heavens fall.[3] Although a court would not grant specific performance of such a promise, the breaching party would still be liable for damages.[4] The theory was that the breaching party should obtain self-protection by negotiating a protective provision in the contract.[5]

Despite this absolute statement of the rule, from early times courts have made two exceptions. One was the case of a promise of personal services made impossible by death or unavoidable illness.[6] A second exception was made where there was a supervening change in the law making performance unlawful and therefore legally impossible.[7]

Starting with the case of Taylor v. Caldwell[8] discussed below,[9] the courts of England and the U.S. have expanded the exceptions to the doctrine. This expansion was articulated in the terms of implied or constructive conditions.[10] The parties were said to have contemplated the continued existence of a particular state of facts. If these facts change so as to render impossible a party's performance, it is often said that the continued existence of the contemplated state of facts is a condition precedent to the promisor's duty under the contract.[11] Another more recent development is that there has been a tendency to relax the standard to one of impracticability rather than impossibility.[12]

The following modern statement of the impracticability doctrine appears in a leading case.[13]

> The doctrine of impossibility of performance has gradually been freed from the earlier fictional and unrealistic strictures of such tests as the "implied term" and the "parties' contemplation." [citations omitted]. It is now recognized that "A thing is impossible in

2. Hyland, Pacta Sunt Servanda, 34 Va. J.Int'l Law 405 (1994). Many legal systems have a more flexible approach. See Perillo, 5 Tul.J.Int'l & Comp.L. 5 (1997).

3. 14 Corbin § 74.2 (Nehf 2001); Paradine v. Jane, Aleyn 26, 82 Eng.Rep. 897 (K.B.1647); Silverman v. Charmac, 414 So.2d 892 (Ala.1982).

4. Rs. 2d, Introductory Note to ch. 11.

5. Paradine v. Jane, Aleyn 26, 82 Eng. Rep. 897 (K.B.1647).

6. 16 Williston § 1931 (3d ed.).

7. Ibid.

8. 122 Eng.Rep. 309 (K.B.1863); Page, The Development of the Doctrine of Impossibility of Performance, 18 Mich.L.Rev. 589 (1920); Annot., 84 ALR2d 12 (1962).

9. See § 13.3 infra.

10. See § 13.20 infra.

11. This is the basic approach taken by the UCC and the Restatement (Second). See § 13.20 infra. There has been some tendency to treat questions of impracticability and frustration as questions of law rather than fact. Rs. (2d), Introductory Note to ch. 11; Butler Mfg. v. Americold, 850 F.Supp. 952 (D.Kan.1994); Central Kansas Credit Union v. Mutual Guaranty, 102 F.3d 1097 (10th Cir.1996); but see Alimenta (U.S.A.) v. Cargill, 861 F.2d 650 (11th Cir.1988); Oosten v. Hay Haulers, Dairy Emp. & Helpers Union, 45 Cal.2d 784, 291 P.2d 17 (1955), cert. denied; Mishara Constr. v. Transit–Mixed Concrete, 365 Mass. 122, 310 N.E.2d 363, 70 ALR3d 1259 (1974); Housing Auth. v. East Tennessee Light & Power, 183 Va. 64, 31 S.E.2d 273 (1944).

12. Both the UCC and the Restatement (Second) speak in terms of impracticability rather than impossibility. See § 13.9 infra.

13. Transatlantic Financing v. U.S., 363 F.2d 312, 315 (D.C.Cir.1966); 41 Tul.L.Rev. 709 (1967); 8 Wm. & Mary L.Rev. 679 (1967).

legal contemplation when it is not practicable; and a thing is impracticable when it can only be done at an excessive and unreasonable cost." [citations omitted]. The doctrine ultimately represents the ever-shifting line, drawn by courts hopefully responsive to commercial practices and mores, at which the community's interest in having contracts enforced according to their terms is outweighed by the commercial senselessness of requiring performance. When the issue is raised, the court is asked to construct a condition of performance based on changed circumstances, a process which involves at least three reasonably definable steps. First, a contingency—something unexpected—must have occurred. Second, the risk of the unexpected occurrence must not have been allocated either by agreement or by custom. Finally, occurrence of the contingency must have rendered performance commercially impracticable.

The case articulated several requirements. One, that the contingency be unexpected, relates to foreseeability and is discussed below.[14] In addition, under modern case law, a promisor must overcome two main hurdles to have the defense of impracticability. Not only must the promisor show impossibility or impracticability but must also show the absence of an assumption of the risk that the event would occur.[15]

All contracts involve risks. Some contracts are almost purely aleatory. If one sells shares of stock on the stock exchange that one does not have—the so-called "short sale"—it is a contract of pure risk and there is no circumstance (absent fraud or the like) in which a court should relieve the seller or buyer from a total loss even if unexpected and unforeseeable events disrupt the market.[16] On the other hand, in the more typical contract involving the sale of goods or services, or the rental of real estate, each party expects to gain from the contract and each party understands that the other party also expects to gain. In such contracts, neither party expects to gain from the other's loss, although both realize that such an imbalance may occur. It is in these situations that the impracticability doctrine may redress the imbalance.

Three kinds of events produce an almost automatic excuse for nonperformance: death of a person who is to personally perform, supervening illegality of a performance, and the destruction of the subject matter. When one goes beyond these three categories, relief is most justified if unexpected events inflict a loss on one party and provide a windfall gain for the other or where the excuse would save one party from an unexpected loss while leaving the other party in a position no worse than it would have without the contract.[17]

---

14. See § 13.18 infra.

15. See 14 Corbin (Nehf 2001); Patterson, The Apportionment of Business Risks, 24 Colum.L.Rev. 335 (1924); Rs. 2d, Introd. Note to ch. 11.

16. General Elec. v. Metals Resources, 293 A.D.2d 417, 741 N.Y.Supp.2d 218 (2002) (commodity swap).

17. See Mark P. Gergen, A Defense of Judicial Reconstruction of Contracts, 71 Ind. L.J. 45, 55 (1995).

§ 13.2   The UCC and the Restatement (Second)

The UCC[1] and the Restatement (Second) make no significant changes in the prior law.

UCC § 2–615 states in part:

> "*Except so far as a seller may have assumed a greater obligation* * * *. (a) Delay in delivery or non-delivery in whole or in part by a seller who complies with paragraphs (b) and (c) is not a breach of his duty under a contract for sale if performance as agreed has *become impracticable* by the occurrence of a contingency the non-occurrence of which was a basic assumption on which the contract was made * * *." (italics supplied).[2]

A careful reading shows that the italicized portions refer to assumption of the risk and impracticability—the two "hurdles" that a party seeking to use the defense of impracticability must overcome. A third element is introduced by the words "by the occurrence of a contingency the non-occurrence of which was a basic assumption on which the contract was made."

This third element relates to the assumption of the risk.[3] The introductory language ("Except so far as a seller may have assumed a greater obligation") also relates to assumption of the risk. How do the two provisions mesh? The introductory language relates to an assumption of risk by the terms of the agreement. The other provision relates to the allocation of the risk imposed by law.

A number of questions must be answered before a party may successfully assert the defense of impracticability. These questions are:

(1) Was there an event that changed a basic assumption shared by both parties on which the contract was made? If the non-occurrence of this event was not a basic assumption of both parties, then the seller does not have the defense of impracticability.

(2) Did that event in fact make performance impossible or at least impracticable? A performance is rendered impracticable if it can be accomplished only with extreme and unreasonable difficulty.[4]

(3) Even if questions (1) and (2) are answered affirmatively, one must still inquire whether the party who seeks to utilize the defense of impracticability assumed this risk by the terms of the contract. If the risk was assumed, there will be no defense of impracticability.

§ 13.2

1. The UCC provisions are again discussed in § 13.22 infra, with emphasis on the *effects* of impracticability rather than its legal existence. See Annot. 55 ALR5th 1 (1998).

2. The revision makes one substantive change. The term "delay in delivery or non delivery" is replaced by "delay in performance or non-performance." A suggested comment points out the seller may have obligations other than delivery.

3. U.S. v. Wegematic, 360 F.2d 674, 676 (2d Cir.1966).

4. See § 13.9 infra.

(4) If the contract does not allocate the risk, to whom should the risk be allocated? Legal and economic analysis requires the answer to two questions before the risk is allocated.[5]

(a) Who was in a better position to prevent the risk from occurring? If one party could have prevented the supervening event, the risk should be allocated to that party. Often, however, when cataclysmic events occur, neither party could have prevented the event, in which case the next question must be tackled.

(b) Who is better able to bear the risk? This is not a test of which of the parties has greater wealth. Rather, who is better able to spread the risk as by insurance, by hedging on the futures market, or by passing on the economic impact of the event to the ultimate consumer.

The Restatement (Second) takes the same impracticability approach as the Code, except it makes explicit, what the Code leaves implicit. A promisor may not benefit from the doctrine of impracticability if the promisor is guilty of contributory fault.[6]

As stated above, "the doctrine ultimately represents the ever-shifting line, drawn by courts hopefully responsive to commercial practices and mores, at which the community's interest in having contracts enforced according to their terms is outweighed by the commercial senselessness of requiring performance."[7]

Although impossibility or impracticability may arise in many different ways, the tendency has been to classify the cases into five categories which are actually convenient groupings rather than conceptually distinct classifications. These are: 1) destruction, deterioration or unavailability of the subject matter or the tangible means of performance; 2) failure of the contemplated mode of delivery or payment; 3) supervening prohibition or prevention by law; 4) failure of the intangible means of performance; and 5) death or illness. Closely related to the doctrine of impracticability is the doctrine of excuse of performance by reasonable apprehension of impracticability or reasonable apprehension of danger to life or health and also the doctrine of frustration of the venture.

§ 13.3 Destruction or Unavailability of the Subject Matter or Tangible Means of Performance

Since Taylor v. Caldwell,[1] the case that gave rise to the modern doctrine of impossibility, it has been held, rather consistently, that

5. We follow here the analysis in Posner, Economic Analysis of Law 102–06 (4th ed. 1992). For a critique of Posner's analysis, however, see Trimarchi, Commercial Impracticability in Contract Law: An Economic Analysis, 11 Int'l Rev. of Law & Ec., 63 (1991); also critical is Gergen, A Defense of Judicial Reconstruction of Contracts, 71 Ind. L.J. 44 (1995), and Wagner, In Defense of the Impossibility Defense, 27 Loyola Chi. L.J. 55 (1995). A different perspective is

provided by Frug, Rescuing Impossibility Doctrine: A Postmodern Feminist Analysis of Contract Law, 140 U.Pa.L.Rev 1029 (1992). The allocation of risks is treated in greater detail in §§ 13.16—13.17 infra.

6. Rs. 2d § 261. See § 13.15 infra.

7. See § 13.1 supra.

§ 13.3

1. 122 Eng.Rep. 309 (K.B.1863).

impossibility is an excuse for non-performance where there has been a fortuitous destruction, material deterioration, or unavailability of the subject matter or tangible means of performance of the contract. The defendant promised, for a consideration, to permit the plaintiff to use a music hall for the giving of concerts. But prior to the time for performance a fire destroyed the hall. The court held that the defendant was excused from performance; that is, the music hall's unavailability was not a breach of contract.[2] The plaintiff was also excused from performance under the doctrine of prospective failure of performance.[3]

Under the analysis of the previous section, the continued existence of the music hall was a basic assumption on which the contract was made. The court also decided that there was impossibility in fact and that defendant had not assumed the risk of the destruction of the music hall. In other words, if the defendant had promised to be liable even though the music hall burned down, the result would be different.

Although the doctrine makes good sense, it was perhaps misapplied in Taylor v. Caldwell. The risk should have been allocated to the defendant who was in a significantly better position to prevent the fire. Second, the plaintiffs were not seeking expectancy relief. They sought only reliance damages. Many American courts today would grant such relief even if the defense were allowed.[4]

Good illustrations of destruction of the subject matter are the numerous crop failure cases.[5] If A promises to deliver 2000 tons of Regent potatoes to be delivered from A's farm, A would be excused from performance if, without any contributory fault, a pestilence destroyed the crop.[6] The case would be somewhat different if A simply promised to deliver 2000 tons of Regent potatoes without specifying where they were to be grown. If the parties assumed as a matter of course that the crops were to be grown on A's farm, the majority of cases would allow the defense of impracticability because the parties by implication agreed that the potatoes were to come from this farm.[7] This is particularly true where the parties made the contract while they were at the farm of the seller.[8] Other courts, however, have taken the absolute language of the contract at face value and have concluded that since the parties did not contract with respect to a particular source of supply, destruction of a

2. See Rs. 2d § 263 and cmt a. In the music hall case the plaintiff had a license rather than a lease. Certain rules of property or sales law may lead to a different result where the subject matter of the contract is destroyed. For a similar case involving "deterioration," see Opera Co. Of Boston, v. Wolf Trap Found. for the Performing Arts, 817 F.2d 1094 (4th Cir.1987) (power failure caused cancelation of a performance).

3. See § 12.2 supra.

4. See § 13.23 infra.

5. See Comment, 22 S.D.L.Rev. 529 (1977).

6. Ontario Deciduous Fruit–Growers' Ass'n v. Cutting Fruit–Packing, 134 Cal. 21, 66 P. 28 (1901); Bruce v. Indianapolis Gas, 46 Ind.App. 193, 92 N.E. 189 (1910) (oil or gas from named well); Ward v. Vance, 93 Pa. 499 (1880) (water from named well); Howell v. Coupland, 1 Q.B.D. 258 (1876), 46 L.J.Q.B. 147 (1876).

7. Rs. 1st § 460; UCC § 2–615 cmts 5 and 9; Rs. 2d § 263 ill. 7.

8. Squillante v. California Lands, 5 Cal. App.2d 89, 42 P.2d 81 (1935); Unke v. Thorpe, 75 S.D. 65, 59 N.W.2d 419 (1953); Snipes Mountain v. Benz Bros. & Co., 162 Wn. 334, 298 P. 714, 74 ALR 1287 (1931).

source does not excuse performance.[9] This result is sometimes based on the parol evidence rule,[10] the theory being that if the contract is expressed in a total integration, an attempt to prove the fact that the parties contemplated a unique source of supply is an impermissible attempt to add a supplementary term.

The situation is somewhat different if the contract is made for the delivery of potatoes but not with a farmer. What if both parties assume as a matter of course that the potatoes are to come from a specific area (e.g., a 100 mile radius) and that entire crop in that area is destroyed? Again there are conflicting cases but the courts seem to be a little more reluctant to reach the conclusion that the defense of impracticability should be granted.[11]

The same problem exists in cases stemming from the destruction of factories. Here, the question is whether the parties contemplated that the goods were to come from the particular factory that has been destroyed or could come from other factories. The same lack of uniformity can be found in the factory cases as in the crop cases.[12] The mere fact that timely performance is rendered impossible by damage to the means of performance by unknown causes was held insufficient to trigger an

9. ConAgra, Inc. v. Bartlett Ptshp., 248 Neb. 933, 540 N.W.2d 333 (1995); accord Whitman v. Anglum, 92 Conn. 392, 103 A. 114 (1918) (failure of milk supply caused by death of cows); Oakland Elec. v. Union Gas & Elec., 107 Me. 279, 78 A. 288 (1910) (failure of electricity supply caused by injury to dam); Anderson v. May, 50 Minn. 280, 52 N.W. 530 (1892) (failure of bean crop). Overall shortages of supply of a given product can constitute a defense. UCC § 2–615 cmt 4; Mansfield Propane Gas v. Folger Gas, 231 Ga. 868, 204 S.E.2d 625 (1974); G.W.S. Serv. Stations v. Amoco, 75 Misc.2d 40, 346 N.Y.S.2d 132 (1973); Note, 1973 Duke L.J. 867. For the burden of proof on the seller ought to meet, see Ohio Turnpike Comm'n v. Texaco, 35 Ohio Misc. 99, 297 N.E.2d 557 (1973).

10. See, e.g., Bunge v. Recker, 519 F.2d 449 (8th Cir.1975); Ralston Purina v. Rooker, 346 So.2d 901 (Miss.1977). Other courts have not considered the parol evidence rule as important on the theory that you cannot tell whether a contract is impossible unless one knows the basis on which the parties contracted. Krell v. Henry (1903) 2 K.B. 740, a "frustration" case, appears to have taken this approach. See also Canadian Indus. Alcohol v. Dunbar Molasses, 258 N.Y. 194, 179 N.E. 383, 80 ALR 1173 (1932). It is clear that this problem may also be approached from the point of view of interpretation. E.g., International Paper v. Rockefeller, 161 A.D. 180, 146 N.Y.S. 371 (1914)

and Rs. 2d § 263 cmt b, which states: "In proving such an understanding, prior negotiations may be used to show the meaning of a writing even though it takes the form of a completely integrated writing."

11. Compare Pearce–Young–Angel v. Charles R. Allen, 213 S.C. 578, 50 S.E.2d 698 (1948) (allowing a defense of impossibility) and Mitchell Canneries v. U.S., 77 F.Supp. 498 (Ct.Cl.1948) with Huntington Beach Union H.S. v. Continental Info. Sys., 621 F.2d 353 (9th Cir.1980) ("Under California law, the seller's inability to acquire the contract item from a third party is no defense to an action for breach unless both parties contemplated that the item would be obtained from that particular source."); Holly Hill Fruit Prods. v. Bob Staton, Inc., 275 So.2d 583 (Fla.App.1973) (even if no particular source is contemplated "Staton's obligation was not to buy fruit wherever one could find it in order to fulfill the contract. His obligation was to find fruit, if possible, even at greater expense than anticipated, in Highlands and Hardee Counties."); and Clark v. Wallace County Coop., 26 Kan.App.2d 463, 986 P.2d 391 (1999).

12. See Stewart v. Stone, 127 N.Y. 500, 28 N.E. 595 (1891); Annot., 12 ALR 1273 (1921); Annot., 74 ALR 1289 (1931); Rs. (2d) § 263 ill. 1. Compare Booth v. Spuyten Duyvil Rolling Mill, 60 N.Y. 487 (1875) with Canadian Indus. Alcohol v. Dunbar Molasses, 258 N.Y. 194, 198–99, 179 N.E. 383, 384 (1932).

excuse.[13]

The allocation of risks of destruction or unavailability is also illustrated in the building contract field. Suppose a contractor agrees to construct a building on land owned by the other party to be completed and delivered on May 5, but on April 30, the nearly completed building is destroyed by fire without the contractor being at fault.[14] As a practical matter, performance is impossible. Yet, although the Restatement of Contracts accepts extreme "impracticability" as the equivalent of "impossibility,"[15] it deals with this situation under the heading of "unanticipated difficulty" which does not provide an excuse for non-performance.[16] In this analysis the Restatement is in accord with the great weight of authority.[17] How can this situation be distinguished from Taylor v. Caldwell?[18] One could say that in Taylor v. Caldwell, the contract related to the existing music hall, while in the construction case the contract related to a completed building constructed on the site, not necessarily the first. The results have been justified by economic analysis,[19] but industry practice is to require the owner to insure the risk of destruction.[20] It is much more realistic to say that the results reached are based on the basic precedents that were decided before Taylor v. Caldwell.

The foregoing situation is further complicated if the building is destroyed or rendered less valuable because of defective plans and specifications supplied by the owner. Earlier cases took the position that the builder by accepting the owner's plans promises to produce the result called for by the plans and accepts the risks attendant on using the owner's specifications.[21] It was believed that the owner relied on the builder's technical knowledge. The modern cases, however, generally hold that the owner warrants that the plans are adequate to produce the desired result.[22] But this rule only applies where the plans are prepared

13. R & B Falcon v. American Exploration, 154 F.Supp.2d 969 (S.D.Tex.2001).

14. School Dist. No. 1 v. Dauchy, 25 Conn. 530, 68 Am.Dec. 371 (1857).

15. Rs. 2d § 261. Compare Rs. 1st § 454.

16. Rs. 1st § 467 ill. 1. The Rs. 2d § 263 ill. 4 reaches the same result. However, there is authority that where the house was essentially completed at the time of the fire, risk of loss shifted to the owner. Baker v. Aetna Ins., 274 S.C. 231, 262 S.E.2d 417 (1980). Often it is provided that the risk of loss is on the contractor until the project is "accepted." Hartford Fire Ins. v. Riefolo Constr., 81 N.J. 514, 410 A.2d 658 (1980). See also Halmar Constr. v. New York State Env. Facilities, 76 A.D.2d 957, 429 N.Y.S.2d 51 (1980), app. denied.

17. School Dist. v. Dauchy, 25 Conn. 530 (1857); Rowe v. Peabody, 207 Mass. 226, 93 N.E. 604 (1911); Tompkins v. Dud-

ley, 25 N.Y. 272, 82 Am.Dec. 349 (1862); see Note, 54 Harv.L.Rev. 106 (1940).

18. 122 Eng.Rep. 309 (K.B.1863) (the music hall case).

19. The result is said to be justified by the greater ability of the contractor to prevent the fire and to insure against the risk. See R. Posner, Economic Analysis of Law 106 (4th ed. 1992).

20. Sweet, Legal Aspects of Architects, Engineering and the Construction Process 603 (3d ed.1985) ("Typically, the owner insures the work in progress while the contractor insures its equipment and the other property that will not go into the project.")

21. Stees v. Leonard, 20 Minn. 494 (1874); Superintendent & Trustees v. Bennett, 27 N.J.L. 513, 72 Am.Dec. 373 (1859); Dobler v. Malloy, 214 N.W.2d 510 (N.D. 1973).

22. U.S. v. Spearin, 248 U.S. 132 (1918); J.L. Simmons v. U.S., 412 F.2d 1360 (Ct.Cl.

by professionals hired by the owner. These rules are overridden when the language of the contract or the circumstances otherwise indicate.[23] "Differing site conditions" clauses are common.[24] But a mere general disclaimer of the accuracy of the information provided may be insufficient to shift the risk to the contractor.[25] Even in cases where the owner is held to warrant the plans, the builder cannot rely on them if the builder has reason to know of their inadequacy.[26] A contractor who furnishes a subcontractor with plans is in a similar position as the owner.[27]

The above analysis also applies to federal government building contracts, but a comparable analysis was held not to apply consequential damages paid by manufacturers who produced Agent Orange pursuant to government specifications.[28]

The parties are free to allocate the risks by agreement. Thus, if the builder expressly warrants that the owner's plans are adequate, the builder has assumed the risk and may not claim the excuse that they are inadequate.[29] If the parties agree on contingency plans or payments in the event of unexpected soil conditions, the agreement will be given effect despite any alleged inadequacy of the specifications, and whether or not the unexpected conditions were grossly outside the reasonable contemplation of the parties.[30] Similarly, even if no contingency plans or payments are contemplated, a contractor may assume the risk of soil conditions even where those conditions are far worse than estimated by the owner.[31]

1969); Simpson Timber v. Palmberg Constr., 377 F.2d 380 (9th Cir.1967); Unnerstall Contr. v. Salem, 962 S.W.2d 1 (Mo. App.1997); State v. Commercial Cas. Ins., 125 Neb. 43, 248 N.W. 807, 88 ALR 790 (1933); MacKnight Flintic Stone v. New York, 160 N.Y. 72, 54 N.E. 661 (1899); 5 Okla.L.Rev. 480 (1930). Some courts appear to proceed on a negligence rather than a warranty theory. In either case it would be relevant to ascertain whether the plans were the proximate cause of the failure to complete. Kinser Constr. v. State, 204 N.Y. 381, 97 N.E. 871 (1912). The defective specifications provide not only an excuse for non-performance, but also a basis for an action for recovery of increased expenses involved in producing the desired result. Montrose Contracting v. Westchester, 80 F.2d 841 (2d Cir.1936), cert. denied; Simpson Timber v. Palmberg supra. See Recent Developments in the Spearin Doctrine, in The Construction Lawyer 3 (August 1994).

23. Compare Faber v. New York, 222 N.Y. 255, 118 N.E. 609 (1918), with Application of Semper, 227 N.Y. 151, 124 N.E. 743 (1919).

24. Beh, Allocating the Risk of the Unforeseen, Subsurface and Latent Conditions, 46 U.Kan.L.Rev. 115 (1997).

25. Morris v. State, 598 N.W.2d 520 (S.D.1999).

26. Montrose Contracting v. Westchester, 94 F.2d 580 (2d Cir.1938), cert. denied; Lewis v. Anchorage Asphalt Paving, 535 P.2d 1188, 73 ALR3d 1196 (Alaska 1975); Banducci v. Frank T. Hickey, 93 Cal.App.2d 658, 209 P.2d 398, 399 (1949); Marine Colloids v. M.D. Hardy, Inc., 433 A.2d 402 (Me.1981); Mayville–Portland School Dist. v. C.L. Linfoot Co., 261 N.W.2d 907 (N.D. 1978).

27. APAC Carolina v. Town of Allendale, 41 F.3d 157 (4th Cir.1994).

28. Hercules, Inc. v. U.S., 516 U.S. 417 (1996).

29. Philadelphia Housing Auth. v. Turner Constr., 343 Pa. 512, 23 A.2d 426 (1942).

30. Simpson Timber v. Palmberg Constr., 377 F.2d 380 (9th Cir.1967); Depot Const. v. State, 19 N.Y.2d 109, 278 N.Y.S.2d 363, 224 N.E.2d 866 (1967).

31. Brown Bros. v. Metropolitan Gov't., 877 S.W.2d 745 (Tenn.App.1993).

The situation is completely different where the owner supplies plans which show the desired end result without indicating the method of completion. In such cases the contractor, as in the early cases, is deemed to promise the result called for by the plans and to shoulder the risks of completion.[32]

Construction contracts with the federal government now routinely include a "changed conditions" clause which provides for an equitable adjustment in price or in time for performance in the event unknown physical conditions occur or are discovered after the contract is entered into.[33] As a result much of the litigation in government contracts cases concerning the issues discussed in this chapter now centers on the interpretation of standard contract provisions.[34]

A contract to repair or alter an existing building is not treated in the same way as a contract to construct a building. A different allocation of risk is made. The continued existence of the building is deemed to be a basic assumption on which the parties contracted and it is impossible to repair a non-existing building. Thus, unless the contractor in fact assumed this risk, the duty to repair or alter a building that has been destroyed after contracting is excused under the doctrine of impracticability.[35] As discussed later, once the contract is discharged because of impracticability, justice may require that the rights of the parties be adjusted.[36] Here, the contractor is entitled to a quasi-contractual recovery.[37] The same concepts have been applied to excuse subcontractors from their duty of performance when a building is destroyed. Here, too, quasi-contractual relief will be awarded.[38] By extension of the reasoning in the repair and the sub-contractor cases, a construction contractor has been excused from performance when the structure being erected was destroyed without the contractor's fault where the owner was cooperating in the project by supplying some labor.[39] A different result has been reached where the owner merely supplied materials.[40]

32. See Coto–Matic v. Home Indem., 354 F.2d 720 (10th Cir.1965). See also § 13.17 infra.

33. Cf. Fattore v. Metropolitan Sewerage Comm'n, 505 F.2d 1 (7th Cir.1974); 35 Geo.Wash.L.Rev. 978 (1967).

34. See, e.g., Beh, Allocating the Risk of the Unforeseen, Subsurface and Latent Condition, 46 U.Kan. L.Rev. 115 (1997) (discussing the "differing site condition" clause).

35. The analysis is based on the explanation offered in § 13.2 supra. But the risk may be shifted by contract. RNJ Interstate v. U.S., 181 F.3d 1329 (Fed.Cir.1999), cert. denied.

36. See § 13.23 infra.

37. Bell v. Carver, 245 Ark. 31, 431 S.W.2d 452, 28 ALR3d 781 (1968). The measure of recovery under the theory of quasi-contract has varied. Under one view,

the contractor's recovery is limited to the value of the fixtures incorporated into the building. Young v. Chicopee, 186 Mass. 518, 72 N.E. 63 (1904). Other cases allow, in addition, the value of materials destroyed at the job site. Haynes, Spencer & Co. v. Second Baptist Church, 88 Mo. 285, 57 Am. Rep. 413 (1885). Still other cases have allowed, in addition, expenses in preparation for performance. Albre Marble & Tile v. John Bowen, 338 Mass. 394, 155 N.E.2d 437 (1959). See also § 13.23 infra.

38. M. Ahern v. John Bowen, 334 Mass. 36, 133 N.E.2d 484 (1956); Hayes v. Gross, 9 A.D. 12, 40 N.Y.S. 1098 (1896), aff'd.

39. Butterfield v. Byron, 153 Mass. 517, 27 N.E. 667 (1891).

40. Vogt v. Hecker, 118 Wis. 306, 95 N.W. 90 (1903).

§ 13.4   Failure of the Contemplated Mode of Performance

In the preceding sections the impediment that resulted in impracticability went to the essence of the contract, but sometimes the impediment is in respect to a matter which, although important, is incidental to the main obligations of each party. Among such incidental obligations are mode of payment and mode of delivery. There is no right of substitution if the performance goes to the essence of the contract,[1] but in situations involving incidental obligations, the question becomes whether a commercially reasonable substitute is available. If so, that substitute should be used and accepted.[2] The defense of impracticability would not be available.

Courts could have applied this logic in a number of cases involving the closing of the Suez Canal in 1956 and again in 1967. They did not. Nevertheless, the courts arrived at similar results, using a different line of reasoning. A leading case is American Trading and Production v. Shell Int'l Marine Ltd,[3] decided in accordance with the rules stated in § 13.2 above, holding that the closing of the Canal was not an event that changed a basic assumption on which the contract was made, and, in addition, the closing of the Canal did not involve impossibility or even impracticability. If the court had used the logic of the prior paragraph it could have reasoned that, although the use of the Canal was impossible, the trip around the Cape of Good Hope was a commercially reasonable substitute. Consequently the owner was obliged to use that route, and the charterer was obliged to pay no more than the contract price.[4]

The UCC specifically deals with failure of the contemplated mode of delivery or payment.[5] The Code was not applicable to the Suez cases, because no sale of goods was in issue. However, the UCC provisions, which are themselves outgrowths of the common law cases cited above, would have been a useful source for reasoning by analogy. This section provides:

> (1) Where without fault of either party the agreed berthing, loading, or unloading facilities fail or an agreed type of carrier becomes unavailable or the agreed manner of delivery otherwise becomes commercially impracticable but a commercially reasonable substitute is available, such substitute performance must be tendered and accepted.

§ 13.4

1. R.C. Craig, Ltd. v. Ships of the Sea, 401 F.Supp. 1051 (S.D.Ga.1975).

2. E.g., Meyer v. Sullivan, 40 Cal.App. 723, 181 P. 847 (1919); Iasigi v. Rosenstein, 141 N.Y. 414, 36 N.E. 509 (1894).

3. 453 F.2d 939 (2d Cir.1972); see also Transatlantic Fin. Corp. v. U.S., 363 F.2d 312 (D.C.Cir.1966); Schlegel, Of Nuts, and Ships, and Sealing Wax, Suez, and Frustrating Things, 23 Rutgers L.Rev. 419 (1969); G.H. Treitel, Frustration and Force Majeure ¶¶ 4–061 to 4–072 (1994).

4. If the contract specifically calls for a Suez passage or a trip around the Cape of Good Hope, then the promise made is alternative. In that situation, both alternatives must become impossible or impracticable before the defense of impracticability is available. Glidden v. Hellenic Lines, 275 F.2d 253 (2d Cir.1960). Transatlantic Fin., note 3 supra, states that "the Cape route is generally regarded as an alternative means of performance."

5. UCC § 2–614 (unchanged in the revision).

(2) If the agreed means or manner of payment fails because of domestic or foreign governmental regulation, the seller may withhold or stop delivery unless the buyer provides a means or manner of payment which is commercially a substantial equivalent. If delivery has already been taken, payment by the means or in the manner provided by the regulation discharges the buyer's obligation unless the regulation is discriminatory, oppressive or predatory.

Subsection 1 would apply to the Suez Canal cases if the contracts involved the sale of goods. It is important that the failure of the mode of delivery not be caused by the party who attempts to substitute for the agreed mode of delivery.[6] An interesting question is whether the ship owners in the Suez cases would be liable because they did not perform on time. Comment 7 to UCC Section 2–615 indicates that the additional time taken should not amount to a breach,[7] but it is not applicable to a ship charter agreement except by analogy.

Subsection 2 applies to the mode of payment. The first part deals with a case where delivery has not yet been made and payment in accordance with the terms of the agreement becomes illegal under the applicable foreign or domestic regulations. In such a case in the language of the statute "the seller may withhold or stop delivery unless the buyer provides a means or manner of payment which is commercially a substantial equivalent." The contract is discharged unless the buyer is able to pay in a substitute manner. The second part of the subsection applies where the goods have already been delivered. Here, the statute provides for "payment by the means or in the manner provided by the regulation * * * unless the regulation is discriminatory, oppressive or predatory."[8]

§ 13.5　Supervening Prohibition or Prevention by Law

If an agreement is illegal when made, the problem is illegality.[1] If instead, an agreement that is legal when made, later becomes illegal, the issue is not illegality but supervening impossibility. Lawful performance becomes impossible.

---

6. S & S v. Plambeck, 478 N.W.2d 857 (Iowa App.1991) (buyer was delicensed).

7. "The failure of conditions which go to convenience or collateral values rather than to commercial practicability of the main performance does not amount to a complete excuse. However, good faith and the reason of the present section and of the preceding one may properly be held to justify and even to require any needed delay involved in a good faith inquiry seeking a readjustment of the contract terms to meet the new conditions."

8. Exceedingly complex problems have arisen in regard to currency regulations of foreign countries. Treaty obligations are often applicable. In the absence of a treaty, traditionally, domestic courts have refused to recognize foreign restrictive regulations on the movement of currency. See Banco Do Brasil v. A.C. Israel Commodity, 12 N.Y.2d 371, 239 N.Y.S.2d 872, 190 N.E.2d 235 (1963), cert. denied; A. Ehrenzweig, Conflict of Laws § 191 (1962); Effros, 9 ICSID Rev. 165 (1994). The Code's recognition of these regulations is open to various interpretations on the question of when the restrictive currency regulation is applicable to the case. This is a question of conflict of laws. Cf. UCC § 1–105; revision § 1–301.

§ 13.5

1. See Chapter 22 infra.

It is well settled that supervening prohibition of performance by law or administrative regulation of the U.S., a state or municipality provides an excuse for non-performance,[2] provided, of course, that all of the other requisites of the doctrine are met.[3] For example, if the law intervenes because of the promisor's fault, the defense is denied because of (1) contributory fault and (2) the impracticability is only subjective.[4] The problem arises typically in a case where a promisor is enjoined from performing. If promisor's wrongdoing is the basis for the issuance of the injunction, the defense is disallowed.[5] Where, however, the order is not caused by the promisor's fault, there is no reason why it should not provide as much an excuse for non-performance as any other kind of legal prohibition.[6] Even if the promisee has improvidently obtained a temporary injunction, upon its dissolution any time periods burdening either party are tolled.[7]

Indeed, non-judicial action by a governmental agency affecting a particular party rather than the public generally has been held to excuse performance. For example, the requisition of a factory for war production has been held to excuse performance of civilian contracts for production at the factory.[8] There is no reason why judicial action affecting a party should not equally be an excuse. The UCC is in accord with the views stated here.[9]

A promisor may assume the risk of a change of law or other government action. Such an assumption will result in a denial of the defense of impracticability.[10]

The early cases generally took the position that prevention or

---

2. Rs. 2d § 284; see Horowitz v. U.S., 267 U.S. 458 (1925); In re Kramer & Uchitelle, 288 N.Y. 467, 43 N.E.2d 493, 141 ALR 1497 (1942), rearg. denied; Cinquegrano v. T.A. Clarke Motors, 69 R.I. 28, 30 A.2d 859 (1943); see also McNair & Watts, The Legal Effects of War 156–202 (4th ed. 1966); Blair, Breach of Contract Due to War, 20 Colum.L.Rev. 413 (1920).

3. Rs. 2d § 264 cmt a; Harwell v. Growth Programs, 451 F.2d 240 (5th Cir. 1971), modified.

4. Klauber v. San Diego Street Car, 95 Cal. 353, 30 P. 555 (1892); Peckham v. Industrial Securities, 31 Del. 200, 113 A. 799 (Super.1921). See § 13.15 infra.

5. Peckham, supra. Sureties will be discharged from a bail bond where the defendant fails to appear because of incarceration in another jail, provided the sureties have not been negligent. State v. Scherer, 108 Ohio App.3d 586, 671 N.E.2d 545 (1995).

6. Boston Plate & Window Glass v. John Bowen, 335 Mass. 697, 141 N.E.2d 715 (1957); Kuhl v. School Dist. No. 76, 155 Neb. 357, 51 N.W.2d 746 (1952); People v. Globe Mut. Life Ins., 91 N.Y. 174 (1883).

7. Syndicom v. Takaya, 275 A.D.2d 676, 714 N.Y.S.2d 256 (2000).

8. Israel v. Luckenbach S.S., 6 F.2d 996 (2d Cir.1925), cert. denied (vessel commandeered); Mawhinney v. Millbrook Woolen Mills, 231 N.Y. 290, 132 N.E. 93, 15 ALR 1506 (1921) (output of factory requisitioned); 28 Yale L.J. 399 (1919). Informal governmental pressure excused late performance in Eastern Air Lines v. McDonnell Douglas, 532 F.2d 957 (5th Cir.1976), and nonperformance in Harriscom Svenska v. Harris Corp., 3 F.3d 576 (2d Cir.1993). But see Hilton Oil Transport v. Oil Transport, 659 So.2d 1141 (Fla.App.1995) (detention of vessel by Honduran government for unknown reasons and its subsequent destruction by storm was foreseeable).

9. UCC § 2–615(a). Rs. 2d § 264 cmt b, is also in accord. The comment adds that it is not necessary that the order be valid, but a party may have a duty to test its validity. Ordinarily if performance is simply made more burdensome, this will not suffice as an excuse. See § 13.9 infra.

10. Rs. 2d § 264 cmt a & ill. 3.

prohibition by *foreign* law was not an excuse for non-performance.[11] Modern cases have discarded this rule.[12] The UCC explicitly equates foreign law with domestic law as an excuse for non-performance.[13] The contract can, however, allocate the risk of change of law or governmental policy to the promisor.[14]

To be distinguished are changes in law that affect government contracts. Legislation that seeks to undo a government's contractual obligation constitutes a breach by repudiation unless the legislation is of such a general nature to to fall under the "sovereign acts" doctrine.[15]

§ 13.6 Failure of the Intangible Means of Performance

The chief illustrations of the failure of the intangible means of performance are prevention under foreign law, discussed in § 13.5, and strikes. This topic was covered in the First Restatement in a section entitled "Non–Existence of Essential Facts Other Than Specific Things or Person."[1] The Second Restatement does not distinguish between tangible and intangible means of performance[2] and even the First Restatement took the position that the same basic rules should apply although the fact patterns may create different types of problems.[3]

This distinction was important when the courts limited the defense of impracticability to situations where "performance is rendered impossible by an act of God, the law, or the other party."[4] This formulation was intended to include the destruction of a specified thing and death or incapacitating illness of a promisor in a contract which has for its object the rendering of personal services. The formulation did not include failure of the intangible means of performance.[5]

Illustrative of the traditional rule is Fritz–Rumer–Cooke v. U.S.[6] The plaintiff agreed to remove certain railroad tracks from an area around a gaseous diffusion plant. The contract specifically provided that

11. Jacobs, Marcus & Co. v. Credit Lyonnais, 12 Q.B.D. 589 (1884); Vanetta Velvet v. Kakunaka & Co., 256 A.D. 341, 10 N.Y.S.2d 270 (1939).

12. Texas Co. v. Hogarth Shipping, 256 U.S. 619 (1921) (ship requisitioned by British Government); Rothkopf v. Lowry & Co., 148 F.2d 517 (2d Cir.1945); Held v. Goldsmith, 153 La. 598, 96 So. 272 (1919) (contract by German to ship goods to U.S. on British vessel discharged by outbreak of war between Germany and Britain); Rs. 2d § 264.

13. UCC § 2–615(a); accord Rs. 2d § 264.

14. Chase Manhattan Bank v. Traffic Stream, 86 F.Supp.2d 244 (S.D.N.Y.2000) (extensive subsequent history omitted).

15. U.S. v. Winstar, 518 U.S. 839 (1996); U.S. v. Westlands Water Dist., 134 F.Supp.2d 1111 (E.D.Cal.2001); see Speidel,

Contract Excuse Doctrine and Retrospective Legislation, 2001 Wis. L.Rev. 795.

§ 13.6

1. Rs. 1st § 461.

2. See Rs. 2d § 261.

3. Rs. 1st § 461 cmts a, b, and c.

4. Fritz–Rumer–Cooke v. U.S., 279 F.2d 200 (6th Cir.1960).

5. Wischhusen v. American Medicinal Spirits, 163 Md. 565, 163 A. 685 (1933); Browne & Bryan Lumber v. Toney, 188 Miss. 71, 194 So. 296 (1940); Ellis Gray Mill. v. Sheppard, 359 Mo. 505, 222 S.W.2d 742 (1949); see also Elsemore v. Inhabitants of Hancock, 137 Me. 243, 18 A.2d 692 (1941) (includes the act "of a public enemy").

6. 279 F.2d 200 (6th Cir.1960); see also Rs. 1st § 461 ill. 7.

the work was to be completed in one month and contained no provision protecting the contractor against a delay caused by strikes. Employees of the gaseous diffusion plant went on strike and the plaintiff's employees refused to cross the picket line. The strike lasted 30 days. The government granted an extension of time. Plaintiff sought to recover damages sustained because of the interruption in the work caused by the strike. The court disposed of the problem by stating what it termed "a well settled rule of law that if a party by a contract charges himself with an obligation possible to be performed, unforeseen difficulties, however great, will not excuse him, unless performance is rendered impossible by act of God, the law, or the other party."[7]

The more modern approach is exemplified by the case of Mishara Construction v. Transit–Mixed Concrete.[8] The plaintiff was a general contractor and the defendant, a sub-contractor, promised to supply ready-mixed concrete. Deliveries were to be made "as required" by plaintiff. A labor dispute disrupted work on the site for a month or so and, although work resumed, "a picket line was maintained on the site until the completion of the project." Defendant failed to make deliveries and plaintiff purchased elsewhere and sued for damages.

Plaintiff sought to exclude any evidence concerning the picket line and sought an instruction that defendant "was required to comply with the contract regardless of picket lines, strikes or labor difficulties." The court analyzed the impracticability problem in more modern terms and concluded that plaintiff's request to charge to the effect that there was no impracticability as a matter of law was incorrect and that the issue was properly submitted to the jury.[9] The court repeats Williston's conclusion that there are "many variables" that bear on the question and that the trend is "toward recognizing strikes as excuses for non-performance."[10]

The Second Restatement omits reference to strikes. The Reporter's Note to § 261 and comment d to the Restatement (Second) state that it "is omitted, because the parties often provide for this eventuality and, where they do not, it is particularly difficult to suggest a proper result without a detailed statement of all the circumstances." As suggested by the quotation, it has become customary to include strike clauses in contracts with the result that there has been a substantial amount of litigation relating to the interpretation of these clauses.[11] The UCC does

---

7. 279 F.2d at 201. The same result has been reached where it is the promisor's employees who are on strike. The theory is that failure to come to terms with employees or to make other arrangements is contributory fault. 14 Corbin § 75.8 (Nehf 2001); McGovern v. New York, 234 N.Y. 377, 138 N.E. 26, 25 ALR 1442 (1923); cf. The Richland Queen, 254 F. 668 (2d Cir. 1918), cert. denied; Empire Transp. v. Philadelphia & R. Coal & Iron, 77 F. 919 (8th Cir.1896); 16 Williston § 1951A (3d ed.).

8. 365 Mass. 122, 310 N.E.2d 363, 70 ALR3d 1259 (1974); see also New York v. Local 333, 79 A.D.2d 410, 437 N.Y.S.2d 98 (1981), aff'd.

9. More often than not, a question of impracticability is looked upon as a question of law. See § 13.1, n.11 supra.

10. 16 Williston § 1951A (3d ed.).

11. See, e.g., Corona Coal v. Robert P. Hyams Coal, 9 F.2d 361 (5th Cir.1925); Davis v. Columbia Coal–Min., 170 Mass. 391, 49 N.E. 629 (1898); J.M. Rodriguez &

not specifically refer to the subject of strikes.[12]

§ 13.7 Death or Disability

Ordinarily the death of the offeror terminates the power of acceptance created by a revocable offer.[1] But the situation is different here, where the death occurs *after* the formation of the contract. Death does not ordinarily discharge a contract.[2] If a contract, however, calls for personal performance by the promisor[3] or a third person,[4] and the person who is to render the performance dies or becomes so ill[5] as to make performance impossible or seriously injurious to his or her health, the promisor's duty is excused unless the risk was assumed.[6] Similarly, a lawyer who is appointed to the judiciary may be disabled from performing contracts with clients or partners.[7] On the other hand, if the performance is delegable, the death or illness of the promisor or of a third party who is expected to perform does not excuse performance.[8]

Some of the normal constraints of the impracticability doctrine are not employed in death or illness cases. Since both death and illness are foreseeable risks, the normal foreseeability test is not applicable. In the case of death by a self-administered overdose of drugs, it was held that the contributory fault of the decedent, River Phoenix, did not bar the impracticability defense raised by his estate.[9]

The personal representative of the deceased employee whose death discharges the contract is entitled to quasi-contractual recovery for the reasonable value of the services rendered. The contract rate is evidence of this value but is not conclusive, except that it sets the upward limit on

Co. v. Moore–McCormack Lines, 32 N.Y.2d 425, 345 N.Y.S.2d 993, 299 N.E.2d 243 (1973); see also § 13.19 infra.

12. But see UCC § 2–615 cmt 4 ("unforeseen shutdown of major sources of supply" may give rise to impracticability).

§ 13.7

1. See § 2.20(c) supra.

2. Thomas Yates & Co. v. American Legion, 370 So.2d 700 (Miss.1979). Thus, a promise to pay money is not made impossible because of the death or illness of either the debtor or creditor. Hasemann v. Hasemann, 189 Neb. 431, 203 N.W.2d 100 (1972).

3. Herren v. Harris, Cortner & Co., 201 Ala. 577, 78 So. 921 (1918); Buccini v. Paterno Constr., 253 N.Y. 256, 170 N.E. 910 (1930); Peaseley v. Virginia Iron, Coal & Coke, 12 N.C.App. 226, 182 S.E.2d 810 (1971), cert. denied; 14 Corbin § 75.2 (Nehf 2001). Conversely, the promisee need not accept a performance tendered by the deceased promisor's personal representative. Ames v. Sayler, 267 Ill.App.3d 672, 205 Ill.Dec. 223, 642 N.E.2d 1340 (1994), app.denied (death of tenant farmer).

4. Spalding v. Rosa, 71 N.Y. 40, 27 Am. Rep. 7 (1877); Phillips v. Alhambra Palace, 1 Q.B. 59 (1901).

5. Strader v. Collins, 280 A.D. 582, 116 N.Y.S.2d 318 (1952) (football coach). Of course, if the illness is relatively minor, there may be only temporary or partial impracticability. See §§ 13.13, 13.14 infra. On the effect of supervening mental illness of a client on the attorney-client relationship, see Donnelly v. Parker, 486 F.2d 402 (D.C.Cir.1973).

6. Mullen v. Wafer, 252 Ark. 541, 480 S.W.2d 332 (1972); Rs. 2d § 262 and cmt a.

7. Cazares v. Saenz, 208 Cal.App.3d 279, 256 Cal.Rptr. 209 (1989).

8. Chamberlain v. Dunlop, 126 N.Y. 45, 26 N.E. 966 (1891). Rs. 1st § 459 cmt c, is perhaps clearer on this relationship than Rs. 2d § 262 cmt a. See §§ 18.25 to 18.32 infra on delegability.

9. CNA Int'l Reinsurance v. Phoenix, 678 So.2d 378 (Fla.App.1996); but see Handicapped Children's Educ. Bd. v. Lukaszewski, 112 Wis.2d 197, 332 N.W.2d 774 (1983) (teacher's hypertension was self-caused).

recovery.[10] Although the death of the employee who is to render personal services is not a breach, a number of jurisdictions have permitted the employer to set off damages for non-performance of the contract against the estate's claim for quasi-contractual recovery for part performance.[11] Such results appear to be sound inasmuch as the parties' own risk allocations ought to be considered a principal guide towards reallocations of the risks necessitated by the doctrine of impracticability.[12]

The same principles should govern the death or serious illness of an employer. If the employee was to work under the direct supervision of the employer, the employer's incapacity makes supervision in accordance with the contract impossible. The employer is discharged because of impracticability and the employee because of employer's prospective inability to perform.[13] Thus, the question is whether the employer's duty and right of supervision are delegable and assignable.[14] Although perhaps most of the cases are reconcilable with this test, too often courts have indulged in sweeping generalizations and have indicated that a rule of mutuality is applied to the effect that since the employee's duties are personal, death of the employer discharges both parties.[15]

§ 13.8   Apprehension of Impracticability or Danger

Closely related to the doctrine of impracticability, is a doctrine that reasonable apprehension of impracticability excuses beginning or continuing performance.[1] The most frequent application of the rule is to situations where the apprehension of impracticability relates to danger to life or health.[2] Thus, an actor is excused from performing if he has symptoms of what may be a serious disease and enters a hospital for an examination. It matters not that the examination reveals that the illness is not serious.[3] A ship owner is excused from sailing into submarine-infested waters to deliver its cargo, although it subsequently is shown that the ship could have arrived at its destination several hours prior to

10. Buccini v. Paterno Constr., 253 N.Y. 256, 170 N.E. 910 (1930). Difficult problems arise where the deceased was to be paid a contingent fee. See Rowland v. Hudson County, 7 N.J. 63, 80 A.2d 433 (1951); see also Morton v. Forsee, 249 Mo. 409, 155 S.W. 765 (1913) (death of attorney); Barnsdall v. Curnutt, 198 Okl. 3, 174 P.2d 596 (1945) (architect to receive percentage of construction costs; plans were incomplete; building never built).

11. Clark v. Gilbert, 26 N.Y. 279, 84 Am.Dec. 189 (1863); Patrick v. Putnam, 27 Vt. 759 (1855); 46 Mich.L.Rev. 401, 421 (1948); see 69 Yale L.J. 1054 (1960).

12. See Burka v. Patrick, 34 Md.App. 181, 366 A.2d 1070 (1976); Perillo, Restitution in a Contractual Context, 73 Colum.L.Rev. 1208, 1224–25 (1973).

13. See Lacy v. Getman, 119 N.Y. 109, 23 N.E. 452 (1890); 14 Corbin § 75.2. Although it is not impossible for the employer to pay, personal supervision is impossible.

14. See Kelley v. Thompson Land, 112 W.Va. 454, 164 S.E. 667 (1932); see also § 18.31.

15. See 16 Williston § 1941 (3d ed.). A mixture of sound analysis and sweeping over-generalizations is often found. See, e.g., Minevitch v. Puleo, 9 A.D.2d 285, 193 N.Y.S.2d 833 (1959).

§ 13.8

1. Rs. 1st § 465 cmt a.

2. Rs. 1st § 465 cmt b.

3. Wasserman Theatrical Enterprise v. Harris, 137 Conn. 371, 77 A.2d 329 (1950). Employee rights in some circumstances are governed by statute and OSHA regulations. See Note, 81 Colum.L.Rev. 544 (1981).

the outbreak of hostilities.[4] An employee is discharged from a duty to work in an area where an epidemic of a serious contagious disease appears to be in progress.[5] The rule applies not only when there is a threatened harm to the promisor but also where the threatened harm relates to others.[6] The doctrine is not ordinarily applied where the danger to be apprehended relates to land or goods because ordinarily that situation will not involve impracticability.[7] "Nevertheless, where the risk of pecuniary loss or harm to land or goods is great and the harm to the promisee caused by failure to perform is not, the risk need not be taken if there is good ground for apprehending that performance will be impossible."[8]

The Restatement (Second) no longer treats cases in this category as representing a separate doctrine, but rather as examples of impracticability.[9] However, it states the same general rules.[10] The Restatement (Second) does add that the promisor must use reasonable efforts to overcome the obstacles to performance.[11]

§ 13.9   Impracticability

(a) Current Doctrine

The law is changing with respect to situations where the performance is not impossible, but is impracticable. Under the more traditional rule performance was required to be literally impossible.[1] Under the more modern view, however, impracticability is sufficient.[2] This modern trend is due to the first Restatement which equated extreme impracticability with impossibility.[3] This trend has continued and has been fortified by the UCC which utilizes the term "impracticable" to encompass "impossible"[4] and the Restatement (Second) which follows the lead of the Code. Chapter 11 of the Restatement (Second) is entitled, "Impracticability of Performance and Frustration of Purpose."

Professor Williston used the term "impracticability" in his 1920 edition as meaning "not obtainable except by means and with an *expense* impracticability in a business sense."[5] The Restatement (Second) speaks

---

4. The Kronprinzessin Cecilie, 244 U.S. 12 (1917).

5. Lakeman v. Pollard, 43 Me. 463, 69 Am.Dec. 77 (1857); see also Hanford v. Connecticut Fair Ass'n, 92 Conn. 621, 103 A. 838 (1918). In all of these cases there may be additional questions such as assumption of the risk, contributory fault and whether the impracticability is temporary. See §§ 13.16 & 13.13 infra.

6. Rs. 1st § 465 cmt f.

7. Rs. 1st § 465 cmt d.

8. Ibid.

9. Rs. 2d § 261.

10. Rs. 2d § 261 cmt a, and ill. 7. Compare Rs. 2d § 262 ill. 5.

11. Rs. 2d § 261 cmt d.

§ 13.9

1. Hudson v. D & V Mason Contr., 252 A.2d 166 (Del.Super.1969).

2. Portland Section v. Sisters of Charity, 266 Or. 448, 513 P.2d 1183 (1973); F.J. Busse v. Dep't of Gen. Servs., 47 Pa. Cmwlth. 539, 408 A.2d 578 (1979).

3. Rs. 1st § 454.

4. UCC § 2–615.

5. 3 Williston § 1963 (1920).

of "extreme or unreasonable difficulty, expense, injury or loss * * *." It adds that "impracticability means more than impracticality."[6]

How much difficulty amounts to impracticability? A mere increase in the expense of performing does not give rise to a defense of impossibility. For example, increases in costs in the amount of 33⅓%, 100%, and 300% have been held to be insufficient.[7] Both Restatements state that a party assumes the risk of increased cost within a normal range but might not assume the risk of "extreme and unreasonable difficulty."[8]

The UCC is more forgiving. An official comment states that "increased cost alone does not excuse performance unless the rise in cost is due to some unforeseen contingency which *alters the essential nature of the performance*. Neither is a rise or a collapse in the market in itself a justification, for that is exactly the type of business risk which business contracts made at a fixed price are intended to cover. But a severe shortage of raw materials or of supplies due to a contingency such as war, embargo, local crop failure, unforeseen shutdown of major sources of supply or the like, which causes a marked increase in cost is within the contemplation of this section."[9]

An illustration of a contingency that alters the essential nature of the performance arose in Mineral Park Land v. Howard.[10] The defendant agreed to fill the requirements of gravel needed for a bridge-building project by removing it from plaintiff's land and to pay for it at a rate of five cents per yard. The defendant removed all of the gravel above water level but refused to take gravel below water level on the grounds that the cost of removal would be ten to twelve times the usual cost, because of the need to use a steam dredge and to employ a drying process. The court held that the defendant was excused from performing. It reasoned that although it was not impossible to remove additional gravel, for practical purposes no additional gravel was available and therefore, performance was excused because of the non-existence, for practical purposes, of the subject matter of the contract. A good number of cases[11] in accord concerning mineral leases have been decided on a variety of grounds, mostly as a matter of interpretation of the lease, but also on grounds of mutual mistake of fact.[12] The case actually involves existing impracticability rather than supervening impracticability.[13]

There are a number of other cases that have used impracticability as the basis for applying the defense where the cost of performance was

6. Rs. 2d § 261 cmt d.

7. American Trading & Production v. Shell Int'l Marine, 453 F.2d 939 (2d Cir. 1972); Publicker Indus. v. Union Carbide, 1975 WL 22890 (E.D.Pa.1975); International Paper v. Rockefeller, 161 A.D. 180, 146 N.Y.S. 371 (1914).

8. See Rs. 2d § 261 cmt d; Rs. 1st §§ 454, 460 ill. 2 and 3. The First Restatement mentions an abrupt ten fold increase.

9. UCC § 2–615 cmt 4.

10. 172 Cal. 289, 156 P. 458 (1916), 4 Cal.L.Rev. 407 (1916).

11. E.g., Swiss Oil v. Riggsby, 252 Ky. 374, 67 S.W.2d 30 (1933); Carozza v. Williams, 190 Md. 143, 57 A.2d 782 (1948); Scioto Fire Brick v. Pond, 38 Ohio St. 65 (1882).

12. Petrey v. John F. Buckner & Sons, 280 S.W.2d 641 (Tex.Civ.App.1955); Paddock v. Mason, 187 Va. 809, 48 S.E.2d 199 (1948).

13. See § 13.11 infra.

considerably increased as a result of the necessity of performing in a manner radically different from what was originally contemplated.[14] There are relatively few cases where impracticability was the foundation of a defense solely on the basis of increased costs.[15] A large number of cases dealing with inflationary rises in cost have reiterated the traditional notion that increased costs alone do not give rise to the defense of impracticability.[16] Similarly, drastic decreases in market prices have not excused contracts made at fixed prices.[17] Contrary to the common law, many legal systems impose price adjustments in cases of unforeseen drastic variations in prices.[18] Many contracts contain price adjustment mechanisms such as indexing or renegotiation clauses.[19]

(b) Foreign and International Trends and Future Development

After World War I, the German economy was devastated by inflation of an almost incredible scale; the mark ultimately sunk to one-trillionth of its former value. Although the German Civil Code explicitly granted relief for hardship only in cases of impossibility, the courts ultimately held that they could give relief for hardship as an emanation of the principle of good faith also found in the German Civil Code. Professor Paul Oertmann developed the theory of the Wegfall der Geschäftsgrundlage—disappearance of the foundations of the contract.[20] Germany's high court seized upon this theory and ruled that legal tender no longer had to be accepted in payment of debts, as no debtor could in good faith

14. Northern v. Chugach Elec. Ass'n, 518 P.2d 76 (Alaska 1974); Vernon v. Los Angeles, 45 Cal.2d 710, 290 P.2d 841 (1955); M.J. Paquet v. New Jersey DOT, 171 N.J. 378, 794 A.2d 141, 794 A.2d 141 (2002).

15. More or less standing alone are AL-COA v. Essex Group, 499 F.Supp. 53 (W.D.Pa.1980); Florida Power and Light v. Westinghouse Elec., 826 F.2d 239 (4th Cir. 1987), cert. denied.

16. Neal–Cooper Grain v. Texas Gulf Sulphur, 508 F.2d 283 (7th Cir.1974); Hudson v. D. & V. Mason Contr., 252 A.2d 166 (Del.Super.1969); Maple Farms v. City School Dist., 76 Misc.2d 1080, 352 N.Y.S.2d 784 (1974); Portland Section v. Sisters of Charity, 266 Or. 448, 513 P.2d 1183 (1973); but see Moyer v. Little Falls, 134 Misc.2d 299, 510 N.Y.S.2d 813 (1986) (price rises caused by governmental action in shutting down competing landfills). There has been much written on this point. See Eagan, The Westinghouse Uranium Contracts, 18 Am. Bus.L.J. 281 (1980); Jaskow, Commercial Impossibility, The Uranium Market and the Westinghouse Case, 6 J. Legal Studies 119 (1976); Schwartz, Sales Law and Inflations, 50 S.Cal.L.Rev. 1 (1976); Wallach, The Excuse Defense in the Law of Contracts, 55 Notre Dame Law. 203 (1979); Note, 50 Notre Dame Law. 297 (1974). See also § 13.16 infra.

17. Northern Ind. Public Service v. Carbon County Coal, 799 F.2d 265 (7th Cir. 1986).

18. Perillo, Force Majeure and Hardship Under the UNIDROIT Principles of International Commercial Contracts, 5 Tul. J.Int'l & Comp.L. 5, 9–10 (1997). Such rules often produce the most efficient result. See Trimarchi, Commercial Impracticability in Contract Law: An Economic Analysis, 11 Int'l Rev. of Law & Ec. 63 (1991).

19. See Bartels, Contractual Adaptation and Conflict Resolution (1985); Draetta, Lake & Nanda, Breach and Adaptation of International Contracts chs. 6 & 7 (1992). See also Glopak v. U.S., 12 Cl.Ct. 96 (1987), aff'd (discussing price adjustment clauses in government contracts); Kentucky Utilities v. South East Coal, 836 S.W.2d 392 (Ky. 1992), cert. dismissed (indexing in long term contract).

20. See Dawson, Judicial Revision of Frustrated Contracts: Germany, 63 B.U.L.Rev. 1039, 1045–46 (1983) (discussing Oertmann's writings).

make such a tender.[21] As the case law has evolved, the party who is unduly burdened because of changed circumstances may obtain a discharge of the contract, or the court can adapt the contract to changed circumstances if both parties want the contract to continue.[22] The changed circumstances must be exceptional and the court must balance the interests of both parties.[23] Courts of other countries have followed the German lead, including Switzerland.[24]

Other countries have reached the same result by legislation, Italy in 1942,[25] Greece in 1946,[26] and more recently the Netherlands.[27] The Netherlands Code provides as follows:

> 1. Upon the demand of one of the parties, the judge may modify the effects of a contract, or he may set it aside in whole or in part on the basis of unforeseen circumstances which are of such a nature that the co-contracting party, according to criteria of reasonableness and equity, may not expect that the contract be maintained in an unmodified form. The modification or the setting aside of the contract may be given retroactive force.

> 2. The modification or the setting aside of the contract is not pronounced to the extent that the person invoking the circumstances should be accountable for them according to the contract or common opinion.

> 3. For the purposes of this article, a person to whom a contractual right or obligation has been transferred, is assimilated to a contracting party.

Thus, the modern trend, exemplified by the Netherlands Code, is to recognize the established doctrines of impossibility of performance and frustration of the venture and to add to them a doctrine of excessive hardship. Under this trend, where, because of changed circumstances, a contract has become excessively burdensome on one of the parties, the party subjected to that burden may request a discharge of the contract, or, alternatively, its modification to reflect an exchange of values in accordance with market values at the time of the changed circumstances.

21. See id. at 1047–48 & n.21 (citing to 107 RGZ 78 and P. Oertmann, Die Aufwertungsfrage 40 (1924)); see also Arthur Nussbaum, Money in the Law 206–11 (1950); Keith S. Rosenn, Law and Inflation 84–94 (1982); John P. Dawson, Effects of Inflation on Private Contracts: Germany 1914–24, 33 Mich. L. Rev. 171 (1935).

22. See Peter Hay, Frustration and Its Solution in German Law, 10 Am. J. Comp. L. 345, 360 (1961).

23. See id.

24. See Hans Smit, Frustration of Contract: A Comparative Attempt at Consolidation, 58 Colum. L. Rev. 287, 289–96 (1958).

25. Codice Civile arts. 1467–1469 (Mario Beltramo et al. trans., 1991).

26. Greek Civil Code art. 388. For an English translation, see Rudolf B. Schlesinger et al., Comparative Law: Cases—Text—Materials 737 (5th ed. 1988).

27. New Netherlands Civil Code Patrimonial Law art. 6:258 (P.P.C Haanappel & Ejan Mackaay trans., 1990); Arthur S. Hartkamp, The Binding Force of Contract in Dutch Law, in Binding Force of Contract, at 41, 46 (Budapest 1991).

The UNIDROIT Principles of International Commercial Contracts reflect the trend started in post World War I Germany. These are its provisions on hardship:

Article 6.2.1 (Contract to be observed)

Where the performance of a contract becomes more onerous for one of the parties, that party is nevertheless bound to perform its obligations subject to the following provisions on hardship.

Article 6.2.2 (Definition of hardship)

There is hardship where the occurrence of events fundamentally alters the equilibrium of the contract either because the cost of a party's performance has increased or because the value of the performance a party receives has diminished, and

(a) the events occur or become known to the disadvantaged party after the conclusion of the contract;

(b) the events could not reasonably have been taken into account by the disadvantaged party at the time of the conclusion of the contract;

(c) the events are beyond the control of the disadvantaged party; and

(d) the risk of the events was not assumed by the disadvantaged party.

Article 6.2.3 (Effects of hardship)

(1) In case of hardship the disadvantaged party is entitled to request renegotiations. The request shall be made without undue delay and shall indicate the grounds on which it is based.

(2) The request for renegotiation does not in itself entitle the disadvantaged party to withhold performance.

(3) Upon failure to reach agreement within a reasonable time either party may resort to the court.

(4) If the court finds hardship it may, if reasonable,

(a) terminate the contract at a date and on terms to be fixed; or

(b) adapt the contract with a view to restoring its equilibrium.

UNIDROIT's definition of hardship is complex, because it not only defines the nature of the burden, but also other factors that must coexist with the burden to make it legally relevant. As a predicate to legally relevant hardship there must have been "the occurrence of events fundamentally altering the equilibrium of the contract either because the cost of a party's performance has increased or because the value of the performance a party receives has diminished. . . ." When is the equilibrium of a contract fundamentally altered? "[A]n alteration amounting to 50% or more of the cost or the value of the performance is likely to involve a 'fundamental' alteration" justifying invocation of the doctrine.[28] Thus, one illustration involves a ten-year contract for the sale of uranium at fixed prices in U.S. dollars payable in New York. The currency in the buyer's country declines to 1% of the value that it had at the time of contracting. The buyer cannot invoke force majeure.[29] Similarly, if the price is increased tenfold because some Texans have almost cornered the market, force majeure is not present.[30] Nonetheless, the buyer may have redress under the hardship provisions. As a factual matter, hardship exists if the "equilibrium of the contract" is "fundamentally altered" by events that occur or become known after contracting.

As with the case of impossibility, hardship as a fact does not automatically trigger the juridical concept of hardship. In addition, it must be shown that the events could not reasonably have been taken into account, are not within the party's control, and the risk was not assumed. Consequently, in the two illustrations just described, prima facie claims of hardship are made out.

There is a trend beyond the UNIDROIT Principles to the effect that excessive hardship is a ground for relief. The Commission on European Contract Law has formulated a rule that is basically the same as UNIDROIT's.[31] In England, perhaps the staunchest bastion of pacta sunt servanda, the Law Commission's proposed "Contract Code," contains a comparable provision.[32] Should we doubt that these documents show the direction of the law of this century?[33]

§ 13.10   Impracticability as an Excuse of Condition

The preceding sections concerned impracticability as an excuse for a failure to perform a promise. Here, we consider the effect of impracticability of complying with a condition. We saw an example of the excuse in the music hall case in which the defendant's promise to license the hall was excused.[1] What if the music hall owner claimed a contractual recovery, arguing that the failure to perform the constructive condition was excused because of impracticability? Such an argument outrages common sense.[2] If accepted, the plaintiffs would be obliged to pay for the use of the music hall even though they had not received what they had bargained for.

---

28. Art. 6.2.2 cmt.2; see also Art. 6.2.3 ill. 1.

29. Art. 7.1.7 ill.1(1). This is not a draconian result if the buyer can pass the inflationary costs onto the ultimate consumer.

30. Art. 7.1.7 ill. 1(3).

31. Principles of European Contract Law Art. 6:111 (2000).

32. Harvey McGregor, Contract Code Drawn up on Behalf of the English Law Commission § 595 (1993).

33. Hillman, Court Adjustment of Long–Term Contracts, 1967 Duke L.J. 1;

Speidel, Court–Imposed Price Adjustments Under Long–Term Supply Contracts, 76 Nw.U.L.Rev. 369 (1981).

§ 13.10

1. See § 13.3 supra.

2. "[W]hile such an impossibility may release the party from liability to suit for non-performance, it does not stand for performance so as to enable the party to sue and recover as if he had performed." Smoot's Case, 82 U.S. (15 Wall.) 36, 46 (1872).

However, at times a condition has been excused because of impracticability. The problem is closely related to § 11.35 supra entitled "Excuse of Conditions Involving Forfeiture." There we discussed the rule that an express condition "may be excused without other reason" if (a) the failure to excuse the condition will result in extreme forfeiture and (b) the condition being excused is not a material part of the agreed exchange.[3] Examples of an immaterial part of the performance are conditions that merely fix the time or manner of performance or provide for giving notice or the supplying of proofs.[4] The same basic rule applies to excusing an express condition on the basis of impracticability except that the Restatement (Second) indicates that the forfeiture need not be extreme.[5]

It should be obvious by now that impracticability may not be used to excuse a constructive condition of performance, because, by definition, such a condition is a material part of the agreed exchange. Thus, in the hypothetical version of the music hall case, above, the condition would not be excused because no forfeiture is involved and the condition is a material part of the agreed exchange.

Both elements of the rule are satisfied in a case where a building contractor who has at least substantially performed cannot produce the certificate of a named architect because of the architect's death or incapacity. The failure to comply with the express condition of the production of the certificate is excused and the contractor may recover on the contract.[6] If the contractor had not substantially performed prior to the death of the architect, presumably the contract would be discharged and the contractor would be limited to a quasi-contractual recovery.[7]

Another instance of excuse of condition is where an insured, because of impracticability, fails to furnish proofs of loss or fails to give notice within the time stated. Some courts have excused the condition, but others have disagreed.[8] However, the situation is different if the insured fails to pay a premium within a stipulated time. The condition relating to the premium is a material part of the agreed exchange and therefore is not excused.[9] There is some contrary authority.[10]

---

3. Rs. 1st § 302; Rs. 2d § 271.

4. See § 11.35 supra; Rs. 2d § 88 cmt d.

5. Rs. 2d § 271 cmt a, suggests that the rule may apply even if the party seeking excuse assumed the risk of the condition, but only if the forfeiture is extreme.

6. Rs. 2d § 271 ill. 1. See also In re Prime Motor Inns, 131 B.R. 233 (Bkrtcy. Fla.1991) (condition that audit by independent CPA be furnished excused where the approved accounting firm ceased to function); U.S. v. Klefstad Eng'r, 324 F.Supp. 972 (W.D.Pa.1971) (condition of certification excused where fire destroyed records kept by registered surveyor).

7. See § 13.23 infra.

8. Semmes v. City Fire Ins., 80 U.S. 158 (13 Wall.) 158 (1871) (excused by Civil War). Compare Rs. 2d § 271 ill. 2, with Clements v. Preferred Acc. Ins., 41 F.2d 470, 76 ALR 17 (8th Cir.1930). See Comment, 34 Mich.L.Rev. 257 (1935).

9. Rs. 2d § 271 ill. 3. See also Thoracic Cardiovascular Assocs. v. St. Paul Fire and Marine Ins., 181 Ariz. 449, 891 P.2d 916 (App.1994) (impracticability of reporting a claim).

10. See Mulligan, Does War Excuse the Payment of Life Insurance Premiums?, 17 Fordham L.Rev. 63, 85 (1948).

Similar problems may also arise in cases involving the sale of goods. Prior to the enactment of the UCC, if goods were to be sold at a price to be fixed by an appraiser, the buyer was excused from performance if the price was not so fixed.[11] If the goods were delivered and accepted, however, the buyer's duty of performance was not discharged, rather the condition to the duty of performance was excused; the buyer was required to pay a reasonable price.[12] The UCC puts cases of this kind on a somewhat different basis.[13] If the price is not fixed in the manner agreed, the contract will be construed to mean that a reasonable price must be paid on delivery. If, however, the parties intended not to be bound unless the price is fixed in the manner agreed on, as when they rely on the unique expertise of the appraiser, the contract is discharged if the appraiser is unable to set the price, even though the goods have been delivered. The buyer must return the goods already received. If this is not possible, the buyer must pay a reasonable price.

§ 13.11 Existing Impracticability

Impracticability may exist at the time of the agreement. The rules stated above with respect to supervening impracticability generally apply equally to existing impracticability.[1] However, there are two major differences. One is that the party seeking to use the doctrine must show the absence of knowledge or reason to know the facts that made performance impossible.[2] In addition, existing impracticability results in a void contract whereas supervening impracticability discharges a contract that has already arisen.[3]

Knowledge of existing impracticability is one way of creating an assumption of risk. A party may also assume the risk of existing impracticability in other ways.[4] One illustration is a case involving technological break-through, discussed below.[5] These cases show that the problem of existing impracticability is closely related to the topic of mistake.[6]

§ 13.12 Frustration of the Venture

What is the difference between impracticability and frustration? A person who is to supply lands, goods or services, but cannot perform, will

11. Louisville Soap v. Taylor, 279 F. 470, 27 ALR 119 (6th Cir.1922), cert. denied (price to be that prevailing on Savannah market; market was inactive); Stern v. Farah Bros., 17 N.M. 516, 133 P. 400 (1913); Oglebay Norton v. Armco, 52 Ohio St.3d 232, 556 N.E.2d 515 (1990); see UCC § 2–305 cmt 4.

12. Hood v. Hartshorn, 100 Mass. 117, 1 Am.Rep. 89 (1868).

13. UCC § 2–305; see § 2.9 supra.

§ 13.11

1. Faria v. Southwick, 81 Idaho 68, 337 P.2d 374 (1959); Briggs v. Vanderbilt, 19 Barb. 222 (N.Y.1855); Housing Auth. v.

East Tenn. Light & Power, 183 Va. 64, 31 S.E.2d 273 (1944); Rs. 2d § 266 cmt a.

2. Reid v. Alaska Packing Ass'n, 43 Or. 429, 73 P. 337 (1903); Rs. 1st § 455; Rs. 2d § 266 cmt a.

3. Mariani v. Gold, 13 N.Y.S.2d 365 (1939); Rs. 2d § 266 cmt a.

4. Rs. 2d § 266 cmt b.

5. See § 13.17 infra.

6. As to mistake see § 9.26 supra and § 13.20 infra.

attempt to use the impracticability defense. A buyer or any party who is obliged to pay will ordinarily attempt to use the defense of frustration. For example, if A agreed to supply B with a number of barges to carry a finished product from B's plant and B promises to pay a fixed sum per barge, and A was unable to supply the barges, A would attempt to use the defense of impracticability. If B had no product to ship, B would attempt to use the frustration doctrine. Impracticability does not apply to B's promise because it is still perfectly possible for B to pay. The problem is that B is getting nothing for the money.[1]

The doctrine of frustration of the venture had its origin in the coronation cases. In Krell v. Henry,[2] the plaintiff had granted the defendant a license to use his apartment for two days to view the coronation procession of King Edward VII and defendant agreed to pay £75 for this privilege. After the agreement was made, the coronation was canceled because the King was stricken by perityphlitis. It was held that the defendant was excused from the duty of payment. Performance was not impossible. Payment could have been made. This and companion cases ushered in a doctrine of frustration.

As is often the case with doctrines believed to be innovative, there were prior decisions in accord which were not perceived as having broken new ground. A perfect example is Miles v. Stevens,[3] where a contract for the sale of lots was premised on the construction of a canal to a particular point. The canal route was shifted. Deciding that the contract was discharged because of mistake, the court said, "where the parties contract, either with a view to existing facts, or facts merely in contemplation between the parties dependent on future events or contingencies [and] the basis of the contract fails without the assent of the parties, to attempt to enforce the agreement is inequitable."[4] Even earlier, a court had held that a municipal contract to pay for the provision of food and lodging to a pauper for a one-year term was discharged by the death of the pauper.[5]

The Restatement (Second) sets forth the same rule for frustration as it does for impracticability.[6] A party must comply with four requirements in order to make out the defense of frustration of the venture. These are: (1) The object of one of the parties in entering into the contract must be frustrated by a supervening event.[7] (2) The other party must also have contracted on the basis of the attainment of this object. The attainment

§ 13.12

1. New York v. Long Island Airports Limousine Serv., 96 A.D.2d 998, 467 N.Y.S.2d 93 (1983), aff'd; Weiskopf, Frustration of Contractual Purpose—Doctrine or Myth?, 70 St. John's L.Rev. 239 (1996).

2. [1903] 2 K.B. 740.

3. 3 Pa. 21, 45 Am.Dec. 621 (1846).

4. 3 Pa. at 37, 45 Am.Dec. at 624–5.

5. Willington v. West Boylston, 21 Mass. 101 (1826). Supervening disabling illness of

a student has been held to be grounds for entitlement to a refund of tuition. Dubrow v. Briansky Saratoga Ballet Center, 68 Misc.2d 530, 327 N.Y.S.2d 501 (1971).

6. Rs. 2d § 265.

7. The government cannot terminate a contract for newly formulated environmental concerns and claim frustration. Everett Plywood v. U.S., 651 F.2d 723 (1981).

of this object was a basic assumption common to both parties.[8] (3) The frustration must be total or nearly total—in more modern terminology the principal purpose of the promisor (the one seeking to use the defense) must be either totally or substantially frustrated.[9] This distinction is akin to the distinction between impossibility and impracticability. (4) The party seeking to use the defense must not have assumed a greater obligation than the law imposes. In addition, as in the case of impracticability, the party seeking to use the defense must not be guilty of contributory fault.[10] Thus, if the promisor was already in material breach at the time of the frustrating event, the defense is not available.[11]

Frequently, a promised performance will become totally useless to the purchaser. Consider a contracted-for wedding dress where the prospective groom is killed in an accident before the wedding. Suppose at the time of the accident the dress is ready but not yet paid for. Clearly, the frustration defense should not be available to the bride. Many explanations can be given for this. We believe the result is based on the fact that there is no unjust enrichment in the case. The tailor who contracts to make the dress employs his or her usual skill, labor, and materials.[12] The licensor of the apartment to view the coronation is, however, charging a very high rate for an extraordinary use of the apartment and this extraordinary use has become worthless. Remember, also, that the King will recover and will be crowned on some other day and the apartment will again command a high rate.[13]

Before successfully asserting a frustration defense, the party must overcome another difficult hurdle—proving that the principal purpose was substantially frustrated.[14] This proposition is well illustrated in the cases in the Prohibition era involving leases.[15] For example, in Doherty v.

8. See Rs. 2d § 265; 14 Corbin §§ 77.1–77.10 (Nehf 2001). It should be noted that as used in England, the term "frustration" today encompasses both frustration of the venture and impracticability of performance.

9. Lloyd v. Murphy, 25 Cal.2d 48, 153 P.2d 47 (1944); North Am. Capital v. McCants, 510 S.W.2d 901, 89 ALR3d 322 (Tenn.1974); Chicago, M., St. P. & P., R.R. v. Chicago & N.W. Transp., 82 Wis.2d 514, 263 N.W.2d 189 (1978). See Rs. 2d § 265 cmt a (the frustration must be substantial and the fact that the transaction became less profitable is insufficient).

10. When a company decides to go out of business, it cannot claim that its contracts are frustrated. Diston v. EnviroPak Medical Prods., 893 P.2d 1071 (Utah App. 1995) (employment contract).

11. Days Inn v. Patel, 88 F.Supp.2d 928 (C.D.Ill.2000) (N.J. Law).

12. An alternative unconvincing explanation is that the continued existence of the groom was not the basis on which the par-

ties contracted. See Farnsworth, Young & Jones, Cases & Materials on Contracts p. 849, problem 2 (2d ed. 1972), and the corresponding portion of the teacher's manual.

13. See Felt v. McCarthy, 78 Wn.App. 362, 898 P.2d 315 (1995), aff'd, holding that a contract for sale of land to a developer is not frustrated when supervening wetlands regulation prohibits development, distinguishing Weyerhaeuser Real Estate v. Stoneway Concrete, 96 Wn.2d 558, 637 P.2d 647 (1981), involving a mineral lease for strip mining arousing intense public opposition causing the lessee to withdraw; the existence of an ongoing relationship between lessor and lessee and other facts showed that both parties shared the same assumption. See also Western Properties v. Southern Utah Aviation, 776 P.2d 656 (Utah App.1989).

14. See note 9 supra.

15. Some cases have doubted whether a lease can ever be discharged by frustration. Viewed as a matter of property law, a lease is a conveyance of an estate in land, perfor-

Monroe Eckstein Brewing,[16] the defendant was in possession under a lease which provided: "It being expressly agreed, that the only business to be carried on in said premises is the saloon business."[17] During the term of the lease a national prohibition law which made the sale of alcoholic beverages illegal was enacted. It was held that the lease was discharged. This is not a case of supervening illegality of the lease; it is not illegal for the tenant to pay rent on unused premises. Rather, there is frustration. Some courts reached the same result even though the defendant could still have used the premises to sell cigars, cigarettes, soft drinks and the like. In such cases, the holding was that the principal purpose (the sale of alcoholic beverages) was totally frustrated.[18] The net result is that where the principal use is completely frustrated, the frustration will be deemed to be total or nearly total, but where the principal use is not completely frustrated the defense of frustration is not available.[19] Even if the purpose is totally frustrated, the party claiming the defense must not have assumed the risk of the supervening event.[20]

In another type of case, a Canadian seller agreed to sell a quantity of lamb pelts to B.[21] Delivery was to be made in Toronto for shipment to Philadelphia. Prior to the delivery date, U.S. government regulations were promulgated under which the importation of lamb pelts of this type was prohibited. The defendant refused to take delivery and asserted the defense of frustration. The court stated that the goods could be shipped anywhere else in the world since shipping instructions are not an essential part of the agreement. Thus, the purpose of the buyer was not substantially frustrated even though the buyer may have suffered a loss.

Unjustifiably, the courts are more inclined to sustain a defense of impracticability than one based on frustration. One law review discussion states that "neither sense nor justice would be served by allowing a

---

mance being complete on the execution of the lease. In Paradine v. Jane, Aleyn 26, 82 Eng.Rep. 897 (K.B.1647), it was held that a lessee was required to pay rent although the premises were allegedly occupied by alien enemies. It is rather clear today, however, that the doctrine applies to leases as well as other kinds of contracts. See Perry v. Champlain Oil, 101 N.H. 97, 134 A.2d 65 (1957); 2814 Food Corp. v. Hub Bar Bldg., 59 Misc.2d 80, 297 N.Y.S.2d 762 (1969). England has not extended the doctrine to leases. See Treitel, Frustration and Force Majeure ¶ ¶ 3–030 to 3–031 (1994).

16. 198 A.D. 708, 191 N.Y.S. 59 (1921).

17. Such a restrictive covenant is often deemed essential to give rise to a question of frustration of a lease.

18. See also The Stratford v. Seattle Brewing & Malting, 94 Wn. 125, 162 P. 31 (1916). Contra, Proprietors' Realty v. Wohltmann, 95 N.J.L. 303, 112 A. 410

(1921). Some courts spoke in terms of supervening illegality.

19. Lloyd v. Murphy, 25 Cal.2d 48, 153 P.2d 47 (1944) (auto dealership); Wood v. Bartolino, 48 N.M. 175, 146 P.2d 883 (1944) (gasoline station); Colonial Operating v. Hannan Sales & Serv., 265 A.D. 411, 39 N.Y.S.2d 217 (1943), appeal granted (auto dealership); Downing v. Stiles, 635 P.2d 808 (1981). For total frustration of a plea bargain, see U.S. v. Thompson, 237 F.3d 1258 (10th Cir.2001), cert. denied.

20. Brenner v. Little Red School House, 302 N.C. 207, 274 S.E.2d 206, 20 ALR4th 295 (1981) (The father paid private school tuition in advance. The mother who had custody sent the child to another school. Tuition not recoverable because the contract allocated the risk.)

21. Swift Canadian v. Banet, 224 F.2d 36 (3d Cir.1955); accord, Bardons & Oliver v. Amtorg Trading, 123 N.Y.S.2d 633 (1948), aff'd; General Electric Supply v.

seller to use a section 2–615 (UCC) defense and simultaneously deny it to the buyer in the same situation."[22] In the language of another, "Buyers and sellers should have the opportunity to claim a section 2–615 excuse when faced with an unduly burdensome and commercially senseless contract. Equity and mutuality support this view."[23]

The UCC contains no explicit provision relating to frustration.[24] However, the Code intends that the common law of frustration should apply.[25] Thus, the point made in these articles would appear to be valid as a universal. A good illustration is the hypothetical case involving the hiring of the barges mentioned at the beginning of this section. If the supplier of barges could have the defense of impracticability for failure to supply barges why couldn't the hirer of the barges have a defense of frustration if without any fault there is no product to ship on the barges? Mississippi seems to have recognized the problem. It has added an additional provision to the UCC which it designated as UCC § 2–617.

Just as there are cases of existing impracticability, there are also cases of existing frustration. An illustration can be found in another one of the coronation cases.[26] In that case there was also an agreement to hire a room to view the coronation procession, but it was made one hour after the decision to operate on the king was made. This is a case of existing mistake.[27]

§ 13.13 Temporary Impracticability or Frustration

Temporary impracticability, such as a temporarily incapacitating illness, may give rise to a prospective inability to perform.[1] Where the promisor encounters temporary impracticability,[2] whether or not the encounter provides an excuse, the prospective inability will normally give the other party a right to suspend performance. However, if the prospective inability created by the temporary impracticability is so serious that there is reasonable probability that substantial performance will not be forthcoming, the other party may cancel the contract.[3]

If the other party does not have a right to terminate the contract or chooses not to, what rules govern the conduct of the party in whose favor the defense of temporary impracticability runs? Obviously this party may suspend performance and later, when the impracticability ceases, usually must perform in full, and is entitled to an appropriate extension of time for performance.[4] Whether there is an obligation to perform in the

---

Gulf Electroquip, 857 S.W.2d 591 (Tex.App. 1993).

22. Comment, 51 Temple L.Q. 518, 548 (1978).

23. Comment, 5 Hofstra L.Rev. 167, 183 (1976); see also UCC § 2–615 cmt 9.

24. See § 13.22 infra.

25. See § 13.22 infra. See also Nora Springs Co-op. v. Brandau, 247 N.W.2d 744, 93 ALR3d 574 (Iowa 1976).

26. Griffith v. Brymer, 19 T.L.R. 434 (K.B.1903).

27. §§ 9.25 to 9.36 supra.

§ 13.13

1. Rs. 1st § 462 cmt a.

2. Colorado Coal Furnace Distribs. v. Prill Mfg., 605 F.2d 499 (10th Cir.1979).

3. See § 12.2 supra. Sutheimer v. Stoltenberg, 127 Idaho 81, 896 P.2d 989 (1995), appears contra and unsound.

4. Specialty Tires v. CIT Group, 82 F.Supp.2d 434 (W.D.Pa.2000); Rs. 2d § 269 cmt a.

aftermath of temporary impracticability depends on whether the delay will make performance substantially more burdensome. If it will, the temporary impracticability not only suspends, but discharges the obligation.[5]

Two illustrations will serve to clarify these rules. A promised to sing the leading female role in a new opera being produced by B. The first performance was to take place on November 28th. On November 23rd, A became ill during a rehearsal. At this time the length of her illness was indefinite and unknown. The only available substitute insisted on being hired for the entire performance and B hired her for the run of the show. A was ready to perform on December 4th at which time she tendered her services which were refused. The jury found as a fact that the engagement of the substitute was reasonable.[6]

A's illness was a defense to any action for breach of contract that B might bring relating to the period of illness. B undoubtedly could suspend its own performance during this period. However, B did more than suspend performance; B chose to terminate the contract. The question was whether B was justified. Conceptually, there was a finding that there was serious prospective inability to perform justifying B's cancellation of the contract. The result, probably would be different if it were clear on November 23 that A's illness would have lasted only two or three days.[7]

The party who has the defense of temporary impracticability may also cancel the contract if the delay will make performance substantially more burdensome. In one case,[8] a movie star under contract with a studio was drafted into the army. Not only was he excused from performing while he was in the army, but was also relieved of all obligations under the contract; delay had made his performance substantially more burdensome.[9] There is some authority that if the impracticability actually extends beyond the contract period termination is automatic.[10] The same rules apply to temporary frustration.[11] Again, the rules are over-ridden if one party has assumed the risk by agreement or otherwise.[12]

§ 13.14 Partial Impracticability

When promisors have the defense of impracticability as to only a

5. Rs. 2d § 269 cmt a; 14 Corbin § 76.7 (Nehf 2001); 18 Williston §§ 1957–58 (3d ed.); Patterson, Temporary Impossibility of Performance of Contract, 47 Va.L.Rev. 798 (1961).

6. Poussard v. Spiers & Pond, 1 Q.B.D. 410 (1876). This case was discussed in § 12.2 supra.

7. See, for example, Bettini v. Gye, 1 Q.B.D. 183 (1876).

8. Autry v. Republic Productions, 30 Cal.2d 144, 180 P.2d 888 (1947).

9. See also Village of Minneota v. Fairbanks, Morse & Co., 226 Minn. 1, 31 N.W.2d 920 (1948). But see Peerless Cas. v. Weymouth Gardens, 215 F.2d 362 (1st Cir. 1954).

10. 14 Corbin § 76.7 (Nehf 2001); but see UCC § 2–615 (excusing delay).

11. Rs. 2d § 269; see Patch v. Solar Corp., 149 F.2d 558 (7th Cir.1945), cert. denied.

12. Rs. 2d § 269 cmt a; see Long Signature Homes v. Fairfield Woods, 248 Va. 95, 445 S.E.2d 489 (1994).

part of their performances they are excused from performing those parts[1] except that, if they can render reasonable substitute performances, they are obliged to do so.[2] If substantial performance is still practicable (taking into account any reasonable substitute performance) performance of the remainder of the contract is required.[3] Performance is deemed impracticable if the partial impracticability has made the remaining performance substantially more burdensome.[4] Even though substantial performance is no longer possible, continuation of performance is required if the other party within a reasonable time promises to perform in full.[5] The other party has a power to cancel the contract if the part that is unperformed prevents, aside from any permitted delay, the possibility of substantial performance.[6]

If the failure to perform the part that is partially impossible does not prevent substantial performance, both parties are obliged to perform the rest of the contract.[7] The party who has a defense is excused as to the partially impossible part and the other party may have a claim for restitution.[8] The various ways in which the rights of the parties may be adjusted after a contract has been terminated by impracticability (including partial impracticability) are discussed below.[9]

§ 13.15 Subjective Impracticability—Contributory Fault

The First Restatement contained a specific section to the effect that a defense of impracticability may not be based on subjective impracticability; objective impracticability was required.[1] The Restatement described the difference between the two as the difference between "the thing cannot be done" and "I cannot do it."[2] As we have seen, if a party who is personally to perform dies, the obligation is discharged by impracticability.[3] The impracticability is not only subjective, but it is also objective; the decedent is the only one who could have performed the duty because a personal performance is non-delegable.[4]

The Restatement (Second), with a somewhat different approach, recognizes that subjective impracticability involves assumption of the

---

§ 13.14

1. Rs. 1st § 463.

2. Meyer v. Sullivan, 40 Cal.App. 723, 181 P. 847 (1919); Rs. 2d § 270 and cmt a; UCC § 2–614 cmt 1.

3. Rs. 2d § 270(a).

4. Rs. 2d § 270 cmt a.

5. Rs. 2d § 270(b) and cmt c; see also Van Dusen Aircraft Supplies v. Massachusetts Port Authority, 361 Mass. 131, 279 N.E.2d 717 (1972).

6. See § 11.18(b) supra.

7. Rs. 2d § 270 cmt b.

8. Ibid.

9. See § 13.23 infra.

§ 13.15

1. Rs. 1st § 455; Ballou v. Basic Constr., 407 F.2d 1137 (4th Cir.1969); Phillips v. Marcin, 162 Ga.App. 202, 290 S.E.2d 546 (1982); Roundup Cattle Feeders v. Horpestad, 184 Mont. 480, 603 P.2d 1044 (1979); Sachs v. Precision Prods., 257 Or. 273, 476 P.2d 199 (1970); Williams v. Carter, 129 Vt. 619, 285 A.2d 735 (1971).

2. Rs. 1st § 455 cmt a; White Lakes Shopping Center v. Jefferson Standard Life Ins., 208 Kan. 121, 490 P.2d 609 (1971); Stone v. Stone, 34 Md.App. 509, 368 A.2d 496 (1977).

3. See § 13.7 supra.

4. Rs. 1st § 455 ill. 4; see § 13.7 supra and § 8.13 infra.

risk or contributory fault.[5] We have already seen that a person who is guilty of contributory fault or who assumes the risk is denied the defense of impracticability.[6] For example, a promisor who is enjoined by a court from performing a promise may be allowed to use the defense of impracticability. However, if the promisor's wrongful conduct was responsible for the injunction, the defense will be disallowed because of contributory fault,[7] but a consent decree or other negotiated settlement may not be conclusive on the question of fault.[8] If a party who is to deliver specific goods on Feb. 1 fails without good cause to deliver them on that date, and the goods are subsequently destroyed, the defense of impracticability will be disallowed because of contributory fault.[9]

Perhaps the most common illustration of assumption of the risk is an impracticability that arises because a promisor is insolvent and is unable to make a scheduled payment. In these circumstances the promisor is not excused irrespective of the reason for the promisor's insolvency.[10] The insolvent party will be deemed to have assumed the risk of becoming insolvent.

The burden of proof is on the party who asserts impracticability.[11] The promisor must show that the task to be done could not be accomplished. *A fortiori*, if a party creates the impracticability by his or her own voluntary act, no excuse is allowed.[12]

§ 13.16   Assumption of the Risk

One of the key issues in any impracticability or frustration case is whether the promisor assumed the risk in question. The very core of contract involves the assumption of risks that the law would not ordinarily impose.[1] The risk of impracticability or frustration can be assumed by contract. Indeed, a contract can provide that the party is responsible for performance come "Hell or high water."[2]

Absent a clear assumption of risk, the court, nonetheless, frequently concludes that the promisor has assumed the risk. A little light is shed

5.   Rs. 2d § 261 cmt e.

6.   See § 13.2 supra.

7.   See § 13.5 supra. Some courts have held that, if an injunction is granted, the party enjoined is automatically guilty of contributory fault. South Memphis Land v. McLean Hardwood Lumber, 179 F. 417 (6th Cir.1910).

8.   General Aniline & Film v. Bayer, 305 N.Y. 479, 113 N.E.2d 844 (1953).

9.   International Paper v. Rockefeller, 161 A.D. 180, 146 N.Y.S. 371 (1914).

10.   Central Trust v. Chicago Auditorium Ass'n, 240 U.S. 581, 591 (1916); Christy v. Pilkinton, 224 Ark. 407, 273 S.W.2d 533 (1954); Baldi Constr. Eng. v. Wheel Awhile, 263 Md. 670, 284 A.2d 248 (1971); 407 East 61st Garage v. Savoy Fifth Ave., 23 N.Y.2d 275, 296 N.Y.S.2d 338, 244 N.E.2d 37

(1968); Title & Trust v. Durkheimer Inv., 155 Or. 427, 451, 63 P.2d 909, 919 (1936); Rs. 2d § 281 cmt b.

11.   Ocean Air Tradeways v. Arkay Realty, 480 F.2d 1112 (9th Cir.1973); 18 Williston § 1978B (3d ed.).

12.   Omni Inv. v. Cordon Int'l, 603 F.2d 81 (9th Cir.1979).

§ 13.16

1.   See Reefer & General Shipping v. Great White Fleet, 1995 WL 575290, 1996 A.M.C. 1254 (S.D.N.Y.1995); see also § 13.2 supra.

2.   For a ferocious example, see Colorado Interstate v. CIT Group/Equipment Fin., 993 F.2d 743 (10th Cir.1993); see also Wheelabrator Envirotech v. Mass.Laborers Dist. Council, 88 F.3d 40 (1st Cir.1996).

on the process by which this conclusion is reached by the case of Transatlantic Financing v. U.S.[3] According to the court, "The doctrine ultimately represents the ever-shifting line, drawn by courts hopefully responsive to commercial practices and mores at which the community's interest in having contracts enforced according to their terms is outweighed by the commercial senselessness of requiring performance."[4] Fundamentally, the issue is one of equitable allocation.[5]

To illustrate, consider variations on the facts underlying Canadian Industrial Alcohol v. Dunbar Molasses.[6] The plaintiff agreed to buy and the defendant, a middleman, agreed to sell approximately 1,500,000 gallons of molasses of the usual run from the National Sugar Refinery in Yonkers.[7] The refinery curtailed its output. As a result, defendant was able to deliver only 344,083 gallons. When sued, the defendant raised the defense of impracticability. The court held, inter alia, that the defendant could not avail itself of that defense because it was guilty of contributory fault in failing to enter into a contract with the refinery.[8]

If the refinery had burned down, despite the absence of a contract between the defendant and the refinery, the court indicates that the defendant would have the defense. In this hypothetical, the fault of the defendant in not entering into the contract would not have contributed to defendant's failure to perform. Rather the proximate cause of nonperformance would have been the destruction of the refinery. The continued existence of the refinery was the basis on which both parties entered into the agreement and defendant did not in fact assume this risk.[9] This seems fair, because the defendant would not have a cause of action against the refinery even if he had contracted with it.

If the defendant had entered into contract with the refinery and the refinery nevertheless voluntarily curtailed its output, should the defendant have the defense of impracticability? The court suggests that the answer would be, no.[10] The reason is that both parties did not enter into

3. 363 F.2d 312, 315 (D.C.Cir.1966).

4. Id.; Noted, 41 Tul.L.Rev. 709 (1967); 8 Wm. & Mary L.Rev. 679 (1967).

5. Quick v. Stuyvesant, 2 Paige's Ch. 84, 92 (N.Y.1830). "Where from any defect of the common law, want of foresight of the parties, or other mistake or accident, there would be a failure of justice, it is the duty of this court to interfere and supply the defect or furnish the remedy."

6. 258 N.Y. 194, 179 N.E. 383 (1932). A similar case in accord is Barbarossa & Sons v. Iten Chevrolet, 265 N.W.2d 655 (Minn. 1978).

7. The court assumes that this is not merely language of description but that the molasses must come from a particular factory.

8. For contributory fault, see § 13.15 supra. Contributory fault exists "if the promisor is in some way responsible for the

event which makes performance of his promise impossible." Appalachian Power v. John Stewart Walker, Inc., 214 Va. 524, 201 S.E.2d 758 (1974); see also Alamance County Bd.of Ed. v. Bobby Murray Chevrolet, 121 N.C.App. 222, 465 S.E.2d 306 (1996); Lowenschuss v. Kane, 520 F.2d 255 (2d Cir.1975); Rs. 1st § 261 cmt d and § 265 cmt b.

9. Center Garment v. United Refrigerator, 369 Mass. 633, 341 N.E.2d 669 (1976); cf. Sunseri v. Garcia & Maggini, 298 Pa. 249, 148 A. 81, 67ALR.1428 (1929).

10. But see Specialty Tires v. CIT Group, 82 F.Supp.2d 434 (W.D.Pa.2000), where defendant contracted to sell machinery both knew to be in the possession of a third party. The person in possession wrongfully refused to surrender possession. Defense upheld. See also Carter Steel & Fab. v. Ohio DOT, 721 N.E.2d 1115 (Ohio

the agreement on the basis of the voluntary continued output of the refinery; the defendant assumed the risk of a voluntary diminution of the refinery's output. The defendant is a middleman and a middleman's role in the economy is to assume such risks. In any event, the result is sensible because defendant, in turn, would have a cause of action against the refinery.[11] But where a governmental unit insists that a contractor deal with a sole-source supplier, the latter's delay has been held to excuse the contractor's late performance despite the ability of the contractor to sue the supplier.[12]

The result would be different in the Molasses case if the parties had agreed that defendant's performance was contingent on the refinery's performance,[13] or if the contract restricted the seller's source of supply to a sole-source and the source fails to deliver, the defendant may be excused[14] absent an assumption of the risk or contributory fault. The parol evidence rule may restrict the ability of the seller to prove that a sole-source supplier had been agreed upon.[15]

In addition, there are cases that conclude from surrounding circumstances that a party assumed a risk that would not be imposed by law.[16] Custom and usage are particularly important in this context. A middleman is expected to lock up a source of supply before committing to a resale. Similarly, an auto dealer should not commit to supply a vehicle that the manufacturer does not make.[17]

§ 13.17 Technological Impracticability—Unforeseen Possibilities

(a) Technological Impracticability

Other illustrations of assumption of the risk are the cases involving technological breakthroughs. In a number of cases, mostly involving government contracts for the manufacture of new products, or the use of new processes, the manufacturer has contended that compliance with

Ct.Cl.1999) (single source supplier delayed delivery).

11. UCC § 2–615 cmt 5 seems to say the defendant should have the defense of impracticability in this case but on the condition of turning over to the buyer "the rights against the defaulting source of supply * * *." But see Alamance County Bd. v. Bobby Murray Chevrolet, 121 N.C.App. 222, 465 S.E.2d 306 (N.C.App.1996), where GM failed to deliver to its dealer; dealer liable to customer although its contract with GM exculpated GM.

12. Carter Steel & Fab. v. Ohio DOT, 721 N.E.2d 1115 (Ohio Ct.Cl.1999). There are contrary cases.

13. Mosby v. Smith, 194 Mo.App. 20, 186 S.W. 49 (1916); Scialli v. Correale, 97

N.J.L. 165, 117 A. 255 (1922); Rs. 1st § 460 ill. 12.

14. Scialli v. Correale, 97 N.J.L. 165, 117 A. 255 (1922); J. Gavigan Corp. v. Wampatuck Country Club, 344 Mass. 762, 183 N.E.2d 880 (1962) Selland Pontiac-GMC v. King, 384 N.W.2d 490 (Mn.App. 1986).

15. Luria Bros. & Co. v. Pielet Bros. Scrap, 600 F.2d 103 (7th Cir.1979).

16. Wills v. Shockley, 52 Del. 295, 157 A.2d 252 (Super.1960); Savage v. Peter Kiewit Sons' Co., 249 Or. 147, 432 P.2d 519 (1967), modified; see also UCC § 2–615 cmt 8.

17. Roy v. Stephen Pontiac–Cadillac, 15 Conn.App. 101, 543 A.2d 775 (1988).

the contract has proved impossible, at least under existing technology. The cases involve existing, not supervening, impracticability.[1]

Generally, the cases have held that the contractor has assumed the risk that production was possible because it knew or should have known of the limits of existing technology.[2] On the other hand, where detailed plans of manufacturing processes, as opposed to goals which the end product must meet, are provided by the government, it has been held that the government assumes the risk because it warrants that the plan will produce the desired result.[3]

Cases involving existing impracticability are closely related to the topic of mistake and this is especially true of the cases involving technological impracticability.[4]

In an interesting and unprecedented case,[5] a contractor agreed to produce artillery shells for the government using a new process. In the course of negotiations the contractor argued that the process would not produce the result desired unless certain machinery were used to remove excess steel. The government, however, insisted that such equipment was not needed. The plaintiff succumbed to the government's insistence and agreed to produce the shells pursuant to the process at a fixed price. After costly experimentation, the government agreed that the process would not work without equipment such as plaintiff had originally urged and permitted the plaintiff to make use of such equipment. The plaintiff sued for extra compensation based on the losses sustained as a result of the added expenses incurred in attempting to make the original specifications work. The court rightly held that the plaintiff could not recover under breach of implied warranty. The specific negotiations concerning the adequacy of the specifications negated any justifiable reliance on them. The court, however, held that the plaintiff was entitled to reformation of the contract on grounds of mutual mistake. The plaintiff and the defendant were required by the court to share the losses as if they had been engaged in a joint venture rather than in a fixed price contract.

The decision received less than favorable comment in the law reviews[6] and the court clearly and admittedly departed from principles ordinarily governing mutual mistake and reformation. Although impracticability was not discussed, it is clear that performance in the manner agreed was in fact impossible. Under traditional analysis, however,

---

§ 13.17

1. See § 13.11 supra.

2. J.A. Maurer v. U.S., 485 F.2d 588 (Ct.Cl.1973); U.S. v. Wegematic, 360 F.2d 674 (2d Cir.1966) (UCC as "federal common law"); Austin Co. v. U.S., 314 F.2d 518 (Ct.Cl.1963), cert. denied; Rolin v. U.S., 160 F.Supp. 264 (Ct.Cl.1958). Contra, Smith Engineering v. Rice, 102 F.2d 492 (9th Cir. 1938), cert. denied (Mont. Law).

3. Coto–Matic v. The Home Indem., 354 F.2d 720 (10th Cir.1965); Helene Curtis Indus. v. U.S., 312 F.2d 774 (Ct.Cl.1963).

Where the government merely suggests rather than requires a given production process, the government does not warrant that the process will produce the desired result. Clark Grave Vault v. U.S., 371 F.2d 459 (Ct.Cl.1967). Compare the construction case discussed in § 13.3 supra.

4. Mistake is discussed in ch. 9 supra.

5. National Presto Indus. v. U.S., 338 F.2d 99 (Ct.Cl.1964), cert. denied.

6. 65 Colum.L.Rev. 542 (1965); 33 Fordham L.Rev. 507 (1965).

impracticability would not have excused performance because the plaintiff foresaw and even complained about the risk. Either the decision will be deemed "wrong" and ignored in the future or it will help point the way to a more flexible allocation of the parties' risks without reference to their agreement.[7]

(b) Unforeseen Possibilities

Sometimes the opposite side of technological development presents a problem. For example, many land owners in the Appalachians conveyed mineral interests to mining companies by "broad form" deeds. Such deeds were executed before strip mining methods and machinery were conceived of, but read literally they permit mining by any means, even if the surface of the land is destroyed. Although the technological breakthrough was outside the contemplation of the parties, the question of whether the deeds should be read to permit strip mining has been treated as a question of interpretation of the deed without the help of any legal doctrine other than the rules and standards of interpretation.[8] Similar questions of omitted terms arose as to the effect of copyright licensing agreements made prior to the development of talking pictures,[9] and after the development of new methods of satellite transmission of television images,[10] and percentage rental agreements made prior to the establishment of state lotteries where the tenant commences to sell lottery tickets.[11]

§ 13.18 Foreseeability

If the event that is the basis of a claim of impracticability or frustration is reasonably foreseeable, according to abundant authority, the defense will be lost because the promisor should have provided for the contingency in the contract.[1] Failure to provide for the foreseeable contingency is deemed to demonstrate that the promisor assumed the risk. This rationale, however, is not applied to cases of death or illness, both of which are quite foreseeable. Those cases historically, and quite properly today, are treated for many purposes as *sui generis*.

Anyone who has read a bit of history can foresee, in a general way, the possibility of war, revolution, embargo, plague, terrorism, hyper-

---

7. The case is read narrowly. Edwards v. U.S., 19 Cl.Ct. 663, 674 (1990).

8. Watson v. Kenlick Coal, 498 F.2d 1183, 1190–91 (6th Cir.1974), cert. denied; Ward v. Harding, 860 S.W.2d 280 (Ky. 1993), cert. denied; see Eardley, 12 J.Nat Resources & Envtl.L. 101 (1996); Phipps v. Leftwich, 216 Va. 706, 222 S.E.2d 536 (1976); Annot., 70 ALR3d 383.

9. Kirke La Shelle v. Paul Armstrong, 263 N.Y. 79, 188 N.E. 163 (1933).

10. Turner Ent. v. Degeto Film, 25 F.3d 1512 (11th Cir.1994).

11. In re Circle K, 98 F.3d 484 (9th Cir.1996).

§ 13.18

1. Bernina Distributors v. Bernina Sewing Machine, 646 F.2d 434 (10th Cir.1981); Butler Mfg. v. Americold, 850 F.Supp. 952 (D.Kan.1994); Associated Grocers v. West, 297 N.W.2d 103 (Iowa 1980); Werner v. Ashcraft Bloomquist, Inc., 10 S.W.3d 575 (Mo.App.2000); Helms Constr. & Development v. State, 97 Nev. 500, 634 P.2d 1224 (1981); Brenner v. Little Red School House, 302 N.C. 207, 274 S.E.2d 206, 20 ALR4th 295 (1981); see also Annot., 89 ALR3d 329 (1979).

inflation, economic depression, global warming or the recurrence of an ice age, among other horrors. Furthermore, if one reads science fiction, one learns of the possibility of new terrors that have not yet afflicted us, but involve possibilities that are not pure fantasy. A sensible approach is to define the unforeseeable in the following way: an event so unlikely to occur that reasonable parties see no need explicitly to allocate the risk of its occurrence, although the impact it might have would be of such magnitude that the parties would have negotiated over it, had the event been more likely.[2]

However, it is difficult to believe that judges in reviewing the "factual" question of foreseeability can refrain from taking into account the larger consequences of a finding of foreseeability. It has been held that the closings of the Suez Canal, America's entry into World War II and OPEC price increases were all reasonably foreseeable.[3] If, for example, in one case, American entry into the second World War had been declared to be unforeseeable, how many thousands, or tens of thousands of contracts would have to be dissolved because of impracticability or frustration? How many shipping and sales contracts would have been thwarted by the Suez closings? How broadly would international trade be disrupted and how much uncertainty would be injected into domestic and international trade? It is no accident that the court is more willing to find an excuse where the supervening event has drastic consequences only for one contract or a small number of contracts than where the supervening event affects an enormous number of transactions.

A few authorities argue that allocation of the risks on the basis of foreseeability should be abandoned or at least modified.[4] The Restatement (Second) states that foreseeability is only one of the factors to be considered in determining whether the defense of impracticability is available.[5] One view is that the promisor should be free to explain why there was no clause in the contract covering the contingency; for example, that the other party was the dominant party and therefore the promisor was forced to sign a standard form contract.[6] There is also authority to the effect that failure to deal with an improbable or

2. Trimarchi, Commercial Impracticability in Contract Law: An Economic Analysis, 11 Int'l Rev. of L. & Ec. 63, 65 n.4 (1991).

3. Transatlantic Fin. Corp. v. U.S., 363 F.2d 312 (D.C.Cir.1966), noted in 41 Tul. L.Rev. 709 (1969) and 6 Wm. & Mary L.Rev. 679 (1967); Glidden v. Hellenic Lines, Ltd., 275 F.2d 253 (2d Cir.1960); Lloyd v. Murphy, 25 Cal.2d 48, 153 P.2d 47 (1944); Publicker Indus. v. Union Carbide, 1975 WL 22890, 17 UCC Rep.Serv. 989 (E.D.Pa.1975).

4. Glenn R. Sewell Sheet Metal v. Loverde, 70 Cal.2d 666, 75 Cal.Rptr. 889, 451 P.2d 721 (1969); Wills v. Shockley, 52 Del.

295, 157 A.2d 252 (1960); Mishara Constr. v. Transit–Mixed Concrete, 365 Mass. 122, 310 N.E.2d 363 (1974); Rs. 1st § 457. UCC § 2–615 cmt 8 states, "Thus the exemptions of this section do not apply when the contingency in question is sufficiently foreshadowed at the time of contracting to be included among the business risks which are fairly to be regarded as part of the dickered terms, either consciously or as a matter of reasonable, commercial interpretation from the circumstances."

5. Rs. 2d § 261 cmt b.

6. L.N. Jackson & Co. v. Royal Norwegian Gov't, 177 F.2d 694 (2d Cir.1949), cert. denied.

insignificant contingency, even though foreseen, should not be deemed to amount to an assumption of the risk.[7]

An even more liberal view has been espoused by a few cases and some commentators.[8] Their notion is that foreseeability is of no importance when it is clear that the parties did not intend that the risk of the occurrence should be assumed by the promisor.[9]

A leading case helps to clarify the point.[10] Defendant contracted to sell certain real property to the plaintiff and to lease it back. As the plaintiff was a tax-exempt charity, the parties believed that certain very substantial tax benefits would accrue to defendant. Plaintiff strongly asserted the opinion to the defendant that these tax advantages would accrue. Under the evidence it is clear that plaintiff knew that the defendant would not have entered into the transaction but for the prospective tax advantages and that the transaction was premised on these advantages. The IRS subsequently issued a revenue ruling disallowing the kinds of tax advantages that the parties expected. The defendant refused to perform and claimed the defense of frustration of the venture.

The court agreed with the defendant that the basis on which both parties contracted was the receipt of tax advantages. However, plaintiff argued that defendant did not have the defense of frustration because it was foreseeable that the IRS might disapprove the tax benefits. Despite this, the court held that the defense was available because it was clear that the parties intended that neither party should assume this risk.[11]

§ 13.19   Force Majeure Clauses

Because most cases have held that failure to cover a foreseeable risk in the contract deprives a party of the defense of impracticability, the best way to protect a client from this rule is to provide against foreseeable risks in the agreement. Such a clause is often referred to as a *force majeure* clause or an excusable delay clause.[1] Subject to the Statute of Frauds, the clause may be oral.[2] Care should be taken, however, lest the clause diminish the availability of an excuse.[3]

7. Ibid; Rs. (2d) § 261 cmts b & c.

8. West Los Angeles Inst. v. Mayer, 366 F.2d 220 (9th Cir.1966), cert. denied; Edward Maurer v. Tubeless Tire, 285 F. 713 (6th Cir.1922); Glenn R. Sewell Sheet Metal v. Loverde, 70 Cal.2d 666, 678 n. 13, 75 Cal.Rptr. 889, 896 n. 13, 451 P.2d 721, 728 n. 13 (1969); Smit, Frustration of Contract. A Comparative Attempt at Consolidation, 58 Colum.L.Rev. 287 (1958); see also Aubrey, Frustration Reconsidered, 12 Int'l & Comp.L.Q. (1963).

9. Western Properties v. Southern Utah Aviation, 776 P.2d 656 (Utah App.1989).

10. West Los Angeles Inst. v. Mayer, n.8 supra.

11. See also Krell v. Henry, [1903] 2 K.B. 740 (C.A.); Quick v. Stuyvesant, 2 Paige Ch. 84 (N.Y.1830).

§ 13.19

1. See Publicker Industries v. Union Carbide Corp., 17 UCCRep.Serv. 989 (E.D.Pa.1975) and Eastern Air Lines v. McDonnell Douglas, 532 F.2d 957 (5th Cir. 1976).

2. InterPetrol Bermuda v. Kaiser Aluminum Int'l, 719 F.2d 992 (9th Cir.1983).

3. E.g., Idaho Power v. Cogeneration, 134 Idaho 738, 9 P.3d 1204 (2000) (clause did not cover frustration).

Drafting such a clause involves number of intricate problems. Specificity may be important. Many courts have concluded that "Exculpatory provisions which are phrased merely in general terms have long been construed as excusing only *unforeseen* events which make performance impracticable * * *. Courts have often held, therefore, that if a party desires to broaden the protections available under the impracticability doctrine, the excusing contingencies should be described with particularity and not in general language."[4]

However, the contingencies need not always be described with particularity. If the risk is unforeseen and unforeseeable then the exculpatory clause that enlarges on excuses provided by law may be phrased in general terms. Yet, even here, the drafter faces a number of problems.

One illustration will suffice.[5] The force majeure clause reads: *"Neither party shall be liable for its failure to perform hereunder* if said performance is made *impracticable due to any occurrence* beyond its reasonable control, including acts of God, fires, floods, wars, sabotage, accidents, labor disputes or shortages, governmental laws, ordinances, rules and regulations." Assume that the event on which the claimed impracticability is based is an act of the OPEC cartel. The italicized introductory language seems broad enough to cover any contingency. However, under a rule of interpretation that passes under the Latin name of *ejusdem generis,* the broad introductory language is cut down by the specific language that follows, so that if the particular risk—act of the cartel—is not indicated in the listing, it will not serve as an excuse unless it is very similar to the specified events. There is some authority that the rule of *ejusdem generis* may be avoided by using the phrase "including but not limited to" rather than simply "including."[6]

Another problem with the force majeure clause in this case is its use of the word "impracticable." If performance is impracticable under existing law, the clause is not needed. If the performance is not impracticable, then the use of the word prevents the clause from applying.[7]

The UCC expresses some limitations on broad exculpatory clauses when it states: "Generally, express agreements as to exemptions designed to enlarge upon or supplant the provisions of this section are to be read in the light of mercantile sense and reason, for this section itself sets up the commercial standard for normal and reasonable interpreta-

---

4. Eastern Air Lines v. McDonnell Douglas, 532 F.2d 957, 990–91 (5th Cir. 1976). For typical cases eviscerating force majeure clauses, see Moncrief v. Williston Basin Interstate Pipeline, 880 F.Supp. 1495 (D.Wyo.1995), affirmed in part, reversed in part and remanded 174 F.3d 1150 (10th Cir.1999); Macalloy Corp. v. Metallurg, 284 A.D.2d 227, 728 N.Y.S.2d 14 (2001); for an arguably too broad interpretation, see Guillory Farms v. Amigos Canning, 966 S.W.2d 830 (Tex.App.1998).

5. Based on Publicker Industries v. Union Carbide Corp., 17 UCC Rep.Serv. 989 (E.D.Pa.1975); see also Kel Kim v. Central Markets, 70 N.Y.2d 900, 524 N.Y.S.2d 384, 519 N.E.2d 295 (1987).

6. Eastern Air Lines v. McDonnell Douglas, 532 F.2d 957 (5th Cir.1976).

7. Publicker Industries v. Union Carbide, 17 UCC Rep.Serv. 989 (E.D.Pa.1975).

tion and provides a minimum beyond which the agreement may not go."[8] This language is far from clear. A leading case rejected the notion that it means that any attempt by a seller to enlarge on the provisions of the statute must be in clear and specific language, since such an intent may also be found by application of trade usage.[9] It is clear that any exemption clause that is manifestly unreasonable, in bad faith, or unconscionable will not be enforced.[10]

§ 13.20 Underlying Rationale

Contract liability is no-fault liability. The fundamental maxim is *pacta sunt servanda*—agreements must be kept. Even if performance is impossible or senseless, the assessment of damages for non-performance remains a possibility. Still, several policy judgments have been made to create the limited excuses for non-performance discussed in this chapter.

The first stems from one of the underpinnings of contract obligations. Contract liability stems from consent.[1] If an event occurs that is totally outside the contemplation of the parties and drastically shifts the nature of the risks ostensibly consented to, is the consent real?[2]

Second, the doctrines of impracticability and frustration are closely allied with the doctrine of mutual mistake.[3] The distinction is that mutual mistake as a doctrine is applicable only if the parties are mistaken as to a vital existing fact, while ordinarily frustration and impracticability relate to future events. As was stated in the discussion of mistake, ideas of unjust enrichment are heavily involved in granting relief for mistake. Before applying the doctrine one must search the facts for unexpected, unbargained-for gain on the one hand and unexpected, unbargained-for loss on the other.[4]

Third, notions of conscionability and fairness tend to support the doctrines. The law deems it to be unconscionably sharp practice to take advantage of the mistake of another. It may equally be deemed uncon-

---

8. UCC § 2–615 cmt 8. See also Northern Ind. Pub. Serv. v. Carbon County Coal, 799 F.2d 265 (7th Cir.1986).

9. Eastern Air Lines v. McDonnell Douglas, 532 F.2d 957 (5th Cir.1976). See also Greer Properties v. LaSalle Nat. Bank, 874 F.2d 457 (7th Cir.1989) (seller could cancel if environmental cleanup turned out to be "economically impracticable" in its "best business judgment"); PPG Indus. v. Shell, 919 F.2d 17 (5th Cir.1990) (can exculpate for inability to perform because of explosions whether or not within its control); Kentucky Utilities v. South East Coal, 836 S.W.2d 392 (Ky.1992).

10. UCC §§ 1–102(3), 1–203, and 2–302; see Greer Properties v. LaSalle Nat. Bank, 874 F.2d 457 (7th Cir.1989).

§ 13.20

1. See § 2.1 supra.

2. See Sharp, The Ethics of Breach of Contract, 45 Int'l J. of Ethics 27, 42–44 (1934).

3. See U.S. v. Gen. Douglas MacArthur Senior Village, 508 F.2d 377 (2d Cir.1974), where the majority discusses frustration and the dissent argues mistake; Cook v. Kelley, 352 Mass. 628, 227 N.E.2d 330 (1967), where the court discusses mistake when the case involved an unexpected future event. See also Chemical Bank v. Washington Public Power Supply Sys., 102 Wn.2d 874, 691 P.2d 524 (1984), cert denied (contracts discharged by frustration and mistake).

4. See § 9–26(b) supra. See also Sharp, supra note 2, at 42–44.

scionable to take advantage of a mistake as to the course of future events.[5]

From the point of view of legal analysis, the doctrine of impracticability and frustration have been explained by a number of conceptual models. The earlier cases talked in terms of the existence of an implied (in fact) term. Thus, in the music hall case[6] the court spoke of "an implied condition that the parties shall be excused in case, before breach, performance becomes impossible from the perishing of the thing" that formed the foundation of the contract. Other cases have talked about the "contemplation of the parties."[7] The notion is that one can infer from the facts that the parties did not intend that performance would have to be rendered if an unexpected event would create a radical change in the nature of the performance. This view still has a strong following in England.[8] It finds support in public international law which has long recognized the principle of *rebus sic stantibus*, an implied term in every treaty is that it will cease to be binding when the facts and conditions on which it was based have fundamentally changed.[9] The full Latin text of the doctrine, freely translated is: "contracts providing for successive acts of performance over a future period of time must be understood as subject to the condition that the circumstances will remain the same."[10]

Later cases speak of the excuse being based on a constructive condition—that is one imposed by law in the interests of justice. The excuse stems from a rule of law rather than inferences drawn from the facts.[11] However, as we have seen, the circumstances or the agreement may indicate that a party has assumed a risk greater than the risk that would be imposed by law.[12]

The most recent explanation is consistent with the earliest American impracticability case.[13] The reasoning is that even though the promise is in terms absolute, it was not intended to cover the situation that in fact arose, and therefore the court is free to supply a term that will do justice.[14] In the words of the Restatement (Second), "since it is the

---

5. See Newman, The Renaissance of Good Faith in Contracting in Anglo–American Law, 54 Cornell L.Rev. 553, 561 (1969); Note, 53 Colum.L.Rev. 94 (1953).

6. Taylor v. Caldwell, 122 Eng.Rep. 309 (K.B.1863).

7. Transatlantic Financing v. U.S., 363 F.2d 312, 315 (D.C.Cir.1966).

8. See Nicholas, Rules and Terms, 48 Tul.L.Rev. 946 (1974); but see Treitel, Frustration and Force Majeure ¶¶ 16–005 to 16–009 (1994).

9. See, e.g., Bederman, The 1871 London Declaration, Rebus Sic Stantibus and a Primitivist View of the Law of Nations, 82 Am.J.Int'l L. 1 (1988).

10. Litvinoff, Force Majeure, Failure of Cause and Théorie de L'Imprévision: Louisiana Law and Beyond, 46 La.L.Rev. 1, 4 (1985).

11. See Quick v. Stuyvesant, 2 Paige Ch. 84, 91–92 (N.Y.Ch.1830), and Turner Ent. v. Degeto Film, 25 F.3d 1512 (11th Cir.1994); see also Farnsworth, Disputes Over Omission in Contracts, 68 Colum.L.Rev. 860 (1968); Patterson, Constructive Conditions in Contracts, 42 Colum.L.Rev. 903, 946–50 (1942); Smit, Frustration of Contract: A Comparative Attempt at Consolidation, 58 Colum.L.Rev. 287 (1958).

12. See § 13.2 supra.

13. Pollard v. Shaaffer, 1 U.S. 210 (1 Dall. 210) (Pa.1787).

14. Watson v. Kenlick Coal, 498 F.2d 1183, 1190–91 (6th Cir.1974), cert. denied; see also Kirke La Shelle v. Paul Armstrong, 263 N.Y. 79, 188 N.E. 163 (1933) discussed in § 11.14 supra.

rationale of this chapter that, in a case of impracticability or frustration, the contract does not cover the case that has arisen, the court's function can be viewed generally as that * * * of supplying a term to deal with the omitted case."[15] Thus viewed, relief for impracticability or hardship does not interfere with freedom of contract.

§ 13.21 Effect of Impracticability On a Prior Repudiation

If A and B enter into an agreement under which A is to serve B for a year and B repudiates before the time for performance arrives and A dies within that time, although A had a cause of action for the repudiation, A's estate could not recover, because it would be necessary to show that A would have been ready, willing and able to perform but for the repudiation.[1]

The converse of this situation exists where, after a party repudiates, events occur that make the repudiator's own performance impossible. Should the subsequent impracticability be taken into account in adjusting the rights of the parties? There are two views. Some have taken the position that it should not because the rights of the parties became fixed by the repudiation.[2] The better rule, however, is that subsequent impracticability will discharge an anticipatory breach and will ordinarily limit damages in the case of a non-anticipatory breach.[3] This view is better because it takes into account all facts known at the time of trial.

Thus, under the better rule, if A repudiated and then died before the time for performance, B would not be entitled to any recovery.[4] If A repudiated and then died one month after performance was to begin, B would be entitled to damages for only one month.[5] So also if A performed for two weeks and A then repudiated and died two weeks later, A would be entitled to damages for the two weeks following the repudiation and preceding A's death.[6]

§ 13.22 Impracticability and Frustration Under the UCC

There are two sections in the Code relating to the subject matter of this chapter.[1] Reference has been made to section 2–614 which governs failure of the contemplated means of delivery or payment.[2] The basic section of the Code governing impossibility, impracticability, and frustra-

15. Rs. 2d § 272 cmt c and Introductory Note to Ch. 11.

§ 13.21

1. See §§ 12.2 and 13.7 supra.

2. Papaioannou v. Sirocco Supper Club, 75 Misc.2d 1001, 349 N.Y.S.2d 590 (1973).

3. Jones v. Fuller–Garvey, 386 P.2d 838 (Alaska 1963); Model Vending v. Stanisci, 74 N.J.Super. 12, 180 A.2d 393 (1962); Fratelli Pantanella v. International Commer-

cial, 89 N.Y.S.2d 736 (1949); 16 Williston § 1967A (3d ed.).

4. Rs. 1st § 457 cmt d.

5. Id. ill. 4.

6. Id. cmt 4.

§ 13.22

1. See Annot., 55 ALR5th 1 (1998). The revised draft of the UCC would make no substantive change.

2. See § 13.4 supra.

tion is § 2–615.[3] The prior discussion of this section will not be repeated here except where it is necessary to understand the new material in the ensuing discussion. It provides:

Excuse by Failure of Presupposed Conditions

Except so far as a seller may have assumed a greater obligation and subject to the preceding section on substituted performance:

(a) Delay in delivery or non-delivery in whole or in part by a seller who complies with paragraphs (b) and (c) is not a breach of his duty under a contract for sale if performance as agreed has been made impracticable by the occurrence of a contingency the non-occurrence of which was a basic assumption on which the contract was made or by compliance in good faith with any applicable foreign or domestic governmental regulation or order whether or not it later proves to be invalid.

(b) Where the causes mentioned in paragraph (a) affect only a part of seller's capacity to perform, he must allocate production and deliveries among his customers but may at his option include regular customers not then under contract as well as his own requirements for further manufacture. He may so also allocate in any manner which is fair and reasonable.

(c) The seller must notify the buyer seasonably that there will be delay or non-delivery and, when allocation is required under paragraph (b), of the estimated quota thus made available for the buyer.

The introductory language and paragraph (a) have already been discussed. Their application requires asking the questions posed in § 13.2. Although the introductory language makes it clear that the seller may assume a greater burden than that imposed by law, it is equally clear that, within limits, the seller may successfully negotiate a diminution of law-imposed obligations by agreement. This is demonstrated by an examination of the legislative history of the Code.[4]

If all of the elements of subsection (a) are met and the seller has not assumed a greater obligation, the seller is excused for a delay in delivery or non-delivery in whole or in part by complying with paragraphs (b) and (c).

Subsection (b) comes into play where the excuse found under paragraph (a) affects only a part of the seller's capacity to perform. The subsection requires the seller to allocate the available supply among its customers in "any manner which is fair and reasonable."[5] The seller in allocating may include regular customers not under contract as well as its own requirements for further manufacture. In addition, under sub-

---

3. See generally, Annot. 93 ALR3d 584.

4. See Eastern Air Lines v. McDonnell Douglas, 532 F.2d 957 (5th Cir.1976); Hawkland, The Energy Crisis and Section 2–615 of the Uniform Code, 79 Com.L.J. 75 (1974). See § 13.19 supra.

5. See UCC § 2–615 cmt 11; see also Cliffstar v. Riverbend Prods., 750 F.Supp. 81 (1990) (seller has broad discretion as to allocation among buyers); Harvey v. Fearless Farris Wholesale, 589 F.2d 451 (9th Cir.1979); Terry v. Atlantic Richfield, 72 Cal.App.3d 962, 140 Cal.Rptr. 510 (1977).

section (c) the seller must notify the buyer in writing of the "estimated quota thus made available for the buyer." When the buyer receives a justified notice of allocation, the buyer may modify the contract by agreeing to take the available quota in substitution or terminate the executory portion of the contract.[6]

Most cases under § 2–615 do not involve an allocation problem. The section also comes into play when there is a material or indefinite delay that is excused under subsection (a). In that case the seller must still give notice and the buyer still has the option to terminate the contract.

UCC § 2–616 contains a provision governing installment contracts. It gives the buyer the option to terminate or modify where the prospective deficiency caused by a material or indefinite delay or an allocation as to any installment substantially impairs the value of the whole contract. If the value of the whole contract is not impaired the buyer would not have that option as to the whole contract but only as the installment or installments involved.[7]

Subsection (3) of UCC § 2–616 provides: "The provisions of this section may not be negated by agreement except in so far as the seller has assumed a greater obligation under the preceding section." This subsection is designed to protect the buyer not the seller.[8]

UCC §§ 2–615 and 2–616 facially set up a rule that gives an excuse only to the seller. Despite this, at least one case has applied the section to a buyer.[9] Even if the Code section is deemed not to apply to buyers it is clear that the pre-Code law would be consulted to supplement the Code in case of a buyer's claim of excuse which most likely would be a claim of frustration.[10]

§ 13.23 Adjusting the Rights of the Parties

The effect of total supervening impracticability or frustration is to discharge the excused party's remaining duties.[1] Simultaneously, the other party is discharged because the performance of the excused party will not be forthcoming.[2] If the supervening impracticability or frustration is only prospective the other party has the same options as in a case where the non-performance would be a breach, except that there will not be a cause of action for breach.[3] We have already discussed the rules

---

6. This rule in the UCC appears to be in substantial accord with prior law. Yuba v. Mattoon, 160 Cal.App.2d 456, 325 P.2d 162 (1958); Mawhinney v. Millbrook Woolen Mills, 234 N.Y. 244, 137 N.E. 318 (1922) (government requisitioned much, but not all, of manufacturer's output); 14 Corbin § 75.10 (Nehf 2001); Rs. 1st § 464; see also UCC § 2–615 cmt 11; cf. Hudson, Prorating in the English Law of Frustrated Contracts, 31 Mod.L.Rev. 535 (1968).

7. See § 11.20(d) supra.

8. UCC § 2–616, comment.

9. Nora Springs Coop. v. Brandau, 247 N.W.2d 744 (Iowa 1976).

10. UCC § 2–615 cmt 9; Note, 105 U.Pa.L.Rev. 880, 904 (1957); see G. Gilmore, Security Interests § 41.7 at 1104–6 (1965); see § 13.12 supra.

§ 13.23

1. Rs. 2d § 261.

2. See § 11.18(b) supra.

3. See § 12.8 supra.

relating to temporary impracticability and partial impracticability.[4]

Where the contract has been discharged for impracticability or frustration, it is often necessary, in the interests of justice, to adjust the rights of the parties.[5] For example, if the excused party has rendered part performance before the impracticability arose, recovery for the part performance may be available under the doctrine of divisibility.[6] The Restatement (Second) suggests that a court may sever a contract in the interests of justice even if the normal tests for divisibility are not met.[7]

If the contract is deemed not to be divisible, another possibility is restitution. However, as demonstrated in the coronation cases, courts have had difficulty in applying the concept of restitution in an impracticability or frustration context. While in Krell v. Henry[8] it was held that the defendant was excused from paying for use of the premises, in the related case of Chandler v. Webster,[9] it was held that a defendant who had made a substantial down payment and had agreed to pay the balance in advance of the coronation, was not entitled to restitution and furthermore was liable to pay the balance. The rule was simply that the parties should be placed in the position they would have been in at the occurrence of the frustrating event.

Chandler v. Webster was subsequently overruled by the Fibrosa case[10] which, however, produced an equally arbitrary rule. In a case involving supervening impracticability, restitution of a down payment was granted, placing the parties in the position they enjoyed prior to contracting. This ruling was not flexible enough to take into account the relative extent to which the parties might be out of pocket by reason of action in reliance on the contract. At the suggestion of the Law Lords in the Fibrosa case, the English Parliament enacted legislation[11] permitting recovery under a contract discharged by reason of impracticability or frustration for the value of benefits received, "if it considers it just to do so, having regard for all the circumstances." Pursuant to this enactment, the court may deduct for expenses incurred in reliance on the contract, taking into consideration the circumstances giving rise to the frustration or impracticability.

In the U.S., courts have generally taken the view that when a contract is discharged by impracticability or frustration, the parties must make restitution for the benefits conferred on them. At times the concept of "benefit" is stretched to include expenses incurred in preparation for performance.[12] However, there is increasing recognition that

---

4. See §§ 13.13 to 13.14 supra.

5. For a detailed discussion of this problem, see Dawson, Judicial Revision of Frustrated Contracts, 64 B.U.L.Rev. 1 (1984).

6. Mullen v. Wafer, 252 Ark. 541, 480 S.W.2d 332 (1972).

7. Rs. 2d § 272 cmt c & ill. 3.

8. [1903] 2 K.B. 740.

9. [1904] 2 K.B. 493.

10. Fibrosa Spolka Akcyjna v. Fairbairn Lawson Combe Barbour, Ltd., H.L., [1943] A.C. 32 (1942), 2 All E.R. 122, 144 ALR 1298; 91 U.Pa.L.Rev. 262 (1942).

11. Law Reform (Frustrated Contracts) Act, 1943, 6 & 7 Geo. 6, ch. 40. For a suggested American statute, see Comment, 69 Yale L.J. 1054 (1960).

12. The American cases are ably analyzed in Comment, 69 Yale L.J. 1054 (1960). A landmark case has recognized explicitly

restitution, when employed to unwind a contract that cannot be performed, is concerned with equitable adjustment of gains and losses sustained by the parties and not merely the redressing of unjust enrichment.[13] In this respect the Restatement (Second) states that the court may grant relief on such terms "as justice requires including protection of the parties' reliance interests."[14] The notion is that gains and losses should be apportioned without concern for conceptual barriers. In addition, the court can supply a term that is necessary for a determination of the parties' rights and duties.[15]

It is even possible to reshape the contract so that the duties of the parties will continue. This may be done by allocation,[16] by the rules governing temporary or partial impracticability[17] or by supplying a term that "is reasonable in the circumstances."[18] The party to whom performance is owed has the power to reshape the contract by waiving restrictive clauses,[19] or substantial non-performance[20] and other obstacles, thereby reinstating the duty of performance, albeit on somewhat different terms.[21] This power demonstrates that one of the bases of the doctrine of impracticability is the unconscionability of insisting on strict performance in the light of radically changed circumstances. There is even some authority for the proposition that a party who has a defense of impracticability may waive it and perform by virtue of a source of supply not contemplated by the contract.[22]

§ 13.24   Risk of Casualty Losses

This topic is only tangentially related to the topic of impracticability. When goods or real property are in the process of being sold, or are under lease or bailment, frequently the question arises as to which of the parties must bear the risk of damage or destruction of the subject matter. Unlike the problems presented earlier in this chapter, the primary question is not whether a promise is sought to be excused. At times, however, both problems may arise because of the destruction of the subject matter.

that "reliance" expenses incurred by the promisee may be recoverable when the equities are on the promisee's side. Albre Marble & Tile v. John Bowen, 338 Mass. 394, 155 N.E.2d 437 (1959), modified 343 Mass. 777, 179 N.E.2d 321 (1962).

13. See Rs. 2d § 272 cmt b; Perillo, Restitution in a Contractual Context, 73 Colum.L.Rev. 1208 (1973).

14. Rs. 2d § 272(2).

15. Rs. 2d § 272 cmt b which references to § 204.

16. See Rs. 2d § 272 ill. 5; see § 13.22 supra.

17. See Rs. 2d § 272 ill. 4; see §§ 13.13 and 13.14 supra.

18. Rs. 2d § 272 cmt c; Unihealth v. U.S. Healthcare, 14 F.Supp.2d 623 (D.N.J. 1998).

19. Lloyd v. Murphy, 25 Cal.2d 48, 153 P.2d 47 (1944); 33 Colum.L.Rev. 397, 423.

20. Rs. 2d § 272 ill. 1.

21. Cf. Northern v. Chugach Elec. Ass'n, 518 P.2d 76 (Alaska 1974), aff'd (defendant's refusal to modify the contract after performance proved impossible, enhanced defendant's liability).

22. International Paper v. Rockefeller, 161 A.D. 180, 146 N.Y.S. 371 (1914). ("We need not say that defendant could not have furnished [like] wood of equal quality from other lands").

The issue of risk of loss can be illustrated by an accidental fire destroys a building between the time a contract for sale is made and the time for the closing of title. There are three views. The majority places the risk of loss on the purchaser by applying the concept of equitable conversion: once the contract is made, the purchaser is regarded by a court of equity as the owner. Under this view, "risk of loss" means that the buyer must pay for the property even though the buyer did not have legal title to it at the time of the casualty. Under a minority view, the buyer does not assume this risk. The seller as legal owner of a property simply loses the seller's own property and is not entitled to look to the buyer for payment.[1] The seller suffers the risk of loss. Under this view, an additional question arises which does relate to the doctrine of impracticability. Must the seller respond in damages for the failure to convey the property? No, because the seller has the defense of impracticability based on the destruction of the subject matter of the contract.[2] A third view, embodied in the Uniform Vender and Purchaser Risk Act, enacted in about ten states, places the risk of loss on a purchaser only if the purchaser is in possession or has legal title.[3]

The UCC governs the similar problem of risk of loss of goods that have been identified to the contract. This is a subject that is traditionally discussed in connection with "sales" law rather than "contract" law, a traditional division based more on academic convenience than on logic.[4]

---

§ 13.24

1. Ross v. Bumstead, 65 Ariz. 61, 173 P.2d 765 (1946) (majority); Rector v. Alcorn, 241 N.W.2d 196 (Iowa 1976); Skelly Oil v. Ashmore, 365 S.W.2d 582 (Mo.1963) (minority). See generally, J. Cribbet, Principles of the Law of Property, 149–154 (2d ed.1975).

2. J. S. Potts Drug v. Benedict, 156 Cal. 322, 104 P. 432 (1909). However, the down payment must be returned. See also Dixon v. Salvation Army, 142 Cal.App.3d 463, 191 Cal.Rptr. 111 (1983).

3. See, e.g., McKinney's N.Y.Gen. Oblig.Law § 5–1311. As to how insurance relates to this problem, see Long v. Keller, 104 Cal.App.3d 312, 163 Cal.Rptr. 532 (1980); Brownell v. Bd. of Educ., 239 N.Y.

369, 146 N.E. 630, 37 ALR 1319 (1925); Suburban v. Cincinnati Ins., 323 Ill.App.3d 278, 256 Ill.Dec. 211, 751 N.E.2d 601 (Ill. App.2001); McCord, Allocation of Loss, and Property Insurance, 39 Ind.L.J. 647 (1964); Comment, 28 Albany L.Rev. 253 (1964). On related problems arising where the land is taken by condemnation, see, e.g., Lucenti v. Cayuga Apartments, 48 N.Y.2d 530, 423 N.Y.S.2d 886, 399 N.E.2d 918 (1979); Chester Litho v. Palisades Interstate Park Comm'n, 27 N.Y.2d 323, 317 N.Y.S.2d 761, 266 N.E.2d 229 (1971); Annot., 27 ALR3d 572 (1969).

4. For risk of loss, see White & Summers ch.5 (4th ed.).

Chapter 14

DAMAGES

Table of Sections

Table of Sections

A. INTRODUCTION

B. NON–COMPENSATORY DAMAGES

C. COMPENSATORY DAMAGES

D. FORESEEABILITY

E. CERTAINTY

A.   INTRODUCTION

Table of Sections

§ 14.1   Damages Defined

The plaintiff's contract rights are primary rights and upon breach by the defendant, these primary rights are discharged and in substitution the law grants the plaintiff secondary rights.[1] The law of remedies defines the scope of these secondary rights. The remedy most often granted by the common law is the remedy of damages;[2] restitution is usually not a satisfactory remedy and specific performance is available only in special circumstances.[3] A brief historical excursion will help understanding of the present law of damages.

In the later stages of the common law writ system, two basic writs were available in contract actions.[4] If the plaintiff had fully performed all or a severable part of the contractual obligation and if the agreed exchange for plaintiff's performance was the payment of money, the writ of *general assumpsit* was available. The plaintiff's recovery was the agreed price, or, if no price had been agreed upon, the reasonable value of the labor or services rendered or the property transferred to the defendant.[5]

When the defendant breached the contract prior to a completed performance by the plaintiff, the appropriate writ was *special assumpsit*. In this case the plaintiff was not entitled to recover the agreed price, but only the amount of the pecuniary injury, if any, plaintiff had suffered.

Modern law has kept the distinction made in these common law writs. This is not necessarily because the common law writs continue to rule us from the grave; rather the distinction makes good economic sense. Both kinds of recovery involve the enforcement of the "performance interest" of the promisee.[6] After having fully performed, the plaintiff has earned the agreed price. The UCC labels a lawsuit seeking this kind of recovery an "action for the price."[7] When the plaintiff has not fully performed, however, it would often be unduly generous to plaintiff and unduly harsh on the defendant to award plaintiff the price. Rather, the inquiry should be and is: what was the extent of the economic injury caused by the breach?[8] Usually, this will be less than the

---

§ 14.1

1. 5 Corbin § 995. The First Restatement, looking at the right-duty relationship from the perspective of the obligor's duty, states that the obligor's contractual duty is discharged and in substitution a duty to make compensation is imposed. Rs. 1st § 399(1). The Second Restatement distinguishes between "rights to performance" (Rs. 2d § 236 cmt b) and "rights to damages." Id. § 346 cmt a.

2. An economic explanation for this preference is proffered by Mahoney, Contract Remedies and Options Pricing, 25 J.Legal Stud. 139 (1995). It is, however, difficult to believe that the preference is rooted in economic incentives. All non-common-law capitalist countries have a preference for specific performance.

3. See chs. 15 (Restitution) and 16 (Specific Performance).

4. A common law pleader would find this statement greatly over-simplified. For a

discussion of the writs formerly available in contract cases, see Shipman, Common Law Pleading 132–169 (3d ed. Ballantine 1923).

5. Although such recovery was sometimes referred to as "damages," e.g., Stephen, Principles of Pleading in Civil Actions 361 (2d ed. Andrews 1901), it is conceptually and practically different from an award of damages as that term is generally understood.

6. Friedmann, The Performance Interest in Contract Damages, 111 L.Q.Rev. 628, 629–30 (1995).

7. UCC § 2–709. Unlike the rule under the common law writs, however, in an action for the price, incidental damages may be recovered in addition to the price. See § 14.25 infra; 5 Corbin § 995.

8. Two kinds of economic harm are usually non-compensable—attorneys' fees (§ 14.35 infra) and attrition of the value of the amount recovered because of inflation.

agreed exchange; but sometimes it will be more. Compensation allowed by law for this injury is known as damages. In addition, two categories of recoveries—nominal damages and punitive damages—have other non-compensatory functions. These play a rather small role in contract actions and will be discussed briefly at the outset of this chapter.

B. NON–COMPENSATORY DAMAGES

Table of Sections

Sec.
14.2 Nominal Damages.
14.3 Punitive Damages.

§ 14.2 Nominal Damages

For every legal wrong there is a legal remedy.[1] Thus, for every breach of contract a cause of action exists. If the aggrieved party has suffered no compensable damages, a judgment for nominal damages will be entered.[2] The usual amount of nominal damages is six cents or one dollar,[3] and symbolizes vindication of the wrong done.

As a practical matter, an award of nominal damages in a contract action may arise in one of two settings. First, the plaintiff may bring an action that may bring only nominal damages in order to establish a precedent in a test case or in a dispute that is likely to recur in a continuing relationship.[4] Today, under modern statutes, one is more likely to bring an action for a declaratory judgment. Second, and more frequently, the plaintiff is likely to institute an action in the belief that substantial damages will be obtained. At trial plaintiff establishes that the contract was breached, but fails to establish actual damages. Thus, plaintiff is entitled to a judgment for nominal damages.[5] Traditionally, since plaintiff has established a cause of action, plaintiff is also entitled to the costs of the action. It is sometimes said that nominal damages is a "peg to hang costs on."[6] This function of nominal damages has been somewhat curtailed. Statutory provisions frequently provide that if the action could have been brought in a court of inferior jurisdiction costs

Hauser, Breach of Contracts Damages During Inflation, 33 Tul.L.Rev. 307 (1959).

§ 14.2

1. Ashby v. White, 92 Eng.Rep. 126 (Q.B. 1703).

2. Freund v. Washington Square Press, 34 N.Y.2d 379, 357 N.Y.S.2d 857, 314 N.E.2d 419 (1974); Taylor v. NationsBank, 365 Md. 166, 776 A.2d 645 (2001); Rs. 2d § 346(2).

3. Nicholas v. Pennsylvania State Univ., 227 F.3d 133 (3d Cir.2000) ($1); Patel v. Howard University, 896 F.Supp. 199 (D.D.C.1995).

4. McCormick, Damages 95–96 (1935).

5. Hydrite Chemical v. Calumet Lubricants, 47 F.3d 887 (7th Cir.1995); Evans v. Werle, 31 S.W.3d 489 (Mo.App.2000); Freund v. Washington Square Press, 34 N.Y.2d 379, 357 N.Y.S.2d 857, 314 N.E.2d 419 (1974). On the additional question of whether a judgment for the defendant will be reversed and remanded when it appears that the plaintiff is entitled to merely nominal damages, see Note, 25 Colum.L.Rev. 963 (1925).

6. Stanton v. New York & E. Ry., 59 Conn. 272, 282, 22 A. 300, 303 (1890); see Camino Real v. Wolfe, 119 N.M. 436, 891 P.2d 1190 (1995)

will not be recovered unless a specified minimum judgment is entered.[7] These statutes are designed to relieve congestion in the major trial courts.

§ 14.3   Punitive Damages

Punitive damages, sometimes known as "exemplary" damages, are granted to punish malicious or willful and wanton conduct.[1] The purpose of such an award is to deter the wrongdoer from similar conduct in the future as well as to deter others from engaging in such conduct. Although such awards are increasingly important in tort litigation, punitive damages are usually not awarded in contract actions, no matter how egregious the breach.[2]

But punitive damages are awarded where the breach constitutes or is accompanied by an independent malicious or wanton tort.[3] They are also awarded where the breach also involves the malicious or wanton violation of a fiduciary duty even where the violation does not constitute an independent tort.[4] Furthermore, some jurisdictions have gone beyond the independent tort and fiduciary violation cases and permit an award of punitive damages where elements of fraud, malice, gross negligence or oppression "mingle" with the breach.[5]

Generally, punitive damages are available against insurance companies for bad faith refusals to settle claims; the breach of the implied

---

7. E.g., McKinney's N.Y.C.P.L.R. 8102; see McCormick, Damages 94–95.

§ 14.3

1. See McCormick, Damages 275–299; Polinsky & Shavell, Punitive Damages: An Economic Analysis, 111 Harv.L.Rev. 869, 936–39 (1998).

2. U.S. v. Merritt Meridian Constr., 95 F.3d 153 (2d Cir.1996); Berkla v. Corel, 302 F.3d 909 (9th Cir.2002); Weber v. Domel, 48 S.W.3d 435 (Tex.App.2001); Francis v. Lee Enter., 89 Hawai'i 234, 971 P.2d 707 (1999); UCC § 1–106(1); § 1–305 (2001 revision); Rs. 2d § 355; 11 Williston § 1340 (3d ed.). In arbitration, see Symposium, 63 Fordham L.Rev. 1571–75, 1651–78 (1995); Ware, Punitive Damages in Arbitration, 63 Fordham L.Rev. 63 (1994); Polak, 10 Ohio St.J.Disp.Resol. 1 (1994). Ex Parte Thicklin, 824 So.2d 723 (Ala.2002) holds that a provision prohibiting punitives in arbitration is unconscionable.

3. Gateway Technologies v. MCI, 64 F.3d 993 (no tort, no punitives); Klingbiel v. Commercial Credit, 439 F.2d 1303 (10th Cir.1971) (breach of contract constituted a conversion); El Ranco v. First Nat. Bank, 406 F.2d 1205 (9th Cir.1968), cert. denied; General Motors v. Piskor, 281 Md. 627, 381 A.2d 16, 93 ALR3d 1097 (1977) (breach of

contract involved false imprisonment and assault). To the effect that this is the only situation in which punitive damages is available in a contract action, see New York University v. Continental Ins., 87 N.Y.2d 308, 639 N.Y.S.2d 283, 662 N.E.2d 763 (1995); see also Ciba–Geigy v. Murphree, 653 So.2d 857 (Miss.1994).

4. Brown v. Coates, 253 F.2d 36, 67 ALR2d 943 (D.C.Cir.1958), 33 N.Y.U. L.Rev. 878 (1958) (real estate broker); cf. International Brotherhood of Boilermakers v. Braswell, 388 F.2d 193 (5th Cir.1968), cert. denied (union wrongfully expelled member); Hoche Productions v. Jayark Films, 256 F.Supp. 291 (S.D.N.Y.1966) (film distributor fraudulently accounted for gross receipts); Wagman v. Lee, 457 A.2d 401 (D.C.App.1983), cert. denied. See Scallen, Promises Broken vs. Promises Betrayed, 1993 U.Ill.L.Rev. 897 (urging expansion of the range of fiduciary relations).

5. Watson v. Johnson Mobile Homes, 284 F.3d 568 (5th Cir.2002) (Miss.); Public Service Co. v. Diamond D. Constr., 131 N.M. 100, 33 P.3d 651 (N.M.App.2001); Beck v. Moishe's Moving & Storage, 167 Misc.2d 960, 641 N.Y.S.2d 517 (1995) (threats to destroy plaintiff's goods); Sullivan, Punitive Damages in the Law of Contract, 61 Minn.L.Rev. 207 (1977); Note, 10 S.C.L.Rev. 444 (1958).

covenant of good faith and fair dealing being treated as if it were a tort.[6] California and Montana had carried this one step further beyond insurance cases, holding that a breach of a covenant of good faith and fair dealing in any contract is tortious and therefore a predicate for punitive damages, but both states have retreated.[7]

C. COMPENSATORY DAMAGES

Table of Sections

§ 14.4   The General Standard

(a) Contracts in General

For breach of contract, the law of damages seeks to place the aggrieved party in the same economic position the aggrieved party would have attained if the contract had been performed.[1] This involves an award of both the "losses caused and gains prevented by the defendant's breach, in excess of savings made possible."[2]

An illustrative case is Lieberman v. Templar Motor Co.[3] The plaintiff contracted to manufacture a number of specially designed automobile bodies. The contract was repudiated by the defendant buyer after production had commenced and about one-quarter of the bodies had been delivered. Since there was no market for auto bodies of this special design, the plaintiff could not mitigate damages by completing the manufacture of the remaining bodies and selling them on the market. It was held that the plaintiff could recover the profit it would have made had the defendant fully performed the contract. The amount of gains prevented was calculated by the difference of what would have been the cost of performance and the contract price. In addition, the plaintiff was permitted to recover for losses sustained. These consisted of payments

---

6. Gruenberg v. Aetna Ins., 9 Cal.3d 566, 108 Cal.Rptr. 480, 510 P.2d 1032 (1973); Miller v. Byrne, 916 P.2d 566 (Colo. App.1995); contra, Shaefer v. Aetna Life & Cas., 910 F.Supp. 1095 (D.Md.1996); see Creedon, Punitive Damages for Breach of Contract—Does the Punishment Fit the Crime?, 1983 Det.C.L.Rev. 1149; Holmes, Is There Life after Gilmore's Death of Contracts?, 65 Cornell L.Rev. 330 (1980); Sykes, "Bad Faith" Breach of Contract by First Party Insurers, 25 J.Leg. Studies 405 (1996); Comment, 76 St. John's L.Rev. 201 (2002).

7. The complete story is detailed in Freeman & Mills v. Belcher Oil, 11 Cal.4th 85, 900 P.2d 669, 44 Cal.Rptr.2d 420 (1995).

A follow-up is Cates Constr. v. Talbot Partners, 21 Cal.4th 28, 86 Cal.Rptr.2d 855, 980 P.2d 407 (1999).

§ 14.4

1. UCC § 1–106; § 1–305 of the revision; 5 Corbin § 992; McCormick, Damages 561; 11 Williston § 1338 (3d ed.).

2. Rs. 1st § 329, see also Rs. 2d § 347.

3. 236 N.Y. 139, 140 N.E. 222, 29 ALR 1089 (1923). The same result would be reached today under UCC § 2–708(2), and its proposed revision (see § 14.27 infra), and under CISG. See Delchi Carrier v. Rotorex, 71 F.3d 1024 (2d Cir.1995).

for labor and material, reasonably made in part performance of the contract, to the extent that these were wasted; that is, to the extent that the labor product and materials could not be salvaged. Also included are "overhead expenses" such as an allocated share of the cost of management, plant, electric power, etc.[4]

There are many rules of damages for particular kinds of contracts, such as contracts for the sale of goods,[5] construction contracts,[6] employment contracts,[7] etc. With only a few exceptions, mainly in the real property area,[8] these specialized rules implement the general standard of gains prevented and losses sustained. Sometimes, because of the particular facts of a case the specialized rule usually applicable does not fulfill its purpose of providing an accurate formula for determining the gains prevented and losses sustained. In such a case the courts will turn to the general standard.[9]

The above analysis is the traditional common-law approach. A more modern analysis of the elements of contract damages has been made.[10] This analysis does not conflict with the gains prevented and losses sustained analysis; it merely represents a different breakdown of the same economic harm suffered. The use of this newer analysis has been widely adopted by theorists, although it has had little impact on the courts.

The more modern analysis divides a contracting party's legally protected interests into three categories: a restitution interest, a reliance interest, and an expectation interest. The restitution interest represents the benefits conferred upon the other party. The reliance interest represents the detriment incurred by changing position. In most cases, reliance interest recovery includes the restitution interest which then is a subspecies of reliance.[11] The expectation interest represents the prospect of gain from the contract. It is not precisely the same as the concept of "gains prevented," because it does not take into consideration "oppor-

---

4. See Conditioned Air v. Rock Island Motor Transit, 253 Iowa 961, 114 N.W.2d 304, 3 ALR3d 679 (1962), cert. denied; accord, UCC § 2–708(2) and its proposed revision.

5. See §§ 14.20 to 14.27 infra.

6. See §§ 14.28 to 14.29 infra.

7. See §§ 14.18 to 14.19 infra.

8. See § 14.30 infra.

9. See, e.g., Great Atlantic & Pac. Tea v. Atchison, T. & S. F. Ry., 333 F.2d 705 (7th Cir.1964), cert. denied; Liberty Navig. & Trading v. Kinoshita & Co., 285 F.2d 343 (2d Cir.1960), cert. denied; DeWaay v. Muhr, 160 N.W.2d 454 (Iowa 1968); Abrams v. Reynolds Metals, 340 Mass. 704, 166 N.E.2d 204 (1960).

10. Fuller & Perdue, The Reliance Interest in Contract Damages (Parts I and II), 46 Yale L.J. 52, 373 (1936–37). See Hudec, Restating the "Reliance Interest," 67 Cor-

nell L.Rev. 704 (1982). The terminology adopted by Fuller & Perdue and its underlying rationale is criticized in Friedmann, The Performance Interest in Contract Damages, 111 L.Q. Rev. 628 (1995)., and in Barnes, The *Net* Expectation Interest in Contract Damages, 48 Emory L.J. 1137, 1149 (1999). These are persuasive criticisms. Barnes at 1150–51 states the process by which almost all damages calculations can be made without resort to interest analysis. As to opportunities forgone and pre-contractual expenditures, see Crespi, Recovering Pre-contractual Expenditures as an Element of Reliance Damages, 49 SMU L.Rev. 43 (1995).

11. In unusual cases, the restitution interest consists also of profits made by the breaching party. In such cases, it is not a subspecies of reliance. See § 15.4 infra.

tunity costs," the value of opportunities forgone because of the contract. An example of an opportunity cost is the rejection of an offer of full-time employment because one has accepted an offer for a different full-time position.[12] An opportunity cost is a reliance cost.

Our legal system starts from the premise that the expectation interest (perhaps better called the "performance interest")[13] of contracting parties is the primary interest deserving protection. In order to protect it to the fullest—that is, in order to put the aggrieved party in the same economic position the party would have attained upon full performance of the contract—the restitution and reliance interests need to be protected as well. The following hypothetical is illustrative:

Purchaser (P) contracts to purchase Blackacre from Vendor (V) for $100,000, subject to obtaining a mortgage loan, paying V $10,000 as a down payment. An appraisal commissioned by P's bank shows that Blackacre has a market value of $120,000. Upon learning of the appraisal, V repudiates. Prior to repudiation, P expended $500 for a survey of Blackacre and $500 for banking fees for a loan application, and, as was foreseen by V, $1,000 for an option to purchase adjoining land which P intended to use to provide additional parking for the structure on Blackacre. P's expectancy of profit is $20,000. The restitution interest is the $10,000 down payment. The reliance interest is $2,000, but the survey and the banking fees were necessary expenses to obtain the expectancy—the property. Thus, the recovery will be $31,000, the expectancy and restitution interests and that part of the reliance interest (the option money) that would not have to be expended toward earning the expectancy.

The term "expectancy interest" (or "expectation interest") is often used in the manner stated in the above hypothetical to separate it from the reliance and restitution interests where elements of all three interests are combined in the judgment. At other times the term "expectancy interest" is used in the broader sense of the amount necessary to put the aggrieved party in the same economic position as performance would have done. Often, this expectation is called "the benefit of the bargain." In this broader sense, the expectancy interest in the hypothetical is $31,000, not $20,000. The analysis is the same, but the vocabulary is employed differently. In this broad sense, a better term would be the "performance interest."

The reliance interest has been divided into two classes. Expenditures made toward performing the contract have been called expenditures in "essential reliance" or "performance costs." Expenditures that are not required by the contract, but in furtherance of it have been labeled as expenditures in "incidental reliance" or "surplus enhancing costs." For example, suppose the defendant promised the plaintiff a franchised outlet. As required by the contract, the plaintiff commenced construction of a building. Although the contract does not require the

---

12. E.g., Grouse v. Group Health Plan 306 N.W.2d 114 (Minn.1981).

13. See Friedmann, supra note 10.

plaintiff to advertise the forthcoming franchise outlet, plaintiff incurs advertising expenditures. The construction involves "essential reliance," the advertising involves "incidental reliance."

In addition to the three interests, just discussed, damages sometimes include a fourth element–breach related costs such as consequential damages and the expenses incurred in minimizing damages.

At times, the expectation (the benefit of the bargain) cannot be recovered because of a lack of probative evidence[14] or for policy reasons.[15] In such instances, the aggrieved party may have recovery based on one or both of the other interests. These themes will be developed at various points in this chapter.

(b) Attorney–Client Retainers

Contracts engender expectations, and contract law generally protects those expectations by rules providing for awarding of damages, restitution, or specific enforcement; moreover, constitutional principles protect these expectations from government interference. Tort law also protects these expectations from interference by third parties.

Consequently, it is somewhat surprising that a lawyer has no expectancy interest in a special retainer contract, that is, a contract retaining a lawyer for a particular case. A leading text echoes the case law: "It is now uniformly recognized that the client-lawyer contract is terminable at will by the client. For good reasons, poor reasons, or the worst of reasons, a client may fire the lawyer."[16] If the client elects to fire the lawyer without cause, the lawyer is entitled to recover in *quantum meruit*, but, subject to a few exceptions, has no right to expectancy damages.[17] Similarly, lawyers may not keep unrefundable retainers.[18] Health care professionals also are inhibited from seeking expectancy damages,[19] but other licensed professionals recover expectancy damages for breach.[20]

14. See § 14.9 infra

15. E.g., certain promissory estoppel decisions, discussed in ch. 6 supra; certain cases where a vendor breaches a contract to convey real property (§ 14.30); certain non-commercial contracts, such as a plastic surgeon's breach of promise to achieve a given result. Sullivan v. O'Connor, 363 Mass. 579, 296 N.E.2d 183, 99 ALR3d 294 (1973). See Rs. 2d § 351(3).

16. Wolfram, Modern Legal Ethics § 9.5.2.(1986). Texas appears to be an exception. Johnson v. California Real Estate Inv. Trust, 912 F.2d 788 (5th Cir.1990).

17. The seminal case is Martin v. Camp, 219 N.Y. 170, 114 N.E. 46, 48 (1916). The Court indicated that damages might be awarded for breach of a general retainer or if the contract induced an attorney to change position.

18. Matter of Thonert, 682 N.E.2d 522 (Ind.1997).

19. A search has turned up no cases where a health care professional has sought damages for breach as opposed to compensation for work done. The closest cases are actions by dentists who have sought and received payment for dentures that were incomplete because of patient non-cooperation. Giering v. Lemoine, 106 So.2d 534 (La.Ct.App.1958); Parvey v. Barasch, 142 A. 230 (R.I.1928). The "Patient's Bill of Rights" of the American Hospital Association provides: "The patient has the right to refuse treatment to the extent permitted by law...." Cyril H. Wecht, Medical Ethics and Legal Liability 337 (1976). It follows that if the patient has this right, the health care professional has no right to expectancy damages.

20. Bernard Tomson & Norman Coplan, Architectural and Engineering Law 233–36 (2d ed. 1967) (listing case briefs of damages recoveries).

D. FORESEEABILITY

Table of sections

§ 14.5 The Rule of Hadley v. Baxendale

(a) Economic Injury

Prior to 1854 there were almost no rules of contract damages. The assessment of damages was for the most part left to the unfettered discretion of the jury.[1] Such broad discretion, however, was unsuited to the newly mature commercial economy of England. In 1854 Hadley v. Baxendale[2] was decided. It has won universal acceptance in the common law world and remains the leading case in the field.[3]

The Hadley plaintiffs operated a grist mill which was forced to suspend operations because of a broken shaft. Plaintiff's employee brought the broken shaft to the defendants for shipment to an engineering company which was to manufacture a new shaft, using the broken one as a model. The defendants inexcusably delayed the shipment for several days. As a result the mill was shut down for a greater period of time than it would have been had the shipment been seasonably dispatched.[4] A jury verdict for the plaintiff included an award of damages for the lost profits of the mill. The trial court's judgment based on the verdict was reversed.

§ 14.5

1. Kuehl v. Freeman Bros. Agency, 521 N.W.2d 714 (Iowa 1994); McCormick, Damages 562–563; Washington, Damages in Contract at Common Law, 47 Law Q.Rev. 345 (1931), 48 Law Q.Rev. 90 (1932).

2. 156 Eng.Rep. 145 (1854). The decision of the case represents a borrowing from the French writer, Pothier. Washington, supra note 1 at 103; see also Danzig, 4 J.Leg.Studies 249, 257–59 (1975). The decision in this celebrated case had been preceded by the adoption of Pothier's formulation by American authors. See, e.g., Chipman, An Essay on the Law of Contracts for the Payment of Specific Articles 122 (1822); Sedgwick, A Treatise on the Measure of Damages 67 (2d ed. 1852).

3. Referring to the Convention for the International Sale of Goods, the court said: "The CISG requires that damages be limited by the familiar principle of Hadley v. Baxendale." Delchi Carrier SpA v. Rotorex,

71 F.3d 1024 (2d Cir.1995). For a critique of Hadley, see Diamond & Foss, Consequential Damages for Commercial Loss: An Alternative to Hadley v. Baxendale, 63 Fordham L.Rev. 665 (1994) (arguing that the rule is both ambiguous and inflexible).

4. There has been confusion as to the facts of the case. According to the reporter's statement of the facts the plaintiff's servant told the clerk that the mill was stopped and the shaft was to be sent immediately. But the opinion of the court states: "We find that the only circumstances here communicated by the plaintiffs to the defendants at the time the contract was made were that the article to be carried was the broken shaft of a mill, and the plaintiffs were millers of that mill." Even as careful a scholar as McCormick, uncritically accepted the reporter's statement of the facts. McCormick, Damages 564; McCormick, The Contemplation Rule as a Limitation upon Damages for Breach of Contract, 19 Minn.L.Rev. 497,

The decision to reverse was clearly based on the policy of protecting enterprises in the then burgeoning industrial revolution.[5] The court laid down two rules which still govern today. First, the aggrieved party may recover those damages "as may fairly and reasonably be considered * * * arising naturally, i.e., according to the usual course of things, from such breach of contract itself." Today, such damages are frequently referred to as general damages. Second, recovery is allowed for damages "such as may reasonably be supposed to have been in the contemplation of both parties, at the time they made the contract, as the probable result of the breach of it."[6]

A delay of several days in the shipment of a shaft does not "in the usual course of things" result in catastrophic consequences. Usually, delay in shipment of a chattel results in a loss of the value of its use for the period of delay, that is, its rental value.[7] Liability for damages in excess of that value, according to the second rule of Hadley v. Baxendale, will only be awarded if such additional damages were in the contemplation of both parties as a probable consequence of a breach. As applied in this case and subsequent cases, this means that such consequences must be foreseeable.[8] Thus, if the shipper had known that the mill was shut down because of the want of the shaft and that no substitute shaft was available, the shipper would have been liable for consequential damages consisting of the lost profits of the mill. To the extent that contracting parties are guided by legal consequences, the rule promotes economic efficiency by giving purchasers of goods and services an incentive to divulge all relevant information to sellers.[9]

509 (1935). A subsequent English case has pointed out the error of reliance on the reporter's statement insofar as it conflicts with the court's analysis of the facts. Victoria Laundry (Windsor) Ltd. v. Newman Indus., [1949] 2 K.B. 528, 537; see Danzig, supra note 2, at 262–63. In this case the court indicated that if the reporter's headnote were correct, the decision would have gone the other way. Unfortunately some cases have relied on the headnote, thereby reaching erroneous results. E.g., Moss Jellico Coal v. American Ry. Exp., 198 Ky. 202, 248 S.W. 508 (1923).

5. Danzig, supra note 2; McCormick, The Contemplation Rule as a Limitation upon Damages for Breach of Contract, 19 Minn.L.Rev. 497 (1935).

6. 156 Eng.Rep. at 151.

7. New Orleans & N.E.R. v. J.H. Miner Saw Mfg., 117 Miss. 646, 78 So. 577 (1918); Chapman v. Fargo, 223 N.Y. 32, 119 N.E. 76 (1918). If, however, the goods are shipped for the purpose of sale, the aggrieved party may recover any depreciation in the market value of the goods which may have occurred between the time the goods should have arrived and the time of their arrival. Ward v. New York Cent. R.R., 47

N.Y. 29, 7 Am.Rep. 405 (1871); The Heron II, [1967] 3 All E.R. 686 (H.L.). But cf. Great Atlantic & Pac. Tea v. Atchison, T. & S.F.Ry., 333 F.2d 705 (7th Cir.1964), cert. denied (no damages awarded where wholesale price declined but goods were resold at price originally contemplated).

8. Rs. 2d § 351. For the intimate relationship between the doctrine of foreseeability and the doctrine of avoidable consequences, see § 14.15 infra. For an argument to the effect that knowledge of the consequences of a breach acquired after contracting should also be relevant, see Samek, The Relevant Time of Foreseeability of Damage in Contract, 38 Austl.L.J. 125 (1964). Such an approach appears to have been adopted by the UCC. See § 14.22 infra. Foreseeability is an ambiguous term. For an attempt to create a trifurcated standard to encompass it, see Diamond & Foss, Consequential Damages for Commercial Loss: An Alternative to Hadley v. Baxendale, 63 Fordham L.Rev. 665 (1994) ("probability," "significant possibility" and "intermediate" standards).

9. Ayres & Gertner, Filling Gaps in Incomplete Contracts: An Economic Theory of

To a certain extent, it is fictional to speak in terms of the damages which are in the subjective contemplation of the parties. When parties enter into a contract their minds are usually fixed on performance rather than on breach.[10] When courts speak in terms of the "contemplation of the parties," they use this terminology within the framework of the objective theory of contracts. Under the first rule of Hadley v. Baxendale, certain damages will so naturally and obviously flow from the breach that every one is deemed to contemplate them. Frequently such damages are known as "general" damages. Under the second rule, less obvious kinds of damages are deemed to be contemplated if the promisor knows or has reason to know the special circumstances which will give rise to such damages. Such damages are frequently known as "special" or "consequential" damages.

A number of English cases subsequently applied a stricter rule than that announced in Hadley v. Baxendale. According to these cases, mere notice of special circumstances is an insufficient basis for imposing liability for consequential damages. These decisions required that the knowledge of special circumstances "must be brought home to the party to be charged under such circumstances that he must know that the person he contracts with reasonably believes that he accepts the contract with the special condition attached to it."[11] In other words, there must be an express or implied manifestation of intent to assume the risk of foreseeable consequential damages. This "tacit agreement" test was adopted by Justice Holmes for the U.S. Supreme Court as Federal common law,[12] but has attracted few followers among the state courts.[13] This additional qualification of the rule of Hadley v. Baxendale appears to have been abandoned in England[14] and has been repudiated by the

Default Rules, 99 Yale L.J. 87, 101–18 (1989).

10. Leonard v. New York, A. & B. Electro–Magnetic Tel., 41 N.Y. 544, 567, 1 Am. Rep. 446 (1870).

11. British Columbia Saw–Mill v. Nettleship, L.R., 3 C.P. 499, 500 (1868); accord, Horne v. Midland R.R., L.R., 7 C.P. 583 (1872), L.R., 8 C.P. 131 (1873). Judge Posner's theory is similar. According to him, this limitation on recovery "induces the party with knowledge of the risk [of special damages] either to take appropriate precautions himself or, if he believes that the other party might be the more efficient preventer or spreader (insurer) of the loss, to reveal the risk to that party and pay him to assume it. Incentives are thus created to allocate the risk in the most efficient manner." Posner, Economic Analysis of Law 127 (4th ed. 1992).

12. Globe Ref. Co. v. Landa Cotton Oil Co., 190 U.S. 540 (1903). See also Hooks Smelting v. Planters' Compress, 72 Ark.

275, 79 S.W. 1052 (1904). In diversity cases the Federal courts must apply state law in such cases. Krauss v. Greenbarg, 137 F.2d 569 (3d Cir.1943), cert. denied.

13. See McCormick, Damages 579–80. It has also been attacked by writers on contracts. 5 Corbin § 1010; 11 Williston § 1357 (3d ed.). It is supported by Bauer, Consequential Damages in Contract, 80 U.Pa. L.Rev. 687 (1931). State courts that had adopted the test, have repudiated it. AM/PM Franchise Ass'n. v. Atlantic Richfield, 526 Pa. 110, 584 A.2d 915 (1990).

14. Victoria Laundry (Windsor) v. Newman Indus., [1949] 2 K.B. 528, seems to have slightly liberalized the Hadley v. Baxendale test. Consequential damages were allowed where the defendant had "reason to know" the special circumstances although these were not communicated by the plaintiff. Accord, Appliances v. Queen Stove Works, 228 Minn. 55, 36 N.W.2d 121 (1949).

UCC[15] and the Restatement (Second).[16] The "tacit agreement" test was based on the dubious assumption that damages for breach of contract are based upon the contracting parties' implied or express promise to pay damages in the event of breach, rather than based upon a secondary duty imposed by law as a consequence of the breach.[17]

(b) Mental Distress and Personal Injury

It is well established that, as a general rule, no damages will be awarded for the mental distress or emotional trauma that may be caused by a breach of contract.[18] While some courts have reached this result because such damages are too remote to have been within the contemplation of the parties,[19] it seems apparent that the courts have forged "a rule of policy defining the limits of business risk."[20] Contrariwise, liability for personal injury may attach even in the absence of foreseeability.[21]

However, courts have made exceptions in situations where "the plaintiff's interests of personality are involved. * * * These are cases of actions for breach of contract for expulsions of guests from hotels, or passengers from trains, or expulsion or refusal of admission to ticket holders in places of public resort or entertainment."[22] Contracts for funeral arrangements are also well within this class,[23] while employment contracts are generally outside it.[24] One case has taken the exception much further. A bank's mismanagement of a construction loan, resulting in the builder putting the money in projects other than building the plaintiffs' residence was held to be a basis for such relief.[25] This takes the exception much further than most cases have been willing to go. One reason for the result may be the special trust customers place in banks.

15. UCC § 2–715 cmt 2 (unchanged in the revision). It seems no longer to be followed by Federal courts in the application of federal law. See, e.g., L.E. Whitlock Truck Serv. v. Regal Drilling, 333 F.2d 488 (10th Cir.1964), overruled on other grounds.

16. Rs. 2d § 351 cmt a, and Reporter's Notes thereto, but there are surviving bunkers. Wolfe v. First Bank, 1999 WL 318034 (Ark.App.1999); Jones v. Lee, 126 N.M. 467, 971 P.2d 858 (1998).

17. See 5 Corbin § 1010; 11 Williston § 1357 (3d ed.).

18. Rs. 2d § 353; Corbin § 1076; McCormick on Damages § 145; Williston §§ 1338, 1341 (3d ed.).

19. Redgrave v. Boston Symphony Orchestra, 855 F.2d 888 (1st Cir.1988); Erlich v. Menezes, 21 Cal.4th 543, 981 P.2d 978, 87 Cal.Rptr.2d 886 (1999) (serious construction defects in new home).

20. McCormick on Damages 593.

21. UCC § 2–715(2)(b) (unchanged by the revision).

22. McCormick, supra note 20 (footnotes omitted); but see Sagnia–Blythe v. Gamblin, 160 Misc.2d 930, 611 N.Y.S.2d 1002 (1994) (no recovery for mental anguish where defendant failed to deliver bridesmaid's dresses in timely fashion); accord Seidenbach's v. Williams, 361 P.2d 185, 88 ALR2d 1360 (Okl.1961).

23. Hirst v. Elgin Metal Casket, 438 F.Supp. 906 (D.Mont.1977); Yochim v. Mt. Hope Cemetery, 163 Misc.2d 1054, 623 N.Y.S.2d 80 (1994); Lamm v. Shingleton, 231 N.C. 10, 55 S.E.2d 810 (1949).

24. See note 19 supra and Nicholas v. Pennsylvania State Univ., 227 F.3d 133 (3d Cir.2000). In England there is a trend toward including employment contracts. See Comment, 55 Can.B.Rev. 169, 333 (1977).

25. Sexton v. St. Clair Fed. Sav. Bank, 653 So.2d 959 (Ala.1995); see Scallen, Promises Broken vs. Promises Betrayed: Metaphor, Analogy, and the New Fiduciary Principle, 1993 U.of Ill.L.Rev. 897; but see Roehm v.Charter Mobile Home Moving, 907 F.Supp. 1110 (W.D.Mich.1993).

Although the courts do not seem to be inclined to enlarge the kinds of cases in which damages for mental distress are given, the recent enlargement of the categories of cases in which punitive damages are granted may be seen as an indirect way of redressing such injuries.[26]

§ 14.6 Application in Carrier and Telegraph Cases

Hadley v. Baxendale itself was a carrier case. It indicated that a carrier will be liable for consequential damages if it is on notice of the particular purpose the cargo will serve and the fact that there is no available substitute for the cargo that is delayed, lost or injured in transit. If there were an available substitute, the aggrieved party, by virtue of the doctrine of avoidable consequences—another name for the principle of mitigation of damages—would not be able to recover those damages that could have been avoided by employment of the substitute.[1]

Applying this test, a carrier is not liable for consequential damages consisting of lost profit when it delays shipment of a motion picture film to a theater if it has no notice that the theater could not procure a substitute film.[2] Similarly a carrier was held not liable for a lost engagement that a vaudeville artist suffered because of a delay in shipment of his baggage; although the carrier knew the contents of the baggage, it did not know that the artist was engaged for a performance at the point of destination.[3]

On the other hand, if the shipment is of such a character that its purpose is obvious and the consequences of non-delivery equally obvious, the carrier will be held liable for consequential damages. Thus, when a carrier undertakes to transport scenery for a road show and knows the date of the scheduled theatrical performance, it will be liable for consequential damages suffered by the road company, as the carrier should be aware that no substitute scenery will be available.[4] In a decision, perhaps more liberal than most, a carrier was held liable for loss of a herd of hogs caused by its delay in the shipment of hog cholera serum.[5] The Court indicated that the carrier should be aware of the probable use and probable consequences of the delay although it did not know, for example, that the consignee was a farmer. A stronger case is made out when the carrier is actually told the special circumstances. Thus, if the carrier is told that an oil well drilling rig is the only one the consignor has and the consequent importance of timely delivery, it is liable for the loss of profit attributable to the lack of prompt delivery.[6] If, however, other rigs

---

26. See discussion in Zimmerman v. Michigan Hospital Service, 96 Mich.App. 464, 292 N.W.2d 236 (1980).

§ 14.6

1. See § 14.15 infra.

2. Chapman v. Fargo, 223 N.Y. 32, 119 N.E. 76 (1918).

3. Rives v. American Ry. Exp., 227 A.D. 375, 237 N.Y.S. 429 (1929).

4. Weston v. Boston & M. R.R., 190 Mass. 298, 76 N.E. 1050, 4 LRA (n.s.) 569 (1906).

5. Adams Exp.v. Allen, 125 Va. 530, 100 S.E. 473 (1919).

6. L.E. Whitlock Truck Serv. v. Regal Drilling, 333 F.2d 488 (10th Cir.1964).

were available on a short term basis on the rental market, the decision would go the other way.

Decisions involving the liability of telegraph companies are closely aligned to those involving carriers. Telegraph companies share with common carriers a duty to serve everyone on an equal basis. In addition, they both receive a relatively small compensation for services which, if not duly performed, could result in catastrophic financial losses to their clients. The courts have been highly reluctant to shift these losses to the carrier in view of the disproportion between the compensation received and the potentially large burden of damages. Thus, the courts have tended towards particular strictness in these classes of cases in applying the test of foreseeability. If a telegraph message clearly indicates the nature of the transaction, the telegraph company is liable for consequential damages flowing from negligence in failing to transmit the message or in transmitting it erroneously.[7] If the message conveys nothing to the company as to the nature of the transaction, clearly there is no liability for consequential damages.[8] Where, as is often the case, the message is obviously a business message, but the nature of the transaction is not clear, there is not a sufficient basis for recovery of consequential damages. "Notice of the business, if it is to lay the basis for special damages, must be sufficiently informing to be notice of the risk."[9]

In any modern case involving a common carrier or telegraph company, an additional factor to be considered is limitations of the carrier's liability under applicable state and federal regulatory legislation.[10] While these statutes do not overrule the contemplation of the parties test, they frequently curtail the amount of recovery by setting a maximum limit, or permit the parties to set such a limit by agreement. Despite much regulatory legislation and limits of liability provisions on bills of lading, these carrier cases are viable precedents in some circumstances.[11]

§ 14.7   Application of the Rule in Other Cases

The doctrine of foreseeability is applicable not only in carrier cases but in all contract cases. The discussion in this chapter dealing with damages in particular kinds of contract actions (§§ 14.18—14.30) will consider both general and consequential damages in such actions.

---

7. Leonard v. New York, Albany and Buffalo Electro–Magnetic Tel., 41 N.Y. 544 (1870) (message as transmitted read, "Send 5,000 casks of salt immediately," instead of "send 5,000 sacks of salt immediately."); Allen v. Western Union, 209 S.C. 157, 39 S.E.2d 257, 167 ALR 1392 (1946).

8. Primrose v. Western Union, 154 U.S. 1 (1894) (message in private code).

9. Kerr S.S. v. Radio Corp., 245 N.Y. 284, 288, 157 N.E. 140, 141, 55 ALR 1139 (1927); accord, Evra v. Swiss Bank., 673 F.2d 951 (7th Cir.1982), cert. denied (bank negligently handled telex message); Einbin-

der v. Western Union, 205 S.C. 15, 30 S.E.2d 765, 154 ALR 704 (1944).

10. Cf. UCC § 7–309 as to carriers' limitations of liability. The official comments cite to other legislation. On federal preemption of state law, see Western Union v. Priester, 276 U.S. 252 (1928); Western Union v. Abbott Supply, 45 Del. 345, 74 A.2d 77, 20 ALR2d 754 (1950).

11. E.g., W.R. Grace & Co. v. Railway Exp., 9 A.D.2d 425, 193 N.Y.S.2d 780 (1959), aff'd (carrier knew that package contained platinum).

It should be noted that the rule is not applied blindly and mechanically. Courts must be aware of the transactional context. Notions of disproportionality between the agreed price and the ensuing loss, relative fault, and the willfulness or innocence of the breach are some of the factors that guide the decisions in a concrete case.[1]

E. CERTAINTY

Table of Sections

§ 14.8   Certainty as a Limitation Upon Damages

Ordinarily, prior to rendering its verdict a jury is charged by the judge to render a decision based on the "preponderance of the evidence."[1] The jury's verdict may be set aside only if the court concludes that no reasonable person would solve the litigation in the way the jury has chosen to do.[2] Frequently, however, a different standard is applied in cases involving contract damages. The jury's verdict will be set aside if the standard of "certainty" is not met. It has been said that the damages "must be certain, both in their nature and in respect to the causes from which they proceed."[3] The certainty doctrine is, thus, in part about causation.[4] It seems to be generally recognized that absolute certainty is not required; "reasonable certainty" will suffice.[5]

Courts do not as a rule stringently impose the requirement of certainty except where the damages in issue involve lost profits on transactions other than the transaction on which the breach occurred.[6] To illustrate, if there is a contract for the delivery of sugar at 60 cents a pound and at the time the buyer learns of the breach the market price is 70 cents, the purchaser has suffered gains prevented in the amount of 10 cents per pound. The courts generally do not insist upon a standard of

§ 14.7

1. Rs. 2d § 351(3); see Stone, Recovery of Consequential Damages for Product Recall Expenditures, 1980 B.Y.U.L.Rev. 485, 528–38.

§ 14.8

1. McCormick, Evidence § 339 (4th ed. 1994).

2. Rapant v. Ogsbury, 279 A.D. 298, 109 N.Y.S.2d 737 (1952).

3. Griffin v. Colver, 16 N.Y. 489 (1858). See Farnsworth, Legal Remedies for Breach of Contract, 70 Colum.L.Rev. 1145, 1210–15 (1970).

4. Point Productions v. Sony, 215 F.Supp.2d 336 (S.D.N.Y.2002), opinion amended on reconsideration 2002 WL 3185695 (S.D.N.Y.2002) (insufficient proof that breach led to plaintiff's bankruptcy), amended.

5. Rs. 2d § 352; McCormick, Damages 401.

6. Corbin §§ 1020–1028; 3 Dobbs on Remedies § 12.4(3); Dunn, Recovery of Damages for Lost Profits (5th ed.1998); McCormick, Damages 104–106; see Todd Marine Enterprises v. Carter Mach., 898 F.Supp. 341 (E.D.Va.1995); Camino Real Mobile Home Park v. Wolfe, 119 N.M. 436, 891 P.2d 1190 (1995).

certainty in establishing this loss even though the market price may be in fact uncertain or fictitious.[7] The 10 cent rise in price represents the purchaser's general damages. The notion of certainty plays a more prominent role for special damages. That is, if the seller has reason to know that the sugar will be used by the buyer for the baking of cakes for resale and no other supply of sugar will seasonably be available to the buyer, the seller may be liable for the profits that would have been made upon resale of the cakes.[8] It is to profits such as these that the standard of certainty most frequently is applied.[9] The baker must show with certainty that he would have made profits on the sale of the cakes; not all bakery operations necessarily result in profits. Although there are cases holding that the amount of such profits must be established with certainty, the trend is clearly in the direction of holding that once the fact of lost profit is established, its amount need not be shown with precision.[10]

There is no satisfactory way of defining what is meant by "certainty" or "reasonable certainty." These terms mean, however, that the quality of the evidence must be of a higher caliber than is needed to establish most other factual issues in a lawsuit. Although the courts have been using more or less the same language for well over a century, the stringency of its application has tended to vary in different decades dependent upon the makeup and philosophy of the bench in a particular jurisdiction at a particular time.[11]

Certain circumstances help determine whether certainty in lost profits can be established. It has usually been held that lost profits caused by a breach of contract to produce a sporting event,[12] theatrical performance or other form of entertainment,[13] are too uncertain for

---

7. See § 14.12 infra. See Blaine Economic Dev. Auth. v. Royal Elec., 520 N.W.2d 473 (Minn.App.1994) (lost profits on construction contract); but see Asibem Assocs. v. Rill, 264 Md. 272, 286 A.2d 160 (1972) (certainty standard applied to property valuation); Wenzler & Ward Plumbing & Heating v. Sellen, 53 Wn.2d 96, 330 P.2d 1068 (1958) (doctrine applicable in determining the value of services).

8. See § 14.20 & 14.22 infra.

9. Compare cases where the lost profits are general damages. E.g, Ballard v. Amana Soc., 526 N.W.2d 558 (Iowa 1995).

10. Typographical Service v. Itek, 721 F.2d 1317 (11th Cir.1983); Mann v. Weyerhaeuser, 703 F.2d 272 (8th Cir.1983); A to Z Rental v. Wilson, 413 F.2d 899, 908 (10th Cir.1969); El Fredo Pizza v. Roto–Flex Oven, 199 Neb. 697, 261 N.W.2d 358 (1978).

11. Compare the liberal attitude and the relaxed standard of certainty in Wakeman v. Wheeler & Wilson Mfg., 101 N.Y. 205, 4 N.E. 264 (1886), with the stringent standard of Judge Cardozo in Broadway

Photoplay Co. v. World Film Corp., 225 N.Y. 104, 121 N.E. 756 (1919), and the return to a relaxed standard in Duane Jones Co. v. Burke, 306 N.Y. 172, 117 N.E.2d 237 (1954); Spitz v. Lesser, 302 N.Y. 490, 99 N.E.2d 540 (1951), 9 Wash. & Lee L.Rev. 75 (1952), and a shift to a rigid standard in Kenford Co. v. Erie County, 67 N.Y.2d 257, 502 N.Y.S.2d 131, 493 N.E.2d 234 (1986). See 3 Dobbs on Remedies § 12.4(3) ("hard and soft approaches").

12. CSC Holdings v. New Information Techs., 148 F.Supp.2d 755 (N.D.Tex.2001) (pay-per-view boxing); Chicago Coliseum Club v. Dempsey, 265 Ill.App. 542 (1932); Carnera v. Schmeling, 236 A.D. 460, 260 N.Y.S. 82 (1932).

13. MindGames v. Wesern Publ'g, 218 F.3d 652 (7th Cir.2000) (promotion of board game); Narragansett Amusement v. Riverside Park Amusement, 260 Mass. 265, 157 N.E. 532 (1927) Willis v. Branch, 94 N.C. 142 (1886); cf. Contemporary Mission. v. Famous Music, 557 F.2d 918 (2d Cir.1977); compare Orbach v. Paramount Pictures, 233 Mass. 281, 123 N.E. 669 (1919) with

recovery. Evidence of profits made by other performances of a similar kind or by the same performance in a different city has been deemed insufficiently probative of whether profits would have been made and, in any event, of the amount which would have been made. Similarly, new businesses have not generally been successful in establishing with certainty what their profits, if any, would have been in cases where the defendant's breach prevented or delayed their opening for business. This has been the result, despite evidence of earnings subsequent to their opening or earnings of similar businesses elsewhere.[14] It is interesting to note, however, that in actions based upon antitrust law violations, new businesses have been awarded damages based upon lost profits.[15] The difference in treatment accorded to contract actions reveals rather clearly that the standard of certainty, like the rule of foreseeability, is based at least partly upon a policy of limiting contractual risks.[16] Nonetheless, today, the new business rule is undergoing a period of relaxation.[17]

Nevertheless, established businesses are allowed to recover lost profits on transactions of a kind in which the particular business has traditionally engaged.[18] Even here, however, a verdict for the plaintiff will be set aside if the court is not convinced that the record contains the best available evidence upon which an informed verdict can be based.[19]

Broadway Photoplay v. World Film, 225 N.Y. 104, 121 N.E. 756 (1919).

14. Benham v. World Airways, 432 F.2d 359 (9th Cir.1970); Allard v. Arthur Andersen & Co., 924 F.Supp. 488 (S.D.N.Y.1996); Thrift Wholesale v. Malkin–Illion, 50 F.Supp. 998 (E.D.Pa.1943); Marvell Light & Ice v. General Elec., 162 Ark. 467, 259 S.W. 741 (1924); Evergreen Amusement v. Milstead, 206 Md. 610, 112 A.2d 901 (1955); Cramer v. Grand Rapids Show Case, 223 N.Y. 63, 119 N.E. 227, 1 ALR 154 (1918); Brenneman v. Auto–Teria, 260 Or. 513, 491 P.2d 992 (1971); Barbier v. Barry, 345 S.W.2d 557 (Tex.App.1961); Country Club Assocs. v. FDIC, 918 F.Supp. 429 (D.D.C. 1996).

15. William Goldman Theatres v. Loew's, 69 F.Supp. 103 (E.D.Pa.1946), aff'd.

16. McCormick, Damages 105; Fuller & Perdue, supra § 14.4 n.10, at 373–77. Indeed, courts have on occasion intermingled the foreseeability and certainty tests into a single doctrine. See Archer–Daniels–Midland v. Paull, 293 F.2d 389 (8th Cir.1961); Note, 48 Iowa L.Rev. 147 (1962); Witherbee v. Meyer, 155 N.Y. 446, 50 N.E. 58 (1898).

17. Humetrix v. Gemplus, 268 F.3d 910 (9th Cir.2001); Excelsior Motor Mfg. & Supply v. Sound Equip., 73 F.2d 725 (7th Cir. 1934); Lakota Girl Scout Council v. Havey Fund–Raising Mgt., 519 F.2d 634 (8th Cir. 1975); Upjohn v. Rachelle Labs., 661 F.2d 1105 (6th Cir.1981); La Societe Generale v. Minneapolis Community Dev. Agency, 827 F.Supp. 1431 (D.Minn.1993), reversed on other grounds. See Wallach, 14 UCC L.J. 236, 265–71 (1982).

18. Natural Soda Prods. v. Los Angeles, 23 Cal.2d 193, 143 P.2d 12 (1943), cert. denied. The cases which are perhaps most cited on the point today are cases involving private actions to recover treble damages under the antitrust laws. Bigelow v. RKO Radio Pictures, 327 U.S. 251 (1946), rehearing denied; Eastman Kodak v. Southern Photo Materials, 273 U.S. 359 (1927). Reliance on the relatively relaxed standard applied in these cases has had a notably liberalizing effect upon contract decisions.

A small number of decisions take the position that lost profits on resale are inherently too speculative for proof and refuse to allow any evidence on the point. See Paris v. Buckner Feed Mill, 279 Ala. 148, 182 So.2d 880 (1966).

19. Center Chem. v. Avril, Inc., 392 F.2d 289 (5th Cir.1968); Alexander's Dep't Stores v. Ohrbach's, 269 A.D. 321, 56 N.Y.S.2d 173 (1945); Allen, Heaton & McDonald v. Castle Farm Amusement, 151 Ohio St. 522, 86 N.E.2d 782, 17 ALR2d 963 (1949); McCormick, Damages 107–10. For a summary of the kind of evidence deemed acceptable, see 14 Minn.L.Rev. 820 (1930). See also Whitman's Candies v. Pet, 974 S.W.2d 519 (Mo.App.1998) (expert testimo-

There are said to be several modifying doctrines of the rule of certainty. Leading among these is the statement that "where the defendant's wrong has caused the difficulty of proof of damage, he cannot complain of the resulting uncertainty."[20] If this statement were literally true, no verdict could be set aside on the ground of uncertainty except in the case where plaintiff's counsel has failed to produce the best available evidence of the fact and amount of lost profits. Yet courts frequently rely on this supposed modifying doctrine.[21] However, it is also clear that they frequently do not.[22] It has been suggested that there is a tendency to relax the rule of certainty and to apply this modifying doctrine where the breach is willful.[23] What is clear is that there is no universal application of the rule of certainty, and that, within a given jurisdiction, case authority which applies a stringent test often exists along with other cases which, in express terms[24] or, in effect, hold that certainty is not a requirement. More commonly than is the case in other fields of contract law, the decision as to a particular set of facts cannot be predicted by the application of abstract legal rules. Official comments to the UCC indicate that in UCC-governed cases the standard of proof must be flexibly applied and certainty will not be insisted upon where the facts of the case do not permit more than an approximation.[25]

If the aggrieved party is unable to prove lost profits with sufficient certainty it does not follow that no recovery is possible. The next three sections will consider alternative measures of recovery where lost profits cannot be established with certainty.

§ 14.9   Alternative: Reliance and Restitution Interests Protected

When the aggrieved party cannot establish its expectancy interest with sufficient certainty, the party may recover expenses of preparation and of part performance, as well as other foreseeable expenses incurred in reliance upon the contract.[1] This relief is awarded on "the assumption

---

ny); Commonwealth Trust v. Hachmeister Lind, 320 Pa. 233, 181 A. 787 (1935).

20. McCormick, Damages 101; see Tagare v. NYNEX Network Sys., 921 F.Supp. 1146 (S.D.N.Y.1996).

21. Bigelow v. RKO Radio Pictures, 327 U.S. 251 (1946), rehearing denied (antitrust case); Milton v. Hudson Sales, 152 Cal. App.2d 418, 313 P.2d 936 (1957); Wakeman v. Wheeler & W. Mfg., 101 N.Y. 205, 4 N.E. 264 (1886).

22. Broadway Photoplay v. World Film, 225 N.Y. 104, 121 N.E. 756 (1919); and see the cases cited at ns.9–13 supra.

23. Perillo, Misreading Oliver Wendell Holmes on Efficient Breach and Tortious Interference, 68 Fordham L.Rev. 1085, 1099–1102 (2000); Rs. 2d § 352 cmt a.

24. Cases which have expressly stated that certainty is not a requirement include

Dominiun Mgt. Serv. v. Nationwide Housing, 195 F.3d 358 (8th Cir.1999) (Cal. law) (standard of reasonable probability); Tobin v. Union News, 18 A.D.2d 243, 239 N.Y.S.2d 22 (1963), aff'd. ("A reasonable basis for the computation of approximate result is the only requisite"). Such cases in the present state of the law should be viewed skeptically.

25. UCC §§ 1–106 cmt 1; 1–305 of the revision; 2–715 cmt 4.

§ 14.9

1. Rs. 2d § 349; Kvaerner, U.S. v. Hakim Plast, 74 F.Supp.2d 709 (E.D.Mich. 1999); Anglia Television v. Reed, 3 All E.R. 690 (C.A.1971). The restitution interest is a sub-set of the reliance interest and may be protected in a conceptually different way. Chodos v. West Pub. Co., 292 F.3d 992 (9th Cir.2002); see ch.15 infra.

that the value of the contract would at least have covered the outlay."[2] Such relief is awardable whether the lost expectancy constitutes general or consequential damages. Such damages are "compensatory" as that term is used in a statute.[3]

Thus, for example, where the defendant's breach of contract prevents the staging of a theatrical event, it is very unlikely that the plaintiff can establish with sufficient certainty the amount of profits that would have made had the performance taken place, but the plaintiff typically will be permitted to recover all expenses in preparation for performance.[4] A farmer who purchases and plants defective seed, may or may not be able to prove the value the crop would have had if the seed had been of merchantable quality.[5] If not, the farmer is permitted to recover the amount paid for the seed, the rental value of the land on which it was sown and the cost of preparing the land and sowing the seed.[6] A distributor whose franchise is wrongfully terminated may or may not be able to prove lost profits; if not, the distributor may elect to claim reliance expenditures.

Such expenditures include not only expenses incurred in part performance and in preparation for performance–sometimes this is described as "essential reliance." But also compensable are such foreseeable collateral expenses as amounts expended in advertising the manufacturer's product[7]–sometimes described as "incidental reliance."

As to consequential damages, the owner of a plant who incurs expenses by building a foundation on which to install machinery may recover these expenses if the machines are not delivered.[8] Of course, to the extent that the reliance expenditures are salvageable, no recovery will be allowed.[9] The mitigation principle is also applicable.[10]

Since the allowance of recovery for reliance expenditures is based on the assumption that the aggrieved party would at least have broken even if the contract had been performed, if it can be shown that the contract

2. McCormick, Damages 586; Holt v. United Security Life Ins. and Trust, 76 N.J.L. 585, 72 A. 301, 21 LRA NS 691 (1909).

3. Nashville Lodging v. Resolution Trust, 59 F.3d 236 (D.C.Cir.1995).

4. Chicago Coliseum Club v. Dempsey, 265 Ill.App. 542 (1932) (promoter's expenses in preparing for boxing match); Bernstein v. Meech, 130 N.Y. 354, 29 N.E. 255 (1891).

5. Farmers have often been successful in proving the value the crop would have had. E.g., C.O. Gore v. George J. Ball, 279 N.C. 192, 182 S.E.2d 389 (1971), 7 Wake Forest L.Rev. 669 (1971); Haner v. Quincy Farm Chemicals, 97 Wn.2d 753, 649 P.2d 828 (1982); but see Albin Elevator v. Pavlica, 649 P.2d 187 (Wyo.1982).

6. Crutcher & Co. v. Elliott, 13 Ky. L.Rep. 592 (1892); 5 Corbin § 1026.

7. Hardin v. Eska Co., 256 Iowa 371, 127 N.W.2d 595 (1964); accord, In re Las Colinas, 453 F.2d 911 (1st Cir.1971), cert. denied (expenditures in reliance upon a promise of financing); Sperry & Hutchinson v. O'Neill–Adams, 185 F.231 (2d Cir.1911) (advertising and other expenses in connection with promotion of product).

8. L. Albert & Son v. Armstrong Rubber, 178 F.2d 182, 17 ALR2d 1289 (2d Cir. 1949).

9. Royce Chem. v. Sharples Corp., 285 F.2d 183 (2d Cir.1960); Gruber v. S–M News, 126 F.Supp. 442 (S.D.N.Y.1954).

10. Wartzman v. Hightower Productions, 53 Md.App. 656, 456 A.2d 82 (1983), Sears Roebuck v. Grant, 49 Wn.2d 123, 298 P.2d 497 (1956).

would have been a losing proposition for that party, an appropriate deduction should be made for the loss which was not incurred. The burden of proof that a loss would have occurred is upon the wrongdoer.[11]

Not all contracting parties contemplate a direct and identifiable profit from the contract. A manufacturer may contract to have a product shipped to a convention for display in the hopes of attracting interest in its product, rather than immediate sales. If the shipper is aware of the manufacturer's purpose, it can foresee that in reliance upon the contract, the manufacturer will rent exhibition space and incur other expenses. In the event of breach such reliance expenditures are recoverable.[12]

The Restatement (Second) suggests that reliance recovery is limited to the contract price, apparently on the theory that, if reliance expenditures exceed the contract price, full performance would have resulted in a losing contract.[13] This reasoning ignores consequential expenditures that could have been recouped if the contract had fully been performed.[14]

The cases are divided on the subject of the recovery of wasted expenditures that were incurred prior to entry into the contract. To the extent that it was foreseeable that these losses would be incurred, recovery should be allowed.[15] Although these expenditures would have been incurred even if the contract had not been entered into, it is not at all clear that they would have been wasted if the contract had not been made. Such recovery would be a surrogate for opportunities forgone in reliance on the contract.[16] Alternatively, one could characterize such recovery as a portion of an expectation measure. Assume zero profits and apply a standard expectation measure of recovery. This measure would include pre-contract expenses and a share of overhead.[17]

§ 14.10   Alternative: Value of a Chance or Opportunity

In Chaplin v. Hicks[1] the plaintiff was one of fifty semifinalists in a beauty contest in which twelve finalists would receive prizes. The defendant, promoter of the contest, breached the contract by failing

11. On the burden of proof of non-salvageability, see L. Albert & Son v. Armstrong Rubber, 178 F.2d 182, 17 ALR2d 1289 (2d Cir.1949); Matter of Yeager, 227 F.Supp. 92 (N.D.Ohio 1963); Brenneman v. Auto–Teria, 260 Or. 513, 491 P.2d 992 (1971); Rs. 2d § 349 cmt a; see 5 Corbin § 1033.

12. Security Stove & Mfg. v. American Ry. Exp., 227 Mo.App. 175, 51 S.W.2d 572 (1932).

13. Rs. 2d § 349 cmt a.

14. See, e.g., Security Stove & Mfg. v. American Ry. Exp., 227 Mo.App. 175, 51 S.W.2d 572 (1932) ($1000 reliance damages; contract price $147); Anglia Televisions v. Reed, 3 All E.R. 690 (C.A.1971) (£2,750 reliance damages; contract price £1,050);

see also Hudec, Restating the Reliance Interest, 67 Cornell L.Rev. 704 (1982).

15. Glendale Fed. Bank v. U.S., 239 F.3d 1374 (Fed.Cir.2001); contra, Drysdale v. Woerth, 153 F.Supp.2d 678 (E.D.Pa. 2001).

16. See Crespi, Recovering Pre-contractual Expenditures, 49 SMU L.Rev. 43 (1995).

17. See Kelly, The Phantom Reliance Interest in Contract Damages, 1992 Wis. L.Rev. 1775.

§ 14.10

1. [1911] 2 K.B. 786. For its present status in England, see Reece, 59 Modern L.Rev. 188 (1996).

properly to notify the plaintiff of the time and place of the competition. The jury assessed the damages at £100, about one quarter of the value of the lowest prize. The judgment entered upon the jury's verdict was affirmed on appeal. It is obvious that not only was the amount of damages uncertain, but also the fact of damage. The court, nonetheless, indicated that the chance of winning had value which could be assessed by the law of averages. The Restatement has accepted the rationale of this decision but only under circumscribed conditions. In general, the Restatement allows recovery for the value of a chance only if the promised performance is aleatory; that is, conditioned upon an event that is not within the control of the parties.[2] As such, its primary fields of applicability are in the cases of contests[3] and in cases of wrongful cancellation of insurance contracts by the insurer.[4] It has also been applied in some cases to contracts to drill exploratory oil or gas wells.[5]

One may well question the wisdom of the limitation imposed upon the doctrine by the Restatement. If damages based upon a theory of probability is a sound approach to aleatory contracts, why is it unsound as to other contracts?[6] For example, if a manufacturer wrongfully terminates a distributorship, it will frequently be impossible to prove that the distributorship would have made a profit and the amount, if any, of such profits. Aside from the possibility of electing to claim merely reliance damages, the distributor in such a case faces an all or nothing prospect: full recovery for the profits that would have been made or merely nominal damages. If, as an alternative, the distributor were permitted to recover the value of the lost opportunity to strive for the profit, the hazards and possible injustice of the all or nothing approach would be reduced. Recovery would be allowed on the basis of the price that a reasonable person would pay for the opportunity.[7] Despite authority for such an approach in an excellently reasoned old American case,[8]

2. Rs. 1st § 332; Rs. 2d § 348(3).

3. The value of a chance in contest cases has been granted in Mange v. Unicorn Press, 129 F.Supp. 727 (S.D.N.Y.1955); Wachtel v. National Alfalfa Journal, 190 Iowa 1293, 176 N.W. 801 (1920); Kansas City, M. & O. Ry. v. Bell, 197 S.W. 322 (Tex.App.1917); contra, Phillips v. Pantages Theatre, 163 Wn. 303, 300 P. 1048 (1931); Collatz v. Fox Wis. Amusement, 239 Wis. 156, 300 N.W. 162 (1941).

4. Caminetti v. Manierre, 23 Cal.2d 94, 142 P.2d 741 (1943); Commissioner of Ins. v. Massachusetts Acc., 314 Mass. 558, 50 N.E.2d 801 (1943); People v. Empire Mut. Life Ins., 92 N.Y. 105 (1883).

5. Because of the speculative nature of exploratory drilling, a wide variety of approaches have been taken toward the assessment of damages. See Ballem, Some Second Thoughts on Damages for Breach of a Drilling Commitment, 48 Can.B.Rev. 698 (1970); Scott, Measure of Damages for Breach of a Covenant to Drill a Test Well

for Oil and Gas, 9 U.Kan.L.Rev. 281 (1961); 5 Corbin § 1093.

6. See Eisenberg, Probability and Chance in Contract Law, 45 UCLA L.Rev. 1005 (1998); Schaefer, Uncertainty and the Law of Damages, 19 Wm. & Mary L.Rev. 719 (1978); Comment, 18 Rutgers L.Rev. 875 (1964).

7. See Kessler, Automobile Dealer Franchises: Vertical Integration by Contract, 66 Yale L.J. 1135, 1188–89 (1957); Comment, 74 Yale L.J. 354 (1964); Annot., 54 ALR3d 324 (1973).

8. Taylor v. Bradley, 39 N.Y. 129, 144, 100 Am.Dec. 415 (1868) where the court said: " * * * he is deprived of his adventure; what was this opportunity which the contract had apparently secured to him worth?" See also Mechanical Wholesale v. Universal–Rundle, 432 F.2d 228 (5th Cir. 1970); Locke v. U.S., 283 F.2d 521 (Ct.Cl. 1960); Air Technology v. General Elec., 347 Mass. 613, 199 N.E.2d 538 (1964).

counsel in this country seem seldom to have made this argument,[9] although this approach is now well accepted in England.[10] Interestingly, it has been applied in a negligence case in which the plaintiff suffered slight permanent damage of her voice which deprived her of the opportunity of commencing a career as an opera singer, a field of endeavor in which the chances of success are speculative and remote.[11]

§ 14.11   Alternative: Rental Value of Property

If the evidence in Hadley v. Baxendale had established that the defendants had sufficient notice to be able to foresee the prolonged shutdown of the mill as a consequence of their breach, plaintiff might have been unable to establish the fact and amount of loss with sufficient certainty. The plaintiff would, however, be able to obtain recovery under an alternative theory, which is based on ample authority,[1] and formulated in the Restatement in the following language: "[i]f the breach is one that prevents the use and operation of property from which profits would have been made, damages may be measured by the rental value of the property or by interest on the value of the property."[2]

F.   THE CONCEPT OF VALUE

Table of Sections

§ 14.12   Market Value as the Usual Standard

One of the most pervasive concepts of law is that of "value." In practically every tort and contract case in which damages are to be assessed there is some reference to value. The concept also is widely used

---

9. The argument is, however, persuasively put forth in McCormick, Damages 117–23.

10. Hall v. Meyrick, [1957] 2 Q.B. 455, rev'd on other grounds; Domine v. Grimsdall, [1937] 2 All E.R. 119 (K.B.); Treitel, The Law of Contract 861–62 (9th ed.1995).

11. Grayson v. Irvmar Realty, 7 A.D.2d 436, 184 N.Y.S.2d 33 (1959); see also Delaney v. Cade, 255 Kan. 199, 873 P.2d 175 (1994) (medical malpractice, loss of chance of recovery). It was rejected in a medical malpractice case. Kramer v. Lewisville Mem. Hosp., 858 S.W.2d 397 (Tex.1993).

§ 14.11

1. New York & Colorado Mining Syndicate v. Fraser, 130 U.S. 611 (1889) (defective machinery rendered silver mill inoperative; rental value of mill calculated at the rate of legal interest on the cost of the mill in absence of other competent testimony of rental value); Witherbee v. Meyer, 155 N.Y. 446, 50 N.E. 58 (1898) (failure to provide sufficient waterpower to a mill; damages awarded for diminution in rental value); Dixon–Woods v. Phillips Glass, 169 Pa. 167, 32 A. 432 (1895) (defective furnace installed; damages awarded for rental value of glass factory); Livermore Foundry & Mach. v. Union Storage & Compress, 105 Tenn. 187, 58 S.W. 270, 53 LRA 482 (1900) (rental value of compressing plant for entire season); see 5 Corbin § 1029; but cf. Natural Soda Prod. v. Los Angeles, 23 Cal.2d 193, 143 P.2d 12 (1943), cert. and rehearing denied.

2. Rs. 1st § 331(2); Rs. 2d § 348(1). Hadley v. Baxendale is discussed in § 14.5 supra.

in cases of condemnation, taxation, quasi contract, administrative rate making, and even in criminal law.

By and large in contract cases, the standard of valuation considered is market value in contradistinction to any peculiar value the object in question may have had to the owner.[1] This standard offers no particular problems as to goods and securities that are actively traded upon stock and commodity exchanges. As to these there is in the literal sense a market place and a market price.[2] However when the standard is applied to other objects, such as commodities and shares of stock that are not actively traded, land, unique chattels, and professional services, the determination of a market value is somewhat fictional. What is actually sought is the sum of money that a willing buyer would pay to a willing seller,[3] although some courts refuse to engage in the use of the fiction and speak of "real" value where there is no market.[4] When market value does not compensate fully for the peculiar use of the property by the owner, "value to the owner" is used as a standard.[5] At times the courts reject any single standard.[6] Whatever standard is chosen, the main issues that arise in making the factual determination of value involve the kind of evidence that may be admitted.

§ 14.13 Proof of Value

Publications reporting the price of goods regularly bought and sold in any established commodity market are admissible as evidence of value.[1] If goods of the kind in issue have not been traded at the relevant time or place, evidence is admissible of prices prevailing at any reasonable times prior or subsequent to the relevant time and at any place which could reasonably serve as a substitute, with due allowance for transportation costs to or from that place.[2]

Other relevant evidence includes expert opinions,[3] original cost less

§ 14.12

1. See McCormick, Damages § 44.

2. But even as to shares of stock listed on stock exchanges, the current price is not necessarily the value if special circumstances exist. Seas Shipping v. C.I.R., 371 F.2d 528 (2d Cir.1967), cert. denied (large block of shares in a corporation whose shares were inactively traded); Kahle v. Mt. Vernon Trust, 22 N.Y.S.2d 454 (1940).

3. Standard Oil v. Southern Pac., 268 U.S. 146 (1925); Heiman v. Bishop, 272 N.Y. 83, 4 N.E.2d 944 (1936) rearg. denied; Allen v. Chicago & N.W. Ry., 145 Wis. 263, 129 N.W. 1094 (1911).

4. See Airight Sales v. Graves Truck Lines, 207 Kan. 753, 486 P.2d 835 (1971).

5. See Alfred Atmore Pope Foundation v. New York, N.H. & H. Ry., 106 Conn. 423, 138 A. 444 (1927) (negligence action; forest attached to forestry school was destroyed by fire).

6. Court View Centre v. Witt, 753 N.E.2d 75 (Ind.App.2001) ("broad evidence rule"); see McAnarney v. Newark Fire Ins., 247 N.Y. 176, 159 N.E. 902, 56 ALR 1149 (1928) (fire insurance on a brewery rendered obsolete by national prohibition).

§ 14.13

1. UCC § 2–724 (revision would include other media).

2. UCC § 2–723 (revision does not change this rule).

3. Standard Oil v. Southern Pac., 268 U.S. 146 (1925). This is said to be the most common sort of evidence of value. McCormick, Damages 175. It is sometime held that an owner is an expert in the evaluation of his or her own property. Pocatello Auto Color v. Akzo Coatings, 127 Idaho 41, 896 P.2d 949 (1995).

depreciation,[4] reproduction cost less an allowance for depreciation,[5] and sales of comparable personalty or realty.[6] Also admissible is the sale price of the property if it was resold to another soon after the breach.[7] Offers to purchase the property are inadmissible, however, on the grounds that the fabrication of such evidence would be too easy.[8] In contrast, offers to sell the property may be introduced in evidence but only as evidence against the offeror.[9] Because tax assessments of real property are notoriously unreliable as indicia of value, the overwhelming weight of authority is to the effect that such evidence is inadmissible.[10] However, the owner's statements to the tax assessing authorities are admissible against the owner, as admissions.[11]

§ 14.14   Value a Variable Concept

It is obvious that property may have more than one market value. There is a wholesale and a retail market for most products. The appropriate market is the one in which the aggrieved party may obtain replacement of the property. Thus, while the retail market is normally the appropriate standard for the consumer, the wholesale market sets the standard for the dealer.[1] Similarly, a given object can have different market values dependent upon its use.[2] A cow may be used for beef

4. Standard Oil v. Southern Pac., 268 U.S. 146 (1925) (ship); Thornton v. Birmingham, 250 Ala. 651, 35 So.2d 545, 7 ALR2d 773 (1948) (price paid for land two years previously). Original cost of goods some years prior to the wrong, standing alone, is not sufficient evidence of value. Some evidence as to depreciation must also be introduced. Rauch v. Wander, 122 Misc. 650, 203 N.Y.S. 553 (1924), as well as evidence of changes in market values, Watson v. Loughran, 112 Ga. 837, 38 S.E. 82 (1901).

5. Standard Oil v. Southern Pac., 268 U.S. 146 (1925); Alabama G. S. R.R. v. Johnston, 128 Ala. 283, 29 So. 771 (1901); Missouri Pac. R.R. v. Fowler, 183 Ark. 86, 34 S.W.2d 1071 (1931).

6. Redfield v. Iowa State Highway Comm'n, 251 Iowa 332, 99 N.W.2d 413, 85 ALR2d 96 (1959); Amory v. Commonwealth, 321 Mass. 240, 72 N.E.2d 549, 174 ALR 370 (1947); Lawrence v. Greenwood, 300 N.Y. 231, 90 N.E.2d 53 (1949). In a substantial minority of jurisdictions, however, such evidence is not admissible as to real property and unique chattels. Walnut Street Fed. S. & L. Ass'n v. Bernstein, 394 Pa. 353, 147 A.2d 359 (1959).

7. Louis Steinbaum Real Estate v. Maltz, 247 S.W.2d 652, 31 ALR2d 1052 (Mo.1952) (fraud case); Williams v. Ubaldo, 670 A.2d 913 (Me.1996); Triangle Waist v. Todd, 223 N.Y. 27, 119 N.E. 85 (1918)

(breach by employee; salary paid by new employer evidence of value of employee's services).

8. Sharp v. U.S., 191 U.S. 341 (1903); Thornton v. Birmingham, 250 Ala. 651, 35 So.2d 545, 7 ALR2d 773 (1948); Fort Worth v. Beaupre, 617 S.W.2d 828, 25 ALR4th 562 (Tex.App.1981), writ ref. n.r.e.

9. Kalb v. International Resorts, 396 So.2d 199, 25 ALR4th 977 (Fla.App.1981), review denied; Cotton v. Boston Elevated Ry., 191 Mass. 103, 77 N.E. 698 (1906) (owner's listing price); McAnarney v. Newark Fire Ins., 247 N.Y. 176, 159 N.E. 902, 56 ALR 1149 (1928).

10. Commonwealth v. Gilbert, 253 S.W.2d 264, 39 ALR2d 205 (Ky.1952).

11. San Diego Land & Town v. Jasper, 189 U.S. 439 (1903).

§ 14.14

1. Ocean Elec. Co. v. Hughes Lab., 636 So.2d 112 (Fla.App.1994); Illinois Cent. R.R. v. Crail, 281 U.S. 57 (1930); Wehle v. Haviland, 69 N.Y. 448 (1877).

2. "A loblolly pine tree at sixty years that would produce a fifty-foot piling would be worth fifty dollars peeled and loaded on a truck, for saw timber it would be worth $4.80." Shirley and Graves, Forest Ownership for Pleasure and Profit 32 (1967); cf. Spink v. New York, N.H. & H.R., 26 R.I. 115, 58 A. 499 (1904) (standing timber de-

production, milk production or primarily for breeding. The aggrieved party is entitled to an evaluation based upon the most profitable use to which that party reasonably could have put the object.[3]

G. AVOIDABLE CONSEQUENCES

Table of Sections

§ 14.15 The "Duty" to Mitigate Damages

Although liability for breach of contract is primarily based on a no-fault principle, the rules for damages are more judgmental, especially in connection with the mitigation principle.[1] As an almost inflexible proposition, a party who has been wronged by a breach of contract may not unreasonably sit idly by and allow damages to accumulate. Such damages are not proximately caused by the breach.[2] The law does not permit the wronged party to recover those damages that "could have [been] avoided without undue risk, burden, or humiliation."[3]

This absence of a right of recovery for enhanced damages, often improperly called a "duty to mitigate,"[4] is at the root of many of the rules of the law of damages. Thus, for example, the rule of Hadley v. Baxendale[5] becomes clearer when viewed in terms of the mitigation principle. Under that decision the defendants would have been liable for the lost profits of the mill if they had had reason to know that no substitute shaft was available. In other words, liability for consequential damages stems from reason to know that the plaintiff will be unable to mitigate damages. The mitigation principle (also known as the doctrine of avoidable consequences) is also an unspoken premise in most rules of general damages. Thus, the rule in sales contracts that damages for breach by the seller are measured by the difference between the market price and the contract price is based on the idea that in the event of breach the plaintiff can minimize damages by purchasing similar goods

stroyed in fire may be valued on the basis of prices for poles and piles rather than cordwood).

3. Campbell v. Iowa Central Ry., 124 Iowa 248, 99 N.W. 1061 (1904) (brood mare); Southwestern Tel. & Tel. v. Krause, 92 S.W. 431 (Tex.App.1906) (milk cows not valued on basis of value of beef cattle).

§ 14.15

1. See Cohen, The Fault Lines in Contract Damages, 80 Va. L.Rev. 1225 (1994).

2. S. J. Groves & Sons v. Warner Co., 576 F.2d 524 (3d Cir.1978).

3. Rs. 2d § 350; see Goetz & Scott, The Mitigation Principle, 69 Va.L.Rev. 967 (1983).

4. McClelland v. Climax Hosiery Mills, 252 N.Y. 347, 358–59, 169 N.E. 605, 609 (1930) (Cardozo, C.J., concurring). Others, using Hohfeld's terminology have referred to a "disability" to recover damages which could have been avoided, rather than the more accurate "no right" to recover. Rock v. Vandine, 106 Kan. 588, 189 P. 157 (1920); Comment, 32 Yale L.J. 380 (1923); 28 Yale L.J. 827 (1920); cf. 5 Corbin § 1039.

5. See § 14.5 supra.

on the open market. Breach of an obligation to register stock is measured by the difference between the highest intermediate price of shares during a reasonable time at beginning of the restricted period and average market price of shares during a reasonable period after restrictions were lifted.

In addition to its role as an implied premise in many other rules and doctrines, the doctrine of avoidable consequences serves as an independent basis for decision. Thus, where an experienced farmer is supplied patently defective seed, the farmer will not be permitted to enhance damages by planting the seed and losing a crop.[6] Similarly, the doctrine is employed in every manner of contract including contracts of employment,[7] sale,[8] construction,[9] and in the U.S., even in cases of breach by anticipatory repudiation.[10] One rare exception exists where continuation of performance cuts down damages. There, the aggrieved party may continue without jeopardizing recovery.[11]

The doctrine of avoidable consequences merely requires reasonable efforts to mitigate damages. Thus, the efforts need not be successful.[12] Many rules address reasonableness. The wronged party need not act if the cost of avoidance would involve unreasonable expense.[13] One need not commit a wrong, as by breaching other contracts, in order to minimize damages,[14] nor need one jeopardize one's credit rating.[15] Where the breaching party gives assurances that performance, though late, will be forthcoming, the wronged party need not take action to minimize damages.[16] The burden is on the breaching party to prove that the aggrieved party failed to mitigate.[17]

One troublesome issue has vexed and divided the courts. Must the aggrieved party accede to a wrongful demand by the wrongdoer if accession would minimize damages? The problem is illustrated in its extreme form in a case where a water company agreed to supply water for a year for $58 payable at the end of the year. The company then unjustifiably asked for installment payments during the year instead of

---

6. Wavra v. Karr, 142 Minn. 248, 172 N.W. 118 (1919).

7. See §§ 14.18 to 14.19 infra.

8. Quality Truck Equip. v. Layman, 51 Ark.App. 195, 912 S.W.2d 18 (1995); see §§ 14.20 to 14.27 infra.

9. See §§ 14.28 to 14.29 infra.

10. See §§ 14.20 & 14.23 infra; § 12.8 supra.

11. F. Enterprises v. Kentucky Fried Chicken, 47 Ohio St.2d 154, 351 N.E.2d 121 (1976); see also § 14.27 infra.

12. Ninth Ave. & Forty–Second St. v. Zimmerman, 217 A.D. 498, 217 N.Y.S. 123 (1926) (unsuccessful suit against third party to clear title); Rs. 2d § 350(2).

13. Taylor v. Steadman, 143 Ark. 486, 220 S.W. 821 (1920); Chambers v. Belmore

Land & Water, 33 Cal.App. 78, 164 P. 404 (1917); 5 Corbin § 1041.

14. Leonard v. New York, Albany and Buffalo Electro–Magnetic Tel., 41 N.Y. 544 (1870); McCormick, Damages, 141; contra, Western Union v. Southwick, 214 S.W. 987 (Tex.App.1919), 33 Harv.L.Rev. 728 (1920), reversed on other grounds.

15. Audiger, Inc. v. Hamilton, 381 F.2d 24 (5th Cir.1967).

16. S.J. Groves & Sons v. Warner Co., 576 F.2d 524 (3d Cir.1978). There is no need to mitigate until there is an actual breach. Carolyn B. Beasley Cotton v. Ralph, 59 S.W.3d 110 (Tenn.App.2000).

17. Webster v. Edward D. Jones & Co., 197 F.3d 815 (6th Cir.1999); Ballard v. El Dorado Tire, 512 F.2d 901 (5th Cir.1975).

payment at the end of the year. The plaintiff, an owner of an irrigated vineyard, refused to accede to this change of company policy. As a consequence, defendant shut off the water and the plaintiff lost his crop. The court ruled that the trivial extra cost (interest on the advance payments) amounting to less than $2, viewed in relation to the large amount of injury foreseeably ensuing, was such that the plaintiff should have acceded to the unjustified demand.[18] But this approach involves only one of three views. On similar facts other courts have disagreed with this court,[19] while still others have let the jury decide whether the plaintiff's refusal was reasonable.[20]

Note, however, the above discussion concerned relatively trivial demands. Where the demand is not trivial in relation to the ensuing damages, most courts have ruled that the plaintiff need not comply with the wrongdoer's demand even if it would have the effect of minimizing damages.[21]

Frequently, the aggrieved party accedes to the demands of the other, because any other course of action would result in a major disruption of business or personal affairs. When this happens, a court may hold that the aggrieved party is without remedy because the accession is a substituted agreement discharging the prior contract.[22] Under the UCC, this result may be avoided by surrendering to the demand while indicating that accession is under protest.[23] If this is not done but the elements of duress[24] or bad faith[25] are present, it may be possible for the aggrieved party to set aside the discharge of rights under the earlier contract.

A traditional exception to the mitigation requirement exists as to leases of real property. Under the orthodox view, upon the tenant's abandonment of the premises, the landlord may elect to terminate the tenancy and sue for damages, or to continue the tenancy. If the landlord elects to continue the tenancy, the landlord may sue for the agreed rent although no effort to mitigate by securing a substitute tenant is made.

---

18. Severini v. Sutter–Butte Canal, 59 Cal.App. 154, 210 P. 49 (1922). The decision was distinguished in a subsequent case involving similar facts except that the water's unjustified demand was in the amount of about $100. The court deemed this to be a substantial rather than trivial demand. Schultz v. Lakeport, 5 Cal.2d 377, 54 P.2d 1110, 108 ALR 1168 (1936).

19. Southwestern Gas & Elec. v. Stanley, 45 S.W.2d 671 (Tex.App.1931), aff'd.

20. Key v. Kingwood Oil, 110 Okl. 178, 236 P. 598 (1924).

21. Coppola v. Marden, Orth & Hastings, 282 Ill. 281, 118 N.E. 499 (1917); Schatz Distributing v. Olivetti, 7 Kan. App.2d 676, 647 P.2d 820 (1982); Seeley v. Peabody, 139 Wn. 382, 247 P. 471 (1926), aff'd; 5 Corbin § 1043; McCormick, Damages § 39. Thus, an employee whose employment is pursuant to an employment contract need not mitigate damages by accepting an offer from his employer for employment in a different position or on other different terms. Billetter v. Posell, 94 Cal. App.2d 858, 211 P.2d 621 (1949); see § 14.18 infra.

22. Stanspec v. Jelco, 464 F.2d 1184 (10th Cir.1972); see Comment, 19 N.C.L.Rev. 59 (1940). Compare the sound result in Dreyfuss v. Board of Ed., 76 Misc.2d 479, 350 N.Y.S.2d 590 (1973), aff'd (no discharge by accepting substitute position).

23. UCC § 1–207; § 1–308 (revision).

24. Austin Instrument v. Loral Corp., 29 N.Y.2d 124, 324 N.Y.S.2d 22, 272 N.E.2d 533 (1971), rearg. denied; see § 9.6 supra.

25. Roth Steel Prods. v. Sharon Steel, 705 F.2d 134 (6th Cir.1983).

This result is based on the property concept that the landlord has conveyed a leasehold to the tenant, thereby performing the agreed exchange.[26] A strong contrary trend is growing.[27]

§ 14.16　Non-exclusive Contracts—An Apparent Exception to the Doctrine of Avoidable Consequences

A full-time employee owes a duty to devote the assigned working hours to the employer's business. If the employee is wrongfully discharged, damages are reduced by any earnings from employment the employee secures or could secure with reasonable diligence during the contract period.[1] If it were not for the breach, such employment ordinarily could not lawfully be obtained because of the full-time nature of the work.

In contrast, if the relation between the parties is such that the wronged party was legally free to enter into similar contracts with others, that subsequent to the breach the wronged party could have or actually has made similar contracts, in no way reduces the entitlement to damages.[2] Thus, for example, if the lessee of automobiles from a car rental breaches the lease, damages will not be reduced by the fact that the lessor leases, or could have leased, the automobiles to another.[3] The lessor was free to obtain as many customers as it was willing and able to secure, provided that as a practical matter it could secure additional automobiles for such customers. On the other hand, if the lease is of a unique chattel such as an ocean-going freighter, the lessor's damages will be reduced by any amount earned or earnable by chartering the ship to another, each ship being regarded as unique.[4] Similar considerations exist where a purchaser breaches a contract for sale.[5] Construction contracts are non-exclusive and a construction contractor's damages are not normally reduced by any earnings attributable to contracts made subsequent to the breach.[6] Similarly, a publisher's damages resulting

26. Enoch C. Richards Co. v. Libby, 136 Me. 376, 10 A.2d 609, 126 ALR 1215 (1940); Holy Properties Ltd. v. Kenneth Cole Productions, 87 N.Y.2d 130, 661 N.E.2d 694, 637 N.Y.S.2d 964 (1995); Comment, 55 Ark. L.Rev. 123 (2002).

27. Sommer v. Kridel, 74 N.J. 446, 378 A.2d 767 (1977); Austin Hill Country Realty v. Palisades Plaza, 948 S.W.2d 293, 75 ALR5th 647 (Tex.1997).

§ 14.16

1. See § 14.18 infra.

2. But where a consultant spent almost full time consulting with the defendant, it was held proper to reduce his claimed damages by amounts earned in a similar role after the breach. Obelisk v. Riggs Nat. Bank, 668 A.2d 847 (D.C.App.1995).

3. Gianetti v. Norwalk Hosp., 64 Conn. App. 218, 779 A.2d 847 (2001), certification granted in part. (surgeon); Jetz Service v. Salina Properties, 19 Kan.App.2d 144, 865 P.2d 1051 (1993) (coin-operated laundry equipment), noted 34 Washburn L.J. 136 (1994); Mount Pleasant Stable v. Steinberg, 238 Mass. 567, 131 N.E. 295, 15 ALR 749 (1921) (teams of horses and wagons); Locks v. Wade, 36 N.J.Super. 128, 114 A.2d 875 (1955) (juke box).

4. Liberty Navigation & Trading v. Kinoshita & Co., 285 F.2d 343 (2d Cir.1960), cert. denied.

5. See generally §§ 14.23 to 14.27 infra.

6. Koplin v. Faulkner, 293 S.W.2d 467 (Ky.1956); M. & R. Contractors and Builders v. Michael, 215 Md. 340, 138 A.2d 350 (1958); Olds v. Mapes–Reeves Constr., 177

from breach of an advertising contract are not to be reduced under the doctrine of avoidable consequences,[7] unless the publication has limited space for advertising, in which case it would be incumbent upon the publisher to attempt to secure additional advertisers to fill the space vacated as a result of the breach.[8]

§ 14.17 Recovery of Expenses Sustained in Avoiding Consequences of a Breach

The doctrine of avoidable consequences is a two-edged sword. That it may reduce the aggrieved party's damages has been considered in the preceding discussion. But the doctrine may also act to provide recovery for certain kinds of expenses not otherwise recoverable. This aspect of the doctrine is strikingly illustrated by a leading tort case.[1] The plaintiff, a steamship flying the neutral flag of Norway during World War I, was accused by the defendant newspaper publisher of carrying on illegal activities for the benefit of the German war effort. In order to protect its reputation, the steamship placed paid advertisements in other newspapers refuting the defendant's libel. The court held that the plaintiff could recover these expenses as a reasonable effort, whether or not successful, to mitigate damages.

The same principle finds wide application in cases involving breach of contract,[2] and is implicitly recognized by the UCC in its provisions regarding "cover"[3] and "incidental" damages.[4] A common law example is the holding that the cost of procuring a substitute outlet for water is recoverable where the defendant breached its contract to allow the use of its ditch.[5] Such reasonable expenditures are recoverable even if hindsight

---

Mass. 41, 58 N.E. 478 (1900). In a celebrated case the court seems inappropriately to have applied the general rule. The plaintiff contracted with X corporation to install certain apparatus in X's plant. X, because of insolvency, repudiated the contract. X's receivers sold the plant to Y corporation. Y contracted with the plaintiff to make the same installation. This contract was performed. Nevertheless, on the ground that it was not a contract for personal services, plaintiff was permitted to recover damages against X's receivers for breach of the first contract without a deduction for the profit made on the second contract despite the fact that but for the breach of the first contract plaintiff could not have entered into the second. Grinnell Co. v. Voorhees, 1 F.2d 693 (3d Cir.1924), 34 Yale L.J. 553 (1925); accord, Olds v. Mapes–Reeves Constr., 177 Mass. 41, 58 N.E. 478 (1900); contra, Canton–Hughes Pump v. Llera, 205 F. 209 (6th Cir.1913); cf. Kunkle v. Jaffe, 71 N.E.2d 298 (Ohio App.1946).

7. Western Grain v. Barron G. Collier, 163 Ark. 369, 258 S.W. 979, 35 ALR 1534 (1924); Western Adv. v. Midwest Laundries, 61 S.W.2d 251 (Mo.App.1933); J.K. Rishel

Furn. v. Stuyvesant Co., 123 Misc. 208, 204 N.Y.S. 659 (1924).

8. Barron G. Collier v. Women's Garment Store, 152 Minn. 475, 189 N.W. 403 (1922).

§ 14.17

1. Den Norske Ameriekalinje Actiesselskabet v. Sun Printing & Publishing Ass'n, 226 N.Y. 1, 122 N.E. 463 (1919); accord, Rs. 2d § 347 cmt c; see 5 Corbin § 1044; McCormick, Damages § 42.

2. See, e.g., Audiger v. Hamilton, 381 F.2d 24 (5th Cir.1967).

3. See § 14.20 infra.

4. See §§ 14.22, 14.25 infra.

5. Hoehne Ditch v. John Flood Ditch, 76 Colo. 500, 233 P. 167 (1925); Spang Indus. v. Aetna Cas. and Sur., 512 F.2d 365 (2d Cir.1975) (overtime labor and other expenses in crash program to pour concrete before freezing weather where supplier delayed delivery of steel); Apex Mining v. Chicago Copper & Chem., 306 F.2d 725 (8th Cir.1962) (defendant failed to deliver ore;

shows that the expenditure exceeds the decrease in damages.[6] Thus, in one case a city, as part of a renewal project, sold land to a restaurateur, promising that the rest of the land would be developed with residential and commercial improvements. However, the voters, in a referendum, forced the city to develop the land as a park. The restaurant tried to make a go of it, but there was no customer base in the vicinity. Among the permissible items of recovery was about $200,000 of "expenses incurred by the plaintiff after the breach in an [unsuccessful] attempt to keep the restaurant afloat."[7]

H.   DAMAGES IN PARTICULAR ACTIONS

Table of Sections

§ 14.18   Wrongful Discharge of Employee

When an employee is wrongfully discharged, the employee is entitled to the salary[1] that would have been payable during the remainder of the term reduced by the income which the employee has earned, will earn, or could with reasonable diligence earn during the unexpired term.[2] This

---

plaintiff purchased jaw crusher to process substitute ore of a different type); see also Northwestern Steam Boiler & Mfg. v. Great Lakes Eng. Works, 181 F.38 (8th Cir.1910).

6. Apex Mining v. Chicago Copper & Chem., 306 F.2d 725 (8th Cir.1962); Hogland v. Klein, 49 Wn.2d 216, 298 P.2d 1099 (1956).

7. West Haven Sound Dev. v. West Haven, 201 Conn. 305, 514 A.2d 734, 743 (1986).

§ 14.18

1. The problem of the valuation of fringe benefits as an element of salary has yet to be explored thoroughly by the courts. See McAleer v. McNally Pittsburg Mfg., 329

F.2d 273 (3d Cir.1964) (no recovery for loss of group life insurance protection); Wyatt v. School Dist., 148 Mont. 83, 417 P.2d 221, 22 ALR3d 1039 (1966) (value of teacher's rent-free quarters); Knox v. Microsoft, 92 Wn. App. 204, 962 P.2d 839 (1998) (stock options).

2. Sutherland v. Wyer, 67 Me. 64 (1877); Hollwedel v. Duffy–Mott Co., 263 N.Y. 95, 188 N.E. 266, 90 ALR 1312 (1933); Godson v. MacFadden, 162 Tenn. 528, 39 S.W.2d 287 (1931); Galveston H. & S.A. Ry. v. Eubanks, 42 S.W.2d 475 (Tex.App.1931), aff'd. If the unexpired term is of lengthy duration, the recovery is to be discounted at a reasonable rate of interest inasmuch as the plaintiff will recover well in advance of

rule takes into consideration the employee's burden of mitigation. In carrying out this burden, however, the employee need not seek or accept a position of lesser rank,[3] or at a reduced salary,[4] or at a location unreasonably distant from the former place of employment,[5] or a position necessitating a residence apart from the employee's spouse.[6] It has been held that an employee must accept an unconditional offer of reinstatement in the absence of special circumstances.[7] If, however, the employee does engage in employment of a different character, damages are reduced by the amount so earned.[8] The authorities agree that an employee has properly mitigated damages by going into business with the knowledge that the prospects for earning from the business are minimal in its initial stages.[9] It was wisely held in one such case, however, that recovery should be reduced by the value of the former employee's services in building up the business.[10]

Sometimes the question arises whether damages should be reduced by the amount of payments that the wronged party has received from some third party such as an insurer. This question arises most frequently in tort cases involving personal injuries where a doctrine known as the "collateral source rule" has evolved. Generally, except where changed by statute, under this rule damages assessed against a tortfeasor are not diminished by any payments received by the injured party from medical insurance, pension and disability plans, or other sources other than the tortfeasor or the tortfeasor's insurer.[11] The corresponding question here is should recovery awarded to a wrongfully discharged employee be

the dates on which future salary payments would have been payable. Hollwedel v. Duffy–Mott Co., supra; Dixie Glass v. Pollak, 341 S.W.2d 530, 91 ALR2d 662 (Tex.App. 1960), aff'd. The discount rate is discussed in Comment, 63 U.Chi.L.Rev. 1099 (1996). A small minority of jurisdictions permit the discharged employee to recover damages suffered only up to the time of trial. The authorities on this question are collected in Dixie Glass v. Pollak, supra, where the minority view is repudiated.

3. Parker v. Twentieth Century–Fox Film, 3 Cal.3d 176, 89 Cal.Rptr. 737, 474 P.2d 689, 44 ALR3d 615 (1970) (actress engaged as lead in musical film need not accept substitute role as lead in a western film); Cooper v. Stronge & Warner Co., 111 Minn. 177, 126 N.W. 541, 27 LRA NS 1011, 20 Am.Ann.Cas. 663 (1910) (department manager need not accept position as sales clerk at same salary); State ex rel. Freeman v. Sierra County Bd. of Ed., 49 N.M. 54, 157 P.2d 234 (1945) (principal need not accept post as teacher at reduced salary); Rudman v. Cowles Communications, 30 N.Y.2d 1, 330 N.Y.S.2d 33, 280 N.E.2d 867, 63 ALR3d 527 (1972); Kloss v. Honeywell 77 Wn.App. 294, 890 P.2d 480 (1995) (nurse need not take a custodial job); contra, Life Care Centers of America v. Charles Town Assocs., 79

F.3d 496 (6th Cir.1996) (Tenn. law); Rs. Agency 2d § 455 cmt d.

4. Billetter v. Posell, 94 Cal.App.2d 858, 211 P.2d 621 (1949); Crabtree v. Elizabeth Arden Sales, 105 N.Y.S.2d 40 (1951), aff'd.

5. American Trading v. Steele, 274 F.774 (9th Cir.1921) (resident of China need not seek employment in U.S.); San Antonio & A.P. Ry. v. Collins, 61 S.W.2d 84 (Tex.App.1933) (resident of Houston need not accept employment in San Antonio).

6. Jackson v. Wheatley School Dist., 464 F.2d 411 (8th Cir.1972).

7. Fair v. Red Lion Inn, 943 P.2d 431 (Colo.1997).

8. Board of Ed. v. Jennings, 102 N.M. 762, 701 P.2d 361 (1985).

9. Ransome Concrete Machinery v. Moody, 282 F.29 (2d Cir.1922); Cornell v. T.V. Dev., 17 N.Y.2d 69, 268 N.Y.S.2d 29, 215 N.E.2d 349 (1966); see Note, 15 Harv. L.Rev. 662 (1902).

10. Kramer v. Wolf Cigar Stores, 99 Tex. 597, 91 S.W. 775 (1906).

11. Helfend v. Southern Cal. Rapid Transit Dist., 2 Cal.3d 1, 84 Cal.Rptr. 173, 465 P.2d 61, 77 ALR3d 398 (1970).

diminished by the amount the employee receives from unemployment insurance[12] or from social security?[13] No consistent answer has been given.[14] There seems to be no justification, however, for the cases allowing for recovery of more money than required to compensate the employee for the injury done.

Generally speaking, a public officer's right to compensation is not dependent upon contract, but on public law. If an officer is wrongfully denied office, the doctrine of avoidable consequences is inapplicable. Therefore, recovery is not diminished by the amount the officer has earned or could have earned during the term of office.[15] Most persons on the public payroll, however, are employees rather than officers[16] and are subject to the doctrine of avoidable consequences.[17]

Special damages are rarely awarded for wrongful discharge. Damages for injury to the employee's reputation are ordinarily said to be too remote and not in the contemplation of the parties,[18] but expenses incurred in an attempt to mitigate damages by securing other employment are recoverable.[19] There is considerable authority in England[20] and some in the U.S. for an award of consequential damage where the contract contemplates that performance will enhance the employee's reputation, as where a script writer is promised screen credits[21] and

12. Diminution was not permitted in Billetter v. Posell, 94 Cal.App.2d 858, 211 P.2d 621 (1949). Contra, Meyers v. Director of Div. of Emp. Sec., 341 Mass. 79, 167 N.E.2d 160 (1960); Corl v. Huron Castings, 450 Mich. 620, 544 N.W.2d 278 (1996); Dehnart v. Waukesha Brewing, 21 Wis.2d 583, 124 N.W.2d 664 (1963). Payments from a fidelity bond that the injured plaintiff bought should not be subtracted from recovery against defalcating employees or their co-conspirators. Pacific Gas and Elec. v. Superior Court, 28 Cal.App.4th 174, 33 Cal.Rptr.2d 522 (1994)

13. Recovery was diminished in United Protective Workers v. Ford Motor, 223 F.2d 49, 48 ALR2d 1285 (7th Cir.1955).

14. Rs. 2d § 347 cmt c; Fleming, The Collateral Source Rule and Contract Damages, 71 Cal.L.Rev. 56 (1983); Note, 48 B.U.L.Rev. 271 (1968); Horstmann v. Nicholas J. Grasso, P.C., 210 A.D.2d 671, 619 N.Y.S.2d 848 (1994) (collateral source rule applied to "lost wages" that were in fact paid); but see Corl v. Huron Castings, 450 Mich. 620, 544 N.W.2d 278 (1996) (collateral source rule inapplicable); see also Inchaustegui v. 666 5th Ave., 96 N.Y.2d 111, 725 N.Y.S.2d 627, 749 N.E.2d 196 (2001) (tenant failed to get insurance but landlord had coverage, collateral source rule applied).

15. Gentry v. Harrison, 194 Ark. 916, 110 S.W.2d 497 (1937); Corfman v. McDev-

itt, 111 Colo. 437, 142 P.2d 383, 150 ALR 97 (1943).

16. For the distinction between public office and public employment, see C.J.S. Officers § 5; Annot., 140 ALR 1076 (1942). See also Punke, Breach of Teacher Contracts, and Damages, 26 Ala.Law. 243, 265–74 (1965).

17. White v. Bloomberg, 501 F.2d 1379 (4th Cir.1974) (postal employee); Stockton v. Department of Employment, 25 Cal.2d 264, 153 P.2d 741 (1944); People v. Johnson, 32 Ill.2d 324, 205 N.E.2d 470 (1965); Spurck v. Civil Service Bd., 231 Minn. 183, 42 N.W.2d 720 (1950); Wyatt v. School Dist. No. 104, 148 Mont. 83, 417 P.2d 221, 22 ALR3d 1039 (1966).

18. Skagway City School Bd. v. Davis, 543 P.2d 218 (Alaska 1975) (overruled on other grounds); Gary v. Central of Ga. Ry., 37 Ga.App. 744, 141 S.E. 819 (1928); Tousley v. Atlantic City Ambassador Hotel, 25 N.J.Misc. 88, 50 A.2d 472 (1947); Amaducci v. Metropolitan Opera, 33 A.D.2d 542, 304 N.Y.S.2d 322 (1969).

19. Wyatt v. School Dist., 148 Mont. 83, 417 P.2d 221, 22 ALR3d 1039 (1966).

20. Tolnay v. Criterion Film Prods., 2 All E.R. 1225 (1936); Marbe v. George Edwardes, Ltd., 1 K.B. 269, 56 ALR 888 (1928).

21. Paramount Productions v. Smith, 91 F.2d 863 (9th Cir.1937), cert. denied.

where a disc jockey is promised exposure to a large audience.[22] Such holdings are consistent with the related rule that if the services to be rendered will be of benefit to the employee as by enhancing the employee's skill or reputation, the employer is obliged not only to pay his salary but also to provide work of the kind contemplated,[23] under conditions that are not intolerable.[24]

§ 14.19 Wrongful Termination by Employee

When an employee breaches a contract by wrongfully quitting, the employer's recovery is measured by the additional market cost of obtaining substitute help for the unexpired contract term; that is, the difference between the market value of such services and the contract rate of compensation.[1] Although courts do not generally deny the possibility of an award of consequential damages against the employee, the rules of foreseeability, mitigation and certainty have been so strictly applied as to indicate a strong policy against such awards against employees.[2]

§ 14.20 Buyer's General Damages for Total Breach

The traditional measure of general damages for a total breach of contract by the seller is the difference between the market price of the goods and the contract price. The UCC continues this rule[1] but has added an alternative measure which will sometimes produce a different result. The buyer may choose to cover; that is, make a good faith purchase or contract to purchase substitute goods without unreasonable delay.[2] The buyer may then recover the difference between the cost of cover and the contract price.[3]

22. Colvig v. RKO General, 232 Cal. App.2d 56, 42 Cal.Rptr. 473 (1965); Annot., 96 ALR3d 437 (1979).

23. Van Steenhouse v. Jacor Broadcasting 958 P.2d 464 (Colo.1998); Sigmon v. Goldstone, 116 A.D. 490, 101 N.Y.S. 984 (1906); Rs. 2d, Agency § 433; Comment, 27 U.Miami L.Rev. 465 (1973).

24. Romano v. Basicnet, 238 A.D.2d 910, 661 N.Y.S.2d 135 (1997); Tennyson v. School Dist., 232 Wis.2d 267, 606 N.W.2d 594 (App.1999), rev. denied.

§ 14.19

1. Roth v. Speck, 126 A.2d 153, 61 ALR2d 1004 (D.C.Mun.App.1956); Triangle Waist v. Todd, 223 N.Y. 27, 119 N.E. 85 (1918); 5 Corbin § 1096; 11 Williston § 1362A (3d ed.).

2. See Reich v. Bolch, 68 Iowa 526, 27 N.W. 507 (1886); Peters v. Whitney, 23 Barb. 24 (N.Y.1856); Winkenwerder v. Knox, 51 Wn.2d 582, 320 P.2d 304 (1958). For rare cases awarding such damages, see Stadium Pictures v. Walker, 224 A.D. 22, 229 N.Y.S. 313 (1928) (actor); Anglia Tele-

vision v. Reed, 3 All E.R. 690 (C.A.1971); R.K. Chevrolet, v. Hayden, 253 Va. 50, 480 S.E.2d 477 (1997) (manager).

§ 14.20

1. UCC § 2–713(1). The Code speaks of this as the remedy "for non-delivery or repudiation." The same measure would apply in case the buyer "rightfully rejects or justifiably revokes acceptance." UCC § 2–711. Revised § 2–713(1)(a) deals with non-delivery, rejection, and revocation of acceptance.

2. UCC § 2–712(1) (the revision clarifies the section).

3. UCC § 2–712(2) (unchanged by the revision); This measure of recovery is available even though the buyer was able to pass on the increased costs to its customers. KGM Harvesting v. Fresh Network, 36 Cal. App.4th 376, 42 Cal.Rptr.2d 286 (1995). A buyer may not "cover" by taking goods out of its own inventory which were purchased at a time when the market was considerably higher. Chronister Oil v. Unocal, 34 F.3d 462 (7th Cir.1994).

While this measure of damages will often produce the same result as the traditional market price minus contract price rule, this will not always be so.[4] In the following circumstances, the cover price minus contract price produces the more reasonable result. When notified of a breach the purchaser may be forced to go outside its normal sources of supply and to pay more than the normal price that constitutes the "market."[5] Or the buyer may pay a higher than market price unaware that the goods were available at the market price from some suppliers; also, if goods of the same quality and specifications are not readily available, and the buyer procures as a reasonable substitute, goods of a somewhat higher quality and cost.[6]

This cover provision, although one of the simplest, is yet one of the most useful innovations to appear in the UCC. In addition to bringing about the more reasonable result, the cover rule obviates the often difficult, expensive, and time consuming task of proving the market price at trial. The provision, however, also creates some new problems. It might appear that if the buyer covers at less than the market price, the buyer's sagacity will redound to the benefit of the seller. The buyer's recovery may be limited to the difference between the cost of cover and the market price plus incidental damages.[7] One complication that is bound to arise is that it may be difficult to determine if and when a buyer has covered. A buyer may have many active accounts with suppliers of similar goods. In the event of breach by one of them, it may be quite difficult to establish that any particular contract entered into after the buyer learns of the breach is the "cover" contract.[8] The potential for vexatious problems is immense if the given market is a fluctuating one.[9]

Although the buyer has an option to cover or not, the choice is not altogether a free one. If the buyer could have avoided consequential

4. Cf. 3 Williston, Sales § 599 (rev.ed. 1948) where the rationale for the older view is expressed: "[I]f the buyer pays more than the market price, it is not the seller's wrong but his own error of judgment which was the cause of the excessive payment."

5. For example, an article in the Financial Section of the New York Times, dated January 1, 1967, discussing the tight supply of sulphur, points out that while two large producers charged $28.50 per ton, "Demand is so strong that some consumers have been paying more than $50 a ton for spot supplies. * * * Authorities said overseas markets had been chaotic and prices had been hard to catalogue. They were reported to have ranged recently from $40 to $65 a ton."

6. Thorstenson v. Mobridge Iron Works, 87 S.D. 358, 208 N.W.2d 715, 64 ALR3d 242 (1973).

7. UCC § 2–713 cmt 5; see White & Summers § 6–4 (4th ed.). Trenchant criticism of the notion of giving the breaching

party the benefit of the aggrieved party's actions cutting losses to below market levels appears in Simon, A Critique of the Treatment of Market Damages in the Restatement (Second) of Contracts, 81 Colum.L.Rev. 80 (1981); Simon & Novak, Limiting the Buyer's Market Damages to Lost Profits, 92 Harv.L.Rev. 1395 (1979). Totally contrary to these two articles is Childres, Buyer's Remedies: The Danger of Section 2–713, 72 Nw.U.L.Rev. 837 (1978) (market price minus contract price never an appropriate measure). See also Wallach, The Buyer's Right to Monetary Damages, 14 UCC L.J. 236, 238–42 (1982); Carroll, A Little Essay in Partial Defense of the Contract—Market Differential as a Remedy for Buyers, 57 S.Cal.L.Rev. 667 (1984).

8. See Jamestown Farmers Elevator v. General Mills, 552 F.2d 1285 (8th Cir.1977) (seller must prove buyer's purchases were intended as "cover").

9. Nordstrom, The Law of Sales 444 (1970).

damages by covering, the buyer's failure to cover will bar recovery of consequential damages.[10] Moreover, replevin[11] and specific performance[12] are not generally available remedies if the disappointed purchaser could have obtained substitute goods elsewhere.

In the event that the buyer does not cover, and utilizes instead the market price minus contract price rule, the relevant price is that which is in effect at the time the buyer learned of the breach.[13] The majority view prior to the UCC was to the contrary, holding that the applicable market price was that of the date on which delivery should have been made.[14] (Revised § 2–713 would restore this rule except as to anticipatory repudiations). The UCC rule arguably makes two significant changes in prior common law. First, (and this is non-controversial), it *postpones* the date on which damages are assessed in cases where the buyer is unaware of the breach until after performance is due; for example, where defective goods are shipped and defects are discovered later.[15] The buyer can cover only after learning of the breach and if the buyer fails to cover, the principle of avoidable consequences does not allow the enhancement of damages caused by standing idly by. Thus, damages are measured as of the time the buyer could have covered. Second, (and this is controversial), the UCC *accelerates* the date on which damages are assessed in cases where there is a breach by anticipatory repudiation.[16] The literal meaning of § 2–713(1) so provides: "[T]he measure of damages for non-delivery or repudiation by the seller is the difference between the market price at the time when the buyer learned of the breach and the contract price. * * * " An initial difficulty with accepting a literal interpretation of this section is that this language requires some creative interpretation when read with § 2–610, which permits the aggrieved party after the repudiation to await performance "for a commercially reasonable time." A logical solution of the difficulty

---

10. UCC § 2–715(2) (unchanged by the revision); Lewis v. Nine Mile Mines, 268 Mont. 336, 886 P.2d 912 (1994); see § 14.22

11. UCC § 2–716(3) (revision has stylistic changes).

12. See UCC § 2–716 cmt 2. This would be changed by the revision if the contract contains a clause consenting to specific performance.

13. UCC § 2–713(1) The revision substitutes date of tender of delivery for the "time when the buyer learned of the breach." However, a separate rule has been crafted for anticipatory breaches.

14. Reliance Cooperage v. Treat, 195 F.2d 977 (8th Cir.1952); Acme Mills & Elevator v. Johnson, 141 Ky. 718, 133 S.W. 784 (1911); Segall v. Finlay, 245 N.Y. 61, 156 N.E. 97 (1927); McCormick, Damages § 175; Rs. 1st § 338. This still appears to be the law in England. See George, Dam-

ages for Anticipatory Breach of Contract, 1971 J.Bus.L. 109.

15. Cf. Perkins v. Minford, 235 N.Y. 301, 139 N.E. 276 (1923) (under prior law).

16. Trinidad Bean & Elev. v. Frosh, 1 Neb.App. 281, 494 N.W.2d 347 (1992). Contrary to the analysis herein is White & Summers, Uniform Commercial Code § 6–7 (4th ed.). Essentially in accord, but urging amendment of the Code, is Nordstrom, The Law of Sales 453–57 (1970). Also in accord is Jackson, "Anticipatory Repudiation" and the Temporal Element of Contract Law: An Economic Inquiry into Contract Damages in Cases of Prospective Non Performance, 31 Stan.L.Rev. 69 (1978) (forward, not spot, price a reasonable time after learning of the repudiation); Leibson, Anticipatory Breach and Buyer's Damages—A Look into How the UCC Has Changed the Common Law, 7 UCC L.J. 272 (1975).

is to conclude that the buyer has "learned of the breach" at the expiration of a commercially reasonable time.[17]

Other difficulties are (1) that early analysts of the Code did not read § 2–713 as overturning precedent in the anticipatory repudiation field,[18] and (2) that there is a conflict between the literal meaning of § 2–713 and a cross reference to the evidentiary rule of § 2–723.[19] Such arguments and other arguments based upon textual exegesis will not solve the problem.

What ought to be determinative is whether the result reached achieves internal consistency with the economic results achievable by other remedies available to the buyer under the Code. Primary among these remedies is the buyer's option to cover and recover any amount paid in excess of the contract price. Under a literal reading, § 2–713(1) measures the difference between contract price and market price as of the time the buyer would reasonably cover. Such a reading has the principle of avoidable consequences built into it. If the buyer does not cover, damages cannot be enhanced by the buyer's remaining idle until the time for delivery under the contract. The same economic harm ought to be measured in essentially the same way no matter which remedial choice is made by the buyer. Consequently, the literal meaning of § 2–713 ought to be and has generally been followed.[20]

The revision of Article 2 provides that when a seller repudiates damages are measured by "the difference between the market price at the expiration of a commercially reasonable time after the buyer learned of the repudiation...."[21]

§ 14.21 Buyers Damages for Breach of Warranty or Fraud

The UCC leaves unchanged the measure of general damages for breach of warranty. The measure is the difference between the value of the goods accepted and the value they would have had if they had been as warranted.[1] In routine cases, the difference in value is established by

---

17. First Nat. Bank v. Jefferson Mtge., 576 F.2d 479 (3d Cir.1978); but see Weiss v. Karch, 62 N.Y.2d 849, 477 N.Y.S.2d 615, 466 N.E.2d 155 (1984).

18. For pre-UCC Law, see Beale, Damages Upon Repudiation of a Contract, 17 Yale L.J. 443 (1908); Note, 24 Colum.L.Rev. 55 (1924).

19. The villain of the piece, § 2–723(1) provides: "If an action based on anticipatory repudiation comes to trial before the time for performance with respect to some or all of the goods, any damages based on market price (Section 2–708 or Section 2–713) shall be determined according to the price of such goods prevailing at the time when the aggrieved party learned of the

repudiation." A literal reading of § 2–713(1) would require that the cross-reference in § 2–723 to § 2–713 be treated as inadvertent surplusage and that § 2–723 is applicable only to a case involving a buyer's repudiation. See § 14.23 infra.

20. Palmer v. Idaho Peterbilt, 102 Idaho 800, 641 P.2d 346 (1982) (collecting cases); Wallach, Anticipatory Repudiation and the UCC, 13 UCC L.J. 48 (1980); Rs. 2d § 350 ill. 17.

21. Revision § 2–713(1)(b).

§ 14.21

1. UCC § 2–714(2) (unchanged in the revision).

showing the reasonable cost of repair.[2]

Value normally is determined, however, at the time and place of acceptance.[3] As indicated in the discussion of the concept of value, barring very special circumstances, the legal system employs an objective "market" standard of value.[4] It has been suggested, however, that a subjective standard of value to the buyer should be applied in connection with breach of warranty where the buyer is able to show that the goods are less valuable in the light of special needs.[5] Such a suggestion seems to be an unnecessary invitation to further confuse the concept of value. Rather, in such circumstances, the buyer's recourse is under the last clause of § 2–714(2), which permits recovery where "special circumstances show proximate damages in a different amount." In addition § 2–715 specifically takes into account the buyer's special needs in allowing for consequential damages, provided that the seller has reason to know of those needs—a complex subjective-objective test. Purely subjective tests ought not to be favored. Recovery of "proximate damages of a different amount" has been allowed in a case in which a painting was sold and there was a breach of warranty of title. The court held that damages should be assessed as of the time the true owner reclaimed the painting from the disappointed buyer—a time at which the painting had greatly enhanced in value.[6]

The UCC provides that remedies for material misrepresentation or fraud shall be the same as for breach of contract.[7] In an action for damages, therefore, the measure of damages would be the same as for breach of warranty. This has the almost unnoticed effect of repealing, at least in the context of sales of goods, the "out of pocket" rule previously applicable to actions for fraud in a number of jurisdictions.[8] Pursuant to that rule, the defrauded purchaser was permitted to recover only the difference between the amount paid and the value of the goods received

2. Bendix Home Sys. v. Jessop, 644 P.2d 843 (Alaska 1982); Lanterman v. Edwards, 294 Ill.App.3d 351, 689 N.E.2d 1221, 228 Ill.Dec. 800 (1998); Malul v. Capital Cabinets, 191 Misc.2d 399, 740 N.Y.S.2d 828 (2002) (full purchase price worthless and irreparable goods); White & Summers § 10–2 (4th ed).

3. UCC § 2–714(2) (unchanged in the revision).

4. See §§ 14.12 to 14.14 supra. On proof of value of a unique computer system, see Chatlos Sys. v. NCR, 670 F.2d 1304 (3d Cir.1982), cert. dismissed.

5. Peters, Remedies for Breach of Contracts Relating to the Sale of Goods Under the UCC, 73 Yale L.J. 199, 269 (1963).

6. Menzel v. List, 24 N.Y.2d 91, 298 N.Y.S.2d 979, 246 N.E.2d 742 (1969); see also Colton v. Decker, 540 N.W.2d 172, 47 ALR5th 951 (S.D.1995) (legal fees as consequential damages for breach of warranty of title); disapproved by Olbrys v. Peterson

Boat Works, 81 F.3d 161 (6th Cir.1996), where the court could have distinguished the cases. The legal fees in Colton were incurred in collateral litigation with a *third party* to clear title.

7. UCC § 2–721 (unchanged in the revision); see Monserud, Measuring Damages After Buyer's Affirmation of an Article 2 Sales Contract Induced by Fraud, 1996 Colum.Bus.L.Rev. 423.

8. The leading cases establishing this rule are Derry v. Peek, L.R., 37 Ch.Div. 541 (1887) and Reno v. Bull, 226 N.Y. 546, 124 N.E. 144 (1919), 5 Cornell L.Q. 167. See McCormick, Damages 448. The contrary "benefit of the bargain" rule adopted by the UCC has support in prior law in a good number of jurisdictions. Hartwell Corp. v. Bumb, 345 F.2d 453, 13 ALR3d 868 (9th Cir.1965), cert. denied. A compromise position is taken in Rs. 2d, Torts § 549.

rather than the difference between the value the goods would have had if they were as represented and actual value.

§ 14.22 Buyer's Consequential and Incidental Damages for Seller's Breach

In the ordinary case the buyer is made whole by application of the rules of general damages. Thus, if the buyer contracted to purchase sugar at 60 cents per pound and the seller breaches when the market price is 70 cents, the purchaser is entitled to damages of 10 cents per pound. This ordinarily provides full compensation because the purchaser may go out into the market and purchase the sugar at no cost except the original contract price plus the damages which can be recovered. Suppose, however, there is no sugar on the market or no sugar available for delivery in time for the purchaser to keep resale commitments to retail outlets or for keeping the buyer's bakery in operation. The lost profits and other proximate damages, as, for example, damages payable to aggrieved retailers, are recoverable only if these were foreseeable to the seller. Prior to the UCC, many cases held that such consequential damages were awardable only if the seller knew two things at the time of contracting: first, the buyer's purpose in making the purchase, and, second, that no substitute would be available to the purchaser in the event of a breach by the seller.[1] The UCC seems to have relaxed the requirement of foreseeability considerably. Section 2–715(2) provides (and is not changed by the revision) that consequential damages include:

> "any loss resulting from general or particular requirements and needs of which the seller at the time of contracting had reason to know and which could not reasonably be prevented by cover or otherwise * * *."

Under the UCC it would seem not to be necessary that the seller have reason to know at the time of contracting that no substitute will be available to the buyer.[2] It is sufficient that at the time of the breach no substitute is reasonably available[3] and that the seller had reason to know the buyer's needs. However, if the seller has such knowledge, liability for all consequential losses does not necessarily follow. For example, where the seller knows that the buyer is purchasing for resale to a sub-vendee, the seller has reason to know that the buyer will suffer a loss of resale

§ 14.22

1. Marcus & Co. v. K.L.G. Baking, 122 N.J.L. 202, 3 A.2d 627 (1939); Czarnikow–Rionda v. Federal Sugar Ref., 255 N.Y. 33, 173 N.E. 913, 88 ALR 1426 (1930); Thomas Raby, Inc. v. Ward–Meehan, 261 Pa. 468, 104 A. 750 (1918).

2. Sun Maid Raisin Growers v. Victor Packing, 146 Cal.App.3d 787, 194 Cal.Rptr. 612 (1983); accord under prior law, Lukens Iron & Steel v. Hartmann–Greiling, 169 Wis. 350, 172 N.W. 894 (1919) (steel shortage occurred after the contract was

formed); cf. Samek, The Relevant Time of Foreseeability of Damage in Contract, 38 Austl.L.J. 135 (1964). The Restatement (Second) appears to take the position that the UCC has not changed the common law as stated above. Rs. 2d § 351 cmt d.

3. As to "reasonable availability," see Oliver–Electrical Mfg. v. I.O. Teigen Constr., 177 F.Supp. 572 (D.Minn.1959) (defendant proved that a substitute supplier was available but failed to prove that plaintiff should have known this).

profits if the seller breaches and the buyer cannot seasonably replace the goods on the market. But ordinarily the seller does not have reason to know that the sub-vendee will cancel its account with the buyer. Absent knowledge of special circumstances tending to show that such a cancellation will occur, the seller will neither be liable for damages caused by the cancellation,[4] nor for a general loss of good will.[5] While an occasional case allows recovery for loss of good will, generally the tests of foreseeability and certainty are applied so stringently as to preclude recovery.[6] Moreover, a court granting lost profits should be careful to ensure that a grant for loss of good will or diminution in value of a business do not duplicate each other.[7]

In addition to obvious cases of market shortages,[8] a seller has reason to know that the buyer cannot obtain substitute goods when the goods are brand name goods and the seller controls the supply of goods bearing that brand[9] or when the goods are made pursuant to a patent exclusively controlled by one of the parties.[10]

Where a seller delivers goods to a manufacturer knowing they are to be used in the manufacturing process, the seller has reason to know that defective goods may cause a disruption of production and a consequent loss of profits. Under the UCC it is clear that the seller is liable for such lost profits.[11] The seller also has reason to know that if a component supplied is defective it may result in an expensive process of product recall and component replacement.[12] As under prior law, consequential damages for breach of warranty also include foreseeable injury to person or property proximately resulting from the breach.[13]

The UCC expressly permits the parties to limit or exclude consequential damages by agreement, unless the limitation or exclusion is unconscionable. But while an attempt to limit damages for injury to the person in connection with a sale of consumer goods is, however, "prima facie unconscionable * * * limitation of damages where the loss is commercial is not."[14]

4. Harbor Hill Lith. v. Dittler Bros., 76 Misc.2d 145, 348 N.Y.S.2d 920 (1973).

5. Neville Chem. v. Union Carbide, 422 F.2d 1205 (3d Cir.1970), cert. denied.

6. See Comments, 23 Baylor L.Rev. 106 (1971); 75 Dick.L.Rev. 63 (1970); Annot., 96 ALR3d 299 (1980).

7. Protectors Ins. Service v. U.S. Fidelity & Guar., 132 F.3d 612 (10th Cir.1998); Kolaski & Kuga, Measuring Commerical Damages Via Lost Profits or Loss of Business Value, 18 J.L. & Comm. 1 (1998).

8. Lukens Iron & Steel v. Hartmann–Greiling, 169 Wis. 350, 172 N.W. 894 (1919).

9. Orester v. Dayton Rubber Mfg., 228 N.Y. 134, 126 N.E. 510 (1920).

10. Booth v. Spuyten Duyvil Rolling Mill, 60 N.Y. 487 (1875).

11. Southern Illinois Stone v. Universal Eng., 592 F.2d 446 (8th Cir.1979); Lewis v. Mobil Oil, 438 F.2d 500 (8th Cir.1971).

12. Taylor & Gaskin v. Chris–Craft, 732 F.2d 1273 (6th Cir.1984).

13. UCC § 2–715(2)(b); see Prosser & Keeton, Torts § 97 (5th ed.1984).

14. UCC § 2–719(3) (unchanged in the revision);. A case considering the conscionability of a limitation of consequential damages to commercial losses is Luick v. Graybar Elec., 473 F.2d 1360 (8th Cir.1973).

Frequently, agreements limit warranties and exclude consequential damages. Typically, in substitution for the broader warranties and damages, the seller promises to repair defects for a given period of time.[15] The UCC permits such agreements. If the seller breaches the promise to repair, however, consequential damages may flow from the breach, as the remedy contractually substituted for UCC remedies has failed of its essential purpose.[16] Some courts have held that the material breach of the contractual substitute entitles the purchaser to excise the remedies clause of the contract and utilize the remedies provisions of the UCC.[17] Where the contract is between merchants, a majority of cases allow a provision excluding consequential damages to stand independently despite a material breach.[18]

The UCC has adopted a category of damages known as incidental damages. Included in this category are "expenses reasonably incurred in inspection, receipt, transportation and care and custody of goods rightfully rejected * * *."[19] Also included in the UCC category of incidental damages are "any commercially reasonable charges, expenses or commissions in connection with effecting cover * * *."[20] In addition, "any other reasonable expenses incident to the delay or other breach" are recoverable as damages.[21]

§ 14.23   Seller's General Damages

The seller's general damages for non-acceptance or repudiation by the buyer is the difference between the market price and the unpaid contract price.[1] However, this measure of damages will not always place the seller in as good a position as performance would have; thus, sometimes a different rule is necessary. For example, if a dealer contracts to sell an automobile at the retail market price of $20,000, upon a breach by the buyer, recovery on the basis of the difference between retail market price and contract price would result in a recovery of only nominal damages. But in fact the dealer has lost the profit on the sale measured by the difference between the contract price and the cost to the dealer of the automobile. In order to give full compensation in such

15. Such a limitation was part of the contract as a trade usage in Figgie Int'l v. Destileria Serralles, 190 F.3d 252 (4th Cir. 1999).

16. UCC § 2–719(2) (unchanged in the revision); Caudill Seed & Warehouse v. Prophet 21, 123 F.Supp.2d 826 (E.D.Pa. 200); RRX Indus. v. Lab–Con, 772 F.2d 543 (9th Cir.1985) (inability to de-bug software); Dowty Communications v. Novatel Computer Sys., 817 F.Supp. 581 (D.Md. 1992), aff'd.

17. E.g., clause forbidding revocation of acceptance, Rose v. Colorado Factory Homes, 10 P.3d 680 (Colo.App.2000) cert. denied.

18. Pierce v. Catalina Yachts, 2 P.3d 618 (Alaska 2000); Rheem Mfg. v. Phelps Heating, 746 N.E.2d 941 (Ind.2001); Int'l Fin. Serv. v. Franz, 534 N.W.2d 261 (Minn. 1995). But see Sunny Indus. v. Rockwell Int'l, 175 F.3d 1021 (7th Cir.1999) (case by case analysis); Krupp PM Eng. v. Honeywell, 209 Mich.App. 104, 530 N.W.2d 146 (1995). See Mather, 38 S.C.L.R. 673 (1988); Note, 74 Cornell L.Rev. 359 (1989).

19. UCC § 2–715(1) (unchanged in the revision).

20. UCC § 2–715(1).

21. UCC § 2–715(1).

§ 14.23

1. UCC § 2–708(1).

cases, the UCC provides that if the difference between the contract price and the market price provides inadequate recovery, "the measure of damages is the profit (including reasonable overhead) which the seller would have made from full performance by the buyer."[2] Recovery of the lost profit would be appropriate in any case in which the seller has, for practical purposes, an unlimited supply of goods of the kind involved in the transaction.[3] The seller's lost profits can be calculated by subtracting the cost to the dealer of the automobile (variable cost) from the contract price. This will give the seller the gross profit which includes both the net profit and an allocation calculated in the contract price for a share of the overhead.[4] Section 2–708(2) ends with the confusing statement that the seller is to allow "due credit for payments or proceeds of resale." Legislative history clarifies this confusing clause, which on its face, appears to undercut the entire thrust of the subsection. "Proceeds of resale" refers not to the proceeds of resale of the subject matter but, in a manufacturing contract, to proceeds of the sale of any components for salvage or junk.[5]

Generally, the appropriate market price is the price at the "time and place for tender."[6] The relationship between this rule and the doctrines of anticipatory breach and avoidable consequences is complex. If the buyer repudiates a contract, what is the relevant time for calculating damages? The UCC provisions have been described as "curiously incon-

---

2. UCC § 2–708(2) (clarifying change in the revision). For a definitive analysis of this provision, see Childres & Burgess, Seller's Remedies: The Primacy of UCC 2–708(2), 48 N.Y.U.L.Rev. 833 (1973), which contradicts much of the analysis contained in Speidel & Clay, Seller's Recovery of Overhead Under UCC Section 2–708(2), 57 Cornell L.Rev. 681 (1972). Also sound is Schlosser, Construing UCC Section 2–708(2) to Apply to the Lost–Volume Seller, 24 Case W.L.Rev. 686 (1973). An alternative analysis, rejecting in this context the general principle that an aggrieved party is entitled to protection of the expectation interest, is Shanker, The Case for a Literal Reading of UCC Section 2–708(2) (One Profit for the Reseller), 24 Case W.L.Rev. 697 (1973); cf. UCC § 1–106 (expectation interest protected). A critical economic analysis of this provision is made in Goetz & Scott, Measuring Seller's Damages: The Lost–Profits Puzzle, 31 Stan.L.Rev. 323 (1979), which is reviewed critically in Sebert, Remedies under Article 2 of the UCC, 130 U.Pa.L.Rev. 360, 386–93 (1981). See, for synthesis, Schlosser, Damages for a Lost Volume Seller, 17 UCC L.J. 238 (1985); Note, 9 Wm.Mitchell L.Rev. 266 (1984). To the effect that an award of lost profits in this context is unfair and unnecessary, see Cooter & Eisenberg, Damages for Breach of Contract, 72 Cal.L.Rev. 1432, 1471–77 (1985).

3. NCI v. Commodore Business Machines, 163 Cal.App.3d 688, 209 Cal.Rptr. 636 (1985); Neri v. Retail Marine, 30 N.Y.2d 393, 334 N.Y.S.2d 165, 285 N.E.2d 311 (1972); see also Jetz Service v. Salina Properties, 19 Kan.App.2d 144, 865 P.2d 1051 (1993), 34 Washburn L.J. 136 (1994) (applied to lessor of equipment).

4. Nordstrom on Sales § 177. Alternatively, net profit would have to be calculated and added to a pro rata share of the seller's fixed overhead. A trial on this basis would involve an expensive and cumbersome clash between the accountants of the parties. See Shanker, supra note 2, at 707–10. For a particularly difficult case, see Automated Medical Labs. v. Armour Pharmaceutical, 629 F.2d 1118 (5th Cir.1980).

5. See authorities collected in Neri v. Retail Marine, 30 N.Y.2d 393, 399 n. 2, 334 N.Y.S.2d 165, 169 n. 2, 285 N.E.2d 311, 314, n. 2 (1972). The revision would eliminate the quoted language and add a clarifying subsection (1)(b).

6. UCC § 2–708(1) (revision is in accord). If the case comes to trial prior to the date for performance, damages will be determined at the time the seller learned of the breach. UCC § 2–723(1). The revision would abolish this rule because it has specific provisions on repudiation.

sistent and almost incoherent in places."[7] The inconsistencies must be resolved by following the UCC's guiding remedial principle: "that the aggrieved party may be put in as good a position as if the other party had fully performed * * *"[8] and its guiding philosophy of requiring commercially reasonable conduct.[9] If the goods are of the kind that the seller normally deals in, and in which there is an active market, e.g., grains, it would be commercially reasonable for the seller to take no action, await the time for performance, and seek damages measured by the contract price minus market price differential as of that date. Of course, there will be actual damages only if the prognosis as to grain prices was correct. Equally reasonable, on learning of the repudiation the seller might enter into a forward contract to sell grain and charge the breaching party with the difference between this resale price and the contract price.[10] If the contract involves the transfer of used machinery which would decline in value merely by aging, and the seller is not a dealer in such machinery, a prompt resale (or action for the price) would seem incumbent upon the seller. The variations are many, but the key goals of protecting the seller's expectancy interest and protecting the breaching party from predatory or other commercially unreasonable retaliation must guide the outcome.

Occasionally the buyer's breach may involve misconduct other than a failure to pay, as where a buyer breaches the duty of cooperation in providing specifications, resulting in delayed production and additional cost to the seller.[11] While the UCC permits the seller to cancel,[12] or to perform in any reasonable manner such as providing the seller's own specifications,[13] it is silent on the situation where the seller exercises patience, awaits the buyer's specifications and thereby suffers a loss. It would seem that the buyer's breach could be deemed a breach of a "collateral" obligation,[14] remedial rights from which are not abrogated by the UCC.[15]

§ 14.24   Seller's General Damages Following Resale

In the event of a breach by the buyer that leaves the goods in the seller's possession or control,[1] the seller may identify the goods to the

7. Jackson, "Anticipatory Repudiation" and the Temporal Element of Contract Law: An Economic Inquiry into Contract Damages in Cases of Prospective Nonperformance, 31 Stan.L.Rev. 69, 103 (1978).

8. UCC § 1–106(1); (§ 1–305 revision). Revised § 2–708(1)(b) would provide that the damages will be calculated "at the expiration of a commercially reasonable period after the seller learned of the repudiation."

9. UCC § 2–708(1) provides that seller's damages are calculated as of "the time and place for tender." Section 2–723, provides that if an action comes to trial before that date damages will be measured as of the time the seller learned of the repudiation. See Roye Realty & Developing v. Arkla, Inc., 863 P.2d 1150 (Okl.1993).

10. On "resale" as a remedy see § 14.24 infra.

11. Kehm v. U.S., 93 F.Supp. 620 (Ct. Cl.1950).

12. UCC § 2–711. The revision clarifies this right.

13. UCC § 2–311 (modest changes in the revision).

14. UCC § 2–701 (unchanged in the revision).

15. Semble: Holmgren v. Rogers Bros., 94 Idaho 267, 486 P.2d 278 (1971).

§ 14.24

1. UCC § 2–706 (clarifying amendments in the revision).

contract[2] and resell them at a private or public sale. The seller may then recover from the buyer the difference between the resale price and contract price,[3] provided the sale is conducted in a commercially reasonable manner and prior notice of the intended resale is given the buyer.[4] This, of course, is the counterpart of the buyer's remedy of cover.[5] The seller need not account to the buyer for any profit made on the resale.[6] The UCC is unclear, however, as to how any part payment made by the buyer is to be allocated. In fairness, such payment ought to be credited to the buyer.[7]

The resale remedy is not exclusive, however. Seller's remedies under the UCC are cumulative[8] in the sense that, although the same economic harm is not to be compensated more than once, recovery under all remedial provisions of the UCC can be had until the aggrieved party is made whole. Thus, for example, if a retailer has an unlimited supply of a given product, the resale of goods at the market price does not make the retailer whole because of the deprivation of a profit on a lost sale. As discussed in connection with damages under UCC § 2–708(1),[9] in such a case the seller may recover "the profit (including reasonable overhead) which the seller would have made from full performance by the buyer."[10]

§ 14.25 Seller's Consequential and Incidental Damages

Subject to one exception, consequential damages are not available to the seller. According to Section 1–106 of the UCC (§ 1–305 of the revision) such damages are not available unless specifically provided for by the UCC or other rule of law and none of the provisions of the UCC dealing with seller's damages allow for the recovery of consequential damages.[1] And under prior case law, the buyer's failure to pay the price—or indeed the failure to pay any liquidated indebtedness, such as a loan[2]—was never a sufficient basis for the award of consequential damages no matter how foreseeable the injury to the creditor. The only recovery allowable was the sum of money owed with interest.[3] Thus, a seller's claim for consequential damages faces difficult obstacles indeed.

2. UCC § 2–704 (stylistic changes in the revision).

3. UCC § 2–706(1); see Shuchman, Profit on Default: An Archival Study of Automobile Repossession and Resale, 22 Stan.L.Rev. 20 (1969).

4. Cook Composites v. Westlake Styrene, 15 S.W.3d 124 (Tex.App.2000).

5. See § 14.20 supra.

6. UCC § 2–706(6) (stylistic changes in the revision)

7. Nordstrom, Seller's Damages Following Resale Under Article Two of the UCC, 65 Mich.L.Rev. 1299 (1967).

8. UCC § 2–703 cmt 1; § 2–706 (7) of the revision.

9. See § 14.23 supra.

10. Neri v. Retail Marine, 30 N.Y.2d 393, 334 N.Y.S.2d 165, 285 N.E.2d 311 (1972); Childres & Burgess, supra § 14.23 n.2, at 870–874.

§ 14.25

1. Northern Helex v. U.S., 524 F.2d 707 (Ct.Cl.1975), cert. denied.

2. Tevdorachvili v. Chase Manhattan, 103 F.Supp.2d 632 (E.D.N.Y.2000).

3. Loudon v. Taxing Dist., 104 U.S. (14 Otto) 771 (1881); 11 Williston § 1410 (3d ed.). Departing from this rule by way of dictum is Salem Eng. & Constr. v. London-

There is one well recognized exception to the common law view precluding consequential damages to aggrieved creditors, including unpaid sellers. Where payment is to be made to a third person, the creditor has been allowed to recover special damages suffered, often consisting of injury to credit and reputation.[4]

While the the UCC precludes recovery for consequential damages suffered by the seller, it expressly permits recovery for incidental damages suffered. These recoverable damages "include any commercially reasonable charges, expenses or commissions incurred in stopping delivery, in the transportation, care and custody of goods after the buyer's breach, in connection with return or resale of the goods or otherwise resulting from the breach."[5] Incidental damages are recoverable whether the seller sues for damages following resale,[6] for damages without reference to resale,[7] or for the price.[8] The proposed revision would, for the first time, allow sellers to claim consequential damages, but not for breach of a consumer contract.[9]

§ 14.26 Seller's Action for the Price

An action by the seller for the price is not an action for damages.[1] Nevertheless, a brief discussion of the issue will round out the discussion of the various kinds of money judgments available to an aggrieved seller. Such an action is available if the goods have been accepted by the buyer.[2] It is also available if the seller identifies the goods to the contract and is unable after reasonable effort to resell them at reasonable price, or if the circumstances reasonably indicate that such effort will be unavailing.[3] In this event, the seller must hold the goods for the buyer, but if resale subsequently becomes practicable the seller may resell them at any time prior to collection of a judgment for the price.[4]

derry School Dist., 122 N.H. 379, 445 A.2d 1091 (1982).

4. Cf. UCC § 4–402 (1990) (liability of bank to depositor for wrongful dishonor). See also Dillon v. Lineker, 266 F. 688 (9th Cir.1920) (damages of $28,000 sustained by failure of defendant to pay off creditor's mortgage of $3,000); Miholevich v. Mid–West Mut. Auto Ins., 261 Mich. 495, 246 N.W. 202, 86 ALR 633 (1933) (liability insurer failed to pay judgment recovered against insured, held liable for damages as a result of a body execution levied on insured).

5. UCC § 2–710; Tuttle v. Equifax Check, 190 F.3d 9 (2d Cir.1999) (cost of collecting bounced check).

6. UCC § 2–706(1) (clarifying changes in the revision).

7. UCC § 2–708(1) & (2) (revision substantially unchanged except as to repudiations).

8. UCC § 2–709(1) (major change in revision; consequential damages also recoverable).

9. Proposed § 2–710(2) & (3).

§ 14.26

1. See § 14.23 supra.

2. UCC § 2–709(1)(a). It is unclear whether this includes the situation where the buyer purports to revoke acceptance because of alleged defects. See White & Summers, § 7–3 (4th ed.); Peters, Remedies for Breach of Contracts Relating to the Sale of Goods Under the UCC; A Roadmap for Article Two, 73 Yale L.J. 199, 241–43 (1963). The revision does not address the issue.

3. UCC § 2–709(1)(b); Northern Trading v. Songo of Maine, 646 A.2d 356 (Me. 1994) (goods could not be sold to others without infringing a trademark); see Annot., 90 ALR3d 1141.

4. UCC § 2–709(2) (stylistic change in the revision).

The seller also has an action for the price if the goods are lost or damaged within a commercially reasonable time after risk of their loss has passed to the buyer.[5] Analysis of this provision would require discussion of the complexities of when risk of loss passes and the relation of these complexities to the question of insurance coverage. This is best left to works on Sales.[6]

§ 14.27 Contracts to Manufacture Special Goods

There is no explicit provision in the UCC measuring damages for repudiation by the buyer of a contract to manufacture special goods. It is clear that if the manufacture is completed the seller may maintain an action for the price if the goods are not reasonably resalable[1] and if resalable, the seller may utilize the resale remedy[2] or maintain an action for damages.[3]

The problem arises where the repudiation occurs prior to completion of manufacture. The UCC has an express provision as to mitigation in this eventuality. The seller "in the exercise of reasonable commercial judgment for the purposes of avoiding loss and of effective realization" has two options.[4] The first option is to complete the manufacture, appropriate the goods to the contract and then exercise the remedy of resale or of an action for the price. The second option is to "cease manufacture and resell for scrap or salvage value or proceed in any other reasonable manner." If the seller exercises this option, the UCC does not specify a remedy. It seems clear, however, that the seller may sue for damages measured by the difference between the market price and contract price plus incidental damages, or for the profit that would have been made.[5] Recovery of profit alone, however, would not compensate for losses sustained. Under prior law in addition to the gains prevented, the seller would have been entitled to losses sustained measured by the expenditures made pursuant to the contract to the extent that the product of such expenditures is not salvageable.[6] The UCC appears to continue to permit such recovery in addition to lost profits by requiring "due allowance for costs reasonably incurred."[7]

5. UCC § 2–709(1)(a) (unchanged in the revision).

6. See Nordstrom, The Law of Sales § 178 (1970); White & Summers § 7–4 (4th ed.)

§ 14.27

1. See § 14.26 supra.

2. See § 14.24 supra.

3. See § 14.23 supra.

4. UCC § 2–704(2) (unchanged in the revision).

5. Anchorage Centennial Dev. v. Van Wormer & Rodrigues, 443 P.2d 596 (Alaska 1968); Detroit Power Screwdriver v. Ladney, 25 Mich.App. 478, 181 N.W.2d 828, 42 ALR3d 173 (1970); see § 14.23 supra.

6. Lieberman v. Templar Motor, 236 N.Y. 139, 140 N.E. 222, 29 ALR 1089 (1923); see § 14.25 supra.

7. UCC § 2–708(2). The revision eliminates the quoted language and substitutes a right to recover consequential damages. For discussions of damages for breach of manufacturing contracts, see Peters, supra § 14.27 n.2, at 273–75.

§ 14.28   Construction Contracts: Contractor's Recovery

The construction contractor is in many respects in the position of a seller of goods. There is, however, a major difference. Unlike the performance of the typical seller, the contractor's performance is affixed to land of another. Thus, such remedies as resale or replevin are unavailable to the aggrieved construction contractor.

Complete performance results in the contractor's unquestionable entitlement to the agreed price.[1] If, however, the contract is repudiated by the owner or if the contractor justifiably cancels the contract because of a breach by the owner, the contractor's remedy is in damages.[2] If no work has been done, the contractor is entitled to the profit that would have been made, measured by the difference between the contract price and the prospective cost of performance.[3] If the contractor is delayed by the breach, recovery for at least the rental value of the equipment tied up during the period of the delay[4] plus increased overhead costs,[5] and higher labor costs may be recovered. At times, consequential damages may be available.[6] If the work has commenced, the contractor is entitled for a total breach to the unpaid contract price less the amount it would have cost to complete performance.[7] Proof of the amount it cost to retain a substitute to complete the job may not be sufficient if the owner fails to prove that the cost was reasonable.[8] This represents his profit and his sunk costs.

The measure of recovery is sometimes expressed in different formulas. Under a second formula, the contractor is entitled to the profit that would have been made plus the cost of work actually performed, less any progress payments received.[9] A third formula has also found judicial approval. This permits the builder to recover "such proportion of the contract price as the cost of the work done bears to the total cost of doing the job, plus, for the work remaining, the profit that would have been made on it."[10] In most cases, each of these formulas yields the same

§ 14.28

1. McCormick, Damages § 640.

2. There is also a remedy in restitution, discussed in § 15.3 infra.

3. McCormick, Damages § 164; 11 Williston § 1363 (3d ed.). For a thorough discussion of the rules discussed in this section, see Patterson, Builder's Measure of Recovery for Breach of Contract, 31 Colum.L.Rev. 1286 (1934).

4. W.G. Cornell Co. v. Ceramic Coating, 626 F.2d 990 (D.C.Cir.1980); Mullinax Eng. v. Platte Valley Constr., 412 F.2d 553 (10th Cir.1969); Studer v. Rasmussen, 80 Wyo. 465, 344 P.2d 990 (1959).

5. Walter Kidde Constr. v. State, 37 Conn.Supp. 50, 434 A.2d 962 (1981); Higgins v. Fillmore, 639 P.2d 192 (Utah 1981).

6. Downey, Inc. v. Bradley Center, 188 Wis.2d 435, 524 N.W.2d 915 (App.1994) (subcontractor recovers from general); Zie-

linski v. Miller, 277 Ill.App.3d 735, 660 N.E.2d 1289, 214 Ill.Dec. 340 (1995) (general recovers from subcontractor).

7. Guerini Stone v. P.J. Carlin Constr., 240 U.S. 264, 280 (1916); Peter Kiewit Sons' Co. v. Summit Constr. Co., 422 F.2d 242 (8th Cir.1969); Millen v. Gulesian, 229 Mass. 27, 118 N.E. 267 (1918).

8. Driver Pipeline v. Mustang Pipeline, 69 S.W.3d 779 (Tex.App.2002).

9. U.S. v. Behan, 110 U.S. 338, 344 (1884); Warner v. McLay, 92 Conn. 427, 103 A. 113 (1918). For a discussion of the similarity of result usually achieved by the application of this and the previous formula, see Petropoulos v. Lubienski, 220 Md. 293, 152 A.2d 801 (1959).

10. McCormick, Damages § 641. Cases utilizing this formula include McGrew v. Ide Estate Inv., 106 Kan. 348, 187 P. 887

result. However, where the contract would have been performed at a loss to the contractor, each of the formulas may produce a different result.[11] However, in the case of a losing contract, the contractor would frequently find that recovery would be greater in an action for restitution than in an action for damages.[12]

§ 14.29   Construction Contracts: Owner's Recovery

As a general rule, an owner whose building contract is defectively performed is entitled to damages measured by the cost of remedying the defect.[1] There are a number of controversial cases where this measure is arguably overly generous to the owner. Consider these facts:

> *Case I*. The contractor inadvertently installs Cohoes brand instead of Reading brand wrought iron pipe into a new house, contrary to the contract specifications. The two brands are regarded in the trade to be equal in quality. The owner discovers the breach only after the walls are plastered. The cost of removing the Cohoes pipe, installing Reading pipe and replastering the walls would be $35,000. The house, as is, is worth $250,000. If the defect is remedied, its market value would be precisely the same.

On facts such as these, courts have refused to apply the usual measure of damages and have held that the owner is entitled to merely the difference between the value of the structure if built to specifications and the value it has as constructed.[2] On the facts of Case I the owner is, therefore, entitled only to nominal damages.

It has been said that the rationale for such cases is to avoid "unreasonable economic waste."[3] The matter, however, is more complex than that. It seems clear that if the owner had an idiosyncratic value attached to Reading pipe (e.g., the owner was an executive of the Reading) and had communicated this to the contractor, a judgment ought to be entered in the amount required to replace the plumbing, regardless of economic waste.[4] Similarly, if the breach were willful (e.g.,

(1920); Kehoe v. Borough of Rutherford, 56 N.J.L. 23, 27 A. 912 (1893).

11. The following illustration is given in McCormick, Damages 642. "Assume an extreme case: The contract price is $10,000, the work already done has cost $5,000, and the unfinished part would cost $10,000 to complete. Here under the three formulas the builder would recover (1) zero, (2) $5,000, and (3) $3,333.33."

12. See § 15.4 infra; Guittard, 32 Texas B.J. 91 (1969).

§ 14.29

1. Shell v. Schmidt, 164 Cal.App.2d 350, 330 P.2d 817, 76 ALR2d 792 (1958); Ervin Constr. v. Van Orden, 125 Idaho 695, 874 P.2d 506 (1993); Greg Allen Constr. v. Estelle, 762 N.E.2d 760 (Ind.App.2002); Prier

v. Refrigeration Eng., 74 Wn.2d 25, 442 P.2d 621 (1968); 5 Corbin § 1089; McCormick, Damages § 168; 11 Williston § 1363 (3d ed). Caveat: if the owner has not fully paid the price and performance by the builder is not substantial, in many jurisdictions the owner need pay nothing, or nothing further, on the contract. See § 11.22 supra.

2. Jacob & Youngs v. Kent, 230 N.Y. 239, 129 N.E. 889, 23 ALR 1429 (1921).

3. 5 Corbin § 1090 at p. 493.

4. Groves v. John Wunder Co., 205 Minn. 163, 286 N.W. 235, 123 ALR 502 (1939) (dissent); Chamberlain v. Parker, 45 N.Y. 569 (1871) (A man may choose "to erect a monument to his caprice or folly on his premises. * * * "). See also Linzer, On the Amorality of Contract Remedies—Effi-

Cohoes pipe was purchased more cheaply at a distributor's distress sale), many courts would award replacement cost rather than difference in value.[5] These elements are absent in case I. There, the owner would doubtlessly pocket the proceeds of a judgment for replacement costs rather than replace the pipes. Such enrichment appears unjust in relationship to the cost to the innocent, albeit breaching, contractor.

> *Case II.* A strip miner contracts to lease 60 acres of farmland, mine it, and restore the surface to specified grades and conditions. The miner mines the land but does not restore it. Restoration would cost $29,000, but the land is worth only $300 less than it would be worth if restored.

The court adjudicating Case II restricted the owners' recovery to $300.[6] There are cases to the contrary[7] and scholars disagree as to the appropriate result.[8] Note that the breach is willful and the strip miner keeps $29,000 that it had committed itself to expend. As one commentator has written:

> "While one might argue for a damage system that neither encourages nor discourages performance, it is difficult to advance reasoned argument in favor of a damage system that affirmatively encourages non performance."[9]

Arguments based on what is the most economically efficient result seem to cancel each other out.[10] The decision in Case II appears plainly wrong when approached from the perspective of the moral obligation created by contractual promises, the policy of discouraging contract breaches and the prevention of unjust enrichment.

> *Case III.* L, a municipality, leased a pier to T for a ten year term at an annual rental of $200,000. T had also agreed to keep the pier in

ciency, Equity, and the Second Restatement, 81 Colum.L.Rev. 111, 117–20, 131–34 (1981); Note, Breach of a Covenant to Restore, 39 S.Cal.L.Rev. 309 (1966); Muris, Cost of Completing or Diminution in Market Value: The Relevance of Subjective Value, 12 J.Leg.Stud. 379 (1983).

5. Shell v. Schmidt, 164 Cal.App.2d 350, 330 P.2d 817, 76 ALR2d 792 (1958), cert. denied; City School Dist. v. McLane Constr., 85 A.D.2d 749, 445 N.Y.S.2d 258 (1981), appeal denied; see generally Marschall, Willfulness: A Crucial Factor in Choosing Remedies for Breach of Contract, 24 Ariz. L.Rev. 733 (1982).

6. Peevyhouse v. Garland Coal & Mining, 382 P.2d 109 (Okl.1962), cert. denied, thoroughly and critically analyzed in Maute, *Peevyhouse v. Garland Coal & Mining Co.* Revisited, 89 Nw.L.Rev. 1341 (1995). The case is alive and strong in Oklahoma. Schneberger v. Apache Corp., 890 P.2d 847 (Okl.1994) (breach of contract to reduce water pollution caused by oil and gas drilling).

7. Groves v. John Wunder Co., 205 Minn. 163, 286 N.W. 235, 123 ALR 502 (1939) (performance of promise to grade gravel and sand pit would cost $80,000; land as restored would be worth $12,000; Emery v. Caledonia Sand and Gravel, 117 N.H. 441, 374 A.2d 929 (1977); American Standard v. Schectman, 80 A.D.2d 318, 439 N.Y.S.2d 529 (1981), appeal denied (contract to demolish and remove foundations to depth of one foot; land levelled but no foundation removed; court awards $90,000 cost of completion rather than $3,000 diminution in value).

8. The discussions are many. For thorough discussions, see Linzer, supra note 4; Marschall, supra note 5; Yorio, In Defense of Money Damages for Breach of Contract, 82 Colum.L.Rev. 1365, 1388–1424 (1982); for England, see Poole, 59 Modern L. Rev. 272 (1996).

9. Vernon, Expectancy Damages for Breach of Contract: A Primer and Critique, 1976 Wash.U.L.Q. 179, 228.

10. See Yorio, supra note 8, at 1388–97.

good repair at T's expense. But at the expiration of the leasehold, L discovered that T had failed to maintain the pier in good repair and that the cost of repair would be about $200,000. Soon thereafter, L, pursuant to a plan known to T at the time of entering into the lease, demolished the pier for replacement by a containership terminal. In an action by L for damages, T argues that L suffered no damages as the pier had long been scheduled for demolition and was, in fact, demolished.

Case III is much like Case II. The primary difference is that it is absolutely clear that repairs will be valueless not only in terms of market value but in terms of any subjective or idiosyncratic value repair might have to L. Repair would be economically inefficient. Nonetheless, judgment was awarded to L for the cost of repairs.[11] While it is clear that L suffered no economic injury by the failure to repair, a judgment for T would have validated T's unjust enrichment. Part of T's bargained-for return was the cost of repairs. There is no economic inefficiency in allocating to L, rather than T, the savings caused by the lack of repair. If T had acted honorably and rationally, it would have offered, during the leasehold period, to renegotiate the lease, offering, perhaps, an additional payment of $5,000 per year in exchange for a release from the covenant to repair. If L acted rationally it would have accepted that offer, or at least made a counter-offer for, say, $10,000 per year. Rather than award L the full cost of repair in Case III the court could have split the windfall between the parties, although few cases have done so.[12]

> *Case IV.* The U.S. chartered a ship from plaintiff, agreeing that, at the end of World War II, it would restore the ship to its original condition. At the end of the War there was a glut of ships and labor and materials costs had risen. As a result, restoration would cost $4,000,000, but the restored ship would be worth only $2,000,000. Unrestored, the ship is valueless except as scrap.

The court, stating that if plaintiff were awarded $4,000,000, the ship "would still rust at anchor,"[13] awarded plaintiff the loss in value ($2,000,000). It deprived plaintiff of what it regarded as a $2,000,000 windfall. In a sense, however, the U.S. received a $2,000,000 windfall by not having to undertake the costs of repair to which it had contractually committed itself. There seems to be no clear-cut answer to the dilemma that Case IV posed. Neither party is dishonorable. They are caught up in a set of circumstances that they did not foresee.

It has been suggested that the court ought to split the difference,[14] but there is little authority for splitting either losses or windfalls.[15] It has

11. Farrell Lines v. New York, 30 N.Y.2d 76, 330 N.Y.S.2d 358, 281 N.E.2d 162 (1972); contra, Associated Stations v. Cedars Realty and Dev., 454 F.2d 184 (4th Cir.1972).

12. Rs. 2d § 351(3) suggests that the court has the power to limit recovery. See Young, Half Measures, 81 Colum.L.Rev. 19 (1981).

13. Eastern S.S. Lines v. U.S., 112 F.Supp. 167, 175 (Ct.Cl.1953).

14. See Yorio, supra note 8, at 1365, 1417–18.

15. See Young, supra note 12.

been suggested that in Cases II, III and IV, the best solution is to order the breaching party to specifically perform.[16] Because the owner prefers money to performance in each of the cases, the parties would then negotiate an economically efficient solution. While this would cut through the conflicting vectors, it faces formidable traditional obstacles against the award of specific performance in construction cases.[17]

It cannot usually be said that there is unreasonable economic waste or windfall recovery if the structure is unusable or unsafe in its present condition. Thus, the owner's measure of damages in such a case is the cost of remedying the defect.[18]

If the builder abandons the construction prior to completion, the measure of damages normally is the reasonable cost of completion,[19] plus any damages suffered by the consequent delay in completion.[20] Damages for delay normally consist of the rental or use value the premises would have had during the period of delay.[21] If the requisite foreseeability and certainty exist, special damages are also recoverable.[22]

§ 14.30 Contracts to Sell Realty: Total Breach

(a) Breach by Vendor

Among the earliest rules of damages laid down in England were those relating to real property.[1] In 1776, it was held in Floreau v. Thornhill[2] that, upon a vendor's breach of a contract because of an inability to convey good title, the vendee may not recover for loss of bargain. About half of the American states have accepted this English rule.[3] In such jurisdictions the vendee generally may recover only the

16. See Linzer, supra note 4.

17. See § 16.5 infra. The obstacles are recognized by the proponent. See Linzer, supra note 4, at 126–30.

18. Bellizzi v. Huntley Estates, 3 N.Y.2d 112, 164 N.Y.S.2d 395, 143 N.E.2d 802 (1957).

19. State v. R.M. Hudson Paving & Constr., 91 W.Va. 387, 113 S.E. 251 (1922); McCormick, Damages § 169.

20. Noonan v. Independence Indem., 328 Mo. 706, 41 S.W.2d 162, 76 ALR 931 (1931).

21. Wing & Bostwick v. U.S. Fidelity & Guar., 150 F. 672 (C.C.W.D.N.Y.1906); Standard Oil v. Central Dredging, 225 A.D. 407, 233 N.Y.S. 279 (1929), aff'd; McCormick, Damages § 170; Lande, Uncle Sam's Right to Damages for Delay, 10 Santa Clara Law. 2 (1969). The owner, however, under the doctrine of avoidable consequences may not enhance damages by prolonging the period of delivery. See Losei Realty v. New York, 254 N.Y. 41, 171 N.E. 899 (1930), a case which pushes the re-

quirement of mitigation to extreme limits, holding that although the defendant did not expressly repudiate the contract and manifested an intention of eventually performing, the plaintiff as a reasonable person should have mitigated damages by putting an end to the contract.

22. Olson v. Quality–Pak, 93 Idaho 607, 469 P.2d 45 (1970); Reilly v. Connors, 65 A.D. 470, 72 N.Y.S. 834 (1901); J.T. Stark Grain v. Harry Bros., 57 Tex.Civ.App. 529, 122 S.W. 947 (1909). Normally, consequential damages will not include injury to one's credit rating. Raymond Le Chase v. Vincent Buick, 77 Misc.2d 1024, 353 N.Y.S.2d 151 (Sup.Ct.1974).

§ 14.30

1. Other early rules limiting damages, not here considered, relate to breaches of covenants in conveyances. See McCormick, Damages § 185.

2. 96 Eng.Rep. 635 (1776).

3. McCormick, Damages §§ 177, 179 (lining up the jurisdictions).

down payment plus the reasonable expenses in examining title.[4]

In its inception, the rationale for the English rule's limitation on vendee's recovery was the difficulty besetting a vendor in ascertaining whether title was marketable in view of the lack of adequate land registries.[5] Although adequate land registries now exist in this country, in those jurisdictions in which the limitation is accepted the rule is so well established and known to the legal profession and to land-owners that any judicial overturning of the rule would be unwarranted.[6] Nevertheless, the original rationale must be strictly borne in mind in applying the rule. The vendor who has good title but refuses to convey will be liable for ordinary contract damages, measured by the difference between the value of the land and the contract price,[7] together with consequential damages.[8] Similarly, the vendor who was aware of the defect in title at the time of contracting will be liable,[9] or if a previously unknown curable defect is discovered and the vendor fails to utilize best efforts to remove the defect, liability will attach.[10] All of these cases are frequently said to come within a "bad faith" exception to the English rule, although in many such cases the question of whether or not the vendor was in bad faith is not so much in issue as is the question of whether the vendor knowingly assumed the risk of acquiring marketable title.[11] In cases where the vendee is permitted to recover for loss of bargain, the vendee may not also recover expenses in examining title,[12] but in a proper case consequential damages will be awarded.[13] Consequential damages may include litigation costs in defending title.[14]

Many jurisdictions follow the "American rule," pursuant to which the vendee is entitled in all cases to recover for the loss of bargain

4. Id. § 182.

5. See Oakley, Pecuniary Compensation for Failure to Complete a Contract for the Sale of Land, 39 Cambridge L.J. 58 (1980).

6. The English rule was overturned in Donovan v. Bachstadt, 91 N.J. 434, 453 A.2d 160, 28 ALR4th 1062 (1982).

7. Soloman v. Western Hills Dev., 110 Mich.App. 257, 312 N.W.2d 428 (1981).

8. Ocean Air Tradeways v. Arkay Realty, 480 F.2d 1112 (9th Cir.1973); Pearce v. Hubbard, 223 Ala. 231, 135 So. 179 (1931); BGW Dev. v. Mt. Kisco Lodge, 247 A.D.2d 565, 669 N.Y.S.2d 56 (1998); Donovan v. Bachstadt, note 6 supra (increased mortgage interest). Of course, as a prerequisite to the recovery of consequential damages the vendee must meet the tests of foreseeability and certainty. Gilmore v. Cohen, 95 Ariz. 34, 386 P.2d 81, 11 ALR3d 714 (1963).

9. Stone v. Kaufman, 88 W.Va. 588, 107 S.E. 295 (1921); Arentsen v. Moreland, 122 Wis. 167, 99 N.W. 790 (1904). See also Potts v. Moran's Ex'rs, 236 Ky. 28, 32 S.W.2d 534 (1930), which collects many of the cases and

adopts a somewhat different view. See Carnahan, 20 Ky.L.J. 304 (1932).

If the vendee is aware of the vendor's lack of marketable title at the time of contracting, as where the vendor merely has a contract to purchase the realty, some cases take the position that since there is a lack of bad faith, the vendor will not be liable for loss of bargain where title cannot be perfected. Northridge v. Moore, 118 N.Y. 419, 23 N.E. 570 (1890). Contra, Edgington v. Howland, 111 Neb. 171, 195 N.W. 934 (1923).

10. Braybrooks v. Whaley, [1919] 1 K.B. 435.

11. See Hammond v. Hannin, 21 Mich. 374, 386–87, 4 Am.Rep. 490 (1870); Arentsen v. Moreland, 122 Wis. 167, 99 N.W. 790 (1904); McCormick, Damages 689–91.

12. Schultz & Son v. Nelson, 256 N.Y. 473, 177 N.E. 9 (1931).

13. Petrie–Clemons v. Butterfield, 122 N.H. 120, 441 A.2d 1167 (1982).

14. Patel v. Anand, 264 Va. 81, 564 S.E.2d 140 (2002).

together with consequential damages pursuant to the general principles of contract damages.[15]

(b) Breach by Vendee

If the vendee breaches, it seems to be the rule everywhere that the vendor may recover standard contract damages: the difference between the contract price and the market value of the real property at the time of the breach.[16] In an appropriate case the vendor may recover consequential damages.[17]

If the breach takes the form of a vendor's delay in conveying, the vendee may recover the rental value of the premises during the period of delay, plus, if the prerequisites exist,[18] consequential damages.[19]

I.   AGREED DAMAGES

Table of Sections

§ 14.31   Liquidated Damages and Penalties

Historically, a rule developed in Equity that courts would not enforce penalties that the parties had agreed on. Later, courts of law adopted equitable rule, which was designed to prevent over-reaching and to give relief from unconscionable bargains.[1] The courts have assiduously

---

15. Doherty v. Dolan, 65 Me. 87, 20 Am.Rep. 677 (1876); McCormick, Damages § 177; Annots., 48 ALR 12 (1927); 68 ALR 137 (1930).

16. Webster v. Di Trapano, 114 A.D.2d 698, 494 N.Y.S.2d 550 (1985); Chris v. Epstein, 113 N.C.App. 751, 440 S.E.2d 581 (1994), rev. denied; but see Kuhn v. Spatial Design, 245 N.J.Super. 378, 585 A.2d 967 (1991) (in a falling market, market price at time of resale).

17. Rogers v. Lockard, 767 N.E.2d 982 (Ind.App.2002); Tague Holding v. Harris, 250 N.Y. 422, 165 N.E. 834 (1929) (vendor had a contract to purchase from the owner, lost profit awarded);

18. See §§ 14.5 to 14.7 supra.

19. Christensen v. Slawter, 173 Cal. App.2d 325, 343 P.2d 341, 74 ALR2d 567 (1959); Bumann v. Maurer, 203 N.W.2d 434 (N.D.1972).

§ 14.31

1. Liquidated damages are discussed in McCormick, Damages §§ 146–157, and the historical development of the doctrine in § 147. See generally Crowley, New York Law of Liquidated Damages Revisited, 4 N.Y.Cont.Leg.Ed. No. 1, 59 (1966); Macneil, Power of Contract and Agreed Remedies, 47 Cornell L.Q. 495 (1962); Sweet, Liquidated Damages in California, 60 Cal.L.Rev. 84 (1972); Comment, 45 Chi.-Kent L.Rev. 183 (1968); Comment, 45 Fordham L.Rev. 1349 (1977) (hereinafter Fordham Comment). Differing analyses of the economic efficiency of rules regarding penalties are given in Rea, Efficiency Implication of Penalties and Liquidated Damages, 13 J.Leg.Stud. 147 (1984); Goetz & Scott, Liquidated Damages, Penalties and the Just Compensation Principle, 77 Colum.L.Rev. 554 (1977); Clarkson, Miller & Morris, Liquidated Damages

continued to refuse enforcement of penalty clauses, though the reason for this has not been obvious. The rule is anomalous, given the deeply rooted principle of freedom of contract and the reluctance of courts to inquire into the wisdom of a bargain except when fraud or something like it is proved.[2] The traditional equitable doctrine of unconscionability has survived in this area as a foundation for the rule against the enforcement of contractual penalties.[3]

While parties are not empowered to provide for penalties in the event of a breach, they can under certain conditions determine in advance what damages will be assessed in the event of a breach. Such a provision is known as a liquidated damages clause.

A penalty is designed to deter a party from breaching the contract and to punish the breacher in the event the deterrent is ineffective.[4] Courts ritualistically list three criteria by which a valid liquidated damages clause may be distinguished from an invalid penalty clause. In order to qualify as a liquidated damages clause: first, the parties must intend to provide for damages rather than for a penalty; second, the injury caused by the breach must be uncertain or difficult to quantify; third, the sum stipulated must be a reasonable pre-estimate of the probable loss. The UCC and the Restatement (Second) have reshaped these criteria somewhat. Under both the traditional and newer formulations the third criterion is generally determinative, but under the newer formulation the question is whether the sum is a reasonable pre-estimate of the probable *or* actual loss.[5]

(a) Intention

That intention is of little moment is indicated by decisions upholding clauses that the parties have labeled as penalty clauses[6] and striking down clauses which parties have labeled as providing for liquidated damages.[7] Moreover, even if it be shown that the parties conscientiously

v. Penalties, 1978 Wis.L.Rev. 351; Comment, 72 Nw.U.L.Rev. 1055 (1978) (hereinafter Northwestern Comment); Note, 50 S.Cal.L.Rev. 1055 (1977).

2. DiMatteo, A Theory of Efficient Penalty: Eliminating the Law of Liquidated Damages, 38 Am.Bus.L.J. 633 (2001) (collecting the literature and proposing a sea change in approach).

3. Fridman, Freedom of Contract, 2 Ottawa L.Rev. 1, 10–11 (1967).

4. Muldoon v. Lynch, 66 Cal. 536, 6 P. 417 (1885); Berger v. Shanahan, 142 Conn. 726, 118 A.2d 311 (1955); Shields v. Early, 132 Miss. 282, 95 So. 839 (1923). Compare the function of punitive damages and the general lack of availability of such damages in contract actions. See § 14.3 supra. Special situations: Continental Turpentine & Rosin v. Gulf Naval Stores, 244 Miss. 465, 142 So.2d 200 (1962) (trade association "fine"); Garrett v. Coast & Southern Feder-

al S. & L. Ass'n, 9 Cal.3d 731, 108 Cal.Rptr. 845, 511 P.2d 1197, 63 ALR3d 39 (1973) ("late charges"); Rye v. Public Service Mut. Ins., 34 N.Y.2d 470, 358 N.Y.S.2d 391, 315 N.E.2d 458 (1974) (penal bond extracted by municipality).

5. This is convincingly demonstrated in McCormick, Damages §§ 148–149; Crowley, supra note 1, at 60–66; see Mobil Oil v. Flores, 175 F.Supp.2d 1080 (N.D.Ill.2001); Wheeling Clinic v. Van Pelt, 192 W.Va. 620, 453 S.E.2d 603 (1994).

6. U.S. v. Bethlehem Steel, 205 U.S. 105 (1907); Pierce v. Fuller, 8 Mass. 223, 5 Am.Dec. 102 (1811); Tode v. Gross, 127 N.Y. 480, 28 N.E. 469 (1891). But see Berger v. Shanahan, 142 Conn. 726, 118 A.2d 311 (1955), where intention is heavily emphasized.

7. Caesar v. Rubinson, 174 N.Y. 492, 67 N.E. 58 (1903); Seeman v. Biemann, 108 Wis. 365, 84 N.W. 490 (1900); but see Oran

intended to provide for liquidated damages, the clause will be struck down if the amount stipulated is out of proportion to the probable or actual injury.[8] Significantly, neither UCC § 2–718 nor Section 356 of the Restatement (Second) considers the question of intention to be relevant on the issue.

(b) Injury Uncertain or Difficult to Quantify

Traditionally courts have stated that as a prerequisite to upholding a liquidated damages clause, damages must be uncertain. Professor Macneill has isolated five kinds of uncertainty:[9]

> (1) Difficulty of *producing proof* of damages from a breach after it has occurred. (2) Difficulty of determining what damages were caused by the breach. (3) Difficulty of ascertaining what damages were contemplated when the contract was made. (4) Absence of any standardized measure of damages for a certain breach. (5) Difficulty of forecasting, when the contract was made, all the *possible* damages which may be caused (or occasioned) by any of the possible breaches.

Despite the wealth of potential that this analysis suggests, the criterion of uncertainty has been little explored and has been seldom decisive. Frequently, liquidated damages clauses have been upheld although actual damages are readily calculable.[10] The language of the UCC and of the Second Restatement speaks not of uncertainty but of "the difficulties of proof of loss."[11] Whether this represents a substantive change from pre-existing law is uncertain.[12] Although not many cases have appeared to turn on the criterion of uncertainty,[13] it is nonetheless true that a liquidated damages clause is most useful to the parties and most likely to be upheld in cases where actual damages are most difficult to prove, as in the case of a covenant not to compete ancillary to the sale of a business.[14]

(c) Reasonableness

A provision containing an unreasonably high liquidated damages

v. Canada Life Assur., 194 Ga.App. 518, 390 S.E.2d 879 (1990), cert. denied (label is important).

8. J. Weinstein & Sons v. New York, 264 A.D. 398, 35 N.Y.S.2d 530 (1942), aff'd; 5 Corbin § 1058.

9. Macneil, supra note 1, at 502 (emphasis in original; footnote omitted).

10. Callanan Road Improv. v. Colonial Sand & Stone, 190 Misc. 418, 72 N.Y.S.2d 194 (Sup.Ct.1947) (excellent discussion); McCormick, Damages 605–06; Clarkson, Miller & Muris, supra note 1, at 354–55; Northwestern Comment, supra note 1, at 1064–65.

11. Rs. 2d § 356(1); UCC § 2–718(1). The revision would limit consideration of

difficulties of proof of loss to consumer contracts.

12. See Fordham Comment, supra note 1, at 1358–63; Northwestern Comment, supra note 1, at 1063–65.

13. See note 10 supra.

14. Jaquith v. Hudson, 5 Mich. 123 (1858), which contains one of the better discussions of the relative significance of intention, uncertainty and disproportion, is such a case. Red Sage v. DESPA, 254 F.3d 1120 (D.C.Cir.2001) (landlord's covenant ancillary to a lease); Henshaw v. Kroenecke, 656 S.W.2d 416 (Tex.1983) (ancillary to partnership agreement); Robbins v. Finlay, 645 P.2d 623 (Utah 1982) (covenant not to use customer leads).

clause is void as a penalty.[15] Until enactment of the UCC there was almost general agreement that ordinarily reasonableness must be judged as of the time of contracting rather than as of the time of the breach. The UCC and the Restatement (Second) take the view that reasonableness should be tested "in the light of the anticipated or actual" loss.[16] Thus, contrary to prior doctrine, there are two moments at which the liquidated damages clause may be judged rather than just one.[17] This change clearly works in favor of more frequent enforceability of agreed damages clauses. Since the doctrine is rooted in unconscionability, an evaluation as of the time of breach is rational.

Under both the more traditional and newer views it would appear that if a substantial agreed damages clause was a reasonable pre-estimate of the harm likely to be caused by a breach, it should be enforced even if no damage ensues. Some cases have so held.[18] Others have ruled that under such extreme circumstances the general rule should not be followed.[19] The Restatement (Second) indicates that the latter cases are sound because the actual loss (or absence of loss) can be readily proved.[20] This indicates that to the restaters the difficulty of proof is to be examined at the time of trial rather than at the time of contracting. Prior law has been in conflict as to the proper moment for testing uncertainty of damages, although the prevailing view appears to have been that the proper moment is the time of contracting.[21]

The phrases "actual harm" or "actual loss" are ambiguous. Do they include injury not compensable as damages because of the rules of foreseeability, certainty and mitigation? There is no definitive answer.[22] It is submitted that "actual harm" means all harm that could not have

---

15. For breach of a commercial real estate sales contract, liquidated damages of 17% was deemed not unreasonable in Wallace Real Estate Inv. v. Groves, 124 Wn.2d 881, 881 P.2d 1010 (1994).

16. UCC § 2–718(1); Rs. 2d § 356(1).

17. Equitable Lumber v. IPA Land Development, 38 N.Y.2d 516, 381 N.Y.S.2d 459, 344 N.E.2d 391, 98 ALR3d 577 (1976).

18. Gaines v. Jones, 486 F.2d 39 (8th Cir.1973), cert. denied (dictum); Southwest Eng. v. U.S., 341 F.2d 998 (8th Cir.1965), cert. denied; Frick Co. v. Rubel Corp., 62 F.2d 765 (2d Cir.1933) (evidence of lack of any actual damages was excluded, an erroneous decision because under any view such evidence should be admissible as bearing on what losses were foreseeable); Guiliano v. Cleo, Inc., 995 S.W.2d 88 (Tenn.1999); McCarthy v. Tally, 46 Cal.2d 577, 297 P.2d 981 (1956), 9 Stan.L.Rev. 381 (1957); see Young Elec. Sign v. United Standard West, 755 P.2d 162 (Utah 1988).

19. Massman Constr. v. Greenville, 147 F.2d 925 (5th Cir.1945) (one factor in decision); Rispin v. Midnight Oil, 291 F. 481, 34

ALR 1331 (9th Cir.1923); Norwalk Door Closer v. Eagle Lock & Screw, 153 Conn. 681, 220 A.2d 263 (1966); McCann v. Albany, 158 N.Y. 634, 53 N.E. 673 (1899). Such cases are criticized in Crowley, supra note 1, at 64; and are discussed with approval in Macneil, supra note 1, at 504–509. Where a real property contract for sale calls for the turning over of possession and payment in installments thereafter, it should be incumbent on the court to determine if an unconscionable forfeiture would result if the seller were to regain possession and retain all payments made as liquidated damages. See Glezos v. Frontier Inv., 896 P.2d 1230 (Utah App.1995).

20. Rs. 2d § 356 ill. 4; but see Reporter's Notes to Comment b.

21. Northwestern Comment, supra note 1, at 1065–69; PacifiCorp Capital v. Tano, Inc., 877 F.Supp. 180 (S.D.N.Y.1995); Fisher v. Schmeling, 520 N.W.2d 820 (N.D. 1994).

22. See Fordham Comment, supra note 1, at 1357.

been minimized under the mitigation principle, whether or not compensable in the absence of an agreed damages clause.[23]

Even if no actual harm flows from the breach, the facts should be scrutinized to determine if the breaching party would be unjustly enriched by the breach,[24] as where a seller has been paid a premium price for prompt delivery, but delivers tardily with no actual injury to the buyer.[25]

It is not a requirement that the liquidated damages clause be expressed by a liquidated sum. A formula for its calculation is sufficient.[26]

When the parties' agreement sets damages at a sum disproportionately *lower* than the foreseeable or actual harm, the clause is not viewed as a penalty.[27] It may, however, be struck down as unconscionable.

It is generally held that the burden of proof that the agreed damages clause is disproportionate to the foreseeable (or actual) harm is on the defendant.[28]

§ 14.32　Two Pitfalls of Draftsmanship

Many contracts contain a number of covenants of varying importance. Damages for breach of each of these covenants may vary greatly. Thus, a lessee may promise to pay rent, maintain fire insurance, keep the corridors lighted, etc. A clause that stipulates that in the event the lessee breaches the lease a given sum will be paid as liquidated damages (or that a given security deposit will be forfeited)—here called a Shotgun Clause—cannot be a reasonable pre-estimate of the loss for breach of each of the lessee's covenants and thus will be deemed a penalty.[1] If such

23. So held in Wassenaar v. Panos, 111 Wis.2d 518, 331 N.W.2d 357, 40 A.L.R.4th 266 (1983); see Vanderbilt University v. DiNardo, 174 F.3d 751 (6th Cir.1999) (indeterminate consequential losses caused by football coach's breach).

24. Berger v. Shanahan, 142 Conn. 726, 118 A.2d 311 (1955).

25. U.S. v. Bethlehem Steel, 205 U.S. 105 (1907). Although it is common to speak of penalty clauses and penalty bonds in government contracts, such clauses are valid in the absence of a specific statute only if they conform to the requirements of liquidated damage clauses generally. DJ Mfg. v. U.S., 86 F.3d 1130 (Fed.Cir.1996); Rye v. Public Service Mut. Ins., 34 N.Y.2d 470, 358 N.Y.S.2d 391, 315 N.E.2d 458 (1974); see Gantt & Breslauer, Liquidated Damages in Federal Government Contracts, 47 B.U.L.Rev. 71 (1967); Peckar, Liquidated Damages in Federal Construction Contracts, 5 Public Contract L.J. 129 (1972).

26. Circle B Enterprises v. Steinke, 584 N.W.2d 97 (1998) ($100 a day for delay plus

payments to any third party to complete the job); see Sweet, supra note 1, at 120–24.

27. UCC § 2–718 cmt 1 (explicit in revised § 2–718(1)); Roscoe–Gill v. Newman, 188 Ariz. 483, 937 P.2d 673 (Ariz.App. 1996); Purcell Tire & Rubber v. Executive Beechcraft, 59 S.W.3d 505 (Mo.2001); Wedner v. Fidelity Security Sys., 228 Pa.Super. 67, 307 A.2d 429 (1973); Rs. 2d § 356 cmt 1; Fritz, "Underliquidated Damages as Limitation of Liability," 33 Texas L.Rev. 196 (1954); Sweet, supra note 1, at 92–93; but see Bonhard v. Gindin, 104 N.J.L. 599, 142 A. 52 (1928).

28. Wasserman's v. Middletown, 137 N.J. 238, 645 A.2d 100 (1994); Continental Ins. v. Hull, 98 Nev. 542, 654 P.2d 1024 (1982); Wasenaar v. Panos, supra note 23.

§ 14.32

1. Seach v. Richards, Dieterle & Co., 439 N.E.2d 208 (Ind.App.1982); H.J. McGrath Co. v. Wisner, 189 Md. 260, 55 A.2d 793 (1947); Wilt v. Waterfield, 273 S.W.2d 290 (Mo.1954); Lenco, Inc. v.

holdings are pressed to their logical conclusions, no liquidated damages clause would be valid because even as to the major covenant a breach may take varying forms.[2] It will often be possible to interpret such a clause so as to confine it to breach of the major covenant, in which event, if the stipulated sum is a reasonable pre-estimate of the loss for the breach of that covenant, the clause will be upheld.[3] So also, under the modern view, it will be upheld if it is reasonable in the light of the actual harm caused by a breach.

Under the flexible formulation of the UCC, the reasonableness of the clause is to be tested by the anticipated or actual harm. Thus, such a clause can be upheld if it bears a reasonable relationship to the actual consequences of the breach.[4] The Restatement (Second) has adopted the formulation of the UCC as had modern cases that confine the inquiry to whether the stipulated sum is disproportionate to the actual or foreseen damages for the breach that has occurred.[5]

Another pitfall into which contract drafters have plunged involves an attempt to fix damages in the event of a breach with an option on the part of the aggrieved party to sue for such additional actual damages that may occur—here called a Have Cake and Eat It Clause. These have been struck down as they do not involve a reasonable attempt definitively to estimate the loss.[6] While this is a logical deduction from the definition of "liquidated damages," it is hard to see how enforcement of such a clause is in any sense a penalty; the results are unwarranted infringements on freedom of contract. Distinguishable are contracts that liquidate some items of prospective damages but not others; such provisions are valid if the liquidation meets the standard criteria.[7]

§ 14.33 Liquidated Damages and Specific Performance

Despite the presence in a contract of a valid liquidated damages clause, if the criteria for equitable relief are met, the court will issue a

Hirschfeld, 247 N.Y. 44, 159 N.E. 718 (1928); Jolley v. Georgeff, 92 Ohio App. 271, 110 N.E.2d 23 (1952); Management, Inc. v. Schassberger, 39 Wn.2d 321, 235 P.2d 293 (1951).

2. Macneil, supra § 14.31 n.1, at 509–13.

3. Hungerford Constr. v. Florida Citrus Exp., 410 F.2d 1229 (5th Cir.1969), cert. denied; Ward v. Haren, 183 Mo.App. 569, 167 S.W. 1064 (1914); Hackenheimer v. Kurtzmann, 235 N.Y. 57, 138 N.E. 735 (1923); Hathaway v. Lynn, 75 Wis. 186, 43 N.W. 956, 6 LRA 551 (1889); cf. Ann Arbor Asphalt Constr. v. Howell, 226 Mich. 647, 198 N.W. 195 (1924).

4. See Fordham Comment, supra § 14.31 n.1, at 1358.

5. Rs. 2d § 356 (1); Truck Rent–A–Ctr. v. Puritan Farms 2nd, 41 N.Y.2d 420, 393 N.Y.S.2d 365, 361 N.E.2d 1015 (1977).

6. MCA Television v. Public Interest, 171 F.3d 1265 (11th Cir.1999) (clearly correct is disallowing double recovery);; Lefemine v. Baron, 573 So.2d 326 (Fla.1991); Catholic Charities v. Thorpe, 318 Ill.App.3d 304, 741 N.E.2d 651, 251 Ill.Dec. 764 (2000); contra, Margaret H. Wayne Trust v. Lipsky, 123 Idaho 253, 846 P.2d 904, 39 A.L.R.5th 817 (1993); cf. In re Plywood Co., 425 F.2d 151 (3d Cir.1970) (court permitted the retention of the agreed amount but disallowed additional damages for the breach). See Fordham Comment, supra § 14.31 n.1, at 1369–71; Comment, 39 Emory L.J. 267, 302 n.165 (1990).

7. J.E. Hathaway & Co. v. U.S., 249 U.S. 460, 464 (1919) (liquidating delay damages only).

decree for specific performance. The fact that damages have been liquidated does not give the party who has promised to pay liquidated damages an option to perform the basic agreement or to pay damages.[1] It has been held, however, that an agreement may be clearly drafted "so as to limit the seller's remedy to retaining the earnest money deposit as liquidated damages."[2] In issuing its decree for specific performance a court of equity may also award damages for injury sustained between the period of the breach and the issuance of the decree.[3]

§ 14.34 Alternative and Miscellaneous Promises Distinguished

If a builder promises to build two houses by a specified day or pay the promisee $4,000, several interpretations of the agreement are possible. The parties may have regarded their agreement as calling for a firm commitment to build the houses, and on default, the builder is to pay $4,000 as (1) damages or (2) as a penalty. But a third interpretation is also possible. The parties may have meant that the builder was to have the privilege of not building; the price of this privilege was fixed at $4,000. Thus interpreted, the agreement would be an option contract, with a price fixed for the exercise of an option to terminate.[1] Courts have sustained such options,[2] but the form of the agreement is not controlling.[3] The court must determine whether the parties actually bargained for an option.[4] If the clause was inserted at the request of the party who wishes to terminate the contract, it is likely that an option was intended.[5] Nonetheless, pre-payment clauses drafted by lenders are commonly upheld against borrowers.[6]

§ 14.33

1. Public Service Co. v. Burlington Northern R.R., 53 F.3d 1090 (10th Cir. 1995); Southeastern Land Fund v. Real Estate World, 237 Ga. 227, 227 S.E.2d 340 (1976); Bauer v. Sawyer, 8 Ill.2d 351, 134 N.E.2d 329 (1956); Rubinstein v. Rubinstein, 23 N.Y.2d 293, 296 N.Y.S.2d 354, 244 N.E.2d 49 (1968); 11 Williston § 1444 (3d ed); Fordham Comment, supra § 14.31 n.1, at 1371–72.

2. Lines v. Idaho Forest Indus., 125 Idaho 462, 872 P.2d 725 (1994). Similarly, clauses permitting a vendor to keep the earnest money deposit must be construed to determine if the clause liquidates damages or permits an action for damages in excess of the deposit. See Annot., 39 ALR5th 33.

3. Wirth & Hamid Fair Booking v. Wirth, 265 N.Y. 214, 192 N.E. 297 (1934).

§ 14.34

1. This was the holding in the fact pattern discussed in the text. Pearson v. Williams' Adm'rs, 24 Wend. 244 (N.Y.1840), which, however, was later affirmed on the theory that the promise to pay was a valid liquidated damages clause. 26 Wend. 630 (N.Y.1841).

2. Pennsylvania Re–Treading Tire v. Goldberg, 305 Ill. 54, 137 N.E. 81 (1922), 32 Yale L.J. 618 (1924) (promise to deliver shares of stock or pay $50,000); Edward G. Acker, Inc. v. Rittenberg, 255 Mass. 599, 152 N.E. 87 (1926) (defendant to give leasehold or pay $4,000); Chandler v. Doran Co., 44 Wn.2d 396, 267 P.2d 907 (1954); see 5 Corbin § 1070.

3. But see James Neff Kramper Family Farm v. Dakota Indus. Dev., 8 Neb.App. 893, 603 N.W.2d 463 (Neb.App.1999).

4. Bradford v. New York Times, 501 F.2d 51 (2d Cir.1974); see Seko Air Freight v. Transworld Sys., 22 F.3d 773 (7th Cir. 1994), where a prepayment was treated as an option for services that were never called upon.

5. Fordham Comment, supra § 14.31 n.1, at 1373.

6. Atlantic Ltd. Ptshp. v. John Hancock Mutual, 95 F.Supp.3d 678 (E.D.Mich.2000).

Early in the process of a negotiation for a corporate acquisition or merger, the parties may agree that if one of the parties withdraws from the negotiation, that party will pay a termination fee. Such a fee may be an unlawful deterrent to withdrawal–a penalty, or it may be a valid liquidation clause tested by the same criteria as other agreed damages clauses.[7]

It is the practice in the oil and gas industry for purchasers (usually pipelines) to promise to take delivery of a specific minimum quantity of gas and to pay for the minimum quantity whether or not they accept delivery. These have consistently been held to be valid alternative promises. These "take or pay" contracts have been justified as meeting the specific economic needs of the industries involved.[8] These contracts generally provide that the purchasers may recoup in a later year the gas that they paid for but did not take.

Other valid agreements that are distinguished from penalties include agreements for severance pay,[9] and "golden parachutes."[10] In common with the other situations discussed in this section, the promisee is not in breach of contract.

§ 14.35 Additional Agreed Damages: Attorney's Fees

In the U.S. an award of damages does not ordinarily include reimbursement of the successful party's attorney's fees. The rationale is that a contrary rule would discourage impecunious plaintiffs from prosecuting meritorious claims.[1] It has become common practice for drafters of leases, notes, and credit sales to provide that if legal fees are incurred in the collection of payments due under the instrument, attorney's fees will also be payable. The majority of jurisdictions uphold such agreements.[2] It has been held, however, that a clause requiring reimbursement of "any loss, cost or expense" did not include attorney's fees.[3] Because attorneys are officers of the court, the reasonableness of the agreed fee can be reviewed by the court.[4]

---

7. Brazen v. Bell Atlantic, 695 A.2d 43 (Del.Super.1997); Comments, 65 Brook. L.Rev. 585 (1999); 70 U.Colo.L.Rev. 341 (1999). In CMG Realty v. Colonnade One, 36 Conn.App. 653, 653 A.2d 207 (1995), a "termination fee" was deemed a penalty.

8. See Brooke, Great Expectations, 70 Texas L.Rev. 1469 (1992); Medina, The Take-or-Pay, 27 Tulsa L.J. 283 (1991).

9. Bradwell v. GAF, 954 F.2d 798, 800 (2d Cir.1992).

10. Koenings v. Joseph Schlitz Brewing, 126 Wis.2d 349, 377 N.W.2d 593 (1985); see also Boyle v. Petrie Stores, 136 Misc.2d 380, 518 N.Y.S.2d 854 (1985).

§ 14.35

1. See Note, 20 Vand.L.Rev. 1218 (1967). Attorneys' fees can be granted to a litigant whose adversary acts in bad faith.

Albee v. Judy, 136 Idaho 226, 31 P.3d 248 (Idaho 2001) (frivolous defense).

2. Wellness Community—National v. Wellness House, 891 F.Supp. 1273 (N.D.Ill. 1995), reversed on other grounds; Roberts v. Adams, 47 P.3d 690 (Colo.App.2001); Jackson v. Hammer, 274 Ill.App.3d 59, 210 Ill.Dec. 614, 653 N.E.2d 809 (1995); Brown v. Johnson, 109 Wn.App. 56, 34 P.3d 1233 (2001) (clause also encompasses fraud claims arising from the contract); Rs. 2d § 356, cmt d.

3. Hunzinger Constr. v. Granite Resources, 196 Wis.2d 327, 538 N.W.2d 804 (App.1995).

4. Allfirst Bank v. Dept. of Health, 140 Md.App. 334, 780 A.2d 440 (2001).

J.   EFFICIENT BREACH THEORY

Sec.

14.36   Should "Efficient Breaches" Be Encouraged?

§ 14.36   Should "Efficient Breaches" Be Encouraged?

The theory of efficient breach holds that if a party breaches, and is still better off after paying damages to compensate the victim of the breach, the result is Pareto superior, that is, considered as a unit, the parties are better off because of the breach and the breach makes no party worse off. Consequently, according to the theory, the party who will benefit from the breach should breach.[1]

Judge Posner, a principal proponent of efficient breach theory, states: "Even if the breach is deliberate, it is not necessarily blameworthy. The promisor may simply have discovered that his performance is worth more to someone else. If so, efficiency is promoted by allowing him to break his promise, provided he makes good the promisee's actual losses. If he is forced to pay more than that, an efficient breach may be deterred and the law doesn't want to bring about such a result."[2] If the law doesn't want to deter efficient breaches, why does it subject the "someone else" to a tort action for inducing the breach,[3] with exposure to a tort measure of damages and punitive damages?[4]

Judge Posner has given this example of an efficient breach: "Suppose I sign a contract to deliver 100,000 custom-ground widgets at 10¢ apiece to A for use in his boiler factory. After I have delivered 10,000, B comes to me, explains that he desperately needs 25,000 custom-ground widgets at once since otherwise he will have to close his pianola factory at great cost, and offers me 15¢ apiece for them. I sell him the widgets and as a result do not complete timely delivery to A, causing him to lose $1,000 in profits. Having obtained an additional profit of $1,250 on the sale to B, I am better off even after reimbursing A for his loss, and B is also better off. The breach is Pareto superior."[5] If B is aware that the sale to him entails the breach of the seller's contract with A, this illustration perfectly illustrates the tort of inducing a breach of contract. Not all such breaches will involve the tort of interference with a

---

§ 14.36

1. Another stream of economic thought, based on the Kaldor–Hicks principle, is unconcerned whether the non-breaching is compensated. If the net gain to the breacher exceeds the loss to the non-breaching party, the result is efficient, because the world is wealthier.

2. Patton v. Mid–Continent Sys., 841 F.2d 742, 750 (7th Cir.1988).

3. See Prosser & Keeton on Torts § 129 (5th ed. 1984). Judge Posner's efficient breach analysis is well-answered by Daniel Friedmann, The Efficient Breach Fallacy,

18 J.Leg. Stud. 1 (1989); Ian R. Macneil, Efficient Breaches of Contract: Circles in the Sky, 68 Va. L.Rev. 947 (1982), and Woodward, Contractarians, Community, and the Tort of Interference with Contract, 80 Minn.L.Rev. 1103 (1996).

4. See Texaco v. Pennzoil, 729 S.W.2d 768 (Tex.App.1987), judgment for $7.3 billion compensatory damages and $3 billion punitive damages reduced by remittitur to $7.3 billion plus $1 billion punitive.

5. Posner, Economic Analysis of Law 119 (4th ed. 1992).

contract, but the fact that some do involve such a tort refutes the idea that the law does not want to deter efficient breaches. Economists have replied that the tort of interference with a contract ought to be abolished or limited to a small number of egregious cases. The illustration is also seriously flawed for another reason. A's recovery is measured by the difference between the market price and the contract price. The transaction has caused the market price to rise to 15¢. B's entire extra profit on the sale to "me," must be disgorged to A.[6]

The efficient breach theory contains a number of simplifying assumptions that do not hold in the real world. First, it assumes the absence of transaction costs—the costs of litigation and negotiation, which is so exceedingly high that aggrieved parties often decline to litigate. Second, the rules of contract damages often fail to compensate for all the losses of the party injured by the breach. For example, the doctrines of foreseeability and certainty are barriers to the recovery of genuine losses. These barriers are justified,[7] but in a calculation of what is Pareto superior, shouldn't these losses be calculated? Moreover, damages for mental distress and the time and effort to scramble for a substitute performance are not compensable.

Healthy business relationships help the market function efficiently and encourage market activity. Such relationships are almost always disrupted by a breach, whether it is efficient or otherwise.[8] Of course, if a party can get a better deal elsewhere, there is no harm in asking the other party to accept a sum of money in substitution for performance; to talk is not to breach. However, if efficient breaches are encouraged, what effect does such encouragement have on trust among actors in the market? Efficient breach theory encourages "breach first, talk afterwards."[9] How would the market appraise the negative drag of law-inspired distrust? As discussed in § 1.4 in this book, there are many reasons why contracts are enforced. Economic efficiency is only one of them. The business community rejects efficient breach theory as a justification for willful breaches,[10] the courts should also.[11]

---

6. See § 14.20 supra.

7. The foreseeability limitation promotes efficiency by encouraging a contracting party with specialized information to convey that information to the other contracting party.

8. An economist would assert that the value of the relationship is a form of capital, the value of which the breacher would take into account when deciding to breach.

9. Macneil, supra note 3, at 968.

10. See Baumer & Marschall, 65 Temple L.Rev. 159 (1992) (analyzing the law in the light of a survey of business executives).

11. To the effect that courts have generally rejected the notion, see Note, 20 Cardozo L.Rev. 321 (1998).

Chapter 15

RESTITUTION AS A REMEDY
FOR BREACH

Table of Sections

---

§ 15.1 Introduction

The aims of damages and restitution differ in an important way. While the aim of the law of contract damages is generally to place the aggrieved party in the same economic position that performance would have provided, the aim of restitution is to place both of the parties in the position they had prior to entering into the transaction.

Quasi-contractual recovery is the principal type of restitutionary recovery at law. In the past, restitutionary recovery of a money judgment for *breach of contract* has been viewed as a type of quasi-contractual recovery. While such recovery for breach is now distinct from quasi-contract, it shares many principles with the law of quasi-contract. Throughout this volume reference has been made to the availability in particular circumstances of a quasi-contractual or other restitutionary recovery. The availability of such remedies has been discussed or alluded to in the context of performance pursuant to agreements that are too indefinite to constitute contracts,[1] agreements made by persons lacking full contractual capacity,[2] contracts that are avoided because of duress, undue influence, misrepresentation or mistake,[3] contracts that are unenforceable because of the Statute of Frauds,[4] contracts that are discharged because of impossibility of performance or frustration,[5] agreements that

<hr>

§ 15.1

1. See § 2.9 supra.
2. See §§ 8.8, 8.13 supra.
3. See ch. 9 supra.

4. See §§ 19.40 to 19.45 infra.
5. See § 13.23 supra.

are illegal,[6] and situations in which a defaulting plaintiff seeks to recover for part performance.[7]

This chapter has a twofold objective: first, to discuss briefly the common principles which underlie the law of restitution;[8] and second, to discuss restitution as an alternative remedy for breach of contract.

§ 15.2 What Is Meant by Restitution? The Concept of Unjust Enrichment

As the term is generally used today, "restitution" has a very flexible meaning.[1] Restitution encompasses recovery in quasi contract in which form of action the plaintiff recovers a money judgment.[2] It is also used to encompass equitable remedies for specific relief such as decrees that cancel deeds,[3] or impose constructive trusts or equitable liens,.

The common thread which draws these actions together is that "one person is accountable to another on the ground that otherwise he would unjustly benefit or the other would unjustly suffer loss."[4] It has been said, somewhat misleadingly, that the core of the law of restitution is the principle that "A person who has been unjustly enriched at the expense of another is required to make restitution to the other."[5] It should be emphasized, however, that this is a principle underlying many particular rules rather than an operative rule.[6] Taken as a rule, it would be both too broad and too narrow. Too broad, because situations exist where one's sense of justice would urge that unjust enrichment has occurred, yet no relief is available. Too narrow, because very often restitution is available where there has been no enrichment of the defendant, but the plaintiff has suffered a loss.[7] For example, where the plaintiff seeks restitution for the value of what the plaintiff has done pursuant to a contract unenforceable under the Statute of Frauds, the measure of recovery is ordinarily the loss sustained by the plaintiff (but not the gains prevented) as a result of the breach.[8] Not infrequently, however, this result is articulated in manipulative terms. The losses sustained by

6.   See ch. 22 infra.

7.   See § 11.22 supra.

8.   On restitution in a contractual setting, see Anderson, The Restoration Interest and Damages for Breach of Contract, 53 Md.L.Rev. 1 (1994); Gergen, Restitution as a Bridge Over Troubled Contractual Waters, 71 Fordham L.Rev. 709 (2002); Kull, Restitution as a Remedy for Breach of Contract, 67 S.Cal.L.Rev. 1465 (1994); Skelton, Restitution and Contract (1998).

§ 15.2

1.   See Comment, Restitution: Concept and Terms, 19 Hastings L.J. 1167 (1968). The leading American treatise on Restitution is Palmer, The Law of Restitution (4 vols. 1978); see also 3 Dobbs on Remedies § 12.7. The English are prolific writers in the field. See Goff & Jones, Law of Restitution (5th ed. 1998); Beatson, The Use and Abuse of Unjust Enrichment (1991); Burrows, Essays on the Law of Restitution (1991).

2.   See § 1.12 supra.

3.   See § 15.5 infra.

4.   See Rs. Restitution p. 1 (1937); see also Rs. 2d, Restitution ch. 1 (Tent.Draft No. 1, 1983).

5.   Rs. Restitution p. 1 (1937).

6.   Rs. Restitution p. 11 (1937).

7.   But see Kull, Rationalizing Restitution, 83 Cal.L.Rev. 1191 (1995) (restitution should be limited to cases of unjust enrichment).

8.   See § 19.44 infra.

the plaintiff are artificially labeled as benefits conferred upon the defendant.[9] In other contexts, however, such as in those limited areas where the plaintiff may recover for benefits conferred upon another without request, courts are rather strict in seeking to limit recovery to the amount by which the defendant has actually been enriched.[10]

§ 15.3   Restitution as an Alternative Remedy for Breach

Restitution is available as a remedy for total breach only, not a partial breach.[1] In the event of total breach, the aggrieved party may cancel the contract and pursue all available remedies, one of which is restitution. An old view of restitution has left its mark on current law. In former times, a suit for damages was deemed to be an action to enforce the contract. A suit for restitution was deemed to be an election to rescind the contract and pursue a quasi-contractual remedy not based on the contract. It has long been recognized that the right to damages or restitution are both remedial rights based on the contract.[2] Nevertheless, the older view still affects the rules governing the availability, and measure, of recovery under this restitutionary remedy. Restitution is available only when the breach is total[3] and the aggrieved party has made two elections. First, the non-breaching party must elect to cancel the contract.[4] Traditionally, notice of cancellation has been called "rescission." The use of the term "rescission" to describe the notice of cancellation of the contract should be avoided. The legal relations

9. See Childres & Garamella, The Law of Restitution and The Reliance Interest in Contract, 64 Nw.U.L.Rev. 433 (1969); Dawson, Restitution without Enrichment, 61 B.U.L.Rev. 563, esp. 577–85 (1981); Galligan, Extra Work in Construction Cases: Restitution, Relationship and Revision, 63 Tul.L.Rev. 799,, 803, 858 (1989); Perillo, Restitution in a Contractual Context, 73 Colum.L.Rev. 1208 (1973); Sullivan, The Concept of Benefit in the Law of Quasi-Contract, 64 Geo.L.J. 1 (1975); Wonnell, Replacing the Unitary Principle of Unjust Enrichment, 45 Emory L.J. 153 (1996).

10. Discussion of recovery for benefits conferred without request is outside the scope of this volume. An illustration of such a recovery is restitution awarded against a parent to one who unofficiously supplies necessaries to an infant. Greenspan v. Slate, 12 N.J. 426, 97 A.2d 390 (1953); Note, 39 Cornell L.Q. 337 (1954). See Dawson, The Self–Serving Intermeddler, 87 Harv.L.Rev. 1409 (1974); Wade, Restitution for Benefits Conferred Without Request, 19 Vanderbilt L.Rev. 1183 (1966); 2 Palmer on Restitution §§ 10–1 to 10–11.

§ 15.3

1. U.S. for Use of Bldg. Rentals v. Western Cas. & Sur., 498 F.2d 335 (9th Cir.

1974); Rudd Paint & Varnish v. White, 403 F.2d 289 (10th Cir.1968); 5 Corbin § 1104.

2. See 5 Corbin § 1106; Woodward, Quasi Contracts § 260 (1913). The question whether an action for restitution based on breach is a contract remedy or a quasi-contractual action is not devoid of practical significance. For example, the U.S. has not waived its immunity under the Tucker Act as to quasi-contractual actions. Knight Newspapers v. U.S., 395 F.2d 353 (6th Cir. 1968). An action for restitution based on breach may, however, be brought under the Act. Acme Process Equip. v. U.S., 347 F.2d 509 (Ct.Cl.1965), on the theory that the action is on the contract. Rev'd on other grounds. For the confused state of the law with respect to restitutionary claims against the government, see Wall & Childres, The Law of Restitution and the Federal Government, 66 Nw.U.L.Rev. 587 (1971).

3. Buffalo Builders' Supply v. Reeb, 247 N.Y. 170, 159 N.E. 899 (1928); Sidney Stevens Imp. v. Hintze, 92 Utah 264, 67 P.2d 632, 111 ALR 331 (1937); Harris v. Metropolitan Mall, 112 Wis.2d 487, 334 N.W.2d 519 (1983); cf. Rosenwasser v. Blyn Shoes, 246 N.Y. 340, 159 N.E. 84 (1927); 5 Corbin § 1104; Woodward, supra n.2, at § 263. For total breach, see § 11.18 supra.

4. Rs. 2d § 373(1).

resulting from a mutual rescission and from a decision by an aggrieved party to cancel the contract are quite distinct, but have often been confused because of the semantic trap caused by utilization of the same term to describe distinct concepts. The UCC avoids this difficulty by adopting the term "cancel."[5] If an election to cancel is not made, the contract continues to bind both parties and the non-breaching party may recover damages for partial breach but not restitution.[6] If cancellation is effective, the non-breaching party generally must next elect to recover either restitution (quantum meruit) or damages; in some cases specific performance may also be an available remedy. The time when such an election must be made depends on the procedural rules of the particular jurisdiction.

In the past, the precondition necessary for the remedy of restitution was determined by whether the action was at law or in equity. At common law, the plaintiff was required to tender[7] back all tangible benefits received pursuant to the contract as a condition to commencement of the action.[8] In equity, however, actual tender was not always required, as a court of equity could condition its decree upon restitution by the plaintiff or offset the value of the benefits retained.[9] Today, a good number of jurisdictions have adopted the equity rule at law.[10] Although the Restatement (Second) § 384 continues to require an offer (but not a tender) by the plaintiff to make restoration, the requirement is mitigated by a number of exceptions.

§ 15.4 Measure of Recovery

The basic aim of restitution is to place the plaintiff in the same economic position as the plaintiff enjoyed prior to contracting.[1] Thus, unless specific restitution is obtained, the plaintiff's recovery is for the reasonable value of services rendered, goods delivered, or property conveyed less the reasonable value of any counter-performance received.[2]

---

5. UCC §§ 2–106(4), 2–703(f), 2–711(1) (no substantive changes by revision); see § 21.2 infra.

6. See § 11.32 supra.

7. Rs. 1st § 349 avoids the term "tender" and requires merely an offer to return. The UCC requires neither a tender nor an offer to return. The buyer must merely hold the goods at the seller's disposition. UCC § 2–602(2)(b) (no substantive change by revision). As to counterfeit goods, see Rice Aircraft v. Grumman Aerospace, 196 A.D.2d 583, 601 N.Y.S.2d 181 (1993).

8. Woodward, supra n.2, at § 265. As a corollary to this rule, a plaintiff who had received intangible benefits, such as services, could not bring an action at law for restitution. This is no longer the prevailing view. Timmerman v. Stanley, 123 Ga. 850, 51 S.E. 760 (1905); Brown v. Woodbury, 183 Mass. 279, 67 N.E. 327 (1903); Bollen-

back v. Continental Cas., 243 Or. 498, 414 P.2d 802 (1966).

9. See Holdeen v. Rinaldo, 28 A.D.2d 947, 281 N.Y.S.2d 657 (1967); Sneed v. State, 683 P.2d 525 (Okl.1983); 5 Corbin §§ 1102–1103, 1115–1116; 12 Williston §§ 1460, 1460A, 1463.

10. See 5 Corbin §§ 1102–1103, 1115–1116; 12 Williston § 1460.

§ 15.4

1. Resolution Trust v. FSLIC, 25 F.3d 1493 (10th Cir.1994).

2. ATACS Corp. v. Trans World Communications, 155 F.3d 659 (3d Cir.1998); Woodward, § 15.3 n.2 supra, at § 268. When an insured sues for restitution of premiums because an insurer wrongfully refuses to pay a claim, the cases are divided on the question of whether a deduction

No unjust enrichment is required here. The plaintiff recovers the reasonable value of the performance whether or not the defendant in any economic sense benefitted from the performance.[3] The quasi-contractual concept of benefit continues to be recognized by the rule that the defendant must have received the plaintiff's performance. Traditionally, it has been said that acts merely preparatory to performance will not justify an action for restitution.[4] "Receipt," however, is a legal concept rather than a description of physical fact. If what the plaintiff has done is part of the agreed exchange, it is deemed to be "received" by the defendant.[5]

As stated elsewhere, the trend of the law is to go beyond the benefit concept:

> When the plaintiff has expended funds, rendered services, or otherwise diminished his or her own estate in performing or preparing to perform an agreement that has since failed, but has not conferred a benefit on the defendant, the cutting edge of the case law has allowed recovery of these expenses. Often courts have accomplished this by legal alchemy, transmuting reliance damages into "benefits conferred" simply by so labeling them. Other courts have, with greater candor, expressly protected the reliance interest in restitution actions.[6] (Citations omitted).

How is reasonable value determined? By the weight of authority the plaintiff is not restricted to the contract rate of payment; however, the contract price is admissible as evidence of the value of the performance.[7] Thus, in Boomer v. Muir,[8] the plaintiff on a construction project justifiably canceled because of the defendant's breach. Upon completion of the work, plaintiff would have been entitled to an additional payment of $20,000, and that would have been plaintiff's recovery in an action for damages. Rather than sue for damages, however, the plaintiff elected to claim restitution. Judgment in the amount of $257,965.06 was affirmed on appeal. Scholars have debated the wisdom of the outcome. Some observers have regarded results such as this as an unwarranted distur-

---

should be made for the value of coverage the insured has had. See Bollenback v. Continental Cas., 243 Or. 498, 414 P.2d 802 (1966) (collecting cases).

3. U.S. v. Zara Contracting, 146 F.2d 606 (2d Cir.1944); Chodos v. West Pub. Co., 292 F.3d 992 (9th Cir.2002); Rogers v. Becker–Brainard Milling Mach., 211 Mass. 559, 98 N.E. 592 (1912); Mooney v. York Iron, 82 Mich. 263, 46 N.W. 376 (1890); Reed v. Reberry, 883 S.W.2d 59 (Mo.App. 1994); Robertus v. Candee, 205 Mont. 403, 670 P.2d 540 (1983); see Rs. 2d § 371; but see Stringer Oil v. Bobo, 320 S.C. 369, 465 S.E.2d 366 (1995), reh. denied (value to the defendant is the measure).

4. Rs. 1st § 348; Rs. 2d § 370.

5. Farash v. Sykes Datatronics, 59 N.Y.2d 500, 465 N.Y.S.2d 917, 452 N.E.2d 1245 (1983); Rs. 1st § 348 cmt a; Rs. 2d § 370 cmt a.

6. Perillo, Restitution in the Second Restatement of Contracts, 81 Colum.L.Rev. 37, 39 (1981). Another example of legal alchemy is Petrie–Clemons v. Butterfield, 122 N.H. 120, 441 A.2d 1167 (1982); see Libassi v. Chelli, 206 A.D.2d 509, 615 N.Y.S.2d 75 (1994) (avoidance for fraud; reliance interest protected).

7. U.S. for the Use of Building Rentals v. Western Cas. & Sur., 498 F.2d 335 (9th Cir.1974). See Palmer, The Contract Price as a Limit on Restitution for Defendant's Breach, 20 Ohio St.L.J. 264 (1959).

8. 24 P.2d 570 (Cal.App.1933), hearing dismissed.

bance of the risks assumed by the parties and argue that the contract rate should set an upper limit[9] or that the claimant be relegated to obtaining expectancy damages.[10] But others have justified such results by pointing out either that the wrongdoer must take the consequences,[11] or that the party who has breached should not be permitted to seek the protection of the contract.[12] Others, reading between the lines, justify the decision on the grounds that the general contractor's delays were responsible for the overrun.[13]

If the plaintiff has made full or part payment for a performance that was not rendered, it is generally agreed that the plaintiff should not be relegated to expectancy damages if plaintiff prefers to seek restitution of its payments.[14] If the plaintiff has performed in whole or in part and the value of the defendant's return promise is too uncertain to be a predicate for expectancy damages, restitution is an available remedy.[15]

The Restatement (Second) states that restitution is available only if the benefit to the defendant is conferred by the plaintiff. "It is not enough that it was simply derived from the breach."[16] The comments offer the illustration of an employee, *A*, who in violation of his obligation to his employer, *B*, not to work for anyone else, takes a part-time job with *C*. *B* cannot recover from *A* the salary paid by *C*, "because it [is] not a benefit conferred by *B*."[17] While the illustration is sound, the rule must be supplemented by exceptions existing beyond the borderland of traditional contract scholarship, such as those contained in the Restatements of Agency and Restitution. Three sections of the Restatement of Agency deal with such exceptions.[18] The rule is that an employer may recover a bribe received by an employee.[19] Employees and others in fiduciary or confidential relationships must disgorge any other benefits received by them in breach of trust.[20] Other exceptions to the "source of benefit" rule exist and, though sporadic, arise frequently enough to suggest that a residuum of cases arise in which the most appropriate remedy is restitution by the breaching party of ill-gotten gains obtained from the breach.[21]

9. Childres & Garamella, The Law of Restitution and the Reliance Interest in Contract, 64 Nw.U.L.R. 433 (1969); Perillo, Restitution in the Second Restatement of Contracts, 81 Colum.L.Rev. 37, 44–45 (1981).

10. Mather, Restitution as a Remedy for Breach of Contract: The Case of the Partially Performing Seller, 92 Yale L.J. 14 (1982).

11. Palmer supra note 7, at 269–73.

12. Gegan, In Defense of Restitution: A Comment on Mather, Restitution as a Remedy for Breach of Contract, 57 S.Cal.L.Rev. 723 (1984).

13. Gergen supra § 15.1 n.8 at 711–13.

14. Bush v. Canfield, 2 Conn. 485 (1818); Sparks v. Farmers Fed. S. & L. Assn., 183 W.Va. 315, 395 S.E.2d 559 (1990).

15. Chodos v. West Pub. Co., 292 F.3d 992 (9th Cir.2002).

16. Rs. 2d § 370 cmt a.

17. Rs. 2d § 370 ill. 4.

18. Rs. 2d, Agency §§ 403, 404, 404A.

19. Lamdin v. Broadway Surface Advertising, 272 N.Y. 133, 5 N.E.2d 66 (1936) (restitution at law); Fuchs v. Bidwill, 31 Ill.App.3d 567, 334 N.E.2d 117 (1975) (constructive trust in equity), reversed on other grounds; Rs. 2d, Agency § 403; Rs., Restitution § 197.

20. Raestle v. Whitson, 119 Ariz. 524, 582 P.2d 170 (1978); Meinhard v. Salmon, 249 N.Y. 458, 164 N.E. 545, 62 ALR 1 (1928); 4 Palmer on Restitution § 21.7.

21. Snepp v. U.S., 444 U.S. 507 (1980); Reeves v. Alyeska Pipeline Service Co., 56 P.3d 660 (Alaska 2002) (disgorgement for breach of a non-disclosure agreement.); EarthInfo v. Hydrosphere Resource Consultants, 900 P.2d 113 (Colo.1995); 4 Palmer

§ 15.5   Specific Restitution

At times, an equitable decree for specific restitution is available for breach of contract. The remedy requires all elements of an action at law for restitution except that it is not a precondition to a suit for specific restitution that the plaintiff have offered to restore what he has received under the contract.[1] However, traditionally, there exists an additional requirement for this equitable remedy. The plaintiff must show the inadequacy of the legal remedy.[2] The Restatement (Second) dispenses with this requirement,[3] but little or no authority exists for this dispensation.

Inadequacy of the legal remedy may exist because property transferred by the plaintiff is unique. But such a showing is more difficult in an action for specific restitution than in an action for specific performance. In the latter case, any real property is treated as unique, but since the plaintiff was willing to part with the property, it normally cannot be said that it has unique value to the plaintiff.[4] Therefore, specific restitution in the form of cancellation of a deed is not normally available[5] against a defaulting purchaser. Another reason commonly given for denial of such relief is that the grantor could have negotiated a condition in the deed or have taken back a purchase money mortgage as security for the purchase price.[6]

Nevertheless, if special circumstances exist—often where the damages suffered are speculative—such relief is available. Thus, if real property is transferred in exchange for a life support promise, specific restitution has generally been permitted for total breach of the promise.[7] Where there has been an agreement to exchange parcels of land, and the legal remedy has been shown to be inadequate, specific restitution has been granted.[8] Also, mineral leases have been canceled where the lessee

---

on Restitution § 4.9; 3 Dobbs on Remedies 174–78; Birks, Restitutionary Damages for Breach of Contract: Snepp and the Fusion of Law and Equity, 1987 Lloyd's Mar. & Com. L.Q. 421; Farnsworth, Your Loss or My Gain?, 94 Yale L.J. 1339 (1985); Jones, The Recovery of Benefits Gained from Breach of Contract, 99 L.Q.Rev. 443 (1983); Kull, Disgorgement for Breach, the "Restitution Interest," and the Restatement of Contracts, 79 Tex.L.Rev. 2021 (2001); Laycock, The Scope and Significance of Restitution, 67 Tex.L.Rev. 177, 1289 (1989). An economic justification for such results is given in Kronman, Specific Performance, 45 U.Chi.L.Rev. 351, 376–82 (1978).

§ 15.5

1.   Rs. 1st § 354(b); see § 15.3 supra.

2.   Rs. 1st § 354.

3.   Rs. 2d § 372, but see cmt b as to land transactions. See Perillo, Restitution in the Second Restatement of Contracts, 81 Co-

lum.L.Rev. 37, 47–49 (1981); 3 Dobbs on Remedies § 12.7(2).

4.   Rs. 1st § 354 cmt b; 5 Corbin § 1120.

5.   12 Williston § 1456.

6.   Cleveland v. Herron, 102 Ohio St. 218, 131 N.E. 489 (1921); see Comment, 46 Chi.-Kent L.Rev. 197 (1969). Similarly a purchaser is usually denied restitution on a real property transaction for failure of title on the ground the purchaser should have negotiated for warranties. Comment, 18 Baylor L.Rev. 92 (1966).

7.   Rs. 2d § 372 ill. 3; Caramini v. Tegulias, 121 Conn. 548, 186 A. 482, 112 ALR 666 (1936); Yuhas v. Schmidt, 434 Pa. 447, 258 A.2d 616 (1969). An equitable lien has sometimes been imposed instead of cancellation of the deed. See Coykendall v. Kellogg, 50 N.D. 857, 198 N.W. 472 (1924).

8.   Rs. 2d § 372 ill. 2; Graves v. White, 87 N.Y. 463 (1882); Piper v. Queeney, 282 Pa. 135, 127 A. 474 (1925).

has breached its promise to develop the tract.[9] In one case where specific restitution was ordered, land had been transferred in exchange for a promise that the land would be subdivided and developed and that a portion of the land would be reconveyed to the original grantor.[10]

Specific restitution of personal property is also available where the legal remedy is inadequate. Thus, where the holder of a patent assigns it to another in consideration of a share of profits to be earned from its exploitation, the assignor may have specific restitution for total breach by the assignee.[11] The remedy of damages would be inadequate because damages cannot be proved with sufficient certainty. Although monetary restitution for the value of the patent is more susceptible to proof, the seller evinced no intent to transfer the patent for a cash price. A denial of specific restitution would transmute the contract into a cash sale. Restitution of shares of stock issued under a stock option plan has been ordered when a contrary result would destroy the purpose of the stock option plan.[12] Such restitution has also been permitted where the transfer of stock has resulted in a change of corporate control.[13] Of course, here, as elsewhere, the breach must go to the essence of the contract.

Often the inadequacy of the legal remedy is predicated upon the insolvency of the defendant and the consequent inability to obtain satisfaction of a money judgment. Equity will grant specific restitution in such cases provided, however, that the interests of other creditors will not be adversely affected.[14] As to sales of goods, the UCC contains specific provisions with respect to insolvency. Section 2–702(2) provides, in part, that:

> Where the seller discovers that the buyer has received goods on credit while insolvent he may reclaim the goods upon demand made within ten days after the receipt, but if misrepresentation of solvency has been made to the particular seller in writing within three months before delivery the ten day limitation does not apply.[15]

The UCC is silent on the question of whether a seller may reclaim goods for reasons other than insolvency and non-payment. As to nonpayment, when payment is due on delivery of goods and payment is demanded, the buyer's "right as against the seller to retain or dispose of them is conditional upon his making the payment due."[16] Consequently, it has been suggested that under this provision if the seller is given a

---

9. Sauder v. Mid–Continent Petroleum, 292 U.S. 272, 93 ALR 454 (1934); Leonard v. Carter, 389 S.W.2d 147 (Tex.Civ.App. 1965), error dismissed.

10. Benassi v. Harris, 147 Conn. 451, 162 A.2d 521 (1960); see also Sneed v. State, 683 P.2d 525 (Okl.1983).

11. Alder v. Drudis, 30 Cal.2d 372, 182 P.2d 195 (1947); Rs. 1st § 354 ill. 7; see also KSL Recreation v. Boca Raton Hotel, 168 Misc.2d 18, 637 N.Y.S.2d 261 (1995) (return of financial and other proprietary records).

12. Maytag v. Alward, 253 Iowa 455, 112 N.W.2d 654, 96 ALR2d 162 (1962).

13. Callanan v. Powers, 199 N.Y. 268, 92 N.E. 747 (1910). See Rs. 2d § 372 ill. 5.

14. Rs. 1st § 354(a) ills. 6, 7.

15. The revision makes two substantive changes. The term "a reasonable time" is substituted for "ten days" and the language concerning "misrepresentation of solvency" is deleted.

16. UCC § 2–507(2) (the revision clarifies some language).

check which is dishonored, the seller may have specific restitution by replevying the goods.[17] Whether, in transactions governed by the UCC, specific restitution is available based on the inadequacy of the legal remedy because the goods are unique is an open question.[18]

Both under common law[19] and under the UCC,[20] a sale of property to a bona fide purchaser for value cuts off rights of specific restitution or, as the UCC puts it, reclamation. If the proceeds can be traced, however, to other property, the court may impose a constructive trust or equitable lien upon the other property.[21]

§ 15.6   Restitution at Law Not Available if a Debt Has Been Created: Severability

It is an anomaly of the law of restitution that if the plaintiff in Boomer v. Muir, discussed in section 15.4, had completed the performance and was aggrieved by the defendant's failure to pay, the maximum recovery would have been $20,000. It is firmly established that if a debt has been created by the plaintiff's full performance,[1] the plaintiff may not have restitution.[2] The creditor is restricted to an action for recovery of the debt. No explanation for this rule appears to exist other than such a result appears to have been established early in the history of the writ of indebitatus assumpsit.[3]

An interesting case pointing up the anomaly is Oliver v. Campbell,[4] in which plaintiff, an attorney, was retained as counsel in a divorce action for the agreed fee of $750. At the conclusion of the divorce trial, but before judgment, plaintiff was discharged without justification. The court found that the reasonable value of the services was $5,000. The majority of the court, however, took the position that plaintiff had fully

---

17. Nordstrom, Sales § 166; White & Summers, Uniform Commercial Code § 3–7 (4th ed.).

18. A negative view is expressed in Nordstrom, Sales § 165 n. 86, apparently on the ground that UCC § 2–703 and related sections contain considered policy decisions as to the rights of sellers, particularly with respect to the rights of other creditors. However, special situations arise that fall outside such considered policy decisions. These can be decided under UCC § 1–103 (revised § 1–103(b)). See, e.g., Alder v. Drudis, 30 Cal.2d 372, 182 P.2d 195 (1947) (restitution of patent rights and patent models; the models are goods and specific restitution is the most rational remedy).

19. Rs. 1st § 354(a).

20. UCC § 2–702(3) (no substantive change by revision)

21. Clark v. McCleery, 115 Iowa 3, 87 N.W. 696 (1901); Matthews v. Crowder, 111 Tenn. 737, 69 S.W. 779 (1902); cf. Rs. 1st § 354 ill. 4 (subrogation); Rs. 2d § 372 cmt a.

§ 15.6

1. Lynch v. Stebbins, 127 Me. 203, 142 A. 735 (1928); Farron v. Sherwood, 17 N.Y. 227 (1858); 5 Corbin § 1110; Rs. 2d § 373(2); Comment, 57 Mich.L.Rev. 268 (1958).

2. Holland v. Tandem Computers, 49 F.3d 1287 (8th Cir.1995); Siebler Heating & Air Conditioning v. Jenson, 212 Neb. 830, 326 N.W.2d 182 (1982); Rs. 2d § 373(2).

3. Keener, Quasi Contracts 301–02 (1893); Woodward, § 15.3 supra n.2, at 415; cf. 5 Corbin § 1110. The Restatement states that the rule makes the court's job easier. Rs. 2d § 373 cmt b.

4. 43 Cal.2d 298, 273 P.2d 15 (1954); Matter of Montgomery's Estate, 272 N.Y. 323, 6 N.E.2d 40, 109 ALR 669 (1936) (plaintiff attorney was promised $5,000 for agreed services; after completing five-sixths of the agreed services he was discharged; recovery of $13,000 was sustained).

performed and thus could recover only $750, while the dissenting judges concluded that he had not fully performed and was, therefore, entitled to $5,000.

It also has been stated to be the rule that if any severable portion of the contract has been performed, the plaintiff may not obtain restitution as to that portion, but only the apportioned price.[5] Conversely, if the contract is severable, the plaintiff may obtain restitution of the materially breached portions without canceling those portions that are performed.[6]

The criteria for severability developed in other contexts have not been mechanically applied in this connection. The mere fact that a unit price has been established by contract per ton of coal delivered or per unit of earth excavated should not result in a finding of severability if it appears that the contract price is based on an average of the estimated future market price which fluctuates seasonally or an average value per unit of excavation of ground of varying difficulty, and the plaintiff's deliveries were made during the period when the market price was highest[7] or the ground excavated was of more than average difficulty.[8] The mere fact that a debt has been created will not bar restitution if the claimant was owed other duties under the contract, such as the continuation of a partnership[9] or a reasonable opportunity to be considered for admission to a partnership.[10]

§ 15.7 Recovery of Both Damages and Restitution

As a general rule, a plaintiff may not recover both restitution and damages for breach of contract.[1] At some stage the plaintiff must elect remedies;[2] the time at which such an election must be made varies with local practice, but the modern tendency is to dispense with the earlier requirement that an election be made in the pleadings.[3]

5. Dibol v. Minott, 9 Iowa 403 (1859); Rs. 1st § 351.

6. Czarnikow–Rionda v. West Market Grocery, 21 F.2d 309 (2d Cir.1927) cert. denied; Portfolio v. Rubin, 233 N.Y. 439, 135 N.E. 843 (1922).

7. Wellston Coal v. Franklin Paper, 57 Ohio St. 182, 48 N.E. 888 (1897) (coal has a higher market value in winter); accord, Clark v. Manchester, 51 N.H. 594 (1872) (contract of employment for one year at $25 per month; plaintiff discharged after working during season when wages were generally highest); see also Davidson v. Laughlin, 138 Cal. 320, 71 P. 345 (1903); Williams v. Bemis, 108 Mass. 91, 11 Am.Rep. 318 (1871).

8. Scaduto v. Orlando, 381 F.2d 587 (2d Cir.1967); Clark v. City of N.Y., 4 N.Y. 338, 53 Am.Dec. 379 (1850); Rs. 1st § 347 ill. 3; see 3 Dobbs on Remedies § 12.7(6); Palmer, The Contract Price as a Limit on Restitution for Defendant's Breach, 20 Ohio St.L.J. 264, 276 (1959).

9. Nelson v. Gish, 103 Idaho 57, 644 P.2d 980 (1982); Bailey v. Interstate Airmotive, 358 Mo. 1121, 219 S.W.2d 333, 8 ALR2d 710 (1949). Not all jurisdictions accept this view. See Comment, 57 Mich. L.Rev. 268 (1958).

10. Kovacic, Applying Restitution to Remedy a Discriminatory Denial of Partnership, 34 Syracuse L.Rev. 743 (1983).

§ 15.7

1. Downs v. Jersey Central Power & Light, 117 N.J.Eq. 138, 174 A. 887 (1934); Pickinpaugh v. Morton, 268 Or. 9, 519 P.2d 91 (1974).

2. For a discussion of what election is most favorable to a plaintiff in one context, see Guittard, Building Contracts: Damages and Restitution, 32 Tex.B.J. 91 (1969).

3. See, e.g. Barron & Holtzoff, Federal Practice and Procedure § 282 (1960); Clark, Code Pleading § 77 (2d ed. 1937); Moore, Federal Practice § 2.06[3] (1967); Wein-

It should carefully be noted, however, that in an award for damages, the plaintiff's restitutionary interest is usually protected.[4] The plaintiff is entitled to losses sustained (benefits conferred on the other and reliance expenditures) as well as gains prevented. Until the advent of the UCC, however, in an action for restitution, the plaintiff's expectation interest usually received no protection. If defective machinery were delivered and the buyer elected to return the machinery, the buyer was entitled to restitution of payments made and often certain reliance expenditures,[5] but received no compensation for any additional cost of replacing the machinery. Under the UCC, however, the buyer may have the remedy of restitution and recover damages as well.[6] For example, a purchaser of goods may revoke acceptance upon discovery of a breach of warranty, offer to return the goods, and recover the purchase price plus damages measured by the expectation and reliance interests.[7]

stein, Korn and Miller, New York Civil Practice § 3002–04 (1998); Rs. 2d § 378.

4. See generally, Fuller & Perdue, The Reliance Interest in Contract Damages, 46 Yale L.J. 52, 373 (1936–37).

5. Freight charges were recovered in International Harvester v. Olson, 62 N.D. 256, 243 N.W. 258 (1932); Houser & Haines Mfg. v. McKay, 53 Wash. 337, 101 P. 894, 27 LRA NS, 925 (1909); but see American Paper & Pulp v. Denenberg, 233 F.2d 610 (3d Cir.1956). Expenses incurred in attempting to utilize defective purchases were recovered in Granette Products v. Arthur H. Neumann & Co., 200 Iowa 572, 203 N.W. 935 (1925), modified 200 Iowa 572, 205 N.W. 205 (1925), aff'd; National Sand & Gravel v. R.H. Beaumont Co., 9 N.J.Misc.

1026, 156 A. 441 (1931). Consequential damages resulting from personal injuries were recovered in Russo v. Hochschild Kohn & Co., 184 Md. 462, 41 A.2d 600, 157 ALR 1070 (1945). See 12 Williston § 1464; Anderson, Quasi Contractual Recovery in the Law of Sales, 21 Minn.L.Rev. 529 (1937); Rooge, Damages upon Rescission for Breach of Warranty, 28 Mich.L.Rev. 26 (1929); Notes, 21 Minn.L.Rev. 111 (1936); 45 Yale L.J. 1313 (1936).

6. UCC § 2–711(1) (substantively unchanged by revision); see Grandi v. LeSage, 74 N.M. 799, 399 P.2d 285 (1965).

7. See Nordstrom, Restitution on Default and Article Two of the UCC, 19 Vand. L.Rev. 1143, 1175 (1966); 1 Palmer on Restitution § 4.15.

Chapter 16

SPECIFIC PERFORMANCE AND INJUNCTIONS

Table of Sections

Table of Sections

A. SUBSTANTIVE BASES FOR EQUITABLE RELIEF

B. DEFENSES

C. COVENANTS NOT TO COMPETE

A. SUBSTANTIVE BASES FOR EQUITABLE RELIEF

Table of Sections

§ 16.1   Inadequacy of the Legal Remedy

A legal system can provide redress of various kinds for breach of contract. It can choose to grant specific performance, an order compelling a defaulting promisor to perform. But while a number of legal systems regard a decree for specific performance to be the ideal and preferred choice, the common law has evolved differently. The primary relief that the Anglo–American legal systems offer is substitutionary relief,[1] normally damages. Under this approach, instead of mandating performance of the promise, the value of the promise is substituted. The next preferred remedy is restitution where the value of what has been given in exchange for the promise is substituted for the performance of the promise.[2]

Specific performance is an extraordinary remedy developed in Courts of Equity to provide relief when the legal remedies of damages and restitution are inadequate.[3] Put another way, equity will give no remedy unless the plaintiff can show that irreparable injury will result if equitable relief is refused. The terms "inadequate" and "irreparable" should be taken with a grain of salt: the accretion of centuries of precedent has given them meanings that would astonish dictionary-makers.[4]

---

§ 16.1

1. See Yorio, Contract Enforcement § 1.2 (the most extensive modern treatment of specific performance); Dawson, Specific Performance in France and Germany, 57 Mich.L.Rev. 495 (1959); Farnsworth, Legal Remedies for Breach of Promise, 70 Colum.L.Rev. 1145, 1145–60 (1970).

2. Delivery Service and Transf. v. Heiner Equip. & Supply, 635 P.2d 21 (Utah 1981); cf. Rs. 2d § 359(3) and cmt c.

3. Maryland and Massachusetts by statute permit specific performance in some cases where, under traditional tests, the legal remedy is adequate. See Van Hecke,

Changing Emphases in Specific Performance, 40 N.C.L.Rev. 1, 9–11 (1961).

4. See Laycock, The Death of the Irreparable Injury Rule (1991); but see Nemer Jeep–Eagle v. Jeep–Eagle Sales, 992 F.2d 430 (2d Cir.1993) (in depth inquiry into adequacy of legal remedy in an unusual context); Zurn Constructors v. B.F. Goodrich Co., 685 F.Supp. 1172 (D.Kan.1988) (same); ER Holdings v. Norton Co., 735 F.Supp. 1094 (D.Mass.1990) (same); American Music v. Higbee, 289 Mont. 278, 961 P.2d 109 (1998) (same); Hovey v. Superior Ct., 165 Ariz. 278, 798 P.2d 416 (1990) (plea bargain).

A decree for specific performance takes many forms. It may order a party affirmatively to carry out contractual duties or enjoin the party from acting where the contract requires forbearance.[5] But at times, a party will merely be enjoined from violating a contract rather than ordered to perform. For example, a seller under an output contract may be enjoined from selling to anyone other than the plaintiff.[6] In such a case the court will not be burdened with supervision of performance, but the seller will have every economic incentive to perform. Although there are a variety of methods of enforcing such a decree, its ultimate force derives from the ability of a court of equity to punish violations of its decrees by fines and imprisonment for contempt of court.[7] Declaratory judgments, the product of modern statutes, are generally deemed to be equitable in nature.[8]

Economic analysts have questioned whether equitable relief produces efficient results. While some analysts stress that specific performance exactly protects the expectancy interest and thus avoids overcompensation and undercompensation,[9] others have warned that the routine grant of specific performance would be inadvisable. They argue that where the cost of full performance exceeds its value to the claimant, the claimant would be in a position to exact "bribe" money for settling the case or, at any rate, that the cost of negotiating a settlement would be excessive and inefficient.[10] But these critics tend to ignore that, in the situation where cost of performance exceeds its value, relieving the breaching party of the duty of performance would result in its unjust enrichment. Why the breaching party's savings should not inure to, or be shared by, the aggrieved party is not at all clear. Whatever the merits of those economic analyses that support the routine grant of equitable relief, the restrictions on equitable relief are so ingrained in our legal system that only a very gradual removal of them is foreseeable.

In those situations where specific performance is routinely given, the claimant's interest in the subject matter is very much akin to a property interest.[11] The other party is not merely subject to a liability to pay damages but must turn over precisely the thing or service promised.

5. Wellness Community—National v. Wellness House, 891 F.Supp. 1273 (N.D.Ill. 1995), reversed on jurisdictional grounds.

6. See Rs. 2d § 357 ill. 1; but see Florida Jai Alai v. Southern Catering Services, 388 So.2d 1076 (Fla.App.1980).

7. See McClintock, Handbook of the Principles of Equity § 17 (2d ed. 1948) [hereinafter McClintock].

8. Reno v. Bossier Parish School Bd., 520 U.S. 471 (1997).

9. Schwartz, The Case for Specific Performance, 89 Yale L.J. 271 (1979); Schwartz, The Myth that Promisees Prefer Supra Compensatory Remedies, 100 Yale L.J. 369 (1990); Linzer, On the Amorality of Contract Remedies—Efficiency, Equity, and the Second Restatement, 81 Colum.L.Rev.

111 (1981); Ulen, The Efficiency of Specific Performance, 83 Mich.L.Rev. 341 (1984); compare Yorio, In Defense of Money Damages for Breach of Contract, 82 Colum.L.Rev. 1365 (1982).

10. Posner, Economic Analysis of Law 130–132 (4th ed.); Kronman, Specific Performance, 45 U.Chi.L.Rev. 351 (1978); Muris, The Cost of Freely Granting Specific Performance, 1982 Duke L.J. 1053. Economic, moral and administrative factors that inform a decision on equitable relief are analyzed in Rendleman, The Inadequate Remedy at Law Prerequisite for an Injunction, 33 U.Fla.L.Rev. 346 (1981).

11. See Kronman, supra n.10.

The rules pertaining to real property have long recognized this phenomenon, developing the doctrine of equitable conversion to account for the contract purchaser's interest in realty.[12]

The next four sections discuss the inadequacy of the legal remedy in contexts where the issue most frequently arises. It should be noted, however, that the legal remedy may be inadequate in any context. Consider the following circumstances.

- A breach of contract to give a film maker screen credits on the film may be redressed by enjoining further release of the film without such credits, partly because the loss of publicity is most difficult to quantify and, if quantified, does not fully repair the injury done.[13]

- A breach of a unilateral obligation to pay money in installments is best redressed by a decree ordering payments to be made as they mature[14] because the legal remedy redresses only past due breaches of such an obligation.[15]

- A pre-marital agreement to appear before a rabbinical tribunal in the event of a civil divorce, in order to release the spouse from the religious tie of marriage, has been specifically enforced.[16] No legal remedy exists for this breach, but without the tribunal appearance, the spouse cannot, consistent with religious conscience, remarry.

- The ETS may be ordered to follow its procedures for reviewing examination scores it questions. If the candidate submits explanatory material for consideration the ETS must examine the material in good faith in accordance with its contract terms.[17]

- An injunction may be issued to protect the status quo pending the resolution of an arbitration where the status quo cannot later be restored.[18]

- No legal remedy exists for a threatened breach. Under the proper circumstances, equity may enjoin a threatened breach. "Should a judge stand idly by, watch a wrongdoer inflict harm, and only later tell him to pay the victim?"[19] Certainly not.

12. See § 16.2 infra; Cunningham, Stoebuck & Whitman, The Law of Property § 10.13 (1984). The consequences of equitable conversion are many. See, e.g., DeShields v. Broadwater, 338 Md. 422, 659 A.2d 300 (1995) (lis pendens filed after a contract to sell is made does not affect contract purchaser's rights).

13. Tamarind Lithography Workshop v. Sanders, 143 Cal.App.3d 571, 193 Cal.Rptr. 409 (1983).

14. Tuttle v. Palmer, 117 N.H. 477, 374 A.2d 661 (1977); Teague v. Springfield Life Ins., 55 N.C.App. 437, 285 S.E.2d 860 (1982).

15. See § 12.9 supra.

16. Minkin v. Minkin, 180 N.J.Super. 260, 434 A.2d 665 (1981); Avitzur v. Avitzur, 58 N.Y.2d 108, 459 N.Y.S.2d 572, 446 N.E.2d 136, 29 ALR4th 736 (1983), cert. denied, 49 Albany L.Rev. 131 (1984), 33 Cath.U.L.Rev. 219 (1983); contra, Aflalo v. Aflalo, 295 N.J.Super. 527, 685 A.2d 523 (1996).

17. Dalton v. ETS, 87 N.Y.2d 384, 663 N.E.2d 289, 639 N.Y.S.2d 977 (1995).

18. Organizing Committee for the 1998 Goodwill Games v. Goodwill Games, 919 F.Supp. 21 (D.D.C.1995).

19. Rendleman, Book Review, 90 Mich. L.Rev. 1642, 1647 (1992); see U.S. Reinsurance Corp. v. Humphreys, 205 A.D.2d 187, 618 N.Y.S.2d 270 (1994) (threat by fiducia-

● Workers' Compensation claims may be adjudicated or reopened years after an injury occurs. Thus, in one case an employer contracted with a Workers' Compensation insurer for coverage with a large deductible. It agreed to provide a letter of credit to ensure its ability to pay the deductibles, but failed to provide the letter of credit. The court enjoined the insurer from cancelling for breach but decreed that the employer furnish the letter of credit.[20]

§ 16.2 Legal Remedy Inadequate—Real Property

In Medieval England, the doctrine became established that each parcel of land and every interest in land was unique. This made sense in a society where one's rank in society was often derived from the nature and quality of one's land holdings. Consequently, the remedy of damages for breach of a contract to convey an interest in land was deemed inadequate.

Today, despite the frequently non-unique character of parcels in housing subdivisions, the medieval doctrine still holds. Every interest in land is conclusively presumed to be unique and a contract to convey will be specifically enforced,[1] even where the presumptive unique value of the land is rebutted as when the vendee has in turn contracted to resell the interest to a third party.[2] The availability of specific performance is so well established that the law of property has come to look at the contract purchaser as the owner under the doctrine of equitable conversion, a doctrine having numerous practical consequences.[3] The uniqueness of real property carries over to contracts with respect to its use. Restrictive covenants with respect to the use of land are often enforced by enjoining nonconforming uses.[4]

Absent an agreement to the contrary, a contract to convey real property contains an implied term that title be "marketable," that is, title must be good. When the vendor's title is discovered to be encumbered, and thus not "marketable," the vendee may nonetheless elect to enforce the contract. The court will decree specific performance with an abatement in price.[5] Although it has been charged that such a decree

ry to utilize plaintiff's trade secrets); New York v. New York Jets, 90 Misc.2d 311, 394 N.Y.S.2d 799 (1977) (injunction against threat to breach lease).

20. The Power P.E.O. v. Employees Ins., 201 Ariz. 559, 38 P.3d 1224 (App. 2002).

§ 16.2

1. Kitchen v. Herring, 42 N.C. (7 Ired Eq.) 190 (1851); Rs. 1st § 360(a) and cmt a; Rs. 2d § 360, cmt e; DeFuniak, Contracts Enforceable in Equity, 34 Va.L.Rev. 637, 643 (1948); Annot., 65 ALR 7, 40 (1930). Contra, Suchan v. Rutherford, 90 Idaho 288, 410 P.2d 434 (1966); Centex Homes v. Boag, 128 N.J.Super. 385, 320 A.2d 194 (1974) (condominium apartment deemed

not unique), noted in 6 St. Mary's L.Rev. 766 (1975), 9 Suffolk L.Rev. 922 (1975); 48 Temple L.Q. 847 (1975); 43 U.Cin.L.Rev. 935 (1974).

2. Justus v. Clelland, 133 Ariz. 381, 651 P.2d 1206 (1982); Rs. 1st § 360 cmt a; Rs. 2d § 360 cmt e. De Funiak, supra n.1, at 643. Contra, Marthinson v. King, 150 F. 48 (5th Cir.1906).

3. See Cunningham, Stoebuck & Whitman, supra § 16.1 n.12.

4. Terrien v. Zwit, 467 Mich. 56, 648 N.W.2d 602 (2002).

5. Wooster Republican Printing v. Channel Seventeen, 682 F.2d 165 (8th Cir. 1982); Fleenor v. Church, 681 P.2d 1351

involves the remaking of the contract, in fact the court is merely tailoring the remedy for breach of contract to fit the situation by enforcing the contract and offsetting damages from the purchase price.[6] Abatements have also been employed where the plaintiff suffered damages from the defendant's fraud.[7] Frequently, however, the court will refuse an abatement where the vendee knew of the defect at the time of contracting[8] (on a theory of assumption of the risk or estoppel) or where the nature of the defect is such that only a radically different kind of estate can be conveyed from that contracted for.[9]

§ 16.3   Legal Remedy Inadequate—Personal Property

The UCC provides in Section 2–716 that "specific performance may be decreed where the goods are unique or in other proper circumstances."[1] This rule represents a departure from the more circumscribed rule previously in effect under the Uniform Sales Act. Clearly, goods are unique if they are "family heirlooms or priceless works of art,"[2] or a stereo system assembled over a period of fifteen years.[3] In addition, goods may be deemed "unique" or "other proper circumstances" may be deemed to exist if there is an inability to cover.[4] Inability to cover may exist because of market shortages[5] or because of a monopoly on the part of the defendant.[6] Normally, however, goods are available in the market and damages is an adequate remedy for breach of a contract to sell goods,[7] but requirements and output contracts have been specifically enforced with some frequency. One reason why this is so is that damages

(Alaska 1984); Atkin v. Cobb, 663 S.W.2d 48 (Tex.App.1983); See Annot. 143 ALR 555 (1943); 5A Corbin § 1160; 11 Williston § 1436; Note, 24 Okl.L.Rev. 495 (1971); Rs. 1st § 365. On rare occasions a *vendor* has been granted specific performance with an abatement in an action against a vendee. See 3 Dobbs, Remedies 323–24 (1993); McClintock at 174–75. See also § 9.26 supra.

6.   McClintock at 175.

7.   Stoll v. Grimm, 681 N.E.2d 749 (Ind. App.1997).

8.   Hughes v. Hadley, 96 N.J.Eq. 467, 126 A. 33 (1924).

9.   In re Estate of Hayhurst, 478 P.2d 343 (Okl.1970), 24 Okla.L.Rev. 495 (1971) (life estate instead of fee); Reid v. Allen, 216 Va. 630, 221 S.E.2d 166 (1976).

§ 16.3

1.   On the background and application of this provision, see Axelrod, Specific Performance of Contracts for Sales of Goods, 7 Vt.L.Rev. 249 (1982); Greenberg, Specific Performance under Section 2–716 of the Uniform Commercial Code, 17 New Eng. L.Rev. 321 (1982); 87 Comm.L.J. 583 (1982).

2.   UCC § 2–716 cmt 1; Ruddock v. First Nat. Bank, 201 Ill.App.3d 907, 147 Ill.Dec. 310, 559 N.E.2d 483 (1990) (rare clock); see 11 Williston § 1419 n. 2; Yorio, Contract Enforcement § 11.2.2.

3.   Cumbest v. Harris, 363 So.2d 294 (Miss.1978).

4.   UCC § 2–716 cmt 2; see Bander v. Grossman, 161 Misc.2d 119, 611 N.Y.S.2d 985 (1994) (Aston–Martin is unique, but plaintiff was guilty of laches).

5.   Laclede Gas v. Amoco, 522 F.2d 33 (8th Cir.1975); Mitchell–Huntley Cotton v. Waldrep, 377 F.Supp. 1215 (D.Ala.1974) (defendant ordered to pick, gin and deliver cotton crop during market shortage); Kaiser Trading v. Associated Metals & Minerals, 321 F.Supp. 923 (N.D.Cal.1970), appeal dismissed; Glick v. Beer, 263 A.D. 599, 33 N.Y.S.2d 833 (1942); Comment, 53 N.C.L.Rev. 579 (1975); King Aircraft Sales v. Lane, 68 Wn.App. 706, 846 P.2d 550 (1993) (planes were rare but not unique).

6.   11 Williston § 1419. On the the seller's right to sue for the price (a form of specific performance at law), see § 14.26 supra.

7.   Pierce–Odom v. Evenson, 5 Ark.App. 67, 632 S.W.2d 247 (1982).

are very difficult to ascertain when goods are to be delivered in installments over a long term.[8]

Contracts for the sale of unique personalty other than goods are also specifically enforceable as the purchaser cannot obtain a substitute performance on the market. Consequently, contracts for the transfer of patents,[9] copyrights,[10] shares in a closely held corporation,[11] or sufficient shares to assure control of a corporation whose shares are publicly traded have been specifically enforced.[12] Contracts for the sale of a business are also often specifically enforced as each business can be deemed unique.[13] For the same reason, a merger agreement can be specifically enforced.[14]

The proposed revision of UCC Article 2 would make a major change with respect to contractual provisions consenting to specific performance. Clauses providing for specific performance in the event of breach have been uncommon. Generally, the courts have ruled that such a clause is ineffective but may be influential in determining how the court will exercise its discretion.[15] Section 2–716 of the UCC revision draft, however, proposes that such clause be binding except in a consumer contract and in cases where the only remaining obligation of the breaching party is to pay money. This would bring the Code into line with Articles 46 and 62 of the United Nations Convention for the International Sale of Goods and with the views of those economists who view specific performance as the most efficient remedy.[16]

Clauses providing that specific performance will not be an available remedy are given effect,[17] but are narrowly construed.[18]

8. Laclede Gas v. Amoco, 522 F.2d 33 (8th Cir.1975); Griffin v. Oklahoma Nat. Gas, 37 F.2d 545 (10th Cir.1930); Hunt Foods v. O'Disho, 98 F.Supp. 267 (N.D.Cal. 1951); Energy Tactics v. Niagara Mohawk Power, 219 A.D.2d 577, 631 N.Y.S.2d 697 (1995); Adalex Labs. v. Krawitz, 270 P.2d 346 (Okl.1954) (exclusive territorial franchise); 5A Corbin §§ 1147, 1149; 11 Williston § 1419B; Van Hecke, Changing Emphases in Specific Performance, 40 N.C.L.Rev. 1, 4–9 (1961); UCC § 2–716 cmt 2.

9. Conway v. White, 9 F.2d 863 (2d Cir. 1925).

10. Benziger v. Steinhauser, 154 F. 151 (S.D.N.Y.1907).

11. Medcom Holding v. Baxter Travenol Labs., 984 F.2d 223 (7th Cir.1993) (stocks not publicly traded, valuation would be imprecise and business is a unique asset), later history omitted; Chadwell v. English, 652 P.2d 310 (Okl.App.1982); Owen v. Merts, 240 Ark. 1080, 405 S.W.2d 273, 28 ALR3d 1390 (1966); Lange v. Lange, 520 N.W.2d 113 (Iowa 1994); see 5A Corbin § 1148; Van Hecke, supra n.8, at 1–3.

12. Armstrong v. Stiffler, 189 Md. 630, 56 A.2d 808 (1948).

13. Wooster Republican Printing v. Channel Seventeen, supra § 16.2 n.5; Leasco v. Taussig, 473 F.2d 777 (2d Cir.1972); Cochrane v. Szpakowski, 355 Pa. 357, 49 A.2d 692 (1946); Van Hecke, supra n.8, at 3–4; Annot. 82 ALR2d 1102.

14. In re IBP, 789 A.2d 14 (Del.Ch. 2001).

15. Macneil, Power of Contract and Agreed Remedies, 47 Cornell L.Q. 495, 520–23 (1962); but see Terex Trailer v. McIlwain, 579 So.2d 237 (Fla.App.1991) ("The parties were free to specify their remedies").

16. See § 16.1 n.10 supra.

17. Sun Bank of Miami v. Lester, 404 So.2d 141 (Fla.App.1981), review denied; Ashley v. Metz, 49 Or.App. 1105, 621 P.2d 671 (1980).

18. Logue v. Seven–Hot Springs, 926 F.2d 722 (8th Cir.1991); S.E.S. Importers v. Pappalardo, 53 N.Y.2d 455, 442 N.Y.S.2d 453, 425 N.E.2d 841 (1981).

The remedy of replevin is a legal rather than an equitable remedy. When employed as a remedy for breach of contract the result is a form of specific enforcement. The UCC, under rather limited circumstances, permits a buyer to replevy goods as a remedy for breach. There are several requirements. The goods must have been identified to the contract. In addition, the buyer must show either (1) that an attempt to cover has been or will be unavailing or (2) that the goods have been shipped to the buyer under reservation (i.e. the seller has reserved a security interest to help assure payment) and the buyer has made or tendered satisfaction of the security interest.[19]

Although the Code liberalizes the availability of specific relief,[20] such relief remains the extraordinary rather than the ordinary remedy. In a market economy, the very existence of a market in most kinds of personalty affords a breaching party an opportunity to cover.[21] This includes a situation in which a lender breaches a contract to lend money.[22] Our legal system will almost always withhold specific relief when the opportunity to cover is present. Yet, the entire picture must be considered. In one striking case, the court granted specific performance of a stock option agreement, although the plaintiff could have purchased equivalent shares on the market. The court ruled that the special treatment the Internal Revenue Code granted to securities purchased under stock options made the remedy at law inadequate.[23]

§ 16.4 Legal Remedy Inadequate—Insolvency

There is a current of authority to the effect that specific performance will be ordered against an insolvent because the legal remedy of damages is inefficacious against a person who is judgment proof.[1] Before a court grants such a remedy, however, it is necessary that care be given to assure that rights of other creditors not be infringed.[2] Note, however, that the specific enforcement of an insolvent's contract does not necessarily curtail the rights of other creditors. For example, a contract by an

---

19. UCC § 2–716(3); see White & Summers, Uniform Commercial Code § 6–6(d)(4th ed.).

20. For some ingenious hypotheticals, see Comment, 33 U.Pitt.L.Rev. 243 (1971).

21. See generally Farnsworth, supra § 16.1 n.1.

22. Annot., 41 ALR 357 (1926). But see First Nat. State Bank v. Commonwealth Fed. S. & L. Ass'n, 610 F.2d 164 (3d Cir. 1979); Vandeventer v. Dale Constr., 271 Or. 691, 534 P.2d 183, 82 ALR3d 1108 (1975). For a debate on the question of whether a lender should be permitted to obtain specific performance of a loan commitment, compare Groot, Specific Performance of Contracts to Provide Permanent Financing, 60 Cornell L.Rev. 718 (1975), with Draper, The Broker Commitment: A Modern View of the Mortgage Lender's Remedy, 59 Cornell L.Rev. 418 (1974); see also Brannon, En-

forceability of Mortgage Loan Commitments, 18 Real Prop.Prob. & T.J. 724 (1983); Mehr & Kilgore, Enforcement of the Real Estate Loan Commitment: Improvement of the Borrower's Remedies, 24 Wayne L.Rev. 1011 (1978).

23. Kentucky Fried Chicken v. Thuermer, unreported case discussed in 22 Vand. L.Rev. 416 (1969).

§ 16.4

1. Rs. 1st § 362; Rs. 2d § 360 cmt d. There is also strong authority to the contrary. See generally, Horack, Insolvency and Specific Performance, 31 Harv.L.Rev. 702 (1918); Note, Specific Performance and Insolvency—A Reappraisal, 41 St. John's L.Rev. 577 (1967); 5A Corbin § 1156.

2. See Rs. 1st § 362 cmts b, c, d and ills. 1, 2; Rs. 2d § 365 cmt b and ill. 4.

insolvent to transfer stock in trade for a fair price will not prejudice other creditors as the decree will be conditioned on the price being paid.[3] The result would be different if the buyer had already paid for the stock in trade. In this case, delivery would give the buyer a preference over other creditors.[4] Therefore, although in some instances insolvency may be the basis for the decree of specific performance, in other instances the defendant's insolvency may be grounds for denying specific performance, as where the decree would give the plaintiff a preference over other creditors.[5] As we shall see below, there are other contexts where the interests of third parties are factors to be considered in granting or withholding equitable relief.[6]

§ 16.5 Service Contracts

No court will order an employee, or other person who is to render personal services, to perform.[1] There are several reasons for this rule. Such an order might well violate the involuntary servitude clause of the thirteenth amendment.[2] Additional reasons are the difficulty of supervising the decree and an unwillingness to force individuals into an unwanted personal association.[3] Nonetheless, courts have "indirectly enforced by injunction"[4] contracts to render personal services by restraining the defendant from working for a competitor.[5] The theory is that the court is merely enforcing an express or implied negative covenant not to work for competitors during the contract term.[6]

Although there is some authority for the proposition that an injunction will not be issued unless the plaintiff employer will suffer irreparable harm from breach of the negative covenant (as by luring clientele to a competitor),[7] the weight of authority is less restrictive. Injunctions have been granted against working for another where the employee's

---

3. Rs. 2d § 360 ill. 9.

4. Rs. 1st § 362 ill. 1.

5. Jamison Coal & Coke v. Goltra, 143 F.2d 889, 154 ALR 1191 (8th Cir.1944), cert. denied.

6. See § 16.13 infra.

§ 16.5

1. Rs. 2d § 367(1), although the lower Court did so order in Pingley v. Brunson, 272 S.C. 421, 252 S.E.2d 560 (1979). The law was not always thus. See Dalton, The Countrey Justice 68–75 (1622 ed.); see also Steyn, Gijzeling 33 (1939) (specific performance of contracts to marry in medieval Holland).

2. See People v. Lavender, 48 N.Y.2d 334, 422 N.Y.S.2d 924, 398 N.E.2d 530 (1979); Stevens, Involuntary Servitude by Injunction, 6 Corn.L.Q. 235 (1921). Military enlistment are, however, specifically enforced. Baldwin v. Cram, 522 F.2d 910 (2d

Cir.1975); Dilloff, 8 U.Richmond L.Rev. 121, 147–48 (1974).

3. 5A Corbin § 1204.

4. Rs. 1st § 380(2).

5. The leading case is Lumley v. Wagner, 42 Eng.Rep. 687 (1852). In depth, but contradictory analyses, of this line of cases include Sterk, Restraints on Alienation of Human Capital, 79 Va.L.Rev. 383 (1993); VanderVelde, The Gendered Origins of the Lumley Doctrine, 101 Yale L.J. 775 (1992); Wonnell, The Contractual Disempowerment of Employees, 46 Stan. L.Rev. 87 (1993).

6. For a discussion of covenants not to compete after the contract term expires, see §§ 16.19 to 16.22 infra.

7. De Pol v. Sohlke, 30 N.Y.Super.Ct. 280 (1867); 5A Corbin § 1206; 11 Williston § 1450 ("In general it is not the mere taking of new employment but unfair competition which equity enjoins"); Stevens, supra note 2, at 265–68.

services are unique and extraordinary.[8] The main applications of the rule have been in the entertainment industry,[9] and in professional sports.[10] The tendency is to regard all professional athletes as possessing unique and extraordinary skills.[11] Injunctive relief frequently appears to be granted against breaching players to preserve the organizational structure of professional athletics, without reference to the question of the degree of injury to the employer by breach of the negative covenant not to work for another.

On occasion an employee has sought specific performance of an employment contract against an employer. Such relief has almost invariably been denied.[12] Such enforcement would not involve questions of involuntary servitude, but would involve difficulty of supervision and, often, forcing the continuance of a distasteful personal relationship. Arbitration awards ordering reinstatement have, however, been specifically enforced,[13] and reinstatements have been ordered under civil service and civil rights legislation.[14] In view of these developments, the reasons behind the traditional bar against a court decree ordering an employer to perform are questionable.[15]

Courts have been reluctant to enforce even non-personal services contracts on grounds of difficulty of supervision.[16] For example, normally courts have not granted specific performance of construction contracts.[17]

8. Since in most cases the purpose of the injunction is to coerce the individual into returning to work, it has been argued that the constitutional provision against involuntary servitude is violated. Stevens, supra n. 2. Contra, McClintock, Equity § 65 (2d ed. 1948). Without taking a position on involuntary servitude, The Rs. 2d § 367 cmt c, opposes injunctions that are designed to coerce performance. Florida by statute focuses on "extraordinary or specialized training". See Cavico, 14 St. Tomas L.Rev. 53 (2001).

9. See Tannenbaum, Enforcement of Personal Service Contracts in the Entertainment Industry, 42 Cal.L.Rev. 18 (1954); Berman & Rosenthal, Enforcement of Personal Service Contracts in the Entertainment Industry, 7 J.Beverly Hills B.A. 49 (1973).

10. See Brennan, Injunction against Professional Athletes Breaching their Contracts, 34 Brooklyn L.Rev. 61 (1967); Notes and Comments 43 Conn.B.J. 538 (1969); 77 Dick.L.Rev. 352 (1973); 6 Tulsa L.J. 40 (1969).

11. See e.g., Central N.Y. Basketball v. Barnett, 181 N.E.2d 506 (Ohio Com.Pl. 1961); Dallas Cowboys Football Club v. Harris, 348 S.W.2d 37 (Tex.Civ.App.1961); Cf. Brennan, supra n. 10, at 70; but see Connecticut Professional Sports v. Heyman, 276 F.Supp. 618 (S.D.N.Y.1967).

12. Kaplan v. Kaplan, 98 Ill.App.3d 136, 53 Ill.Dec. 449, 423 N.E.2d 1253 (1981); see 5A Corbin § 1204.

13. Staklinski v. Pyramid Elec., 6 N.Y.2d 159, 188 N.Y.S.2d 541, 160 N.E.2d 78 (1959) (reinstatement of production manager); see also R.P.T. of Aspen v. Innovative Communications, 917 P.2d 340 (Colo. App.1996) (broad powers of arbitrators to fashion remedies). Numerous cases of arbitrator-ordered reinstatement are discussed in Elkouri & Elkouri, How Arbitration Works 939–43 (5th ed. 1997).

14. See, e.g., McKinney's N.Y.Civ.Serv. Law. § 75; Brown v. Trustees of Boston Univ., 891 F.2d 337 (1st Cir.1989), cert. denied (sex discrimination); Hopkins v. Price Waterhouse, 920 F.2d 967 (D.C.Cir. 1990).

15. So held in American Ass'n of University Professors v. Bloomfield College, 136 N.J.Super. 442, 346 A.2d 615 (1975); State ex rel. Wright v. Weyandt, 50 Ohio St.2d 194, 363 N.E.2d 1387 (1977).

16. See § 16.10 infra.

17. Northern Delaware Indus. Dev. v. E.W. Bliss Co., 245 A.2d 431 (Del.Ch.1968); Bissett v. Gooch, 87 Ill.App.3d 1132, 42 Ill.Dec. 900, 409 N.E.2d 515 (1980) (contract to build and convey); London Bucket v. Stewart, 314 Ky. 832, 237 S.W.2d 509 (1951). See 5A Corbin § 1172; 11 Williston

However, they have granted such relief where particularly compelling circumstances have made the remedy at law particularly inadequate. For example, where a defendant agreed to construct a building in a shopping center and lease it to the plaintiff, specific performance was granted.[18] Plaintiff's damages would have been entirely speculative and the land site was unique in the ordinary, as well as the legal, sense of the word. In the ordinary building or repair contract, however, where construction is to be on plaintiff's land, a substitute contractor can be called in and damages ascertained with relative certainty; consequently, specific performance normally will be denied. No matter what the nature of the construction contract, however, arbitration awards of specific performance will be enforced.[19]

Service contracts other than for construction or personal services can be specifically enforced if grounds for equitable intervention exist. The remedy at law must be inadequate. If the service is unique so that a substitute performance would not make the plaintiff whole, specific performance will be granted.[20] Despite the difficulty of supervision, a court has found a state executive department in contempt of a settlement agreement and has appointed a receiver to take over the main functions of the department.[21] In addition, there are cases not involving uniqueness where damages are inadequate. For example, the promisee in a contract made for a third party donee beneficiary ordinarily will suffer no pecuniary injury by the breach. Consequently, the remedy of specific performance may be available to the promisee.[22] Also, insurance policies that are wrongfully cancelled before the insured event occurs may be specifically enforced because of the speculative nature of damages in such a case.[23]

§ 16.6 Mutuality as a Basis for Equitable Relief

The "mutuality of remedy" doctrine was in vogue in equity jurisprudence for a considerable period of time. The most important use of the

§ 1422A; Axelrod, Judicial Attitudes toward Specific Performance of Construction Contracts, 7 U.Dayton L.Rev. 33 (1981); Barnicle, Expediting Construction by Enjoining Performance, 21 Prac.Law (No. 5) 59 (1975); Note, 47 Notre Dame Law. 1025 (1972).

18. City Stores v. Ammerman, 266 F.Supp. 766 (D.D.C.1967), aff'd 394 F.2d 950, 38 ALR3d 1042 (D.C.Cir.1968); accord, O'Neil v. Lipinski, 173 Mont. 332, 567 P.2d 909 (1977); cf. Besinger v. National Tea Co., 75 Ill.App.2d 395, 221 N.E.2d 156 (1966); see also Hamilton West Dev. v. Hills Stores, 959 F.Supp. 434 (N.D.Ohio 1997); McDonough v. Southern Or. Min., 177 Or. 136, 159 P.2d 829, 164 ALR 788 (1945), reh. denied; but see CBL Assocs. v. McCrory Corp., 761 F.Supp. 807 (M.D.Ga.1991).

19. Grayson–Robinson v. Iris Constr., 8 N.Y.2d 133, 202 N.Y.S.2d 303, 168 N.E.2d

377 (1960), rearg. denied, noted in numerous law reviews.

20. See American Brands v. Playgirl, 498 F.2d 947 (2d Cir.1974) (is the back cover of "Playgirl" unique as an advertising medium?); Wilson v. Sandstrom, 317 So.2d 732 (Fla.1975), cert. denied (contract to furnish greyhounds for racing).

21. Judge Rotenberg Educ. Center v. Commissioner, 424 Mass. 430, 677 N.E.2d 127 (1997).

22. Drewen v. Bank of Manhattan, 31 N.J. 110, 155 A.2d 529, 76 ALR2d 221 (1959). See § 17.11 infra; 5A Corbin § 1200; Yorio, Contract Enforcement § 2.4 (Supp. by Thel).

23. Burnet v. Wells, 289 U.S. 670 (1933); Annot., 34 ALR3d 245 § 8.

doctrine was to deny specific performance in certain cases. This will be discussed below.[1] But the doctrine also had an affirmative side. It provided that a plaintiff could obtain specific performance if the defendant could have obtained specific performance if the plaintiff were the breaching party. Consequently, a vendor of land was permitted to obtain specific performance against the vendee although the vendee's performance (payment) is not unique because the vendee could have obtained specific performance had the vendor breached. Also, a seller of a unique chattel was able to obtain specific performance against a purchaser. The affirmative rule of mutuality seems not to have been applied to service contracts.

Today, the doctrine of mutuality as a basis for denying relief has been exploded.[2] Nevertheless, the rule remains that a vendor of real property or a seller of unique goods may obtain specific performance. Scholarly attempts have been made to base this rule on the inadequacy of the legal remedy.[3] Yet it cannot be said in each such case that the legal remedy is inadequate.[4] The availability of specific performance in such instances continues to be based on precedents formulated under the mutuality doctrine.[5]

B.   DEFENSES

Table of Sections

§ 16.7   Discretionary Nature of Equitable Relief

The historical foundation of equity has left its residue on today's equitable jurisprudence. Historically, an appeal to equity was a petition

---

§ 16.6

1. See § 16.11 infra.

2. See § 16.11 infra.

3. Walsh, Equity § 68 (1930).

4. Inadequacy on specific facts was shown in Shuptrine v. Quinn, 597 S.W.2d 728 (Tenn.1979).

5. McClintock at 185. Rs. 2d § 360 cmt c, regards the doctrine as discarded. While Corbin regards the doctrine as innocuous (5A Corbin § 1179), Richards urges its abolition. Richards, Mutuality of Remedy—A Call for Reform, 13 Memphis St.L.Rev. 1 (1982).

to the chancellor. It was normally a request for grace based on "reason and conscience," rather than for the implementation of a rule of law.[1] Today, equitable discretion is no longer based on the chancellor's conscience, but consists of a sound discretion, based upon precedents, principles and doctrines that have to a large extent hardened over the last two centuries.[2] These will be considered in the discussion which follows. The maintenance of the distinction between defenses available in an equity case and in a law case may to a large extent be an historical anomaly,[3] but at least one observer justifies the distinction on the grounds that these defenses minimize court coercion and allow for a middle ground solution.[4]

§ 16.8 Validity, Enforceability, and Definiteness of the Contract

For the equitable remedy of specific performance to be granted there usually must be a valid and enforceable contract.[1] The one exception to this rule is that if a contract for the sale of real property does not satisfy the Statute of Frauds, equity may grant specific performance under the part performance doctrine,[2] although traditionally there has been no legal enforcement remedy.[3] Promissory estoppel also can be invoked to compel specific performance of an otherwise unenforceable contract.[4]

The standard for definiteness is higher in equity than in law.[5] Since a violation of an equitable decree may be punishable by contempt, the parties must know with reasonable certainty what is expected of them. Still, before a contract is denied specific enforcement on grounds of indefiniteness, all applicable gap fillers should be used[6] and parol evidence considered to clarify any indefinite provisions.[7] Following a recent trend in actions at law, courts of equity, in deciding specific performance cases have adopted a more flexible attitude toward the validity of contracts containing some indefinite terms.[8] A standard of reasonable

---

§ 16.7

1. For a history of equity, see Walsh, Equity §§ 1–7 (1930). On equitable discretion, see 5A Corbin § 1136; 11 Williston §§ 1425, 1425A; Rs. 2d § 357 cmt c.

2. Van Wagner Advertising v. S & M Enterprises, 67 N.Y.2d 186, 501 N.Y.S.2d 628, 492 N.E.2d 756 (1986); County of Lincoln v. Fischer, 216 Or. 421, 339 P.2d 1084 (1959); Rs. 1st § 359 cmt a; Rs. 2d § 357 cmt c; 5A Corbin § 1136; 11 Williston §§ 1425, 1425A.

3. Laycock, The Irreparable Injury Rule (1991); Sherwin, Law and Equity in Contract Enforcement, 50 Md.L.Rev. 253 (1991), both contend that some justifications exist in several typical situations, but these should be faced overtly.

4. Yorio, A Defense of Equitable Defenses, 51 Ohio St.L.J. (1990).

§ 16.8

1. Rs. 1st § 358 cmt e.

2. See § 19.15 infra.

3. Rs. 2d § 129 cmt c; see § 19.15 infra.

4. See § 19.48 infra.

5. Sweeting v. Campbell, 8 Ill.2d 54, 132 N.E.2d 523, 60 ALR2d 247 (1956); Dewey v. Wentland, 38 P.3d 402 (Wyo.2002); Rs. 2d § 362; Yorio, Contract Enforcement § 3.3.

6. See Squillante, Specific Performance of Indefinite Contracts, 72 Com.L.J. 12 (1967).

7. E.g., Travellers Int'l v. Trans World Airlines, 722 F.Supp. 1087, 1105 (S.D.N.Y. 1989) (course of dealing); McClintock § 56.

8. See § 2.9 supra; Rs. 2d § 362 cmt b; Yorio, Contract Enforcement § 3.4.4.

certainty has replaced an earlier standard of precision.[9] Indeed, in a significant case an "agreement to agree" was granted specific performance by a decree ordering negotiations with the help of a court appointed mediator.[10]

§ 16.9 Consideration in Equity

The rules for the presence or absence of consideration are basically the same in equity as in law.[1] The question of whether nominal consideration is sufficient to support a contract is controversial.[2] Assuming its sufficiency, equity will generally refuse specific performance.[3] Similarly, equity will not enforce a promise if its validity is based solely on the fact that it is under seal or in writing.[4] Such refusals are often stated in maxims such as "equity disregards the form" and "equity will not aid a volunteer."[5]

There are important exceptions to the rule refusing enforcement. Where a contract, such as an option contract, is supported by nominal consideration, a seal, or a writing, and looks to a further performance that constitutes a fair exchange as a condition to the defendant's duty, equity will enforce it.[6] Moreover, if past consideration has been given, a new promise supported by a statutory writing, a seal, or nominal consideration, or rules dispensing with consideration will be specifically enforced.[7]

The degree to which equity will examine the adequacy of the consideration is discussed below.[8]

§ 16.10 Difficulty of Supervision

In many cases, courts have refused to grant specific performance on grounds that supervision of performance would involve an undue investment of judicial time and effort.[1] This has particularly been true in cases

9. Rs. 2d § 362; Furuseth v. Olson, 297 Minn. 491, 210 N.W.2d 47 (1973); Manassas v. Board of County Sup'rs, 250 Va. 126, 458 S.E.2d 568 (1995) (agreement to make good faith efforts); see Yorio, Contract Enforcement § 3.4; Note, 5 UCLA–Alaska L.Rev. 122 (1975); but see Plantation Land v. Bradshaw, 232 Ga. 435, 207 S.E.2d 49 (1974).

10. Oglebay Norton v. Armco, 52 Ohio St.3d 232, 556 N.E.2d 515 (1990).

§ 16.9

1. This has not always been so. See Pound, Consideration in Equity, 13 Ill. L.Rev. 667 (1919).

2. See § 4.6 supra.

3. George W. Kistler, Inc. v. O'Brien, 464 Pa. 475, 347 A.2d 311 (1975).

4. Id.; Rs. 1st § 366; Rs. 2d § 364 cmt b.

5. McClintock § 55.

6. Rs. 1st § 366 and cmt b; 5A Corbin § 1165. Cf. Rs. 2d § 87(1)(a) and cmt b, § 88(a) and cmt a. See § 4.6 supra.

7. McCrilles v. Sutton, 207 Mich. 58, 173 N.W. 333 (1919); accord, Speelman v. Pascal, 10 N.Y.2d 313, 222 N.Y.S.2d 324, 178 N.E.2d 723 (1961), rearg. denied (an assignment; statutory writing coupled with past consideration).

8. See § 16.14 infra.

§ 16.10

1. Western & Southern Life Ins. v. Crown American, 877 F.Supp. 1041 (E.D.Ky.1993); Peachtree on Peachtree Investors v. Reed Drug, 251 Ga. 692, 308 S.E.2d 825 (1983); but see Hamilton West Dev. v. Hills Stores, 959 F.Supp. 434 (N.D.Ohio 1997).

seeking specific performance of construction contracts,[2] as well as contracts requiring continuing services of various kinds, and contracts requiring long term delivery of goods. This last category has been overturned by the UCC,[3] where it had not already been overturned by judicial decision.[4] Indeed, there is an increasing realization that in many cases the difficulties have been overstated.[5] Indeed, the willingness of courts of equity in recent decades to take on supervision of complex school desegregation and legislative reapportionment plans, would indicate that supervision of contract performance is a burden that courts can deal with.

§ 16.11   Mutuality of Remedy

In 1858, an English scholar, Fry, published a treatise on specific performance, stating a rule of mutuality of remedy to the effect that specific performance will not be granted unless from the outset (in the event of breach) the remedy is available against both parties.[1] He listed several exceptions. Subsequent scholars added to the list of exceptions.[2] Except in states that have adopted the rule by statute,[3] the requirement of mutuality generally has been abandoned.[4]

An important core of the doctrine, however, has been preserved. The Restatement (Second) has adopted the rule's common sense rationale that a defendant should not be compelled to perform without an assurance that the plaintiff will perform. It provides: "Specific performance or an injunction may be refused if a substantial part of the agreed exchange for the performance to be compelled is unperformed and its performance is not secured to the satisfaction of the court."[5] Thus, for example, a vendor who has contracted to convey on deferred payment terms, can be compelled to convey, but the court may condition relief on the purchaser's execution of a mortgage to secure payment.[6]

2. See § 16.5 supra.

3. See § 16.3 supra.

4. See, e.g., Fleischer v. James Drug Stores, 1 N.J. 138, 62 A.2d 383 (1948).

5. See 5A Corbin §§ 1171–1172; Van Hecke, supra § 16.3 n.8, at 13–16; Rs. 1st § 371 cmt a; Rs. 2d § 366.

§ 16.11

1. Fry, Specific Performance § 460 (1858). For earlier statements of a rule of mutuality, see Parkhurst v. Van Cortlandt, 1 Johns.Ch. *273, *280 (N.Y.Ch.1814) reversed 14 Johns. 15 (1816) (dictum by Chancellor Kent); Hutcheson v. Heirs of McNutt, 1 Ohio 14, 20 (1821).

2. 11 Williston § 1434 lists seven exceptions to the former rule.

3. Note, Mutuality of Remedy in California under Civil Code Section 3386, 19 Hastings L.J. 1430 (1968).

4. Stamatiades v. Merit Music Service, 210 Md. 597, 124 A.2d 829 (1956); Vanzandt v. Heilman, 54 N.M. 97, 214 P.2d 864, 22 ALR2d 497 (1950). For its rise and fall in one typical jurisdiction, see Austin, Mutuality of Remedy in Ohio, 28 Ohio St. L.J. 629 (1967); see also Walsh, Equity § 70 (1930). Where the doctrine has not been abandoned "it has been practically nullified by exceptions." McClintock, at 181. Its final abandonment is urged in Richards, Mutuality of Remedy—A Call for Reform, 13 Memphis St.L.Rev. 1 (1982).

5. Rs. 2d § 363. This appears to be the core of what Cardozo, C.J., meant when he wrote that, "What equity exacts today as a condition of relief is the assurance that the decree, if rendered, will operate without injustice or oppression either to plaintiff or defendant." Epstein v. Gluckin, 233 N.Y. 490, 494, 135 N.E. 861, 862 (1922).

6. Rs. 2d § 363 ill. 1. See Carman v. Gunn, 198 So.2d 76 (Fla.App.1967) (court

In cases where the performances of the parties are to be concurrent, the defendant is protected by the rules concerning concurrent conditions.[7] In other cases, the respective rights of the parties can be protected by the great flexibility of the equitable decree. It can be conditioned not only on some performance or security to be rendered by the plaintiff,[8] but also upon acts of persons not parties to the litigation.[9] There are cases where the decree cannot assure the defendant that return performance will be rendered.[10] This is particularly true in cases where the plaintiff is to render personal services in the future in exchange for a conveyance or other immediate performance. More often than not, specific performance is denied in such circumstances.[11]

§ 16.12 Plaintiff in Default—Relief From Forfeiture

In an action at law, whenever there has been a failure of express condition to the defendant's obligation or a material breach by the plaintiff, there can be no successful action for breach of contract,[1] although quasi-contractual relief is available in some jurisdictions.[2] Generally, the same rule prevails in equity.[3] There is, however, a different rule with respect to the plaintiff's readiness, willingness and ability to perform. In an action at law, the burden is on the plaintiff to prove that she or he would have been ready, willing and able to perform but for the defendant's breach. In an action for specific performance, however, the plaintiff must additionally show that she or he continues to be ready, willing and able.[4]

There is one other major difference in the treatment of conditions in law and equity expressed by the maxim "equity abhors a forfeiture." The main application of the maxim has been in contracts for the sale of land where a plaintiff in default has made substantial payments toward the purchase price. Such a plaintiff may obtain specific performance on condition that future payments are well secured to the satisfaction of the court and on condition that damages be paid to the defendant.[5] In a

imposes an equitable lien as security); see also Rego v. Decker, 482 P.2d 834 (Alaska 1971).

7. Walsh, Equity 349 (1930). See §§ 11.6, 11.17 supra.

8. See Dillon v. Cardio–Kinetics, 52 Or. App. 627, 628 P.2d 1269 (1981) (conditions of decree not complied with).

9. Safeway System v. Manuel Bros., 102 R.I. 136, 228 A.2d 851 (1967).

10. Stenehjem v. Kyn Jin Cho, 631 P.2d 482 (Alaska 1981).

11. See 5A Corbin § 1184.

§ 16.12

1. See §§ 11.9, 11.12, 11.18 supra.

2. See § 11.22 supra.

3. Rs. 2d § 369.

4. Allen v. Nissley, 184 Conn. 539, 440 A.2d 231 (1981); Hadcock Motors v. Metzger, 92 A.D.2d 1, 459 N.Y.S.2d 634 (1983). While some cases require a formal tender to put the defendant into breach, Derosia v. Austin, 115 Mich.App. 647, 321 N.W.2d 760 (1982); Century 21 v. Webb, 645 P.2d 52 (Utah 1982), others excuse tender even in the absence of repudiation. Fleenor v. Church, 681 P.2d 1351 (Alaska 1984); Tantillo v. Janus, 87 Ill.App.3d 231, 42 Ill.Dec. 291, 408 N.E.2d 1000 (1980).

5. Rs. 1st §§ 374(2), 375(3); see Reporter's Notes to Rs. 2d § 369; McClintock §§ 75, 117; 5A Corbin § 1177; 11 Williston § 1425B; Dillingham Commercial v. Spears, 641 P.2d 1 (Alaska 1982); Berry v. Crawford, 237 Ark. 380, 373 S.W.2d 129 (1963); MacFadden v. Walker, 5 Cal.3d 809, 97 Cal.Rptr. 537, 488 P.2d 1353, 55 ALR3d 1 (1971) (despite wilfulness of the breach),

number of jurisdictions where the practice of selling real property for installment payments is ingrained, statutes have been enacted to regulate the matter.[6] Another application of the doctrine has been in the area of options to renew or to purchase ancillary to a lease. Courts have permitted late acceptance of such options where the tenants would otherwise forfeit fixtures and good will built up during the leasehold period.[7]

§ 16.13   Impracticability, Effect on Third Persons or the Public

The rules on impossibility have a particular effect on the availability of specific performance. Under certain circumstances, a party's contractual duty is discharged when its performance becomes impossible or impracticable.[1] There are many circumstances, however, where impossibility does not discharge a duty, for example, where the impossibility has been caused by the obligor.[2] When this occurs, the obligor is liable at law, but no decree of specific performance will be issued.[3] For example, where a contract vendor of land breaches a contract by conveying to a bona fide purchaser for value, the vendor is liable for damages but a decree for specific performance will not be granted against the vendor.[4]

A court in determining whether to grant the discretionary relief of specific performance may consider the effect of specific performance on third persons.[5] Persons on an equal footing will be treated alike. Suppose, for example, a seller contracts to sell 500 bushels of seed to X and 500 bushels to Y but is able to deliver only a total of 500 bushels because of a market shortage under conditions that do not excuse him. In a suit by X for specific performance, the court may properly limit X's relief to a decree requiring delivery of 250 bushels plus compensatory damages.[6]

The court may also consider the public interest.[7] Courts have applied this factor to deny relief in cases where railroads have contracted to

---

noted in 5 Loyola U.L.Rev. 435 (1972); Kaiman Realty v. Carmichael, 65 Haw. 637, 655 P.2d 872 (1982); Christiansen v. Griffin, 398 So.2d 213 (Miss.1981); see Annot., 55 ALR3d 10 (1974).

6. See Lee, Remedies for Breach of the Installment Land Contract, 19 U.Miami L.Rev. 550, 562 (1965); Annot., 55 ALR3d 10, § 5b (1974).

7. Xanthakey v. Hayes, 107 Conn. 459, 140 A. 808 (1928); Holiday Inns of America v. Knight, 70 Cal.2d 327, 74 Cal.Rptr. 722, 450 P.2d 42 (1969); J.N.A. Realty v. Cross Bay Chelsea, 42 N.Y.2d 392, 397 N.Y.S.2d 958, 366 N.E.2d 1313 (1977); see also Schlegel v. Hansen, 98 Idaho 614, 570 P.2d 292 (1977) (lessee in arrears exercised option to purchase); see supra § 11.35; 1 Corbin § 2.15 (Perillo 1993).

§ 16.13

1. See ch. 13 supra.

2. See § 13.15 supra.

3. Brand v. Lowther, 168 W.Va. 726, 285 S.E.2d 474 (1981); Rs. 1st § 368; Rs. 2d § 364 cmt a; see Bogdan & Faist v. CAI Wireless, 295 A.D.2d 849, 745 N.Y.S.2d 92 (2002) (stock was eliminated by bankruptcy reorganization).

4. Flackhamer v. Himes, 24 R.I. 306, 53 A. 46 (1902); see also Rs. 1st § 368 ill. 1.

5. Thus specific performance with an abatement was denied where the rights of contingent remaindermen would be adversely affected. Hawks v. Sparks, 204 Va. 717, 133 S.E.2d 536 (1963), 5 Wm. & Mary L.Rev. 290 (1964).

6. Cf. Rs. 1st § 368 ill. 1.

7. City of London v. Nash, 3 Atk. 512 (Ch. 1747); Peachtree on Peachtree Investors v. Reed Drug,, 251 Ga. 692, 308 S.E.2d 825 (1983); see Note, 72 Tex.L.Rev. 849

maintain grade crossings or stations at places inconvenient to the public[8] and to grant relief, despite the difficulty of supervision, of a contract by a railroad to elevate its tracks.[9] Specific performance of a contract to sell land has also been denied because of the public interest in the esthetic appearance of an art museum,[10] and the maintenance of a public school.[11] It has also been refused where enforcement would cause employees of the defendant to go out on strike, thereby inconveniencing the public.[12] An oil supplier was enjoined from breaching its contract to supply a public power company with fuel, despite the availability of cover at a substantially higher price, because of the adverse effect any power interruption would have on the public.[13] Specific performance of a contract to deliver ball bearings was decreed where the withholding of delivery would have an adverse effect on the Chinese public and China's economy.[14]

§ 16.14 Harshness, Inequitable Conduct, and Other Forms of Unconscionability; Balancing

As indicated in an earlier chapter,[1] the concept of unconscionability constitutes the foundation stone of much of equitable doctrine. The effect of unconscionability depends on its context. In some areas of the law of contracts, such as mistake and penalty clauses, the concept has been used to set aside contracts or contractual clauses. In the context of specific performance, it has frequently been used merely as a basis for denying the remedy, leaving the contract intact.[2] Few rules can be stated in the area. Refusal of enforcement, states the Restatement, depends "upon the moral standards of enlightened judges."[3]

As indicated elsewhere, equity generally requires as a prerequisite to specific performance that there be free and open disclosure of all pertinent facts.[4] For example, in one case, specific performance was

(1994) (public interest as a "wild card" in preliminary injunctions).

8. See Rs. 1st § 369 and ills. 1 & 2; Rs. 2d § 365 and ill. 2; see also Seaboard Air Line Ry. v. Atlanta, B. & C.R.R., 35 F.2d 609 (5th Cir.1929), cert. denied; 14 Minn. L.Rev. 580 (1930); City of N.Y. v. N.Y. Central R.R., 275 N.Y. 287, 9 N.E.2d 931 (1937), 38 Colum.L.Rev. 914 (1938).

9. Pennsylvania R.R. v. Louisville, 277 Ky. 402, 126 S.W.2d 840 (1939), 26 Va. L.Rev. 116 (1939). See also Laclede Gas v. Amoco, 522 F.2d 33 (8th Cir.1975) (public interest in propane gas); Wilson v. Sandstrom, 317 So.2d 732 (Fla.1975).

10. Rockhill Tennis Club v. Volker, 331 Mo. 947, 56 S.W.2d 9 (1932), 18 Minn. L.Rev. 90 (1933); 47 Harv.L.Rev. 141 (1932).

11. Wheeler v. Standard Oil Co., 263 N.Y. 34, 188 N.E. 148 (1933).

12. Gulf, M. & N.R. v. Illinois Cent. R.R., 21 F.Supp. 282 (W.D.Tenn.1937), appeal dismissed.

13. Orange & Rockland Util. v. Amerada Hess, 67 Misc.2d 560, 324 N.Y.S.2d 494 (1971); see also Laclede Gas v. Amoco, 522 F.2d 33 (8th Cir.1975) (propane requirements).

14. Danieli & C. Officine Meccaniche v. Morgan Constr., 190 F.Supp.2d 148 (D.Mass.2002).

§ 16.14

1. See §§ 9.37 to 9.40 supra.

2. For an argument that equity should not refuse enforcement of valid contracts, despite the case law to the contrary, see Patterson, Equitable Relief for Unilateral Mistake, 28 Colum.L.Rev. 859, 899 (1928).

3. Rs. 1st § 367 cmt b; see Rs. 2d § 364; 5A Corbin § 1164.

4. See § 9.20 supra.

denied because the vendor failed to inform the vendee of an underground water course. In the same case, however, the vendee was not permitted to avoid the contract with the result that the vendor was permitted to retain the down payment and seek damages.[5] Similarly, to obtain specific performance, the purchaser of land must have disclosed the existence of mineral deposits known to the purchaser on the land contracted to be sold,[6] or that the value of the land exceeds the purchase price,[7] but the purchaser need not disclose the purchaser's plan to make improvements in the area that will enhance the value of the land.[8]

While law has only recently recognized unilateral mistake as grounds for avoidance of a contract,[9] equity has long refused to grant specific performance where one party was under a material mistake. Such refusal is by no means automatic. The mistake must be viewed in the light of the harshness of enforcement, any change of position by the other party, any hint of unfair conduct by that party and the nature and degree of any negligence by the mistaken party.[10] Although unilateral mistake is now grounds for avoidance at law, a mistake of a kind that would not permit avoidance of the contract, may permit denial of specific performance.[11]

Equity does examine the adequacy of consideration,[12] but there is no consensus on how much weight courts should give to the inadequacy of consideration. Many cases state that inadequacy of consideration, standing alone, is not a basis for denying specific performance,[13] but is only a factor to be considered to determine if the agreement was obtained inequitably.[14] Others have said that inadequacy of consideration is some evidence of fraud, overreaching, sharp practice, lack of mental capacity, undue influence or the like.[15] Other courts have indicated that gross inadequacy of consideration, standing alone, is sufficient to deny specific enforcement.[16] It is difficult to assess where the weight of authority lies,

---

5. Kleinberg v. Ratett, 252 N.Y. 236, 169 N.E. 289 (1929). The double standard of morality in law and equity is criticized in Newman, The Renaissance of Good Faith in Contracting in Anglo–American Law, 54 Cornell L.Rev. 553 (1969).

6. Schlegel v. Moorhead, 170 Mont. 391, 553 P.2d 1009 (1976). The rule is stated and criticized as based on "sentiment." McClintock at 201. See also 11 Williston § 1426.

7. Margraf v. Muir, 57 N.Y. 155 (1874).

8. See § 9.20 supra.

9. See § 9.27 supra.

10. See 11 Williston § 1427; McClintock § 74; Rs. 1st § 367(c) and cmt a; Rs. 2d § 364 cmt a; Annot., 65 ALR 7, 97–102 (1930).

11. See Clayburg v. Whitt, 171 N.W.2d 623 (Iowa 1969) (seller's action for specific performance dismissed; counter-claim based on "rescission" denied); Double AA v. New-

land & Co., 273 Mont. 486, 905 P.2d 138 (1995) (vendor contracted to sell because of erroneous tax advice; specific performance denied but damages awarded); Bailey v. Musumeci, 134 N.H. 280, 591 A.2d 1316 (1991).

12. See Annot., 65 ALR 7, 86–96 (1930).

13. Ligon v. Parr, 471 S.W.2d 1 (Ky. 1971).

14. See, e.g., Schiff v. Breitenbach, 14 Ill.2d 611, 153 N.E.2d 549 (1958).

15. Musser v. Zurcher, 180 Neb. 882, 146 N.W.2d 559 (1966); 5A Corbin § 1165.

16. Margraf v. Muir, 57 N.Y. 155 (1874); Wagner v. Estate of Rummel, 391 Pa.Super. 555, 571 A.2d 1055, 1059 (1990); Hodge v. Shea, 252 S.C. 601, 168 S.E.2d 82 (1969). In some jurisdictions this rule is codified. See O'Hara v. Lynch, 172 Cal. 525, 157 P. 608 (1915); Moody v. Mendenhall, 238 Ga. 689, 234 S.E.2d 905 (1977) (plaintiff must show that contract is fair).

as it is a rare case indeed where inadequacy of consideration is not the fruit of inequitable dealing.[17]

Such cases do, however, exist. In one fascinating case, the court found that the defendant had invented a device and fuel which would enable an automobile to run 400 miles to the gallon. The fuel could be manufactured for 1 cent per gallon. The defendant in a complicated transaction, stripped to its essentials, agreed to transfer a 49% interest in the process and control over its marketing for a sum of $50,000. Plaintiff's experts testified that the process was worth from $20,000,000 to $1,000,000,000. Specific performance was denied on the grounds of inadequacy of consideration.[18]

Apart from the adequacy of the consideration, the court will examine the entire transaction to determine whether it is so grossly one-sided as to be oppressive.[19] Consider the case of a carrot farmer who had contracted to sell carrots. Under the contract, the purchaser was free, under certain circumstances, to refuse to accept the carrots. Furthermore, if the purchaser exercised this option, the farmer was not permitted to sell the carrots to others without the purchaser's consent. This clause coupled with other one-sided clauses in a contract of adhesion led the court to a finding of unconscionability.[20]

There is considerable, but not unanimous, authority to the effect that a contract fair and conscionable when made will not be specifically enforced if supervening events have rendered the contract so unfair as to shock the conscience.[21] A sharp increase or decrease in the market value of the subject matter, however, standing alone is not grounds for denying specific performance.[22]

Equity will balance the hardship to the defendant against the benefit to the plaintiff that would ensue from the enforcement of the contract. If the benefit to the plaintiff will be slight, and the hardship to the defendant relatively great, specific enforcement will be refused.[23]

§ 16.15　Laches—Prejudicial Delay

Equity will not allow a party to sleep on his or her rights, at least

17. 11 Williston § 1428; McClintock § 71; Rs. 2d § 364(1)(c) ("grossly inadequate").

18. Weeks v. Pratt, 43 F.2d 53 (5th Cir. 1930). Anyone having information about the whereabouts of this process, please contact the authors!

19. McKinnon v. Benedict, 38 Wis.2d 607, 157 N.W.2d 665 (1968).

20. Campbell Soup v. Wentz, 172 F.2d 80 (3d Cir.1948).

21. 3615 Corp. v. N.Y. Life Ins., 717 F.2d 1236 (8th Cir.1983) (serious damage to building); Jensen v. Southwestern States Management, 6 Kan.App.2d 437, 629 P.2d 752 (1981); Hart v. Brown, 6 Misc. 238, 27 N.Y.S. 74 (1893); 5A Corbin § 1162; 3 Pomeroy Specific Performance 452, 457 (3d ed. 1926); Annot., 65 ALR 7, 72–75 (1930).

22. County of Lincoln v. Fischer, 216 Or. 421, 339 P.2d 1084 (1959); see Annot., 11 ALR2d 390 (1950).

23. Rs. 1st § 367(b); Rs. 2d § 364(1)(b); Patel v. Ali, [1984] 1 All.E.R. 978, noted in 134 New L.J. 927 (1984); Kakalik v. Bernardo, 184 Conn. 386, 439 A.2d 1016 (1981); Smith v. Meyers, 130 Md. 64, 99 A. 938 (1917); Miles v. Dover Furnace Iron, 125 N.Y. 294, 26 N.E. 261 (1891); Parolisi v. Beach Terrace Imp. Assn., 463 A.2d 197 (R.I.1983).

where such slumber is prejudicial to the other party.[1] Thus a court will deny specific performance where such prejudicial delay occurs. The prejudice may involve a change of position by the defendant,[2] the loss of evidence or the death of witnesses.[3] Similarly, a court of equity will not grant specific performance to a plaintiff who bides time until the subject matter significantly increases or decreases in value.[4] Delay that is nonprejudicial, however, does not bar equitable relief.[5]

§ 16.16   Unclean Hands

A plaintiff who comes into court with "unclean hands" will be denied equitable relief.[1] In cases of this kind, as in cases of nonenforcement of illegal contracts,[2] the rationale is not injury to the defendant, but rather a policy of keeping the courts respectable.[3] This principle has been used very broadly to encompass cases where the plaintiff has been guilty of inequitable conduct such as misrepresentation and nondisclosure.[4] More narrowly the doctrine applies to conduct bordering on illegality. An example would be where plaintiff conveys real property to defendant on the defendant's promise to reconvey at a later date. The purpose of the conveyance is to defraud plaintiff's creditors. Plaintiff may not obtain specific performance because plaintiff comes into court with unclean hands.[5]

The doctrine is flexible and often difficult to apply. For example, a professional team signs up a collegiate sports star, and in violation of collegiate rules, the parties agree that the contract is to be kept secret until the end of the season, and the star will continue to play collegiate

---

§ 16.15

1. Laches may be an available defense in an action for declaratory judgment. See UTI v. Fireman's Fund Ins., 896 F.Supp. 362 (D.N.J.1995).

2. Lake Caryonah Imp. Assn. v. Pulte Home, 903 F.2d 505, 510 (7th Cir.1990) (payment of taxes and other charges for 11 years); Tom Doherty Assocs. v. Saban Entertainment, 869 F.Supp. 1130 (S.D.N.Y. 1994), aff'd (license arrangements were made for Power Rangers, plaintiff remained inert); Seifert v. Seifert, 173 Mont. 501, 568 P.2d 155 (1977); O'Dette v. Guzzardi, 204 A.D.2d 291, 611 N.Y.S.2d 294 (1994) (defendant made $18,000 of improvements).

3. Hungerford v. Hungerford, 223 Md. 316, 164 A.2d 518 (1960).

4. Welborne v. Preferred Risk Ins. Co., 232 Ark. 828, 340 S.W.2d 586 (1960); Commonwealth v. Pendleton, 480 Pa. 107, 389 A.2d 532 (1978); Gaglione v. Cardi, 120 R.I. 534, 388 A.2d 361 (1978); Crawford v. Workman, 64 W.Va. 10, 61 S.E. 319 (1908); cf. Amoco v. Kraft, 89 Mich.App. 270, 280 N.W.2d 505 (1979) ("unclean hands").

5. Shell v. Strong, 151 F.2d 909 (10th Cir.1945); Hochard v. Deiter, 219 Kan. 738, 549 P.2d 970 (1976); McClintock § 28.

§ 16.16

1. Royce v. Duthler, 209 Mich.App. 682, 531 N.W.2d 817 (1995); see McClintock § 26.

2. See § 22.1 infra.

3. See Stringfellow, Who Comes into Equity Must Come with Clean Hands, 1 Ala.Lawyer 248 (1940); but see Chafee, Coming into Equity with Clean Hands, 47 Mich.L.Rev. 877, 1065 (1949).

4. So used in 5A Corbin § 1168, and in many cases. E.g., Merimac Co. v. Portland Timber & Land Holding, 259 Or. 573, 488 P.2d 465 (1971).

5. MacRae v. MacRae, 37 Ariz. 307, 294 P. 280 (1930); cf. Seagirt Realty v. Chazanof, 13 N.Y.2d 282, 246 N.Y.S.2d 613, 196 N.E.2d 254 (1963), 66 W.Va.L.Rev. 333 (1964).

ball until that time. While one court has found this to be a classic example of unclean hands,[6] another has disagreed.[7]

The doctrine of unclean hands cannot be invoked unless the inequitable conduct relates to the same transaction. Thus, in a partnership accounting action, the trial judge ascertained that the partnership books were intentionally inaccurate to evade taxes and dismissed the case with the statement: "why should this court give aid to crooks?" The appellate court, reversing, held that the illicit conduct was not directly related to the subject matter of the litigation and therefore did not trigger the doctrine.[8]

It has been held that inequitable conduct after the contract has been entered into does not give rise to the doctrine,[9] but there is no unanimity on this point.[10] At any rate, even if the doctrine is technically inapplicable, the new emphasis of the UCC[11] and the Restatement (Second)[12] on good faith in the performance of a contract is, of course, applicable in equity and in law.

§ 16.17   Effect of Denial of Specific Performance or Injunction

A denial of specific performance, whether on the ground that the legal remedy is adequate or on the basis of the plaintiff's inequitable conduct, does not void the contract. The plaintiff may still enforce the contract in an action for damages or seek restitution. Frequently, however, this option is of little comfort to the plaintiff because damages may be merely nominal[1] or may be too speculative to be susceptible to proof.[2] Under many modern procedural codes, the court is empowered, when denying specific performance, to grant damages, thereby avoiding the necessity of commencing a new action.[3] However, if specific performance is denied on a ground that would bar an action for damages as well, (e.g.,

---

6. New York Football Giants v. Los Angeles Chargers, 291 F.2d 471 (5th Cir.1961). The doctrine is not limited to contract cases. See, e.g., Consolidated Aluminum v. Foseco Int'l, 910 F.2d 804 (Fed.Cir.1990) (patent invalid for unclean hands in its procurement).

7. Houston Oilers v. Neely, 361 F.2d 36 (10th Cir.1966), cert. denied.

8. Dinerstein v. Dinerstein, 32 A.D.2d 750, 300 N.Y.S.2d 677 (1969); cf. Al–Ibrahim v. Edde, 897 F.Supp. 620 (D.D.C.1995) (agreement to defraud the IRS); see McClintock at 163–64.

9. Meis v. Sanitas Service, 511 F.2d 655 (5th Cir.1975).

10. Saudi Basic Indus. v. Exxonmobil, 194 F.Supp.2d 378 (D.N.J.2002) (one joint venturer allegedly overcharged the other); Myers v. Smith, 208 N.W.2d 919 (Iowa 1973); Lazy M Ranch, Ltd. v. TXI Operations, 978 S.W.2d 678 (Tex.App.1998) (deliberate breach, even if immaterial, constitutes unclean hands).

11. UCC §§ 1–201(19), 1–203, 2–103(1)(b).

12. Rs. 2d § 205.

§ 16.17

1. Margraf v. Muir, 57 N.Y. 155 (1874).

2. See Frank & Endicott, Defenses in Equity and "Legal Rights," 14 La.L.Rev. 380 (1954).

3. Sundstrand Corp. v. Standard Kollsman Indus., 488 F.2d 807 (7th Cir.1973); Charles County Broadcasting v. Meares, 270 Md. 321, 311 A.2d 27 (1973); Lane v. Mercury Record, 21 A.D.2d 602, 252 N.Y.S.2d 1011 (1964), aff'd, Noted, 31 Brooklyn L.Rev. 428 (1965).

invalidity of the contract), a subsequent action at law would be barred on grounds of res judicata.[4]

§ 16.18   Relationship to Damages; Agreed Remedies

Clearly, a decree for specific performance is generally inconsistent with a judgment for damages. If the plaintiff receives the very performance bargained for, plaintiff should not also be compensated for the value of the defendant's promise. There are occasions, however, where the court may properly award some damages in addition to equitable relief. Where there is a breach of a valid covenant not to compete, an injunction will issue coupled with damages incurred during the period between the breach and the issuance of the injunction.[1] Where a conveyance is decreed, damages for delay may also be awarded.[2] Similarly, where a court orders personalty to be delivered, delay damages may be awarded as well.[3] As discussed elsewhere, the existence of a liquidated damages clause is no bar to an action for specific performance.[4] The uncertainty of damages can be one basis for the grant of equitable relief.[5]

Contracts that either provide for the remedy of specific performance or that bar such relief are discussed in § 16.3.

C.   COVENANTS NOT TO COMPETE

Table of Sections

§ 16.19   Agreements Not to Compete

Although agreements not to compete are not exclusively of equitable cognizance, most of the litigation concerning them has arisen in equita-

---

4. Rs. Judgments § 65 cmt e. See Annot. 38 ALR3d 323 (1971).

§ 16.18

1. See § 14.33 supra.

2. Reis v. Sparks, 547 F.2d 236 (4th Cir.1976) (Hadley v. Baxendale not applicable to damages from higher interest rate); Turley v. Ball Assocs., 641 P.2d 286 (Colo. App.1981) (damages from higher interest rate); Bostwick v. Beach, 103 N.Y. 414, 9 N.E. 40 (1886) (accounting for rents and profits or value of use and occupation); Brockel v. Lewton, 319 N.W.2d 173 (S.D. 1982); cf. Pirchio v. Noecker, 226 Ind. 622, 82 N.E.2d 838, 7 ALR2d 1198 (1948) (loss of resale opportunity not compensable); Ma-

trix Properties v. TAG Investments, 644 N.W.2d 601 (N.D.2002) (post appeal ancillary proceedings upheld).

3. Winchell v. Plywood Corp., 324 Mass. 171, 85 N.E.2d 313 (1949); cf. Owen v. Merts, 240 Ark. 1080, 405 S.W.2d 273, 28 ALR3d 1390 (1966); Virginia Pub. Service v. Steindler, 166 Va. 686, 187 S.E. 353, 105 ALR 1413 (1936) (depreciation in value not compensable).

4. See § 14.33 supra.

5. See the mention of output contracts in § 16.3 supra; Frierson v. Delta Outdoor, 794 So.2d 220 (Miss.2001)

ble actions to enjoin violations of such agreements[1] and, in general, the rules concerning these agreements preserve an equitable flavor.[2] An agreement by a person to refrain from exercising his or her trade or calling, standing alone, is viewed as being illegal and contrary to public policy because it is inimical to the interests of society in a free competitive market and to the interests of the person restrained in earning a livelihood.[3] Thus, such agreements are viewed from the perspectives of both illegality and unconscionability. But if a covenant not to compete forms part of a legitimate transaction, a different problem is presented. Such a covenant is often described as an "ancillary restraint" to indicate its connection with a legitimate transaction. The legitimate transactions to which such restraints are most frequently connected are sales of business and employment contracts.[4]

(a) Covenant by a Seller of a Business Not to Compete

It is common in the purchase of a business to buy its "good will" along with the business' other assets in the expectation that the customers of the business will patronize the new owners. Therefore it is common to provide that the seller shall not reopen a business in competition with the business sold.[5] Such a provision raises the question of whether the common law policy against unreasonable restraints of trade is violated.

English cases made the question of legality depend upon whether the restraint imposed was "general" or "limited."[6] In some of the early cases in the U.S., applying two versions of this test, a restraint that covered an entire state was deemed to be per se illegal,[7] and in others a restraint that did not cover the entire country was deemed to be limited and therefore legal.[8] The English test has now generally been abandoned and the test is whether the restraint of trade is unreasonable.[9] Thus, if

§ 16.19

1. But see Van Dyck Printing v. DiNicola, 43 Conn.Sup. 191, 648 A.2d 898 (1993) (damages); Weber v. Tillman, 259 Kan. 457, 913 P.2d 84 (1996) (liquidated damages).

2. See Intagliata v. Peelle Co., 227 A.D.2d 450, 642 N.Y.S.2d 914 (1996).

3. Rs. 2d § 187; U.S. v. Addyston Pipe & Steel, 85 F. 271 (6th Cir.1898), mod and aff'd 175 U.S. 211 (1899); 6A Corbin §§ 1379–1384; Handler & Lazaroff, Restraint of Trade and the Restatement, Second, Contracts, 57 N.Y.U.L.Rev. 669 (1982).

4. See Watson, Enforceability of Covenants Not To Compete in Mississippi, 64 Miss.L.J. 703 (1995). This chapter discusses covenants not to compete ancillary to sales of going businesses and ancillary to employment contracts. Rules similar to those applicable to these transactions have been forged for other ancillary restraints, such as restraints ancillary to the sale of corporate shares (6A Corbin § 1388), ancillary to the

sale or lease of real property (6A Corbin § 1389; 14 Williston § 1642), ancillary to partnership agreements (14 Williston § 1644), and ancillary to stock option agreements. Fox v. Avis Rent–A–Car, 223 Ga. 571, 156 S.E.2d 910 (1967). Some of these are discussed in depth in Handler & Lazaroff, supra note 3, at 678–714.

5. LDDS Communications v. Automated Communications, 35 F.3d 198 (5th Cir. 1994): Aviation Assocs. v. TEMSCO Helicopters, 881 P.2d 1127 (Alaska 1994).

6. Mitchel v. Reynolds, 24 Eng.Rep. 347 (Ch. 1711).

7. Parish v. Schwartz, 344 Ill. 563, 176 N.E. 757, 78 ALR 1032 (1931).

8. Diamond Match v. Roeber, 106 N.Y. 473, 13 N.E. 419 (1887).

9. Coffee System of Atlanta v. Fox, 226 Ga. 593, 176 S.E.2d 71 (1970), appeal after remand 227 Ga. 602, 182 S.E.2d 109 (1971); Grempler v. Multiple Listing Bur., 258 Md.

the business is national in extent, a covenant not to compete anywhere in the nation may be upheld if otherwise reasonable.[10] A seller's covenant not to lure away employees of the business sold is enforceable and if materially breached is a failure of constructive condition.[11]

Unreasonable restraints of trade are void. "A promise by a seller not to compete with the buyer is illegal and unenforceable insofar as the restraint is in excess of the extent of the good will purchased."[12] Thus, if the restraint covers territory in which the seller has no good will, it is an unreasonable restraint of trade, and the same is true if the restraint covers lines of trade in which the seller was not engaged.[13] Many cases however have held or intimated that the covenant may validly embrace the area of probable expansion of the business sold.[14]

Although there are a number of cases to the effect that the duration of the restrictive covenant is immaterial,[15] the better view is that a restraint is invalid if it is to continue "for a longer time than the good will built up by the seller and sold to the buyer can reasonably be expected to continue."[16]

(b) Covenant by an Employee Not to Compete

An employee's covenant not to compete after termination of employment, as is the case with contracts generally, requires consideration. If the covenant is agreed on when the employee is hired, consideration presents no problem. It can be problematic if an employee whose hiring is at will signs such a covenant after being hired. Some cases hold that the covenant agreed to in such circumstances is void for lack of consideration.[17] But even where there is consideration for the covenant, a serious question of public policy must be confronted.

419, 266 A.2d 1, 45 ALR3d 180 (1970); Jewel Box Stores v. Morrow, 272 N.C. 659, 158 S.E.2d 840 (1968); Rs. 2d § 188.

10. Voices v. Metal Tone Mfg., 119 N.J.Eq. 324, 182 A. 880 (1936), aff'd, cert. denied; Diamond Match v. Roeber, 106 N.Y. 473, 13 N.E. 419 (1887) (where, however, Nevada and Montana were excluded from the restraint).

11. Prince William Professional Baseball Club v. Boulton, 882 F.Supp. 1446 (D.Del.1995), opinion withdrawn.

12. 6A Corbin § 1387. "When a business is sold with its good will, but without any express promise not to compete, the seller is privileged to open up a new business in competition with the buyer; but he is under obligation not to solicit his former customers or to conduct his business under such a name and in such a manner as to deprive the buyer of the 'good will' that he paid for." 6A Corbin § 1386.

13. Schultz v. Johnson, 110 N.J.Eq. 566, 160 A. 379 (Ct.Err. & App.1932); Purchasing Assocs. v. Weitz, 13 N.Y.2d 267, 246

N.Y.S.2d 600, 196 N.E.2d 245 (1963), reargument denied.

14. Schnucks Twenty–Five v. Bettendorf, 595 S.W.2d 279 (Mo.App.1979); see Handler, Blake, Pitofsky, Goldschmid, Trade Regulation—Cases and Materials 46 (1975).

15. Beatty v. Coble, 142 Ind. 329, 41 N.E. 590 (1895).

16. 6A Corbin § 1391.

17. Hollingsworth Solderless Terminal v. Turley, 622 F.2d 1324 (9th Cir.1980); Heatron v. Shackelford, 898 F.Supp. 1491 (D.Kan.1995) (continued employment and promotion); but see NBZ v. Pilarski, 185 Wis.2d 827, 520 N.W.2d 93 (Wis.App.1994) (continued employment is not consideration). On the diverse views concerning consideration and the at-will employee, see Abel v. Fox, 274 Ill.App.3d 811, 211 Ill.Dec. 129, 654 N.E.2d 591 (1995); Ackerman v. Kimball Int'l, 652 N.E.2d 507 (Ind.1995); Central Adjustment Bureau v. Ingram, 678 S.W.2d 28 (Tenn.1984)

An employee's promise not to compete is treated differently from that of a seller of a business. Frequently, an employee promises the employer that upon the completion of the employment the employee will not compete with the employer either as an entrepreneur, or by working for a competitor.[18] If the employee learns no secrets and does not have any contact with the customers of the employer, there is no reason for enforcing such a restrictive covenant and the covenant should be struck down as it imposes an undue hardship upon the person restricted and deprives the public of the employee's skills.[19]

While a covenant by a seller of a business is tested by the reasonableness of its duration, geographic extent and scope of activity, different criteria apply to employment restraints. To uphold an employment covenant the employer must show special circumstances such as close customer contact, trade secrets or other confidential information.[20] It is generally agreed that, if an employee learns a trade secret or confidential information, a promise not to disclose it or use it will be enforced.[21] Indeed, even in the absence of an express covenant, employees may not, even after termination of employment, disclose or make use of trade secrets, including secret customer lists.[22] Enforcement by injunctions of reasonable covenants not to compete where the former employee has learned trade secrets goes one step beyond this rule, as it eliminates the *potential* for misuse or wrongful disclosure.[23]

Covenants not to compete are frequently upheld where the former employee has had contact with the employer's customers under circumstances where the employee may have obtained the good will of the customers, a good will that is likely to follow the employee. The present tendency is to enforce the covenant only in cases where the customers were developed over a period of time with great effort. If the customers were such as are listed in standard directories, enforcement is refused.[24]

---

18. See generally, Blake, Employee Covenants Not to Compete, 73 Harv.L.Rev. 625 (1960); Hutter, Drafting Non–Competition Agreements to Protect Confidential Business Information, 45 Albany L.Rev. 311 (1981); Wetzel, Employment Contracts and Non-competition Agreements, 1969 U.Ill. L.F. 61. In some Jurisdictions the matter is governed by statute. See 19 Fla.St.U.L.Rev. 1105 (1992). Covenant entered into with a non-employer may not be valid even if the relationship later becomes one of employment. Pitney Bowes v. Berney Office Solutions, 823 So.2d 659 (Ala.2001).

19. Vencor v. Webb, 33 F.3d 840 (7th Cir.1994) (Ky.law); E.L. Conwell & Co. v. Gutberlet, 429 F.2d 527 (4th Cir.1970); Geritrex v. Dermarite Indus., 910 F.Supp. 955 (S.D.N.Y.1996); Rs. 1st § 515(b); Rs. 2d § 188.

20. Central Water Works Supply v. Fisher, 240 Ill.App.3d 952, 181 Ill.Dec. 545, 608 N.E.2d 618 (1993). For a critique of this requisite, see Arnow–Richman, Bar-

gaining for Loyalty, 80 Ore.L.Rev. 1163 (2001).

21. Uncle B's Bakery v. O'Rourke, 920 F.Supp. 1405 (N.D.Iowa 1996) (secrets of making bagels); McCall Co. v. Wright, 198 N.Y. 143, 91 N.E. 516 (1910); J. & K. Computer Systems v. Parrish, 642 P.2d 732 (Utah 1982).

22. Mixing Equipment v. Philadelphia Gear, 436 F.2d 1308 (3d Cir.1971); Town & Country House & Home Serv. v. Newbery, 3 N.Y.2d 554, 170 N.Y.S.2d 328, 147 N.E.2d 724 (1958). Cf. In re Uniservices, 517 F.2d 492 (7th Cir.1975) (implied contract theory).

23. Business Intelligence Services v. Hudson, 580 F.Supp. 1068 (S.D.N.Y.1984).

24. American Hardware Mut. Ins. v. Moran, 705 F.2d 219 (7th Cir.1983); Ivy Mar v. C.R. Seasons, 907 F.Supp. 547 (E.D.N.Y.1995); Microbiological Research v. Muna, 625 P.2d 690 (Utah 1981); Rubin &

However, there are many cases to the contrary.[25] In short, the customer list must be akin to a trade secret. In addition, as in the cases involving the sale of a business, if the restraint in space and time is greater than is necessary to protect the employer, it will be deemed overbroad.[26] Similarly the restraint is overbroad if it covers a line of endeavor not engaged in by the employer[27] or a line of work for the competitor that is different from the employee's job with the former employer.[28]

A number of cases have intimated that there is a third circumstance in which a covenant not to compete will be upheld; that is, where the employee's services are "unique" or "extraordinary."[29] Such unsound intimations have been borrowed uncritically from cases in which an employee has been enjoined from competing during the term of employment.[30] After the employment term is terminated the general principle of free competition supersedes any interest the employer has in preventing competition from unique and extraordinary individuals.[31] It is only where the employer has a legitimate interest in self protection from the possibility of tortious or near tortious conduct by the former employee that a restraint should be upheld. It is primarily to protect this legitimate interest that injunctions are issued in the trade secret and customer contact cases despite the principle of free competition.[32]

Although the cases generally fall into the categories discussed above, the modern approach is to utilize an overall standard of reasonableness. Among the factors to be considered, for example, is whether the employee has received adequate additional compensation for the non-competi-

Shedd, Human Capital and Covenants Not to Compete, 10 J.Leg.Stud. 93 (1981).

25. Murray v. Lowndes County Broadcasting, 248 Ga. 587, 284 S.E.2d 10 (1981); Dana F. Cole & Co. v. Byerly, 211 Neb. 903, 320 N.W.2d 916 (1982); Rental Uniform Service of Florence v. Dudley, 278 S.C. 674, 301 S.E.2d 142 (1983); Roanoke Engineering Sales v. Rosenbaum, 223 Va. 548, 290 S.E.2d 882 (1982).

26. Purchasing Assoc. v. Weitz, 13 N.Y.2d 267, 246 N.Y.S.2d 600, 196 N.E.2d 245 (1963); Jones v. Deeter, 112 Nev. 291, 913 P.2d 1272 (1996) (five years is too long); Eastern Business Forms v. Kistler, 258 S.C. 429, 189 S.E.2d 22 (1972); Matlock v. Data Processing Security, 618 S.W.2d 327 (Tex.1981). A restraint unlimited in time may be valid if otherwise reasonable. Karpinski v. Ingrasci, 28 N.Y.2d 45, 320 N.Y.S.2d 1, 268 N.E.2d 751, 62 ALR3d 1006 (1971); 40 Fordham L.Rev. 430 (1971).

27. Thus a covenant not to practice dentistry in a given area is too broad where the employment related only to oral surgery. Karpinski v. Ingrasci, 28 N.Y.2d 45, 320 N.Y.S.2d 1, 268 N.E.2d 751 (1971); 40 Fordham L.Rev. 430 (1971); accord, Faces Bou-

tique v. Gibbs, 318 S.C. 39, 455 S.E.2d 707 (App.1995).

28. Modern Environments v. Stinnett, 263 Va. 491, 561 S.E.2d 694 (2002).

29. E.L. Conwell & Co. v. Gutberlet, 429 F.2d 527 (4th Cir.1970); Purchasing Assocs. v. Weitz, 13 N.Y.2d 267, 246 N.Y.S.2d 600, 196 N.E.2d 245 (1963), rearg. denied. Contra and sound is Nigra v. Young Broadcasting of Albany, 177 Misc.2d 664, 676 N.Y.S.2d 848 (1998) (television personality).

30. See § 16.5 supra.

31. See Kniffin, Employee Noncompetition Covenants: The Perils of Performing Unique Services, 10 Rutgers–Camden L.J. 25 (1978).

32. See Diaz v. Indian Head, 402 F.Supp. 111 (N.D.Ill.1975), aff'd. For discussions of covenants not to compete from the viewpoint of legal policies furthering competition, see, Goldschmid, Antitrust's Neglected Stepchild: A Proposal for Dealing with Restrictive Covenants under Federal Law, 73 Colum.L.Rev. 1193 (1973); Sullivan, Revisiting the "Neglected Stepchild:" Antitrust Treatment of Postemployment Restraints of Trade, 1977 U.Ill.L.F. 621.

tion covenant.[33] As put by the Texas court:

> "A determination of the reasonableness of territorial restraints upon non-competition contracts requires a balance of the interests of the employer, the employee, and the public while being mindful of the basic policies of individual liberty, freedom of contract, freedom of trade, protection of business, encouragement of competition and discouragement of monopoly."[34]

Covenants not to compete in contracts employing lawyers or in law partnership agreements are in violation of professional ethics and void because they deprive clients of freedom of choice.[35] This exceptional rule seems to apply to no other profession.[36]

Assume that an employee has entered a *valid* covenant that meets the tests of consideration and public policy and suffers from no infirmity such as fraud. Assume further, that the term of employment is at will or for a term that has expired, and that the employee is discharged without cause. Will the covenant be enforced? Would not such enforcement be unconscionably abusive? The answer of classical contract law is that a valid contract exists and should be enforced.[37] Yet, very many cases have employed flanking devices such as artful interpretation,[38] the exercise of equitable discretion,[39] and the stretching of the equitable doctrine of "unclean hands."[40] Other courts basically have sputtered that enforce-

---

33. Bradford v. New York Times, 501 F.2d 51 (2d Cir.1974).

34. Matlock v. Data Process Security, supra n. 26.

35. Jacob v. Norris, McLaughlin & Marcus, 128 N.J. 10, 607 A.2d 142 (1992); see Perillo, The Law of Lawyers' Contracts Is Different, 67 Fordham L.Rev. 443, 477–80 (1998).

36. As to physicians, see Annots., 62 ALR3d 918, 970, 1014 (1975); accountants, see Schuhalter v. Salerno, 279 N.J.Super. 504, 653 A.2d 596 (A.D.1995).

37. Robert S. Weiss & Assocs. v. Wiederlight, 208 Conn. 525, 546 A.2d 216 (1988). (employee's four-year term of employment expired; held that the expiration activated the covenant.); Orkin Exterminating v. Harris, 224 Ga. 759, 164 S.E.2d 727, 728–29 (1968) (The agreement provided: " '[t]hese covenants (restrictive) on the part of the employee shall be construed as an agreement independent of any other provision in this agreement, and the existence of any claim or cause of action of the employee against the company whether predicated on this agreement or otherwise, shall not constitute a defense to the enforcement by the Company of said covenants.' "); Gomez v. Chua Medical, 510 N.E.2d 191, 195 (Ind. App.1987) (where an at-will employment was terminated by the employer the cove-

nant would be enforced even if the firing were "essentially arbitrary").

38. In Derrick, Stubbs & Stith v. Rogers, 256 S.C. 395, 182 S.E.2d 724, 726 (1971), it was held that termination of the contract of employment also terminated the covenant. Many covenants are written to prevent such a holding. In Grant v. Carotek, 737 F.2d 410 (4th Cir.1984), very strict construction was given to the covenant making it unreasonable and unenforceable.

39. Frierson v. Sheppard Bldg. Supply, 247 Miss. 157, 154 So.2d 151, 155 (Miss. 1963). "Had the chancellor found that appellant's discharge was arbitrary, capricious, or in bad faith, he could have refused to lend the aid of equity in enforcing the contract." Bishop v. Lakeland Animal Hosp., 268 Ill.App.3d 114, 205 Ill.Dec. 817, 644 N.E.2d 33 (1994) (breach of covenant of good faith); Ma & Pa v. Kelly, 342 N.W.2d 500 (Iowa 1984), (the cause for the termination was only one factor in determining whether an injunction should issue); Security Services v. Priest, 507 S.W.2d 592, 595 (Tex.Civ.App.1974) ("equity may deny enforcement of the covenant if the employer acts arbitrarily and unreasonably in discharging the employee.")

40. Chicago Towel v. Reynolds, 108 W.Va. 615, 152 S.E. 200 (W.Va.1930). The employee was discharged without notice on

ment would be unjust.[41]

The doctrine of abuse of rights, if recognized, would explain why such a covenant will not be enforced by either law or equity where the employee is discharged for the convenience of the employer.[42] The shared purpose of an employment agreement containing a covenant not to compete is to protect the employer from conduct that is in the penumbra of unfair competition, while assuring the employee a means of practicing the trade or profession for which the employee is trained. The employee's purpose in agreeing to the covenant is to practice this trade or profession with the employer who has now destroyed the assurance of a job while seeking to prevent the employee from working at such a job elsewhere. Such enforcement would be a grave abuse of rights.

§ 16.20 Equitable Discretion and Remedy at Law

Even if the employee's covenant meets the standards of validity, equity may nonetheless refuse injunctive relief if such relief will result in disproportionate hardship to the defendant[1] or failure to issue the injunction will cause no irreparable harm to the plaintiff.[2] Where injunctive relief is sought, the entire array of equitable defenses is, of course, available.[3] As Corbin states, "Before granting an injunction preventing an employee from earning his living in his customary trade or employment, the court should make sure, not only that he contracted to forbear and is guilty of a breach, but also that the former employer is suffering substantial harm, that the employee is soliciting former customers or otherwise depriving his employer of business good will that he has paid wages for helping to create, and that the employee will not be deprived

---

the ground that his salary was too high. The court denied an injunction on the basis of the "unclean hands" doctrine.

41. In Bailey v. King, 240 Ark. 245, 398 S.W.2d 906, 908 (1966), the court said: "Of course, if an employer obtained an agreement of this nature from an employee, and then, without reasonable cause, fired him, the agreement would not be binding. In other words, an employer cannot use this type of contract as a subterfuge to rid himself of a possible future competitor."

In Post v. Merrill, Lynch, Pierce, Fenner & Smith, 48 N.Y.2d 84, 421 N.Y.S.2d 847, 849, 397 N.E.2d 358, 361 (1979), the court said "[w]here the employer terminates the employment relationship without cause, however, his action necessarily destroys the mutuality of obligation on which the covenant rests as well as the employer's ability to impose a forfeiture. An employer should not be permitted to use offensively an anticompetition clause coupled with a forfeiture provision to economically cripple a former employee and simultaneously deny other potential employers in his services." The attempt to base the result on mutuality of

obligation is like the flailing of a non-swimmer. First, mutuality of obligation is an obsolete and abandoned doctrine. See § 4.12(c) supra; 2 Corbin ch. 6. Second, in the typical at-will employment, there is no obligation on the employee, except perhaps the covenant itself. A theory of abuse of rights is inherent in the rest of this quotation.

In Dutch Maid Bakeries v. Schleicher, 58 Wyo. 374, 131 P.2d 630, 636 (1942) the court said that the employer's conduct "savored with injustice."

42. See § 11.39 supra.

§ 16.20

1. Mixing Equipment v. Philadelphia Gear, 436 F.2d 1308 (3d Cir.1971) (dissenting opinion); Cogley Clinic v. Martini, 253 Iowa 541, 112 N.W.2d 678 (1962); 48 Iowa L.Rev. 159 (1962); Standard Oil v. Bertelsen, 186 Minn. 483, 243 N.W. 701 (1932).

2. Menter Co. v. Brock, 147 Minn. 407, 180 N.W. 553, 20 ALR 857 (1920).

3. See §§ 16.7 to 16.18 supra.

of opportunity to support himself and his family in reasonable comfort."[4] As usual, all of the facts and circumstances should be considered in making this determination of unreasonable hardship.[5]

Because there is likely to be greater hardship on an employee than on the seller of a business, courts have stated on a number of occasions that they are more reluctant to uphold and to enforce covenants not to compete entered into by employees than those agreed to by sellers of businesses.[6] The cases are divided on the question as to whether covenants not to compete attached to partnership agreements are to be treated on a par with employment agreements or sales of businesses.[7]

Where the covenant is valid, but an injunction is denied on equitable principles, damages may be awarded to the plaintiff.[8] Damages are also available in addition to an injunction for injury done between the time of the breach and the time the injunction is issued.[9]

§ 16.21 Limited Enforcement of Overbroad Restraints

In the past, the standard approach to an unreasonable covenant not to compete was to strike the entire covenant.[1] The rule of total invalidity was mitigated by the "blue pencil" rule, which has its basis in the doctrine of severability as applied to illegal contracts.[2] Under the rule, the courts would, if grammatically feasible, sever some words of the covenant, leaving intact those parts of the covenant that were reasonable. For example, in one case the employee agreed not to compete in 46 named counties. The court granted an injunction against competing in 31 of the named counties.[3]

4. 6A Corbin § 1394; see Taylor Freezer Sales v. Sweden Freezer Eastern, 224 Ga. 160, 160 S.E.2d 356 (1968).

5. Solari Indus. v. Malady, 55 N.J. 571, 264 A.2d 53 (1970); Note, 17 Drake L.Rev. 69 (1967).

6. Day Companies v. Patat, 403 F.2d 792 (5th Cir.1968), cert. denied; H & R Block v. Lovelace, 208 Kan. 538, 493 P.2d 205, 50 ALR3d 730 (1972); Morgan's Home Equip. v. Martucci, 390 Pa. 618, 136 A.2d 838 (1957).

7. Compare Millet v. Slocum, 4 A.D.2d 528, 167 N.Y.S.2d 136 (1957), aff'd (employment) with Scott v. McReynolds, 36 Tenn. App. 289, 255 S.W.2d 401 (1952) (business); cf. Bradford v. Billington, 299 S.W.2d 601 (Ky.1957) (sui generis) and Abrams v. Liss, 53 Mass.App.Ct. 751, 762 N.E.2d 862 (2002) (implied covenant).

8. Tull v. Turek, 38 Del.Ch. 182, 147 A.2d 658 (1958); see Comment, 15 So.Tex. L.J. 289 (1974).

9. See § 16.18 supra.

§ 16.21

1. Some examples are Welcome Wagon v. Morris, 224 F.2d 693 (4th Cir.1955); Rec-

tor–Phillips–Morse v. Vroman, 253 Ark. 750, 489 S.W.2d 1, 61 ALR3d 391 (1973); Kolani v. Gluska, 64 Cal.App.4th 402, 75 Cal.Rptr.2d 257 (1998); Weatherford Oil Tool v. Campbell, 161 Tex. 310, 340 S.W.2d 950 (1960); 40 Tex.L.Rev. 152 (1961).

In one case, the consideration for the covenant was found to be so interwoven with the entire agreement that the agreement as a whole was deemed invalid. Alston Studios v. Lloyd V. Gress & Assoc., 492 F.2d 279 (4th Cir.1974).

2. Smart Corp. v. Grider, 650 N.E.2d 80 (Ind.App.1995); see § 22.6 infra.

3. Thomas v. Coastal Indus. Services, 214 Ga. 832, 108 S.E.2d 328 (1959). Georgia has subsequently abandoned the "blue pencil" rule and has refused to adopt the concept of limited enforcement Amstell, Inc. v. Bunge Corp., 213 Ga.App. 115, 443 S.E.2d 706 (1994), but accepts limited enforcement as to covenants ancillary to sales of businesses. Jenkins v. Jenkins Irrigation, 244 Ga. 95, 259 S.E.2d 47 (1979). Applications of the blue pencil rule include Hartman v. W.H. Odell & Assocs., 117 N.C.App. 307, 450 S.E.2d 912 (1994).

A more modern approach that represents the weight of recent authority is that an overbroad covenant will be enforced by the issuance of an injunction limited to the area, time, or calling as to which the covenant is reasonable, regardless of whether a grammatical severance is possible.[4] This modern approach is based upon a realization that an equitable decree is a flexible instrument and that such flexibility need not be based on a theory of severability.[5] While this approach has much to commend it, it doubtless has the effect of encouraging employers to draft overbroad covenants not to compete that have *in terrorem* effect on employees who can only ascertain their rights by costly litigation.[6] Therefore, it has been held that enforcement will be totally denied where the employer has made no effort to protect the legitimate interests of the employee.[7]

§ 16.22 Anti-competition Conditions Distinguished From Covenants

Although *covenants* not to compete must meet the standards of reasonableness, the weight of authority automatically upholds anti-competition *conditions* without regard to reasonableness. In the typical case a pension plan or other form of deferred compensation provides that rights under the plan are conditioned upon the ex-employee's refraining from entering into competitive employment. On the dubious ground that the employee is not restrained from entering into competing employment, but has a choice whether to compete or not, such conditions have generally been upheld.[1] Federal law now severely restricts the validity of such pension forfeitures.[2]

---

4. Solari Indus. v. Malady, 55 N.J. 571, 264 A.2d 53 (1970); Karpinski v. Ingrasci, 28 N.Y.2d 45, 320 N.Y.S.2d 1, 268 N.E.2d 751 (1971); Jacobson & Co. v. International Env., 427 Pa. 439, 235 A.2d 612 (1967); Weatherford Oil Tool v. Campbell, 161 Tex. 310, 340 S.W.2d 950 (1960), 40 Tex.L.Rev. 152 (1961); see 6A Corbin §§ 1390, 1394; 14 Williston §§ 1659, 1660; contra Varsity Gold v. Porzio, 202 Ariz. 355, 45 P.3d 352 (App.2002) (limited enforcement would encourage employers to draft overbroad covenants).

5. For an example of such flexibility, see Electronic Data Systems v. Kinder, 497 F.2d 222 (5th Cir.1974); see also CAE Vanguard v. Newman, 246 Neb. 334, 518 N.W.2d 652 (1994) (refusing to "reform" the covenant, applying the "minority view").

6. See Blake, supra § 16.19 n.17, at 683–84; Rector–Phillips–Morse v. Vroman, 253 Ark. 750, 489 S.W.2d 1, 61 ALR3d 391 (1973) (adhering to traditional view).

7. Insurance Center v. Taylor, 94 Idaho 896, 499 P.2d 1252 (1972); Terry D. Whit-

ten v. Malcolm, 249 Neb. 48, 541 N.W.2d 45, 48 (1995) ("it is not the function of courts to reform unreasonable covenants for the purpose of make them enforceable"); see Comment, 15 Columb.J.L. & Soc. Problems 181, 222–31 (1979); Rs. 2d § 184(2) and cmt b.

§ 16.22

1. Rochester Corp. v. Rochester, 450 F.2d 118 (4th Cir.1971). The vitality of a leading case, Kristt v. Whelan, 4 A.D.2d 195, 164 N.Y.S.2d 239 (1957), aff'd, was questioned in Bradford v. New York Times, 501 F.2d 51 (2d Cir.1974); but see Diakoff v. American Re–Insurance, 492 F.Supp. 1115 (S.D.N.Y.1980). For a critical appraisal of the covenant-condition distinction, see Goldschmid, Anti-trust's Neglected Stepchild, 73 Colum.L.Rev. 1193, 1196–1200 (1973).

2. See Note, Erisa's Restrictions on the Use of Postemployment Anticompetition Covenants, 45 Albany L.Rev. 410 (1981).

Chapter 17

THIRD PARTY BENEFICIARIES

Table of Sections

---

§ 17.1   History and Introduction

It was firmly established in the nineteenth century that only a person in "privity" could sue on the contract. Although the word "privity" is used in several senses, in this context it refers to those who exchange the promissory words or those to whom the promissory words are directed.[1]

Some earlier cases had been to the contrary. In Dutton v. Poole,[2] the defendant had promised his father to pay defendant's sister £1000 if the father would forbear from selling certain property. When defendant's sister sought to enforce this promise, defendant took the position that his sister could not succeed because she was not in privity. However, because of the close relationship between the father, the promisee, and his daughter, the beneficiary, the court sustained the action even though there was no privity.

In the language of this chapter, the defendant is the promisor, the father is the promisee, and the plaintiff is the alleged beneficiary. On the

§ 17.1

1.   4 Corbin § 778.

2.   83 Eng.Rep. 523 (K.B.1677), aff'd 83 Eng.Rep. 156 (Ex.Ch. 1679).

facts of Dutton v. Poole, the relationship that was important was the relationship between the promisee (father) and the beneficiary (daughter). In the terminology of this chapter the plaintiff is a donee beneficiary.[3] This means that the father, by the contract he made with his son, intended to and did confer on his daughter a gift in the form of a promise. This gift does not require delivery because it was purchased by the consideration furnished by the father.[4]

In every bilateral contract there are at least two promisors. Why then should the defendant be called the promisor? The simple answer is that the promisor has made the promise that a third party seeks to enforce. Usually, only one of the promisors has made a promise that benefits the third party. However, it is conceivable that both parties made a promise beneficial to the beneficiary. In such a case *the* promisor would be the party against whom enforcement is sought.

Later English cases repudiated Dutton v. Poole. However, Parliament reinstated the doctrine in 1999.[5] In contrast, third party beneficiary doctrine has received a much warmer reception in the U.S. Lawrence v. Fox is the landmark decision.[6] The promisee, Holly owed $300 to Lawrence. Fox promised Holly to pay this debt in exchange for a loan of $300 that Holly made to Fox. Since the agreement was between Holly (promisee) and Fox (promisor), Lawrence was not in privity. Although there was some discussion of trusts and agency[7] in the decision, ultimately the case held that Lawrence could recover because it was manifestly just that he should. While Dutton v. Poole involved a donee beneficiary, Lawrence v. Fox permitted recovery to a beneficiary known as a creditor beneficiary because the promisee's purpose was to have a creditor paid.[8]

In a case such as Lawrence v. Fox, the beneficiary, Lawrence could have sued his debtor, Holly, who in turn could have impleaded the promisor, Fox. However, there may sometimes be jurisdictional or other procedural impediments that would prevent such a procedure. At any rate, it is certainly more efficient to allow a direct action between the beneficiary and the promisor.

---

3. See § 17.2 infra.

4. Byron Chamber of Commerce v. Long, 92 Ill.App.3d 864, 48 Ill.Dec. 77, 415 N.E.2d 1361 (1981); Estate of Sheimo, 261 Iowa 775, 156 N.W.2d 681 (1968); Continental Bank v. Barclay Riding Acad., 93 N.J. 153, 459 A.2d 1163 (1983), cert. denied.

5. Contracts (Rights of Third Parties) Act of 1999; see Merkin, Privity of Contract (2000).

6. 20 N.Y. 268 (1859). Generally complimented as an innovative case, but see Karsten, the "Discovery" of Law by English and American Jurists of the Seventeenth,

Eighteenth and Nineteenth Centuries: Third-Party Beneficiary contracts as a Test Case, 9 Law & Hist. Rev. 327 (1991).

7. The concurring judges preferred to rely on an agency theory; that is, that Holly was acting as an agent for Lawrence. This theory was of doubtful validity. See Rs. 2d § 302 cmt f. This was the approach taken in Massachusetts which refused to recognize the third party beneficiary doctrine until the case of Choate, Hall & Stewart v. SCA Serv., 378 Mass. 535, 392 N.E.2d 1045 (1979).

8. See § 17.2 infra.

§ 17.2   The First Restatement

The First Restatement, based on Dutton v. Poole and Lawrence v. Fox and other similar precedents, utilized terminology under which two types of third party beneficiaries have enforceable rights—creditor beneficiaries and donee beneficiaries. Others who will benefit from the contract but who have no enforceable rights are labeled incidental beneficiaries. Under this approach, the third party who is a creditor or a donee beneficiary qualifies as a third party beneficiary, but an incidental beneficiary's action is doomed to failure.[1]

The First Restatement focuses on the purpose of the promisee in obtaining the promise for the beneficiary. It set out three categories. (1) If the purpose is to confer a gift, the third party is a donee beneficiary. In making this determination the terms of the agreement and the surrounding circumstances should be taken into account.[2] (2) If the purpose of the promisee in obtaining the promise is to discharge "an actual or supposed or asserted duty of the promisee to the beneficiary," the beneficiary is a creditor beneficiary.[3] (3) A third person who will benefit by performance of the contract, but does not fall into either of these two categories, is called an incidental beneficiary and may not enforce the promise.[4]

§ 17.3   The Test of Intent to Benefit

Many courts have avoided the terminology of the First Restatement and have expressed a test of "intent to benefit."[1] There are two key questions that often receive different answers. Whose intent do we seek and what evidence is admissible on the issue of intent?

Some cases stress the intent of the promisee[2] but others have indicated that the intention of the promisor is equally important.[3] The first group of cases are sounder because the real question is why did the

§ 17.2

1. See Rs. 1st § 133; Williams v. Fenix & Scisson, 608 F.2d 1205 (9th Cir.1979).

2. See Rs. 1st § 133(a); People ex rel. Resnik v. Curtis & Davis, 78 Ill.2d 381, 36 Ill.Dec. 338, 400 N.E.2d 918 (1980).

3. Rs. 1st § 133(b). The effect of a supposed obligation is also discussed in sections 17.4 and 17.6 infra. In addition, this provision states that a person may qualify as a creditor beneficiary even though the claim against the promisee "has been barred by the Statute of Limitations or by a discharge in bankruptcy, or which is unenforceable because of the Statute of Frauds." Id. This is discussed in § 17.4 infra.

4. See Rs. 1st § 133(c); Young Ref. v. Pennzoil, 46 S.W.3d 380 (Tex.App.2001).

§ 17.3

1. Detroit Institute v. Rose, 127 F.Supp.2d 117 (D.Conn.2001); Centennial Mortgage v. Blumenfeld, 745 N.E.2d 268 (Ind.App.2001); Powers, Expanded Liability and the Intent Requirement in Third Party Beneficiary Contracts, 1993 Utah L.Rev. 67.

2. See Norfolk & Western v. U.S., 641 F.2d 1201 (6th Cir.1980); Sazerac Co. v. Falk, 861 F.Supp. 253 (S.D.N.Y.1994); Ins. Co. of North America v. Waterhouse, 424 A.2d 675 (Del.Super.1980); Owner–Operator Indpt. Drivers v. Concord EFS, 59 S.W.3d 63 (Tenn.2001).

3. See Holbrook v. Pitt, 643 F.2d 1261, 1270–1271 n. 17 (7th Cir.1981); Hylte Bruks Aktiebolag v. Babcock & Wilcox, 399 F.2d 289, 292 (2d Cir.1968); accord, Eisenberg, Third Party Beneficiaries, 92 Colum.L.Rev. 1358, 1377 (1992); but see Simmons v. Charleston Housing Auth., 881 F.Supp. 225 (S.D.W.Va.1995).

promisee extract the promise in question. When we speak of the admissibility of evidence we should recall that the intention of the parties is a question of interpretation[4] and that all of the questions discussed in that context again become relevant. Thus, we are again confronted with the plain meaning rule[5] and its opposite, ambiguity,[6] and the admissibility of extrinsic evidence,[7] including evidence of subjective intent.[8] Again, there is the question of whether the issue is a question of fact or question of law.[9]

The "intent to benefit test" is largely a fiction, except in cases of pure donative intent.[10] Yet, the term is commonly used and has acquired a doctrinal content. First, note that "intent to benefit" does not connote benevolent intent. One can contract that a hated creditor will receive a benefit.[11] As aptly put by one court: "Payment direct to the third person is, of course, a benefit to him [or her], and, if that is required by a contract, the intent to so benefit is beyond question."[12] Thus, a property owner's medical coverage for injured persons, payable without respect to fault, creates third party beneficiary rights.[13] An arbitration clause that expressly includes a third party is enforceable by that party.[14] Because the rights of third parties are derivative, defenses and limitations created by such clauses are effective against beneficiaries as well.[15]

The presumption is that the parties contract for their own benefit and not for the benefit of a third person.[16] However, if the parties explicitly agree that a third party shall have an enforceable right, their

4. See ch. 3 supra.

5. Talman Home Fed. S. & L. v. American Bankers Ins., 924 F.2d 1347 (5th Cir. 1991); First Hartford Realty v. Corporate Property Investors, 12 Mass.App.Ct. 911, 423 N.E.2d 1020 (1981).

6. Wilson v. General Mtge., 638 S.W.2d 821 (Mo.App.1982).

7. See Garcia v. Truck Ins. Exchange, 36 Cal.3d 426, 682 P.2d 1100, 204 Cal.Rptr. 435 (1984); Lane v. Aetna Cas. & Sur., 48 N.C.App. 634, 269 S.E.2d 711 (1980), rev. den.

8. See Local 80 v. Tishman Constr., 103 Mich.App. 784, 303 N.W.2d 893 (1981); Kary v. Kary, 318 N.W.2d 334 (S.D.1982).

9. See Hylte Bruks Aktiebolag v. Babcock & Wilcox, 399 F.2d 289 (2d Cir.1968), noted 37 Fordham L.Rev. 291 (1968); Clarke v. ASARCO, 124 Ariz. 8, 601 P.2d 612 (App.1978), vacated 123 Ariz. 587, 601 P.2d 587 (1979); Concrete Contractors v. E.B. Roberts Constr., 664 P.2d 722 (Colo. App.1982), aff'd.; Cutler v. Hartford Life Ins., 22 N.Y.2d 245, 292 N.Y.S.2d 430, 239 N.E.2d 361 (1968).

10. See Eisenberg, supra note 3, at 1378–85.

11. Gateway v. DiNoia, 232 Conn. 223, 654 A.2d 342 (1995).

12. Lenz v. Chicago & N.W. Ry., 111 Wis. 198, 86 N.W. 607 (1901); see Gateway v. DiNoia, supra ("intent to assume a direct obligation" to the creditor); Ridgway v. Ford Dealer Computer Serv., 114 Fed.3d 94 (6th Cir.1997) (promise of severance pay made to predecessor corporation enforceable by employee); Stine v. Stewart, 80 S.W.3d 586 (Tex.2002) (promise in divorce settlement to repay joint debt to mother-in-law).

13. Harper v. Wasau Ins., 56 Cal. App.4th 1079, 66 Cal.Rptr.2d 64 (1997)

14. Ex parte Stamey, 776 So.2d 85 (Ala. 2000).

15. Jansen v. Salomon Smith Barney, 342 N.J.Super. 254, 776 A.2d 816 (2001). see § 17.10 infra.

16. Liquid Drill v. U.S. Turnkey Exploration, 48 F.3d 927 (5th Cir.1995); Choi v. Chase Manhattan, 63 F.Supp.2d 874 (N.D.Ill.1999); Little Rock Wastewater Utility v. Larry Moyer Trucking, 321 Ark. 303, 902 S.W.2d 760 (Ark.1995); National Bd. of Examiners v. American Osteopathic Ass'n, 645 N.E.2d 608 (Ind.App.1994).

express agreement on this point will be given effect.[17] Similarly, if their agreement states that no third party will have an enforceable right, that express intent will be honored.[18] In the absence of an expressed intent to benefit, such an intent is established if it is clear that the promisor's performance is to run directly to the beneficiary.[19] This test of to whom is the performance to run has been used in many cases even though, at times, it is not clear to whom the performance is to run.[20] Under this test, if it is decided that the performance is to run directly to the promisee, the third party is ordinarily an unprotected incidental beneficiary.[21] Thus, for example, if a bank promised A a loan with which to pay creditors, the creditors would be deemed incidental beneficiaries,[22] but if the bank's promise was to pay the money directly to the creditors, they would be classified as intended beneficiaries.[23]

Frequently property owners retain maintenance companies to keep their property in good enough shape to prevent accidental injuries. Security companies are retained, among other reasons, to prevent assaults, robberies and other crimes against patrons or other invitees. In either case, the property owner may have a duty of care to such third persons. In contracting to maintain the premises or to keep the premises secure, has the promisor made itself liable for injuries to patrons or other invitees? Some cases hold that the patron is a third party creditor beneficiary of the promise.[24] The premise of the holding is that the owner owes a duty to patrons to use due care to prevent criminal activity.

However, this is not the only test employed. For example, in Lucas v. Hamm,[25] a lawyer promised to draft a will for the testator in which the

17. Seaboard Constr. v. Continental Mtge. Inv., 298 F.Supp. 579 (S.D.Ga.1969).

18. Jordan v. Caswell, 264 Ga. 638, 450 S.E.2d 818 (1994); Indiana Gaming v. Blevins, 724 N.E.2d 274 (Ind.App.2000); Sokoloff v. Harriman Estates, 275 A.D.2d 317, 712 N.Y.S.2d 60 (2000) reversed on other grounds MCI Telecom. v. Texas Utilities Elec., 995 S.W.2d 647 (1999).

19. Fourth Ocean Putnam v. Interstate Wrecking, 108 A.D.2d 3, 487 N.Y.S.2d 591 (1985) aff'd; Starrett v. Commercial Bank, 226 Ga.App. 598, 486 S.E.2d 923 (1997); Vikingstad v. Baggott, 46 Wn.2d 494, 282 P.2d 824 (1955).

20. See Ossining Union Free School Dist. v. Anderson LaRocca Anderson, 73 N.Y.2d 417, 539 N.E.2d 91, 541 N.Y.S.2d 335 (1989) ("bond between them so close as to be the functional equivalent of contractual privity;" consulting engineers retained by architects liable to school district).

21. McConnico v. Marrs, 320 F.2d 22 (10th Cir.1963); Fidelity & Deposit v. Rainer, 220 Ala. 262, 125 So. 55 (1929); Carson Pirie Scott & Co. v. Parrett, 346 Ill. 252, 178 N.E. 498, 81 A.L.R. 1262 (1931); Tomaso, Feitner and Lane v. Brown, 4 N.Y.2d

391, 175 N.Y.S.2d 73, 151 N.E.2d 221 (1958); Vikingstad v. Baggott, 46 Wn.2d 494, 282 P.2d 824 (1955); but see Grossoehme v. Cordell, 904 S.W.2d 392 (Mo.App. 1995) (drunken driver is given probation on condition he pay victim $4,000 a year for ten years; held victim has no enforceable rights).

22. See Mortgage Assocs. v. Monona Shores, 47 Wis.2d 171, 177 N.W.2d 340 (1970). Compare Hamill v. Maryland Cas., 209 F.2d 338 (10th Cir.1954).

23. See Apex Siding & Roofing v. First Fed. S. & L., 301 P.2d 352 (Okl.1956). As to the unreliability of this test, see Eisenberg, supra n.3 at 1380–81.

24. L.A.C. v. Ward Parkway Shopping Ctr., 75 S.W.3d 247 (Mo.2002) (minor was raped; security company sued); cf. James v. Jamie Towers, 294 A.D.2d 268, 743 N.Y.S.2d 85 (2002) (security company not liable for assault where absence of guard was pursuant to the contract); Espinal v. Melville Snow Contr., 98 N.Y.2d 136, 773 N.E.2d 485, 746 N.Y.S.2d 120 (2002) (snow plow contractor not liable for icy condition where it did not have control of premises).

25. 56 Cal.2d 583, 15 Cal.Rptr. 821, 364 P.2d 685 (1961), cert. denied; accord, Jew-

plaintiffs (third parties) were named as distributees. Because the will was improperly drawn, the plaintiffs received $75,000 less from the testator's estate than the testator had intended. The court recognized that the performance (drawing the will) was to run to the testator, but rejected this test. It stated, "Insofar as intent to benefit a third person is important in determining his [or her] right to bring an action under a contract, it is sufficient that the promisor must have understood that the promisee had such intent."[26]

This test stresses the intent of the promisee but also indicates that the promisor must also have reasonably understood this intent. Although the will was drawn for the testator, the ultimate intended beneficiaries of a will are the distributees named in the will.

The two tests can produce contrasting results. Although the test of to whom is the performance to run is a more mechanical one, the other test is better because it is based on the intention of the parties. The more modern cases are heading in the direction of the test in Lucas v. Hamm.[27] The test is particularly appropriate where the promisee's motive is donative.

Consider cases where a party has made a promise to obtain liability insurance for another party. Suppose O, the owner of property, obtained a mortgage loan from B Bank. As part of the mortgage agreement, B promised to obtain liability insurance to cover the premises. B failed to keep this promise. Plaintiff was injured as a result of O's negligence in the maintenance of the property. May plaintiff successfully sue B as a result of B's failure to keep its promise made to O? A number of cases have so held even though B's promised performance (to obtain the insurance) ran to O and to the insurance company that was to receive a premium.[28]

ish Hospital v. Boatmen's Nat. Bank, 261 Ill.App.3d 750, 199 Ill.Dec. 276, 633 N.E.2d 1267 (1994); American Centennial Ins. v. Canal Ins., 843 S.W.2d 480 (Tex.1992); Weiner v. Physicians News Serv., 13 A.D.2d 737, 214 N.Y.S.2d 474 (1961) (insurance case); see Note, 72 U.Det. Mercy L.Rev. 327 (1995); Annots. 61 ALR4th 464, 615; Comment, 23 J.Leg.Prof. 273 (1999); see also U. S. v. Carpenter, 113 F.Supp. 327 (E.D.N.Y. 1949) (agreement between exporters and U.S. importer to restrict use of potatoes imported into U.S. for seed purposes, the U.S. Government held to be an intended beneficiary); TSS Sportswear, Ltd. v. The Swank Shop (Guam), 380 F.2d 512 (9th Cir.1967) (agreement between seller and buyer of stock that corporate debtor would no longer owe any money to seller or firms controlled by him). Contra to Lucas is Estate of Pascale, 168 Misc.2d 891, 644 N.Y.S.2d 887 (1996).

26.   15 Cal.Rptr. at 825, 364 P.2d at 689 (1961).

27.   See Guy v. Liederbach, 501 Pa. 47, 459 A.2d 744 (1983); Matter of Gosmire's Estate, 331 N.W.2d 562 (S.D.1983); Feinman, Attorney Liability to Nonclients, 31 Tort & Ins.L.J. 735 (1996); but see Estate of Pascale, 168 Misc.2d 891, 644 N.Y.S.2d 887 (1996). According to some authorities the action may be brought on either a tort or a contract theory. Heyer v. Flaig, 70 Cal.2d 223, 226, 74 Cal.Rptr. 225, 227, 449 P.2d 161, 163 (1969), overruled on other grounds.

28.   See Johnson v. Holmes Tuttle Lincoln–Mercury, 160 Cal.App.2d 290, 325 P.2d 193 (1958); Khalaf v. Bankers & Shippers Ins., 404 Mich. 134, 273 N.W.2d 811 (1978); Pappas v. Jack O.A. Nelsen Agency, 81 Wis.2d 363, 260 N.W.2d 721 (1978); contra Caswell v. Zoya Int'l, 274 Ill.App.3d 1072, 211 Ill.Dec. 90, 654 N.E.2d 552 (1995);

The test of intent to benefit is not applied uniformly.[29] The courts do not always decide cases solely on the basis of the intent of the parties. The courts openly or covertly have employed third party beneficiary doctrine to advance social and economic policies.[30] For example, consider a provision for the support of a child living with a custodial parent under a separation agreement. It would be poor policy to have the payment made directly to the child.[31] However, if the parent refuses to take the money and the children are not being supported, that is a different matter.[32]

At times, recognition of a third party's right of action has no real effect on the promisor's burden. For example, if A is indebted to B, and thereafter C agrees with A, for a consideration, to pay the amount of this debt directly to B, B is a third party beneficiary.[33] This does not change C's burden because even if B were not a third party beneficiary B could sue A and A could in turn sue C. The efficiency of judicial administration may be slightly increased by permitting B to sue C.[34]

A donee beneficiary situation is quite different. Ordinarily, the donee beneficiary has no claim against the promisee and the promisee ordinarily has little or no financial incentive to sue the promisor, and even if the promisee obtained restitution, the goals of the contract would have been thwarted.[35] Therefore, justice requires that an intended donee beneficiary have a direct claim against the promisor.[36]

However, there are cases where the third party beneficiary doctrine could be used to impose a crushing burden on a promisor. Consider the case of H.R. Moch Co. v. Rensselaer Water Co.[37] The defendant promised the City of Rensselaer to supply water at fire hydrants at a specified pressure. Plaintiff's building caught fire and was destroyed because of the breach of defendant's promise. Plaintiff was not a creditor beneficiary[38] and the court treated the owner as a potential donee beneficiary. The court, however, concluded that the owner was not an intended beneficiary in part because the defendant could have been destroyed financially if, for example, the entire city had been destroyed by this fire.

Schell v. Knickelbein, 77 Wis.2d 344, 252 N.W.2d 921 (1977).

29. See Note, 54 Va.L.Rev. 1166 (1968).

30. See § 17.7 nn.11–13 infra.

31. See Forman v. Forman, 17 N.Y.2d 274, 270 N.Y.S.2d 586, 217 N.E.2d 645, 34 ALR3d 1351 (1966); cf. Astle v. Wenke, 297 A.2d 45 (Del.Supr.1972); Stichter v. Zuidema, 269 Ill.App.3d 455, 206 Ill.Dec. 929, 646 N.E.2d 296 (1995) (antenuptial agreement); Ferro v. Bologna, 31 N.Y.2d 30, 334 N.Y.S.2d 856, 286 N.E.2d 244 (1972).

32. E.C. Ernst v. Manhattan Constr., 551 F.2d 1026 (5th Cir.1977); Bethune v. Bethune, 96 Misc.2d 507, 413 N.Y.S.2d 800 (1976), reinstated. But see Percival v. Luce, 114 F.2d 774 (9th Cir.1940).

33. Starrett v. Commercial Bank, 226 Ga.App. 598, 486 S.E.2d 923 (1997).

34. See Shingleton v. Bussey, 223 So.2d 713 (Fla.1969); contra, Commonwealth v. Celli–Flynn, 115 Pa.Cmwlth. 494, 540 A.2d 1365 (1988).

35. See §§ 17.13 to 17.14 infra.

36. See, e.g., Seaver v. Ransom, 224 N.Y. 233, 120 N.E. 639, 2 ALR 1187 (1918).

37. 247 N.Y. 160, 159 N.E. 896, 62 A.L.R. 1199 (1928); contra, Weinberg v. Dinger, 106 N.J. 469, 524 A.2d 366 (1987) (tort liability found).

38. See discussion in § 17.7 infra.

Again, this involves a policy consideration. Here, the law of contracts overlaps the law of torts.[39] In the Moch case, a cause of action based on tort was also rejected. Extensive attention to policy considerations that underlie tort law in general and to the economic and social impact of extended liability in the particular area of the economy involved will produce sounder analysis than an attempt to fathom the intention of the parties.[40] Nonetheless, the mechanical test of "to whom does the performance of the promise run" is consistent with the outcome. The water was to be supplied to the city's fire hydrants and not to the plaintiff.

The difficulty of fathoming the intention of the parties in the construction industry has led courts to hesitate to find third party beneficiaries. This is so, according to these courts "because of the multiple contractual relationships involved and because performance ultimately, if indirectly, runs to each party of the several contracts."[41] In construction projects, owners, tenants, general contractors, sub-contractors and suppliers are enmeshed in a network of contracts, though privity may not exist between two given parties.[42] For example, should an owner be deemed to be a third party beneficiary of a contract between a general contractor (promisee) and a sub-contractor (promisor)? Should a sub-contractor be treated as a beneficiary of the owner's (promisor's) promises to the general contractor (promisee)? In the past, most cases answered both questions in the negative.[43] Recent cases indicate a trend toward permitting such actions, thus indicating disagreement with the bases of the earlier cases.[44] Multiple prime contractors on the same

39. See, e.g., McDonald v. Amtel, 633 P.2d 743 (Okl.1981); see Eisenberg, supra n.3 at 1407–12.

40. For sophisticated analyses of such considerations as to one profession, see Katsoris, Accountants' Third Party Liability, 36 Fordham L.Rev. 191 (1967); Comment, Title Abstractor's Liability in Tort and Contract:, 22 Am.U.L.Rev. 455 (1973). As to home inspectors retained by a relocation company, see Real Estate Support Services v. Nauman, 644 N.E.2d 907 (Ind.App.1994); contra, Meininger v. Henris Roofing, 137 Or.App. 451, 905 P.2d 861 (1995); as to a physician assigned by an H.M.O, see St. Charles v. Kender, 38 Mass.App.Ct. 155, 646 N.E.2d 411 (1995).

41. Port Chester Elec. Constr. v. Atlas, 40 N.Y.2d 652, 655–56, 357 N.E.2d 983, 986, 389 N.Y.S.2d 327, 330 (1976); see also Tampa v. Thornton–Tomasetti, P.C., 646 So.2d 279 (Fla.App.1994).

42. See generally, Feinman, Economic Negligence: Liability of Professions and Businesses to Third Parties for Economic Loss (1995).

43. See Joest Vibratech, Inc. v. North Star Steel, 109 F.Supp.2d 746 (N.D.Ohio 2000); A.R. Moyer, Inc. v. Graham, 285 So.2d 397, 65 ALR3d 238 (Fla.1973); John Day Co. v. Alvine & Assoc., 1 Neb.App. 954, 510 N.W.2d 462 (1993); Faist v. Garslip Constr., 220 A.D.2d 718, 633 N.Y.S.2d 327 (1995); Thomson v. Espey Huston & Assocs., 899 S.W.2d 415 (Tex.App.1995); but see Midwest Dredging v. McAninch Corp., 424 N.W.2d 216, 226 (Iowa 1988); Halamicek Bros. v. R & E Asphalt Serv., 737 S.W.2d 193 (Mo.App.1987); see also Eisenberg, supra n.3, at 1402–06; Comment, 40 Fordham L.Rev. 315 (1971).

44. See Sears, Roebuck & Co. v. Jardel Co., 421 F.2d 1048 (3d Cir.1970); Comment, supra note 43, at 326–32. Holding that an architect could be sued by a party not in privity, see Seiler v. Levitz Furniture, 367 A.2d 999 (Del.1976) and Davidson & Jones v. New Hanover, 41 N.C.App. 661, 255 S.E.2d 580 (1979), cert. denied; see also Rowe v. Akin & Flanders, 240 Ga.App. 766, 525 S.E.2d 123 (1999); Paukovitz v. Imperial Homes, 271 Ill.App.3d 1037, 208 Ill.Dec. 417, 649 N.E.2d 473 (1995) (owner is beneficiary of contract between contractor and supplier of plans and shell); Board of Managers v. Carol Management, 214 A.D.2d 380, 624 N.Y.S.2d 598 (1995) (liability of

project are generally deemed to be third party beneficiaries of the owner's contracts with other prime contractors.[45]

Similar problems of analysis surface in other kinds of service contracts. A bank makes a commitment to a borrower to make a construction loan. The bank agrees to disburse the proceeds to the general contractor as the work progresses. The bank retains an appraiser to monitor and report on the degree of progress. The appraiser negligently overestimates the degree of progress. The funds are depleted and the contractor becomes insolvent prior to completion. It has been held that the borrower has an action against the appraiser.[46] This result is based on the second of the two tests of intent to benefit discussed above. Clearly, the bank (the promisee) does not owe the borrower the appraisal service. Neither does it have donative intent. On the other hand, contracts between property owners or commercial tenants and security services are generally construed not to give a crime victim a claim against the security service as a third party beneficiary.[47] A balloting agent in a bankruptcy proceeding has been held to owe a duty to the creditors who cast votes.[48] An organization that supervises car racing and contracts with racetrack owners to assure safety precautions are in place has been held liable to an injured race car driver whose injuries were caused by inadequate precautions.[49] The issues in cases such as these are similar to the issues in products liability cases, although courts have generally been more willing to find liability for defective products than for defective services.

Another potentially important factor in the third party beneficiary area is the element of reliance. Thus, where a law firm prepares an opinion letter for a client, knowing that a potential lender will rely on the content of the letter, the firm is liable for its negligent preparation.[50]

architect, management company and construction manager); Finch, Pruyn & Co. v. M. Wilson Control Services, 239 A.D.2d 814, 658 N.Y.S.2d 496 (1997) (liability of sub); Indiana Ins. v. Erhlich, 880 F.Supp. 513 (W.D.Mich.1994) (sub a beneficiary of a "waiver of subrogation clause"). Adhering to the need for privity is Fleischer v. Hellmuth, Obata & Kassabaum, 870 S.W.2d 832 (Mo.App.1993). Privity between sub and owner was found in C & W Enterprises v. Sioux Falls, 635 N.W.2d 752 (S.D.2001).

Some cases have allowed recovery by subcontractors under a sometimes fictional theory that a "liquidating agreement" allows the general contractor to obtain a subcontractor's damages from the owner on a "pass through" basis, irrespective of whether the general is liable to the sub. See Barry, Bette & Led Duke, Inc. v. State, 169 Misc.2d 594, 645 N.Y.S.2d 713 (Ct.Cl.1996).

45. Little Rock Wastewater Utility v. Larry Moyer Trucking, 321 Ark. 303, 902

S.W.2d 760 (Ark.1995); Eisenberg, supra n.3, at 1400–02.

46. Vogan v. Hayes Appraisal Assocs., 588 N.W.2d 420 (Iowa 1999).

47. Anderson v. Atlanta Committee for Olympic Games, 273 Ga. 113, 537 S.E.2d 345 (2000): Krass v. Tri–County Sec., 233 Mich.App. 661, 593 N.W.2d 578 (Mich.App. 1999); Hudson v. Riverport Perf. Arts Ctr., 37 S.W.3d 261 (E.D.Mo.2000); Hoisington v. ZT–Winston–Salem Assocs., 133 N.C.App. 485, 516 S.E.2d 176 (N.C.App.1999) (collecting cases).

48. Internationale Nederlanden (U.S.) v. Bankers Trust, 261 A.D.2d 117, 689 N.Y.S.2d 455 (1999).

49. Wolfgang v. Mid–America Motorsports, 111 F.3d 1515 (10th Cir.1997).

50. Prudential Ins. v. Dewey, Ballantine, Bushby, Palmer & Wood, 80 N.Y.2d 377, 590 N.Y.S.2d 831, 605 N.E.2d 318 (1992); See Comment, 54 Va.L.Rev. 1166 (1968); Rs. 2d § 302 cmt d, discussed in § 17.4 infra.

It is possible that, in a contract where the promisor makes a number of promises, the third party may be the beneficiary of one promise but not of another. For example, in the Moch[51] case, although the plaintiff was not a beneficiary of the defendant's promise to supply water at fire hydrants, the plaintiff was a third party beneficiary of the promise specifying the maximum rates to be charged for its own consumption.[52]

A person may qualify as a third party beneficiary even if the person is not named, identifiable, or even in being at the time of contracting. It is sufficient that the third party be identifiable when the time arrives for the performance of the promise made for the benefit of the third party.[53] The Restatement (Second) adds, however, that this is one of the factors to be considered in determining whether the beneficiary is an intended or incidental beneficiary.[54]

A good number of states have enacted statutes governing the question of third party beneficiaries. By and large, the questions which arise and the solutions reached are the same as those in non-statutory states.[55]

In corporate law a doctrine of *successor liability* is emerging. If a corporation merges with another, or enters into a de facto merger, the successor corporation is generally held liable for the obligations of the entity that has disappeared. There are other instances of successor liability, especially for products liability. The rights of third party creditors or tort victims are very much the same as those of a third party beneficiary. Treatment of this topic is best left to works on corporations.[56]

At the beginning of this section it was stated that many courts have emphasized the test of "intent to benefit." Some courts have used this test as a sole test[57] but others have looked to see, in addition, if the third party qualifies as a creditor or a donee beneficiary.[58] The Restatement (Second) on this point is discussed in the next section.

§ 17.4   The Second Restatement

The Restatement (Second) has articulated a new formulation of the doctrine of third party beneficiary but the new formulation certainly has

---

51. See note 37 supra.

52. See § 17.7 infra; Northwest Airlines v. Crosetti Bros., 258 Or. 340, 483 P.2d 70 (Or.1971).

53. See Beverly v. Macy, 702 F.2d 931 (11th Cir.1983); U.S. v. State Farm, 455 F.2d 789 (10th Cir.1972); Keith v. Schiefen-Stockham Ins. Agency, 209 Kan. 537, 498 P.2d 265 (1972); Associated Teachers v. Board of Ed., 33 N.Y.S.2d 229, 306 N.E.2d 791, 351 N.Y.S.2d 670 (1973). Rs. 1st § 139; but see Data Proc. Fin. & Gen. v. I.B.M., 430 F.2d 1277 (8th Cir.1970).

54. Rs. 2d § 308 cmt a.

55. A table of statutes appears in 2 Williston § 367 (3d ed.). For a discussion see id. § 365; Note, 57 Colum.L.Rev. 406, 414–15 (1957).

56. See Blumberg & Strasser, The Law of Corporate Groups: Enterprise Liability ch. 20 (1998).

57. Whether the third person is a creditor or donee beneficiary is relevant in determining the issue of intent to benefit, see Broadway Maintenance v. Rutgers, 90 N.J. 253, 447 A.2d 906 (1982), and on the question of vesting. See § 17.11 infra.

58. See, e.g., Seaver v. Ransom, 224 N.Y. 233, 120 N.E. 639 (1918) (court stressed that there was not only an intent to benefit but also a close family relationship between the promisee and the beneficiary.)

its roots in the past. It avoids the use of the terms "donee" and "creditor" beneficiaries because they "carry overtones of obsolete doctrinal difficulties" and adopts the test of intent to benefit which we have just explored.[1]

However, in order to qualify as an intended beneficiary, the third party must meet two requirements; otherwise the third party is only an incidental beneficiary.[2] First, the third party must show that recognition of a right to performance in the beneficiary "is appropriate to effectuate the intention of the parties." And second, the party must show one of the following: (a) "the performance of the promise will satisfy an obligation of the promisee to pay money to the beneficiary" *or* (b) "the circumstances indicate that the promisee intends to give the beneficiary the benefit of the promised performance."

The first requirement clearly relates to intent to benefit. It does not attempt to solve the many inherent problems of the phrase that have already been discussed.[3]

Because the Restatement (Second) avoids the use of the terms "donee" and "creditor" beneficiary, the alternatives that the second requirement sets forth are somewhat surprising. The first alternative is that the claimant be a creditor beneficiary; the second alternative is that the claimant be a donee beneficiary. But instead of using the words "creditor" and "donee" the Restatement (Second) refers to a promise under (a) as a "promise to pay the promisee's debt" and a promise under (b) as a "gift promise."[4]

In the case of a promise "to pay the promisee's debt," the Restatement (Second) makes some significant changes. Contrary to the First Restatement which stated that a person qualified as a third party beneficiary even if there was only a *supposed* obligation owing from the promisee to the beneficiary,[5] the Second Restatement requires an *actual* obligation owing from the promisee to the beneficiary.[6] Thus, a person who was classified as a creditor beneficiary under the First Restatement will in these circumstances be characterized as a donee beneficiary under the Second Restatement.[7]

Subsection (b) relates to a "gift promise" or, under the old terminology, a donee beneficiary. Notice that there are no restrictions on a donee

---

§ 17.4

1. Rs. 2d Introductory Note to Ch. 14 and Reporter's Note to § 302. See § 17.3 supra. It should be recalled that the First Restatement did not employ the test of intent to benefit but rather decided cases based on three categories—creditor, donee and incidental beneficiaries. See § 17.2 supra.

2. See Rs. 2d § 302(2); Reidy v. Macauley, 57 N.C.App. 184, 290 S.E.2d 746 (1982), review denied.

3. See § 17.3 supra.

4. Rs. 2d § 302 cmts (b) and (c).

5. See § 17.2 supra.

6. Rs. 2d § 302 cmt (b). However, a suretyship relation may exist even though the duty of the promisee is voidable or unenforceable by reason of the statute of limitations or the Statute of Frauds. See § 17.2 n.3 supra.

7. See Rs. 2d § 302 cmt b; Rae v. Air-Speed, 386 Mass. 187, 435 N.E.2d 628 (1982).

beneficiary, as for example, the requirement of a close family relationship between the promisee and the beneficiary.[8]

The Restatement (Second) also states that a third party who does not qualify as an intended beneficiary under the rules stated above may qualify as an intended beneficiary "if the beneficiary would be reasonable in relying on the promise as manifesting an intention to confer a right on him [or her] * * *."[9] The comment does not speak in terms of actual reliance but rather in terms of whether reliance would be reasonable. The illustrations, however, involve actual reliance.[10]

Parenthetically, it may be noted that the Restatement (Second) agrees that the parties may agree as they wish on the issue of third party beneficiaries so long as the agreement is not contrary to public policy.[11]

§ 17.5 Third Party Beneficiaries and the Statute of Wills

Under the Statute of Wills and its modern descendants, a testamentary disposition must usually be in writing, signed and witnessed in a rather rigidly specified manner. If a contract for the benefit of a third party makes the beneficiary's rights conditional on surviving the promisee, some courts have held that the promisee acquires no rights because the contract creates a testamentary disposition and fails to comply with the Statute of Wills.[1] This is clearly incorrect. The promisee is not disposing of an existing right by will but is creating a present conditional right by contract.[2] If compliance with the Statute of Wills were required, no life insurance policy would be enforceable.

§ 17.6 The Mortgage Assumption Cases

Third party beneficiary law is invoked when a promisor who buys property that is encumbered by a mortgage promises the seller to pay off the mortgage loan. A mortgage is a security interest in real property typically given in exchange for a loan. The loan is usually evidenced by a bond or note that creates a personal obligation. Suppose that A, in exchange for a loan, gives a bond and mortgage to B and later sells the

---

8. Rs. 2d § 302. Some cases hold, or intimate, that such a relationship is needed. E.g., Seaver v. Ransom, 224 N.Y. 233, 120 N.E. 639 (1918); but this view is obsolete outside the mortgage assumption cases, § 17.6 infra.

9. Rs. 2d § 302 cmt d. See Aronowicz v. Nalley's, 30 Cal.App.3d 27, 106 Cal.Rptr. 424 (1972). The reliance referred to here is the reliance of the beneficiary and not the reliance of the promisee. See Overlock v. Central Vt. Pub. Serv., 126 Vt. 549, 237 A.2d 356 (1967); Loews v. Sperry, 86 A.D.2d 221, 449 N.Y.S.2d 715 (1982). See Note, 6 Val.U.L.Rev. 353 (1972).

10. See Rs. 2d § 302 ills. 11, 12.

11. Rs. 2d § 302.

§ 17.5

1. Coley v. English, 235 Ark. 215, 357 S.W.2d 529 (1962); McCarthy v. Pieret, 281 N.Y. 407, 24 N.E.2d 102 (1939), rearg. denied; cf. Freer v. J.G. Putman Funeral Home, 195 Ark. 307, 111 S.W.2d 463 (1937); In re Estate of Hillowitz, 22 N.Y.2d 107, 291 N.Y.S.2d 325, 238 N.E.2d 723 (1968).

2. If, however, the promisor undertakes by contract to provide for the beneficiary by will, in some jurisdictions the Statute of Frauds provides that the promise must be in writing. See McKinney's N.Y. E.P.T.L. 13–2.1(2). A number of peculiar rules govern contracts to make wills. See Marosites v. Proctor, 59 N.C.App. 353, 296 S.E.2d 526 (1982); Note, 18 Hastings L.J. 423 (1967).

mortgaged property to C. The transaction in the past could be negotiated in two ways.[1] C could "assume" the mortgage, which in common usage means that C promises A to pay the mortgage indebtedness to B. In such a case, the situation is in essence the same as Lawrence v. Fox.[2] It is generally agreed that B is a third party beneficiary of C's promise made to A.[3] Continuing with this illustration, if C conveyed the property to D who validly assumed the mortgage, B would be a third party beneficiary of D's promise to C.[4]

If, in the conveyance, C had merely taken "subject to" the mortgage, that is, recognized that there was a security interest in the land, but assumed no personal obligation in regard to the indebtedness, B would not be a third party beneficiary since C has not promised to pay any debt.[5] Suppose, however, C, despite the absence of a personal obligation, in a subsequent conveyance to D, causes D to assume the mortgage. This was the situation in Vrooman v. Turner.[6]

The court ruled that D's promise to pay the indebtedness was not enforceable by B. It held that before a party can qualify as a third party beneficiary two requirements must be met. First, there must be an intent to benefit, which the court apparently found to exist, and, second, there must be an obligation owing from the promisee to the beneficiary. The second requisite was missing because C, the promisee, had no obligation with respect to the indebtedness.[7]

An interesting question with respect to cases such as Vrooman v. Turner, is why did C, who was under no personal liability to B, extract a promise of assumption from D? In most cases there is no basis for a finding that C's purpose was to confer a gift on B.[8] Nor will it usually be concluded that the assumption clause was included inadvertently or by mistake.[9] Rather, generally it will be deemed that C's purpose was to

---

§ 17.6

1. In modern days what is said here is often irrelevant because a "due on sale" clause is commonly inserted in the mortgage loan documents. Under this clause, when the property is sold, the entire amount due becomes due and payable. For the most part these clauses have been sustained as written. See Income Realty & Mtge. v. Columbia S. & L., 661 P.2d 257 (Colo.1983); First Federal S. & L. v. Wick, 322 N.W.2d 860 (S.D.1982); Annot., 22 ALR4th 1266 (1983).

2. 20 N.Y. 268 (1859), discussed in § 17.1 supra.

3. See Burr v. Beers, 24 N.Y. 178, 80 Am.Dec. 327 (1861); 4 Corbin § 796; 2 Williston § 383. Notice that this is a case where the promise is to pay directly to the third party. See § 17.3 supra.

4. See The Home v. Selling, 91 Or. 428, 179 P. 261, 21 ALR 403 (1919). On the facts B would have a cause of action for breach against A, C and D but would be entitled to only one satisfaction. See § 17.13 infra.

5. See Schewe v. Bentsen, 424 F.2d 60 (5th Cir.1970) (nor may the vendor sue the vendee for failing to pay the mortgage debt as the vendee has made no promise).

6. 69 N.Y. 280, 25 Am.Rep. 195 (1877).

7. Notice that the Court posits a second requirement in addition to intent to benefit. See § 17.4 supra.

8. In some cases such a motive can be found. See Schneider v. Ferrigno, 110 Conn. 86, 147 A. 303 (1929); Federal Bond & Mtge. v. Shapiro, 219 Mich. 13, 188 N.W. 465 (1922) (promisee wished to protect the second mortgage on the premises).

9. Parol evidence is admissible to strike out an assumption clause on grounds of mistake, to reform the instrument, or to show that the clause was inserted in the deed without the promisor's assent. See Blass v. Terry, 156 N.Y. 122, 50 N.E. 953

guard against a supposed liability.[10]

The court in Vrooman v. Turner decided that B was not a third party beneficiary, because an *actual* obligation owing from the promisee to the beneficiary is required to create a creditor beneficiary. A large number of cases are in accord with this conclusion.[11] As we have seen, however, the First Restatement disagreed.[12] It took the position that a *supposed* obligation is sufficient. The Second Restatement concludes that the plaintiff in Vrooman v. Turner qualifies as a third party *donee* beneficiary.[13] It indicates that the plaintiff is in fact an intended beneficiary or at least should be treated as an intended beneficiary under the theory of reliance.[14] Plaintiff cannot qualify as a creditor beneficiary under the Restatement(Second) because it requires an *actual* obligation owing from the promisee to the beneficiary to qualify as a creditor beneficiary.[15]

It is difficult to reconcile Vrooman v. Turner with decisions such as Rouse v. U.S.,[16] which are generally recognized to be sound even in states that follow Vrooman v. Turner.[17] In the Rouse case the plaintiff's assignor sold an oil burner to B on credit. When B sold the house, the defendant purchaser agreed to assume the payments still due on the oil burner contract. The defendant failed to make payment and sought to interpose as a defense that plaintiff's assignor had breached a warranty made to B. One would expect that in states that follow Vrooman v. Turner the defendant would be permitted to raise this defense; he attempted to show that there was no obligation owing from the promisee to the beneficiary. The court, however, ruled that the defendant, by his assumption, promised to pay irrespective of any defense the promisee might have. This is the usual holding in a case where there is an assumption of a specific alleged debt.[18]

The rationale employed by the court in Vrooman v. Turner is no longer accepted in New York where the case was decided. It is obvious that if there must an obligation owing from the promisee to the beneficiary, a donee beneficiary could not qualify as a protected beneficiary. However, a few years after the decision in Vrooman v. Turner it was held in New York that a donee beneficiary may recover if there is a close family relationship between the beneficiary and the promisee.[19] Subsequent cases have erased the necessity for such a relationship.[20] This is

(1898) (no assent); Kilmer v. Smith, 77 N.Y. 226, 33 Am.Rep. 613 (1879) (clause stricken out); cf. Ross v. Warren, 196 Iowa 659, 195 N.W. 228 (1923) (insufficient evidence to justify reformation).

10. See 2 Williston § 386A (3d ed.).

11. See 4 Corbin § 796, at 151.

12. See § 17.2 supra.

13. Rs. 2d § 302 cmt d; Rs. 2d § 304 cmt c, ill. 2.

14. Rs. 2d § 302 cmt d; see § 17.6 supra.

15. See § 17.4 supra.

16. 215 F.2d 872 (D.C.Cir.1954); accord, Rs. lst § 144; Rs. 2d § 140(3).

17. E.g., Bennett v. Bates, 94 N.Y. 354 (1884) (invalidity of mortgage); see 4 Corbin §§ 821–822; 2 Williston § 399.

18. The Rs. 2d takes the same position in § 144, cmt b.

19. Seaver v. Ransom, 224 N.Y. 233, 120 N.E. 639 (1918).

20. Oxford Commercial v. Landau, 12 N.Y.2d 362, 239 N.Y.S.2d 865, 190 N.E.2d 230 (1963); Lait v. Leon, 40 Misc.2d 60, 242 N.Y.S.2d 776 (1963).

the prevailing view in the country,[21] although occasional decisions to the contrary may be found.[22]

The result in Vrooman v. Turner, still accepted by a large number of jurisdictions,[23] is best looked at as a living fossil, limited to mortgage assumption cases and surviving from the era when there was great uncertainty as to the limits of the then radical third party beneficiary doctrine. An attempt at an analytic reconciliation of the case with prevailing principles, however, can possibly be made. Unlike the situation in Rouse v. U.S., there was no antecedent promise running from the promise to the beneficiary. Restated, Vrooman v. Turner may be said to require that for an intended creditor beneficiary to recover there must be at least an ability by the supposed creditor to show the color of a claim against the promisee. The Restatement (Second) provides a basis for reconciling the two lines of cases. It attaches great significance to the question of whether the promisee is a surety. It reasons that where the duty of the promisee is voidable (as in Rouse) or unenforceable, the promisee is still a surety; even though the purchaser's promise would satisfy only a voidable duty of the promisee, the beneficiary is treated as an intended beneficiary. In the Vrooman case the promisee is not a surety.[24]

§ 17.7 Public Contracts

Is an inhabitant of a governmental unit a third party beneficiary of a contract made by the governmental unit?[1] In a sense every contract made by a governmental unit is made for the benefit of its inhabitants. If a city contracts to have a police station, fire house, or park built, it does so to enhance the general welfare and, thus, to benefit the public. The ultimate question is whether there was an intent to benefit the inhabitants in the sense that individual inhabitants have the right to enforce the contract. In such an action, contrary to a taxpayer's action, the recovery goes to the individual rather than to the public treasury. Although the courts often purport to employ the same rules as are applied to private contracts, they are reluctant to find that such rights exist.[2]

---

21. See Rs. 1st § 133.

22. West v. Norcross, 190 Ark. 667, 80 S.W.2d 67 (1935); Scheidl v. Universal Aviation Equip., 159 N.Y.S.2d 278 (Sup.Ct. 1957).

23. According to 2 Williston § 386A the majority of cases are in accord. But see 4 Corbin § 796, at 151, stating that the majority of cases have held for the beneficiary. There is a fairly even split and certain distinctions are sometimes made within a given jurisdiction. See Schneider v. Ferrigno, 110 Conn. 86, 147 A. 303 (1929) ("The cases which deny liability . . . do not seem fully to recognize the extent and force of the rule which permits a third party benefi-

ciary to sue upon a contract as it has now been developed.")

24. Rs. 2d § 133 cmt a; § 144 cmt a.

§ 17.7

1. See Rs. 2d § 313. "The rules stated in this Chapter apply to contracts with a government or governmental agency except to the extent that application would contravene the policy of the law authorizing the contract or prescribing remedies for its breach." Rs. 2d § 313(1). It has been held that a non-inhabitant of the political unit in question may qualify as a third party beneficiary. Wilson v. Oliver Costich Co., 231 A.D. 346, 247 N.Y.S. 131 (1931), aff'd.

2. Luhnow v. Horn, 760 N.E.2d 621 (Ind.App.2001); Hagan v. Comstat Security,

Nevertheless, an individual inhabitant may be deemed to be a third party beneficiary of a public contract. The first arises where the promisor agrees to perform services for the governmental unit which the unit is under a legal duty to perform to individual members of the public. In such a case, it is held that the individuals may recover from the promisor if the promisor breaches. Obviously, the key question is when is a governmental unit under a duty to an individual member of the public? When or whether such a duty exists involves questions of tort law and, at times, requires the interpretation of statutes.[3] The successful plaintiffs in this kind of case have traditionally been called creditor beneficiaries.[4]

Individuals are sometimes intended donee beneficiaries of a contract between the governmental unit and the promisor. A good illustration is La Mourea v. Rhude.[5] The defendant contractor promised the City of Duluth "to do certain work of sewer construction." The contract contemplated "the use of heavy charges of explosives." Defendant agreed to be "liable for any damages done to the work or other structures or public or *private property* and injuries sustained by persons." (Emphasis supplied). Plaintiff's property was injured by the blasting. The court treated the plaintiff as a donee beneficiary and decided that the language manifested an intent to benefit plaintiff directly because damages were to be paid directly to private property owners; the promised performance ran directly to the plaintiff.[6]

This case should be compared with H.R. Moch Co. v. Rensselaer Water Co.[7] Defendant, Water Company, had promised the City of Rensselaer to furnish the City with water at its hydrants. Plaintiff, a property owner, sued when his building was destroyed by the failure to have sufficient water pressure at the hydrant. Again, the issue was whether the plaintiff was an intended donee beneficiary. The court concluded that the promised performance ran to the City and that therefore the plaintiff was an incidental beneficiary. Clearly part of the reason for the decision was one grounded in public policy. In the words of the court if plaintiff were permitted to recover the defendant's "field of obligation

214 A.D.2d 435, 625 N.Y.S.2d 196 (1995); see Rs. 1st § 145; Rs. 2d § 313(2), also discussed in the next section.

3. New Hampshire Ins. v. Madera, 144 Cal.App.3d 298, 192 Cal.Rptr. 548 (5th Dist. 1983); St. Joseph Light & Power v. Kaw Valley Tunneling, 589 S.W.2d 260 (Mo. 1979).

4. See § 17.2 supra. However, whether these plaintiffs would be considered to be creditor beneficiaries under the Second Restatement is a more difficult matter. Under the Second Restatement to qualify as a

creditor beneficiary there must be an actual obligation on the part of the promisee to pay *money* or its equivalent to the beneficiary. See § 17.4 supra. Is a breach of a duty that results in a money judgment a duty to pay money within the meaning of the Second Restatement? See the specific language of Rs. 2d § 313.

5. 209 Minn. 53, 295 N.W. 304 (1940).

6. See the discussion of to whom is the performance to run in § 17.3 supra.

7. 247 N.Y. 160, 159 N.E. 896 (1928), discussed in § 17.3 supra.

would be expanded beyond reasonable limits."[8] The majority of the cases are in accord. As previously indicated, courts are reluctant to find that an inhabitant qualifies as a third party beneficiary of a public contract.[9]

If, in the Moch case, the Water Company also promised the City to limit the prices charged the property owners, the performance would run to the individual; therefore the plaintiff could qualify as a third party beneficiary. Many cases are in accord.[10] Notice that in this situation there was no possibility of the crushing burden as there was in the branch of the case relating to the fire hydrant.

Often, it is quite clear that a decision rests primarily on policy grounds. For example, a Delaware Court ruled that a federal prisoner kept in a Delaware state prison under a contract between the state and the U. S. is a third party beneficiary of that contract, permitting the prisoner to recover for injuries suffered from an assault in the prison. The decision, circumventing Delaware's rule of sovereign immunity in the tort area,[11] was based in part on giving the prisoner rights similar to those in federal prisons, who may sue the federal government under the Federal Tort Claims Act.[12] Third party beneficiary theory has also been employed as the basis for the advancement of a social policy of racial equality.[13] In some cases, it is quite clear that the government intended to give a class of persons rights they can enforce, as in the case of contracts between a state and nursing homes concerning the treatment of medicaid patients.[14] However, tenants in a federally subsidized housing project were not held to be third party beneficiaries when it was alleged that private defendants were illegally siphoning federal funds and the U. S. was acquiescing in this illegal conduct.[15]

---

8. 247 N.Y. at 164, 159 N.E. at 897 (1928).

9. Drummond v. Univ. of Pa., 651 A.2d 572 (Pa.Cmwlth.1994). This is further illustrated by the cases where contractors have promised a governmental unit to repair or maintain highways. See Davis v. Nelson–Deppe, 91 Idaho 463, 424 P.2d 733 (1967). See also Kornblut v. Chevron Oil, 48 N.Y.2d 853, 424 N.Y.S.2d 429, 400 N.E.2d 368 (1979). Contra, Potter v. Carolina Water, 253 N.C. 112, 116 S.E.2d 374 (1960); but see Matternes v. Winston–Salem, 286 N.C. 1, 209 S.E.2d 481 (1974). See § 17.8 infra.

10. See, e.g., Bush v. Upper Valley Tele-cable, 96 Idaho 83, 524 P.2d 1055 (1973); Rochester Tel. v. Ross, 195 N.Y. 429, 88 N.E. 793 (1909); Pond v. New Rochelle Water, 183 N.Y. 330, 76 N.E. 211 (1906). So also a contract with a municipality and a tract developer as to compliance with subdivision regulations has been held to give enforceable rights to a purchaser of a house within the tract. Ogden v. Earl R. Howarth & Sons, 58 Misc.2d 213, 294 N.Y.S.2d 430 (1968).

11. The doctrine of sovereign immunity was also a prime factor in extending third party beneficiary recovery in Visintine & Co. v. New York, C. & St. L.R.R., 169 Ohio St. 505, 160 N.E.2d 311 (1959).

12. See Blair v. Anderson, 325 A.2d 94 (Del.1974).

13. Olzman v. Lake Hills Swim Club, 495 F.2d 1333 (2d Cir.1974) (statute forbidding discrimination in contracting on racial grounds forbids discrimination against contracting party's guest at swimming pool; guest is a third party beneficiary); see also Bossier Parish School Bd. v. Lemon, 370 F.2d 847 (5th Cir.1967), cert. denied.

14. Smith v. Chattanooga Medical Invs., 62 S.W.3d 178 (Tenn.App.2001); similar cases, Stewart v. Jackson, 804 So.2d 1041 (Miss.2002); Elie v. St. Barnabas Hosp., 283 A.D.2d 364, 724 N.Y.S.2d 749 (2001).

15. Falzarano v. U.S., 607 F.2d 506 (1st Cir.1979); Martinez v. Socoma Cos., 11 Cal.3d 394, 113 Cal.Rptr. 585, 521 P.2d 841 (1974); see Note, 35 J.Urb. & Contemp.L. 203 (1989). See also Waters, The Property in the Promise: A Study of the Third Party Beneficiary Rule, 98 Harv.L.Rev. 1109 (1985).

§ 17.8 Promises of Indemnity

Indemnification is a vast and complicated subject. Here, we are concerned only with the question of whether a third party qualifies as a third party beneficiary of a promise of indemnification against loss or a promise of indemnification against liability.[1]

In essence, a promise of indemnity against loss is a promise by the indemnitor to reimburse the indemnitee after the indemnitee has paid the third party. For example, A Corp. (indemnitee) obtained a policy of fidelity insurance from I (indemnitor) under which I agreed to reimburse (indemnify) A against any loss which A might sustain through the fraudulent or dishonest acts of any of its own employees. C, a third party, has a claim against A for the dishonest acts of an employee. The question is may C successfully sue I on a third party beneficiary theory? The answer is clearly no, because I need not perform until A has paid. The promised performance runs to A and not C.[2]

The situation is somewhat different in the case of indemnity against liability—a situation in which I (indemnitor) promises A (indemnitee) to discharge A's legal liability in the event that A becomes liable to the third party.[3] This is the situation presented under a liability insurance policy. It is often held that the third party may not recover from the indemnitor until a valid judgment has been obtained against the indemnitee.[4] Under this holding in effect the third party is not a third party beneficiary until a judgment has been obtained. This conclusion is, however, usually based on specific language in the insurance contract providing that no action shall be brought against the insurer[5] but also often as a result of a policy against having the jury be aware that an insurer will ultimately pay the damages the jury assesses.[6] In the absence of such language, a promise of an indemnity against liability easily qualifies as a promise for the benefit of a third person.[7]

§ 17.8

1. The distinction is well set out in the case of Sorensen v. Overland Corp., 142 F.Supp. 354 (D.Del.1956), aff'd.; Rs. Security § 82 cmt l.

2. Ronnau v. Caravan Int'l, 205 Kan. 154, 468 P.2d 118 (1970).

3. Sisters of St. Joseph v. Russell, 318 Or. 370, 867 P.2d 1377 (Or.1994).

4. See Jefferson v. Sinclair Ref., 10 N.Y.2d 422, 223 N.Y.S.2d 863, 179 N.E.2d 706 (1961); Snyder Plumbing & Heating v. Purcell, 9 A.D.2d 505, 195 N.Y.S.2d 780 (1960); Smith v. King, 52 N.C.App. 158, 277 S.E.2d 875 (1981). There are contrary cases. See Annot., 64 ALR3d 1207 (1975); Beneficiary status was refused in Kilpatrick v. Ogden Enter., 745 So.2d 492 (Fla.App. 1999).

5. Litigation concerning the validity and effect of such language has been especially prolific in conflict of laws cases. For discussions of the problems of contract law and

conflict of laws, see MacDonald, Direct Action Against Liability Insurance Companies, 1957 Wis.L.Rev. 612; Notes, 57 Colum.L.Rev. 256 (1957); 74 Harv.L.Rev. 357 (1960). For a decision holding that such contractual language is void because it impedes the effectiveness of the remedies of an injured party, see Shingleton v. Bussey, 223 So.2d 713 (Fla.1969).

6. See Morton v. Maryland Cas., 1 A.D.2d 116, 148 N.Y.S.2d 524 (1955), aff'd. This policy has been somewhat relaxed in New York, but only as to cases in which the law of another jurisdiction is applicable. See Oltarsh v. Aetna Ins., 15 N.Y.2d 111, 256 N.Y.S.2d 577, 204 N.E.2d 622 (1965); for another situation see Garcia v. Lovellette, 265 Ill.App.3d 724, 203 Ill.Dec. 376, 639 N.E.2d 935 (1994).

7. Stilley v. James, 345 Ark. 362, 48 S.W.3d 521 (2001).

Despite the discussion above stating that a promise of indemnity against loss does not give rise to a third party beneficiary situation, there are a significant number of municipality cases to the contrary. A typical illustration will suffice. A, a municipality, owes a duty to the public to keep its streets in good repair.[8] B promises A to keep the streets in good repair and also promises to indemnify A against loss if it fails to keep the streets in good repair. B breaches its promise to keep the streets in good repair and as a result C is injured.

There are a number of cases that have held that C is a third party beneficiary.[9] This is in part due to the influence of the original Restatement which did not employ the test of intent to benefit, but rather allowed third parties to sue if they were creditor or donee beneficiaries.[10] The point of the illustration is that although there is no intent to benefit C, under the facts asserted, C is a creditor beneficiary. Thus, under the analysis of the First Restatement, C is an intended creditor beneficiary and, as we have seen, courts have followed this analysis.[11]

The Restatement (Second) takes pains to indicate its disapproval of this approach. Instead, it sets forth a more flexible rule. It states that where, as here, the municipality is under a duty to C, C may bring an action against the promisor if the action "is consistent with the terms of the contract and with the policy of the law authorizing the contract and prescribing remedies for its breach."[12] The Restatement (Second) lists as factors which may make an action against the promisor inappropriate: "arrangements for governmental control over the litigation and settlement of claims, the likelihood of impairment of service or of excessive financial burden, and the availability of alternatives such as insurance."[13]

§ 17.9   The Surety Bond Cases

When a general contractor undertakes substantial construction for a private owner or a public works project for the U.S. or other political body, it is common to require the general contractor to obtain a surety bond from a bonding company.[1] The general contractor and the surety company are the promisors, the owner is the promisee and the potential beneficiaries are those named in the bond.[2] Among those normally named are workers, subcontractors, and suppliers.

---

8. See § 17.7 at n.9 supra where street repair cases are discussed.

9. See O'Connell v. Merchants' & Police Dist. Tel., 167 Ky. 468, 180 S.W. 845 (1915); Rigney v. New York Cent. & Hudson River R.R., 217 N.Y. 31, 111 N.E. 226 (1916); Stewart v. Sullivan County, 196 Tenn. 49, 264 S.W.2d 217 (1953); cf. Coley v. Cohen, 169 Misc. 933, 9 N.Y.S.2d 503 (1939), aff'd. But see Silton v. Kansas City, 446 S.W.2d 129 (Mo.1969) (indemnity against loss provision held to be solely for the benefit of the promisee).

10. See § 17.2 supra.

11. See § 17.7 n.9 supra and Blair v. Anderson, 325 A.2d 94 (Del.1974).

12. Rs. 2d § 313(2)(b).

13. Rs. 2d § 313 cmt a; see also id. ill. 5.

§ 17.9

1. Surety bonds are also used in non-construction contexts. These require interpretation. Helmsman Management Servs. v. Colorado Dep't of Labor, 31 P.3d 895 (Colo. App.2000).

2. The language of the bond must be read with great care. See, e.g., Home Indem. v. Daniels Constr., 285 Ala. 68, 228

There are various types of bonds that may be used singly or in conjunction with others. The one that is most likely to create a third party beneficiary situation is a payment bond. Such a bond is "conditioned to be void" on payment by the contractor to those named in the bond, usually subcontractors, suppliers and workers. The surety company promises to pay if the contractor fails to pay.[3]

The question is whether these parties are third party beneficiaries of the payment bond. In the case of a private owner these parties, if not paid, can file mechanics' liens against the owner's property.[4] However, public property is generally exempt from mechanics' liens. As a result, the U.S. and other public entities have enacted statutes requiring a payment bond in favor of these parties.[5] Since the purpose of the statutes is to protect these parties. It has generally been held that they are third party beneficiaries of bonds given pursuant to these statutes.[6]

The situation is a little more complicated in the case of a private owner. In this case, it has often been concluded that the owner's intent is to protect against mechanics' liens and therefore these parties are incidental beneficiaries.[7] However, other courts have recognized that the owner is protected if these parties are looked on as third party beneficiaries because, in such a case, the promisors will be bound to pay them and that payment will extinguish the possibility of a mechanics' lien.[8]

The problem is further complicated when a subcontractor furnishes the general contractor with a payment bond. The question again is

So.2d 824 (1969) (language of the bond held to include all of the subcontractors of the general contractor but not subcontractors of subcontractors). Ordinarily the bond will include subcontractors of subcontractors and laborers and suppliers.

3. Since the courts are reluctant to conclude that parties not in privity are third party beneficiaries of a construction contract, the parties named in the bond ordinarily will not be third party beneficiaries of any other contract. See Superior Glass v. First Bristol County Nat. Bank, 380 Mass. 829, 406 N.E.2d 672 (1980). See § 17.3 supra. In suretyship terms the general contractor is the principal debtor, the bonding company is the surety and the parties named in the bond are the creditors. See Lybeck & Shreves, The Law of Payment Bonds (1998).

4. This means that even if there is no personal obligation on the part of the owner to pay these parties there is a lien on his property that may be foreclosed. Generally the subcontractor will have no in personam action against the owner.

5. See, e.g., Miller Act, 40 U.S.C.A. §§ 270a–270e. A Miller Act payment bond covers only (1) those suppliers, laborers and contractors who deal directly with a prime contractor and (2) those suppliers, laborers and contractors who have a direct relationship with a subcontractor. Those in the second category must give written notice to the contractor within 90 days after the date on which such claimant performed the last of the labor or delivered the last of the material for which the claim is made. See Clifford F. MacEvoy v. U.S., 322 U.S. 102 (1944).

6. A.E.I. Music v. Business Computers, 290 F.3d 952 (7th Cir.2002) (contract liability for failure to require a bond); Acoustics v. Hanover Ins., 118 N.J.Super. 361, 287 A.2d 482 (1971); Carolina Builders v. AAA Dry Wall, 43 N.C.App. 444, 259 S.E.2d 364 (1979); cf. Boren v. Thompson & Assocs., 999 P.2d 438 (Okla.2000) (negligence liability for failure to require a bond).

7. Ross v. Imperial Constr., 572 F.2d 518 (5th Cir.1978); Fidelity & Deposit v. Rainer, 220 Ala. 262, 125 So. 55 (1929).

8. Ogden Dev. v. Federal Ins., 508 F.2d 583 (2d Cir.1974); Socony–Vacuum Oil v. Continental Cas., 219 F.2d 645 (2d Cir. 1955); Daniel–Morris v. Glens Falls Indem., 308 N.Y. 464, 126 N.E.2d 750 (1955); General Acc. Ins. v. Parker, 445 Pa.Super. 300, 665 A.2d 502 (1995); 2 Williston § 372 (3d ed.); Rs. 2d § 302, ill. 12; Mungall, 11 Vill. L.Rev. 41, 42–43 (1965).

whether the parties named are third party beneficiaries of this bond.[9] Much has been said as to whether the beneficiaries under a payment bond are creditor or donee beneficiaries.[10] Where a statute requires the delivery of a payment bond, it is clear that the situation is *sui generis* and does not fit within the categories previously developed. This is so, because a private owner does not owe a personal obligation to the alleged beneficiaries but the owner's land is burdened by their liens. The situation is more analogous to a creditor beneficiary situation.[11] This situation is not the same as Vrooman v. Turner discussed above, because in that case not only did the promisee not owe a personal obligation to the beneficiary, in addition, when he conveyed the property to the party who assumed, he was no longer concerned with the lien of the mortgage.[12] It is primarily because of the *sui generis* nature of surety bonds that the Restatement (Second) dropped the terminology of "donee" and "creditor" as adjectives for beneficiaries.

A *performance* bond is different. It assures payment of damages to the owner in the event of the contractor's non-performance or payment of damages to a contractor by a subcontractor.[13] Parties not in privity are not beneficiaries of a performance bond.[14] However, the argument is often made that what is labeled as a performance bond is by virtue of the language therein also a payment bond.[15]

There are also bonds that are expressly labeled as joint performance—payment bonds. The decisions in this situation have not been harmonious.[16] A leading case has indicated that where there is a performance—payment bond, at least presumptively the bond is intended to inure solely to the benefit of the promisee-owner; otherwise the bond might be dissipated in paying the third party beneficiaries without paying the promisee.[17]

9. An intent to benefit the named beneficiaries was found in Daniel–Morris v. Glens Falls Indem., 308 N.Y. 464, 126 N.E.2d 750 (1955). If the named parties are already protected under another bond, there is a split of authority as to whether they are protected. Compare Socony–Vacuum Oil v. Continental Cas., 219 F.2d 645 (2d Cir.1955) with Treasure State Indus. v. Welch, 173 Mont. 403, 567 P.2d 947 (1977) and McGrath v. American Sur., 307 N.Y. 552, 122 N.E.2d 906 (1954).

10. Compare 2 Williston § 372 (3d ed), with 4 Corbin § 802 (1951).

11. See Holiday Dev. v. J.A. Tobin Constr., 219 Kan. 701, 549 P.2d 1376 (1976). Under the Rs. 2d, is there an actual obligation to pay money or its equivalent when a lien exists? See Rs. 2d § 302 cmt d, ill. 12.

12. See § 17.6 supra.

13. Nebraska Beef v. Universal Surety, 9 Neb.App. 40, 607 N.W.2d 227 (2000) (but

owner may have a subrogation claim against subcontractor).

14. See Frommeyer v. L. & R. Constr., 139 F.Supp. 579 (D.N.J.1956); Scales–Douwes v. Paulaura Realty, 24 N.Y.2d 724, 301 N.Y.S.2d 980, 249 N.E.2d 760 (1969); Rs. Security § 166.

15. See, e.g. Cretex Companies v. Constr. Leaders, 342 N.W.2d 135 (Minn. 1984); Novak & Co. v. Travelers Indemnity, 56 A.D.2d 418, 392 N.Y.S.2d 901 (1977), app. denied.

16. See 4 Corbin §§ 799–803; 2 Williston § 372 (3d ed.). This is often called a "faithful performance bond." See Sweet, Legal Aspects of Architecture, Engineering and the Construction Process § 37.10 (4th ed.1989).

17. Fosmire v. National Sur., 229 N.Y. 44, 127 N.E. 472 (1920) remit. amend. & rearg. denied; but see Johnson Serv. v. E.H. Monin, Inc., 253 N.Y. 417, 171 N.E. 692, 77 ALR 214 (1930). These and subsequent

§ 17.10   Promisor's Defenses and Counterclaims

A party who qualifies as a third party beneficiary may still lose the case. The rights of the beneficiary stem from the contract between the promisor and the promisee.[1] For this reason, the general rule is that the promisor may assert against the beneficiary any defense that the promisor can assert against the promisee.[2]

Thus, for example, if A promises not to cut down certain timber in exchange for B's promise to pay C $1,000 and A cuts down the timber, C, although qualifying as a third party beneficiary, may not successfully sue B, because B has the defense of non-performance against A.[3] In other words, the rights of the beneficiary generally do not exceed those of the promisee. As such the result would be the same, for example, if the promisor's defense against the promisee is fraud,[4] mistake,[5] lack of consideration,[6] illegality,[7] or the statute of limitations.[8] If the contract contains an arbitration clause, the beneficiary will be bound by the clause unless it provides otherwise.[9]

There are a number of exceptions to the general rule. The first is where the parties agree that the beneficiaries will have an enforceable

New York cases are discussed in Note, 41 Cornell L.Q. 482 (1956); Comment, 27 Fordham L.Rev. 262 (1958). Contra, Byram Lumber and Supply v. Page, 109 Conn. 256, 146 A. 293 (1929); Seubert Excavators v. Eucon, 125 Idaho 409, 871 P.2d 826 (1994); Neenah Foundry v. National Sur., 47 Ill. App.2d 427, 197 N.E.2d 744 (1964). The presumption discussed in Fosmire may be rebutted if the bond specifically states that it is for the benefit of these third parties or if the bond is given pursuant to a statute which permits such suits. Even in these cases, however, the third party is obliged to show that the promisee has received substantial performance or that the bond is sufficient to cover the claims of the promisee and the beneficiaries. It is also possible that the promisee has a cause of action on behalf of the third parties as a trustee but the question remains whether the promisee is obligated to bring such an action. See Comment, 27 Fordham L.Rev. 262 (1958); see also Scales–Douwes v. Paulaura Realty, 24 N.Y.2d 724, 301 N.Y.S.2d 980, 249 N.E.2d 760 (1969).

§ 17.10

1. See Rotermund v. U.S. Steel, 474 F.2d 1139 (8th Cir.1973); Willis v. Hamilton Mut. Ins., 614 S.W.2d 251 (Ky.App.1981).

2. See Punikaia v. Clark, 720 F.2d 564 (9th Cir.1983), cert. denied. This general rule applies to both creditor and donee beneficiaries. See Rs. 2d § 309; Blue Cross v. Ayotte, 35 A.D.2d 258, 315 N.Y.S.2d 998 (1970); Texas Farmers Ins. v. Gerdes, 880 S.W.2d 215 (Tex.App.1994). Naturally the

promisor may also assert any wrongful conduct on the part of the beneficiary. Rs. 2d § 309; Dorman v. Pan–American Investments, 625 F.2d 605 (5th Cir.1980).

3. Stratosphere Lit. v. Grand Casinos, 298 F.3d 1137 (9th Cir.2002); Sedgwick v. Blanchard, 170 Wis. 121, 174 N.W. 459 (1919).

4. While the beneficiary's rights are subject to the defense of fraud, the promisor may not retain the benefits of the transaction while relying on the defense. See Arnold v. Nichols, 64 N.Y. 117 (1876).

5. See Page v. Hinchee, 174 Okl. 537, 51 P.2d 487 (1935).

6. See Western Farm Bureau Mut. Ins. v. Barela, 79 N.M. 149, 441 P.2d 47 (1968). But see Bass v. John Hancock Mut. Life Ins., 10 Cal.3d 792, 518 P.2d 1147, 112 Cal.Rptr. 195 (1974); Lawhead v. Booth, 115 W.Va. 490, 177 S.E. 283 (1934).

7. See Burns Jackson Miller Summit & Spitzer v. Lindner, 59 N.Y.2d 314, 464 N.Y.S.2d 712, 451 N.E.2d 459 (1983); Lawhead v. Booth, 115 W.Va. 490, 177 S.E. 283 (1934).

8. Allgor v. Travelers Ins., 280 N.J.Super. 254, 654 A.2d 1375 (A.D.1995) (even where beneficiary is a minor); Lynbrook Glass & Architectural Metals v. Elite Assocs., 215 A.D.2d 453, 626 N.Y.S.2d 543 (1995).

9. Lewis v. CEDU Educational Serv., 135 Idaho 139, 15 P.3d 1147 (2000).

right despite any defense which the promisor has against the promisee.[10] This occurs frequently in fire insurance contracts containing "the standard mortgagee clause" which provides that a mortgagee (3rd party) may recover on the policy despite any act or neglect of the mortgagor-promisee. Under this clause, it is possible for the mortgagee to recover from the insurer despite fraud or non-payment of premiums by the promisee.[11] This standard clause protects lenders against the misconduct or defaults of borrowers with respect to their insurance policies.

There are occasional cases that violate the general rule for special policy reasons. Thus, in collective bargaining agreements it has been held that the employer may not use against its employees a defense that it has against the union.[12] A collective bargaining agreement is not a typical third-party beneficiary situation and policy considerations prevail. At times, it has been held that a beneficiary under a payment bond[13] has rights against the surety even though the surety would have a defense against the owner.[14] At times, the promisor will be estopped from asserting defenses that would be available against the promisee by virtue of reliance on the part of the beneficiary.[15] Still another exception to this rule exists under the confusing label of vesting, the subject of the next section.

There are very few cases dealing with the question of whether the promisor may assert counterclaims against the beneficiary which might be asserted against the promisee. The general answer is that the promisor may assert a counter-claim that arises out of the same transaction but not a claim arising out of other transactions. The counter-claim acts only as a defense and the promisor cannot recover affirmatively on the counter-claim.[16]

10. See Schneider Moving & Storage v. Robbins, 466 U.S. 364 (1984).

11. Standard Federal Sav. Bank v. State Farm Fire & Cas., 248 Neb. 552, 537 N.W.2d 333 (Neb.1995); Goldstein v. Nat. Liberty Ins., 256 N.Y. 26, 175 N.E. 359 (1931); Prudential Ins. v. Franklin Fire Ins., 180 S.C. 250, 185 S.E. 537 (1936).

12. See Lewis v. Benedict Coal, 361 U.S. 459 (1960); Alaska Trowel Trades Pension Fund v. Lopshire, 855 F.Supp. 1077 (D.Alaska 1994), modified.

13. See § 17.9 supra.

14. See School Dist. v. Livers, 147 Mo. 580, 49 S.W. 507 (1899); Doll v. Crume, 41 Neb. 655, 59 N.W. 806 (1894). But see Rumsey Elec. v. Univ. of Delaware, 358 A.2d 712 (Del.Super.1976); Camelot Excavating v. St. Paul Fire & Marine Ins., 410 Mich. 118, 301 N.W.2d 275 (1981); Haakinson & Beaty v. Inland Ins., 216 Neb. 426, 344 N.W.2d 454 (1984).

15. See Levy v. Empire Ins., 379 F.2d 860 (5th Cir.1967) (beneficiary who purchased debentures in reliance on terms of written contract permitted to recover although the written contract was subject to conditions precedent not stated in the writing); Simmons v. Western Assurance, 205 F.2d 815 (5th Cir.1953); Aetna Ins. v. Eisenberg, 188 F.Supp. 415 (E.D.Ark.1960), aff'd (insurance policy covering furs stored by customers of furrier where furrier and insured cooperated in advertising coverage not avoidable against customers although furrier failed to comply with policy conditions); but see U.S. Pipe and Foundry v. U.S. Fidelity and Guar., 505 F.2d 88 (5th Cir.1974).

16. See Rs. 2d § 309 cmt c; U.S. v. Indus. Crane & Mfg., 492 F.2d 772 (5th Cir.1974).

§ 17.11   Vesting

Assume that A is a third party beneficiary of a contract between B (promisee) and C (promisor). Can B and C by an agreement subsequent to the contract destroy or curtail A's rights? This may not be done if the rights of the beneficiary have vested before the second agreement was made.[1] The question then becomes, when do the rights of the beneficiary vest? There are several views.

According to the original Restatement, which distinguishes between donee and creditor beneficiaries, the rights of a creditor beneficiary vest when the beneficiary brings an action to enforce the contract or otherwise materially changes position before learning of the discharge or the modification. This view requires injurious reliance on the part of the beneficiary before the beneficiary's rights vest.[2]

Another view is that the rights of a creditor beneficiary vest on learning of the initial contract and assenting to it.[3] The second view seems preferable in that once the creditor beneficiary has assented to the contract there is likely to be reliance in subtle ways, not easily provable, on the security of the contract.[4]

When the beneficiary is a donee, according to the original Restatement, the rights of the beneficiary vest immediately on the making of the contract.[5] This view is supported by a good number of life insurance cases[6] and only a few other decisions.[7] A large number of cases, however, have questioned the soundness of the original Restatement's position on the theory that a donee beneficiary should not have greater rights than a creditor beneficiary.[8] Thus, the trend today is to apply the rules original-

§ 17.11

1. See Rs. 2d § 311(2).

2. See Sears, Roebuck v. Jardel Co., 421 F.2d 1048 (3d Cir.1970); Morstain v. Kircher, 190 Minn. 78, 250 N.W. 727 (1933); Rs. 1st §§ 142–143; accord, Crowell v. Currier, 27 N.J.Eq. 152 (1876), aff'd (rescission permitted, no change of position); cf. Hartman v. Pistorius, 248 Ill. 568, 94 N.E. 131 (1911) (rescission permitted, creditor beneficiary's rights do not vest while the performances running between promisee and promisor are still executory, unless the beneficiary changes position in reliance on the contract).

3. See Palmer v. Radio, 453 F.2d 1133 (5th Cir.1971); Copeland v. Beard, 217 Ala. 216, 115 So. 389 (1928) (on theory that creditor's assent makes the beneficiary a party to the contract); Gifford v. Corrigan, 117 N.Y. 257, 22 N.E. 756 (1889). Sometimes assent is presumed. See Lawrence v. Fox, 20 N.Y. 268 (1859) (dictum, presumption of assent). This is especially true if the beneficiary is an infant. See Rhodes v. Rhodes, 266 S.W.2d 790, 44 ALR2d 1266 (Ky.1953); Plunkett v. Atkins, 371 P.2d 727

(Okl.1962). But see Spates v. Spates, 267 Md. 72, 296 A.2d 581 (1972); Rs. 2d § 311 cmt d.

4. See Gifford v. Corrigan, 117 N.Y. 257, 22 N.E. 756 (1889); Rs. 2d § 311 cmt h (analogy to the law of offer and acceptance).

5. Rs. 1st § 142.

6. See, e.g., Ford v. Mut. Life Ins., 283 Ill.App. 325 (1936); Whitehead v. New York Life Ins., 102 N.Y. 143, 6 N.E. 267 (1886); Vance, The Beneficiary's Interest in a Life Insurance Policy, 31 Yale L.J. 343 (1922).

7. See Plunkett v. Atkins, 371 P.2d 727 (Okl.1962); Logan v. Glass, 136 Pa.Super. 221, 7 A.2d 116 (1939), aff'd (following Restatement); Tweeddale v. Tweeddale, 116 Wis. 517, 93 N.W. 440 (1903).

8. See, e.g., McCulloch v. Canadian Pac. Ry., 53 F.Supp. 534 (D.Minn.1943) (reliance required); Lehman v. Stout, 261 Minn. 384, 112 N.W.2d 640 (1961); Salesky v. Hat Corp., 20 A.D.2d 114, 244 N.Y.S.2d 965 (1963); see Page, The Power of the Contracting Parties to Alter a Contract for Rendering Performance to a Third Person, 12 Wis.L.Rev. 141 (1937).

ly applied to creditor beneficiary to donee beneficiaries.[9]

The Restatement (Second) has noted these criticisms and has set forth a rule that applies equally to donee and creditor beneficiaries.[10] Under the rule of the Second Restatement, the rights of a beneficiary vest as provided in the contract or when the beneficiary "materially changes . . . position in justifiable reliance on the promise or brings suit on it or manifests assent to it at the request of the promisor or promisee."[11]

The parties may, by agreement, determine the issue of vesting such as the creation of a right in the beneficiary that may not be varied by a subsequent agreement without the beneficiary's consent.[12] Conversely, the parties may by agreement reserve "a power to discharge or modify the promisor's duty."[13] This is nearly always done in modern life insurance policies,[14] employee death benefits plans[15] and the like.

The rights of the named irrevocable beneficiary in a life insurance policy may also be defeated by a provision in the contract that allows the insured promisee to borrow against it. In such a case, the beneficiary may not complain if the promisee reduces or destroys the beneficiary's rights by borrowing pursuant to the terms of the contract.[16]

The doctrine of vesting constitutes an exception to the general rule that the promisor may assert against the beneficiary any defense which the promisor could assert against the promisee.[17] After the rights of the beneficiary have vested, the promisor may not raise any defense stemming from a subsequent agreement or consensual discharge made with the promisee.

As to other defenses, the topic of vesting is irrelevant. Assume the promisee agrees not to cut down certain timber and the promisor in exchange promises to pay $1,000 to the beneficiary and the promisee breaches. Assume also that the law of the jurisdiction is that the rights of the beneficiary vest immediately. The last statement is irrelevant because the case does not involve a situation where the promisee and the promisor attempt to vary or discharge the rights of the beneficiary. Since the topic of vesting is irrelevant, it is clear that this case is governed by the general rule stated in the preceding section, that is, the promisor

---

9. See, e.g., Blackard v. Monarch's Mfrs. and Distribs., 131 Ind.App. 514, 169 N.E.2d 735, 97 ALR2d 1255 (1960); Comment, 57 Colum.L.Rev. 406, 418–420 (1957); see Eisenberg, § 17.3 n.3 supra, at 1414–21 (both restatements are too favorable to beneficiaries); cf. Bain v. Pioneer Plaza, 894 P.2d 47 (Colo.App.1995) (reliance was not justifiable as a matter of law).

10. Rs. 2d § 311.

11. Rs. 2d § 311(1) & (2) & cmts a and b; see Detroit Bank & Trust v. Chicago Flame Hardening, 541 F.Supp. 1278 (N.D.Ind.1982); Matter of Cohen, 83 N.Y.2d 148, 629 N.E.2d 1356, 608 N.Y.S.2d 398 (1994).

12. See Rs. 2d § 311. This broad statement is limited by considerations of fairness. Rs. 2d § 311 cmt j.

13. Rs. 2d § 311 cmts c and e; New York Life Ins. v. Cook, 237 Mich. 303, 211 N.W. 648 (1927).

14. See New York Life Ins. v. Cook, 237 Mich. 303, 211 N.W. 648 (1927).

15. See Salesky v. Hat Corp., 20 A.D.2d 114, 244 N.Y.S.2d 965 (1963).

16. Fankuchen v. Fankuchen, 63 Misc.2d 348, 311 N.Y.S.2d 704 (1970).

17. See Rs. 2d § 309.

may assert against the beneficiary any defense that the promisor could assert against the promisee.

Another interesting question is whether and when a third party beneficiary may disclaim the rights created by the contract between the promisor and the promisee. The rule is that the beneficiary may within a reasonable time after learning of the contract for his or her benefit "render any duty to himself [or herself] inoperative from the beginning by disclaimer."[18] However, "once the beneficiary has manifested assent, disclaimer is operative only if the requirements are met for the discharge of a contractual duty."[19]

§ 17.12 May a Promisor Raise the Promisee's Defenses?

In section 17.10, the question was whether the *promisor* can assert against the beneficiary a defense the *promisor* has against the promisee. Here the question is whether the promisor may assert against the beneficiary a defense that the *promisee* has against the beneficiary.

Rouse v. United States illustrates this problem.[1] The plaintiff's assignor sold an oil burner to B on credit. When B sold the house, the defendant purchaser agreed to assume the payments still due on the oil burner contract. The defendant failed to pay and sought to interpose as a defense that plaintiff's assignor had breached a warranty made to B.

The issue is whether the promisor (defendant) may assert against the beneficiary (plaintiff) a defense (breach of warranty) that B has against the plaintiff. The court held that the issue was one of interpretation and states that there are two possible interpretations. One is that the promisor promises to pay whatever the promisee owes. Under this interpretation the promisor is permitted to use the defense.

The other possible interpretation is that the promisor promises to pay irrespective of the liability of the promisee to the beneficiary. Under this understanding, clearly the defendant may not assert the defense that the promisee has against the beneficiary. The court then held that the promise to assume was a promise to pay irrespective of the liability of the promisee.[2] This is a logical interpretive choice. The promisee has paid for the assumption by crediting the unpaid installments toward the promisor's purchase price of her house.

The court assumed that the plaintiff was an intended third party beneficiary.[3] Would this be true in a jurisdiction that followed the rule of

---

18. Rs. 2d § 306.

19. Rs. 2d § 306 cmt b. This means that there must be consideration or its equivalent. There are complicated questions as to the effect of a disclaimer by the beneficiary on the rights of the promisee and third parties. See Rs. 2d § 306 cmts c and d. See also Rs. 1st § 356.

§ 17.12

1. 215 F.2d 872 (D.C.Cir.1954); accord, Joyner v. Vitale, 926 P.2d 1154 (Alaska 1996), but see Eisenberg, § 17.3 n.3 supra, at 11421–28.

2. See Rs. 2d § 312.

3. Under the two Restatements, a plaintiff, situated as was the plaintiff in the Vrooman case qualifies as a third party beneficiary. Both make the point that this

Vrooman v. Turner?[4] The rule of that case is that the third party does not qualify as a third party creditor beneficiary unless there is an obligation owing from the promisee to the beneficiary. In the Rouse case, was the promisee under an obligation to the plaintiff within the meaning of the Vrooman case? The answer appears to be in the affirmative.[5] This does not mean that Vrooman v. Turner has been overruled on its own facts because in the Rouse case the promisee made a voidable promise; in Vrooman the promisee, having taken subject to the mortgage, made no promise whatsoever.

§ 17.13 Rights of the Beneficiary Against the Promisee

Assuming the existence of a valid contract creating a third party beneficiary, the question here is whether the beneficiary also has a claim against the promisee. In this context, the distinction between a creditor and a donee beneficiary is important.

Assume a case in which C is indebted to A. B for a consideration assumes this indebtedness.[1] A is an intended creditor beneficiary and as such has a cause of action against B.[2] A does not, however, thereby lose rights against C. The original obligation continues unimpaired.[3] The net result is that A may obtain a judgment against both C and B but is entitled to only one satisfaction.[4]

As between C and B the relationship is principal-surety. B is the principal and C the surety.[5] The main consequence of this relationship is that if C is compelled to pay the indebtedness, C may proceed against B for reimbursement.[6]

In contrast to a creditor beneficiary, a donee beneficiary ordinarily has no rights against the promisee. By definition, there is no antecedent obligation owing from the promisee to the beneficiary and the promisee

---

result is not changed if the promisor has a defense of Statute of Limitations or Statute of Frauds against the promisee. See §§ 17.2 and 17.4 supra.

4. See § 16.6 supra.

5. See Bennett v. Bates, 94 N.Y. 354 (1884); 4 Corbin, §§ 821–822; 2 Williston § 399.

§ 17.13

1. If there was no consideration from C for B's promise, B could assert the lack of consideration against A. See § 17.10 supra.

2. See § 17.6 infra.

3. See § 18.25 infra. If A discharges C in exchange for B's assumption of the obligation there is a novation; B becomes liable and C is discharged. Notice that the discharge arises by virtue of an agreement between A and C. See § 21.8 infra. If there were only a promise to discharge, there would not be a novation but rather an executory accord. See § 21.8 infra. Some

courts have erroneously held that when B assumes the obligation A releases C by proceeding against B. Conversely, A releases B by proceeding against C. See, e.g., Henry v. Murphy, 54 Ala. 246 (1875). Contra and sound is Modern Photo Offset Supply v. Woodfield Group, 663 N.E.2d 547 (Ind.App. 1996).

4. See Copeland v. Beard, 217 Ala. 216, 115 So. 389 (1928); Vulcan Iron Works v. Pittsburg–Eastern, 144 A.D. 827, 129 N.Y.S. 676 (1911); Erickson v. Grande Ronde Lumber, 162 Or. 556, 94 P.2d 139 (1939); see also Rs. (2d) § 310(1). It will generally be possible for the beneficiary to join the original debtor and the assuming promisor as defendants in the same action.

5. See Rs. 2d § 314; id. § 310 cmts a & b.

6. See 4 Corbin § 825. Generally speaking a surety is also entitled to exoneration and subrogation.

undertakes no obligation to the beneficiary by virtue of the contract. However, there is authority to the effect that where the promisee receives consideration for a promise to discharge or modify the promisor's duty, a donee beneficiary may have an interest in the consideration received by the promisee. According to the First Restatement, the beneficiary was required to elect whether to assert a right against the consideration so received or whether to pursue the promisor.[7] Under the Restatement (Second), the requirement for an election is eliminated[8] and substituted therefor is a rule of what is equitable under the circumstances.[9]

§ 17.14   Rights of the Promisee Against the Promisor

The question posed here is whether the promisee may sue the promisor for breach even though the beneficiary has a cause of action against the promisor based on the same breach. The majority view is that the promisee may maintain such an action and this is logically correct because the promise breached was made to the promisee.[1]

The problem is not significant in a donee beneficiary situation because ordinarily the promisee will not suffer any compensatory damages,[2] and if so, these will not duplicate the damages suffered by the beneficiary.[3] Since the promisee's action for damages would ordinarily provide inadequate relief, the promisee may bring an action for specific performance.[4] An action for restitution may also be available.[5]

The situation is substantially different in a creditor beneficiary situation. Under the majority view, the breach of the promise to pay the debt permits the promisee to recover the amount of the debt.[6] Since the beneficiary may do the same, the possibility of a double recovery exists. To avoid this possibility, some courts have ruled that the promisee may recover the debt only if the promisee has paid the creditor.[7] Of course, the promisor may protect against double recovery by paying the creditor beneficiary prior to judgment. In addition, the promisor may ordinarily ensure that both the promisee and the creditor participate in the same

---

7. Rs. 1st § 142.

8. Rs. 2d § 311(4).

9. Id. § 311(4) cmt j.

§ 17.14

1. See In re Spong, 661 F.2d 6, 69 ALR Fed. 394 (2d Cir.1981); Heins v. Byers, 174 Minn. 350, 219 N.W. 287 (1928); Rs. 1st §§ 135(b), 136(1)(b). The Rs 2d continues the same rule in § 305.

2. Hawkins v. Gilbo, 663 A.2d 9 (Me.1995)(promisee not entitled to damages); see Rs. 2d § 305; Rs. 1st § 345.

3. See discussion in § 17.3 supra. See also Vineyard v. Martin, 29 N.Y.S.2d 935 (1941).

4. See Drewen v. Bank of Manhattan, 31 N.J. 110, 155 A.2d 529, 76 ALR2d 221 (1959); Croker v. New York Trust, 245 N.Y. 17, 156 N.E. 81 (1927); Lehmann v. Lehmann, 182 Misc.2d 22, 696 N.Y.S.2d 663 (1999); Yorio, Contract Enforcement § 2.4.5 (Supplement by Thel).

5. See Rs. 1st § 136 cmt c; id. § 356.

6. See 11 Williston § 1408; Rs. 2d § 305.

7. See White v. Upton, 255 Ky. 562, 74 S.W.2d 924 (1934) (promisee, however, may sue the promisor to compel payment of the debt). Other courts have held that the promisee holds the proceeds in trust for the creditor and that the promisor can compel the promisee to pay the money to the beneficiary. See Gustafson v. Koehler, 177 Minn. 115, 224 N.W. 699 (1929).

action by utilizing interpleader procedure or other procedural techniques. In the event this is not done, the remote possibility of a double recovery can be avoided by the flexibility possessed by a modern court in which law and equity are merged; for example, the court may order the judgment be payable to the creditor even if the action is brought by the promisee,[8] or the court may accept payment into court to be held until the rights of the parties can be sorted out.[9]

8. See Heins v. Byers, 174 Minn. 350, 219 N.W. 287 (1928). It has also been suggested that the promisor may enjoin the action by the promisee but the injunction will be conditioned on payment of the debt to the creditor. Simpson, Suretyship 202.

9. See Lewis v. Germantown Ins., 251 Md. 535, 248 A.2d 468 (1968).

Chapter 18

ASSIGNMENT AND DELEGATION

Table of Sections

Table of Sections

A. INTRODUCTION

B. ASSIGNMENTS—GENERAL BACKGROUND

C. DEVIANTS FROM THE NORM

D. NON–ASSIGNABLE RIGHTS

A.   INTRODUCTION

Table of Sections

§ 18.1   Terminology—Relationship to Prior Chapter

Just as the chapter on third party beneficiaries employs the terminology of promisor, promisee and beneficiary, this chapter employs similar terminology.[1]

Suppose A promises to pay Runner $30,000 if Runner wins the Boston Marathon. Runner now assigns to Creditor this conditional right to payment. Runner is an assignor and Creditor is an assignee. A's label is less clear. Before Runner runs the race, A is a promisor, but after Runner wins the race, A is an obligor because Runner has performed and A is now obligated to pay. A could be referred to as a promisor or an obligor depending on whether or not performance has already occurred. For the balance of the chapter we will ignore the distinction made here

§ 18.1

1.   See § 17.1 supra.

and simply refer to A as the obligor. Thus, A is the obligor, Runner is the obligee-assignor (we will generally refrain from using the term "obligee") and Creditor is the assignee.

Although this illustration is a unilateral arrangement, the illustration could just as easily have been a bilateral contract. In such a case who is the obligor? The answer is—the party who owes the obligation sought to be enforced by the assignee or alleged assignee. Although there are two obligors, we are concerned only with the obligation of the party who is an assignor.

The title of this chapter—"Assignment and Delegation"—needs to be explained. The distinction between the two terms stems from the distinction between rights and duties. An assignment transfers rights.[2] A delegation, in contrast, is the appointment of another to perform one's duties.[3] Courts and lawyers generally are not always careful to make this distinction and are prone to use the word "assignment" (a word of art) inartfully, frequently intending to encompass the distinct concepts of assignment and delegation.[4]

Our discussion of delegation will, to some extent, overlap some of what was discussed in the chapter on third party beneficiaries. In that chapter, we spoke of a situation where A owes B $100 and C for a consideration agrees to assume A's obligation. B is a third party beneficiary of C's promise to A.[5] In terms of this chapter, A has delegated to C the duty of paying $100 to B.[6] Because C assumed this duty, B is a third party beneficiary of C's promise to A. Not all delegations are accompanied by an assumption of duties by the delegate.[7] For example, C could be a messenger delegated to deliver $100 of A's money to B or a carpenter hired by a contractor to install windows.

Lawyers sometimes confuse the concepts of assignment and third party beneficiary. Although both involve rights of a person who was not a party to the contract, the concepts differ as to the origin of the third party's rights. The rights of a third party beneficiary are created by the contract of the two parties to the contract. The rights of an assignee, in contrast, only arise when a party who has rights under a contract transfers to an assignee the rights that had previously been created.

§ 18.2 History

Very early in the common law an attempted assignment of a contract right was ordinarily ineffective.[1] It was believed that the con-

---

2. See § 18.3 infra.

3. See § 18.25 infra.

4. A classic article that has helped to unsnarl the terminological confusion in this area is Corbin, Assignment of Contract Rights, 74 U.Pa.L.Rev. 207 (1926), Selected Readings on The Law of Contracts 718 (1931); see also Rs. 2d § 328 cmt a and § 316 cmt c.

5. See § 17.6 supra.

6. See § 18.25 infra. For the terminology of delegation, see § 18.31 infra.

7. See § 18.26 infra.

§ 18.2

1. The historical background of the law of assignments is traced in Bailey, Assignments of Debts in England from the Twelfth to the Twentieth Century, 47 L.Q.Rev. 516 (1931), 48 L.Q.Rev. 248, 547

tractual relation was too personal to permit the interjection of a third person into the relationship without the consent of the obligor. This idea was reinforced by the law's policy against maintenance and champerty—crimes related to the stirring up of litigation.[2] In time, the rule against assignments was circumvented by the use of powers of attorney. The assignee was appointed as agent of the assignor and eventually was permitted to sue in the name of the assignor and retain the proceeds.[3] Under this approach, the agency of the assignee was terminated by the assignor's revocation of the agency or the assignor's death or bankruptcy.[4] In time, equity held that such an assignment was not terminable.[5] The law courts eventually followed suit,[6] although it was generally necessary for the assignee to sue in the assignor's name and to make the assignor a party to the action.[7] Most states abolished this requirement in the nineteenth century by statutes permitting the assignee to sue as the real party in interest.[8]

The history of the law of assignments is an interesting illustration of the struggle between commercial needs and the tenacity of legal conceptualism. The common law developed when wealth was primarily land and, secondarily, chattels. Intangibles hardly mattered. In a developed economy, however, wealth is primarily represented by intangibles: bank accounts, securities, accounts receivable, etc. The free alienability of these assets is essential to commerce, a necessity the UCC recognizes fully.[9] An early assignment enthusiast wrote: "If we are asked–who made the discovery which has most deeply affected the fortunes of the human race? We think, after full consideration, safely answer–The man who first discovered that a Debt is a Saleable Commodity."[10]

(1932); Holdsworth, The History of the Treatment of Choses in Action by the Common Law, 33 Harv.L.Rev. 997 (1920), Selected Readings 706. There were some exceptions to the rule of non-assignability, such as assignments by the government. These are but of historical interest. Under the Law Merchant, bills and notes were transferable. These mercantile instruments continue to be governed by a separate body of law, presently largely by Article 3 of the UCC. See Gilmore, The Commercial Doctrine of Good Faith Purchase, 63 Yale L.J. 1057 (1954).

2. Lord Coke utilized this rationale to explain the rule against assignments. See Lampet's Case, 77 Eng.Rep. 994, 997 (K.B. 1613).

3. See Mallory v. Lane, 79 Eng.Rep. 292 (Ex.Ch.1615). An interesting historical parallel is found in Roman law. The Roman rule against assignments was circumvented in the same manner. M. Radin, Roman Law 53, 290–92 (1927).

4. Potter v. Turner, 124 Eng.Rep. 7 (K.B.1622).

5. Peters v. Soame, 2 Vern. 428, 23 Eng. Rep. 874 (Ch. 1701).

6. See Cook, The Alienability of Choses in Action, 29 Harv.L.Rev. 816 (1916), Selected Readings 738; Williston, Is the Right of an Assignee of a Chose in Action Legal or Equitable?, 30 Harv.L.Rev. 97 (1916), Selected Readings 754, and 31 Harv.L.Rev. 822 (1918), Selected Readings 790.

7. The equity courts, however, held that the assignee could sue in the assignee's own name. See Cook, The Alienability of Choses in Action, 29 Harv.L.Rev. 816, 820, (1916), Selected Readings 738, 742 (1931).

8. See Clark & Hutchins, The Real Party in Interest, 34 Yale L.J. 259 (1924). The introductory note to Ch. 15 of the Rs. 2d analyzes the state real party in interest statutes.

9. UCC § 9–318(4) (pre 1999), § 9–406(d) (1999), § 2–210(2), discussed at §§ 18.10, 18.16 infra. Revised § 2–210(1)(a) is substantively the same but clarified.

10. Macleod, Principles of Economical Philosophy 481 (2d ed. 1872), quoted in Kastely, Post, & Hom, Contracting Law 1136 (1996).

B. ASSIGNMENTS—GENERAL BACKGROUND

Table of Sections

§ 18.3 Nature of an Assignment

Ordinarily, parties to an assignment have one of two purposes in mind. They may intend an outright transfer of the right in question, or they may intend that the right be transferred as collateral security for a debt. An assignment made as collateral security creates a security interest in the assignee,[1] a property interest comparable to that which a mortgage lender obtains in mortgaged real estate. This text is not generally concerned with security assignments which are covered in works on secured transactions, but the two kinds of assignments are so intertwined that some mention must be made of them. At times, questions of fact arise as to whether the parties intended an outright transfer or merely the creation of a security interest. The parol evidence rule does not bar evidence of this intention.[2]

We are primarily concerned with outright assignments. An outright assignment may be defined as a manifestation of intent by the holder of a right—an obligee—to the assignee[3] to make a present transfer of the right to the assignee.[4] For example, if A in a signed writing states, "I sell and transfer this account against David Mead to William Richardson," an assignment is created, a manifestation of intent by the assignor (A) to presently transfer a right that A has against David Mead (obligor) to William Richardson (assignee).[5] The fact that the word "assign" was not used is not important; any language of present transfer will do.[6] As elsewhere in contract law, there must be an objective manifestation; an intent to assign is insufficient.[7]

Ordinarily, an outright assignment extinguishes the right in the assignor and transfers it to the assignee.[8] The word "ordinarily" is used because even if the transaction meets the definition of assignment, the

---

§ 18.3

1. See International Harvester v. Peoples Bank & Trust, 402 So.2d 856 (Miss. 1981).

2. U.S. v. G & T Enter., 978 F.Supp. 1232 (N.D.Iowa 1997), aff'd; U.S. v. Poling, 73 F.Supp.2d 882 (S.D.Ohio 1999).

3. See Rs. 1st § 149; Rs. 2d § 317. The manifestation may be made to a third person on the assignee's behalf. Rs. 2d § 324.

4. See Matter of Boyd's Estate, 606 P.2d 1243 (Wyo.1980).

5. Richardson v. Mead, 27 Barb. 178 (N.Y.1858).

6. Cobb v. Baxter, 292 P.2d 389 (Okla. 1956).

7. Property Asset Mgt. v. Chicago Title Ins., 173 F.3d 84 (2d Cir.1999).

8. See Continental Oil Co. v. U.S., 326 F.Supp. 266 (S.D.N.Y.1971). When this results, it is sometimes referred to as an "effective assignment." Rs. 2d § 317 cmt a; Rs. 1st § 150.

assignor's powers are not fully extinguished where the assignment is gratuitous (Section 18.7), voidable (Section 18.8), or equitable (18.9). An outright assignment ordinarily carries with it rights, remedies and benefits that are incidental to the thing assigned.[9] For example, the assignment of a bond carries with it a security interest such as a mortgage.[10]

Because an assignment is a present transfer—an executed transaction—a promise to do something in the future cannot be an assignment because a promise is executory. Thus, a promise to pay money when the promisor collects it from a specified source is not an assignment.[11] There is no present transfer. The same is true of a promise to assign at some future time a right that the promisor presently owns.[12] However, because the promise can be specifically enforced, the promisee in such a case has an equitable assignment or an equitable lien.[13]

An order to pay is not usually an assignment. If D owes C $1,000 and C writes D, "Please pay T $1,000 out of the amount you owe," this does not amount to an assignment.[14] Therefore, T acquires no rights under the order issued by C to D. However, if D paid T, D's debt would be discharged.[15]

The situation is somewhat different if C delivered this order to T. There is authority that the instrument amounts to an assignment because it is conditioned on the duty of D to C and because C manifests an intention that a person other than C is to receive the performance.[16] But a check—an order to the bank—is not an assignment even if it is delivered to the payee.[17]

An authorization to a health care provider to collect from one's insurer is not an assignment, and is similar to an order to pay.[18] The authorization is an appointment of the provider as an agent to collect and vests no property interest in the agent.

9. Kintzel v. Wheatland Mut. Ins., 203 N.W.2d 799, 65 ALR3d 1110 (Iowa 1973); National Loan Investors v. Heritage Square Assocs., 54 Conn.App. 67, 733 A.2d 876 (1999) (assignee gets assignor's favorable statute of limitations).

10. South End Plaza Ass'n v. Cote, 52 Conn.App. 374, 727 A.2d 231 (1999).

11. Bass v. Olson, 378 F.2d 818 (9th Cir.1967); Donovan v. Middlebrook, 95 A.D. 365, 88 N.Y.S. 607 (1904); 4 Corbin § 877.

12. See Kansas City v. Milrey Dev., 600 S.W.2d 660 (Mo.App.1980); Lauerman Bros. v. Komp, 156 Wis. 12, 145 N.W. 174 (1914). An assignment of a right not presently owned is discussed in § 18.9 infra.

13. See Morrison Flying Serv. v. Deming Nat. Bank, 404 F.2d 856 (10th Cir. 1968), cert. denied; but see Monegan v. Pacific Nat. Bank, 16 Wn.App. 280, 556 P.2d 226 (1976); see § 18.9 infra.

14. Twin Valley Motors v. Morale, 136 Vt. 115, 385 A.2d 678 (1978); (instructions to attorney to pay debt are revocable); Rs. 2d § 325 cmt a; but see Leon v. Martinez, 84 N.Y.2d 83, 638 N.E.2d 511, 614 N.Y.S.2d 972 (1994) (attorney who drafts instructions for both parties owes a fiduciary duty to both).

15. See Edmund Wright Ginsberg Corp. v. C.D. Kepner Leather, 317 Mass. 581, 59 N.E.2d 253 (1945).

16. See Delbrueck & Co. v. Manufacturers Hanover Trust, 609 F.2d 1047 (2d Cir. 1979); Gingold v. State Farm Ins., 168 Misc.2d 62, 642 N.Y.S.2d 812 (1996); Rs. 2d § 325(1).

17. UCC § 3–409(1); § 3–408 of the 1990 revision.

18. Kelly Health Care v. Prudential Ins., 226 Va. 376, 309 S.E.2d 305 (1983).

§ 18.4 Coverage of This Chapter—Impact of UCC

The coverage of this chapter is primarily concerned with outright assignments.[1] Specifically, it focuses on outright assignments of contractual rights—the assignment of intangible rights that arise by contract.[2] This chapter will discuss the common law rules governing the assignment of these contractual rights as affected by statute.

The most relevant legislation is Article 9 of the UCC. It might occur to the reader to ask, how this could be? Article 9 of the UCC governs security transactions! Its title is "Secured Transactions." However, Article 9 also covers outright assignments for value[3] of "accounts" and "chattel paper."[4] The 1999 revision extends its reach also to "payment intangibles," and promissory notes and an array of other rights.[5]

Article 9 underwent major revisions in 1972. Other revisions were approved later to conform it to the adoption of Article 2A dealing with leases, and to revisions of Articles 5 & 8, and the deletion of Article 6. Other unrelated revisions have also been made. Adoption of these revisions by the states has been far from uniform. The Uniform Commissioners approved an overall revision of Article 9 in 1999. Citations to the UCC in this text will be to the official text of the 1999 revisions. The 1999 revised text has been widely adopted in a short period of time.

An account is a right to payment. Notice that there is an account only when there is a right to payment. Thus, a right to receive goods or services does not amount to an account. Also, not all rights to payment are accounts. The term is limited to rights to payment for (1) goods sold, (2) goods leased, or (3) services rendered. Such a right to payment is an account whether or not it has yet been earned by performance. The 1999 revision broadens the kinds of monetary obligations that constitute accounts to a large array of rights to payment, while making certain exceptions.[6] However, the right to payment is not an account, under either the pre or post 1999 versions, if the obligation is evidenced by an instrument or chattel paper.

The word "instrument" refers to a negotiable instrument and certain specialties.[7] "Chattel paper" is a writing or other record that evidences both a monetary obligation and a security interest in or a lease of specific goods.[8] Chattel paper is generally used in a consumer sale where the consumer buys goods on credit–the consumer promises to pay

§ 18.4

1. See § 18.3 supra.

2. For the same approach, see Rs. 2d § 316 cmt a. It suggests that the rules stated here may apply to non-contractual choses in action. These include intangible property rights (e.g., patents and copyrights) and intangible tort rights. See Rs. 2d, Intro. Note to Ch. 15; Rs. 2d § 316 cmt a.

3. The term "for value" is defined in § 18.7 infra.

4. See UCC § 9–109 (1999)

5. UCC § 9–109 (a) (1999).

6. UCC § 9–109 (1999).

7. § 9–102(a)(47) (1999).

8. UCC § 9–102(a)(11) (1999). For a more detailed and nuanced definition, consult the statute.

for the goods purchased by executing a promissory note. In addition, the seller retains a security interest in the goods.

Article 9 of the UCC applies to outright assignments of accounts and chattel paper because of their more frequent assignments as financing devices.[9] It is logical that certain outright assignments that fit the definition of an account or chattel paper would be eliminated from the coverage of Article 9 because they clearly do not have a financing character. Exclusions from Article 9 include any outright assignment in connection with the sale of a business from which the rights assigned arose, an assignment for the purposes of collection only, a transfer of rights to an assignee who is also to perform under the contract, and a variety of other transactions including "a transfer" of a "single account to an assignee in whole or partial satisfaction of a pre-existing indebtedness."[10] Article 2 of the UCC also contains provisions relating to assignments that apply only if the assignment arises out of a sales transaction.[11]

When a transaction is excluded from the coverage of the UCC, common law rules govern the transaction; however, other statutory enactments must also be consulted.

§ 18.5 Formalities

In the absence of an applicable statute, the manifestation of intent required for an assignment need not be in writing.[1] Unlike the common law, Article 9 of the UCC heavily emphasizes the requirement of a writing. A "security interest" governed by Article 9 of the UCC is generally not enforceable against the debtor or third persons unless the debtor has authenticated a "security agreement"[2] or unless the assignee has possession or control of the collateral.[3] The statute performs the function of a Statute of Frauds.[4] If the assignment is not governed by Article 9, a provision of Article 1 requires written evidence of an assignment of personal property (e.g., patents, copyrights, royalties) where enforcement would be of the amount or value exceeding $5,000.[5] If revised Article 1 is adopted this provision is repealed. The 1999 revision of Article 9, however, subjects them to the rules of Article 9; former Article 9 excluded them from coverage.

The primary concern of this chapter is the outright assignment of accounts. An outright assignment of an account is unenforceable unless

---

9. See 1 G. Gilmore, Security Interests in Personal Property § 10.5 (1965).

10. UCC § 9–109(d) (1999).

11. UCC § 2–210. This provision is discussed in several of the sections that follow. See particularly § 18.16.

§ 18.5

1. See Anaconda Aluminum v. Sharp, 243 Miss. 9, 136 So.2d 585, 99 ALR2d 1307 (1962); Jemison v. Tindall, 89 N.J.L. 429, 99 A. 408 (1916); Brown v. Fore, 12 S.W.2d 114, 63 ALR 435 (Tex.Com.App.1929); Rs.

2d § 324 cmt a; Rs. 1st § 157; 4 Corbin § 879.

2. UCC § 9–203 (1999).

3. Id. This is an attempt to simplify a complicated provision. Collateral is defined in UCC § 9–102 (a)(12) (1999).

4. § 9–203 cmt 4; Scott v. Cushman & Wakefield, 249 Ga.App. 264, 547 S.E.2d 794 (Ga.App.2001).

5. UCC § 1–206(1) (pre-revision).

it is evidenced by an authenticated security agreement authenticated by the assignor,[6] or is one of the kinds of assignments excluded from Article 9's coverage.

C. DEVIANTS FROM THE NORM

Table of Sections

§ 18.6 Introduction

Ordinarily, an outright assignment terminates a right in the assignor and transfers it to the assignee.[1] There are, however, situations where an assignment may be terminable or revocable. In these situations, the assignor retains certain powers, while the rights of the assignee are in limbo for a period of time. We discuss here three of these situations.

18.7 Gratuitous Assignments

An assignment is an executed transaction and therefore there is no requirement that it be supported by consideration. Nevertheless, assignments are divided into two categories—gratuitous assignments and assignments for value. An assignment is for value if the assignee parts with consideration or if the assignment is taken as security for or in total or partial satisfaction of a pre-existing debt.[1] If the assignment is not for value then it is gratuitous.

To start with, the obligor cannot defend a claim by the assignee by pointing out that the assignment was gratuitous.[2] It is an issue only when raised by the assignor, the assignor's successors, or other competing claimants to the obligor's performance.

A gratuitous assignment is terminable by the death of the assignor, by a subsequent assignment of the same right, or by a notice of termination communicated by the assignor to the assignee or to the obligor.[3] However, a gratuitous assignment need not remain terminable

---

6. Under Article 9 a writing must ordinarily be filed in a designated public office to protect the assignee against third parties. There is an exception to the filing requirement where an assignment of accounts do not alone or in conjunction with other assignments transfer a significant part of the outstanding accounts or. payment intangibles. UCC § 9–309(2) & cmts 2, 4 (1999).

§ 18.6

1. See § 18.3 supra.

§ 18.7

1. See Rs. 2d § 332(5); UCC § 1–201(44); revised § 1–204 contains substantially the same definition but adds that "value" is also given in a third situation: where a buyer by taking delivery under a pre-existing contract converts a contingent into a fixed obligation.

2. GMAC v. Scio Volunteer Fire Dept., 191 A.D.2d 981, 595 N.Y.S.2d 145 (1993).

3. Rs. 2d § 332.

in perpetuity. The gift of the right may be completed in a variety of ways. Thus, whether the gratuitous assignee will have rights under the assignment depends on which occurs first, the terminating event or the completion of the gift.

What events complete the gift of the assignment? The law applicable to gifts of chattels requires that a gift be completed by delivery.[4] Since a right cannot be physically delivered, the law has validated certain substitutes for delivery. The assignee can complete the gift by obtaining payment from, or a judgment against, the obligor, or by entering into a substituted contract with the obligor—that is, a binding agreement with the obligor to pay the assignee or to substitute some other performance.[5]

The gift is also deemed to be completed if the right assigned is evidenced by a writing that the creditor is required to surrender on payment (what is called a symbolic writing) and the writing is delivered to the assignee.[6] Writings in this class include bonds and mortgages, savings account books, life insurance policies, and stock certificates.[7] The Restatement (Second) adds that this rule should be extended to include the delivery of an evidentiary writing—an integration that embodies the contract.[8] A number of cases have adopted the same basic position in holding that the delivery of the contract embodying a right is sufficient delivery even though it is not a symbolic writing.[9]

In jurisdictions that continue to recognize the efficacy of a seal, an assignment may be completed by a deed of gift, that is a written instrument under seal.[10] In other states, it has generally been held that the delivery of a signed writing expressing an intent to assign makes a gratuitous assignment irrevocable.[11] For the most part, these cases have required delivery.[12] New York has enacted a statute that provides: "An

---

4. See Adams v. Merced Stone, 176 Cal. 415, 178 P. 498, 3 ALR 928 (1917); Biehl v. Biehl's Adm'x, 263 Ky. 710, 93 S.W.2d 836 (1936); Cook v. Lum, 55 N.J.L. 373, 26 A. 803 (1893); Williston, Gifts of Rights under Contracts in Writing by Delivery of the Writing, 40 Yale L.J. 1 (1930); Bruton, The Requirement of Delivery as Applied to Gifts of Choses in Action, 39 Yale L.J. 837 (1930).

5. Rs. 1st § 158; Rs. 2d § 332. However, a gratuitous assignment bars action by the assignor unless and until the assignor effectively terminates the assignment.

6. See Rs. 1st § 158(1)(b); Rs. 2d § 332(1)(b); Farrell v. Passaic Water, 82 N.J.Eq. 97, 88 A. 627 (1913).

7. See Brooks v. Mitchell, 163 Md. 1, 161 A. 261, 84 ALR 547 (1932) (delivery of suitcase containing savings bank book sufficient delivery to create assignment of bank account); 4 Corbin §§ 915–920; 3 Williston §§ 438A–440 (3d ed.).

8. See Rs. 2d § 332 cmt d.

9. See In re Huggins' Estate, 204 Pa. 167, 53 A. 746 (1902) (gift of rights under a

contract for the sale of real property effected by delivery of the written contract); Rs. 2d § 332 cmt d; contra, Rs. 1st § 158 ill. 2.

10. See Sweeney v. Veneziano, 70 N.J.Super. 185, 175 A.2d 241 (1961); Rs. 2d § 332(1)(a); Rs. 1st § 158(1)(a).

11. See Berl v. Rosenberg, 169 Cal. App.2d 125, 336 P.2d 975 (1959); Smith v. Smith, 313 S.W.2d 753 (Mo.App.1958); Thatcher v. Merriam, 121 Utah 191, 240 P.2d 266 (1952); 4 Corbin § 921; 3 Williston § 438A (3d ed.).

12. See Biehl v. Biehl's Adm'x, 263 Ky. 710, 93 S.W.2d 836 (1936); Cooney v. Equitable Life Assur. Soc., 235 Minn. 377, 51 N.W.2d 285 (1952); Williston, Gifts of Rights under Contracts in Writing by Delivery of the Writing, 40 Yale L.J. 1 (1930).

Another question is whether delivery of such a writing is sufficient to complete the gift when the right to be transferred is embodied in a symbolic writing. Should not the symbolic writing be delivered? In Thatcher v. Merriam, 121 Utah 191, 240

assignment shall not be denied the effect of irrevocably transferring the assignor's rights because of the absence of consideration if such an assignment is in writing and signed by the assignor, or by the assignor's agent."[13]

The doctrine of estoppel may also render a gift irrevocable. If the assignor should reasonably foresee that the assignee will injuriously change position in reliance on the assignment and such reliance does occur, the assignment is irrevocable.[14]

§ 18.8   Voidable and Conditional Assignments

Just as a contract may be voidable,[1] an assignment may be voidable. For example, an assignment may be voidable because of infancy, insanity, duress or fraud.[2] In the case of a voidable assignment, the assignment does not necessarily extinguish the rights of the assignor because the assignor has a power to avoid the assignment pursuant to the rules generally applicable to consensual transactions.[3]

Where an assignment is voidable, the obligor's duty to the assignor is discharged if the obligor pays the assignee in good faith without notice of the defect that made the assignment voidable. If the obligor pays the assignee with reason to know that the assignment is voidable, however, the obligor does so at the obligor's own peril and is vulnerable to a judgment for a second payment.[4]

A conditional assignment of a right is another situation where the rights of the assignor are not extinguished by the assignment.[5] The Restatement (Second) gives the following illustration. A has a right against B to payment of $400, and assigns the right to C. The assignment is in payment for an automobile delivered by C on condition that the car runs 1000 miles without needing repairs. Although there is an assignment, if repairs are needed within the 1000–mile test period, the right to $400 belongs to A, and not to C.[6] Thus, the rights of A are not extinguished on the occurrence of the assignment. They are extinguished only when the event specified occurs or is excused.[7]

§ 18.9   Assignments of Future Rights

The word "assignment" carries the connotation of a present transfer. Here, we are concerned with the present assignment of a future

---

P.2d 266 (1952) the court held that the symbolic writing need not be delivered. This decision is to be applauded. The delivery of the informal writing is a sufficient evidentiary basis for a finding of a completed gift.

13. McKinney's N.Y.Gen.Oblig.L. § 5–1107; see Speelman v. Pascal, 10 N.Y.2d 313, 222 N.Y.S.2d 324, 178 N.E.2d 723 (1961).

14. See Rs. 2d § 332(4); Rs. 1st § 158(1)(c).

§ 18.8

1. See Chapters 8 and 9 supra.

2. See Rs. 2d § 338 cmt g.

3. See Chapters 8 and 9 supra.

4. See Rs. 2d § 338 cmt g.

5. See Rs. 2d § 331.

6. See Rs. 2d § 331 ill. 1.

7. See Rs. 2d § 331 cmt b.

right as opposed to the assignment of a present right. The cases have been in confusion as to the distinction between the two. An illustration will help clarify the distinction.

Suppose a builder under an existing contract is entitled to progress payments of $1,000 per month, conditioned on performance of a specified amount of work each month. There is no question that an assignment by the contractor at the end of the first month amounts to a present assignment.[1] The question that has in the past created the greatest problem is whether an assignment at the end of the first month of the money to be earned in the second month amounts to the assignment of a present or future right? The modern law takes the view that this is an assignment of a present right because the right to the second month's payment arises under an existing contract. Today, the concept of the assignment of a future right is applicable only when the assignment is of a right under a contract that is not in existence but that the assignor expects to enter into.[2]

The notion of assignment of a future right has presented a conceptual difficulty. In the past, it has often been stated that it is impossible for a person to transfer a right that is not yet in existence.[3] In time, it was held that the assignment of a right under a contract not yet in existence amounted to an equitable assignment.[4] Thus, the assignee would ordinarily have rights superior to the assignor and was entitled to demand performance from the obligor.[5]

However, the assignee of a future right has rights inferior to a number of potential third party claimants. Thus, in the case of a double assignment, the second assignee who is a good faith purchaser for value, and who has obtained payment or other satisfaction, would prevail over the equitable assignee.[6] In addition, it has been held that an attaching creditor of the assignor prevails over the equitable assignee if the rights of the creditor attach after the right has arisen and before the assignor has made a present assignment.[7] Moreover, the equitable assignee's rights will be subordinated to the rights of the assignor's trustee in bankruptcy.[8]

§ 18.9

1. See Rs. 2d § 321 cmt a.

2. See Rs. 1st § 154(2); Rs. 2d § 321(2); Comment, 27 Fordham L.Rev. 579 (1959). However, in the case of a continuing relationship where there is no contract, for example, the relationship between a supplier and a construction contractor, the situation is often treated as involving a present transfer. See Rs. 2d § 321 cmt c.

3. See Rs. 2d § 331 cmt b. The same conceptual problem arose with respect to a mortgage on after-acquired property. See G. Osborne, Mortgages § 39 (2d ed. 1970).

4. Rs. 2d § 330 cmt c and § 321 cmt d.

5. See Speelman v. Pascal, 10 N.Y.2d 313, 222 N.Y.S.2d 324, 178 N.E.2d 723 (1961); Rs. 2d § 321 cmt d.

6. See State Factors v. Sales Factors, 257 A.D. 101, 12 N.Y.S.2d 12 (1939); Axelrod, Successive Assignments—Conflicting Priorities, 14 U. Dayton L. Rev. 295 (1989).

7. See Harold Moorstein & Co. v. Excelsior Ins., 31 A.D.2d 177, 296 N.Y.S.2d 2 (1968), aff'd; Rs. 2d § 330 cmt d. There are contrary cases. See 1 G. Gilmore, supra § 18.4 n.9 at § 7–12.

8. See Manchester Nat. Bank v. Roche, 186 F.2d 827 (1st Cir.1951).

The UCC has changed these common law rules to the extent of its coverage. Generally speaking, if the assignee files a financing statement, or otherwise perfects its interests, and if Article 9 of the UCC applies, the assignee will prevail.[9] In addition, UCC § 9–204 expressly validates a floating lien on shifting accounts and on shifting stocks of goods. A creditor is permitted to obtain from the debtor a lien on the debtor's shifting stock in trade (merchandise) and a security interest in the debtor's shifting accounts receivable. To achieve this result, the agreement should provide that the creditor's lien automatically attaches to newly acquired stock in trade and to newly created accounts. In addition, the creditor must file a financing statement. If Article 9 applies and is complied with, an assignment of a future right has the same consequences as an assignment of a present right.

D. NON–ASSIGNABLE RIGHTS

Table of Sections

§ 18.10 Introduction

In contrast with the earlier law,[1] the modern view is emphatically to the effect that rights are ordinarily assignable.[2] However, there are exceptions. Both Restatements[3] and Article 2 of the UCC provide that a right is not assignable in the following circumstances: (1) if the assignment would materially change the duty of the obligor; (2) if the assignment would increase materially the burden or risk imposed on the obligor by the contract; or (3) if the assignment would impair the obligor's chance of obtaining return performance[4] or, according to the

---

9. See UCC § 9–204 (1999) (excluding certain consumer contracts).

§ 18.10

1. See § 18.2 supra.

2. See Macke Co. v. Pizza of Gaithersburg, 259 Md. 479, 270 A.2d 645, 53 ALR3d 461 (1970); S. & L. Vending v. 52 Thompkins Ave. Restaurant, 26 A.D.2d 935, 274 N.Y.S.2d 697 (1966); Willow City v. Vogel, Vogel, Brantner & Kelly, 268 N.W.2d 762 (N.D.1978); Weathers v. M.C. Lininger & Sons, 68 Or.App. 30, 682 P.2d 770 (1984), rev. denied. Free assignability is deemed to be good public policy. See Augusta Med. Complex v. Blue Cross, 230 Kan. 361, 634 P.2d 1123 (1981); but see Parrish Chiropractic Centers v. Progressive Cas. Ins., 874 P.2d 1049 (Colo.1994). If a right to payment could not be assigned, the credit system employed in our civilization could not exist. H. Macleod, Principles of Economical Philosophy 481 (2d ed. 1872). See also § 18.2 note 10 supra.

3. See Rs. 2d § 317(2)(a); Rs. 1st § 151(a).

4. See UCC § 2–210(2); § 2–210(1)(b) of the revision is substantially the same.

Second Restatement, if the assignment would materially reduce the value of the return performance to the obligor.[5] In addition, on various policy grounds, the law restricts the assignability of certain kinds of rights.[6] Generally, the obligor can waive the non-assignability of a right created by contract.

§ 18.11   Assignment Materially Changing the Obligor's Duty

Almost any assignment changes, to a degree, the duty of the obligor. Nevertheless, it is generally recognized that in practically every case a right to payment of money is assignable.[1] So too is a right to delivery of goods that have been paid for.[2] But if A agreed to paint B's portrait for a fee, B could not, by assignment of the right to C, obligate A to paint C's portrait. A's duty would be materially changed. The situation would be different if B assigned to C the right to receive B's portrait after it was painted. What is and what is not a material change of duty is obviously a question of degree.[3]

A good illustration of this problem arises in the area of requirements contracts. The key issue in each case should be whether the requirements of the assignee would approximate the requirements of the assignor. Thus, while, in the past, it was sometimes held that the right to receive one's requirements was not assignable, there were contrary cases.[4] The cases were not necessarily in conflict because of factual differences among them.

Under the UCC, the requirements buyer may generally assign the right to purchase. An official comment states: the "requirements in the hands of the new owner continue to be measured by the actual good faith * * * requirements under the normal operation of the enterprise prior to sale."[5] The "good faith" is that of the assignee, granting to the assignee an element of personal discretion. However, this element of personal discretion is carefully circumscribed by supplying the objective criterion of "the normal operations of the enterprise prior to sale."

---

5. See Rs. 2d § 317(2)(a).

6. See 18.15 infra; see also § 18.16 infra which discusses the extent to which an agreement may prevent assignment, and § 18.32 infra, dealing with the assignability of option contracts.

§ 18.11

1. American Litho. v. Ziegler, 216 Mass. 287, 103 N.E. 909 (1914); Booker v. Everhart, 294 N.C. 146, 240 S.E.2d 360 (1978). But see Bondanza v. Peninsula Hospital & Med. Ctr., 23 Cal.3d 260, 152 Cal.Rptr. 446, 590 P.2d 22 (1979).

2. Rochester Lantern v. Stiles & Parker Press, 135 N.Y. 209, 31 N.E. 1018 (1892); UCC § 2–210(2). A change in delivery terms, however, may constitute a repudiation. S & S v. Meyer, 478 N.W.2d 857 (Iowa App.1991).

3. Some of these problems are discussed in § 18.12 infra.

4. See Matson v. White, 122 Colo. 79, 220 P.2d 864 (1950); C.H. Little Co. v. Cadwell Transit, 197 Mich. 481, 163 N.W. 952 (1917).

5. UCC § 2–306 cmt 4 (unchanged by revision).

§ 18.12 Assignment Materially Increasing the Obligor's Burden or Risk

In this section, the assumption is that the the assignment has not materially changed the obligor's duty, but the obligor's burden or risk has materially increased. A simple illustration is a purported assignment of a fire insurance policy. If A owns a building that X insurance company insures against loss by fire, and A sells it to B, may A assign the insurance coverage to B?

Clearly, the assignment would not change the obligor's duty. The insurer's obligation is to pay in the event of fire. It is equally clear that the insurer's risk will be increased if B is a less careful person than A or has a history of fire losses. However, the insurer is not required to deal with B even if B could prove that he or she is the most careful person in the world. The insurance company may reject the assignment because the risk *may* be different.[1] Any other result would force the insurer to weigh in every case the care that would be used by the assignor and the assignee. In actual practice, consent of the insurer is sought and is frequently obtained. Non-assignability is a protection that the obligor may waive.

§ 18.13 Assignment Materially Impairing the Other Party's Chance of Obtaining Return Performance

When an assignor assigns rights under a contract, the assignor loses some of the incentive to perform because the consideration that was to come to the assignor is now to go to the assignee. However, it is generally held that this reduction in incentive would not impair the other party's chance of obtaining return performance.

Suppose S agrees to sell and deliver 1,000 bushels of potatoes to B in exchange for B's promise to pay $10,000 on delivery. S, for a consideration, prior to delivery assigns the right to payment to T. As a result of the assignment S undoubtedly loses some incentive to perform because on delivery the $10,000 goes to T. Nevertheless, the assignment is effective.[1] S has a sufficient incentive to perform because failure to perform will result in liability to both B and the assignee.[2]

The primary kind of case where the assignment would materially impair the other party's chance to obtain return performance is where

---

§ 18.12

1. See Central Union Bank v. New York Underwriters' Ins., 52 F.2d 823, 78 ALR 494 (4th Cir.1931). This view has been expressed in the prior editions of this book and criticized by Professors Murray and Farnsworth without any direct authority to support their positions. See Murray, Contracts § 138(A)(7) (3d ed.1990) cf. § 138 (A)(4) (4th ed.); Farnsworth, Contracts § 11.4 (2d ed.1990). The issue is mooted by

standard non-assignability clauses. Couch on Insurance § 35:3.

§ 18.13

1. See Rockmore v. Lehman, 129 F.2d 892 (2d Cir.1942), cert. denied; but see Paper Prods. Mach. v. Safepack Mills, 239 Mass. 114, 131 N.E. 288 (1921), criticized in 4 Corbin § 865 ns. 13 and 14, a decision that is probably obsolete.

2. See 4 Corbin § 869.

the assignment is coupled with an improper delegation. There are two kinds of improper delegations. The first is where the duty is non-delegable. This type of duty and the effect of an attempted delegation are discussed below.[3] The second kind of improper delegation is where the delegate is unqualified. As an example of the second kind, the assignor was the exclusive distributor in Texas for Nexxus hair products. The assignor sold its business to a subsidiary of Nexxus's major competitor and purported to assign its Nexxus contract to the buyer and delegated its duties under the contract to the assignee. The assignment was void, as the assignee owed a duty of best efforts to the obligor's competitor, necessarily placing it in a conflict of interest.[4] The coupling of an improper delegation with an assignment results in an assignment that is void.

§ 18.14   Attempted Transfer of a Non-assignable Right

The attempted assignment of a right that is not assignable need not be honored by the obligor.[1] However, the obligor may waive the fact of non-assignability and the assignor may not object.[2] It is generally held that the assignment of a non-assignable right does not amount to a material breach unless the assignor insists that the improper assignment be accepted.[3]

The assignor does not impliedly warrant that the right purported to be assigned is assignable. Therefore, the assignee does not have a claim against the assignor if the right assigned is not assignable,[4] except perhaps a claim for restitution based on voiding the transaction for mistake of law.[5] Thus, it is the obligor who is generally empowered to raise the defense of non-assignability against the assignee.

§ 18.15   Assignment Prohibited by Statute or Public Policy

By statute, many states have outlawed or restricted certain types of

---

3. See § 18.28 to 18.31 infra.

4. Sally Beauty v. Nexxus Products, 801 F.2d 1001 (7th Cir.1986); accord, Berliner Foods v. Pillsbury, 633 F.Supp. 557 (D.Md. 1986); but see Judge Posner's strong dissent in Sally Beauty.

§ 18.14

1. Under UCC § 2–609 discussed in § 12.2(b) supra, the obligor has a right to demand assurances against the assignor before asserting the right not to honor the assignment. This right is one of the factors to be considered in determining whether the assignment impairs the obligor's chance of obtaining return performance. In addition, in making this determination, any security that the obligor has should be taken into account. UCC § 2–210(5), also relating to security, is discussed below, § 18.31.

2. See Citibank, N.A. v. Tele/Resources, 724 F.2d 266 (2d Cir.1983); Metropolitan Life Ins. v. Dunne, 2 F.Supp. 165 (S.D.N.Y. 1931); Sillman v. Twentieth Century–Fox Film, 3 N.Y.2d 395, 165 N.Y.S.2d 498, 144 N.E.2d 387 (1957); Rs. (2d) § 322(2) and cmt d; Rs. 1st § 176. An assignor may not complain the right assigned is not assignable. State Farm Fire & Cas. Ins. v. Farmers Ins. Exch., 489 P.2d 480 (Okl.1971).

3. See Mitsui & Co. v. Puerto Rico Water Resources Auth., 528 F.Supp. 768 (D.P.R.1981); 3 Williston § 420 (3d ed.); but see Forest Commodity v. Lone Star Indus., 255 Ga.App. 244, 564 S.E.2d 755 (2002) (improper assignment is a repudiation).

4. Farnsworth, Contracts § 11.4 n. 6 (2d ed.).

5. See § 9.28 supra.

assignments.[1] For example, at the time of enactment of the UCC, most states regulated wage assignments by outright prohibition or by limiting their duration or effect.[2] The FTC has since outlawed such assignments in consumer transactions.[3] Such prohibitions are designed to prevent a wage earner from, in effect, mortgaging his or her wage-earning capacity.[4] Similar concerns arise where a tort victim attempts to assign rights in a structured settlement.[5] Federal statutes and some state statutes forbid, with some exceptions, the assignment of a right to payment under a public contract,[6] and regulate the assignment of rights in veterans' life insurance policies.[7]

Even if the assignment of a right is not prohibited by statute, it may still be ineffective because it violates public policy.[8] The most common illustrations are the non-assignability in most jurisdictions of the salary or other remuneration of a public officer[9] that has not yet been earned,[10] the non-assignability of government pensions,[11] and unmatured alimony claims.[12] This chapter deals with the assignability of rights stemming from contract and does not consider the assignability of tort claims,[13] patents, trademarks, etc.

The securing of assignments for the purpose of stirring up litigation is also against public policy.[14] This is especially true if the assignee is a lawyer.[15] However, this is not true if the attorney has a legitimate interest in acquiring the assignment.[16] The majority of jurisdictions regard the assignment of lawyer-malpractice claims to be against public policy.[17]

§ 18.15

1. See Rs. 2d § 317(2)(b) cmt e; Rs. 1st § 547.

2. See Rs. 2d Chapter 15, Introductory Note.

3. 16 C.F.R. § 444.2.

4. See In re Nance, 556 F.2d 602 (1st Cir.1977).

5. In re Nitz, 317 Ill.App.3d 119, 250 Ill.Dec. 632, 739 N.E.2d 93 (2000); Singer Asset Finance Co. v. CGU Life Insurance Co., 275 Ga. 328, 567 S.E.2d 9 (Ga.2002); In re Spinelli, 353 N.J.Super. 459, 803 A.2d 172 (2002) (statute requires court approval of assignment). Structured settlements often have anti-assignment clauses. See Crespi, Selling Structured Settlements, 28 Pepp. L.Rev. 787 (2001).

6. 31 U.S.C.A. § 3727; 41 U.S.C.A. 15. See Poorvu v. U.S., 420 F.2d 993 (Ct.Cl. 1970) and 44 ALRFed. 775 (1979).

7. Funeral Fin. Sys. v. U.S., 234 F.3d 1015 (7th Cir.2000).

8. Rs. 2d § 317(2)(b) cmt e.

9. There is no unanimity on the question of who is a "public officer." Compare Bliss v. Lawrence, 58 N.Y. 442, 17 Am.Rep. 273 (1874) with Kimball v. Ledford, 13 Cal. App.2d 602, 57 P.2d 163 (1936).

10. Kaminsky v. Good, 124 Or. 618, 265 P. 786 (1928); 3 Williston § 417 (3d ed.). The rationale is the protection of the public by protecting those engaged in performing public duties. See Bliss v. Lawrence, 58 N.Y. 442, 17 Am.Rep. 273 (1874). Compare Community State Bank v. U.S., 493 F.2d 908 (5th Cir.1974) (held that there was a question of fact as to whether the assignment deprived the public officer of the means of support).

11. See 5 U.S.C.A. § 8346(a).

12. See Welles v. Brown, 226 Mich. 657, 198 N.W. 180 (1924).

13. See INS Investigations Bureau v. Lee, 709 N.E.2d 736 (Ind.App.1999) (most tort claims now assignable).

14. See Kenrich Corp. v. Miller, 377 F.2d 312 (3d Cir.1967) (in form, involved a power of attorney rather than an assignment). The obligor's defense of champerty was sustained.

15. See § 22.10 infra.

16. Capobianco v. Halebass Realty, 72 A.D.2d 804, 421 N.Y.S.2d 924 (1979).

17. Quinn, On the Assignment of Legal Malpractice Claims, 37 S. Tex. L.Rev. 1203 (1996); Beck, Assignment of Legal Malprac-

§ 18.16 Clause Prohibiting or Authorizing an Assignment

Sometimes a contract contains a provision prohibiting assignment. The question here is the validity and effect of such a provision. A minority of cases have held that a contractual provision prohibiting the assignment of rights created by the contract is an unlawful restraint on alienation.[1] The great majority of cases, however, have reached a contrary conclusion refusing to interfere with the parties' freedom of contract in such an explicit manner.

The courts' ostensible deference to freedom of contract did not always lead to the effect intended by the parties. The courts have tended to find that the particular provision before the court was not drafted with sufficient clarity to accomplish its purpose of prohibiting assignment. They have often emasculated the provision by holding it to be merely a promise not to assign.[2] Under such a construction an assignment is effective, but the obligor has a cause of action against the assignor for breach of contract.[3] Since damages for such a breach ordinarily will be merely nominal, the anti-assignment provision is of no practical value. If, however, the provision expressly states that any assignment shall be void, or uses other equivalent language, the courts have generally held that the purported assignment is ineffective,[4] unless the obligor consents to the assignment.[5]

The UCC has two provisions that limit the effectiveness of an anti-assignment clause. One is in Article 2 and the other in Article 9. Section 2–210(2) provides that an anti-assignment clause in a sale of goods contract will not render ineffective an assignment of a right to damages for a total breach. It also provides that it cannot prohibit the assignment of a right arising out of the assignor's due performance, that is, the right to payment for goods delivered and the right to receive delivery of goods that have been paid for. The revision is in accord.

tice Claims, 43 Baylor L.Rev. 193 (1991); Comment, 59 U.Chi. L.Rev. 1553 (1992).

§ 18.16

1. Portuguese–American Bank v. Welles, 242 U.S. 7 (1916), 26 Yale L.J. 304 (1917).

2. See Randal v. Tatum, 98 Cal. 390, 33 P. 433 (1893); Portland Elec. & Plumbing v. Vancouver, 29 Wn.App. 292, 627 P.2d 1350 (1981); but see Parrish Chiropractic Ctrs. v. Progressive Cas. Ins., 857 P.2d 540 (Colo. App.1993). aff'd on different grounds.

3. See Hull v. Hostettler, 224 Mich. 365, 194 N.W. 996 (1923). It has been held that there is no breach of an anti-assignment clause when the assignment is made because of a change in the assignor's business, as where an individual forms a corporation and assigns personal contractual rights to the corporation. Ruberoid v. Glassman Constr., 248 Md. 97, 234 A.2d 875 (1967); TXO Prod. v.M. D.Mark, Inc., 999 S.W.2d 137 (Tex.App.1999), 53 Baylor L. Rev. 489 (2001) (subsidiary merged into parent). The cases are not uniform. See Ballew, 38 Bus. Law 45 (1982); Note, Effect of Corporate Reorganization on Nonassignable Contracts, 74 Harv.L.Rev. 393 (1960).

4. See Allhusen v. Caristo Constr., 303 N.Y. 446, 103 N.E.2d 891, 37 ALR2d 1245 (1952); Rs. 2d § 317(2)(c) and cmt c; Rs. 1st § 151(c). However, the clause does not prohibit an assignment of a claim for damages for breach of contract. See Paley v. Cocoa Masonry, 433 So.2d 70 (Fla.App.1983).

5. Grady v. Commers Interiors, 268 N.W.2d 823 (S.D.1978); see § 18.14 supra.

Section 9–318(4) has adopted the rule that an anti-assignment clause is ineffective to prohibit the assignment of an "account"[6] and the 1999 revision continues and expands the ability of the creditor to assign despite attempted restrictions or hurdles.[7]

Thus, both Article 2 and Article 9 invalidate a clause that seeks to prevent the assignment of a right to the payment of money.[8] The Article 2 provision, however, covers only rights to payment that have been fully earned by performance, while Article 9 makes ineffective a prohibition of the right to payment whether or not the right has been fully earned. This appears to create a potential conflict. As one writer has stated, it appears that the two provisions "were drafted by different groups for different purposes."[9]

Article 2 of the UCC also contains a provision relating to interpretation of anti-assignment clauses. It provides that a clause in a sales contract prohibiting assignment of "the contract" should be, unless the circumstances indicate the contrary, construed as barring only the delegation of duties.[10] The Restatement has a provision in accord which has been followed by the courts,[11] but anti-assignment clauses in contracts between patients and their H.M.O.'s are generally upheld.[12]

Following the lead of the UCC, courts in the application of the common law are now tending to hold that anti-assignment clauses are ineffective unless the obligor has a legitimate interest in non-assignability.[13]

A provision *permitting* assignment, will be honored (except in the case of an illegal assignment)[14] even if the rights under the contract would be otherwise non-assignable.[15] However, very often a clause appears in a contract to the effect that the contract shall inure to the benefit of the heirs and assigns of the parties. Such a clause normally is not directed at the issue of assignability and unless there is some other manifestation of intent of assignability, it will not be taken into account on this issue.[16]

6. See Mississippi Bank v. Nickles & Wells Constr., 421 So.2d 1056 (Miss.1982). Account is defined in § 18.4 supra.

7. UCC § 9–406(d) (1999).

8. A right to damages for breach is assignable despite a broad anti-assignment clause. Folgers Architects v. Kerns, 262 Neb. 530, 633 N.W.2d 114 (2001).

9. Nordstrom, Sales § 45; Revised Article 9 and proposed revised Article 2 are more mindful of the problem of coordination.

10. UCC § 2–210(3); § 2–210(4) of the revision; Union Bond & Trust v. M & M Wood Working, 256 Or. 384, 474 P.2d 339 (1970).

11. Rs. 2d § 322(a); Bel–Ray v. Chemrite (Pty), Ltd., 181 F.3d 435 (3d Cir.1999); but see Riley v. Hewlett–Packard Co., 36 Fed.Appx. 194 (6th Cir.2002).

12. Somerset Orthopedic v. Horizon Blue Cross, 345 N.J.Super. 410, 785 A.2d 457 (A.D.2001) (collecting cases).

13. Wonsey v. Life Ins., 32 F.Supp.2d 939 (S.D.Mich.1998) (assignment of rights in a structured tort settlement); contra, Grieve v. American Life Ins., 58 F.Supp.2d 319 (D.Vt.1999) (legitimate interest found); cf. Rumbin v. Utica Mutual, 254 Conn. 259, 757 A.2d 526 (2000) (clause valid but violation does not void assignment).

14. See § 18.15 supra.

15. Washington Capitols Basketball Club v. Barry, 304 F.Supp. 1193 (N.D.Cal. 1969), aff'd (player's contract); see Rs. 2d § 323(1); Rs. 1st § 162(1); 3 Williston § 423 (3d ed.).

16. See Standard Chautauqua Sys. v. Gift, 120 Kan. 101, 242 P. 145 (1926); Paige

With some frequency, commercial leases, franchises, and other agreements will contain a clause forbidding assignment without the consent of the landlord, franchisor or other obligor. There is a growing trend to holding that consent cannot arbitrarily be withheld with impunity.[17]

E.   DEFENSES OF THE OBLIGOR

Table of Sections

§ 18.17   Defenses of the Obligor Against the Assignee

We saw in the previous chapter the general rule that a promisor may assert against a third party beneficiary any defense that the promisor could have asserted against the promisee.[1] A similar rule prevails here. The obligor may generally assert against the assignee the defenses the obligor could have asserted against the assignor.[2] For example, S and B enter into a contract for the sale and purchase of goods. S, before delivery, assigns the rights under the contract to T who gives notice of the assignment to B. S fails to deliver. In an action by T, B has the defense of non-performance.[3] The same rule applies to lack of consideration, illegality, Statutes of Frauds, incapacity, duress, or any other doctrine that makes the contract void, voidable or unenforceable.[4]

However, just as in a third party beneficiary context there is an exception under the doctrine of "vesting,"[5] a related exception exists in the area of assignments. An assignee is not bound by any defense resulting from an agreement reached between the obligor and the

---

v. Faure, 229 N.Y. 114, 127 N.E. 898, 10 ALR 649 (1920); Rs. 2d § 323 cmt b; but see Baum v. Rock, 106 Colo. 567, 108 P.2d 230 (1940).

17. Kendall v. Ernest Pestana, Inc., 40 Cal.3d 488, 495, 220 Cal.Rptr. 818, 822, 709 P.2d 837, 841 (1985) (in bank) ("A growing minority of jurisdictions now hold where a lease provides for assignment only with the prior consent of the lessor such consent may be withheld *only where the lessor has a commercially reasonable objection to the assignment.*") (court's emphasis); see Perillo, Abuse of Rights: A Pervasive Legal Concept 27 Pac. L.J. 37, 81 (1995); Note, 23 J.Corp.L. 135 (1997).

§ 18.17

1. See § 17.10 supra.

2. Fajen v. Powlus, 98 Idaho 246, 561 P.2d 388 (1977); McIntyre v. ILB Inv., 172 N.J.Super. 415, 412 A.2d 810 (1979); Citizens Fed. Bank v. Brickler, 114 Ohio App.3d 401, 683 N.E.2d 358 (1996) (unwritten modification). This is true even if the assignee did not know of the defenses at the time of assignment and even if the defenses came into existence subsequent to the assignment. UCC § 9–404(1999); James Talcott, Inc. v. H. Corenzwit & Co., 76 N.J. 305, 387 A.2d 350 (1978).

3. See Sponge Divers' v. Smith, Kline & French, 263 F. 70 (3d Cir.1920); First Inv. v. Andersen, 621 P.2d 683 (Utah 1980).

4. For an exception regarding fraudulently over-billing the government, see Note, 65 Harv.L.Rev. 1448 (1952).

5. See § 17.11 supra.

assignor or payment made to the assignor after the obligor has notice of the assignment.[6] Notice received by the obligor of the assignment vests the rights of the assignee in the sense that after notice the assignee's rights are not defeasible by agreement of the original contracting parties or by payment made by the obligor to the assignor.[7] Notice is not necessary to the validity of an assignment.[8] Although an assignment is effective without notice, the failure to give notice may destroy the rights of the assignee. The assigned rights will not vest. Therefore the assignee's rights can be destroyed by an agreement between the obligor and the assignor or payment by the obligor to the assignor

It should be stressed that the doctrine of vesting becomes relevant only when notice has been given and a defense is based on a subsequent agreement between the obligor and the assignor or payment made by the obligor to the assignor. For example, if S and B enter into a contract for the sale of goods and S assigns the rights under the contract to T who gives notice of the assignment, a subsequent modification of the agreement by S and B will not be effective against T.[9] To some extent this rule has been changed by Article 9.

In the illustration used in the first paragraph of this section, although notice vested T's rights, vesting is irrelevant because the defense is failure to perform and does not stem from an agreement between the obligor and the assignor or by payment made by the obligor to the assignor.

The UCC has several provisions that govern vesting. Some of these provisions continue the common law rules, others clarify them, and others make radical changes. Article 9 provides that the obligor may continue to pay the assignor until receipt of notice of the assignment and of the duty to pay the assignee.[10] This is in accord with the common law rule. The UCC has clarified the question of the kind of notice required.

6. Welch v. Mandeville, 14 U.S. (1 Wheat.) 233 (1816) (assignor may not release obligor after notice of the assignment); Credit General Ins. v. NationsBank, 299 F.3d 943 (8th Cir.2002); Terino v. LeClair, 26 A.D.2d 28, 270 N.Y.S.2d 51 (1966); Charlotte–Mecklenburg Hospital Auth. v. First of Georgia Ins., 340 N.C. 88, 455 S.E.2d 655 (1995), reh. denied (obligor may not pay assignor after notice of assignment);. Until receipt of notice, the obligor is free to deal with the assignor. See Van Keuren v. Corkins, 66 N.Y. 77 (1876) (payment after assignment of bond and mortgage, recording is not notice to obligor); Rs. 2d § 338(1); UCC § 9–406(a) (1999). A gratuitous release (one not supported by consideration or its equivalent, see § 21.10 infra) given by the assignor to the obligor even prior to notice does not affect the rights of the assignee unless the assignment is revocable or voidable, in which case the gratuitous release would revoke or avoid the assignment. See §§ 18.7 and 18.8 supra.

7. See Equilease v. State Federal S. & L., 647 F.2d 1069 (10th Cir.1981); Citizens & Southern Nat. Bank v. Bruce, 562 F.2d 590 (8th Cir.1977).

8. Broyles v. Iowa Dep't of Social Services, 305 N.W.2d 718 (Iowa 1981); Commonwealth v. Baldassari, 279 Pa.Super. 491, 421 A.2d 306 (1980).

9. See Brice v. Bannister, 3 Q.B.D. 569 (1878). This does not prevent the obligor and the assignor from making a new agreement if the assignor was guilty of a material breach.

10. UCC § 9–406(a) (1999). UCC § 1–201(25), and § 1–204 of the revision define notice. On the assignee's acquiescence to payments to the assignor after notification, see Abrams & Co. v. ITS Equip. and Leasing, 216 A.D.2d 503, 628 N.Y.S.2d 784 (1995).

First, the notice must "reasonably identify" the rights assigned.[11] Moreover, if requested by the obligor, the assignee must furnish proof that the assignment was made and failure to do so permits the obligor to pay the assignor.[12]

A significant change in the UCC from the common law is a provision that despite notification of the assignment to the obligor, the original contracting parties may agree to modify or substitute[13] the contract in good faith and in accordance with reasonable commercial standards, provided the assigned contract right has not been earned by full performance. The assignee is bound by the modification but acquires rights under the modified or substituted contract.[14] These provisions constitute a radical departure from the traditional common law rule. The drafters of the UCC obviously felt that the traditional common law rule on vesting was too rigid and not suited to the realities of commerce. However, the obligor and assignor can agree that a modification or substitution is a breach.[15]

An illustration of the UCC rule is furnished by a hypothetical case. A county contracted with C for the construction of a courthouse for the sum of $55,000,000. C assigned its rights under the contract to T, a bank, which agreed to extend to C a line of credit to be drawn on as C purchases supplies and pays subcontractors and workers. Because of complaints by its citizens, the county renegotiated the contract with C. The modification agreement called for a smaller courthouse at a price of $35,000,000. It would seem that the modification was made in good faith and according to reasonable commercial standards.[16] Thus, T's rights were effectively curtailed. T would have rights as assignee of the modified or substituted contract.[17] It should be noted that T was not injured by the change if it could locate other creditworthy borrowers at the same or higher rate of interest.

Since it is a general rule that the obligor may assert against the assignee any defense that the obligor can assert against the assignor, it is often stated that "an assignee stands in the shoes of the assignor."[18]

11. See UCC § 9–406(b) (1999); Uniform Commercial Credit Code § 3.406 (1968); National Consumer Act § 2.408; Bank of Salt Lake v. Corporation, 534 P.2d 887 (Utah 1975).

12. UCC § 9–406(c) (1999). On the question of bank deposits and commercial instruments, see also Rs. 2d § 339 cmt c.

13. It is generally believed that the words "modifying or substitute" include the concept of "termination." See Rs. 2d § 338 ill. 6.

14. UCC § 9–405(a) (1999); accord Rs. 2d § 338(2). For a detailed discussion, see Gilmore, The Assignee of Contract Rights and His Precarious Security, 74 Yale L.J. 217 (1964).

15. UCC § 9–405(a) (1999). The assignee becomes a third party beneficiary of the provision.

16. The general contractor may also make appropriate arrangements with subcontractors without getting the permission of the assignees of the subcontractor. Rs. 2d § 336(4); see Babson v. Ulysses, 155 Neb. 492, 52 N.W.2d 320 (1952).

17. There may be factual questions if a second contract is indeed a substituted contract or an entirely different arrangement. See FDIC v. Registry Hotel, 658 F.Supp. 311 (N.D.Tex.1986).

18. James Talcott, Inc. v. H. Corenzwit & Co., 76 N.J. 305, 387 A.2d 350 (1978); Pioneer State Bank v. Johnsrud, 284 N.W.2d 292 (N.D.1979); Aird Ins. Agency v.

The assignee has no better rights than the assignor.[19] This is another way of saying that, even if the assignee is a good faith purchaser for value, the assignee's rights are subject to the legal rights of third parties in the assigned rights.[20]

We have already seen that the doctrine of vesting is an exception to the general rule that the assignee stands in the shoes of the assignor.[21] There are other exceptions. One occurs under the ubiquitous doctrine of estoppel.[22] Suppose that A assigns and delivers a savings bankbook to C. In turn, C assigns to D, but D allows C to retain the book. The bank pays C in good faith before notice of assignment from D, but does not require surrender of the book. Subsequently, C assigns and delivers the book to E who is a bona fide purchaser for value. The bank is liable to E because of its failure to require production of a symbolic writing;[23] its failure to do so estops it from asserting its payment to C against E.[24] In addition, there are statutes under which an assignee may have greater rights than the assignor, for example, the real property recording acts.

Financial institutions are unhappy with the general rule that they are bound by the defenses that the consumer has against the retailer. One prominent branch of their business is the financing of retailers by lending on the security of their accounts receivable. One vehicle of escape from the general rule was the furnishing for use by retailers of a negotiable instrument to be signed by the customer. By use of such an instrument the financial institution could qualify as a holder in due course and thus under the law of negotiable instruments would be free of the customers' defenses.[25]

The financial institutions also devised another way to circumvent the rule that the obligor may assert against the assignee any defense that the obligor had against the assignor. They did this by having the retailer include in the contract with the consumer a provision that reads substantially as follows:

> "Buyer hereby acknowledges notice that the contract may be assigned and that the assignees will rely on the agreements contained in this paragraph, and agrees that the liability of the Buyer to

Zions First Nat. Bank, 612 P.2d 341 (Utah 1980).

19. See Fox–Greenwald Sheet Metal v. Markowitz Bros., 452 F.2d 1346 (D.C.Cir. 1971); Morse Electro Prods. v. Beneficial Indus. Loan, 90 Wn.2d 195, 579 P.2d 1341 (1978).

20. See Gilmore, The Commercial Doctrine of Good Faith Purchase, 63 Yale L.J. 1057 (1954); as to equitable, as opposed to legal, rights of third parties, see § 18.20.

21. See § 18.17 supra.

22. See Dimmitt & Owens Financial v. Realtek Indus., 90 Mich.App. 429, 280 N.W.2d 827 (1979).

23. On the meaning of "symbolic writings" see § 18.7 supra.

24. Assets Realization v. Clark, 205 N.Y. 105, 98 N.E. 457 (1912); see Rs. 2d § 338 cmt h and ill. 12.

25. If an instrument is negotiable and negotiated to a transferee (holder), the transferee will qualify as a holder in due course if the instrument is taken in good faith and without notice that it is overdue, or has been dishonored, or that there is a defense against it or claim to it. In that event the holder in due course takes free of personal defenses (e.g. breach of warranty) but subject to real defenses (e.g. illegality). See UCC §§ 3–302—3–305 (original and revised).

any assignee shall be immediate and absolute and not affected by any default whatsoever of the Seller signing this contract."[26]

If such a clause is valid, it would effectively eliminate the rule that the obligor may assert against the assignee any defense that the obligor has against the assignor; the rights of the assignee would resemble those of a holder in due course.[27] The argument in favor of the effectiveness of such a clause is the policy of freedom of contract. The argument on the other side is that it is unfair that the consumer must pay even though the consumer has a defense against the assignor and is particularly unfair where the assignor has become insolvent. There are jurisdictions that have held, as a common law proposition, that such clauses are invalid[28] but the majority of courts have sustained them.[29]

The UCC validates such "hell or high water" clauses where the assignee takes in good faith for value without notice of the defense but not with respect to defenses that would be denominated as real defenses to a negotiable instrument.[30] The UCC, however, subordinates this provision to any consumer protection law or decision.[31] There are statutes that make the waiver of defense clause a nullity;[32] others have provided that the buyer (obligor) may preserve defenses by giving notice within a specified time.[33]

Some decisions have held that when there is a close or continuing relationship between the assignor and the assignee, the assignee cannot claim to be in good faith and without notice of the obligor's defenses.[34]

The FTC has also addressed this problem. It has promulgated a rule that abolishes the holder in due course rule in the case of consumer paper and prohibits retail installment sales agreements, and leases that contain provisions destroying the consumer's rights against either the seller or the seller's assignee.[35] The rule applies only to a consumer, defined as "a natural person who seeks or acquires goods for personal, family, or household use." Thus, the rule would not protect a business obligor.

---

26. This is the language of the instrument in Unico v. Owen, 50 N.J. 101, 106, 232 A.2d 405, 408 (1967).

27. See note 25 supra.

28. Fairfield Credit v. Donnelly, 158 Conn. 543, 264 A.2d 547, 39 ALR3d 509 (1969); Quality Fin. v. Hurley, 337 Mass. 150, 148 N.E.2d 385 (1958); Motor Contract v. Van Der Volgen, 162 Wash. 449, 298 P. 705, 79 ALR 29 (1931).

29. See U.S. v. Troy-Parisian, 115 F.2d 224 (9th Cir.1940), cert. denied.

30. UCC § 9–403(b)(4) (1999); see Benedictine College v. Century Office Prods., 866 F.Supp. 1323 (D.Kan.1994). "Real defenses" are infancy, lack of legal capacity, duress, illegality, fraud in the factum, and discharge by reason of insolvency. See White & Summers § 14.10.

31. UCC § 9–403 (e) (1999).

32. See 1 CCH Consumer Credit Guide ¶ 4380 (1969).

33. See, e.g., UCCC. § 3.406 (1968); Nat. Consumer Act § 2.406; Model Consumer Credit Act § 2–601 (1973); Meyers v. Postal Fin., 287 N.W.2d 614 (Minn.1979).

34. See Rehurek v. Chrysler Credit, 262 So.2d 452, 54 ALR3d 1210 (Fla.App.1972), cert. denied; Massey–Ferguson v. Utley, 439 S.W.2d 57 (Ky.1969); Unico v. Owen, 50 N.J. 101, 232 A.2d 405 (1967); contra, Fidelity Bank v. Avrutick, 740 F.Supp. 222 (S.D.N.Y.1990); Murphy, Another "Assault Upon the Citadel": Limiting the Use of Negotiable Notes and Waiver-of-Defense Clauses in Consumer Sales, 29 Ohio St.L.J. 667 (1968).

35. See 16 C.F.R. 433.

§ 18.18 Defenses of the Assignor Against the Assignee

This topic has been covered in a number of prior sections—18.5, which relates to an assignment that contravenes the Statute of Frauds, gratuitous assignments (18.7), voidable assignments and conditional assignments of rights (18.8), and assignments of future rights (18.9). None of these sections involve a void assignment. However, it seems clear that, generally speaking, a void assignment should be governed by the rules relating to void contracts.[1]

F. COUNTERCLAIMS, SET OFF, AND RECOUPMENT

Table of Sections

§ 18.19 Counterclaims Against the Assignee

Section 18.17 discussed whether the obligor may assert against the assignee a defense that the obligor has against the assignor. Here, the same question is presented concerning counterclaims. Counterclaims are of two types—recoupment and set-off.[1]

A recoupment is a counterclaim that arises out of the assigned contract. The common law rule is that the obligor may use the assignor's breach against the assignee whether or not the claim arose prior to the notice of assignment.[2] The obligor's claim may only be used in diminution of the assignee's claim. That is, the obligor cannot use the claim to obtain a money judgment against the assignee,[3] unless the obligor has a claim of its own directly against the assignee.[4] The UCC is in accord.[5]

A counterclaim in the nature of a set-off involves a claim that does not arise out of the assigned agreement. It may arise out of another agreement between the same obligor and assignor. Before the UCC, this

§ 18.18

1. See §§ 1.08(b) & 4.12 supra.

§ 18.19

1. See First Nat. Bank v. Master Auto Service, 693 F.2d 308 (4th Cir.1982).

2. American Bridge v. Boston, 202 Mass. 374, 88 N.E. 1089 (1909); Cronkleton v. Hastings Theatre & Realty, 134 Neb. 168, 278 N.W. 144 (1938); Seibert v. Dunn, 216 N.Y. 237, 110 N.E. 447 (1915). The assignor's failure to perform would amount to a breach of warranty. See § 18.24 infra.

3. Rs. 2d § 336.

4. This could occur where the assignee has assumed the assignor's duty. See § 18.26 infra. Some cases hold that if the obligor pays the assignee before learning of the defense, the obligor is entitled to restitution even if the payment was negligent, provided the assignee has not changed position in reliance on the payment. Farmers Acceptance v. DeLozier., 178 Colo. 291, 496 P.2d 1016 (1972); contra, Irrigation Ass'n v. First Nat. Bank, 773 S.W.2d 346 (Tex.App. 1989).

5. UCC § 9–404(a)(1)(1999); see Fall River Trust v. B.G. Browdy, Inc., 346 Mass. 614, 195 N.E.2d 63 (1964) (remand to determine whether the counterclaim arose out of the same contract, or if from different contracts, to determine when was notice received); In re Calore Exp., 288 F.3d 22, 45 (1st Cir.2002).

topic was governed for the most part by statute. These statutes vary and in non-UCC cases must be taken into account. The UCC takes the position that if the set-off accrues before the obligor receives notice of assignment, it may be used against the assignee. Conversely, if the claim accrued after notice of the assignment, it may not be used.[6] Again, the obligor may only utilize the set-off by way of subtraction from the assignee's claim and may not obtain a judgment against the assignee for any excess over the assignee's claim.[7] The obligor may obtain a judgment against the assignee only if the obligor has an unrelated claim against the assignee.[8]

The UCC rules, adopted by the Restatement (Second), also apply to sub-assignees—that is, subsequent assignees of the original assignee.[9] The contrary rule of the original Restatement[10] was eliminated to bring the Restatement (Second) into harmony with the interpretation of the UCC.[11]

G.   OTHER POSSIBLE LIMITATIONS
ON THE ASSIGNEE'S RIGHTS

Table of Sections

§ 18.20   Latent Equities

A "latent equity" is an equity, not known by the assignee held by a party other than the obligor or the assignor. The issue is who owns the assigned right, the assignee or some third party. This in turn depends on whether the assignee's rights are subordinate to "latent equities."

An illustration will help clarify the discussion. A is obligated to B who, induced by C's fraud, assigns to C who then assigns to D who takes in good faith, for value and without notice of B's right to avoid the assignment to C. The question is whether or not D takes subject to B's latent equity.[1] The result depends on whether D qualifies as a purchaser for value. We have already seen that an assignee does not usually qualify

---

6.   UCC § 9–404(a)(2)(1999); accord Rs. 2d § 336(2). See Seattle–First Nat. Bank v. Oregon Pac. Indus., 262 Or. 578, 500 P.2d 1033 (1972).

7.   UCC § 9–404(b); Rs. 2d § 336 cmt d.

8.   The obligor's right to counterclaim on an unrelated transaction may be limited for trial convenience by procedural rules. See Rs. 2d § 336 cmt c.

9.   First New England Fin.v.Woffard 421 So.2d 590 (Fla.App.1982), interpreting former UCC § 9–318(1)(b) which is moved to § 9–404; Rs. 2d § 336 cmt e.

10.   Rs. 1st § 167(3).

11.   See Rs. 2d § 336 cmt e and Reporter's note.

§ 18.20

1.   Rs. 1st § 174.

as a purchaser for value.[2] The reason for this is that historically an assignee was looked on as having only an equitable right; to qualify as a purchaser for value one had to receive a legal title.[3] If this approach is followed, B will prevail.[4]

However, the modern approach is to consider an assignment as vesting a legal interest in the assignee. Under this approach, in the above illustration, D would qualify as a purchaser for value and defeat B's claim.[5]

§ 18.21 Priorities Between Successive Assignees

Suppose A assigns to B a right of payment of $1,000 that X owes to A. If A subsequently assigns the same right to C, who prevails?[1] A has obviously acted unlawfully in making the second assignment, and if solvent and brought to justice, can be made to pay for the wrongful act.[2] But, as between the two innocent assignees, there are essentially three views on the question of priority.

The English view is that as between successive assignees the last will prevail if this party is the first to give notice and acts without notice of any prior assignment and pays value.[3] The rule is designed to encourage assignees to give prompt notice to the obligor so that the obligor is in a position to answer inquiries as to who owns the claim. The failure to give such notice is looked on as negligence.[4] This would not be a satisfactory rule for the U.S. in the light of the very common use of non-notification financing here.

The New York rule gives priority to the first assignee. Under this rule, the first assignee may recover from the second assignee even if the second assignee, who the obligor has paid was the first to give notice.[5]

---

2. We have already seen that the assignee stands in the shoes of the assignor and that this means that the assignee does not qualify as a purchaser for value. See § 18.17 supra.

3. Holt v. American Woolen, 129 Me. 108, 150 A. 382 (1930); McClintock, Equity 69–71 (1948). As between two competing equities the rule is that prior in time is prior in right. Id. at 52. For "value" see § 18.7 supra.

4. See Owen v. Evans, 134 N.Y. 514, 31 N.E. 999 (1892). This view is strongly supported by 3 Williston § 447 (3d ed.), stating that it is supported by the weight of authority. See also 3 Williston § 438 (3d ed.). His policy rationale, stated in § 447, ("it is to be observed that intangible choses in action are not primarily intended for merchandising, as chattels are") is no longer an accurate statement of commercial practice.

5. See Glass v. Springfield L.I. Cemetery Soc'y., 252 A.D. 319, 299 N.Y.S. 244 (1937), appeal denied; Rs. 2d § 343; Rs. 1st § 174. Corbin describes this as the prevailing view. 4 Corbin § 900. See Comment, 20 U.Chi.

L.Rev. 692 (1953). This rule is not applied where the protection of the purchaser would impair the rights of the obligor. Rs. 2d § 343 cmt b.

§ 18.21

1. See generally, Axelrod, Successive Assignment—Conflicting Priorities, 14 U. Dayton L. Rev. 295 (1995).

2. See § 18.24 infra relating to the warranties of the assignor. The second assignment may even constitute larceny. People v. Schwartzman, 24 N.Y.2d 241, 299 N.Y.S.2d 817, 247 N.E.2d 642 (1969).

3. Graham Paper v. Pembroke, 124 Cal. 117, 56 P. 627 (1899); Anaconda Aluminum v. Sharp, 243 Miss. 9, 136 So.2d 585, 99 ALR2d 1307 (1962). On the meaning of "value" see § 18.7 supra.

4. Dearle v. Hall, 38 Eng.Rep. 475 (Ch. 1827).

5. Superior Brassiere v. Zimetbaum, 214 A.D. 525, 212 N.Y.S. 473 (1925). The recovery is quasi-contractual.

Under this rule, however, the obligor is discharged by payment to the second assignee.[6] The rationale of the New York rule is that, as between two competing claims of title, first in time is first in right.[7] It is based on the axiom, *"Nemo dat quod non habet"*—no one gives what one does not have. Having assigned once, there is nothing left for the assignor to assign.[8]

The Restatements have adopted an intermediate third view—the so called "Massachusetts" or "four horsemen" rule. Under this rule, the first assignee prevails unless a second assignee who pays value in good faith without notice (a) obtains payment from the obligor; (b) recovers judgment; (c) enters into a new contract with the obligor; or (d) receives delivery of a tangible token or writing, the surrender of which is required by the obligor's contract (a symbolic writing).[9] According to the Restatement (Second) the justification for the rule is that the second assignee takes a legal title and qualifies as a purchaser for value.[10] The rule relating to a symbolic writing is based on the doctrine of estoppel.[11]

Even in states that adopt the New York rule, which favors the first assignee, the second assignee will prevail under certain circumstances. One is where the first assignment was voidable or was a gratuitous uncompleted gift.[12] A second is, if the necessary elements of estoppel are present, the first assignee may be estopped from asserting priority as, for example, by failure to take possession of a symbolic writing.[13] Third, the second assignee may also prevail under certain statutes, as for example, the Real Property Recording Act. Finally, the same is true in the case of an assignment of a future right (except if the UCC applies) and the second assignment is legal and the assignee pays value and takes without notice.[14]

The problem of successive assignments is not extremely important in itself, since such conduct is rare. Yet there has been a highly dramatic side effect of the rule governing successive assignments. In Corn Exchange National Bank & Trust Co. v. Klauder, the U.S. Supreme Court ruled that assignments of accounts receivable in Pennsylvania, where the English rule prevailed, were not "perfected" liens within the protection of the Bankruptcy Act.[15] This was because it was possible that a second hypothetical assignee could, under the Pennsylvania law, obtain priority over the first assignee. This means that the first assignee was

---

6. This is because the obligor has not received notice from the first assignee. See § 18.20 supra.

7. Salem Trust v. Manufacturers' Fin., 264 U.S. 182, 31 ALR 867 (1924).

8. See note 5 supra.

9. Rs. 2d §§ 342, 332 cmt c; Rs. 1st § 173(b); see Rabinowitz v. People's Nat. Bank, 235 Mass. 102, 126 N.E. 289 (1920).

10. Rs. 2d § 342 cmt e.

11. Rs. 2d § 342 cmt f. As to symbolic writings, see § 18.7 and § 18.17 supra.

12. See McKnight v. Rice, Hoppner, Brown & Brunner, 678 P.2d 1330 (Alaska 1984); Rs. 2d § 342 cmt d; cf. Perkins v. City Nat. Bank, 253 Iowa 922, 114 N.W.2d 45 (1962).

13. See note 9 supra.

14. See § 18.20 supra.

15. 318 U.S. 434 (1943). The "four horsemen" rule, however, was held to perfect the assignment within the meaning of the Bankruptcy Act. In re Rosen, 157 F.2d 997 (3d Cir.1946), cert. denied.

not protected under the Bankruptcy Act and thus became an unsecured creditor. The legislative response was prompt and a majority of states enacted legislation to protect the security interest that the assignee received by virtue of the assignment. Some enacted the New York rule; some adopted a system of marking the debtor's books; others instituted a filing system.[16]

Against this background, the UCC provided for a filing system whereby notice of the assignment is filed in a public record office. However, as we have seen, certain outright assignments are excluded from the coverage of Article 9.[17] In addition, the filing provisions of Article 9 are inapplicable "to an assignment of accounts that does not alone or in conjunction with other assignments to the same assignee transfer a significant part of the outstanding accounts of the assignor."[18]

If the filing provision of Article 9 applies, as between two assignees for value, the one who first files a financing statement will prevail.[19] This allows a party to rely on the filing system. However, the assignment of an account excluded from Article 9 will be covered by the common law rules discussed above. Where the right assigned is covered by the UCC but is excluded from the filing provision of the UCC, the assignee's right is perfected without filing and thus the first assignee will prevail if the formalities described in § 18.5 are met.[20]

§ 18.22 Assignee Versus an Assignor's Attaching Creditor

An assignee clearly has rights superior to the general creditors of the assignor. A general creditor does not have a security interest in any property of the debtor. An assignee has a property interest in the right assigned. Thus, an assignee will almost always prevail over a general creditor. However, a general creditor may, in a variety of ways, obtain a security interest in specific property of the debtor. One of these ways is by attaching an asset of the debtor (obligor).

Assume that a creditor attaches the same right that has been assigned. If the creditor attached this right prior to the assignment, the attaching creditor has priority over the assignee.[1] The converse is usually true. An assignment that precedes an attachment will have priority over the attachment.[2]

---

16. The statutes are analyzed in Comment, 67 Yale L.J. 402 (1958).

17. See § 18.4 supra.

18. UCC §§ 9–109 & 9–110 (1999). See § 18.4 supra.

19. UCC § 9–322 (1999). This is true even if the second assignee has knowledge of the first assignment. This allows a party to rely on the filing system.

20. See UCC §§ 9–203, 9–309 & 9–310 (1999); Annot., 85 ALR3d 1050.

§ 18.22

1. Rs. 2d § 341(1).

2. Stathos v. Murphy, 26 A.D.2d 500, 276 N.Y.S.2d 727 (1966), aff'd; 4 Corbin § 903; 3 Williston § 434 (3d ed.). As to an assignment of future rights, see Harold Moorstein & Co. v. Excelsior Ins., 25 N.Y.2d 651, 254 N.E.2d 766, 306 N.Y.S.2d 464 (1969) (non-UCC); Parker Roofing v. Pacific First Fed. Sav. Bank, 59 Wn.App. 151, 796 P.2d 732 (1990) (UCC); § 18.21 supra.

The rule last stated, if absolute, could work to the prejudice of the debtor (obligor). It is therefore held that under certain circumstances the assignee is estopped from asserting priority.[3] The issue arises in relation to the failure of the assignee to give the obligor timely notice of the assignment.[4] There are two versions as to what is timely notice. One version bars the claim of the assignee unless the obligor receives notice in time to call the assignment to the attention of the court in the attachment proceeding and thus prevent a judgment in favor of the attaching creditor in those proceedings.[5] Other cases have held that even though judgment has been entered in the attachment proceedings in favor of the attaching creditor, the rights of the assignee will not necessarily be barred. For the assignee to prevail, two conditions must be met. The assignee must give notice to the obligor (debtor) prior to payment of the judgment entered as a result of the attachment proceedings. Second, under the applicable procedure, the *obligor* must still be able to use the assignment to defeat the claim of the attaching creditor.[6]

The UCC, to a large extent, resolves the priority problem discussed here by its filing system. Thus, if the assignment is of the kind that comes under the filing provisions, and the assignment is filed prior to the attachment, the assignment takes priority over the lien of the subsequent attachment.[7] Conversely, if the attachment arises before the filing occurs, the attaching creditor (lien creditor) will prevail.[8] If the assignment is governed by Article 9 but is excluded from the filing provisions of the UCC, the assignment is perfected without filing and thus the assignee will prevail over a subsequent lien creditor if the formalities described in § 18.5 are met.[9] If the assignment is excluded from Article 9, then the common law rules apply.

§ 18.23　Partial Assignments

At early common law, a partial assignment was unenforceable over the objection of the obligor because of the rule against splitting a cause of action.[1] Moreover, because procedure at law limited any suit to two parties, the obligor would be subject to multiplicity of suits.[2] In time, however, partial assignments were recognized in equity because the

---

3. Rs. 2d § 341 cmt b.

4. Since a creditor does not qualify as a purchaser for value by an attachment, the creditor can obtain priority over an assignee only by an estoppel or by the terms of a statute. Rs. 2d § 341 cmt a. However, an attaching creditor who is subsequent to an assignee will have superior rights if the assignment is terminable or voidable. Rs. 2d § 341 cmt b; cf. Rs. 1st § 172(1).

5. Rs. 1st § 172(2).

6. See McDowell, Pyle & Co. v. Hopfield, 148 Md. 84, 128 A. 742, 52 ALR 105 (1925); Goldfarb v. C & K Purchasing, 170 Misc. 90, 9 N.Y.S.2d 952 (1939); see also Rs. 2d § 341(2).

7. DuBay v. Williams, 417 F.2d 1277 (9th Cir.1969). In the terminology of the UCC, an attaching creditor is a "lien creditor." UCC § 9–102 (52) (1999).

8. UCC § 9–317(a)(2) (1999).

9. Id.

§ 18.23

1. Standard Discount v. Metropolitan Life Ins., 321 Ill.App. 220, 53 N.E.2d 27 (1944).

2. Andrews Elec. v. St. Alphonse Catholic Total Abstinence Soc'y, 233 Mass. 20, 123 N.E. 103 (1919).

obligor could join all of the partial assignees in one law suit.[3] Today, the majority view, often as a result of procedural codes, is that the equity rule applies not only in equity but also at law.[4] Thus, the partial assignee may sue at law provided that all of the interested parties have been joined, or the assignee complies with procedural rules that dispense with the necessity of joining other partial assignees because it is fair to do so under the circumstances.[5]

H. RIGHTS OF THE ASSIGNEE AGAINST THE ASSIGNOR

Table of Sections

Sec.
18.24 Warranties of the Assignor.

§ 18.24 Warranties of the Assignor

If the assignee has any rights against the assignor, it is likely to be on a warranty theory. What does an assignor warrant when making an assignment? The parties may agree that the assignment is without warranty.[1] If an express warranty is made, it will be enforced.[2]

If an assignment is for value,[3] and the parties are silent on the subject, three warranties are implied:[4] (1) the right exists and is subject to no defenses or limitations except as stated or apparent;[5] (2) the assignor will do nothing to defeat or impair the value of the assignment and has no knowledge of any fact that would do so; and (3) documents delivered as part of the transaction are genuine (not a forgery). The assignor does *not* warrant that the obligor is solvent or that the obligor will perform.[6] In the absence of a contrary manifestation of intention,

3. See National Exch. Bank v. McLoon, 73 Me. 498, 40 Am.Rep. 388 (1882); see also Annot., 80 ALR 413 (1932).

4. See Schwartz v. Horowitz, 131 F.2d 506 (2d Cir.1942); Zurcher v. Modern Plastic Mach., 24 N.J.Super. 158, 93 A.2d 778 (1952), aff'd; Prudential Fed. S. & L. v. Hartford Acc. & Indem., 7 Utah 2d 366, 325 P.2d 899 (1958); 4 Corbin § 889; cf. 3 Williston §§ 442–43 (3d ed.); Terino v. LeClair, 26 A.D.2d 28, 270 N.Y.S.2d 51 (1966) (obligor who continued to pay assignor after notice of the partial assignment held liable to the assignee); Clark v. New York, N.H. & H.R., 279 A.D. 39, 107 N.Y.S.2d 721 (1951) (specific performance of partial assignment of right to purchase land); contra, Space Coast Credit Union v. Walt Disney World, 483 So.2d 35 (Fla.App.1986) (not enforceable if obligor objects).

5. Staples v. Rush, 99 So.2d 502 (La. App.1957); In re Fine Paper Litigation, 632 F.2d 1081 (3d Cir.1980); Rs. 2d § 326(2).

§ 18.24

1. Brod v. Cincinnati Time Recorder, 82 Ohio App. 26, 77 N.E.2d 293 (1947); Rs. 2d § 333 cmt b.

2. Bradley Factor v. U.S., 86 F.Supp.2d 1140 (M.D.Fla.2000); Rs. 2d § 333(3).

3. Assignments "for value" and gratuitous assignments are distinguished in § 18.7 supra.

4. Lonsdale v. Chesterfield, 99 Wn.2d 353, 662 P.2d 385 (1983); Rs. 2d § 333(1); Rs. 1st § 175.

5. In the absence of a binding disclaimer, this warranty is violated if the obligor has a defense or a counterclaim against the assignor that may be used against the assignee. See §§ 18.17 and 18.19 supra.

6. Rs. 2d § 333; Rs. 1st § 175.

the express or implied warranties of an assignor do not run to a sub-assignee.[7]

I. DELEGATION

Table of Sections

§ 18.25   Introduction

We have already mentioned the importance of the distinction between assignment and delegation. Rights are assigned; duties are delegated.[1] When a right is assigned, the assignor ordinarily no longer has any interest in the claim.[2] When a duty is delegated, however, the delegating party (delegant) continues to remain liable.[3] If this were not so, every solvent person could obtain freedom from debts by delegating them to an insolvent. Delegation involves the appointment by the obligor-delegant of another to render performance on the obligor's behalf. It does not free the obligor-delegant from the duty to see to it that performance is rendered,[4] unless there is a novation.[5]

Although an obligor is not liable in respondeat superior for the negligence of independent contractors to whom the party has delegated contractual duties, the original obligor is liable to the other contracting party for work that is negligently performed.[6]

§ 18.26   Liability of the Delegate

The concept of delegation was touched on in Chapter 17—Third Party Beneficiaries. If A owes B $1,000 and C, for a consideration, agrees

---

7. Rs. 2d § 333(4).

§ 18.25

1. See § 18.1 supra.

2. See § 18.3 supra. If the assignment is revocable, voidable, unenforceable or conditional, the assignor retains some interest in the right assigned. Also, if the assignment is for security, the assignor retains an interest in the account. See §§ 18.6 to 18.9 supra.

3. Callon Petroleum v. Big Chief Drilling, 548 F.2d 1174 (5th Cir.1977), reh. denied; Epland v. Meade Ins. Agency, 564 N.W.2d 203 (Minn.1997); Cuchine v. H. O. Bell, Inc., 210 Mont. 312, 682 P.2d 723

(1984); Rosenberg v. Son, Inc., 491 N.W.2d 71 (N.D.1992); Baker v. Weaver, 279 S.C. 479, 309 S.E.2d 770 (1983).

4. UCC § 2–210(1) restates the common law when it says: "No delegation of performance relieves the party delegating of any duty to perform or any liability for breach." § 2–10(2)(a) restates the same language. See also 3 Williston § 419 (3d ed.); Rs. 1st § 160(4).

5. See §§ 18.26, 21.8 infra.

6. Gordon v. Sanders, 692 So.2d 939 (Fla.App.1997).

with A to assume that duty, there are a number of consequences that flow from the transaction. 1) There is a delegation of A's duty to C (the delegate) because A has appointed C to pay the money on A's behalf. 2) B is a third party beneficiary of the agreement between C and A.[1] 3) Since A continues to remain liable and C is liable to B under a third party beneficiary theory, it follows that B has a claim against both A and C but is entitled to only one satisfaction.[2] 4) The delegate (C) is not only liable to B on a third party beneficiary theory but is also liable to A because the promise to assume was made to A.[3] 5) A continues to remain liable in the absence of a novation.[4] A novation would occur if B discharged A in consideration of C's assumption of A's duty.[5]

In the above hypothetical, A delegates the duty and C, the delegate, assumes the duty. This is only one of the ways in which delegation can take place. Instead, A and C may agree that C's promise to A with respect to the delegated duty runs only to A and not to B, who then would at most be an incidental beneficiary of the promise.[6]

It is also possible for A to delegate the duty to C by giving C the option of performing the duty if C wishes. In such a case, C is liable to neither A nor B if C does not perform.[7]

In the illustration given at the beginning of this section, C *expressly* assumed A's duty. It is also possible to have an *implied* assumption of a duty by conduct. For example, in Epstein v. Gluckin,[8] the court held that the assignee of a right to purchase property, who had not assumed the duty at the time of the assignment, assumed it subsequently by bringing an action for specific performance. In a later case, the same court held that the purchaser of a building who has taken subject to a lease of air conditioners impliedly assumed the obligation by refusing to allow the lessor of air conditioners to remove them.[9]

§ 18.27   Problems of Interpretation

At times, it is unclear whether a party intends to assign rights or delegate duties or both.[1] The issue then becomes one of interpretation. A

---

§ 18.26

1. See § 17.6 supra.

2. See § 17.13 supra.

3. See § 17.14 supra.

4. See § 17.13 supra.

5. See § 17.13 supra and § 21.8 infra; Tony & Leo v. U.S. Fidelity and Guaranty, 281 N.W.2d 862 (Minn.1979). The assumption of a duty, standing alone, does not give rise to a novation. Mt. Wheeler Power v. Gallagher, 98 Nev. 479, 653 P.2d 1212 (1982). However, the original contract may provide that if the rights are assigned and the duties delegated, the assignment and delegation will discharge the assignor-delegant. Won's Cards v. Samsondale/Haverstraw Equities, 165 A.D.2d 157, 566 N.Y.S.2d 412 (1991).

6. Lewis v. Boehm, 89 Wn.App. 103, 947 P.2d 1265 (1997); see §§ 17.2–17.3 supra; 4 Corbin §§ 779D, 779E.

7. Rs. 2d § 318 cmt b; Rs. 1st § 160(2).

8. 233 N.Y. 490, 135 N.E. 861 (1922); cf. Kneberg v. H. L. Green Co., 89 F.2d 100 (7th Cir.1937) (no implied assumption where assignee sues for restitution).

9. Conditioner Leasing v. Sternmor Realty, 17 N.Y.2d 1, 266 N.Y.S.2d 801, 213 N.E.2d 884 (1966), rearg. denied; cf. Fleming v. Wineberg, 253 Or. 472, 455 P.2d 600 (1969).

§ 18.27

1. Where there is both an assignment of a right and a delegation of a duty, a word on terminology is in order. Assume that S

common question of interpretation arises when a party to a bilateral contract uses general language such as, "I assign this contract," or "all my rights under this contract." Although the question should be treated as a question of interpretation of the language in the light of the particular circumstances of the case,[2] it has frequently been treated as if it were governed by the mechanics of *stare decisis*.

While some courts have adhered to the rule that such phraseology creates merely an assignment of rights,[3] a more modern view is that the probable intention is to create not only an assignment of rights but also a delegation and assumption of duties.[4] The sales article of the UCC adopts the latter presumption.[5] The presumption can, of course, be overcome if the language or the circumstances indicate the contrary.[6] For example, if the assignment is for security, the circumstances would rebut the presumption.[7]

§ 18.28   Non-delegable Duties

Just as some rights cannot be assigned, some duties are not delegable. Again the modern law has come a long way from the era when contractual relations were deemed strictly personal. *Delectus Personae* was the Law Latin catch phrase to indicate that a party had a right to choose the persons with whom to deal. Today, however, the general proposition is that, subject to exceptions, duties are delegable.

A duty is non-delegable where performance by the delegate would vary materially from performance by the obligor.[1] The test is whether

promises to deliver goods to B in exchange for B's promise to pay $1,000, and S assigns the right to payment and delegates the duties to T. When S assigns rights, S is the assignor and T is the assignee. B is the obligor because B has the duty of paying $1,000. As to S's duty to deliver the goods, S is the delegant, and T is the delegate. In this phase of the transaction, B is often referred to as "the other party." See also § 18.31 infra.

2. This was admirably done in Chatham Pharmaceuticals v. Angier Chemical, 347 Mass. 208, 196 N.E.2d 852 (1964).

3. Loegler v. C. V. Hill & Co., 238 Ala. 606, 193 So. 120 (1940); Pumphrey v. Kehoe, 261 Md. 496, 276 A.2d 194 (1971); Meyer v. Droegemueller, 165 Minn. 245, 206 N.W. 391 (1925); State ex rel. Hoyt v. Shain, 338 Mo. 1208, 93 S.W.2d 992 (1936); Langel v. Betz, 250 N.Y. 159, 164 N.E. 890 (1928). See generally Grismore, Is the Assignee of a Contract Liable for the Non-Performance of Delegated Duties? 18 Mich. L.Rev. 284 (1920), Selected Readings 802; 4 Corbin § 906; 3 Williston § 418A (3d ed.).

4. Nofziger Communications v. Birks, 757 F.Supp. 80 (D.D.C.1991); Newton v. Merchants & Farmers Bank, 11 Ark.App.

167, 668 S.W.2d 51 (1984); Rose v. Vulcan Materials, 282 N.C. 643, 194 S.E.2d 521, 67 ALR3d 1 (1973). See Art Metal Constr. v. Lehigh Structural Steel, 116 F.2d 57 (3d Cir.1940), after trial it was found as a fact that no assumption was intended. 126 F.2d 134 (3d Cir.1942) cert. denied; Rs. 1st § 164. The Rs. 2d § 328, which is generally in accord, points out, however, that the overwhelming weight of authority in land contract cases is in accord with Langel v. Betz, supra note 3, and refrains from taking any position with respect to land contracts. For a rationalization of an exception for land contracts see Rs. 2d § 328 cmt c.

5. UCC § 2–210(4); accord, § 2–210 (3) of the revision & Rs. 2d § 328; see DiMatteo Depersonalization of Personal Services Contracts, 27 Akron L.Rev. 407 (1994).

6. UCC § 2–210(4); § 2–210(3) of the revision.

7. UCC § 2–210 cmt 5; § 2–210(3) of the revision is explicit.

§ 18.28

1. Overseas Development Disc v. Sangamo Constr., 686 F.2d 498 (7th Cir.1982); Boswell v. Lyon, 401 N.E.2d 735 (Ind.App.

performance by the delegating party (delegant), or under this party's personal supervision, has been bargained for.[2] The UCC expresses the same thought in the following language: "A party may perform his [or her] duty through a delegate * * * unless the other party has a substantial interest in having his [or her] original promisor perform or control the acts required by the contract."[3] The same formulation is found in the Restatement (Second).[4]

The test is necessarily imprecise. Equally imprecise is a phrase that is often used—"a personal service contract."[5] The phrase implies that the "other party" to the contract relies on the personality of the delegant and that therefore any attempted delegation is improper. Personality comprises many ingredients including honesty, skill, reputation, character, ability, wisdom and taste.[6] Thus, if the contract is premised on the artistic skill or unique abilities of a party, the duties are not delegable. Clearly, there is no objective standard by which the performance of the delegate can be determined to be the equivalent of the delegant's if the performance is to paint a portrait[7] or to produce an entertainment.[8] Also non-delegable are duties that involve a close personal relationship, such as the duties owed by an attorney to a client,[9] or a physician to a patient.[10] In addition it is often held that a party to a contract who has expressly or impliedly promised to act in "good faith" or to use "best efforts" may not delegate that duty even though the duty might otherwise be delegable.[11]

There are several categories of performances that generally are deemed to be delegable. It is generally held that duties under a construction contract are delegable, because it is contemplated that the work will be performed by a person other than the obligor. This result has been based on the well-known custom of general contractors to delegate to

---

1980); Devlin v. New York, 63 N.Y. 8 (1875); Rs. 1st § 160.

2. Devlin v. New York, 63 N.Y. 8 (1875).

3. UCC § 2–210(1); accord, § 2–210(a) of the revision.

4. Rs. 2d §§ 318(2) and 319(2).

5. Loftus v. American Realty, 334 N.W.2d 366 (Iowa App.1983).

6. 4 Corbin § 866.

7. See Taylor v. Palmer, 31 Cal. 240 (1866) ("[a]ll painters do not paint portraits like Sir Joshua Reynolds, nor landscapes like Claude Lorraine, nor do all writers write dramas like Shakespeare or fiction like Dickens. Rare genius and extraordinary skill are not transferable, and contracts for their employment are therefore personal, and cannot be assigned [correction, delegated]. But rare genius and extraordinary skill are not indispensable to the workmanlike digging down of a sand hill or the filling up of a depression to a given level, or the construction of brick sewers with manholes and covers, and contracts for such work are not personal, and may be assigned [delegated])."

8. Standard Chautauqua Sys. v. Gift, 120 Kan. 101, 242 P. 145 (1926). A song publisher's duties to publish and promote a song have, however, been held to be delegable. Nolan v. Williamson Music, 300 F.Supp. 1311 (S.D.N.Y.1969), aff'd 499 F.2d 1394 (2d Cir.1974).

9. Corson v. Lewis, 77 Neb. 446, 109 N.W. 735 (1906); In re Zacoum's Estate, 115 N.Y.S.2d 42 (1952). Delegation without client consent would also violate disciplinary rules. See Perillo, The Law of Lawyers' Contracts is Different, 67 Fordham Law Review 443, 460–66 (1998).

10. Kovacs v. Freeman, 957 S.W.2d 251 (Ky.1997) (surgery performed by substitute constitutes battery); Deaton v. Lawson, 40 Wash. 486, 82 P. 879 (1905).

11. Sally Beauty v. Nexxus Products, 801 F.2d 1001 (7th Cir.1986); Wetherell Bros. v. U.S. Steel, 200 F.2d 761 (1st Cir. 1952).

subcontractors.[12] Similarly, duties under other contracts calling for mechanical skills that can be tested by objective standards are generally delegable,[13] at least where it is not contemplated that a given individual perform or supervise the work.[14] A seller's duty to deliver goods is also generally delegable.[15]

A duty to pay money is delegable. It is immaterial if the delegate is less creditworthy than the delegant because the delegant continues to remain liable.[16] If, however, one of the duties sought to be delegated is the execution of a promissory note or other instrument of credit, the delegation is ineffective[17] unless the delegate is willing and able to tender cash in place of the instrument of the delegant (delegating party).[18]

It has been intimated that the duty of a corporation is always delegable because a corporation's performance necessarily involves a delegation of duties to individuals.[19] This is too broad a statement. It is possible to conceive of a contract with a corporation under which the basis of the bargain is the personal performance of particular individuals within the corporate structure and delegation to another corporation or person would be ineffective. For example, a corporation producing motion pictures for a distribution company could not delegate its duties to another corporation producing motion pictures if the effect of the delegation is to deprive the other party to the contract of the contemplated performance of famous "stars," directors, or key figures within the delegating corporation's structure.[20]

If the delegant has a right or a duty to control or supervise the performance of the delegate, this may, in a close case, lead to a decision in favor of delegability.[21] Conversely, if the delegant goes out of business, this will ordinarily lead to the conclusion that the duty is non-delegable.[22] In such a case, the delegant is no longer in a position to supervise. This may also lead to a situation where the delegant, who is still liable despite the delegation, is no longer in a position to fulfill that obligation.[23]

---

12. New England Iron v. Gilbert El. R.R., 91 N.Y. 153 (1883); 4 Corbin § 865.

13. Devlin v. New York, 63 N.Y. 8 (1875) (duty to clean streets); British Waggon v. Lea & Co., 5 Q.B.D. 149 (1880) (duty to keep railway cars in repair).

14. Rs. 2d § 318 cmt c and ill. 7; Swarts v. Narragansett Elec. Lighting, 26 R.I. 388, 59 A. 77 (1904), reh. denied; Johnson v. Vickers, 139 Wis. 145, 120 N.W. 837 (1909).

15. UCC § 2–210(1); accord, § 2–210(2)(a) of the revision.

16. See § 18.25 supra.

17. E. M. Loews v. Deutschmann, 344 Mass. 765, 184 N.E.2d 55 (1962).

18. Cochran v. Taylor, 273 N.Y. 172, 7 N.E.2d 89 (1937); as to option contracts, see § 18.32 infra.

19. New England Iron v. Gilbert Elev. R.R., 91 N.Y. 153, 167 (1883).

20. CNA Int'l Reinsurance v. Phoenix, 678 So.2d 378 (Fla.App.1996); cf. Emerald Christmas Tree v. Bedortha, 66 Or.App. 425, 674 P.2d 76 (1984). But see N.Y. Bank Note v. Hamilton Bank Note Engraving & Printing, 180 N.Y. 280, 73 N.E. 48 (1905); Note, 74 Harv.L.Rev. 393 (1960).

21. Arnold Prods. v. Favorite Films, 298 F.2d 540 (2d Cir.1962).

22. New England Cabinet Works v. Morris, 226 Mass. 246, 115 N.E. 315 (1917).

23. Wetherell Bros. v. U.S. Steel, 200 F.2d 761 (1st Cir.1952); N.Y. Bank Note v. Hamilton Bank Note Engraving & Printing, 180 N.Y. 280, 293, 73 N.E. 48, 52 (1905). Both cases involve the liquidation of a corporation. This situation is quite similar to

A delegation of particular duties may be prohibited by statute, a rule, or by public policy.[24] In addition, the contract itself may contain a provision against delegation. In contrast with rules favoring free alienation of rights that limit the validity of clauses purporting to prohibit assignments,[25] there seems to be no restriction on the parties' ability to provide in their contract that duties are non-delegable.[26] Once more, it should be recalled that it is common for contract draftsmen to utilize the word "assignment" where "delegation" is meant. Taking notice of this proclivity, the UCC provides: "Unless the circumstances indicate the contrary, a prohibition of assignment of 'the contract' is to be construed as barring only the delegation to the assignee of the assignor's performance."[27]

§ 18.29 Attempted Delegation of a Non-delegable Duty

If the delegant delegates a delegable duty to a delegate and the delegate performs, the duty of the delegant will be discharged. This also implies that the other party must accept the performance of the delegate and that a refusal to do so is a repudiation.[1]

However, if the duty is non-delegable, the other party may refuse to proceed. This does not mean that the attempted delegation of a non-delegable duty amounts to a repudiation. In legal effect, an attempted delegation of a non-delegable duty amounts to nothing more than an offer to waive non-delegability.[2] This offer will be accepted if the other party assents, as for example, by dealing with the delegate. If the other party refuses to accept the offer and the delegant refuses to honor the contract unless the other party assents to the delegation, the delegant is guilty of a repudiation.[3] If the other party consents to the delegation, this consent, standing alone, does not result in a novation.[4]

the cases discussed in § 18.30 infra, where the delegating party repudiates. However this rule may not apply to a transaction that amounts to a consolidation or a merger or where the purchasing corporation is merely a continuation of the selling corporation. Fisher v. Berg, 158 Wash. 176, 290 P. 984 (1930); see § 18.16 n.3 supra.

24. Rs. 2d §§ 318(1), 319(1); Rs. 1st § 160(3)(b).

25. See § 18.16 supra.

26. UCC § 2–210(1) accord § 2–210(2)(d) of the revision & Rs. 2d §§ 318(1), 319(1); Rs. 1st § 160(3)(c). They may also provide that the duties are delegable. Baum v. Rock, 106 Colo. 567, 108 P.2d 230 (1940). However, a routine provision to the effect

that a party's successor is bound by the contract does not make a duty delegable. Standard Chautauqua Sys. v. Gift, 120 Kan. 101, 242 P. 145 (1926). There is a similar rule with respect to assignments of rights. See § 18.16 supra.

27. UCC § 2–210(3); accord, § 2–210 (4) of the revision. Rs. 2d § 322(a).

§ 18.29

1. Devlin v. New York, 63 N.Y. 8 (1875).

2. 4 Corbin § 867.

3. American Colortype v. Continental Colortype, 188 U.S. 104 (1903); Rs. 2d § 329(2).

4. Clark v. General Cleaning, 345 Mass. 62, 185 N.E.2d 749 (1962).

§ 18.30   Effect of Repudiation by Delegating Party

In the preceding section, we saw that an attempted delegation of a non-delegable duty does not amount to an offer of novation.[1] Here, the question is whether a repudiation by the delegating party may amount to an offer of novation.

When the delegating party delegates a duty, the delegant's liability continues unless there is a discharge by the other party in consideration of the delegate's assumption of the delegant's duty.[2] That would be a novation. But what if the delegating party delegates a duty and asserts that his or her liability is now at an end? For example, A and B enter into a bilateral contract. B delegates the duties to C who agrees to assume B's duties. B then tells A to look solely to C for performance. B's statement has been regarded as an offer of novation—an offer to A to substitute the liability of C for that of B,[3] although a better analysis would describe the statement as an immaterial breach that ripens into a repudiation if persisted in. A need not accept the supposed offer. If A does not accept and B insists on the position of non-liability, B becomes guilty of a repudiation.[4]

But what if A deals with C with knowledge of the delegation and opportunity to reject performance? There is substantial authority to the effect that B's offer of novation has been accepted when A deals with C.[5] But even if this is a logical approach, it seems unfair that B should be released by B's own repudiation when there is no actual agreement to release B. The logic of the approach stems from the faulty premise that a repudiation constitutes an offer rather than a breach. The Restatements have softened the rigor of this regrettable rule by indicating that A may defeat the occurrence of a novation by notifying either B or C of an intention to retain the contract rights.[6]

§ 18.31   Assignment Coupled with Delegation

This chapter first discussed assignments and later, delegation. In many cases, however, a transaction will do both, simultaneously assigning rights and delegating duties under the contract. This section is designed to show how such a situation should be approached. This will be done by analyzing a number of concrete cases. In addition, some questions not previously mentioned will be introduced into the discussion. In this discussion the terminology used is based on Section 18.1 supra.

§ 18.30

1. Crane Ice Cream v. Terminal Freezing & Heating, 147 Md. 588, 128 A. 280, 39 ALR 1184 (1925).

2. See § 18.26 supra.

3. See § 18.26 supra.

4. Consolidated Edison v. Charles F. Guyon, Inc., 98 A.D.2d 483, 471 N.Y.S.2d 269 (1984); 4 Corbin § 870; 3 Williston § 420 (3d ed).

5. Western Oil Sales v. Bliss & Wetherbee, 299 S.W. 637 (Tex.Com.App.1927). A similar problem arises when the delegating party is a corporation and is dissolved. See § 18.28 nn.23, 24 supra; 4 Corbin § 865. As to the effect of the insolvency of the assignor, see UCC § 2–609; 3 Williston § 420 (3d ed.); 6 Williston § 880 (3d ed.).

6. Rs. 2d § 329(2) & cmt c; Rs. 1st § 165.

In a well-known case,[1] defendant (Pizza) entered into an arrangement with Virginia Coffee under which Virginia was to supply cold-drink vending machines to defendant's pizza parlors. Virginia also agreed to keep machines in good repair and stocked with merchandise and to pay a percentage of income to Pizza. During the term of the contract, Virginia assigned its rights and delegated its duties to the plaintiff, Macke. When this occurred, defendant terminated the contract. It argued that the duty was non-delegable.

The first step to take in analyzing such a case is to determine the rights and duties of Virginia. Here, Virginia's rights were to install machines on Pizza's premises and to get the proceeds. These rights, are assignable.[2] Virginia's duty was to install and leave the machines, stock them with merchandise, make repairs and pay a percentage of the gross to Pizza. Thus, the issue is whether these duties are delegable.

The court stated the issue to be whether this was "a personal service contract"[3] and concluded that it was not, since the duties of Virginia were mechanical in nature and performance by Macke was not significantly different from performance by Pizza.[4] This conclusion was not changed by the fact that Pizza had dealt with Macke before and had chosen Virginia because Pizza liked the way in which Virginia did business.[5] Macke prevailed because Pizza's termination of the contract was a repudiation.[6]

The court also mentioned UCC § 2–210(5). This section, which has not previously been discussed,[7] provides that the "other party may treat any assignment which delegates performance as creating reasonable grounds for insecurity and may without prejudice to his [or her] rights against the assignor demand assurances against the assignee." There is no requirement, however, in the statute that "the other party" must proceed by way of demanding assurances. Presumably, the "other party" (Pizza) could also demand assurances under the general provision granting the right to demand and receive assurances.[8] Pizza made no demand against either the assignor or the assignee.

In another case,[9] plaintiff entered into a contract with the defendant, Bates Studio, for dance lessons. Bates, assigned its rights and delegated its duties to the Dale Studio. Again, we must differentiate the rights from the duties. Bates' right was to receive money and this right is normally assignable. The duty was to give dance lessons. Again the

---

§ 18.31

1. Macke Co. v. Pizza of Gaithersburg, 259 Md. 479, 270 A.2d 645 (1970).

2. See § 18.11 supra.

3. See § 18.28 supra.

4. See § 18.28 supra.

5. This seems to be the generally accepted view. C.H. Little Co. v. Cadwell Transit, 197 Mich. 481, 163 N.W. 952 (1917). An opposite view was reached by the much criticized case of Boston Ice v. Potter, 123 Mass. 28, 25 Am.Rep. 9 (1877). In determining the issue of delegability, the nature of the duty is important. However, in some cases the "personality" of the delegant is also important. See § 18.28 supra.

6. It should be recalled that an attempt to delegate a non-delegable duty amounts only to an offer to waive the non-delegability, or, more accurately, an immaterial breach. However, if the delegant persists in the delegation after the other party refuses, there is a repudiation. See § 18.29 supra.

7. We, however, previously discussed UCC § 2–609 (demanding assurances) as it relates to assignments. See § 18.14 supra. The UCC Section quoted in the text is in the revision as 2–210(2)(d).

8. UCC § 2–609 (stylistic changes in the revision); see § 12.2 supra.

9. Seale v. Bates, 145 Colo. 430, 359 P.2d 356 (1961).

question is whether this duty was delegable. This court again inquires whether this was a "personal service contract" and concludes that it was. Therefore, the plaintiff was not required to take lessons from Dale. Bates would have been guilty of a repudiation if it continued to insist on the delegation of this non-delegable duty. Moreover, the assignment which was coupled with an improper delegation would also have failed; plaintiff would have had no obligations to the assignee.

However, after the delegation, the plaintiff took lessons for a period of time at the Dale Studios. According to the court, this amounted to a waiver of non-delegability and thus plaintiff was bound to continue to take lessons from Dale.[10] However, there was no novation and Bates continued to remain liable.[11]

A case that shows the importance of clearly distinguishing between rights and duties is Paige v. Faure.[12] The defendant gave Paige and Linder, jointly, an exclusive agency in return for their promise of best efforts to promote the defendant's product. Subsequently Linder assigned his rights and delegated his duties under the contract to Paige. The court held the assignment ineffective stating broadly: "Rights arising out of a contract cannot be transferred if they are coupled with liabilities."[13] The court's reasoning was defective because, as we have seen in the cases above, the assignment of an assignable right is not rendered ineffective even if it is coupled with the delegation of a duty if the duty is delegable. Here the duty was non-delegable, at least in part, because of the duty to use "best efforts."[14] The more accurate generalization would have been "rights arising out of a contract cannot be transferred if the transfer is coupled with the delegation of non-delegable duties."[15]

The cases discussed thus far have related primarily to issues of delegation of duties. Let us discuss one case that can be discussed in terms of assigning rights. The defendant, Sisco, entered into a contract of employment with Gas & Chemicals.[16] The employment contract contained a provision that the employee would not compete with the employer within a 50–mile radius for 5 years after the termination of the contract. A provision permitted the employer to terminate the contract by giving 30 days notice. Gas & Chemicals assigned its rights and delegated its duties to the plaintiff, Empire Gas. The plaintiff, relying on

---

10. See § 18.30 supra.

11. See § 18.30 supra.

12. 229 N.Y. 114, 127 N.E. 898 (1920).

13. 229 N.Y. at 118, 127 N.E. at 899 (1920).

14. See § 18.28 supra (if there is a duty to act in "good faith" or to use "reasonable efforts," a court will often hold the duty to be non-delegable).

15. E.g., Arkansas Valley Smelting v. Belden Mining, 127 U.S. 379 (1888) (contract for the purchase of ore not assignable

when coupled with the delegation of the purchaser's obligation to pay upon the purchaser's assay of the value of the ore).

16. Sisco v. Empiregas, 286 Ala. 72, 237 So.2d 463 (1970); see Eisner Computer Sol. v. Gluckstern, 293 A.D.2d 289, 741 N.Y.S.2d 511 (2002); cf. Cooper v. Gidden, 515 So.2d 900 (Miss.1987) (assignment of a covenant not to compete attached to the sale of a business).

the non-competition clause, sought to enjoin Sisco from working for a new employer.

Could Gas & Chemicals effectively assign its rights to Sisco's services to Empire?[17] The court held that the contract was a personal service contract and therefore, non-assignable. However, it did not say that a right to an employee's services is never assignable.[18] It pointed out the significance of the coupling of the non-competition clause coupled with the notice of termination provision.[19]

Thus, it would appear that the employee would prevail. However, Sisco worked for Empire for a period of time after the improper assignment. The court said that this gave rise to the possibility that Sisco consented to and adopted the assignment, or that as a result of Sisco's continued work, Empire entered into a contract that contained all of the terms of the contract between Sisco and the original employer. The same thought could possibly be expressed by saying that there was a waiver of the right's non-assignability. The same type of problem arose in Seale v. Bates (the dance studio case) except in that case the issue was delegation rather than assignment.

Some cases hold that the right to an employee's services may be assigned even if the contract contains a non-competition clause.[20] The factual setting of each case is all important, and includes whether the assignee is in a loose sense an *alter ego* of the assignor, as for example as a result of a consolidation or a merger.[21]

§ 18.32 Option Contracts: Assignment and Delegation

An offer can be accepted only by the person or persons to whom it is made.[1] It follows that an offer is not assignable. This prohibition is based, at least in part, on the notion that everyone has the privilege of choosing with whom to contract.[2] This is true whether the offer looks to a bilateral or a unilateral contract, and even though the offeree is only to pay money. Thus, if A offers to sell a car to B for $25,000, the offer

17. Some cases would have asked whether Gas & Chemicals could delegate its duty of supervision. There is no question that the duty to pay wages could be delegated.

18. Compare Sevier Ins. Agency v. Willis Carroon Corp., 711 So.2d 995 (Ala.1998) (successor corporation can enforce non-solicitation agreement); see DiMatteo Depersonalization of Personal Services Contracts, 27 Akron L.Rev. 407 (1994).

19. The court reasoned that no employee would sign such an agreement without having great trust and confidence in the employer. Also, Sisco had worked for this employer for a period of time before signing this contract.

20. Torrington Creamery v. Davenport, 126 Conn. 515, 12 A.2d 780 (1940); Sickles

v. Lauman, 185 Iowa 37, 169 N.W. 670, 4 ALR 1073 (1918).

21. But see Evening News v. Peterson, 477 F.Supp. 77 (D.D.C.1979) where it was held that the services of a newscaster-anchorman were assignable even though the new owner was not an alter ego of the delegant. See also Munchak Corp. v. Cunningham, 457 F.2d 721 (4th Cir.1972); 4 Corbin § 865. Notice the similar problem with respect to delegation. See § 18.28 supra.

§ 18.32

1. See § 2.14 supra.

2. This privilege is not absolute. Antitrust and civil rights legislation forbid some discriminatory refusals to deal.

cannot be accepted by C. But once an offer has ripened into a contract, the rights created are usually assignable.[3]

This seeming anomaly is at least partially explainable. An assignor by an assignment divests rights, but one cannot unilaterally divest duties. While a person may sometimes delegate duties, the delegant remains liable for their due performance.[4] The other contracting party is thus not deprived of having the right to enforce the contract against the person whose credit and reputation were relied on in entering into the contract.[5]

In discussing the assignability of an option contract it must be recalled that an option contract gives the optionee the option of accepting or rejecting the terms of the underlying offer.[6] Whether the optionee may assign the rights in the underlying contract to a third party depends on a number of factors including whether the underlying contract is unilateral or bilateral.[7] Suppose A offers to sell property to B in exchange for B's promise to pay $100,000. A asks B for $1,000 to keep the offer open for 10 days, which B pays, creating an option contract. The offer in the underlying contract is an offer looking to a bilateral contract and can be accepted only by B's promise. If B does not make the promise, there is no possibility of the underlying contract being effectively assigned. A is entitled to B's promise because A relied on B's credit.[8] If B makes that promise, then the right to receive a deed would be assignable and the duty to pay money would be delegable.[9]

The situation is obviously different if the underlying contract is unilateral. Here, B need not make a promise in order to make any attempted assignment effective. The only issues are whether the right is assignable and whether the act of acceptance is delegable. Let us assume that A promised to convey on receipt of $10,000 within 10 days and $100 was paid to keep the offer open, and B assigned the right to purchase and delegated the conditional duty to pay to C. B's right is still assignable. B has no unconditional duty because B has the option of buying or not buying. The question, then, is not whether the *duty* is delegable but rather whether the *act of acceptance* is delegable. The rules as to delegability are the same in this situation as when B is under a duty.[10]

3. See § 18.10 supra. Thus, even if an option contains a valid anti-assignment clause, the optionee can accept and assign the newly created contract rights. LG & E Capital v. Tenaska VI, 289 F.3d 1059 (8th Cir.2002).

4. See § 18.25 supra.

5. This rule also explains the liability of an agent for an undisclosed principal. See Seavey, Agency § 123 (1964). However, it does not explain why an offer is not assignable if all that is required of the offeree is payment in cash.

6. See § 2.25 supra.

7. 1 Corbin § 3.3.

8. 1 Corbin § 3.3; see also Rs. 2d § 152 and cmt a; Rs. 1st § 155.

9. Another issue is whether the parties intended the option to be limited to the optionee. Masterson v. Sine, 68 Cal.2d 222, 65 Cal.Rptr. 545, 436 P.2d 561 (1968); Campbell v. Campbell, 313 Ky. 249, 230 S.W.2d 918 (1950). A right of first refusal is assignable, Kennedy v. Dawson, 296 Mont. 430, 989 P.2d 390 (1999), but was not properly assigned in First Illinois Nat. Bank v. Knapp, 246 Ill.App.3d 152, 185 Ill.Dec. 780, 615 N.E.2d 75 (1993).

10. See § 18.28.

On the other hand if B was to pay by rendering personal services, the act would be non-delegable although the right would be assignable.[11] A is not required to accept C's services in substitution because they are personal.[12] C may, however, enforce the underlying contract if B performs the services.[13]

11. Rs. 2d § 319.

12. Franklin v. Jordan, 224 Ga. 727, 164 S.E.2d 718 (1968); Lojo Realty v. Isaac G. Johnson's Est., 253 N.Y. 579, 171 N.E. 791 (1930).

13. Cochran v. Taylor, 273 N.Y. 172, 183, 7 N.E.2d 89, 92–93 (1937); 1 Corbin § 3.3; 4 Corbin § 883.

Chapter 19

STATUTE OF FRAUDS

Table of Sections

I. WHEN A RECORD IS NECESSARY

II. SUFFICIENCY AND EFFECT OF A RECORD

III. RESTITUTIONARY REMEDIES

IV. ESTOPPEL

I. WHEN A RECORD IS NECESSARY

I. WHEN A RECORD IS NECESSARY

F.   RELATIONSHIP AMONG THE VARIOUS PROVISIONS

§ 19.1   The Statute, E–Sign, and UETA

(a) The Original Writing Requirement

At early common law, oral promises were generally not enforced by the King's courts, but this changed with the advent and gradual expansion of the writ of assumpsit.[1] When oral promises became enforceable, perjury and subornation of perjury appear to have become commonplace.[2] In 1677 Parliament enacted an Act for the Prevention of Fraud and Perjuries.[3] This Statute contained twenty-five sections which dealt with conveyances, wills, trusts, judgments and executions in addition to contracts.[4] Only two sections, the fourth and the seventeenth are important for contract purposes.

These sections singled out certain kinds of contracts and imposed a writing requirement. The selected agreements had to be in writing or, alternatively, a note or memorandum of the agreement would suffice. The agreement or memorandum had to "signed by the party to be charged" or the party's agent. Section 4 singled out for the writing requirement the following kinds of contracts for the writing requirement:

- (1) a promise by an executor or administrator to answer damages out of his own estate;

- (2) a promise to answer for the debt, default or miscarriage of another person;

- (3) an agreement made in consideration of marriage;

- (4) any contract for the sale of land or interests in land;

- (5) any agreement that is not to be performed within the space of one year from the making thereof.

Section 17 imposed a similar requirement for the sale of goods for the price of ten pounds sterling or more, but also provided for ways other than written evidence of satisfying the Statute. While the equivalent of Section 4 is on the books in almost every American jurisdiction, the provision regarding the sale of goods has been thoroughly revamped by the UCC.

While the writing requirement was imposed in large part to obviate perjury, it is clear that other policy bases for the requirement exist. An agreement reduced to writing promotes certainty; false testimony stems

---

§ 19.1

1. See 4 Corbin § 12.1 (Brown 1997); Teeven, Seventeenth Century Evidentiary Concerns and the Statute of Frauds, 9 Adelaide L.Rev. 252 (1983–85).

2. See 6 Holdsworth, A History of English Law 379–97 (1927).

3. 29 Car. II, c. 3, 8 Stat. at Large 405.

4. See Hamburger, The Conveyancing Purposes of the Statute of Frauds, 27 Am.J.Legal Hist. 354 (1983).

from faulty recollection as well as from faulty morals. In addition, the required formality of a writing "promotes deliberation, seriousness, * * * and shows that the act was a genuine act of volition."[5] While all will agree that to a lesser or greater extent these are desirable goals, it is obvious that the carrying out of these goals may well frustrate honesty and fair dealing. As with the case of a strict application of the parol evidence rule, the quest for certainty and deliberation involves the exclusion of evidence of what the parties may have actually agreed to. Oral agreements are made and are performed. If the oral agreement is within the Statute of Frauds and the Statute is enforced with vigor, the expectations of the person who had performed would be frustrated and the person who had breached the oral agreement would be unjustly enriched. If such were the result, the Statute would encourage fraud and sanction unethical conduct.

The ability of the Statute to cause injustice has had a strong impact on judicial decisions. Often the courts have viewed the Statute with disfavor and have tended to give it a narrow construction as to the kinds of contracts covered. In addition, they have developed devices for "taking the contract outside" the Statute. Finally, a variety of legal and equitable remedies have been forged to grant relief to a party who has performed an oral agreement within the statutory terms. Other courts have tended to view the basic policy of the Statute as sound and have given it a broad construction. It is not surprising that the decisions rendered throughout its 325 year history are not entirely harmonious. In 1954 Parliament repealed all but the provisions with respect to real property and suretyship.[6] Similar repeal in the U.S. is, however, not considered likely within the foreseeable future. Indeed, in the U.S. the policy of requiring a writing has been extended by legislation to other areas. For example, the policy of the statute has been extended in some jurisdictions to contracts to leave property by will, contracts to pay a broker a commission,[7] and a promise to pay a debt contracted during infancy.[8] More recently, many jurisdictions have enacted legislation requiring that agreements to lend money must be in writing.[9] In addition, many statutes and regulations requiring government contracts to be in writing are in the Statute of Frauds tradition.[10]

Writing requirements serve numerous important functions.[11] Many observers have suggested, however, that the tri-centenarian Statute of Frauds in its present form has outlived its usefulness.[12] The kinds of

5. Rabel, The Statute of Frauds and Comparative Legal History, 63 L.Q.Rev. 174, 178 (1947).

6. 2 & 3 Eliz. II, c. 34.

7. Eastern Commercial Realty v. Fusco, 654 A.2d 833 (Del.Super.1995).

8. See Rs. 2d, Statutory Note to Ch. 5; Note, 50 Fordham L.Rev. 239 (1981).

9. Budnitz, The Law of Lender Liability, Exhibit 5.1 (looseleaf 1996).

10. See U.S. v. American Renaissance Lines, 494 F.2d 1059 (D.C.Cir.1974), cert. denied; Veling v. Kansas City, 901 S.W.2d 119 (Mo.App.1995).

11. See Fridman, The Necessity for Writing in Contracts Within the Statute of Frauds, 35 U. Toronto L.Rev. 43 (1985); Perillo, The Statute of Frauds in the Light of the Functions and Dysfunctions of Form, 43 Fordham L.Rev. 39, 43–68 (1974).

12. Id. at n. 232.

transactions selected to be put in writing do not seem to constitute a rational catalog of transactions which ought to be singled out for formalization. The consequences of non-compliance appear too drastic. Most importantly, the volume of litigation involving questions of whether the transaction is within the Statute and if it is, whether it fits within one of the judge-made exceptions is enormous. Also, in many cases, there is evidence of the contract in a record and the litigation focuses on the sufficiency of the record rather than on the crux of the dispute between the parties.[13] Reform is needed. The UCC adopted a modernized version of the Statute of Frauds for sales and certain other transactions.[14] The UCC eliminates many of the dysfunctional aspects of the original statute and could provide a guide for modernization of the Statute as a whole.[15]

(b) Electronic Communication—E–Sign and UETA

In modern commerce, e-mail, EDI, and programmed trading in commodities frequently replace hard-copy records. Congress recognized this by enacting the Electronic Signatures in Global and National Commerce Act (E–Sign). This law allows states to preempt it by the enactment of UETA, the Uniform Electronic Transactions Act. Most states have enacted UETA, so it is the key law governing electronic contracting. UETA does not affect basic contract doctrine. It dwells on the use of electronics to communicate. If a law, such as the Statute of Frauds, requires a writing, it provides that an electronic record will satisfy the requirement. An electronic record is "information that is inscribed on a tangible medium or that is stored in an electronic or other medium and is retrievable in perceivable form." If the law requires a signature, UETA provides that an electronic signature will satisfy the law's requirement. However, these rules apply only to "transactions," a term that refers "the conduct of business, commercial, or governmental affairs."[16] This is perhaps an unfortunate limitation; many contracts made within the family or with non-profit institutions can only with difficulty be defined as a "business or commercial" transaction. This discussion of UETA is limited to the effect it has on the Statute of Frauds; it affects many other transactions and, as one would expect, contains exceptions.

A. SURETYSHIP CONTRACTS

§ 19.2 Promise by Executor or Administrator

A promise by an administrator or executor "to answer damages out of his own estate" is "within" the Statute of Frauds. The term "within the Statute of Frauds" means that the Statute requires a record for this kind of transaction. The clause is somewhat unclear because it does not

---

13. See §§ 19.26 to 19.39 infra.

14. See § 19.34 infra.

15. But see Cunningham, A Proposal to Repeal Section 2–201, 85 Com.L.J. 361 (1980).

16. UETA § 2(16).

state what or whose damages the executor or administrator is promising to pay. The cases have made it clear, however, that the Statute applies only where the executor or administrator promises to be personally liable for a debt of the deceased.[1] It does not apply to promises to pay debts of the deceased out of the assets of the estate.[2]

Since this is the accepted view of the meaning of this section, this provision is merely a particular application of the second subsection relating to promises to answer for the debt, default or miscarriage of another and what is said with reference to that subsection is applicable here.[3]

§ 19.3 Special Promises to Answer for the Debt, Default or Miscarriage of Another[1]

The task here is to determine which oral promises[2] contravene this section of the Statute and which promises are not condemned by the Statute even though they are oral. When a promise contravenes this section because it is not evidenced by a record, it is said to be collateral; when it does not, it is called original. These words are generally used to express a result and do not help in ascertaining which promises are enforceable.[3]

It is apparent from the wording of the section that almost all of the factual situations governed by it will be tripartite. One party has made the promise and now pleads the Statute as a defense. Since the promisor is invariably the defendant in these cases we will refer to this party by the letter D. The person to whom the promise is made we will refer to as the creditor (C). Invariably C will be the plaintiff in the action. The person for whom the promisor promises we shall refer to as the third party (TP). This terminology is used rather than P (principal) and S (surety) to minimize the possibility of begging the question by assuming that one of the parties is the principal and another the surety.[4]

At the outset a distinction must be drawn between cases where there is no prior obligation owed by the third party (TP) to the creditor

§ 19.2

1. Mackin v. Dwyer, 205 Mass. 472, 91 N.E. 893 (1910); Bellows v. Sowles, 57 Vt. 164, 52 Am.Rep. 118 (1884).

2. Piper v. Goodwin, 23 Me. (10 Shep.) 251 (1843); Norton v. Edwards, 66 N.C. 367 (1872).

3. Bellows v. Sowles, 57 Vt. 164 (1884); 2 Corbin § 346; Rs. 2d § 111 and cmt a.

§ 19.3

1. Much of this discussion is based on Calamari, The Suretyship Statute of Frauds, 27 Fordham L.Rev. 332 (1958). Although the word "special" may have had a particular meaning when the statute was

originally enacted, see Hening, 57 U.Pa. L.Rev. 611 (1909), today it is used "to restrict the statutory provision to promises in fact made." 4 Corbin § 15.2 (Brown 1997).

2. A number of states have extended the Statute of Frauds by providing that there shall be no liability for a misrepresentation as to the credit of a third person unless the representation is in a signed record. See Tenna Mfg. v. Columbia Union Nat. Bank & Trust, 484 F.Supp. 1214 (W.D.Mo.1980); Taylor, 16 U.C.L.A. L.Rev. 603 (1969).

3. 3 Williston § 463 (3d ed.); 4 Corbin § 15.3 (Brown 1997); see Kutilek v. Union Nat. Bank, 213 Kan. 407, 516 P.2d 979 (1973).

4. See § 19.4 nn.12–20 infra.

(C) to which D's promise relates, and cases where there is such a prior obligation.[5] This distinction is of extreme importance, since, as we shall see, there are different rules governing the two situations. We shall discuss first the cases where there is no prior obligation. The word "obligation" is used to include all duties recognized by law, whether contractual or not.

§ 19.4 Where There Is No Prior Obligation Owing From TP to C

An illustration will serve to bring this category of cases into focus. D says to C, "Deliver these goods to TP and I will see that you are paid." C delivers the goods. Is D's promise enforceable? This depends on the answers to a number of questions, some of contract, some of suretyship. In a case where there is no prior obligation owing from TP to C, for the promise to be collateral TP must come under at least a voidable obligation to C; there must be a principal-surety relationship between TP and D; and C must know or have reason to know of the principal-surety relationship.[1] In addition some courts hold that the promise must not be joint.[2] Moreover the main purpose rule must not apply. Each of these facets of the problem will now be explored.

(a) TP Must Come Under at Least a Voidable Obligation to C

D's promise can be collateral only where TP eventually[3] comes under an obligation to C. If TP does not come under an obligation to C, the promise must be original because D is not promising to pay the debt of another, there being no other debt. It would appear, then, that the first inquiry which must be made is whether TP eventually came under at least a voidable obligation to C. For the purposes of this rule, a voidable obligation is an obligation, but a void obligation is not.[4]

In the illustration given, did TP come under any such obligation to C? The first requisite for any contract is that the offeror manifest a contractual state of mind, and this is a key to determining whether TP came under an obligation to C. This explains why the courts place so much emphasis on the question of whether C extended credit to TP,[5] for this is merely another way of inquiring whether C manifested an intention to contract with TP. In other words, if credit is extended only to D, D's promise is original.[6] Charging TP as a debtor on C's books is

---

5. 4 Corbin § 15.5 (Brown 1997); 3 Williston § 462 (3d ed.).

§ 19.4

1. Rs. 2d § 112.

2. Id. § 113(b) and cmt b.

3. It is arguable that D's promise has to be original since at the time of making the promise there is no obligation owing from TP to C. This contention was rejected in the early case of Jones v. Cooper, 98 Eng.

Rep. 1058 (K.B.1774). See 4 Corbin § 15.5 (Brown 1997); 3 Williston § 461 (3d ed.).

4. 4 Corbin § 15.11 (Brown 1997); Simpson, Suretyship 126–27 (1950); 3 Williston § 454 (3d ed.).

5. See General Elec. v. Hans, 242 Miss. 119, 133 So.2d 275 (1961).

6. See J. J. Brooksbank Co. v. American Motors., 289 Minn. 404, 184 N.W.2d 796 (1971), noted in 56 Minn.L.Rev. 281 (1971).

strong evidence that credit was extended to TP[7] but is not conclusive.[8] The question is ordinarily one of fact.[9] The fact that C did not charge TP is some evidence that credit was not extended to TP, but is not considered strong evidence.

If C has extended credit to TP, obviously the only remaining question to determine whether TP came under an obligation to C is to ascertain whether TP accepted C's offer. In many of the reported cases[10] there is no discussion of what transpired after D made the promise to C. Nevertheless, whether TP accepted C's offer must be determined under the already discussed rules relating to acceptance by silence or exercise of dominion, as well as other forms of manifestation of assent by conduct.[11]

An instructive case on the question of who is TP is Mease v. Wagner.[12] The defendant (D), a friend of the deceased, Mrs. Bradley, told the plaintiff (C), an undertaker, to bury Mrs. Bradley in a certain manner and to charge the estate of Dr. Bradley (TP) (the husband of Mrs. Bradley who had predeceased her) or a certain nephew (also TP) of Mrs. Bradley and "if they don't pay I will." It may be assumed that the plaintiff extended credit to the estate of Dr. Bradley and to the nephew. However the estate of Dr. Bradley never became liable because it did nothing to manifest an acceptance and would not otherwise be liable. The estate of a deceased husband is not ordinarily liable even for the necessaries of a wife. His death, generally speaking, terminates his duty to support.[13] Although the nephew promised to pay after the services were rendered, he never became liable because of the familiar doctrine that past consideration is not consideration. However, under long established principles of quasi contract the estate of a decedent is liable for burial expenses.

The court concluded that since neither the estate of Dr. Bradley nor the nephew came under an obligation to the plaintiff, the promise of the defendant had to be original and therefore was enforceable notwithstanding the absence of a record. The court did not consider whether the estate of Mrs. Bradley became liable.[14] The theory was that it is "settled doctrine that when no action will lie against the party undertaken for, it is an orignal [sic] promise."[15] Here the third parties were the estate of

---

7. Lusk v. Throop, 189 Ill. 127, 59 N.E. 529 (1901); Wood v. Dodge, 23 S.D. 95, 120 N.W. 774 (1909); Simpson, Suretyship 124 (1950).

8. Hammond Coal v. Lewis, 248 Mass. 499, 143 N.E. 309 (1924); Annot., 99 ALR 79, 83 (1935).

9. Lawrence v. Anderson, 108 Vt. 176, 184 A. 689 (1936); 4 Corbin § 15.7 (Brown 1997); Burdick, 20 Colum.L.Rev. 153, 155 (1920).

10. For example, this is true of all of the cases in Simpson, Cases on Suretyship 1–10 (1942) which deal with this problem.

11. See §§ 2.18, 2.19 supra.

12. 12 S.C.L. (1 McCord) 395 (1821).

13. Wilson v. Hinman, 182 N.Y. 408, 75 N.E. 236 (1905).

14. Cape Girardeau Bell Tel. v. Hamil, 160 Mo.App. 521, 140 S.W. 951 (1911); Annots., 35 ALR2d 1399 (1954); 82 ALR2d 873 (1962). This liability would exist even if the undertaker did not specifically intend to charge her estate but only whomever proved ultimately responsible. Rs, Restitution § 113 cmt e.

15. Mease v. Wagner, 12 S.C.L. (1 McCord) 395, 396 (1821); cf. Crawler Parts v. Hill, 441 So.2d 1357 (Miss.1983); Four Winds Hosp. v. Keasbey, 59 N.Y.2d 943, 466

Dr. Bradley and the nephew. Because they did not come under an obligation. the promise is original,[16] irrespective of whether the estate of Mrs. Bradley became liable. In a word, for the purpose of the Statute of Frauds,[17] TP is the person for whom the defendant undertakes.

To use a simpler illustration, where a man orally retains a law firm to represent his daughter in an action to enforce her divorce decree, the promise is original, but if he guaranties payment, the promise is collateral[18] To summarize: in the category of cases under discussion, the courts reason that if TP does not come under an obligation (at least voidable) to C, the promise is original.[19] If TP does come under obligation, *so far as we know now*, the promise is collateral.[20] However, the promise, due to factors discussed below, may still be original.

There is another contract question which must be considered. It can perhaps best be introduced by a simple illustration. D says to C, "Deliver these goods to TP and, provided you extend credit to TP, I will pay if TP does not." Assume that the goods are delivered to TP but that C extends no credit to TP. Is D liable to C?

It is clear under the rules previously considered that D's promise is original because TP never came under an obligation to C. D should not be liable to C since, in failing to extend credit to TP, C has not accepted D's offer. In the logical order, of course, this question should be considered before adverting to whether the promise is original or collateral, for if there is no contract between C and D the question of whether the promise is original or collateral under the Statute of Frauds can only be of academic interest.

This simple illustration makes clear that in every case it is important to determine whether C has accepted D's offer and performed.[21] Some authorities do not emphasize this in the least and seem to imply that C in every case is free to extend or not extend credit.[22] The better view, however, is that such a determination must be made; in the ordinary case whether D has insisted as a condition precedent to liability

N.Y.S.2d 300, 453 N.E.2d 529 (1983) (question of fact).

16. Simpson, Suretyship 125 (1950).

17. On the assumptions made, the defendant would be a non-consensual surety in relation to the estate of Mrs. Bradley. Mathews v. Aikin, 1 N.Y. (1 Comst.) 595 (1848); Campbell, Non–Consensual Suretyship, 45 Yale L.J. 69 (1935).

18. Schier, Deneweth & Parfitt v. Bennett, 206 Mich.App. 281, 520 N.W.2d 705 (1994) (original); see also Gallagher, Langlas & Gallagher v. Burco, 587 N.W.2d 615 (Iowa App.1998) (collateral); Walker v. Elkin, 758 N.E.2d 972 (Ind.App.2001) (original and joint).

19. Cf. Highland Park v. Grant–Mackenzie, 366 Mich. 430, 115 N.W.2d 270

(1962) (employer's promise to pay hospital for bills in excess of employee's insurance coverage is original).

20. Fendley v. Dozier Hardware, 449 So.2d 1236 (Ala.1984); Drummond v. Pillsbury, 130 Me. 406, 156 A. 806 (1931); Builders Supply v. Carr, 276 N.W.2d 252 (S.D. 1979); Johnson Co. v. City Cafe, 100 S.W.2d 740 (Tex.App.1936).

21. See Kerin Agency v. West Haven Painting and Decorating, 38 Conn.App. 329, 660 A.2d 882 (1995).

22. See Simpson, Suretyship 125; 4 Corbin § 15.8 (Brown 1997); see also Lawrence v. Anderson, 108 Vt. 176, 184 A. 689 (1936).

that credit be extended to TP or that TP come under an obligation to C is a question of interpretation and very often a jury question.[23]

In summary, the first inquiry to be made in this type of case (one where TP is not under a prior obligation to C at the time D makes the promise to C) is whether TP eventually comes under an obligation to C. If TP does not, the promise is original. If TP does, the promise is collateral unless it is rendered original for one of the reasons now to be discussed.

(b) TP and D Must Be in a Principal–Surety Relationship

Even though TP comes under an obligation to C, D's promise will still be original if there is not a principal-surety relationship[24] between TP and D.[25] To illustrate, assume that TP makes a purchase from C and at the same time D guaranties payment, and credit is extended to TP who becomes obligated. The case is still within the first category, for if TP and D became bound at the same time, there was no prior obligation on the part of TP to C at the time that D made the promise. Under the rules thus far considered, D's promise would be collateral. But if it were established that TP was acting as D's agent in this transaction, would D's promise be collateral? The answer is in the negative.[26] As pointed out above, for D's promise to be collateral there must not only be an obligation on the part of TP but there must also be a principal-surety relationship between TP and D. Here, that relationship does not exist. Here, under the assumption made, TP would be liable to C as an agent for an undisclosed principal.[27] TP is the agent and D is the principal. Though it is probably true that as between the two, D should ultimately pay,[28] so that there may be additionally a principal and surety relationship under the Restatement definition, still the relationship between TP and D is not principal and surety but surety and principal. When the rule states that there must be a principal-surety relationship between TP and D it means that TP must be the principal and D the surety and not vice versa.

(c) C Must Have Reason to Know of the Relationship

Even if TP comes under an obligation to C and there is in fact a principal-surety relationship between TP and D, D's promise will still be original if C does not know or have reason to know of the relationship.[29]

23. Duca v. Lord, 331 Mass. 51, 117 N.E.2d 145 (1954); Simpson, Suretyship 273–77; 3 Williston § 454 (3d ed.).

24. Rs. 2d § 112. Rs. 3d Suretyship & Guaranty § 1 (1996) defines suretyship.

25. 4 Corbin § 15.4 (Brown 1997).

26. Lesser–Goldman Cotton v. Merchants' & Planters' Bank, 182 Ark. 150, 30 S.W.2d 215 (1930); cf. Bartolotta v. Calvo, 112 Conn. 385, 152 A. 306 (1930).

27. Ferson, Principles of Agency § 170 (1954).

28. Thomas J. Nolan, Inc. v. Martin & William Smith, 193 Misc. 877, 85 N.Y.S.2d 380 (1949), aff'd. An agent for an undisclosed principal does not have the defense of Statute of Frauds. Savoy Record v. Cardinal Export., 15 N.Y.2d 1, 254 N.Y.S.2d 521, 203 N.E.2d 206, (1964).

29. Rs. 2d § 112; 4 Corbin § 15.17 (Brown 1997); 3 Williston § 475 (3d ed.).

One illustration will suffice.[30] When goods are being purchased from C, D promises to pay and TP guaranties D's payment. C is informed that the goods are to be delivered to D. Assume that the arrangement between TP and D is that D shall turn the goods over to TP and this is done. Credit is extended to both. Though TP came under an obligation to C and there is a principal-surety relationship between TP and D, D's promise is still original because C did not know or have reason to know of the principal-surety relationship between TP and D. In the illustration, TP would also be liable to C, but TP is the principal debtor because TP received the goods and, as between TP and D, TP should ultimately pay.

C knows that there is a principal-surety relationship but C thinks TP is the surety and that the defendant (D) is the principal. The rule means that before the promise of the defendant (D) can be collateral, the creditor must know, or have reason to know, that the defendant (D) is the surety. This only is fair, otherwise the creditor, even if knowledgeable of the Statute of Frauds, might not require a record. This result is at times explained by saying that the sale to D makes D the principal, "[a]nd ordinarily it makes no difference what he did with the goods after conveyance to him; he may have destroyed, sold or given them away, yet he remains a debtor notwithstanding."[31]

(d) The Promise Must Not Be Joint

By the great weight of authority,[32] even though TP comes under an obligation to C and there is a principal-surety relationship between TP and D and C knows of this relationship, D's promise is still original if the promise and TP's promise are joint.[33] The theory of these cases is that since the promise is joint there is only one obligation (a joint one) and that, therefore, the obligation *in toto* must be original.[34] The rule does not apply where the obligation is joint and several because in such a case more than one obligation results.[35]

(e) Summary

From what has been said it is concluded that where there is no prior obligation on the part of TP to C to which D's promise relates at the

---

30. Rs. 1st § 112 ill. 11; 4 Corbin § 15.10 (Brown 1997), particularly Colbath v. Everett D. Clark Seed, 112 Me. 277, 91 A. 1007 (1914).

31. 4 Corbin § 15.10 (Brown 1997). This is undoubtedly what the Restatement means when, after giving the illustration, it states that D's promise is not subject to the Statute of Frauds, "since the duty to pay is in truth his." Rs. 2d § 112 ill. 11; see also id. § 112 ill. 10.

32. Fluor v. U.S., 405 F.2d 823 (9th Cir.1969), cert. denied; Boyce v. Murphy, 91 Ind. 1, 46 Am.Rep. 567 (1883); Rs. 1st

§ 181; 4 Corbin § 15.16 (Brown 1997); 3 Williston § 466 (3d ed.); contra, Walker v. Elkin, 758 N.E.2d 972 (Ind.App.2001).

33. The rules which establish when a promise is joint, joint and several, or several, are discussed in 4 Corbin §§ 923–42; 2 Williston §§ 316–46 (3d ed.); § 20.2 infra.

34. The joint nature of the promise does not prevent a surety relationship from arising. Simpson, Contracts §§ 136–43 (2d ed. 1965).

35. Simpson, Suretyship 132 (1950).

time that D's promise is made, the promise will be original unless all of the following conditions concur:

1.   TP comes under at least a voidable obligation to C.

2.   There is a principal-surety relationship between TP and D.

3.   C knows or has reason to know of the principal-surety relationship between TP and D.

4.   The promise is not joint (in jurisdictions which posit this requirement).

5.   The main purpose rule is not satisfied.

If all of these conditions concur the promise is collateral; otherwise it is original. The main purpose rule is discussed in § 19.6.

§ 19.5   Where There Is a Prior Obligation Owing From TP to C

In the previous section attention was directed to the case where there is no obligation owing from TP to C at the time that D makes the promise. Here the we discuss the rules covering the situation where TP was obligated to C.

It is clear that the Statute applies to this situation. It is not surprising, therefore, to find that where TP is obligated to C at the time of D's promise, the promise will be held to be collateral[1] and therefore subject to the requirement of a record, unless it falls within one of a number of recognized exceptions to the Statute which will now be discussed. There are also problems of consideration associated with such promises.[2]

(a) Novation

The first exception which is universally recognized arises where there is a novation.[3] This is so whether the novation be denominated legal or equitable.[4] A practical reason for the exception is that if the promise of D causes TP's obligation to be discharged and if D's promise were held to be collateral, C would be in the unfortunate position of being unable to collect the obligation from either TP or D. The legal reason usually given is that advanced by Lord Mansfield in Anstey v. Marden:[5] "I did not see how one person could undertake for the debt of

§ 19.5

1. Colpitts v. L.C. Fisher Co., 289 Mass. 232, 193 N.E. 833 (1935); Lou Atkin Castings v. M. Fabrikant & Sons, 216 A.D.2d 111, 628 N.Y.S.2d 98 (1995); 4 Corbin § 15.5 (Brown 1997); 3 Williston § 469 (3d ed.).

2. E.g., Strong v. Sheffield, 144 N.Y. 392, 39 N.E. 330 (1895); see § 4.12 supra.

3. Hill v. Grat, 247 Mass. 25, 141 N.E. 593 (1923); Annot., 74 ALR 1025 (1931); 4 Corbin § 15.20 (Brown 1997). For example,

if D says to C, "release TP and I will pay," and C releases TP, D's promise is original. But if C does not release TP other problems arise. If the arrangement between C and D were bilateral, D undoubtedly could sue for specific performance and TP might have rights as a third party beneficiary.

4. 3 Williston § 477 (3d ed.); see § 21.8 infra.

5. 1 Bos. & Pul. (N.R.) 124, 127 Eng. Rep. 406 (C.P.1804).

another, when the debt, for which he was supposed to undertake, was discharged by the very bargain."[6]

(b) Where the Promise to Pay Is Made to TP

The second exception arises where D makes the promise to TP rather than to C.[7] A typical illustration is the situation where the assuming grantee (D) promises the grantor (TP) to pay a mortgage debt to the mortgagee (C). In that case, C may ordinarily enforce D's promise made to TP under the theory of third party beneficiary[8] or, in some jurisdictions, under the theory of equitable subrogation.[9] The Statute of Frauds provision under discussion is not a defense to D.[10] The best reason given as to why this should be is that as a result of the promise D becomes the principal debtor and is, therefore, merely promising to pay his or her own debt.[11] For the same reason, a liability insurer's oral settlement agreement with an injured party (C) is not within the Statute.[12]

(c) Where the Promise Is Made to C but Is Co-Extensive with D's Obligation to C

The question then arises as to what extent a promise made by D to C, after D's promise to TP, is enforceable. Assume C is an at-will employee of TP who owes C wages of $1000. TP enters into an agreement with D whereby TP agrees to turn the business over to D in consideration *inter alia* of D's promise to pay TP's obligation to C. As we have seen, D's promise made to TP to pay C is enforceable by C.

But suppose that one week later D personally promises C to pay C. Is this promise enforceable? So far as the Statute of Frauds is concerned the promise is original.[13] Since D is already the principal debtor,[14] D is merely promising to pay a pre-existing debt. This is a situation where the promise is enforceable without consideration.[15]

Suppose that D promises TP to pay TP's wages to C out of profits and that D later makes the same promise to C. Both of these promises are enforceable despite the absence of a record.[16] When D promises TP, D

---

6. Id. at 131, 127 Eng.Rep. at 409; Henry C. Beck Co. v. Fort Wayne Structural Steel, 701 F.2d 1221 (7th Cir.1983).

7. Magrann v. Epes, 646 So.2d 760 (Fla. App.1994); People's State Sav. Bank v. Cross, 197 Iowa 750, 198 N.W. 70 (1924); Rs. 2d § 123; 4 Corbin § 357.

8. Osborne, Mortgages § 261 (2d ed. 1970); see § 17.6 supra. Of course, under the orthodox view (§ 4.9) there must be consideration for the assumption. Trans–State v. Barber, 170 Ga.App. 372, 317 S.E.2d 242 (1984).

9. Osborne, note 8 at § 262.

10. Walter E. Heller & Co. v. Video Innovations, 730 F.2d 50 (2d Cir.1984); Langman v. Alumni Ass'n, 247 Va. 491, 442

S.E.2d 669 (1994). In some states a promise to assume a mortgage must be in record because of a different statute. See, e.g., McKinney's N.Y.Gen'l Obl.Law § 5–705.

11. Aldrich v. Ames, 75 Mass. (9 Gray) 76 (1857).

12. Carter v. Allstate Ins., 962 S.W.2d 268 (Tex.App.1998).

13. Rs. 2d § 114.

14. Rs. 2d § 119.

15. See § 5.3 supra.

16. Contra, Ackley v. Parmenter, 98 N.Y. 425, 50 Am.Rep. 693 (1885). Cases where TP has not consented to D's promise to pay from property of TP under D's con-

becomes the principal, and when D makes the same promise to C, D is merely promising to pay D's own debt. For the same reason, where one of several co-partners promises personally to pay the whole debt of the partnership, the promise is not within the Statute of Frauds.[17]

Suppose further in the illustration given that when D makes the promise to TP, D promises to pay C out of proceeds. Subsequently, D says to C, "If you agree to continue the work that you were doing for TP for six months, I promise to pay you $1,000 per week and to pay TP's debt to you after one month."[18] C accepts the offer. There is consideration for D's promises. Though there may be other reasons why there is consideration, it is clear that C, in promising to work six months when the original hiring by TP was at will, is suffering detriment. Is the promise to pay TP's debt after one month original? If not, is the other promise to pay $1,000 per week enforceable, or must both promises stand or fall together? The answer to these questions depends in part on the so-called main purpose rule which is discussed in the next section.[19]

§ 19.6 The Main Purpose (or Leading Object) Rule

The main purpose rule may be stated as follows: "Where the party promising has for his object a benefit which he did not enjoy before his promise, which benefit accrues immediately to himself, his promise is original, whether made before, after or at the time of the promise of the third party, notwithstanding that the effect is to promise to pay or discharge the debt of another."[1] The main purpose rule applies whether or not there was a prior obligation owing from TP to C to which the promise relates.[2]

Two elements are necessary for the main purpose rule to apply: (a) there must be consideration for D's promise and (b) the consideration must be beneficial to D. The benefit to be obtained has been described by adjectives such as personal, immediate, pecuniary and direct.[3]

It is obvious that this rule involves difficult distinctions as to the degree of benefit and as to purpose and motive. The application of the rule may ultimately be a question of fact.[4] No extended discussion of

trol have not been uniform. See 4 Corbin § 15.18 (Brown 1997).

17. For this and other cases where this principle applies, see 4 Corbin § 16.21 (Brown 1997).

18. Facts suggested by Belknap v. Bender, 75 N.Y. 446, 31 Am.Rep 476 (1878), modified 76 N.Y. 633.

19. See also § 19.36 infra.

§ 19.6

1. Nelson v. Boynton, 44 Mass. (3 Metc.) 396 (1841); accord, Burlington Indus. v. Foil, 284 N.C. 740, 202 S.E.2d 591 (1974);

Austford v. Smith, 196 N.W.2d 413 (N.D. 1972).

2. See §§ 19.4 and 19.5 supra.

3. Warner–Lambert v. Sylk, 471 F.2d 1137 (3d Cir.1972); Hurst Hardware v. Goodman, 68 W.Va. 462, 69 S.E. 898 (1910); but see General Electric v. Gate, 273 S.C. 88, 254 S.E.2d 305 (1979). Rs. 2d § 116 states the rule in terms of whether the promisor desires his own "economic advantage." Yet not every interest or economic advantage will trigger the rule. See Walton v. Piqua State Bank, 204 Kan. 741, 466 P.2d 316 (1970).

4. Alexander, Corder et al. v. Jackson, 811 So.2d 506 (Ala.2001).

these matters is possible here.[5] However, a few typical situations will be discussed in the next section.

§ 19.7   Some Illustrations

If TP is indebted to C and C has a lien on TP's property and D promises to pay the debt in order to discharge the lien of the property, does the main purpose rule apply? The answer is that it depends on whether D has some interest to protect as would be the case where D had taken subject to a mortgage.[1] It is otherwise however, if the lien surrendered is on property in which D has no interest to protect as, for example, where D is a first mortgagee and has no other reason to promise to pay the second mortgagee.[2]

Another common situation involving the main purpose rule occurs when a stockholder of a corporation makes a promise to a creditor of the corporation that induces action that at least indirectly benefits the stockholder. For example, in one case[3] defendant was a substantial stockholder in a corporation and the plaintiff, a creditor, had been furnishing merchandise to the corporation which had not paid its bills. Defendant promised to be responsible for these bills and for future deliveries if the plaintiff would continue to supply the corporation, which plaintiff did. The court held that the main purpose rule did not apply because stock ownership is too indirect and remote to satisfy the main purpose rule. This is the orthodox view.[4] Where the defendant was the sole stockholder, the cases are not in harmony but the better view is that the main purpose rule applies.[5]

A number of cases have arisen where D, the owner of unimproved realty, employs TP, a general contractor, to build a house for D on the latter's land. TP orders material from C who makes deliveries for which TP fails to pay. C tells TP that C will not fill further orders, but subsequently agrees to fill further orders to TP when D agrees to pay the overdue debt of TP and to pay for subsequent deliveries. C fills the orders. TP does not pay. C sues D who sets up the defense of Statute of Frauds. Is the Statute in whole or in part a defense?

5. See 4 Corbin §§ 16.1 to 16.7.

§ 19.7

1. Kahn v. Waldman, 283 Mass. 391, 186 N.E. 587, 88 ALR 699 (1933).

2. Griffin v. Hoag, 105 Iowa 499, 75 N.W. 372 (1898).

3. Hurst Hardware v. Goodman, 68 W.Va. 462, 69 S.E. 898 (1910).

4. Richardson Press v. Albright, 224 N.Y. 497, 121 N.E. 362, 8 ALR 1195 (1918); Mid–Atlantic Appliances v. Morgan, 194 Va. 324, 73 S.E.2d 385, 35 ALR2d 899 (1952); Note, 54 N.Car.L.Rev. 117 (1975); but see Pravel, Wilson & Matthews v. Voss, 471 F.2d 1186 (5th Cir.1973) (question of fact);

Nelson v. TMH, 292 N.W.2d 580 (N.D. 1980); Armbruster, Inc. v. Barron, 341 Pa.Super. 409, 491 A.2d 882 (1985).

5. Davis v. Patrick, 141 U.S. 479 (1891); T.L. Swint Indus. v. Premiere Sales Group, 16 F.Supp.2d 937 (N.D.Ill.1998); Eastern Wood Prods. v. Metz, 370 Pa. 636, 89 A.2d 327 (1952); cf. Adams v. H & H, 41 S.W.3d 762 (Tex.App.2001) (substantial minority shareholder and employee); contra, Bulkley v. Shaw, 289 N.Y. 133, 44 N.E.2d 398 (1942); Goldie–Klenert Distrib. v. Bothwell, 67 Wn. 264, 121 P. 60 (1912). See 4 Corbin § 16.7; Simpson, Suretyship § 38.

There are three views. One view is that the promise to pay for past deliveries is unenforceable but the promise to pay for future deliveries is enforceable.[6] Under this view the promises are said to be severable. The Restatement (Third) of Suretyship and Guaranty rejects the doctrine of severability and carries the main purpose rule to its logical conclusion when it holds both promises enforceable because of the benefit conferred.[7] New York, for reasons to be discussed in the next section, holds both promises to be unenforceable.[8]

§ 19.8 The Peculiar New York Rule

The New York main purpose rule is different from the main purpose rule as it exists elsewhere.[1] A discussion of this difference begins with a review of the landmark cases,[2] culminating in the decision of White v. Rintoul.[3] Leonard v. Vredenburgh[4] held that so long as the promisor (D) received new consideration for the promise the promise was original. The fallacy of this position was demonstrated in Mallory v. Gillett[5] where the plaintiff (C) had made repairs on the boat of TP and therefore had a lien.[6] D went to C and promised to pay for the repairs if C would surrender possession of the boat. C surrendered possession. D did not pay and C brought this action against D. Under the test of Leonard v. Vredenburgh the promise would be original because D's promise to pay is supported by consideration. The surrender of the boat and the lien is consideration. The court pointed out that to say the new consideration makes the promise original effectively eliminates the Statute of Frauds since consideration is necessary to support the new promise in any event. The court added that for the main purpose rule to apply not only is consideration for D's promise necessary but in addition the consideration must be directly beneficial to the promisor. At this point New York had adopted the main purpose rule in its generally accepted form.[7]

6. Peterson v. Paxton–Pavey Lumber, 102 Fla. 89, 135 So. 501 (1931).

7. § 11 ill. 20 (1996). See Rs. 2d § 116 ill. 3; Wilson Floors v. Sciota Park, Ltd., 54 Ohio St.2d 451, 377 N.E.2d 514 (1978) (bank guarantied that subcontractor would be paid after general contractor defaulted); Haas Drilling v. First Nat. Bank, 456 S.W.2d 886 (Tex.1970), 2 St. Mary's L.J. 267 (1970); Gulf Liquid Fertilizer v. Titus, 163 Tex. 260, 354 S.W.2d 378 (1962) (incoming partner agreed to pay outstanding debts of partner so that future credit deliveries will be made); cf. Abraham v. H.V. Middleton, Inc., 279 F.2d 107 (10th Cir. 1960).

8. Witschard v. A. Brody & Sons, 257 N.Y. 97, 177 N.E. 385 (1931); Worlock Paving v. Camperlino, 207 A.D.2d 975, 617 N.Y.S.2d 87 (1994).

§ 19.8

1. Conway, 22 Fordham L.Rev. 119 (1953). Compare Martin Roofing v. Goldstein, 60 N.Y.2d 262, 469 N.Y.S.2d 595, 457

N.E.2d 700 (1983), cert. denied, and Capital Knitting Mills v. Duofold, 131 A.D.2d 87, 519 N.Y.S.2d 968 (1987), appeal withdrawn, with White Stag Mfg. v. Wind Surfing, 67 Or.App. 459, 679 P.2d 312 (1984), and Century 21 Products v. Glacier Sales, 74 Wn. App. 793, 875 P.2d 1238 (1994), reversed on other grounds.

2. Conway, note 1, at 124–30 has an extended discussion of these cases.

3. 108 N.Y. 222, 15 N.E. 318 (1888).

4. 8 Johns. 29, 5 Am.Dec. 317 (N.Y. 1811).

5. 21 N.Y. 412 (1860).

6. McKinney's N.Y. Lien Law § 80.

7. Conway, note 1, at 125.

In Brown v. Weber[8] the Court of Appeals introduced a third element to the content of the New York law when it stated as dictum:

> The language shows that the test to be applied to every case is, whether the party sought to be charged is the principal debtor, primarily liable, or whether he is only liable in case of the default of a third person; in other words, whether he is the debtor, or whether his relation to the creditor is that of surety to him for the performance, by some other person, of the obligation of the latter to the creditor.[9]

The Court of Appeals explained, or attempted to explain, the meaning of this language in the leading case of White v. Rintoul. In that case, Wheatcroft and Rintoul (TP) made two notes in favor of the plaintiff (C). Before the maturity date of the notes, D, who was the father of one of the members of the firm, requested that C forbear collection and stated that if C would do so he would see that C was paid. D was a secured creditor of the firm. C complied with D's request and sought to recover from D on this promise. It is apparent that the court might simply have stated that the promise was collateral because the consideration for the promise of D was not sufficiently beneficial to D. The benefit was to TP and not D. However, the court reviewed the earlier cases and concluded as follows:

> These four cases, advancing by three distinct stages in a common direction, have ended in establishing a doctrine in the courts of this state which may be stated with approximate accuracy thus, that where the primary debt subsists and was antecedently contracted, the promise to pay it is original when it is founded on a new consideration moving to the promisor and beneficial to him, and such that the promisor thereby comes under an independent duty of payment irrespective of the liability of the principal debtor.[10]

A reading of this language compels the conclusion that three elements must be satisfied before the main purpose rule will apply:

(a) there must be consideration;

(b) it must be beneficial to the promisor; and

(c) the situation must be such that "the promisor thereby comes under an independent duty of payment irrespective of the liability of the principal debtor."

The same thought is expressed in different language in Richardson Press v. Albright,[11] when the Court of Appeals said that D's promise "is regarded as original only where the party sought to be charged clearly becomes, within the intention of the parties (TP and D) a principal debtor primarily liable."

---

8. 38 N.Y. 187 (1868).

9. Id. at 189. Thus where a corporate officer promises to be primarily liable for the corporation's legal fees, no record is required. Lederer v. King, 214 A.D.2d 354, 625 N.Y.S.2d 149 (1995).

10. White v. Rintoul, 108 N.Y. 222, 227, 15 N.E. 318, 320 (1888).

11. 224 N.Y. 497, 502, 121 N.E. 362, 364 (1918).

In New York the promise of an owner to pay a subcontractor for goods delivered by the general contractor has the defense of Statute of Frauds since the main purpose rule does not apply.[12] The reason is that the the third element of White v. Rintoul is not satisfied. It is difficult to determine what this requirement means because of the paucity of cases which have decided that this requirement is satisfied.[13]

§ 19.9 Promises of Indemnity

The overwhelming weight of authority is to the effect that a promise of indemnity, whether it is a promise to indemnify against loss or against liability, is not within the Statute of Frauds.[1]

A problem which has divided the courts is a four party situation where the defendant requests the plaintiff to become a surety on the obligation of TP to C and orally promises the plaintiff that if plaintiff is forced to pay, the defendant will reimburse the payment. If the plaintiff complies and is compelled to pay, may plaintiff recover on the oral promise or is the promise collateral? Some courts have concluded that the promise is original, as one of indemnity, because the promise was made to a debtor, the surety.[2] However, as some courts have pointed out, the surety is also a creditor, for the surety has a right to reimbursement from the principal; these courts conclude that the promise is collateral.[3]

However, when a promise is made to a creditor it is very difficult to determine whether the promise is one of indemnity or one of suretyship (a promise to answer for the debt, default or miscarriage of another). Part of the difficulty stems from the fact that the authorities are not in total accord on the test to be used in making this determination. Williston states that there is suretyship and not indemnity where the parties, the plaintiff (C) and defendant (D), expect that a third party (TP) will come under an obligation to C.[4] Corbin states that there is a promise of indemnity where the contract is made solely for the benefit of the promisee (C) and not for the accommodation or benefit of some third

---

12. See note 1.

13. This requirement was held to be satisfied in Raabe v. Squier, 148 N.Y. 81, 42 N.E. 516 (1895) and Rosenkranz v. Schreiber Brewing, 287 N.Y. 322, 39 N.E.2d 257 (1942). These cases are analyzed extensively in Calamari, The Suretyship Statute of Frauds, 27 Fordham L.Rev. 332 (1958). See also Biener Contracting v. Elberon Restaurant, 7 A.D.2d 391, 183 N.Y.S.2d 756 (1959), 28 Fordham L.Rev. 384 (1959); Leonard Lang, Ltd. v. Birch Holding, 72 A.D.2d 806, 421 N.Y.S.2d 921 (1979). This last case might better have been decided under the rule stated in § 19.5(b) supra.

§ 19.9

1. Villarreal v. Metropolitan Bank & Trust, 277 Ill.App.3d 188, 213 Ill.Dec. 812, 660 N.E.2d 69 (1995); Corbin, Contracts of Indemnity and the Statute of Frauds, 41 Harv.L.Rev. 689 (1928); Rs. 3d Suretyship and Guaranty § 11(d).

2. Rs. 2d § 118; see Rosenbloom v. Feiler, 290 Md. 598, 431 A.2d 102, 13 ALR4th 1140 (1981); Steinberger v. Steinberger, 252 A.D.2d 578, 676 N.Y.S.2d 210 (1998); Newbern v. Fisher, 198 N.C. 385, 151 S.E. 875, 68 ALR 345 (1930). See § 19.5 supra.

3. Rs. 2d § 118; see Green v. Cresswell, 10 Ad. & El. 453, 113 Eng.Rep. 172 (1839).

4. 3 Williston § 482 (3d ed.).

person.[5] Corbin, in answering the question of whether a third party was being accommodated, places great weight on whether the third party is an indeterminate third person or a specific third person.[6]

A good illustration of the difference in approach is a case of credit insurance. According to Williston, credit insurance involves suretyship and not indemnity because the parties expect that a third party will come under an obligation.[7] Under Corbin's view a contract of credit insurance would be a contract of indemnity because the contract is for the benefit of the promisee and not for the accommodation of a third person.[8] Both agree that a contract of collision insurance involves indemnity[9] and that a contract of fidelity insurance involves suretyship.[10] It might also be noted that if the contract is one of suretyship, the premium received by the insurance company does not bring the case within the main purpose rule.[11]

§ 19.10   The Promise of the Del Credere Agent

A del credere agent is one who receives possession of the goods for sale on commission and who guaranties to the principal that buyers on credit will pay. The Statute of Frauds problem arises when the principal seeks to enforce the oral promise of the del credere agent. In the terminology that has been employed herein, the agent is D, the principal is the creditor (C) and the TP's are the unknown persons to whom the agent sells.

It is uniformly held that the oral promise of the del credere agent is not within the Statute of Frauds.[1] A variety of reasons are assigned for the holding. Thus, for example, Corbin explains the result on the ground that this is a promise of indemnity because it is not for the accommodation or benefit of the third parties.[2] Williston explains the case by saying that the guaranty is merely incidental to the agency in that it is part and parcel of the arrangement for compensation.[3]

§ 19.11   The Assignor's Guaranty of Performance

The promise of an assignor to the assignee guarantying performance by the obligor is not within the Statute of Frauds.[1] Here the obligor is TP, the assignee is C and the assignor is D. Here again Corbin explains the result on the theory that this is a promise of indemnity,[2] and

---

5. 4 Corbin §§ 16,16, 16.18 (Brown 1997).

6. Id.

7. See n.4.

8. See n.5.

9. See nn.4 & 5.

10. 4 Corbin § 16.6 and n.4.

11. 3 Williston § 472 (3d ed.); Rs. 2d § 116 cmt c.

§ 19.10

1. 4 Corbin § 16.19 (Brown 1997); Rs. 2d § 121(2).

2. Id.

3. 3 Williston § 484 (3d ed.).

§ 19.11

1. 4 Corbin § 16.20 (Brown 1997); Rs. 2d § 122.

2. Id.

Williston again explains it by saying that the guaranty is incidental to a larger contract.[3]

§ 19.12 A Promise to Buy or Assume a Claim

If A owes B one hundred dollars and B promises to assign the right to payment to C, and C promises to pay a stated sum for the assignment, it is clear that C's promise to pay is not a promise to answer for the debt, default or miscarriage of another. C is not promising to pay the debt, but rather it is contemplated that the claim will continue with C as the holder of the claim.[1]

A different situation arises if D promises C to assume TP's debt for a consideration. Thus, when plaintiff agreed with the National Football League to assume a bankrupt's debt to the League in exchange for a license to sell football cards, D could enforce the contracts.[2] There are two reasons. First, under the main purpose rule, D's purpose was to benefit itself. Second, the suretyship Statute is designed to protect guarantors, not creditors.

B. CONTRACTS IN CONSIDERATION OF MARRIAGE

§ 19.13 When the Statute of Frauds Applies

The Statute of Frauds covers "any agreements made on consideration of marriage." It has consistently been held, however, that the Statute does not apply to mutual promises to marry.[1] This is not inherent in the language of the Statute but rather appears to be a policy decision,[2] although there is some indication that the drafters of the act did not intend to encompass mutual promises to marry within this terminology.[3] However it does apply to promises to give money or property or anything else in exchange for marriage or a promise of marriage,[4] including a promise to support a child of the prospective spouse.[5] It would even apply to a negative covenant given in exchange for the consideration of marriage.[6]

---

3. See § 19.10 n.3 supra.

§ 19.12

1. Chester Nat. Bank v. Rondout Marine, 46 A.D.2d 985, 362 N.Y.S.2d 268 (1974), appeal denied; 3 Williston § 480 (3d ed.); Rs. 2d § 122.

2. Power Entertainment v. National Football League Prop., 151 F.3d 247 (5th Cir.1998).

§ 19.13

1. Clark v. Pendleton, 20 Conn. 495 (1850); Blackburn v. Mann, 85 Ill. 222 (1877); Brock v. Button, 187 Wn. 27, 59 P.2d 761 (1936).

2. Short v. Stotts, 58 Ind. 29 (1877); Kellner v. Kellner, 196 Misc. 774, 90 N.Y.S.2d 743 (1949).

3. See Costigan, Has There Been Judicial Legislation in the Interpretation and Application of the "Upon Consideration of Marriage" and Other Contract Clauses of the Statute of Frauds?, 14 Ill.L.Rev. 1 (1919).

4. Chase v. Fitz, 132 Mass. 359 (1882).

5. Byers v. Byers, 618 P.2d 930 (Okl. 1980), or to adopt, Maddox v. Maddox, 224 Ga. 313, 161 S.E.2d 870 (1968).

6. Williams v. Hankins, 75 Colo. 136, 225 P. 243 (1924).

But the courts have held that the Statute does not apply if the promise is made merely in contemplation of marriage, that is, if marriage is not a consideration for the promise but is merely an occasion for the promise, or a condition of it.[7] The same is true if marriage is merely an incident of the contract and not the end to be attained.[8] A promise made by a third party in consideration of the marriage of two other persons is within this subsection of the Statute of Frauds.[9]

The fact that the marriage ceremony has taken place is not sufficient performance to make the promise enforceable.[10] If there has been additional part performance the unperformed part of the contract may become enforceable.[11] If not, restitutionary remedies may be available.[12] As usual, full performance on both sides eliminates any question of the Statute of Frauds.[13]

Of late, many courts have begun to recognize the validity of express contracts between unmarried cohabitants.[14] Perhaps anomalously such contracts are not subject to this provision of the Statute of Frauds.[15]

C.   CONTRACTS FOR THE SALE OF REALTY

§ 19.14   Contracts for the Sale of Land

(a) Introduction

The original Statute by its terms applied to "any contract or sale of lands, tenements or hereditaments, or any interest in or concerning them." This language would appear to encompass both the conveyance of an interest in land and an executory contract to transfer an interest in land.[1] However, other sections of the original Statute covered conveyances, and it is common even today to find conveyances governed by a separate statute. The clause under discussion has been interpreted as if it had said "contract for the sale of land" and this is the wording which is commonly adopted today. The phrase "tenements or hereditaments" is not of great significance today and many of the modern Statutes do

---

7. Riley v. Riley, 25 Conn. 154 (1856); Rs. 2d § 124 ill. 5.

8. Bader v. Hiscox, 188 Iowa 986, 174 N.W. 565, 10 ALR 316 (1919).

9. In re Peterson's Estate, 55 S.D. 457, 226 N.W. 641 (1929); Rs. 2d § 124.

10. Busque v. Marcou, 147 Me. 289, 86 A.2d 873, 30 ALR2d 1411 (1952).

11. Rs. 2d § 124 cmt d; see Ferrell v. Stanley, 83 Kan. 491, 112 P. 155 (1910); Thompson v. St. Louis Union Trust, 363 Mo. 667, 253 S.W.2d 116 (1952).

12. In re Marriage of Heinzman, 198 Colo. 36, 596 P.2d 61 (1979); see §§ 19.40 to 19.46.

13. McDonald v. McDonald, 215 Ala. 179, 110 So. 291 (1926); Bernstein v. Pru-

dential Ins., 204 Misc. 775, 124 N.Y.S.2d 624 (1953); see Annot. 30 ALR2d 1419 (1953).

14. See § 22.1 n.6 infra.

15. Morone v. Morone, 50 N.Y.2d 481, 429 N.Y.S.2d 592, 413 N.E.2d 1154 (1980); see Levin & Spak, Judicial Enforcement of Cohabitation Agreements: A Signal to Purge Marriage from the Statute of Frauds, 12 Creighton L.Rev. 499 (1978).

§ 19.14

1. A revocation of an offer to sell land need not be in a record. Board of Control v. Burgess, 45 Mich.App. 183, 206 N.W.2d 256 (1973).

not use this phraseology.[2]

(b) A Promise to Pay for an Interest in Real Property

Setting aside questions of part performance which are discussed later,[3] one of the most troublesome questions has been whether the Statute, which obviously applies to a promise to transfer an interest in land, also applies to a promise to pay for the interest. There is substantial authority for the proposition that a contract for the purchase and sale of an interest in realty is unenforceable against either the purchaser or the vendor absent a sufficient record signed by the party to be charged.[4] This is because, as we shall see, contracts, rather than promises, are within the Statute of Frauds.[5] However, under the wording of some Statutes, the contract to be enforceable must be signed by the "vendor" rather than the "party to be charged." Under such Statutes it would seem clear that the purchaser's promise could be enforced without a record signed by the purchaser.[6]

(c) Interests in Land

(1) In General

A difficult question is whether the subject matter of a particular contract constitutes an interest in land.[7] Some problem areas are discussed below. Not only is a promise to transfer a legal estate in lands covered but also a promise to create, or transfer or assign a lease,[8] or easement,[9] or rent,[10] or according to the majority view, a restriction on land.[11] Unlike an easement, a license is not within the Statute.[12] Also included are transactions relating to equitable interests in land including

2. 4 Corbin § 17.1 (Brown 1997).

3. See § 19.15 infra. See also Hamburger, the Conveyancing Purposes of the Statute of Frauds, 27 Am.J.Legal Hist. 354 (1983).

4. Rs. 2d § 125 cmt d; 4 Corbin § 17.2 (Brown 1997).

5. See §§ 19.22 & 19.36 infra.

6. Krohn v. Dustin, 142 Minn. 304, 172 N.W. 213 (1919). Some courts have held that in such a case the vendor must have signed and delivered a record to the purchaser or show that the purchaser otherwise accepted the record as correct. Geraci v. Jenrette, 41 N.Y.2d 660, 394 N.Y.S.2d 853, 363 N.E.2d 559 (1977). Cf. Thomas v. Dickinson, 12 N.Y. (2 Kern.) 364 (1855).

7. For a listing of interests in land, see 3 Williston § 491 (3d ed.).

8. Most statutes exclude a lease of short duration—usually from one to three years—from the operation of this subsection of the Statute. 4 Corbin § 17.7 (Brown 1997); Rs. 2d § 125 cmt b. On special problems concerning leases, see Volkmer, 6 Creighton

L.Rev. 342 (1973); Note, 27 Clev.St.L.Rev. 231 (1978).

9. Dougan v. Rossville Drainage Dist., 270 Kan. 468, 15 P.3d 338 (2000); Berg v. Ting, 125 Wn.2d 544, 886 P.2d 564 (1995).

10. "The common law regarded rent as 'issuing from the land.' Although the conception is artificial, an agreement to transfer the right to rent must, in many jurisdictions, be in writing; but a promise by an assignee of a lease to assume payment of rent need not be." 3 Williston § 491 (3d ed.) (footnotes omitted).

11. Sargent v. Leonardi, 223 Mass. 556, 112 N.E. 633 (1916); Kincheloe v. Milatzo, 678 P.2d 855 (Wyo.1984) (majority view); Thornton v. Schobe, 79 Colo. 25, 243 P. 617 (1925) (minority). Rs. 2d § 127 cmt b is in accord with the majority view.

12. Kitchen v. Kitchen, 465 Mich. 654, 641 N.W.2d 245 (2002); Moon v. Central Builders, 65 N.C.App. 793, 310 S.E.2d 390 (1984); 4 Corbin § 17.9 (Brown 1997); Rs. 2d § 127 cmt b.

the assignment of a contract of sale.[13] An option to buy an interest in realty is clearly within the Statute.[14] A settlement agreement that involves a promise to transfer real property is also within the Statute.[15] The ultimate answer to the question of what is an interest in land is found generally in the law of property,[16] but policy concerns may dictate deviations. For example, it has been held that shares in a cooperative apartment constitute real property.[17]

(2) Liens

A promise to give a mortgage or other lien as security for money loaned has ordinarily been held to be within this section of the Statute of Frauds even though the Statute refers to the "sale" of land.[18] But the Statute does not apply to an interest in land that arises by operation of law; for example, a grantor's lien or a constructive trust.[19] However, once a mortgage is created, a promise to assign it is not considered by most courts as the sale of an interest in land, but rather as the assignment of a chose in action since the assignment is ordinarily in connection with the transfer of the debt which the mortgage secures.[20]

(3) Fructus Industriales

Products of the soil, such as annual crops, obtained by the labor and cultivation of humans are not considered interests in land even though at the time of the making of the contract the crops are attached to the soil. "It has also been held to be true of crops that are gathered annually even though borne on perennial trunks or stems, such as apples, small fruits, and hardy shrubs and bulbs."[21] The Sales Article of the UCC adopts this approach. An official comment states, "[t]he concept of 'industrial' growing crops has been abandoned, for under modern practices fruit, perennial hay, nursery stock and the like must be brought within the scope of this Article."[22] The UCC is also specific that "the unborn young of animals" are to be considered goods.[23]

13. Traiman v. Rappaport, 41 F.2d 336, 71 ALR 475 (3d Cir.1930).

14. Michel v. Bush, 146 Ohio App.3d 208, 765 N.E.2d 911 (2001); Coombs v. Ouzounian, 24 Utah 2d 39, 465 P.2d 356 (1970).

15. FDIC v. Altholtz, 4 F.Supp.2d 80 (1998).

16. Rs. 2d § 127 cmt a.

17. Lebowitz v. Mingus, 100 A.D.2d 816, 474 N.Y.S.2d 748 (1984); contra Firth v. Lu, 146 Wn.2d 608, 49 P.3d 117 (2002).

18. Nixon v. Nixon, 100 N.J.Eq. 437, 135 A. 516 (1927); Sleeth v. Sampson, 237 N.Y. 69, 142 N.E. 355, 30 ALR 1400 (1923); Lambert v. Home Fed. S. & L. Assn., 481 S.W.2d 770 (Tenn.1972); contra, Bigelow v. Nottingham, 833 P.2d 764 (Colo.App.1991) (a lien-theory mortgage is not an interest in land).

19. 4 Corbin § 17.6 (Brown 1997); accord, Remmick v. Mills, 165 N.W.2d 61 (N.D.1968) (alfalfa).

20. Osborne, Mortgages § 65 (2d ed. 1970); Citizens United Bank, N.A. v. Pearlstein, 733 F.2d 28 (3d Cir.1984) (agreement to accept substitute performance to discharge mortgage). A promise to release property from the lien of a mortgage has been held not to be within the Statute of Frauds. Nye v. University Dev., 10 N.C.App. 676, 179 S.E.2d 795 (1971), cert. denied. But see Eastgate Enterprises v. Bank & Trust, 236 Pa.Super. 503, 345 A.2d 279 (1975) (promise not to foreclose is within the Statute).

21. 4 Corbin § 17.11 (Brown 1997).

22. UCC § 2–105 cmt 1 (unchanged by the revision).

23. Id. § 2–105(1) (unchanged by the revision).

(4) Other Things Attached to the Earth

The UCC,[24] provides: "A contract for the sale of minerals or the like (including oil and gas) or a structure or its materials to be removed from realty is a contract for the sale of goods within this Article if they are to be severed by the seller * * *."[25] "If the buyer is to sever, such transactions are considered contracts affecting land * * *."[26]

The UCC further provides: "a contract for the sale apart from land of growing crops or other things attached to realty and capable of severance without material harm thereto but not described in subsection (1)[27] or of timber to be cut is a contract for the sale of goods within this Article whether the subject matter is to be severed by the buyer or by the seller even though it forms part of the realty at the time of contracting, and the parties can by identification effect a present sale before severance."[28]

(5) Miscellaneous Excluded Items

If the subject matter of the contract is not the transfer of an interest in realty, it does not come within the Statute, even if the end result would be an interest in land. For example, a contract to build a building or to do work on land is not within the Statute,[29] and the same would be true of a contract to lend money to buy land,[30] and of a contract between partners to buy and sell real estate and to divide the profits.[31] It should also be noted that the fact that the consideration on one side of a contract is an executed interest in land does not bring the agreement within the Statute.[32] Boundary line and partition contracts are generally held to be within this section of the Statute of Frauds.[33]

A promise to pay a broker a commission for finding a purchaser is not within the traditional Statute of Frauds.[34] Several states, however,

24. Compare Baird v. Elliott, 63 N.D. 738, 249 N.W. 894, 91 ALR 1274 (1933) with Home Owners' Loan v. Gotwals, 67 S.D. 579, 297 N.W. 36 (1941) and with Slingluff v. Franklin Davis Nurseries, 136 Md. 302, 110 A. 523 (1920).

25. UCC § 2–107(1) (unchanged by the revision).

26. Id. § 2–107 cmt 1; see Bell v. Hill Bros. Constr., 419 So.2d 575 (Miss.1982).

27. Set forth in the preceding paragraph in the text.

28. UCC § 2–107(2) (unchanged by the revision).

29. Plunkett v. Meredith, 72 Ark. 3, 77 S.W. 600 (1903); McCaffrey v. Strainer, 81 A.D.2d 977, 439 N.Y.S.2d 773 (1981), app. dismissed; Scales v. Wiley, 68 Vt. 39, 33 A. 771 (1895).

30. Horner v. Frazier, 65 Md. 1, 4 A. 133 (1886).

31. Anderson v. Property Developers, 555 F.2d 648 (8th Cir.1977); Evanovich v. Hutto, 204 So.2d 477 (Miss.1967); Pace v. Perk, 81 A.D.2d 444, 440 N.Y.S.2d 710 (1981); see 4 Corbin § 17.12 (Brown 1997); contra, Rice v. Barnes, 149 F.Supp.2d 1297 (M.D.Ala.2001). A joint venture agreement that contemplates the transfer of land owned by one of the parties is within the Statute. Dobbs v. Vornado, 576 F.Supp. 1072 (E.D.N.Y.1983).

32. Byers v. Locke, 93 Cal. 493, 29 P. 119 (1892).

33. Rs. 2d § 128(1); but see Norwood v. Stevens, 104 Idaho 44, 655 P.2d 938 (App. 1982); DeWitt v. Lutes, 581 S.W.2d 941 (Mo.App.1979); Norberg v. Fitzgerald, 122 N.H. 1080, 453 A.2d 1301 (1982).

34. Atlantic Coast Realty v. Robertson, 240 Fed. 372 (4th Cir.1917).

have enacted a separate statute requiring such a contract to be in a record.[35]

§ 19.15   Enforceability Because of Part Performance

Prior to enactment of the Statute of Frauds a permissible method of conveyance of land was "livery of seisin," an oral transfer accompanied by a symbolic handing over of a twig or clump of earth in the presence of witnesses.[1] Within a decade of enactment of the Statute, the Chancellor ruled that where a grantee had been put into possession of land the Statute of Frauds was inapplicable as the transaction was "executed."[2] Consequently, the grantee was entitled to specific performance in the face of the grantor's attempt to regain possession.

Later courts, losing sight of the historical origins of the part performance doctrine, required more than possession, insisting on some conduct "unequivocally referable" to the alleged oral agreement. In Cardozo's words, there must be "performance which alone and without the aid of words of promise is unintelligible or at least extraordinary unless as an incident of ownership, assured if not existing * * *. [W]hat is done must itself supply the key to what is promised. It is not enough that what is promised may give significance to what is done."[3] In short, the conduct must convincingly evidence the existence of the agreement.[4] This occurs in some jurisdictions where there is payment and the making by the vendee of valuable improvements on the land with the consent of the vendor.[5] But in other jurisdictions these elements are not necessary[6] although it is clear that these are always important factors to be considered.[7] The "unequivocally referable" test, or some variation of

---

35. See, e.g., Pine–Wood, Ltd. v. Detroit Mtge. & Realty, 95 Mich.App. 85, 290 N.W.2d 86 (1980).

§ 19.15

1. See 14 Powell on Real Property ¶ 895 (1997).

2. Butcher v. Stapley, 1 Vern. 363, 23 Eng.Rep. 524 (Ch. 1685); see Pound, The Progress of the Law, 1918–1919, Equity, 33 Harv.L.Rev. 929–944 (1920).

3. Burns v. McCormick, 233 N.Y. 230, 232, 135 N.E. 273, 273 (1922). Cardozo may well have been influenced by Pound, n.2, at 944. For stringent application of the rule, see Wilson v. La Van, 22 N.Y.2d 131, 291 N.Y.S.2d 344, 238 N.E.2d 738 (1968), noted in 35 Brooklyn L.Rev. 301 (1969); Gilbride, The Part Performance Exception in New York, 26 Brooklyn L.Rev. 1 (1959). For analyses in other states, see Comment, 8 Idaho L.Rev. 205 (1971); Comment, 14 Kan. L.Rev. 647 (1966); Note, 9 Utah L.Rev. 91 (1964). For its application to leases, see Comment, 28 Baylor L.Rev. 413 (1976).

4. Anostario v. Vicinanzo, 59 N.Y.2d 662, 463 N.Y.S.2d 409, 450 N.E.2d 215 (1983); Eggers v. Rittscher, 247 Neb. 648, 529 N.W.2d 741 (1995); Nashan v. Nashan, 119 N.M. 625, 894 P.2d 402 (App.1995).

5. Pfeifer v. Raper, 253 Ark. 438, 486 S.W.2d 524 (1972); [but see Langston v. Langston, 3 Ark.App. 286, 625 S.W.2d 554 (1981)]; Baker v. Rice, 37 So.2d 837 (Fla. 1948); Weale v. Massachusetts Gen'l Housing, 117 N.H. 428, 374 A.2d 925 (1977); Sharp v. Stacy, 535 S.W.2d 345 (Tex.1976); Bradshaw v. McBride, 649 P.2d 74 (Utah 1982); Jasmin v. Alberico, 135 Vt. 287, 376 A.2d 32 (1977). Two requisites are considered in Note, 22 Baylor L.Rev. 588 (1970); Note, 22 Baylor L.Rev. 361 (1970).

6. Zukowski v. Dunton, 650 F.2d 30 (4th Cir.1981); Smith v. Cox, 247 Ga. 563, 277 S.E.2d 512 (1981); Recker v. Gustafson, 279 N.W.2d 744 (Iowa 1979); Tsiatsios v. Tsiatsios, 140 N.H. 173, 663 A.2d 1335 (1995); Spears v. Warr, 44 P.3d 742 (Utah 2002); Powers v. Hastings, 93 Wn.2d 709, 612 P.2d 371 (1980). See 4 Corbin § 18.15 (Brown 1997).

7. Bear Island Water Ass'n v. Brown, 125 Idaho 717, 874 P.2d 528 (1994); Stackhouse v. Cook, 271 S.C. 518, 248 S.E.2d 482 (1978).

it has been applied also to other provisions of the Statute.[8] A very small number of states do not recognize the doctrine of part performance.[9]

The doctrine is strictly a doctrine of equity, the available remedy being specific performance and not damages.[10] Under the equitable notion of mutuality, if the circumstances are such that the purchaser might obtain specific performance under the part performance doctrine, the vendor is entitled to demand specific performance.[11]

It is well settled that if the vendor fully performs by conveying to the vendee, the oral promise of the vendee is enforceable unless payment is to be by transfer of an interest in land.[12] On the other hand, full payment by the purchaser does not justify enforcement of the contract because the purchaser has the restitutionary remedy of quasi-contract.[13]

As discussed later the doctrine of promissory estoppel is fast making inroads on enforcement of oral contracts within the Statute of Frauds.[14] As this doctrine gains greater acceptance, the various technical requirements of the part performance doctrine applied in many states are giving way to a broader principle of promissory estoppel.

D. CONTRACTS FOR THE SALE OF GOODS: THE UCC

§ 19.16   Contracts for the Sale of Goods

(a) Introduction

Prior to enactment of the UCC, the Uniform Sales Act was the law of sales prevailing generally throughout the U.S. Section 2–201 of the UCC is to a large extent a restatement of the Sales Act provision with modifications and clarifications.[1] To a large extent, therefore, cases decided under the Sales Act continue to be authoritative.

---

8. Marta v. Mutual Life Ins., 887 F.Supp. 722 (D.Del.1995) (provision with respect to a promise of a non-consumer loan in excess of $100,000); Netteland v. Farm Bureau Life Ins., 510 N.W.2d 162 (Iowa App.1993) (one-year section), disapproved 567 N.W.2d 405 (Iowa 1997); Friedman & Fuller v. Funkhouser, 107 Md.App. 91, 666 A.2d 1298 (1995) (same); but see Pavel Enterprises v. A.S. Johnson Co., 342 Md. 143, 674 A.2d 521 (1996).

9. Mississippi, North Carolina and Tennessee. See 4 Corbin § 18.24 (Brown 1997). But see Baliles v. Cities Service, 578 S.W.2d 621 (Tenn.1979) (estoppel).

10. Cain v. Cross, 293 Ill.App.3d 255, 227 Ill.Dec. 659, 687 N.E.2d 1141 (1997); McKinnon v. Church of Jesus Christ of Latter–Day Saints, 529 P.2d 434 (Utah 1974); 4 Corbin § 17.10 (Brown 1997); Rs. 2d § 129 cmt c; Comment, 47 Can.B.Rev. 644 (1969). For a break-through case holding that because of the merger of law and equity, damages are now available, see Mil-

ler v. McCamish, 78 Wn.2d 821, 479 P.2d 919 (1971), 47 Wn.L.Rev. 524 (1972); see also Clay v. Bradley, 74 Wis.2d 153, 246 N.W.2d 142 (1976) (damages awarded; no discussion of remedy).

11. Walter v. Hoffman, 267 N.Y. 365, 196 N.E. 291, 101 ALR 919 (1935). See § 16.6 supra.

12. Rs. 2d § 125(3); Wiggins v. White, 157 Ga.App. 49, 276 S.E.2d 104 (1981); Dangelo v. Farina, 310 Mass. 758, 39 N.E.2d 754 (1942); Fox v. Bechthold, 37 P.3d 966 (Okla.App.2001); Allen v. Allen, 550 P.2d 1137 (Wyo.1976).

13. Rs. 2d § 129 ill. 1; Pugh v. Gilbreath, 571 P.2d 1241 (Okl.App.1977); but see Kartes v. Kartes, 195 Mont. 383, 636 P.2d 272 (1981).

14. See § 19.48 infra.

§ 19.16

1. Section 2–201 of the UCC provides:

(b) Price or Value

The Sales Act applied to goods "of the *value* of five hundred dollars or upwards," while the UCC refers to "the *price* of $500 or more." (The revision would raise the price threshold from $500 to $5,000). To what extent the codifiers intended a substantive change from the Sales Act is unclear. In ordinary speech "price" is far less vague a term than "value" and thus it may be that the codifiers intended to eliminate problems of (1) whether the Statute of Frauds applies when goods are sold for a price less than their value and (2) when, in addition to a monetary consideration, other benefits are conferred on the seller.[2] The resolution of the second of these problems, however, is complicated by § 2–304(1) which provides that: "the price can be made payable in money or otherwise."[3] This definition makes clear that the Statute of Frauds continues to apply if goods are exchanged not for money but for other property or services of a value of five hundred dollars or more.[4]

The UCC offers no solution to a recurring problem under pre-existing law. Often parties contract for the exchange of a number of chattels having an aggregate value in excess of five hundred dollars but which individually have a value below this statutory amount. The test, often difficult to apply, is whether there is one contract or several.[5]

Formal Requirements; Statute of Frauds

(1) Except as otherwise provided in this section a contract for the sale of goods for the price of $500 or more is not enforceable by way of action or defense unless there is some writing sufficient to indicate that a contract for sale has been made between the parties and signed by the party against whom enforcement is sought or by an authorized agent or broker. A writing is not insufficient because it omits or incorrectly states a term agreed upon but the contract is not enforceable under this paragraph beyond the quantity of goods shown in such writing.

(2) Between merchants if within a reasonable time a writing in confirmation of the contract and sufficient against the sender is received and the party receiving it has reason to know its contents, it satisfies the requirements of subsection (1) against such party unless written notice of objection to its contents is given within ten days after it is received.

(3) A contract which does not satisfy the requirements of subsection (1) but which is valid in other respects is enforceable

(a) if the goods are to be specially manufactured for the buyer and are not suitable for sale to others in the ordinary course of the seller's business and the seller, before notice of repudiation is received and under circumstances which reasonably indicate that the goods are for the buyer, has made either a substantial beginning of their man-

ufacture or commitments for their procurement; or

(b) if the party against whom enforcement is sought admits in his pleading, testimony or otherwise in court that a contract for sale was made, but the contract is not enforceable under this provision beyond the quantity of goods admitted; or

(c) with respect to goods for which payment has been made and accepted or which have been received and accepted (Section 2–606).

The revision would change the threshold amount to $5,000, substitute "record" for writing, provide that the one-year provision of the Statute of Frauds in inapplicable, and make some minor other changes.

This statute is also discussed in § 19.34 infra. The rationale for such a provision is the subject of: Johnston, The Statute of Frauds and Business Norms: A Testable Game–Theoretic Model, 144 U.Pa.L.Rev. 1859 (1996); and Posner, Norms, Formalities, and the Statute of Frauds, 144 U.Pa. L.Rev. 1971 (1966).

2. See Hawkland, Sales and Bulk Sales 33 (1958).

3. Stylistic change only in the revision.

4. This was the weight of authority under the Sales Act. Misner v. Strong, 181 N.Y. 163, 73 N.E. 965 (1905).

5. See Williston, Sales § 70 (rev.ed. 1948).

(c) Goods

The UCC provision with respect to manufactured goods is largely based on the compromise solution enacted in the Sales Act. A contract for sale of goods to be manufactured is within the Statute, unless "the goods are to be specially manufactured for the buyer and are not suitable for sale to others in the ordinary course of the seller's business and the seller, before notice of the repudiation is received and under circumstances which reasonably indicate that the goods are for the buyer, has made either a substantial beginning of their manufacture or commitments for their procurement."[6] Under the UCC, the seller need not be the manufacturer, but may be a third party. The UCC exemption applies, however, only if the seller has acted in reliance on the contract by making a substantial beginning toward manufacturing or by making commitments for the procurement of the goods.

Things that are realty or interests in realty are not included in the term "goods."[7] A vexatious problem is the mixed contract involving the sale of goods and transfer of real property, the rendition of services, or the transfer of intangibles. It is well established that a contract to furnish labor and materials in erecting a structure or repairing a chattel is not within the Statute unless there is a transfer of title to goods prior to annexation.[8] Some courts have sought to find the "essence" of the transaction, and to classify the transaction as "essentially" a sales rather than a service transaction.[9] Others have looked to the dominant purpose of the transaction.[10] These tests seem to be different terms for the same analysis.

(d) Choses in Action

The Statute of Frauds provision of the Uniform Sales Act specifically encompassed choses in action (intangible personal property) as well as goods. Section 2–201 of the UCC applies solely to contracts for the sale of goods. Three sections of the original UCC governed writing requirements in connection with transfer of choses in action. Section 8–319 related to investment securities, but has since been excised from revised Article 8.[11] Section 9–203 continues to govern the writing requirement for the creation of security interests and the assignment of contract rights.[12]

---

6. UCC § 2–201(3)(a); see 4 Corbin § 2–201(3)(a) (Brown 1997). On the distinction between stock items and specially manufactured goods, see Annot., 45 ALR4th 1126 (1981).

7. See § 19.14 supra.

8. 2 Corbin § 476 (1950); Marshall, The Applicability of the Uniform Commercial Code to Construction Contracts, 28 Emory L.J. 335 (1979); Annot., 5 ALR4th 501 (1981).

9. Robertson v. Ceola, 255 Ark. 703, 501 S.W.2d 764 (1973); see Note, 28 Md.L.Rev. 136 (1968).

10. United Industrial Syn. v. Western Auto Supply, 686 F.2d 1312 (8th Cir.1982); Ogden Martin Sys. v. Whiting, 179 F.3d 523 (7th Cir.1999) ("predominant thrust"); Colorado Carpet Install. v. Palermo, 668 P.2d 1384, 45 ALR4th 1113 (Colo.1983); 4 Corbin § 21.1 (Brown 1997).

11. UCC § 8–113(1994).

12. See § 18.5 infra. See also UCC § 5–104 (letters of credit).

Section 1–206 governs all contracts for the sale of personal property not specifically governed by the other writing or electronic recording requirements of the Code.[13] It requires a record signed by the party to be charged for a contract relating to the sale of a chose in action if the amount sought to be enforced in court exceeds $5,000. Principally, this section is intended to govern the assignment of rights known as general intangibles (e.g. patent rights)[14] that are not governed by Article 8 or 9 of the Code. Since outright assignments of general intangibles were not covered by the original Article 9 they were covered by this section,[15] as is the sale of a franchise.[16] Revised Article 1 would repeal this section without replacing it. "General intangible" is, however, now defined in § 9–102(a)(42) and its assignment is now covered by revised Article 9.

(e) Part Performance

The original sales Statute of Frauds and the later Sales Act provided that no writing was required if the buyer accepted or received the goods or gave something in earnest to bind the bargain or made a part payment. The UCC has made significant departures from preexisting law.[17] The UCC provision with respect to specifically manufactured goods is discussed above.[18]

(1) Accept and Receive

Prior to the UCC, the entire oral contract was enforceable if the buyer had accepted and received part of the goods.[19] Acceptance related to title[20] and receipt had to do with possession.[21] The UCC continues preexisting law only in part. The requirement of a record is dispensed with only as to those items which have been received and accepted.[22] Receipt continues to mean the taking of physical possession of the goods.[23] Acceptance, however, has a somewhat different meaning under the UCC. It is not a question of whether the buyer accepted title to the goods but whether the buyer has indicated an intention to keep the goods.[24] This represents a shift in emphasis from a legal conclusion to a factual one. The rationale for the "accept and received" exception as

---

13. See Comment, 70 Yale L.J. 603 (1961).

14. Goldsmith v. Income Properties, 31 N.Y.2d 1023, 341 N.Y.S.2d 898, 294 N.E.2d 657 (1973).

15. See Grappo v. Alitalia, 56 F.3d 427, 62 ALR5th 805 (2d Cir.1995) (applying the provision to a non-exclusive license of a copyright).

16. Ackerman Buick v. General Motors, 66 S.W.3d 51 (Mo.App.2001).

17. See 4 Corbin § 2.16 (Brown 1997).

18. See text at n.6 supra.

19. Uniform Sales Act § 4(1). This was true although the buyer denied contracting for any quantity beyond that which had been accepted and received. John Thallon &

Co. v. Edsil Trading, 302 N.Y. 390, 98 N.E.2d 572 (1951).

20. See Rs. 1st § 201.

21. See id. § 202.

22. UCC § 2–201(3)(c); see Bagby Land & Cattle v. California Livestock Comm'n, 439 F.2d 315 (5th Cir.1971); In re Nelsen's Estate, 209 Neb. 730, 311 N.W.2d 508 (1981); Gardner & Beedon v. Cooke, 267 Or. 7, 513 P.2d 758 (1973).

23. UCC § 2–103(1)(c) (unchanged in the revision) provides: " 'Receipt' of goods means taking physical possession of them."

24. The concept of acceptance is discussed in § 11.20 supra. For a typical Statute of Frauds acceptance case, see Pride Lab. v. Sentinel Butte Farmers Elevator, 268 N.W.2d 474 (N.D.1978).

well as for the exception discussed in the next paragraph is that "[r]eceipt and acceptance either of goods or of the price constitutes an unambiguous overt admission by both parties that a contract actually exists."[25] It should be noted, however, unlike the exception to the real property Statute of Frauds, there is no requirement that the part performance be "unequivocally referable" to the alleged contract.[26]

(2) Payment or Earnest

"Something in earnest," a phrase used in the original Statute of Frauds and in the Sales Act, sounds rather remote from modern commercial practice. The phrase has reference to an old custom of giving a sum of money or some tangible object to cement a bargain. "Earnest" is not part payment as it is not applied to the price.[27] Because of the disappearance or, at least, rarity of this practice, the UCC has abolished this exception to the requirement of a record.

Under prior law if payment in whole or in part was made by the buyer and accepted by the seller, the entire contract was enforceable.[28] The UCC, if taken literally, seems to have significantly changed this rule by providing that the contract is enforceable only as to "goods for which payment has been made and accepted."[29] Part payment, therefore, would seem to give rise only to partial enforcement.[30] However, the commentators and some decisions take the position that if a just apportionment can be made it should be made; if not, part payment should make the entire contract enforceable.[31] The UCC also indicates that the part payment may be made by money, check, goods or services so long as the money, check, goods or services have been accepted.[32]

(f) Admission in Court

The UCC expressly provides that a contract is enforceable "if the party against whom enforcement is sought admits in his pleading, testimony or otherwise in court that a contract for sale was made, but

---

25. UCC § 2–201 cmt 2.

26. Hofmann v. Stoller, 320 N.W.2d 786 (N.D.1982); Gerner v. Vasby, 75 Wis.2d 660, 250 N.W.2d 319, 97 ALR3d 897 (1977).

27. See 2 Corbin § 494 (1950); 3 Williston § 564 (3d ed.). Some cases have held that "earnest" and part payment are the same thing. Scott v. Mundy & Scott, 193 Iowa 1360, 188 N.W. 972, 23 ALR 460 (1922).

28. 2 Corbin § 495 (1950); 3 Williston § 565 (3d ed.); Rs. 1st § 205.

29. UCC § 2–201(3)(c) (1950); see Gray v. Wilbanks, 646 So.2d 152 (Ala.Civ.App. 1994) (check for full payment which was stopped); Huyler Paper Stock v. Information Supplies, 117 N.J.Super. 353, 284 A.2d 568 (1971).

30. Williamson v. Martz, 11 Pa.D. & C.2d 33 (1958).

31. Nordstrom, Sales § 27, at 69–72 (1970); see Lockwood v. Smigel, 18 Cal. App.3d 800, 96 Cal.Rptr. 289 (1971); Thomaier v. Hoffman Chevrolet, 64 A.D.2d 492, 410 N.Y.S.2d 645 (1978) (both hold that a small down payment permitted proof that a contract was made for the sale of a car). See, Beane, The Partial Payment Exception to the UCC Sale of Goods Statute of Frauds, 13 UCC L.J. 135 (1980); Note, 20 U.Kan.L.Rev. 538 (1972). See also UCC § 2–201 cmt 2.

32. UCC § 2–201 cmt 2; see Kaufman v. Solomon, 524 F.2d 501 (3d Cir.1975) (receipt and retention of a check).

the contract is not enforceable under this provision beyond the quantity of goods admitted."[33]

This provision is new, although to some extent the problems it concerns itself with were raised in prior case law.[34] The principal question the UCC provision raises is whether and to what extent the party against whom enforcement is sought can be compelled to admit the existence of the oral contract either during the trial or in pre-trial proceedings. That is, may the party charged object to the question on the grounds that the Statute of Frauds has been raised as an affirmative defense? It has been held that, under the UCC, it is no longer possible to dismiss a complaint that on its face alleges an oral contract within the Statute of Frauds because the defendant may conceivably admit the existence of the contract at trial, and such holdings appear to be quite consistent with the legislative intention behind the UCC provision.[35] For this exception to apply, it is essential that the person testifying be, at the time of testifying, the party to be charged or an agent still having authority to bind the principal.[36] Of course, a pleading that references the oral contract is a sufficient admission.[37]

(g) Memoranda, Confirmations, and Estoppel

These topics are discussed below.[38]

E. CONTRACTS NOT PERFORMABLE WITHIN A YEAR

§ 19.17 Computation of the One Year Period

The original Statute of Frauds embraced within its terms "an agreement that is not to be performed within the space of one year from making thereof." The test is not how long the performance will take, but

---

33. Id. § 2–201(3)(b). There was a similar provision in § 8–319(d). Cf. Martocci v. Greater New York Brewery, 301 N.Y. 57, 92 N.E.2d 887 (1950). UCC § 2–201 cmt 7 adds: "Under this section it is no longer possible to admit the contract in court and still treat the statute as a defense. However, the contract is not thus conclusively established. The admission so made by a party is itself evidential against him of the truth of the facts so admitted and of nothing more, as against the other party, it is not evidential at all." See also, Blankenfeld v. Smith, 290 Minn. 475, 188 N.W.2d 872 (1971); Rs. 2d § 133 cmt d; Herbert, Procedure and Promise: Rethinking the Admissions Exception to the Statute of Frauds, 45 Okla. L.Rev. 203 (1992); Stevens, Ethics and the Statute of Frauds, 37 Cornell L.Q. 355 (1952).

34. See 4 Corbin §§ 14.1 & 14.21 (Brown 1997); Note, 38 Cornell L.Q. 604 (1953).

35. Roth Steel v. Sharon Steel., 705 F.2d 134 (6th Cir.1983); Garrison v. Piatt, 113 Ga.App. 94, 147 S.E.2d 374 (1966); Lewis v. Hughes, 276 Md. 247, 346 A.2d 231, 88 ALR3d 406 (1975); Weiss v. Wolin, 60 Misc.2d 750, 303 N.Y.S.2d 940 (1969); contra, Triangle Marketing v. Action Indus., 630 F.Supp. 1578 (N.D.Ill.1986). See, Duesenberg, 33 Bus.Law. 1859 (1978); Yonge, 33 Wn. & Lee L.Rev. 1 (1976); Notes, 65 Cal.L.Rev. 150 (1977); 3 J.L. & Com. 167 (1983); 56 Tex.L.Rev. 915 (1978); 32 U.Fla.L.Rev. 486 (1980); Annot., 88 ALR3d 416 (1978).

36. Miller v. Sirloin Stockade, 224 Kan. 32, 578 P.2d 247 (1978).

37. Synergistic Tech. v. IDB Mobile Comm., 871 F.Supp. 24 (D.D.C.1994).

38. See § 19.34 (sufficiency of the record); §§ 19.47, 19.48 (estoppel).

when will it be complete. Thus, if on December 10, 2003, A in a bilateral contract promises to make a one hour television appearance on February 1, 2005, the contract is within the Statute.[1]

If A contracts to work for B for one year, the work to begin more than one day after making the agreement, the contract is within the one-year section;[2] but if the work is to begin the very next day the contract is not within the Statute. The theory is that the law disregards fractions of a day.[3] If the contract is restated at the beginning of the work and the restatement can be regarded as the making or remaking of the contract, the year starts to run from that time. "Courts have been very liberal in holding that the restatement was itself a contract."[4]

It is difficult to discern a rationale for the one year provision of the Statute of Frauds. It has been speculated that "as in the case of the other subsections the draftsmen had in mind a transaction type: employment and similar relationships, such as apprenticeships and fiduciary retainers. The common law rule was that a general hiring was presumed to be for a one year term."[5] Some have thought that its purpose was "not to trust to the memory of witnesses for a longer time than one year."[6] However, "[t]here is no necessary relationship between the time of the making of the contract, the time within which its performance is required and the time when it might come to court to be proven."[7] Because of the lack of discernable rationale, the tendency has been to give the provision a narrow construction.[8]

§ 19.18 Possibility of Performance Within One Year

The one-year section of the Statute of Frauds has never been a favorite of the courts; it has been interpreted in such a way as to narrow its scope as much as possible. Thus, it is has been interpreted to mean that it only applies to a promise or agreement[1] which by its terms does not admit of performance within one year from the time of its making. If by its terms, performance is possible within one year, however unlikely or improbable that may be, the agreement or promise is not within this subsection of the Statute of Frauds.[2] Thus a promise made in October

§ 19.17

1. See Lund v. E.D. Etnyre & Co., 103 Ill.App.2d 158, 242 N.E.2d 611 (1968). For unilateral contracts see § 19.24 infra.

2. Sinclair v. Sullivan Chevrolet, 31 Ill.2d 507, 202 N.E.2d 516 (1964); Jennings v. Ruidoso Racing Ass'n, 79 N.M. 144, 441 P.2d 42 (1968).

3. Rs. 1st § 198 cmt d; 4 Corbin § 19.4 (Brown 1997); 3 Williston § 502 (3d ed.).

4. 4 Corbin § 19.5 (Brown 1997); see also 3 Williston § 503 (3d ed.); Rs. 2d § 130 cmt c.

5. Perillo, The Statute of Frauds in the Light of the Functions and Dysfunctions of Form, 43 Fordham L.Rev. 39, 77 n.214 (1974).

6. Smith v. Westall, 1 Ld. Raym. 316, 317, 91 Eng.Rep. 1106, 1107 (1697).

7. D & N Boening v. Kirsch Beverages, 63 N.Y.2d 449, 454, 483 N.Y.S.2d 164, 165, 472 N.E.2d 992, 993 (1984).

8. Explicitly so stated in, e.g., Ohanian v. Avis Rent A Car System, 779 F.2d 101, 106 (2d Cir.1985).

§ 19.18

1. Whether "promises" or "agreements" are within this subsection of the Statute of Frauds is discussed in § 19.22 infra.

2. C.R. Klewin, Inc. v. Flagship Properties, 220 Conn. 569, 600 A.2d 772 (1991); Davidson v. Holtzman, 47 S.W.3d 445 (Tenn.App.2000).

1920 to cut down and deliver certain timber on or before April 1, 1922 is not within the Statute.[3] It is immaterial whether or not the actual period of performance exceeded one year.[4] The same is true of a promise to build a house within fifteen months.[5] A promise to perform on completion of a dam is not within the Statute although it is contemplated that the dam will be completed in three years and in fact completion takes three years.[6] In general, contracts of indefinite duration are not within this provision of the Statute.[7] In short, the question is, *would it be a breach of contract to perform in less than a year; only then is the contract within the one-year section.* A distinct minority of cases have taken into account how the parties intended and expected that the contract would be performed, and if they expect performance to endure beyond a year from the making of the contract it is held to be within the Statute.[8]

Despite its narrow construction, there *are* contracts that are within the Statute of Frauds. A promise by A to work for B for a period in excess of one year[9] or a promise not to compete for two years is within the Statute, although there are contrary cases.[10] The theory of the contrary authorities is that although the contract cannot by its terms be performed or even terminated within a year, its purpose would be attained within a year if the promisor were to die. A promise by B to pay in monthly installments extending over a period of two years is definitely within the Statute.[11]

It has generally been held that a contract whereby an employee is to be paid a bonus or commission on an annual basis but which cannot be calculated and paid until after the books have been closed is not within

3. Gallagher v. Finch, Pruyn & Co., 211 A.D. 635, 207 N.Y.S. 403 (1925), amended 212 A.D. 847, 207 N.Y.S. 403 (1925). Numerous cases in accord are collected in 4 Corbin § 19.1 (Brown 1997).

4. In re Estate of Hargreaves, 201 Kan. 57, 439 P.2d 378 (1968).

5. Plimpton v. Curtiss, 15 Wend. 336 (N.Y.1836); Rs. 2d § 130 cmt a; but see J.R. Loftus, Inc. v. White, 85 N.Y.2d 874, 649 N.E.2d 1196, 626 N.Y.S.2d 52 (1995) (contract to build a house with a one year warranty from completion would be within the Statute).

6. Gronvold v. Whaley, 39 Wn.2d 710, 237 P.2d 1026 (1951); accord, Walker v. Johnson, 96 U.S. (6 Otto) 424 (1877); C.R. Klewin, Inc. v. Flagship Properties, 220 Conn. 569, 600 A.2d 772 (1991); Augusta Bank & Trust v. Broomfield, 231 Kan. 52, 643 P.2d 100 (1982); Chesapeake Fin. v. Laird, 289 Md. 594, 425 A.2d 1348 (1981); Thompson v. Stuckey, 171 W.Va. 483, 300 S.E.2d 295 (1983); contra Doyle's Constr. & Remodeling v. Wendy's Int'l, 144 F.Supp.2d 969 (N.D.Ill.2001).

7. Joe Regueira, Inc. v. American Distilling, 642 F.2d 826 (5th Cir.1981); Adell

Broadcasting v. Cablevision Indus., 854 F.Supp. 1280 (E.D.Mich.1994); Garland v. Branstad, 648 N.W.2d 65 (2002); Weiner v. McGraw–Hill, 57 N.Y.2d 458, 457 N.Y.S.2d 193, 443 N.E.2d 441, 33 ALR4th 110 (1982); Rs. 2d § 130 cmt a.

8. Krueger v. Young, 406 S.W.2d 751 (Tex.App.1966); 4 Corbin § 19.3 (Brown 1997); 3 Williston § 500 (3d ed.). On the peculiar line of New York cases in agency situations see § 19.24 infra.

9. Carroll v. Palmer Mfg., 181 Mich. 280, 148 N.W. 390 (1914); Feinerman v. Russ Togs, 37 A.D.2d 805, 324 N.Y.S.2d 855 (1971); Chase v. Hinkley, 126 Wis. 75, 105 N.W. 230 (1905).

10. Higgins v. Gager, 65 Ark. 604, 47 S.W. 848 (1898); McGirr v. Campbell, 71 A.D. 83, 75 N.Y.S. 571 (1902). Contra, Doyle v. Dixon, 97 Mass. 208, 93 Am.Dec. 80 (1867); Rs. 2d § 130, ill. 4; see 4 Corbin § 19.10 (Brown 1997); 3 Williston § 497 (3d ed.). See § 19.20 infra.

11. Sophie v. Ford, 230 A.D. 568, 245 N.Y.S. 470 (1930); Thompson v. Ford, 145 Tenn. 335, 236 S.W. 2 (1921). But see Rs. 2d § 130 cmt d.

the Statute although the bonus cannot be calculated until after the end of the year.[12]

§ 19.19   Performance Conditioned on an Uncertain Event

Contracts of indefinite duration are not within the one-year section. If A contracts to pay B $10,000 on the sale of certain property, it is not within the Statute because the act of payment can be performed within a year and it is possible that the condition will occur within a year.[1] Insurance contracts for more than one year are generally not within the one-year section because the contingency on which payment is promised may occur within the year.[2] A warranty that a pressure cooker will not explode is not within the one year provision even if the explosion on which suit is brought occurs two years after the making of the warranty.[3] Also, it has been held that an oral promise made by a railroad to maintain a switch so long as the plaintiff needed it is enforceable twenty-two years after it was made.[4]

So too, the one year provision does not bar enforcement of a contract to leave a bequest by will[5] or to pay a sum at the death of a named person,[6] or a contract for lifetime employment.[7] The contingency of death could occur within the year and therefore it is immaterial whether it occurred within the year or many years later. It should be noted, however, that legislation in some jurisdictions has extended the Statute of Frauds to contracts which are not performable before the end of a lifetime and to contracts to make testamentary dispositions.[8]

§ 19.20   A Promise Terminable on an Uncertain Event

If A promises to supply B with services for the duration of the war, A's promise is not within the Statute because the war might have ended

---

12. White Lighting v. Wolfson, 68 Cal.2d 336, 66 Cal.Rptr. 697, 438 P.2d 345 (1968); Dennis v. Thermoid, 128 N.J.L. 303, 25 A.2d 886 (1942); Cron v. Hargro Fabrics, 91 N.Y.2d 362, 670 N.Y.S.2d 973, 694 N.E.2d 56 (1998); Robertson v. Pohorelsky, 583 S.W.2d 956 (Tex.App.1979).

§ 19.19

1. Sullivan v. Winters, 91 Ark. 149, 120 S.W. 843 (1909); Bartlett v. Mystic River, 151 Mass. 433, 24 N.E. 780 (1890).

2. Sanford v. Orient Ins., 174 Mass. 416, 54 N.E. 883 (1899); International Ferry v. American Fidelity, 207 N.Y. 350, 101 N.E. 160 (1913); Struzewski v. Farmers' Fire Ins., 179 A.D. 318, 166 N.Y.S. 362 (1917) reversed on other grounds; 4 Corbin § 19.2 (Brown 1997); Hollman, Insurance and the Statute of Frauds, [1977] Ins. L.J. 143. But if there is a promise to pay premiums over a number of years, this promise is within the one-year section of the Statute of Frauds. Hummel v. Hummel, 133 Ohio St. 520, 14 N.E.2d 923 (1938).

3. Joseph v. Sears, Roebuck, 224 S.C. 105, 77 S.E.2d 583, 40 ALR2d 742 (1953).

4. Warner v. Texas and P. Ry., 164 U.S. 418 (1896).

5. Dixon v. Lamson, 242 Mass. 129, 136 N.E. 346 (1922); Carlin v. Bacon, 322 Mo. 435, 16 S.W.2d 46, 69 ALR 1 (1929). It, however, may be within the real property provision. See § 19.14 infra.

6. Riddle v. Backus, 38 Iowa 81 (1874).

7. Shaw v. Maddox Metal, 73 S.W.3d 472 (Tex.App.2002) (lifetime annuity); Wior v. Anchor Indus., 641 N.E.2d 1275 (Ind. App.1994), reversed because contract was for 20+ years. 669 N.E.2d 172 (1996); contra McInerney v. Charter Golf, 176 Ill.2d 482, 680 N.E.2d 1347, 223 Ill.Dec. 911 (1997), noted 43 St.Louis L.J. 137 (1999) (pointing out that Illinois is lonely on this point); Boyle v. Tyler Pipe Indus., 6 S.W.3d 593 (Tex.App.1999).

8. See Note, 50 Fordham L.Rev. 239 (1981).

within a year.[1] So too, if A promises to support X for life or to employ X for life, the promise is not within the Statute. It is not for a fixed term and X may die within a year.[2] These cases should be compared with cases cited in § 19.18 at n.9. There, it is said that if A promised to work for B for two years, the contract is within the Statute of Frauds. But it is quite possible that A might die within a year and the contract discharged under the doctrine of impossibility.[3] Nonetheless, the courts hold that where the contract is phrased in terms of a number of years rather than in terms of a lifetime, death operates as a *defeasance* of the contract rather than as its fulfillment.[4] Where the contract is phrased in terms of a specific number of years with an express provision for termination at death, the authorities are not harmonious as to the proper result.[5]

In Duncan v. Clarke[6] a promise was made to pay for the support of a child by paying sixty dollars per month until the child became twenty-one. At the time of the promise the child was four years of age. The majority opinion held that if the child were to die the agreement would have been fully performed and since the child could have died within a year the promise by its terms might have been performed within a year.[7] The contrary argument, that appears to have been accepted by the court below, is death would have resulted in the defeasance of the contract and not the attainment of its essential purpose.

§ 19.21   Alternative Performances; Options to Terminate or Extend

Where a contracting party promises one of two or more performances in the alternative, the promise is not within the one-year section if any of the alternatives can be performed within one year from the time of the making thereof. It does not matter which party has the right to name the alternative.[1]

If A and B enter into an oral contract by the terms of which A promises to perform services for B for five years and B promises to pay

§ 19.20

1. Canister v. National Can, 63 F.Supp. 361 (D.Del.1945), motion denied.

2. Quirk v. Bank of Commerce & Trust, 244 F. 682 (6th Cir.1917); Kitsos v. Mobile Gas Service, 404 So.2d 40 (Ala.1981); Hobbs v. Brush Elec. Light, 75 Mich. 550, 42 N.W. 965 (1889); Bussard v. College of St. Thomas, 294 Minn. 215, 200 N.W.2d 155 (1972); Fidelity Union Trust v. Reeves, 96 N.J.Eq. 490, 125 A. 582 (1924), aff'd; Young v. Ward, 917 S.W.2d 506 (Tex.App.1996); contra, Quinn v. Workforce 2000, 887 F.Supp. 131 (E.D.Tex.1995) (lifetime employment is within the Statute); see Comment, 50 Baylor L.Rev. 493 (1998).

3. See § 13.7 supra.

4. See 4 Corbin § 19.4 (Brown 1997).

5. Compare Gilliam v. Kouchoucos, 161 Tex. 299, 340 S.W.2d 27, 88 ALR2d 693 (1960) with Silverman v. Bernot, 218 Va. 650, 239 S.E.2d 118 (1977); see Rs. 2d § 130 cmt b.

6. 308 N.Y. 282, 125 N.E.2d 569, 49 ALR2d 1287 (1955); accord In re Marriage of Strand, 86 Ill.App.3d 827, 42 Ill.Dec. 37, 408 N.E.2d 415 (1980).

7. 4 Corbin § 19.3 (Brown 1997); see Rs. 2d § 130 cmt b.

§ 19.21

1. Hill v. GMAC, 207 Mich.App. 504, 525 N.W.2d 905 (1994) (five-year lease with option to purchase in first year); 4 Corbin § 19.3 (Brown 1997); but see § 19.36 infra, which states a different rule for the other subsections of the Statute of Frauds.

for the services at a fixed rate over that period and one or both have the right by the terms of the contract to terminate the contract as for example by giving 30 days notice within the year, is the one-year section a defense? The majority view is that the Statute is a defense because although *defeasance* is possible within a year *performance* is not.[2]

The other view is that the contract is not within the Statute of Frauds.[3] It is reasoned that alternative promises are provided: (1) either to perform for the full period or (2) to perform up to the time of election and then exercise that option to cancel.[4] As we have seen, the general rule is that if one of the alternative promises may be performed within a year the one-year section does not apply. A peculiar variation on this approach has been made by the New York courts. It is held that the Statute does not apply if the option of termination is bilateral or if the option is in the defendant, but that the Statute would be a defense if the option of termination is only in the plaintiff. "For in such cases defendant's liability endures indefinitely subject only to the uncontrolled voluntary act of the party who seeks to hold the defendant. Under such circumstances it is illusory, from the point of view of the defendant, to consider the contract terminable or performable within one year."[5]

Options to extend or renew present similar problems. The same split of authority evidenced in the option to terminate cases also appears here.[6] Again, New York takes a peculiar position. If the option to extend or renew that could require performance for more than one year is held by the plaintiff, the contract is within the Statute. If the option is bilateral or is held by the defendant alone, the contract is outside the reach of the Statute.[7]

§ 19.22   Multiple Promises in One Contract

Where any of the promises on either side of a bilateral contract cannot be fully performed within one year from the time of the formation of the contract, the entire contract is within the one-year section of the Statute of Frauds.[1] This means that the contract is unenforceable by

2. Coan v. Orsinger, 265 F.2d 575 (D.C.Cir.1959); Barth v. Women's City Club, 254 Mich. 270, 236 N.W. 778 (1931); Deevy v. Porter, 11 N.J. 594, 95 A.2d 596 (1953); see 3 Williston §§ 498A–498B (3d ed.); Rs. 2d § 130 cmt b. However, comment b goes on to say that the "distinction between performance and non-performance is sometimes tenuous; it depends on the terms and the circumstances, particularly on whether the essential purpose of the parties will be attained." Illustrations 6 and 7 appear to be contradictory.

3. Fothergill v. McKay Press, 361 Mich. 666, 106 N.W.2d 215 (1960); see 4 Corbin §§ 19.6 & 19.2 (Brown 1997).

4. Hopper v. Lennen & Mitchell, 146 F.2d 364, 161 ALR 282 (9th Cir.1944); Johnston v. Bowersock, 62 Kan. 148, 61 P.

740 (1900); Blake v. Voight, 134 N.Y. 69, 31 N.E. 256 (1892).

5. Harris v. Home Indem., 6 A.D.2d 861, 175 N.Y.S.2d 603 (1958).

6. Hand v. Osgood, 107 Mich. 55, 64 N.W. 867 (1895) (the Statute is a defense). Contra, Ward v. Hasbrouck, 169 N.Y. 407, 62 N.E. 434 (1902); see 4 Corbin § 19.7 (Brown 1997).

7. See Belfert v. Peoples Planning, 22 Misc.2d 753, 199 N.Y.S.2d 839 (1959), aff'd.

§ 19.22

1. 4 Corbin § 19.13 (Brown 1997); Rs. 1st § 198; Rs. 2d § 130(1) and cmt d. However, see the rule stated for alternative promises in § 19.21 and § 19.36.

either party in the absence of a sufficient record or in the absence of performance, the effect of which is discussed in the next section. Other qualifications of the rule are discussed in § 19.36.

§ 19.23　Performance Under the One–Year Section

Courts have had to deal with the question of part and full performance on one side under each subsection of the Statute of Frauds. Different doctrines have been forged for many of these subsections. Under the majority view, full performance on one side renders a contract within the one-year section enforceable.[1] Some of the jurisdictions adopting this view, however, qualify this position by requiring that the performance must have actually taken place within one year from the making of the contract.[2] A minority of jurisdictions, however, hold that performance is ineffective to render the contract enforceable, restricting the performing party to a quasi-contractual remedy.[3]

Traditionally, part performance on one side does not entitle either party to sue to enforce the contract,[4] unless according to some authorities, the contract is divisible.[5] Traditions change and there is contrary case law.[6] Quasi-contractual recovery is available to the performing party.[7] There are also a number of cases in which enforcement has been granted on the basis of estoppel.[8]

§ 19.24　Unilateral Contracts

There is a great deal of authority to the effect that unilateral contracts are enforceable without reference to the one-year Statute of Frauds.[1] This stems in part from the majority rule that where the plaintiff has fully performed, the one year provision of the Statute is not a defense.[2]

Even in jurisdictions adopting the minority view, however, it is still arguable that a unilateral contract would not ordinarily be within the

§ 19.23

1. Ortega v. Kimbell Foods, 462 F.2d 421 (10th Cir.1972); Emerson v. Universal Prods., 35 Del. 277, 162 A. 779 (Super.1932); Glass v. Minnesota Protective Life Ins., 314 N.W.2d 393 (Iowa 1982); McElwee v. Estate of Joham, 15 S.W.3d 557 (Tex.App.2000); Lambousis v. Johnston, 657 P.2d 358 (Wyo.1983); 4 Corbin § 19.13 (Brown 1997); Rs. 2d § 130 and cmt d; Annot., 6 ALR2d 1111 (1949).

2. See 4 Corbin § 19.14 (Brown 1997).

3. Montgomery v. Futuristic Foods, 66 A.D.2d 64, 411 N.Y.S.2d 371 (1978).

4. Advocat v. Nexus Indus., 497 F.Supp. 328 (D.Del.1980); Chevalier v. Lane's, 147 Tex. 106, 213 S.W.2d 530, 6 ALR2d 1045 (1948); Rs. 2d § 130 cmt e.

5. Blue Valley Creamery v. Consolidated Prods., 81 F.2d 182 (8th Cir.1936) (install-

ment sales of dairy products); Murphy v. CNY Fire Emergency Servs., 225 A.D.2d 1034, 639 N.Y.S.2d 628 (1996); but see § 19.36 infra.

6. Schnider v. Carlisle, 65 S.W.3d 619 (Tenn.App.2001).

7. See §§ 19.40 to 19.46 infra.

8. See §§ 19.47 & 19.48 infra.

§ 19.24

1. Hartung v. Billmeier, 243 Minn. 148, 66 N.W.2d 784 (1954) ("You boys stick with me for five years and I will give you a hundred dollars a year bonus."); John William Costello Assocs. v. Standard Metals, 99 A.D.2d 227, 472 N.Y.S.2d 325 (1984); Auerbach's v. Kimball, 572 P.2d 376 (Utah 1977); Rs. 2d § 130 cmt a; 4 Corbin § 19.14 (Brown 1997).

2. See § 19.23 supra.

Statute of Frauds. If A said to B, "if you walk across Brooklyn Bridge three years from today, I promise to pay you $100 immediately after you walk," the promise logically would not be within the one year provision of the Statute because, by its terms, its performance is to take place immediately after the contract is made.[3] The result would logically be different if A's promise was to pay more than one year after B performed the act that created the contract.[4]

A series of decisions in New York, a minority jurisdiction, are of interest in this context. Among the more interesting of these cases is Martocci v. Greater N.Y. Brewery.[5] The defendant had promised to pay the plaintiff a 5% commission on all sales made by the defendant to P. Lorillard & Co., if the plaintiff introduced P. Lorillard & Co. to the defendant. The plaintiff performed and the defendant set up the defense of the one year provision of the Statute of Frauds.

There are a number of preliminary observations to be made. First the plaintiff had completely performed, and, therefore, under the majority view the Statute of Frauds would have been satisfied.[6] Second, the contract was unilateral as it did not arise until the plaintiff had performed.

The Court of Appeals held, however, that the defendant's promise was within the Statute, stating:

"If the terms of the contract here had included an event which might end the contractual relationship of the parties within a year, defendant's possible liability beyond that time would not bring the contract within the [S]tatute. Since, however, the terms of the contract are such that the relationship will continue beyond a year, it is within the [S]tatute, even though the continuing liability to which defendant is subject is merely a contingent one. The endurance of the defendant's liability is the deciding factor. The mere cessation of orders from Lorillard to defendant would not alter the contractual relationship between the parties; it would not constitute performance; plaintiff would still be in possession of his contractual right, though it may have no monetary value, immediately or ever."[7]

---

3. This is logical where the Statute speaks in terms of an "agreement," but not necessarily so when it speaks in terms of a "promise." That is to say the issue is whether in the case of a unilateral contract the year is to be measured from the making of the promise or the making of the contract.

4. See Simpson, Contracts 172 (2d ed. 1965); Rs. 2d § 130 cmt c.

5. 301 N.Y. 57, 92 N.E.2d 887 (1950), motion denied 301 N.Y. 662, 93 N.E.2d 926 (1950). This and subsequent New York cases are discussed in Comment, 25 Fordham L.Rev. 720 (1957).

6. See the similar sales commission case of McIntire v. Woodall, 140 N.H. 228, 666 A.2d 934 (1995).

7. 301 N.Y. at 62–63, 92 N.E.2d at 889; accord, Zupan v. Blumberg, 2 N.Y.2d 547, 161 N.Y.S.2d 428, 141 N.E.2d 819 (1957) (commission payable to salesman on any account he brought in so long as account remained active); Nurnberg v. Dwork, 12 A.D.2d 612, 208 N.Y.S.2d 799 (1960), aff'd (commission on percentage of sales if at any future time plaintiff obtains concessions for defendant at designated stores); contra, Crabb v. Mid–American Dairymen, 735 S.W.2d 714 (Mo.1987).

The contract was treated as of perpetual rather than of indefinite duration.[8] The court here distinguished the kind of case typified by a promise to deliver services for the duration of the war. In such a case the contingency is expressed in the contract and the contingency terminates the contractual relationship; thus, the promise by its terms may be performed within a year. In a case such as Martocci, the promise endures continuously into the future. The court does not take into account the possibility that P. Lorillard may cease to exist within a year. We have previously seen that if a promise is limited by the life of a person, or even if the essential purpose of the contract for a period of years is attained on the death of a person, it is not within the one-year section.[9] In the Martocci case, however, it is quite clear that by its terms the performance of the defendant was not limited by the life of the customer, P. Lorillard & Co. Had it been, the problem would be that stated in § 19.22. It would also appear that the essential purpose of the parties would not be achieved if the corporation ceased to exist.

In a later case,[10] the plaintiff, pursuant to an oral agreement, was promised the exclusive distributorship of the defendant's beer in a specified area for as long as defendant sold beer in the area.[11] Two years later the defendant designated a new distributor. Plaintiff sued for breach and defendant set up as a defense the one-year section of the Statute of Frauds. The Court held that the Statute was not a defense, indicating that since by the terms of the contract the defendant could at any time discontinue its beer sales in the area, the defendant could perform in less than a year by withdrawing its products from the market in the area.

The Court distinguished the Martocci case by saying that there the plaintiff had completely performed and therefore there was greater opportunity for fraud in that type of case, and, secondly, that in the Martocci case the agreement by its terms could not be terminated by either party to the contract, whereas here at least the defendant had a right to terminate the arrangement. The court treated the defendant's right to discontinue doing business in the locality as an option to terminate and it then followed the traditional New York rule that a right held by a defendant to terminate within a year takes the contract outside of the Statute of Frauds.[12]

8. The distinction under Florida law is discussed in Joe Regueira, Inc. v. American Distilling, 642 F.2d 826 (5th Cir.1981).

9. See § 19.20 supra. To be distinguished are cases where there is an offer looking to a series of contracts. Here each contract should be treated individually to see if it violates the one-year section of the Statute of Frauds. See Nat Nal Serv. Sta-

tions v. Wolf, 304 N.Y. 332, 107 N.E.2d 473 (1952); Rs. 2d § 130 ill. 10.

10. North Shore Bottling v. C. Schmidt & Sons, 22 N.Y.2d 171, 292 N.Y.S.2d 86, 239 N.E.2d 189 (1968).

11. The language would seem to raise a consideration problem but this was not discussed. See § 4.12(b)(4) supra.

12. See § 19.21 supra.

F. RELATIONSHIP AMONG THE VARIOUS PROVISIONS

§ 19.25 Relationship Among the Various Provisions

A contract may be within one or more sections of the Statute of Frauds. Ordinarily the various clauses of the Statute of Frauds are considered separately and the most restrictive is applied. However, where a land contract is specifically enforceable under the doctrine of part performance, the other clauses of the Statute do not prevent enforcement.[1] The traditional view has been that the one-year section applies to all contracts no matter what their subject matter.[2] Thus, for example, it has been held that a contract for the sale of goods must comply with both the one-year and the sale-of-goods provisions of the Statute.[3] The weight of recent authority, however, holds that if a contract for the sale of goods satisfies the UCC's Statute of Frauds, it need not satisfy the one-year section even if performance is not performable within a year from the making of the contract.[4] According to the weight of authority, mutual promises to marry not performable within one year are within the one-year provision,[5] although not within the consideration-of-marriage subsection.[6]

II. SUFFICIENCY AND EFFECT OF A RECORD

Table of Sections

§ 19.25

1. Rs. 2d § 129 cmt f. See § 19.15 supra.

2. Rs. 2d § 130 cmt f; see Haire v. Cook, 237 Ga. 639, 229 S.E.2d 436 (1976) (apply the more rigorous one-year provision to real property contract).

3. Seaman's Direct Buying Service v. Standard Oil, 36 Cal.3d 752, 206 Cal.Rptr. 354, 686 P.2d 1158 (1984), overruled on other grounds; Bryant v. Credit Service, 36 Del. 360, 175 A. 923 (1934); contra, Roth Steel Prod. v. Sharon Steel, 705 F.2d 134 (6th Cir.1983) (need satisfy only UCC).

4. Rosenfeld v. Basquiat, 78 F.3d 84 (2d Cir.1996); AP Propane v. Sperbeck, 77 N.Y.2d 886, 568 N.Y.S.2d 908, 571 N.E.2d 78 (1991). The revision in § 2–201(4) explicitly provides that the one-year section is not applicable to sales of goods.

5. 4 Corbin §§ 19.12, 20.2 (Brown 1997).

6. See § 19.13 supra.

Sec.

19.39   Formal Contracts and Promises to Execute a Record.

§ 19.26   Introduction

Assuming that a contract is within the Statute of Frauds, it is enforceable if the contract itself is in a record or a memorandum is recorded. In a general way this was foreshadowed by Section 4 of the English Statute which made the contract enforceable if "the agreement * * *, or some memorandum or note thereof, shall be in writing, and signed by the party to be charged therewith, or some other person thereunto by him lawfully authorized." The substance of this language has been adopted by most of the states. However, there are variations from state to state. The variations are not so great as to prevent general discussion but in every case the words of the particular statute should be considered.

§ 19.27   Parol Evidence and the Record

The relationship between the parol evidence rule and the Statute of Frauds is wrapped in much the same controversy and confusion as the parol evidence rule itself.[1] It is clear that a record sufficient to satisfy the Statute of Frauds need not be an integration.[2] Yet the distinction between an integrated record and a nonintegrated record is important in at least one respect.

Where the record is not integrated it may be shown that the oral agreement contained essential terms different from or additional to those stated in the record. When the record is thus exposed as inaccurate, the party sought to be charged may obtain a dismissal of the case because the record does not contain the essential terms of the agreement[3]—one of the more bizarre results of the often criticized Statute of Frauds.[4] However, if there is a total integration, the record may not be varied, contradicted or supplemented in order to show that it is inaccurate.[5]

The situation is quite different when a party seeks to introduce oral evidence in order to establish terms not found in the record for the purpose of enforcing those terms. But here, consistent additional non-essential oral terms may be shown unless there is a total integration.[6]

§ 19.27

1. See Ch. 3.

2. See Drury v. Young, 58 Md. 546, 42 Am.Rep. 343 (1882) where the memorandum was made by defendant for his records without plaintiff's knowledge.

3. 4 Corbin §§ 22.1, 23.1 (Brown 1997); 4 Williston § 575 (3d ed.); Rs. 2d § 131 cmt g. The statement does not take into account the possibility of a court of equity granting reformation. See § 19.28.

4. See 4 Corbin § 12.1 (Brown 1997); see also 4 Williston § 599 at 275 n. 12 (3d ed.) (urging a uniform liberalized statute).

5. Lyon v. Big Bend Dev., 7 Ariz.App. 1, 435 P.2d 732 (1968); N.E.D. Holding v. McKinley, 246 N.Y. 40, 157 N.E. 923 (1927); Rs. 1st § 131 ill. 11. The possibility of reformation is considered at § 19.28 infra.

6. See Lynch v. Davis, 181 Conn. 434, 435 A.2d 977 (1980); Lane v. Floorcraft Clyde Beherens, Ltd., 29 P.3d 1092 (Okla. App.2001); 4 Williston § 575 (3d ed.); cf. 4 Corbin § 527; A.B.C. Auto Parts v. Moran, 359 Mass. 327, 268 N.E.2d 844 (1971).

Moreover extrinsic evidence should be admissible in aid of interpretation unless it is excluded by the rules of interpretation set forth in Chapter 3.[7]

§ 19.28 Reformation and the Statute of Frauds

The great majority of cases have held that if the equitable relief of reformation is sought, the Statute of Frauds does not exclude parol evidence tending to prove that an agreement in a record or conveyance is at variance with the parties' prior oral agreement.[1]

A minority of jurisdictions have refused to admit such evidence on the ground that the admission of such evidence would fly in the face of the statutory ban against the enforcement of oral agreements.[2] The majority answers, however, that by the process of reformation the court is not enforcing an oral agreement but is rectifying the record to conform it to what the parties thought they were recording. "The correction of erroneous instruments therefore does not rest necessarily upon any assumption that a prior completed oral contract is being enforced."[3]

It is very important to remember that if the alleged contract is within the Statute of Frauds, the record as reformed must satisfy the statutory requirements. It should also be recalled that terms intentionally omitted may not be added by a decree of reformation.[4] In addition, reformation is not permitted except on clear and convincing evidence.[5] With these three safeguards in mind, it would be incorrect to state that the policy of the Statute is violated by permitting reformation.

In New York a peculiar distinction has been made. It has been held that although a written contract may be reformed,[6] a memorandum of a contract may not be reformed.[7] This rule apparently stems from confusion between the exclusionary rules of the Statute of Frauds and the parol evidence rule.[8]

---

7. See § Ch. 3(C) supra; Koedding v. Slaughter, 634 F.2d 1095 (8th Cir.1980); Marsico v. Kessler, 149 Conn. 236, 178 A.2d 154 (1962); Stanley v. A. Levy & J. Zentner, 60 Nev. 432, 112 P.2d 1047, 158 ALR 76 (1941); Jacobson v. Gulbransen, 623 N.W.2d 84 (S.D.2001); § 19.29 infra. For purposes of interpretation, Williston treats a record under the Statute of Frauds as if it were an integration. See § 3.11 supra.

§ 19.28

1. World of Sleep v. Seidenfeld, 674 P.2d 1005 (Colo.App.1983); Slipp v. Stover, 651 A.2d 824 (Me.1994); Grappo v. Mauch, 110 Nev. 1396, 887 P.2d 740 (1994); Rs. 2d § 156; see Palmer, Reformation and the Statute of Frauds, 65 Mich.L.Rev. 421 (1967). Such a result has even been reached under a statute requiring contracts hiring school superintendents to be in writing and

filed. Hampton School Dist. v. Phillips, 251 Ark. 90, 470 S.W.2d 934 (1971).

2. The minority position had been accepted in part by Rs. 1st § 509. Rs. 2d § 156 embraces the majority view.

3. 9 Wigmore, Evidence § 2417 (Chadbourn rev. 1981).

4. See § 9.33 supra; Rs. 2d § 156 cmt a. Thus, a signature, inadvertently omitted can be supplied by court decree. Lane v. Spriggs, 71 S.W.3d 286 (Tenn.App.2001).

5. See § 9.31 supra.

6. Brandwein v. Provident Mut. Life Ins., 3 N.Y.2d 491, 168 N.Y.S.2d 964, 146 N.E.2d 693 (1957).

7. Donald Friedman & Co. v. Newman, 255 N.Y. 340, 174 N.E. 703, 73 ALR 95 (1931).

8. See Palmer, note 1, at 437–40.

§ 19.29　The Contents of the Record

The record[1] must state with reasonable certainty: (a) the identity of both contracting parties; however, the party need not be named if the record sufficiently describes the party; extrinsic evidence to clarify the description is admissible;[2] (b) the subject matter of the contract so that it can be identified either from the record alone or with the aid of extrinsic evidence;[3] and (c) the essential "terms and conditions of all the promises constituting the contract and by whom and to whom the promises are made."[4] If the consideration is executed (e.g., payment has been made), it is still in dispute whether the consideration must be stated.[5]

It should be repeated that the "essential terms"—a term of considerable flexibility itself—must be stated with only "reasonable" certainty.[6] A leading case which illustrates this rule is Marks v. Cowdin.[7] In 1911 the plaintiff was employed under a written contract for two years as "sales manager." When this period expired the parties made an oral agreement for further employment. The memorandum, signed some time later read: "It is understood. that the arrangements made for employment of L. Marks in our business on January 1, 1913, for a period of three years from that date at a salary of $15,000 per year plus 5 percent of the gross profits earned in our business which we agree shall not be less than $5,000 per year—continues in force until Jan. 1, 1916."

It is apparent that the record did not state the nature of the employment to be performed by Marks, the plaintiff. The court held that the record was sufficient to permit the plaintiff to show that he had been employed as a "sales manager" and that the employment had been continued. The court stated that "the statute must not be pressed to the

§ 19.29

1. If the statute reads that the contract must be in writing or in a record, a memorandum is insufficient. Rs. 2d § 131 cmt a.

2. Rs. 1st § 207(a); Rs. 2d § 131(b) adds that the memorandum should indicate that a contract has been made or that the signer has made an offer. See Rs. 2d § 131 cmt f and ill. 10; Arcuri v. Weiss, 198 Pa.Super. 506 & 608, 184 A.2d 24 (1962); cf. Carter v. Murphey, 256 Ga.App. 150, 567 S.E.2d 326 (2002) (signed guaranty insufficient that does not bear the name of the principal debtor); Kenby Oil v. Lange, 42 P.3d 201 (Kan.App.2002) (same).

3. C–470 Joint Venture v. Trizec Colorado, 176 F.3d 1289 (10th Cir.1999); Hackal v. Adler, 234 A.D.2d 341, 650 N.Y.S.2d 792 (1996) ("my property—house and land" sufficient to sustain an option); Swan Kang v. Tae Sang Kang, 243 Ga.App. 684, 534 S.E.2d 145 (2000) (postal address sufficient); Owen v. Hendricks, 433 S.W.2d 164, 30 ALR3d 929 (Tex.1968); Wozniak v. Kuszinski, 352 Mich. 431, 90 N.W.2d 456 (1958); ("your 960 acres in Dallam County" may be sufficient); but see Martin v. Seigel,

35 Wn.2d 223, 212 P.2d 107, 23 ALR2d 1 (1949) (street address insufficient); Moudy v. Manning, 82 S.W.3d 726 (Tex.App.2002). See Rs. 1st § 131(a); 4 Corbin § 22.12 (Brown 1997).

4. Rs. 1st § 207(c); Rs. 2d § 131(c); Slotkin v. Willmering, 464 F.2d 418 (8th Cir.1972); Botello v. Misener–Collins, 469 S.W.2d 793 (Tex.1971). Terms implied in law are part of the record even if the implied term has been agreed to. Rs. 2d § 131 cmt g. But see Morris Cohon & Co. v. Russell, 23 N.Y.2d 569, 297 N.Y.S.2d 947, 245 N.E.2d 712 (1969).

5. 4 Corbin § 22.4 (Brown 1997); see Rs. 2d § 131, particularly cmt h and the reporter's notes to cmts a & h.

6. Rs. 1st § 207; Rs. 2d § 131 cmt g. See Fruin v. Colonnade One, 38 Conn.App. 420, 662 A.2d 129 (1995) (real property contract—contingency could lower the price to an unknown extent), aff'd; Morris Cohon & Co. v. Russell, 23 N.Y.2d 569, 297 N.Y.S.2d 947, 245 N.E.2d 712 (1969); Pick v. Bartel, 659 S.W.2d 636 (Tex.1983).

7. 226 N.Y. 138, 123 N.E. 139 (1919).

extreme of a literal and rigid logic * * *. The memorandum which it requires, like any other memorandum, must be read in the light of reason." In addition the nature of the employment was stated in a notice sent during the first period of employment to sales representatives describing plaintiff as "sales-manager."[8]

§ 19.30 The Form and Timing of the Record—Delivery

(a) Writing

The record that satisfies the Statute need not have been made to satisfy the Statute.[1] It may be a receipt[2] or a telegram[3] or an exchange of correspondence[4] or the record books of a business,[5] or a check,[6] or a letter that acknowledges the contract and repudiates it,[7] a written offer that has been orally accepted[8] or even a suicide note.[9] It may be in the form of a written statement addressed to a stranger to the contract,[10] or a last will and testament.[11] For the record to be sufficient it must "amount to acknowledgment by the party to be charged that he [or she] has assented to the contract that is asserted by the other party."[12]

The record need not be prepared with the purpose of satisfying the Statute,[13] nor at the same time that the contract is made; but, according to the first Restatement, it must be made before the suit is instituted.[14] It is also generally agreed that the record need not be delivered.[15] Of course a deed must be delivered to be effective as a deed but there is no

---

8. Accord, Lloyd v. Grynberg, 464 F.2d 622 (10th Cir.1972); Jennings v. Ruidoso Racing Ass'n, 79 N.M. 144, 441 P.2d 42 (1968).

§ 19.30

1. Rs. 2d § 131 cmt d.

2. Goetz v. Hubbell, 66 N.D. 491, 266 N.W. 836 (1936).

3. Brewer v. Horst–Lachmund, 127 Cal. 643, 60 P. 418 (1900).

4. U.S. v. New York, 131 F.2d 909 (2d Cir.1942), cert. denied; Aragon v. Boyd, 80 N.M. 14, 450 P.2d 614 (1969) (letters after oral agreement).

5. Al–Sco Realty v. Suburban Apt., 138 N.J.Eq. 497, 48 A.2d 838 (1946), aff'd.

6. See Annot., 9 ALR4th 1009 (1981).

7. See Rs. 1st § 209; Rs. 2d § 133 and cmt c; Commonwealth Aluminum v. Stanley Metal, 186 F.Supp.2d 770 (W.D.Ky.2001) (letters trying to work out problems); Schmoll Fils & Co. v. Wheeler, 242 Mass. 464, 136 N.E. 164 (1922); Webb v. Woods, 176 Okl. 306, 55 P.2d 959 (1936); Bailey v. Sweeting, 142 Eng.Rep. 332 (1861).

8. Donovan v. RRL, 26 Cal.4th 261, 109 Cal.Rptr.2d 807, 27 P.3d 702 (2001); Lang v. Oregon–Idaho Ann. Conf., 173 Or.App. 389, 21 P.3d 1116 (2001).

9. Petition of Schaeffner, 96 Misc.2d 846, 410 N.Y.S.2d 44 (1978).

10. Morris Cohon & Co. v. Russell, 23 N.Y.2d 569, 297 N.Y.S.2d 947, 245 N.E.2d 712 (1969); Bunbury v. Krauss, 41 Wis.2d 522, 164 N.W.2d 473 (1969).

11. Newman v. Huff, 632 N.E.2d 799 (Ind.App.1994); see Annot., 94 ALR2d 921 (1964).

12. 4 Corbin § 22.9 (Brown 1997); see § 19.29 supra & § 19.33 infra.

13. Annot., 85 ALR 1184, 1215 (1933); see Rs. 2d § 133 which makes an exception for a contract in consideration of marriage.

14. Rs. 1st §§ 214, 215; accord, Watson v. McCabe, 527 F.2d 286 (6th Cir.1975); The Rs 2d omits § 215 of the original Restatement "as procedural, and as contrary to the spirit of modern procedural reforms." (§ 136 Reporter's Note).

15. Mirchel v. RMJ Securities, 205 A.D.2d 388, 613 N.Y.S.2d 876 (1994) (documents in defendant's own files); Rs. 2d § 133 cmt b; see Kludt v. Connett, 350 Mo. 793, 168 S.W.2d 1068, 145 ALR 1014 (1943). Contra, Main v. Pratt, 276 Ill. 218, 114 N.E. 576 (1916).

such requirement for it to be effective as a record. It is also clear that the record need not be in existence at the time of suit; it is sufficient that it existed at one time.[16]

(b) Recordings, Electronic Messages and Oral Stipulations

A considerable number of transactions are agreed to by various forms of electronic communication.[17] As stated above, E–Sign and UETA provide that such forms of communication satisfy the requirements of the Statute of Frauds.[18] Naturally, such a communication must suitably memorialize the agreement.

It is well settled that an oral stipulation made in open court satisfies the Statute of Frauds even though the record is not signed by the party to be charged.[19] A signed fax satisfies the Statute.[20] Whether a tape recording of a conversation in which an oral contract is made can be deemed a record has not received a uniform response.[21]

(c) Admissions

As we have seen, an admission in pleadings or in court satisfies the sale of goods requirement for a record even if the admission is compelled by cross-examination.[22] Of late, a number of courts have applied the same rule to other provisions of the Statute of Frauds.[23]

(d) Usage, Course of Dealing and Course of Performance

A number of cases have confronted the question of whether a trade usage, a course of dealing or a course of performance can override the requirements of the Statute of Frauds.[24] As an abstract proposition the

---

16. Hiss v. Hiss, 228 Ill. 414, 81 N.E. 1056 (1907); 4 Corbin § 23.10 (Brown 1997); Rs. 2d § 137.

17. See Robertson, Electronic Commerce on the Internet and the Statute of Frauds, 49 S.C.L.Rev. 787 (1998); Symposium: Digital Signature and Electronic Document Verification, 17 J. Marshall J.Computer & Info. L. 721 (1999); Horning, 12 Santa Clara Computer & High Tech L.J. 253 (1996); Morrison, 14 Geo. Mason U.L.Rev. 637 (1992); Note, 14 Cardozo Arts & Ent. L.J. (1996); Comment 41 U.Kan.L.Rev. 403 (1993); Note, 13 J.L. & Com. 143 (1993).

18. See § 19.1 supra.

19. Scarbrough v. Long, 112 F.Supp.2d 609 (S.D.Miss.2000); Farrell v. Farrell, 661 So.2d 1257 (Fla.App.1995); Fuchs v. Fuchs, 65 A.D.2d 595, 409 N.Y.S.2d 414 (1978); Estate of Eberle, 505 N.W.2d 767 (S.D. 1993).

20. Den Norske v. Hydrocarbon Processing, 992 F.Supp. 913 (S.D.Tex.1998).

21. Ellis Canning v. Bernstein, 348 F.Supp. 1212 (D.Colo.1972) (yes); Sonders v. Roosevelt, 64 N.Y.2d 869, 487 N.Y.S.2d 551, 476 N.E.2d 996 (1985) (no); Dzek v. Desco Vitroglaze, 285 A.D.2d 926, 727 N.Y.S.2d 814 (2001) (yes); see Misner, 61 Iowa L.Rev. 941 (1976).

22. See § 19.16(f).

23. Gibson v. Arnold, 288 F.3d 1242 (10th Cir.2002); Posner v. Marcus & Millichap, 180 F.Supp.2d 529 (S.D.N.Y.2002) (N.Y.'s one year provision); Stoetzel v. Continental Textile, 768 F.2d 217 (8th Cir. 1985); Anchorage–Hynning & Co. v. Moringiello, 697 F.2d 356 (D.C.Cir.1983); Wolf v. Crosby, 377 A.2d 22 (Del.Ch.1977) (real property); Smith v. Boyd, 553 A.2d 131 (R.I.1989) (real property). The traditional and contrary view is expressed in Pierce v. Gaddy, 42 N.C.App. 622, 257 S.E.2d 459 (1979), cert. denied; Shedd, The Judicial Admissions Exception to the Statute of Frauds, 12 Whittier L.Rev. 131 (1991); Note, 67 Iowa L.Rev. 551 (1982) (exceptional statute in Iowa).

24. Wholesale Materials v. Magna, 357 So.2d 296 (Miss.1978), cert. denied (course of dealing); Farmers Co-op. Ass'n v. Cole, 239 N.W.2d 808 (N.D.1976) (usage).

Statute of Frauds cannot be waived by an actual or imputed agreement;[25] however, a consistent usage or course of dealing can be the basis of an estoppel[26] and a course of performance may modify a contract.[27]

§ 19.31 Signed by the Party to Be Charged

The term "signature" includes any mark or sign, written, printed, stamped, photographed, engraved, or otherwise placed on any record with intent to execute or authenticate the record.[1] The important thing is that the instrument be authenticated by the party to be charged.[2] Authentication means that the signer assents to and adopts the record.[3] If the name is inscribed at the end, that constitutes prima facie evidence of authentication. "If the name is inscribed elsewhere * * * the contrary presumption may arise, making other evidence requisite to convince the court that the inscribed name was intended to be a signature."[4] If, however, the record indicates it is not binding unless signed by an officer of the company, the pre-printed company name on the form is insufficient.[5] A better analysis would have been that there was no contract.

Some states, as to some or all provisions of the Statute of Frauds, have imposed the requirement that the record be "subscribed" rather than "signed." Some courts have held that because of this language the record must be signed at the end.[6] Others, however, have held that "subscribed" and "signed" are basically synonymous.[7]

The record need not be signed by both parties, it need only be signed by the party to be charged.[8] The party to be charged is ordinarily the defendant, but in case of a counterclaim it is the plaintiff.[9] Since the record need be signed only by the party to be charged, there will be situations where the contract is enforceable against one party and not the other as, for example, where one party sends an offer in a signed

25. See UCC § 1–205 cmt 4.

26. Northwest Potato Sales v. Beck, 208 Mont. 310, 678 P.2d 1138 (1984); H.B. Alexander & Son v. Miracle Recreation Equipment, 314 Pa.Super. 1, 460 A.2d 343 (1983).

27. Farmers Elevator v. Anderson, 170 Mont. 175, 552 P.2d 63 (1976).

§ 19.31

1. See McKinney's N.Y. Gen.Constr. Law § 46 which restates the common law; 4 Corbin § 23.4 (Brown 1997); Rs. 2d § 134 and cmt a; UCC § 1–201(39) (defined in the revision as "any symbol executed or adopted with present intention to adopt or accept a writing"); Hillstrom v. Gosnay, 188 Mont. 388, 614 P.2d 466 (1980) (typewritten signature on telegram); Hansen v. Hill, 215 Neb. 573, 340 N.W.2d 8 (1983) (same).

2. Scheck v. Francis, 26 N.Y.2d 466, 311 N.Y.S.2d 841, 260 N.E.2d 493 (1970).

3. Rs. 2d § 134. It has been held that the automatic imprinting, by a fax machine, of the sender's name at the top of the pages

transmitted, is not an authentication. Parma Tile Mosaic & Marble v. Estate of Short, 87 N.Y.2d 524, 640 N.Y.S.2d 477, 663 N.E.2d 633 (1996).

4. 4 Corbin § 23.4 (Brown 1997).

5. Toppings v. Rainbow Homes, 200 W.Va. 728, 490 S.E.2d 817 (1997).

6. 300 West End Ave. v. Warner, 250 N.Y. 221, 165 N.E. 271 (1929); see R.C. Durr Co. v. Bennett Indus., 590 S.W.2d 338 (Ky.App.1979); Venable v. Hickerson, Phelps, Kirtley & Assoc., 903 S.W.2d 659 (Mo.App.1995) (letterhead not a signature).

7. California Canneries v. Scatena, 117 Cal. 447, 49 P. 462 (1897); Butler v. Lovoll, 96 Nev. 931, 620 P.2d 1251 (1980); see 4 Corbin § 23.4 (Brown 1997).

8. Ullsperger v. Meyer, 217 Ill. 262, 75 N.E. 482 (1905); but see Hemingway v. Gruener, 106 Idaho 422, 679 P.2d 1140 (1984).

9. Rs. 2d § 135 cmt a.

record and the other party orally accepts.[10] Some statutes do not use the phrase signed "by the party to be charged" but rather use the phrase "signed by the vendor or lessor." Under such statutes it would appear that the vendee's promise could be enforced without a record but most courts have held that the vendor must prove delivery of a signed record to the purchaser or that the purchaser otherwise accepted the record as correct.[11]

The original Statute of Frauds expressly provided that a memorandum is sufficient if signed by an authorized agent of the party to be charged. Generally, the American statutes have expressly or implicitly continued this rule.[12] By the great weight of authority, the agent's power to sign a record need not be conferred by a record;[13] an oral grant of authority is sufficient. A number of states, however, have by statute provided that if the contract is within the Statute of Frauds, the agent's authority must be evidenced by a record.[14] Often, however, this requirement is limited to the real property Statute of Frauds.[15] If property is jointly owned, the signature of only one party is sufficient.[16]

§ 19.32   The Record in Auction Sales

If goods having a price of $500 or more, or real property, are sold at auction, the Statute of Frauds must be satisfied. It is well established that the auctioneer is authorized to sign a record of sale on behalf of both parties.[1] This authority is limited and expires soon after the sale has been made.[2] According to some authorities, the buyer or seller has the power to terminate the auctioneer's authority to sign a record between the time of the fall of the hammer and the signing of the

---

10. Hagan v. Jockers, 138 Ga.App. 847, 228 S.E.2d 10 (1976); Tymon v. Linoki, 16 N.Y.2d 293, 266 N.Y.S.2d 357, 213 N.E.2d 661 (1965); Kitchen v. Stockman Nat. Life Ins., 192 N.W.2d 796 (Iowa 1971).

11. Schwinn v. Griffith, 303 N.W.2d 258 (Minn.1981); Geraci v. Jenrette, 41 N.Y.2d 660, 394 N.Y.S.2d 853, 363 N.E.2d 559 (1977). Rs. 2d § 133 cmt b.

12. Rs. 2d § 135 cmt b; Vickers v. North American Land Dev., 94 N.M. 65, 607 P.2d 603 (1980).

13. See 4 Corbin § 23.7 (Brown 1997); Seavey, Agency § 19F (1964); but see Cincinnati Ins. v. Talladega, 342 So.2d 331 (Ala.1977). The problems of the relationship between rules governing agents for undisclosed principals, the Statute of Frauds and the parol evidence rule are not considered in this book. On the subject, see Dodge v. Blood, 299 Mich. 364, 300 N.W. 121, 138 ALR 322 (1941), noted in 42 Colum.L.Rev. 475 (1942) and 40 Mich.L.Rev. 900 (1942); cf. Jaynes v. Petoskey, 309 Mich. 32, 14 N.W.2d 566 (1944).

14. See 4 Corbin § 23.7 (Brown 1997).

15. E.g., McKinney's N.Y.Gen. Oblig.Law § 5–703; see Commission on Ecumenical Mission v. Roger Gray, Ltd., 27 N.Y.2d 457, 318 N.Y.S.2d 726, 267 N.E.2d 467 (1971); Ripple v. Pittsburgh Outdoor Adv., 280 Pa.Super. 121, 421 A.2d 435 (1980); for extremely narrow construction of such a statute, see Nelson v. Boone, 78 Haw. 76, 890 P.2d 313 (1995).

16. Muscatello v. Artco Chemical, 251 A.D.2d 882, 674 N.Y.S.2d 518 (1998).

§ 19.32

1. Schwinn v. Griffith, 303 N.W.2d 258 (Minn.1981); Rs. 2d § 135 cmt b; Rs. 2d Agency § 30 cmt f; Rs. 1st § 213 (2); 4 Corbin § 23.6 (Brown 1997); 4 Williston § 588 (3d ed.); Note, 9 U.W.Austl.L.Rev. 70 (1969). For a statutory rule to this effect, affecting goods, see McKinney's N.Y.Gen. Oblig.L. § 5–701(a)(6).

2. The cases quoted in 4 Williston § 588 (3d ed.) speak in terms of signing "immediately" after the sale. The Rs. 2d, Agency § 30 cmt f, speaks of "a reasonable time during the day of the sale." Cf. 4 Corbin § 23.6 (Brown 1997) (reasonable time).

record.[3] The Restatement, however, regards the auctioneer's authority as irrevocable.[4]

If the auctioneer is the seller, the auctioneer cannot satisfy the Statute of Frauds by signing on the purchaser's behalf.[5] The auctioneer's clerk, however, can satisfy the statute by signing on behalf of the buyer.[6] The memorandum must meet the requisites of a sufficient record.[7]

§ 19.33   Record Quilted from Several Records

If there is more than one record and all of the records are signed by the party to be charged and it is clear by their contents that they relate to the same transaction, no problems other than those previously discussed are present.[1]

But if the party to be charged has signed only one of the documents comprising the record, the matter becomes a little more complicated. Two issues are present—the connection between the documents and the existence of assent to the unsigned document. When the unsigned document is physically attached to the signed document at the time it is signed, the Statute is satisfied.[2] This is also true when the signed document by its terms expressly refers to the unsigned document.[3]

However the cases are in conflict where the signed document is not attached to or does not expressly refer to the unsigned papers. One view is that in such a situation the unsigned document is not sufficiently authenticated.[4] The other and better view is that even if the signed document does not expressly refer to the unsigned document or if the unsigned document is not attached, it is still sufficient if the documents by internal evidence refer to the same subject matter or transaction; in that event, extrinsic evidence is admissible to help show the connection between the documents and the assent of the party to be charged.[5]

---

3. 4 Williston § 588 (3d ed.) and cases therein cited. Rs. 1st § 212(2) was in accord.

4. Rs. 2d, Agency § 30 cmt f.

5. Rs. 2d, Agency § 24 and cmt b; 4 Williston § 588 (3d ed.). The rule is acknowledged but criticized in 4 Corbin § 23.6 (Brown 1997).

6. Romani v. Harris, 255 Md. 389, 258 A.2d 187 (1969).

7. Sims v. Broughton, 225 Ill.App.3d 1076, 168 Ill.Dec. 656, 589 N.E.2d 1056 (1992); Maddox v. Cosper, 25 S.W.3d 767 (Tex.App.2000).

§ 19.33

1. Jennings v. Ruidoso Racing Ass'n, 79 N.M. 144, 441 P.2d 42 (1968); Central Power & Light v. Del Mar Conservation Dist., 594 S.W.2d 782 (Tex.App.1980).

2. Tallman v. Franklin, 14 N.Y. (4 Kern) 584 (1856).

3. Leach v. Crucible Center, 388 F.2d 176 (1st Cir.1968); Tampa Shipbldg. & Eng'r v. General Constr., 43 F.2d 309, 85 ALR 1178 (5th Cir.1930).

4. Ezzell v. S.G. Holland Stave, 210 Ala. 694, 99 So. 78 (1924); Young v. McQuerrey, 54 Haw. 433, 508 P.2d 1051 (1973); Hoffman v. S V, 102 Idaho 187, 628 P.2d 218 (1981), 18 Idaho L.Rev. 133 (1982); Owen v. Hendricks, 433 S.W.2d 164, 30 ALR3d 929 (Tex.1968).

5. Crabtree v. Elizabeth Arden Sales, 305 N.Y. 48, 110 N.E.2d 551 (1953); Greenberg v. Bailey, 14 N.C.App. 34, 187 S.E.2d 505 (1972); Pentax v. Boyd, 111 Nev. 1296, 904 P.2d 1024 (1995); Rs. 2d § 132 cmts a, b, and c. Unsigned memoranda prepared by the plaintiff do not ordinarily bind the defendant. Karlin v. Avis, 457 F.2d 57 (2d Cir.1972), cert. denied. But see § 19.34, and Pentax. See also Intercontinental Planning v. Daystrom, 24 N.Y.2d 372, 300 N.Y.S.2d 817, 248 N.E.2d 576, 47 ALR3d 125 (1969),

Even under this view, it is necessary that the signed document evidence a contractual relationship. Thus, a signed cover letter transmitting an unsigned proposed contract is not a sufficient basis for treating the unsigned document as a sufficient record.[6]

§ 19.34　The Record Under UCC § 2–201

Section 2–201 of the UCC introduces several innovations with respect to the contents of a record signed by the party to be charged. Only two definite and invariable requirements as to the record are made by this subsection. First, it must evidence a contract for the sale of goods; second, it must be "signed," a word that includes any authentication identifying the party to be charged.[1] According to most interpretations of the statute, the record must contain a third requisite, a quantity term.[2] A sounder reading of the provision is that if the record contains a quantity term, it is unenforceable beyond the quantity stated.[3]

The UCC provision represents a significant relaxation of the requirement of a record.[4] According to Comment 1 to UCC § 2–201, all that is required is that there is some writing [record] sufficient to indicate that a contract for sale has been made. Thus, it is not necessary that all essential terms be included. "It need not indicate which party is the buyer and which the seller * * *. The price, time and place of payment or delivery, the general quality of the goods, or any particular warranties may be omitted * * *." According to this official comment, "if the 'price' consists of goods rather than money the quantity of goods must be stated."[5]

As a general rule, under the traditional Statute of Frauds, it may be shown that the oral agreement contained terms not set forth in the record, with the result that the record is insufficient (unless a court would grant reformation based on misconduct or mistake).[6] In contrast, under the UCC, if the record is in error as to any term, other than the

rearg. denied; Morris Cohon & Co. v. Russell, 23 N.Y.2d 569, 245 N.E.2d 712, 297 N.Y.S.2d 947 (1969). A record that is subsequent to the signed record may be considered part of the signed record. Rs. 2d § 132 cmt d.

6. Scheck v. Francis, 26 N.Y.2d 466, 311 N.Y.S.2d 841, 260 N.E.2d 493 (1970); cf. Pirilla v. Bonucci, 320 Pa.Super. 496, 467 A.2d 821 (1983) (minutes and letter of intent); Tiverton Estates Ltd. v. Wearwell Ltd., [1974] 1 All E.R. 209, noted in [1974] Cambridge L.J. 42 and 37 Mod.L.Rev. 695 (1974).

§ 19.34

1. UCC § 1–201(39). A letter of intent may not be enough to evidence a contract. Flameout Design and Fab. v. Pennzoil Caspian, 994 S.W.2d 830 (Tex.App.1999).

2. See Southwest Eng'r v. Martin Tractor, 205 Kan. 684, 473 P.2d 18 (1970); see

White & Summers, Uniform Commercial Code § 2–4 (4th ed.).

3. 4 Corbin § 21.2 pp. 661–67 (Brown 1997).

4. See Comment, 4 U.S.F.L.Rev. 177 (1969).

5. UCC § 2–201 cmt 1; Derden v. Morris, 247 So.2d 838 (Miss.1971); Harry Rubin & Sons v. Consolidated Pipe, 396 Pa. 506, 153 A.2d 472 (1959), overruled on other grounds; Julian C. Cohen Salvage v. Eastern Elec. Sales, 205 Pa.Super. 26, 206 A.2d 331 (1965). However, a notation on a check stating "tentative deposit on tentative purchase," is not a sufficient record as it shows a lack of commitment to the purchase. Arcuri v. Weiss, 198 Pa.Super. 506, 184 A.2d 24 (1962). See, Rs. 2d § 131 cmt b.

6. See § 19.28 supra; 4 Corbin § 12.13 (Brown 1997).

quantity term, extrinsic evidence is admissible to correct the error.[7] The Statute explicitly states: "A writing [record] is not insufficient because it omits or incorrectly states a term agreed upon but the contract is not enforceable under this paragraph beyond the quantity of goods shown in such writing [record]." If the quantity term is not accurately stated, recovery is limited to the amount stated, unless the court reforms the record.[8]

The UCC's apparent insistence that the record contain a quantity term creates difficulties in contracts containing open quantity terms, such as requirement or output contracts, distributorships and the like. The UCC's substantive provisions encourage flexibility rather than rigidity.[9] It would be unfortunate if a rigid application of the quantity requirement of the Statute of Frauds were to subvert the substance of the UCC.[10]

When merchants[11] have concluded an oral contract it is quite common for one to send to the other a letter of confirmation, or perhaps a printed form of contract. This confirmation, if sent will serve as a record and will be signed only by the party who sent it, thus, under the old version of the Statute, leaving one party at the mercy of the other. The UCC remedies this situation by providing: "Between merchants if within a reasonable time a writing [record]in confirmation of the contract and sufficient against the sender is received and the party receiving it has reason to know its contents, it satisfies the requirement of subsection (1) against such party unless ~~written~~ notice of objection [in a record] to its contents is given within ten days after it is received."[12] This means that the receiver of the record is in the equivalent position of having signed it so that it may be enforced against the receiver.[13] However, the party alleging the contract still has the burden of proving the oral agreement that the record purports to confirm.[14]

7. 2 Corbin § 531 (1950).

8. The revision draft is in accord.

9. E.g., UCC § 2–204 discussed in § 2.9 supra; PMC v. Houston Wire & Cable, 147 N.H. 685, 797 A.2d 125 (N.H.2002) ("major portion" of buyer's needs is a sufficient term).

10. Rigid cases include Cox Caulking & Insulating v. Brockett Distrib., 150 Ga.App. 424, 258 S.E.2d 51 (1979) ("2.62 per bag for the above project," not a sufficient indication of quantity term). Flexibility is shown in Riegel Fiber v. Anderson Gin, 512 F.2d 784 (5th Cir.1975); Omega Engineering v. Eastman Kodak, 908 F.Supp. 1084 (D.Conn. 1995). For thorough analysis, see Bruckel [now Brown] The Weed and The Web: Section 2–201's Corruption of the UCC's Substantive Provisions—The Quantity Problem, 1983 U.Ill.L.Rev. 811.

11. Merchant is defined in § 1.7 supra. The revision in § 2–104 makes stylistic changes.

12. UCC § 2–201(2). On what constitutes a notice of objection, see Simmons Oil. v. Bulk Sales, 498 F.Supp. 457 (D.N.J. 1980).

13. C.I.F. Productions v. Burlington Coat Factory, 881 F.Supp. 104 (S.D.N.Y. 1995); Herman Oil v. Peterman, 518 N.W.2d 184 (N.D.1994) (invoice satisfies the Statute). See 4 Corbin § 21.3 pp. 669–85 (Brown 1997). "Reasonable time" is usually a question of fact. St. Ansgar Mills v. Streit, 613 N.W.2d 289 (Iowa 2000).

14. I.S. Joseph v. Citrus Feed, 490 F.2d 185 (5th Cir.1974), rehearing denied; Perdue Farms v. Motts, 459 F.Supp. 7 (N.D.Miss.1978) (thorough discussion); Azevedo v. Minister, 86 Nev. 576, 471 P.2d 661 (1970); but see Shpilberg v. Merrill Lynch, Pierce, Fenner & Smith, 535 S.W.2d 227 (Ky.1976) (confirmation treated as a total integration); contra, Khoshnou v. Paine, Webber, Jackson & Curtis, 525 So.2d 977 (Fla.App.1988); Matter of Marlene In-

Finally, this section of the UCC provides that the agreement is enforceable despite the absence of a record "if the party against whom enforcement is sought admits in his pleading, testimony or otherwise in court that a contract for sale was made, but the contract is not enforceable under this provision beyond the quantity of goods admitted."[15]

§ 19.35   Effect of Non–Compliance—Unenforceability

The many Statutes of Frauds which have been adopted have not been uniform in describing the effect of non-compliance with the Statute. The fourth section of the English Statute says "no action shall be brought," the seventeenth section says "no action shall be allowed to be good." The UCC states that the oral contract "is not enforceable by way of action or defense."[1] Some statutes say that the oral contract is "void"[2] and at least one statute talks in terms of admissibility of evidence.[3]

Partly as a result of the difference in wording, and partly as a result of judicial interpretation, the effect of non-compliance has not always been deemed to be the same.[4] Despite the differences in wording, the tendency of the decisions is to avoid literal construction of the Statute. The majority view is to treat the oral contract as unenforceable rather than void, even when the Statute uses the term "void."[5] The vast majority of the cases which have held that the Statute merely makes the contract unenforceable hold that the oral contract is operative for a wide variety of purposes.[6] However, the courts which say that the oral contract is void or that the oral contract is not admissible have held that the oral contract is inoperative at least for some of these purposes.[7]

This difference probably can be best understood in the light of a few illustrations. We have already seen that under the majority view if the record is signed by only one party it is enforceable against that party.[8] However, under the minority view since the return promise of the unsigned party is not sufficient consideration, being void, the entire contract is unenforceable under the doctrine of mutuality.[9]

---

dus., 45 N.Y.2d 327, 408 N.Y.S.2d 410, 380 N.E.2d 239 (1978).

15. See § 19.16(f); see 4 Corbin §§ 21.5 (Brown 1997).

§ 19.35

1. UCC § 2–201(1).

2. E.g., McKinney's N.Y.Gen.Oblig. Law § 5–701. But see n.5.

3. Iowa Code Ann., § 622.32.

4. See Note, 14 Cornell L.Q. 102 (1928).

5. Borchardt v. Kulick, 234 Minn. 308, 48 N.W.2d 318 (1951); Crane v. Powell, 139 N.Y. 379, 34 N.E. 911 (1893).

6. 4 Corbin § 12.5 (Brown 1997) lists ten purposes for which the oral contract is effective under this view. See also, UCC § 2–201 cmt 4; Daugherty v. Kessler, 264 Md. 281, 286 A.2d 95 (1972). Under Pennsylvania law, the Statute of Frauds applies only to an action for specific performance and not to a suit for damages for breach of an oral contract respecting real estate. Polka v. May, 383 Pa. 80, 118 A.2d 154 (1955). On the distinction between void, voidable and unenforceable, see § 1.08 supra.

7. 4 Corbin §§ 12.19, 12.13 (Brown 1997).

8. See § 19.31 supra

9. Wilkinson v. Heavenrich, 58 Mich. 574, 26 N.W. 139 (1886); Burg v. Betty Gay of Wn., 423 Pa. 485, 225 A.2d 85 (1966), noted in 71 Dick.L.Rev. 494 (1967).

Again under the majority view the Statute of Frauds must be pleaded as an affirmative defense.[10] However under the minority view since the oral agreement is no contract at all, this may be shown under a general denial,[11] or, if no record is pleaded, a motion to dismiss for failure to state a cause of action.[12] But even here it cannot be raised for the first time on appeal.[13]

Again where the contract has been fully performed on both sides it is unanimously agreed that the Statute has no effect, thus indicating that the oral agreement is not void.[14] So also the general rule is that the Statute of Frauds is personal to the party to the contract and those in privity; a third party may not assert its invalidity, thus indicating that the oral agreement is not void.[15] However, the opposite result has been reached where the Statute was deemed to make the contract void.[16]

Finally, the oral contract is shown to be unenforceable rather than void by the rule that the record may be made at a time other than the time of contracting.[17] However, if the oral contract was "void" the record would have to come into existence at the same time as the agreement or at least while both parties were still in agreement.[18]

§ 19.36 Effect of Part of a Contract Being Unenforceable

Where one or more of the promises in a contract are within the Statute and others are not, the general rule is that no part of the contract is enforceable.[1] Any other approach would be unfair. There is, of course, predictable difficulty in determining whether the proffered testimony relates to a part of the contract or a separate contract.[2] A large number of cases have applied the same rule even though the contract might be considered divisible.[3] But contrary cases hold that if the

---

10. Raoul v. Olde Village Hall, 76 A.D.2d 319, 430 N.Y.S.2d 214 (1980); Adams v. H. & H., 41 S.W.3d 762 (Tex.App. 2001).

11. Jones v. Pettigrew, 25 S.D. 432, 127 N.W. 538 (1910).

12. Leonard v. Martling, 378 Pa. 339, 106 A.2d 585 (1954).

13. Iverson v. Cirkel, 56 Minn. 299, 57 N.W. 800 (1894).

14. E.g., Blackwell v. Blackwell, 196 Mass. 186, 81 N.E. 910 (1907); Rs. 2d § 145.

15. Friedman v. Jackson, 266 Cal. App.2d 517, 72 Cal.Rptr. 129 (1968) (tortious interference with contractual relation); B.D.S. v. Gillis, 477 A.2d 1121 (D.C. 1984); Pasquay v. Pasquay, 235 Ill. 48, 85 N.E. 316 (1908); Blue Valley Turf Farms v. Realestate Marketing and Dev., 424 N.E.2d 1088 (Ind.App.1981); Amsinck v. American Ins., 129 Mass. 185 (1880); Clements v. Withers, 437 S.W.2d 818 (Tex.1969), 21 Baylor L.Rev. 402 (1969); Rs. 2d § 144; but see Trammell Crow v. Harkinson, 944 S.W.2d 631 (Tex.1997). A party in privity,

such as a subsequent contract vendee of real property may invoke the Statute. O'Banion v. Paradiso, 61 Cal.2d 559, 39 Cal.Rptr. 370, 393 P.2d 682 (1964), 5 Santa Clara L.Rev. 87 (1964).

16. Gerndt v. Conradt, 117 Wis. 15, 93 N.W. 804 (1903).

17. See § 19.30 supra.

18. Wilkinson v. Heavenrich, 58 Mich. 574, 26 N.W. 139 (1886).

§ 19.36

1. Blanchard v. Calderwood, 110 N.H. 29, 260 A.2d 118 (1969); Rs. 2d § 147(3). Contra, White Lighting v. Wolfson, 68 Cal.2d 336, 66 Cal.Rptr. 697, 438 P.2d 345 (1968).

2. Compare Austin v. Montgomery, 336 So.2d 745 (Miss.1976) with Kristinus v. H. Stern Com. E. Ind., 466 F.Supp. 903 (S.D.N.Y.1979).

3. Hornady v. Plaza Realty, 437 So.2d 591 (Ala.Civ.App.1983); Hurley v. Donovan, 182 Mass. 64, 64 N.E. 685 (1902).

contract is divisible and the part that is not within the Statute is performed, the corresponding promise may be enforced.[4] Moreover, according to some cases, substantial performance takes the contract outside of the Statute.[5]

There are exceptions to the general rule stated above. The first is where all of the promises that are within the Statute have been performed, then all of the other promises become enforceable.[6] The second exception occurs where the party who is to receive the performance under the only promise or promises within the Statute agrees to abandon that part of the performance.[7] Moreover, where a promisor makes a promise of alternative performances, one of which is within the Statute and the other without, it is generally held that the promisee may enforce the promise that is without the Statute.[8] It should also be recalled that under some of the sections of the Statute of Frauds full performance or even part performance may make the contract enforceable.

§ 19.37　Oral Rescission or Modification

As a general rule, a contract made in a record may be rescinded or modified orally. The usual question presented is one of consideration.[1] Does the same rule apply when a contract is within the Statute of Frauds and is evidenced by a sufficient record? The majority rule is that an executory contract that satisfies the Statute of Frauds may be rescinded orally,[2] thus inducing some contracting parties to draft clauses that purport to forbid oral rescissions.[3]

There are some cases which hold that when a contract is within the Statute of Frauds and is in a record, it may not be modified by an oral agreement.[4] The better rule, however, is that if the new agreement is not within the Statute of Frauds, it is not only enforceable without a record, but also serves to discharge the previous agreement.[5] Moreover, if the

4. Vanston v. Connecticut Gen'l Life Ins., 482 F.2d 337 (5th Cir.1973); Blue Valley Creamery, v. Consolidated Prods., 81 F.2d 182 (8th Cir.1936); Belleville Lumber & Supply v. Chamberlin, 120 Ind.App. 12, 84 N.E.2d 60 (1949); Murphy v. CNY Fire Emergency Servs., 225 A.D.2d 1034, 639 N.Y.S.2d 628 (1996).

5. Vada v. Harrell, 156 Ga.App. 137, 273 S.E.2d 877 (1980).

6. Rs. 2d § 147(2).

7. Rs. 1st § 221. Rs. 2d § 147(1) states that the exception "does not apply to a contract to transfer property on the promisor's death."

8. Chandler v. Doran, 44 Wn.2d 396, 267 P.2d 907 (1954); Annot., 13 ALR 267 (1921). But see § 19.21 which states a different rule in effect in some jurisdictions for the one-year section of the Statute of Frauds.

§ 19.37

1. See §§ 4.9, 5.14 supra.

2. Annot., 42 ALR3d 242 (1972); Fidelity & Deposit v. Tom Murphy Constr., 674 F.2d 880 (11th Cir.1982); Strychalski v. Mekus, 54 A.D.2d 1068, 388 N.Y.S.2d 969 (1976); Investment Properties v. Allen, 281 N.C. 174, 188 S.E.2d 441 (1972), vacated on other grounds; 2 Corbin § 13.2 (Brown 1997); Rs. 2d § 148 which adds, "the Statute may, however, apply to a contract to rescind a transfer of property." Holding to the contrary, that a contract within the Statute may not be rescinded orally. Givens v. Dougherty, 671 S.W.2d 877 (Tex.1984); Strevell–Paterson v. Francis, 646 P.2d 741 (Utah 1982).

3. See § 5.14.

4. Bradley v. Harter, 156 Ind. 499, 60 N.E. 139 (1901).

5. Norris, Beggs & Simpson v. Eastgate Theatres, 261 Or. 56, 491 P.2d 1018 (1971); ABC Outdoor Advertising v. Dolhun's Marine, 38 Wis.2d 457, 157 N.W.2d 680 (1968); Rs. 1st § 222; 4 Corbin § 13.2 (Brown

agreement as modified is within the Statute, the original contract evidenced by a record, coupled with the modification, constitutes the contract. If the original record sufficiently evidences the contract, there is no need for the modification to be evidenced in a record.[6]

If the modified agreement is within the Statute of Frauds and is unenforceable because it is insufficiently memorialized, the former contract remains enforceable,[7] unless the new agreement takes precedence under the doctrines of waiver and estoppel.[8] But the waiver may be retracted by reasonable notice that strict performance will be required of any term waived, "unless the retraction would be unjust in view of a material change of position in reliance on the waiver."[9]

This last situation is illustrated by the case of Imperator Realty v. Tull.[10] There, the parties agreed to exchange two pieces of real property. The contract contained a provision that each seller would clear any violations. The plaintiff alleged that prior to the time for performance the parties orally agreed that either party instead of clearing a violation could deposit with a third party a sum of money sufficient to clear the violation. The plaintiff tendered performance under the oral modified agreement; the defendant refused to accept the performance. The court held that although the defendant could have withdrawn his consent to the modification before a change of position by the plaintiff, it could not do so after the plaintiff changed its position.[11] The defendant was estopped from taking advantage of the fact that the plaintiff had not complied with the written agreement,[12] and the oral agreement was enforced despite the Statute of Frauds.

§ 19.38 Defensive Use of an Unenforceable Contract

The general rule is that a contract that is not enforceable because of the Statute of Frauds may not be used "by way of action or defense."[1]

1997); 4 Williston § 592 (3d ed.). As to realty contracts, see Rs. 2d § 149 and cmt a; Annot., 42 ALR3d 242 (1972).

6. 4 Corbin § 13.1 (Brown 1997); see Flowers Ginning v. Arma, Inc., 106 F.3d 390 (4th Cir.1997); White & Summers 31–32 (4th ed.); Comment, 21 Campbell L.Rev. 307 (1999).

7. Rouse v. Boston Seafood, 894 S.W.2d 190 (Mo.App.1995); Cox v. Venters, 887 S.W.2d 563 (Ky.App.1994); Lieberman v. Templar Motor, 236 N.Y. 139, 140 N.E. 222, 29 ALR 1089 (1923).

8. Van Iderstine v. Barnet Leather, 242 N.Y. 425, 152 N.E. 250, 46 ALR 858 (1926); Rs. 2d § 149(2); see UCC § 2–209(4). The new agreement contravening the Statute of Frauds may still have effect under the doctrines of waiver and estoppel. Cf. Finer v. Loeffler–Green Supply, 456 P.2d 534 (Okl. 1969) (oral modification fully performed by vendor); Fisher v. Fisher, 907 P.2d 1172 (Utah App.1995).

9. UCC § 2–209(5); Double–E Sportswear v. Girard Trust Bank, 488 F.2d 292 (3d Cir.1973), noted in 15 Wm. & Mary L.Rev. 699 (1974); see Eisler, Oral Modification of Sales Contracts: The Statute of Frauds Problem, 58 Wn.U.L.Q. 277 (1980); Note, 21 Drake L.Rev. 593 (1982). See also §§ 19.47 & 19.48 infra.

10. 228 N.Y. 447, 127 N.E. 263 (1920).

11. Rs. 2d § 150. See § 11.31 supra and §§ 19.47 & 19.48 infra. But see Callender v. Kalscheuer, 289 Minn. 532, 184 N.W.2d 811 (1971).

12. Accord, Johnston v. Holiday Inns, 565 F.2d 790 (1st Cir.1977); Ball v. Carlson, 641 P.2d 303 (Colo.App.1981); Thoe v. Rasmussen, 322 N.W.2d 775 (Minn.1982); North v. Simonini, 142 Vt. 482, 457 A.2d 285 (1983).

§ 19.38

1. UCC § 2–201(1); Rs. 1st § 217.

Thus, the oral contract may not be used by way of set-off. Nonetheless, if the plaintiff is suing on an oral contract and has a sufficient record signed by the defendant alone, the defendant may still use any defense arising out of the terms and conditions of the contract, including a counterclaim in the nature of recoupment.[2]

There are a number of other exceptions to the general rule, some of which are discussed in the sections that follow. One occurs when the plaintiff is suing in quasi contract but is in default, and the defendant is not, and has never refused to sign a sufficient record when requested.[3] This is discussed in more detail in § 19.41.

So also, an agreement that is unenforceable because of the Statute of Frauds may operate to prevent a tort from occurring.[4] For example, if A has entered into possession under an unenforceable contract or lease, A is not a trespasser until the vendor or lessor gives notice of repudiation.[5]

§ 19.39 Formal Contracts and Promises to Execute a Record

The Statute of Frauds does not apply to formal contracts. Included in the concept "formal contracts" are contracts under seal, recognizances and negotiable instruments.[1] If a contract is within the Statute of Frauds, an oral promise to execute a sufficient record is not enforceable for the simple reason that, if it were, the very purpose of the Statute could be circumvented.[2]

III. RESTITUTIONARY REMEDIES

Table of Sections

2. Oxborough v. St. Martin, 169 Minn. 72, 210 N.W. 854, 49 ALR 1115 (1926); Rs. 2d § 140 cmt b & ill 2.

3. Rs. 1st § 217(1)(b); Rs. 2d § 138 cmts b and c. For the refusal to sign a record see Rs. 2d § 141 cmt b.

4. Rs. 1st § 217(1)(c); Rs. 2d § 142.

5. Rosenstein v. Gottfried, 145 Minn. 243, 176 N.W. 844 (1920).

§ 19.39

1. 4 Corbin § 12.6 (Brown 1997); see Owens v. Lombardi, 41 A.D.2d 438, 343 N.Y.S.2d 978 (1973), app. denied.

2. McKinnon v. The Church of Jesus Christ of Latter–Day Saints, 529 P.2d 434 (Utah 1974); 4 Corbin § 12.8 (Brown 1997); Rs. 2d § 141 cmt b. However, the Restatement suggests that such a promise may be enforced under the doctrine of promissory estoppel. Rs. 2d § 110 cmt d. See also Rs. 1st §§ 138, 141 cmt b; Medesco v. LNS Int'l, 762 F.Supp. 920 (D.Utah 1991); and § 19.48 infra.

§ 19.40　Introduction

It is neither illegal nor against public policy to enter into an oral agreement of the kind governed by the Statute of Frauds. A party who in whole or part performs under such an agreement is not an outlaw. On the contrary, it has been suggested that a defendant's attorney who automatically raises the defense of the Statute in any case in which it is applicable may be guilty of unethical conduct.[1] Thus, the courts have developed doctrines under which the oral agreement will be enforced if sufficient performance has been rendered on one side.[2] The circumstances under which performance will be a sufficient predicate for enforcement of the contract varies with respect to the particular subsection of the Statute in question and from jurisdiction to jurisdiction.[3]

A plaintiff who has rendered some performance and has not defaulted may recover in quasi contract for the value of the benefits conferred on the defendant,[4] other expenditures in reliance on the contract,[5] and in some instances, specific restitution.[6] The majority of such cases involve a performance that is not sufficient to bring into operation the rules permitting enforcement of the contract. There is substantial authority, however, to the effect that even in a case in which the plaintiff could secure enforcement of the contract on grounds of performance, the plaintiff may elect a restitutionary remedy.[7] Restitutionary remedies include quasi-contractual relief in which the recovery is always and solely for a sum of money. Also included are equitable remedies in which specific restitution is granted, such as by cancellation of a conveyance or imposition of a constructive trust or an equitable lien, and the legal remedy of replevin.

Apparently very few cases have considered the question of whether a third party beneficiary may recover in quasi contract for the value of the performance rendered by the promisee under an unenforceable contract. Recovery has been denied on the ground that the plaintiff had conferred no benefit on the defendant.[8] The same theory led a court to grant

---

§ 19.40

1. Stevens, Ethics and the Statute of Frauds, 37 Cornell L.Q. 355 (1952).

2. See § 19.15 (real property); § 19.23 (the one-year section), § 19.16(e) (goods).

3. Annot., 21 ALR3d 9 (1968).

4. Fischer v. First Chicago, 195 F.3d 279 (7th Cir.1999); Grappo v. Alitalia, 56 F.3d 427 (2d Cir.1995); Cato Enterprises v. Fine, 149 Ind.App. 163, 271 N.E.2d 146 (1971); Ricks v. Sumler, 179 Va. 571, 19 S.E.2d 889 (1942); Rs. 2d § 375; 4 Corbin § 14.3 (Brown 1997); 3 Williston § 534 (3d ed.).

5. See Perillo, Restitution in a Contractual Context, 73 Colum.L.Rev. 1208, 1221–22 (1973); Rs. 2d § 139 is in accord but regards such recovery as analytically distinct from the restitutionary remedy of quasi contract. See Perillo, Restitution in the Second Restatement of Contracts, 81 Colum.L.Rev. 37 (1981); see § 19.44 infra.

6. 4 Corbin § 14.5 (Brown 1997); 3 Williston § 535 (3d ed.); see § 19.46 infra.

7. Id.

8. Pickelsimer v. Pickelsimer, 257 N.C. 696, 127 S.E.2d 557 (1962), noted in 41 N.C.L.Rev. 890 (1963); but see Rowell v. Plymouth–Home Nat. Bank, 13 Mass.App. Ct. 1044, 434 N.E.2d 648 (1982) (dictum).

restitution to the promisee under an oral contract for the conveyance of land to a third person.[9]

§ 19.41 The Plaintiff Must Not Be in Default

According to the great weight of authority, a plaintiff who is entitled to restitution for his performance under an unenforceable contract must not be in default under the agreement,[1] which of course means that the defendant must have repudiated or otherwise materially breached the agreement.[2] It is obvious that proof of the oral agreement is admissible to establish the obligations of the parties, otherwise a breach could not be proved.

In a minority of jurisdictions, under the doctrine of Britton v. Turner,[3] a defaulting party may have quasi-contractual relief under an enforceable contract. It logically follows that in such jurisdictions a defaulting party may have quasi-contractual relief under a contract unenforceable under the Statute of Frauds.[4] The same result has been reached in a number of other jurisdictions on the theory that if the decision were made to turn on which party was in default, the court would be indirectly enforcing the contract.[5]

§ 19.42 Effect of Restoration of the Status Quo

According to the Restatement,[1] if the defendant tenders restoration of specific property delivered to the defendant pursuant to an unenforceable contract, the plaintiff's right to quasi-contractual relief is divested. This is on the theory that the defendant's obligation is primarily that of making specific restitution.[2] There is a paucity of case authority on the point and the leading case is to the contrary.[3] The Restatement rule would clearly be unsound if the value of the specific property is speculative and has declined in value at the time of the tender.

---

9. Graham v. Graham, 134 A.D. 777, 119 N.Y.S. 1013 (1909). Cf. Rs. 1st § 356.

§ 19.41

1. Betnar v. Rose, 259 Ark. 820, 536 S.W.2d 719 (1976); Watkins v. Wells, 303 Ky. 728, 198 S.W.2d 662, 169 ALR 185 (1946); Bendix v. Ross, 205 Wis. 581, 238 N.W. 381 (1931); 4 Corbin §§ 14.5, 14.6 (Brown 1997); 3 Williston § 538 (3d ed.). See also Keener, Quasi Contracts 234–39 (1893); Woodward, Quasi Contracts § 98 (1913).

2. Rs. 1st § 355(4); accord, Rs. 2d § 141 (but qualified by § 374).

3. 6 N.H. 481 (1834), 26 Am.Dec. 713; see § 11.22 supra.

4. 3 Williston § 538 (3d ed.); see Rs. 2d § 374.

5. Freeman v. Foss, 145 Mass. 361, 14 N.E. 141 (1887); accord, Reedy v. Ebsen, 60 S.D. 1, 242 N.W. 592 (1932), on the additional ground that in South Dakota an oral contract within the Statute of Frauds is void rather than unenforceable. Contra, Rowell v. Plymouth–Home Nat. Bank, 13 Mass.App. 1044, 434 N.E.2d 648 (1982). The South Dakota statute has been changed. Braunger v. Snow, 405 N.W.2d 643 (1987).

§ 19.42

1. Rs. 1st § 355(2); accord, Rs. 2d § 372(3).

2. Keener, Quasi Contracts 285–89 (1893); 3 Williston § 535 (3d ed.).

3. Hawley v. Moody, 24 Vt. 603 (1852); accord, 4 Corbin § 14.6 (Brown 1997).

§ 19.43 Restitution Sometimes Denied on Policy Grounds

According to the Restatement, "[t]he remedy of restitution is not available if the Statute that makes the contract unenforceable so provides, or if the purpose of the Statute would be nullified by granting such a remedy."[1] This exception to the general rule does not apply to the original Statute of Frauds nor to the re-enactment of its basic provisions.[2] The exception seems to have been confined largely to statutes enacted in a number of jurisdictions requiring a promise to pay a commission for services as a real estate broker to be in a record. The courts in these jurisdictions have generally refused quasi-contractual recovery to the broker who alleges performance under an oral agreement.[3] Although no right to restitution exists, a subsequent promise to pay may be enforced under the moral obligation doctrine.[4]

§ 19.44 Measure of Recovery

In quasi contract cases it is usually stated that the plaintiff's recovery is the value of "benefits conferred" on the defendant.[1] As discussed elsewhere in this book,[2] the concept of "benefit" is so flexible as to be misleading. Indeed, the weight of decided cases supports a rule to the effect that the measure of recovery is the injury incurred by the plaintiff in reliance on the contract.[3]

Typical of the cases that wrestle with the concept of benefit is Fabian v. Wasatch Orchard.[4] The plaintiff was employed as a sales representative on commission basis under an oral contract not performable within one year. Acting under the contract the plaintiff procured a number of orders that were filled by the defendant. In an action by the plaintiff for quasi-contractual relief, the defendant argued that the products were sold at a loss and therefore it had not received a benefit. The court, however, ruled that any performance rendered pursuant to

§ 19.43

1. Rs. 1st § 355(3).

2. 4 Corbin § 14.6 (Brown 1997).

3. Baugh v. Darley, 112 Utah 1, 184 P.2d 335 (1947); Hale v. Kreisel, 194 Wis. 271, 215 N.W. 227, 56 ALR 780 (1927); accord, under a statute limited to certain business brokerage contracts, McKinney's N.Y.Gen.Oblig. Law § 5–701(10); contra, Cassidy & Pinkard v. Jemal, 899 F.Supp. 5 (D.D.C.1995); Felland v. Sauey, 248 Wis.2d 963, 637 N.W.2d 403 (2001).

4. See § 5.9 supra.

§ 19.44

1. See generally, Jeanblanc, Restitution Under the Statute of Frauds: Measurement of the Legal Benefit Unjustly Retained, 15 Mo.L.Rev. 1 (1950); Jeanblanc, Restitution Under the Statute of Frauds: What Constitutes an Unjust Retention, 48 Mich.L.Rev. 923 (1950); Jeanblanc, Restitution Under the Statute of Frauds: What Constitutes a Legal Benefit, 26 Ind.L.J. 1 (1950).

2. See § 15.4 supra.

3. Trollope v. Koerner, 106 Ariz. 10, 470 P.2d 91, 64 ALR3d 1180 (1970); Farash v. Sykes Datatronics, 59 N.Y.2d 500, 452 N.E.2d 1245, 465 N.Y.S.2d 917 (1983); 3 Williston § 536 at 830 n. 6 (3d ed.) (collecting cases); Fuller and Perdue, The Reliance Interest in Contract Damages: 2, 46 Yale L.J. 373, 394 (1936); Perillo, Restitution in a Contractual Context, 73 Colum.L.Rev. 1208 (1973).

4. 41 Utah 404, 125 P. 860, LRA 1916D,892 (1912). But see Baugh v. Darley, 112 Utah 1, 184 P.2d 335 (1947).

the oral agreement and accepted by the defendant constituted a benefit whether or not it resulted in economic enrichment.[5]

Many courts have gone beyond the concept of benefit and have frankly permitted recovery for reliance losses in actions for restitution or on a theory of promissory estoppel.[6] One of the earlier cases in which the reliance interest was openly protected was Riley v. Capital Airlines.[7] Plaintiff entered into an oral contract to supply defendant's requirements of methanol for a five year period. On the defendant's repudiation of the agreement, the plaintiff was permitted to recover his losses based on expenditures made as a necessary prerequisite to performance. The plaintiff had purchased special tanks and pumps to produce and store the methanol and was forced by the breach to resell these at a loss. In no sense were these losses a benefit to the defendant. Both of the leading contract treatises assert, without qualification, that in the absence of receipt by the defendant of the plaintiff's property or services, no quasi-contractual relief is possible.[8] Yet, decisions like Riley are now made with some frequency[9] and demonstrate attempts by the courts to prevent the Statute of Frauds from operating as an instrument of injustice.

§ 19.45   Contract Price as Evidence of Value

If A orally agrees to perform services for a two year period in return for B's promise to pay $20,000 at the end of the period, the contract is within the Statute of Frauds. If B discharges A at the end of six months, may A introduce the contract price as evidence of the value of the services? The great weight of authority is to the effect that the price is admissible into evidence[1] despite the fact that in many cases the jury's verdict will often be the equivalent of what it would have been in an action on the contract.

If the preceding sections have not made it clear, however, it should be explicitly stated that in many instances the plaintiff's judgment in an

---

5.   Accord, Matousek v. Quirici, 195 Ill. App. 391 (1915) (required to pay reasonable rental value of premises orally leased although lessee never occupied the premises); Randolph v. Castle, 190 Ky. 776, 228 S.W. 418 (1921) (employees may recover for value of their time while on the job site although they performed no services).

6.   See §§ 19.47, 19.48 infra.

7.   185 F.Supp. 165 (S.D.Ala.1960).

8.   4 Corbin § 14.9 (Brown 1997); 3 Williston § 536 at 832 (3d ed.).

9.   See authorities cited in note 3.

§ 19.45

1.   Grantham v. Grantham, 205 N.C. 363, 171 S.E. 331 (1933) [but see Doub v. Hauser, 256 N.C. 331, 123 S.E.2d 821 (1962)]; Bennett Leasing v. Ellison, 15 Utah 2d 72, 387 P.2d 246, 21 ALR3d 1 (1963); Cochran v. Bise, 197 Va. 483, 90 S.E.2d 178 (1955); 4 Corbin § 14.10 (Brown 1997); 3

Williston § 536 at 838 (3d ed.); Rs. 1st § 217(2); Rs. 2d § 143. Contra, Blanchard v. Calderwood, 110 N.H. 29, 260 A.2d 118 (1969). The reader is warned to beware of statements couched in terms of "weight of authority." Consider that in one jurisdiction the following cases deem the contract price admissible: Leahy v. Campbell, 70 A.D. 127, 75 N.Y.S. 72 (1902); Gall v. Gall, 27 A.D. 173, 50 N.Y.S. 563 (1898), app. dismissed; In re Schweizer's Estate, 231 N.Y.S.2d 534 (1962), and the following cases deem it inadmissible: Zaitsev v. Salomon Bros., 60 F.3d 1001 (2d Cir.1995); Erben v. Lorillard, 19 N.Y. 299 (1859); Schlanger v. Cowan, 13 A.D.2d 739, 214 N.Y.S.2d 784 (1961); Parver v. Matthews–Kadetsky, 242 A.D. 1, 273 N.Y.S. 44 (1934); Black v. Fisher, 145 N.Y.S.2d 142 (1955). See also Galvin v. Prentice, 45 N.Y. 162, 6 Am.Rep. 58 (1871).

action for quasi contract may differ markedly from the result which would be obtainable if the contract were enforceable in an action for damages. One illustration may suffice. Suppose an uncle orally promised his nephew to devise to him all of his real property in exchange for the nephew's promise to take care of him for life.[2] Suppose further that several weeks later the uncle repudiated and soon thereafter died. In a quasi-contractual action for the value of his services, the nephew may realistically hope to recover several hundred or perhaps even several thousand dollars. In an action for damages to enforce the contract, he would be entitled to the benefit of his bargain; that is, the value of the real property, conceivably millions of dollars, with a deduction for the expenses saved as a result of the repudiation.

On the other hand, in an action for restitution, the plaintiff's recovery may sometimes be greater than would have been available in an action on the contract for damages. Thus, an employee who alleged that he was hired for a three year period under an oral agreement and had been compensated at the rate of $18 to $25 per week before his wrongful discharge was permitted to plead and prove that the value of the services rendered was $50 per week.[3]

§ 19.46 Specific Restitution in Equity

Equity has forged an armory of remedies to aid a deserving petitioner. One recurring fact pattern will be considered to suggest the kind of analysis utilized in equity in cases involving specific restitution.

Frequently a grantor conveys land to the defendant on the defendant's *oral*[1] promise to reconvey it to the grantor on demand or to hold it in trust for the grantor or some third person.[2] The oral promise may be within the Statute of Frauds provision regarding the transfer of interests in land. In addition, in most jurisdictions there is a specific provision of the Statute of Frauds requiring a record for the creation of express

---

2. It is generally held that a promise to leave real property by will is within the real property Statute of Frauds. See 4 Corbin § 17.3 (Brown 1997). Some jurisdictions have a specific provision of the Statute of Frauds applicable to contracts to make a testamentary disposition. E.g., McKinney's N.Y. Est. Powers & Trusts Law § 13–2.1(2). Thus, under the majority view that if any part of the contract is within the Statute, the entire contract must satisfy the Statute (§ 19.36); a promise to leave "all my property" is within the Statute if the promisor owns any real property. Blanchard v. Calderwood, 110 N.H. 29, 260 A.2d 118 (1969).

3. McGilchrist v. F. W. Woolworth, 138 Or. 679, 7 P.2d 982 (1932); accord, Schanzenbach v. Brough, 58 Ill.App. 526 (1895) (contract price does not set a maximum); Grossberg v. Double H. Licensing, 86 A.D.2d 565, 446 N.Y.S.2d 296 (1982); Ricks v. Sumler, 179 Va. 571, 19 S.E.2d 889 (1942). For a criticism of this rule, see Perillo, Restitution in the Second Restatement of Contracts, 81 Colum.L.Rev. 37, 44–45 (1981).

§ 19.46

1. If the promise is in a sufficient record, specific restitution is available under the rules discussed in § 15.5 supra.

2. Sometimes this is done to defraud creditors, in which case the grantor is faced with the additional difficulty of recovering under an illegal bargain. See Wantulok v. Wantulok, 67 Wyo. 22, 214 P.2d 477, 21 ALR2d 572 (1950), rehearing den., noted in 37 Va.L.Rev. 455 (1951) and 5 Wyo.L.J. 152 (1951).

trusts.[3] It is obvious that the oral promise cannot be enforced as such without conflicting with the Statute. It is also obvious that the grantee who violates the oral agreement has been unjustly enriched and the grantor unjustly impoverished.

Equity in such a case may impose a constructive trust on the land or, if the grantee has sold the land, the proceeds. The trust is said to be "constructive" because it is not based on the agreement but is imposed by law to avoid unjust enrichment and inequitable conduct. The conditions under which the constructive trust will be imposed, however, is a matter of dispute. The weight of authority supports the imposition of a constructive trust: (1) where the conveyance was procured by fraud, misrepresentation, duress, undue influence or mistake; (2) where the transferee is a fiduciary; or (3) where the transfer was made as security only.[4] A minority of jurisdictions will construct a trust in any case where there is a violation of an oral agreement to convey.[5] The majority rule is based on traditional grounds for the existence of equity jurisdiction. Since the merger of law and equity, most jurisdictions have taken the view that merger merely brought procedural unification.[6] Massachusetts appears to stand alone in refusing to construct a trust for violation of an oral promise, relegating the grantor to a quasi-contractual action for the value of the land.[7]

While the Restatement of Restitution states that one of the grounds for the imposition of a constructive trust, where there has been a violation of an oral agreement to reconvey, is the existence of a "fiduciary" relation,[8] many of the cases go well beyond this and hold that any pre-existing confidential relationship is sufficient. This would include such a relationship as husband and wife, father and son, brother and sister, lawyer and client, doctor and patient, priest and parishioner.[9]

It is generally recognized that in order to obtain relief of the kind described here the plaintiff must establish his case by more than the preponderance of the evidence. The cases speak in terms of clear and

---

3. See 4 Corbin § 17.6 (Brown 1997).

4. Moses v. Moses, 140 N.J.Eq. 575, 53 A.2d 805, 173 ALR 273 (1947); Rs. Restitution § 182(c); Rs. Trusts § 44. On conveyances made for purposes of security, see Straight v. Hill, 622 P.2d 425 (Alaska 1981); Fogelman, The Deed Absolute as a Mortgage in New York, 32 Fordham L.Rev. 299 (1963).

5. Orella v. Johnson, 38 Cal.2d 693, 242 P.2d 5 (1952), 40 Calif.L.Rev. 621 (1952).

6. For a convincing argument that a substantive merger of equitable and legal principles ought to extend the range of constructive trusts, see Newman, Some Reflections on the Function of the Confidential Relationship Doctrine in the Law of Trusts, in Perspectives of Law 286, 300–01 (1964).

7. Kemp v. Kemp, 248 Mass. 354, 142 N.E. 779 (1924).

8. Rs. Restitution § 182.

9. These relationships are specifically enumerated in Fraw Realty v. Natanson, 261 N.Y. 396, 402, 185 N.E. 679, 680 (1933). These are not, however, exclusive. See generally Newman, note 6; Talbott, Restitution Remedies in Contract Cases: Finding a Fiduciary or Confidential Relationship to Gain Remedies, 20 Ohio St.L.J. 320 (1959). "A confidential relationship exists when one person relies upon and trusts the other with the management of his [or her] property and attendance to his [or her] business affairs, thereby creating some degree of fiduciary obligation." Paletta v. Mercantile Bank, 889 S.W.2d 58, 61 (Mo. App.1994). quoting an earlier case.

convincing evidence or of establishing the oral promise beyond a reasonable doubt.[10]

The Restatement (Second) has dramatically enlarged the availability of specific restitution. A party who is entitled to monetary restitution and is not in breach is entitled to specific restitution unless it would "unduly interfere with the certainty of title to land or otherwise would cause injustice."[11] Since restitution is readily available for performances rendered under unenforceable contracts, acceptance of this rule would greatly advance the availability of specific restitution.

IV. ESTOPPEL

Table of Sections

§ 19.47   Equitable Estoppel and the Statute of Frauds

Most jurisdictions recognize that if the elements of equitable estoppel are present, the party to be charged will not be permitted to raise the defense of the Statute of Frauds.[1] It will be recalled that equitable estoppel requires justifiable injurious reliance on a factual representation or conduct of the other. Thus, if the Statute of Frauds of a given jurisdiction requires that an agent's authority be granted in a record, the principal will be estopped from asserting this Statute as a defense if the principal has indicated to the other contracting party that the agent is duly authorized to act[2] provided, of course, that the representation produced injurious reliance.[3] So also if the party to be charged, by words or conduct, represents that he or she has signed a record of the contract, this representation can be the basis of an estoppel to plead the Statute.[4] A representation that a three-year oral contract was binding has been held to be a predicate for an estoppel.[5]

---

10. E.g., for an especially strong statement, Strype v. Lewis, 352 Mo. 1004, 180 S.W.2d 688, 155 ALR 99 (1944), where it was said that the evidence must be so clear, cogent and convincing as to exclude every reasonable doubt from the chancellor's mind.

11. Rs. 2d § 372(1).

§ 19.47

1. Tidewater Beverage Services, v. Coca Cola, 907 F.Supp. 943 (E.D.Va.1995); Burdick, A Statute for Promoting Fraud, 16 Colum.L.Rev. 273 (1916); Note, 66 Mich. L.Rev. 170 (1967); But see Ozier v. Haines, 411 Ill. 160, 103 N.E.2d 485 (1952), which requires deceit on the part of the defendant; Polka v. May, 383 Pa. 80, 118 A.2d 154 (1955), rejecting the notion that the

doctrine of estoppel may be invoked against the operation of the Statute of Frauds, but allowing reliance damages.

2. Fleming v. Dolfin, 214 Cal. 269, 4 P.2d 776, 78 ALR 585 (1931), noted in 20 Cal.L.Rev. 663 (1932); Levy v. Rothfeld, 271 A.D. 973, 67 N.Y.S.2d 497 (1947), app. dismissed.

3. Coombs v. Ouzounian, 24 Utah 2d 39, 465 P.2d 356 (1970).

4. Owens v. Foundation for Ocean Research, 107 Cal.App.3d 179, 165 Cal.Rptr. 571 (1980), overruled on other grounds; cf., McKay Prods. v. Jonathan Logan, Inc., 54 Misc.2d 385, 283 N.Y.S.2d 82 (1967), aff'd; Rs. 1st § 178 cmt f.

5. Lago & Sons Dairy v. H.P. Hood, Inc. 892 F.Supp. 325 (D.N.H.1995), modified.

Some courts have gone far beyond the traditional notions and have used the label of equitable estoppel where the claimant has suffered an unconscionable injury by reliance on an oral or insufficiently memorialized contract. Cases such as these have led to the widespread adoption of promissory estoppel to defeat a plea of the Statute of Frauds.

§ 19.48   Promissory Estoppel

The first edition of this hornbook, published in 1970, predicted "a major new approach" towards the interrelationship between promissory estoppel and the Statute of Frauds,[1] basing this prediction on relatively few cases.[2] Since that time, there has been widespread application of promissory estoppel to cases in which it would be inequitable to allow the Statute of Frauds to defeat a meritorious claim. The older view took the position that "[s]uch a holding is clearly impossible of justification on any theory, in view of the language of the statute."[3] This suggestion appears to be based on a misunderstanding of the relationship between common law doctrines and legislation. The doctrine of estoppel, promissory or otherwise, is as much a part of our law as the Statute of Frauds. It is for the courts to harmonize the Statute and common law doctrine into a coherent and just pattern within our legal system—certainly a difficult task.[4] Until the Statute of Frauds is reformed so as to take into account the many problems that more than three hundred years of history have shown were unforeseen by its draftsmen, the courts should be encouraged in their creative work of doing justice by utilizing all doctrines available to them.

The First Restatement's only use of the term "promissory estoppel" appears in the context of a promise to make a record which "if * * * relied on, may give rise to an effective promissory estoppel if the Statute would otherwise operate to defraud."[5] Thus, we find courts that have not fully embraced promissory estoppel nevertheless applying the doctrine as to such cases.[6] The Restatement (Second) broadly enlarged the availabili-

---

§ 19.48

1. Calamari & Perillo, Contracts § 327 (1970).

2. Alaska Airlines v. Stephenson, 15 Alaska 272, 217 F.2d 295 (9th Cir.1954); Monarco v. Lo Greco, 35 Cal.2d 621, 220 P.2d 737 (1950); Boesiger v. Freer, 85 Idaho 551, 381 P.2d 802 (1963); Miller v. Lawlor, 245 Iowa 1144, 66 N.W.2d 267, 48 ALR2d 1058 (1954); Somerset Acres West Homes Ass'n v. Daniels, 191 Kan. 583, 383 P.2d 952 (1963); Vogel v. Shaw, 42 Wyo. 333, 294 P. 687, 75 ALR 639 (1930), 29 Mich.L.Rev. 1075 (1931).

3. Grismore on Contracts § 284 (rev'd 2d ed. 1965) (this statement does not appear in the current edition known as Murray on Contracts) (4th ed 2001). Compare Ozier v. Haines, 411 Ill. 160, 103 N.E.2d 485 (1952). But see Loeb v. Gendel, 23 Ill.2d 502, 179 N.E.2d 7 (1961).

4. See Smith v. Ash, 448 S.W.2d 51 (Ky. 1969), in which the court refused to invoke an estoppel because of the plaintiff's misrepresentations (coupled with other equities against the plaintiff) despite the plaintiff's extensive acts of reliance on defendant's oral promise. See also Brooks v. Cooksey, 427 S.W.2d 498 (Mo.1968) where an estoppel was denied partly on the ground that defendant did not benefit from plaintiff's change of position; Williams v. Denham, 83 S.D. 518, 162 N.W.2d 285 (1968) where an estoppel was denied because acts in reliance took place after defendant repudiated the oral contract.

5. Rs. 1st § 178 cmt f; accord Landry v. Landry, 641 A.2d 182 (Me.1994).

6. Johnson v. Gilbert, 127 Ariz. 410, 621 P.2d 916 (App.1980); Leach v. Conoco, 892 S.W.2d 954 (Tex.App.1995); see Klinke v.

ty of the doctrine in Statute of Frauds cases, following the lead of cases such as Alaska Airlines v. Stephenson.[7] The plaintiff had been employed as a pilot with Western Airlines, a position affording a good deal of employment security. He then accepted a position as general manager of the defendant airline. The oral agreement was to the effect that the plaintiff would take a six-month leave of absence from Western to work for the defendant and, if the defendant received a franchise to fly from Seattle to Alaska, the plaintiff would receive a written contract for two years employment. The plaintiff moved his family from California to Alaska, abandoned his tenure rights with Western and occupied the position of defendant's general manager. When the franchise was obtained, no written contract was forthcoming. Instead, the plaintiff was discharged. The court in ruling for the plaintiff explicitly based its decision on promissory estoppel, suggesting that this approach "will generally be followed throughout the country."[8]

The Alaska court's suggestion that the nation's courts would follow its lead has largely proved to be correct,[9] although a few courts have rejected promissory estoppel as a device to overcome the requirements of the Statute of Frauds.[10] Although the use of the doctrine for this purpose has been largely accepted, it is marked by what has been labeled as a "remarkably incoherent body of case law."[11] The widespread use of the doctrine in this context is in its infancy, therefore its analytic structure is not yet mature. Factors that go into a finding that the doctrine applies include unconscionable injury, unjust impoverishment not fully redressable by restitution, and the extent to which conduct in reliance on the contract corroborates the making of the agreement.[12]

Conduct corroborating the existence of the agreement is, of course, at the root of the part performance doctrine applied mainly in real property cases.[13] These cases, although stemming from different princi-

Famous Recipe Fried Chicken, 94 Wn.2d 255, 616 P.2d 644 (1980).

7. 15 Alaska 272, 217 F.2d 295 (9th Cir.1954).

8. 217 F.2d at 298. Promissory estoppel is discussed in 4 Corbin § 12.8 (Brown 1997). For its relation to the one-year section, see id. § 19.15.

9. MacEdward v. Northern Elec., 595 F.2d 105 (2d Cir.1979) (Vt. law); Gray v. Mitsui & Co., 434 F.Supp. 1071 (D.Or. 1977); Ralston Purina v. McCollum, 271 Ark. 840, 611 S.W.2d 201 (App.1981); Meylor v. Brown, 281 N.W.2d 632 (Iowa 1979); Decatur Co–op. Ass'n v. Urban, 219 Kan. 171, 547 P.2d 323 (1976); Hickey v. Green, 14 Mass.App.Ct. 671, 442 N.E.2d 37 (1982), rev. denied; Lovely v. Dierkes, 132 Mich. App. 485, 347 N.W.2d 752 (1984); Alpark Distrib. v. Poole, 95 Nev. 605, 600 P.2d 229 (1979); Jamestown Terminal Elev. v. Hieb, 246 N.W.2d 736 (N.D.1976); Buddman Distrib. v. Labatt Importers, 91 A.D.2d 838,

458 N.Y.S.2d 395 (1982); T * * * v. T * * *, 216 Va. 867, 224 S.E.2d 148 (1976); B & W Glass v. Weather Shield Mfg., 829 P.2d 809 (Wyo.1992); see Annot., 54 ALR3d 715 (1974); Comment, 44 Fordham L.Rev. 114 (1975); but see Time Warner Sports Merch. v. Chicagoland Processing, 974 F.Supp. 1163 (N.D.Ill.1997).

10. Collected and rejected in Alaska Democratic Party v. Rice, 934 P.2d 1313 n. (Alaska 1997).

11. Metzger & Phillips, Promissory Estoppel and Section 2–201 of the Uniform Commercial Code, 26 Vill.L.Rev. 63, 64 (1980).

12. Rs. 2d § 139. As discussed in § 6.4 supra, the doctrine allows for flexibility of remedy. See Midwest Energy v. Orion Food Sys., 14 S.W.3d 154 (Mo.App.2000) (damages limited to reliance interest); Comment, 58 J.Mo.B. 132 (2002).

13. See § 19.15 supra.

ples, can be looked at as promissory estoppel cases because relief is granted where a party has taken concrete action in reliance on a promise.[14] Although the part performance doctrine has its own particularized set of rules, there is a tendency to depart from the narrower doctrines of part performance and to base a decision on grounds of estoppel whenever the plaintiff's equities are so great as to make a contrary decision unconscionable.[15] In a few jurisdictions, such as California, the tendency to rely on estoppel is so great as to result in the obliteration of the doctrine of part performance and its incorporation into the more generalized doctrine of estoppel.[16]

Some courts have refused to recognize the applicability of promissory estoppel to cases involving the sale of goods reasoning that UCC § 2–201 provides such a thorough catalog of ways to satisfy the Statute of Frauds that adding to it would be an act of judicial usurpation.[17] In so holding they have seemingly overlooked UCC § 1–203 (1–103(b) of the revision) which provides that "the principles of law and equity, including * * * estoppel * * * shall supplement * * *" the provisions of the Act.

---

14. Durkee v. Van Well, 654 N.W.2d 807 (S.D.2002) discusses the common elements of the part performance and estoppel rationales.

15. D. C. Housing Fin. Agcy. v. Harper, 707 A.2d 53 (D.C.App.1998); Boesiger v. Freer, 85 Idaho 551, 381 P.2d 802 (1963) (part performance insufficient, but other actions in reliance raised an estoppel); Somerset Acres West Homes Ass'n v. Daniels, 191 Kan. 583, 383 P.2d 952 (1963); Barber v. Fox, 36 Mass.App. 525, 632 N.E.2d 1246 (1994); Vogel v. Shaw, 42 Wyo. 333, 294 P. 687, 75 ALR 639 (1930), 29 Mich.L.Rev. 1075 (1931); In re Estate of Gorton, 167 Vt. 357, 706 A.2d 947 (1997). See 4 Corbin § 18.21 (Brown 1997); 3 Williston § 533A (3d ed); Annot., 56 ALR3d 1037 (1974).

16. Redke v. Silvertrust, 6 Cal.3d 94, 98 Cal.Rptr. 293, 490 P.2d 805 (1971), cert. denied; Monarco v. Lo Greco, 35 Cal.2d 621, 220 P.2d 737 (1950); Seymour v. Oelrichs, 156 Cal. 782, 106 P. 88 (1909); but see Itek

v. RCA, 32 N.Y.2d 730, 344 N.Y.S.2d 365, 297 N.E.2d 100 (1973) (California law). See also Bunbury v. Krauss, 41 Wis.2d 522, 164 N.W.2d 473 (1969); Steadman v. Steadman, [1974] 3 W.L.R. 56, noted in 90 L.Q.Rev. 433 (1974).

17. E.g., C.R. Fedrick v. Borg–Warner, 552 F.2d 852 (9th Cir.1977), noted in 9 Rut.-Cam.L.J. 387 (1977) and 18 Santa Clara L.Rev. 837 (1978); C.G. Campbell & Son v. Comdeq, 586 S.W.2d 40 (Ky.App. 1979); contra, Allen M. Campbell Co. v. Virginia Metal Indus., 708 F.2d 930 (4th Cir.1983), noted in 41 Wn. & Lee L.Rev. 588 (1984); Meylor v. Brown, 281 N.W.2d 632 (Iowa 1979); Decatur Co–op. Ass'n v. Urban, 219 Kan. 171, 547 P.2d 323 (1976), noted in 26 U.Kan.L.Rev. 327 (1978); Potter v. Hatter Farms, 56 Or.App. 254, 641 P.2d 628, 29 ALR4th 997 (1982); B & W Glass v. Weather Shield Mfg., 829 P.2d 809 (1992); Metzger & Phillips, Promissory Estoppel and Section 2–201 of the Uniform Commercial Code, 26 Vill.L.Rev. 63 (1980).

Chapter 20

JOINT AND SEVERAL CONTRACTS

Table of Sections

Table of Sections

A. MULTIPLE OBLIGORS

A.   MULTIPLE OBLIGORS

Table of Sections

§ 20.1　Multiple Promisors

This chapter is concerned with rights and duties created by multiple promises of the *same* performance. It is not concerned with multiple promises of *different* performances. Whether or not multiple promises refer to the same performance or to different performances is a question of interpretation.[1]

For example, if A and B each promise to pay C $500, they are promising different performances. However, if A and B each promise to pay C a total of $1,000 so that each is liable for $1,000, but C is entitled to collect only once, they are promising the same performance.

We are concerned here with the old common law concepts of joint, joint and several, and several obligations.[2] These concepts are not engaged unless the promises relate to the same performance. The question is whether multiple promisors of the same performance have promised as a unit (jointly), or have promised the same performance separately (severally), or both as a unit and separately (jointly and severally). Having made this determination, the question then is the effect at common law of joint, joint and several, or several obligations, and finally what changes have been made (ordinarily by statute) in the arbitrary and unfortunate common law rules.[3]

§ 20.2　Promisors Bound Jointly, Severally, or Jointly and Severally

The old common law rule strongly favored a finding of joint promises. The rule was to the effect that promises of the same performance were joint[1] "unless the promises took a linguistic form appropriate to several duties."[2] Thus if A & B as promisors stated, "we jointly promise to pay the same obligation," there would be nothing to overcome the presumption of a joint obligation. However, if A & B stated "each of us independently promises to pay the obligation," the presumption of a

---

§ 20.1

1. Rs. 2d ch. 13, Introductory Note; id. § 288. Illustrative of promises of different performances is Over the Road Drivers v. Transport Ins. Co., 637 F.2d 816 (1st Cir. 1980).

2. There are similar problems where a promise is made to multiple promisees. See §§ 20.7 to 20.11 infra.

3. See Werner, Shared Liability: An Alternative to the Confusion of Joint, Several and Joint and Several Obligations, 42 Albany L.Rev. 1 (1977); see also Bromberg, Enforcement of Partnership Obligations—Who Is Sued for the Partnership, 71 Neb. L.Rev. 143 (1992).

§ 20.2

1. Rs. 2d § 289(2); 4 Corbin § 425.

2. Rs. 2d § 289 cmt b; see Clayman v. Goodman Properties, 518 F.2d 1026 (D.C.Cir.1973).

joint obligation would be overcome by the words of severance.[3] If A & B promised by saying, "we bind ourselves and each of us promise to pay," the obligation is joint and several[4] and the same is true where two or more persons promise in the first person singular.[5] In the case of a joint and several obligation involving two promisors there are three obligations, the joint obligation and the two several obligations.

The old common law tended to view the problem "as a deduction from legal concepts."[6] However, the more modern approach is that the question is one of the intention of the parties and, although the presumption in favor of joint liability continues to exist, it is more easily overcome.[7]

The fact that one of the parties is a principal and the other a surety does not change these rules,[8] and the same is true even where the parties have agreed *inter se,* unknown to the promisee, that each will be liable to the promisee for an aliquot share of the undertaking.[9]

Many state statutes provide that promises which would be joint under the common law rules should be treated as if they were joint and several.[10]

§ 20.3   Consequences of Joint Liability

There are at least five common law doctrines relating to joint obligations that have proved disgracefully unsatisfactory.[1] These are: 1)

3. Rs. 2d § 289, ill. 7. Subscription contracts, that is, promises in one instrument to make individual payments, are held to be several even though reading, "We, the undersigned, subscribe and promise to pay the amounts set opposite our names." 4 Corbin § 927.

4. Lorimer v. Goff, 216 Mich. 587, 185 N.W. 791 (1921); Guynn v. Corpus Christi Bank & Trust, 620 S.W.2d 188 (Tex.Civ. App.1981) ("We or either of us promise to pay").

Language of joint and several liability creates an "obligation in solido" under the Louisiana Code, with consequences that are not quite the same as in other states. Tramonte v. Palermo, 640 So.2d 661 (La.App. 1994).

5. UCC § 3–118(e), § 3–116(a) of the 1990 revision; Rs. 1st § 115; Continental Ill. Bank & Trust Co. v. Clement, 259 Mich. 167, 242 N.W. 877 (1932).

6. Rs. 2d § 289 cmt b.

7. Rs. 2d § 289 cmts b and c; 4 Corbin § 925; Douglas v. Bergere, 94 Cal.App.2d 267, 210 P.2d 727 (1949); Schubert v. Ivey, 158 Conn. 583, 264 A.2d 562 (1969); Falaschi v. Yowell, 24 Wn.App. 506, 601 P.2d 989 (1979). However the vitality of the common

law presumption of joint liability should not be underestimated. See Mileasing Co. v. Hogan, 87 A.D.2d 961, 451 N.Y.S.2d 211 (1982); Vermeer Industrial v. Bachmeier, 486 N.W.2d 506 (N.D.1992) (credit sale "sold to 80% Lance * * * & 20% Don" does not overcome presumption); 2 Williston § 320 (3d ed.); but see Brokerage Resources v. Jordan, 80 Ill.App.3d 605, 400 N.E.2d 77, 35 Ill.Dec. 940 (1980) (statutory change).

8. Rs. 2d § 289, cmt c; Philadelphia v. Reeves, 48 Pa. 472 (1865).

9. Knowlton v. Parsons, 198 Mass. 439, 84 N.E. 798 (1908).

10. The statutes are collected in the Rs. 2d of Contracts, Introductory Note to ch. 13, as well as in 2 Williston §§ 336–336A (3d ed.); but see Uniform Partnership Act § 15 of 1914 as to a partner's liability for partnership obligations, which in most instances is joint, but in some instances joint and several. The 1997 Uniform Partnership Act § 306 provides for joint and several liability. See 2 Bromberg & Ripstein, Partnership § 5.08(b) (looseleaf).

§ 20.3

1. See Braucher, Freedom of Contract and the Second Restatement, 78 Yale L.J. 598, 608 (1969) ("Rules and results * * *

compulsory joinder of joint promisors; 2) the discharge of other joint promisors by a judgment against one; 3) a judgment against joint promisors must be a joint one; 4) the rule of survivorship which barred an action against the estate of a deceased joint obligor; and 5) the rule that a discharge of one joint promisor released the others. These doctrines will now be considered seriatim.

(a) Compulsory Joinder of Joint Promisors

If A & B are joint obligors and C, the obligee, brought a suit against A, at early common law it was held that A could demur to the declaration and the demurrer would be sustained. This was true even though B was insolvent or beyond the jurisdiction. The theory was that A and B had promised as a unit and therefore had to be sued as a unit.[2]

In time the rule was modified so that the fact of non-joinder could be raised only by a plea in abatement (motion to dismiss), unless the non-joinder appeared on the face of the declaration,[3] and in the U.S. at least, the plea could be defeated if the joint obligor not joined was not alive, or not subject to process.[4]

The rule of compulsory joinder continues to be the general rule in the U.S. today in the absence of a statute,[5] but exceptions have also been made "for dormant partners, bankrupt co-promisors, and promisors against whom a claim is barred by the statute of limitations."[6]

The statutes referred to above have changed the common law rule in a variety of ways. One type of statute allows less than all of the joint obligors to be sued (provided all are named) in the discretion of the court. These statutes further provide that the judgment binds the joint property of all of the joint obligors but the separate property only of those served.[7] A second type of statute is similar to the first except that it eliminates the requirement that all of the joint obligors be named. Another type of statute permits an action against those served without any necessity for naming the other obligors or without any element of discretion in the judge. Many states also have statutes which permit partners to be sued in the firm name irrespective of whether the obligation is joint.[8]

(b) Discharge of Joint Promisors by a Judgment Against One

outraged both common and commercial sense."). On the general topic, see Griffith, Joint Rights and Liabilities (1897); Williams, Joint Obligations (1949); Evans, Contractual Joint Rights and Duties in Kentucky and the Restatement, 18 Ky.L.J. 341 (1930).

2. 4 Corbin § 929; 2 Williston § 327 (3d ed.); see generally, Reed, Compulsory Joinder of Parties in Civil Actions, 55 Mich. L.Rev. 327 (1927).

3. Rice v. Shute, 96 Eng.Rep. 409 (1770); see Koffler & Reppy, Common Law Pleading § 208 (1969).

4. Camp v. Gress, 250 U.S. 308 (1919); but see Turner Outdoor Adv. v. Old South, 185 Ga.App. 582, 365 S.E.2d 149 (1988); see Koffler & Reppy, Common Law Pleading § 208 (1969).

5. Rs. 2d § 290.

6. Rs. 2d § 290 cmt c.

7. See, e.g., McKinney's NY CPLR. § 1501.

8. See Bromberg & Ripstein, Partnership § 5.08(c) (looseleaf); Crane and Bromberg, Partnership § 60 (1968); 2 Rowley, Partnerships § 49.3 (2d ed.1960).

In subsection (a) we discussed the common law rule whereby a joint obligor could object to the non-joinder of other joint obligors and cause the action to be dismissed. Absent an objection, the action would proceed to judgment. Where the judgment is in favor of the plaintiff and against the joint obligor or obligors served, the result was that the judgment merged the entire claim so that no further action could be maintained against the other joint obligors, even though the parties against whom judgment had been obtained proved to be insolvent.[9] In time, exceptions came to be made in the case of promisors who were out of the jurisdiction, for foreign judgments, for cases of estoppel, and for judgments on promises given as conditional payment or collateral security.[10] But old concepts have tenacity. In Bank of the West v. Burlingame,[11] a judgment was obtained against one co-guarantor. This apparently was permissible. However, a discharge of the judgment was held to discharge the entire claim, discharging the other guarantor.

Today there are many statutes providing that a judgment against a joint promisor or promisors does not bar an action against other joint promisors, and some have permitted the joint property of those not served to be bound subject to later proceeding wherein they may be required to show cause why they should not be bound.[12]

(c) Only a Joint Judgment Can Be Entered Against Joint Promisors

Here the question is the effect of a judgment in favor of one of the joint obligors served. The common law took the position that against joint obligors only a joint judgment could be entered. This meant that it was impossible to have a verdict against the plaintiff in favor of one promisor and in favor of the plaintiff against another promisor. In other words, if the plaintiff lost to one joint obligor the plaintiff must lose to all.[13]

Eventually an exception was made where a defendant won the case because of a personal defense as, for example, lack of capacity, discharge in bankruptcy or the statute of limitations.[14]

The Restatement (Second) in § 291 sets forth the modern rule when it states: "In an action against promisors of the same performance, whether their duties are joint, several, or joint and several, judgment can properly be entered for or against one even though no judgment or a different judgment is entered with respect to another, except that a

9. Ward v. Johnson, 13 Mass. 148 (1816); Mitchell v. Brewster, 28 Ill. 163 (1862).

10. Rs. 2d § 292 cmt b; 2 Williston § 327 (3d ed.).

11. 134 Or.App. 529, 895 P.2d 1367 (1995).

12. The statutes are collected in the Introductory Note to § 288 of the Rs. 2d of Contracts.

13. Simpson, Contracts § 137 (2d ed.1965). Although the judgment is joint, a successful plaintiff could levy against the individual assets of any joint obligor who was served, although many courts require that joint assets be exhausted first.

14. Rs. 2d § 291 cmt a; Eastern Elec. Co. v. Taylor Woodrow Blitman Constr. Co., 11 Mass.App.Ct. 192, 414 N.E.2d 1023 (1981), rev. denied; Seafirst Center. v. Erickson, 127 Wn.2d 355, 898 P.2d 299 (1995).

judgment for one and against another is improper where there has been a determination on the merits and the liability of one cannot exist without the liability of the other."[15] It is often held that joint property must be exhausted before individual property may be levied upon.[16]

(d) The Rule of Survivorship

At early common law if a joint obligor died, the decedent's estate could not be sued. The creditor could proceed only against the surviving co-obligors.[17] If all of the joint obligors died only the estate of the last one to die was liable to the creditor.[18] Obviously this rule worked unfairly particularly where the remaining obligor or obligors were insolvent. The Courts of Chancery did not rigidly apply this doctrine and invented various procedures in order to do justice.[19] Today, whether by statute or by case decisions this rule has been abolished in most states.[20] However, there are still some decisions to the effect that a surety who is a joint obligor is discharged by death.[21]

(e) A Discharge of One Joint Obligor Discharges the Others

The joint nature of a joint obligation also led the common law courts to hold that a discharge of one or more joint obligors discharged the other joint obligors.[22] This was true whether the discharge occurred by virtue of release, rescission, or accord and satisfaction, and irrespective of the intention of the parties.[23] Because the rule operated very unfairly, some of the courts held that the rule operated only in the case of a formal release under seal.[24] The harsh common law was soon circum-

---

15. Accord, 4 Corbin § 929. The exception at the end of the statement is based on principles of res judicata or collateral estoppel by judgment.

16. Wayne Smith Constr. Co. v. Wolman, Duberstein & Thompson, 65 Ohio St.3d 383, 604 N.E.2d 157 (1992). In agreement on this point, while disagreeing as to others is Thompson v. Wayne Smith Constr. Co., 640 N.E.2d 408 (Ind.App.1994).

17. Davis v. Van Buren, 72 N.Y. 587 (1878); McLaughlin v. Head, 86 Or. 361, 168 P. 614 (1917); 2 Williston § 344 (3d ed.); Annot., 67 ALR 608 (1930). The fact the deceased joint obligor's estate was no longer liable to the creditor did not affect the estate's obligation of contribution to a joint obligor who had been compelled to pay.

18. Rs. 1st § 126.

19. 4 Corbin § 930; 2 Williston § 344 (3d ed.); Note, 2 Mich.L.Rev. 216 (1903).

20. Rs. 2d § 296 cmt b; see Nadstanek v. Trask, 130 Or. 669, 281 P. 840, 67 ALR 599 (1929). A statutory table appears in 2 Williston § 344A (3d ed.).

21. 4 Corbin § 930.

22. North Pacific Mtge. Co. v. Krewson, 129 Wn. 239, 224 P. 566, 53 ALR 1416 (1924); 4 Corbin § 931; 2 Williston § 333 (3d ed.); see generally Havighurst, The Effect of a Settlement With One Co–Obligor upon the Obligations of the Others, 45 Cornell L.Q. 1 (1951); Williston, Releases and Covenants Not To Sue Joint, or Joint and Several Debtors, 25 Harv.L.Rev. 203 (1912), Selected Readings 1179.

23. Rs. 1st § 294; Brooks v. Neal, 223 Mass. 467, 112 N.E. 78 (1916); Pacific Southwest Trust & Sav. Bank v. Mayer, 138 Wn. 85, 244 P. 248 (1926); 2 Williston § 333A (3d ed.). Illustrative of the purity of the logic and the barbarity of the results that marked this era is Jenkins v. Jenkins, [1928] 2 K.B. 501, 14 Cornell L.Q. 215 (1928). One of the co-obligors of a note was appointed executor of the payee's estate. His appointment had the effect of discharging him under the doctrine of merger. (See § 21.13 & 21.14, infra). It was held that other co-obligors who were jointly and severally liable with the executor were also discharged.

24. Deering v. Moore, 86 Me. 181, 29 A. 988 (1893); Line v. Nelson, 38 N.J.L. 358 (1876); 2 Williston § 333A (3d ed.).

vented by using a covenant not to sue.[25] While a release is an executed transaction, a covenant not to sue is executory and even when it is breached it is not specifically enforced in favor of the covenantee, and so it is held that a covenant not to sue is not a defense either to the covenantee or the other joint obligors. The covenantee may be sued but is protected by the court's requiring the creditor to refrain from levying against the property of the covenantee.[26]

Another device to circumvent the rule was a release containing a reservation of rights against the other obligors.[27] Such a reservation of rights caused the release to be interpreted as a covenant not to sue, provided that it was concurrent with the purported release and in the same instrument.

The Restatement (Second) adopts the common law rule but adds: "Modern decisions have converted it from a rule defeating intention to a rule of presumptive intention," and adds that where a contrary intention is manifested the release or discharge should be treated as a covenant not to sue.[28] The requirement that the reservation of rights must be in writing and concurrent stems from the parol evidence rule.[29]

A more modern approach is that the release of one obligor, releases no others from liability unless the terms so provide.[30]

There are also many states that have changed the common law rule by statute. For example, the Model Joint Obligations Act provides that a release or discharge of one or more of joint, joint and several, or several obligors does not discharge co-obligors against whom rights are reserved in writing and as part of the same transaction.[31] If there is no reservation of rights, then if the obligee knows or has reason to know "that the obligor released or discharged did not pay so much of the claim as he was bound by his contract or relation with that co-obligor to pay, the obligee's claim against that co-obligor shall be satisfied to the amount

---

25. Marret v. Scott, 212 Ga.App. 427, 441 S.E.2d 902 (1994); Seafirst Center. v. Erickson, 127 Wn.2d 355, 898 P.2d 299 (1995); 4 Corbin § 932; 2 Williston §§ 338, 338C (3d ed.).

26. Rs. 1st § 124; Rs. 2d § 295. See § 21.10 infra.

27. 4 Corbin § 933; 2 Williston § 338 (3d ed.).

28. Rs. 2d § 294 cmt a; accord, Community School Dist. v. Gordon N. Peterson, Inc., 176 N.W.2d 169 (Iowa 1970) (collecting cases supporting the modern view); Deblon v. Beaton, 103 N.J.Super. 345, 247 A.2d 172 (1968).

29. Oxford Commercial Corp. v. Landau, 12 N.Y.2d 362, 239 N.Y.S.2d 865, 190 N.E.2d 230, 13 ALR3d 309 (1963); see 4 Corbin § 934.

30. Hermes Automation Tech. v. Hyundai Electronics Indus., 915 F.2d 739 (1st Cir.1990) (prognosticating Mass. law); Sims v. Honda Motor Co., 225 Conn. 401, 623 A.2d 995 (1993) (statutory rule); Breen v. Peck, 28 N.J. 351, 146 A.2d 665, 73 ALR2d 390 (1958), aff'd; Seafirst Center v. Erickson, 127 Wn.2d 355, 898 P.2d 299 (1995).

31. See, e.g., McKinney's N.Y.Gen. Oblig. L § 15–104. In January 2003, this Act was in effect in Hawai'i, Maine, Nevada, New York, Utah and Wisconsin. A similar rule exists in the Uniform Contribution Among Tortfeasors Act in effect in Arizona, Colorado, Florida, Massachusetts, Nevada, North Carolina, North Dakota, Ohio, Oklahoma, South Carolina and Tennessee. The interpretations of the Act have varied. See Annot., 6 ALR5th 883 (1992). The enactments have varied also.

which the obligee knew or had reason to know that the released or discharged obligor was bound to such co-obligor to pay."[32]

For example, X, Y and Z are jointly obligated to C in the sum of $180,000, that is, there is one debt of $180,00 and each is liable to C for the full amount of the debt. Assume that they have agreed *inter se* that X will be liable for ½ and Y for ¼. If C knows this and releases X, then Y and Z will be liable for only $90,000.

The statute goes on to say that if C did not know or have reason to know of the agreement of the parties *inter se* then Y and Z will be discharged to the extent of the lesser of two amounts:[33] (1) "the amount of the fractional share of the obligor released or discharged," which on the facts in the illustration is $60,000, that is ⅓ (since there are three co-obligors involved) of $180,000; (2) "the amount that such obligor was bound by his contract or relation with his co-obligor to pay" which on the facts is $90,000.

Since the lesser sum is $60,000, C could still proceed against Y and Z for $120,000. ($180,000–$60,000); if Y and Z paid the $120,000, they should still be entitled to collect $30,000 from X, $15,000 each.

The rules just stated do not apply in a suretyship context. A principal and a surety may promise as joint promisors; normally, the same rules will apply despite the principal-surety relation.[34] However, it is a rule of suretyship law, that has not been changed by statute or by case law, that a creditor who releases a principal with knowledge of the suretyship relation releases the surety in the absence of a reservation of rights.[35] Conversely, a discharge of a surety does not discharge the principal debt.[36]

§ 20.4   Consequences of Joint and Several Liability

If A and B promise jointly and severally, there are three liabilities, the several liability of A, the several liability of B, and the joint liability of A and B.[1] Therefore, many of the problems that exist in joint liability situations also exist with respect to joint and several liability. To start with, each of the obligors is liable for the full amount of the obligation.[2]

---

32. See, e.g., McKinney's N.Y.Gen.Obligations Law § 15–105(1); cf. McKinney's N.Y.Gen.Obligations Law § 15–108(a) (applicable to joint tortfeasors).

33. See, e.g., McKinney's N.Y.Gen.Obligations Law § 15–105(2).

34. See § 20.2 supra.

35. Rs. 3d Suretyship & Guaranty § 39(b).

36. Rs. 2d § 294(1) (a). The principal is ordinarily credited with any consideration that the surety pays. The surety is entitled to reimbursement for the part payment, and on full payment, is in addition entitled

to be subrogated. If there is an agreement that the payment by the surety is not to be credited on the obligation, the surety loses the right of reimbursement. Rs. 2d § 294(3) cmt g.

§ 20.4

1. See § 20.2 supra. On the common law of joint and several liability, see generally, Chaney, Liability of Parties Who Are at the Same Time Both Jointly and Severally Liable Ex Contractu, 57 Cent.L.J. 283 (1903).

2. Pekofsky v. Nanuet Auto Parts, 210 A.D.2d 208, 619 N.Y.S.2d 740 (1994).

On the question of joinder, the rule was that the plaintiff could elect to sue one, or plaintiff could elect to sue all, but could not elect to sue more than one unless all were joined.[3] Thus, if the creditor sued one of the obligors on the several promises and recovered, there was no merger and separate actions and separate judgments could be obtained against the others.[4] But, if the creditor brought suit against more than one and less than all of the obligors, the rule of a merger with respect to joint obligors would apply.[5]

If the creditor sues one of the several obligors without joining the other obligors and loses, the doctrine of merger would not apply and the creditor's only problem would be under the doctrine of collateral estoppel by judgment.[6] The result would be otherwise if more than one were sued or if all were sued, in which event the rule with respect to joint obligors would obtain.[7]

The common law doctrine of survivorship that applied to joint obligations did not apply to joint and several obligations; the creditor could sue the representative of the deceased obligor on the several obligation.[8] But, where the creditor sought to sue the representative of the deceased obligor along with other co-obligors, the action could be resisted by the representative.

As we have seen, the general common law rule is that a voluntary release of one joint obligor releases the others.[9] The same rule[10] was applied to a joint and several obligation.[11]

Just as the rules with respect to joint obligations have been changed by statute and court decisions,[12] so the rules as to joint and several obligations that followed the joint obligations rules have also been changed.

§ 20.5 Consequences of Several Liability

There is very little to be said concerning the consequences of several liability because none of the consequences that arose with respect to joint and joint and several liability arise here except where suretyship principles may be involved.[1] Indeed, since the obligations were consid-

---

3. Koenig v. Currans Restaurant & Baking Co., 306 Pa. 345, 159 A. 553 (1932). This common law rule has been largely eliminated by modern rules of procedure. 4 Corbin § 937.

4. Gruber v. Friedman, 104 Conn. 107, 132 A. 395 (1926).

5. Rs. 2d § 291 cmt a.

6. 4 Corbin § 937.

7. Rs. 2d § 292 cmt a.

8. Eggleston v. Buck, 31 Ill. 254 (1863).

9. Fisher v. Chadwick, 4 Wyo. 379, 34 P. 899 (1893).

10. See § 20.3 supra.

11. Dwy v. Connecticut Co., 89 Conn. 74, 92 A. 883 (1915), but changed by statute; Dccse v. Mobley, 392 So.2d 364 (Fla. App.1981) (rule survives but is affected by Art. 3 of UCC).

12. See § 20.3 supra; see also United Pacific Ins. Co. v. Lundstrom, 77 Wn.2d 162, 459 P.2d 930 (1969) (release of one joint and several obligor does not discharge others unless intention to discharge is manifested.)

§ 20.5

1. Simpson, Contracts § 139 (2d ed.1965).

ered separate, at common law it was not possible to join the several obligors in one action. If the plaintiff joined several obligors in one action and at trial demonstrated that the defendants were severally liable, judgment would be entered against the plaintiff because only joint or joint and several obligors could be joined as defendants.[2] Under modern procedural statutes several obligors can generally be joined as defendants.[3]

§ 20.6   Relation of Co-obligors to Each Other—Contribution

The question here is the rights and liabilities of the co-obligors *inter se*. This does not depend on whether the liability of the co-obligors is joint, joint and several, or several but depends on suretyship principles.[1] Any payment, whether full or partial, by any co-obligor will inure to the benefit of the other co-obligor in the sense that there is a partial discharge of the obligation.[2] An agreement to the contrary is not effective.[3]

If C builds a structure for X and Y at an agreed price of $180,000 and X pays the full $180,000, X may recover $90,000 from Y in the absence of any contrary agreement between X and Y. A co-obligor who has paid more than a proportionate share is entitled to contribution.[4] What is the proportionate share of a co-obligor depends on the agreement between or among the co-obligors and, if there is no such agreement, on equitable principles. Thus, in the illustration given, in the absence of an agreement, X and Y as between themselves would be liable for $90,000 each.[5] But if X and Y agreed between themselves that X was responsible for ⅔ and Y for ⅓, X would be entitled to only $60,000 from Y.[6]

The situation would be different if C lent $180,000 to X that X and Y agreed to repay. Here although X and Y are co-obligors, X is the

---

2. Jones and Carlin, Non–Joinder and Misjoinder of Parties—Common Law Actions, 28 W.Va.L.Q. 266, 266–76 (1922); see also Air Engineers v. Reese, 283 Ala. 355, 217 So.2d 66 (1968), indicating that this rule prevails in Alabama in attenuated form.

A plaintiff who alleges joint liability but proves that liability is several may be nonsuited because of a variance between pleading and proof. Wheatley v. Carl M. Halvorson, Inc., 213 Or. 228, 323 P.2d 49 (1958).

3. See Clark, Code Pleading §§ 60–61 (2d ed.1947).

§ 20.6

1. Aspinwall v. Sacchi, 57 N.Y. 331 (1874); 2 Williston § 345 (3d ed.).

2. 4 Corbin § 936.

3. Rs. 2d §§ 294(3), 295(3). The only exception, as we have seen, is where the payment comes from a surety and it is expressly agreed that the amount paid should not be credited against the obligation. In such an event, the surety loses the right to reimbursement to the extent that the surety agrees that the amount paid shall not be credited to the obligation. See § 20.3 supra.

4. UCC § 3–116(b) (1990 revision); First American Bank v. Fallova Shredder Co., 155 Misc.2d 143, 587 N.Y.S.2d 119 (1992); Simpson, Contracts § 143 (2d ed.1965).

5. As to C, of course, we are assuming that both X and Y are liable for the full $180,000.

6. 2 Williston § 345 (3d.); Rs. Restitution § 81 (1937).

principal and, Y the surety.[7] Therefore, when X pays the $180,000, X is not entitled to contribution.[8] The situation would also be different if the loan was to Y, in which event X would be the surety. Here X would not be entitled to contribution ($90,000), but to reimbursement ($180,000).[9] In addition, X would be entitled to all other rights that a surety has, including the right of exoneration,[10] which is enforced by an equitable decree compelling the principal to fulfill the obligation to the creditor.[11]

In a sense, there is also suretyship involved in the original illustration (where C built a house for X and Y). As between X and Y, X is primarily liable for $90,000 and Y is surety for that $90,000. Conversely Y is primarily liable for $90,000 and X is surety for that $90,000.[12] Thus, X is only entitled to be reimbursed for the $90,000 on which he or she is a surety; X is not entitled to recover the $90,000 for which he or she is the principal.[13]

B.   MULTIPLE OBLIGEES

Table of Sections

§ 20.7 Multiple Promisees

We are not concerned with promises that promise different performances to multiple promisees, but rather are concerned with promises that promise the *same* performance to multiple promisees. As is the case with obligations, "rights may be either 'joint' or 'several' or some combination"[1] Under the modern view, at least, the question is one of intention, and where the intention is not clearly shown the rights of

---

7. Y is the surety because, as between X and Y, X is the one who should ultimately pay because X received all of the consideration. Rs. 3d Suretyship & Guaranty § 1, ill. 4.

8. Obviously the principal debtor does not have rights against the surety.

9. Rs. 3d Suretyship and Guaranty §§ 22, 23.

10. Rs. 3d Suretyship and Guaranty § 21(2) & cmt i.

11. Glades County v. Detroit Fidelity & Sur. Co., 57 F.2d 449 (5th Cir.1932); D'Ippolito v. Castoro, 51 N.J. 584, 242 A.2d 617, 38 ALR3d 672 (1968).

12. Lorimer v. Julius Knack Coal Co., 246 Mich. 214, 224 N.W. 362, 64 ALR 210

(1929); Wold v. Grozalsky, 277 N.Y. 364, 14 N.E.2d 437, 122 ALR 518 (1938).

13. See notes 7 and 8 supra.

§ 20.7

1. Rs. 2d § 297 cmt a. The Reporter's Note to § 297 confusingly states that "[r]eferences to 'several' rights and 'joint and several' rights are omitted." At the same time illustration 3 to the section concludes: "D has a several right." Cf. Braucher, supra § 20.3 n.1, at 610, stating: " * * * the original Restatement provided that co-promisees of the same performance might have a 'joint' right, 'several' rights, or 'joint and several' rights. But nothing of substance seemed to turn on this terminology and the Second Restatement refers only to 'joint' rights."

obligees of the same performance are deemed to be joint except where "the interests of the obligee in the performance or in the remedies for breach are distinct."[2] This means that the surrounding circumstances will be considered to determine whether or not promisees have distinct interests or a unitary interest in the promised performance.[3]

Thus, if A promised to pay B and C $1,000 for work to be done by B and C, the question of whether B and C are joint promisees is resolved by interpreting the wording of the contract in the light of the nature of the relationship between B and C. If they are partners, they have a community of interest in the profits and losses of the transaction and as a matter of law their rights are joint.[4] If they were not partners, in a formal sense, but joined together for this particular project with an intention to share profits and losses, the same result would follow.[5] Here too, they would be operating as a business organization even if on an ad hoc basis.[6] If, however, B and C were merely employees of A, there would be no community of interest between B and C. Their rights would be several.

In a leading case,[7] A, B, and C promised to care for D's herd of cattle for two years and D promised to pay them one-half of the selling price in excess of $36,000. Although the promise in form might appear to have been made to the promisees jointly, the court took note of the fact that the promisees were but employees and had no community of interest in any capital investment and would not share any losses and held that B could sue separately for a one-sixth interest in the excess more than $36,000.

Similarly, where a coal merchant in a single document promised to take all of its requirements from three coal companies in equal shares, it was held that each of the coal companies was a several obligee, there being no connection between them other than the contract itself.[8] If each of the coal companies desired to join in one action against the merchant, however, there is little question that the action should be permitted even in the face of a statute which permits joinder of plaintiffs only when they have a "joint" right.[9] If necessary, the rights of the obligees should be

---

2. Rs. 2d § 297; see 4 Corbin §§ 939–940; 2 Williston § 321 (3d ed.).

3. St. Regis Paper Co. v. Stuart, 214 F.2d 762 (1st Cir.1954), cert. denied.

4. Crane and Bromberg, Partnership § 57 (1968).

5. Id. at § 35.

6. Apparently, the intent of the Restatement (Second) is to reach the same result, but it characterizes cases such as this as involving promises of separate performances. Rs. 2d, Reporter's Note to § 297. But see ill. 3 thereto.

7. Beckwith v. Talbot, 95 U.S. (5 Otto) 289, 24 L.Ed. 496 (1877); accord, St. Regis Paper Co. v. Stuart, 214 F.2d 762 (1st Cir.

1954), cert. denied (two sales representatives worked as a team and were promised a team commission; despite absence of words of severability, one of them could bring an action for a share of the commission).

8. Shipman v. Straitsville Cent. Min. Co., 158 U.S. 356 (1895); cf. Donzella v. N.Y. State Thruway Auth., 7 A.D.2d 771, 180 N.Y.S.2d 108 (1958).

9. See 4 Corbin § 940. Today, almost everywhere several obligees of the same performance are now permitted to join as plaintiffs.

classified as "joint" for permitting joint action by them and "several" for the purpose of permitting separate actions by them.

§ 20.8 Compulsory Joinder of Joint Obligees

Where there are multiple promisees and they have a joint right, the promisor has an interest in not being harassed by a multiplicity of actions.[1] Thus, where less than all of the joint promisees bring an action, the defendant, as a common law proposition, may raise this issue and prevent a judgment.[2] Statutes that have relaxed the rule of compulsory joinder of joint obligors, generally also relax the rule as to joint obligees.[3] A joint obligee who refuses to join in the action may be joined as a plaintiff or an additional party defendant.[4] The fact that one of the joint obligees is out of the jurisdiction does not vary the situation because any joint obligee should be able to sue in the name of all of the joint obligees.[5]

But the old rule is tenacious. In McClain v. Buechner,[6] an attorney was allegedly negligent in allowing a default judgment to be entered against a client, a partnership. The partnership sued.[7] At least one of the six partners was named as a plaintiff as well. Discovering the mistake of law, the other partners moved to intervene in the action. It was held that because the statute of limitations had passed, they could not intervene. Because they were necessary parties, the action was dismissed—not sound law for a civilized society.

§ 20.9 Discharge by One Joint Obligee

One joint obligee has the power to act for the others and may discharge the rights of the co-obligees, for example, by accepting payment,[1] by an accord and satisfaction, or by release.[2] The rule as to negotiable instruments is statutory.[3] An exception occurs where the discharge is in violation of a duty to a co-obligee who may then avoid the discharge to the extent necessary for self protection "except to the extent that the promisor has given value or otherwise changed his

§ 20.8

1. 4 Corbin § 939; see generally, Reed, supra § 20.3 n.2.

2. Lee v. Ricca, 29 Ariz. 309, 241 P. 508 (1925); Dakin v. Greer, 685 S.W.2d 276 (Mo.App.1985).

3. See, e.g., Fed.R.Civ.P. 19; McKinney's N.Y.C.P.L.R. 1001; § 20.3 supra.

4. Hand v. Heslet, 81 Mont. 68, 261 P. 609 (1927).

5. Jackson Mfg. Co. v. U.S., 434 F.2d 1027 (5th Cir.1970). There are exceptions to this rule in the case of negotiable instruments, where the joint obligees have made a contrary agreement, or where bringing the action would amount to the violation of a duty to a co-obligee. Rs. 2d § 298(2).

6. 776 S.W.2d 481 (Mo.App.1989).

7. In most jurisdictions, partnerships are not entities. They are aggregations of individuals who act jointly or jointly and severally.

§ 20.9

1. Hutchens v. U.S., 5 Cl.Ct. 524 (1984), aff'd 755 F.2d 908 (Fed.Cir.1985).

2. Rs. 2d § 299; Cayce v. Carter Oil Co., 618 F.2d 669 (10th Cir.1980).

3. UCC § 3–116; UCC § 3–110 (1990 revision).

position in good faith and without knowledge or reason to know of the violation."[4]

Inconsistent with the general rule that one joint obligee may discharge a joint obligation, is the holding that a repudiation by one of the parties who jointly held rights and obligations under a bilateral contract does not create an anticipatory breach,[5] and that one joint obligee cannot exercise an option to accelerate.[6]

§ 20.10　Survivorship of Joint Rights

The rule of survivorship with respect to joint obligors also applied to joint obligees.[1] If a joint promisee died, the decedent's executor no longer had any right to sue the obligor for a money judgment.[2] If all of the joint obligees died, the personal representative of the last survivor could alone sue the obligor.[3] Ordinarily, at least, the death of a joint obligee would not deprive the estate of the right to an accounting from the co-obligee who received performance or settled the claim.[4] This rule has not been changed and is justified as a matter of convenience because "it is unnecessary to join the personal representative of a deceased co-obligee in an action for a money judgment."[5]

§ 20.11　Multiple Offerees or Optionees

An offer made jointly to a group of six offerees cannot be accepted by two of them.[1] Similarly, an offer made to two joint lessees cannot be accepted by either of them individually.[2] A purported exercise of an option by one of three multiple optionees is not a good acceptance.[3] This is especially true where there is a credit term in the offer.[4] But even in the absence of a credit term, an optionor would be exposed to the

4. Rs. 2d § 300(2). Thus if the obligor knows that the released obligee is violating a duty to the co-obligees, the release is effective only to the extent of the released obligee's share of the performance. An exhaustive review of the authorities appears in Freedman v. Montague Assocs., 18 Misc.2d 1, 187 N.Y.S.2d 636 (1959) (which, however, reached a contrary conclusion), rev'd 9 A.D.2d 936, 195 N.Y.S.2d 392 (1959), app. denied.

5. Link v. Weizenbaum, 229 Va. 201, 326 S.E.2d 667 (1985).

6. Lapidus v. Kollel Avreichim Torah Veyirah, 114 Misc.2d 451, 451 N.Y.S.2d 958 (1982).

§ 20.10

1. See § 20.3 supra.

2. Israel v. Jones, 97 W.Va. 173, 124 S.E. 665 (1924).

3. Rs. 2d § 301.

4. Hill v. Breeden, 53 Wyo. 125, 79 P.2d 482 (1938). Thus, for example, in a partner-

ship, only the surviving partners may enforce partnership claims, but the estate of the deceased partner has a beneficial interest in the proceeds of the litigation. Contrariwise, on the death of a joint tenant, the estate of the deceased tenant has no such beneficial interest. The results turn on the substantive law of partnership and property, rather than on merely procedural rules.

5. Rs. 2d § 301 cmt b. This comment adds: "Where equitable relief is sought, joinder of such a representative is permitted and when necessary to complete adjudication is required."

§ 20.11

1. Meister v. Arden–Mayfair, 276 Or. 517, 555 P.2d 923 (1976).

2. Spitalnik v. Springer, 59 N.Y.2d 112, 463 N.Y.S.2d 750, 450 N.E.2d 670 (1983), rearg. denied.

3. Clayman v. Goodman Properties, 518 F.2d 1026 (D.C.Cir.1973).

4. Ibid.

possibility of litigation by selling to one of multiple optionees.[5] Of course, if the one offeree or optionee has authority to bind the others and exercises that authority, the result would be different.[6]

5. Spitalnik v. Springer, note 2, supra.

6. See, e.g., Crane & Bromberg, Partnership §§ 49, 50 on the authority of a partner.

Chapter 21

DISCHARGE OF CONTRACTS

Table of Sections

Table of Sections

Sec.
21.1 Introduction.

I. CONSENSUAL DISCHARGES

A. RESCISSION

21.2 Mutual Rescission.

B. DESTRUCTION OR SURRENDER

21.3 Cancellation or Surrender.

C. EXECUTORY ACCORD—ACCORD AND SATISFACTION— SUBSTITUTED AGREEMENT

21.4 Background of these Doctrines.
21.5 Difference Between an Accord and a Substituted Contract.
21.6 Distinguishing an Accord From a Substituted Contract.
21.7 Offer to a Unilateral Accord.

D. THREE PARTY SITUATIONS

21.8 Assignment, Beneficiary Contract, and Novation.

---

§ 21.1 Introduction

The First Restatement of Contracts listed 22 ways in which a contract may be discharged.[1] Some of these have been discussed previously. Included in this category are "occurrence of a condition subsequent";[2] "breach by the other party or failure of consideration, or frustration";[3] "exercise of the power of avoidance if the duty is avoidable";[4] "impossibility";[5] "illegality of a contract or of its enforcement";[6] "the failure of a condition precedent to exist or to occur";[7] "incapacity of the parties to retain the right duty relationship";[8] and "the rules governing joint debtors."[9] Two of the methods of discharge listed, "res judicata" and "the rules governing sureties," are beyond the scope of

§ 21.1

1. Rs. 1st § 385. The Restatement (Second) contains no such catalog, but see Introductory Note to its Ch. 12.

2. See § 11.7 supra.

3. See ch. 13 supra.

4. See, e.g., § 8.4 supra.

5. See ch. 13 supra.

6. See ch. 22 infra.

7. See § 11.15 supra.

8. See Rs. 1st § 450 (discharge by marriage; an obsolete provision).

9. See ch. 20 supra.

this treatise. The remaining twelve, some of which have been mentioned elsewhere, will be discussed briefly here.

I. CONSENSUAL DISCHARGES

A. RESCISSION

Table of Sections

Sec.
21.2 Mutual Rescission.

§ 21.2 Mutual Rescission

If A and B enter into an executory bilateral contract, they are free to rescind the agreement by a mutual agreement. The surrender of rights under the original agreement by each party is the consideration for the mutual agreement of rescission.[1] Formerly, a sealed instrument could be discharged by a subsequent agreement only if the later agreement was also under seal. Today, however, the prevailing view in jurisdictions which have retained the seal is that an agreement under seal may be modified, rescinded or substituted by an oral agreement or an unsealed written agreement.[2]

Sometimes a contract provides that it cannot be rescinded except in a writing signed by the contracting parties. But are such clauses effective? As a common law proposition, such a provision is ineffective as the parties cannot restrain their future ability to contract with each other in the future.[3] However, the UCC[4] and some state statutes of general applicability[5] give efficacy to such provisions.

If the original agreement has been performed in part by one of the parties before the agreement of mutual rescission, a question that frequently arise is whether the performance that has been rendered should be paid for. The issue is one of the intention of the parties.[6] Very often, however, the parties have expressed no intention on the matter, expressing themselves in broad terms such as "Let's call the whole deal off."

The courts are split on this issue. Some courts have ruled that in such a case a promise to pay for the performances rendered should be

---

§ 21.2

1. Smith & Smith Building v. DeLuca, 36 Conn.App. 839, 654 A.2d 368 (1995); Kirk v. Brentwood Manor Homes, 191 Pa.Super. 488, 159 A.2d 48 (1960).

2. Kirk v. Brentwood Manor Homes, supra; Rs. 1st § 407 cmt c; 5A Corbin § 1236; 6 Corbin § 1316; 15 Williston §§ 1834–36 (3d ed.); see § 7.8 supra and § 21.3 infra.

3. ABC Outdoor Advertising v. Dolhun's Marine, 38 Wis.2d 457, 157 N.W.2d 680 (1968).

4. UCC § 2–209(2), discussed at § 5.14(b) supra.

5. E.g., Cal.Civ.Code § 1698; McKinney's N.Y.Gen.Oblig.Law § 15–301. As to the effect of the Statute of Frauds, see § 19.37 supra.

6. Rs. 2d § 283 cmt c; Rs. 1st § 409; 5A Corbin § 1236; 15 Williston § 1827 (3d ed.).

implied.[7] Others, however, have indulged in the presumption that unless an affirmative agreement to the contrary appears the parties intended that payment need not be made for services rendered prior to rescission.[8] As in any case involving intention, stare decisis should only play a suggestive role and each case should be decided on its facts.[9]

A similar problem arises where a party cancels the contract because of a material breach.[10] The UCC provides that "Unless the contrary intention clearly appears, expressions of 'cancellation' or 'rescission' of the contract or the like shall not be construed as a renunciation or discharge of any claim in damages for an antecedent breach."[11] The Code language and comment make it clear that this provision applies after a breach and is designed to avoid an involuntary loss of a remedy for breach by the use of language by the aggrieved party to the effect that the contract is called off. The Code primarily addresses itself to a number of unsound decisions that have held that, when a contract is canceled for breach, it is logically impossible to permit an action on the contract since the contract is nonexistent; therefore, only quasi-contractual relief is available.[12] The Code takes cognizance of the fact that the term "rescission" is often used by lawyers, courts and businessmen in many different senses, for example, termination of a contract by virtue of an option to terminate in the agreement, cancellation for breach, and avoidance on the grounds of infancy or fraud.[13] In the interests of clarity of thought—as the consequences of each of these forms of discharge may vary—the UCC carefully distinguishes three circumstances. "Rescission" is utilized as a term of art to refer to a mutual agreement to discharge contractual duties.[14] "Termination" refers to the discharge of duties by the exercise of a power granted by the agreement.[15] "Cancellation" refers to the putting an end to the contract by reason of a breach by the other party.[16] The UCC, however, takes into account that the parties do not necessarily use these terms in this way. The parties' label is not conclusive; the context determines the legal effect of bringing the contract to an end.

To return to the topic of mutual rescission, if one of the parties has fully performed under a bilateral contract or as offeree of a unilateral

---

7. Anderson v. Copeland, 378 P.2d 1006 (Okl.1963); Johnston v. Gilbert, 234 Or. 350, 382 P.2d 87 (1963).

8. Coletti v. Knox Hat, 252 N.Y. 468, 169 N.E. 648 (1930).

9. Rs. 1st § 409; 5A Corbin § 1236; 15 Williston § 1827 (3d ed.); see Montgomery v. Stuyvesant Ins., 393 F.2d 754 (4th Cir. 1968); Copeland Process v. Nalews, 113 N.H. 612, 312 A.2d 576 (1973).

10. See §§ 11.18, 11.33 supra.

11. UCC § 2–720 (unchanged in the revision)

12. Walter–Wallingford Coal v. A. Himes Coal, 223 Mich. 576, 194 N.W. 493

(1923); Thackeray v. Knight, 57 Utah 21, 192 P. 263 (1920); see Woodward, Quasi Contracts, ch. 19 (1913); 5A Corbin § 1237; Annot., 1 ALR2d 1084 (1948).

13. See, e.g., Annot., 1 ALR2d 1084 (1948) ("Notice of Rescission as Irrevocable Election When Other Party Refuses to Assent Thereto"), where the annotator brings together cases involving significantly different issues merely because the court utilized the term "rescission."

14. UCC § 2–209 cmt 3.

15. UCC § 2–106(3) (unchanged in the revision).

16. UCC § 2–106(4); (unchanged in the revision).

contract, a mutual agreement to put the contract to an end is ineffective. The party whose duties remain executory has incurred no detriment and therefore the promise of the party who has performed is not supported by consideration. Under some circumstances this purported rescission may be effective as a "release," a concept discussed below.[17] But generally speaking, as we have seen, if a party who has completely performed, promises to surrender or purports to surrender the correlative rights under the contract, in the absence of consideration or of a statute providing otherwise, or in the absence of a completed gift, the transaction is ineffective.[18]

Thus, it is a general rule that an attempt to discharge a duty that has arisen by complete or substantial performance requires consideration.[19] It must be stressed that we are not talking about a waiver of condition, which is discussed in Chapter 11, or renunciation of a right to damages for breach, which occurs before there has been complete performance, or renunciation of a right to recover for partial performance, which is discussed below.[20]

Rescission also occurs where the parties enter into a new contract which is substituted for the original contract. The old agreement is discharged but the parties are still bound contractually. At times new terms are added to an existing contract. It is obvious that the lines between three situations are indistinct:

(1) Unconditional rescission of an existing contract followed by a subsequent entering into of a new agreement.

(2) Rescission of an existing contract contemporaneous with and conditioned on the entering into of a new agreement.

(3) Retention of an existing contract with a modifying agreement as to new terms.

The manner of distinguishing among these situations cannot be authoritatively answered and it may be that the variation in factual settings is so extensive that no test can be formulated, yet one court has made a good attempt: "An alteration of details of the contract which leaves undisturbed its general purpose constitutes a modification rather than a rescission of the contract."[21] The necessity for distinguishing these categories is not merely academic. For example, the presence or absence of consideration,[22] the necessity of complying with the Statute of Frauds,[23] the survival of provisions in the first agreement[24] and the

---

17. See § 5.16 supra and § 21.10 infra.

18. See §§ 4.9, 5.14, 5.16 supra. On the gift of a debt, see also Annot., 63 ALR2d 259 (1959) and § 21.3 infra.

19. As stated in § 4.10 supra, the question of discharge of duties as an original proposition could have been distinguished and exempted from the requirement of consideration. But this is not how the law has developed.

20. See § 21.10 infra.

21. Travelers Ins. v. Workmen's Comp. Appeals Bd., 68 Cal.2d 7, 17, 64 Cal.Rptr. 440, 446, 434 P.2d 992, 998 (1967); see Dime Sav. Bank v. Montague St. Realty Assocs., 90 N.Y.2d 539, 686 N.E.2d 1340, 664 N.Y.S.2d 246 (1997) (new lease is subject to an intervening mortgage, a modified lease is not).

22. See § 4.9 supra.

23. See § 19.37 supra.

24. Eslon Thermoplastics v. Dynamic Systems, 49 S.W.3d 891 (Tex.App.2001).

applicable law,[25] may vary, dependent upon the category into which the transaction falls. Moreover, if the agreement falls into the third of these categories, the original agreement is not discharged.[26]

Although rescissions are ordinarily explicitly expressed, a good number of cases involve implied rescissions. For example, a mutual failure of the parties to cooperate in the performance of a contract,[27] or concurrent breaches by both parties[28] or repudiation by one and acquiescence by the other, may be deemed an implied rescission. Where the parties are in dispute as to the mechanics of implementing their contract, the failure of one party to reply to the other's offer to rescind may give rise to an implied rescission.[29] An unsuccessful attempt to re-negotiate a contract may be found to constitute an implied rescission.[30] Material mutually agreed revisions of contractual terms may constitute such a rescission, sometimes called a "cardinal change."[31] In some jurisdictions, implied rescissions are classified as abandonments,[32] a concept that comes from property rules concerning the relinquishment of leaseholds or other interests in land. The equating of implied mutual rescission and abandonment of a property interest is a source of confusion since distinct rules apply.[33]

B. DESTRUCTION OR SURRENDER

Table of Sections

§ 21.3   Cancellation or Surrender

At early common law, the normal method of discharging a formal obligation was the cancellation of the instrument by its physical destruction or mutilation.[1] The theory was that the instrument itself was the

---

25. Chapman's Golf Center v. Chapman, 524 N.W.2d 422 (Iowa 1994).

26. Kimball Investment Land v. Chmela, 604 N.W.2d 289 (S.D.2000).

27. Admiral Plastics v. Trueblood, 436 F.2d 1335 (6th Cir.1971); 2 Black, Rescission of Contracts and Cancellation of Written Instruments § 533 (2d ed.1929); 15 Williston § 1826 (3d ed.).

28. Gentry v. Smith, 487 F.2d 571 (5th Cir.1973).

29. Sweetarts v. Sunline, 423 F.2d 260 (8th Cir.1970).

30. Minnesota Ltd. v. Public Utilities Comm'n, 296 Minn. 316, 208 N.W.2d 284 (1973).

31. R.M. Taylor, Inc. v. General Motors, 187 F.3d 809 (8th Cir.1999), cert. denied

(abandonment not found); L.K. Comstock & Co. v. Becon Constr., 932 F.Supp. 906 (E.D.Ky.1993), aff'd ("abandonment" and "cardinal change" discussed but not found); Douglas Constr. v. Marcais, 239 A.D.2d 803, 657 N.Y.S.2d 835 (1997) ("abandonment" found).

32. AEB & Assocs. v. Tonka Corp. 853 F.Supp. 724 (S.D.N.Y.1994); In re Marriage of Christensen, 543 N.W.2d 915 (Iowa App. 1995); 2 Black, supra note 27 at § 532; C.J.S. Contracts § 412.

33. See Jakober v. E.M. Loew's Capitol Theatre, 107 R.I. 104, 265 A.2d 429 (1970).

§ 21.3

1. Ames, Specialty Contracts and Equitable Defences, 9 Harv.L.Rev. 49 (1895).

obligation and not merely evidence of the obligation; therefore, cancellation of the instrument discharged the obligation irrespective of the intention of the parties. Conversely, surrender, e.g., handing it over to the debtor, without destruction of the formal instrument did not amount to a discharge even if the parties intended a discharge.[2] However, under present law, a formal instrument, such as a negotiable instrument,[3] insurance policy or instrument under seal, may be discharged by either cancellation or surrender provided that the party having the right intends to discharge the duty.[4] No consideration is required. Surrender or cancellation of an informal contract may be evidence of an intent to discharge[5] but, in addition, consideration, or one of its substitutes, or the elements of a gift, would be required.[6]

C.   EXECUTORY ACCORD—ACCORD AND SATISFACTION—SUBSTITUTED AGREEMENT

Table of Sections

§ 21.4   Background of these Doctrines

A bilateral executory accord is "an agreement that an existing claim shall be discharged *in the future* by the rendition of a substituted performance."[1] For example, C (creditor) writes D (debtor), "I promise to discharge the debt you owe me upon delivery of your black Mercedes if you promise to deliver the Mercedes to me within a reasonable time." D promises. Their agreement is a bilateral executory accord.

---

2.   15 Williston § 1876 (3d ed.).

3.   UCC § 3–605(1) (§ 3–604 of the 1990 revision) (negotiable instruments). But if a negotiable instrument is discharged by surrender, a subsequent holder in due course will be permitted to enforce the instrument. UCC § 3–602, (§ 3–601(b) of the 1990 revision).

4.   Rs. 2d § 274; 15 Williston § 1878 (3d ed.); 5A Corbin § 1250. If the formal instrument is bilateral, both parties must join in or consent to cancellation. Rs. 1st § 432(2).

5.   If the contract is bilateral and executory on both sides, surrender or cancellation joined in by both parties would result in a mutual rescission. See Schwartzreich v. Bauman–Basch, 231 N.Y. 196, 131 N.E. 887 (1921), rearg. denied.

6.   See chs. 4, 5, & 6 supra; 5A Corbin § 1250; 15 Williston §§ 1876, 1879 (3d ed.); see § 21.2 supra.

§ 21.4

1.   Alaska Creamery Prods. v. Wells, 373 P.2d 505, 511 (Alaska 1962) (emphasis supplied); see also Rs. 2d § 281(1); 6 Corbin § 1268. See generally, Gold, Executory Accords, 21 Boston U.L.Rev. 465 (1941); Havighurst, Reflections on the Executory Accord, in Perspectives of Law; Essays for Austin Wakeman Scott 190 (1964); Comment, Executory Accord, Accord and Satisfaction, and Novation—The Distinctions, 26 Baylor L.Rev. 185 (1974).

If D delivers the Mercedes and C accepts it, there is an accord and satisfaction. The agreement is the accord. Its performance is the satisfaction.[2] We have already seen that an accord and satisfaction supported by consideration discharges a claim.[3]

Formerly, an executory bilateral accord was without any effect even if, as in the illustration given, it was supported by consideration. An executory accord could not be used as a defense nor did its breach give rise to a cause of action.[4] The reason for the rule is purely historical. Informal contracts supported by consideration were not recognized under the early common law and so it was very often held that an executory bilateral accord was not enforceable. Even when informal bilateral contracts came to be enforced, apparently the courts failed to recognize that an executory bilateral accord was nothing more nor less than a bilateral contract, and continued to apply the old rule of unenforceability to them.[5] Modern changes to this rule will be discussed below.

An executory bilateral accord must be distinguished from a substituted agreement. Even now, the two kinds of transactions produce significantly different results. If we change slightly the illustration previously given, we can also illustrate a substituted agreement. C (creditor) writes to D (debtor), "If you will promise to deliver your black Mercedes within 30 days I will immediately treat the debt you owe me as satisfied and discharged." D accepts the offer. Here we have a substituted agreement. It operates immediately to discharge C's claim. Because the discharge is immediate, the substituted contract is frequently called an accord and satisfaction. This terminology is not used here because it may prove confusing.[6] This situation is factually distinct from an accord and satisfaction created by the performance of an executory accord. In the absence of a statute, either kind of agreement can be oral.[7]

The two illustrations given above are quite similar. First, we note that both are bilateral and supported by consideration.[8] The essential difference, however, is that in the second case, where a substituted agreement is created, C asks for and accepts D's new promise in satisfaction of the original claim. In the first illustration, however, C

---

2. Jon–T Chemicals v. Freeport Chemical, 704 F.2d 1412 (5th Cir.1983); 6 Corbin § 1269. In the cases discussed in § 4.11, the cashing of the check manifests the assent of the creditor to the accord and also simultaneously operates as the satisfaction.

3. See § 4.11 supra.

4. Reilly v. Barrett, 220 N.Y. 170, 115 N.E. 453 (1917); see also Larscy v. T. Hogan & Sons, 239 N.Y. 298, 146 N.E. 430 (1925).

5. 6 Corbin § 1271; 15 Williston §§ 1839–40 (3d ed.); Gold, supra n.1, at 465–71.

6. Other classifications of such an agreement are "novations," "compromise and settlement" and "accord accepted in satisfaction." As to the use of "novation," see § 21.8 infra.

7. Lynch, Inc. v. SamataMason, Inc., 279 F.3d 487 (7th Cir.2002); Tabler v. Industrial Comm'n, 202 Ariz. 518, 47 P.3d 1156 (App.2002).

8. In this context as in others, promissory estoppel may substitute for consideration. Boshart v. Gardner, 190 Ark. 104, 77 S.W.2d 642, 96 ALR 1130 (1935) (an executory accord mistakenly labeled a "novation," but treated as an executory accord; expenses incurred in reliance on the accord a substitute for consideration).

made it clear that the original claim will not be discharged until the debtor performs the new agreement.[9] An executory accord is created.

The common law rule making executory accords unenforceable has been overturned by judicial decisions in so many states, that today they are generally deemed to be enforceable.[10] In New York, the common law rule has been changed by statute, but only where such an agreement is in writing and signed by the party "against whom it is sought to enforce the accord," "or by his [or her] agent."[11]

§ 21.5　Difference Between an Accord and a Substituted Contract

An enforceable executory accord has considerably different effects from a substituted agreement. The original obligations of the parties are, by definition, not satisfied until the bilateral executory accord is performed.[1] Under the view which seems to have gained general acceptance, the executory accord has a suspensive effect on the prior obligations.[2] In the event the debtor materially breaches the agreement, the prior obligation revives and the creditor has the option of enforcing the original claim or the executory bilateral accord.[3] Part performance by the debtor, followed by unjustified failure to complete, does not prevent an action by the creditor on the original claim,[4] but a three day delay in

---

9. 1937 N.Y.Law Rev.Comm.Rep. 214–218.

10. Very v. Levy, 54 U.S. (13 How.) 345 (1851); Markowitz & Co. v. Toledo Met. Housing Auth., 608 F.2d 699 (6th Cir.1979); Estate of Knapp v. Newhouse, 894 S.W.2d 204 (Mo.App.1995); Trenton St. Ry. v. Lawlor, 74 N.J.Eq. 828, 71 A. 234 (Ct.Err. & App.1908); Dobias v. White, 239 N.C. 409, 80 S.E.2d 23 (1954); Ladd v. General Ins., 236 Or. 260, 387 P.2d 572 (1963); Browning v. Holloway, 620 S.W.2d 611 (Tex.Civ.App. 1981); Rs. 2d § 281; Rs. 1st § 417; 6 Corbin §§ 1271–73; 15 Williston § 1845 (3d ed.). The common law view retains some adherents. Karvalsky v. Becker, 217 Ind. 524, 29 N.E.2d 560, 131 ALR 1074 (1940); Bartlett v. Newton, 148 Me. 279, 92 A.2d 611 (1952); Watkins v. Williams, 265 Mont. 306, 877 P.2d 19 (1994).

11. McKinney's N.Y.Gen.Oblig.Law § 15–501. This statute has been characterized as a provision of the Statute of Frauds. Condo v. Mulcahy, 88 A.D.2d 497, 454 N.Y.S.2d 308 (1982). Earlier statutes in California and other states adopting a civil code are collected in 1937 N.Y.L.Rev.Comm. Rep. 241–44.

§ 21.5

1. Both types, of course, require offer and acceptance. Merely sending a check

with a statement as to how it was calculated does not operate as an offer to an accord. Wallace v. United Mississippi Bank, 726 So.2d 578 (1998).

2. Rs. 2d § 281(2). A tripartite accord, although not denominated as such, suspending a mortgagee's right to foreclose, was found in Bank of Fairbanks v. Kaye, 16 Alaska 23, 227 F.2d 566 (9th Cir.1955).

3. Paramount Aviation v. Agusta, 178 F.3d 132 (3d Cir.1999), cert. denied; Markowitz & Co. v. Toledo Met. Housing Auth., 608 F.2d 699 (6th Cir.1979); Mitchell Properties v. Real Estate Title, 62 Md.App. 473, 490 A.2d 271 (1985); Browning v. Holloway, 620 S.W.2d 611 (Tex.Civ.App.1981). Plant City Steel v. National Mach. Exch., 23 N.Y.2d 472, 297 N.Y.S.2d 559, 245 N.E.2d 213 (1969) (creditor need not elect between the original obligation and the executory accord until after all the evidence has been adduced.). But if the creditor brings an action solely on the original claim, it has been held that the election is binding. Rist v. Comi, 250 A.D.2d 966, 672 N.Y.S.2d 961 (1998). After judgment has been entered on the executory accord, the creditor is precluded from suing on the original claim. Coffeyville State Bank v. Lembeck, 227 Kan. 857, 610 P.2d 616 (1980).

4. Stratton v. West States Constr., 21 Utah 2d 60, 440 P.2d 117 (1968).

making a final payment is not a material breach of the accord, and even if it were, the creditor's acceptance of the payment is a waiver.[5]

If the creditor breaches, as by refusing the debtor's tender, a similar rule exists. The debtor may raise the executory accord as a defense against an action by the creditor on the original claim,[6] and may maintain an action for specific performance of the accord.[7] Instead, the debtor may seek damages for total or partial breach.[8]

As previously indicated,[9] a substituted contract immediately discharges the prior claim which is merged into the new agreement. Consequently, in the absence of an express agreement to the contrary, the original claim can no longer be enforced. In the event of a breach, any action would have to be brought on the substituted agreement.[10] If, however, the substituted agreement is unenforceable or voidable, the original claim either remains unimpaired or is revived by avoidance of the new agreement.[11] An occasional case has held that upon a material breach of the substitute contract, the aggrieved party may cancel it, reviving the original claim.[12] The Restatement (Second) disapproves such a result,[13] even though the result is achieved by normal principles regarding cancellation for material breach followed by restitution.[14]

If such a result were to be widely accepted, it would, for most practical purposes, erase the distinction between executory accords and substituted contracts. The concept of "substituted contract" was created largely to circumvent the unsatisfactory rules that until recently governed executory accords.[15] Now that these rules have been modernized, the next step should be the reabsorption of the substituted contract into the executory accord. Of course, under the general principle of contractual freedom, the parties would continue to be free to articulate the intention that the prior claim is for all purposes and in all circumstances discharged. However, the untidy distinction between executory accords and substituted contracts should not be allowed to complicate litigation about routine claim settlements.

---

5. Associated Builders v. Coggins, 722 A.2d 1278 (Me.1999).

6. Clark v. Elza, 286 Md. 208, 406 A.2d 922 (1979); Bestor v. American Nat. Stores, 691 S.W.2d 384 (Mo.App.1985).

7. Union Central Life Ins. Co. v. Imsland, 91 F.2d 365 (8th Cir.1937). See Corbin, Recent Developments in the Law of Contracts, 50 Harv.L.Rev. 449, 466 (1937).

8. Rs. 2d § 281(3) cmt c.

9. Sections 21.4, 21.5 supra.

10. Moers v. Moers, 229 N.Y. 294, 128 N.E. 202, 14 ALR 225 (1920); Paul Dean Corp. v. Kilgore, 252 Ga.App. 587, 556 S.E.2d 228 (2001); Golden Key Realty v. Mantas, 699 P.2d 730 (Utah 1985); see Rs. 2d § 279(2); 15 Williston § 1846 (3d ed.).

11. Rs. 2d § 279 cmt b. See also § 19.37 supra.

12. See Publicker Indus. v. Roman Ceramics, 603 F.2d 1065 (3d Cir.1979); Seitz v. Industrial Com'n, 184 Ariz. 599, 911 P.2d 605 (App.1995); Christensen v. Hamilton Realty, 42 Utah 70, 129 P. 412 (1912); see also 6 Corbin § 1293 at 196; Annot., 94 ALR2d 504 (1964); Gold, supra § 21.4 n.1, at 487–88.

13. Rs. 2d § 279(2); accord, P.L.A.Y. v. Nike, 1 F.Supp.2d 60 (D.Mass.1998).

14. Murray v. Crest Constr., 900 S.W.2d 342 (Tex.1995).

15. See, e.g., 6 Corbin § 1274 n. 55 ("by the device of calling an accord executory a substituted contract."); Gold, supra § 21.4 n.1, at 475–76.

§ 21.6   Distinguishing an Accord From a Substituted Contract

The distinction between executory accords and substituted contracts is often crucial to a determination of the rights of the parties. It is often difficult, however, to classify a given agreement as one or the other. The question is said to be one of the intentions of the parties and is sometimes treated as a question of fact.[1] Where the parties have not expressed themselves on the matter, the courts often emphasize the fact that the burden of proof of discharge of a claim is on the party asserting the discharge.[2] This is the equivalent of holding that the agreement is presumed to be an executory accord that merely suspends the claim.

This is sound and not only for formalistic reasons. It is usually unlikely that the claimant intended to surrender a claim for a yet unperformed promise.[3] Contrariwise, it is often held that if the claim is disputed or unliquidated, the presumption is that there is a substituted agreement.[4] This is because it is assumed that the creditor enters into the new agreement to obtain the certainty of a promise rather than the uncertainty of an unliquidated claim. Even in such a case, however, the determination may turn on the degree of deliberation and formalization which has gone into the agreement. An agreement made with little deliberation and formality is not likely to be deemed to discharge the prior claim.[5] In cases involving a liquidated and undisputed obligation it will generally be presumed that the creditor did not intend to surrender prior rights unless and until the new agreement is actually performed.[6]

§ 21.7   Offer to a Unilateral Accord

Although most accords are bilateral, it is possible to have an offer of accord looking to a unilateral contract. For example, to vary the illustration previously used in § 21.4 supra, C writes to D, "If you deliver your black Mercedes within a reasonable time, I promise to discharge your debt." If D tendered the Mercedes and C accepted it, there would be an accord and satisfaction. If D tendered the Mercedes and C refused it, setting aside questions of accord, there would be a unilateral contract.[1]

§ 21.6

1. Warner v. Rossignol, 513 F.2d 678 (1st Cir.1975); Johnson v. Utile, 86 Nev. 593, 472 P.2d 335 (1970); Moers v. Moers, 229 N.Y. 294, 128 N.E. 202, 14 ALR 225 (1920); Golden Key Realty v. Mantas, 699 P.2d 730 (Utah 1985).

2. Constitution Bank v. Kalinowski, 38 F.Supp.2d 384 (E.D.Pa.1999); Lipson v. Adelson, 17 Mass.App.Ct. 90, 456 N.E.2d 470 (1983); Rhea v. Marko Constr., 652 S.W.2d 332 (Tenn.1983).

3. Board of Managers v. Broadway/72d Assocs., 285 A.D.2d 422, 285 A.D.2d 422, 729 N.Y.S.2d 16 (2001).

4. Rudick v. Rudick, 403 So.2d 1091 (Fla.App.1981); Rs. 2d §§ 279 cmt c, 281

cmt e. But see, McFaden v. Nordblom, 307 Mass. 574, 30 N.E.2d 852 (1941).

5. Goldbard v. Empire State Mut. Life Ins., 5 A.D.2d 230, 171 N.Y.S.2d 194 (1958). The formality of the proceeding which preceded the settlement agreement was a factor in classifying it as a substituted contract in National American Corp. v. Federal Republic of Nigeria, 597 F.2d 314 (2d Cir. 1979).

6. Rs. 2d §§ 279 cmt c, 281 cmt e; 15 Williston § 1847 (3d ed.); 6 Corbin §§ 1268, 1271, 1293.

§ 21.7

1. See ch. 2 supra.

Until quite recently, however, the rule was that C was free to reject the tender without being guilty of any legal wrong.[2] This result has been changed by the modern authorities[3] and in New York by statute if the offer is in writing and signed by the offeror or the offeror's agent.[4] Under the modern view, the debtor could sue for damages for breach of the accord, or in a proper case, could sue for specific performance of the accord by keeping the tender good. Specific enforcement of the accord would obviously defeat an action upon the original claim, as would allowing the accord to be pleaded and proved as an affirmative defense, provided the debtor continues ready to perform.[5]

D. THREE PARTY SITUATIONS

Table of Sections

§ 21.8 Assignment, Beneficiary Contract, and Novation

The common characteristic of the kinds of transactions grouped under this heading is that three parties are involved.

Assignments were discussed in chapter 18. Subject to the qualifications stated in that chapter, an effective assignment transfers the assignor's interests to the assignee and thereby discharges the obligor's duty to the assignor.

Contracts for the benefit of a third person were discussed in chapter 17. The making of such a contract creates new duties and often discharges prior duties. If D owes C $100 and they enter into a contract whereby D promises to pay this sum to T, a duty to pay T is substituted for the duty to pay C. C, as promisee, has an interest in the performance of this contract, but this interest now stems not from the original contract but from the substituted contract.[1]

The word "novation" is used in a variety of senses. Courts frequently use it as synonymous with "substituted contract."[2] Most academic writers[3] and both contracts' restatements,[4] however, restrict its use to describe a substituted contract involving at least one obligor or obligee

2. Harbor v. Morgan, 4 Ind. 158 (1853); Kromer v. Heim, 75 N.Y. 574, 31 Am.Rep. 491 (1879); see generally 1937 N.Y.Law Rev.Comm.Rep. 212, 233–35.

3. Rs. 1st § 417 cmt a.

4. McKinney's N.Y.Gen.Oblig.Law § 15–503.

5. Cf. Rs. 1st § 417(d).

§ 21.8

1. Rs. 1st § 426; Rs. 2d § 280 cmt d.

2. E.g., Jakobi v. Kings Creek Village Townhouse Ass'n, 665 So.2d 325 (Fla.App. 1995); Powell v. Norman Electric Galaxy, 229 Ga.App. 99, 493 S.E.2d 205 (1997); Mello v. Coy Real Estate, 103 R.I. 74, 234 A.2d 667 (1967). Most of the cases in the Decennial Digests under the heading "Novation" appear to be of this kind. See also Comment, Executory Accord, Accord and Satisfaction, and Novation—The Distinctions, 26 Baylor L.Rev. 185 (1974).

3. E.g., 6 Corbin § 1297; 15 Williston § 1865 (3d ed.).

4. Rs. 1st § 424; Rs. 2d § 280.

who was not a party to the original contract. A contract is a novation in the restricted sense if it does three things: (a) discharges a duty immediately, (b) creates a new duty (or a good faith claim), and (c) includes a new obligor or obligee.[5] An assignment is not a novation because it is an executed transaction rather than a contract.[6] A tripartite agreement between the obligor, obligee and assignee is a novation if it discharges a right the assignee has against the obligee, but is not commonly denominated as such.[7] Some third party beneficiary contracts are novations,[8] but are not usually so labeled. Indeed, the utility of the classification of novation is doubtful. Its legal effect is that of a substituted contract.[9] The development of a separate category under the rubric "novation" is doubtless traceable to problems of consideration formerly thought to be present in such contracts because of the former common law rule that consideration must be supplied by the promisee.[10] This rule has long been laid to rest almost everywhere.

It is necessary to distinguish an executory accord from a novation. A novation is a substituted contract which operates immediately to discharge an obligation. However, if the discharge is to take place upon performance, the tripartite agreement is merely an executory accord.[11] An obligor may be discharged by an actual performance by a third person, accepted by the obligee in full or partial satisfaction of the claim.[12] This is not a novation but an executed accord and satisfaction.

5. Rs. 1st § 424; Rs. 2d § 280; see Perry Drug Stores v. CSKG, 83 F.Supp.2d 873 (E.D.Mich.2000); McGlothin v. Huffman, 94 Oh.App.3d 240, 640 N.E.2d 598 (1994); Eagle Industries v. Thompson, 321 Or. 398, 900 P.2d 475 (1995); cf. Kinsella v. Merchants Nat. Bank & Trust, 34 A.D.2d 730, 311 N.Y.S.2d 759 (1970).

6. See § 18.3 supra.

7. Compare Rs. 1st § 424 cmt c, with 15 Williston § 1867A (3d ed.).

8. Rs. 1st § 426; Rs. 2d § 280 cmt d. The mere assumption of a duty by a new obligor with the consent of the obligee is not a novation since no duty is discharged by such an assumption unless the obligee also agrees to discharge the original obligor. See U.S. v. Nill, 518 F.2d 793 (5th Cir. 1975); Mansfield v. Lang, 293 Mass. 386, 200 N.E. 110 (1936); Credit Bureaus Adjustment Dep't v. Cox Bros., 207 Or. 253, 295 P.2d 1107, 61 ALR2d 750 (1956); and § 18.25 supra. Cf. Navine v. Peltier, 48 Wis.2d 588, 180 N.W.2d 613 (1970).

9. Extensive discussions of novations in 6 Corbin §§ 1297–1302 and 15 Williston

§§ 1865–75 (3d ed.) are valuable for their analyses of the variety of factual situations in which a novation has been or is alleged to have been created. For a discussion of one common situation involving the assignment of rights and assumption of duties by a stranger to the contract coupled with a repudiation by the assignor, see § 18.30 supra.

10. See 15 Williston § 1866 (3d ed.).

11. See Trudeau v. Poutre, 165 Mass. 81, 42 N.E. 508 (1895) (question of fact whether agreement was to discharge original obligor immediately or only on condition that new obligor perform a promise to execute mortgages); see generally 6 Corbin § 1300.

12. Jackson v. Pennsylvania R.R., 66 N.J.L. 319, 49 A. 730, 55 LRA 87 (1901); Rs. 1st § 421; Rs. 2d § 278 cmt b. See King, Accord and Satisfaction by a Third Person, 15 Mo.L.Rev. 115 (1950); Gold, Accord and Satisfaction by a Stranger, 19 Can.B.Rev. 165 (1941).

E. ACCOUNT STATED

Table of Sections

§ 21.9 Account Stated

An account stated arises where there have been transactions between debtor and creditor resulting in the creation of matured debts and the parties by agreement compute a balance which the debtor promises to pay and the creditor promises to accept in full payment for the items of account.[1] The account stated operates as a new contract; a promise to pay a pre-existing debt being binding without new consideration.[2] Few of the reported cases involve express agreements. Instead, many of the cases involve the rendition of a statement of account by the creditor followed by a part payment by the debtor. On these facts, some courts find that an account stated is formed as a matter of law;[3] others hold that part payment permits a jury to infer an account stated.[4] More frequently the cases involve an implied agreement arising when the debtor or creditor sends an itemized account to the other who retains it without objection for more than a reasonable time.[5] The debtor's silence is equivocal, however, giving rise to a rebuttable inference of assent which when controverted, as by a prior disagreement between the parties as to the amount of the debt, gives rise to a question of fact.[6] Because of the fiduciary relationship between attorney and client, courts appear reluctant to find assent to an attorney's bill.[7]

An account stated cannot be the origin of a debtor-creditor relationship. There is no duty to reply to a bill from a person with whom one has no debtor-creditor relation.[8]

§ 21.9

1. Rs. 1st § 422; Rs. 2d § 282; 6 Corbin § 1303; Freeland v. Heron, Lenox & Co., 11 U.S. (7 Cranch) 147 (1812); West v. Holstrom, 261 Cal.App.2d 89, 67 Cal.Rptr. 831 (1968).

2. Egles v. Vale, Cro.Jac. 70, 79 Eng. Rep. 59 (1606); see § 5.3 supra.

3. Jannuzzo v. de Cuevas, 216 A.D.2d 37, 627 N.Y.S.2d 919 (1995); Stan's Lumber v. Fleming, 196 Wis.2d 554, 538 N.W.2d 849 (App.1995).

4. University of So. Alabama v. Bracy, 466 So.2d 148 (Ala.Civ.App.1985); Chieffe v. Alcoa Bldg. Prods., 168 Ga.App. 384, 309 S.E.2d 167 (1983).

5. First Commodity Traders v. Heinold Commodities, 766 F.2d 1007 (7th Cir.1985); Griffith v. Hicks, 150 Ark. 197, 233 S.W. 1086, 18 ALR 882 (1921); R.E. Tharp, v. Miller Hay, 261 Cal.App.2d 81, 67 Cal.Rptr. 854 (1968); Meagher v. Kavli, 251 Minn. 477, 88 N.W.2d 871 (1958); Rice's Feed Service v. Dodson, 904 S.W.2d 475 (Mo.App. 1995); Johnson v. Tindall, 195 Mont. 165, 635 P.2d 266 (1981); Marchi et al. v. All-Star Video, 107 A.D.2d 597, 483 N.Y.S.2d 707 (1985).

6. Sunshine Dairy v. Jolly Joan, 234 Or. 84, 380 P.2d 637 (1963); see also Hunt Process v. Anderson, 455 F.2d 700 (10th Cir.1972); Truestone v. Simi West Indus. Park II, 163 Cal.App.3d 715, 209 Cal.Rptr. 757 (1984); Old West Enterprises v. Reno Escrow, 86 Nev. 727, 476 P.2d 1 (1970).

7. Davis & Cox v. Summa, 751 F.2d 1507 (9th Cir.1985) (presumption of undue influence); Trafton v. Youngblood, 69 Cal.2d 17, 69 Cal.Rptr. 568, 442 P.2d 648 (1968). Compare American Druggists Ins. v. Thompson Lumber, 349 N.W.2d 569 (Minn. App.1984) with Roehrdanz v. Schlink, 368 N.W.2d 409 (Minn.App.1985) (attorney and client); but see Werner v. Nelkin, 206 A.D.2d 422, 614 N.Y.S.2d 66 (1994).

8. Big O Tire Dealers v. Big O Warehouse, 741 F.2d 160 (7th Cir.1984); Whelan's v. Bob Eldridge Constr., 668 S.W.2d 244 (Mo.App.1984) (bill for unrequested services). Where the agent is an attorney retaining a court reporter or expert witness for a disclosed client, most cases hold the

The chief advantage of an account stated from the plaintiff's point of view is the facility of the requirements of pleading and proof.[9] In an action on the account, the creditor need not plead and prove the making and performance of each contract (goods sold and delivered, money lent, services rendered, etc.) which went into the account.[10] Moreover, since an account stated is a new contract, the statute of limitations commences upon assent to the account.[11]

In its narrowest sense an account stated involves mere computation of liquidated debits and credits. It is not a compromise agreement.[12] No consideration is present in striking such a balance. The account is supported by the survival in this area of the common law rule that a pre-existing debt is consideration for a promise to pay the debt.[13] Such a promise, however, can be avoided for fraud, mistake or other grounds on which a contract may be avoided. Indeed it may be shown that the account contradicts the contractually agreed upon method of computation.[14] If the computation is incorrect, the primary effect of an account stated is merely to shift the burden of going forward with the evidence to the party who claims the account is incorrect.[15] If, however, a party has changed position in reliance upon the account, the other party is estopped from proving that the account was in error.[16] Another effect of an account stated is that it is often held that the account is enforceable even as to items it contains which would otherwise be unenforceable because of the statute of limitations or Statute of Frauds.[17]

Despite its typical inclusion in a chapter on discharge, an account stated does not discharge the antecedent obligations. The creditor may opt to pursue a claim on the original obligations or on the account stated.[18]

attorney liable. McCullough v. Johnson, 307 Ark. 9, 816 S.W.2d 886 (1991); Copp v. Breskin, 56 Wn.App. 229, 782 P.2d 1104 (1989); contra, Free v. Wilmar J. Helric Co., 70 Or.App. 40, 688 P.2d 117 (1984), rev. denied.

9. Cf. Telefunken Sales v. Kokal, 51 Wis.2d 132, 186 N.W.2d 233 (1971).

10. Karrh v. Crawford–Sturgeon Ins., 468 So.2d 175 (Ala.Civ.App.1985); Andrews Elec. v. Farm Automation, 188 Neb. 669, 198 N.W.2d 463 (1972); Onalaska Elec. Heating v. Schaller, 94 Wis.2d 493, 288 N.W.2d 829 (1980); but see Neil v. Agris, 693 S.W.2d 604 (Tex.App.1985).

11. Zinn v. Fred R. Bright Co., 271 Cal. App.2d 597, 76 Cal.Rptr. 663, 46 ALR3d 1317 (1969); see Schapiro, Mutual, Open and Current Accounts, Book Accounts, Accounts Stated and the Statute of Limitations, 11 Cal.L.Rev. 12 (1922).

12. 6 Corbin § 1312.

13. See § 5.3 supra.

14. Hopwood Plays v. Kemper, 263 N.Y. 380, 189 N.E. 461 (1934); Norfolk Hosiery & Underwear Mills v. Westheimer, 121 Va. 130, 92 S.E. 922 (1917); 11 ALR 597 (1924); 75 ALR 1287 (1931).

15. Ally & Gargano v. Comp. Accounting, 615 F.Supp. 426 (S.D.N.Y.1985); Home Health Services v. McQuay–Garrett, Sullivan & Co., 462 So.2d 605 (Fla.App.1985); Dodson v. Watson, 110 Tex. 355, 220 S.W. 771, 11 ALR 583 (1920); 6 Corbin §§ 1307, 1308, 1310, 1311.

16. First Nat. Bank v. Williamson, 205 Iowa 925, 219 N.W. 32 (1928).

17. 6 Corbin § 1309; 15 Williston § 1863 (3d ed.). The result in any given jurisdiction is often dependent in part on statutory interpretation. See Boatner v. Gates Bros. Lumber, 224 Ark. 494, 275 S.W.2d 627, 51 ALR2d 326 (1955).

18. Newburgh v. Florsheim Shoe, 200 F.Supp. 599 (D.Mass.1961); 6 Corbin § 1314.

F.   RELEASE AND COVENANT NOT TO SUE

Table of Sections

§ 21.10   Release

Historically, the term "release" referred to a formal sealed instrument that in ritual words expressed an intent to discharge an obligation.[1] Because it was under seal, no consideration was necessary to support the discharge.[2] This same result obtains today in jurisdictions that have retained the common law seal.[3] Several jurisdictions that have abolished or downgraded the legal effect of the seal have enacted statutes giving effect to written releases irrespective of the presence or absence of consideration.[4] Some jurisdictions require a release to be supported by consideration.[5]

Most current definitions of "release" indicate that a release must be in writing.[6] Courts, however, not infrequently state that a release supported by consideration may be oral; these cases, analytically, are really accords and satisfactions.[7] A "release," written or oral, supported by consideration and operative under the laws of a jurisdiction that has abolished the effect of the seal, is an accord and satisfaction.[8] At common law, the release under seal, a species of deed, was ineffective without delivery.[9] Today, a "release" supported by consideration would no more have to be delivered than an accord and satisfaction.[10] A release unsupported by consideration[11] may be validated by the releasee's injurious reliance upon it.[12] Despite the absence of conceptual differences between many accords and satisfactions, and releases, practitioners tend to use

§ 21.10

1. Agnew v. Dorr, 5 Whart. 131, 34 Am. Dec. 539 (Pa.1840); Eastman v. Grant, 34 Vt. 387 (1861).

2. See ch. 7 supra.

3. E.g., England. See Guest, Anson's Law of Contracts 429 (26th ed. 1984).

4. See, e.g., UCC §§ 1–107 (1997 revision § 1–306), 3–605 (1990 revision § 3–604); McKinney's N.Y.Gen.Oblig.Law § 15–303; Rs. 2d § 284, Reporter's Note.

5. Fedder v. McClennen, 959 F.Supp. 28 (D.Mass.1996); White v. Homewood, 256 Ill. App.3d 354, 195 Ill.Dec. 152, 628 N.E.2d 616 (1993); Barnes v. Ricotta, 142 Ohio App.3d 560, 756 N.E.2d 218 (2001).

6. 5A Corbin § 1238; Rs. 1st § 402(1); Rs. 2d § 284(1).

7. Reserve Ins. v. Gayle, 393 F.2d 585 (4th Cir.1968); Bank of U.S v. Manheim, 264 N.Y. 45, 189 N.E. 776 (1934).

8. See §§ 21.4—21.7 supra.

9. See Rs. 2d § 284(2). UCC §§ 1–107 and 3–605 impose delivery requirements for releases unsupported by consideration. The revision § 1–306 replaces 1–107 and dispenses with the delivery requirement and allows for an electronic record. The 1990 revision of Article 3, § 3–604, dispenses with the delivery requirement.

10. Industrial Heat Treating v. Industrial Heat Treating, 104 Ohio App.3d 499, 662 N.E.2d 837 (1995). See n.6 supra.

11. Rs. 2d § 284 appears to provide that a written unsealed release is valid without consideration. This reading is undercut, however, by cmt b. Cf. 5A Corbin § 1238.

12. Southern Furniture Mfg. v. Mobile, 276 Ala. 322, 161 So.2d 805 (1963); Fried v. Fisher, 328 Pa. 497, 196 A. 39, 115 ALR 147 (1938).

forms entitled "release" for some discharges and contractual documents for other discharges, perhaps more out of habit than necessity.

A release may be conditional.[13] If the condition is precedent, the discharge is effective upon the happening of the condition.[14] If the condition is subsequent, the release operates as a covenant not to sue unless and until the condition occurs.[15] A condition precedent which is not contained in the release is also effective. The parol evidence rule does not bar evidence of the condition.[16] A conditional release may be used to circumvent[17] the common law rule that the release of one joint obligor releases the others.[18]

Much litigation centers on the scope of releases, that is, the extent of the claims that are discharged. This is a question of interpretation.[19] The doctrine of mistake is also frequently invoked when a general release discharges claims that were unknown to the releasor.[20] Releases of rights under Federal employment laws must be knowing and voluntary.[21] As in the case of other consensual transactions, a release may be voidable for fraud.[22]

§ 21.11   Covenant Not to Sue

A release is an executed transaction. A covenant not to sue is a promise by the creditor not to sue either permanently or for a limited period.[1] If the promise is one never to sue, it operates as a discharge just as does a release.[2] The theory is that should the creditor sue despite the promise not to, the debtor has a counterclaim for damages for breach of the creditor's covenant not to sue which is equal to and cancels the original claim. To avoid circuity of action, despite the promissory form, the promise is given the effect of a discharge of the claim.[3] The main reason this kind of instrument is used instead of a release is to circum-

---

13. Rs. 2d § 284 cmt b.

14. Rs. 1st § 404(1); Johnson v. Pickwick Stages Sys., 108 Cal.App. 279, 291 P. 611 (1930); 19 Geo.L.J. 378 (1931).

15. Rs. 1st § 404(2); Robinson v. Thurston, 248 F. 420 (9th Cir.1918); but see, 19 Geo.L.J. 378 (1931).

16. Schoeler v. Roth, 51 F.Supp. 518 (S.D.N.Y.1942); Kitchens v. Kitchens, 142 So.2d 343 (Fla.App.1962); see § 3.7(b) supra.

17. See Johnson v. Pickwick Stages Sys., 108 Cal.App. 279, 291 P. 611 (1930); 19 Geo.L.J. 378 (1931).

18. See § 20.3 supra.

19. See, e.g., Virginia Impression Prods. v. SCM, 448 F.2d 262 (4th Cir.1971), cert. denied; Damron v. Norfolk & Western Ry., 925 F.Supp. 520 (N.D.Ohio 1995); Pokorny v. Stastny, 51 Wis.2d 14, 186 N.W.2d 284 (1971); 15 Williston § 1835 (3d ed.).

20. See §§ 9.26(d) & 20.3 supra.

21. See § 9.26(e) supra.

22. Goney v. E.I. Du Pont., 144 F.S.2d 1286 (M.D.Fla.2001).

§ 21.11

1. On distinguishing a release and a covenant not to sue, see Nassif, When is a Release Not a Covenant (Parts I & II), 34 J.Mo.Bar 12, 102 (1978); Sade v. Hemstrom, 205 Kan. 514, 471 P.2d 340 (1970). The Uniform Contribution Among Tortfeasors Act abolishes the distinction between a release and a covenant not to sue. See Ottinger v. Chronister, 13 N.C.App. 91, 185 S.E.2d 292 (1971).

2. Seligman v. Pinet, 78 Mich. 50, 43 N.W. 1091 (1889).

3. Rs. 1st § 405 cmt a; 5A Corbin § 1251.

vent past and present rules holding that the release of one joint obligor releases all of them.[4]

The release of one of a number of joint obligors containing a reservation of rights against the others is treated as a covenant not to sue.[5] However, in this situation, and in the case of an express covenant not to sue one joint obligor, the creditor is permitted to sue the "released" obligor despite the covenant not to sue,[6] but is precluded from levying execution.[7] The reason for this rule is to be found in the historical and present intricacy of the rules concerning joint obligors, especially the rule that all joint obligors are necessary parties to an action on the obligation.[8]

If the covenant is not to sue for a limited time, the modern view is that the covenant may be raised as an affirmative defense to any action brought in violation of the covenant. The only exception is, as explained above, in the case of joint obligors.[9]

G. GIFT, RENUNCIATION, AND REJECTION OF TENDER

Table of Sections

§ 21.12   Gift, Renunciation, and Rejection of Tender

(a) Gift

A gift normally requires delivery of the subject matter and a manifestation of donative intent.[1] If, however, the subject matter is personal property already in the possession of the donee, delivery is not needed.[2] Thus, if B pays $5,000 to S for future delivery of an identified automobile, B's subsequent statement to S that S may keep the car as a birthday present perfects the gift.[3] The result would be the same if S were in possession of a symbolic writing of the kind that ordinarily is deemed to incorporate a debt and B manifested an intention to give the rights symbolized by the writing to S.[4]

---

4. Leon v. Parma Community General Hospital, 140 Ohio App.3d 95, 746 N.E.2d 689 (2000).

5. See § 20.3 supra.

6. Annot., 53 ALR 1461 (1928).

7. Rs. 2d § 285(3); 5A Corbin § 1239.

8. See § 20.3 supra.

9. Rs. 2d § 285 cmt a.

§ 21.12

1. R. Brown, Personal Property chs. 8 & 9 (3d ed. 1975).

2. Rs. 2d § 276; Rs. 1st § 414.

3. Rs. 2d § 276, ill. 1; R. Brown, Personal Property § 7.8 (3d ed. 1975); 5 Williston § 727 (3d ed.).

4. Rs. 1st § 414; Rs. 2d § 276; R. Brown, Personal Property § 8.5 (3d ed. 1975).

A gift of a right not incorporated into a symbolic writing is a more complex issue. As we know, the discharge of an obligation generally requires consideration.[5] There is a vast number of cases holding that part payment of a debt is not consideration for a purported discharge.[6] The purported discharge is not seen as a manifestation of donative intent. Where the purported discharge is manifested in a spirit of liberality rather than settlement, however, there is a completed gift.[7]

(b) Renunciation

A renunciation is a gratuitous statement purporting to surrender a right. Under the majority view, a renunciation is generally ineffective because of the absence of consideration.[8]

There is, however, support for the effectiveness of a renunciation in several contexts. The first context merely is a sub-species of gift. When a contract is still executory in whole or in part on both sides, there is authority to the effect that one party may discharge the other from all or part of his or her obligations under the contract. In essence, despite the absence of consideration, a party may modify *downwards* the performance owed. This rule is supported by both contracts restatements,[9] but does not appear to be supported by much case authority except for cases where the downward modification is actually executed, as in rent reduction cases.[10]

The second context where a renunciation may be effective is where a contract is canceled for material breach. If the cancellation is accompanied by a renunciation of the right to damages, such a renunciation is effective.[11] UCC § 2–720 adopts the better common law cases when it states:

> "Unless the contrary intention clearly appears, expressions of 'cancellation' or 'rescission' of the contract or the like shall not be construed as a renunciation or discharge of any claim in damages for an antecedent breach." (Unchanged by the revision).

The third context involves a renunciation of damages for partial breach where the renunciation is prior to or upon acceptance of a deficient performance.[12] Under the UCC there are instances where such

---

5. See § 4.10 supra.

6. See § 4.10 supra.

7. Gray v. Barton, 55 N.Y. 68, 14 Am. Rep. 181 (1873); see 5A Corbin § 1247.

8. Burns v. Beeny, 427 S.W.2d 772 (Mo. App.1968); 5A Corbin §§ 1240–1241.

9. Rs. 2d § 275; Rs. 1st § 416; see 5A Corbin §§ 1248, 1249; 15 Williston §§ 1829–1831 (3d ed.).

10. Collected in 5A Corbin § 1249; see also Ottenberg v. Ottenberg, 194 F.Supp. 98 (D.D.C.1961) (waiver of contractual duty to support mother).

11. 5 Williston §§ 700–744 (3d ed.); Rs. 1st § 410. The Restatement, Second § 277, agrees only if the renunciation is in a signed writing.

12. Rs. 2d § 277(2); Rs. 1st § 411; 5 Williston §§ 700–744 (3d ed.); see Schmeck v. Bogatay, 259 Or. 188, 485 P.2d 1095 (1971) (acceptance of a deficient performance without a renunciation does not discharge); accord, Aubrey v. Helton, 276 Ala. 134, 159 So.2d 837 (1964).

a renunciation is implied from silence.[13]

Last, the Restatement (Second) adopts the rule that a written renunciation signed and delivered to the breaching party, even after accepting performance, discharges a claim for damages.[14] In some jurisdictions even broader results are available by utilizing the device of a gratuitous written release.[15]

(c) Rejection of Tender

A wrongful refusal of tender of performance of an obligation is a breach and frequently is so material as to justify cancellation of the contract by the party tendering.[16] If the tendering party's obligation is unilateral, as in the case of services paid for in advance, there is authority to the effect that if the services are rejected the obligation is discharged.[17] Such a holding should be reached only if material prejudice results from the refusal of tender. At any rate, it is clear that a refusal of tender of payment of a debt does not discharge the debt, although it may have the effect of cutting off further accrual of interest.[18] For this result to obtain, many authorities hold that the tender must be kept good;[19] i.e., that the amount tendered be segregated from the debtor's other funds. However, if Article 3 of the UCC governs the debt, such segregation is not required. A proper tender[20] also has the effect of discharging a mortgage or other lien which secures the debt.[21]

H. MERGER

Table of Sections

§ 21.13 Merger

The term "merger" may be used in a broad or narrow sense. In a broad sense any time a contract supersedes and incorporates all or part

---

13. UCC § 2–605; see § 11.20 supra.

14. Rs. 2d § 277(2).

15. See §§ 21.10, 21.11 supra. As to commercial paper, see UCC § 3–605, § 3–604 of the 1990 revision.

16. Liddle v. Scholze, 768 A.2d 1183 (Pa.Super.2001); Perlman v. M. Israel & Sons, 306 N.Y. 254, 117 N.E.2d 352 (1954); 5 Williston §§ 743–744 (3d ed.); 6 Williston §§ 832–833 (3d ed.).

17. See 15 Williston §§ 1817–1818 (3d ed.); Rs. 1st § 415. See the enigmatic reference to § 415 in Rs. 2d, Ch. 12, Reporter's Notes, p. 364.

18. See 5A Corbin §§ 1232–1235. The rule is codified in UCC § 3–604 (§ 3–603 of the 1990 revision).

19. See 5A Corbin § 1235; 15 Williston § 1816 (3d ed.).

20. For the requisites of a valid tender of money see 5A Corbin § 1235; 15 Williston §§ 1810–1819 (3d ed.). The technical requisites are waived if the creditor does not base the refusal on noncompliance with them. See, e.g., UCC § 2–511(2); Geary v. Dade Dev., 29 N.Y.2d 457, 329 N.Y.S.2d 569, 280 N.E.2d 359 (1972). On refusal of a check or draft as payment, see § 11.20(e) supra.

21. Kortright v. Cady, 21 N.Y. 343, 78 Am.Dec. 145 (1860); but see Geary v. Dade Dev., 29 N.Y.2d 457, 329 N.Y.S.2d 569, 280 N.E.2d 359 (1972).

of an earlier agreement, it may be said that the earlier agreement is merged into the later. In this sense a substituted contract results in a discharge by merger.[1] Also an earlier tentative agreement is merged into an integration.[2]

In the narrower sense, a common law rule emerged in the 1600's to the effect that a merger occurred if a "lower form" of obligation was superseded by a "higher form."[3] Thus, for example, where an obligation arising under a contract is reduced to judgment the only remaining obligation is the judgment.[4] Also, where the obligation created by an informal contract is superseded by a sealed instrument or other specialty, the informal contract is discharged by merger.[5] The primary effect of such a discharge of the earlier obligation was an almost total exclusion of parol evidence of the prior contract in an attempt to vary or contradict the higher obligation, or indeed even to explain it.[6] The judgment or specialty was itself the obligation and not merely evidence of it. This early rule of integration preceded the parol evidence rule as applied to informal integrations. Today, the merger of an informal contract into a specialty raises basically the same problem as the merger of an informal contract into an integration; that is, the extent to which the prior expressions of agreement are admissible into evidence. Thus, the existence of a separate heading of "discharge by merger" in Restatements, treatises, and texts is largely an anachronism.[7] What is involved is merely a substituted obligation.

Although a negotiable instrument is regarded as a specialty and is a "higher" form of obligation, it has generally been held that the acceptance of a negotiable instrument from the obligor does not discharge the underlying obligation unless it is given and accepted in satisfaction of the underlying obligation. This rule created a good deal of litigation as to the factual question of whether or not the instrument was accepted in satisfaction. The UCC makes it clear that in the usual case, the instrument acts as an executory accord, suspending the underlying obligation. In the event the instrument is dishonored, the obligee may sue on the instrument or the prior obligation.[8]

§ 21.13

1. See § 21.6 supra; Bonastia v. Berman Bros., 914 F.Supp. 1533 (W.D.Tenn.1995) (stressing that the rights in the original contract no longer exist).

2. See ch. 3 supra.

3. The historical development and effect of this rule is exhaustively treated in 9 Wigmore, Evidence § 2426 (3d ed.1940); see also 15 Williston §§ 1874–1875C (3d ed.).

4. Rs. 1st § 444. An arbitration award has the same effect. Id. § 445.

5. Rs. 1st § 446. There is generally stated to be a presumption that a contract is merged in a deed but the question ordinarily is one of intent and a question of fact. Webb v. Graham, 212 Kan. 364, 510 P.2d 1195 (1973); see Dunham, Merger by Deed—Was it Ever Automatic, 10 Ga.L.Rev. 419 (1976); but see Warner v. Estate of Allen, 776 N.E.2d 422 (Ind.App.2002).

6. See 9 Wigmore, Evidence § 2426 (3d ed. 1940).

7. The topic is omitted in the Rs. 2d. See Ch. 12, Reporter's Note, p. 363.

8. UCC § 3–802. The 1990 revision, § 3–310, is to the same effect except that certified checks and the like are excepted. See also § 2–511(3).

Merger by judgment is today largely considered as one aspect of the doctrine of res judicata and treated in depth in works on judgments and civil procedure.

I.   UNION OF RIGHT AND DUTY IN THE SAME PERSON

Table of Sections

§ 21.14   Debtor's Acquisition of the Correlative Right

Closely analogous to merger is a discharge by the union of right and duty in the same person. The first Restatement stated the general rule as follows: "Where a person subject to a contractual duty, or to a duty to make compensation, acquires the correlative right in the same capacity in which he [or she] owes the duty, the duty is discharged."[1] The simplest illustration is where a creditor assigns a claim against a debtor to the same debtor.[2] The Restatement rule, however, is to be disapproved as an overly sweeping generalization. Especially in the field of mortgages, difficult questions arise as to merger of the right-duty relation in the same person and often enough that person's intention to keep the two aspects of the relation separate will be given effect.[3] The Restatement (Second) is less dogmatic, but too vague to provide guidance, stating: "where one party to a contract becomes both obligor and obligee and there are no other parties to the contract, the contract is not necessarily deprived of all legal consequences."[4]

II.   DISCHARGES BY OPERATION OF LAW

J.   ALTERATION

Table of Sections

§ 21.15   Discharge by Alteration

At early common law, any material alteration of a written contract whether or not fraudulent and whether caused by the obligee or not,

§ 21.14

1. Rs. 1st § 451.

2. Wright v. Anderson, 62 S.D. 444, 253 N.W. 484, 95 ALR 81 (1934).

3. See Reeves v. Sanderlin, 249 Ga.App. 882, 549 S.E.2d 837 (2001); Kissinger v. Genetic Eval. Center, 260 Neb. 431, 618 N.W.2d 429 (2000) (intent of the mortgagee); Miller v. Martineau & Co., 983 P.2d 1107 (Utah App.1999) (where merger would be against the interests of the party holding the fee and the mortgage).

4. Rs. 2d § 9 cmt a.

resulted in a discharge.[1] Under modern law, however, an alteration by a third person or by accidental means does not discharge a written contract.[2] The general rule is that a material alteration of a writing by one who asserts a right under it extinguishes his or her rights and discharges the obligation of the obligor if the alteration is made by the obligee with fraudulent intent.[3] An alteration is material if the rights or duties of the obligee would be varied.[4] The Restatements take the position that the rule applies only to sealed instruments, integrations, or memoranda required by the Statute of Frauds.[5] Article 3 of the UCC contains a rule that governs commercial paper much like the general rule stated above.[6]

A discharge caused by an alteration is nullified by a subsequent assent to or forgiveness of the alteration even though the promise to forgive is not supported by consideration.[7] Similarly, if the contract is bilateral and the innocent party knowing of the alteration asserts rights under the contract, the duties of both parties are revived.[8] If the arrangement is unilateral, alteration discharges the rights of the party who is guilty of the alteration but does not discharge the rights of the other party who must, however, as a condition to the assertion of rights perform all conditions to these rights.[9]

K.   BANKRUPTCY

Table of Sections

§ 21.16   Bankruptcy

In a liquidation proceeding, a bankrupt is discharged by operation of law with respect to provable debts. The cases sometimes indicate that merely the remedy is barred or suspended by the decree in bankruptcy;[1] but others speak in terms of an actual discharge.[2] But these differences in theory are no longer relevant in current law.[3]

§ 21.15

1. 15 Williston § 1881 (3d ed.); Williston, Discharge of Contracts by Alteration (Pts. I & II), 18 Harv.L.Rev. 105, 165 (1904–05), Selected Readings 1221, 1232.

2. Litton Industries Credit v. Plaza Super of Malta, 503 F.Supp. 83 (N.D.N.Y. 1980); Kelley v. Kelley, 435 So.2d 214 (Ala. 1983).

3. Knapp v. Knapp, 251 Iowa 44, 99 N.W.2d 396 (1959); First Nat. Bank v. Hull, 189 Neb. 581, 204 N.W.2d 90 (1973); Rs. 1st § 434; Rs. 2d § 286(1); cf. Moving Picture Mach. Operators Union v. Glasgow Theaters, 6 Cal.App.3d 395, 86 Cal.Rptr. 33 (1970) (voidable at option of innocent party).

4. Rs. 2d § 286(2).

5. Rs. 1st § 435; Rs. 2d § 286(1); 6 Corbin § 1317.

6. UCC § 3–407 (old version and 1990 revision).

7. Rs. 2d § 287.

8. Rs. 2d § 287.

9. 6 Corbin § 1317.

§ 21.16

1. Zavelo v. Reeves, 227 U.S. 625 (1913).

2. Henry v. Root, 33 N.Y. 526 (1865).

3. See § 5.6 supra.

L. PERFORMANCE

Table of Sections

§ 21.17 Performance of the Duty—To Which Debt Should Payment Be Applied?

A contractual duty is discharged by performance.[1] A frequent method of performance is payment—the delivery of money or its equivalent in specific property or services by one from whom it is due to another person to whom it is due.[2] Unless the contract indicates otherwise, payment is to be made in legal tender—greenbacks. Significant payments, however, are not usually made in legal tender. Thus, Section 2–511(2) of the UCC provides: "Tender of payment is sufficient when made by any means or in any manner current in the ordinary course of business unless the seller demands payment in legal tender and gives any extension of time reasonably necessary to procure it." The giving of one's own negotiable instrument does not constitute payment unless the instrument is accepted as payment.[3]

When the debtor owes the creditor more than one debt, to which debt should a payment be applied? Except as later indicated, there are three possible scenarios: (1) if the debtor manifests an intention in this respect at or before the time of payment, the creditor must apply the payment in accordance with the debtor's directions;[4] (2) if the debtor makes no manifestation, the creditor may within a reasonable time make the application;[5] (3) if neither the creditor nor the debtor makes a seasonable manifestation, the law will apply the payment in the manner that is most equitable.[6]

There is an exception to the rule stated in (1). Where the payor is under a duty to a third person, for example, a surety, to apply the money to a particular debt and the creditor knows or has reason to know of the facts which create the duty, the creditor must apply the payment in discharge of the debt in which the third party is interested.[7]

§ 21.17

1. Rs. 2d § 235.

2. Sizemore v. E.T. Barwick Indus., 225 Tenn. 226, 465 S.W.2d 873 (1971).

3. U.S. v. Heyward–Robinson, 430 F.2d 1077 (2d Cir.1970), cert. denied; Boynton v. Law Offices, 294 A.D.2d 778, 742 N.Y.S.2d 713 (2002); 15 Williston § 1875A (3d ed.); UCC § 3–310 (former § 3–802(1)(b)).

4. Schreiber v. Armstrong, 70 N.M. 419, 374 P.2d 297 (1962); Rs. 2d § 258. A manifestation once made cannot be changed without the consent of the other party.

5. J. & G. Constr. v. Freeport Coal, 147 W.Va. 563, 129 S.E.2d 834 (1963); Debelak Bros. v. Mille, 38 Wis.2d 373, 157 N.W.2d 644 (1968); Rs. 2d § 259.

6. Carozza v. Brannan, 186 Md. 123, 46 A.2d 198 (1946); Rs. 2d § 260.

7. School District v. Transamerica Ins., 633 S.W.2d 238 (Mo.App.1982); Bounds v. Nuttle, 181 Md. 400, 30 A.2d 263 (1943); Rs. 2d § 258(2); contra, Uhl Constr.v. Fidelity & Deposit, 371 Pa.Super. 520, 538 A.2d 562 (1988); cf. Greens at Hilton Run I v. Rollin Bldg. Supply, 87 Md.App. 220, 589 A.2d 536 (1991).

There are also exceptions to the rule stated in (2). The creditor may not apply the payment to a claim that is disputed, illegal or unmatured and must apply it to a debt which if not paid by the debtor will result in a forfeiture or violate a duty owed by the debtor to a third party, provided the creditor knows or has reason to know of this duty.[8] Aside from these restrictions, the creditor is permitted to serve its own best interests as by applying a payment to an unsecured rather than secured debt, to interest rather than principal,[9] to an open account rather than an account that had been sent to a collection agency,[10] and to an unenforceable rather than an enforceable debt.[11] The creditor may apply involuntary payments, e.g., the foreclosure of collateral, to any debt secured by the collateral.[12]

8. Rs. 2d § 259(2), (3).

9. City Coal v. Noonan, 434 Mass. 709, 751 N.E.2d 894 (2001).

10. Boynton v. Law Offices, 294 A.D.2d 778, 742 N.Y.S.2d 713 (2002).

11. In re Applied Logic, 576 F.2d 952 (2d Cir.1978); 5A Corbin § 1231; 15 Williston § 1796 (3d ed.).

12. Baxter State Bank v. Bernhardt, 985 F.Supp. 1259 (D.Kan.1997).

Chapter 22

ILLEGAL BARGAINS

Table of Sections

§ 22.1 What Makes a Bargain Illegal?

The first Restatement of Contracts attempted to define "illegal bargain" with analytic rigor, providing that a bargain is "illegal * * * if either its formation or its performance is criminal, tortious or otherwise opposed to public policy."[1] The Restatement (Second) avoids the term "illegal" and subsumes all such unenforceable bargains under the amorphous but ubiquitous concept of "public policy," the "unruly horse"[2] of the law. Under the Restatement (Second) approach, a contract that violates the criminal law is not necessarily against public policy. This approach is well supported by the cases.[3] The thrust of the Restatement (Second)'s rules is to allow judicial flexibility in weighing the strength of legally recognized policies against the effect of declaring a particular bargain to be against public policy.[4]

§ 22.1

1. Rs. 1st § 512.

2. Richardson v. Mellish, 2 Bing. 229, 252, 130 Eng.Rep. 294, 303 (1824).

3. See, e.g., cases cited at note 37 infra. Also supporting this position are cases that reason that although a particular contract is illegal, it may nevertheless be enforced. See § 22.4 infra.

4. Rs. 2d § 178. See Northern Indiana Public Service v. Carbon County Coal, 799 F.2d 265, 273–74 (7th Cir.1986) (Posner, J.).

As one court stated, "public policy can be enunciated by the Constitution, the legislature or the courts at any time and whether there is a prior expression or not the courts can refuse to enforce any contract which they deem to be contrary to the best interests of citizens as a matter of public policy."[5] Public policy has been the announced rationale for striking down contracts or contract clauses on grounds of immorality,[6] unconscionability,[7] economic policy,[8] unprofessional conduct,[9] the prevention of obstruction of justice,[10] paternalism,[11] and diverse other criteria, including government or corporate contracts that are ultra vires[12] and contracts between parents that prejudice their children's rights to support.[13]

The various kinds of contracts or contract clauses that have been struck down on grounds of public policy will not be discussed here. This chapter will be limited to considering the consequences of a bargain contaminated in whole or in part by the presence of an actual or contemplated violation of the law of crimes or torts, or a collision with other public policies.[14]

5. Anaconda Fed. Credit Union v. West, 157 Mont. 175, 178, 483 P.2d 909, 911 (1971); accord, J.S. Alberici Constr. v. Mid-West Conveyor, 750 A.2d 518 (Del.Super.2000) (choice of law clause where foreign law was against public policy); Rome v. Upton, 271 Ill.App.3d 517, 208 Ill.Dec. 163, 648 N.E.2d 1085 (1995) (contingent fee for enactment of legislation); Quiring v. Quiring, 130 Idaho 560, 944 P.2d 695 (Idaho 1997) (property settlement in consideration of not reporting sexual contact with a minor). See Gellhorn, Contracts and Public Policy, 35 Colum.L.Rev. 679 (1935); Greenhood, The Doctrine of Public Policy in the Law of Contracts—Reduced to Rules (1886); Stone, Social Dimensions of Law and Justice 182–198 (1966); Strong, The Enforceability of Illegal Contracts, 12 Hastings L.J. 347 (1961); Symmons, The Function and Effect of Public Policy in Contemporary Common Law, 51 Aust.L.J. 185 (1977).

6. Casad, Unmarried Couples and Unjust Enrichment: From Status to Contract and Back Again, 77 Mich.L.Rev. 47 (1978); Dwyer, Immoral Contracts, 93 L.Q.Rev. 386 (1977); Note, 37 Brandeis L.J. 245 (1998). On the effect of changing attitudes towards sexual morality and their impact on contract law, compare Wilcox v. Trautz, 427 Mass. 326, 693 N.E.2d 141 (1998), with Hewitt v. Hewitt, 77 Ill.2d 49, 31 Ill.Dec. 827, 394 N.E.2d 1204, 3 ALR4th 1 (1979), and County of Dane v. Norman, 174 Wis.2d 683, 497 N.W.2d 714 (1993).

7. E.g., rules pertaining to liquidated damages, §§ 14.31 to 14.35 supra.

8. E.g., Rs. 2d §§ 186–188 (contracts in restraint of trade).

9. E.g., fee splitting between licensed attorneys, Scolinos v. Kolts, 37 Cal.App.4th 635, 44 Cal.Rptr.2d 31 (1995); between doctor and supplier, Harris v. Gonzalez, 789 So.2d 405 (Fla.App.2001), between doctor and university, Odrich v. Columbia Univ., 193 Misc.2d 120, 747 N.Y.S.2d 342 (2002), between unlicensed and licensed broker, Kirkpatrick v. Lawrence, 908 S.W.2d 125 (Ky.App.1995), and rules pertaining to maintenance and champerty. See § 22.10 infra.

10. Fomby–Denson v. Dep't of the Army, 247 F.3d 1366 (Fed.Cir.2001).

11. See Kronman, Paternalism and The Law of Contracts, 92 Yale L.J. 763 (1983); cf. Kennedy, Distributive and Paternalist Motives in Contract and Tort Law, 41 Md. L.Rev. 563, 624–649 (1982).

12. Failor's Pharmacy v. Dept. Of Social and Health Services, 125 Wn.2d 488, 886 P.2d 147 (1994); Bank One v. Rouse, 181 Ariz. 36, 887 P.2d 566 (App.1994). In Gladsky v. Glen Cove, 164 A.D.2d 567, 563 N.Y.S.2d 842 (1991), app. denied, an *ultra vires* contract was said to be illegal, but the promisee was permitted to recover reliance expenditures.

13. Straub v. B.M.T., 645 N.E.2d 597 (Ind.1994); Pecora v. Cerillo, 207 A.D.2d 215, 621 N.Y.S.2d 363 (1995).

14. See 6A Corbin; 4 & 6 Williston (4th ed.).

The starting point for a discussion of illegality is the maxim, *in pari delicto potior est conditio defendentis*—in a case of equal fault the condition of the defending party is the better one. In short, the court will leave the parties where it finds them.

Two basic policies underlie this principle. First, a refusal to enforce a contract that is against public policy will deter the making of such contracts in the future.[15] The second rationale has to with the dignity of the court. "The policy against enforcing a contract calling for an illegal performance is a simple one and does not require extensive comment. It accomplishes very little in discouraging the performance of illegal acts but it keeps the courts respectable."[16] This policy is often colorfully expressed. For example, we read "no polluted hand shall touch the pure fountains of justice."[17] Courts state that they refuse to act "as paymasters of the wages of crime."[18] One court pithily put it this way: "[s]traight shooters should always win, but when there are none, bad guys need not look to us for help."[19]

The courts could have made other policy choices, for example, confiscation of the proceeds of illegality by the state,[20] restoration of the status quo ante,[21] or a decree ordering payment of illicit proceeds to charity.[22] Nonetheless, the choice made by the common law is in accord with that of many legal systems.[23]

As a general rule an illegal bargain is unenforceable[24] and, often void.[25] This last result has often been described as stemming from the principle that a valid bilateral contract requires that both parties furnish consideration.[26] If A promises to do something lawful and B promises to do something unlawful, there can be no action for breach on either side. B may not sue because B's illegal promise does not constitute consideration for A's promise and A may not sue, even though A promises to do something lawful, because of the requirement of mutuality of consideration.[27]

---

15. Weil v. Neary, 278 U.S. 160, 173–74 (1929); Sirkin v. Fourteenth St. Store, 124 A.D. 384, 108 N.Y.S. 830 (1908).

16. Havighurst, The Nature of Private Contract 53 (1961). Thus, the court may raise the issue of illegality *sua sponte.* Quiring v. Quiring, 130 Idaho 560, 944 P.2d 695 (Idaho 1997).

17. Collins v. Blantern, 2 Wils.K.B. 347, 350, 95 Eng.Rep. 850, 852 (1767).

18. Stone v. Freeman, 298 N.Y. 268, 271, 82 N.E.2d 571, 572, 8 ALR2d 304 (1948).

19. Certa v. Wittman, 35 Md.App. 364, 370 A.2d 573 (1977). Perhaps fictionally, "A dirty dog will get no dinner from the courts." A.P. Herbert, Case 52, in Uncommon Law.

20. See Civil Code of the R.S.F.S.R. Art. 49 (Gray & Stults Trans. 1965); cf. Carr v. Hoy, 2 N.Y.2d 185, 158 N.Y.S.2d 572, 139 N.E.2d 531 (1957).

21. Mexican Civ. Code Art. 2239 (M. Gordon Trans. 1980); see Enonchong, Effect of Illegality: French and English Law, 44 Int'l & Comp.L.Q. 196 (1995).

22. Portuguese Civ. Code Art. 692 (1879 ed.).

23. Von Mehren, A General View of Contract § I–42, in VII International Encyclopedia of Comparative Law (1982).

24. Rs. 2d § 178. Valenza v. Emmelle Coutier, 288 A.D.2d 114, 733 N.Y.S.2d 167 (2001) is a ferocious example. An off-the-books employee was not permitted to sue the employer.

25. Rs. 1st §§ 598, 607.

26. See § 4.12 supra.

27. Rs. 1st § 607 cmt a; cf. 6A Corbin § 1523; Buckley, Illegality in Contract and Conceptual Reasoning, 12 Anglo–Am.L.Rev. 280 (1983).

While this analysis suitably explains cases of hard core illegality (e.g., a promise to pay in exchange for a promise to commit murder), it fails to account for the numerous cases where one of the contracting parties may enforce the agreement despite its illegal taint.[28] As one writer has aptly stated: "contracts are not legal or illegal in the same way that eggs are good or bad."[29] The decision to award or withhold a remedy is based on policy choices and precedents, not only on concepts. The Restatement (Second) rejects consideration analysis of contracts against public policy. Under its analysis, A's promise to murder X is indeed consideration for B's promise to pay A $10,000.[30] B's promise is unenforceable, not because of the lack of consideration, but because it is illegal. This is one of many attempts of the Restatement (Second) to free the concept of consideration from excess baggage.

Even assuming an agreement involves some actual or contemplated conduct that violates statutory law or other public policy, the courts do not automatically brand the agreement as illegal. There are countless statutes prohibiting criminal activity. There is a vast array of administrative regulations, the violation of which are penalized. If the legislature states the effect of a violation of a criminal statute upon a contract, that expression of intention must of course be followed.[31] Legislatures, however, do not usually provide for the civil consequences of the violation of the criminal law. In such cases, the matter is one for judicial determination. An English judge has made sound observations in this regard. Judge Devlin in St. John Shipping Corp. v. Joseph Rank Ltd.,[32] stated: "Caution in this respect is, I think, especially necessary in these times when so much of commercial life is governed by regulations of one sort or another, which may easily be broken without wicked intent * * *. Commercial men who have unwittingly offended against one of a multiplicity of regulations may nevertheless feel that they have not thereby forfeited all right to justice."

Illustrative of the problem are statutes penalizing commercial bribery. In 1905, New York became one of the first common law jurisdictions to enact a statute making the bribery of purchasing agents a crime.[33] The penalty was a fine of no more than $500 and imprisonment for no more than a year. In Sirkin v. Fourteenth Street Store,[34] plaintiff delivered hosiery to the defendant pursuant to a contract plaintiff had obtained by bribing defendant's purchasing agent. The court refused to enter a judgment for the purchase price even though the statute was silent as to the civil effects of its violation. A dissenting opinion accused the majority of judicial legislation and of permitting the unjust enrichment of the defendant.

28. See § 22.4 infra.

29. Anson's Law of Contract 384 (Guest's 25th ed.).

30. Rs.2d § 72 cmt d.

31. Anderson v. Frandsen, 36 Wn.App. 353, 674 P.2d 208 (1984) (statute prohibits contractor from recovering).

32. [1957] 1 Q.B. 267, 288, 289.

33. 1905 N.Y.Laws ch. 136. On commercial bribery, see Note, 108 U.Pa.L.Rev. 848 (1960).

34. 124 A.D. 384, 108 N.Y.S. 830 (1908). See Annot., 55 ALR2d 481 (1957).

The debate between the majority and the dissenter is repeated in countless cases. While some cases state the general rule is that the contract will be enforced despite a statutory violation,[35] others state that the general rule provides for non-enforcement.[36] The probability is that the varieties of illegality are too multifarious to be stated in one rule. However, a party who has performed under the agreement tainted with illegality may recover if the offense is merely *malum prohibitum* "and the denial of relief is wholly out of proportion to the requirements of public policy or appropriate individual punishment."[37] While the result is often couched in terms of ascertaining legislative intent, the courts often determine this intent from the degree of hostility manifested by the legislature against the practice it has forbidden.[38] In Sirkin, the court made quite clear the legislature's (and its own) hostility to commercial bribery.

§ 22.2   Recovery on an Illegal Executory Bilateral Contract

Even if an agreement is illegal, there are a number of situations in which a party may recover for breach of an illegal executory bilateral contract.

(a) Ignorance of Facts and Law

If a party enters into an illegal bargain and is justifiably ignorant of the facts creating the illegality and the other is not, the innocent party may recover on the contract by showing a readiness, willingness and ability to perform but for the illegality.[1] A simple illustration is the case of a married man who promises to marry another woman. She, assuming her ignorance of his marital status, could bring an action for breach of a contract to marry, provided that she is in a state that still recognizes such an action.[2] It has been held that a plaintiff could recover from an unlicensed trucking company for breach of a contract of carriage where

---

35. Ets–Hokin & Galvan v. Maas Transport, 380 F.2d 258 (8th Cir.1967), cert. denied.

36. Mascari v. Raines, 220 Tenn. 234, 415 S.W.2d 874 (1967); but see Gene Taylor & Sons Plumbing v. Corondolet Realty Trust, 611 S.W.2d 572 (Tenn.1981).

37. John E. Rosasco Creameries v. Cohen, 276 N.Y. 274, 278, 11 N.E.2d 908, 909, 118 ALR 641, 644 (1937); see also Gates v. Rivers Constr., 515 P.2d 1020 (Alaska 1973); M. Arthur Gensler, Jr. & Assocs. v. Larry Barrett, Inc., 7 Cal.3d 695, 103 Cal. Rptr. 247, 499 P.2d 503 (1972), Measday v. Sweazea, 78 N.M. 781, 438 P.2d 525, 26 ALR3d 1386 (App.1968) (contractor complied with building code but had no building permit); Spadanuta v. Rockville Centre, 15 N.Y.2d 755, 257 N.Y.S.2d 329, 205 N.E.2d 525 (1965); but see Joe O'Brien Investiga-

tions v. Zorn, 263 A.D.2d 812, 694 N.Y.S.2d 216 (1999) (no contractual recovery but quantum meruit allowed).

38. See the cases in n.37 and U.S. v. Acme Process Equipment, 385 U.S. 138 (1966); Annot., 55 ALR2d 481 (1957); Rupert's Oil Service v. Leslie, 40 Conn.Supp. 295, 493 A.2d 926 (1985) (no recovery for unmetered deliveries of fuel oil); Baierl v. McTaggart, 245 Wis.2d 632, 629 N.W.2d 277 (2001) (lease with illegal attorneys' fees provision cannot be enforced).

§ 22.2

1. Symcox v. Zuk, 221 Cal.App.2d 383, 34 Cal.Rptr. 462 (1963).

2. Rs. 2d § 180. On the illegality of such a promise made with knowledge of the facts, see Sanders v. Gore, 676 So.2d 866 (La.App.1996), writ denied.

the plaintiff had no knowledge that the defendant was unlicensed.[3] A seller of land was permitted to recover damages for breach of a contract which was illegal because the purchaser was an enemy alien, where the seller was ignorant of the purchaser's nationality.[4]

These cases do not violate the general rule that ignorance of the law is no excuse.[5] They involve ignorance of facts. There is even an exception to the general rule that ignorance of the law is no excuse where the illegality is minor and the party who is ignorant of the illegality justifiably relies upon an assumed special knowledge of the other of the requirements of law. This usually occurs where the other is in the business to which the contract relates.[6]

(b) Bargain Illegal by Virtue of Wrongful Purpose

Some bargains are illegal by reason of the wrongful purpose of one or both of the parties. The mere fact that an innocent party knows of the illegal purpose of the other does not bar the innocent party from recovering for breach of contract[7] unless the intended purpose involves serious moral turpitude or this party takes action to further the illegal purpose of the other. In the leading case, the plaintiff, a resident of France, contracted to sell a quantity of tea to the defendant, knowing of defendant's intent to smuggle the tea into England. The English court permitted the plaintiff to recover.[8] Soon thereafter, the court denied recovery where the seller had packed the goods in such a way as to facilitate the smuggling operation.[9] A landlord who knowingly leases

---

3. Archbolds (Freightage) Ltd. v. Spanglett Ltd., [1961] 2 W.L.R. 170 (C.A.); accord, Hedla v. McCool, 476 F.2d 1223 (9th Cir.1973) (architect not known to be unlicensd); Commercial Trust & Savings Bank v. Toy Nat. Bank, 373 N.W.2d 521 (Iowa App.1985) (bank exceeded its lending limits); but see Castro v. Sangles, 637 So.2d 989 (Fla.App.1994) (owner knew contractor was unlicensed).

4. Branigan v. Saba, [1924] N.Z.L.R. 481 (1923); see also Eastern Expanded Metal v. Webb Granite & Constr., 195 Mass. 356, 81 N.E. 251 (1907); Hoekzema v. Van Haften, 313 Mich. 417, 21 N.W.2d 183 (1946); Millin v. Millin, 36 N.Y.2d 796, 369 N.Y.S.2d 702, 330 N.E.2d 650 (1975). See also the licensing cases at § 22.7 infra.

5. 6A Corbin § 1539.

6. Rs. 2d § 180; National Conversion v. Cedar Bldg., 23 N.Y.2d 621, 298 N.Y.S.2d 499, 246 N.E.2d 351 (1969) (action on landlord's warranty that lease did not violate zoning requirements); Harrison v. Flushing Nat. Bank, 83 Misc.2d 658, 370 N.Y.S.2d 803 (1975) (bank issued certificates at illegally high rate).

7. Gold Bond Stamp v. Bradfute, 463 F.2d 1158 (2d Cir.1972) (trading stamp company supplies prizes for illegal lottery);

Watkins v. Curry, 103 Ark. 414, 147 S.W. 43 (1912) (sale of automobile used as prize in illegal lottery); Howell v. Stewart, 54 Mo. 400 (1873) (loan to enable defendant to smuggle cattle from Texas to Missouri); San Benito Bank & Trust v. Rio Grande Music, 686 S.W.2d 635 (Tex.App.1984) (bank knew of borrower's illegal purpose); Rs. 2d § 180; but see Access Telecom v. MCI, 197 F.3d 694 (5th Cir.1999) (action for tortious interference with Texas contract to facilitate violation of Mexican law).

8. Holman v. Johnson, 1 Cowp. 341, 98 Eng.Rep. 1120 (K.B.1775); accord, Graves v. Johnson, 179 Mass. 53, 60 N.E. 383 (1901) (sale of liquor in Massachusetts knowing the buyer intended to resell in Maine); authorities in n.7.

9. Biggs v. Lawrence, 3 T.R. 454, 100 Eng.Rep. 673 (K.B.1789); accord Hull v. Ruggles, 56 N.Y. 424 (1874) (packaging in aid of a lottery). For variations on this problem, see Williams Mfg. v. Prock, 184 F.2d 307 (5th Cir.1950) (amusement machines offering free plays to winner); Hart Publications v. Kaplan, 228 Minn. 512, 37 N.W.2d 814 (1949) (contract to print lottery tickets); Carroll v. Beardon, 142 Mont. 40, 381 P.2d 295 (1963) (contract to sell house

property for a purpose forbidden by the zoning laws cannot enforce the tenant's promise to pay rent.[10]

Penal statutes that have expanded the concept of criminal facilitation broaden the category of illegal agreements in jurisdictions that have enacted them. For example, New York outlaws "conduct which provides [another] with the means or opportunity to commit a crime" when he or she believes it probable that the other intends to commit a crime.[11] This expansion of criminal liability naturally leads to the expansion of cases where recovery on an agreement is barred.

(c) Where the Parties Are Not In Pari Delicto

Some statutes are designed to protect one class of persons against another. In a case involving a lottery-office keeper, Lord Mansfield stated: "The statute itself * * * *has marked the criminal.* For the penalties are all on one side; upon the office keeper."[12] While most of the civil litigation concerning agreements made in violation of such statutes are actions for restitution[13] there are cases in which damages for breach have been awarded. For example, rent control legislation is designed to protect tenants. Consequently, a tenant may bring an action for damages for breach of a lease despite the violation of rent regulations by terms in the lease.[14] A rule designed to protect customers against brokers by limiting the extension of credit does not bar the customer from enforcing the agreement by an action for damages.[15] An investigator was not in pari delicto with a lawyer in a fee-splitting arrangement, but such a holding appears aberrant.[16] It has been suggested that an action for specific performance of an agreement that violates a rule designed to protect a class of persons should be available in a proper case to a member of the protected class.[17] An action for damages is certainly

to be used for prostitution); Fineman v. Faulkner, 174 N.C. 13, 93 S.E. 384 (1917) (contract to sell phonograph to prostitute); Hendrix v. McKee, 281 Or. 123, 575 P.2d 134 (1978) (contract to design illegal gambling machines).

10. McMahon v. Anderson, Hibey & Blair, 728 A.2d 656 (D.C.App.1999).

11. McKinney's N.Y. Penal Law Art. 115 (the quoted language appears in a number of sections in this article); Frohlich & Newell Foods v. New Sans Souci Nursing Home, 109 Misc.2d 974, 441 N.Y.S.2d 335 (1981) (no recovery for sales of food where plaintiff overbilled to enhance purchaser's reimbursement from the State).

12. Browning v. Morris, 2 Cowp. 790, 793, 98 Eng.Rep. 1364, 1365 (K.B.1778) (emphasis supplied).

13. See § 22.7 infra.

14. Steinlauf v. Delano Arms, 15 A.D.2d 964, 226 N.Y.S.2d 862 (1962).

15. Pearlstein v. Scudder & German, 429 F.2d 1136 (2d Cir.1970), cert. denied. This S.E.C. rule has been changed to mark both broker and customer as offenders. See Note, 50 Notre Dame Law. 136 (1974); see also Bateman Eichler, Hill Richards v. Berner, 472 U.S. 299 (1985) (insider trading).

16. Shimrak v. Garcia–Mendoza, 112 Nev. 246, 912 P.2d 822 (1996) (investigator). Cases disallowing recovery: Trotter v. Nelson, 684 N.E.2d 1150 (Ind.1997) (clerical employee); Kalled v. Albee, 142 N.H. 747, 712 A.2d 616 (1998) (suspended lawyer); Ungar v. Matarazzo, Blumberg, 260 A.D.2d 485, 688 N.Y.S.2d 588 (1999) (lay law firm administrator); Plumlee v. Paddock, 832 S.W.2d 757 (Tex.App.1992) (ambulance company owner); Rs. Law Governing Lawyers § 10(3). As to fee splitting between attorneys, see id. § 47 and Perillo, The Law of Lawyers' Contracts is Different, 67 Fordham L.Rev. 443, 460–66 (1998).

17. 6A Corbin § 1540.

available.[18] There are times when the same sort of reasoning surfaces in a holding that the party most responsible for the illegal agreement is estopped from raising the defense of illegality.[19] Where an action is allowed to enforce an illegal contract, it has been held that the guilty party cannot rely on protective clauses in the contract.[20]

(d) Severance

An illegal provision does not necessarily render the entire contract unenforceable. If the illegal provision is not central to the agreement and does not involve serious moral turpitude, the illegal portion of the agreement is disregarded and the balance of the agreement is enforceable.[21] We have seen examples of this rule earlier. Thus, contracts containing illegal covenants not to compete are enforced. The illegal covenant is disregarded or curtailed.[22] Contracts containing illegal penalty clauses[23] or illegal exculpatory clauses[24] are enforced. The illegal clauses are in effect deleted.

There are other examples of severance outside of these standardized situations. One, it has been held that if a contract contains an illegal provision whereby a party surrenders the right to appeal, the balance of the contract is enforceable.[25] Two, provisions in a contract unlawfully circumventing the powers of corporate directors have been disregarded where the primary purpose of the contract would not be defeated.[26] Three, a contractual clause that violates state antitrust law by fixing prices to be paid by customers other than the plaintiff may be severed and the plaintiff's promise to purchase enforced.[27] Four, where the legislature authorized agreements with respect to rehabilitation for those convicted of alcohol-related crimes instead of jail time, a provision in such an agreement providing for jail time was deleted.[28] Five, a contract containing an illegal price term can be salvaged by excising the price term and supplying "market price" as an implied-in-fact term.[29]

18. Bolivar v. Monnat, 232 A.D. 33, 248 N.Y.S. 722 (1931) (action for breach of implied warranty of bootleg alcohol); State v. Haid, 325 Mo. 949, 30 S.W.2d 100 (1930) (statute forbidding receipt of deposits except at bank does not void a deposit taken elsewhere); see the licensing cases at § 22.3 nn.9, 10 infra.

19. Russo v. Carey, 271 A.D.2d 889, 706 N.Y.S.2d 760 (2000).

20. John Hancock–Gannon Joint Venture v. McNully, 800 So.2d 294 (Fla.App. 2001).

 21. Rs. 2d § 184.

 22. See § 16.21 supra.

 23. See § 14.31 supra.

 24. See § 9.44 supra.

25. Marshall v. Wittig, 213 Wis. 374, 251 N.W. 439 (1933); see also Wright v.

Robinson, 468 So.2d 94 (Ala.1985) (illegal confession of judgment clause).

26. Jones v. Gabrielan, 52 N.J.Super. 563, 146 A.2d 495 (A.D.1958); Triggs v. Triggs, 46 N.Y.2d 305, 413 N.Y.S.2d 325, 385 N.E.2d 1254 (1978), rehearing denied.

27. Rose v. Vulcan Materials, 282 N.C. 643, 194 S.E.2d 521, 67 ALR3d 1 (1973); see X.L.O. Concrete v. Rivergate, 83 N.Y.2d 513, 611 N.Y.S.2d 786, 634 N.E.2d 158 (1994) (question of fact whether the contract was integrally related to antitrust violations).

28. State v. Crum, 270 Kan. 870, 19 P.3d 172 (Kan.2001).

29. Barrett Refining v. U.S., 242 F.3d 1055 (Fed.Cir.2001).

Cases where illegal provisions have been severed or disregarded are many.[30] What criteria should be used to determine whether the primary purpose of the agreement will be defeated by severance of illegal provisions? Primarily, the criterion would appear to be whether the parties would have entered into the agreement irrespective of the offending provisions of the contract.[31] This can usually be determined by weighing the equality of the agreed exchange before and after the proposed severance.[32] Where the illegality permeates the entire agreement, severance is generally not permitted.[33] Even here, however, the degree of forfeiture and unjust enrichment[34] will be taken into consideration to determine whether severance will be granted.[35]

(e) Purposeful Interpretation and Reformation

If an agreement can be read so that either a legal or illegal meaning can be attributed to it, courts will prefer the interpretation giving the agreement a legal meaning.[36] In addition to the applicability of this rule of interpretation, the possibility of reformation of a written contract exists, although there are very few cases in which the remedy of reformation has been granted.

In one case, the parties entered into an agreement for a mortgage loan, which a title insurance company reduced to writing at their request. The title company made use of a printed form which provided for compound interest in the event of default, a provision that rendered the agreement usurious. It was held that the agreement could be reformed by excision of the offending clause.[37] With the general recognition and gradual expansion of the idea that reformation is available for mistake of law and, in particular, mistake as to the legal effect of a writing,[38] the road is now open to reformation of writing where the parties have inadvertently strayed beyond the boundaries of legality.

De facto reformation often occurs under the doctrines of severance[39] and divisibility.[40] In addition, there are cases where the court essentially rewrites the contract to conform to the law relying on no particular doctrine.[41]

30. Ferro v. Bologna, 31 N.Y.2d 30, 334 N.Y.S.2d 856, 286 N.E.2d 244 (1972) (note also parties were not in pari delicto); Petty v. El Dorado, 270 Kan. 847, 19 P.3d 167 (2001) (plea bargain with illegal jail time); Schue v. Jacoby, 162 N.W.2d 377 (N.D. 1968); Osgood v. Central Vt. R.R., 77 Vt. 334, 60 A. 137 (1905).

31. Cf. Marsh, The Severance of Illegality in Contract (pts. 1 & 2), 64 L.Q.Rev. 230, 347 (1948).

32. Rs. 2d § 184 cmt a.

33. Hall v. Hall, 455 So.2d 813 (Ala. 1984); Hanley v. Savannah Bank & Trust, 208 Ga. 585, 68 S.E.2d 581 (1952); Kukla v. Perry, 361 Mich. 311, 105 N.W.2d 176 (1960); Schara v. Thiede, 58 Wis.2d 489, 206 N.W.2d 129 (1973).

34. Murray Walter, Inc. v. Sarkisian Bros., 107 A.D.2d 173, 486 N.Y.S.2d 396 (1985).

35. Rs. 1st § 603.

36. Rs. 1st § 236(a); Rs. 2d § 203(a).

37. First American Title Ins. & Trust v. Cook, 12 Cal.App.3d 592, 90 Cal.Rptr. 645 (1970).

38. See § 9.34 supra.

39. See § 22.2(d) supra.

40. See § 22.6 infra.

41. E.g., Coronet Ins. v. Ferrill, 134 Ill. App.3d 483, 89 Ill.Dec. 691, 481 N.E.2d 43 (1985); but see Flatt v. Country Mut. Ins., 289 Ill.App.3d 1097, 225 Ill.Dec. 151, 682 N.E.2d 1228 (1997).

(f) Making the Case Without Showing the Illegality

It is the rule in England that if a plaintiff can make out a claim without showing the illegality, the plaintiff can recover for breach of contract even if plaintiff is in *pari delicto* with the defendant.[42] This rule is devoid of any policy content and is purely formalistic. Nevertheless, it has some adherents in the U.S.[43]

§ 22.3   Effect of Licensing Statutes

The violation of licensing statutes is governed by the same general principles that govern other kinds of illegal conduct. However, certain specific distinctions have been made in this class of case. Practicing a trade or profession without a license, where a license is required, is often a criminal offense, but the question remains whether an unlicensed person who does services is entitled to recover for the services done. The primary distinction, which seems, however, to be eroding, has been between licensing statutes that are merely revenue raising and licensing statutes that are designed to certify the skills or moral fitness of licensees.[1] If the licensing statute is merely a revenue raising measure, recovery is permitted, but no recovery is allowed if the statute is in the latter category.[2] Thus, a person who practices a profession such as law without a license is ordinarily denied a recovery.[3] A contract that in essence allows an unlicensed party to utilize the license of another is equally illegal.[4] Still, even here some cases show flexibility in allowing an out of state attorney to recover where the services in the state are occasional.[5] A court may refuse to enforce a contract if the licensing laws

---

42. Tinsley v. Milligan, [1993] All E.R. 65 (H.L.).

43. Northland Transp. v. McElhose Trucking, 3 Neb.App. 650, 529 N.W.2d 809 (1995); see 6A Corbin § 1533.

§ 22.3

1. Cope v. Rowlands, 2 M & W 149, 150 Eng.Rep. 707 (Exch.P.1836) (stockbroker; no recovery); Birbrower et al. v. Santa Clara County Superior Court, 17 Cal.4th 119, 70 Cal.Rptr.2d 304, 949 P.2d 1 (1998) (out-of-state attorneys); 50 Ala.L.Rev. 535 (1999); Solomon v. Gilmore, 248 Conn. 769, 731 A.2d 280 (1999) (mortgage lender).

2. Colston v. Gulf States Paper, 291 Ala. 423, 282 So.2d 251 (1973); Howard v. Lebby, 197 Ky. 324, 246 S.W. 828, 30 ALR 830 (1923) (building contractors' licensing fees were an occupation tax); Benjamin v. Koeppel, 85 N.Y.2d 549, 626 N.Y.S.2d 982, 650 N.E.2d 829 (1995) (attorney registration fee is for revenue); 6A Corbin § 1512; Annots., 82 ALR2d 1429 (1962), 44 ALR4th 271 (1986).

3. U.S. Nursing v. Saint Joseph Med. Center, 39 F.3d 790 (7th Cir.1994); Lozoff v. Shore Heights, 35 Ill.App.3d 697, 342

N.E.2d 475 (1976), aff'd; Spivak v. Sachs, 16 N.Y.2d 163, 263 N.Y.S.2d 953, 211 N.E.2d 329 (1965), 33 Fordham L.Rev. 483 (1965); Business Brokerage Centre v. Dixon, 874 S.W.2d 1 (Tenn.1994); see 11 ALR3d 907 (1967).

4. Déjà Vu v. Talayna's Laclede's Landing, 34 S.W.3d 245 (Mo.App.2000).

5. Spanos v. Skouras Theatres, 364 F.2d 161 (2d Cir.1966), cert. denied (out of state attorney handling federal antitrust case); see also Food Industries Res. & Eng. v. Alaska, 507 F.2d 865 (9th Cir.1974) (out of state engineers); Warde v. Davis, 494 F.2d 655 (10th Cir.1974) (out of state landscape architect); Costello v. Schmidlin, 404 F.2d 87, 32 ALR3d 1139 (3d Cir.1968); Winer v. Jonal, 169 Mont. 247, 545 P.2d 1094, 78 ALR3d 1112 (1976); Furr v. Fonville Morisey Realty, 130 N.C.App. 541, 503 S.E.2d 401 (1998) (real estate broker). A contrary result was reached in Marcus & Nocka v. Julian Goodrich Architects, 127 Vt. 404, 250 A.2d 739 (1969), but note court's close attention to legislative intent.

of the place of performance are violated.[6] Substantial compliance with a licensing law has been held to permit recovery.[7] A construction contractor can promise the services of licensed plumbers, electricians and engineers without violating public policy.[8]

The test of revenue raising as opposed to exercise of police power is no longer regarded as an absolute test and today it is regarded as one indicium of legislative intent.[9] Beyond legislative intent, modern courts have been concerned that the windfall to the defendant may be too great and the penalty too high, if no recovery is permitted for services rendered by an unlicensed person. There are cases permitting recovery where the lack of a license caused no harm to the defendant and posed no grave threat to the public.[10] Partly on these considerations some courts have allowed recovery where the defendant was not a member of the general public but was engaged in the same line of business as the plaintiff.[11] The Restatement (Second) encourages the courts to balance the equities in the light of the public policy served.[12]

Because police power licenses are designed to protect the public, the parties are not in pari delicto.[13] Consequently, where an unlicensed professional makes a bargain with a member of the public, the professional will be liable for damages in cases of malpractice.[14] An unlicensed

6. Escobio v. American Int'l Group, 262 F.3d 1207 (11th Cir.2001) (Chile); Lehman Bros. v. Minmetals Int'l, 2000 WL 1702039 (S.D.N.Y.2000) (China); Madison Realty v. Neiss, 253 A.D.2d 482, 676 N.Y.S.2d 672 (1998) (Florida).

7. McCormick v. Reliance Ins., 46 P.3d 1009 (Alaska 2002); Asdourian v. Araj, 38 Cal.3d 276, 211 Cal.Rptr. 703, 696 P.2d 95 (1985) [since changed by statute]; contra, Cevern v. Ferbish, 666 A.2d 17 (D.C.App. 1995) (entered into home improvement contract 8 days before being licensed).

8. Charlebois v. J.M. Weller Assocs., 72 N.Y.2d 587, 531 N.E.2d 1288, 535 N.Y.S.2d 356 (1988).

9. John E. Rosasco Creameries v. Cohen, 276 N.Y. 274, 11 N.E.2d 908, 118 ALR 641 (1937) (unlicensed milk dealer permitted recovery); cf. Carmine v. Murphy, 285 N.Y. 413, 35 N.E.2d 19 (1941) (unlicensed liquor dealer not permitted to recover). As to real estate brokers, see Galbreath–Ruffin v. 40th & 3rd, 19 N.Y.2d 354, 280 N.Y.S.2d 126, 227 N.E.2d 30 (1967), reargument denied. For an excellent case attempting to carry out legislative intent and policy, see Keller v. Thornton Canning, 66 Cal.2d 963, 59 Cal.Rptr. 836, 429 P.2d 156 (1967) (carrier had no permit, recovery permitted). See also T.E.C. & Assoc. v. Alberto–Culver, 131 Ill.App.3d 1085, 87 Ill.Dec. 220, 476 N.E.2d 1212 (1985) (unlicensed employment agency); Moffit v. Sederlund, 145 Mich.App. 1,

378 N.W.2d 491 (1985) (state securities act); Matter of Migdal Plumbing & Heating, 232 A.D.2d 62, 662 N.Y.S.2d 106 (1997), lv. denied (unlicensed plumber).

10. See notes 4–8. See also Land Ocean Logistics v. Aqua Gulf, 68 F.Supp.2d 263 (W.D.N.Y.1999) (unlicensed transport broker); Hiram Ricker & Sons v. Students Int'l Meditation Soc., 342 A.2d 262 (Me.1975), app. dismissed (expiration of innkeeper's license should not result in forfeiture of $65,000); Town Planning & Eng. Assocs. v. Amesbury Specialty, 369 Mass. 737, 342 N.E.2d 706 (1976) (head of engineering firm unlicensed); Association Group Life v. Catholic War Veterans, 120 N.J.Super. 85, 293 A.2d 408 (A.D.1971), modified 61 N.J. 150, 293 A.2d 382 (1972) (insurance brokerage firm unlicensed but employees were licensed).

11. Gene Taylor & Sons Plumbing, v. Corondolet Realty Trust, 611 S.W.2d 572 (Tenn.1981); Fillmore Products v. Western States Paving, 561 P.2d 687 (Utah 1977).

12. Rs. 2d § 181; Domach v. Spencer, 101 Cal.App.3d 308, 161 Cal.Rptr. 459 (1980); Grenco R.E.I.T. v. Nathaniel Greene Dev., 218 Va. 228, 237 S.E.2d 107 (1977).

13. See § 22.2 supra.

14. Hedla v. McCool, 476 F.2d 1223 (9th Cir.1973); Cohen v. Mayflower, 196 Va. 1153, 86 S.E.2d 860 (1955); see § 22.2 supra.

party who works in association with a licensed party may hope for recovery if the public interest is not subverted.[15]

It should be noted that, although the unlicensed professional may be precluded from recovering, if the client has paid, the unlicensed party can generally successfully defend an action by the payor for restitution,[16] but here, too, there is no unanimity.[17]

§ 22.4   Remoteness of the Illegality

In Sirkin v. Fourteenth Street Store, discussed above,[1] the plaintiff's additional argument was that the illegality was too remote. Plaintiff contended that, although the agreement between the plaintiff and the purchasing agent was illegal, the contract for the sale of hosiery was perfectly legal. The court disagreed, pointing out that the illegal bribe was an inducing cause of the hosiery contract and therefore tainted the contract.[2]

According to the first Restatement,[3] without support in the cases,[4] a legal contract could also become illegal if it were *performed* in an illegal manner. The first case of consequence to agree was Tocci v. Lembo.[5] The plaintiff made a lawful contract to construct a house for defendant. In constructing the house, plaintiff failed to get approval of a federal agency that allocated scarce materials in the period immediately following World War II. Plaintiff's action for the balance of the price was denied. The court relied heavily on Williston's theory that the essential reason for denying recovery on a contract in the context of illegality is the refusal of the courts to reward illegal conduct.[6]

Tocci was followed in McConnell v. Commonwealth Pictures,[7] where defendant retained the plaintiff to obtain certain motion picture distribution rights, promising a commission. Plaintiff obtained the rights by bribing an agent of the motion picture producer. It was held that plaintiff could not recover the promised commission despite the obvious benefits received by the defendant.

Assuming these cases are sound, their rationale should be applied only to conduct that is illegal in a significant way. A contract to

15.   Quartey v. AB Stars Prods., 260 A.D.2d 39, 697 N.Y.S.2d 280 (1999).

16.   Anderson v. Frandsen, 36 Wn.App. 353, 674 P.2d 208 (1984).

17.   Winer v. Ceslik, 66 Conn.App. 842, 786 A.2d 516 (2001).

§ 22.4

1.   See § 22.1 at n.34 supra.

2.   See also Thomas v. Ratiner, 462 So.2d 1157 (Fla.App.1984), appeal denied (attorney procured retainer in hospital in violation of statute; no recovery of fee).

3.   Rs. 1st § 512.

4.   See Comment, 41 Marq.L.Rev. 34 (1957); Notes, 46 Va.L.Rev. 1601 (1960); 25 Albany L.Rev. 146 (1961); 8 U.C.L.A.L.Rev. 638 (1961) and especially 49 Geo.L.J. 362 (1960). More recently, see Haberman v. Elledge, 42 Wn.App. 744, 713 P.2d 746 (1986).

5.   325 Mass. 707, 92 N.E.2d 254 (1950), noted 31 B.U.L.Rev. 108 (1951).

6.   15 Williston § 1761 (3d ed.); see, essentially contra, 6A Corbin § 1529.

7.   7 N.Y.2d 465, 166 N.E.2d 494, 199 N.Y.S.2d 483 (1960). This case is a basis for Rs. 2d § 178, ill. 14, a rare instance in which the new Restatement agrees with Williston's rather than Corbin's position.

transport goods should not be deemed to have been transmuted into an illegal transaction because the trucker exceeded the speed limit.[8]

There are miscellaneous instances of remote illegality. Where a party gained possession of a ring from its owner under an illegal agreement and pawned it, the true owner was permitted to reclaim it from the pawnbroker. Although the defense of illegality would have applied in litigation between the owner and the other party to the illegal agreement, it was too remote to be raised by the pawnbroker.[9] Similarly, a purchaser on credit cannot raise as a defense that the seller has reached illegal contracts with other purchasers but not with it.[10] How remote is "too remote" is obviously a question of degree. "The line of proximity varies somewhat according to the gravity of the evil apprehended."[11]

§ 22.5   Depositaries and Agents

If a person gets funds by illegal conduct and deposits them in a bank, the bank cannot resist repayment to the depositor. The illegal conduct is simply too remote to be an appropriate defense by the bank.[1]

More difficult to explain are the cases in which *A* pays money to *B*, in *B's* capacity as agent for *C*. If the payment is the fruit of an illegal transaction one would expect that *C* could not recover the amount from *B*; recovery would in effect be the successful culmination of *C's* unlawful conduct. Nonetheless, many cases permit recovery by *C*.[2] Although various theories have been expressed to explain such holdings, including remoteness, the only tenable explanation is that *B's* fiduciary obligation as agent is regarded as stronger than the policies against enforcement of illegal agreements.

The principle does not apply where the agent or depositary is an active party to the illegal transaction. Thus, where the plaintiff, a clothing jobber, advanced money to the defendant broker to be used to bribe purchasing agents and plaintiff sought restitution of funds that

---

8. Yankee Microwave v. Petricca Comm. Sys., 53 Mass.App. 497, 760 N.E.2d 739 (2002); Annot., 26 ALR3d 1395 (1969).

9. Pelosi v. Bugbee, 217 Mass. 579, 105 N.E. 222 (1914).

10. Roux Laboratories v. Beauty Franchises, 60 Wis.2d 427, 210 N.W.2d 441 (1973); see also O'Brien v. O'Brien Steel Constr., 440 Pa. 375, 271 A.2d 254 (1970) (failure to report transaction to taxing authority); Seagirt Realty v. Chazanof, 13 N.Y.2d 282, 246 N.Y.S.2d 613, 196 N.E.2d 254 (1963) (plaintiff lost the deed received in culmination of a successful scheme to defraud creditors; action to quiet title permitted).

11. Rs. 1st § 597 cmt b; see also Rs. 2d § 178 cmt d; 6A Corbin § 1529; Robertson

v. Town of Stonington, 253 Conn. 255, 750 A.2d 460 (2000) (taxpayer who hired non-attorney to challenge assessment not barred from continuing proceeding).

§ 22.5

1. An hypothetical case based on Southwestern Shipping v. National City Bank, 6 N.Y.2d 454, 190 N.Y.S.2d 352, 160 N.E.2d 836 (1959), cert. denied.

2. E.g., McBlair v. Gibbes, 58 U.S. (17 How.) 232 (1854); Sheahan v. McClure, 199 Mich. 63, 165 N.W. 735 (1917); Murray v. Vanderbilt, 39 Barb. 140, 152 (N.Y.Sup. 1863); see 6A Corbin §§ 1530, 1531; cf. Rs. 2d, Agency § 412 (1958).

had not been expended, the court held that the defendant was not a mere depositary and therefore could use the defense of illegality.[3]

§ 22.6   Divisibility of Illegal Bargains

Earlier we looked at the idea of divisibility pursuant to which a party in material breach of a contract could nonetheless recover for performance of divisible portions of the contract.[1] A similar, but not identical, idea permits recovery where part of the contract is illegal. For example, plaintiff, an unlicensed plumber, entered into a contract with defendant to do certain plumbing work for an agreed sum. Plaintiff performed, but because of the lack of a license could not recover the price. The court, however, permitted recovery for the materials furnished but not for labor performed.[2] The court thus severed the furnishing of materials from the services rendered although the contract was entire and not divisible in the sense that term is used in § 11.23 supra. This kind of decision tends to show that divisibility is not determined by fixed rules, but by the judicial instinct for justice.[3]

Where a contract is divisible in the sense in which it is used in § 11.24, the rule is that a promise that is legal and has its own separately apportioned consideration is enforceable except where the rest of the bargain is criminal or immoral to a high degree.[4] When a non-essential clause in the contract, is illegal, for example a penalty clause or an overbroad covenant not to compete, the illegal clause is severed and the balance of the contract is enforced.[5]

§ 22.7   Restitutionary Recovery—Not in Pari Delicto

We have previously considered cases where parties may sue to enforce an illegal bargain.[1] A party who is in pari delicto is also estopped from claiming restitution. However, the class of cases in which a party may recover in restitution for performances under illegal bargains is broader than the class of cases in which an illegal executory bargain can

3. Stone v. Freeman, 298 N.Y. 268, 82 N.E.2d 571 (1948). Cases to the contrary exist. See Annot., 8 ALR2d 307 (1949). As to the doctrine of locus poenitentiae, see § 22.8 infra.

§ 22.6

1. See §§ 11.23—11.24 supra.

2. Lund v. Bruflat, 159 Wn. 89, 292 P. 112 (1930); but see American Store Equip. & Constr. v. Jack Dempsey's Punch Bowl, 174 Misc. 436, 21 N.Y.S.2d 117 (1939), aff'd; cf. Birnbaum v. Schuler, 56 A.D.2d 556, 391 N.Y.S.2d 601 (1977). Agreement with respect to illegal cohabitation was severed from the rendition of construction work and business services in Mason v. Rostad, 476 A.2d 662 (D.C.1984) and McCall v. Frampton, 81 A.D.2d 607, 438 N.Y.S.2d 11 (1981).

3. See 6A Corbin § 1520; Rs. 2d § 183.

4. Hill v. Schultz, 71 Idaho 145, 227 P.2d 586 (1951) (mortgage and lease on gambling promises severed; mortgage enforced as it was in consideration of a loan; lease not enforced as it was in consideration of a percentage of gambling revenues); Ingle v. Perkins, 95 Idaho 416, 510 P.2d 480 (1973); Lacks v. Lacks, 39 A.D.2d 485, 336 N.Y.S.2d 874 (1972), appeal dismissed; In re Craig's Estate, 298 Pa. 235, 148 A. 83 (1929); Rs. 1st §§ 606–607; Rs. 2d § 183.

5. See, e.g., Weissman v. Transcontinental Printing, 205 F.Supp.2d 415 (E.D.Pa. 2002).

§ 22.7

1. See § 22.4 supra.

be enforced. In particular, the doctrine of "not in pari delicto" embraces a larger group of claimants than in cases of enforcement of executory agreements. This is often appropriate because denial of relief would result in the unjust enrichment of the party who has received the benefit of the performance and the forfeiture of property or services furnished by the other.[2] Pursuant to the same policies, recovery of fees paid to an unlicensed professional is generally denied.[3]

A party who has performed under an illegal bargain and who was not guilty of serious moral turpitude and, who, although blameworthy, is not as equally guilty as the other party to the illegal bargain, is entitled to restitution.[4] What constitutes serious moral turpitude is obviously a question of degree.[5] A person who bribes or attempts to bribe a public official or agent is usually believed to be guilty of serious moral turpitude.[6] Yet, context can be important too. In a case in which the plaintiff, a Jewish refugee, gave jewels to the defendant to be used in bribing the Portuguese Consul to issue a visa so that plaintiff could escape Hitler's death camps, it was held that the plaintiff might recover the value of the jewels from the defendant as he was not in pari delicto.[7] The court refused to attach the stigma of moral turpitude to an agreement made by a person in dire necessity and motivated by the instinct of self-preservation.[8]

The cases which allow recovery on the ground that the performing plaintiff is not equally at fault tend to come within several flexible categories. Foremost among these categories are cases in which the transaction is outlawed in order to protect a class of persons of which the plaintiff is a member.[9] Thus, a borrower may recover excess interest paid, and often a penalty as well, from a usurer.[10] Antitrust laws are

---

2. See Rs. 2d, Introd. Note Ch. 8, Topic 5; see also GMB Enterprises v. B–3 Enterprises, 39 Wn.App. 678, 695 P.2d 145 (1985) (although the parties are in pari delicto, restitution is in the public interest).

3. Remsen Partners v. Stephen A. Goldberg Co., 755 A.2d 412 (D.C.2000).

4. Rs. 2d § 198(b); Rs. 1st § 604; see generally, 2 Palmer on Restitution § 8.6 (1978); Grodecki, In Pari Delicto Potior est Conditio Defendentis, 71 L.Q.Rev. 254 (1955); Higgins, The Transfer of Property Under Illegal Transactions, 25 Modern L.Rev. 149 (1962); Wade, Restitution of Benefits Acquired through Illegal Transactions, 95 U.Pa.L.Rev. 261 (1947); Note, 42 Notre Dame Law. 46 (1966).

5. William J. Davis, Inc. v. Slade, 271 A.2d 412 (D.C.1970).

6. State v. Strickland, 42 Md.App. 357, 400 A.2d 451 (1979).

7. Liebman v. Rosenthal, 185 Misc. 837, 57 N.Y.S.2d 875 (1945) aff'd 269 A.D. 1062, 59 N.Y.S.2d 148 (1945). See 6A Corbin § 1536. Sometimes the doctrine is worded

in terms that the plaintiff "is not in particips criminis."

8. Emergency measures to avoid imminent injury may be taken, under modern criminal codes, despite the fact that such measures under ordinary circumstances would constitute a criminal act. See Model Penal Code § 3.02; McKinney's N.Y. Penal Law § 35.05.

9. Stenger v. Anderson, 66 Cal.2d 970, 59 Cal.Rptr. 844, 429 P.2d 164 (1967) (statutes governing pre-paid life care are for the benefit of the aged); Neil v. Pennsylvania Life Ins., 474 P.2d 961 (Okl.1970); Jipac v. Silas, 800 A.2d 1092 (Vt.2002); 27 Modern L.Rev. 225 (1964); 6 Corbin § 1540; Wade, supra n.4, at 270–72; § 22.2(c) supra.

10. Trapp v. Hancuh, 530 N.W.2d 879 (Minn.App.1995) CIGNA Ins. v. TPG Store, 894 S.W.2d 431 (Tex.App.1995). Statutory usury laws vary. Under some, the borrower can walk away with the money with impunity. Seidel v. 18 E. 17th St. Owners, 79 N.Y.2d 735, 586 N.Y.S.2d 240, 598 N.E.2d 7 (1992).

aimed, in large part, at enterprises enjoying considerable market power, in order to protect enterprises having a significantly lesser amount of market power. Therefore, it will usually be held that a dealership is not in pari delicto with the manufacturer although the contracts between the manufacturer and its dealers contain illegal provisions in restraint of trade.[11] In some jurisdictions, it has been held that a bettor is not in pari delicto with a professional bookmaker as the gambling laws are aimed primarily against organized gambling.[12] A municipality has recovered amounts paid to a construction contractor where the contract was procured by collusive and fraudulent bidding.[13]

A party is not in pari delicto when "induced to participate in the illegality by fraud or duress or by the use of influence derived from superior knowledge, mental power, or economic position."[14] Certainly an insurance company has superior knowledge about insurance law.[15] A famous series of cases involving the Buckfoot gang illustrates this proposition. The gang had various operatives whose business was to lure wealthy westerners to their headquarters at an athletic club in Missouri. One of their techniques was to induce their guests into betting on races allegedly "fixed" in their favor, when actually they were "fixed" against them. The courts allowed recovery against the gang on the grounds that the parties were not on an equal footing. These highly organized frauds, arranged with consummate skill, were no match for the relatively naive bettors.[16] Similar considerations provide the foundation for the rule that when an illegal agreement is made between parties in a fiduciary relation such as attorney-client, it will be held that the client is not in pari delicto with the fiduciary,[17] at least where the client is acting on the advice of the fiduciary.[18] Intertwined in these cases are consideration of

---

11. Perma Life Mufflers v. Int'l Parts, 392 U.S. 134 (1968) [overruled on other grounds; Copperweld v. Independence Tube, 467 U.S. 752 (1984)]; see Comment, 60 Cal.L.Rev. 572 (1972); Note, In Pari Delicto: The Consumer's Best Friend, 30 Ohio St.L.J. 332 (1969). For another example of legislation designed to protect a class, see McAllister v. Drapeau, 14 Cal.2d 102, 92 P.2d 911, 125 ALR 800 (1939) (mortgage in violation of H.O.L.C. Act).

12. Watts v. Malatesta, 262 N.Y. 80, 186 N.E. 210, 88 ALR 1072 (1933); contra, Elias v. Gill, 92 Ky. 569, 18 S.W. 454 (1892) (professional permitted to set off losses).

13. Christ Gatzonis Elec. Contr. v. School Constr. Auth., 297 A.D.2d 272, 745 N.Y.S.2d 914 (2002).

14. 6A Corbin § 1537; see Southwestern Underground Supply v. Amerivac, 894 S.W.2d 15 (Tex.App.1994). However it is often urged that this exception should be confined to cases in which the defendant misled the plaintiff into believing that the transaction would be lawful. American Mu-

tual Life Ins. v. Bertram, 163 Ind. 51, 70 N.E. 258 (1904); Cooper v. Gossett, 263 N.Y. 491, 189 N.E. 562 (1934).

15. Dornberger v. Metropolitan Life Ins., 961 F.Supp. 506 (S.D.N.Y.1997) (policy set aside as illegal).

16. Stewart v. Wright, 147 F. 321 (8th Cir.1906), cert. denied; Lockman v. Cobb, 77 Ark. 279, 91 S.W. 546 (1905); Hobbs v. Boatright, 195 Mo. 693, 93 S.W. 934 (1906); Falkenberg v. Allen, 18 Okl. 210, 90 P. 415 (1907); see also Catts v. Phalen, 43 U.S. (2 How.) 376 (1844); Grim v. Cheatwood, 208 Okl. 570, 257 P.2d 1049 (1953); Annot., 39 ALR2d 1213 (1955).

17. Singleton v. Foreman, 435 F.2d 962 (5th Cir.1970); Berman v. Coakley, 243 Mass. 348, 137 N.E. 667, 26 ALR 92 (1923); 32 Yale L.J. 745 (1923); Place v. Hayward, 117 N.Y. 487, 23 N.E. 25 (1889); Peyton v. Margiotti, 398 Pa. 86, 156 A.2d 865 (1959).

18. The parties are in pari delicto where the client is the "dominant mind" in the transaction. Schermerhorn v. De Chambrun, 64 F. 195 (2d Cir.1894).

the superior influence which an attorney may exercise on clients as well as the consideration that attorneys must not be permitted to abuse their quasi-public status.

A person entering into an illegal transaction under duress may not be in pari delicto with the party exercising the coercion.[19] This occurs most often in case where a plaintiff seeks restitution of a payment that was made in consideration for the defendant's agreement not to press criminal charges against the plaintiff or against the plaintiff's close relative. The majority of these cases have indicated that, absent special circumstances, the parties are in pari delicto and the plaintiff may have no recovery whether or not the defendant has kept the illegal promise.[20] The same policy leads to the rule that the promise not to press charges is unenforceable.[21] A number of cases have indicated, however, that restitution is available if the party was innocent of the crime for which prosecution was threatened.[22]

Restitution has generally been allowed in cases in which a debtor has been coerced secretly to pay a creditor more than the agreed proportion under a composition agreement with creditors.[23] The degree of duress in such cases is doubtless no stronger than in the cases involving threatened criminal prosecutions. The different degrees of moral turpitude are, we believe, the basis for the differing results.

§ 22.8 Restitution—Locus Poenitentiae

The doctrine of locus poenitentiae is another exception to the general rule that the court leaves the parties to an illegal bargain where it finds them. Even if the plaintiff is in pari delicto and therefore as blameworthy or more blameworthy than the defendant, the plaintiff is entitled to disaffirm the bargain and obtain restitution by acting in time to prevent the attainment of the illegal purpose for which the bargain was made, unless the mere making of the bargain involves serious moral turpitude.[1]

---

19. Karpinski v. Collins, 252 Cal.App.2d 711, 60 Cal.Rptr. 846 (1967) (dairyman permitted to recover kick-backs paid to president of supplier where no other supply of milk was available); 6A Corbin § 1537; Wade, supra n. 4, at 272–76.

20. Baker v. Citizens Bank, 282 Ala. 33, 208 So.2d 601 (1968); Union Exch. Nat. Bank v. Joseph, 231 N.Y. 250, 131 N.E. 905, 17 ALR 323 (1921); Ellis v. Peoples Nat. Bank, 166 Va. 389, 186 S.E. 9 (1936); contra, Gorringe v. Read, 23 Utah 120, 63 P. 902 (1901). The mere fact that an agreement is made to make restitution for a criminal act does not make the agreement illegal. A promise to stifle prosecution is required. Blair Milling v. Fruitager, 113 Kan. 432, 215 P. 286, 32 ALR 416 (1923). See also § 9.4 supra.

21. Cariveau v. Halferty, 83 Cal.App.4th 126, 99 Cal.Rptr.2d 417 (App.2000).

22. Sykes v. Thompson, 160 N.C. 348, 76 S.E. 252 (1912). Restitution may be granted if the person exercising the duress did not believe in the charge. Union Exch. Nat. Bank v. Joseph, 231 N.Y. 250, 131 N.E. 905 (1921) (dictum).

23. Batchelder & Lincoln v. Whitmore, 122 F. 355 (1st Cir.1903); Brown v. Everett–Ridley–Ragan, 111 Ga. 404, 36 S.E. 813 (1900).

§ 22.8

1. Woel v. Griffith, 253 Md. 451, 253 A.2d 353 (1969); Rs. 2d § 199(a); 6A Corbin § 1541; 2 Palmer on Restitution § 8.7 (1978).

The doctrine has been justified on the grounds that it frustrates the carrying out of illegal schemes[2] and that in fairness and morality the plaintiff should have an opportunity to repent. Repentance in a moral sense is not, however, usually required and the courts will not generally inquire into what motivated the plaintiff in repudiating the bargain.[3] Indeed, in cases for restitution of money deposited with a stakeholder for wagering purposes it is often held that the repenting bettor may recover even after the event wagered upon has occurred.[4] In such cases, it is usually apparent that the plaintiff does not repent having violated the law but repents only having lost the wager.

The plaintiff is generally not permitted to withdraw if any part of the illegal performance is consummated.[5] Some cases, however, permit withdrawal any time before the illegal aspects are substantially performed.[6]

Although restitution is generally not granted when the bargain involves moral turpitude, at least one jurisdiction has made a strong case to the contrary,[7] arguing that the basis of the doctrine is:

> to protect society from the influence of contracts made in disregard of the public weal by reducing the number of such transactions to a minimum, and by interrupting the progress of illegal undertakings before the evil purpose has been fully consummated. To hold that the hand of the court is stayed merely because of the pernicious character of the illegal promise, or solely because its performance was not sooner arrested seems like a perversion of the real purpose of the doctrine * * *. The real question at issue in any particular case is whether the ends of the law will be furthered or defeated by granting relief.

Although it is generally said that repentance comes too late if it comes only after the other party to the bargain has reneged, or attainment of the unlawful purpose is seen to be impossible,[8] this rule also finds its exceptions.[9]

---

2. Cleveland C., C. & St. L. Ry. v. Hirsch, 204 F. 849 (6th Cir.1913); Harrington v. Bochenski, 140 Md. 24, 116 A. 836 (1922).

3. See Aikman v. Wheeling, 120 W.Va. 46, 195 S.E. 667, 669 (1938); but see Adams–Mitchell v. Cambridge Distributing, 189 F.2d 913 (2d Cir.1951).

4. Lewy v. Crawford, 5 Tex.Civ.App. 293, 23 S.W. 1041, 1043 (1893) ("not a question of sorrow and repentance, but one of disaffirming and destroying a contract made in violation of law and morals."); 6A Corbin §§ 1484, 1541.

5. See Stone v. Freeman, 298 N.Y. 268, 82 N.E.2d 571, 8 ALR2d 304 (1948) (part of the bribe money reached its destination);

but cf. Gehres v. Ater, 148 Ohio St. 89, 73 N.E.2d 513, 172 ALR 693 (1947) (recovery permitted for value of bond deposited as security for payment of a gambling debt).

6. Kearley v. Thomson, [1870] 24 Q.B.D. 742, 747 (C.A.); Ware v. Spinney, 76 Kan. 289, 91 P. 787 (1907).

7. Meredith v. Fullerton, 83 N.H. 124, 139 A. 359, 365 (1927); accord, Greenberg v. Evening Post Ass'n, 91 Conn. 371, 99 A. 1037 (1917).

8. Bigos v. Bousted, [1951] 1 All E.R. 92 (K.B.); 6A Corbin § 1541.

9. Liebman v. Rosenthal, 185 Misc. 837, 57 N.Y.S.2d 875 (1945), aff'd 269 A.D. 1062, 59 N.Y.S.2d 148 (1945) (alternative ground).

§ 22.9 Change of Law or Facts After the Bargain Is Made

If A and B enter into a legal contract that subsequently becomes illegal, the issue is impossibility of performance.[1] A different problem is presented if the contract is illegal when formed but subsequently contracts of that type become legal as a result of a change in fact or a change in law. The general rule is that a change of law does not validate a contract that was originally illegal and unenforceable.[2] However, the contract may be ratified.[3] Moreover, there are exceptions when the repealing statute expressly so states or where this is implied as for example "when the policy underlying the original statute or the extent of its prohibition is doubtful."[4]

Where the bargain is illegal and a change of facts removes the cause of the illegality the contract does not thereby become enforceable except where either party did not know or have reason to know of the illegality.[5] Where a change in fact occurs that removes the cause of the illegality the parties may subsequently ratify the agreement.[6]

22.10 Illegality in Attorney Contracts

Lawyers have always needed fees to survive, but medieval society frowned on lawyers' marketing their services. Indeed, the ban on lawyers' marketing was stringently enforced by leaders of the profession until recent decades. However, illicit marketing in medieval times did not take the form of advertising.[1] Rather, it was the financing of litigation that was disquieting and prohibited. Blackstone described a triad of related crimes: barratry,[2] maintenance, and champerty, where the "offender," he laments, "(as is too often the case) belongs to the profession of law."[3] These offenses involved the stirring up of litigation

---

§ 22.9

1. See § 13.5 supra.

2. Fitzsimons v. Eagle Brewing, 107 F.2d 712, 126 ALR 681 (3d Cir.1939); Reno v. D'Javid, 42 N.Y.2d 1040, 399 N.Y.S.2d 210, 369 N.E.2d 766 (1977); but see Bloch v. Frankfort Distillery, 273 N.Y. 469, 6 N.E.2d 408 (1936).

3. TCA Bldg. v. Northwestern Resources, 922 S.W.2d 629 (Tex.App.1996).

4. 6A Corbin § 1532 (e.g., Sunday law statutes and usury statutes); Goldfarb v. Goldfarb, 86 A.D.2d 459, 450 N.Y.S.2d 212 (1982); cf. Teh, the Subsequent Validation of Illegal Contracts, 9 Irish Jurist 42 (1974) (distinguishing void and unenforceable contracts). The problem here discussed is but one aspect of the general problem of the retroactive applicability of civil legislation. For a thorough survey centered on corporation laws, see McNulty, Corporations and the Intertemporal Conflict of Laws, 55 Calif.L.Rev. 12 (1967).

5. Rs. 1st § 609.

6. 6A Corbin § 1532.

§ 22.10

1. Lawyers' advertising was a violation of the Code of Professional Responsibility. However, the ban on advertising was held to be a violation of the first amendment's free speech clause in Bates v. State Bar of Arizona, 433 U.S. 350 (1977). Later cases have broadened further the advertising rights of lawyers. See Shapero v. Kentucky Bar Ass'n, 486 U.S. 466 (1988).

2. Blackstone calls it "barretry," but his spelling appears aberrant. IV W. Blackstone, Commentaries on the Laws of England 133–34 (1769).

3. Id. Although these offenses are not limited to lawyers, two centuries after Blackstone, a commentator notes that the terms champerty and maintenance "have come to be applied almost exclusively to the activities of lawyers." MacKinnon, Contingent Fees for Legal Services: Report of the American Bar Foundation 37 (1964). Interestingly, the Saladini case, cited below, ap-

(barratry), the financing of litigation (maintenance), and splitting the fruits of litigation (champerty).

This arcane chapter of the law is rarely, if ever, played out in the criminal courts. Rather, the issue usually surfaces by way of a defense of illegality to a claim for payment of a fee or for breach of contract. There is an obvious tension between the growth of free assignability of assets and the doctrine of champerty. There is also tension between the legality of contingent fees and the illegality of the barratry, maintenance, and champerty triad. The triad has become incoherent.[4] Corbin squares the prohibition against champerty and the legality of the contingent fee in this language: "a bargain is not champertous if the contingent fee is not a share of the money or other thing recovered but is merely measured by a specified percentage of the value of the recovery."[5] This nicely finesses the issue, but when one recalls that the lawyer has a charging lien in the sum recovered, Corbin's distinction becomes rather flimsy. Indeed, many jurisdictions hold that, although a lawyer cannot enforce a champertous contract, the lawyer may recover the reasonable value of his or her services in quasi contract for services rendered under such a contract.[6] The Massachusetts Supreme Judicial court abolished the triad of offenses in 1997.[7] In so doing, it quoted from an earlier decision which had noted that "the decline of champerty, maintenance, and barratry as offences is symptomatic of a fundamental change in society's view of litigation from 'a social ill, which like other disputes and quarrels, should be minimized' to 'a socially useful way to resolve disputes.'"[8]

The Restatement of the Law Governing Lawyers provides for a limited survival of the ban on champerty. Lawyers may not acquire a proprietary interest in the client's cause of action.[9] The Restatement, however, does not forbid the assignment of a cause of action by a client to the client's lawyer provided that the lawyer had not represented the client in asserting the claim.[10] As to maintenance, it authorizes lawyers to advance litigation expenses on behalf of clients, even on a contingency

---

pears to involve only lay persons. The case of Accrued Fin. Services v. Prime Retail, 298 F.3d 291 (4th Cir.2002), dismissing a suit as champertous. apparently involved accountants.

Although lawyers may have been the major culprits in Blackstone's time, it is likely that the first rules against maintenance were aimed at the rich and powerful. Champerty as We Know It, 13 Memphis State L.Rev. 139 (1983) (concentrating on champerty and real property rules); Maintenance by Champerty, 24 Cal. L.Rev. 48 (1935); Winfield, The History of Maintenance and Champerty, 35 L.Q. Rev. 50 (1919).

4. Incoherent, but not dead. If the precise terms of the rule in a particular jurisdiction are violated, the champertous agreement will not be enforced. Thus, where a counterclaim was assigned to a defendant

who could pursue the counterclaim at his own expense and retain a portion of the proceeds, the counterclaim was dismissed. Kenrich v. Miller, 377 F.2d 312 (3d Cir. 1967); see also Ehrlich v. Rebco Ins. Exch., 225 A.D.2d 75, 649 N.Y.S.2d 672 (1996).

5. 6A Corbin on Contracts § 1422.

6. Application of Kamerman, 278 F.2d 411 (2d Cir.1960) (collecting authorities).

7. Saladini v. Righellis, 426 Mass. 231, 687 N.E.2d 1224 (Mass.1997) (financier agreed to furnish funds to allow defendant to pursue certain claims in return for reimbursement from proceeds of the claim and 50% of the net recovery).

8. Id. at 1226. The internal quotes are from MacKinnon, supra note 3 at 210.

9. Rs. § 36(1).

10. Id. cmt. b.

fee basis.[11] The commentary to the Restatement's rules on champerty and maintenance warns the lawyer that its provisions may conflict with state laws.

The Restatement treats the client's grant to the lawyer of literary or media rights with respect to the representation as a "forbidden" "financial arrangement."[12] Such a direct or indirect grant would give the lawyer the incentive to generate the maximum publicity about and suspense surrounding the representation. It would also involve the possible disclosing of confidential information. The Restatement does not indicate the consequences of the violation of the prohibition. Presumably, the intention is to render such a grant void. The case law has not dealt with the respective rights of lawyer and client to the client's story under such a grant. Rather, the issue has played out in criminal cases on the question of effectiveness of counsel, and in disciplinary proceedings.[13]

Because of the disciplinary rule and the criminal cases where the client's grant of media rights to the lawyer provoked disturbances in otherwise normal proceedings, courts will almost certainly declare such grants to be against public policy and void. Once again, we see a situation in which a different legal regime exists for lawyers than for anyone else. While contract law generally holds that agreements against public policy are void, here, a rule of public policy has been created that applies only to lawyers. This time, members of the bar are burdened with a prohibition that applies to no other group.

---

11. Id. § 48(2)(a).

12. Id. § 48(3); accord, Model Rule 1.8(d), and DR 5–104(B).

13. The case law is described in John Gibeaut, Defend and Tell: Lawyers Who Cash in on Media Deals for Their Clients' Stories may Wish They'd Kept their Mouths Shut, 82 A.B.A. J. 64 (Dec. 1996).

Appendix

RESEARCHING CONTRACT LAW ON WESTLAW®

Analysis

Section 1. Introduction

Contracts provides a strong base for analyzing even the most complex problem involving issues related to contracts. Whether your research requires examination of case law, statutes, expert commentary, or other materials, West books and Westlaw are excellent sources of information.

To keep you informed of current developments, Westlaw provides frequently updated databases. With Westlaw, you have unparalleled legal research resources at your fingertips.

Additional Resources

If you have not previously used Westlaw or if you have questions not covered in this appendix, call the West Reference Attorneys at 1–800–REF–ATTY (1–800–733–2889). The West Reference Attorneys are trained, licensed attorneys, available 24 hours a day to assist you with your Westlaw search questions. To subscribe to Westlaw, call 1–800–344–5008 or visit westlaw.com at **www.westlaw.com**.

Section 2. Westlaw Databases

Each database on Westlaw is assigned an abbreviation called an *identifier*, which you can use to access the database. You can find identifiers for Westlaw databases in the online Westlaw Directory and in the printed *Westlaw Database Directory*. When you need to know more detailed information about a database, use Scope. Scope contains coverage information, lists of related databases, and valuable search tips.

The following chart lists selected Westlaw databases that contain information pertaining to the law of contracts. For a complete list of contract law databases, see the online Westlaw Directory or the printed *Westlaw Database Directory*. Because new information is continually being added to Westlaw, you should also check the tabbed Westlaw page and the online Westlaw Directory for new database information.

Selected Contract Law Databases on Westlaw

Database	Identifier	Coverage
Federal and State Case Law Combined		
Federal and State Case Law	ALLCASES	Begins with 1945
Federal and State Case Law–Before 1945	ALLCASES–OLD	1789–1944
Federal Case Law		
Federal Commercial Law and Contracts–Cases	FCML–CS	Begins with 1789
Federal Commercial Law and Contracts–Supreme Court Cases	FCML–SCT	Begins with 1790
Federal Commercial Law and Contracts–Courts of Appeals Cases	FCML–CTA	Begins with 1891
Federal Commercial Law and Contracts–District Courts Cases	FCML–DCT	Begins with 1789

Federal Statutes and Regulations

Database	Identifier	Coverage
Federal Commercial Law and Contracts– U.S. Code Annotated	FCML–USCA	Current data
Uniform Computer Information Transactions Act	UCITA	Current data
Uniform Electronic Transactions Act	UETA	Current data
Uniform Laws Annotated®	ULA	Current data
Federal Commercial Law and Contracts– Code of Federal Regulations	FCML–CFR	Current data
Federal Commercial Law and Contracts– Federal Register	FCML–FR	Begins with July 1980
Legislative History– U.S. Code, 1948 to Present	LH	Begins with 1948

State Materials

Database	Identifier	Coverage
Multistate Commercial Law and Contracts Cases	MCML–CS	Varies by state
Individual State Commercial Law and Contracts Cases	XXCML–CS (where XX is a state's two-letter postal abbreviation)	Varies by state
State Statutes– Annotated	ST–ANN–ALL	Varies by jurisdiction
Individual State Statutes–Annotated	XX–ST–ANN (where XX is a state's two-letter postal abbreviation)	Current data

Uniform Commercial Code (UCC) Materials

Database	Identifier	Coverage
Uniform Commercial Code Cases	UCC–CS	Begins with 1898
Uniform Commercial Code Cases Plus	UCC–CS+	Begins with 1898
Uniform Commercial Code Official Text	UCC–TEXT	Current data
Uniform Commercial Code–Revised Article 9. Secured Transactions	UCC–SECTR	2002 revision

Database	Identifier	Coverage
Uniform Commercial Code Records– Combined	UCC–ALL	Current data
Uniform Commercial Code Records– Individual State	UCC–XX (where XX is a state's two-letter postal abbreviation)	Current data
UCC, Lien, and Civil Judgment Records– Combined	ULJ–ALL	Varies by source
UCC, Lien, and Civil Judgment Records– Individual State	ULJ–XX (where XX is a state's two-letter postal abbreviation)	Varies by source
Anderson on the Uniform Commercial Code	ANDR–UCC	Third edition
Tennessee Practice Series: Uniform Commercial Code Forms	TNPRAC–UCC	Current data
Uniform Commercial Code Series (Hawkland)	HAWKLAND	Current data
Uniform Commercial Code Law Letter	UCCLAWLET	Begins with January 2002
Uniform Commercial Code Official National Forms	UCC–ART9FM	Current data
Uniform Commercial Code Permanent Editorial Board Commentary	UCC–PEB	Current data
Uniform Commercial Code State Variation Service	UCC–VAR	Current data
West's® McKinney's® Forms–Uniform Commercial Code	MCF–UCC	Current data
White and Summers' Uniform Commercial Code	WS–UCC	Current data

Legal Texts, Periodicals, and Practice Materials

Commercial Law and Contracts–Law Reviews, Texts, and Bar Journals	CML–TP	Varies by publication
Calculating Construction Damages	JW–CCD	Current edition

Database	Identifier	Coverage
Commercial Arbitration	CMLARB	Current data
Commercial Ground Leases	PLIREF–COMLEAS	Current data
Construction Lawyer	CONSLAW	Selected coverage begins with 1987 (vol. 7)
Domke on Commercial Arbitration	DCMLARB	Current data
E–Commerce Law and Strategy	ECOMLS	Begins with March 1995
Fifty State Construction Lien and Bond Law	JW–CLBL	Current edition
Journal of Law and Commerce	JLCOM	Selected coverage begins with 1984 (vol. 4); full coverage begins with 1993 (vol. 13)
Law of Fraudulent Transactions	FRAUDTRAN	Current data
Law of Product Warranties	PRODWARR	Current data
Modern Law of Contracts	MODCON	Current data
PLI Commercial Materials from Both Course Handbooks and Reference Books	PLICOMM–ALL	Current data
Restatement of the Law–Contracts	REST–CONTR	1981 and updating appendixes
Syracuse Journal of International Law and Commerce	SYRJILC	Selected coverage begins with 1983 (vol. 10); full coverage begins with 1994 (vol. 20)
Williston on Contracts 4th	WILLSTN–CN	Current data
Williston on Contracts 4th–Forms	WILLSTN–FM	Current data
Williston on Contracts 4th–Treatise and Forms	WILSTN–ALL	Current data

News and Information

Westlaw Topical Highlights–Commercial Law	WTH–CML	Current data

Database	Identifier	Coverage
Westlaw Topical High-lights—E–Commerce	WTH–ECOMM	Current data

Directories		
West Legal Directo-ry®–Commercial	WLD–CML	Current data
West Legal Directory–Construction	WLD–CST	Current data

Section 3. Retrieving a Document with a Citation: Find and Hypertext Links

3.1 Find

Find is a Westlaw service that allows you to retrieve a document by entering its citation. Find allows you to retrieve documents from any-where on Westlaw without accessing or changing databases. Find is available for many documents, including case law (state and federal), the *United States Code Annotated*®, state statutes, administrative materials, and texts and periodicals.

To use Find, simply type the citation in the *Find this document by citation* text box on the tabbed Westlaw page and click **GO**. The following list provides some examples:

To Find This Document	Access Find and Type
Mobil Oil Exploration and Producing Southeast, Inc. v. United States 120 S. Ct. 2423 (2000)	**120 sct 2423**
Hawkins v. McGee, 146 A. 641 (N.H. 1929)	**146 a 641**
15 U.S.C.A. § 1635	**15 USCA 1635**
48 C.F.R. § 52.203–8	**48 cfr 52.203–8**
Cal. Civ. Code § 1689.5	**CA civ § 1689.5**
N.Y. U.C.C. Law § 2–106	**ny ucc § 2–106**

For a complete list of publications that can be retrieved with Find and their abbreviations, click **Find** on the toolbar and then click **Publications List**.

3.2 Hypertext Links

Use hypertext links to move from one location to another on Westlaw. For example, use hypertext links to go directly from the statute, case, or law review article you are viewing to a cited statute, case, or article; from a headnote to the corresponding text in the opinion;

or from an entry in a statutes index database to the full text of the statute.

Section 4. Searching with Natural Language

Overview: With Natural Language, you can retrieve documents by simply describing your issue in plain English. If you are a relatively new Westlaw user, Natural Language searching can make it easier for you to retrieve cases that are on point. If you are an experienced Westlaw user, Natural Language gives you a valuable alternative search method to the Terms and Connectors search method described in Section 5.

When you enter a Natural Language description, Westlaw automatically identifies legal phrases, removes common words, and generates variations of terms in your description. Westlaw then searches for the concepts in your description. Concepts may include significant terms, phrases, legal citations, or topic and key numbers. Westlaw retrieves the documents that most closely match the concepts in your description, beginning with the document most likely to match.

4.1 Natural Language Search

Access a database, such as the Multistate Commercial Law and Contracts Cases database (MCML–CS). Click **Natural Language** and type the following description in the text box:

when is promissory estoppel an exception to the statute of frauds

4.2 Browsing Search Results

Best Mode: To display the best portion (the portion that most closely matches your description) of each document in a Natural Language search result, click the **Best** arrows at the bottom of the right frame.

Term Mode: Click the **Term** arrows at the bottom of the right frame to display portions of the document that contain your search terms.

Previous/Next Document: Click the left or right **Doc** arrow at the bottom of the right frame to view the previous or the next document in the search result.

Citations List: The citations list in the left frame lists the documents retrieved by the search. Click a hypertext link to display a document in the right frame.

4.3 Next 20 Documents

Westlaw displays the 20 documents that most closely match the concepts in your Natural Language description, beginning with the document most likely to match. If you want to view an additional 20 documents, click the right arrow in the left frame.

Section 5. Searching with Terms and Connectors

Overview: With Terms and Connectors searching, you enter a query, which consists of key terms from your issue and connectors specifying the relationship between these terms.

Terms and Connectors searching is useful when you want to retrieve a document for which you know specific details, such as the title or the fact situation. Terms and Connectors searching is also useful when you want to retrieve all documents containing specific terms.

5.1 Terms

Plurals and Possessives: Plurals are automatically retrieved when you enter the singular form of a term. This is true for both regular and irregular plurals (e.g., **child** retrieves *children*). If you enter the plural form of a term, you will not retrieve the singular form.

If you enter the nonpossessive form of a term, Westlaw automatically retrieves the possessive form as well. However, if you enter the possessive form, only the possessive form is retrieved.

Compound Words, Abbreviations, and Acronyms: When a compound word is one of your search terms, use a hyphen to retrieve all forms of the word. For example, the term **non-compensatory** retrieves *non-compensatory, noncompensatory,* and *non compensatory.*

When using an abbreviation or acronym as a search term, place a period after each of the letters to retrieve any of its forms. For example, the term **u.c.c.** retrieves *UCC, U.C.C., U C C,* and *U. C. C.* Note: The abbreviation does not retrieve *uniform commercial code,* so remember to add additional alternative terms such as **"uniform commercial code"** to your query.

The Root Expander and the Universal Character: When you use the Terms and Connectors search method, placing the root expander (!) at the end of a root term generates all other terms with that root. For example, adding the ! to the root *promis* in the query

promis! /s note

instructs Westlaw to retrieve such terms as *promise, promised, promising,* and *promissory.*

The universal character (*) stands for one character and can be inserted in the middle or at the end of a term. For example, the term

withdr*w

will retrieve *withdraw* and *withdrew*. Adding three asterisks to the root *elect*

elect* * *

instructs Westlaw to retrieve all forms of the root with up to three additional characters. Terms such as *elected* or *election* are retrieved by this query. However, terms with more than three letters following the root, such as *electronic,* are not retrieved. Plurals are always retrieved, even if the plural form of the term has more than three letters following the root.

Phrase Searching: To search for an exact phrase, place it within quotation marks. For example, to search for references to *equitable* estoppel, *type **"equitable estoppel"**. When you are using the Terms and Connectors search method, you should use phrase searching only if you are certain that the terms in the phrase will not appear in any other order.*

5.2 Alternative Terms

After selecting the terms for your query, consider which alternative terms are necessary. For example, if you are searching for the term *constitutional*, you might also want to search for the term *unconstitutional*. You should consider both synonyms and antonyms as alternative terms. You can also use the Westlaw thesaurus to add alternative terms to your query.

5.3 Connectors

After selecting terms and alternative terms for your query, use connectors to specify the relationship that should exist between search terms in your retrieved documents. The connectors are described below:

Type:	To retrieve documents with:	Example:
& (and)	both terms	**offer & acceptance**
or (space)	either term or both terms	**assent acceptance**
/p	search terms in the same paragraph	**past /p consideration**
/s	earch terms in the same sentence	**material! /s alter!**
+s	the first search term preceding the second within the same sentence	**freedom +s contract**
/n	search terms within *n* terms of each other (where *n* is a number)	**detrimental /5 reliance**
+n	the first search term preceding the second by *n* terms (where *n* is a number)	**third-party +3 beneficiary**
" "	search terms appearing in the same order as in the quotation marks	**"parol evidence"**

Type:	To exclude documents with:	Example:
% (but not)	search terms following the % symbol	**fraud % "statute of frauds"**

5.4 Field Restrictions

Overview: Documents in each Westlaw database consist of several segments, or fields. One field may contain the citation, another the title, another the synopsis, and so forth. Not all databases contain the same fields. Also depending on the database, fields with the same name may contain different types of information.

To view a list of fields and their contents for a specific database, see Scope for that database. Note that in some databases not every field is available for every document.

To retrieve only those documents containing your search terms in a specific field, restrict your search to that field. To restrict your search to a specific field, type the field name or abbreviation followed by your search terms enclosed in parentheses. For example, to retrieve a U.S. Supreme Court case titled *Mobil Oil Exploration and Producing Southeast, Inc. v. United States*, access the Federal Commercial Law and Contracts–Supreme Court Cases database (FCML–SCT) and search for your terms in the title field (ti):

ti("mobil oil" & southeast)

The fields discussed below are available in Westlaw case law databases you might use for researching issues related to contract law.

Digest and Synopsis Fields: The digest (di) and synopsis (sy) fields, added to case law databases by West's attorney-editors, summarize the main points of a case. The synopsis field contains a brief description of a case. The digest field contains the topic and headnote fields and includes the complete hierarchy of concepts used by West's editors to classify the headnotes to specific West digest topic and key numbers. Restricting your search to the synopsis and digest fields limits your result to cases in which your terms are related to a major issue in the case.

Consider restricting your search to one or both of these fields if

- you are searching for common terms or terms with more than one meaning, and you need to narrow your search; or

- you cannot narrow your search by using a smaller database.

For example, to retrieve state cases that discuss detrimental reliance as a substitute for consideration, access the Multistate Commercial Law and Contracts Cases database (MCML–CS) and type the following query:

sy,di(detriment! /p reli! rely /p consideration)

Headnote Field: The headnote field (he) is part of the digest field but does not contain topic numbers, hierarchical classification information, or key numbers. The headnote field contains a one-sentence summary for each point of law in a case and any supporting citations given by the author of the opinion. A headnote field restriction is useful when you are searching for specific statutory sections or rule numbers. For example, to retrieve headnotes from federal cases that cite 15 U.S.C.A. § 637, access the Federal Commercial Law and Contracts–Cases database (FCML–CS) and type the following query:

he(15 +s 637)

Topic Field: The topic field (to) is also part of the digest field. It contains hierarchical classification information, including the West digest topic names and numbers and the key numbers. You should restrict search terms to the topic field in a case law database if

- a digest field search retrieves too many documents; or

- you want to retrieve cases with digest paragraphs classified under more than one topic.

For example, the topic Contracts has the topic number 95. To retrieve federal courts of appeals cases that discuss rescission of a contract based on fraud, access the Federal Commercial Law and Contracts–Courts of Appeals Cases database (FCML–CTA) and type a query like the following:

to(95) /p rescission rescind! /p fraud! misrepresent!

To retrieve cases classified under more than one topic and key number, search for your terms in the topic field. For example, to retrieve recent federal cases discussing rescission, which may be classified to Consumer Rights (92B), Contracts (95), Sales (343), or Vendor and Purchaser (400), among other topics, access the Federal Commercial Law and Contracts–Cases database (FCML–CS) and type a query like the following:

to(rescission) & da(aft 2000)

For a complete list of West digest topics and their corresponding topic numbers, access the Custom Digest by choosing **Key Numbers and Digest** from the *More* drop-down list on the toolbar.

Note: Slip opinions and cases from topical services do not contain the West digest, headnote, and topic fields.

Prelim and Caption Fields: When searching in a database containing statutes, rules, or regulations, restrict your search to the prelim (pr) and caption (ca) fields to retrieve documents in which your terms are important enough to appear in a section name or heading. For example, to retrieve federal regulations regarding procedures for bidding on Department of Defense contracts, access the Federal Commercial Law and Contracts–Code of Federal Regulations database (FCML–CFR) and type the following:

pr,ca(department /s defense & contract! & bid!)

5.5   Date Restrictions

You can use Westlaw to retrieve documents *decided* or *issued* before, after, or on a specified date, as well as within a range of dates. The following sample queries contain date restrictions:

da(2003) & "parol evidence"

da(aft 1998) & avoid! /s contract /s mistake

da(10/30/2000) & specific /5 performance

You can also search for documents *added to a database* on or after a specified date, as well as within a range of dates, which is useful for updating your research. The following sample queries contain added-date restrictions:

ad(aft 1999) & "statute of frauds"

ad(aft 12/4/2001 & bef 6/3/2002) & third-party /s beneficiary

Section 6. Searching with Topic and Key Numbers

To retrieve cases that address a specific point of law, use topic and key numbers as your search terms. If you have an on-point case, run a search using the topic and key number from the relevant headnote in an appropriate database to find other cases containing headnotes classified to that topic and key number. For example, to search for Florida cases containing headnotes classified under topic 95 (Contracts) and key number 211 (Time as of the Essence of the Contract), access the Florida Commercial Law and Contracts Cases database (FLCML–CS) and enter the following query:

95k211

For a complete list of West digest topics and their corresponding topic numbers, access the Custom Digest by choosing **Key Numbers and Digest** from the *More* drop-down list on the toolbar.

Note: Slip opinions and cases from topical services do not contain West topic and key numbers.

6.1 Custom Digest

The Custom Digest contains the complete topic and key number outline used by West attorney-editors to classify headnotes. You can use the Custom Digest to obtain a single document containing all case law headnotes from a specific jurisdiction that are classified under a particular topic and key number.

Access the Custom Digest by choosing **Key Numbers and Digest** from the *More* drop-down list on the toolbar. Select up to 10 topics and key numbers from the easy-to-browse outline and click **GO**. Then follow the on-screen instructions.

For example, to research issues involving contracts, scroll down the Custom Digest page until topic 95, *Contracts*, is displayed. Click the plus symbols (+) to display key number information. Select the check box next to each key number you want to include in your search, then click **GO**. Select the jurisdiction from which you want to retrieve headnotes and, if desired, select a date restriction and type additional search terms. Click **Search**.

6.2 KeySearch

KeySearch is a research tool that helps you find cases and secondary sources in a specific area of the law. KeySearch guides you through the selection of terms from a classification system based on the West Key Number System® and then uses the key numbers and their underlying concepts to formulate a query for you. To access KeySearch, click

KeySearch on the toolbar. Then browse the list of topics and subtopics and select a topic or subtopic to search by clicking the hypertext links. For example, to search for cases that discuss an issue related to the transfer of electronic funds, click **Commercial Law and Contracts** at the first KeySearch page. Then click **Electronic Funds Transfers** on the next page. Select the source from which you want to retrieve documents and, if desired, type additional search terms. Click **Search**.

Section 7. Verifying Your Research with Citation Research Services

Overview: A citation research service, such as the KeyCite service, is a tool that helps you ensure that your cases, statutes, regulations, and administrative decisions are good law; helps you retrieve cases, legislation, articles, or other documents that cite them; and helps you verify that the spelling and format of your citations are correct.

7.1 KeyCite for Cases

KeyCite for cases covers case law on Westlaw, including unpublished opinions. KeyCite for cases provides the following:

- direct appellate history of a case, including related references, which are opinions involving the same parties and facts but resolving different issues

- negative indirect history of a case, which consists of cases outside the direct appellate line that may have a negative impact on its precedential value

- the title, parallel citations, court of decision, docket number, and filing date of a case

- citations to cases, administrative decisions, secondary sources, and briefs on Westlaw that have cited a case

- complete integration with the West Key Number System so you can track legal issues discussed in a case

7.2 KeyCite for Statutes and Federal Regulations

KeyCite for statutes and federal regulations covers the *United States Code Annotated* (USCA®), the *Code of Federal Regulations* (CFR), and statutes from all 50 states. KeyCite for statutes and regulations provides

- links to session laws or rules amending or repealing a statute or regulation

- statutory credits and historical notes

- citations to pending legislation affecting a federal statute or a statute from California or New York

- citations to cases, administrative decisions, secondary sources, and briefs that have cited a statute or regulation

7.3   KeyCite for Administrative Materials

KeyCite for administrative materials includes the following:

- National Labor Relations Board decisions beginning with 1935
- Board of Contract Appeals decisions (varies by agency)
- Board of Immigration Appeals decisions beginning with 1940
- Comptroller General decisions beginning with 1921
- Environmental Protection Agency decisions beginning with 1974
- Federal Communications Commission decisions beginning with 1960
- Federal Energy Regulatory Commission (Federal Power Commission) decisions beginning with 1931
- Internal Revenue Service revenue rulings beginning with 1954
- Internal Revenue Service revenue procedures beginning with 1954
- Internal Revenue Service private letter rulings beginning with 1954
- Internal Revenue Service technical advice memoranda beginning with 1954
- Public Utilities Reports beginning with 1966
- U.S. Merit Systems Protection Board decisions beginning with 1979
- U.S. Patent and Trademark Office decisions beginning with 1984
- U.S. Tax Court (Board of Tax Appeals) decisions beginning with 1924
- U.S. patents beginning with 1976

7.4   KeyCite Alert

KeyCite Alert monitors the status of your cases, statutes, regulations, and administrative decisions and automatically sends you updates at the frequency you specify when their KeyCite information changes.

Section 8. Researching with Westlaw—Examples
8.1   Retrieving Law Review Articles

Recent law review articles are often a good place to begin researching a legal issue because law review articles serve 1) as an excellent introduction to a new topic or review for an old one, providing terminology to help you formulate a query; 2) as a finding tool for pertinent primary authority, such as rules, statutes, and cases; and 3) in some instances, as persuasive secondary authority.

Suppose you need to gain background information on implied contracts in at-will employment situations.

Solution

- To retrieve recent law review articles relevant to your issue, access the Commercial Law and Contracts–Law Reviews, Texts, and Bar Journals database (CML–TP). Using the Natural Language search method, enter a description like the following:

implied contracts in at-will employment

- If you have a citation to an article in a specific publication, use Find to retrieve it. For more information on Find, see Section 3.1 of this appendix. For example, to retrieve the article found at 45 UCLA L. Rev. 817, access Find and type

45 ucla l rev 817

- If you know the title of an article but not which journal it appeared in, access the Journals and Law Reviews database (JLR) and search for key terms in the title field. For example, to retrieve the article "The Implied-in-Fact Contract Exception to At–Will Employment: A Call for Reform," type the following Terms and Connectors query:

ti(implied-in-fact & exception & reform)

8.2 Retrieving Case Law

Suppose you need to retrieve New York cases dealing with breach of an agreement not to compete.

Solution

- Access the New York Commercial Law and Contracts Cases database (NYCML–CS). Type a Terms and Connectors query such as the following:

breach! /s agreement covenant /s compete non-compete

- When you know the citation for a specific case, use Find to retrieve it. For more information on Find, see Section 3.1 of this appendix. For example, to retrieve *Sager Spuck Statewide Supply Co. v. Meyer*, 751 N.Y.S.2d 318 (N.Y. App. Div. 2002), access Find and type

751 nys2d 318

- If you find a topic and key number that is on point, run a search using that topic and key number to retrieve additional cases discussing that point of law. For example, to retrieve New York state cases containing headnotes classified under topic 95 (Contracts) and key number 202(2) (Restriction of Competition), access NYCML–CS and type the following query:

95k202(2)

- To retrieve cases written by a particular judge, add a judge field (ju) restriction to your query. For example, to retrieve New York state cases written by Justice Spain that contain headnotes classified under topic 95 (Contracts), access NYCML–CS and type the following query:

ju(spain) & to(95)

- You can also use KeySearch and the Custom Digest to retrieve cases and headnotes that discuss the issue you are researching.

8.3 Retrieving Statutes and Regulations

Suppose you need to retrieve federal statutes and regulations addressing advertising requirements for public contracts.

Solution

- Access the Federal Commercial Law and Contracts–U.S. Code Annotated database (FCML–USCA). Search for your terms in the prelim and caption fields using the Terms and Connectors search method:

pr,ca(public /s contract! & advertis!)

- When you know the citation for a specific statute or regulation, use Find to retrieve it. For example, to retrieve 41 U.S.C.A. § 5, access Find and type

41 usca 5

- To look at surrounding sections, use the Table of Contents service. Click the **TOC** tab in the left frame. To display a section listed in the Table of Contents, click its hypertext link. You can also use Documents in Sequence to retrieve the section following section 5 even if that subsequent section was not retrieved with your search or Find request. Select **Docs In Seq** from the drop-down list at the bottom of the right frame and click **GO**.

- When you retrieve a statute or federal regulation on Westlaw, it will contain a red or yellow KeyCite status flag in the document header if the statute or regulation has been affected. Click the flag to display a citation to the document affecting it in the left frame.

8.4 Researching Uniform Commercial Code (UCC) Issues

Suppose you want to retrieve sections of the Uniform Commercial Code (UCC) dealing with contracts with open or missing terms.

Solution

- Access the Uniform Laws Annotated database (ULA) and type a Terms and Connectors query such as the following:

contract /s open missing incomplete /s term

- When you know the citation for a specific section of the UCC, use Find to retrieve it. For example, to retrieve section 2–206 of the UCC, access Find and type

ucc 2–206

- To determine whether a particular state has adopted the UCC and made any changes to the uniform version, access the ULA database and type the following Terms and Connectors query:

ci(ucc) & "table of jurisdictions"

- To search for case law from several states that cite a particular UCC section, access the Uniform Commercial Code Cases (UCC–CS) or Uniform Commercial Code Cases Plus (UCC–CS+) database. Standard UCC section numbers follow the state section numbers in your retrieved documents. For example, to retrieve references to section 2–206, type the following query:

2–206

8.5 Using KeyCite

Suppose one of the cases you retrieve in your case law research is *Grundstad v. Ritt*, 166 F.3d 867 (7th Cir. 1999).

Solution

- Use KeyCite to retrieve direct and negative indirect history for *Grundstad v. Ritt*.

- Use KeyCite to display citing references for *Grundstad v. Ritt*.

8.6 Following Recent Developments

If you are researching issues related to contract law, it is important to keep up with recent developments. How can you do this efficiently?

Solution

One of the easiest ways to follow recent developments in contract law is to access the Westlaw Topical Highlights–Commercial Law database (WTH–CML). The WTH–CML database contains summaries of recent legal developments, including court decisions, legislation, and materials released by administrative agencies in the area of contract law. When you access WTH–CML, you automatically retrieve a list of documents added to the database in the last two weeks.

You can also use the WestClip® clipping service to stay informed of recent developments of interest to you. WestClip will run your Terms and Connectors queries on a regular basis and deliver the results to you automatically. You can run WestClip queries in legal and news and information databases.

*

Table of Cases

Besco, Inc. v. Alpha Portland Cement Co., 619 F.2d 447 (5th Cir.1980)—§ **4.12, n. 47.**

Besinger v. National Tea Co., 75 Ill.App.2d 395, 221 N.E.2d 156 (Ill.App. 1 Dist. 1966)—§ **16.5, n. 18.**

Besser v. K. L. T. Associates, Inc., 42 A.D.2d 725, 345 N.Y.S.2d 659 (N.Y.A.D. 2 Dept.1973)—§ **2.8, n. 17.**

Bestor v. American Nat. Stores, Inc., 691 S.W.2d 384 (Mo.App. E.D.1985)—§ **21.5, n. 6.**

Betaco, Inc. v. Cessna Aircraft Co., 32 F.3d 1126 (7th Cir.1994)—§ **3.6, n. 7.**

Bethlehem Steel Co., United States v., 205 U.S. 105, 27 S.Ct. 450, 51 L.Ed. 731 (1907)—§ **14.31, n. 6, 25.**

Bethlehem Steel Corp., United States v., 315 U.S. 289, 62 S.Ct. 581, 86 L.Ed. 855 (1942)—§ **9.2, n. 10.**

Bethpage Theatre Co., Inc. v. Shekel, 133 A.D.2d 62, 518 N.Y.S.2d 408 (N.Y.A.D. 2 Dept.1987)—§ **11.32, n. 21.**

Bethune v. Bethune, 96 Misc.2d 507, 413 N.Y.S.2d 800 (N.Y.Sup.1976)—§ **17.3, n. 32.**

Betnar v. Rose, 259 Ark. 820, 536 S.W.2d 719 (Ark.1976)—§ **19.41, n. 1.**

Bettancourt v. Gilroy Theatre Co., 120 Cal. App.2d 364, 261 P.2d 351 (Cal.App. 1 Dist.1953)—§ **2.9, n. 26.**

Bettendorf Ed. Ass'n v. Bettendorf Community School Dist., 262 N.W.2d 550 (Iowa 1978)—§ **11.29, n. 4.**

Betterton v. First Interstate Bank of Arizona, N.A., 800 F.2d 732 (8th Cir. 1986)—§ **4.9, n. 21.**

Bettini v. Gye, 1 Q.B.D. 183 (1876)— § **11.18, n. 12.**

Betz Laboratories, Inc. v. Hines, 647 F.2d 402 (3rd Cir.1981)—§ **3.6, n. 6.**

Beverage v. Harvey, 602 F.2d 657 (4th Cir. 1979)—§ **11.29, n. 4.**

Beverage Distributors, Inc. v. Olympia Brewing Co., 440 F.2d 21 (9th Cir. 1971)—§ **2.6, n. 25.**

Beverly v. Macy, 702 F.2d 931 (11th Cir. 1983)—§ **17.3, n. 53.**

BGW Development Corp. v. Mount Kisco Lodge No. 1552 of Benev. and Protective Order of Elks of the United States of America, Inc., 247 A.D.2d 565, 669 N.Y.S.2d 56 (N.Y.A.D. 2 Dept.1998)— § **14.30, n. 8.**

Bickerstaff v. Gregston, 604 P.2d 382 (Okla. App. Div. 1 1979)—§ **6.3, n. 35.**

Biehl v. Biehl's Adm'x, 263 Ky. 710, 93 S.W.2d 836 (Ky.1936)—§ **18.7, n. 4, 12.**

Biener Contracting Corp. v. Elberon Restaurant Corp., 7 A.D.2d 391, 183 N.Y.S.2d 756 (N.Y.A.D. 1 Dept.1959)— § **19.8, n. 13.**

Bier Pension Plan Trust v. Estate of Schneierson, 546 N.Y.S.2d 824, 545 N.E.2d 1212 (N.Y.1989)—§ **4.12, n. 6.**

Big Diamond Mill. Co. v. Chicago, M. & St. P. Ry. Co., 142 Minn. 181, 171 N.W. 799 (Minn.1919)—§ **5.7, n. 17.**

Bigelow v. Nottingham, 833 P.2d 764 (Colo. App.1991)—§ **19.14, n. 18.**

Bigelow v. RKO Radio Pictures, 327 U.S. 251, 66 S.Ct. 574, 90 L.Ed. 652 (1946)— § **14.8, n. 18, 21.**

Biggs v. Lawrence, 3 T.R. 454, 100 Eng. Rep. 673 (K.B.1789)—§ **22.2, n. 9.**

Bigos v. Bousted, 1 All E.R. 92 (1951)— § **22.8, n. 8.**

Big O Tire Dealers, Inc. v. Big O Warehouse, 741 F.2d 160 (7th Cir.1984)— § **21.9, n. 8.**

Bilbie v. Lumley, 2 East 469, 102 E.R. 448 (KBD 1802)—§ **9.28, n. 1.**

Bill Brown Const. Co., Inc. v. Glens Falls Ins. Co., 818 S.W.2d 1 (Tenn.1991)— § **6.1, n. 4.**

Billetter v. Posell, 94 Cal.App.2d 858, 211 P.2d 621 (Cal.App. 2 Dist.1949)— § **14.15, n. 21; § 14.18, n. 4, 12.**

Bill's Coal Co., Inc. v. Board of Public Utilities of Springfield, Mo., 682 F.2d 883 (10th Cir.1982)—§ **12.1, n. 2.**

Binks Mfg. Co. v. National Presto Industries, Inc., 709 F.2d 1109 (7th Cir. 1983)—§ **3.2, n. 16.**

Birbrower, Montalbano, Condon & Frank v. Superior Court, 70 Cal.Rptr.2d 304, 949 P.2d 1 (Cal.1998)—§ **22.3, n. 1.**

Bird Lakes Development Corp. v. Meruelo, 626 So.2d 234 (Fla.App. 3 Dist.1993)— § **3.4, n. 34.**

Birmingham, City of v. Cochrane Roofing & Metal Co., Inc., 547 So.2d 1159 (Ala. 1989)—§ **7.8, n. 6.**

Birmingham Television Corp. v. Water Works, 292 Ala. 147, 290 So.2d 636 (Ala. 1974)—§ **9.42, n. 13.**

Birnbaum v. Schuler, 56 A.D.2d 556, 391 N.Y.S.2d 601 (N.Y.A.D. 1 Dept.1977)— § **22.6, n. 2.**

Birsner v. Bolles, 20 Cal.App.3d 635, 97 Cal.Rptr. 846 (Cal.App. 1 Dist.1971)— § **3.4, n. 43.**

Birznieks v. Cooper, 405 Mich. 319, 275 N.W.2d 221 (Mich.1979)—§ **2.23, n. 3.**

Bishop v. Eaton, 161 Mass. 496, 37 N.E. 665 (Mass.1894)—§ **2.15, n. 7.**

Bishop v. Lakeland Animal Hosp., P.C., 268 Ill.App.3d 114, 205 Ill.Dec. 817, 644 N.E.2d 33 (Ill.App. 2 Dist.1994)— § **16.19, n. 39.**

Bishop v. Washington, 331 Pa.Super. 387, 480 A.2d 1088 (Pa.Super.1984)—§ **9.39, n. 22.**

Bissenger v. Prince, 117 Ala. 480, 23 So. 67 (Ala.1898)—§ **2.9, n. 51.**

Bissett v. Gooch, 87 Ill.App.3d 1132, 42 Ill.Dec. 900, 409 N.E.2d 515 (Ill.App. 2 Dist.1980)—§ **16.5, n. 17.**

C

D

Ercanbrack v. Crandall–Walker Motor Co., Inc., 550 P.2d 723 (Utah 1976)—**§ 2.18, n. 19.**

ER Holdings, Inc. v. Norton Co., 735 F.Supp. 1094 (D.Mass.1990)—**§ 16.1, n. 4.**

Erickson, In re Estate of, 202 Mich.App. 329, 508 N.W.2d 181 (Mich.App.1993)—**§ 8.10, n. 17.**

Erickson v. Goodell Oil Co., 384 Mich. 207, 180 N.W.2d 798 (Mich.1970)—**§ 1.8, n. 12.**

Erickson v. Grande Ronde Lumber Co., 162 Or. 556, 94 P.2d 139 (Or.1939)—**§ 17.13, n. 4.**

Erlich v. Menezes, 87 Cal.Rptr.2d 886, 981 P.2d 978 (Cal.1999)—**§ 14.5, n. 19.**

Erling v. Homera, Inc., 298 N.W.2d 478 (N.D.1980)—**§ 11.20, n. 43.**

Ervin Const. Co. v. Van Orden, 125 Idaho 695, 874 P.2d 506 (Idaho 1993)—**§ 14.29, n. 1.**

Eschenbacher v. Anderson, 306 Mont. 321, 34 P.3d 87 (Mont.2001)—**§ 12.2, n. 4.**

Escobio v. American Intern. Group, Inc., 262 F.3d 1207 (11th Cir.2001)—**§ 22.3, n. 6.**

E.S. Herrick Co. v. Maine Wild Blueberry Co., 670 A.2d 944 (Me.1996)—**§ 4.11, n. 23.**

Eslamizar v. American States Ins. Co., 134 Or.App. 138, 894 P.2d 1195 (Or.App. 1995)—**§ 9.15, n. 1.**

Eslon Thermoplastics v. Dynamic Systems, Inc., 49 S.W.3d 891 (Tex.App.-Austin 2001)—**§ 21.2, n. 24.**

Espinal v. Melville Snow Contractors, Inc., 746 N.Y.S.2d 120, 773 N.E.2d 485 (N.Y. 2002)—**§ 17.3, n. 24.**

Estate of (see name of party)

Esterces & Associates v. Coastal Communications Corp., 271 A.D.2d 286, 707 N.Y.S.2d 62 (N.Y.A.D. 1 Dept.2000)—**§ 11.7, n. 12.**

Estes v. Republic Nat. Bank of Dallas, 462 S.W.2d 273 (Tex.1970)—**§ 3.7, n. 23; § 9.42, n. 40.**

Ets–Hokin & Galvan, Inc. v. Maas Transport, Inc., 380 F.2d 258 (8th Cir.1967)—**§ 22.1, n. 35.**

Evanovich v. Hutto, 204 So.2d 477 (Miss. 1967)—**§ 19.14, n. 31.**

Evans v. Morgan, 69 Miss. 328, 12 So. 270 (Miss.1891)—**§ 8.6, n. 4, 8.**

Evans v. Oregon & W. R. Co., 58 Wash. 429, 108 P. 1095 (Wash.1910)—**§ 4.9, n. 38.**

Evans v. Waldorf–Astoria Corp., 827 F.Supp. 911 (E.D.N.Y.1993)—**§ 9.6, n. 6.**

Evans v. Werle, 31 S.W.3d 489 (Mo.App. W.D.2000)—**§ 14.2, n. 5.**

Evening News Ass'n v. Peterson, 477 F.Supp. 77 (D.D.C.1979)—**§ 18.31, n. 21.**

Everett Plywood Corp. v. United States, 227 Ct.Cl. 415, 651 F.2d 723 (Ct.Cl. 1981)—**§ 13.12, n. 7.**

Evergreen Amusement Corp. v. Milstead, 206 Md. 610, 112 A.2d 901 (Md.1955)—**§ 14.8, n. 14.**

Everlite Mfg. Co. v. Grand Valley Mach. & Tool Co., 44 Wis.2d 404, 171 N.W.2d 188 (Wis.1969)—**§ 4.9, n. 36.**

Ever–Tite Roofing Corp. v. Green, 83 So.2d 449 (La.App. 2 Cir.1955)—**§ 2.10, n. 12.**

Evra Corp. v. Swiss Bank Corp., 673 F.2d 951 (7th Cir.1982)—**§ 14.6, n. 9.**

Examination Management Services, Inc. v. Kirschbaum, 927 P.2d 686 (Wyo.1996)—**§ 3.13, n. 6.**

Excelsior Motor Mfg. & Supply Co. v. Sound Equipment, Inc., 73 F.2d 725 (7th Cir. 1934)—**§ 14.8, n. 17.**

Executive Leasing Associates v. Rowland, 30 N.C.App. 590, 227 S.E.2d 642 (N.C.App.1976)—**§ 2.23, n. 11.**

Ex parte (see name of party)

Ezzell v. S.G. Holland Stave Co., 210 Ala. 694, 99 So. 78 (Ala.1924)—**§ 19.33, n. 4.**

F

Faber v. City of New York, 222 N.Y. 255, 118 N.E. 609 (N.Y.1918)—**§ 13.3, n. 23.**

Fabian v. Wasatch Orchard Co., 41 Utah 404, 125 P. 860 (Utah 1912)—**§ 19.44; § 19.44, n. 4.**

Faces Boutique, Ltd. v. Gibbs, 318 S.C. 39, 455 S.E.2d 707 (S.C.App.1995)—**§ 16.19, n. 27.**

Factor v. Peabody Tailoring System, 177 Wis. 238, 187 N.W. 984 (Wis.1922)—**§ 2.9, n. 20.**

Fada v. Information Sys. & Networks Corp., 98 Ohio App.3d 785, 649 N.E.2d 904 (Ohio App. 2 Dist.1994)—**§ 9.26, n. 4.**

Failor's Pharmacy v. Department of Social and Health Services, 125 Wash.2d 488, 886 P.2d 147 (Wash.1994)—**§ 22.1, n. 12.**

Faimon v. Winona State University, 540 N.W.2d 879 (Minn.App.1995)—**§ 6.1, n. 12.**

Fair v. Red Lion Inn, 943 P.2d 431 (Colo. 1997)—**§ 14.18, n. 7.**

Fairbanks, Morse & Co. v. Consolidated Fisheries Co., 190 F.2d 817 (3rd Cir. 1951)—**§ 9.44, n. 11.**

Fairchild Warehouse Associates, LLC v. United Bank of Kuwait, 285 A.D.2d 444, 727 N.Y.S.2d 153 (N.Y.A.D. 2 Dept. 2001)—**§ 5.14, n. 36.**

Fairfax County Redevelopment and Housing Authority v. Worcester Bros. Co., Inc., 257 Va. 382, 514 S.E.2d 147 (Va. 1999)—**§ 11.28, n. 20.**

G

I

J

L

N

Pugh v. Gilbreath, 571 P.2d 1241 (Okla. App. Div. 1 1977)—§ **19.15, n. 13.**

Pumphrey v. Kehoe, 261 Md. 496, 276 A.2d 194 (Md.1971)—§ **18.27, n. 3.**

Punikaia v. Clark, 720 F.2d 564 (9th Cir. 1983)—§ **17.10, n. 2.**

Purcell Tire & Rubber Co., Inc. v. Executive Beechcraft, Inc., 59 S.W.3d 505 (Mo. 2001)—§ **14.31, n. 27.**

Purchasing Associates, Inc. v. Weitz, 246 N.Y.S.2d 600, 196 N.E.2d 245 (N.Y. 1963)—§ **16.19, n. 13, 26, 29.**

Purvis v. United States for Use and Benefit of Associated Sand & Gravel Co., 344 F.2d 867 (9th Cir.1965)—§ **2.9, n. 11.**

Putnam v. Time Warner Cable of Southeastern Wisconsin, Ltd. Partnership, 255 Wis.2d 447, 649 N.W.2d 626 (Wis. 2002)—§ **9.28, n. 9.**

Pym v. Campbell, 6 El.& Bl. 370 (Q.B. 1856)—§ **3.7, n. 13.**

Q

Quake Const., Inc. v. American Airlines, Inc., 141 Ill.2d 281, 152 Ill.Dec. 308, 565 N.E.2d 990 (Ill.1990)—§ **2.6, n. 24.**

Quality Finance Co. v. Hurley, 337 Mass. 150, 148 N.E.2d 385 (Mass.1958)— § **18.17, n. 28.**

Quality Motors v. Hays, 216 Ark. 264, 225 S.W.2d 326 (Ark.1949)—§ **8.2, n. 10;** § **8.6, n. 9.**

Quality Sheet Metal Co., Ltd. v. Woods, 2 Haw.App. 160, 627 P.2d 1128 (Hawai'i App.1981)—§ **2.1, n. 1.**

Quality Truck Equipment Co. v. Layman, 51 Ark.App. 195, 912 S.W.2d 18 (Ark. App.1995)—§ **14.15, n. 8.**

Quartey v. AB Stars Productions, S.A., 260 A.D.2d 39, 697 N.Y.S.2d 280 (N.Y.A.D. 1 Dept.1999)—§ **22.3, n. 15.**

Quattlebaum v. Gray, 252 Ark. 610, 480 S.W.2d 339 (Ark.1972)—§ **4.2, n. 12.**

Quazzo v. Quazzo, 136 Vt. 107, 386 A.2d 638 (Vt.1978)—§ **4.2, n. 12;** § **9.3, n. 1.**

Queen City Farms, Inc. v. Central Nat. Ins. Co. of Omaha, 126 Wash.2d 50, 882 P.2d 703 (Wash.1994)—§ **3.13, n. 24.**

Quick v. Stuyvesant, 2 Paige Ch. 84, 2 N.Y. Ch. Ann. 823 (N.Y.Ch.1830)—§ **13.18, n. 11;** § **13.20, n. 11.**

Quigley v. Wilson, 474 N.W.2d 277 (Iowa App.1991)—§ **4.9, n. 4.**

Quillen v. Twin City Bank, 253 Ark. 169, 485 S.W.2d 181 (Ark.1972)—§ **9.42, n. 25.**

Quinn v. Workforce 2000, Inc., 887 F.Supp. 131 (E.D.Tex.1995)—§ **19.20, n. 2.**

Quiring v. Quiring, 130 Idaho 560, 944 P.2d 695 (Idaho 1997)—§ **22.1, n. 5, 16.**

Quirk v. Bank of Commerce & Trust Co., 244 F. 682 (6th Cir.1917)—§ **19.20, n. 2.**

R

Raabe v. Squier, 148 N.Y. 81, 42 N.E. 516 (N.Y.1895)—§ **19.8, n. 13.**

Rabinowitz v. People's Nat. Bank, 235 Mass. 102, 126 N.E. 289 (Mass.1920)— § **18.21, n. 9.**

Radford & Guise v. Practical Premium Co., 125 Ark. 199, 188 S.W. 562 (Ark.1916)— § **2.20, n. 65.**

Raffles v. Wichelhaus, 159 Eng.Rep. 375 (Ex.1864)—§ **3.10, n. 22;** § **3.11;** § **3.11, n. 14.**

Rae v. Air–Speed, Inc., 386 Mass. 187, 435 N.E.2d 628 (Mass.1982)—§ **17.4, n. 7.**

Raestle v. Whitson, 119 Ariz. 524, 582 P.2d 170 (Ariz.1978)—§ **15.4, n. 20.**

Raffles v. Wichelhaus, 159 Eng.Rep. 375 (Unknown Court 1864)—§ **3.11, n. 14.**

Ragan v. Williams, 220 Ala. 590, 127 So. 190 (Ala.1930)—§ **8.8, n. 4, 7.**

Ragland v. Sheehan, 256 Mont. 322, 846 P.2d 1000 (Mont.1993)—§ **4.2, n. 1.**

Rague v. New York Evening Journal Pub. Co., 164 A.D. 126, 149 N.Y.S. 668 (N.Y.A.D. 2 Dept.1914)—§ **2.16, n. 8.**

Raible v. Puerto Rico Indus. Development Co., 392 F.2d 424 (1st Cir.1968)—§ **2.19, n. 6.**

Rainbow Const. Co., Inc. v. Olsen, 64 Or. App. 699, 669 P.2d 814 (Or.App.1983)— § **3.4, n. 36.**

Ralph Shrader, Inc. v. Diamond Intern. Corp., 833 F.2d 1210 (6th Cir.1987)— § **2.21, n. 20.**

Ralston v. Mathew, 173 Kan. 550, 250 P.2d 841 (Kan.1952)—§ **4.8, n. 6.**

Ralston Purina Co. v. McCollum, 271 Ark. 840, 611 S.W.2d 201 (Ark.App.1981)— § **19.48, n. 9.**

Ralston Purina Co. v. Rooker, 346 So.2d 901 (Miss.1977)—§ **13.3, n. 10.**

Ram Development Corp. v. Siuslaw Enterprises, Inc., 283 Or. 13, 580 P.2d 552 (Or.1978)—§ **11.8, n. 4.**

Ramirez v. Autosport, 88 N.J. 277, 440 A.2d 1345 (N.J.1982)—§ **11.20, n. 6, 11, 14.**

Ramp Buildings Corp. v. Northwest Bldg. Co., 164 Wash. 603, 4 P.2d 507 (Wash. 1931)—§ **9.7, n. 1.**

Randal v. Tatum, 98 Cal. 390, 33 P. 433 (Cal.1893)—§ **18.16, n. 2.**

Randall v. Sweet, 1 Denio 460 (N.Y.Sup. 1845)—§ **8.8, n. 23.**

Randolph v. Castle, 190 Ky. 776, 228 S.W. 418 (Ky.1921)—§ **19.44, n. 5.**

Randolph v. Randolph, 937 S.W.2d 815 (Tenn.1996)—§ **9.20, n. 38.**

Randon v. Toby, 52 U.S. 493, 11 How. 493, 13 L.Ed. 784 (1850)—§ **6.2, n. 50.**

Raner v. Goldberg, 244 N.Y. 438, 155 N.E. 733 (N.Y.1927)—§ **4.12, n. 65.**

Rann v. Hughes, 7 T.R. 350, 101 Eng.Rep. 1014 (Ex.1778)—§ **5.1, n. 4.**

S

U

Walter E. Heller & Co. v. Aetna Business Credit, Inc., 158 Ga.App. 249, 280 S.E.2d 144 (Ga.App.1981)—§ **2.16, n. 2.**

Walter E. Heller & Co. v. Video Innovations, Inc., 730 F.2d 50 (2nd Cir.1984)— § **19.5, n. 10.**

Walter Kidde Constructors, Inc. v. State, 37 Conn.Supp. 50, 434 A.2d 962 (Conn.Super.1981)—§ **14.28, n. 5.**

Walters v. Marathon Oil Co., 642 F.2d 1098 (7th Cir.1981)—§ **6.3, n. 41.**

Walter–Wallingford Coal Co. v. A. Himes Coal Co., 223 Mich. 576, 194 N.W. 493 (Mich.1923)—§ **21.2, n. 12.**

Walton v. Bank of California, Nat. Assoc., 218 Cal.App.2d 527, 32 Cal.Rptr. 856 (Cal.App. 1 Dist.1963)—§ **9.26, n. 7.**

Walton v. Denhart, 226 Or. 254, 359 P.2d 890 (Or.1961)—§ **11.18, n. 26.**

Walton v. Piqua State Bank, 204 Kan. 741, 466 P.2d 316 (Kan.1970)—§ **19.6, n. 3.**

Wantulok v. Wantulok, 67 Wyo. 22, 214 P.2d 477 (Wyo.1950)—§ **19.46, n. 2.**

Ward v. Goodrich, 34 Colo. 369, 82 P. 701 (Colo.1905)—§ **4.12, n. 17.**

Ward v. Harding, 860 S.W.2d 280 (Ky. 1993)—§ **13.17, n. 8.**

Ward v. Haren, 183 Mo.App. 569, 167 S.W. 1064 (Mo.App.1914)—§ **14.32, n. 3.**

Ward v. Hasbrouck, 169 N.Y. 407, 62 N.E. 434 (N.Y.1902)—§ **19.21, n. 6.**

Ward v. Johnson, 13 Mass. 148 (Mass. 1816)—§ **20.3, n. 9.**

Ward v. New York Cent. R. Co., 47 N.Y. 29 (N.Y.1871)—§ **14.5, n. 7.**

Ward v. Vance, 93 Pa. 499 (Pa.1880)— § **13.3, n. 6.**

Warde v. Davis, 494 F.2d 655 (10th Cir. 1974)—§ **22.3, n. 5.**

Warden v. E.R. Squibb & Sons, Inc., 840 F.Supp. 203 (E.D.N.Y.1993)—§ **3.13, n. 19.**

Ware v. Mobley, 190 Ga. 249, 9 S.E.2d 67 (Ga.1940)—§ **8.2, n. 20.**

Ware v. Spinney, 76 Kan. 289, 91 P. 787 (Kan.1907)—§ **22.8, n. 6.**

Warner v. Estate of Allen, 776 N.E.2d 422 (Ind.App.2002)—§ **21.13, n. 5.**

Warner v. McLay, 92 Conn. 427, 103 A. 113 (Conn.1918)—§ **14.28, n. 9.**

Warner v. Rossignol, 513 F.2d 678 (1st Cir. 1975)—§ **21.6, n. 1.**

Warner v. Texas & P. Ry. Co., 164 U.S. 418, 17 S.Ct. 147, 41 L.Ed. 495 (1896)— § **19.19, n. 4.**

Warner Bros. Pictures v. Brodel, 31 Cal.2d 766, 192 P.2d 949 (Cal.1948)—§ **8.2, n. 16.**

Warner–Lambert Pharmaceutical Co. v. John J. Reynolds, Inc., 178 F.Supp. 655 (S.D.N.Y.1959)—§ **2.9, n. 70.**

Warner–Lambert Pharmaceutical Co. v. Sylk, 471 F.2d 1137 (3rd Cir.1972)— § **19.6, n. 3.**

Warren v. Hodge, 121 Mass. 106 (Mass. 1876)—§ **4.10, n. 2.**

Warrior Constructors, Inc. v. International Union of Operating Engineers, Local Union No. 926, AFL–CIO, 383 F.2d 700 (5th Cir.1967)—§ **2.8, n. 2.**

Wartzman v. Hightower Productions, Ltd., 53 Md.App. 656, 456 A.2d 82 (Md.App. 1983)—§ **14.9, n. 10.**

Warwick Municipal Employees Credit Union v. McAllister, 110 R.I. 399, 293 A.2d 516 (R.I.1972)—§ **8.4, n. 14.**

Washington Capitols Basketball Club, Inc. v. Barry, 304 F.Supp. 1193 (N.D.Cal. 1969)—§ **18.16, n. 15.**

Wassenaar v. Panos, 111 Wis.2d 518, 331 N.W.2d 357 (Wis.1983)—§ **14.31, n. 23.**

Wasserman's Inc. v. Township of Middletown, 137 N.J. 238, 645 A.2d 100 (N.J. 1994)—§ **14.31, n. 28.**

Wasserman Theatrical Enterprise v. Harris, 137 Conn. 371, 77 A.2d 329 (Conn. 1950)—§ **13.8, n. 3.**

Water Street Development Corp. v. City of New York, 220 A.D.2d 289, 632 N.Y.S.2d 544 (N.Y.A.D. 1 Dept.1995)—§ **4.12, n. 39.**

Wat Henry Pontiac Co. v. Bradley, 202 Okla. 82, 210 P.2d 348 (Okla.1949)— § **9.17, n. 7.**

Watkins v. Curry, 103 Ark. 414, 147 S.W. 43 (Ark.1912)—§ **22.2, n. 7.**

Watkins v. Wells, 303 Ky. 728, 198 S.W.2d 662 (Ky.1946)—§ **19.41, n. 1.**

Watkins v. Williams, 265 Mont. 306, 877 P.2d 19 (Mont.1994)—§ **21.4, n. 10.**

Watkins & Son v. Carrig, 91 N.H. 459, 21 A.2d 591 (N.H.1941)—§ **4.9, n. 23;** § **4.10, n. 7.**

Watson v. Billings, 38 Ark. 278 (Ark. 1881)—§ **8.7, n. 7.**

Watson v. Johnson Mobile Homes, 284 F.3d 568 (5th Cir.2002)—§ **14.3, n. 5.**

Watson v. Kenlick Coal Co., Inc., 498 F.2d 1183 (6th Cir.1974)—§ **13.17, n. 8;** § **13.20, n. 14.**

Watson v. Loughran, 112 Ga. 837, 38 S.E. 82 (Ga.1901)—§ **14.13, n. 4.**

Watson v. McCabe, 527 F.2d 286 (6th Cir. 1975)—§ **19.30, n. 14.**

Watson Clinic, LLP v. Verzosa, 816 So.2d 832 (Fla.App. 2 Dist.2002)—§ **9.30, n. 2.**

Watters v. Lincoln, 29 S.D. 98, 135 N.W. 712 (S.D.1912)—§ **2.20, n. 57.**

Watts v. Malatesta, 262 N.Y. 80, 186 N.E. 210 (N.Y.1933)—§ **22.7, n. 12.**

Wavra v. Karr, 142 Minn. 248, 172 N.W. 118 (Minn.1919)—§ **14.15, n. 6.**

Wax v. Northwest Seed Co., 189 Wash. 212, 64 P.2d 513 (Wash.1937)—§ **2.20, n. 16.**

Way v. Sperry, 60 Mass. 238 (Mass.1850)— § **5.5, n. 4.**

Wayne J. Griffin Elec., Inc. v. Dunn Const. Co., 622 So.2d 314 (Ala.1993)—§ **3.13, n. 7.**

Wells v. Hartford Acc. & Indem. Co., 459 S.W.2d 253 (Mo.1970)—§ **4.2, n. 8.**

Wells Fargo Bank v. Arizona Laborers, Teamsters and Cement Masons Local No. 395 Pension Trust Fund, 201 Ariz. 474, 38 P.3d 12 (Ariz.2002)—§ **11.38, n. 41.**

Wellston Coal Co. v. Franklin Paper Co., 57 Ohio St. 182, 48 N.E. 888 (Ohio 1897)—§ **15.6, n. 7.**

Welsh v. Loomis, 5 Wash.2d 377, 105 P.2d 500 (Wash.1940)—§ **4.10, n. 15.**

Wender Presses, Inc. v. United States, 170 Ct.Cl. 483, 343 F.2d 961 (Ct.Cl.1965)—§ **2.24, n. 1.**

Wender & Roberts, Inc. v. Wender, 238 Ga.App. 355, 518 S.E.2d 154 (Ga.App. 1999)—§ **9.23, n. 15.**

Wendling v. Cundall, 568 P.2d 888 (Wyo. 1977)—§ **11.38, n. 23.**

Weng v. Allison, 287 Ill.App.3d 535, 223 Ill.Dec. 123, 678 N.E.2d 1254 (Ill.App. 3 Dist.1997)—§ **9.17, n. 7.**

Wenzel–Gosset by Gaukler, Estate of v. Nickels, 575 N.W.2d 425 (N.D.1998)—§ **9.10, n. 9, 12.**

Wenzler & Ward Plumbing & Heating Co. v. Sellen, 53 Wash.2d 96, 330 P.2d 1068 (Wash.1958)—§ **14.8, n. 7.**

Werner v. Ashcraft Bloomquist, Inc., 10 S.W.3d 575 (Mo.App. E.D.2000)—§ **13.18, n. 1.**

Werner v. Nelkin, 206 A.D.2d 422, 614 N.Y.S.2d 66 (N.Y.A.D. 2 Dept.1994)—§ **21.9, n. 7.**

Werner v. Norwest Bank South Dakota, N.A., 499 N.W.2d 138 (S.D.1993)—§ **2.9, n. 6.**

West v. Holstrom, 261 Cal.App.2d 89, 67 Cal.Rptr. 831 (Cal.App. 5 Dist.1968)—§ **21.9, n. 1.**

West v. Hunt Foods, 101 Cal.App.2d 597, 225 P.2d 978 (Cal.App. 1 Dist.1951)—§ **6.3, n. 47.**

West v. Norcross, 190 Ark. 667, 80 S.W.2d 67 (Ark.1935)—§ **17.6, n. 22.**

West American Ins. Co. v. Band & Desenberg, 925 F.Supp. 758 (M.D.Fla.1996)—§ **3.13, n. 34.**

Western Advertising Co. v. Midwest Laundries, 61 S.W.2d 251 (Mo.App.1933)—§ **14.16, n. 7.**

Western Airlines, Inc. v. Lathrop Co., 499 P.2d 1013 (Alaska 1972)—§ **2.9, n. 87.**

Western and Southern Life Ins. Co. v. Crown American Corp., 877 F.Supp. 1041 (E.D.Ky.1993)—§ **16.10, n. 1.**

Western Farm Bureau Mut. Ins. Co. v. Barela, 79 N.M. 149, 441 P.2d 47 (N.M. 1968)—§ **17.10, n. 6.**

Western Grain Co. v. Barron G. Collier, Inc., 163 Ark. 369, 258 S.W. 979 (Ark. 1924)—§ **14.16, n. 7.**

Western Hills, Oregon, Ltd. v. Pfau, 265 Or. 137, 508 P.2d 201 (Or.1973)—§ **11.11, n. 1; § 11.37, n. 5, 18.**

Western Mfg. Co. v. Cotton & Long, 126 Ky. 749, 104 S.W. 758 (Ky.1907)—§ **9.42, n. 24.**

Western Oil & Fuel Co. v. Kemp, 245 F.2d 633 (8th Cir.1957)—§ **4.13, n. 22.**

Western Oil Sales Corporation v. Bliss & Wetherbee, 299 S.W. 637 (Tex.Com.App. 1927)—§ **18.30, n. 5.**

Western Properties v. Southern Utah Aviation, Inc., 776 P.2d 656 (Utah App. 1989)—§ **13.12, n. 13; § 13.18, n. 9.**

Western Sav. Fund Soc. of Philadelphia v. Southeastern Pennsylvania Transp. Authority, 285 Pa.Super. 187, 427 A.2d 175 (Pa.Super.1981)—§ **2.25, n. 18.**

Western Sign, Inc. v. State, 180 Mont. 278, 590 P.2d 141 (Mont.1979)—§ **4.13, n. 1.**

Western Transmission Corp. v. Colorado Mainline, Inc., 376 F.2d 470 (10th Cir. 1967)—§ **11.33, n. 3.**

Western Union Telegraph Co. v. Cowin & Co., 20 F.2d 103 (8th Cir.1927)—§ **2.24, n. 9.**

Western Union Telegraph Co. v. Gardner, 278 S.W. 278 (Tex.Civ.App.-Dallas 1925)—§ **2.23, n. 30.**

Western Union Telegraph Co. v. Priester, 276 U.S. 252, 48 S.Ct. 234, 72 L.Ed. 555 (1928)—§ **2.24, n. 12; § 14.6, n. 10.**

Western Union Telegraph Co. v. Southwick, 214 S.W. 987 (Tex.Civ.App.-Amarillo 1919)—§ **14.15, n. 14.**

Western Waterproofing Co., Inc. v. Springfield Housing Authority, 669 F.Supp. 901 (C.D.Ill.1987)—§ **3.13, n. 39.**

West–Fair Elec. Contractors v. Aetna Cas. & Sur. Co., 638 N.Y.S.2d 394, 661 N.E.2d 967 (N.Y.1995)—§ **11.10, n. 5.**

West Gate Bank of Lincoln v. Eberhardt, 202 Neb. 762, 277 N.W.2d 104 (Neb. 1979)—§ **4.4, n. 22.**

West Hartford, Town of v. Rechel, 190 Conn. 114, 459 A.2d 1015 (Conn.1983)—§ **11.29, n. 6.**

West Haven Sound Development Corp. v. West Haven, 201 Conn. 305, 514 A.2d 734 (Conn.1986)—§ **14.17, n. 7.**

Westhill Exports, Limited v. Pope, 240 N.Y.S.2d 961, 191 N.E.2d 447 (N.Y. 1963)—§ **11.28, n. 10.**

West India Industries, Inc. v. Tradex, Tradex Petroleum Services, 664 F.2d 946 (5th Cir.1981)—§ **4.9, n. 13.**

Westinghouse Broadcasting Co., Inc. v. New England Patriots Football Club, Inc., 10 Mass.App.Ct. 70, 406 N.E.2d 399 (Mass. App.Ct.1980)—§ **2.25, n. 14.**

West Ky. Coal Co. v. Nourse, 320 S.W.2d 311 (Ky.1959)—§ **9.38, n. 14.**

Westlands Water Dist., United States v., 134 F.Supp.2d 1111 (E.D.Cal.2001)—§ **13.5, n. 15.**

X

Y

Table of Uniform Commercial Code Sections

*

Index

References are to Pages

---

†